Contemporary Literary Criticism

Contemporary Literary Criticism

Excerpts from Criticism
of the Works of Today's
Novelists, Poets, Playwrights,
and Other Creative Writers

Dedria Bryfonski
Editor

Gale Research Company
Book Tower
Detroit, Michigan 48226

STAFF

Dedria Bryfonski, *Editor*

Laurie Lanzen Harris, *Associate Editor*
Laura A. Buch, Dennis Poupard, Jean C. Stine,
Carolyn Voldrich, *Assistant Editors*

Phyllis Carmel Mendelson, *Contributing Editor*

Sharon R. Gunton, *Production Editor*

Linda M. Pugliese, *Manuscript Coordinator*
Thomas E. Gunton, *Research Coordinator*
Emily W. Barrett, Jeanne A. Gough, Tom Ligotti,
James E. Person, Jr., *Editorial Assistants*

L. Elizabeth Hardin, *Permissions Coordinator*
Dawn L. McGinty, *Permissions Assistant*

Contents

Authors in this volume:

Preface

Literary criticism is indispensable to the layman or scholar attempting to evaluate and understand creative writing—whether his subject is one poem, one writer, one idea, one school, or a general trend in contemporary writing. Literary criticism is itself a collective term for several kinds of critical writing: criticism may be normative, descriptive, interpretive, textual, appreciative, generic. Conscientious students must consult numerous sources in order to become familiar with the criticism pertinent to their subjects.

Until now, there has been nothing resembling an ongoing encyclopedia of current literary criticism, bringing together in one series criticism of all the various kinds from widely diverse sources. *Contemporary Literary Criticism* is intended to be such a comprehensive reference work.

The Plan of the Work

Contemporary Literary Criticism presents significant passages from the published criticism of work by well-known creative writers—novelists and short story writers, poets and playwrights. Some creative writers, like James Baldwin and Paul Goodman, are probably better known for their expository work than for their fiction, and so discussion of their nonfiction is included.

Contemporary Literary Criticism is not limited to material concerning long-established authors like Eliot, Faulkner, Hemingway, and Auden, although these and other writers of similar stature are included. Attention is also given to two other groups of writers—writers of considerable public interest—about whose work criticism is hard to locate. These are the newest writers (like Robert M. Pirsig, Erica Jong, and William Kotzwinkle) and the contributors to the well-loved but nonscholarly genres of mystery and science fiction (like Georges Simenon, Agatha Christie, Robert Heinlein, and Arthur C. Clarke).

The definition of *contemporary* is necessarily arbitrary. For purposes of selection for *CLC,* contemporary writers are those who are either now living or who have died since January 1, 1960. Contemporary criticism is more loosely defined as that written any time during the past twenty-five years or so and currently relevant to the evaluation of the writer under discussion.

Each volume of *CLC* lists about 150 authors, with an average of about five excerpts from critical articles or reviews being given for the works of each author. Altogether, there are about 1100 individual excerpts in each volume taken from about 200 books and several hundred issues of some one hundred general magazines, literary reviews, and scholarly journals. Each excerpt is fully identified for the convenience of readers who may wish to consult the entire chapter, article, or review excerpted. Each volume covers writers not previously included and also provides significant new criticism pertaining to authors included in earlier volumes.

Beginning with Volume 10, *CLC* contains an appendix which lists the sources from which material has been reprinted in that volume. It does not, however, list every book or periodical consulted for the volume.

A Note on Bio-Bibliographical References and Page Citations

Notes in many entries directing the user to consult *Contemporary Authors* for detailed biographical and bibliographical information refer to a series of biographical reference books published by the

Gale Research Company since 1962, which now includes detailed biographical sketches of about 50,000 authors who have lived since 1962, many of whose careers began during the post-World War II period, or earlier.

Beginning with *CLC*, Volume 5, the method for referring to pages in the original sources has been standardized. Page numbers appear after each fragment (unless the entire essay was contained on one page). Page numbers appear in citations as well only when the editors wish to indicate, with an essay or chapter title and its *inclusive* page numbers, the scope of the original treatment.

Acknowledgments

The editors wish to thank the copyright holders of the excerpts included in this volume for their permission to use the material, and the staffs of the Detroit Public Library, Wayne State University Library, and the libraries of the University of Michigan for making their resources available to us.

Authors Forthcoming in *CLC*

With the publication of *Contemporary Literary Criticism,* Volume 12, the series will expand its scope to encompass songwriters, screenwriters, cartoonists, and other creative writers whose work is often evaluated from a literary perspective. These writers will take their place with the novelists, poets, dramatists, and short story writers who will continue to be the primary focus of *CLC.* Volume 12 is designed to be of special interest to young adult readers. Volume 13 will include criticism on a number of authors not previously listed, and will also feature new criticism of newer works of authors included in earlier editions.

To be Included in Volume 12

Maya Angelou (Black American novelist, poet, playwright) Author of *I Know Why the Caged Bird Sings*

Judy Blume (American young adult novelist) Author of *Are You There God? It's Me, Margaret* and *Forever. . .*

Mel Brooks (American screenwriter, director, and comedian)

Carlos Casteneda (Brazilian-born American anthropologist and nonfiction writer) Author of *The Teachings of Don Juan*

E. E. Cummings (American poet)

Bob Dylan (American songwriter and novelist)

Esther Forbes (Newbery Award-winning American young adult novelist and biographer) Author of *Paul Revere and the World He Lived In*

Leon Garfield (British young adult novelist, short story writer, and nonfiction writer) His *The God Beneath the Sea* won the 1971 Carnegie Medal

Christie Harris (Canadian young adult novelist and short story writer) Best known for her adaptations of Indian legends

Jamake Highwater (Native American young adult novelist and nonfiction writer) Author of *Anpao: An American Indian Odyssey*

Jim Jacobs and Warren Casey (American playwrights) Their *Grease* is currently Broadway's longest-running play

Norman Lear (Emmy Award-winning American screenwriter and television producer)

John Lennon and Paul McCartney (British songwriters) One-half of The Beatles

Carson McCullers (American novelist and short story writer) Author of *The Heart Is a Lonely Hunter*

Joni Mitchell (Canadian songwriter)

Andre Norton (American science fiction writer)

J. D. Salinger (American novelist and short story writer) Author of *The Catcher in the Rye*

John R. Tunis (American young adult sports writer)

Garry Trudeau (American Pulitzer Prize-winning cartoonist)

Kurt Vonnegut, Jr. (American novelist and short story writer) Author of *Slaughterhouse-Five*

To be Included in Volume 13

Alice Adams (American short story writer and novelist) Will feature criticism on new collection of short stories, *Beautiful Girl*

A. Alvarez (British essayist, poet, and novelist) Will feature criticism on new novel, *Hunt*

Kingsley Amis (British novelist, short story writer, poet, and essayist) Will feature criticism on new novel, *Jake's Thing*

Donald Barthelme (American short story writer and novelist) Will feature criticism on new collection of short stories, *Great Days*

Ann Beattie (American short story writer and novelist) Will feature criticism on new collection of short stories, *Secrets and Surprises*

Marie-Claire Blais (French-Canadian novelist and poet)

Jorge Luis Borges (Argentine short story writer, poet, and essayist)

Anthony Burgess (British novelist and essayist) Will feature criticism on new novel, *Abba Abba*

Arthur C. Clarke (British science fiction writer) Will feature criticism on new novel, *The Fountains of Paradise*

Lawrence Durrell (British novelist and essayist) Will feature criticism on new novel, *Livia; or Buried Alive*

T. S. Eliot (Anglo-American Nobel-Prize-winning poet and critic)

Carlos Fuentes (Mexican novelist, poet, and short story writer) Will feature criticism on new novel, *The Hydra Head*

Doris Grumbach (American novelist and critic) Will feature criticism on new novel, *Chamber Music*

Elizabeth Hardwick (American critic and novelist) Will feature criticism on new novel, *Sleepless Nights*

John Irving (American novelist and short story writer) Will feature criticism on new novel, *The World According to Garp*

André Malraux (French novelist and essayist)

Edna O'Brien (Irish novelist and short story writer) Will feature criticism on new collection of short stories, *A Rose in the Heart*

Flannery O'Connor (American short story writer, essayist, and novelist) Will feature criticism on her collected letters, *The Habit of Being*

Bernard Pomerance (American dramatist) Will feature criticism on Tony Award-winning play, *The Elephant Man*

Katherine Anne Porter (American Pulitzer-Prize-winning short story writer, essayist, and novelist)

Ishmael Reed (Black American novelist and poet)

Susan Sontag (American novelist, essayist, and short story writer) Will feature criticism on new collection of short stories, *I, etcetera*

Muriel Spark (Scottish novelist, poet, and dramatist) Will feature criticism on new novel, *Territorial Rights*

John Updike (American novelist, short story writer, and essayist) Will feature criticism on new novel, *The Coup*

Yevgeny Yevtushenko (Russian poet)

A

ACHEBE, Chinua 1930-

Achebe, a Nigerian-born novelist, poet, short story writer, and author of children's books, is considered one of the finest contemporary African writers. In his works Achebe explores traditional tribal values and the cataclysmic cultural changes invoked through the influence of European colonization. Achebe is recognized as a consummate craftsman for his innovative use of language, notably his use of traditional Ibo proverbs given in literal English translation, evoking the clash between the two cultures. (See also *CLC*, Vols. 1, 3, 5, 7, and *Contemporary Authors*, Vols. 1-4, rev. ed.)

ARTHUR RAVENSCROFT

[*Things Fall Apart*] is a short and extraordinarily close-knit novel which in fictional terms creates the way of life of an Ibo village community when white missionaries and officials were first penetrating Eastern Nigeria. The highly selective details with which Achebe represents the seasonal festivals and ceremonies, the religion, social customs, and political structure of an Ibo village create the vivid impression of a complex, self-sufficient culture seemingly able to deal in traditional ways with any challenge that nature and human experience might fling at it. . . . [The] greatest strength of *Things Fall Apart* is the tragic 'objectivity' with which Achebe handles a dual theme.

There are two main, closely intertwined tragedies—the personal tragedy of Okonkwo, 'one of the greatest men in Umuofia', and the public tragedy of the eclipse of one culture by another. (pp. 8-9)

Things Fall Apart is impressive for the wide range of what it so pithily covers, for the African flavour of scene and language, but above all for the way in which Achebe makes that language the instrument for analyzing tragic experience and profound human issues of very much more than local Nigerian significance. . . .

Superficially *No Longer at Ease* seems merely to carry the themes of [*Things Fall Apart*] into the 1950s, but the differences of approach and treatment should warn against pressing the outward resemblances too far. Its austere contemporaneity, its insistence upon the ordinariness of a young man's failure to live up to his untried ideals of conduct, allow for none of the glamour that many readers have found in *Things Fall Apart*. (p. 18)

No Longer at Ease seems to be too socially satirical to be able to carry off convincingly the tragic effect Achebe gives us reason to think he is striving for. What one misses is the artistically cohesive tension between chief character and setting that occurs in *Things Fall Apart*. (p. 20)

In *Arrow of God* there is the same kind of traditionalism expressed through Ibo proverbs as in *Things Fall Apart*, but the linguistic texture is richer and there is a new dimension in the use of the proverbs. The fuller scale on which the novel is conceived allows for greater elaboration in the descriptions of ceremonies as well as domestic life and personal relations. . . .

In *Arrow of God* Achebe has clearly returned to the African past with relish and a new confidence in his ability to evoke a way of life with which the legends of his childhood had familiarized him. (p. 30)

A Man of the People is a very different kind of novel—a satirical farce about corrupt politicians cynically exploiting a political system inherited from the departed imperial power. So disillusioned is the *exposé* that the author would hardly seem to escape a charge of personal cynicism. (pp. 31-2)

A Man of the People is a sparkling piece of satirical virtuosity, yet we feel throughout that deep anger, bitterness and disillusion are never far beneath the surface. The novel prompts one to ask: Is it too savage, too despairing, too Swiftian? Many readers find it so, but the skill with which Odili's dual function is controlled and the hints at other criteria of judgement . . . do pose values other than those of the 'eat-and-let-eat' politicians. (pp. 35-6)

> *Arthur Ravenscroft, in his* Chinua Achebe (© *Arthur Ravenscroft 1969; Longman Group Ltd., for the British Council), British Council, 1969.*

GERALD MOORE

[Achebe] has recreated for us a way of life which has almost disappeared, and has done so with understanding, with justice and with realism. . . .

Achebe's *Things Fall Apart*, which appeared in 1958, was the first West African novel in English which could be applauded without reserve. (p. 58)

[*Things Fall Apart*] is an extremely well-constructed short novel, fully equal to its theme and written with confidence and precision. Achebe's theme is suggested in the Yeatsian title, but although he sees the disintegration of Ibo society as a communal and personal tragedy for those who lived through it, this does not in any way obscure his objectivity in describing that society as it was. (pp. 58-9)

Achebe's brief, almost laconic style, his refusal to justify, explain or condemn, are responsible for a good deal of the book's success. The novelist *presents* to us a picture of traditional Ibo life as just as he can make it. The final judgement of that life, as of the life which replaced it, is left to us. Only Achebe insists that we should see it as a life actually lived by plausible men and women before we dismiss it, with the usual shrug, as nothing but ignorance, darkness and death. His people win, and deservedly win, our full respect as individuals whose life had dignity, significance and positive values. (p. 59)

In dealing with Iboland sixty or more years ago [as he did in *Things Fall Apart*], Achebe could at least describe a single society, intact at first, and later only beginning to disintegrate. To write of modern Nigeria means writing of a country in which many different societies are flowing into each other, each at a different level of internal change, each dominated and confused by the presence of western standards and values. To make out of this boiling hotch potch a coherent social context for a novel calls for exceptional qualities of organization and selection. And this is the task which Achebe tackles in his second novel, *No Longer at Ease*. (pp. 65-6)

With his larger range of characters, and within the space of a very short novel, Achebe does not succeed in touching all of them into life. (p. 68)

No Longer at Ease is bound to create a certain sense of diffuseness and slackness after the austere tragic dignity of *Things Fall Apart*, a dignity which recalls Conrad, who is in fact one of Chinua Achebe's mentors. The fluid world of Obi Okonkwo [the protagonist of *No Longer at Ease*] is simply not susceptible of the same classic treatment, and to have captured it at all is an achievement of sympathy and imagination. Achebe measures the decline in the simple contrast of Obi and his grandfather [the protagonist of *Things Fall Apart*]; the grandson has more humanity, more gentleness, a wider awareness, but he lacks the force and integrity of his ancestor. He measures it also in a certain slackness of language, which compares sadly with the strong, spare certainty of the speeches of Umuofia's vanished elders. (pp. 68-9)

If *No Longer at Ease* is something less than a tragedy, it is because Achebe does not see Obi Okonkwo as a tragic hero. The pressures that pull and mould him are all pressures making for compromise and accommodation; these are not the stuff of tragedy but of failure and decline. The alien forces that destroyed old Okonkwo were mysterious and inexorable, but still largely external and dramatic. (p. 70)

Gerald Moore, "Chinua Achebe: Nostalgia and Realism," in his Seven African Writers *(© Oxford University Press 1962; reprinted by permission of Oxford University Press), revised edition, Oxford University Press, London, 1970.*

R. ANGOGO

In his two books, *Things Fall Apart* and *Arrow of God*,

Achebe uses a language I would like to refer to as 'Ibo in English'. Both these books share a rural side setting. They describe a relationship between society and individual. Achebe shows us how important communal life in Ibo was. We are presented with people who when supported by the society continue to live profitable and progressive lives, yet when they act as individuals, they meet with dead ends.

To show that the situation he is describing needs more than one person, Achebe in his two novels employs the style of conversation, which would be termed linguistically as casual-register. The casuality is seen through use of vocabulary that would be well known and recognised by everyone in the Ibo society. The imagery is local. (p. 2)

The adoption of casual conversational style gives the *Oral literature* taste, to Achebe's work. As a matter of fact, Achebe is recording the History of the Ibo. A lot of values found in the two novels mentioned above cannot be found in the society today. . . .

Sometimes Achebe uses Ibo words with English sentences. Such form of style reminds us again and again that we are reading an Ibo story and that the Ibo vocabulary is not limited in explaining the Ibo Culture. (p. 3)

The ability to shape and mould English to suit character and event and yet still give the impression of an African story is one of the greatest of Achebe's achievements. It puts into the reader a kind of emotive effect, an interest, and a thirst which so to say awakens the reader. (pp. 3-4)

Achebe integrates character and incident through imagery that is tropical. Okonkwo's character is compared to roaring thunder; flamer of fire; as contrasted to Unoka the weakling who dies through ailing and Nwoye who is compared to 'Cold Ash', and a bowl of foo foo could throw him down. The positive abilities of Okonkwo show us the importance the Ibo attached to physical strength. It is through the use of proverb and similes that Achebe develops his theme on this subject. (p. 4)

Arrow of God has taken the same 'Ibo in English' dialogue-like style [as *Things Fall Apart*]. In fact Achebe's wise invention of the [District Commissioner's] book gives a setting for *Arrow of God*; because that is when the British Government has taken root in Nigeria and the D.C.'s book is being used for guidance in administration. It can be noted Achebe attaches a lot of importance to dialogue when he is representing a traditional Ibo society. Where dialogue fails, the means of communication is cut and destruction follows. Ezeulu's failure can be traced through the failure of *proper dialogue* between him and his own people and also between him and the white man. Achebe may be saying that a society that compromises at the expense of their own values leads to destruction. We see this through the destruction of Ezeulu who symbolically stands for the society of Umuoro, since he is their head, by virtue of being the priest of the great snake cult of the village. (p. 5)

Achebe changes style from that of dialogue in the two books to prose narration [in *No Longer at Ease*]. We find no fault in such a change, because his story and time in history also change. We expect language also to change, because language is very much a human phenomenon and entirely belongs to the shaping of the human beings.

The story takes the form of a flash back. It begins with Obi's conviction and then the rest of the book is the unfolding of the episodes that led to Obi's fate. The nature of the modernity and the urban setting of the story is seen through Achebe's use of pidgin English, which is characteristic of urbanization in West Africa. (p. 7)

In a way, I think what Achebe is emphasizing in the plot of *No Longer at Ease* is that intellectual insight without moral support to sustain it is not worthy the effort. In suiting language to character and time, I do not have a quarrel with Achebe, but as to the claims that he attained a piece of work equivalent to his novel, I would not say that. I find his protagonist Obi too weak. Achebe does not find strong enough words with which to present Obi. He makes him a weakling in every aspect. . . .

Achebe maintains his use of Ibo Proverbs and Idioms which make the story interesting and moving. Accompanying the urban theme are the English social, political as well as christian axioms and maxims which all together add to Achebe's intelligence and mastery over the English language.

A Man of the People portrays Achebe the satirical-author. In this novel Achebe decides that he has been soft long enough to his people and now he must lash them if a word of mouth has failed. Achebe's use of irony in *A Man of the People* surpasses that of any other of his books. (p. 8)

Apart from the prose irony, another feature that Achebe employs in *No Longer at Ease* and *A Man of the People* is pidgin English. This is proper because pidgin is the lingua franca of the urbanized West Africans as contrasted with pure Ibo that Achebe uses in *Things Fall Apart* and *Arrow of God*. Achebe lets the pidgin suit the characters and the situation. . . .

All the four novels of Achebe are full of proverbs and similes. Each of the proverbs is always said at an appropriate time to explain a situation. Achebe has been described as an author who has the talent of knowing where things are supposed to be and placing them there. Achebe uses proverbs to sound, reiterate or clarify a situation that he is describing. (p. 10)

All the proverbs have African environment and imagery. They not only symbolise the vitality of the Ibo life, but also the heroism of Achebe the translator. Achebe has the ability to create a sense of real life, real issues of the Ibo society in an impressive turn of English. He lets his words speak. . . . All in all, Achebe's manipulation of English language to suit situations he is describing raises him far above other African writers. By use of idioms, proverbs, emotive words, action, he manages to put vividness and memorable drama into his writing. . . . Achebe takes an account of interlingual differences of syntax and idiom; of the functions of style and theme and the emotions and ideas and associations which the Ibo would have. (pp. 13-14)

> *R. Angogo, "Achebe and the English Language," in* Busara, *Vol. 7, No. 2, 1975, pp. 1-14.*

PHILIP ROGERS

In Chinua Achebe's view, the African writer of our time must be accountable to his society. . . . To Achebe, it is 'simply madness' to think of art as pure and autonomous, happening by itself in an aesthetic void. . . . Each of Achebe's four novels has had an obvious (but never obtrusive) purpose. *Things Fall Apart* and *Arrow of God* both aim to show that the African past 'with all its imperfections—was not one long night of savagery from which the first Europeans, acting on God's behalf, delivered [Africans]'. The public problems of bribery and the *osu* caste are examined in *No Longer at Ease; A Man of the People*, his most purposeful novel, was written with the deliberate aim of providing 'a serious warning to the Nigerian people' about corruption in government and the cynicism of the masses. . . . Written during and shortly after the Nigerian Civil War, the poems [of *Beware, Soul-Brother*] are centrally concerned with the regeneration of belief after the blight of war. . . . In 'Beware, Soul-Brother' and implicitly throughout the collection he identifies the enemies of the public spirit and admonishes his readers to beware. And in the more personal poems of the collection, which dramatize the rebirth in the poet himself of hope for love, new life, and order, Achebe creates a representative spokesman, an exemplary persona whose experience realizes the goal Achebe seeks for his society as a whole, 'the regeneration of its deepest aspirations'. (pp. 1-2)

Achebe's recovery of spirit is sustained more through desiccating irony and indignation than a positive faith, and in the sequential ordering of the poems, is achieved only after an ordeal of horror, disgust, and cynicism.

The poems are arranged so as to suggest a chronological unfolding of perceptions, beginning with 'The First Shot' of the revolution. . . . The poem sharply contrasts the human time of historical 'first shots' with the mechanical time of real bullets. . . . Achebe foresees the moment when it will lodge 'more firmly than the greater noises ahead' (real bullets) 'in the forehead of memory', where of course, it will resume the pace of human 'striding' in the 'nervous suburb' of the mind. The contrast of historical and mechanical forces announces a central concern of these poems, exploring the kinship of things human and inhuman.

'Air Raid' further defines the contrasting modes of time seen in 'The First Shot'. 'A man crossing the road / to greet a friend / is much too slow', 'His friend [is] cut in halves' by the 'bird of death' from the 'evil forest' of technology. The poem's juxtapositions are immediately and simply effective: the potential unity of two men coming together, crossing the road that separates all men, is set off against abrupt, literal division as the friend is cut in half; the flying shadow from technology's evil forest eclipses the full light of noon; human slowness is contrasted with the dreadful quickness of mechanism. (p. 2)

'Refugee Mother and Child' and 'Christmas in Biafra' are longer, more ambitious poems that attempt to evoke pathos through direct description of civilian casualties—mothers and starving children. . . . Although 'Refugee Mother and Child' and 'Christmas in Biafra' are perhaps the least successful poems in the collection, they are nonetheless important to its central themes. . . . Seen against the plaster immortality of the rosy-cheeked Jesus, the perishing child becomes 'a miracle of its own kind': his mortality emphasizes the vital humanity of his mother's devotion. The spectacle arouses in Achebe a 'pure transcendental hate'. 'Pure' and 'transcendental' are more than casual intensifiers; they suggest a loftiness of feeling from which any hint of self-blame is absent. As in 'Air Raid', evil is perceived as external; the poet sees that war cuts men in half and starves babies, but he believes in the purity of the man's friendship and the mother's love. In the poems that follow, his confidence steadily wanes.

In 'Mango Seedling' ... similar themes appear, but in a different and more effective mask. The poem is loosely allegorical. A mango seedling sprouts incongruously on the concrete ledge of a modern office building. A suggestive emblem of vital, human birth, 'purple, two-leafed, standing on its burst black yolk', the seedling is doomed because it cannot put down roots. Like the starving babies, perhaps the revolution, or even the persona himself, it feeds on its own substance, ultimately starves, and dies.... For the first time in *Beware, Soul-Brother* the persona stands inside the world of the poem. He, too, is entombed in the sarcophagus, remote from the nourishing earth, his tone as detached and distant as his vantage point two stories above, where he observes the seedling through a glass pane. In this sterile place and age, he can believe none of the myths of fertility.... But in the concluding line, the last two words, 'passionate courage', suddenly break the emotional distance the persona has maintained so far. A 'tiny debris' is all that remains of the seedling's 'passionate courage', but the poet's commitment to the significance of perishing courage is unequivocal. Like the dying babies, the withered seedling represents a last vestige of rapidly diminishing human values.

Achebe's confidence in such redeeming human values disappears completely in the next two poems. 'Vultures' and 'Lazarus' reveal the nadir of the poet's spirits. Both explore the idea that good and evil are inextricably linked; the very germ from which new growth may come is tainted with evil.... As in 'Mango Seedling', the moment of birth is blighted, but now the blighting force can no longer be dismissed as external.

The poet's recovery from this spiritually arid, cynical cast of mind is seen in 'Love Song' and 'Answer'. The transition is marked by two significant changes in the persona's stance: unlike the earlier poems, which relate to public scenes and historical moments of the recent past, 'Love Song' is personal in tone, addressed to 'my love' rather than 'my people', and looks to the future. (pp. 3-5)

The moment of recovery looked forward to in 'Love Song' takes place in 'Answer', which dramatizes 'a dramatic descent', the rooting of a new conception of the persona's self in the 'trysting floor' of the earth.... The metaphor of his re-emergence into 'proud vibrant life' is that of the seedling, bursting out of the darkness of its confining hull and sending the 'twin cotyledons' of his hands upward, his feet as roots drawn downward to the earth. (p. 5)

The implications of the symbolic action in 'Love Song' and 'Answer' are elaborated more discursively in the title poem of the collection. 'Beware, Soul-Brother' shapes the personal experience of these poems into a warning to writers, the 'men of soul'. In the central metaphor of the poem, writers are dancers; the earth of the dancing ground is their inspiration and their responsibility. (pp. 5-6)

'Beware, Soul-Brother' may seem too confident in its laying down the law for the arts, but it can easily be seen that Achebe has himself experienced the sense of disinheritance he warns against. He numbers himself among the soul-brothers, and in 'Answer' reveals a moment when he felt obliged to try to recover a lost vitality. Other poems in the collection also betray the uneasiness of one who cannot simply draw away from the 'departed dance' of the African past, even though he has committed himself to catching up to 'the dance of the future'. In three poems, 'Penalty of Godhead', 'Lament of the Sacred Python', and 'Dereliction' Achebe looks back to the world of his ancestors, not to worship at their shrines, or even to lament their passing, but only to express the pain he feels in abandoning them. The inevitable penalty of Godhead is to be left behind. (p. 6)

But the uneasy sense of having betrayed the past is balanced in the final poems of *Beware, Soul-Brother* by a healthy scorn for the uncommitted, whose prudence and insensitivity shield them from the ambivalent emotions of engagement. The restored Achebe asserts his judgments to bring his collection to an angry close. In contrast to the 'pure transcendental hate' of 'Christmas in Biafra', the emotion of these concluding poems is 'seminal rage', a committed hatred that fertilizes and sustains his regenerated spirit. 'NON-commitment' and 'We Laughed at Him', the most important of these poems, are built on contrasting images of defence and penetration.... [The eye] is the primary metaphor of these poems. The uncommitted do nothing and feel nothing chiefly because their imagination is timorous and they find sight excruciatingly painful.... The final poem of *Beware, Soul-Brother* ['We Laughed at Him'], is, of course, a defence of poetry and the poet's role in a society blinded by conventionality and contemptuous of the arts. (pp. 7-8)

Philip Rogers [Harper College, SUNY], "Chinua Achebe's Poems of Regeneration," in Journal of Commonwealth Literature *(© Oxford University Press 1976; reprinted by permission of the author), April, 1976, pp. 1-9.*

SOLA SOILE

[In] *Things Fall Apart* the society is forced to give way to an inevitable change because of its violent collision with an alien institution. In *Arrow of God*, however, we have a more explosive situation of a society cleaving apart largely from its own internal strain. The latter novel illustrates the classic situation of a house divided against itself which, with or without any assistance from an external force, must collapse. To be sure the destructive colonial forces that we encounter in the first novel are still very much alive and thriving, but they now stand on the periphery of the doomed society, waiting on the wing to swoop down, like vultures, the moment the society commits *harakiri*. In this particular sense *Arrow of God* is more truly the tragedy.... (p. 283)

[The] central irony in [*Things Fall Apart* is the] paradox between what the society seems to encourage and what it can actually permit. In *Arrow of God*, Achebe brings out more elements in the Ibo society which help to sustain the internal cohesion of the clan but are at the same time responsible for its ultimate disintegration. This ambiguity is at the center of the tragedy of the hero, Ezeulu, the chief priest of Ulu. As the high priest of Umuaro, Ezeulu is the political and spiritual leader of the community and its most able protector against contamination from internal and external sources, and yet he becomes the unwitting cause of some of the society's woes. The germ of this paradox is built into the very function of the chief priest. As the Ezeulu his role involves the symbolic cleansing of the whole clan of all its abominations.... It is a psychically demanding function, but Ezeulu has gladly accepted this symbolic role of the scapegoat on whose head the sins of the village are periodically heaped. . . . (pp. 283-84)

The chief priest is described by the author as an intellectual, someone who goes to the root of things and thinks about why they happen. He is the archetypical philosopher-king. His broad vision and comprehensive outlook on the world are his strength and at the same time . . . the main source of his tragic weakness.

The action in *Arrow of God* centers around Ezeulu's running battle against two threats to himself and his clan. As the chief priest of the god Ulu, he locks horns with reactionary elements within the clan who, for various reasons, want to displace him and the deity he represents from the long-established hierarchy of the village deities. This represents what one might call the home front of the war. . . . From the outside come the forces of the European colonial institutions represented by the District Officer, Captain Winterbottom. The forces here are initially less threatening, but in the structure of the novel Ezeulu's success on this external front largely depends on the degree of his success on the other front. Achebe carefully balances the two battles side by side, allowing the external situation to impinge on the internal only when the latter permits it.

In these battles Ezeulu naturally relies on the power of his god, but his conception of this power is tragically faulty. His attempt to probe too closely into the mystery of an essentially sacrosanct phenomenon first reveals Ezeulu's intellectual pride, that error of judgment for which he is later punished by Ulu. . . . Ezeulu's intellectual pride makes him attempt a definition of his individual will in relation to the sacred power of which he is only a custodian. The same presumption leads him later to second-guess the god and confuse personal revenge with divine justice by actually refusing to name the day for the harvest, thereby taking upon himself what is properly the prerogative of the deity.

Ezeulu's intellectual pride is, however, only a personal flaw that will partly account for his own individual tragedy. The central action involves the clan as a whole, and what really prompts Ezeulu to examine the nature of his power is the growing schism between rival factions in the community. . . . [In effect], the battle is really between the two gods, Ulu and Idemili, with their respective priests as the human protagonists. (pp. 284-86)

Ezeulu is the agent and champion of change. From the obscurity of the future he discerns the pattern of things to come. The essence of his leadership draws on this power to foresee future events. (p. 286)

His prophetic acumen in rightly guessing the necessity of learning the ways of white men leads him to think that he can similarly foresee and provide for every contingency. . . . [Too] often Ezeulu is blind to [his] limitation. (p. 287)

A superficial reading of the novel and a literal interpretation of the role of Ezeulu as just a mere arrow in the bow of his god might give the unwary the erroneous impression that the chief priest is an amoral agent of the deity. Of course, Ezeulu himself believes this. . . . I think that by relying so dangerously on Ezeulu's own analysis of the god's injunction, an analysis that can hardly be described as objective, [one] fails to recognize the necessary ambiguous role of the god and other divine elements in the novel, and thus misses the central irony. In an interview . . . , Achebe himself comes out with a clear statement of his intention in *Arrow of God*. "I am handling a whole lot of . . . complex themes, like the relationship between a god and his priest . . . and I am interested in this old question of who decides what shall be the wish of the gods, and . . . that kind of situation." That, precisely, is the core of the ambiguity in the novel which must be analyzed before any valid statement can be made about Ezeulu's motivation.

Achebe's enigma is posed right from the beginning with the lack of a precise definition of the nature and extent of the power of the chief priest. (p. 292)

There is little doubt that Ulu himself is visiting the sins of the people on their heads. What Ezeulu and [some critics] confuse is the human revenge of the chief priest and the divine justice of the deity. Ezeulu forgets that revenge is not justice but an unreasonable human retribution which has a way of getting out of proportion to the original offence and thereby constituting a new crime. Thus we hear Ezeulu lament that Umuaro's present suffering is not just temporary but will be for all time. Ironically, Ezeulu feels a sense of community with the people in their suffering as a result of his vengeance, seeing his own participation in the general distress as part of his function as the priest who pays the debt of every man, woman, and child in Umuaro. But in his interpretation of the god's justice he temporarily forgets this responsibility and remembers only his power. He comes to look at divine justice through his flawed vision as something from which he is excluded because of his earlier rectitude. . . . He says to Ulu in effect, "I have done no evil, therefore I must not suffer." He fails to see that true justice is a mysterious order in which the sins of individuals within a community are visited on the whole community; an order in which the sins of the guilty are visited on all—guilty and innocent alike. Ezeulu defines justice in non-personal terms, calling on Ulu, "Let justice be done—on others!" He forgets that far from being outside of this moral, if unfathomable order, far from being a mere spectator, a mere arrow in the bow of the deity, an unimplicated executioner, he is the pivot on which the whole order rotates. He is the Chief Priest of Ulu. . . . The incomprehensibility of the whole mystery of this order of justice remains with Ezeulu to the end. (pp. 293-94)

He looks at himself as the accuser but fails to see that he is also the accused. And without the recognition of this paradox there can be no proper grasp of the concept of justice and the proper role of the scapegoat, which is the office of Ezeulu.

The novel closes as it does with Ezeulu's dementedness because he fails to accept his own moral responsibility for the general sin of the clan. For it is our willingness to accept such guilt that leads to self-knowledge. . . . Although Ezeulu has sinned against the gods, his tragedy is not really a matter of crime and punishment, but a failure of moral self-recognition. (p. 295)

Sola Soile, "Tragic Paradox in Achebe's 'Arrow of God'," in PHYLON: The Atlanta University Review of Race and Culture *(copyright, 1976, by Atlanta University; reprinted by permission of* PHYLON*), Vol. XXXVII, Third Quarter (September, 1976), pp. 283-95.*

AKHMATOVA, Anna (pseudonym of Anna Andreyevna Gorenko)　1889?-1966

Poet, translator, and essayist, Akhmatova is often seen as Pasternak's successor in the Silver Age of Russian poetry and is generally considered the finest woman poet Russia has produced. Participating with the Acmeists in a reaction against symbolist poetry, she wrote in a concise and accessible style. Words are used logically, imagery is concrete. Hers is an intimate and authentic poetry, showing a love of art, of nature, of Russia, and of love itself. Though intensely personal, it achieves a sense of universal statement through a wide range of moods. The darker side of Akhmatova's work reflects the struggle of Russia under siege, the unhappiness of the people, the suffering of her own family, the war. Akhmatova was expelled from the Writer's Union under Stalin's rule, and her work was considered subversive and banned from publication until after Stalin's death. (See also *Contemporary Authors*, Vols. 19-20; obituary, Vols. 25-28; *Contemporary Authors Permanent Series*, Vol. 1.)

SAM N. DRIVER

In [Akhmatova's] four collections after *Rosary,* the love theme remains dominant despite the cataclysm of war and revolution, and the total destruction of the world that [she] had known. If the tone of these volumes reflects the turmoil of the times and becomes less capricious and more austere, the focus remains inward, on a woman's ill-starred love. (p. 55)

It is interesting to note that even in Akhmatova's very earliest work (two poems from the first copy book), desertion and abandonment provide the setting. (p. 58)

In the later volumes, the motif of tragic love escapes oversentimentality in its expression through an almost calm, epic resignation before suffering. In the earliest work, however, the *persona* is more often unreconciled to love's pain, and the lyrical statement lacks the indirection characteristic for more restrained works of the later period. (pp. 59-60)

It is the stance or point of view of the *persona*—somehow apart from herself, observing herself—which is most unusual. The peculiar stance permits an emotional distance, a degree of restraint and a certain objectivity in the expression of intense lyrical emotion. This device, with its shifts in grammatical person and the unusually infrequent use of the first person, is one of the principal reasons that Akhmatova's almost exclusive treatment of the difficult subject of love's pain avoids any impression of mawkishness. (pp. 62-3)

[Akhmatova uses this device in a variety of ways:] direct lyrical statement may be combined with the description of a dramatic scene in which the *persona* is a figure; the description of an interior may serve both to state the *tema* and to provide a setting in which the persona observes herself; in another setting, she may stand entirely apart. (p. 63)

To some extent, it is the sensitivity to furnishings and décor, and certainly the attention to details of feminine attire and coiffure which reminds us constantly that it is a woman who is speaking in Akhmatova's poetry. It would be mistaken, however, to interpret the prominence of such details simply as a preoccupation with traditionally feminine concerns. These necklaces and embroidery frames, painted chests and scarves are the materials from which Akhmatova's poems are constructed, and reflected the Acmeist love

of concrete things. Akhmatova is highly selective in her choice of concrete objects, and items of dress and décor are two categories on which she typically draws. They occur so frequently that they present in themselves minor motifs. (pp. 63-4)

[It is in the] rapid focusing on concrete detail that Akhmatova's practice and Acmeist theory most effectively coincide. Given this focus, ordinary objects are "perceived anew," are evoked in their solidity, their texture, their mass. While they serve to communicate emotions which are often quite unrelated to them, they are not symbolic, but remain themselves, the Acmeist "things."

The most common household objects—although unusual ones in poetry, appear in extraordinary juxtapositions. . . . The poems are set for the most part within the house (and the garden wall the outermost limit); often there is a specific location within a particular room: entrance hall or bedroom, parlor or dining room. The effect of such settings is to create an atmosphere of intimacy, as well as to suggest a specific, concrete background for the brief and rapidly developed dramatic scenes. With the Acmeist fondness for the concrete, Akhmatova includes minor details of the rooms, and the physical setting is often fixed in time as well as place. All this is done with a maximum verbal economy. (p. 65)

Given the frequency of rooms and interiors in Akhmatova's poetry, it is perhaps not surprising that "house" should be one of the commonest words in her lexicon. There is a reflection here of the Acmeist fondness for architectonic imagery, but the house has a more complex function than merely providing concrete background. The house is also symbolic, on this level intimately related to the major motif. One of the aspects in which Akhmatova sees tragic love, for example, is as imprisonment; the house without love is a prison. . . .

If the major motif is often represented by the *tema* of imprisonment, it is much more frequently conceived in terms of abandonment. Quite often, the motif is stated through imagery of the house. The abandoned house signifies the abandoned heart. . . . (p. 66)

Although contemporary concerns did not ordinarily penetrate the intimate world of Akhmatova's lyrics, the threat to her homeland struck deep into her poetic consciousness; she produced a small number of highly moving poems concerning Russia during World War I, and later, in revolution. (p. 70)

The austere, solemn poetic person of the war poems, and those which forcefully reject the emigration . . . , are not typical for the war period. . . . National themes are secondary to the love motif; sometimes . . . they are congruent. . . . (p. 73)

In Akhmatova's poetry, one is constantly reminded of the city [Petersburg] she calls "the murkiest of capitals." Fragmentary views of the city seem to register involuntarily in the mind of the preoccupied poetic person. . . .

Akhmatova's attitude toward the city is, on the one hand, traditional: the mystique of the city permeates her poems, and grandeur past and present is frequently evoked. On the other hand, the attitude is familiar and proprietary. (p. 75)

While there are some points for comparison between Akhmatova and the Symbolist poets with regard to urban themes, there is a fundamental difference in attitudes. Where the city is secondary to the dominant motif of love in Akhmatova's poetry, it is often the poetic subject for the Symbolists. If the city is illusory in Symbolist poetry, it is concrete in Akhmatova's. For the Symbolists, the city is sinister and otherworldly, but Akhmatova approaches it with fondness and familiarity. The ugliness of modernity holds a morbid attraction for the Symbolists; Akhmatova prefers to see Petersburg's historical beauty. (p. 76)

It is the old Petersburg, the familiar Petersburg, the Petersburg of history which captures the imagination of the poet, not the modernity of the contemporary metropolis which so intrigued, in different ways, the Symbolists and the Futurists. . . .

Akhmatova is extremely receptive to the Petersburg mystique, to the great literary tradition and the rich and colorful cultural history of the city. Unlike the Symbolists, however, she does not proceed from mystique to mystery. Her direction is opposite, toward the simplicity and clarity of concrete images. While the grandeur and magnificence—and the malevolence—are deeply sensed, Akhmatova's predominant attitude is a familiar one, even proprietary. It is "my" city; "our" city. (p. 77)

Not only in the quick impressions of the cities of Russia does Akhmatova capture—often in one expressive and picturesque epithet—the feeling of her country, but also by the briefest suggestion she can convey the limitless expanse of rural Russia. (p. 82)

Akhmatova draws upon [the] earlier, richly colorful level of culture for much of her thematic material and imagery. . . . [A] constant backward glance toward Russia's cultural and historical past is necessary to the interpretation of many poems. (p. 83)

[There] are many *personae* in Akhmatova's poems. . . . Some seem almost identifiable with the poet herself, while others can be quite remote from the real person. It is true that an important and most interesting *persona* is the one in whom "there flows a drop of Novgorod blood, like a piece of ice in frothy wine," . . . and whose attitudes are fixed in the patterns of a rich cultural inheritance. It is nevertheless also true that the *persona* may appear as a fashionable lady in a feathered hat riding through the Bois de Boulogne, as a literary figure from the Bohemian world of pre-Revolutionary Petersburg; or as a provincial girl daydreaming in a hammock. She may be haughty or humble, forgiving or malicious, austere or frivolous—and to attempt to reconcile the many poetic persons is both unnecessary and misleading. (p. 84)

Akhmatova's cultural and historical imagery, which strikes her fellow-countrymen as extraordinarily "Russian," is not restricted to immediately recognizable national themes: the so-called "patriotic" poems about Russia in war or Revolution, the urban poetry with its peculiar blend of historical grandeur and lyrical emotion, or the relatively few poems which portray provincial Russia. Nor is this imagery represented principally by the motifs and devices borrowed from Russian folk poetry; her folk settings are always highly stylized and indicate poetic sophistication rather than some uncomplicated spiritual kinship with the Russian folk singer. While these elements in Akhmatova's poetry lend a specifically Russian flavor to many poems, it is the atti-

tudes and roles frequently given the *persona* which suggest most effectively the older, submerged level of Russian culture.

Frequently, for example, the heroine who has been cast aside by her lover is given the role of a homeless wanderer. If . . . the love motif and the imagery of the house are inseparably intertwined, the symbol of homelessness is a potent one in Akhmatova's poetry. (pp. 84-5)

The image of the weeping woman in Akhmatova's poetry is not a simple device to create sympathy for the heroine; if this were the case, a kind of commiseration would be achieved at best—and at worst, embarrassment on the part of the reader. The homeless, destitute wanderer meekly resigned to her fate must be seen in terms of Old Russian attitudes if her reactions are to be understood.

In Old Russian society, a prime virtue was charity. Its innocently unsophisticated interpretation was pity for the unfortunate. . . . (pp. 85-6)

By using the convention of attitudes drawn from the Russian past, Akhmatova is permitted an extraordinary compression in her poetry. Within a single couplet, she can suggest love lost, consequent renunciation of the world, and the life of a pilgrim or anchorite: "And long since have my lips / Not kissed, but they prophesy." . . . (p. 86)

[The] pattern of love lost, meek acceptance, complete forgiveness, rejection of home and worldly possessions, and ultimately an aimless wandering forms the basis for many of Akhmatova's poems. (p. 87)

[The] suggestion of a nun is inescapable among all these images of self-denial, renunciation of the world, triumphant suffering and poverty, humility, and meek resignation. What is remarkable is that Akhmatova keeps the suggestion a suggestion; the heroine is never cast in the role of a nun. (p. 89)

[Akhmatova's] vocabulary is rich in Biblical and liturgical words: chasubles, icons, King David, angels and archangels, incense, St. Eudoxia, crucifix. (p. 94)

When unmistakably religious imagery is employed, and even when Akhmatova makes use of Old Russian images of martyrdom, humility, poverty, pilgrimage, and so forth, it is obvious that the poet is expressing something quite different from religious sentiment. (pp. 95-6)

The majority of religious references . . . suggest a Russian society of earlier days, permeated with Orthodox expressions and symbols. (p. 97)

The Old Russian flavor of the religiosity Akhmatova employs in her imagery is complemented by the frequent evocation of ancient folk superstitions, which along with Orthodoxy were part and parcel of the Old Russian culture. In many poems, there is the suggestion of the folk *dvoeverie* ("double belief," that is, in both religion and superstition). . . .

For the most part, like the superficial elements of religiosity, superstition is part of the cultural pattern which colors Akhmatova's verse. At times, however, an awareness of supernatural phenomena seems to spring from a deeper level. When the poet adopts the role of prophetess, the quality of real superstitious belief is felt. (p. 98)

If Akhmatova draws on peasant traditions for many images, it is not surprising that she should also draw on the lyric genre of Russian folk songs. In Russian folk tradition, the lyric song is exclusively the women's genre. Its subject matter is very close to Akhmatova's own: the cruel husband, the unfaithful lover, the abandoned girl or wife. (pp. 99-100)

Akhmatova, however, was not a folk mannerist; that is to say, she did not attempt to create "folk poetry." She borrowed a few fixed forms from the tradition, a number of settings, images, symbols, but ignored the rigidly fixed rules of the genre. In most cases, the sophisticated, experimental poet can be seen through the colorful but inevitable pattern of the folk lyric. Her *Pesenka* is typical; the folk flavor of the song is inescapable, yet scarcely any of the rules of composition for such songs are followed—notably the syntactical parallelisms, in which a line or couplet is drawn from nature and the succeeding one describes the heroine; more importantly, the highly personal ending is entirely atypical of the folk genre. (p. 100)

[It is the single theme of love] which gives such an extraordinary unity to each of Akhmatova's volumes, and indeed, to the whole series of works published between 1912 and 1922. To Eykhenbaum, Akhmatova's poetry seemed "something like a long novel." The success of Akhmatova's extreme verbal economy depends in large part on the conventions she has gradually established in the "long novel"; many poems would be impossible to interpret fully without them. The unique motif, and the single point of view toward it, provide integration for countless disconnected secondary motifs, which may range widely from details of dress and interiors, through Russia's great cities, and endless open plains, through the history and culture of a people. (p. 102)

The sense of history is strong in Akhmatova. Not only do her fragile love lyrics evoke the great Russian past, but they are a kind of poetic chronicle of the cataclysmic events of the decade 1912-1922. If national reminiscence has become a major motif in Akhmatova's recent work, her poems of this fateful decade register directly her contemporary Edwardian world—and its total destruction. (p. 115)

Where historical and cultural impressions were in the early poems fused with the intensity of the lyrical moment, in later works the historical moment itself is often the source of the lyrical emotion. (p. 116)

The Seventh Book, representing the post-1940 period, shows many of the tendencies exhibited in one or the other of the long poems [*Requiem* or *Poem Without a Hero*]. The tendency to greater length is observed, for example in "Pre-History" (1945), which is one of Akhmatova's most successful later poems; and there is a trend toward length in the grouping of shorter poems into discreet cycles.

In the poems of greater length, too, there is a tendency to draw on the general, European cultural and literary traditions, rather than the almost strictly Russian associations characteristic of much of the earlier poetry. Together with this there is a greater intellectual weight than Akhmatova chose to give the early works. (p. 118)

In the sense of history and time, *Poem Without a Hero* is the most comprehensive, and any discussion of Akhmatova's later poetry must include some commentary on at least the nature of this remarkable work. It is a puzzling one. . . .

It is a private poem, a laying to rest of old ghosts, an exorcism of present terrors, a catharsis. (p. 119)

Also puzzling is the very construction of the poem. "The Petersburg Tale" is a complete work in itself, and in itself, beautifully structured. The next two parts, however, seem to have only tangential relationships with it and with each other. (p. 120)

[What Akhmatova creates in *Poem Without a Hero*] is her sense of the time—the feeling of apprehension, impermanence and unreality. The "characters" are shades and shades of shades, masks, mirror images, portraits stepping from their frames, figures perhaps glimpsed in darkened windows. It is a shadow-play, a "hellish harlequinade," a "Hoffmaniana"—a Symbolist's, not an Acmeist's Petersburg. The ghosts of the past swarm unbidden before the poet and are finally laid to rest. The "Petersburg Tale" is ended. (p. 122)

The "Epilogue," or Part III, returns to Peter's city, this time in the present (1942), when Leningrad lay in ruins and Akhmatova was far away from it—evacuated during the siege to Tashkent. The "Epilogue" is dedicated "To My City," and begins with a farewell to it. As the Russian army fell back before the German offensive it seemed that all Russia was going into exile.

Although Akhmatova continued work on the *Poem* for another twenty years, it is at this indecisive historical moment that she fixed for the ending of the "Epilogue": an open point in time, with no finality such as the end of the war or the return to Leningrad. The sense is not of history past, but of time in an unending continuum. (pp. 124-25)

This suspension, rather than the finality of a different kind of conclusion, may be unsatisfying, but it suits Akhmatova's purpose in her new conception of time.

> As the future ripens in the past,
> So does the past moulder in the future.

These lines, which are central to the *Poem Without a Hero,* might serve as an epigraph for a collection of the later poems, including the other major work undertaken in that same year of 1940: *Requiem.*

Unlike the *Poem Without a Hero, Requiem* is not a private poem. It is not so much a new experiment in Akhmatova's poetry as a culmination of a style perfected over the decades preceding; Akhmatova organizes her characteristic devices and techniques into an amazingly powerful statement which requires no elaboration or "explanation."

Neither is the *Requiem* a private poem in the sense that the subject, unlike that of the "Petersburg Tale," is immediately accessible to anyone with a knowledge of Russia's recent history—and all too well-known to those who lived in Russia during the late 1930's. The poem is, if not private, deeply personal: but Akhmatova is able to generalize her own shattering experience into an epic cry for her people. (p. 125)

[The] structural divisions in the poem are quite complex. There is the prose "In Place of an Introduction," a dedication, a poetic "Introduction," and then a series of ten lyrical poems, not directly related to one another, and employing a variety of styles and moods, but each representing a step in a progression which replaces the usual poetic narrative. The two epilogues follow, returning from the lyric to

the epic stance of the "Dedication" and "Introduction."
. . .

From the general and epic tone of the prefatory pieces, the first poem of the cycle shifts to the specific and individual, a short lyric with the distinctive marks of Akhmatova's style. . . . (p. 127)

After a complete emotional break in Akhmatova's poems, we have come to expect a quick return to calm. In the early lyrics, it is often the calm of resignation, or that brought on by force of will. In the later poetry, there is the suggestion of an unnatural calm, a calm that is not quite sane. It is as though the mind, to protect itself, loses touch with reality and its unbearable grief. The tendency in some early poems for the *persona* to stand aside and apparently observe herself as a separate person is even more marked in the later poetry. Here, the separation can become complete. (p. 129)

For the central poem in her long work, Akhmatova chooses restraint where one might expect a complete breakdown or histrionics. . . .

In "The Sentence," however, there is extreme understatement, a simple, workaday vocabulary and tone. It is not simply epic calm in the face of tragedy, or a kind of resignation and acceptance. The intensity of the moment is increased many times by the pathetic effort of the will to overcome a grief that borders on madness.

In the context of all Akhmatova's poetry up to this point, the poet's very own familiar devices and symbols, already perfected in less tragic days, lend an extraordinary pathos. The conversational tone, the stone imagery, the suggestion of clairvoyance, the peculiar use of bright/radiant, the pervasive symbol of the empty or abandoned house—all these things were once, after all, the stock-in-trade of the "gay little sinner of Tsarskoe Selo." Their reappearance here subtly compounds the emotional charge of this "restrained" lyric. (p. 131)

It is early in time for any attempt at a final assessment of Akhmatova's work, or for trying to define her place in the history of Russian poetry. Her influence—and example—continue as a productive force in the poetry of some of Russia's most outstanding young poets. Among them is a small group which was very close to Akhmatova during the last decade of her life. It is therefore quite possible that Akhmatova may one day be recognized not only for her own work, but also as a direct link between what has been called the "Silver Age" of Russian poetry and another flowering of Russian verse. (p. 133)

> *Sam N. Driver, in his* Anna Akhmatova *(copyright 1972 by Twayne Publishers, Inc.; reprinted with the permission of Twayne Publishers, A Division of G. K. Hall & Co., Boston), Twayne, 1972.*

JOHN FULLER

The 'I' of [Akhmatova's] poems is without egotism, though autobiography is her natural medium. How can we fail to be moved by the story of the victimisation, silence and persistence of a poet who loved her country but not the revolution? Her work survives on memory ('Flaubert, insomnia, the smell of lilacs') as Eliot's does, and it is a poetry of that social class. Indeed, Acmeism has clear affinities with Imagism. But unlike H. D., Akhmatova's perspective is stoical and humanistic. She too appeals for the preservation of her language, but in her case it is so that it may be 'fit for

the songs of our children's children, / pure on their tongues, and free'. She too writes of the London blitz, but typically evokes not Karnak but Shakespearean tragedy. (pp. 230-31)

> *John Fuller, in* New Statesman *(© 1974 The Statesman & Nation Publishing Co. Ltd.), February 15, 1974.*

JOHN BAYLEY

Akhmatova was a very unselfconscious poet in many ways; she had qualities of elemental force, utterance haunted and Delphic; yet these went together with elegance and sophistication, even a certain kind of mirror-gazing and a cunning which is *chétif,* or, as the Russians say *zloi.* She is not in the least like Blake or Eliot, and yet those are the English poets—different as they are—who offer some sort of parallel with her finest work. The incongruity in coupling such names shows how exceptional is her own poetic being. . . .

Strangely enough she has as a poet more in common with what are—in a degraded form—Soviet ideals: restraint, correctness, propriety. Her poetry is dignified in the grandest sense without pretending to dignity, an equivalent in art of what she called the severe and shapely spirit of Russian orthodoxy. . . .

The role of conscience in her poetry reminds us how unfamiliar such a possession is to most poets, whose natural tendency in the Nietzschean and modern era is to say that "such as I cast out remorse". She was deeply religious, and religion—as Dr Johnson noted—does not come over in poetry, but conscience, its precursor and attendant, can and does.

It figures largely, and strangely, in *Poem Without a Hero,* whose title itself suggests the collapse of a Nietzschean world in which men of action, or the hero as poet and seer, could play a part. Its denizens, including Blok, including the poet herself, are in one sense poor creatures, not the heroic figures into whom an intense vision of the past transmutes so many. For this is a poem about remorse, and about a past "in which the future is rotting".

Thus although it is arbitrary to attach a single life and its interior shaping, as Akhmatova does, to the ordeal of Russia in the revolution, to the years of terror and invasion, the theme of remorse—for one and for all—unites these things as they could not have been united in any artificial poem in which such events were directly lamented or celebrated. . . .

Poem Without a Hero was more than twenty years in the writing, and appeared to the poet, during that time, as a recurrent and inescapable malady. On its smaller scale *The Waste Land* had the same characteristic of a visitation, painful to suffer, more painful to evade. And another phenomenon is significantly true of both poems: they derive their status from the reality of the *fait accompli.* Though critics may seek to demonstrate after the event their underlying "unity" and so forth, such poems only now seem so inevitable and so public because they made a total success of being so private and so arbitrary.

As might be expected of Akhmatova, however, *Poem Without a Hero* is extremely literal, as concerned with place and event as a Hardy poem, and closely connected to the poet's life in pre-war St Petersburg. . . . Her poetry at this time has an unstylized purity, sometimes simplistic, absorbed in what might be called the moral nature of things, and assuming its own kind of confidence from them. (p. 450)

Akhmatova calls [*Poem Without a Hero*] a Chinese box "with a triple base", and its numerological patterning is as complex as its references to real people, events, works of art. But it is essentially a voice poem, in that tradition which Pushkin stylized in the figure of the "Improvisatore" in *Egyptian Nights*, who denies any idea of how complex verse comes to him suddenly, rhymed and in regular feet, so that it can be instantly declaimed. Like so many Russian masterpieces the poem has the form of an open secret, at once spontaneous and enigmatic. (p. 451)

> *John Bayley, "Fury and Elegance," in* The Times Literary Supplement *(© Times Newspapers Ltd. (London) 1976; reproduced from* The Times Literary Supplement *by permission), April 16, 1976, pp. 450-51.*

*   *   *

ALBEE, Edward   1928-

Albee, an American dramatist, poet, and novelist, has also adapted several novels for the stage. An innovative stylist, he emerged in the 1960s as one of the most important figures in contemporary drama. His plays are noted for their powerful and brilliant language and reveal a fine sense of dramatic tension. Thematically, Albee is concerned with the sense of alienation and loneliness inherent in modern life. He was twice the recipient of the Pulitzer Prize in Drama. (See also CLC, Vols. 1, 2, 3, 5, 9, and Contemporary Authors, Vols. 5-8, rev. ed.)

RICHARD SCHECHNER

Albee gratifies an adolescent culture which likes to think of itself as decadent.

We want to believe that we are living in the last days, that the world is falling in on our heads, that only our sickest illusions are able to offer us any reason for living. Everyone wants to be Nero watching Rome burn. To attend the last orgy, to be part of it, this is a comfortable and exciting escape from reality—the child's way out. Albee's characters, like the playwright himself, suffer from arrested development. They play the game of decadence, just as he plays the game of creativity. There is no real, hard bedrock of suffering in *Virginia Woolf*—it is all illusory, depending upon a "child" who never was born: a gimmick, a trick, a trap. And there is no solid creative suffering in the writer who meanders through a scene stopping here and there for the sake of a joke or an easy allusion that *almost* fits.

But even more, the values of *Virginia Woolf* are perverse and dangerous. Self-pity, drooling, womb-seeking weakness, the appeal to a transcendent "god" who is no God, the persistent escape into morbid fantasy—all these things are probably too close to our *imagined* picture of ourselves. It is the game of the child who thinks he is being persecuted, who dreams up all kinds of outrages, and who concludes finally that his parents found him one day on the doorstep. Albee wants us to indulge in this same game, this cheap hunt for love; he wants us to point to the stage and simper: "Oooo, there we are! How pitiable, how terrible!" The danger is that Albee may succeed; we are on the verge of becoming the silly role we are playing. (p. 63)

Albee makes dishonesty a virtue, perversion a joke, adul-

tery a simple party game. In honest play-writing if man is mocked he is mocked before God, before the human condition; in Albee's play man is mocked before Oswald Spengler. Sartre once described the life of bad faith as a living lie —of actually believing an untruth and then acting on that false belief. Albee is not conscious of his own phoniness, nor of the phoniness of his work. But he has posed so long that his pose has become part of the fabric of his creative life; he *is* his own lie. If *Virginia Woolf* is a tragedy it is of that unique kind rarely seen: a tragedy which transcends itself, a tragedy which is bad theatre, bad literature, bad taste—but which *believes* its own lies with such conviction that it indicts the society which creates it and accepts it. *Virginia Woolf* is a ludicrous play; but the joke is on all of us. (pp. 63-4)

Virginia Woolf is doubtlessly a classic: a classic example of bad taste, morbidity, plotless naturalism, misrepresentation of history, American society, philosophy, and psychology. There is in the play an ineluctable urge to escape reality and its concomitant responsibilities by crawling back into the womb, or bathroom, or both. . . .

We must not ignore what Albee represents and portends, either for our theatre or for our society. The lie of his work is the lie of our theatre and the lie of America. The lie of decadence must be fought. (p. 64)

> *Richard Schechner, "Who's Afraid of Edward Albee?" in* The Tulane Drama Review *(copyright, © 1963, The Tulane Drama Review), Spring, 1963 (and reprinted in* Edward Albee: A Collection of Critical Essays, *edited by C.W.E. Bigsby, Prentice-Hall, Inc., 1975, pp. 62-5).*

ALAN SCHNEIDER

Without attempting to enthrone Albee alongside anyone (though I personally admire him above all other Americans now writing for the stage), or to hail *Virginia Woolf* as a classic of the modern theatre (which I have no doubt it will become), I would only state that, in my experience, a more honest or moral (in the true sense) playwright does not exist —unless it be Samuel Beckett. To blame Albee for the "sickness" of his subject matter is like blaming the world's ashcans on the creator of Nagg and Nell—which has been done [Schneider is referring to an essay by Richard Schechner; see excerpt above]. And if what Albee is doing is giving us a "sentimentalized" view of ourselves rather than one as harshly and starkly unsentimental as any I know, why didn't those theatre party ladies buy it up ahead of time as they do all those other technicolor postcards which pass for plays? Or is Albee not rather dedicated to smashing that rosy view, shocking us with the truth of our present-day behavior and thought, striving to purge us into an actual confrontation with reality? Anyone who has read any portion of any play he has ever written surely must sense the depth of his purpose and recognize, to some extent, the power of the talent which is at his disposal; certainly no intelligent, aware individual today can fail to recognize somewhere in Albee's characters and moods the stirring of his own viscera, the shadow of his own self-knowledge.

If the child in *Virginia Woolf* is merely a "gimmick," then so is the wild duck, the cherry orchard, that streetcar with the special name, even our old elusive friend Godot. But Albee's play is not about the child—just as *Godot* is not about Godot but about the waiting for him—but about the people who have had to create him as a "beanbag" or crutch for their own insufficiencies and failures, and now are left to find their own way, if there is to be a way, free of him. If truth and illusion are not exactly original themes, any more than they were for O'Neill, the test is not *what* but *how* and how specifically the writer illuminates the immediacy of human life. If Albee's particular choice is more lacking in plot than our editor wishes, its reality is based upon a classic simplicity, a contemporary feeling unmatched in our theatre, a musical economy—in spite of its length—and an ability to hold and shatter his audience.

What baffles me is why the Editor is making such a fuss. . . . Would the American theatre be better off, would it be less voracious, corrupt, morally blind, and perverse, had the play never been written or presented? (pp. 67-8)

That *The Tulane Drama Review* is against the voracity and hypocrisy of Broadway has always been evident—till now. And when a play which, like it or not as you will, is serious, literate, individual in style, ablaze with talent, and written without concern for Broadway values (it was originally intended for off-Broadway); when such a play is presented with taste and economy, without abdicating to the star-system, the theatre-party system, the fancy-advertising system; when the combined talents of a remarkable cast working together in a way Broadway casts rarely do serve to lift the work to "success" over the normal run of machine-made mediocrities which reign supreme in our commercial theatre, it seems to me cause for rejoicing rather than wailing and gnashing of teeth. . . .

It is possible, as the Editor says, that *Who's Afraid of Virginia Woolf?* is "bad theatre, bad literature, bad taste"; it is also at least equally possible that it is good theatre, good literature, good taste. Only time will tell. (p. 68)

> *Alan Schneider, "Why So Afraid?" in* The Tulane Drama Review (*copyright,* © *1963, The Tulane Drama Review*), *Spring, 1963 (and reprinted in* Edward Albee: A Collection of Critical Essays, *edited by C.W.E. Bigsby, Prentice-Hall, Inc., 1975, pp. 66-8).*

JOHN SIMON

The origin of Edward Albee's *Tiny Alice* seems to be the old homosexual joke about the identity of God, whose punch line is "Actually, she is black." Since, however, it is no longer safe socially, let alone financially, to be jocular about Negroes, the God of *Tiny Alice* is, outwardly at least, white. But she is a bitch. (pp. 62-3)

It has been contended that *Tiny Alice* is based on Manichaeanism, or on Genet's notions of evil being good, and good evil. Accordingly, Alice may be God, or the devil, or both in one; she may also be anything one wants her to be (the lawyer explains that we do not get what we want but want what we get); or she may not be at all. (p. 63)

The time, place and duration of the action are left deliberately vague, with contradictory hints about each; the concentric castles, moreover, are supposed to suggest worlds within worlds, each repeating the other. Typically, Albee has already instructed us to enjoy ourselves without trying to understand, but that we can do just as well without seeing the play, if not better. . . .

Tiny Alice fails as symbolism because of its inconsistency and incredibility on the literal level; without firm footing in

literalness, there is no working metaphor—just as without viable dramatic characters, there are no compelling symbols. But the work fails also as pure fantasy, because it lacks even that homogeneity that lends dreams, hallucinations and fairy tales their own kind of logic. . . . Above all, if we were to follow Albee's jesuitic advice, and merely let the play envelop us and wash over us, how would we cope with the gritty nodules of realism and grating dialectical rugosities that refuse to dissolve in the bath water?

Even hostile critics, however, have joined Albee in admiring his play's language—he went so far as to insist on English actors as alone capable of doing justice to his linguistic demands. Actually, the language leaves much to be desired. Thus Albee uses "replica" for both enlargement and miniature, though it can mean only exact duplication. We are given "removed people" for remote or withdrawn, "quixotic" for perverse or capricious. (p. 64)

But the awkwardness is not limited to words alone. Some scenes—almost all of act three, in fact—are so attenuated as to float off before our very eyes into nothingness; others, like the conclusion of act two, are crammed so full as to fall resoundingly flat. (p. 65)

There is, moreover, a homosexual strain running through *Tiny Alice*, but remaining just barely supraliminal and certainly unintegrated; it thus adds considerably to the general confusion. The butler and the lawyer address each other as darling and dearest, there is much hinting about the cardinal's and Julian's being "buddies," the sexuality of the play is largely oral, and there is throughout that suggestive waspishness that characterizes many homosexual relationships. . . . Is all this relevant to the main theme or not? Or is it, perhaps, the main theme? Is the whole play a piece of camp metaphysics or metaphysical camping?

A line in *Tiny Alice* about "the same mysteries, the evasions, the perfect plot" describes not only the play but also the stratagems surrounding it and the utterances of Albee and his associates concerning it. (pp. 65-6)

It may be that Albee is the victim of self-delusion and genuinely thinks that he has made a meaningful statement. It seems at least as likely that he is being a *fumiste*, giving vent to his scorn for the great washed. But neither private masturbation nor public provocation is in itself so dramatically adequate that it can dispense with significant form. (p. 66)

> *John Simon, "'Tiny Alice'" (1965), in his* Uneasy Stages: A Chronicle of the New York Theater, 1963-1973 (*copyright* © *1975 by John Simon; reprinted by permission of Random House, Inc.*), *Random House, 1976, pp. 62-6.*

JOHN SIMON

If Albee were not so arrogant, one would view his desperate stratagems with pity. When you have failed with every kind of play, including adaptations of novels and other people's plays, the last remaining maneuver is the nonplay. Finding himself in a box, Albee has contrived two interlocking nonplays, based, apparently, on a mathematical error: it is by multiplying, not by adding, minuses that you get a plus. *Box* and *Quotations from Chairman Mao Tsetung*, when run together like two ink blots of different colors, raise the Rorschach test to new dramatic heights. (p. 157)

Rather than as a fugue, the exercise struck me as a piece of vocal *cadavre exquis,* without even the amusing *trouvailles* bequeathed by chance on that famous surrealist parlor game. One can perhaps extract some quasi-meanings (like teeth from a toothless mouth): the commonplaces of communism vs. the banalities of the bourgeoisie; the parallel miseries of the rich and the poor; the shibboleths of Mao's gospel vs. the silences of the man of God. But these are not so much legitimate explications as counsels of despair. In a fugue, in any case, there is development. Here, once the quartet is visually and vocally presented, there is nowhere to go. (p. 158)

We get the same ambitious, artificial, circumlocutory prose Albee keeps elaborating in his later, sterile works. It consists of false starts, emendations, indirections, apologies, and general syntactic deviousness. One guesses that Albee imagines this to be some wonderful cross between Beckett and Joyce; in fact, it is a barren, puerile mannerism. It suggests a kind of doddering pedantry that Albee might attribute to a particular character—if it were not so often out of character.... And always that pathetic intellectual climbing of the (insufficiently) self-educated: "They didn't know who Trollope was!—that is a life for you," complains the LWL, and one winces for Albee. For behind such outcries we have come to recognize the genteel author's feelings of superiority over, and especially *against,* the unwashed that surround him, or that he chooses to surround himself with. (pp. 158-59)

But suppose it were the character that is being ridiculed. So much the worse for play and playwright; it would mean that they are suffering from delusions of being Beckett, who alone can get away with this sort of thing by virtue of much greater sensitivity to words and to the essential foibles of human nature. (p. 159)

As for Albee, where does he go from here? He could perhaps eliminate the third dimension from his box, or have us sit in a voiceless dark. We'll get to the grass roots of theater yet, even if it means burrowing underground like a mole. (p. 160)

> *John Simon, "'Box' and 'Quotations from Chairman Mao Tse-Tung'" (1968-69), in his* Uneasy Stages: A Chronicle of the New York Theater, 1963-1973 *(copyright © 1975 by John Simon; reprinted by permission of Random House, Inc.), Random House, 1976, pp. 157-60.*

ROBBIE ODOM MOSES

All Over confronts, as the title suggests, the endemic trait of all living organisms. Death, the great leveler to a poet like William Cullen Bryant, is, for Albee, man's final confrontation with life. In the play, death is tantamount to a metaphysical conceit, with the death of the body being but one thematic strain. The famous man, whose dying is both a public event for the press and the crowd awaiting word of his demise, and a private ritual for the circle of intimates assembled for the vigil, is the instrument through which Albee explores some issues attendant to dying and death. The age at which a person becomes aware of death is an idea examined that is important to the development of psychological maturity. Knowing her husband as a thorough man with almost as much knowledge about law as Best Friend, Wife forces the lawyer into a deeper meaning of death when she dismisses fifteen, "the age we all become philosophers," as the age when he became aware of per-

sonal extinction: "No, no, when you were aware of it for yourself, when you knew you were at the top of the roller-coaster ride, when you knew half of it was probably over and you were on your *way* to it.'' ... (p. 67)

The modern tendency to dehumanize death is another issue broached in the play. The man's removal from the hospital to his former residence, Mistress relates, occurred in obedience to his instructed need to die in familiar surroundings.... (p. 68)

Besides confronting basic issues dealing with death and portraying encounters with the experience of death, Albee's *All Over* exposes a more insidious kind of death. In the play, Mistress' relation of her lover's objection to the use of the verb "to be" in connection with death is no mere semantic indulgence on the part of the playwright. Her report of their conversation provides valuable insights into Albee's concern with death:

> He put down his fork, one lunch, at *my* house ... what had we been talking about? Maeterlinck and that plagiarism business, I seem to recall, and we had done with that and we were examining our salads, when all at once he said to me "I wish people wouldn't say that other people 'are dead.'" I asked him why, as much as anything to know what had turned him to it, and he pointed out that the verb to be was not, to his mind, appropriate to a state of ... non-being. That one cannot ... *be* dead. He said his objection was a quirk—that the grammarians would scoff—but that one could be dying, or have died ... but could not ... be ... dead. ...

Death in this play encompasses those who have died, those who are dying, and those who *are* dead to life. Albee's deathbed scene shares traits that Carla Gottlieb has found to be characteristic of twentieth-century paintings interpreting death by depicting the deceased in the background with the survivors occupying the foreground, and by showing the participants turned away from the dead person and from one another. "Faced with death," Gottlieb concludes, "the family bonds fall apart, revealing their superficial character." In *All Over,* death is a mirror reflecting family ties built upon rancor, resentment, and rivalry. (pp. 73-4)

Long before the dying man expires, rigor mortis has overtaken the attendants. Although the names of the characters represent human relationships, they also signify in this play a cessation of growth. Receiving identity only through their relationship with the dying man, they have become rigid in their unchanging roles. (p. 74)

On one level, the death of the Husband-Father-Lover-Best Friend in *All Over* is the climax to a death watch characterized by friction and hostility among the enlarged family preoccupied with recollections of deaths and dying. On another level, the play uses death as a mirror reflecting the extent of life within the survivors. For Albee, death, then, is a metaphor for the quality of life. The irony in this play is that there is more life in the dead man than in the survivors. If all reports are true, the dying man exhibits a healthy attitude toward death that reflects a genuine, loving assumption of the moral condition.... Death, in *All Over,* is a measurement of life. (p. 76)

Robbie Odom Moses, "Death as a Mirror of Life: Edward Albee's 'All Over'," in Modern Drama *(copyright © 1976, University of Toronto, Graduate Centre for Study of Drama; with the permission of* Modern Drama*), March, 1976, pp. 67-77.*

THOMAS P. ADLER

Counting the Ways is hardly even a play in any traditional understanding of the term. But then, Albee's works have come more and more of late to resemble musical compositions, and this is no exception; as he says of it: "What I intended was something like a set of piano pieces by Satie."

If in *Seascape,* his most recent full-length play, there was still a conflict eventuating in one of Albee's typical highly charged climaxes, here one can just barely discern the outlines of a conflict, and certainly nothing resembling a resolution. The movement (not progression, mind you) of this two-character play is circular: at the opening, She demands, "Do you love me?"—the same question He puts at the end.

The work's subtitle, "A Vaudeville," indicates what the audience should expect: a series of skits, or turns, twenty or so. . . . Several of these brief scenes, which more than one London critic aptly compared to animated *New Yorker* or Thurber cartoons, are duets, some—including a memorable one about the time She received twin gardenia corsages for a dance—are monologues, while at least one is wordless. . . .

He and She, who resemble a sketchier but slightly more hopeful Tobias and Agnes from *A Delicate Balance,* pursue the author's recurrent concerns in an appropriately wistful mood: the death of sexual ardor (they have exchanged their double bed for twins); the waning of culture and civilization; the advancing existential void. But mostly, it is about the difficulty—the impossibility—of "counting the ways," of telling how we love, or even that we love, now that the words we have for expressing things of the heart have been so debased that they appear no more honest than the shopworn formulas on greeting cards. Yet Albee's own poetic dialogue runs the same risk, and cannot always avoid seeming too studied, too precious. (p. 407)

A major dramatic work like *Who's Afraid of Virginia Woolf?* or *A Delicate Balance*? Hardly. Destined to be a commercial or critical success? Never. And yet, accepted on its own terms, this entertaining "diversion"—for that seems an apt classification—can delight with its considerable charm and wit and occasional beauties of language. (pp. 407-08)

Thomas P. Adler, in Educational Theatre Journal *(© 1977 University College Theatre Association of the American Theatre Association), October, 1977.*

JOAN S. FLECKENSTEIN

Listening, a play with more substance, cohesiveness, and bite [than *Counting the Ways*], concerns three characters who meet in a garden to exchange insights, reminiscences, and insults until one of them, who is insane, commits suicide. Although sounding some echoes of *The Zoo Story* (an apparently insane person elicits truth from an apparently sane one and then dies), *Listening* slowly, painstakingly, and with some surprises uncovers powerful and revealing

relationships while playing with the nuance and pretense of language. Indeed, it is the play's emphasis on language that creates both its strengths and its weaknesses.

Listening begins with the extended, solitary musings of a man who wonders about the garden's history, purpose, and effect, thereby suggesting that the setting has some significance. Once the "trimmed and clipped" setting for flirtations and assignations, now a quiet refuge at an institution, it will become the site for the exploration of three souls. The opening speech, however, due to its repetitiveness of phrase and rhythm, seems contrived, and this sense of contrivance straining for significance increases as the characters repeat certain lines, echoing, reiterating, magnifying meaning. But the lines are ordinary (the most repeated is "You're not listening") and their meaning obvious. Thus, although their repetition suggests pregnant significance about to give birth to symbol, that significance never appears.

Misdirected to symbol-searching, one is further misled by an offstage voice which sequentially announces the numbers one through twenty, apparently to emphasize certain moments of the play. But these emphasized moments are also obscure. There appears to be an inadvertent irony resulting in *Listening*—a play which exposes pretense and delusion is pretentious in some of its devices. (p. 408)

Joan S. Fleckenstein, in Educational Theatre Journal *(© 1977 University College Theatre Association of the American Theatre Association), October, 1977.*

*   *   *

AUDEN, W(ystan) H(ugh)   1907-1973

An Anglo-American poet, essayist, playwright, critic, editor, librettist, scriptwriter, and translator, Auden has exerted a major influence on the poetry of the twentieth century. His poetry centers around moral issues, and evidences Auden's strong political, social, and psychological orientation. The teachings of Marx and Freud weigh heavily in his early work, but later give way to religious and spiritual influences. Auden was an antiromantic, a poet of analytical clarity. He sought for order, for universal patterns of human existence. For this reason, some of his work has been criticized as overly detached and facile. Auden's poetry is versatile and inventive, ranging from the tersely epigrammatic to book-length verse, and incorporating his vast scientific knowledge. He has collaborated with Christopher Isherwood and Louis MacNeice, and has joined with Chester Kallman to create libretti for works by Benjamin Britten, Stravinsky, and Mozart. He received the Pulitzer Prize in Poetry in 1948, and the National Book Award in 1956. (See also *CLC*, Vols. 1, 2, 3, 4, 6, 9, and *Contemporary Authors*, Vols. 9-12, rev. ed.; obituary, Vols. 45-48.)

ROBERT BLOOM

The various characteristics that [Randall Jarrell in his essay "Changes of Attitude and Rhetoric in Auden's Poetry," see *CLC*, Vol. 2] lists in order to describe the style of 1930 —so many of them involving ellipsis: the omission of articles, demonstrative adjectives, subjects, conjunctions, relative pronouns, auxiliary verbs—form a language of extremity and urgency. Like telegraphese, with which it has sometimes been compared, it has time and patience only for the most important words in the most kinetic, if not the best, order. . . . Behind this linguistic urgency lies Auden's sense of the immense peril in which the whole human enterprise stands as the hour comes round for a decaying civilization either to renew itself or die. Man, the evolutionary adventurer in Auden's biological-political- economic-psychological-social, Darwinian-Marxist-Freudian universe, must either move forward, or destroy himself, or both. The stripped, laconic language of those early poems is nicely calculated to convey this extremity and imperative without limiting the scope, the universality of reference. Auden deals easily in this stark style with men in general, where a more fully articulated syntax might involve him in the shades and modulations of the particular and the peripheral.

Auden's shift to the "rhetorical" mode a decade later is, among other things, a humanization of his style—an attempt to bring the modulated, civilized life of urban man more closely to bear on the language and feeling of his poems, a readiness to place all things as closely and vividly in relation to particularized human experience as possible. . . . Again and again the adjectives, far from being [in Jarrell's words] "abstract," "critical," "technical," and "nonpoetic," assign or withhold human capacities, dispositions, or valuations to or from non-human nouns, so that in effect we have a traditional anthropocentric poetic device wielded by a far-reaching, audacious, but fastidious imagination—a kind of Pathetic Fallacy by Incongruity or Denial: "the shining neutral summer"; "a new imprudent year"; "the small uncritical islands"; "the rare ambiguous monster"; "weep the non-attached angels"; "the hot incurious sun"; and "the undiscriminating sea." The measure, in each case, is man, and the dominant effect is not so much abstraction as animation. (p. 446)

Auden's intent, even in the examples that Jarrell quotes, is to flesh out his abstractions with that touch of the mundane, the outrageous, the incorrigible which brings them alive and kicking into the human fold. . . . (p. 447)

[The] type, or trait, or differentiating characteristic is often a human quality, and . . . the classes and categories that Auden creates in this way are often composed of human beings who share that quality. In *Another Time,* these examples occur:

> As a rule
> It was the pleasure-haters who became unjust. . . .

> . . . among the Just
> Be just, among the Filthy filthy too. . . .

So used, the definite article makes a demand on our powers of recognition and validation; it assumes the existence of a class whose reality we consent to in the very act of learning that it exists. As a result Auden has us trafficking heavily in the ascription and distribution of quantities of human stuff undergoing reordering. A poem like "Spain 1937" in *Another Time* . . . , with its extensive lists of the human activities, each preceded by its definite article, which are meant cumulatively to represent the whole of the human past, along with a somewhat derogatory hypothesis about the whole of the human future, depends heavily on some such power of recognition and consent in the reader. . . . "Spain 1937," however, calls for a more subtle response as well. Its refrain, "But to-day the struggle," which . . . occurs frequently throughout the whole poem, makes its own demand for recognition; indeed, if the poem is to succeed at all, "*the* struggle" must be more deeply apprehended and

subscribed to than anything else in it, and much of this actuality and consent must be accomplished by the definite article, with its presumption of a known and significant undertaking. . . . There is . . . a hierarchy of realities and recognitions governed, to some degree, by the proposing and disposing of the definite article. (pp. 447-48)

The periphrases that Auden often uses when he alludes to the great in the poems of the middle period invariably introduce us to a human being caught in the toils, relations, and achievements of his life rather than to a mere abstract, impersonal, celebrated name. Instead of simply designating "Dante," Auden speaks of "That lean hard-bitten pioneer / Who spoiled a temporal career / And to the supernatural brought / His passion, senses, will and thought . . .". . . . The device eschews the primitive pleasure in naming, with its delusion of mastery of the thing named, and substitutes for it the more civilized pleasure of knowing, experiencing, and valuing. Or, to view it another way, it allows for a renaming in more personal, intimate, unique terms. The flatly generalized emotive adjectives that are at the opposite pole from those that Auden sets in incongruous juxtapositions with their nouns—"lovely," "marvelous," "wonderful," "lucky"—allow him to deal in those states of feeling that are familiar enough to all men so that they can safely be pointed to rather than enacted, or presented, or evoked. Coming as they do from out of some *Spiritus Mundi* of the feelings, they manifest a shared humanity that Auden counts on. . . . Those similes "blunt, laconic, and prosaic enough to be startling" are yet another way of dealing with this order of common experience; by juxtaposing two unrelated kinds of ordinariness, Auden creates the incongruity that is a root principle of his work in the period. . . . (p. 448)

Exciting and original as [the poems of the early thirties] unquestionably were when they first appeared, one suspects that at least a part of Auden's early triumph was extraliterary, as that of any real or assumed spokesman of the left would inevitably be in a time of widespread political, social, and economic discontent. For all of their urgency about the plight of man in a decadent, depressed capitalist culture, Auden's Hopkinsesque, Anglo-Saxon, elliptical eccentricities are today a little stony and, sometimes, odd just beyond their need to be odd. . . . The contorted or abbreviated syntax is often effective, but sometimes results in an exaggeration rather than an intensification of feeling, as it does, occasionally, in Hopkins himself. And, as with Hopkins, the impenetrability into which the style tends to spill over is too high a price to pay, even for intensity. . . . [Even in "Doom is dark and deeper than any sea-dingle," an incontestable triumph of Auden's elliptical style,] we may observe another aspect of this early idiom which should give pause to the critic with a thoroughly twentieth-century sensibility, if artificiality and obscurity do not. The very bareness of the language creates an air of the abstract, the representative, the nakedly archetypal. Where Auden's heavy reliance on the definite article in his middle period often obligates him to begin with the concrete and particular before he can generalize it into a class—"the Filthy," "the pleasure-haters"—the essentially article-less style of the early period encourages a pervasive referential typicality. The fine poem in question—and it is no less fine, certainly, for this—offers us an Everyman of the Generalized Quest moving through a Universal Landscape of the Strange, the Lonely, and the Intimidating. . . . (pp. 449-50)

[*Look, Stranger!* (1936) reveals] the movement toward a rational lucidity of surface. . . . The time is as unpromising as ever—more so now that Fascism is consolidating itself by successfully exploiting the economic depression—but there is a new willingness in Auden to face its dangers and failures directly in an open, reflective, reasoned, fully syntactic speech rather than cower before them in the gnomic, archaic, ominous mannerisms and fantasies of many of the early poems. In *Look Stranger!* Auden has left behind forever the grunts of a Hopkinsesque-Eliotic sibyl and allowed a full-throated, implicated, moving human voice to emerge —a voice concerned not with extravagance or exaggeration, but with facing the truth and accounting for it. (p. 450)

The presiding presence now is Yeats, rather than Langland, Skelton, or Hopkins—the Yeats who steadfastly refused to surrender traditional syntax in the face of the Symbolist poetics that carried the French late nineteenth and the Anglo-American early twentieth century day, and who used it instead to fashion an elevated meditative style capable of dealing with this world while it suggested knowledge of another. . . . Auden catches this eloquent, personal, manly idiom in a number of the important poems in *Look, Stranger!* . . . (pp. 450-51)

This style allows Auden to comment and reflect on public events from a personal standpoint without suffering the earlier melodramatic fantasized involvement of Airman, Spy, or Scoutmaster. The shift is from a dream of participation in 1930—"Leave for Cape Wrath tonight"—to a reasoned desire to extend his knowledge of and sympathy for humanity without blinking incompatibilities. . . .

If Yeats is the source of one form of eloquence in *Look, Stranger!*, there is another form which owes nothing to anyone. Lofty, hieratic, even vatic, its syntactic sweep and complexity are a kind of spiritual affirmation of the capacity and promise of man. (p. 451)

There are a number of other triumphant stylistic innovations as well in *Look, Stranger!*—possibilities largely unglimpsed in 1930. The ballad, "O What is that sound which so thrilled the ear," . . . is, in its expression of terror and the expectation of rape and degradation, its innerving rhythm, and its brilliantly versified dialogue, one of the most perfect and moving poems Auden has written. . . .

There are also three songs descanting somberly but exquisitely on the perils of the human condition, each finding the courage to face such truths in its own lyricism. (p. 452)

The title poem of the volume, "Look, Stranger, at this island now," . . . is a song, as well, and stands in an illuminating relationship to the poetry of the early period. Like the Hopkinsesque Anglo-Saxonish poems in *Poems* (1930) or *The Orators*, its sounds are important—it is full of alliteration, assonance, internal rhyme, and onomatopoeia—but it employs them to achieve beauty of texture rather than reckless intensity; limpidity is all. . . . (p. 453)

And, finally, there are a half-dozen love poems that exhibit a new intimacy and power, even when they deal with abortive and painful relationships. Auden appears willing to express more of his personal feeling and experience in them than he has hitherto utilized openly. . . . Often—in four of the six love poems—the most moving lines are those in which Auden utilizes the landscape metaphor, which appears either to summon, or arise from, powerful personal

feeling. . . . [Most] sustained, most moving, and most personal is the landscape, or seascape, that concludes "The earth turns over, our side feels the cold." . . . Here Auden proceeds from the "shore where childhood played" through the "archipelago" of youth into a rough sea and thence, hopefully, to a far shore of love fulfilled and past recaptured, reconciled, incorporated—guided only by submission to feeling, an uninsistence on outcomes. . . . The landscape metaphor allows Auden to condense a whole Wordsworthian arc of development into two stanzas without any sacrifice of clarity or power. The amplitude of feeling and imagery in these lines is quite beyond that of *Poems* (1930), which is emotionally, as it is stylistically, crabbed. Auden rightly sensed the need to relinquish his earlier fierce language, of which so many of his admirers had grown so fond, and to put in its place a more tempered, civilized, and memorable speech. All things considered—the deeply moved and moving humanity most of all—*Look, Stranger!* introduced to the world, as nothing else of Auden's yet had, the finest English poet born in the twentieth century. (pp. 453-54)

Robert Bloom, "The Humanization of Auden's Early Style," in PMLA, 83 *(copyright © 1968 by the Modern Language Association of America; reprinted by permission of the Modern Language Association of America), June, 1968, pp. 443-54.*

JAMES D. BROPHY

In a century of the symbolist, surreal, and absurd, W. H. Auden is essentially a poet of the reasonable. "Coming out of me living is always thinking," a line from one of his early poems, is perceptive comment indeed by a poet whose difficult passages, while innovative in syntax and diction, usually yield a logical resolution. (p. 3)

All readers of Auden note a change in his work after 1939, a change some critics interpret as a retreat from the liberal commitment of his poetry in the thirties. The change in style is undeniable—from stressed ellipsis not unlike Hopkins' sprung rhythm to a more relaxed discursiveness. (p. 5)

Auden's recognition of complexity in all things is the basis of his analytical moderation and accounts for other important characteristics of his poetry: his humility and defense of the privacy of others, a great interest in the variety of form and genre (especially light verse), and a penchant for verbal surprise. (p. 7)

["The Letter" (1928) is a work] which demonstrates his early—and late—technique of the skillful collocation of the unusual with the traditional. Of course, the achieved effect would not be surprising without the contrast with the formal and the accepted. And this may be a reason why Auden is such a devotee of so many traditional forms such as the ballad, sonnet, ode, and villanelle. Also in his search for what he calls "curious prosodic fauna" he is understandably led to bacchics, choriambs, and alcaics of the classical past which today are both unknown and unused. . . . The search for what is new or what appears new almost always rejects the work of the immediately preceding generation (Auden, for all his praise of Eliot, did not continue Eliot's or Pound's style which dominated the twenties), but in so doing frequently returns to language and technique of the more distant past. (pp. 8-9)

Auden's language in "The Wanderer," aside from being evocatively alliterative, is also redolent of loneliness and typically eccentric in its Anglo-Saxon strangeness (to modern ears):

> . . . lonely on fell as chat
> By pot-holed becks
> A bird stone-haunting, an unquiet bird.

The poem—as with others of Auden's—gains its power by conjoining the remoteness of Anglo-Saxon tone and vocabulary with the modern idiom. The combination is effective: the use of Old English allusively supports the nature of the poem, the synthesis heightens and gives dignity to the modern situation. (p. 9)

[Especially] prominent in the early poetry [is] the omission of expected monosyllables, particularly the articles necessary to an uninflected language, [creating] a stressed and anxious tone. The opening stanza of "The Exiles" (1934) is an example of this frequent practice of Auden's:

> What siren zooming is sounding our coming
> Up frozen fjord forging from freedom
> What shepherd's call
> When stranded on hill,
> With broken axle
> On track to exile?

The absence of "the" before "hill" and "track" and the omission of "a" before "broken" suggest the same kind of breathless urgency that similar ellipsis of Hopkins' "sprung rhythm" also creates. The conjunction of "siren" and "zooming" in the opening line is another illustration of Auden's accomplished integration of the old ("siren" evokes the Homeric world) and the new. The contrast is startling, energizing yet organically apposite within the poem that describes the modern predicament with "the gun in the drawer" and in which "our nerves are numb" as "the old wound." (pp. 9-10)

The unusual aspects of Auden which characterize almost every one of his poems are not always . . . of a high order of difficulty. And many of them are simple and even conventional. (p. 13)

The later poetry of W. H. Auden, that is, his work after 1939, is remarkably similar to the earlier in asserting the unusual. Only in the realm of syntactical distortion is there a change. The later Auden considerably tempers the elliptical tension of his lines that link him so closely with Hopkins and the Old English poets. He becomes more discursive, and like Eliot's transition from the style of *The Waste Land* to the *Four Quartets* there is more philosophy and somewhat less difficulty (although Auden is not so difficult as Eliot in either period). (p. 14)

[In] no aspect of his work is Auden's multiplicity more evident than in his talent for writing brilliant light or humorous verse concurrently with his serious. No other poet of our century has been able to combine these talents so successfully. (p. 17)

Yet Auden has developed a philosophy of the comic that integrates it with life as it has developed in modern times. . . . The essential element in the comic, according to Auden, is a sense of individuality in conflict with immutable forces. . . . The challenge of immutable laws is involved in a tragic situation also, but in the world of tragedy it is always assumed that deviation from those laws, certainly a kind of uniqueness, is wrong. In Auden's work, as well as

in his definition of the comic, the uniqueness of the individual is honored, and its clash with the immutable laws of society, therefore, can be something less than tragic. . . . (pp. 17-18)

Although much of Auden's poetry, both light and serious, may be basically comic in a philosophical perspective, there is nothing frivolous about his light verse. It is not written, for example, solely for amusement as the appellation "light" generally signifies (especially in disapprobation). (p. 18)

There is . . . in every ballad something anomalous and ironic, which is perhaps one reason why Auden has used the style so frequently—and so successfully. The form accommodates his sense of contrast and balance, the tension of reality as he understands it. (p. 19)

Auden's humor is frequently ironic . . . and depends on brevity and immediately confuting juxtaposition. In [this stanza from "Victor"],

> He stood there above the body,
> He stood there holding the knife;
> And the blood ran down the stairs and sang;
> "I'm the Resurrection and the Life,"

the conjunction of "knife" and "Life," especially where "Life" is the essence of existence as God, is humorous, for it fulfills one of the essential characteristics of the comic which is conflict. In this instance the comedy, regardless of its near blasphemy and involvement with the bloody details of the murder, helps to diminish some of Victor's guilt—first, because it distances us somewhat from the terror of the act, and second, because its substance recalls to us the evangelical conditioning of Victor's childhood. (pp. 21-2)

"O What is that Sound which so Thrills the Ear" may be Auden's best-known and most widely anthologized ballad. . . . Although its stanza form,

> O what is that sound which thrills the ear
> Down in the valley drumming, drumming?
> Only the scarlet soldiers, dear,
> The soldiers coming,

is not that of the traditional ballad, its narrative presentation, rhyme, repetition, and musical insistence suggest that it is a ballad altered by Auden's interest in metrical innovation and variety. The poem—essentially more serious than either "Miss Gee" or "Victor"—is important to discuss because it demonstrates even more clearly than those ballads how subtle and flexible Auden's comic mode can be.

Auden accomplishes a remarkable feat in this poem by developing the terror of the invading soldiers at the same time that several ironies impart a vein of comedy to the speakers, a husband who answers his wife's questions about the approaching force of redcoats. From the outset there is a basis for irony in "thrills," for by the end of the poem the sound chills. . . . Without diminishing the terror Auden dramatizes through comedy how ignorance of the military and abandonment of personal vows of love are part of the world in which force breaks the lock and splinters the door. The deft audacity with which Auden does this contributes to the unique satisfaction which this and other light works of Auden's give. (pp. 22-3)

To Auden the truth about love or anything, in serious or light verse, must have the stamp of uniqueness on it or it will not satisfy him. This is why he is so attached to the comic mode; essentially he defines the comic situation as the individual in conflict with the traditional. (p. 26)

[Auden] thinks that the concept of the *engagé* artist is untenable, that "the political and social history of Europe would be what it has been if Dante, Goethe, Titian, Mozart, Beethoven, *et al.* had never existed." Yet Auden is not so devastatingly restrictive on art's influence and role as this statement might first indicate. . . . Auden's aims for art are modest. Rather than make things "happen," which implies direct significant action, art is involved with more subtle actions: persuading and teaching. Its sphere of action is within the individual, not the political world. (p. 28)

Auden's sense of humility is an important factor in his poetry, because not only does it contribute to his work its characteristic moderation, but it also is responsible for his concern for the individual. (p. 30)

Auden continually uses islands to symbolize refuges that beckon to man, but he categorically rejects such a choice, however alluring it may be. His "Paysage Moralisé" (1933), a seminal poem in Auden's canon, the title of which names Auden's special skill of giving landscapes appropriate meanings, concludes with the wish that "we rebuild our cities, not dream of islands." In Auden's appreciative metaphorical landscape no one becomes an island: Edward Lear, for example, becomes "a land," and Yeats possesses "provinces," "squares," and "suburbs." Nor does his long dramatic poem *The Sea and the Mirror,* which portrays the mutual needs of Prospero and Caliban, a theme which honors all reality, support the symbolic isolation of islands.

Auden's recognition of Caliban as well as Prospero, the primary world as well as the secondary, illustrates an important facet of his recognition of the individual—his informing humility. (p. 34)

As at the outset of his career when (in "The Letter") he expressed the will to be "decent with the seasons," Auden still seeks a harmony analogous to that statement rather than a mindless surrender to Nature. Nature gives him metaphors of order, a paradigm which assigns meaning to the individual, but Man must also be apart from the natural world in many ways. (p. 35)

[In] its description of the vision of the Old Masters, ["Musée des Beaux Arts"] embodies Auden's own concepts of poetry as a reconciliation of the various and the contradictory. . . .

It is Brueghel's *Icarus,* however, that Auden particularly describes: how the disappearing white legs are casually ignored or unnoticed by all in the scene. Auden does not indicate approval of each case of indifference; that the "expensive delicate ship . . . Had somewhere to get to and sailed calmly on" clearly conveys a tone of critical irony. But to Brueghel—as well as to Auden—such is the composition of reality. Much of Auden's technique—his irony and his use of the odd, for example—is the embodiment or portrait of the dichotomous and opposing variety which fills his own perspective.

Auden's "full view" results in a tempered tone (to use the musical sense of "temper" as "adjust to harmony") which, judging from "The Horatians" (a poem of 1969 that describes temperaments like his), also appears to be Horatian.

The term is useful to apply to Auden, not only because it originates from his own work, but also because of its association with satire. And the very concept of mild, that is, Horatian, satire in itself reconciles contradictory aspects. Auden is and always has been a moderate poet—where "moderate" is a position between extremes. (pp. 38-9)

Borders, divisions, and limits to personal freedom are central concerns of the three plays which Auden wrote in the middle thirties with Christopher Isherwood. (p. 40)

Auden has had [a long] fascination with the city as a metaphor for the environment which he posits as good for man. "To build the city" was the closing plea of *On the Frontier,* and in "City Without Walls" thirty-one years later he still reveals his commitment. The new poem, moreover, in its dramatic presentment of three voices without direct comment from the poet still shows the interest that led him to write three plays with Isherwood. Auden has worked frequently in collaboration (also with MacNeice and Chester Kallman), perhaps because it is in itself a dramatic and moderating activity. (p. 43)

Auden's salient characteristic, then, the one that explains his important qualities of uniqueness and gaiety within the drab and sober, a continuing interest in privacy and the individual, and the preference for the comic, is a temperament disposed toward balance. . . .

[In] the final analysis, Auden resists rigid classification. His "full view" is too comprehensive to submit completely to the traditional term. Any poet deserves to be treated on his own terms, but none perhaps so much as Auden who has no peer in our time as a defender of the individual and whose work is nothing if not brilliantly unique. (p. 46)

> *James D. Brophy, in his* W. H. Auden (*Columbia Essays on Modern Writers Pamphlet No. 54; copyright © 1970 Columbia University Press; reprinted by permission of the publisher*), *Columbia University Press, 1970.*

PETER E. FIRCHOW

The usual notion that the earliest Auden is apolitical, as voiced by Jarrell or Spender (e.g., in the famous remark that Auden "came to politics by way of psychology"), is true only in a very qualified sense: that is, by excluding his political poems from consideration. . . .

The reason why Auden came to politics by way of psychology is that Auden's pre-1932 psychology contained a very powerful political element. It was a psychology that definitely preferred action to contemplation. . . . (p. 256)

To be sure, the psychopolitics of *Poems* (1928 and 1930) tend to be of a rather odd sort. Much of the earlier volume is incorporated into the later one, which, while generally speaking more descriptive and less violent than its predecessor, is still full of birds, unidentified interlocutors, ill-defined frontiers, and quarrels over unnamed issues. The framework, however—the sociopolitical framework—for both volumes is chiefly the school or the "gang." While evident throughout, it rises most closely to the surface in the long opening charade of *Poems* (1930), "Paid on Both Sides," a piece that might almost equally well have fitted into *Stalky & Co.* Again and again the reader is confronted with plots and counterplots, attacks and counterattacks by gangs of juveniles who seem to be quite sure of what they are doing, even if no one else is.

To some not easily definable degree, these "gang" fantasies form an image of the Auden group. This is true not merely on the level of a shared group fantasy, . . . but also in the more mundane aspects of the day-to-day lives of Auden and his friends. There is, for example, Auden's trick of keeping a gun in his desk; or the way he thought about his friends, as a "gang" into which new members were periodically recruited. Or there is the way each member of the gang seemed to know instinctively his place in relation to the others, with Isherwood looking up to Upward, Auden to Isherwood, and Spender to Auden. In part at least, Auden's early poems are merely a working out in public of the experiences and fantasies of his own and his friends' private lives. One recalls in this connection the prefatory verses to *The Orators* (1932):

> Private faces in public places
> Are wiser and nicer
> Than public faces in private places.

Inevitably, the carrying over of private preoccupations into a public act like writing and publishing poetry brings with it confusion and misunderstanding. Hence, the early Auden is a difficult and obscure poet. Of no work is this more true than *The Orators,* the most extended of the group fantasies of the early Auden. So obscure is it that critics have been at a loss even for what to call it. Is it a "poem" or a fairy tale or a joke or a story or a collage? Or something else? . . . This confusion reflects a confusion of Auden's, very likely an intentional one. The title of the work suggests that it is intended to be read as an "oration," an intention that seems confirmed by the opening "Address for a Prize Day." But this address, with its direct echoes of Dante's purgatory and indirect ones of Milton's infernal revolutionaries, suggests that Auden's orators are engaged not merely in speechifying but also in prayer. The root meaning of oratory—and its original English meaning, according to Auden's favorite reference work, the *OED*—is, after all, "prayer," and it is unlikely that Auden would not have known this and meant his readers to interpret his title in its dual significance. Indeed, the Prologue to *The Orators* becomes comprehensible only if one reads it with this secondary sense of oration in mind, and the final ode of Book III, the last segment of *The Orators* proper, is unquestionably a prayer. This ambiguity is admittedly confusing, but confusing in a way, I submit, that enriches rather than impoverishes the work as a whole. The same is true of Auden's subtitle, "An English Study," which adds an essayistic, perhaps even a "scientific," dimension to a work that is already self-avowedly rhetorical and religious. . . . [The] primary meaning is surely a "study" of England, as carried out in a quasi-essayistic fashion in "Argument" and other sections of the work. . . . Finally, *The Orators* is also a poem, though this seems to have occurred to Auden only as an afterthought when he included the whole of *The Orators* in his *Poems* (1934). But it is precisely this afterthought that more than any official title provides the reader of *The Orators* with the necessary hint that it is, or is supposed by its author to be, an integrated work of art.

The hint, alas, is only too necessary, as Auden himself is quite aware. "'O where are you going?' said reader to rider," begins the Epilogue to *The Orators,* and the pun on rider/writer is clearly intentional. Finding one's way through this poetical-rhetorical-religious-scientific mirkwood is much like venturing past malodorous middens,

loathsome birds, and twisted trees, over the pass and into the valley where all will become clear. In fact, it resembles that journey so closely that Auden's reader, like the reader in the Epilogue, is left behind unilluminated in the company of horror and fearer (or furor?), while the mysterious writer rides contemptuously away. . . . In any event, it is undeniable that the obfuscation of *The Orators* is deliberate and that, if Auden's "idea" is hidden behind a verbal smokescreen, it is because Auden wanted it to be. (pp. 256-58)

The early Auden's language is to a marked degree an ingroup dialect, intentionally designed to be incomprehensible to outsiders. . . . *The Orators* . . . is a very "young" book full of animosity against an "Enemy" who is undoubtedly square. (p. 258)

The Airman is the most fully developed and important symbolic figure in [*The Orators*], a character whose closest literary analogue is Kipling's Stalky, a kind of authoritarian antiauthoritarian, a paranoic. . . . Though like the other orators in the book he is more of a planner and self-exhorter—and windbag—than he is a doer, this airborne Stalky has proved to be by far the most controversial feature of *The Orators.*

While it bears repeating that the ["Journal of an Airman,"] along with the rest of *The Orators,* is on some level simply an adolescent hoax, this particular hoax has overtones that prevent one from laughing too heartily. (pp. 258-59)

The Airman's uncritical glorification of action, his denigration of reason, his thinking in terms of abstract enemies and friends rather than individuals—"much more research needed into the crucial problem—group organization (the real parts)" is another cryptic entry in the journal—all these are highly suspect to ears that have heard similar sentiments in other contexts.

It is hard to believe that Auden was not originally aware that *The Orators* and especially the "Journal of an Airman" contained Fascist elements. (p. 259)

This is not to say that Auden *was* a Fascist. . . . After all, the Airman does see the error of his ways and in the end repents his violent fantasies. The "enemy," he comes to realize, is always the enemy within, never the enemy without. The real enemy is always some part of oneself. Auden's real aim, I suspect, in "Journal of an Airman" is to show the fallacy of Fascism as a force that always seeks an external enemy, a scapegoat. Certainly such a case could be made, all the more so because that is precisely what Auden does in *The Dance of Death.* But granting this intention, the realization is, to say the least, ambiguous, and it is, perhaps, ultimately to this ambiguity that Auden refers when he calls *The Orators* a "fair notion fatally injured." A number of important questions remain unanswered, such as why Book III takes up the Airman's fantasies of destruction all over again and why the Epilogue, with its clear preference for action over contemplation, confirms them. And why does the preoccupation with groups and strong leaders in *The Orators* dovetail so neatly with a similar preoccupation of Auden and his friends in real life? And why does Auden revert repeatedly to sympathetic portrayals of young, dynamic, charismatic leaders as a major feature of his work, such as Sir Francis Crewe in *The Dog beneath the Skin* (1935) or Michael Ransom in *The Ascent of F6?*

The answer to these questions, I suspect, involves positing

an Auden who, while never a Fascist, came at times remarkably close to accepting some characteristically Fascist ideas, especially those having to do with a mistrust of the intellect, the primacy of the group over the individual, the fascination with a strong leader (who expresses the will of the group), and the worship of youth. (p. 261)

The Auden group is probably the main reason for Auden's complex game of intellectual hide-and-seek in *The Orators*. But there are also other reasons. One of them, surely, is the fun of the game itself, the pure pleasure of not being found out—and of providing his reader with the creative happiness of trying to solve the riddle. This was perhaps especially true of a game where one of the answers was homosexuality. As we have seen, Auden nowhere makes either the Airman's or his own homosexuality explicit. . . . [Critics are] wrong in saying that the obscurity of Auden's early poetry is attributable exclusively to its homosexual content, but . . . not altogether wrong. (p. 268)

How seriously should we take [the Airman's Christian] conversion? Very seriously indeed, on one level; very lightly, on another. "A clean shirt, collar and handkerchief each morning till the end" is one of the last resolutions of the Airman who had turned into a square. . . .

In the end, then, what are we to make of the Airman and his friends? Are they simply intellectual Peter Pans, permanent adolescents flying off to a semifascist, quasi-socialist Neverland? Or are they airmen-artists, descendants of Daedalus (or of Stephen Dedalus?) flying off into new realms of conscience and consciousness, exploring new modes of being? Or are they just lame ducks waddling down the corridors of English literature as an in-group joke of Auden and company? The answer to all of these questions, I suggest, is "Yes." For that is precisely what makes the young Auden's poetry so baffling, so annoying, so pretentious, so brilliant, and so irrepressibly alive. (p. 270)

> *Peter E. Firchow, "Private Faces in Public Places: Auden's 'The Orators'," in* PMLA, *92 (copyright © 1977 by the Modern Language Association of America; reprinted by permission of the Modern Language Association of America), March, 1977, pp. 253-72.*

DAVID PERKINS

Above all I was charmed in Auden by what to me, when I first read him, seemed the ultimate sophistication, which was not disillusion but instead minimal expectations. More exactly, it was the combination of unillusioned insight, antiromantic and scientifically objective, with the ability to believe in and feel, however mutedly, the traditional positives. . . . Such poems as "Lay your sleeping head, my love," seemed a fascinating poetry of deflated affirmation, in which the lover expects little of himself or of human nature and sees through romantic love, and yet also sees that it has a kind of reality and value.

In the 1930s an eddy of criticism rose over the political commitment that was thought to run through his writing. In retrospect his attitudes seem much more complex, divided, and ambiguous. He had a horror of dictators, yet voiced the hope for a strong leader or saviour. He suspected that wars are fought so gunmakers may profit and was antimilitarist, but ready to make exceptions for the just or necessary war ("Spain, 1937"). He was against any crude nationalism, but tenderly loved "our little reef" of England. He explored

the industrial decay in images of "silted harbor" and "derelict works"; he dwelt powerfully on the contrast of the jobless and brutalized poor with the pleasure-seeking rich "constellated at reserved tables" and subject to "immeasurable neurotic dread" and death wishes; he conveyed the gathering international threat in images of secret agents and secret police; and he proclaimed the need of renovation, occasionally promising a better "tomorrow." Yet the utopian note was rarely sounded with much conviction, and his state of mind was much too changing and uncertain to be partisan. Feelings of guilt, battle, and doom were constant in his poetry, but who was guilty and doomed was a question. . . . Nevertheless, there was the anxious thought that one ought to be joining the fight. . . .

His poetry alternated between socio-political and psychological modes of analysis, and he was likely to think that psychological ills are basic, political and social wrong derived from them. The process of diagnosis and healing, with which Auden was always so much concerned, had to start not with social institutions but with the human heart. Primarily he was a moralist, and the chief importance for him of psychological and sociological modes of thought was that they provided criteria of the good. (pp. 731-33)

The amount of Auden's poetry in the thirties was remarkable—nine volumes in ten years. In relation to this poetry, and especially in view of the original contribution he was making, the charges that have since been so often leveled against him—carelessness, manneredness, obscurity, cliquishness, muddled thinking, frivolity, glibness, and a habit of amputating his own past, so that, the argument goes, he achieved virtuosity in different roles or styles rather than cumulative growth—seem either less warranted or less important. He created a style that was completely his own. His penchant for comic entertainment and for song, his ability to write at times with open perspicuity, his informality and imperfection widened the possibilities of poetry for other writers. He was wholly a poet of the contemporary situation, not only by topical allusion and reportage, but also because he explored and expressed the ground feelings of vague guilt, anxiety, isolation, and fear that so many shared. He was never without something to say. However pessimistic the poems might be, the general spirit of his poetry was adventurous, experimental, buoyant, full of intellectual gusto. He was the most significant new voice of the thirties, and because he was so young, he seemed boundlessly promising. But Auden's poetry changed in ways that disappointed most of his readers.

Between 1941 and 1947 he produced four long poems—"New Year Letter" (1941), "The Sea and the Mirror" (1944), "For the Time Being" (1944), and *The Age of Anxiety* (1947). Composed with skill and wit, they did not resolve the apparently unresolvable problem of creating in the modern world an effective form for an extended poetic statement. They lacked, moreover, much of the tension and self-conflict of Auden's former poetry. (pp. 733-34)

In some respects this verse of his last twenty-five years continued tendencies I have already noticed. It was colloquial, meditative, and generalizing in manner. He was fascinated by technical problems. The light touch was almost omnipresent. Yet when compared with Auden's poetry in the early thirties, the style had changed *toto caelo*. The velocity and compression, the sudden shifts of tone or direction, the ambiguity, ellipsis, and wrenched grammar had vanished and been replaced by a way of speaking that was leisurely, fully articulated, and perspicuous. It is a style without depths, so to speak. Everything that is to be understood is said. . . . Who—this perhaps was the first impression of most readers—would have thought Auden could be dull? Of course, he was far from dull, but as one goes from the early to the later work, radical readjustments of expectations and reading habits must be made, and in particular one must read more rapidly. Auden's poems were now, more than ever, written for cultivated people to enjoy without much effort. Approached that way, they are continually amusing and interesting. They show no loss of mastery. But the style is less ambitious. It is also less impersonal. The graceful and charming personality of the speaker counts for more in the total effect. And increasingly Auden referred more openly to himself. To some extent his style had simply moved with the times; he adopted in his own way the suburban blandness of much poetry in the fifties and the confessional mode of the sixties. But the change in style was accompanied by a refocusing of attitudes.

At first impression it might seem that the political concern of the thirties had vanished. The poet who now jocularly identified himself as an Arcadian rather than a Utopian, or who called neither for a change of society nor a change of heart but for a defense of the modes and declensions of grammar . . . was by the light of the thirties trivial, if not something worse. Yet in another sense political feelings were more than ever present in his poetry. The sense of personal helplessness that runs through it catches the mood of the fifties and sixties just as earlier it had caught that of the thirties. As long ago as 1939, faced with the political realities of those days, Auden had asserted that "poetry makes nothing happen." More exactly, it can redirect the way we feel about events but not the events themselves. He now added that nothing in the sense of betterment ever happens anyway. The ills and crimes of the world go on just the same from age to age, and though there are many revolutions, there is no reform. For a poet this means, among other things, that different ages can be coalesced, and this technique, which Auden had always exploited, became more central now. "The Shield of Achilles," for example, pictured simultaneously the world of Homer, of Imperial Rome, and the modern world, all equally brutal. As he looked on these and similar scenes there was an emotional detachment and a wide, impartial gaze (and neither of these were new in his work), noticing in one view the diverse goings-on of human life and the unchanging natural environment. . . . We are utterly vulnerable before the violence of history, but he now accepted this with humorous resignation. . . . (pp. 734-36)

What was missing, in other words, was the feeling that he or "we" ought to be doing something about it, ought at least to be "taking sides." There was, in fact, no side to take. The poetry is the record of a civilized intelligence that found itself in a crass, overwhelming, and nonsensical society. A recurrent symbol was the Roman empire in a late period, with its poets and cultivated minds trying as best they could to keep up civilized tradition, scattered and "ironic points of light" amid the dark, as Auden had expressed it in 1939. Amid windy Caesars, neanderthal generals, bored and overworked civil servants, press agents, ideologues, and barbarians, what could such a person do? He could *cultiver son jardin,* which meant, for Auden, first

of all the *jardin* of the English language and of literary tradition. The more difficult the form, the more fantastic and *recherché* the vocabulary, the more the poet was asserting, with a kind of heroic foppery, his values of civilized wit and sanity. (p. 736)

Along with [an] interest in deflating the pretentious and the falsely imposing, went a quiet appreciativeness of the minor decencies of cultivated living, a tendency that reached its climax in the series of poems called "Thanksgiving for a Habitat." . . . (p. 737)

I have been trying to give the impression of a retreat, for perfectly understandable reasons, into the minor and unpretentious in subject matter and style. This poetry disarms criticism or else puts it on the defensive, helpless before charm and unwilling to seem to prefer "haphazard oracular grunts." And yet, intelligent, amusing, graceful, and gracious as it is, it is not very exciting. To the extent that Auden's poetry survives, it will be mainly the poetry of the thirties. (pp. 737-38)

> *David Perkins, in* The Southern Review *(copyright, 1977, by David Perkins), Vol. XIII, No. 4, Autumn, 1977.*

DAVID LEHMAN

Ever the schoolboy poet, whose mixed blessing it was to have authored juvenilia of such intellectual force and genius of craft that the best of his last writings must inevitably seem a trifle anticlimactic, Auden never was deserted by his adolescent brilliance; and though this may seem something of a left-handed compliment, it was actually his precocious Oxford arsenal of cleverness, cheek, voracious erudition, and ambition . . . that enabled him to produce a body of work more various, prolific, and substantial than that of any of his contemporaries. . . . Skillful practitioner of *ottava rima* . . . , of the sonnet sequence and calypso song, oratorio and eclogue, early Skeltonics and the chatty meditations of middle age, moralized landscapes and secular prayers, the *spezzatura* of the concealed rhyme scheme and the overtly merry *Academic Graffiti,* here was a poet who could make all the old fashions of verse, and the new ones of prose, attractive to any individual talent, wedded to modernity or living in sin with it. . . . (p. 159)

The *Collected Poetry* of 1945 featured Auden at his most capricious, arbitrarily ordering the poems alphabetically by first lines; for the occasion, he conferred upon many of the poems temporary new titles, which usually consisted of a campy colloquialism, in ironic reply to the poems' once and future titles. (p. 160)

Although the differences between early and late Auden tend to overshadow the similarities, one can't help but be struck by how consistently Auden's voice gravitated to the oratorical mode of discourse, how capable he was of making poetic capital out of the meta-languages of sermon, lecture, epistle, toast, and valedictory address, and of the rituals and events that occasion them. In a century that has prized the intimacy of the poetic act, how splendid it is to read poems as comfortable in a crowd as the *Horae Canonicae,* the Phi Beta Kappa poems at Harvard and Columbia, the narrator's speeches in *For The Time Being,* and Caliban's magnificent soliloquy, a triumphant synthesis of creation and commentary, for which Auden devised the masterstroke of assigning to Shakespeare's definitive savage the elegance and syntactical complexity of Henry James. (p. 162)

[As we read the posthumous *Collected Poems,* we] watch the early Auden, for whom the definite article often seemed mere excess verbiage, gradually acquire the habits of his maturity.... Full of espionage missions and medieval initiation rites, as though the romance of being alive consisted in equal measure of tourney and quest, the dashing poems of early career stun with their clipped Icelandic rhythms, their affinity with the projects of Gertrude Stein.... (p. 163)

Upon turning his energies from manner to matter, having decided that life's meaning was "Something more than a mad camp", Auden began to apply to his poetry his extraordinarily analytical cast of mind, and to indulge his remarkable appetite for the capital letters that give his work some of the qualities of allegory; yet he never stops being the virtuoso performer of stylistic arabesques....

[There] can scarcely exist a more pressing need than the example of this dazzlingly urbane man, who would teach us that the manipulation of language is the beginning of all literature, that observation must not exist without an effort of intellection, that patient study of the world may yet permit us to read it like a landscape, a habitat, or a book that "calls into question / All the great powers assume." (p. 164)

> *David Lehman, "The Uncollected Auden," in* Poetry *(© 1977 by The Modern Poetry Association; reprinted by permission of the Editor of* Poetry*), December, 1977, pp. 159-64.*

*　　*　　*

AYMÉ, Marcel　　1902-1967

Aymé was a French dramatist, novelist, short story writer, journalist, and writer of books for children. His fictional subject is often the common man, his fictional setting, a simple rural one. Aymé was able to integrate the supernatural into the fabric of everyday reality, offering a flight into the imaginary and the absurd. He experimented with a variety of narrative styles, revealing a strong imagination and independence of thought.

GERMAINE BRÉE and MARGARET GUITON

A distinguishing characteristic of Marcel Aymé, when set beside other contemporary novelists in France, is the fact that he neither comes from nor has ever really been assimilated to the Paris bourgeoisie.... He is most at home within the microcosm of the small provincial village, where peasants, animals and small-scale local powers achieve a healthy, if somewhat uninspiring, pattern of existence. (p. 89)

It is not difficult to see why [*La Jument verte*] was, and still is, a best-seller in France. Aymé knows how to tell a story, to arouse our attention and curiosity.... Aymé, moreover, is on extremely intimate terms with life, its material necessities, difficulties and pleasures. A man in full possession of his five senses, he ... is gifted with a direct, almost physical flair for the elementary and generally unacknowledged motives of human behavior. He has a fertile and salty imagination. The supernatural, a frequent element in Aymé's early novels and his later stories, has none of the dream-like, otherworldly qualities of the surrealists but is firmly planted in the terrestrial logic of everyday events. Finally, and most important, Aymé is a novelist who can make his reader laugh out loud. (p. 91)

> *Germaine Brée and Margaret Guiton, "Marcel Aymé: Epilogue," in their* An Age of Fiction: The French Novel from Gide to Camus *(copyright © 1957 by Rutgers, The State University; reprinted by permission of the Rutgers University Press), Rutgers, 1957.*

CHARLES ROLO

Aymé has never become involved in literary and ideological cults; he is an old-fashioned individualist, more interested in people than in ideas. He is, moreover, a born storyteller, one of the best practicing in any language, and even in translation his prose is elegant and extremely readable.... Aymé's satire and farce grow out of a profound and tolerant cynicism. He distrusts or finds ridiculous high-minded idealists, revolutionary middle-class intellectuals—in fact, people of all kinds who want to remake the human animal or bowdlerize the truth about his nature. For Aymé, hypocrisy is more vicious than the natural vices of man, and one senses in his work a strong affection for life as it is. Within this framework, his range is wide. In addition to being consistently amusing, he can be gay, tender, cruel, horrifying, or sardonic.

A couple of stories in [*The Proverb and Other Stories*] are memorable examples of Aymé's distinctive combination of fantasy and down-to-earth realism. (p. 102)

There are twelve stories in the book, and more than half of them are outstanding. Among the readers who have so far missed Aymé's work, there must be a good many who would find this volume an entertaining introduction to the fictional world of a first-rate writer. (p. 103)

> *Charles Rolo, "A French Satirist," in* The Atlantic Monthly *(copyright © 1961 by The Atlantic Monthly Company, Boston, Mass.; reprinted with permission), June, 1961, pp. 102-03.*

HENRI PEYRE

Marcel Aymé ... brought to French literature an earthy sense of the life of the peasantry, a robust attachment to the concrete, a vigorous hatred of all escapisms, be they philosophical, esthetic, or political, and an admirably pungent gift of style. It is doubtful whether the success of his novels like "The Green Mare" and "The Second Face" will outlast his generation. They already seem strained and affected in their coarseness or in their fantasy. And Marcel Aymé, who is close to his sixtieth year, is hardly likely to acquire now the poetical touch that alone would have imposed upon disbelieving audiences his play about changing human creatures into birds. But he is today unequaled in France as a writer of racy and humorous short stories. A dozen of his best ones are collected [in "The Proverb and Other Stories"]....

The butts of Marcel Aymé's satire are the savagery of human beings when their welfare is at stake, as was the case during the years of rationing and of starvation; the selfishness of the middle class and its lack of idealism and of charity; the pomposity of the intellectuals and of the politicians, who disguise their greed for power or for importance under fake and pretentious posturing; the injustice of much French, or human, justice. The author is a fierce conservative in politics, as many satirists have been, for it is always easier to mock the new in the name of the old. He is quick to detect corruption everywhere, especially among the Parisian middle class. And if he is less severe on the farmers, he does not idealize them as did Giono or Ramuz. These pungent, entertaining stories à la Maupassant leave an aftertaste of bitterness. There is far more idealistic optimism among the existentialists whom Marcel Aymé likes to deride. And the comic vein may be a thin one, after all, in prosperous and hard-working Europe.

Henri Peyre, "Realism a la Maupassant," in Saturday Review (© 1961 by Saturday Review, Inc.; reprinted with permission), July 22, 1961, p. 25.

DOROTHY BRODIN

In a country where most writers belong to the intellectual classes, Aymé did not conform to the general pattern. He was not shaped by the classical and humanistic disciplines, or fashioned according to the usual university mold; and he steadfastly refused to be considered an intellectual or to belong to any literary school or movement. His experience of the world and his transposition of this experience were always essentially pragmatic and strikingly individualistic, but he appeals to readers of all kinds because of his vivid and unusual style, his extraordinary ability to put words through their paces, and especially because of the fresh and unexpected quality of his vision. His imagination created a new and wonderful world which allows a momentary escape from the one we know. Then we can come back to reality somehow refreshed and perhaps see it in a new light and therefore appreciate it better. (p. 3)

Some critics have described Aymé as essentially a fabulist. He did, in fact, like La Fontaine and Charles Perrault, often use allegory and fable to speak of the world and its inhabitants. His *Contes du Chat perché* (1939) is a collection of ironical tales of children and animals on a typical French farm. Through the device of a nonrealistic, purely imaginative story, the fabulist pokes fun at prejudices and conventions, and indirectly, almost casually, points up a lesson.

Although Aymé's world is not the "comédie aux cent actes divers" which we find in La Fontaine, we nevertheless can discover in his animal kingdom the image of a human world with the stratification, preconceived ideas, clichés, and pomposity of men engaged in the postures of social relations. To that world and society children bring the freshness of doubt. They are not convinced by the teaching of adults. (p. 5)

Aymé's theatre also offers moral lessons. *Vogue la galère* (1944), for instance, takes up . . . the themes of change, of freedom, and of the tendency we have to sacrifice them for the animal comfort of knowing what is expected of us and what the next day will bring. (p. 9)

The play, besides being a commentary on man's reactions to freedom and change, suggests that a society cannot subsist without discipline, common sense, and a kind of moderate conservatism. The idealism of Barrals [a nobleman condemned to death for religious reasons], who preaches friendship and brotherhood, not only dooms his mutiny to failure because of his basic ineffectiveness; worse than that, it nearly causes the loss of the galley with all on board. By his well-intentioned bungling, the young man causes more bloodshed and death than the brutally efficient convict who finally takes over and salvages the ship and its crew. (p. 10)

Men as individuals or men in society, whether through ignorance, stupidity, malice, or selfishness, can deform or flout certain natural laws and in so doing engender suffering. Most of Aymé's fables contain this truth. He presents these natural laws, which should govern human relations and which must enter into account if men and societies are to be saved, in a cosmos often quite different from that of our daily lives. Indeed the supernatural and the mechanisms of science fiction and of surrealism are frequently the chief ingredients of his universe. His characters move in a world where reality extends beyond the limits we usually assign to it. There, animals and human beings undergo varied and striking metamorphoses. (pp. 10-11)

Aymé was primarily concerned with man and with the society and relationships man has created. Whether he presented his characters in a world of fantasy and the supernatural where imagination rules and makes its own laws or whether, on the contrary, he had them move in the ordinary world we know, he always expressed through them his interest in mankind. He looked about him and described what he saw, often in very amusing terms, sometimes with caustic and bitter irony or under the guise of "black humor." In his first books, his verve was exercised mostly at the expense of peasants and artisans, castigating the mores of those who live in small towns and villages. Even in his later stories (*La Jument verte, La Vouivre*), country people were the target of a good deal of his banter. (p. 14)

[When Aymé left the country for the city, his] writing was to reflect the change in his surroundings. From country settings he passed to stories with the city as a background; and, as he began to concentrate on the bourgeoisie, his attitude became more caustic. Unlike Maupassant, who had also satirized both peasant milieus and city-dwellers, Aymé did not create a cohesive universe based on a naturalistic and pessimistic point of view. He merely described the people he saw and remembered.

In such works as *Le Moulin de la Sourdine* (1936) and *Uranus* (1948), the novelist dealt with the *petite bourgeoisie* of small towns; in *Maison basse* (1935), *Travelingue* (1941), and *Le Chemin des écoliers* (1946), he dealt with that of big cities. (p. 16)

On the whole, although Aymé's irony is particularly sharp when it is directed against self-satisfied moralists who consider themselves the allies of Providence, what he criticized in American civilization he criticized everywhere. . . . Aymé mistrusted and disliked power, powerful individuals and powerful collectives. . . . As for bad taste, Aymé did not consider it an American monopoly. (p. 35)

He was perhaps even less sanguine when he discussed nationalism and war, for he saw in them the outgrowth of basic human defects—vanity, smugness, pettiness, as well as savagery and the urge to kill—which have characterized men throughout the centuries and will probably continue to do so in that future era portrayed in *La Convention Belzébir*. (pp. 35-6)

Like most satirists, Marcel Aymé wrote about and against man's vices and illusions. He denounced envy, vanity, pride, prejudice, snobbery, bigotry, egoism, lack of charity, foolishness, all the inner evils that plague mankind. He was especially outspoken against moral blindness and hypocrisy. (p. 36)

[In Aymé's tales, animals] may be cruel, or vain, or envious. They may present all the defects common to men, but they are generally true to their own nature, and this is a saving grace. We cannot really condemn the wolf for his voracity, nor the peacock for his vanity. There is a certain guilelessness in the animals' conduct even when it is most reprehensible.

Human beings, on the other hand, far from measuring up to their real or imagined dignity, seem to spend much of their time and energy deluding themselves and deceiving others. (p. 37)

Aymé repeatedly attacked hypocrisy in its myriad forms, and did so with increasing indignation as he treated of its large-scale public manifestations. . . . In the novel *Uranus*, which has been called "a mirror of modern hypocrisy," almost every character is a hypocrite, but it is among those who are leaders in their social or political spheres that the vice is best exemplified and indeed becomes a way of life. (p. 39)

The postwar novels and plays of Aymé are often savagely sarcastic and contain gruesome accounts of stonings, lynchings, hideous massacres of helpless people, brutal useless acts committed under the mantle of patriotism. The author, when asked about the shocking scenes he described, said that he had not invented them, and indeed could not have done so; that "civilized" men and women had in fact sadistically participated in those violent events or stood by without protest while the mob killed its victim, because they "wanted to be on the side of morality." (p. 40)

[Critics have] accused him of subscribing to a "morale de l'indifférence" and of seeing only self-interest, hypocrisy, depravity, and hatred in an absurd world where norms and values are either inexistent or false. Such a reaction to his work is understandable, but it is as unjustified as the equally one-sided view that he was no more than a tender and amusing storyteller. The truth is more complex. Criticism of hypocrisy and evil in the societies, institutions, and professions of men has been traditionally the affair of writers through the ages; Aymé's satire cannot fairly be singled out as more violent a denunciation than most. Bitterness, moreover, is far from being the only element to be found in his work. It must be remembered that in *Uranus*, for instance, there appears the luminous character of Watrin, and that even in *Silhouette du scandale*, a book which contains some of the author's most indignant statements, there is the thought that we human beings are not absolutely shockproof but can at length be roused from our "morale de l'indifférence," our lethargic acquiescence, when events become scandalous enough.

However caustic Marcel Aymé may have been when he spoke of the smug Pharisaic powers of society, he always dealt gently with the humble unpretentious creatures whose candor and occasional stupidity make us laugh. His sympathy went to animals, children—especially country children and poor children—and those adults who are true to their own nature. He could understand and forgive weakness, and he pitied men and women who are sometime led by their senses, but are redeemed by their capacity to love. (pp. 40-1)

Whereas Marcel Aymé's popularity can undoubtedly be attributed to the richness of his imagination and his ability to tell even the most fantastic and unbelievable tale convincingly and entertainingly, he was much more than a popular author of entertaining books and plays. He could bring to vigorous life all sorts of characters, ranging from the most commonplace to the most extraordinary. He possessed, moreover, a wonderfully supple and vivid style, a brilliantly inventive and amusing way of writing. He used all kinds of literary devices, freely inventing new words and spellings and indulging in many forms of verbal acrobatics.

The names he imagined for the people and places he described, and indeed for the books and stories he wrote, were highly evocative. Such titles, for instance, as "Les Sabines," *Le Chemin des écoliers, Les Quatre Vérités,* and *Les Tiroirs de l'inconnu* are closely akin to puns; and *Travelingue* is a particularly appropriate name for a novel about people interested in the motion picture world and pseudo-American, "arty" attitudes. (pp. 41-2)

At times the author achieved striking effects through lists and enumerations, malapropisms, misunderstandings, and the deliberate association of incongruous terms or incongruous acts. He was very apt to use parody, imitating with signal success all types of literary styles in prose and poetry. . . . He liked to take over the point of view of others, of animals—dogs and wolves and pigs, or even a green mare—and of people—murderers and judges, soldiers, civil servants, children, hypocrites and saints.

Perhaps the most famous and the most fully developed of Aymé's accounts made from the vantage point of someone else's outlook are the "Propos de la Jument" scattered through *La Jument verte*. (pp. 43-4)

Marcel Aymé had a highly developed sense of the incongruous and the paradoxical, creating a world of the absurd which functions according to its own very special brand of logic. (p. 44)

Aymé was primarily a man of imagination. Freely he created new situations where the laws of our cosmos are abrogated or suspended. His creatures move about with an imperturbable logic of their own, forcing our assent. We are freed from our hidebound concepts of time and space, cause and effect; and we can appraise characters and events with a fresh outlook. Like La Fontaine, he composed fables and apologues; like Swift and Lewis Carroll, he invented strange new worlds. There are in his work distant echoes of many famous writers, and critics have often compared him with the great authors of the past, with Rabelais and Voltaire in his use of language, with Molière, Balzac, Stendhal, Proust, and others, because of his interest in society and the human comedy. (p. 45)

[However,] what is a conscious and systematic process with a Balzac or a Rabelais or a Queneau is incidental and transitory with Aymé. He may be a novelist of mores, but he is not a sociologist, and if his works often possess documentary value it is because of his remarkably keen perception of significant traits. Like Queneau he coined new and amusing words and resorted to unconventional spellings, but there is no such thing as a theory of language in his works. He wrote in one manner or another according to the necessities of his subject and, although he himself did not deny the possibility of having been influenced by his readings, that influence, if it did exist, was largely unconscious. He was above all an individualist, curiously old-fashioned at times in his attachment to the values of individualism itself. He was perfectly capable of rising in anger at the abuses he saw about him, but he was unable or unwilling to sustain his indignation in the manner of a true satirist. Bitterness and anger mark only part of his work. He was undoubtedly mercurial and outspoken, but there was about him a gentle quality more often reminiscent of La Fontaine than of Voltaire. Much of the time he appears primarily as a witty, entertaining writer who thoroughly enjoyed his life and his work.

Aymé cannot easily be classified. Perhaps this is a weakness, in that his very versatility, his lack of identification with any single genre, may lead some readers to think of him as a pleasant literary dilettante rather than a serious critic of his times. But if the purpose of art is to touch and to please, Aymé was an artist and a good one. Neither a realist nor a surrealist, he usually looked at life with tolerant amusement, and he varied his style and his approach with his particular mood and the needs of the story he wished to tell. His bittersweet, tragicomic world contains a wealth of gayety, imagination, and lusty good fun. (pp. 45-6)

> *Dorothy Brodin, in her* Marcel Aymé *(Columbia Essays on Modern Writers Pamphlet No. 38; copyright © 1968 Columbia University Press; reprinted by permission of the publisher), Columbia University Press, 1968.*

*   *   *

AZORÍN (pseudonym of José Martínez Ruiz) 1874-1967

A Spanish novelist, essayist, and dramatist, Azorín was one of the central figures in Spain's literary "Generation of '98." His style is concise and sensitive, with great attention to detail and to the commonplace. The pseudonym Azorín was derived from a character of the author's own invention. Fictional and real merged, with José Martínez Ruiz becoming Azorín in private as well as public life. He has also written under the names of Cándido and Ahriman.

MIRELLA D'AMBROSIO SERVODIDIO

The evolution and crystallization of Azorín's attitudes vis-à-vis Spain and her "problem" are revealed with unusual clarity in a given number of Azorín's short stories. These stories point to the change from youthful nonconformity regarding existing social and political conditions to serene conciliation with tradition, and they lay bare the complete *volte face* effected by Azorín with regard to both the letter and spirit of some of his earlier writings. . . .

Even prior to the disaster of 1898, the early stories of *Bohemia* (1897) denote rabid dissatisfaction with Restoration Spain symbolized in part, by the "vida oficial" of Madrid. Rather than formulating general principles of national policy or studying the position of Spain at large, the stories of *Bohemia* strike out at the immediate society on the premise that minor social ailments may be symptomatic of widespread national disease. (p. 55)

Stories such as "La Ley" and "Envidia" represent outspoken clamorings against church and state; in both, the law is found wanting, and an inadequate vehicle for defending human rights. As he views the corruption and stagnancy around him, Azorín's criticism often hits a strident note. The stance of the writer is uncompromising, and social conventions and laws are swept aside. . . . Although the difficulties impinging on the role of social reformer are studied tangentially in several stories, the thrust of Azorín's criticism, at this juncture, lies more in the direction of dis-

closing social ills rather than in introducing concrete proposals for change. Always, the stories of *Bohemia* reveal restlessness and concern with the social order. However, Azorín's vision of Spain is not yet crystallized. His position is an iconoclastic one as he joins the other "angry young men" in agitation for change at any cost.

With the advent of the crisis of '98, full vent and expression are given to projects of reform. The general orientation is towards Europe, and the underlying attitude is ferociously critical. . . . It is in the political arena that Azorín and his companions sharpen and perfect their literary tools and develop critical acumen. Moreover, the threshold between theory and practice is crossed, and overt action is taken in several directions by Maeztu, Baroja and Azorín, commonly known as "los tres." . . . National preoccupation colors the books produced by Azorín at this time. . . . In *Los Pueblos,* he strikes out against the bureaucracy, the poverty and the hopeless agricultural situation afflicting Andalusia. . . . In this early period, Azorín reaches a high point of bitterness, inner convulsion and pessimism. This will be followed by gradual and subtle change.

The seeds for change are implanted as early as 1901. . . . Although Azorín continues to desire social and agrarian reform and educational and cultural improvement, the type of renovation he now seeks ceases to be iconoclastic in nature. More importance is attached to a spiritual renaissance of Spain. . . . Azorín's changing position is not attained without conflict, however: he feels the pull of the past, on the one hand, yet he recognizes the need for change, on the other. Azorín will compromise by looking to reform within the already existing scheme of things—progress and growth within tradition. (pp. 56-9)

As a study of numerous short stories will show, a more objective period ensues in which Azorín correlates patriotism with knowledge, and in which the writer reiterates his conviction that the key to the present may be found in history and tradition. The story significantly entitled "La continuidad histórica" . . . clearly supports these beliefs. (p. 59)

The story "Con La Señora Du Gast" . . . is also highly consonant with the line of thinking of this period. Outlined with schematic clarity are the ingredients which blend into a composite of Spain's essence. History, literature, landscape and popular types are intimately correlated, with one springing from the other. A note of tragedy and melancholy seeps through, denoting a love of Spain. . . . (p. 60)

With time, Azorín inches farther and farther away from his former position regarding method and degree of reform needed in Spain. Earlier zeal is replaced by a more contemplative attitude. In the story "Las Fiestas en el Campo" . . . , he speaks skeptically of projects of renovation and reveals his distrust of politicians and parliamentarians. . . . (pp. 60-1)

Azorín withdraws from his earlier European position and comes to deny the idea of a past decadence. (p. 61)

It is the story "La Seca España" . . . , however, that exemplifies with stunning clarity the complete ideological reversal made by Azorín with regard to Spain. Moving from radicalism to moderation to arch-conservatism, a complete *volte face* has been effected by the writer. The protagonist of the story is Silvino Poveda, a landowner from Alicante, and philosophically, a replica of Azorín. His property, "El Secanet," where only dry farming is possible, is symbolic of all of Spain. Spain is arid and in need of agricultural improvement. In Paris, Povedo encounters a manual illustrating methods of discovering and tapping hidden water resources. This information places Poveda in a conflict situation, and forces him to review his sentiments regarding Spain and her role. By means of Poveda's reflections, Azorín is enabled to rescind the ideas he espoused in his younger days. . . . Given the choice between progress and economic advancement or remaining rooted to the *status quo,* Poveda decides in favor of the latter; the past triumphs irrevocably over the present. The "secanet" will stay as it is—and in a larger scheme, Spain too will hold firm. . . . And Poveda, like Azorín, taking refuge in his dreams, will see this as the best of all possible ways. . . . (pp. 62-3)

> *Mirella D'Ambrosio Servodidio, "Azorín: A Changing Vision of Spain," in* Revista de Estudios Hispanicos, *January, 1971, pp. 55-63.*

JULIAN PALLEY

In *Doña Inés* there is the Nietzschean Eternal Return; there is the Proustian evocation of the past through a physical sensation; there is an historical or demiurgic . . . vision of change and the passage of time; there is time as duration, in the Bergsonian sense; and there are many other variations on the temporal theme in this short, poetic and eloquent novel. . . . There are also, of course, the *things* that Azorín loved and described so well with his hawklike vision. In *Doña Inés* the things themselves are images or symbols of the various aspects of time; they are the objective correlatives (in Eliot's sense) of the emotions that the contemplation of time and its effects produces in the author. (pp. 250-51)

Chapter II contains a detailed and loving description of the protagonist in the year of the novel, 1840. . . . At the end of the chapter the point of view shifts to the present, as the narrator, in his own voice, examines a daguerreotype that was made of her in 1840. . . . The faded daguerreotype symbolizes the passage of time, and the difficulty of evoking a life lived a century ago. The daguerreotype produces in the author the emotion of *le temps perdu,* of an irretrievable past; the object itself is the correlative, the image of that emotion.

The print of Buenos Aires that hangs in Doña Inés' room is one of those things, objects, that evoke in Azorín various emotions. . . . Within the structure of the work, the print of Buenos Aires also symbolizes the past and the future, the simple story out of which the novel is woven. It is the past of Diego el de Garcillán, who was raised in the Argentine capital; and it is the future of Doña Inés herself, who will pass her last years in Argentina, not far from the great city. (p. 251)

El tío Pablo appears to be a somewhat deformed self-portrait of the author. He is the personage most aware of the passage of time, of time as duration. . . .

One of the most striking "images of time," in these chapters devoted to Don Pablo, and in the work itself, is that which Azorín calls *el tiempo cristalizado.* It refers to the experience of meeting someone after years of absence or separation; we have before us simultaneously, on such occasions, the reality of the present and the image in our memory; as the two are superimposed, we have the crystallization of time, a true portrait of time and its effects. (p. 252)

The story of Doña Beatriz is spread over six or seven chapters, and it culminates in the striking Nietzschean vision of Chapter XXXVII, "Los dos besos." This chapter is the climax of the book's action, and it brings together the love story—of Diego el de Garcillán and Doña Inés—with the theme of Eternal Return. (p. 253)

The story of the medieval Doña Beatriz and her infatuation with the young page parallels, in many ways, that of Doña Inés and her love of Diego. Moreover, Don Pablo has noted the physical resemblance between the two women, separated by centuries. The reclining statue of Doña Beatriz in the Cathedral is the source for the portrait of Inés drawn by Taroncher. . . . Inés visits the chapel of the reclining statue. She is drawn to the marble features, and in one hallucinatory moment, she presses her lips against those of Doña Beatriz. . . . In this kiss is crystallized the theme of the Eternal Return. It is followed immediately by a second kiss, that of Diego, who discovers Inés in the Cathedral. The theme of Eternal Return is reinforced by the second kiss, since to the physical resemblance between the two women is added the circumstances of their loves. (pp. 253-54)

The final chapter, the Epilogue, reserves for us still two more images of time. Doña Inés has grown old in an orphanage which she has founded near Buenos Aires. The ombú of the Argentine pampa (mentioned earlier in XXV as Diego recalls his youth) has accomplished a strange transformation: it has marched toward the city. . . . This beautiful image of the ombú "moving" toward the city is a fitting finale for this novel whose protagonist is neither Inés, nor Don Pablo, nor Diego, but Time itself.

But there remains yet another vision of the Eternal Return, whose evocation formed the climax, and central theme, of the work. In Azorín's story "Las nubes" (from *Castilla)* the young lovers Calisto and Melibea, to the reader's agreeable surprise, marry and start to raise a family. At the end their daughter meets a young man who invades their garden, in search of his falcon: the myth of *La Celestina* begins again in circular repetition. Thus at the end of *Doña Inés* the narrator suggests that the poet Diego is born again. . . . (pp. 254-55)

Critics have overemphasized the static nature of Azorín's fiction. In *Doña Inés,* at least, there is considerable dynamism, movement and drama, in small but significant things. In a gesture of Inés as she opens a letter or walks down a street in the *barrio* of Segovia in Madrid; in the hands of Segovia, moving across centuries; in the furious *tolvanera* that causes windows to slam, trees to bend, clouds to scud across the sky; in the psychological and emotional drama of Inés, portrayed largely by external things; above all, in the silent flow of time that pervades the entire novel. (p. 255)

> *Julian Palley, "Images of Time in 'Doña Inés'," in* Hispania *(© 1971 The American Association of Teachers of Spanish and Portuguese, Inc.), May, 1971, pp. 250-55.*

LEON LIVINGSTONE

Azorín's overall note of serenity masks a deep-seated disquietude. (pp. 6-7)

Despite their ideological association in the cultural revolution of the "Generation of 1898", Unamuno and Azorín have been generally considered virtually diametric opposites, separated, as one critic has recently reiterated, by a deep distance between their spiritual and literary styles. So firmly entrenched is this view that to seek to equate in any way the creator of the "delights of the commonplace"—as Ortega y Gasset characterized the art of Azorín in a now-celebrated, and somewhat oversimplified, phrase—with the existential anguish of the tormented philosopher of Salamanca can at first blush seem only an extravagant pretension, if not a veritable contrasense. For how can one bridge the gap between the tortured expression of the conflict of existence of the Basque and the affectionate cultivation of minute details of the Alicantine impressionist; between the poetics of dynamic self-creation and the static "esthetic of repose"; between the conversion of the novel into a vehicle of heroic self-pursuit and its unpretentious reduction to "algunas notas vivaces e inconexas—como lo es la realidad", as Azorín proposed in one of his early novels? The unheroic cultivation of the casual in Azorín is too obvious to ignore and in fact seems clearly confirmed by the author himself.

Azorín's first effort to counteract the constant erosion of temporal flux is to attribute to the past a solidity of permanence by "actualizing" it as he relives his former life. In this revitalization of the past, its resuscitation and restoration to a living present which salvages from oblivion that part of himself which antedates his current existence, the author seeks a firm foundation of self-consciousness on which to build his present identity. However, while the nostalgic tone of these personal reminiscences is in one sense an emotional cementing of the two time zones of being, in another it aggravates the cleavage between them as it establishes a sentimental gulf between the now and the then. And what is even more startling a revelation, between the now and the now! Indeed, an apt and adequate description of the fundamental tone of Azorín's expression would be "a nostalgia for the present". . . . [The] relentless retrogression . . . forces on us the realization that life, both of man and his environment, is a continuous process of dying. In Azorín the bitter acceptance of this truth produces a deep and tragic melancholy . . . which is hauntingly expressed in the first novels. If the lyrical response provides a type of spiritual release it is clear that it is also a continuous reminder of the insufficiency of the proposed solution.

The real issue that Azorín faces in seeking to retrieve present reality from the engulfing current of time is clearly the need to impart to the fugitive moment a quality of eternity. By thus seeking to restore to the ever-receding past a status of presence through the revivifying effect of memory Azorín attempts to make reality impervious to the onslaught of change, to immortalize it in an aspect of timelessness that will place it beyond the reach of all-corrupting temporality. (pp. 9-10)

As a satisfactory solution to the problem of time continues to elude the author, the attendant failure to provide the necessary clue to an undivided identity in turn produces a psychological insecurity that is reflected in the characters who, like their creator, are caught in a helpless contemplation of their own schismatic personalities. (p. 14)

[It is in *The Voluntad,*] in the confrontation of the "I" and the "me" in a destructive stalemate, that the movement of time acquires a sudden terrifying reality. Time had been there all along but the abrupt realization that life is con-

stantly slipping by has the force of a conversion no less epochal for Azorín than was Unamuno's traumatic realization of the reality of death. Henceforth, the problem of identity will be indissolubly linked in Azorín's consciousness to that of time. (p. 15)

In the balanced attraction of consciousness and unconsciousness lies the path to identity. In other words, identity is the net result of the interplay between the development of personality and an intentional depersonalization, between the cult of self and of selflessness, of time and timelessness.

These conflicting directions in Azorín are the result of a synchronic dual movement of extroversion and introversion, towards and away from external reality, a veritable cult of the world of objects in all their pristine solidity that is counteracted by a quasi-mystic revulsion against the physical in an unceasing aspiration to free the spirit from the constraints of the material world. (p. 18)

Certainly a dual track of precise realism and antirealistic abstraction is starkly characteristic of the art of Azorín himself. (p. 19)

In Azorín's art the realization of the fundamentally enigmatic nature of self, which fosters in us, and is actually reinforced by, the desirability of the loss of self as an antidote to the pain of self-consciousness, is productive of a peculiar narrative technique of concealment in which the nature of the action, the exact identification of the character, are intentionally withheld from the reader. Azorín is one of the first of the Spanish novelists of the twentieth century (if not the very first) to use this procedure of delayed disclosure, from which the later "neo-realists" will derive the maximum usage. (pp. 19-20)

[The role of plot is consequently relegated by Azorín] to a level of inferiority to that of the pursuit of identity by the characters, an activity now conceived as a paradoxical cultivation of a selfless self-awareness. The technique of narrative concealment fits admirably into this scheme as it stimulates the sense of self precisely by withholding the clue to the character's identity.

The technique of concealment is obviously not a merely decorative stylistic device but a procedure integral to the identity-orientation of the novel. Moreover, it is not a negative element, for the evasion of plot-narration, as the reader must draw inferences from tangential allusions, employs a language of metaphoric and symbolic reference which reaches the height of the genuinely poetic. (p. 21)

The interrelationship of content and form, the intimate fusion of the theme of the pursuit of identity and a subtle, evocative style that embraces a wide range of artistic techniques, provides the key to the structure of the Azorinian novel, but it does not take into account the ultimate dimension of significance of the creative act itself. The distinction is between degree and nature: between the *extent* of the stylistic intricacies which serve as the vehicle of expression of a fundamental preoccupation with identity and the *nature* of the nuclear role of novelistic creativity in the development of self-awareness. It is on this issue that Azorín joins hands with Unamuno: the formation of identity is inseparable from artistic creativity. That is the ultimate explanation of why the Azorinian novel is characteristically the novel of the art of novelizing and its central figure the writer struggling with the pains of literary gestation. In this sense all of Azorín's fiction could appear under the generic title borne by one of his novels: *El escritor* (1942). That means in the last analysis that the autobiographic element of Azorín's art is not a *terminus a quo* but *ad quem;* not the point of departure of the novel but its ultimate goal. The function of the novel is not to reproduce the personal experiences of the author—or where it does, to make of this reconstruction only a means towards an end—; not to reveal to himself his already-formed identity, but to enable him to give a specific direction or directions to the potentialities of his self.

The autobiographical trilogy that deals with Azorín's childhood, adolescence, and youth thus has the force of a *Bildungsroman,* but of a special kind, one in which the interaction of the real and the imagined results in notable modulations in the personality of the writer. In *Las confesiones de un pequeño filósofo* (1904) and *Antonio Azorín* (1903) the childhood, adolescence, and early youth of the author are recalled more or less factually, although with an increasing element of fiction in the latter, but in both cases the recollections are permeated by a sentimental nostalgia that colors gray facts with a poetic glow. Furthermore, they do not have a systematically chronological structure, but consist largely of somewhat random vignettes whose non-linear arrangement is dictated by sensibility rather than by temporal progression. (pp. 22-3)

To the invasion of the factual by the fictional, as in this redirection of the writer's life and reconstruction of his identity through the example of his literary projection, is added a further dimension of complication of the autobiographic in the elusiveness of time. Time recollected is also time transformed. For, as Azorín insists in his *Memorias inmemoriales,* the remembrance of things past is always colored by the sensibility of the present. (p. 24)

Autobiography as thus conceived is obviously not simply an historically-based, objective self-reproduction but an intricate fusion of the historical and the fictional, of past and present, of fact and imagination, in which the recalled self is influenced by its potential evolution. The "real" self visualizes imaginative possibilities of itself which then serve to modify the original identity of the creator. Author and character act as mutual catalysts to produce in the artist a constant and unceasing self-revelation and self-creation, precisely as Unamuno had insisted.

This underlying and unifying concept is recurrent in Azorín's fiction from its first encapsulated formulation in *Diario de un enfermo* to *El enfermo,* in both of which works the central figure is a writer struggling with the same subject as the author, and in both of which, as their very titles indicate, the question of self-creation through art is intentionally related to the problem of physical and mental health. . . .

The relationship of creativity to identity and of identity to mental alienation is manifested in two ways: in the alternation between artistic inspiration and sterility, equivalent in human terms to the achievement and loss of identity; and in the unrelieved pressure of the need of creative activity to keep alive the sense of self. (p. 25)

[All] of Azorín's novels have a characteristic aspect of anticipated form, of incompletion, and this is in conformity with the conviction that the process of creativity—which carries with it the task of self-creativity—must perforce be continuously self-renewing. . . . The parallel between esthetic creation and the evolution of identity is clear, for the aspiration to form which wilfully impedes its own realization is exactly that of the synchronic striving for self and for selflessness. (pp. 26-7)

[With] the termination of each artistic assignment comes a sensation of personal emptiness which demands the discovery of a new theme around which the revived and revised personality of the author must crystallize for him to survive, for creation is synonymous with life itself; the sense of personal being equivalent to the reality of poetry. . . .

What interests Azorín in the new experimental novelistic phase [which begins with *El cabellero inactual*] is not really so much the cultivation of the literary mode of surrealism, which he interprets in his own fashion, as the attainment of a super-reality (*Superrealismo* is the original title of *El libro de Levante,* one of the novels in this group), a created reality which can be reached only through the subconscious, where the demarcation between separate and mutually-exclusive spatio-temporal zones is obliterated to give the desired illusion of a freedom from the limitations of space and time. (p. 29)

But in this there is an anguish that adulterates the pleasure of creativity, for in the indiscriminate mingling of all planes of time and space in the inner consciousness, as the present becomes indistinguishable from the past and even from the future, the feeling of excessive, of unbridled, freedom from the limitations of fixed, material reality threatens to disintegrate the sense of unified being. The artist's loss of his sense of control over his own world is accompanied by the feeling that the mastery of his material is deserting him. . . . (p. 33)

In the experience of artistic gestation, as plenitude again alternates with aridity, the full realization of self is further contaminated by the fearful attraction of this possibility of the loss of identity. For not only does the dissolution of self loom as an ever-present threat but the impending descent into non-being actually exerts on us the irresistible fascination of a death-wish. (p. 34)

The compulsive thrust towards the annihilation of self at the very height of creative fever is confirmed in a new stylistic element of abstractness that eliminates personal pronouns, especially those copious "I's" so characteristic of the earlier novels, in favor of impersonal infinitives and gerundial constructions. But what is most significant in this irresistible fascination for the depersonalization of self is the role it plays in the repetitive cycle of creativity. (p. 35)

The ceaseless recommencement of creative activity, the beginning over and over of new themes that guarantee the reformulation of our personal consciousness, involves only a fragmentation into a disconnected series of selves without inherent continuity. But without continuity there can be no true identity. . . . [Azorín] seeks to counterbalance the forward projection of self-creation with the cumulative weight of lived reality in a return, even beyond memory, to the atavistic past, far beyond the known historical, as he links the melancholy of the poet with that of his primeval ancestor. . . . (pp. 35-6)

[For Azorín] all existence is a creative process, a fiction, the living of the novel of one's life (or lives), an unceasing dialogue between reality and imagination. In this sense we are all inventors of our own identities; the poet merely the most articulate and sensitive formulator of a universal self-creativity. (pp. 38-9)

Leon Livingstone, "Self-Creation and Alienation in the Novels of Azorín," in Journal of Spanish Studies: Twentieth Century *(copyright © 1973 by the* Journal of Spanish Studies: Twentieth Century*), Spring, 1973, pp. 5-43.*

B

BARNES, Djuna   1892-

An American novelist, dramatist, short story writer, poet, and journalist, Barnes has been as highly unconventional and independent in literature as in lifestyle. She has drawn much of her fiction from her bohemian background, but has colored it surrealistically. Her works are filled with the abnormal, the alienated, the grotesque, and often evoke a nightmarish horror. Their scope, however, extends to portray larger themes of human suffering and alienation. Barnes's style is elegant and lucid, mingling black comedy and satire with the richness of Elizabethan prose and French Modernist poetry. Her attention to rhythm and word sounds has brought T. S. Eliot to say of *Nightwood* that "only sensibilities trained on poetry can wholly appreciate it." Also trained as an artist, Barnes has illustrated several of her own books, including *Ryder* and *The Ladies' Almanack*. *Nightwood* is generally considered her major work. (See also *CLC*, Vols. 3, 4, 8, and *Contemporary Authors*, Vols. 9-12, rev. ed.)

ROBERT L. NADEAU

[*Nightwood*] has attracted a small circle of admirers who have been awed by Barnes's extraordinary ability to infuse macabre or grotesque subject matter with haunting beauty, but the general consensus seems to be, with a few notable exceptions, that an excessive lack of verisimilitude makes it something less than a masterpiece. *Nightwood* has not yet been recognized as a truly great piece of American fiction simply because we have failed to fully appreciate the fact that it does not depict human interaction on the level of conscious, waking existence. It is rather a dream world in which the embattled forces of the human personality take the form of characters representing aspects of that personality at different levels of its functioning. (p. 159)

Barnes's treatment of character seems quite consistent with Freud's conception of the nature of the three divisions in our mental life [ego, superego, and id]. She does not present us with allegorical figures who take on "all" the characteristics of one mode of functioning, but rather with representatives of the interior workings of the human mind at different points along the continuum of psychic experience. (pp. 159-60)

The parallels between Barnes's characterization of Robin and Freud's description of the dynamics of the interior life on the level of the id are simply too extensive to ignore.

The id, which Freud associated with the more vestigial portion of the brain's anatomy, is the place where man's primitive instincts originate. It also functions as a kind of psychic energizer which compels the individual to take action. It is, says Freud, "a chaos, a cauldron of seething excitement," and has "no organization and no unified will, only an impulse to obtain satisfaction for the instinctual needs, in accordance with the pleasure principle." Analytical or logical thought cannot occur in the id because the "laws of logic—above all, the law of contradiction—do not hold for processes in the id." . . . The last of the parallels hardly needs mentioning—sexual desire is the overt manifestation of an instinctual need which the id seeks uncompromisingly to gratify. (p. 160)

Felix's unremitting efforts to mold himself in terms of his idealized conception of his father suggests that the superego is clearly dominant in his personality. The exaggerated interest in societal forms is also commensurate with Felix's role in the novel in that one of the primary functions of the superego is to represent internalized cultural values. . . .

Viewed on the continuum of psychic experience Jenny is a superego type like Felix. She suffers "from some elaborate denial" . . . and is incapable of deriving any real pleasure from the sexual act. . . . The influence of the superego is not as great, however, in Nora's psyche. She feels, for example, no obligation to make moral judgments and no sense of being related to or defined by society. . . . Her vague sense that there is something wrong or reprehensible in Robin's behavior suggests that the superego is more active in her consciousness than it is in Robin's, and it is this which leads Nora to seek advice and counsel from Dr. Matthew O'Connor.

Functioning like a Greek chorus made up of terribly astute analysts with a penchant for poetic statement, Dr. O'Connor comments upon the behavior of others with a precision that invokes both fright and awe. Intimately acquainted with the irrational and yet fully conscious of the dictates of society, O'Connor, like the Freudian ego, strives to establish equilibrium between the two warring factions. One of the fundamental differences between the ego and the id, says Freud, is that the ego has "a tendency to synthesize its contents, to bring together and unify its mental processes which is entirely absent from the id." . . . [O'Connor] incessantly attempts to "synthesize" or "unify" the various levels of mental functioning he sees in operation within himself and others. (p. 161)

Feeling defeated in his effort to make Nora appreciate the dangers involved in maintaining any ties with Robin, O'Connor begins to lose his own tenuous psychic balance. Freud asserted that when the ego is forced to recognize its weakness in the face of the passions of the id it breaks out into neurotic anxiety. . . . When O'Connor is last seen in the narrative, drunk and despondent in his favorite Parisian cafe, he is showing all the signs of neurotic anxiety. . . .

Freud's allegedly pessimistic conclusion in *Civilization and Its Discontents* [is] that the dictates of society will inevitably frustrate the gratification of instinctual needs, and that man is, therefore, a creature divided against himself. Although *Nightwood* is not written in the didactic mode, Barnes appears to have arrived at the same understanding of this very basic human dilemma. In the dream world of the novel Robin does have the opportunity to gratify her instinctual needs with minimal observance of the forms of society, and the consequences are clearly disastrous. All major characters are drawn irresistably to the level of experience which Robin represents, and each suffers some irremedial loss. After she divests herself of the demands of the superego, or that whole complex of forms and values known as "civilization," she simply returns to that state of being which our apish ancestors must have known before any of those forms and values evolved in the first place—she is intensely aware of and responsive to physical stimuli but has apparently lost all capacity to "think." She is an animal—pure and simple. (p. 162)

> *Robert L. Nadeau, "'Nightwood' and the Freudian Unconscious," in* The International Fiction Review, *July, 1975, pp. 159-63.*

ELIZABETH POCHODA

[*Nightwood*] is most often remembered for its high reputation with writers like T. S. Eliot. Apart from this sort of recognition it is examined either as a cache of modernism or, because it is rather tangled and obscure, it is sometimes rewarded with an extravagant *explication de texte*. In short, it has not been much appreciated by critics while among novelists, notably Hawkes and Pynchon, it resonates. Hawkes picks up on the blighted landscape and the fictive detachment which allows Barnes to make comedy of violence, and Pynchon parodies her style in *V* while attending closely to her view of history as a bowdlerized version of human damnation. (p. 179)

Throughout *Nightwood* the theme of de-evolution or of bowing down ("Bow Down" is the title of the first section and was originally meant to be the title for the whole book) has implications for the act of writing. The book itself moves backward. Beginning with an amusing historical flourish in its famous first sentence it eventually turns its back on history, on faith in coherent expression, and finally on words themselves. The novel bows down before its own impotence to express truth; its author wrote no successors. (pp. 179-80)

[The] celebrated obscurities of *Nightwood* would be less troublesome if readers would take hold of the novel by the handle of its wit, for it is a tremendously funny book in a desperately surgical sort of way. Its only warmth and capacity to move us after every conventional response has been cut away arise paradoxically from the ashes of its wit,

but this is not so surprising since it is paradox in general which holds the book together as much as it is paradox which leaves it in tatters at the end. Paradox and contradiction *are* wit. . . . [The witty dissection of honesty and hoax is done] in the novel at large over and over again until actions of every sort are reduced to their initial hoax. Only then is sympathy allowable. The apparently touching love story of Robin and Nora is also a kind of hoaxing, and we are not permitted to weep with Nora over her loss. Once the bloodthirsty nature of such love is uncovered we are allowed the sympathy appropriate to such an inevitable delusion.

Nor is the novel itself immune to the paradox of honesty and hoax. Here is the description of Felix watching the [doctor's] theft of [Robin's] money: "With a tension in his stomach, such as one suffers when watching an acrobat leaving the virtuosity of his safety in a mad unravelling whirl into probable death, Felix watched the hand descend, take up the note, and disappear into the limbo of the doctor's pocket." . . . The aspiration, transcendence, and risk which inevitably accompany our more venal acts are here in this language. And what of this style which soars with breathtaking virtuosity at the same time that it is yoked to a tawdry deed? It is sublimely out of whack with its subject matter. . . . What is most impressive in this writing is also most gratuitous. The style has usually been taken straight when in fact it is deliberately and gorgeously overambitious; it strives to dazzle onlookers in the manner of circus people, whom Barnes describes elsewhere as knowing "that skill is never so amazing as when it seems inappropriate." . . . We shall see more instances of the celebrated style making nothing or as near to nothing as it can of itself. Only by doing so, by assigning the novel's best effects to the inappropriate, is the novelist free to indulge in beautiful writing. (pp. 180-81)

[The horror which has turned all gesture to hoaxing and all style to jocular masquerade] is the unspoken groundwork for some unpleasant comedy, and by leaving it unnamed reinvests it with the enormous impact it deserves. O'Connor's monologues do center on the unnameable atrocity, and their obscurity is partially the result of the notion that the horror is so pervasive that it can and must be taken for granted; it is too large for naming and too well known to need it. But Miss Barnes's early stories are not nearly so reticent about the specific nature of these dark truths of existence, and while the stories are less convincing for that reason, they are at the same time a useful shortcut in talking about the ideas which underlie *Nightwood*. (p. 182)

[An example is "The Doctors," in which] the nightmare landscape and its horrors are the result of some terrible impertinence, or "impudence," to use the word that occurs to [the protagonist] Katrina Silverstaff. . . . This is the impudence corrected by the text of Ecclesiastes 3 verses 18 and 19, a text which "dogs" the pages of *Nightwood*: "I said in mine heart concerning the estate of the sons of men, that God might manifest them, and that they might see that they themselves are beasts. / For that which befalleth the sons of men befalleth beasts . . . so that a man hath no preeminence above a beast; for all is vanity." The impudence of vivisection stands in small for all the acts of estrangement and violation committed in the name of human nature (as something distinct from and above the bestial).

The impudence is arbitrary, unwarranted, and hideous, but it is not until we get to *Nightwood* that Miss Barnes's art rescues it from the melodrama of [her stories] by recognizing that above all the human impertinence is ultimately comic because ultimately futile. It is not simply that *Nightwood* engages and satirizes a world, but it has . . . found a way for satire and the apocalypse to merge so that even the novel must bow down and acknowledge the impertinence of prophesying doom. It does indeed assume the prophetic role in reverse, scraping away at all pretensions. What begins as a joke at the expense of the characters' personal styles ends by swallowing the novel as well. (pp. 182-83)

Miss Barnes has expended a good deal of wit in . . . passages where personal style tries to cloak the knowledge of the night. Style as raiment clogs the action of the principal figures, all of whom are arrested in the museums of their own existences; in one way or another they all resemble Felix Volkbein, who dresses in expectation of participating in some great event "though there was no function in the world for which he could be said to be properly garbed; wishing to be correct at any moment, he was tailored in part for the evening and in part for the day." . . . (p. 183)

It is easy to see the impertinence of style in Nora's existence, since she more than anyone lives for the day in defiance of her night self. The style of Nora and the American ancestors whose fortitude she recalls prompts a more subtle wit from the author. Nora is the avatar of those enemies of darkness who crossed the American plains. . . . As Nora pounds the pavements of Paris at night in search of Robin, she repeats the efforts of her forebears, but it is a faded repetition, a moldering recollection of forgiveness and absolution no longer possible. Nora's honesties are the honesties of love; they are prepared in the style of the saint and are the hoax whereby her love for Robin conceals its own attraction to degradation, evil, suffering, and especially to the death of the beloved as the only secure means of possession. In the paradox of her passion she is indeed "bloodthirsty with love." . . . The language of the passages about Nora's passion appears moving until one realizes that it is heightened just enough to suggest melodrama. Like the exaggerated gestures of the magician, the heightened language suggests that it is a cover for something else. It is not meant to be taken straight. (pp. 183-84)

Nora's love is a stylized lament with the conceit of her own honesty to keep her from knowing that her desire for Robin is as much a desire for the domestication of her own savagery as it is love of the other for the other's sake. (p. 184)

There are no important moral distinctions to be made between the deceptions practiced by Nora and those more obvious and ludicrous gestures of disguise practiced by Felix and Jenny. Passages dealing with Jenny, "one of the most unimportantly wicked women of her time," are invariably amusing, but they do not set her ploys off from those of the other characters except by revealing their laughable transparency. Ultimately, as O'Connor points out, one's heart has to ache "for all creatures putting on the dog. . . .'" . . . All the characters are damned by their willful singularity, by the excrescence of style which sits between them and their recognition of the universal malady of guilt. (pp. 184-85)

[The] doctor is also aware of the final hopelessness of his striving to go backward through the target of personality toward anonymity and the night. While the other characters overindividuate themselves, he dons the universal garment and becomes temporarily both man and woman, youth and age. But in doing so he also becomes more recognizably eccentric. This is an impasse and a paradox which only death can solve, and it helps to explain why he enjoys speaking of himself as if he were a dead soul guiding us through hell. The novel dwells with some amusement upon the visual effects of the doctor's getup, so that even the shadows cast by the interior of his sausage curls do not escape our attention, and he, poor thing, is far from escaping the paradox of his striving. He hoaxes us whether he wishes to or not.

And so does the novel up to a point, for while it is engaged in an experiment to dismantle narrative, to invent a prose which will be indefinite enough to include more of the world than it excludes, the result is not inclusiveness or featurelessness but this eccentric volume which calls attention to its own singularity. (pp. 186-87)

[For Miss Barnes] the experiment with fictional forms is a moral necessity. This is not mere faddishness; her idea is that the conventions of realistic fiction are the familiar clothes which too easily conceal violence, horror, and impertinence. Miss Barnes pursues her own methods with quite as much courage as O'Connor does his monologues, and his monologues are, in fact, the primary agents by which she unravels her novel. . . . At times O'Connor reminds his listeners that he lies. His lies have implications for the structure of the novel. Since we never know when he is lying, we have no handle on the objective movement of the book, but more important than this is the fact that lying is a special form of bowing down for the novelist and her character. Her idea is not so much that the road to truth is paved with error as that the submission to our own error, uncertainty, illogic, and confusion is a necessary part of bowing down. The logical progression of the novel's internal coherence appears to be undercut by O'Connor's monologues, which defy logical penetration; there is a paradox at the core of every important utterance whether it is his or the novelist's. (p. 187)

"The Possessed," the section which follows "Go Down Matthew" and concludes the novel, seems an anticlimax. . . . That Robin should end groveling with a dog makes perfect sense in terms of the ideas which the novel has been developing, but the presentation seems faulty; it is devoid of the wit and energy of the earlier sections. . . . There is nowhere for the prose to go. The end is factual and brief. Only despair remains. Robin's journey into anonymity ends with her ludicrous attempt to crawl back into the beast world. The novel ends in wordlessness and failure, with the impasse of life intact and its contradictions nicely exposed. . . .

From the beginning the novel has embraced more than the destruction of its own stylistic beauties. It has assaulted the very notion of history and with it narrative progression and memory, those staples of plot and characterization. . . . This is a trip like Dante's where all history is present at once so that the distinctions between man and man, and between time and time, can be obliterated in an awareness of the universal malady. The central image in *Nightwood* is that of the circus, where the leveling of all distinctions and the ultimate containment of all aspiration can be shown with some wit. History is an amusement; the circus is a version of history which cancels history out. In addition to the efforts to obliterate distinctions between men and beasts by getting them to perform each other's tricks, the ring itself contains all time at once—there is movement but no progression. It is here, in the feats of the aerialist, that we see the dazzle of human transcendence which is nevertheless tied to the ground. (p. 188)

Even the notion that art with its beauty can transcend the horror it describes proves false. The novel is inseparable from the cruelties it has in fact created. . . .

If history only conceals the horrors which comprise it, it is because memory itself is suspect. The novel moves toward a confusion of times of which the doctor's allusion to his attending Catherine the Great is the most extreme example. Memory, which differentiates and expurgates and dignifies the individual past, is as detrimental to personal history as it is to the history of peoples. (p. 189)

Since there is nothing that does not bear going into to uncover the hoax, nothing that we can take at face value, there is no way for feeling to organize the experience of the novel. As the doctor so often says, none of us suffers or loves as much as we say, and the stripping away of feeling during his talks with Felix and Nora leaves us with no way to orient ourselves with respect to the incidents of the plot. We are not meant to take Nora's loss and suffering at face value, or Felix's; every decent emotion is denied us until at the last the only appropriate response to the absence of any trustworthy tears is pity, despair, wailing, and gnashing of teeth—the reinvention of feeling by the annihilation of conventional response. (pp. 189-90)

> *Elizabeth Pochoda, "Style's Hoax: A Reading of Djuna Barnes's 'Nightwood',"* in Twentieth Century Literature *(copyright 1976, Hofstra University Press), May, 1976, pp. 179-90.*

*   *   *

BECKETT, Samuel   1906-

A Nobel Prize-winning dramatist, novelist, poet, essayist, critic, short story writer, and translator, Beckett was born in Ireland, and currently resides in Paris. His cryptic, often nightmarish vision creates a world of insignificance and nothingness. Mixing comic elements with tragic, he parallels the helpless plight of his characters with a disintegration of language and form. Philosophically, Beckett has been linked with Sartre, Camus, and Kafka, while stylistically some have compared him with James Joyce. (See also *CLC*, Vols. 1, 2, 3, 4, 6, 9, 10, and *Contemporary Authors*, Vols. 5-8, rev. ed.)

A. J. LEVENTHAL

One has to go back to Samuel Beckett's first published fictional work to find the image that is to figure almost continuously in the novels as well as in the plays, to find the character round which the Beckett world moved. The collection of short stories which make up the volume called *More Pricks than Kicks* relates the adventures of Belacqua. . . . Here is a stasis that was to pursue (or should it be pin down) those creations that were to stand out in so markedly an individual manner.

Nor was it by chance that the hero in this book was named Belacqua. The Dante in the title of the first story gives the clue. The name comes straight out of the *Purgatorio*. Little seems to be known about him in real life except that he was

a lute maker in Florence, a friend of Dante and notorious for his indolence and apathy. He comes into the fourth canto of the *Purgatorio*. . . . [Dante's lines describing Belacqua] are reflected in the position taken up by Beckett's hero near the end of the story called "A Wet Night": "[he] disposed himself in the knee-and-elbow position on the pavement." . . . [Finally] he creeps with his poor trunk parallel to the horizon. Here we have the mode of locomotion that was to be repeated by characters in subsequent novels and in his . . . work *Comment c'est* where we are introduced to a painful cyclical crawl, symbolizing, perhaps, among other things, the slow progression of mankind. However, in "A Wet Night" Belacqua desists out of weariness from this method of self-propulsion and takes up the position I mentioned earlier, disposing himself in the knee-and-elbow position on the pavement.

It was thus that Botticelli depicted Belacqua in his drawing to illustrate this canto of the *Purgatorio*. I have seen it in a reproduction, showing him with his head between his clasped knees and with one eye fixed on Dante and Virgil, suggesting that he is even too weary to raise his head or to join his indolent companions in their mockery of the two poet visitors. (pp. 37-40)

When Beckett changes to writing his novels in French he leaves behind him much of the humor, grim as it was, in his previous work. He has less interest in making his characters indulge in games to pass the time as in *Waiting for Godot*. They are now concentrating on their *pénible* task of dying. In the opening passage of *Molloy*, the narrator says that what he wants to speak of are the things that are left, "say my goodbyes, finish dying." He remembers "in the tranquility of decomposition the long confused emotion that was my life." (May I point out the cynical echo of the well-known Wordsworth definition of poetry as "emotion recollected in tranquility"). . . . [There is little doubt] that there is an evolutionary process from Dante to the Belacqua of *More Pricks than Kicks* and through the various stages as manifested by the Murphys, Molloys, Morans, Watts, Estragons, Hamms, culminating in the Pims of *Comment c'est*.

Beckett has not given up the Belacqua picture. The embryo has haunted him to such an extent that in the final novel of his trilogy, the one called *L'Innommable*, he tries, in a frenzy of self-examination, to find out who these heroes of his are. He ranges over the characters he has created, Murphy, Watt, Malone, Molloy, Mahood and picks on a new one whom he calls Worm. He wants to reduce them all to silence. He wants to reduce himself to silence and for a moment he finds solace in the thought of Worm. He would rather that Worm took over from the others with whom he frankly identifies himself. To be Worm means to be away from the world, away from all the other characters who have taken possession of him and at last to think nothing, to feel nothing. For this is himself, himself in embryo—literally in embryo. Many pages are given up to the description of womb life, that is life in the womb, if you can call it life. He would rather not call it by that name. There he cannot stir even though he suffers as a result. Indeed with bitter Beckettian irony he declares that "it would be to sign his life-warrant to stir from where he is." It is again Belacqua's weary phrase: *"L'andare in su che porta?"* What's the use in going up? Never in the history of literature (at least as I know it) has there been so poignant, so despairing a description of birth. Surely no one has ever dared to speak out of the womb as Beckett does here. Perhaps psychoanalysts may be able to send their recumbent patients sufficiently far back into their unconscious to imagine their unborn state but at the very most it could scarcely be much more than a blur—a clouded image based on knowledge acquired in life itself. Thus in the *L'Innommable* we are back to the foetal image of the unborn, the Botticelli drawing of Belacqua, Dante's Florentine friend, the lazy lute maker.

I referred earlier to the evolutionary process in the Beckett characters but the word "evolutionary" is hardly the right one in this connection, for it is normally associated with progression, with a series of biological changes, each improving on the previous condition. In Beckett's world the subject who has begun his fictional existence with his head on his knees ends in *Comment c'est* with his face in the mud. (pp. 42-3)

Stasis, or near stasis, is an outstanding characteristic of Beckett's creations. "*Cette inertie immortelle*" is how Beckett himself makes obeisance to human beings immobilized. Yet the febrile argumentation of his *personae* gives them a dynamic quality—a quality that sometimes borders on delirium. . . . They suffer, not gladly, but inevitably, accepting the ignominious situation, the insult, and turn more and more to the haven of their minds, finding their being as much in the mind's solace as in its *souillures*. (p. 43)

[In Beckett's plays] the very simplicity of the words is disarming and at first sight incompatible with the tragic import of the situations in which the characters find themselves. Soon however it becomes clear that the sparse, bare vocabulary is giving profundity to the statement. So that if, for example, there are many meanings read into *Waiting for Godot* there is none to say which is the inevitable one. The very fact that it lends itself to a religious interpretation that spells hope, the eternal expectation of a messiah, or its opposite, the futility of such an expectation, surely reflects the ambivalence of the human situation. Nothing is clear cut. Nothing can be known absolutely. (p. 46)

Never, in fiction, have so many words been used as by Beckett to underline the inefficiency of language and never, by his very language, has anyone disproved the point so brilliantly. In his French trilogy: *Molloy, Malone Meurt,* and *L'Innommable,* words, words, and more words pour themselves out in a cascade of affirmation and denial. It is an effort to stay the fleeting thought, to capture winging silences. Again and again he challenges the value of his own verbal descriptions, impugning their accuracy, offering another verb, another noun, and finally dismissing them all as being as worthless as the thoughts whose messengers they are. . . . (pp. 46-7)

The question of reality is to be found everywhere in the Beckett *oeuvre*. Beckett understands how Dante can condemn sinners to a limitless stagnation; to this, however, he adds the bewilderment of his *personae* when they become the victims of some luckless fate that brings other suffering. (p. 47)

Beckett seems to have carried with him something of the punning echoing system that he found in James Joyce. Everybody knows how the Joycean mind enjoyed the rather schoolboyish humor of what I might call the physical pun.

Visitors to Joyce's flat in Paris were asked to admire a picture of the city of Cork—a picture which he had decided could be framed in only one substance—cork. Harmless enough as a joke—but it is possible to relate an idiosyncrasy of this kind to the complicated literary apparatus of *Finnegans Wake*.

In the same way there is a certain esoteric quality hidden skeletally in Beckett's work. It is not essential to the work itself but an awareness of its existence can be helpful. We know that a great number of his heroes have names that begin with M. There can be few authors or for that matter doctors who write a more illegible hand than does Sam Beckett. With most people signatures are difficult to read but knowing the identity of the writer one can make out the name Sam that concludes the communication. The S is so formed that it looks like an M standing on its side. And therefrom stem the dissyllables Murphy, Molloy, Malone, Mahood which echo the two syllabled "Beckett." There are monosyllable names like Pim, Pam, Bim, Bom which echo "Sam," while the name Sam itself, which may well refer to the author, occurs in *Watt*. Watt is not only another monosyllable echo but also throws light on his character. If one reads it as an interrogative, visually inserting an h and dropping a t, the quality of curiosity in the creation is pinpointed. In this connection I recall a conversation with the author who was at the time having difficulty in finding a publisher for his novel *Watt*. He cheered up considerably when he heard word from the literary agents to whom he had submitted the work that they were prepared to find a publisher. It was not so much because the agents were hopeful of placing the novel that Beckett was cheered but because *Watt* was to be handled by a firm called Watt and Watt. This comes near to Joyce's cork-framed Cork.

This is not meant to be a key to any symbolism that may run through the novels and plays. As I have probably said already the individual will read his particular reaction or that of a trusted critic into the significance of the text. I am just looking for clues to clearer understanding. And in the light of our familiarity so far with the fact that nomenclature plays a kind of secret part in fixing the sources of the characters it becomes possible to draw tentatively some elementary conclusions.

Let us look at the names of the characters in *Waiting for Godot*: Estragon, Vladimir, Pozzo, Lucky. Estragon is French, Vladimir, Russian, Pozzo, Italian, Lucky, English. . . . It occurs to me that if the names are not adventitious (and Beckett weighs all his words) it means that we are asked to think of this play, not as an isolated piece of inaction in a corner of France, or if you like Ireland, but as a cosmic state, a world condition in which all humanity is involved. (pp. 48-9)

The written word is not enough. His public (be it ever so small) must not be spared. He is bold enough to give physical form to his maimed characters. It is not enough that they are apprehended through the mind in the reading, they must be seen on the stage. The horror of Nagg and Nell immured (No, that's not the word) shall we say jack-boxed into dustbins! Never, since Swift, has there been what the French call "*humour noir*" in such cruel measure as in the dialogue between Hamm's parents. Their joking brings tears. Nor have I referred to his last play *Happy Days*. Photographs of his theatrical scene makes joyous copy for news editors. A woman buried up to the neck in a high mound in a barren landscape—even the Godot tree has vanished—can hold the attention of the student of the form of horses or of the vacillations on the stock market for a second or two, either to be puzzled or annoyed or extract a jocular remark. But the picture is that of Mother Earth tugging with Newtonian gravity to take her own to her bosom. How gaily our heroine carries on up to the end. As long as we have arms free (as in the first act) we can tinker with our handbag, color our lips, put a fine face on things, and chatter. Talk, talk, talk to anybody, to oneself, above all to one's self. Beckett's characters can only be silenced by death. But we rarely see them die. Only in *Comment c'est* do we meet executioner and victim; they are shown to us as undergoing what Mrs. Rooney in *All That Fall* calls a "lingering dissolution." (p. 50)

A. J. Leventhal, "The Beckett Hero" (copyright © 1963 by A. J. Levanthal), a lecture delivered at Trinity College, Dublin, Ireland, in June, 1963 (and reprinted in Samuel Beckett: A Collection of Critical Essays, edited by Martin Esslin, Prentice-Hall, Inc., 1965, pp. 37-51).

DAVID HAYMAN

Beckett's trilogy [*Molloy, Malone Dies,* and *The Unnamable*] is for all its apparent formlessness a close-knit structural unit, though the novels are related to each other more through their form and direction than through any obvious system of interrelated characters or events. All of them are narrated in the first person. Each of them deals with a figure or figures whose condition is purged of the specific, that is, of those qualities which would detract from his universality or from his status as a metaphor for some aspect of human experience. The heroes of the trilogy are all artists, all writers and hence creators; yet they all exhibit a disgust for life to be matched only by the tenacity with which they hold on to it. All of them are models of the egocentric, but as the series progresses toward *The Unnamable* the narrators' worlds tighten and shrink. It is almost as if Beckett were examining layer by layer the mind of the artist and the sources of his inspiration. It follows that the Unnamable speaks from within the cave of the self in the voice of some obscene male sibyl. He spews upon the receptive page a steady stream of heavily-punctuated but almost disembodied thought.

In terms of our own experience this third novel is the monologue of a deaf mute who is at least partially blind and totally incapable of movement. Unfortunately for him, this seemingly hermetic existence is only semi-autonomous.... With his range of choice reduced to an almost absolute minimum, he persists in choosing and speculating. If the Unnamable has a body, he has no senses which would enable him to feel it. Nevertheless, he hears voices which assure him of his physical existence. In response to these he pours his being by turns into idealized creations of his fancy. In the past he has identified with the heroes of Beckett's other novels, Murphy, Watt, Molloy, and Malone; now he becomes or posits [Mahood or Worm].... On one level of interpretation we see these two suffering creatures as projections of the psyche of a suffering god whom we must identify with the Unnamable himself. They are screens for the essential formlessness of the hero, shapes given to the half-formed doubts and the torment of the nameless and the inarticulate.

In this connection the reader familiar with the earlier novels *Murphy* and *Watt* will recall Murphy's favorite patient at the Magdalen Mental Mercyseat, Mr. Endon, the psychotic whose name and condition suggest his function. Mr. Endon is Murphy's ideal, the perfect closed system, impervious to outside influence. His successor, Watt's employer, the godlike Mr. Knott, is in some ways even more so. Consciously or not, all of Beckett's characters are approaching this state. In the trilogy, Molloy is in quest of the womb, Moran is in quest of the Molloy in himself; the bedridden Malone writes out his days from the shelter of a sort of improvised room-womb. But the Unnamable's position is clearly the zenith. It is characteristic of Beckett's humor that this creature, situated on the brink of nirvana, yearns after the world of objects. In him the extremes meet. Paradise leans close to hell. (pp. 130-31)

Although to Beckett's mind all mankind is in purgatory, each of the books in the trilogy contains ironically presented elements of all three of man's postmortal states. Furthermore, each of the three novels puts the ironic emphasis upon one of these states. *Molloy* is infernal, *Malone Dies* is purgatorial, and *The Unnamable* is paradisal. However, paradox is Beckett's stock in trade, and though *The Unnamable* as a novel depicts an ostensibly ideal state, the novel's central figure is in purgatory. Embodying as he does both the unmerited punishment of Worm and the equally unmerited rewards of Mahood, he is seen as forming a middle ground between heaven and hell.

In his article "Dante ... Bruno. Vico ... Joyce," Beckett defines hell as "the static lifelessness of unrelieved viciousness. Paradise the static lifelessness of unrelieved immaculation. Purgatory a flood of movement and vitality released by the conjunction of these two elements."

Although the preceding passage was designed to explain Joyce's concept of existence, Beckett seems also to be defining his own view. We need not be surprised therefore that at each stage in his heroes' adventures apparent hell and apparent heaven give way to the only reality which man knows, that is, the constant purgatory of existence.... Thus the questing creatures, Beckett's tormented heroes, can, in spite of their apparent progress toward the pure state of bodilessness, do nothing more than accomplish the purgatorial spiral, moving ever inward—toward the immaculate and endless purgatory of *The Unnamable.* His latest full-length narrative, *How It Is,* deals finally with hell, portraying a nameless creature crawling endlessly through primeval muck and experiencing grotesquely sadistic pleasures with others of his kind. Figuratively the spiral has begun to unwind. (pp. 132-33)

The most complex of the novels in Beckett's French-Irish trilogy is *Molloy,* the bicyclical tale of two quest-heroes [Molloy and Moran], active seekers after the nameless joys of salvation. The novel is sharply divided into two first-person narratives of equal length. The two wheels of the bicycle are connected by a messenger and steered by the divine will. (p. 134)

My belief is that Molloy's mother, Molloy, Moran, and Moran's son all inhabit the same body; further, the events described in the two narratives are simultaneous and identical though viewed from different angles and differently ordered. Since the narrators are by their own admission untrustworthy to the point of absurdity, it seems probable that they are actually rationalizing the behavior of a posited third force (Youdi or Jacques Junior?) over whom they have progressively lost their power. It is by virtue of this third force that Molloy and Moran are able to interpenetrate, and their two accounts overlap in predictable but nevertheless striking ways. (pp. 135-36)

[*Molloy*] has been described as an anti-novel in the tradition of Rabelais, Sterne, and Joyce and indeed we are aware that the form of the conventional novel is being satirized. But the term "anti-novel" is not descriptive. It would be more like Beckett to write an ante-novel and more appropriate to say that all of his books are what Northrop Frye calls Menippean Satires (a variety of sophisticated farce). At any rate in *Molloy* we are struck by the fact that nothing much is happening. Two vaguely insignificant quest heroes, two suffering clowns are decomposing: the one a noman, the other an everyman. Here is a deliberate reversal of pattern characteristic of Beckett's art. The quest hero is generally conceived of as going into the darkness to retrieve the light and achieve a meaningful existence. In *Molloy* shabby versions of the shining knight-errant achieve deeper darkness and meaninglessness.

Molloy's two parts are intimately linked, a complementary or an ironic couple contributing to a fascinating portrait of the universal man and an ingenious satire of his aspirations and accomplishments. Hence, it can be shown that every event and object described by Molloy is viewed from a different point of vision by Moran. But these relationships are screened by the paradox implicit in the identification of two such disparate creatures, by the displacement which events undergo in the mind of Molloy which knows neither time nor place and finally by the sublimation or distortion of Molloy-like ideas in the narrative of Moran. In one sense the reader is being willfully misled. Only after a second or third reading do we recognize the affinities beneath the contradictions: realizing, for example, that Molloy's vision of the black sheep and their shepherd at the beginning of his narrative is exactly contemporaneous with Moran's vision of them near the end of his tale, that their different reactions are consistent with their different and complementary roles as representatives of the extremes of chaos and order. (pp. 140-41)

[On the most literal level, Jacques Junior] represents, first, hope in the future, being released energy, youth, and apparent freedom; second, despair, being doomed, as Moran indicates, to continue the cycle or spiral of existences. At any rate we may consider him to be the first term of the series concluding with the Unnamable. It is worth noting that only in terms of this sort of development at once temporal and psychic can we account for Jacques Junior's behavior and existence. The more commonly held belief in the inverted order of the narrative accounts neither for the role of the boy nor for the parallelism of the events, nor for the exact equivalence of the two narratives' lengths, nor for the obviously complementary vision of the two narrators. Furthermore, it implies a somewhat simple-minded gimmickry on the part of Beckett whose irony is more subtle. I would suggest that it should stand as a red-herring solution but that we would gain much by tracing the progression, not through Jacques to Moran to Molloy to Malone to the Unnamable but rather through Jacques to the tandem Molloy-Moran or better still through Jacques/Molloy-Moran.

Beckett, using the simplest of tools, a basic French or Eng-

lish vocabulary, a handful of allusions, some standard humorous devices, succeeds in evoking for each of his characters innumerable identities and for his book an interlace pattern as complex as those in the Irish book of Kells or as the Daedalian labyrinth. (pp. 144-45)

Beckett is applying as a principle and with telling effect the idea that opposites are equal, that extremes meet, and that all existence is "a kitten chasing its tail." This principle is drawn in part at least from the teaching of James Joyce's favorite philosopher-heretic, Giordano Bruno, whose theories Beckett outlines in the following passage from his early Joyce article:

> There is no difference, says Bruno between the smallest possible chord and the smallest possible arc, no difference between the infinite circle and the straight line. The maxima and minima of particular contraries are one and indifferent. . . . The principle (minimum) of one contrary takes its movement from the principle (maximum) of another. Therefore not only do the minima coincide with the minima, the maxima with the maxima, but the minima with the maxima in the succession of transmutations. . . . And all things are ultimately identified with God, the universal monad, Monad of monads.

Beckett applies this view to every line, every identity, every concept, analogy, character, image, and book of his trilogy. Hence, the cycles within cycles that characterize its structure, the logical and valid contradictions evident everywhere, the improbable identifications. Hence the flux of movement in the brain of Beckett's readers. . . . Molloy, the Morans (father and son), and Malone are all simply puppets motivated by the static mind of the Unnamable, that symbol of the dubious upper and lower reaches of existence. [The] seemingly endless permutations create the kaleidoscopic effects which are enriched and multiplied by seemingly endless analogical identities, which, like the coincidence of Jacques Junior's name, should, to paraphrase Moran, lead to no confusion.

We find, for example, parallels drawn from Plato, Descartes, Nietzsche, and Bergson; from Freud and Jung; from Christianity, Judaism, Hinduism and the sacred texts; from myth cycles and literature. Each of these contains along with its grain of truth a large pinch of the burlesque, both of which are complicated when the systems are brought into conjunction. Molloy may be seen as Christ (or one of the thieves), Descartes's mind as distinguished from matter, Bergson's creative imagination welling up from a time-free matrix, Plato's deathless soul, and we may say that these metaphors are at once apt and improper. (pp. 146-48)

> *David Hayman, "'Molloy' or the Quest for Meaninglessness: A Global Interpretation," in* Samuel Beckett Now, *edited by Melvin J. Friedman (reprinted by permission of The University of Chicago Press; © 1970 by The University of Chicago), University of Chicago Press, 1970, pp. 129-56.*

ROBERT WILCHER

Just as the 'quality of language' in Proust was more important than 'any system of ethics or aesthetics' [according to Beckett], so the quality of an experience in Beckett's theatre becomes more important than any system of 'meaning' that might be extracted from the words of the text or from the 'symbolism' of the sets, characters, and actions. A dramatic art is created that is 'symbolic without symbolism'.

The purpose of this article is to explore further the implications of [his] statement 'form *is* content, content *is* form' for Beckett's drama and to show that the allegorical approach, which is misleading when applied to the novels, is even less appropriate as a response to the plays. (p. 12)

For all his obvious familiarity with a wide range of philosophical speculation, Beckett has persistently rejected the philosopher's quest for a systematic statement about the nature of reality. . . . It is by the operation of habit, he argues in *Proust,* that man contrives to ignore changes both internal and external, and so imposes a system upon the flux of experience. He insists that 'the creation of the world did not take place once and for all time, but takes place every day', and glosses 'habit' as 'the generic term for the countless treaties concluded between the countless subjects that constitute the individual and their countless correlative objects. The countless selves that constitute 'the individual' no more add up to a fixed, knowable subjective entity than the fleeting impressions we receive from the external world cohere into an objective system. As Malone puts it, he has been 'nothing but a series or rather a succession of local phenomena all my life, without any result.'

Along with his distrust of the intellect and the generalising tendency of language goes a rejection of the 'grotesque fallacy' of realistic art, which subscribes to a conceptual, and hence expressible, view of reality. For the writer, realism is 'the penny-a-line vulgarity of a literature of notations'. . . . In his earliest works of fiction, *More Pricks than Kicks* and *Murphy,* Beckett makes many of the 'concessions required of the literary artist by the shortcomings of the literary convention.' His technique for evading these shortcomings is the simple and clumsy one of occasionally emphasising the essential unreality of what is presented according to the convention as real. (pp. 12-13)

Early on, Beckett made a number of attempts to establish a distinction between conceptual clarity and the immediacy of experience as it happens. This distinction, between the separation of form and content and the complete fusion of form and content, between the 'literature of notations' and the 'revelation of a world', is present in the first paragraph of his first published fiction, the story 'Dante and the Lobster' which opens *More Pricks than Kicks.* Belacqua is reading Dante. He is 'stuck in the first of the canti of the moon', Canto II of *Il Paradiso,* where Beatrice is explaining to the poet the nature of the spots on the moon. . . . The mental processes implied by the words *explanation, demonstration, proof* both bog Belacqua down and bore him. He wants to finish this passage of conceptual argument, in which Beatrice transforms the simple visual phenomenon of spots on the moon's surface into an elaborate system of heavenly science, and pass on to the Piccarda sequence. . . . The meeting with Piccarda is a direct encounter, an experience; Beatrice's lecture on the moon resorts to 'analysis and abstraction'. Disembodied meaning is opposed to embodied experience in the two contrasting episodes. The gap between form and content in the Beatrice passage is stressed in the continuation of the paragraph:

> Still he pored over the enigma, he would not concede himself conquered, he would understand at least the meanings of the words, the order in which they were spoken and the nature of the satisfaction that they conferred on the misinformed poet. . . .

Belacqua is here struggling with the difficulty of reading Italian, so that the enigma is partly linguistic on a simple level. But it is also partly a difficulty arising from the difference between the language of Metaphysics and the language of Poetry. Later Beckett heroes still feel a sharp distinction between these two kinds of language, but tend more and more to abandon the attempt to 'understand at least the meanings of the words', often preferring to pay attention to their quality as sounds and to 'the order in which they were spoken' and deriving a satisfaction from them which does not depend on a grasp of their conceptual dimension. (pp. 13-14)

In *More Pricks than Kicks* and *Murphy,* Beckett is still struggling with 'the shortcomings of the literary convention', still to a large extent using words to talk about the distinction between the conceptual and the experiential apprehension of living, and it is here that [a] view of Beckett as an allegorical novelist might be substantiated. In his third fiction, *Watt,* he begins to exploit the qualities of words to narrow the gap between form and content, to break down the conceptual element of language and to deflect attention from the desire to interpret to the 'ebb and flow of action' in the process of reading the words themselves.

The crucial episode is that of the visit of the piano-tuners, 'the Galls, father and son', which is offered as a paradigm of 'all the incidents of note proposed to Watt during his stay in Mr Knott's house.' The visit of the Galls resembled the other 'incidents of note':

> in the sense that it was not ended, when it was past, but continued to unfold, in Watt's head, from beginning to end, over and over again, the complex connexions of its lights and shadows, the passing from silence to sound and from sound to silence, the stillness before the movement and the stillness after, the quickenings and retardings, the approaches and the separations, all the shifting detail of its march and ordinance, according to the irrevocable caprice of its taking place. . . .

What happens in this passage is that the clear outline and the firm substance of the event disintegrate into the assortment of sense impressions that made it up. In the process of reading this extraordinary prose, which eschews the shaping device of the semi-colon and which rocks us back and forth between opposing forces of sound, sight, and movement, we are absorbed into a rhythmic but directionless experience and share in 'the irrevocable caprice of its taking place'. Form and content fuse; the words begin to vibrate 'at a lower frequency, or a higher, than that of ratiocination.' We enter into the quality of Watt's experience of the visit of the Galls. . . . [As] Watt's mind—and Beckett's prose—breaks down the significant shape of the sense impressions into an unshaped assembly of lights, sounds, and movements the recognizable incident 'became a mere example of light commenting bodies, and stillness motion, and silence sound, and comment comment.' This loss of 'outer meaning' is very disturbing to Watt.... Watt's difficulty is that of the mind which cannot face the possibility that all occurrences in the outer world may be totally random, and that order, meaning, significant and knowable shape may be simply the projection of an inner need which tries to impose its structures on material which does not operate according to the mind's habits.... Watt is an embodiment of the dominant scientific-rationalist view of reality, the inductive method of reasoning which leaves Final Causes—'what they really meant'—on one side, and pursues explanations of physical happenings that can be induced by observation and ingenious ratiocination.... Answers are indicated in *Murphy:* this pursuit of meaning is the pursuit of a chimaera, and it tends to the idolatry of a false god.... Beckett returns to this distrust of conceptual thinking frequently in the novels.... In *The Unnamable* Beckett suggests that the need to reduce experience to clear and distinct notions, the need to think that we know, is the inevitable result of our ignorance and isolation.... The clarity with which [Beckett maintains] art has nothing to do is conceptual clarity—'notions clear and distinct'—the clarity demanded by such questions as 'What's it meant to mean?' The clarity that Beckett's art aims at is the clarity of felt experience, of something undergone though not understood. The incident of the Galls is again central: an incident 'that is to say of great formal brilliance and indeterminable purport'.... [Although] the mind cannot impose a shape on the event, and so render it graspable by the intellect, a series of physical phenomena had taken place.... The nearest language, with its curse of philosophical abstraction and generalisation, can get to expressing it is to say that 'nothing *had happened*'. As Hamm frequently says, 'Something is taking its course'—the 'something' or the 'nothing' cannot be conceptualised, but there is activity which can be suggested by the verbal constructions of *Watt* or by the combination of words and actions in *Endgame*. As the narrator, Sam, says later in the novel, having attempted some explanation of how Mr Knott's powers operate: 'But that does not at all agree with my conception of Mr Knott. But what conception have I of Mr Knott? None.' ... Many of Beckett's plays, like the episode of the Galls, offer passages of dialogue and sequences of stage activity which have 'the utmost formal distinctness'. They provide the audience with an experience, but it is not possible to extrapolate a meaning from the experience in generalised and abstract terms. An allegorical reading is thwarted. *Something* takes its course in the spectator as well as on the stage, but like Watt we are unable to say what has happened. (pp. 16-19)

As Beckett has proceeded as a dramatist, he has deprived would-be interpreters of as many of the possibilities for conceptualising his 'stage machines' as he can. Compared with *Waiting for Godot*, it is much more difficult to suggest esoteric significance of a social, metaphysical, or psychological kind in the characters or their physical situation in *Play*. (p. 20)

[Various allusions] serve an unusual purpose. Rather than cohering into a satisfying pattern which carries in symbolic fashion the message of the play, they lead the interpreter up a series of blind alleys.... This frustration of the curious intellect is itself part of the experience the play provides, making the audience feel the inadequacy of approaching reality by trying to impose systems upon the minute-by-

minute flux of sense impressions. At times, indeed, Beckett plays with the audience's desire to read symbolic meanings into his text. (p. 21)

Krapp's Last Tape, Happy Days, Play, and *Not I* ... reveal Beckett's continuing exploration of the nature of theatre as a means of avoiding definition and of achieving that union of form and content which has been the constant aim of his art. The kind of progression discernible in all the plays from *Waiting for Godot* onwards is similar to that followed in the novels from *Murphy* to *How It Is,* and was already implicit in Beckett's aesthetic theory at the very start of his career.... The audience is still partly free to hold itself aloof from the deprivation shown and talked about on the stage [in *Waiting for Godot* and *Endgame*] and to interpret the 'stage picture' as an image of want and sterility, although the long silences and periods of inactivity begin the process of drawing us into an actual experience of deprivation as an audience. In the later plays Beckett becomes more and more successful at breaking down the distinctions between the objective 'stage picture' of deprivation, the deprivation imposed upon the actors, and the deprivation imposed upon the spectators. (pp. 22-3)

The first play in which light becomes a major ingredient in the overall dramatic effect is *Krapp's Last Tape,* in which the visible action is confined to a pool of light directed onto a desk. 'Rest of stage in darkness' reads the direction for the set. As an audience we are not permitted to see the whole acting area. Any curiosity we might feel about what lies beyond the circle of light is aggravated when Krapp 'goes with all the speed he can muster backstage into darkness. Ten seconds. Loud pop of cork. Fifteen seconds. He comes back into light carrying an old ledger and sits down at table.' Those two periods of silence, of absence of all happening on the part of the stage that we can see—ten seconds and fifteen seconds are a long time in the theatre—do not have quite the same quality as the silences in *Waiting for Godot*. Added to our waiting for something to happen is the provocation of frustrated curiosity. What is he doing back there? ... We simply want to see, and we are not allowed to.

The central episode of the play is an extension into drama of the pattern of contrasting apprehensions of reality.... First of all there is [on the tape] a moment of insight—the 'vision at last'—when he 'saw the whole thing'. He understood, the taped voice leads us to believe, what the meaning of it all was. But such expressions as 'the belief', 'in reality', and 'the whole thing', which suggest a systematic shaping of experience, should put us on our guard, and indeed Krapp is not interested in listening to the vision achieved by his earlier self. What he suddenly *saw*, what became *clear to him at last*, what was revealed to him on that stormy night through *the light of the understanding and the fire* has no relevance for him now. It was just another hypothesis that has collapsed with the passage of time.... The final comment by the recorded voice reinforces [a] sense of complete isolation from 'extracircumferential phenomena'—from the 'big blooming buzzing confusion': 'Past midnight. Never knew such silence. The earth might be uninhabited. *Pause*. Here I end—'. This is the goal of all Beckett's heroes: total blackness, silence, stillness, nothingness—the end—the 'wandering to find home' over.... This quest of the intellect for meaning is relegated to insignificance.... (pp. 23-4)

For the audience in the theatre, the crucial thing is not the possible allegorical equation of tapes and memory processes, but the moment by moment experience of listening to the recorded voice and looking at the figure of Krapp isolated in his pool of light. We hear the passage about the two people in the punt three times, but the striking fact is not that this repetition symbolizes 'the mechanization of the mechanism of memory', but that each time we listen our response is different. On the first occasion, we receive only direct physical impressions. . . . The second time through, we are given some precise information as to the context. . . . And more importantly, because this radically influences the way in which we respond to the incident, we learn the narrative context—it is the end of a love affair: 'it was hopeless and no good going on.' The pure experience —almost like Molloy's 'pure sounds, free of all meaning', except that here sounds are replaced by the physical sensations of touch and movement—is being contaminated by more and more information, so that we begin to replace an experience created by words with ideas about that experience. The timeless and spaceless moment is invaded by time and space. We are diverted from *feeling* to *knowing about* the incident. This is the exact reverse of the process that took place in the treatment of the visit of the Galls in *Watt*. There, an apparently definable and knowable event disintegrated into its random sensuous components; here, the pure sensuous components arc organized and trapped into a rigidly defined narrative episode. More than one critic has demanded a similar definition for the whole play. . . . The gradual accretion of descriptive and narrative details which destroy the purity of the experience in the punt is Beckett's dramatization and rejection of the habit of mind—the demand for realism—that lies behind such criticism. (pp. 25-6)

[The third] time Beckett allows us to hear the closing section, from where it was cut off the first time at 'Here I end —':

> Here I end this reel. Box—*(pause)*—three,
> spool—*(pause)*—five. *(Pause.)* . . .

The mystery that surrounded the words 'Here I end—', seeming to reinforce the imagery of silence and darkness and utter solitude, is drained away by the mundane completing phrase: 'Here I end this reel.' And the whole experience which was so striking and disturbing on first hearing is further reduced by the pigeon-holing precision of 'Box three, spool five.' One is reminded of Clov's remark about putting things in order: 'I love order. It's my dream. A world where all would be silent and still and each thing in its last place, under the last dust.' . . . Once things have been put in order, they are dead. Only the experiential moment is alive. Once an experience is past, it is filed away in the tapes of memory or in the words of a book. The tragedy of Krapp lies not in the loss of the fire of vision and certainty, but in the fact that that very fire of the understanding which creates an ordered view of existence precludes the entry into the experience which we have been enabled to share in our first fragmentary hearing of the punt episode. (pp. 26-7)

[In *Happy Days*] the dramatist has not simply presented the audience with an image of confinement, but has taken us, in the transition from Act One to Act Two, through an experience of being deprived. The range of our response has noticeably deteriorated during the course of the play, but the quality of our response has intensified. In making his actress shrink 'from the nullity of extracircumferential phenomena', Beckett has made it possible for the audience to be 'drawn in to the core of the eddy.' A 'stage machine' which is 'excavatory, immersive, a contraction . . . a descent'—Winnie visibly sinking into the earth—carries a responsive spectator with it into an experience of immersion and contraction. (pp. 28-9)

Happy Days does not simply offer us a representation of frustration; it puts us through an experience of frustration. 'Here form *is* content, content *is* form.' We can attempt to divorce one from the other if we must. There is just enough information in the text to make it possible for Alvarez to interpret it as 'a sour view of a cosy marriage', but such an interpretation has very little relevance to the experience of watching the play in performance.

One episode in particular challenges the audience to interpret: the spontaneous combustion of the parasol. Could it mean anything? What could it mean? . . . It is Watt's problem of trying to discover a system which will account for the facts as he experiences them. . . . Something has seemed to occur: the audience has seen the sunshade go up in smoke. But that something is only an event in the theatre about which it is pointless to theorize. It has happened because Beckett put it in the script, just as Winnie appears to be trapped in the mound because Beckett's stage directions require it. It might be said of the entire play—of any play— that 'nothing has occurred', although Beckett has contrived that something should appear to have occurred 'with the utmost formal distinctness'. Only the 'grotesque fallacy of realistic art' demands that stage facts should pretend to be facts that belong to the world outside the theatre. When the stage directions call for 'Blazing light' there is no necessity for us to interpret that light as sunlight or as the light of Hell as some critics have done. Just as the rapidly rising 'moon' at the end of each Act of *Waiting for Godot* demonstrates the nature of theatrical illusion, using electricity to parody thc activities of heavenly bodies, so the blazing light of *Happy Days* is known by the audience to be just as much an artificial non-reality qua sunlight as the spontaneous combustion of the parasol is known to be a piece of technical trickery, dependent not on a changed set of natural laws but on the expertise of the stage technicians. And a parasol will be there again for the next Act, provided by the property department in accordance with the requirements of the playwright. (pp. 29-30)

Beckett has a scrupulous sense of the essential nature of each art form he adopts, and his later stage plays never abandon the three basic requirements of drama (as distinct from radio-play or mime): an audience that both listens and watches; an actor who can be both seen and heard; and some kind of interaction both on the stage and between the figure(s) on the stage and the spectators in the auditorium. In *Krapp's Last Tape* there is interaction between the Krapp on the stage and the younger Krapps on the tape; and an important part of the play's effect derives, as we saw, from our frustrated desire to see what Krapp is doing at the back of the stage in darkness. Put this on radio and one whole dimension of the experience of performance is lost. In *Play*, Beckett works with even more meagre resources than he permitted himself in *Happy Days,* but still produces an essentially theatrical drama. There is no longer, in the visual dimension of the play, even the minimal facial mobility left to Winnie. Her comic and tragic masks and her eye movements are now seen to have been extremely expressive compared with these unmoving faces, 'so lost to age and aspect as to seem almost part of urns.' No expression is allowed to the voices, which must adopt a 'toneless' delivery. There is no interaction between the three figures, who are oblivious of each other's proximity. But this does not mean that Beckett has provided no interaction on the stage: it is there in the relationship between the probing spotlight and the faces. He achieves this by reversing the usual theatrical convention that the lighting technician is subordinate to the actors. Instead of the light being there to serve the performer, the performer is in bondage to the light. The actors must take their cue from the moving spotlight, rather than the spotlight follow the lead of the actors. In this way the light becomes a dynamic property and the necessary on-stage tension is achieved. (pp. 30-1)

The story—husband, wife, and other woman—is so hackneyed, and the style is so riddled with the clichés of romantic fiction . . . that no intellectual effort is required to follow it. But the method of delivery, the toneless gabble of the voices and the unpredictable switching from one face and one version of the story to another, demands concentrated attention of both eye and ear to piece it together. The play's difficulty lies in the mechanics of perception not in the mental acrobatics of interpretation. The situation in the theatre has been pared down to the fundamental confrontation of perceiver and perceived.

The repetition of the entire play is a necessary part of the process. The first time through we still have curiosity: we listen carefully to make out the story, to catch on to the conventions being used. The second time through, we are deprived even of that curiosity. We are forced simply to watch and listen to what we have already watched and listened to, so that there are no surprises, no revelations. We become 'pure spectators', uncontaminated by the need to do anything but look at and listen to meaningless figures who are there to be perceived.

In *Not I,* the deprivation has gone even further. Now there is one source of words, not three; there is no movement in the light; and there is no face to look at, no eyes with or without expression; there is merely a mouth, spotlit. The need for on-stage interaction is not forgotten, but it is reduced to an absolute minimum: an unspeaking and only dimly seen Auditor, who reacts four times with a gesture of compassion, each one less expansive than the one before, so that the last movement is 'scarcely perceptible'. The dynamic relationship between Mouth and Auditor distracts our attention from the flow of words less each time this movement occurs, so that we participate in a process of the dwindling away of extracircumferential phenomena and are drawn further into the core of the eddy of speech. (pp. 31-2)

Because the audience has nothing else to look at, except for the tiny distractions of the Auditor's movements, it concentrates obsessively on the mouth, the lips, the teeth, the tongue. The extraordinary effect of watching this play is that the mouth seems to grow larger and larger as the performance proceeds, and one becomes aware of the amazingly expressive physical properties of the speech organs themselves. One becomes rivetted by the spectacle of the red tongue moving between the two rows of white teeth, and the pursing and elongating of the lips as different

sounds are produced. It is as if we are given a physical, visual accompaniment to the enjoyment of 'pure sounds'; sounds take on almost tactile properties. (p. 32)

'In the ordinary way' we do not notice the actual word-producing machinery, because we are busy interpreting the product of speech, looking for meaning. But speech has now become for us, as we watch as well as listen, a matter of the physical 'contortions' of lips, cheeks, jaws, tongue. A different order of intentness is demanded by this performance. We are drawn—not suddenly, but gradually, as the nature of the experience grows upon us—into 'feeling'. Like *Krapp's Last Tape* and *Play,* this drama would lose most of its impact on the radio. We must *see* it in order to *feel* it. If we only heard, or read, the text, we would have to conceptualise the references to oral anatomy rather than experience them directly and take part physically in the performance.

Later in the play, Beckett directs attention to the other side of the language machine: the receiver, the ear and what it does with the sounds that come to it. . . . On the purely mechanical level—in theatrical performance—the ear does not catch all of what is said. It hears a stream of words, which at the start and end of the play are required to be completely 'unintelligible', and it has 'no idea what she's saying'. (p. 33)

Beckett provides for his audience an experience of the formal distinctness of words rising from the buzzing confusion of sound and then subsiding again into unintelligibility. He makes us aware once again that the work of art itself presents us with a 'face' which can be distinct without being open to systematic interpretation in conceptual terms, 'symbolic without symbolism'. (p. 34)

> Robert Wilcher, "'What's It Meant to Mean?':
> An Approach to Beckett's Theatre," in Critical
> Quarterly, *Summer, 1976, pp. 9-37.*

LAURA BARGE

The most basic questions [in criticism] have to do with what in conventional literature would be called character and setting. But Beckett's reduction has robbed us of the use of these terms; at best we can speak only of the person or persons described in the pieces and the various places occupied. Who are the persons and where are the places? . . . [The Beckettian hero] is Everyman on his way from womb to tomb, traveling a journey not of his own choosing, but one thrust upon him by some obscure bungler who seems to be in charge of things. . . . [Each] is man suffering the absurdity of being forced to live on the planet Earth.

That the particular area of suffering is the hero's mind is suggested by a correspondence between some of the places occupied and the imagined interior of the human skull. But this correspondence is not needed to establish the sphere of human consciousness as the place described in each piece. Since Watt's futile struggle with the macrocosm, the successive heroes (except for the distraught protagonist of *From an Abandoned Work*) have descended ever deeper into the recesses of the microcosm. It is hardly possible that the surreal landscapes and interiors of this fiction are anything other than soulscapes of the mind. That the slime of *How It Is* and the sulfurous light of *The Lost Ones* resemble Dante's hell implies nothing more than Beckett's conviction that to be conscious is to be in a kind of hell. Descartes' *cogito* undergirds all of Beckett's work, and the assertion in *Proust* that "the world" is "a projection of the individual's consciousness" . . . is reinforced by Beckett's observation concerning Marcel's grandmother that "the dead are only dead in so far as they continue to exist in the heart of the survivor." . . . While care must be taken not to assign indiscriminately every Proustian concept discussed in *Proust* to Beckett, this view of the macrocosm's assuming reality only as it is assimilated into the microcosm obviously holds for both writers. Beckett joins Proust in accepting "Baudelaire's definition of reality as 'the adequate union of subject and object'." . . . This place within the human consciousness is the world of the imagination, but *it is not an imaginary world:* it alone defines reality. . . . The protagonists of these pieces are suspended, as it were, in the sphere of their own consciousness, between the false heaven of the macrocosm and the unplummeted hell of the microcosm. This sphere becomes a place of crucifixion where man as victim endures the suffering of self-perception. . . . (pp. 274-75)

The images in the soulscapes of the mind are those of stillness because what Beckett is depicting is an intensifying of the descent inward toward the core of consciousness, the innermost fountainhead of being.

The heroes have progressively moved toward stillness in order to escape the suffering experienced in macrocosm. The Unnamable, as he tries to descend into an area beneath the speaking consciousness, realizes that he is not in orbital motion, as he has previously thought, but that he is "fixed," . . . and the voice of *Texts* possesses no body with which to move. Reinstated in a body cursed with frenzied motion in a violently unstable world, the protagonist of *From an Abandoned Work* hates movement of all kinds but has a "Great love" in his heart "for all things still and rooted." . . . The whiteness as a symbol of non-movement in this unfinished tale foreshadows the white stillness of *Imagination Dead Imagine* and *Ping,* where only minimal movements occur. The heart of the "little body" in *Lessness* is beating, but otherwise there is "no stir" in this landscape. Because the earth and sky are merged into one gray infinity, there is no space through which to move, and, because the scene is timeless, with no "passing light" of night and day, there is no time during which to move. Therefore, in this place of "endlessness," movement defined as motion through space and time is negated. . . . All verbs and references to movement belong to another world, that of the macrocosm. (p. 276)

[The last searcher in *The Lost Ones*] "finds at last his place and pose whereupon dark descends and . . . the temperature comes to rest not far from freezing point." . . . All previous movement is essentially a last struggle, the death throes of this final stillness. . . . Because Beckett has stated that *Ping* was written "in reaction to" *The Lost Ones,* it is possible to surmise that this last searcher becomes the motionless white body of the white enclosure of *Ping.* In negating the entire episode of *How It Is,* the final voice cancels all the preceding descriptions of movement. There has never been "any procession no nor any journey." . . . Of course, if the cancellation of movement is taken too literally, the entire three-part episode disappears with it, and we have no novel called *How It Is.* Perhaps it is wiser to see the nightmarish travels of Pim and Bom as a final struggle also—a desperate effort by a consciousness, now denied even its own voice, to unlock with a can opener the inner being of some other who, in all probability, is the elusive self, and thus to initiate the motionless crucifixion of further search into the soul.

The underlying theme of all of Beckett's work is this search of the heroes for whatever constitutes metaphysical reality, for the ground of being which is the essence of truth at the core of human experience. Obsessed with this search and supposing its object to be hidden in the recesses of the human consciousness, the heroes turn with an ascetic's scorn from the macrocosm and descend ever deeper into the microcosm. . . . Ignoring *From an Abandoned Work,* we may say that *Texts* is the last fiction to describe the search from the vantage point of the macrocosm. Because no possibility exists that the quest can be completed (its course is, by definition, an asymptotic progression toward zero), the self of the hero, in its plunge into the microcosm, encounters only what must be defined as nothingness. However, since what is being sought is very definitely *something that is there,* it is paradoxically not only negative but also positive—a Plenum-Void. (pp. 276-77)

Beginning with *How It Is,* the situation is no longer the macrocosm as the setting for an alienated microcosm, a human consciousness so separated from the outer world that it has shed its body, or even its voice. Instead, the landscape or interior *is* the microcosm, which is inhabited by the inner self, now split into a condition either of already being (in *Imagination Dead Imagine, Ping,* and *Lessness*) or of becoming (in *How It Is* and *The Lost Ones*), a duality that conveniently may be described as the self-as-subject and the self-as-object. Thus the inner self, alienated from its own body and voice and having retreated from the macrocosm, becomes the object of its own perception in the confines of the mind. The perception is one of suffering because the self that is perceived (the objective self) is never found to be the true core of selfhood sought by the perceiving self (the subjective self). . . .

[One can speculate on] the interesting possibility that Beckett's core of the self is not the essence of reality, that the search is actually for something that would have to be called God, although a God is as impossible in Beckett's world as in Sartre's. (p. 277)

This quest for what the heroes assume to be the true core of the self can hardly be overemphasized in Beckett's fiction. Whatever the object of the quest is, to find this object would provide an answer to the riddle of what life is all about and would serve as a point of reference for human experience. Therefore, the continuing, futile search of the subjective self through layer after layer of objective selfhood becomes a suffering so acute that it can be termed a crucifixion. This observation points toward answers to questions raised in recent criticism concerning the Christ imagery in *Ping.* These images (*nails, hair fallen, scars invisible, flesh torn of old* . . .) are obviously references to the victimized god-man (of Dostoevsky and Hemingway), who, for Beckett, is the only Christ with any validity. Beckett's most exact depiction of this Christ occurs in *Watt.* Bloody and disheveled in the asylum garden, Watt is likened to Bosch's Christ (probably the figure of *Christ Mocked* in the National Gallery in London), who suffers universal crucifixion all men endure for Beckett's universal sin—that of having been born. In the late fiction the Calvary (skull-place) becomes the soulscape of the microcosm, and, specifically in *Ping,* a Christ-body suffers for all the lost ones.

Particular care must be taken, in considering the question of consciousness in these pieces, not to equate the descent toward the core of the microcosm with a loss of self-awareness. Although the divided inner self can no longer communicate its experiences to the outside world (including us as readers), an intensification, not a lessening, of self-perception takes place. That a self that cannot voice *I* can nevertheless suffer the anguish of being is only to be expected in Beckett's world. The subjective self is acutely aware (as the impersonal narrator makes quite clear) of its terrifying descent inward and of its futile search for the true core of the self. The ascesis is a fleeing from macrocosmic consciousness trapped in the absurdity of time and space or in the meaningless flow of speech, but it is not a search for nonselfhood or oblivion. The goal is the seemingly impossible one of authentication, not annihilation, of being. There is nothing in any of the pieces to indicate that any figure has found release from the burden of self-awareness. . . . Any attempt, then to equate [these characters'] states of consciousness with stages of or lapses into oblivion or physical death is misleading. The stillness indicates the nonmovement of ascesis, not the absence of self-awareness. (p. 278)

The subjecting of any figure to darkness corresponds to that figure's terrifying descent inward, the agony of the approach toward nothingness. When Beckett uses darkness metaphorically or symbolically, it is nearly always in association with something that is unclear or irrational, or something that causes suffering. (pp. 278-79)

A knowledge of qualities such as truth, beauty, love, and justice is reason enough for man to expect the world to be a place where the realization of such qualities is at least possible, but Beckett's world is no such place. In this later fiction, as in the earlier, this macrocosm of false promise is symbolized by a nature . . . that wears a mask of order and beauty hiding a reality of suffering and death. Functioning as symbol, nature becomes essentially ironic—a symbol of a nonexistent Eden that man somehow senses should be his birthright and for which he intuitively longs, but which he can never possess. In these pieces nearly every infusion of macrocosmic light into the dark worlds of the microcosm is described in natural imagery, thus suggesting the suffering of being unable to escape an awareness of an environment that cannot deliver what it seems to promise of happiness. (p. 281)

Beckett's designation of residua for *Imagination Dead Imagine* and *Ping* is a particularly apt term for all this later fiction, but not if the word is taken to mean something extraneous that remains or what is left over as dregs when the main substance is removed. In spite of stripped form and condensed wording, these pieces are the concentrated essence, the quintessence, of the entire Beckettian oeuvre. Although Beckett is endlessly finding new forms for his art, the expression of that art remains the same—"a tale . . . signifying nothing." But we must not be deceived concerning the significance of these tales. As Beckett's heroes and Democritus know quite well—"nothing is more real than nothing." (p. 283)

Laura Barge, "'Coloured Images' in the 'Black Dark': Samuel Beckett's Later Fiction," in PMLA, 92 (copyright © 1977 by the Modern Language Association of America; reprinted by permission of the Modern Language Association of America), March, 1977, pp. 273-84.

TED L. ESTESS

John Calder has estimated that, if the present production of books continues unabated, Beckett will by the year 2000 rank fourth behind Jesus, Napoleon, and Wagner among the most written about persons in the world! While it is understandable that the puzzles of this very puzzled man would provoke such a plethora of books and articles, it is rather ironic that a writer who is "at home on the path of silence" would command such a talkative audience. (p. 5)

Beckett is not fully appreciated as what he is: a player. Persons who have noted the element of play in Beckett have tended to construe play as merely one dimension among others in Beckett's vision. A more adequate reading locates in "existence is play" the foundational metaphor of his entire literary cosmos. (pp. 5-6)

Playing . . . is the principal strategy by which Beckett's people establish existential meaning, however ephemeral and truncated, in a time when all inherited paradigms of meaning have dissolved into nothingness. Shuttled against the collapse of what Beckett terms the "teleological hypothesis" as legitimation for existence, Beckett's characters find a way of continuing a-telic play. . . . Through play, his characters go on *after* the old structures of meaning have paled into insignificance and *before* new structures—e.g., Godot, the self, the end—have appeared. Whether these new structures of human significance will emerge is a moot question in Beckett's world; what is important is that play provides a modicum of meaning in the *mean*-time. (p. 8)

Play in Beckett's world combines within itself several important dimensions which, while separable to the analytical eye, function integrally in the literature itself. On one level, play involves turning from the circumstances which circumscribe one's normal life situation. . . . [*Divertissement*] is the way of turning from (*di-vertere*) an insufferable situation. (pp. 8-9)

While the diversionary dimension of play activity is important in Beckett's literature, we should not forget that play has an important temporal dimension as well. In play one leaves the burden of ordinary time and enters into a different temporal framework in which things have their meaning, not within the *chronos* of clock-time, but in terms of the *kairos* of the play world. (p. 9)

Having no action to provide content to the temporal horizon of existence, [Beckett's] characters find in play a means to structure and to pass time. (p. 10)

The activities of both Watt and Malone are mere pastimes which provide a minimal structure to temporal existence, much like the simple tick-tock of the clock.

Malone . . . brings to our attention a fundamental characteristic of all play activity when he acknowledges that he counted "for no reason, for the sake of counting." In contrast with other forms of activity, play is distinctive in having no purpose outside the doing of the activity itself. (pp. 10-11)

[In] Beckett's literature "existence is play" is an expansive metaphor, bringing within its purview all activities which the characters initiate. It is not a matter of some activities being play in Beckett's world and others not being play; it rather is a matter of seeing all activities *as if* they were play. In his study of Proust, Beckett comments that "the Proustian world is expressed metaphorically by the artisan because it is apprehended metaphorically by the artist.'' . . . So it is with Beckett: the artisan (the craftsman) expresses his world through the metaphor of play because the artist (the seer) apprehends his world *sub specie lūdi.*

This vision of things means that finally in Beckett's world the primary model of the self is that of player. In what we might term a psychosocial dimension, Beckett's characters typically understand themselves and their relationships with others in terms of play. With regard to self-understanding, it is important to note that whatever fragile identity Beckett's characters have is secured through make-believe. This motif, which emerges at many points, is especially prominent in the trilogy, where the artist-heroes relentlessly search for self-identity through assuming various roles. The characters which populate the fragments of stories in the trilogy are *personae* which the narrators assume in a attempt to arrive at some response to the question of self-identity. . . . Sapo, Malone, Macmann, Mahood, Worm, Molloy are fictions invented by a character seeking to understand himself; they are epiphenomena hovering above an internal Other that is unable to coalesce and to be with psycho-ontological stability; they are ploys in the game, Who am I. (pp. 12-13)

Beckett's use of "Unnamable" to designate the final narrator of the trilogy signals an admission that the internal Other cannot emerge into the light as a stable identity, but must remain unnamed in the depths, unable to be born and unable to die. With the model of the self as player, Beckett suggests that the particular formulation or name with which we attempt to capture the self is inevitably inadequate. If one says that he is Molloy, then he immediately senses a component of himself that is not Molloy. If one masquerades as Moran or Malone or Watt, then he becomes painfully aware that aspects of the self lie beneath these appearances. The self is ever receding beyond the names with which we attempt to establish it in secure identity. All we know about the self is the disguises that it assumes, the masks with which it confronts the world, the lies which it tells itself and the world.

For all the intensity of self-excavation which Beckctt's literature commands, Beckett's characters finally are not solitary players. They typically have companions with whom, and for whom to play. One form of their playing with and for others involves the notion of *theatrum mundi.* Hamm is a principal manifestation of this type of play. . . . Much like Pozzo in *Waiting for Godot,* Hamm's existence is that of a ham-actor, who performs invented roles in lieu of a more authentic life to live. (pp. 13-14)

In seeing the psychosocial dimension of play in Beckett, it is important to distinguish between playing with another person so as to enjoy his presence and to sympathize with his distress, and gaming with another so as to exercise victimizing power and to gain unfair advantage. The first of these patterns of relationships is more closely aligned to the companionship of Vladimir and Estragon who, while they bicker and insult each other, are nonetheless compassionate fellow-sufferers who assist each other to endure through the long waiting period. In contrast, the relationships which obtain between Pozzo and Lucky and between Hamm and the other characters in *Endgame* tend more toward a tyrannous control without special concern for the suffering of the other. (pp. 15-16)

[Beckett's people] are not only playing; they are played. Play emerges as something which is done to or through the characters, not merely something that they do. This suggests that play is in Beckett a metaphor with ontological import. . . . The play motif moves in the imagination of Beckett from a metaphor by which to construe ordinary time-structuring activities, to a metaphor by which to understand the self and its relationship with others, to a metaphor by which to picture the nature of reality itself. Reality in Beckett's world shows itself as play, and play is that in which Beckett's characters are implicated by virtue of the primordial "sin of having been born." . . . (p. 16)

The brief drama *Play* is . . . helpful in our seeing the ontological dimension of play. The characters speak only when they are provoked by the spotlight. As the fourth character in the play, the light relates to the others as victimizer to victim, as inquisitor to defendant, as eye to object. The characters envisage themselves as involved in a process which they hope will end when the light hears what they may be concealing; or when the light sees what it desires to find; or when they themselves relinquish the desire to understand their plight. Just as the characters see their previous lives as play, so do they understand that they presently are involved in the play of the light. . . . The light is at play, and the characters are contained by that play. They *are* in the play of the light. (pp. 16-17)

It matters little whether that which plays with man is imaged as God, or time, or Godot, or death, or meaning, the result is the same: Beckett's characters are the playthings in a game the rules of which are beyond their control.

Several elements of Beckett's literature reinforce the impression that play is an ontological metaphor of the type I here suggest. The first is the presence of several allusions to the Tantalus mythologem, which is the structural and thematic basis of the mime *Acts Without Words I.* The dramatic tension which propels this brief mime and the tension which keeps Vladimir and Estragon returning to the stage each day is the tension that resides in the realm between expectation and accomplishment, promise and fulfillment, anticipation and actualization. The Tantalus mythologem, which has the same tensive components, may well be Beckett's "representative anecdote" of the human condition, for it gathers together disparate motifs and visualizes in pristine form the fundamental nature of man's situation in Beckett's world. And that situation is one in which man is the plaything of a desire, or a force, or a being, or a situation against which he cannot prevail. (pp. 17-18)

The play of reality is at times like the play of Vladimir and his friend Estragon—genial, surprisingly compassionate, comically amusing; but the play of reality is also like the play of Pozzo with Lucky—cruel, fickle, destructive, angry. The vision is that of Plautus . . . "In strange ways the gods make sport of men." All the dimensions of play come into sharper focus when we realize that a vision of reality as at play informs the entirety of Beckett's world. The simple diversions and time-passing activities, the multiple roles of the self, the image of social relationships as playing—all these are grounded in the prior ontologic vision of all reality as at play.

As is always the case, one's ontology predetermines his espistemology, hence we should not be surprised to discover that Beckett explores the epsitemological dimensions of a play vision of reality. *Watt* is the paradigm for this dimension of play. . . . In form and content the composition is epistemological gamesmanship, for the fundamental question of *Watt* is What. Through intricate and humorous cerebrations, often involving ridiculous permutations and combinations, the protagonist attempts to make sense of the baffling world of Mr. Knott (not, knot). . . . Watt futilely persists in the game of knowing, despite the continual alteration of the reality which he is attempting to know. The exercises of logic, deductive and inductive, rational and empirical, while not giving a final understanding of the reality at play, do provide a temporary surcease of questioning. . . . The existence of man and the final nature of reality remain shrouded in mystery, as much concealed as revealed in the game of knowing. (pp. 19-21)

Parodoxically, Beckett plays against language, attempting to do something that words intractably will not do: he seeks to speak and yet to say nothing. If playing is doing nothing, then writing, when viewed as play, must attempt to say nothing.

In this attempt to render writing as a form of play, Beckett moves art toward abstract painting in which the pictorial images are severed from representational significance; he edges his art toward music in which the delight is not in referential meaning, but in the playful relationships among sounds in time. (p. 21)

Instead of playing tricks with language as did the early narrators of Beckett, the narrators of the trilogy are tricked by language into saying things they do not wish to say. . . . Words do things to Beckett's narrators: they keep them in conscious existence; they cause them to say something when they wish to say nothing. The only way to avoid being the plaything of language is to move, as Beckett does in his later fiction fragments, toward silence. (pp. 23-4)

His art is not merely about people who play, nor is it about a vision of play: his art takes the form of play in order to speak a vision of play. We find in the circular construct of *Godot* and *Play* the finely chiselled form of a game which can be repeated over and over; in *Endgame* we discover the structure of a chess game in which the gradual attrition of pieces brings the game to the tensive moments just prior to the checkmate; in the trilogy we see the amorphous, unpredictable shape of solitary play in which all the rules of standard game-forms are dysfunctional. In Beckett, as he observes of Joyce, "Form is content, content *is* form. . . . His writing is not about something; *it is that something itself.*" Beckett's writing is not about play; it is play itself. (p. 24)

> *Ted L. Estess, "Dimensions of Play in the Literature of Samuel Beckett," in* Arizona Quarterly *(copyright © 1977 by Arizona Board of Regents), Vol. 33, No. 1, Spring, 1977, pp. 5-25.*

MAUREEN HOWARD

All the literary turns of [Beckett's] work never obscure his vital presence for me—that of an Irishman talking on and on, endlessly imagining forms, his words, pauses, silences mysteriously reinventing our sense of reality and time. No one writing today takes such complete pleasure in language as Beckett. No one is as conscious of the responsibility and delight of passing that pleasure on to his audience. (p. 58)

> *Maureen Howard, in* The New York Times Book Review *(© 1977 by The New York Times Com-*

pany; reprinted by permission), December 4, 1977.

HUGH KENNER

"A unique moral figure," I wrote of [Beckett] five years ago, "not a dreamer of rose gardens but a cultivator of what will grow in the wasteland, who can make us see the exhilarating design that thorns and yucca share with whatever will grow anywhere." It's 30 years—is that conceivable?—since he wrote "Godot," a play still perfectly vital, its eloquence spare then, still spare now, het positively garrulous by the standards he sets himself today. In the late months of his 72d year, he bends more and more effort on fewer and fewer words, still pursuing his impossible ambition of making silence sing. The most frequent stage direction in "Godot" was "*Pause.*" Last year in "Footfalls," a play like a late Beethoven quartet, the most eloquent voice was that of a girl not speaking, simply pacing, pacing, very possibly a girl not there, since the last spills of light did not show her at all. Beckett's words, some for her, some to her, some about her, were uttered by a mouth we could not see, and were never more beautiful.

This gentle, generous, punctilious man appears on no talk shows, offers no opinions, grants no interviews, and writes sentences. I could show you a Beckett sentence as elegant in its implications as the binomial theorem, and another as economically sphynx-like as the square root of minus one, and another, on trees in the night, for which half of Wordsworth would seem a fair exchange. The declarative sentence, he makes you suppose, is perhaps man's highest achievement, as absolute as the egg was for Brancusi. That hens lay eggs round the clock the way grocers utter sentences renders neither Brancusi's nor Beckett's preoccupation trivial. We have an obligation to speak with the tongues of angels, as if we could, and a man who won't tire of confronting this obligation can remind us all of our calling. (p. 58)

> *Hugh Kenner, in* The New York Times Book Review *(© 1977 by The New York Times Company; reprinted by permission), December 4, 1977.*

LEONARD MICHAELS

Among living writers, I most admire Samuel Beckett because he is the least living of them. "Imagination Dead Imagine," he says, as if he already speaks to us from the other side. Nothing in his work is the least fashionable, and yet no other writer—not even Virgil or Dante—has been more avant-garde than Beckett. And very few writers—excepting Swift and Kafka—have been so funny and terrifying at once as Samuel Beckett. The great ones always speak from the other side. . . .

As for his language—the basic and ultimate test of a writer's value—Beckett compares well even with great modern poets. For this I admire him most of all. (p. 62)

> *Leonard Michaels, in* The New York Times Book Review *(© 1977 by the New York Times Company; reprinted by permission), December 4, 1977.*

*   *   *

BEHAN, Brendan   1923-1964

Behan was an Irish dramatist, novelist, and essayist. His

work was often drawn from his own involvement in the political struggles of contemporary Ireland and reflects a compassion that transcends partisanship. Critics have consistently remarked on the uneven quality of Behan's work, praising the vitality of his dramatic language while noting his weakness in plot and character development. (See also *CLC*, Vols. 1, 8, and *Contemporary Authors*, Vols. 73-76.)

JOHN RUSSELL TAYLOR

[The characters of Behan's *The Quare Fellow*] are not very precisely individualized, for Behan's style is essentially more narrative than strictly dramatic and he could hardly be farther from psychological drama, but all are observed with a rich, all-embracing humanity. . . . (p. 103)

[The principle upon which the play is built is that] in prison, even when an execution is imminent, comedy and tragedy are inextricably mixed, as everywhere else in life, and the *memento mori* is seldom without its gruesome humour. Murder is horrible, and legalized murder, in cold blood, with the best of intentions, is even more horrible, but the direct attack is not always the most effective, and Behan invites us not only to pray at this funeral, but to drink as well, to laugh and shout and sing as well as to weep and wail and shudder. His theme, basically, is the inalienable dignity of man—inalienable, that is, in that nobody can take it away from him except himself—and the fact that he chooses his examples from what would normally, with some reason, be regarded as the dregs of humanity makes the lesson all the more potent. A note in the programme said: 'This is not a play about prisons, but a play about people.'

The play . . . is not only vividly alive from moment to moment . . . , but also it has a finely coherent overall structure, in which the absence of conventional plot development is to a large extent compensated for by the skill in which the various themes are brought to the fore, held in the background, or ingeniously woven together as the play progresses, linking scene with scene and establishing a gradual, orderly progression to the inevitable end within the framework provided by the recurrent refrain of a song from an unseen prisoner doing solitary in the basement.

On the whole these qualities do not occur in Behan's second play *The Hostage*, though they are replaced by others which, to first acquaintance at least, may seem almost as satisfactory. In *The Quare Fellow* the tragic undertones are always present, and though they are seldom insisted on we are conscious throughout of a sensation in the comedy akin to that of dancing on a coffin-lid. In *The Hostage*, however, though the underlying tragic theme is still there, there are whole stretches in which it is thrust altogether out of sight and rather wild, uncontrolled, and in some cases essentially irrelevant bouts of farcical humour take its place. . . . Ultimately, in fact, the second play is far less disciplined than the first; at times it looks like going off the rail altogether in its quest for the easy laugh or the rather facile shock effect, and the wholesale introduction of music-hall techniques, direct addresses to the audience, songs with self-conscious cues to the accompanist in the orchestra pit, even a bit of dialogue ribbing the author . . . , savours at times of the self-indulgence inherent in all thoroughgoing 'director's theatre'. (pp. 104-05)

[*The Hostage*] appears finally, for all its surface pleasures and occasional deeper insights, a far less substantial and effective play than *The Quare Fellow*, and one rather fears that the wide initial encouragement Behan received as a result of it to rant and roar, to make us laugh instead of being serious (rather than, as in *The Quare Fellow*, when at his most serious of all), and to be as much of a wild Irish 'character' on stage as he was known to be in his not-so-private life, may turn out in the long run to have set him off in quite the wrong direction. Obviously he could, if he so wished, go on pouring out this sort of thing, more or less shaped into plays, until Doomsday, which, if this were all he had to offer, would be acceptable enough. But in *The Quare Fellow* he showed he had more, and so he did in *The Hostage*, even if it sometimes looked in danger of drowning in a sea of swirling words. (pp. 107-08)

> *John Russell Taylor, "Brendan Behan," in his* Anger and After: A Guide to the New British Drama *(© 1962 by John Russell Taylor; reprinted by permission of A D Peters & Co Ltd), Methuen and Co. Ltd., 1962, pp. 101-08.*

BENEDICT KIELEY

[Behan's] I.R.A. activities brought him at an absurdly early age to an English prison and a Borstal institution, gave him the makings of his best book ["Borstal Boy"], which either as autobiography or as part of the literature of penology has established itself as a classic, and inspired him for various reasons with a healthy respect and a liking for the English people. (p. 5)

For all previous sharp statements about the neighbours he made amends in the character of Leslie Williams, the hostage [in "The Hostage"], also a voice from a prison, an ordinary young English boy caught fatally and wonderingly in a situation he cannot hope to understand. Teresa, that sweet young country girl . . . , an orphan as the hostage is, tells him that Monsewer, the old mad owner of the house in which he is held, is an English nobleman: "he went to college with your king."

> *Soldier* [i.e. Leslie]: We ain't got one.
>
> *Teresa:* Maybe he's dead now, but you had one one time, didn't you?
>
> *Soldier:* We got a duke now. He plays tiddly winks.
>
> *Teresa:* Anyway, he [i.e. Monsewer] left your lot and came over here and fought for Ireland.
>
> *Soldier:* Why, was somebody doing something to Ireland?
>
> *Teresa:* Wasn't England, for hundreds of years?
>
> *Soldier:* That was donkey's years ago. Everybody was doing something to someone in those days.

Caitlin Ni Houlihan and John Bull have never spoken so simply, so comically nor so wisely to each other as in that passage. (p. 6)

Monsewer has a dual, lunatic significance: the house he owns and in which the young hostage is held and accidentally killed by his rescuers is, as Pat the caretaker says, a "noble old house that had housed so many heroes" and is, in the end, "turned into a knocking shop." It is also romantic, idealistic Ireland fallen on sordid, materialistic days, and that a madman of that most romantic people, the English, should in his imagination, lead the last Irish Rebellion, playing the pipes and making heroines out of . . . whores, would seem to be a fair chapter of our national story. But the house is more than heroic Ireland down in the dumps; it is the world in a mess and God gone off his rocker: the very first stage direction says: "the real owner isn't right in the head." Monsewer, in fact, is one of Behan's visions of God, and as he parades, salutes, plays the pipes and sings of tea and toast and muffin rings, the old ladies with stern faces and the captains and the kings, he falls into line with images of the Divinity that appear elsewhere in the plays and prose. (pp. 6-8)

Borrowing a sentence from the lingo of his beloved Dublin streets, [Brendan] was fond of saying that every cripple had his own way of walking. It is also true that every writer has his own way of writing, and . . . how wonderful it was that so much good writing came out of Brendan's gregariousness and chronic restlessness. His great kindly spirit had to express itself in every possible way, and what was writing —if it didn't go on too long—but another form of movement. "Borstal Boy," "The Quare Fellow," "The Hostage" and the better portions of the notebooks or sketchbooks are the considerable achievement that he has left us. . . . (pp. 8-9)

> Benedict Kieley, "That Old Triangle: A Memory of Brendan Behan," in The Hollins Critic (copyright 1965 by Hollins College), February, 1965, pp. 1-12.

PAUL M. LEVITT

Brendan Behan's *The Hostage* is a frenetic play, difficult to sum up and easy to distort. . . . There is about it an effortless air of madcap fun, which at first reading is rather deceptive. Because of the frolicking atmosphere of jigs and reels, set in the midst of apparently unconnected scenes, the play appears to be a kind of light variety show or vaudeville. However, the riotous nature of the work has obscured its underlying seriousness. . . . Behan, rather than reinforce Irish devotion to Ireland, examines and reveals the debilitating nature of their senseless idealism. In *The Hostage* . . . Behan attacks the traditional Irish dependence on the past.

The title of the play has several meanings and provides a key to understanding Behan's attitude toward tradition and, in particular, the relation of past to present. The title, *The Hostage,* ostensibly refers to Leslie Williams, the young English soldier who has been taken prisoner by the Irish Republican Army (I.R.A.). (p. 401)

Leslie is a victim of history and patriotism, of romance and nationalism; he is a victim of the I.R.A. dream to unite Ireland—north and south—and drive the British out. In other words, Leslie is a hostage to those who are victims of an historical obsession. (p. 402)

The brothel [the setting of the play] can be read as a metaphorical comment on the value of the old cause in the present. Consider for a moment: a man will go to a brothel to escape present misery. Love with a prostitute is a temporary game of make-believe, played for a fee, and the satisfaction received depends on one's ability to forget himself in a moment of illusion. Similarly, the old cause of the I.R.A. is a romantic illusion, dependent on a fanatical be-

lief in the past and a blindness to the reality of the present. (p. 403)

Pat [manager of the brothel] is clearly the most complex and interesting character in the play; metaphorically, he is the hostage of the title and the hero of the play. He embodies the intellectual and emotional struggle of present day Ireland; he is torn between the romance of the past and the reality of the present. . . . Intellectually, Pat is able to distinguish between the illusions of the past and the facts of the present, and is able sensibly to evaluate the significance of the cause. But emotionally, he claims a share in the patriotic glamour of the past. (pp. 403-04)

Significantly, both Leslie and Teresa [with whom Leslie is imprisoned] are orphans—and thus symbolically free from allegiances to the past. For this reason, they are the only characters in the play who dream of a future. . . . In the midst of the depravity of the brothel, the two orphans make love and plan to see each other again. The act of love, which is literally and figuratively at the center of the play, can be read as Behan's comment on the possibility of transcending the past by means of love. Teresa, a convent-trained girl, willingly accepts Leslie, a Protestant, English soldier. Two people who, in the context of English-Irish relations, would normally be irreconcilable are, in fact, not, because they have neither an historical sense of past injury nor a present desire to maintain old arguments. It would seem, then, that Behan is saying that if we can dissociate ourselves from the past—become orphans, as it were—we might have some chance of getting on together and, consequently, settling our differences. (p. 405)

Unfortunately for the two orphans, they are surrounded by the past and cannot escape its murderous effects. The idea of encirclement is to be found throughout the play, providing an apt metaphor of history as a prison. The young are entrapped by their elders. In fact, Leslie is forced to stand within a circle drawn on the floor. When Leslie is shot, attempting to escape the circle and free himself, the dramatic metaphor is complete. The hostage Leslie Williams is, in effect, executed in reprisal for the death of the boy in Belfast Jail. The war between England and Ireland goes on. The circle is unbroken. That Leslie dies accidentally is important, because his death suggests not only the carelessness in thought and deed of the I.R.A. fanatics, but also the danger of pretense. In this latter regard it is instructive to look at Pat. He is the moral touchstone in the play. He is literally a "good" man fallen among thieves; and we wait and watch to see what he will do. When he apologizes for Leslie's death on the grounds that it was unintentional, and then proceeds implicitly to defend what has happened, we know the price of pretense. . . . We become what we pretend to be. Surrounded (the encirclement idea again) by narrow-minded patriots, degenerates, and impractical dreamers, Pat becomes one of them. By pretending that he and the others are hostage-bound to the old cause, until such time as Ireland, north and south, is united, Pat unwittingly contributes to the death of Leslie. The point is clear. By condoning madness, Pat, the "good" man, is largely responsible for what happens to Teresa and Leslie, innocent lovers, like Romeo and Juliet, who, victimized by an irrational and romantic pride in a heritage of calamitous fighting, are, finally, sacrificed to a past they neither care about nor understand. (p. 406)

> Paul M. Levitt, "Hostages to History: Title as

Dramatic Metaphor in 'The Hostage'," in Die Neueren Sprachen, *October, 1975, pp. 401-06.*

*   *   *

BERGER, Thomas   1924-

An American novelist, short story writer, playwright, and editor, Berger is best known for his satiric caricatures of American life. He deals often with paradox, exploring man's struggle with absurdity, America's myths, and the deceptiveness of modern society. Fantasy, hyperbole, attention to detail, and a love of language are important elements in Berger's style. *Little Big Man* **is generally considered his best work. (See also** *CLC,* **Vols. 3, 5, 8, and** *Contemporary Authors,* **Vols. 1-4, rev. ed.)**

LEONARD MICHAELS

Thomas Berger's fifth novel ["Who Is Teddy Villanova?"] is mainly a parody of detective thrillers; his well-known "Little Big Man" was a parody of Westerns. According to the jacket copy, in "Who Is Teddy Villanova?" we will recognize the familiar "seedy office," "down-at-the-heels shamus," "procession of sinister, chicane, or merely brutal men and scheming, vicious, but lovely women" and a "sequence of savage beatings." All this is true. The novel contains much that is conventional in detective thrillers. Still, one needn't know the books of Dashiell Hammett or Raymond Chandler in order to appreciate Berger's witty burlesque of their characters and situations.

Berger's style, which is one of the great pleasures of the book, is something like S. J. Perelman's—educated, complicated, graceful, silly, destructive in spirit, and brilliant—and it is also something like Mad Comics—densely, sensuously detailed, unpredictable, packed with gags. Beyond all this, it makes an impression of scholarship—that is, Berger seems really to know what he jokes about. This includes not only Hammett and Chandler, but also Racine, Goethe, Ruskin, Elias Canetti, New York and the way its residents behave. Essentially, then, Berger's style is like itself insofar as it is like other styles. And his whole novel —in its wide ranging reference to cultural forms both high and pop—is like a huge verbal mirror. Its reflections are similar to what we see in much contemporary literature—hilarious and serious at once. (p. 1)

On some occasions in the novel, the vulgar material slightly overwhelms Berger's wit, but this is inevitable. The book deals with certain well-known and oppressive banalities; now and then it must descend to mere seriousness.

Before looking at a particular instance, it should be said that Berger's detective hustles about Manhattan from one highly offensive personal experience to another, and this is a little reminiscent of the plot of another novel, Saul Bellow's "detective novel," "Mr. Sammler's Planet." Mr. Sammler, like Berger's detective Russel Wren, is a literate anachronism, a hero who reads books and, by his very nature, too much suffers the life of the mind. (p. 25)

Both novelists also notice murderous violence, Manhattan's dog-zoo of excremental streets, ubiquitous and matter-of-fact sexual perversity, and other features in the gruesome apocalypse of New York. Naturally both novelists make their theme the staggering insufficiency of an educated intelligence to such modern circumstances. Berger's detective, while investigating the mystery in this novel, stops to analyze events and clues. He is meticulous and

exceedingly logical. As a result, he never understands anything until, at last, everything is merely explained to him by the master criminal who then blithely gets away. . . .

As for the mystery itself—the thing this book is about—it seems to lie exactly in Russel Wren's own literary head, his only office, the place where he lives and works. It is a place full of words, but it can neither effectively communicate with the world nor understand its deeply criminal nature. If the novel is hilarious, it is also sometimes a little sad in the sweet, strangely amazing way of Charlie Chaplin. . . .

Still, the novel has an important connection with life, because aside from the pleasure you take in reading it, you will have the wonderful pleasure of reading parts of it aloud to friends and watching the effects in their faces. Terrific comedians always make us "die laughing." Given the alternatives today, we should be grateful. (p. 26)

> *Leonard Michaels, in* The New York Times Book Review *(© 1977 by The New York Times Company; reprinted by permission), March 20, 1977.*

CURT SUPLEE

For a thousand years the Arthurian legends have endured undiminished by progress or pessimism, and in this triumphant comic reaffirmation by Thomas Berger, they will continue to enthrall readers. . . .

Of course, to portray a mortal man in a mythic situation is to invite comedy. And as John Barth did in *Chimera,* Berger [in *Arthur Rex*] exploits the humorous human potential to the fullest, but without compromising the integrity of the original legends—Gawaine and the Green Knight, or the tryst of Tristram and Isolde.

Instead, Berger enriches the texture of the tradition by speculating on the background of each knight—Percival's upbringing as a sissy in girls' clothes, Gawaine's fantastic carnal appetites, Launcelot's ascetic monasticism. . . .

The familiar tales are told in a style as deliberately atavistic as that employed by the translators of the King James Bible in 1611, and to the same purpose: to give the whole a venerable aura and impact. Berger's 15th-century syntax, although inconsistently sustained, succeeds in giving the book both a self-mocking playfulness and a seeming gravity, according to his needs.

But even an imaginative retelling in antique language is less than Berger intends. . . .

Berger's world of the Round Table and its comic-heroic exploits is more obstinately complex, less susceptible to moral redaction [than the earlier versions of the Arthurian legend told by Sir Thomas Malory, Tennyson, or T. H. White]. He knows that all true myths are ritual reenactments of timeless human dilemmas, endlessly suggestive, ultimately inscrutable.

Thus his very human heroes constantly find themselves trapped in ambiguity, and live their comic lives against a background of serious problems perplexingly unresolved: the nature of sin; the spirit versus the letter of the law; how to fulfill God's perfect will in man's fallen world; and how to maintain the artificial virtue of civilization without relapsing into primitive patterns. . . .

Finally, the reader can only sympathize with Launcelot in his confusion: that if living is full of moral complexities, "it was because chivalry in general was more complicated than it seemed, for it is not easy always to know what is the noble thing, or what is brave and generous or even simply decent."

By having the confidence to leave an evocative story alone, and the courage to elaborate when appropriate, Thomas Berger synthesizes the disparate Arthurian romances into a splendid, consistent narrative—and makes them speak eloquently to a modern audience.

Moreover, he even provokes an unexpected nostalgia for that imaginary age in which honor was at stake in every daily act. . . .

> *Curt Suplee, "Knights to Remember," in* Book World—The Washington Post *(© 1978 The Washington Post), September 17, 1978, p. E8.*

GARRETT EPPS

Thomas Berger might be called the Green Knight of American fiction: a mysterious, protean outsider whose pose of destructiveness masks a fierce reverence for form and meaning. . . .

Arthur Rex, a massive retelling of the Camelot legend, may be Berger's most ambitious book, at least in size and literary scale. . . . [Despite his] careful scholarship, despite a prose style which borders on genius, despite many funny moments and a few painfully sad ones, *Arthur Rex,* in the end, remains less than the sum of its parts. (p. 34)

Arthur Rex is not a spoof. Much of its narrative— the adulterous love of Launcelot and Guinevere, the parallel tragedy of Tristram, Isold, and Mark, Sir Gawaine's rise from lechery and fall into vengeance—is seriously intended and often quite moving. The central tragedy in the book is that of Arthur, who attempts to found his table on pure virtue. The book's subtitle is "A Legendary Novel"; taking this term in its oldest meaning, we might consider it as the life story not primarily of a King, but of a saint. For all Arthur's goofiness, his ability to take a pratfall when the author requires it, I think Berger may intend to show Arthur as exactly that: a man who aspires to Godliness with his whole being, a seeker of selflessness who suffers the defeat of those who try for perfection.

Berger ascribes a larger role in the story to God than did the reverent but skeptical Malory. The author of *Arthur Rex* takes a dark, deeply Protestant view of life: God gives to each of us a nature, with strengths and flaws we are powerless to change. . . . The end of life is not happiness or triumph, for our sinful natures preclude these; we must simply do the best we can with what we are given, and lose. We can lose honorably or otherwise—that is our only choice.

This dark parable emerges from a 500-page narrative which is jumbled, fragmented, almost formless. Given Berger's consistent record of literacy and care, I think we can assume this is not unintentional. (pp. 34-5)

One can even theorize that this jumbled effect—this deliberate splintering of character, narrative, and structure— might be Berger's mode of attack on the T. H. White novel, an attempt to erase the sanitized Camelot of *The Once and Future King* and restore the legend's mystery; to remind us that *Le Morte d'Arthur* continues to fascinate us because it is huge, redundant ("God's plenty," as Dryden called it)

inconsistent—in fact, not a novel in the formal sense at all. (p. 35)

[Most] readers of this book will be familiar with White, and will measure *Arthur Rex* against it. And despite Berger's intelligence, wit, and integrity, the new novel loses the contest. . . .

Berger's book is much concerned with the problem of evil and the power that the wicked wield in this world. "Evil," he writes, "is always more easily managed than virtue." But his villains do not scare us, and this is a serious flaw. White's Mordred was a real figure of dread, the whining, injured little rotter we all hate and fear in ourselves; but Berger, who teams Mordred up with Morgan la Fey, manages only to produce a semi-comic medieval Boris and Natasha, energetically wicked without real menace.

The best characters in Berger's work continue to live in the reader's mind long after he has closed the book (I think particularly of Ralph Sandifer, the horny teenager of *Sneaky People*). Those in *Arthur Rex,* I predict, will fade. Readers will laugh at parts of this book, feel despair and grief at others; but after they have finished, it will be White's pompous, pacifistic Arthur, not Berger's doomed saint, who lingers in their minds. (p. 36)

> *Garrett Epps, in* The New Republic *(reprinted by permission of* The New Republic; *© 1978 by The New Republic, Inc.), October 7, 1978.*

JOHN ROMANO

Thomas Berger belongs, with Mark Twain and Mencken and Philip Roth, among our first-rate literary wiseguys. Savvy and skeptical, equipped with a natural eloquence and a knack for parody, he has been expertly flinging mud at the more solemn and self-important national myths for 20 years. . . . Mr. Berger's method . . . is to set [down his mythical landscapes] in his droll, relentlessly straight-faced prose, so as to empty them of romance, and let the brutal/crummy facts stare out. His pages swarm with bawdy puns and slapstick and bookish in-jokes; but even at his most absurd, his intrinsic tone is that of a hard-nosed realist who won't let the myths distort his essentially grouchy idea of the way things really are. . . .

Doing good in a world that is mostly bad can have bizarre or disastrous consequences. This wry paradox is at the heart of Mr. Berger's interest in Good King Arthur and his Knights of the Round Table, and in their incorrigibly noble chivalric code. "Arthur Rex," Mr. Berger's newest novel, is his splendid, satiric retelling of the legend of Camelot. (p. 3)

Mr. Berger's masterpiece, it may be, is his treatment of Sir Launcelot, who unwittingly destroys the Round Table by his affair with Arthur's Queen Guinevere; and it's there, too, that Mr. Berger's command of the complex and contradictory traditions of these stories is most evident. . . . In older versions—the Arthur legend first turns up in a 12th-century manuscript—Launcelot was a shadowy, reluctant paramour, and Mr. Berger draws expertly on the earlier version to make good comic use of Launcelot's bloodless melancholy. . . .

But it is in Mr. Berger's power, apparently, to be both farcical and moving at once. His hapless, retiring Launcelot is finally more likeable than the charm-boy of recent tradition. . . .

The tragedy of Tristran and Isolde gets a lengthy but uninspired retelling, and the adventures of Sir Gawain in Liberty Castle are a good deal less powerful, less sexy, in Mr. Berger's version than in the original. The curious truth is that Mr. Berger's revisions are most authentic, most profound, when the admixture of parody is strongest. At those times—a good three-fourths of the book—he is never merely a parodist after all, but also a compelling yarnspinner in his own right: a Tolkien for the worldly. Indeed, stripped of their 19th-century sentiment by the author's deeply anti-Romantic ways, the stories have a leaner, more strident look than they have had in a long time. Not T. H. White's "The Once and Future King," nor John Steinbeck's mostly antiquarian version, but Thomas Berger's "Arthur Rex" is the Arthur book for our time. (p. 62)

> *John Romano, "Camelot and All That," in* The New York Times Book Review *(© 1978 by The New York Times Company; reprinted by permission), November 12, 1978, pp. 3, 62.*

*   *   *

BIENEK, Horst   1930-

Bienek is a Polish-born novelist, poet, essayist, and screenwriter now living in West Germany. Formerly a student of Bertolt Brecht, Bienek writes an experimental fiction, at times mingling narrative, poetic, and documentary styles. The effects of four years spent in a Siberian labor camp can often be felt in his work. (See also *CLC*, Vol. 7, and *Contemporary Authors*, Vols. 73-76.)

PADDY BEESLEY

[Horst Bienek's determination in *Bakunin: An Invention*] to level stridently with the reader at every turn reminds one most of the Pompidou Centre: all the lines of construction, all the cables and conduits bringing essential supplies, are deliberately displayed and painted vivid colours. Nothing is hidden, nothing extenuated: we follow the author as he visits Neuchâtel to research into the great anarchist writer, as he interviews people who fail to remember anything, writes chivvying notes to himself, makes lists of further reading, examines his own motives, quotes from Bakunin and Turgenev's *Rudin,* then loses interest and sends his books back to the library. There is some play between the anarchist's vigour and idealism and the present writer's lassitude, but little else within the knowing and self-conscious shell of the form. A bookseller who is interviewed remarks at one point that the artist who really wants something new must be an anarchist; and it's more than possible that Bienek, by writing a book about not being able to write a book, is trying to create the first example of anarchist fiction. He certainly knows how to lob a bomb at the powers of concentration. (p. 407)

> *Paddy Beesley, in* New Statesman *(© 1977 The Statesman & Nation Publishing Co. Ltd.), March 25, 1977.*

MICHAEL PORTER

Bienek is a typical example of the type of author who feels compelled to write because he ponders about some extraordinary personal experience and its consequences—in his case, the loss of freedom and the reduction to sub-human conditions during a four-year stay in a Russian prison camp in the early fifties.... [In *Gleiwitzer Kindheit: Gedichte aus zwanzig Jahren*] this event lingers on and works as a

structuring element.... Unfortunately, though, Bienek's talent is not great enough to transform personal experiences into excellent poetry. Literarily, almost everything in this volume is secondhand and has been said more convincingly by somebody else.... Even worse, the further Bienek leaves his prison time behind, the less he has to say; and so he wanders about trying desperately to find messages, some kind of important revelation that nature might have to give him. For the reader, this search turns out to be repetitive and boring.... (p. 273)

> *Michael Porter, in* Books Abroad *(copyright 1977 by the University of Oklahoma Press), Vol. 51, No. 2, Spring, 1977.*

PETER LEWIS

Bakunin defies categorization, but Horst Bienek's description of it as 'An Invention' is preferable to other possible labels, such as "non-fiction fiction", "fictional non-fiction", "documentary novel" or "anti-novel". Its structure is poetic rather than conventionally novelistic, and although it contains a narrative it is really a collage, consisting of passages from Bakunin's own writings, books about him, historical studies of Tsarist Russia, nineteenth-century memoirs, Turgenev's *Rudin* (with its fictional portrait of Bakunin), and even a Berlin police report on him, not to mention left-wing slogans ..., a passage written in verse, and the narrative itself complete with transcripts of conversations. Bienek's "invention" ... records the failed attempt of a modern German anarchist to discover the whole truth about Bakunin, especially his "retirement" from revolutionary politics towards the end of his life, and to write his biography. This is why it sometimes reads like a piece of research in progress or notes for a Ph.D. thesis. In his quest for Bakunin, the modern anarchist visits places where the great Russian anarchist lived, especially Neuchâtel in Switzerland, and tries to find people who can shed even a dim light on events a century earlier. As the "invention" progresses, the contemporary anarchist merges to some extent with his quarry (both are referred to as 'he') and the gradual abandonment of his self-imposed task together with his growing political disillusionment seem to parallel Bakunin's own failures, disappointments, and eventual exclusion from the movement he had done so much to create. In his adherence to anarchism the modern German is pledging his commitment to a philosophy of action, but he finds himself trapped in a world of words, of revolutionary rhetoric and slogans, of books and libraries, and fails to act when the opportunity presents itself.... We finally see him deliberately breaking a beer glass in his hands at a café and cutting himself badly; his one act of "liberating" violence is directed against himself. Not for him the anarchist martyrdom of an heroic death in an assassination attempt but a self-inflicted wound apparently born of despair about the very possibility of revolution. (p. 59)

Amongst other things, *Bakunin* is a critique of biography and history. Its failure to provide a coherent biography of Bakunin ... amounts to a recognition that the search for historical truth founders on the impossibility of ever being able to know the whole truth and that the biographer or historian is a fabricator who deceives us into believing that his "lies" are truths. Bienek, on the other hand, is a self-confessed inventor who offers us the "lies" of fiction as a better way of approaching the truth, about both Bakunin and modern revolutionaries; the truest poetry is, after all, the most feigning. More importantly, the "invention" is an exploration of Bakunin's ideas and idealism, and of their relevance today. Historically the concept of "revolution", as opposed to "rebellion", is recent, and this book is about the current crisis in revolutionary thought and action at a time when it is no longer possible to be politically romantic or naïve except by almost wilful self-blinding or irrational doublethink. . . . Bienek illuminates the paralysis afflicting many intellectual revolutionaries today, aware of the ease with which Western society accommodates and sterilizes revolutionary ideas, even turning revolutionaries into harmless bourgeois cult figures—the book contains a fine ironic passage about Bakunin being a suitable subject for an exciting Hollywood historical romance. The resulting frustration can easily lead to nihilism, a betrayal and perversion of the revolutionary ideal in that it releases the violence of despair, not the violence of liberation. . . . *Bakunin* ends, like much of Brecht's work, not with assertions but with a challenge. Bienek's elliptical and "experimental" methods certainly justify themselves, and he succeeds in putting into just over a hundred pages what a more conventional treatment would not have done in five or even ten times the space. (p. 60)

> *Peter Lewis, in* Stand *(copyright © by* Stand*), Vol. 18, No. 3 (1977).*

*   *   *

BIRNEY, (Alfred) Earle   1904-

A Canadian poet, short story writer, novelist, critic, and editor, Birney is one of the most important Canadian poets of his generation. Many of his poems have been inspired by extensive foreign travel, and exotic settings share the stage with Canadian in his collected works. Birney's studies in Old and Middle English poetry are reflected in both the form and language of his verse. Many of his poems are sardonic depictions of contemporary life. (See also *CLC*, Vols. 1, 4, 6, and *Contemporary Authors*, Vols. 1-4, rev. ed.)

BRUCE NESBITT

"Revolution is revolution", Leon Trotsky noted in his autobiography, "only because it reduces all contradictions to the alternative of life or death". And so Gordon Saunders, the haunted "summer-time rebel" of *Down the Long Table,* emerges as a failed revolutionary, unable to accept the ultimate implications of his evolving commitments. . . . [The] novel forces each reader to challenge his or her own abilities to understand—and withstand—the social forces wrenching us away from our own places and lovers, dissociating both from our individual minds and wills. . . .

Birney's novel brings together forty years by posing two related questions: what is the cost of emotional integrity, and what is the price of intellectual honesty? In the answers lies one of the particular strengths of *Down the Long Table.*

Gordon Saunders, the questing, questioning, naive and anguished academic is the centre of it all: a success at the opening and closing of the novel, but essentially a man tortured by his idiosyncratic past. . . . What sustains him, and our interest, is Birney's dextrous manipulation of Saunders' interior dialogue, the real working out of the novel. (p. 35)

That Gordon Saunders appears to act throughout the novel in response to the confusing melange of minor characters is not fortuitous. As he is a man of his times, so his acquaint-ances collectively embody the conglomerate spirit which was determined by both the urgency and lethargy of the Depression. (p. 36)

The documentary chapters are an integral part of the plot of the novel, commenting on the necessary trivia and the larger horrors of the Depression, occasionally revealing the fate of the characters, and always expanding the irony which is the dominant mood of the novel. (p. 38)

The patterns of the novel are easily discernible: the trials and debates; the recurring presence of an amoral natural world; frequent literary allusions and quotations, especially from Early and Middle English; and the newspaper reports and headlines. . . . And all are evident in his poetry, for through them, among others, Birney has explored one of his most consistent preoccupations as a literary artist. Central to his poetry, poetic drama, and *Down the Long Table* itself is his definition of man's place in a world blind to the ironic consequences of the simultaneity of time. Variations on the nature of that time, then, provide a structural principle; the interplay between time lost and imaginatively recovered, between exorcised ghosts and inescapable memory, is the source of the philosophical irony and Birney's irony of manner. Both, in turn, suggest a further strength of the novel, its verbal irony through Birney's experimentation with varieties of Canadian dialect and speech rhythm, both oral and written. The letters, dramatic dialogues, conversations, internal monologues—these *are* in a sense the atmosphere of the times. . . . While *Down the Long Table* records the failure of a revolutionary, it is also a manifesto for humanism, the "tranced dancing of men," a muted celebration for a cause. (pp. 38-9)

> *Bruce Nesbitt, "'Down The Long Table': A Retrospective Review," in* West Coast Review *(copyright © January, 1975, West Coast Review Publishing Society), January, 1975, pp. 35-9.*

D. G. JONES

[*The Collected Poems of Earle Birney* is an important publication.] Here we find two or three dozen of our most eloquent poems, plus Birney's summing up of half a century of his development and ours.

Birney is a man who grew up backwards. He appears to get younger and gayer with every year. (The collection ends with a spatter of concrete and several new love poems.) Also, he is a man who has spent the past thirty years getting out of the things many spend their lives getting into: the University of Toronto, the Army, the CBC, the Chairmanship of his own Creative Writing Department. . . .

[He] has preferred to remain simply a poet, which for Canadians, says Birney, means being "their eternally invisible Stranger."

It has been said, in fact, that Birney is very much at home abroad because he has always been a stranger at home. Certainly he is a very peripatetic and critical poet. Since the new collection is arranged in an order that is partly chronological and partly geographical, one may note that nearly half, including some of the most lively, writing was inspired by his experience outside the country. The various satirical squibs beginning with "Canada: Case History: 1945" and ending with "Canada: Case History: 1973" may partly explain why.

A good deal of Birney's best work is satire, and a fair portion of that is aimed at Canada. He may celebrate the land and a few individuals, but the cities are damned. . . . (p. 51)

Birney is the frustrated nationalist of a Canada that doesn't exist. . . . He accuses us of hypocrisy, lethargy, meanness, "of failure to become something else-than a dozen separatisms united only by a common war / on our own central government / & by common exploitation / of our poor by our rich," of not creating "the *real* civilization / there may just be time / to glimpse before our species / crawls off to join the dinosaurs."

Birney's vision of the world is an extended variation on Mathew Arnold's "Dover Beach," except that the ignorant armies that clash in the night have a new technological glitter, and the sense of time and space is more Laurentian, cosmic or primordial. It is often closer to the spirit of the Anglo-Saxon "Wanderer." (p. 52)

Birney's heroes too are often skilled and independent wanderers or loners: mountain climbers, like David, or the real-life Conrad Kain; explorers, like Captain Cook and Vitus Bering; the "gentleman geologist," Hiram Bingham, "a believer in myth," who discovered Macchu Picchu. They may be anonymous like the carpenter in the painting of the crucifixion in "El Greco: Espolio," or the two men from Kashmir training a bear to dance in the Delhi road, or the beldams of Tepoztlan, who bargain in three languages: English, Spanish and Aztec. Despite their readiness, they often get it in the neck. The mountain-man is bushed; David is smashed on the finger; Cook gets a spear in the back; Bering is frozen in some Aleutian island. Still, they demonstrate a mixture of self-reliance and selflessness, of patience and passion, even downright stubbornness, that Birney admires.

What Birney celebrates is the creative spark in an indifferent universe, especially the human spark (when man is not "a snow"). It is above all the moment of recognition, of real communion, when people give themselves freely—which, as Birney suggests in the grave rhetoric and particular perspective of "Pacific Door," is rare. . . . The various poems written during Birney's travels round the world are often as satirical as any set in Canada (and sometimes funnier), but often enough too, they are accounts of real human meeting. . . . [Straightforward], concrete, technically precise yet metaphorical language . . . remains basic to much of Birney's best work. During the forties, Birney amplified that voice in two ways: through the use of old English diction and verse forms and through the cultivation of more deliberate rhetoric. . . . The result, when the rhetoric does not simply blur, is a certain gravity and elevation of tone characteristic of many poems written during the war years and of some of Birney's most memorable lines. The racy colloquial language characteristic of much of Birney's later work is essentially a development of the late fifties and sixties. Flat "Upper Canadian" talk, lively American speech, a Mexican mixture of English and Spanish, an Australian or New Zealand accent or a Japanese intonation lend a startling immediacy to many poems. These and the language of advertising and guide books are typically used for hilarious and often brilliant satirical effect. It is a short step to a kind of Joycean play with language and the collage and concrete poems of recent years, which lead Birney almost out of the verbal and into a purely visual expression, as in the delightful "loon about to laugh." . . .

Certainly *The Collected Poems* mirrors a world of increasing cultural collision and what has been called linguistic or literary extraterritoriality. Though Birney may have found his "voice" quite early, he has given it expression in a great variety of language. (p. 53)

> D. G. Jones, "Eternally Invisible Stranger," in Canadian Forum, *December-January 1975/76, pp. 51-3.*

SAM SOLECKI

[I don't particularly like either of Birney's two novels] yet I find that each has a facet which is of real interest. *Down the Long Table,* for example, despite certain structural flaws which Birney has acknowledged, is still an interesting novel if only because of the quality of the insight it provides into the politics of the Thirties. My response to *Turvey* is divided in a similar way. Turvey himself is an almost moronic character. In *The Creative Writer* Birney describes him as a "dumb backwoods private . . . with the intellectual and soldierly capacity of a farmyard duck," and overall Turvey's responses to the absurd and predictable situations in which he is placed are about as compelling and, with a few exceptions, as funny as those of an intellectual duck. The novel fails because the central character is not complex enough to engage the reader's interest for almost three hundred pages. Only in the novel's final and more solemn section do I find myself responding to Birney's depiction of the war years, and at that point Turvey himself is essentially a distraction.

But what orginally kept me reading the novel was the fact that Birney was attempting to deal with the lower class characters, life and, above all, language. *Turvey* is a loosely organized, overly repetitive, and often tedious whole but some of its dialogue is the best record we have in our fiction of what certain Canadian dialects sound like. . . . Birney's soldiers come alive in and through their speech and the fact that they do so makes the restoration of the "obscene" words even more important: a novel dealing with polite society can be authentic without them, but one depicting lower class life is inevitably marred if the essentials of the speech of that life—slang etc.—are missing. (p. 56)

This facet of *Turvey* does not make it a successful novel but it does give it a sociological significance. In fact, I suspect that both of Birney's novels will be read eventually less for the aesthetic satisfaction they provide—or rather fail to provide—than for the insights they give us into the Canadian situation at a particular place and time. (pp. 56-7)

> Sam Solecki, "Topsy Turvey, Again," in Canadian Forum, *June-July, 1976, pp. 56-7.*

WARREN TALLMAN

There is [a] personal factor that enters into Birney's relations with the west coast Modernists, indeed with the world at large. I [mention] his touchiness, which stems from a deeply experienced supersensitivity, the source doubtless of his art. Generous, democratic, open-handed to other poets he certainly is, traits of the eclectic man. But he is also the isolato, the loner, and for this reason the wanderer. Able to draw on a wide range of influences, he is not inclined to join in, and much of his poetry which takes Canada as its occasion testifies how alien he feels in his own country. It is when Birney is on the road, in Mexico, China, India, where he *is* an alien, recognized as such, that he seems to relax into his finest delicate-eared, quick-eyed poems. His 'Canadian' poems reveal not only the pain but the writing strain of the alienation he feels. Modernist art, in which the self is subject and the ultimate object to live all you can, calls not simply for approval from the correspondent, the other, whether he be teacher, writer or reader. But for a joining in. Because Birney is not a joiner, few of the poets were able to experience a Birney-in-themselves. Aware as they were of his benevolence, few of them were able to take him in as a source for their poetry. (pp. 193-94)

> *Warren Tallman, "Wonder Merchants: Modernist Poetry in Vancouver During the 1960's" (1973), in* Open Letter *(copyright © 1976 by Warren Tallman), Winter, 1976-77, pp. 175-207.*

GEORGE WOODCOCK

[*Ghost in the Wheels*] is obviously Birney's own selection of the poems he likes best—"none I think great and none I hope bad," as he wryly adds. (p. 95)

Birney accompanies these poems with a brief preface, in which—as always—he notes that critics have misunderstood him and have not allowed for the inventive element in poems that—like "David"—sound personal—have not, in other words, reckoned with the difference between the poet in the act of experiencing and the poet in the act of imaginative transformation. It is a valid plea, though one may justly wonder whether—in the guerrilla war that Birney has carried on for so many years with his reviewers—he has not sometimes missed those occasions when a perceptive critic will detect a nuance of true meaning that misses the poet when he becomes his own reader. (pp. 95-6)

Birney's preface also contains the announcement that he no longer wishes to be called a *poet,* but a *maker,* and that he prefers his poems themselves should be described as *makings.* (p. 96)

[In] the description of poems as makings, there is something especially appropriate to Birney's way of working. For he has never regarded a poem, once put into print, as an inviolable art object. In fact he does not seem to regard a poem of his as finally completed while he himself remains active, but rather as a work in the process of becoming which the maker is entitled to change as he himself changes. And so there are some of Birney's poems, appearing first in early collections like *The Strait of Anian* thirty years ago, which have gone through many changes over the years. The process is indicated in the dates at the end of the poems that appear in the *Collected* and also in *Ghost in the Wheels.* In some cases the time span is enormous. "Once High upon a Hill" was begun in San Francisco in 1930, but the version we now have was completed in 1970, forty years later; in the process it has changed from a poem about recent experience to a poem of distant memory, its whole tone and perspective altered and its viewpoint enriched by the depth of time. . . . Now, in 1977, it seems as though Birney regards the canon of his work as finally set, for none of the poems which received their last revision for inclusion in the *Collected* of 1975 shows any sign of having been further changed.

What is the significance of this revisionist urge in terms of Birney's achievement? Has it really involved a progression in his art as a poet? I think not. Some of his finest poems remain among his earliest and unchanged works. . . . And I find it interesting that the poems which I still admire most

in rereading them in *Ghost in the Wheels* were all written over short periods . . . and were not later changed: poems like . . . the magnificent meditation, perhaps the best of Birney's poems and one of the best of all Canadian poems, "November Walk near False Creek Mouth." (pp. 96-7)

If one can judge from such a reaction, it would seem that Birney's best poems were those stirred by an inspiration strong enough for them to be quickly completed, and those which allowed themselves to be worked on over the years were and remain the less successful. Perhaps one can go further, and say that the really effective Birney poems seem to be those motivated by a physical or emotional experience that is unrepeatable, and that the less effective are the intellectual ones to which much thought has been given and which involve tricky and deliberate intellectual structures, like "Alaska Passage," "Window Seat," etc., where the visual aspect of the poem on the page becomes more important than the sound or than the visual images it arouses in the inner mind. Birney rarely goes all the way with the concrete poets, but he goes far enough in some poems to negate the wonderful natural lyricism, the melancholic or sometimes joyful irony, and the satiric anger that are his best qualities.

How does *Ghost in the Wheels* stand as a late selection—which one imagines is meant as a definitive one—of Birney's lifelong poetic output? It seems to me at least as good as anyone else might make. All the very good poems are there (the score or so that are needed to make a major poet), and enough of the rest to represent the experiences that have been imaginatively significant to Birney and also the changes in his craftsmanship that have taken place over the years. . . . Birney may sustain his ritual antagonism to the critics, but in this selection he shows himself a first-rate self-critic.

Certainly Birney's hope that none of these poems is *bad* is vindicated; one wishes every Canadian poet had been as sensitively selective in presenting his work. His thought that none of them is "great" may be more open to question. Greatness is in practice a relative term—relative to the temporal and the cultural contexts. . . . Birney, there is no doubt, has been one of the Canadian poets whose work has been remarkable in its own right and also significant in its sensitivity to the Canadian setting and to Canadian attitudes. I would suggest, then, that his best poems are great by both standards; they are likely to be remembered as long as anything written at this time and place, and they are significant as reflections of the mind of a notable Canadian who has never been insular in his loyalties: who has indeed made the world his pearly and productive oyster. (pp. 97-8)

> *George Woodcock, "Birney's Makings," in* The Ontario Review *(copyright © 1978 by The Ontario Review), Fall-Winter, 1978-79, pp. 95-8.*

*   *   *

BÖLL, Heinrich   1917-

Böll is a West German novelist, short story writer, playwright, translator, and essayist. Böll's literary philosophy, emerging from the environment of post-war Germany, called for the creation of a new literature, one that manifested a radical change in both style and moral content. The simple, laconic prose characteristic of his work is a direct reaction against the stylistic complexity of classical German literature. Consistent with his dedication to the development of a new

literature, Böll does not dwell on the past with despair. Rather, he finds hope in the lives and actions of individuals. With biting satire, Böll exposes the meaninglessness of political and religious dogmas, contrasting their emptiness with the private acts of love and sacrifice which rebuild the spiritual strength of a people. Böll received the Nobel Prize for Literature in 1972. He has collaborated with his wife, Annemarie, on translations of the works of several contemporary writers. (See also *CLC*, Vols. 2, 3, 6, 9, and *Contemporary Authors*, Vols. 21-24, rev. ed.)

D. J. ENRIGHT

'What portion in the world can the artist have,' asked Yeats, 'but dissipation and despair?' Hans Schnier, the hero of Heinrich Böll's ... *The Clown,* doesn't take to dissipation—he is an innocent, a pure person, irretrievably monogamous, and cognac costs money—nor completely to despair. The book ends with him begging outside Bonn Railway Station, the first coin falling into his hat. Charity? But he is singing for his supper. And rather the charity of passing individuals than a retainer, a grant, a subsidy. For this way no group, no institution, no party is buying the clown and his services. (p. 196)

Lacking action in the usual sense of the word, yet *The Clown* moves with a remarkable purposiveness, its constituents working singlemindedly together. Possibly for this reason it may not prove altogether acceptable. The sensitive contemporary reader prefers to be knocked flat by a velvet glove and there is perhaps too much iron in evidence here. I think it is the case that the irony is rather too insistent. (pp. 196-97)

Böll takes his epigraph from Romans XV. 'To whom he was not spoken of, they shall see: and they that have not heard shall understand.' Paul had been preaching the gospel where Christ's name was unknown, where he could not build upon another man's foundation. Schnier is a gifted mime, he could make an excellent living in Leipzig with his 'Cardinal' or 'Board Meeting' turn, and in Bonn with his 'Party Conference Elects its Presidium' or 'Cultural Council Meets' act. But the trouble is, he wants to do the latter numbers in Leipzig and the former in Bonn: he apparently lacks 'audience-sense'. 'To poke fun at Boards of Directors where Boards of Directors don't exist seems pretty low': and the same with Elections of Presidiums where presidiums are not elected. There is an obvious parallel here with Schrella's story in Böll's previous novel, *Billiards at Half-past Nine.* A refugee from the Nazis, Schrella was imprisoned in Holland for threatening a Dutch politician who said that all Germans ought to be killed. When the Germans came in they freed him, a martyr for Germany, but then realized that he was on their list of wanted persons, so he had to escape to England. In England he was imprisoned for threatening an English politician who said that all Germans should be killed and only their works of art saved. The clown's job is not to confirm but to disturb, to preach to the unconverted. Böll's further gloss on the text from Romans would seem to have it that, in the world as it is, *real* Christian feeling exists outside the Churches, *real* socialism outside the socialist parties, *real* concern for racial harmony and *real* chances of it outside the Executive Committee of the Societies for the Reconciliation of Racial Differences. ... And, perhaps, *real* married love outside the marriage certificate.

Schnier then is an active non- or anti-party man, not merely

an elegant ironist on the side-line. How he behaves as an artist consorts exactly with how he feels as a man. (pp. 197-98)

The rhetorician seeks to deceive his neighbour, Yeats said, the sentimentalist to deceive himself. Böll deals nimbly with his rhetoricians, but his clown is something of a sentimentalist, perhaps, a little too sorry for himself. In his lamentations for Marie he grows maudlin: a clown should be able to cut his losses, to shoulder a broken heart and march on. But the sorrows of unrequited monogamy are a rare phenomenon in current fiction, and it may be that our conditioning inevitably makes them seem embarrassing. Elsewhere I am more sure that Böll's tact has forsaken him. Our sympathies go astray when Schnier informs us that his mother (on whom we are already fully informed) was a ban-the-bomb campaigner for three days until a business friend told her this policy would lead to a slump in the stock market. At times Böll can be strident, as when Schnier thinks of the people who helped Marie and him in their hard times 'while at home they sat huddled over their stinking millions, had cast me out and gloated over their moral reasons'. Possibly explicitness of this order, this insistence, is intended as a guard against a self-indulgent or merely self-protective irony, against that habit of 'keeping your superiority feelings fresh in a refrigerator of irony', as a character in *Billiards at Half-past Nine* puts it. Böll doesn't want his novel read as a cosy, remote 'allegory', a mere parable about The Creative Artist in Relation to Church and State in an Age of Technology (to borrow a lecture-title from his earlier book, *Tomorrow and Yesterday*) or the Condition of Twentieth-Century Man (who is never you or me). Every now and then a clown must be allowed to be very simple and straightforward and unsophisticated.

Böll has something to say, and not of course merely something about the Germans. He says it several times. A common weakness of writers with something to say is their inability to understand that saying it four times is not necessarily four times as effective as saying it once. But to have something to say—how rare this is! Unlike Uwe Johnson in *Speculations about Jakob,* Böll doesn't erect reading-difficulty into a law; although retaining the flashback technique of *Billiards at Half-past Nine,* this new novel is less gratuitously involuted, with a positive stylishness of clarity and competency, and free from fussiness. Unlike Günter Grass, Böll doesn't obscure his real meaning with a barrage of private emblems. Unlike certain British contemporaries, he doesn't seek to obscure the absence of meaning with an aura of bogus 'symbolism', to disguise as high metaphysics a bedroom farce or an Arabian Nights' sexual dream. 'I would rather read Rilke, Hofmannsthal and Newman one by one than have someone mix me a kind of syrup out of all three,' remarks Schnier apropos of a sermon by an 'artistic' prelate. There are few novels coming out these days which aren't either a kind of syrup or a kind of emetic. *The Clown,* I have omitted to mention, besides being one of these few, is at times very funny, as well as sad, as well as salutary. (pp. 199-200)

> *D. J. Enright, in his* Conspirators and Poets (© *D. J. Enright 1966*), *Chatto & Windus, 1966.*

W. E. YUILL

Heinrich Böll was born in the last year of the Kaiser's reign and the first of the Russian revolution. Almost all of his stories have the local and topical affinities that this suggests: they are mostly set in the city of his birth and deal with the tumultuous era of European history that coincides with his life. Like a character whom he describes in one of his short stories he is "as old as the hunger and the filth in Europe, and the war".

The local associations of Böll's work go beyond mere setting and local colour, for, as a writer, he displays many of the attributes of his fellow-citizens: traditional Catholic faith, unquestioned but not unquestioning, level-headedness and practicality, humour and a drastic wit. He has the disrespect for authority and the sound political sense that prompted the Cologne crowds to greet Hitler not with flowers but with flower-pots; he has, too, the introspective and faintly melancholy temperament that characterizes what he calls "the gin-drinker's Rhine"—the part of the river that extends from Bonn to the mists of the North Sea. For Böll, however, Cologne is not simply an urban landscape: the dimensions of space merge for him into that of time, for he is constantly aware of the past that literally and metaphorically lies buried beneath the present—not only the past of his own experience but the remote past of Roman settlers. The past is not thought of in terms of a "cultural heritage" but rather as a continuity of human experience linking the Roman colonist with the modern artisan or clerk. Certainly Böll's fascination by the past is not of the kind that one would expect to issue in the form of historical novels or stories that are quaintly local; it is an aspect rather of his imaginative insight into basic human situations—and perhaps also of his belief in the ultimate timelessness of human existence.

Böll has always been more than a local writer: he is concerned with the fate and experience of a whole generation of Germans and of the individual in the great materialistic urban societies of the modern world. It was as the spokesman of his own generation that Böll first came into prominence; he subsequently developed into a mentor and critic of all those who seemed to forget too easily the sufferings of that generation and the causes of that suffering. . . . The tone of Böll's early war stories is certainly not nostalgic or romantic, but neither is it as hysterical as that of Borchert's play *Draussen vor der Tür:* the writer's reaction is one of sober, sombre, seemingly dispassionate disgust. . . . It is only in . . . *Entfernung von der Truppe,* that Böll, looking back over twenty years, can see his experience of war in a satirical and at times scurrilously comic light. In the early stories, when memories were still painfully fresh, there was no room for humour. In an age of conscription and mechanization war had lost whatever glamour it might formerly have had, and was unmitigated by heroism. There is certainly nothing romantic or heroic about the soldiers in *Der Zug war pünktlich* and *Wo warst du, Adam?* They are cannon-fodder. The railway station, which in Böll's stories so often epitomizes the impersonality, restlessness and rootlessness of modern life, becomes in war-time the antechamber of fate. Men are driven by "the grey authoritarian scourge" of loudspeakers into trains which, as symbols of destiny, carry them unresisting to a punctual death. Scarcely one figure in these early stories eludes death. Feinhals, in *Wo warst du, Adam?,* escapes until the last moment, only to be blown to pieces—by a random German shell—on the threshold of his own home. The stories are not designed, however, as hair-raising accounts of the horrors of battle, for the writer is concerned with deeper issues than physical ordeal and destruction. . . . It is the demoral-

ization and degradation, the spiritual maiming and blinding that are emphasized. The killing of men's bodies is not the worst; their souls are enthralled or crushed by mindless discipline. (pp. 141-43)

Böll's stories are full of war-wounded and convalescents in the figurative sense, people for whom the war can never be "over"—not only the physically handicapped or the manifestly neurotic, but also those who are simply demoralized. The returning soldier and his attempts to adjust himself to life in post-war Germany naturally figure prominently in the stories. These "Heimkehrer" are not burdened like Beckmann, the hero of *Draussen vor der Tür,* with a sense of guilt, they do not succumb to hysterical despair. They suffer, rather, from an inarticulate malaise, a paralysis of will and feeling. (p. 143)

[The characters from Böll's early novels] are moody and uncommunicative. It is symptomatic of their alienation that they prefer to speak on the telephone rather than face to face. They turn their backs on the reviving world around them and, young as they are, live in their memories. Reminiscence is the characteristic dimension of Böll's writing. He is fascinated by the counterpoint of time and place and by the changes worked through time and circumstance. (p. 144)

It is not unnatural that the drastic disruption of their lives by the war made the whole of Böll's generation obsessively conscious of a pattern of change and continuity. For characters like Albert and Nella in *Haus ohne Hüter* time is out of joint in a special sense. For them the past is the time before the war, the present is the time since, and between past and present lies a limbo, a gulf that has swallowed what might have been. Besides the actual past and present there is in their minds a potential time, "le temps perdu", "the third level", as Böll calls it. He is continually seeking metaphors to express all this: in *Haus ohne Hüter,* three "times" are visualized as discs superimposed upon one another and revolving eccentrically. . . .

Many of Böll's introspective characters, like the young widow Nella, cannot shake off the nostalgia for what might have been. They are haunted by the memory of a turning point in their lives. For these people time is essentially private and cannot be divorced from inner experience. (p. 145)

Hypnotized by the notion of time, [Böll's characters] often see in habit a means of arresting its flow. In the sacramental form of ritual, habit is a legitimate escape from time, an access to eternity, the rituals of his Church playing a large part in Böll's stories. In a secular context, however, habit can be a baleful force. The attempt to resurrect the past by repetition may have harrowing effects: Hans Schnier in *Ansichten eines Clowns* describes his abortive experiments in this respect and confesses that moments cannot be repeated. Habit can be an aid to survival, but it may also be an inert weight that crushes individuality and impoverishes life. In the story entitled *Über die Brücke,* the narrator, passing years later over a railway bridge he regularly used to cross, observes with mingled relief and dismay that the windows of a house are being cleaned in exactly the same sequence as before the war: the daughter, having taken over from her mother, the hypnotic routine of the "Putzplan" is becoming the same kind of household drudge. It may be that Böll has here put his finger on a particular weakness of his nation—the fondness for ceremony and regulated routine. (pp. 146-47)

The part played by time, memory and habit in Böll's works points to a concentration on emotion and inner sensation rather than on action. Only the satirical short stories tend to have definable plots: many others simply trace the changes of emotional climate in a character or the evolution of attitudes from a germ of experience. Even in the novels the external action—as distinct from reminiscence—rarely occupies more than a few hours. There is little of what one might call epic objectivity: frequently the author identifies himself with the protagonist, while the more complex works are built up from a series of private views.

The tone of the first person narrative so common in Böll is generally subdued, resigned, melancholy, often with a hint of the morbid. . . . To the ideal of frantic activity for which his countrymen are renowned Böll opposes the ascetic motto of *memento mori*. Too few of his compatriots, he asserts, are capable of melancholy—the mark of humility and hence of true humanity. . . .

Although often struck, this muted note is by no means the only one in the register of Böll's work. In many of his stories, particularly since about 1952 when symptoms of over-indulgence began to appear in German society, Böll looks round him with a critical eye, and the tone becomes ironical, sometimes hilariously satirical. (p. 148)

Böll tends to dwell in the minds of his characters, to convey his own view in their reflections and utterances. But it is not only their minds that he inhabits but their bodies as well. He sees with their eyes—it is perhaps significant that, when he describes the appearance of his protagonists, he often does so through the reflection in a mirror. Even more characteristically, he feels with them in the physical as well as the emotional sense: he feels the itch of stiff new uniforms, registers the peptic climate of his characters, is aware of their defective teeth. Above all, particularly in the later works, he seems to be sharply conscious of everyday smells. . . . (p. 149)

Few German writers have evoked so effectively the familiar texture and repetitive patterns of ordinary urban life. His meticulous descriptions have a certain aura of professional craftsmanship about them. . . . His technique might in a specific sense be called "realistic", but his realism is not simply objective, does not consist only in accumulation of detail. It is largely subjective: physical reality is nearly always apprehended through the senses and minds of characters in the stories. Nearly always it is restricted to features within the purview of one individual; we do not often find extensive description of landscape, setting or background. The author identifies himself with figures moving in urban surrounds—often precisely named real localities—so familiar or so restricted that the wider background is taken for granted. He operates, as it were, with a very short focal length, sometimes creating an effect that is almost obsessive or claustrophobic. One might perhaps detect in Böll an absorption in familiar things and in particular a leaning towards the drab and sordid that almost constitutes a kind of inverted romanticism with which readers of Graham Greene will be acquainted.

Böll's realism might be described as poetic as well as subjective. A poetic quality is manifested on two levels. In the first place, Böll imparts to the perceptions of the people in his stories the awareness of an urban poet, a sense of the intrinsic strangeness of familiar things. Secondly, as author,

he invests objects with symbolic significance and employs them in thematic patterns. The sharp contours of everyday objects in the stories often give the impression that these items of reality have been torn from their context by the prehensile mind of the observer—it is not the natural coherence or proportions of things in themselves that matters but their emotional or emblematic associations. Familiar actions—the making of a telephone call, for instance—may be seen in close-up or slow motion, as it were, because the moment is fraught with emotional significance. Trivial objects acquire meaning as the evidence of fateful events: Bruno Schneider in *Die Postkarte* pores over the scrap of paper that changed the course of his life—the registration slip from his calling-up papers. . . . The relationship, at once spiritual and physical, between a man and a woman, between Schnier and Marie Züpfner, is commemorated in a mosaic of trivial objects and gestures. One of the charges that Schnier levels at Catholics is precisely that they "have no sense of detail". It is in keeping with Schnier's character that the obsession with what the song-writer calls "these foolish things" descends into near-maudlin sentimentality; for Böll, as a writer a concern with the details of ordinary living is linked with his awareness that man is a psychosomatic entity, that the soul inhabits a body and must express itself in a world that is physically real. Mundane things and actions can readily acquire a sacramental significance: the sensuous pleasure of eating fresh bread so exactly described in *Das Brot der frühen Jahre* has sacramental implications. (pp. 149-51)

This kind of symbolism is one of the features that give Böll's stories depth and make them much more than evocations of mood and setting. Many are mounted on a framework of parable: singly and together marking out a moral universe which has the objective coherence that the physical world they describe seems to lack. Behind the topicality is a timeless reality. In the grouping of characters and in typical experiences they undergo one may detect a kind of theology: figures superficially somewhat diverse fall into opposing categories that have the unambiguity of those in a morality play. (p. 151)

The division of characters into opposite moral types is not in itself an artistic weakness. However, the difference of approach to the two fundamental types, a consequence of Böll's theological view, might be considered an aesthetic drawback. It possibly deprives the stories of balance and involves a danger of oversimplification. The reluctance to fathom the "evil" character, or even to see him as problematic, and the habit of seeing him through the eyes of his anti-type suggest a certain limitation in the writer's imaginative range. The sympathetic characters, although superficially diverse, tend to share a resigned and inhibited temperament. Nevertheless, Böll's later works, particularly *Entfernung von der Truppe*, do suggest that he is acquiring more insight into bitterly rebellious or sardonic characters. (p. 152)

Böll's criticism of the political aspect of Roman Catholicism may be less specific than the much-publicized attack launched by Hochhuth in *The Representative;* it is hardly less outspoken and all the more impressive in that it is based on the personal experience of a sincere and thoughtful Catholic. *Brief an einen jungen Katholiken* embodies the first direct attack on the political attitude of the Church. Böll notes that the Vatican was the first foreign state to seek an understanding with Hitler and recalls the religious instruction which he himself received as a conscript. This instruction was concerned almost solely with sexual morality never referring to the real moral dangers threatening young men pressed into the service of an evil totalitarian system; the concept of conscience hardly entered into it. In post-war Germany Böll sees the Church again in danger of becoming too closely identified with the Establishment, of ceasing to be a theological and moral power and becoming instead a political pressure group.

In the novels and stories true faith is seldom linked with efficiency, success and prosperity, and is not found in the loveless organizational religion of Frau Franke and her like. Faith is most authentic in failure, in squalid surroundings or where it verges on despair—a paradoxical truth familiar to readers of Graham Greene. (pp. 153-54)

It is in keeping with the theological implications of Böll's works that many of his central characters have a strong impression that their lives are pre-ordained, that they are in some cases subject to supernatural guidance. . . .

Andreas in *Der Zug war pünktlich* has a premonition of his death, a premonition that is punctually fulfilled, but in most of the stories it is love which strikes the hero with the force of revelation. . . . The kind of love shown in these encounters is not narrow and selfish; it initiates a reconciliation with mankind at large. Love emancipates the individual from isolation and imagined self-sufficiency, [and] breaks down a psychic blockage. . . . (p. 154)

Love, in Böll's view, even in its basest manifestations is never totally devoid of a sacramental element. Its true culmination, however, is in marriage and family life. Marriage is not simply a social institution; it is a sacrament as distinct from a ceremony, a communion of souls ordained in heaven and independent of—even on occasion in contravention of —social sanction. The harmony of souls in marriage is a facet of the divine cosmic order. (p. 155)

Among the writers of post-war Germany Heinrich Böll has earned a prominent place as a literary artist and moralist. His works appeal not only as authentic renderings of atmosphere, setting and mood, but also because they clearly embody emblematic characters and situations demonstrating moral problems and truths. They deal with ideas and experiences that are none the less profound because they can be understood by the great majority of people. In this, as in more obvious senses, Böll is a democrat. Unlike many German writers he is not hampered by philosophical systems or fettered by a pretentious "literary" tradition. It is hardly a compliment to a writer to say that his language is "simple", but Böll's idiom is at any rate not obscure or difficult: "workmanlike" might be the best word to describe it. Clear it certainly is and always to the point. That he is capable, however, of considerable sophistication is evident from the stories written in a parodistic style and also from the complex structure of works like *Billard um halbzehn* and *Entfernung von der Truppe*. Although his themes and settings may not be very diverse, the range of Böll's technique is in fact much wider than it might appear at first sight. The form in which Böll is most obviously at home is the short story, and even the novels, with their brief span of "real" time and their episodic structure, have the economy of short stories. Nevertheless, within the novels and in individual short stories there is a considerable variety of idiom,

ranging from laconic description of incident, through impressionistic evocation of atmosphere to the regular structure of *Novellen* like *Die Waage der Baleks* or *Wir Besenbinder,* forming altogether a body of work remarkable for humour and perceptiveness.

As a Christian moralist Böll tries to apply the values of a traditional faith to the problems of modern man, isolated as he often is in an over-populated environment where economic considerations are paramount. The moral issues of the urban lower and middle classes with which Böll principally deals are not sensational. Men are corrupted in a banal fashion, "as in second-rate films". (pp. 155-56)

Böll wishes men to cleanse themselves of the grimy sediment that is deposited in an atmosphere of mere "respectability", he wishes to lead them back to a positive faith, to the humanistic nucleus of Christianity, to charity. Where he satirizes the social provisions of our industrial society it is because he fears their dehumanizing influence. Where he criticizes his Church it is because he fears that it is falling into dogmatism, working for sectional interests, becoming modish rather than modern. The motive behind much that Böll writes is compassion. In this compassion there is an element of sentimentality that has led one critic to speak of "allegorical confectionery", but nearly everywhere—and particularly in his latest works—the sweetness is neutralized by the acid of satire. It is the critical vein in Böll's writing as well as his technical skill that has kept him in the *avant-garde* of German writing and given him an appeal and authority far beyond the membership of his Church. (pp. 156-57)

W. E. Yuill, "Heinrich Böll," in Essays on Contemporary German Literature: German Men of Letters, Vol. IV, *edited by Brian-Keith Smith (© 1966 Oswald Wolff), Oswald Wolff, 1966, pp. 141-58.*

H. M. WAIDSON

[*Gruppenbild mit Dame*] might well be called a "Zeitroman", a panoramic social novel which traces the impact of public events upon private lives. It is a novel form which may encourage a historical conspectus in which individual problems may be subordinated to the pattern of known, outward happenings. . . . Böll succeeds in embodying the moods of past times with the emotional tensions of the principal characters. Yet though poignant feeling is often present, the wider vistas of the "Zeitroman" contribute to preventing the reader from coming so constantly close to anyone in *Gruppenbild mit Dame* as he does to Hans Schnier, the first-person narrator and central figure of *Ansichten eines Clowns*. At the same time the later work can be regarded as a "Bildungsroman", as the author has indicated. He points out that his heroine learns what is inwardly relevant to her, while rejecting much else, and that the novel is about the formation of a woman's personality, in the sense of what she acquires in the way of traditional cultural-educational material and also of the manner in which she develops as an individual.

Gruppenbild mit Dame sums up within itself a whole range of action and feeling that has affinities with moods and motifs in others of the author's works. As Böll sees it, this novel, or parts of it, are almost like a summary, or a further development, of earlier ones. Certainly this is not the first time that he has described the reactions of young people to the anticipation and arrival of the war in 1939; the experiences of the war-years in a large urban centre like Cologne are given with detailed particulars, probably more fully than in any of Böll's preceding writings. (p. 124)

Heinrich Böll's heroines, from Olina in *Der Zug war pünktlich* . . . onwards, have by now become an impressive series of figures, comparable in their gradations of variety and consistency with the young women of Hardy's novels. But sometimes we see relatively little of them, and their personality has to come through obliquely and at rare intervals, as in the case of Edith (*Billard um halbzehn*) and Henriette (*Ansichten eines Clowns*). Now in *Gruppenbild mit Dame* it seems as if Leni Pfeiffer is to be brought before us as a full-length portrait. The novelist has expressed his aim as being "to describe or write about the fate of a German woman in her late forties" whose whole life has had to cope with the burden of the history of those years. . . . However, the reader does not come as close to Leni's own thinking and feeling or indeed her outward presence as might be expected, even though the narrative keeps circling round her, and the variety and liveliness of the information about her and her environment are impressive.

In its narrative method *Gruppenbild mit Dame* is reasonably accessible, certainly in comparison with *Billard um halbzehn,* where the analytical approach seems to cause the principal characters to be particularly deliberate and inward looking. Very early on in *Gruppenbild mit Dame* the narrator disclaims anything like total insight into Leni's outward or inner life. His aim, he states in this first intervention, is to acquire "what is called factual information", supporting his evidence by giving his source and mentioning not only the name of the informant but also some particulars about him. The narrator—"Der Verf." as he calls himself—is a self-appointed research worker who has taken on the task of collecting together all possible material that will contribute to a study of Leni Pfeiffer, reproducing written documents, taking down the statements of those who knew her, and interpolating summaries of what people generally think of her, as well as making his own comments. . . . The reader is indeed completely dependent upon the narrator for access to Leni and to the various people who have known her and talk about her. However, as the narrator is anxious to communicate and to take the reader into his confidence, it seems that there should not be many problems in this respect. There is certainly a wealth of information. Movement in time and place can be instantaneous, as the informants' memories take their impressions from one association to another. But the narrator, while allowing a free rein to his interviewees, and to himself, does keep in view a steady movement forward in time. (pp. 125-26)

The period of Leni's fulfilment is the axis of the novel. It could almost form a separate, rounded tale of its own; chapters V-IX . . . give this essential unit. What came earlier was preparation, and Leni's later life is revealed as clearly less memorable. (p. 126)

The flowering of love between Leni and Boris takes place paradoxically in an environment of death. Throughout 1944 and in the first months of 1945 the aerial bombardment of the urban centre is no small threat The two young people work together at the preparation of tributes to the dead. Their relationship is politically forbidden, and its discovery would probably lead to their execution. But when there are daylight raids, they can retreat alone to someone's family vault in the nearby cemetery. Within the episode of Leni's

union with Boris there is one inset period which forms the core, between February 20 and March 7 1945, when the lovers and their closest acquaintances and friends live underground in catacomb-like conditions in the cemetery. . . . The analogies with the conditions of early Christians in Rome or of life before the fall of man and the social contract offer themselves. . . .

Although we are told quite a lot about Leni, it is reporting and hearsay for the most part. We see her from the outside and do not come close to her. She is not particularly talkative, and her love for Boris has certain linguistic limitations in any case. We depend on the narrator, and he depends on his various informants, since he has no direct personal contact with Leni. (p. 127)

Apart from a satirical episode relating her contact with the Communist Party . . . there is little about Leni until the incidents of 1970 which form the final crisis. Now Leni is to be evicted from her flat by the Hoysers (grandfather and two grandsons), but her friends and admirers form a "Leni in Not—Helft Leni-Kommittee" and the narrator agrees to put the findings of his researches at the committee's disposal. Leni's association with "Gastarbeiter", her failure to charge her sub-tenants a sufficiently high rent, the imprisonment of her son Lev on account of the illegal way in which he has tried to assist his mother pay her debts, her pregnancy, and her marriage to the Turk Mehmet (who is already married with four children)—these are the tensions of 1970 which have become exacerbated to their critical point in the course of the time that the narrator has been writing about Leni. The happy ending demonstrates that the threat to the anarchist sub-culture which has been building up around Leni and the immigrant workers was only a passing one. In 1945 the spontaneously formed social group in the catacombs was clandestine and short-lived, but 25 years later a fresh community is emerging, which, although seriously threatened, survives the crisis and can maintain its essential self-expression. (p. 128)

Yet we are still some way from Leni, though the narrator meanwhile has been acquiring a profile of his own. While she remains distant, he comes closer and absorbs more of the reader's attention. If some authors, for instance in the nineteenth century, would begin a work with a substantial framework narrative but then let the device lapse, Böll directs attention increasingly to the narrator and his activities as the novel hurries along to its end. He opts for a casework approach to the characters whom he interviews, offering to give statistics about their size and weight if they are among the more prominent in the narrative. Most of the information provided by the various interviewees is handed on to the reader verbatim, and letters and other documents are also passed on. He informs us that, feeling himself to be in no position to meditate on tears, he has had recourse to encyclopaedia definitions . . . which lead him to a series of bumbling but affecting abbreviations. He offers alternative hypotheses concerning the fate of his heroine if her husband Alois Pfeiffer had not been killed in Russia during the war, or if five other eventualities involving Alois, Erhard and/or Heinrich had come about. . . . The presence of such interferences is to indicate that "many questions remain open". . . . He may become "extremely confused" if an interviewee unexpectedly shows strong emotion. . . . He is a heavy smoker . . . and has got behind with his researches through watching the Clay-Frazier boxing-match on television. . . .

These and the like may be playful ornamentations on the framework, but when the narrator visits Rome to find out more about Sister Rahel Maria Ginzburg, once a mentor of Leni's at her convent school, he and his interviewee, Sister Klementina, fall in love at first sight. This scene is an idyllic counterpart to the corresponding scene between Leni and Boris. Like Leni's act of offering a cup of coffee, Sister Klementina's request for a cigarette from the narrator takes on ritual significance, but at a correspondingly lighter level. (pp. 128-29)

The crisis of Leni's imminent eviction is clearly a much less dramatic and serious threat than was the sequence of events culminating in her and Boris' withdrawal to the catacombs twenty-five years earlier. The objective reasons for her way of life being in jeopardy at this time in the history of the Federal Republic are evidently more slender than the much closer presence of immediate and irreparable disaster in 1944-45. The main impact of poignant, sombre tension must come at the earlier time, while the narrator can step more into the foreground as the action of the novel and the passing of time, bringing with it an increasing remoteness of the war years and of youth, would allow the heroine to occupy a less central position, while permitting a lightening of the novel's texture and its permeation with even more freely ranging fantasy. Alternatively one could emphasize that the heightening crises and the formation of the two spontaneous groupings correspond to the times of Leni's two pregnancies; the birth of her second child is likely to be accompanied by a renewed and, we assume, possibly less precariously balanced fulfilment of her being.

These points concerning the roles of Leni and the narrator will by no means explore completely the possibilities of interpretation in a novel which is the author's most extended to date and where there is frequently a combination of exuberance and fantasy. What might be seen as the secularisation and sexualisation of the way in which human relationships are presented, by comparison with some earlier works of Böll, might well be looked at more closely, not to speak of the functions of the various other characters. (pp. 130-31)

> *H. M. Waidson, "Heroine and Narrator in Heinrich Böll's 'Gruppenbild Mit Dame'," in* Forum for Modern Language Studies *(copyright © by Forum for Modern Language Studies and H. M. Waidson), April, 1973, pp. 125-31.*

W. G. CUNLIFFE

The German novelist, Heinrich Böll, reflects a striking change in West German attitudes that has taken place since the end of World War II, when Böll started writing. The change concerns a basic dilemma of modern, Western society: the incongruity between man as a private individual and as a citizen of the state. This liberals' dilemma is expressed clearly in the first chapter of *Emile,* where Rousseau explains that a true conformity between the two is impossible, and that, therefore, the decision must be made whether to educate the individual as a private person (homme) or as a citizen of the state (citoyen). (p. 473)

Böll, too, is caught up in this dilemma, which we see him pursuing through his works. In the early works he is firmly on the side of the private individual, but later he becomes less certain of individual values without being able to embrace supraindividual values. Unlike Rousseau, Böll attempts to find a compromise between "homme" and "ci-

toyen," an attempt which results in the eccentric rebels characteristic of his later work.

In his early works, however, Böll has little doubt what to choose. In this he is typical of the German writers returning from the war. For them, the individual and his private life were far more important than any public cause, inevitably associated with totalitarian government. For years the cause of the *polis* had been advanced and the rights of the individual ruthlessly trampled underfoot. . . . The most private of private lives, that of the petit-bourgeois, was often seen as the bravest assertion of these rights, all the braver for its touching vulgarity disguising a tough core of passive resistance to authority. (pp. 473-74)

The early Böll is equally vehement in his praise of the petit-bourgeois private individual, with an added insistence on his mildness and lack of harmful drive or ambition. The mild-mannered hero of *Wo warst du, Adam? (Adam, Where Art Thou?),* the former architect Feinhals, passes through war and battle, noisy historical events, dazed and indifferently contemptuous. His one wish, as he explains when the closing stages of the war bring him from the Balkans to the Rhine, is to return to his nearby home where he can resume a useful, unpretentious life. He makes a final confession of this longing for home in a kitchen, a last haven before he meets his death on his own doorstep. (p. 474)

But it is not only under the extreme conditions of war and totalitarian rule that stuffy middle-class values provide a form of resistance in Böll's works against the ruthless world of affairs. In the early post-war stories, too, in *Und sagte kein einziges Wort* (1953) *(Acquainted with the Night),* *Haus ohne Hüter* (1954) *(The Unguarded House),* and *Das Brot der frühen Jahre* (1955) *(The Bread of our Early Years),* the humble private virtues are a shield against the blandishments of the new prosperity. (p. 475)

The post-war world of affairs and business is condemned, as the war had been, from the point of view of a utopian petit-bourgeois. This point of view is exemplified in satirical sketches, such as the radio play *Zum Tee bei Dr. Borsig* (1955) *(Tea with Dr. Borsig).* Commerce is depicted here as the sale of grotesque and spurious patent medicines, and Borsig takes refuge from it in a petit-bourgeois haven, a cheap apartment near the railway station and a girl-friend who steals an afternoon from work to go with him to the movies. She does this as a matter of principle, as a way of protecting the claims of private life against a soulless community, and she may be considered as an early, slight exemplar of Böll's rebels. (p. 476)

This kind of resistance to the norms of a complacently prosperous society depends on private integrity and humanitarian non-conformity. These qualities, however, have become illusory in the post-war world. As Böll explains in a revelatory essay on Brendan Behan, this is an age in which the lower middle classes self-consciously ape the clichés of high society, because "striving for dull freedom out of dull bondage, [they] cannot get rid of their lower middle class clichés and believe they can, they ought to play at being sophisticated by 'sinning'—often without really enjoying it."

In other words, the rejection of old-fashioned petit-bourgeois integrity has, as Böll is forced to recognize, become a petit-bourgeois cliché. (pp. 476-77)

Böll's dissatisfaction with the virtues of individualism is revealed in *Billard um halbzehn* (1959) (*Billiards at Half-past Nine*). Up to then, the typical Böll hero had been a harmless victim, whose fate can be summed up in the last sentence of the short story "Der Mann mit den Messern"/ "The Knife Thrower": " I was the man they threw knives at." Whether in war-time (*The Train Was on Time; Adam, Where Art Thou?*) or in the post-war period (*Acquainted with the Night, The Unguarded House*), decent, long-suffering humanity is the prey of the nameless forces of history. It is in *Billiards* that Böll introduces active critics of society and abandons, as Reich-Ranicki puts it, "inwardness and disguised lyricism." The passive character, the hotel page-boy Hugo, exists only in the margin. The central figure, Robert Fähmel, blows up an abbey designed by his father because it is a breeding-place of Fascism or, in the religious terminology of this novel, "the sacrament of the buffalo" is observed there. After the war he still wishes to eradicate all traces of the past, although he is caught in a web of inactivity relieved only by a tender concern for the "lamb" Hugo. It is his mother, Johanna, who emerges as the first of Böll's eccentric rebels, for Robert's act of destruction is a symbolical act. For years, Johanna has sought oblivion in the "enchanted castle" of a sanatorium, a means of escaping from the outside world. Now, on the day in 1958 which covers the foreground of the plot, she emerges from this refuge and becomes an activist. She is, however, an eccentric, almost comic activist—an old lady who, on a day's outing to visit her family, shoots at and wings a prominent political personage who is watching a political procession from a hotel balcony.

Böll is expressing the humanitarian liberal's dilemma by creating characters who are activists, feeling responsibility for the community, yet at the same time individualists, not subscribing to any ideology. They find a solution in eccentric rebellion which, from now on, is a recurring element in Böll's work. In *Die Ansichten eines Clowns* (*The Clown*), published in 1963, by which time the official Church has lost its integrity and is firmly entrenched in the ruling classes, the eccentric position of the hero is acknowledged in the epithet "clown." (pp. 477-78)

Rebellion through play-acting is the essential theme of the next novels, *Entfernung von der Truppe* (1964) (*Absent without Leave*) and *Ende einer Dienstfahrt* (1966) (*End of a Mission*). The hero of the former chooses the role of latrine orderly in the *Wehrmacht* and uses the noisome adjuncts of his calling to keep the world at bay. The latter centers around an act of defiance whereby the Gruhls, father and son, set fire to an army jeep in protest against a system that encourages official wastefulness, yet penalizes the honest, old-fashioned carpenter's business of Gruhl senior. The protest touches on big issues, but Böll keeps it at local level with the protesters anything but professional agitators, for Böll makes much play in this novel with the pleasures of the table and domestic happiness. In Böll's . . . *Gruppenbild mit Dame* (1971) (*Group Portrait with Lady*), the individualistic revolt is carried back to the war period, during which Böll's heroes had behaved so passively. Now we read of two young soldiers executed during the war for resistance activities, their resistance taking the eccentric form of offering an anti-aircraft gun to Danish partisans. One of the accused, we are told, claimed at the court-martial that they were dying for an honorable profession, the arms trade. (p. 478)

In moving from the passive hero to the eccentric rebel who is no longer satisfied with the virtues of the lamb, Böll has reflected an important change in German attitudes since the war. (p. 479)

W. G. Cunliffe, "Heinrich Böll's Eccentric Rebels," in Modern Fiction Studies (© copyright 1975, by Purdue Research Foundation, West Lafayette, Indiana), Autumn, 1975, pp. 473-79.

MICHAEL BUTLER

Although he began writing before the Second World War, Böll's published work coincides almost exactly with the history of the Federal Republic, and there can be few more instructive documents on the extraordinary growth and success, doubts and strains, of this fledgling democracy. The sweep of Böll's narrative world—from the bleak anecdotes of the immediate post-war years, via the artistic turning-point of *Billard um halb zehn* to the controlled bitterness of *Die verlorene Ehre der Katharina Blum* and the complex irony of *Gruppenbild mit Dame*—illuminates the social, economic and political development of West Germany. . . .

When all allowances have been made for Böll's characteristic weaknesses—a certain stylistic banality and an occasional tendency towards sentimentality—the presentation of his complete narrative *oeuvre* underlines not only the astonishing consistency and inventiveness but also the humane warmth of a writer who has never wavered in his defence of the disadvantaged and inarticulate—those products of society so often dismissed as *Abfall*. Even without the counterbalancing record of his personal involvement in the political and social issues of his time . . . Böll's creative work of the past thirty years stands as a clear and impressive testament to the writer's commitment to the individual and his vital needs in the face of the manifold pressures of an increasingly abstract and anonymous society.

Michael Butler, "For the Defence," in The Times Literary Supplement (© Times Newspapers Ltd. (London) 1978; reproduced from The Times Literary Supplement by permission), June 30, 1978, p. 730.

DIANA ROWAN

Reading a novel by Heinrich Böll is to pick through a pile of rubble with a teaspoon, or with bare hands. Shards of domestic pottery, bits of cloth almost unrecognizable as clothing, a doll with no face, half a singed photograph emerge slowly and painfully from a great deal of disintegrated brick and plaster. These shattered fragments just begin to suggest the outlines of a former life, when the grim weight of detail renders us numb, and the ponderous but relentless pace with which Böll forces it all into our attention makes a bilious taste of resentment rise in our throats. We were, after all, here to be entertained by good literature.

Yet we cannot stop; the shreds and shards look ominously familiar. The jaunty archaeological dig in some other era, in other people's lives is over. Too late, we realize that the author has us exactly where he wants us—staring at some scrap in the pile of debris with the full shock of recognition.

At times, in the many novels and stories of this prolific writer, one feels manipulated, occasionally duped. The procession of characters, battered so hard by events that they no longer comprehend or even care about the forces which shaped their lives, almost becomes predictable and almost loses the original impact. Almost, but not quite. Böll . . . usually proves too much a master for that.

We might not immediately connect with this novel of postwar Germany "[And Never Said a Word"] . . . but the cumulative emotional impact is still there. In this tale, narrated alternately by an estranged husband and wife, the actual shock of war still lingers. . . .

Between this couple, no longer young, lie 15 years of tangled history—the ordinary personal strengths and failings warped and magnified by the horror of war and its aftermath, poverty and hopelessness. . . .

Where has the violence and despair in him come from? From the war? Or has some shard of violence, apathy, and greed in a score or legion of hearts as ordinary as his lead to the cataclysm of this latest war in an endless cycle of wars? The subtitle of one of Böll's best-known works, "The Lost Honor of Katherina Blum," underscores the intensity of Böll's concern with this massive theme; "How Violence Develops and Where it Leads." He tracks it ruthlessly and his writing reaches a scalding brilliance when he comes close to isolating something unnameable. (p. 18)

Böll's characters, and the shape of the social and emotional terrain in his fiction, may seem compulsively grotesque; but so are the realities with which he deals. He grapples with, and uncovers the substance of these people, not to exploit or condemn their grotesqueness, but in order to explore the possible sources of their dis-ease, which seems, by inheritance or by nature, to be ours as well.

He presents no answers, only the acrid questions of a survivor; but he also presents the few broken clues he has found, and keeps finding, in the wreckage. (p. 19)

Diana Rowan, "Living in War's Landscape" in The Christian Science Monitor *(reprinted by permission from* The Christian Science Monitor; © *1978 by The Christian Science Publishing Society; all rights reserved), July 12, 1978, pp. 18-19.*

*   *   *

BOWEN, Elizabeth   1899-1973

Bowen was an Anglo-Irish novelist, short story writer, essayist, critic, editor, and author of several autobiographical and historical works, and books for children. The inevitable disillusionment inherent in human relationships is a recurrent theme in Bowen's work. The plots of her novels often revolve around conflicts of innocence and experience, usually depicted through the painful experiences of love in a young female character. Bowen defined the novel as the "non-poetic statement of a poetic truth," and in her straightforward, unadorned prose she achieves this verisimilitude. She received the C.B.E. (Commander, Order of the British Empire) in 1948. (See also *CLC*, Vols. 1, 3, 6, and *Contemporary Authors*, Vols. 17-18; obituary, Vols. 41-44, rev. ed.; *Contemporary Authors Permanent Series*, Vol. 2.)

PAUL A. PARRISH

[*The Last September, The House in Paris, The Death of the Heart,* and *Eva Trout* are each] concerned with a young romantic female awakening to life and love and [have] certain central scenes which focus on the imagination of these young innocents. Readers of Elizabeth Bowen have too easily concentrated on the inherent sympathy in the por-

trayals of these characters and have too seldom recognized that to Miss Bowen the inexorable romantic mind is doomed, as well as, in its own way, admirable. The scenes which unite the elements of nature, love, and idealism are themselves reminiscent of the Edenic myth and the Garden where reality, in the form of a serpent, sin, and death, intrudes and ultimately destroys the perfection which has been realized. Adding to a sense of the tragic destiny of the inflexible romantic is the paradox that the young idealist commands the greatest sympathy precisely at the moment that the futility of her romanticism is most fully recognized. As Lois, Karen, Portia, and Eva strive to claim their loves and to live with their lovers in an alien world, the reader is emotionally bound up in their efforts but intellectually certain of their inevitable failure. These young idealists fail because they cannot distinguish between the external world and the Edenic world of their imaginations. . . . Unless a person feels, he is not really alive, but if that feeling distorts or falsifies external reality, death, either spiritual or physical, is the ultimate consequence. The dream of an Eden is at once appealing and impossible, the romantic herself sympathetic and doomed. (pp. 86-7)

[In *The Last September*] the conjunction of nature, love, and imagination possesses characteristics quite unlike the pattern found in the other three novels. . . . The most distinctive feature of *The Last September* is the presence of a prominent, older male romantic, Hugo Montmorency, as well as a young female innocent, Lois Farquar. The most dramatic scene in which nature, love, and imagination conjoin is the mill scene in Chapter Seven of Part II, in which Lois is primarily an observer, not a participant. Hugo acts and feels: he is in love, and his mind captures the importance of the moment by its imaginative participation with nature. (p. 87)

Hugo is here the romantic mind *in extremis,* projecting onto nature his feelings and imagination. That his love is, from its very conception, unrealizable seems obvious. What is more important is that Lois has an opportunity to *witness* a romantic mind in love and in nature, unique among Miss Bowen's romantic heroines. . . .

But if she observes and learns, if it is true, as Marda tells her, that "nothing gets past . . . [her] imagination," . . . her education and imagination push her further into the extremes of idealism. . . . As she reads a letter from Gerald she thinks of their relationship as "perfect." At that moment the perfection seems to be confirmed by the appearance of a ray of sunshine which alters "the room like a revelation." . . . Even as she is witnessing it, the room ominously suggests that she is deceived: "Noiselessly, a sweet pea moulted its petals on to the writing table, leaving a bare pistil. The pink butterfly flowers, transparently balancing, were shadowed faintly with blue as by an intuition of death." . . . Between this moment and their final meeting in the garden of Danielstown (their only memorable scene in a natural environment), the "intuition of death," not the sunshine, prevails.

The garden at Danielstown, unlike the mythic one, admits no perfection. Nature here implies no sanction of their love; to Lois it is, in fact, severe and limiting. . . . When Gerald leaves she can remember only his seemingly innocent act, during a former meeting, of pulling the leaves from the hedge, "scattering them on the grass and throwing them over her." . . . The experience smothers her, and like the snail she is crushed, not by the hand of another person, but by the destruction of her romantic vision. When the necessary reconciliation with the world of reality is not accomplished, the death of the spirit is the inevitable result. (pp. 88-9)

The effect of the weather [in *The House in Paris*] is felt most acutely in the scene at Hythe, a scene in which we again see that particular conjunction of love, nature, and imagination. (pp. 89-90)

Even during [Karen's and Max's] first meeting nature and the sun seem to be offering their sanction of the relationship. As in *The Last September*, a garden is the setting. . . . (p. 90)

Later, when Karen and Max walk after their dinner and talk, the sun is oppressive; they seek the comfort of the shade. The oppression is only physical; it does not affect the imagination of either. The sun is still felt to be that third presence which contributes to their association. Its absence from Hythe causes a disturbance not felt at Boulogne.

Rain casts a literal and spiritual shadow over the meeting of Karen and Max at Hythe. There she "cannot divide the streets from the patter of rain and rush of rain in the gutters." . . . Something is wrong imaginatively. Although physically the rain is no more harmful than is the sun, they recognize the latter's absence as that of a god which has previously watched over them and blessed their union. (pp. 91-2)

Karen falls victim to the false conception she has of her love and its future. . . .

Lois Farquar suffers because she has required of her relationship with Gerald a perfectability it cannot attain. Karen, on the other hand, is crushed because that very perfection of love, so apparently attainable in her life and Max's, is not to be realized in a world of sin and death; it reaches fulfillment only in a world of isolation and imagination. (p. 93)

Portia's imagination is only barely active in "The World," the first part of *The Death of the Heart*. But she exhibits one characteristic not possessed by Lois or Karen: a vivid memory of love, not for a man, but for her mother. . . . The evocative power of nature is apparent as she associates with this past relationship "the pension on the crag in Switzerland, that had been wrapped in rain the whole afternoon." (pp. 93-4)

With the exception of such isolated instances Portia reveals little active imagination until she meets Eddie. . . . Portia exhibits a sensitivity to natural surroundings as she recognizes her growing fondness for Eddie. (p. 94)

To both Eddie and Portia the country has an obvious unreality because it is not the kind of life they know. Its effect on Portia is the stimulation of her imagination and emotions, in which she can maintain her own unrealities. The effect on Eddie is more simple. He tries to get away with actions he cannot perform in London and, at the same time, wants to cancel any effect the setting might have on Portia's mind.

By the time Portia and Eddie are alone in a natural setting, that scene which she has so long anticipated, much has happened to affect the focus of it. . . . [The] climax is withheld until that most important scene in the woods. There,

where love and imagination can mingle in nature, Portia's commitment to a false conception of love is evident.

The scene, of course, does not conform to Portia's preconception of it: the lovers walk to the woods, not by the sea. (p. 95)

[Portia's] romantic will asserts itself most inflexibly when she feels that it is being threatened. Just as Karen first fears, then ignores, the threat of rain to her romantic vision, so Portia first distrusts, then accepts, the woods as a setting proper to their love.

The falsifying vision causes Portia's spiritual death; the bubble of her romantic will must burst. . . . Portia's imagination has made of the scene and of Eddie something they are not. . . . Like Lois and Karen before her, Portia is defeated by the reality she must finally face. The death of the heart and of the romantic imagination is again the result.

[In *Eva Trout*,] separated from *The Death of the Heart* by thirty years, the surface characteristics of its heroine are similar to those of the figures we have considered. Eva is young and romantic; she is concerned about love and is acutely aware of her surroundings. As with Portia, the early hints of Eva's imagination are vague and inconclusive. We see an indication in the importance of the castle setting in her memory. (pp. 96-7)

Not until she senses her growing love for Henry does [Eva] begin to mingle in her imagination the image of Henry with the surroundings in which he is seen. Her habit is first revealed as she relives the day she has just spent with him at Cambridge. Nature relates to her sense of his presence to give that day and that sensation an eternal quality. . . .

The most important scene in *Eva Trout* is the final appearance of Eva and Henry together at the castle. The natural setting provides an immediate atmosphere of tranquility for the lovers; it is, again, a modern-day Eden. (p. 97)

The change in setting and the change in Henry's mood are simultaneous. In observing the prematurity of the wild roses, Henry confirms the increasing stimulation of his emotions by asking bluntly: "What's supposed to be going to happen, Eva?" Her response is uncertain and shy, not because she does not know her own feelings, but because she does not know Henry's. She accentuates her uncertainty by seeking refuge in nature, retreating because she fears the reality which Henry may reveal; even a briar bush, with its tearing and grabbing spines, is a "sanctuary" when she is confronted with a reality which may hurt more severely. Her fear is not justified; Henry acknowledges his deep feeling, if not love, for her, and she comes away from her sacred isolation.

The escape of Eva to the briar bush is symbolic of the larger escape that she and Henry participate in at the castle. When confronted with the demands of the real world, the romantic mind must seek refuge in nature. But Eva fails to make the necessary distinction between the idyllic world of the castle and her imagination and the world outside the Garden. To her what can be expressed and realized in the one can be realized in the other. (p. 98)

Eva's commitment to her romantic vision is complete. Desiring an ideal marriage to Henry, she is willing to reconcile herself to a marriage of pretense. Both solutions are dreams; neither is realizable in a world alien to the romantic. Eva, like Lois, Karen, and Portia, is never to experience the kind of love she has conceived in her imagination. She is struck down at the very height of her joyful anticipation. Unlike the other three, she never knows the misery of spiritual desolation. Her death, a physical death, is the most certain of all. In *Eva Trout* a new foe strikes down the romantic protagonist. Not only the outside world, but also fate, accident, chance—it goes by many names—is an enemy of the totally romantic will. . . . The hopes and joys of the romantic will are never to be realized. As in the other novels we are left simply with death.

One might, of course, argue that we are left with more than death in these novels. Particularly with Lois, Karen, and Portia the spiritual death may be a prelude to a more informed and more fully conscious resurrection. (pp. 98-9)

[The] emphasis in the novels lies clearly on the loss the protagonist experiences, not on the recovery she may make in the future. . . . [In] many scenes which involve nature, love, and idealism [there] is an allusion to the mythic Eden whose Garden is a symbol both of the perfection man once had and of the loss he has sustained. In these novels the perfection of the myth is available only to an isolated imagination; it clearly does not exist in truth. Because the ideal conception of love is not possible in the world since the Fall, the romantic protagonist must re-enact the Genesis story and fall again. That may not, of course, be the end of the story, but for the reader of Elizabeth Bowen's novels the second part of the Christian view of man is left largely to hope and speculation. Eden is certain; the Resurrection not so clear. The romantic protagonists in three of these novels may recover; they do, of a certainty, fall. (pp. 99-100)

> *Paul A. Parrish, "The Loss of Eden: Four Novels of Elizabeth Bowen," in* Critique: Studies in Modern Fiction *(copyright © by Critique 1973), Vol. XV, No. 1, 1973, pp. 86-100.*

EDWIN J. KENNEY, JR.

[In] the stylishness of Elizabeth Bowen's art, one senses the dislocated child who is urgently seeking an identity as a means of survival, and who sometimes strikes that "kind of *farouche* note which one associates with teen-age delinquents about to break prison—that is, leave home," as her friend Sean O'Faolain said. As Miss Bowen asserts in her most famous novel, *The Death of the Heart,* "Illusions are art . . . and it is by art that we live, if we do." The recurrent theme of Elizabeth Bowen's fiction is man's primary need for an illusion, an image of himself, in order for him to be. Her fascination with problems of identity has its source in the experience of her early life, and it often finds its expression in allusions to the story of the early life of man, the story of the fall from the garden of Eden; for both are stories of the need to be, the loss of innocence, the acquisition of knowledge through loss, and the entrance into selfhood. (p. 18)

She showed her own fascination with [her background as a motherless only child, shuffled between England and Ireland,] by writing three works of nonfiction specifically about it—*Seven Winters* (1943), "a fragment of autobiography" . . . describing her life with her mother and father in Dublin until she was seven; *Bowen's Court* (1942, 1964), a history of her family home, where she spent her summers; and *The Shelbourne Hotel* (1951), a history of the cosmo-

politan focus of Anglo-Irish life—and one early novel, *The Last September,* set during the Troubles. The biographical and historical experiences described in these books inform all of Miss Bowen's fiction. (p. 20)

Her sense of Ireland was not a literary or intellectual one of revived myths and celebrated national heroes; Ireland always existed for her literally in the land itself and in the image of Bowen's Court, behind its demesne walls, at the end of a long avenue, set on the land in its circle of trees. (p. 21)

Miss Bowen's whole conception of the Anglo-Irish naive dignity and tragedy implies and depends on a sense of betrayal, a feeling that the best intentions of the best of her class were somehow betrayed both by others of that class and by the native Irish. . . . This view of the Anglo-Irish in Ireland is also Elizabeth Bowen's view of having been brought up to be Anglo-Irish, and ultimately her view of life itself. (p. 23)

The experience of unknowing separation from vital goings-on that is most often violated by a sudden knowledge of betrayal fraught with tragic consequences is what Miss Bowen sees in the history of her class in Ireland and in her being brought up to the expectations of that class at the time she was. This is what she describes as child-like; this is what she felt made her a "nomad" in her travels between Ireland and England, and this is, not surprisingly, the story of her relations with her mother and father, both of whom seemed to abandon and at the same time to implicate her. (p. 24)

In *The Last September,* Miss Bowen's first important novel, she deals directly with the crisis of being Anglo-Irish at a time of national crisis, called the Troubles. Just as her early stories were written about her childhood at the time of her transition to adulthood, this work, too, marks another stage of transition in her life. (p. 31)

The achievement of this novel . . . is the complementarity it creates between the adolescent crisis of its heroine, Lois Farquar, . . . and the cultural and political crisis of the Anglo-Irish in 1920. The Anglo-Irish are seen now as being not just only children but adolescent only children. The suspension between being English and Irish finds its complement in the suspension between being a child and being an adult because this is the time when one feels it most confusedly, as Elizabeth Bowen herself did. Miss Bowen said that this novel was of all her books the one "nearest her heart" and that it had a "deep, unclouded spontaneous source" in her own experience. (p. 32)

Our loss of innocence is the business of Elizabeth Bowen's fiction. Her novels create, obsessively, a sense of insecurity. One is made to feel that life itself cannot be trusted; those we love are taken away by obscure, arbitrary forces such as death, or they betray us. The experience of Miss Bowen's fiction is similar to her description of the experience of Ireland: it tends to drive one "back on oneself." (p. 40)

In her novels she is . . . as much or more concerned with the self's response to the experience of loss as she is with the loss itself. Like her admired friends E. M. Forster and Virginia Woolf, she regarded the surface of life as a fragile crust saving us from the bottomless abyss below, and she said that "the more the surface seems to heave or threaten to crack, the more its actual pattern fascinates me." Once "the crack appears across the crust of life," Miss Bowen is concerned with how her characters work around it, for ultimately there is no making the crack go away or pretending it is not there. If one tries not to acknowledge it, one risks self-destruction; one falls into the abyss. This horrible alternative to creating a new pattern that includes the knowledge of life's evils is explored in *To The North*.

Neither *To The North* (1932) nor Miss Bowen's preceding novel, *Friends and Relations* (1931), should be ranked among her best works. Despite moments of fine writing and comic effect, both are rather static books with diagrammatic design the execution of which seems to have squeezed the life out of them. In *To The North* this design is that of melodramatic tragedy.... [Emmeline is] at the center of the tragic action [in *To The North*], and her capacity for feeling places her there. This quality is part of her innocence and her fatality because she does not see the dangers, within and without, that threaten her. She is characterized as nearsighted and, although she requires glasses, she chooses not to wear them on social occasions, times of most perilous encounters.

What makes Emmeline transcend the archetypal innocent is the way Elizabeth Bowen shows how Emmeline has coped with her situation though her disability goes unrecognized by all those around her. Emmeline is unlike Miss Bowen's other heroines who have nothing to do, or who have only those "deliberate interests" for young ladies that provide excuses for luncheons. (pp. 40-2)

Emmeline, the orphan, the dislocated child, is characterized by Miss Bowen as "the stepchild of her uneasy century." This is Elizabeth Bowen's vision of herself, and Emmeline's attraction to travel, like Miss Bowen's, is an expression of this dislocation and an attempt at accommodation with the condition of it. (p. 43)

The importance of fictive concords to overcome the fragmentariness of life and the self is nowhere more poignantly expressed by Miss Bowen than in the disjointed *The House in Paris* (1935).... As in *The Hotel* and *The Last September*, Miss Bowen uses the architectural framework of the house in Paris as a structure for her fiction, an enclosure for her characters, and an emblem of their lives. But this novel is distinguished by her use of the child as a vantage point for viewing the conduct of the adults and by her bold division of the book into three sections that juxtapose time in such a way as to express the separation between child and adult. (p. 46)

The child's loneliness, often caused by deaths or separation of parents or abandonment by them, is for Elizabeth Bowen a metaphor for all human loneliness caused by the combination of fate, of external circumstances, and innocence. The child is alone because he does not know what is going on outside of and often within himself; in this sense the child is an outsider to any family, community, or place, whose tacit organization, conduct, and values he does not understand. In this same sense we are all outsiders at times, all children and innocents. This explains why the metaphor of the child can be so easily substituted for or combined with Miss Bowen's other favorite metaphor for her life and the human condition, that of the alien, the traveler. (p. 48)

In *The Death of the Heart* (1938), the child becomes not only a focal point for viewing the adults but also the heroine

of the novel. This work is the culmination of Elizabeth Bowen's treatment of the theme of youthful innocence confronting the risks of life in a world of unsympathetic, "fallen" adults, the finest of her novels, and a significant achievement in modern fiction. It is a triumph of the "well-made" realistic novel, in which the conception, organization, and realization of each of the parts and characters and their relations to one another and to the settings are in perfect accord. Miss Bowen's own ambivalence is here given its fullest expression in the familiar oppositions between child and adult, innocence and experience, past and present, man and woman.

The Death of the Heart is Elizabeth Bowen's most complete statement of the way the child's expectations and desires must confront and become transformed into the style and art of the adult, and of the way this process at the same time vitalizes and humanizes the artfulness of the adults, saving them from corruption and death. The title of the novel is slightly ambiguous because there is no final death of the heart either in the child or the adults; there is rather a transference of the innocence of heart from the child to the adult and of the restraints of the heart from the adult to the child. There must be, Miss Bowen tells us, a death of our innocence, but we must not lose heart if we are to survive. (pp. 53-4)

Elizabeth Bowen knows hope is only an illusion necessary for life to go on; this is why she never represents actual reconciliation in her novels. She cannot because she does not really believe in its efficacy in solving or illuminating the problems of human life, and she is too honest and tough-minded to say otherwise. (p. 64)

[The] anguished time [of the war years] was crucial to Miss Bowen, but it was crucial not so much because it was a terrifying shock to the ordinary illusions of security as because it confirmed her earlier experiences, personal and fictional, that there is no security. All of her writing done at this time has a coherence in its repeated emphasis on what she now called fantasy and hallucination, the strongest expression of what had always been Miss Bowen's main subject—illusion. These works, written during and reflecting the most awful happenings, show, in the face of the extremity of actual catastrophe, the instinctive and great power of the human imagination to create and sustain new images of peace and immunity that allow life to go on. (p. 65)

[Both *Bowen's Court* and *English Novelists* point] out again the connection between private imaginative fantasy and art that she felt in her own life. This connection explains why she wrote some of her best short stories at this time. (p. 66)

Because disruption, dislocation, and destruction are the actual condition of all life in *The Heat of the Day*, the legitimate terrors of darkened, bombed-out London during the war justify the characters' intensified feelings of insecurity, and the machinations of spy, counterspy intrigue exaggerate their feelings of conspiracy, plot, and betrayal. In this novel Elizabeth Bowen's language of violence, destruction, and conspiracy is literal; it is no longer metaphoric. The outward order of time and space is destroyed and life goes on in a vacuum; the war is a sea of horror through which the characters move, like fish in "shoals," among shored-up ruins. (p. 68)

With her history of the Bowens in Ireland, this is Miss

Bowen's most "comprehensive" work; it is her most ambitious attempt to connect her personal and imaginative concern with private worlds of illusion to the larger public life of national politics and international ideals. (p. 74)

A World of Love is generally considered the least successful and least popular of all Miss Bowen's works; it is a difficult novel because Miss Bowen was deliberately striving for a more elaborate "poetic" style to create the effects of "mirage-like shimmer" that she found in Ireland's light-consumed distances, and of fantasy that would permit spiritual presences to move in and out of life. The problem with the novel, despite the narrator's clear judgments at certain moments, is the fundamental ambiguity about what is going on. The novel makes the best critical sense when viewed as another exploration of the characters' fantasies, their "queered" relations to the past. But just as there are some real ghosts in *The Demon Lover* stories, so, too, are there moments in *A World of Love* when it seems that Miss Bowen ought to be, because she seems to desire to be, writing a straight mystery story about unambiguous spiritual presences, real mediums, and true possession. One feels that this language is not just a convenient vocabulary for Miss Bowen, not just available metaphor, but a genuine possibility. The difficulty of excessive style in the novel seems to be caused by Miss Bowen's not making up her mind about which way the story should go and trying, therefore, to have it both ways. Uncertainty permeates this novel and epitomizes the inescapable ambivalence of her Anglo-Irish sensibility.

A World of Love and *The Last September* are the only novels to be set entirely in Ireland and to focus on isolated big house life. In *The House in Paris* and *The Heat of the Day,* Ireland exists as a world apart from the central focus of the characters' lives; it is a world of escape, apparently out of time, eternal, and out of the spaces of Paris and London, more an image or ideal than an actual place. As its title suggests, *A World of Love* makes this quality of unreality the entire "world" of the novel. . . . Montefort, the small country house in the novel, is further a world of illusion created by love, for as Miss Bowen has demonstrated in her earlier works, the world of love is always a world of illusion. (pp. 78-9)

The idea for *The Little Girls* may have come to Miss Bowen in writing *A World of Love,* for the relations of Jane, Antonia, and Lilia to Guy, to the past, and to one another are similar to the relations among the three women of *The Little Girls*. But there is nothing uncertain or overly elaborate about this book; it is Elizabeth Bowen's wittiest and funniest novel, and it retains the sense of mystery she sought in *A World of Love*. . . . [In] this novel someone in the present seeks out the past, rather than, as in *A World of Love*, someone from the past seeking out the present. . . . The women in *The Little Girls* are seen by one another and their author as the witches in *Macbeth;* they come together not to announce Macbeth's fate, but because they are one another's fate. Chance not choice brings them together. This is the discovery of the novel both for the characters and the reader, but it is a discovery that reveals a fundamental, impenetrable mystery about human life. (pp. 86-7)

[Again] the power of illusion, of love, and of art continues to fascinate Elizabeth Bowen's imagination, but the language of aesthetic creation now merges with that of witchcraft and magic. What remains constant is Miss Bowen's

consciousness of her own metaphor-making and her frequent desire—in *The Little Girls* her brilliant source of comic irony—to make the reader share in her own spellcasting by undercutting it with commonplace utterances and occurrences. If on one level we are invited to see these women and their shared power as the witches from *Macbeth,* we are also forced at the same time but on another level to see them as just naughty little girls. (pp. 89-90)

In *The Little Girls,* when the women return to the grounds of the vanished St. Agatha's, Miss Bowen says "There is seldom anything convulsive about change. What is there is there; there comes to be something fictitious about what is not." This is the sense one gets from the revised edition of *Bowen's Court* [in which the house is destroyed]; the book had been written as history and memory and it had now become pure image, pure art. The house reached its apotheosis through its destruction. (pp. 94-5)

[Miss Bowen's] tenth and last novel, *Eva Trout* (1969) . . . is a recapitulation of all Miss Bowen's personal and fictional experiences of anguished insecurity. It is the only novel whose title is that of the name of the main character, and Eva Trout is Miss Bowen's only full-scale treatment of a truly neurotic heroine. In Eva Trout, all of the isolated and isolating, the self-destructive and destructive capacities of all her innocent heroines are concentrated and exaggerated. She is that most distinct and proverbial alien, a fish out of water, desperately and recklessly flopping about for survival.

Eva Trout, like Miss Bowen's other heroines, is defined by the disordered circumstances of her parents' lives. She is first of all, an only child, and she is alone because she is an orphan. These are the primary conditions and metaphors for Miss Bowen's consideration of the crisis of identity which recurs throughout her work. (pp. 95-6)

Another condition of Eva's situation is a complement to the others and still another of Miss Bowen's metaphors for life. Just as Eva cannot make connections among the places she has been to give her a sense of meaningful continuity in her life, so, too, she cannot make connections among her thoughts and feelings or between herself and others through language. . . . More than any of Miss Bowen's other innocents, Eva literally can find no language in which to speak on her own terms, and she does not resign herself to being translated imperfectly. Rather, she seeks what she imagines to be the perfection of "normal" patterns of behavior and speech in order to overcome her psychic fragmentation. . . . (p. 97)

[The] violently melodramatic conclusion to the novel has produced the harshest criticism of Miss Bowen's late fiction. But *Eva Trout* is a projection of psychic forces, which are by nature both violent and melodramatic. Miss Bowen's out-sized heroine, so rich and autonomous, so imperious even in her attempts to reduce herself to normal size, demands the elaborate sets of "changing scenes," the novel's subtitle, and theatrical moments such as the book's grand finale. The operatic names of the other characters and their controverted passions are the necessary complements to the desperate alienation of Eva. This is a Dickensian novel in its claustrophobia and also in its feelings of possession, of . . . "dynamic energy seeking an outlet." This outlet is identity; it is what Eve and Eva had to be. What this novel, with its black humor, mischievous puns, and its own imperious willingness to ignore the conventional expectations for the realistic novel, conveys is that identity is energy. This is the final significance of Eva's last name; she is a fish out of water and that is precisely what makes her so difficult to handle. We cannot get hold of her until she is dead, until she is just an image. This is Elizabeth Bowen's final statement of her recurrent subject, "what a slippery fish is identity; and what *is* it besides a slippery fish?" (pp. 103-04)

> *Edwin J. Kenney, Jr., in his* Elizabeth Bowen *(© 1975 by Associated University Presses, Inc.), Bucknell University Press, 1975.*

WALTER SULLIVAN

At the end of her career Elizabeth Bowen's work was in a state of decline. Like a baseball pitcher who starts aiming for the plate, Miss Bowen in her closing years was trying to achieve by main force the drama and ambiguity and profundity that accrued naturally to her work in her finest days. *A World of Love* was a shadow, an anemic imitation of the best of her novels, and *The Little Girls* and *Eva Trout* were tours de force which did not succeed. (p. 142)

According to her own testimony her fictional process, the manner of her creating, always started with place. Other novelists might begin with a concept of character or with a germ of a story or with a human situation that they feel compelled to probe. But with Elizabeth Bowen there was first the deliberate limning of the landscape or the drawing-room or the street or the park. Of all the places that she described, houses were obviously her favorites. . . . Though her characters move about—there are sequences which take place in Ireland and England in *The House in Paris*—it is impossible to read Miss Bowen and not be aware of how architecture and topography give weight to her fiction and contribute actively to the development of plot and theme.

The estate in *The Last September* is not only the center of the action but a symbol of what the action is about. The house, patterned obviously after Bowen's Court, is the locus of the main characters—the Naylors and the Montmorencys and Lois—and of Marda Naylor. From here the grounds reach out and the action follows. . . . Even when the plot of the narrative takes us to the army barracks or to the nearby city, the presence of Danielstown encroaches on the action, representing as it does the troubles of that time. (p. 143)

The static quality of Mme. Fisher's bedroom in *The House in Paris,* as Miss Bowen points out in *Pictures and Conversations,* exerts a kinetic force on the characters in the book. The chamber and its dying occupant are the stillness at the center, the heart of the story without which nothing else could take place. . . .

The Heat of the Day is a slightly different matter, for the damages of war are not to be avoided: ruins, like ghosts or corpses, carry their own power, set their own mood. But, of course, Elizabeth Bowen knew this, and what she attains in this otherwise flawed novel is the sense of places as yet unexploded; we see their wholeness as a reflection of the encompassing threat. (p. 144)

Elizabeth Bowen was a novelist of manners, and one of the principal problems for the reader with this sort of artist is to discover the public dimension in the author's work. In *The Last September,* which in my judgment is the first of Miss

Bowen's major novels, the solution is conventional. Like the people in the time of Noah who continue to the end eating and drinking and giving in marriage, the characters at Danielstown go their ways, generally indifferent to the clouds that gather, though the clouds are undeniably, palpably there. (pp. 144-45)

[Like] all good novelists of manners, [Elizabeth Bowen] was aware that small actions are reflections of a larger context: events in the drawing-room mirror those in parliament and courtroom and cathedral. Thus the apparent stability of the Naylors and the uncertainty of the Montmorencys combine to make an image of the contradictions of the human state in general and of this particular time and place. . . .

The Last September is exquisitely of a piece; every stroke of the conclusion, every nuance of the denouement is totally prepared for; nothing is taken for granted or left to chance. (p. 145)

Miss Bowen was to do better. *The Death of the Heart* is generally thought to be her masterpiece, and I make no cavil at this judgment, but *The House in Paris* is almost as fine. The superiority of *The Death of the Heart* results, perhaps, from the fullness of the characterization of Portia and from the novel's larger scope. But much of the restriction that *The House in Paris* suffers from the narrowness of its boundaries is offset by the tightness of its structure and the dramatic intensity of its scenes. . . .

At the beginning and end of this novel there are touches that show Elizabeth Bowen at her particular best. Henrietta, child and female, utterly ignorant but intuitively wise, breaks by her presence one of fiction's traditional conventions: she is an extra character; she has no stake in the action; what happens to Leopold and the others is none of her affair. Yet she is the first character we meet, and her humane concern for the dispossessed Leopold is our concern, the world's concern. More than anyone else she endows the book with its breadth and depth; on her own small shoulders she bears the burden of doing for *The House in Paris* what was done for *The Last September* by the war. (p. 146)

The Heat of the Day presented Elizabeth Bowen with new fictional problems, which, as I have indicated, she did not fully solve. For one thing she was attempting to work on a more public, if not a larger, scale. The novel takes place in London during World War II; the basic plot is built around Stella Rodney's discovery that her lover is a traitor to his country, a Nazi spy. This kind of material involved Miss Bowen in the sort of thing that she was least fitted for—discussions of ideologies, questions of political right and wrong. Because of the historical context, she was forced to start with the general: wartime London, global conflict, competing moral philosophies; and work toward the particular. . . . (p. 148)

The characters are delineated well by ordinary standards, but they are not so good as those in Miss Bowen's earlier work. Some of her English critics, who lived through the enveloping action of the novel, were pleased with the author's evocation of atmosphere, the spirit of wartime England. But this world, however accurately it is depicted, is not Elizabeth Bowen's world; and the society, the organization of western culture which supported and informed her best efforts, was not, in her lifetime, to be found again. (pp. 148-49)

Walter Sullivan, "A Sense of Place: Elizabeth Bowen and the Landscape of the Heart," in Se-wanee Review (reprinted by permission of the editor; © 1976 by The University of the South), Winter, 1976, pp. 142-49.

HERMIONE LEE

The opening of *To the North* is deceptive: leaving Italy is not, in itself, to be of importance. Cecilia Summers, the 'young widow' waiting for the train, is not to be the heroine. Its tone is significantly odd and ambiguous. The satirical treatment of a carefully demarcated social world is apparently anticipated, and this is borne out by the ensuing emphasis on manner and properties. . . . Affluent people lunch, dine, and go to parties; we are often told what they are wearing. The fashions are exactly registered. . . . (pp. 129-30)

Nevertheless, there is a discomforting tone to the first paragraph of the novel, strongly suggesting that the material world in which it has its being is to be undermined. The knowing information about the Anglo-Italian express sounds a little ominous. The season, like the travellers, is 'uncertain'. Suspended between anticipation and loss, they lunch 'uneasily', awaiting their journey to the north. They are not moving yet, but the . . . violent, repetitive images precipitate them towards movement, and, even, with 'brass-barred' and 'girdle', towards an idea of imprisonment. That they sit 'facing the clock' hints most forcibly of all at the idea of a train journey as a journey out of life, into the after-world. . . . There is no doubt (we are told that 'neither had nice characters') that Cecilia and Markie are a punishment to one another for being what they are. The image of a journey in hell is not insistent, but the language keeps edging into unaccountable ferocity. . . . The climactic last page of the novel, Emmeline's desperate drive with Markie (whom she loves and who has betrayed her) 'to the north' and to their deaths, is prefigured in the oddly sinister tone, the incipient violence of the first chapter.

[Violent deaths] are symptoms of betrayal in Elizabeth Bowen's work, and mark the passing of innocence, whether personal or national. In order that their moral significance should not be blurred by the dramatic shock of feeling the deaths evoke, Elizabeth Bowen establishes from the start a pattern of images which will necessitate them. That the pure-hearted Emmeline should be driven to what is, in effect, murder and suicide, is a badge of her innocence. But the ending of this novel is not therefore grotesquely sensational, as Elizabeth Bowen sometimes chooses to be in horror stories like 'The Cat Jumps'. Rather it has an air of classical formality: the motifs are seen to accumulate and finally cohere in a formulation which is at once simple and extreme.

Unlike her sister-in-law, Emmeline is not quite of this world. She is ethereal, angelic, 'pale and clear', 'more than half transparent materially'. (pp. 130-31)

On the other hand, Markie, as Cecilia perceives at their first meeting, is Satanic. (She notices at once that he has the 'quick-lidded eyes of an agreeable reptile'.) He is the familiar modern anti-hero who has lost touch with the sources of faith and idealism. Reason is his God. . . . He is an 'uneasy moralist', who, for hedonistic ends, has repressed his sensibilities. Elizabeth Bowen's moral hostility to this character is as pronounced as Henry James's for Gilbert Osmond or D. H. Lawrence's for Gerald Crich,

with whom Markie has similarities. . . . But while her repugnance for Markie is evident, Elizabeth Bowen shares the ability of those greater writers to persuade the reader of what it feels like to be a damned soul. . . . The sense of strain [felt at times in the novel]—too much ice, too many mannered pairings [of images] . . .—is caused by the effort to impose the images necessary to the novel's formal organization on Emmeline's train of thought. This is a risk inherent in the plan to load Emmeline and Markie's relationship with elemental imagery and ominous images of travel. But at the two points of greatest intensity in the affair, the week-end of Emmeline's seduction in Paris, and their final car-drive together, the patterning of images contributes to a satisfying aesthetic logic. (pp. 131-33)

Emmeline and Markie, though inside a partly comic novel, are thus implacably directed by the author to their end as tragic protagonists. The strict formality of the plot—two women, two lovers, Henry's death before the start and Emmeline's and Markie's in conclusion, a journey to begin with and a journey to end with—undermines the characters' opportunities for free choice, in the same way as the relentless patterning of the images which dominate them. Even when the emphasis is on the comic world (traditionally one of choice and self-improvement, as in Jane Austen and Forster) the freedom of the will seems no more than a toy. . . . (p. 134)

[Markie's fear of Emmeline's innocence and idealism] leads into a histrionic, grotesque passage on Tragedy which removes the novel to its furthest point from realism and formalizes the characters into aspects of a genre:

> Here figures cast unknown shadows; passion knows no crime, only its own movement; steel and the cord go with the kiss. Innocence walks with violence; violence is innocent, cold as fate; between the mistress's kiss and the blade's is a hair's-breadth only, and no disparity; every door leads to death. . . . The curtain comes down, the book closes—but who is to say that this is not so?
>
> (p. 135)

The high ritual tone is not a success. It sounds like an affected pastiche of the elements of Jacobean tragedy. But the passage, unusually choric, is evidently intended as a major statement of the novel's ontology. When an implacable idea of necessity is combined with a romantic belief in the personal existence of goodness and innocence, extreme characters must answer to extreme destinies.

The combination is bound to create a problem of realism. Sometimes the tragic formality to which the story aspires is laid bare, as in the passage just quoted; sometimes, as in the opening paragraph, realism is used as a cloak. In other ways too, Elizabeth Bowen has surprisingly little difficulty in making an extreme relationship work at the level of the possible. . . . The transcendental qualities which we have to allow Emmeline are . . . offset by her relationship to characters who exist on a more moderate plane.

It is, however, the treatment of place which provides the most versatile, complex vehicle for the novel's deeper meanings. This is not to imply a 'staticness' (which is, as Elizabeth Bowen calls it, a 'dead weight' if scene setting is undramatic). When she says that 'Nothing can happen nowhere', she points to her interest in places which do not readily qualify as 'somewhere'. Boarding houses, shut-up homes, empty villas, obscure shops one can never find again, parks at dusk—places where people have stopped living or are on their way to somewhere else—such settings (particularly in the short stories) are always at the heart of what is odd or ominous in 'the Bowen terrain'. They attract people who have lost their homes or their way. . . . They are places for 'the disinherited', like the all-night road house in the story of that name. . . . Similar venues occur in *To the North,* from the station at Milan to the 'jaded glare of an all night café', glimpsed by Markie on the final journey. Travel, which provides the *raison d'être* for such settings, has a moral as well as a symbolic significance, caricatured in a comic platitude by Lady Waters: '*This* age . . . is far more than restless; it is decentralized'. Markie's sinister flat, cut off at the top of his sister's 'very high, dark-red house in Lower Sloane Street' with its shadowy corners and its invisible cook whose 'reedy, ghostly whistle' makes Emmeline jump, is the major example of such impermanent 'nowhere' places, symptoms of deracination. Set against them are places offering peace and stability. But all are potentially lost paradises; a careful colouring of anticipated nostalgia fills the descriptions. (pp. 135-38)

Emmeline's betrayal is . . . intended not simply as a melodramatic romance or as the working-out of a theory of extremes (the angelic and the daemonic) confronting each other, but as a symptom of a more general, historical state of loss and dereliction. The emphasis on material things, as well as being necessary for the novel's social, comic vein, justifies itself morally by being emblematic. Sheltered, gracious living in a place with its own past is considered not only as a good thing in itself but also as a symbol of innocence. This implies, naturally enough, an opposition between rural and urban values which, while it casts a cold eye on modern life, is compatible with the tradition of Jane Austen and Forster. Oudenarde Road is as much of a secret grove as one can find in London; its peace is destroyed by Markie, an essentially cosmopolitan villain.

To strengthen the novel's broader meanings, landscapes of dereliction, which are not required as locales for the action, are imported as illustrations of or metaphors for states of mind. Certainly the consistently suggestive use of place gives these passages homogeneity with the rest of the novel, but they are intended to strike a strange note, and indeed stand out like miniature short stories—the more so since they anticipate so many of the settings, the sinister, autumnal, suburban villas, found in *The Cat Jumps* (1934) or *Look at all Those Roses* (1941). (p. 139)

The emotional deprivations from which Elizabeth Bowen's characters suffer (either as a temperamental disability or in response to blows of fate) are so consistently formalized as localities that an eerie overlap between interior and exterior landscapes results. A set piece of description [in *To the North*], looked at again, is revealed as a Homeric metaphor for the state of a soul:

> When a great house has been destroyed by fire . . . the master has not, perhaps, the heart or the money to rebuild. Trees that were its companions are cut down and the estate sold up to the speculator. Villas spring up in red rows, each a home for someone. . . . Life here is liveable, kindly

and sometimes gay; there is not a ghost of space or silence; the great house with its dominance and its radiation of avenues is forgotten. When spring is sweet in the air . . . something touches the heart, someone, disturbed, pauses, hand on a villa gate. But not to ask: What was here?

> With the quick fancy, the nerves and senses Cecilia could almost love. . . . With her, the gay little streets flourished, but, brave when her house fell, she could not regain some entirety of spirit. Disability seems a hard reward for courage. . . .

Such an ornate analogy turns the dramatic, personal material of the story into a casebook on the effects of loss. The author's romantic language cloaks her disenchanted vision. (Sean O'Faolain rightly calls the novels 'exquisitely composed logs of disaster'.) The ruined lives with which we are invited to sympathize are reduced to symptoms of an 'uneasy century'—so that there is a tension between the violent, passionate elements in their experience and the clinical use to which they are put by the author. The effect is not a cosy or an endearing one. . . . But it shows that it is not enough to treat Elizabeth Bowen as merely a writer of sentimental romances. . . . The losses she chronicles are more than personal. (pp. 140-42)

> *Hermione Lee, "The Placing of Loss: Elizabeth Bowen's 'To the North'," in* Essays in Criticism, *April, 1978, pp. 129-42.*

*   *   *

BRATHWAITE, Edward   1930-

Brathwaite is a Barbadian poet, playwright, editor, historian, and critic. His novels are united by a thematic concern with the West Indian black's quest for an identity. (See also *Contemporary Authors,* Vols. 25-28, rev. ed.)

[*Rights of Passage* reminds] one of the difficulty of all long poems: how to control pace, mood and matter consistently enough to hold the reader's attention. . . .

[Brathwaite's] theme is that of the West Indian, modern and ancestral, in slavery, emigrating, suffering, resilient but melancholy. It is potentially a striking and exciting theme, but Mr. Brathwaite's technique and verbal control do not match his ambition. One can imagine that it might—given the right voice, the right production, and the right mood— make a powerful radio performance, at least in part: but it makes very flat reading on the page. (p. 125)

> The Times Literary Supplement (© *Times Newspapers Ltd. (London) 1967; reproduced from* The Times Literary Supplement *by permission), February 16, 1967.*

JULIAN SYMONS

[Brathwaite's] poems are about typical West Indian experiences of life in [the West Indies, England, America, and Ghana], and they are written in a free slangy language similar to that of blues songs. Attitudes change, children mock their father's Uncle Tom deference, negroes live up to the white conception of them, 'black skin red eyes broad back big you know what'. The total effect is impressive. The poems [in *Rights of Passage*] have a sense of the present, a feeling for the past, above all an awareness of a world changing, sometimes chaotically. This—I mean no disrespect to Mr. Brathwaite—is Commonwealth poetry. (p. 479)

Julian Symons, in New Statesman (© 1967 The Statesman & Nation Publishing Co. Ltd.), April 7, 1967.

LEWIS TURCO

[*Rights of Passage*] is the first part of a poem titled "Masks." . . . "Masks" would appear to be an epic-length work of the sort established by Whitman in "Song of Myself," and continued by Pound and Williams in "The Cantos" and "Paterson" respectively. But perhaps "established" isn't the right word, for the form remains vague and personal, even if the general direction of such poems seems to be the discovery of self and national identity by means of catalogues derived from a physical and intellectual environment. (pp. 31-2)

If in such poems as this there is no narrative involving several characters besides the author, then there must be style. This is present in Whitman, Pound, and Williams, but we do not seem to find it in Mr. Brathwaite. What we have instead is sociology and journal entries in a generalized, contemporary, sometimes jazzy free verse, and that is not enough. (p. 32)

Lewis Turco, in Saturday Review (© 1967 by Saturday Review, Inc.; reprinted with permission), October 14, 1967.

LAURENCE LIEBERMAN

[In *Masks* Edward Brathwaite] has been able to invent a hybrid prosody which, combining jazz/folk rhythms with English speaking meters, captures the authenticity of primitive African rituals in a way that the translations of the Trask anthology are rarely able to do. The author is totally immersed both in the expressive resources of the English tongue and in the firsthand spiritual dynamics of primitive living—a rare combination of proficiencies with lucky dividends for contemporary readers. Brathwaite's success in this long verse-quartet is advanced by his skill in assimilating without strain numerous proper nouns and idioms of the Ghanian vernacular into the poem's fluid English base. . . . *Masks* demonstrates that the primitive impulse must be filtered through the linguistic tactility of a single totally operative artistic intelligence, a consciousness fully in touch with our moment, if it is to become experiencable to us as readers. (pp. 56-7)

Laurence Lieberman, in Poetry (© 1969 by The Modern Poetry Association; reprinted by permission of the Editor of Poetry), April, 1969.

HAYDEN CARRUTH

To convey a sense of the quality of Edward Brathwaite's poetry is difficult. Let me suggest a distinction between poetry that is moving and poetry that is stirring. . . . H. D.'s poems are the former kind; Brathwaite's are the latter. I don't mean like a Sousa march either, though I've no objection to Sousa. It is a question of vigor and a certain fibrous resiliency. Brathwaite, who is the foremost poet of the English-speaking Caribbean and at least in some sense a revolutionary, is never shrill, is always keen to the pathos of his people's plight, yet the basic exuberance of his feeling cannot be doubted. In part it is revolutionary optimism, in part a closeness to his sources in folk culture. Brathwaite has said that the chief literary influence on his work has been the poetry of T. S. Eliot, but if this is so it has been an influence almost entirely limited to matters of organization and structure, and perhaps to Eliot's manner of rhyming, though this could have come from anywhere. In texture, in verbal technique, in almost everything, nothing could be further from Eliot's poetry than Brathwaite's. Brathwaite has made his reputation on three long poems, *Rights of Passage* (1967), *Masks* (1968), and *Islands* (1969). Now they have been published in one volume, *The Arrivants: A New World Trilogy*, and it is a book everyone should read. Brathwaite uses many voices, ranging from standard English to dialects of several kinds, and in many rhythms, from subdued free cadence to calypso. Not all passages are equally successful; sometimes his jazz tempos remind us too much of Lindsay's "Congo" or his dialect slips too far toward the type of Auden's ballads. But in general he has been remarkably successful in reproducing black speech patterns, both African and Caribbean, in English syntax, using the standard techniques of contemporary poetry, and he has been equally successful in suggesting to an international audience the cultural identities and attitudes of his own people. To my mind his best writing is in *Masks,* a poem which explores the poet's longing to discover his own roots in the culture and history of the Ashanti Federation, written as a consequence of his living and working in Ghana for a number of years. In the end his seeking was, and had to be, a failure, as he acknowledges, but it produced magnificent poetry. . . . (pp. 317-18)

[There] is no way to suggest in a small space the density, variety, wisdom, and fervor of Brathwaite's poems. . . . [He] is a poet of real accomplishment by any standards, to whom we must give not only our attention but our admiration. (p. 320)

Hayden Carruth, in The Hudson Review (copyright © 1974 by The Hudson Review, Inc.; reprinted by permission), Vol. XXVII, No. 2, Summer, 1974.

*   *   *

BROPHY, Brigid   1929-

Brophy is a British novelist, playwright, critic, short story writer, and journalist. She often incorporates elements of farce and of word play into her work. Strongly influenced by both Freud and Shaw, she creates witty social satires around themes of middle-class morality and hypocrisy. (See also *CLC*, Vol. 6, and *Contemporary Authors*, Vols. 5-8, rev. ed.)

JOSEPH WOOD KRUTCH

One expects the fantasy-with-a-moral to be written by a mature sage like Voltaire, Samuel Johnson, or Anatole France. . . . Nevertheless, it will have to be admitted that Brigid Brophy not only writes with a great deal of delicate skill, but gets away very nicely with the air of mellow wisdom. "As old as the world" she would have us believe, and there are moments when the illusion is quite convincing. (p. 36)

Certainly there is a good deal of originality in ["Hackenfeller's Ape," the tale of] a scientist with emotional conflicts who was trying to understand animals, humanity, and possibly even God by observing the behavior of [an ape, the] creature whom he believed to be just at the beginning of that dubious development in the course of which esthetic and moral preferences, undefinable desires, and a sense of sin spoil the animal without . . . quite succeeding in turning him into anything which we have any real right to call satisfactory as a human being. (pp. 36-7)

Miss Brophy's tale is richly ornamented with witty turns, it is full of events, and by no means all of the surprises are to be anticipated. . . .

But just what the main point is or, for that matter, whether a sharply defined main point is intended, is not sure. If a single lesson is implicit, perhaps it is kept a bit too completely in solution. . . . If Miss Brophy stands anywhere, it seems to be on the contention that this is a sorry world we never made and that it's not likely to better until we come a long way further from the apes than we are now. (p. 37)

> *Joseph Wood Krutch, "Spoiled Ape," in Saturday Review (copyright © 1954 by Saturday Review, Inc.; reprinted with permission), June 12, 1954, pp. 36-7.*

DAN WICKENDEN

Beyond the haunting title of Brigid Brophy's second novel lies a tale as strange and original as the one she told three years ago in "Hackenfeller's Ape." Like that small, remarkable book, "The King of a Rainy Country" is youthful, glittering, a little perverse; and it is written in the same immaculate prose. . . .

[It] is brittle, sparkling stuff. Lacking the pointed satire and the allegorical overtones that enlarged the scope of "Hackenfeller's Ape," one is left with the feeling that Miss Brophy hasn't, this time, found a theme to match her exceptional talent. The fact remains that "The King of a Rainy Country" exerts a strong fascination, and provides a brand of entertainment for which the best word is exquisite, in all its connotations.

> *Dan Wickenden, "An Original Tale, Comic, Brittle, Sad and Sparkling," in New York Herald Tribune Book World (© 1957, New York Herald Tribune Inc.), February 17, 1957, p. 3.*

BARBARA SCHILLER

As in her previous books, Brigid Brophy has written a self-assured, spirited and elegant novel ["Flesh"], gleaming with perverse wit and classic style. Further, she is able to draw her characters' family background colorfully yet sparingly, to understate yet understand subtle psychological relationships. . . . But where is the theme for these talents, and why does one think of Miss Brophy as a young novelist of promise when this is in fact her fifth book? A writer who can do so much so well forces her readers to demand the most and the best. However, if this ultimate satisfaction is missing, and it is, one can still be very pleased with the delights that are present.

> *Barbara Schiller, "Male Pygmalion," in New York Herald Tribune Books (© 1963, New York Herald Tribune Inc.), July 7, 1963, p. 7.*

MANFRED WOLF

[In *Flesh* Brigid Brophy] traces the relationship of two young people, first in courtship, then in marriage. Marcus, passive and anxiety-ridden, is transformed by Nancy into assertiveness and independence, while Nancy gradually loses the energy and control that once marked her. This kind of short novel, with its paucity of characters and its relentless concentration on them, is rather more popular in Europe than it is here, and *Flesh* shows once again what is wrong with the type: the range is so narrow that to be satisfactory the work must be perfect. The relationship of Nancy and Marcus gives the impression of a preliminary sketch for a larger novel. More important, the relationship itself is inadequately drawn, and the book's conclusion is noticeably hurried. . . .

The best and worst one can say about this novel is that it is well written. Miss Brophy has the enviable knack of combining precision with suggestiveness, as when she says about Nancy that "in direct personal relationships she had a habit not of failing to see nuances but of naming and discussing them—a sort of coarseness of mind sometimes found in nurses . . ." This talent gives to parts of the book, especially to the character of Nancy, a certain astringent charm. But most of the time her gift for observation obtrudes rather ludicrously. . . . Descriptions of chairs, carpets, *objets d'art* abound, giving the book an unpleasantly snobbish air. Even worse than the descriptions are the conversations about furniture; those who do not furnish tastefully are damned.

Miss Brophy's attitude does not appear to differ from that of her characters. Such lack of distance between author and characters is a common feature of this type of fiction; it has the unfortunate effect here of making their snide cleverness, their fake psychologizing, and their languid despair all the more annoying for being taken so seriously. In addition, Nancy and Marcus display an almost adolescent rebelliousness against their Jewish background, which manifests itself in nasty remarks about parents, Jews, North London, and so forth. All this is supposed to be sophistication, but *Flesh* would have been a better book if the author had not been so thoroughly taken in by it.

> *Manfred Wolf, "A Passion for Decor," in Saturday Review (copyright © 1963 by Saturday Review, Inc.; reprinted with permission), July 27, 1963, p. 29.*

JEREMY TREGLOWN

[*Palace without Chairs*] starts as a what's-going-on, develops into a what's-it-all-about and ends as a so-what. It's a modishly fanciful piece about a palace revolution in a never-never land called Evarchia, where none of the dying King's heirs is willing or able to succeed him. Full of sharp details and elegantly written, it's largely composed of interminably proliferating fantasy sequences long out-Pythoned. There is a Meaning, of course, revealed in advance on the jacket but otherwise available, as the blurb promises, to the persistent reader. . . .

Brophy calls it 'A Baroque Novel', and the title and epigraphs come from works by her art-historian husband. The trouble with analogies between painting and literature, of course, is that paintings—however rich in narrative content or intricately decorative—have an immediate completeness of impact which the tantalising serialism of fiction denies. (p. 566)

> *Jeremy Treglown, in New Statesman (© 1978 The Statesman & Nation Publishing Co. Ltd.), April 28, 1978.*

MARY HOPE

Brigid Brophy writes with such style, elegance and wit that it is quite possible to read [*Palace Without Chairs*] without pausing to fathom the fable. It should first be said that this is often a very, very *funny* book, and also an extremely clever one. Whether it is the lethal exactitude of a pithy narrative phrase, a description of the setting-up of a committee to consider the provision of chairs in the uncomfortably unsedentary palace, or the consideration of the payment and nonproductivity of writers, . . . it all sparkles. The story is simple enough. . . . It is a fable of social and personal change and family responsibility. But, though the meaning is important, like all the best allegorists, Miss Brophy has created a wholly 'real' parallel world which it is a pleasure to enjoy just for itself. (p. 29)

> *Mary Hope, in* The Spectator (© *1978 by* The Spectator; *reprinted by permission of* The Spectator*),* May 6, 1978.

JOSH RUBINS

[*Palace Without Chairs* is] another of Brigid Brophy's "baroque" fictions—baroque in its droll verbal tap-dancing . . . and in its contrapuntal, obliquely affecting arrangements of unconnected tableaux: a taut debate on criminal insanity between a prosecutor and a psychiatrist; tea with Evarchia's only great novelist; a lecture on security at the Academy of Advanced Military Studies. Stacked up by a less crafty architect, such interludes might work only as satiric or didactic digressions. Here they bounce off one another with little pings of irony and gentle thuds of regret, reflecting Brophy's essentially compassionate and cautiously optimistic view of humanity caught between the death instinct —one by one the Evarchian royals succumb—and the Life Force.

But Brophy never writes a dry novel of ideas. The Life Force in *Palace Without Chairs* is embodied in the massive, teen-age princess, Heather. An unself-consciously hoydenish, unneurotic lesbian, she survives the collapse of Evarchia's monarchy and is last seen being clumsily seductive in a London bar. With such a warm-blooded center for the swirl of icy wit, Brophy has spun out one of her most appealing essay-entertainments. (p. 34)

> *Josh Rubins, in* Saturday Review (© *1978 by Saturday Review Magazine Corp.; reprinted with permission),* July 8, 1978.

*   *   *

BUCK, Pearl S(ydenstricker)   1892-1973

Buck was an American novelist, short story writer, playwright, essayist, editor, biographer, autobiographer, author of juvenile literature, and translator. The daughter of Presbyterian missionaries, Buck spent almost forty years in China, and in her published work strove to interpret China for the Western world. Her work has generally been regarded as skillful in its portrayal and interpretation of Oriental life, but weak artistically. A champion of many humanitarian causes, Buck often allowed a didactic quality to override artistic objectivity in her work. Her third book, *The Good Earth*, was both a popular and critical success, however, winning for the author the Pulitzer Prize in 1932. Buck was awarded the Nobel Prize for Literature in 1938, becoming the first American woman to achieve that honor. In addition to her novels of Chinese life, Buck wrote several novels with an American setting under the pseudonym of John Sedges. (See also *CLC*, Vol. 7, and *Contemporary Authors*, Vols. 1-4, rev. ed.; obituary, Vols. 41-44, rev. ed.)

PHYLLIS BENTLEY

[It is] as novelist, as pure literary artist, that Mrs. Buck regards herself and prefers to be regarded. It seems worth

while, therefore, to consider her books as novels, works of art, to analyze them as fiction, without prejudging them by applying any label. Let us, that is, for a moment forget that Mrs. Buck is famous as "the novelist of China," "the author of those Chinese books," and inquire simply, as with any unknown novelist, into her choice of material and her technique. Such an analysis is in her case difficult, for there is a firm unity in her work which makes its component parts not easily distinguishable, but I am sure that the degree of permanence to be achieved by any fiction can only be ascertained by assessing it as a work of art. (p. 791)

Mrs. Buck's chosen scene—and it is part of our scheme to state it thus coolly—is modern China. There are parts of that vast country where modern China means the same as ancient China; there are parts where the change of date implies a profound social change. These two Chinas, the old and the new, form the material for Mrs. Buck's art. . . .

[The] attempt is made to present China from within, as the Chinese see it. . . . [The] landscape in Mrs. Buck's novels is always presented as seen by familiar eyes. Now this is one of the great difficulties of the novelist who chooses to write about a land not native to him; he is likely to write of the scenery as he, the stranger, sees it, not as the man who has lived with it all his life; the dawns are lurid with beauty to the stranger, where the native sees the coming of rain or the rising of a wind. . . . Mrs. Buck has lived in China so long that she really knows the landscape, and she never once, in all the volume of her work, forgets it and goes into raptures as over an alien scene. (p. 792)

In the same way Mrs. Buck aims to present the Chinese customs as familiar, natural and correct, because so would her characters regard them. The customs at birth and death and marriage and new year, the earthen gods, the family ceremonial, the slavery of women, are all copiously illustrated, but always presented, as it were, unself-consciously, as part of the natural process of living; never by the slightest word or turn of phrase does Mrs. Buck call our attention to the difference of these customs from our own. This may be thought a commonplace, but, in fact, an identification with one's characters so complete and so well sustained is rare in fiction; nor is this an unimportant matter, but a quality which goes far in welding the firm unity we have already mentioned. Her picture of the Chinese civilization is highly remarkable, then; for she presents to us China as the Chinese see it, but in language (of both lip and mind) which we understand. (p. 793)

[The] language in which Mrs. Buck presents this material shares the same dual character. It is English—very plain, clear English; yet it gives the impression that one is reading the language native to the characters all the time. This is very largely due, I think, to the entire absence of Chinese words in the prose. . . . The prose which is broken by many foreign words in italics accentuates our sense of being English-speaking people reading a book written in English about an alien race. Especially is this the case when the foreign word is followed by an explanation of its meaning. Pearl Buck never uses a Chinese word, never needs to explain one. Even "Mah-Jongg," for example, is called "sparrow dominoes"—and very rightly, since that is what the Chinese word means to the Chinese. On the other hand, Mrs. Buck never, I think, uses a word for which a literal translation into Chinese could not be found. The effect of her prose is to translate what the Chinese mean into language which means that to us. That it is also exceedingly beautiful prose is just our luck, so to speak, and a remarkable instance of Mrs. Buck's skill. The grave, quiet, biblical speech, full of dignity, in which Mrs. Buck, without ever "raising her voice," is able to render both the deepest and the lightest emotions—the feeling of a mother over her dead child and the excitement of an old man over his tea—is a fine example of an instrument perfectly adapted to its task. (pp. 793-94)

Mrs. Buck's main characters in each novel, always Chinese, always belong to one family, the action being seen through the eyes of that family alone.... There are other characters, but they are subsidiary; the main drama is not that of clash between house and house, but consists in the varying fortunes and happiness of one house alone. This is probably deeply true to Chinese life, and forms part of Mrs. Buck's essential theme. It does not result, however, in a limitation of scope; indeed, our author's range of character is remarkable. She is equally successful with characters of every age, sex, class, and type, and in the indication of the differences between these various types. (pp. 794-95)

Her presentation of character is objective; that is to say, she does not color her characters too much with her own feelings about them, but allows them to be just and right- eous, even though she disapproves of them, and a little peevish and weak, even though they be her heroes.... The parents who cling to the old ways, the children who revolt to the new, are each presented sympathetically; and it is this impartiality which helps to make of Mrs. Buck a novel- ist, instead of a mere propagandist writer on China. (p. 795)

This reveals itself, too, in her treatment of the minor char- acters who are present, plentifully though not confusingly, in all her books. The reader feels always that these charac- ters are not in any way to be despised or thought of as less important; they are just as alive as the major persons and have their own deeply interesting story somewhere about them. We do not hear it only because at the moment we chance to be busy with something else.... They add their separate life to the book and enrich its substance. (pp. 795- 96)

We may, I think, perceive one or two indications of Mrs. Buck's methods. She observes external appearances close- ly, and presents them with a detailed accuracy....

Mrs. Buck observes with equal clearness the personal mannerisms of her characters, how they speak and walk and eat and cough. (p. 796)

Any young writer desirous of improving his characteriza- tion could learn volumes from Mrs. Buck's choice of verbs, adverbs and adverbial expressions....

An aspect of Mrs. Buck's skill in this branch of her art which cannot be illustrated within the limits of an article because the examples are ... so closely woven into the text, is her handling of the moods and changes of mind of her characters. How Yuan in *A House Divided* cannot make himself love the girl revolutionist and yet cannot free himself from her; how Wang Lung slips into bondage to Lotus out of sheer *ennui;* the fatal quarrel over a mere length of blue-cotton cloth between the Mother and her husband—these deserve study for their beautifully living quality. One thing buds from another, and the mood grows, as is only possible in living organisms.

One of the severest tests of a writer's power of characteri- zation is his handling of heredity. Does he portray children as the mechanical duplicates of their parents, or as having no resemblance to them at all ...? Mrs. Buck's success in this difficult task is well known. The Mother's lads, though so different, are truly brothers; and every child of the horde which crowd the Wang courts is the child of his father and mother, the descendant of Wang and O-Lan, yet a separate person too....

This careful and vigorous presentation of the power of he- redity is an essential part of Mrs. Buck's true theme. (p. 797)

Her stories take the epic rather than the dramatic form; that is to say, they are chronological narratives of a piece of life, seen from one point of view, straightforward, without de- vices; they have no complex plots, formed of many strands skilfully twisted, but belong to the single-strand type, with the family, however, rather than the individual, as unit. *East Wind: West Wind* tells, it is true, the tales of two mar- riages in modern China.... Both tales, however, are seen and told by the girl who has bound feet, and are thus wound into a single strand....

It is now time for us to seek the figure in Mrs. Buck's car- pet, the theme on which she threads her pearls.

Is it her deep intention to present China to the West? Yes, I suppose it is; and she succeeds in it to admiration. But I do not feel that this is the only figure in the carpet; indeed, at times I feel that China makes the colors of her design rather than the pattern. (p. 798)

Is it her aim to present China in contact with Western civi- lization, China in revolution, the transition, in a word, from the old China to the new? Yes, I suppose it is; though per- sonally I do not feel this to be the most successful part of her work. In *East Wind: West Wind,* and still more in *A House Divided,* some of her truest art is lacking. (p. 799)

For my part I consider that the figure in Mrs. Buck's car- pet, her true theme, is the continuity of life.

One aspect of this continuity is beautifully revealed in that miniature masterpiece, *The Mother.* All the characters in this novel remain anonymous, it will be remembered.... [What] they say and do is deeply true to all human motive, so that we sympathize and understand. This again is a hall- mark of quality in a novelist; for those only tell the truth who make us feel the biological certainty that all men are made of the same elements, differently arranged.

Another aspect of this continuity is the one most generally recognized in Mrs. Buck's work—the passing of life on from generation to generation. The sense of this continuity is strongly present in every detail of our author's work, as has already emerged in our discussion of plot and charac- ter. It is especially strong in the *Good Earth* trilogy, and is summed up for us in *Sons,* where Wang the Tiger is riding to his father's funeral. "Riding thus at the head of his cav- alcade," writes Mrs. Buck, "his women and his children, Wang the Tiger took his place in the generations.... he felt his place in the long line of life." (pp. 799-800)

[For] the interest of her chosen material, the sustained high level of her technical skill, and the frequent universality of her conceptions, Mrs. Buck is entitled to take rank as a considerable artist. To read her novels is to gain not merely knowledge of China but wisdom about life. (p. 800)

Phyllis Bentley, "The Art of Pearl S. Buck," in English Journal (copyright © 1935 by The National Council of Teachers of English), December, 1935, pp. 791-800.

MALCOLM COWLEY

["The Good Earth" is] a parable of the life of man, in his relation to the soil that sustains him. The plot, deliberately commonplace, is given a sort of legendary weight and dignity by being placed in an unfamiliar setting. The biblical style is appropriate to the subject and the characters. If we define a masterpiece as a novel that is living, complete, sustained, but still somewhat limited in its scope as compared with the greatest works of fiction—if we define it as "Wuthering Heights" rather than "War and Peace"—then ["The Good Earth" is a masterpiece].

But it wasn't intended to stand alone.... Miss Buck planned to write three novels that would fit together and become a sort of Chinese "Buddenbrooks."

"Sons," the second novel, is a long step toward achieving this purpose. Considered by itself, I'm not sure that it isn't even better than "The Good Earth." ... Once again the plot falls into a legendary pattern, since the career of Wang the Tiger is based on one of the oldest and most exciting stories in Chinese folklore, that of the Good Bandit.... Besides this drama, the book has a quality that one doesn't associate with Pearl Buck—a rather earthy humor, most of it rising from the contrast between the traditional place of Chinese women—who are supposed to be household slaves —and the real power that they exercise over their lazy and self-indulgent husbands.

But "A House Divided" is a different story. It doesn't matter whether you judge it by itself or by what it contributes to the trilogy; in either case it is surprisingly inferior....

Its most obvious weakness is its style. In the course of the three novels, Miss Buck has changed her setting from past to present, from an old walled city to modern Shanghai.... Meanwhile her style has remained the same; if anything, her mannerisms out of the King James Version have become exaggerated. They seemed appropriate to Wang the Farmer and even Wang the Tiger, both figures in a legend; but they are out of place in the Shanghai drawing room of Wang the Landlord. (p. 24)

And the plot of "A House Divided" is essentially even weaker than its style. Miss Buck has always had trouble constructing a novel that deals with contemporary material, partly because of her strong sense of fidelity to the events that actually happened; she refuses to rearrange them into a harmonious pattern. Her best books have been parables or legends. But even a writer used to inventing plots would have been baffled by the problem she set herself in "A House Divided." She explains in the foreword ... that she wanted to trace the original vigor of Wang Lung as it reappeared in his descendants. "That vigor, first found in one figure, is dissipated, as time goes on, into many sons and many places. In 'A House Divided' the vigor seems quite scattered." But how could anybody make a unified novel out of such material? ... The truth is that her trilogy does not end at all. It declines into mere scaffolding, then stops in the middle like a great unfinished bridge. (pp. 24-5)

"The Patriot," is based on the same material as "A House Divided." ...

From the very first, "The Patriot" seems a better novel, partly because Miss Buck is now writing modern prose, with extreme simplicity as its only mannerism, but also because of a greater subtlety and detachment in handling her material. The Wu family seems to belong in Shanghai—unlike the Wangs—and the political background is more credible. The second part of the novel, which passes in Japan, is an even greater improvement over "A House Divided." Miss Buck does something here that very few Western novelists would even attempt: she describes the impressions of a Chinese visitor to Japan and his courtship of a Japanese woman. Without being able to pass on the ultimate truth of her picture, I found it altogether convincing. ...

"A House Divided" is a failure that ought to be destroyed. In its place, Miss Buck should put "The Patriot"; she would have to change the names of the characters and their family trees, but not much else. (p. 25)

Malcolm Cowley, "Wang Lung's Children" (reprinted by permission of the author; renewal copyright 1967 by Malcolm Cowley), in The New Republic, May 10, 1939, pp. 24-5.

PAUL A. DOYLE

East Wind: West Wind [Pearl Buck's first book] is usually spoken of as a novel, but, actually, it consists of two definite short stories with a decided break between them. The first narrative is more poetic and romantic; the second, more sparse and moralistic. The Dreiser influence, which we are to see displayed particularly in The Good Earth, is non-existent in this book.

East Wind: West Wind is written in a much more delicately wrought and self-conscious style than is found in the later works of Pearl Buck. While basically simple in form, the style in this work is somewhat artificial. The style tends to be choppy, slow-paced, heavily romantic, often strikingly exotic, reminiscent in many of its colorful images of Edward Fitzgerald's translation of The Rubaiyat of Omar Khayyam. The prose is often too consciously flowery, and several "purple passages" also appear too obviously calculated for effect. The framework of having Kwei-lan write the details of the story to the foreign lady who has lived in China becomes increasingly artificial, forced, and wearisome as the narrative progresses.

A certain amount of extraneous description occurs; for example, there are some rather unnecessarily detailed portraits of the concubines in Kwei-lan's father's house. Such descriptions are yanked into the narrative for evident background and coloring, but the majority of Miss Buck's descriptions serve the useful purpose of enumerating the manners of aristocratic Chinese families and of underscoring the complete differences in customs between China and the West. Here the book is most successful. Both the situation and the reality of the problem present themselves in a credible fashion, and the book does manage to convey a definite flavor of setting, scene, and authenticity of locale—later a basic characteristic of Pearl Buck's fiction.

At times sentimentalism predominates.... Perhaps Miss Buck overlabors the point that, in their basic emotions and feelings people the world over are, regardless of race, much alike.

In spite of its deficiencies, East Wind: West Wind contains

several effective passages, and the theme is meaningful. The characters are caught in a modern dilemma, and the happy resolution in Kwei-lan's case and the semi-tragic resolution in her brother's are convincingly rendered. The objections of the Chinese mother and father to a foreign daughter-in-law strike a common chord, and the tensions produced from their prejudices and instinctive attitudes bring focus to the problem. Truth is at the core of *East Wind: West Wind,* but at times the veneer of romanticism and sentimentalism blurs and softens this truth.

In an overall view, *East Wind: West Wind* remains more interesting for its promise than for its effectiveness as a book in its own right. Although it reveals several weaknesses—uncertainty in handling a story framework, tendencies to stylistic artificiality, and a pronounced sentimentality—it points up the fact that Miss Buck has a thorough knowledge of her subject and possesses a fundamental narrative sense. Her first book of fiction also demonstrates that she is a novelist who is in the happy position of understanding both sides in various conflicts between two different worlds, and between the old and new customs. Miss Buck has established a solid hook on which she can hang innumerable stories revolving around these themes.

Perhaps the most important aspect of *East Wind: West Wind* was that it gave Pearl Buck the necessary confidence to continue in the field of fiction since she now realized that a market for stories using Chinese materials was available. (pp. 33-4)

The impetus for [*The Good Earth*] was the anger she had experienced because the common people of China were so often oppressed and abused.

When she was prepared to write *The Good Earth,* she acknowledges that "there was no plot or plan. Only the man and the woman and their children stood there before me." Later, she came to realize, however, that these people were not just Chinese; they were representative of farming people the world over. They were universal in their struggles, in their joys, in their disappointments. (p. 37)

A vividness of both character and scene . . . distinguishes *The Good Earth.* . . .

Part of the reason for this vividness rests in the universality of the novel's various portraits. (p. 38)

[Portrayed] with graphic authority is the ebb and flow of life, its change and perpetual movements, not only seasonally from spring to winter, from seed planting to harvest, but also a cycle of both family and humanity. Past links with present, and present links with future. . . . [A] sense of "being shaped by eternities" is one of the characteristics of *The Good Earth.* (pp. 38-9)

In addition, careful handling and emphasis on both the precise and the appropriate descriptive details . . . enhance the [universality] of experience. . . . The descriptions are never overdrawn or excessive; their conciseness always centers on concrete, closely observed, "essential" details; and, although the scene which we behold is unfolding in a distant land and many of the practices and traditions are exotic or picturesque, we see the essential logic and reality of these customs in their time and place. In its economy and in its laconic but vital lyricism, the descriptive passages in *The Good Earth* often remind us of Ernest Hemingway's writing. The style bears no dross; only descriptive details necessary to convey the scene or to reinforce the mood are recorded.

The style of *The Good Earth* is one of the novel's most impressive characteristics. This style is based on the manner of the old Chinese narrative sagas related and written down by storytellers and on the mellifluous prose of the King James version of the Bible. (pp. 39-40)

Pearl Buck's writing in *The Good Earth* is characterized by simplicity, concreteness, a stress on long serpentine sentences, parallelism, balance, and repetition of words. Although the majority of the sentences are lengthy, they break into shorter, sometimes choppy, segments of thought which undulate in movement. The style, generally slow-paced, evinces a quiet stateliness and seriousness. It does not at all rival the color or richness of the biblical imagery, principally because it follows the simplicity of word choice of the Chinese saga rather than the more imaginative and exotic coloring of the Old and New Testaments. At certain times Miss Buck's style achieves poetical suggestion, but never is the imbalance between the normal and the more poetic so pronounced as to produce isolated "purple passages," as was the case in *East Wind: West Wind.*

The style of *The Good Earth* is unusually appropriate for the saga story. The simplicity and the slow but steady movement of the prose fit harmoniously the heroic and epic-like qualities of the narrative. (pp. 40-1)

In structure, *The Good Earth* uses a chronological form which proceeds at a fairly regular pace. Some climaxes occur, although they do not reach too much higher than the normal incidents in the story. The movement is slower and somewhat less arresting after O-lan's death, but some slackening is inevitable in a *roman-fleuve.* (p. 42)

Although *The Good Earth* places much emphasis on the family unit, and the analysis of the family fortunes is pivotal, the main characters are studied in detail. The portrayal of Wang Lung's character is starkly frank. His strengths and weaknesses are candidly examined and bared before the reader; and while, on the basis of a superficial reading, he might appear to be a one-dimensional figure, he actually runs the whole gamut of human emotions. (pp. 42-3)

Mention should be made of the haze of romanticism which hovers over and about the novel. Miss Buck has wisely avoided the artificial romanticism and the obvious sentimentalism which marred *East Wind: West Wind.* Yet the story of *The Good Earth,* although it maintains a convincing realism, takes on a certain exotic remoteness which lends additional charm to its episodes. The strange is made familiar, and the familiar is made pleasantly strange. . . . The faraway coloring of *The Good Earth* lights the familiar elements with new freshness and appeal. Realism and romanticism blend in just the right proportions. Life is given the glow of legend, and legend is given the aura of life. (pp. 44-5)

Pearl Buck has acknowledged the influence of Zola, and it is almost immediately evident. Certainly *The Good Earth* is Naturalistic in many ways: in its documentary approach to its material, in its detached and objective presentation, in its stress on factors of environment and heredity, in its accuracy of setting and descriptive details, and in its interest in impoverished and earthy people who dwell on the lower strata of social class. Yet, at the same time, several differences exist between Miss Buck's approach and Zola's. She is much less interested in sordidness, brutality, and squalor; and her emphasis on these factors arises out of a more balanced and wholesome interest in things as they are than from a deliberate stress on the seamier aspects of life in order to shock and horrify. (p. 46)

Realism rather than Naturalism would be a more accurate term to apply to Pearl Buck's work. The pessimism and despair of a writer like Zola are far removed from Miss Buck's more affirmative approach to things as they exist and from the basic meliorism which her writing in general displays. She stands as an optimist rather than as a pessimist, although she often hears and records the "eternal note of sadness." (p. 47)

As a novel, *Sons* [sequel to *The Good Earth*] labors under the handicap which all sequels to famous books must face. A narrative to equal *The Good Earth* would have to be more powerful and absorbing than *Sons*. Yet, within its own limitations, *Sons* is an interesting, worth-while novel and a work of no mean effort. It perhaps suffers in that the emphasis on brigands and war lords, on their characteristics and activities, seems somewhat remote to a Western audience. (p. 59)

The fundamental defect of *Sons* is the weakness of the characterization of Wang the Tiger. (pp. 59-60)

In contrast to [actual war lords throughout Chinese history], Wang the Tiger is a considerably more limited and colorless individual. Although the reader comes to know him quite well, a particular remoteness about him persists. His motives and behavior are analyzed at some length, but he does not come fully alive as a flesh and blood character. And he does not arouse interest or sympathy as Wang Lung and O-lan do. (p. 60)

It is difficult to sense tragedy here, at least from the way the story and characters present themselves.

The style of *Sons* follows the same biblical-Chinese saga influence displayed in *The Good Earth,* and, in general, repeats this pattern beneficially. Many of the long sweeping sentences are especially lyrical and mellifluous, and numerous passages of thoughtful beauty recur. . . . [However, in] *The Good Earth,* the style was absorbed in the humanity of the characters and their difficulties; consequently, the style took on a special life and feeling. In *Sons,* Wang the Tiger does not maintain the same interest to carry along the style with him. Thus, the prose of *Sons* occasionally seems utilitarian, a mere archaic-flavored ordering and recital of events. While it may not actually be determined that Pearl Buck felt her story and people more deeply and more vibrantly in *The Good Earth* than in *Sons,* this conclusion is strongly suggested by the style and characterization of *Sons.*

Sons, of course, possesses social and historical value as an illustration of a way of life in China. . . . The novel also has merit as a pointed, ironic commentary on the differences between generations in the same family. . . . The individual differences between Wang Lung's sons and their wives display a universality which rings true and is an easily remembered aspect of the story.

But, in the final analysis, *Sons* falls short of *The Good Earth* because it does not have the same universal quality of timelessness, the same inevitable moment of birth and death, of success and failure, of tragedy and of joy. Universality has been narrowed to the rise of a war lord and the subsequent—but never powerfully felt by the reader—misunderstanding between father and son. Even the time movement of Wang Lung's descendants seems to sink into secondary significance in the emphasis given to the story of one rather colorless military chief. (pp. 63-4)

A House Divided [the final volume of the trilogy], which studies the development of one young man's mind during a turbulent and crucial period of modern Chinese history and also probes the changes wrought in one family over a period of several generations, is actually the weakest volume in the *House of Earth* trilogy. Part of the reason for this situation is that Yuan does not hold the same reader interest as did Wang Lung or even Wang the Tiger. Yuan does not come alive as a believable individual. None of the characters in *A House Divided* arouses any particular interest; and, while much happens, the events do not involve the reader in the action.

As an examination of one man's mind, *A House Divided* fails to be appealing primarily because Miss Buck's technique is not thorough and conclusive enough in its introspective probing. Yuan seems to wear his heart on his sleeve, and his sudden shifts of emotion and feeling are not presented logically. . . . Miss Buck's technique is more effective in analyzing external events and elements than in presenting internal aspects. Too much explaining of Yuan's thoughts and character occurs. (pp. 68-9)

The reader is also too conscious of authorial manipulation in the handling of Yuan's character. He is a puppet who dances the same tunes on constantly shifting strings, strings which are observed by the audience. The romance between Yuan and Meiling is, for instance, shamelessly managed and rigged by the author. . . .

Further, the book wanders about somewhat aimlessly. *A House Divided* treats of a number of places and a number of events, and its canvas often becomes episodic and unwieldy. Malcolm Cowley has observed that the material in this last volume of the trilogy is too scattered and does not progress to any significant conclusion [see excerpt above]. (p. 69)

Miss Buck's style, effective in the early scenes when Yuan returns to his grandfather's earthen house, often appears flat and ordinary—a mere recording of events. The prose of *A House Divided* is, in general, much too dull and undistinguished to do more than merely tell a story. A particularly heavy burden is placed on the style to describe internal events; and while at times some poetry filters through the external description, the style is not adequate to the needs of so much internal analysis. (pp. 69-70)

A House Divided has appeal as the final view of a family that we have seen at its best and at its worst. . . . Yet, while [its] events themselves have great significance, the people in *A House Divided* who participate in them appear awfully pallid and lifeless in comparison.

In 1934, between the publication of the second and third volumes of her *House of Earth* trilogy, Pearl Buck issued one of her most unusual novels, *The Mother*. This narrative was intended to give a universal portrait of the eternal mother, to present the various cycles of her life, and to capture some of the timelessness of her existence. In a sense, this novel was attempting to describe one woman in the same manner that *The Good Earth* had endeavored to analyze one particular family. (pp. 70-1)

The Mother is an extremely important work in the canon of Pearl Buck's writing. The never-ending cycle of birth and death and the eternal round of a mother's life with its joys and sorrows stir the reader because of their proportions and the novelist's insight into life. Here is a portrait of a perennial mother, with universal implications. (pp. 72-3)

In many ways *The Mother* is one of Miss Buck's finest books. It possesses many distinctions: for example, the cyclical flow of time, the eternal *mater dolorosa* caught in this movement, the tragedies and hardness of existence, the mistakes and crises revolving around the life of a mortal woman. Nevertheless, in an overall estimate, one comes to admire the book for its ambitious attempt rather than for its complete realization of achievement. Several reasons support this viewpoint.

In the first part of the novel, description predominates, and the mother speaks very little. In the latter part, however, she becomes, comparatively at least, quite garrulous and even naggish. While this change is logical under the impact of increasing age and sorrow, it tends to forfeit reader sympathy.... [Her] failings can be justified on the basis that such events happen in life, but in the novel they tend to emphasize the main character's weaknesses and, hence, to diminish sympathy. (p. 73)

A prime weakness exists in the failure to involve the reader in a sense of the mother's toughness and power of endurance.... The basic fault with the mother is that she becomes too much a type and too little a realized individual. (pp. 73-4)

Pearl Buck seems to feel that her mother character was too far removed from common experience to be popular.... If characterization is vivid, complete, and penetrating [however], the strangeness of person and subject matter is conquered. In her portrayal of the mother, Miss Buck has not succeeded in rendering her character with accuracy and thorough discernment.

The prose of *The Mother* is reduced to the barest simplicity. It is less rich, poetic, and varied than *The Good Earth;* it possesses an economy which, while it often approaches biblical phrasing and is often pleasingly lyrical, eventually becomes monotonous. Although the style is deliberately reduced to the utmost simplicity in order to balance with the stark and basic movement of time and with the plight of the universal mother caught in this movement, about halfway through the novel one realizes that the prose is too plain and too sparse for the theme; more richness and variety are needed—more poetry, more of the coloring found in *The Good Earth*. The style found in *The Mother* suggests that the biblical-Chinese saga style, which Pearl Buck has often used very effectively, can be drawn too thin or be too simple in a lengthy narrative and, hence, lacks a vital heightening and variety of tone and harmony.

In general, *The Mother* is an interesting, ambitious attempt to effect a monumental achievement in both theme and style. The attempt does not succeed, but the effort was desirable. The theme is worthy of a truly great work, and the material is there; but Miss Buck has miscalculated the stylistic effects, and she has not thought out nor developed

thoroughly enough the characterization of her central figure. In addition, the reader is told about a great many things happening too suddenly in the universal movement of time. This suddenness is not prepared for and seems incongruous. *The Mother* definitely needed more patient revision. (pp. 74-5)

The Nobel Committee citation, which accompanied [Pearl Buck's Nobel award] read: "For rich and generous epic description of Chinese peasant life and masterpieces of biography." Selma Lagerlöf, the Swedish novelist ... who was a member of the Nobel Committee, revealed that she cast her vote in favor of Pearl Buck because of the excellence of Miss Buck's biography of her father. These two facts indicate the importance of what may be called, with incontrovertible accuracy, the Nobel Prize biographies: *The Exile,* a study of Miss Buck's mother, and *Fighting Angel,* a portrait of her father. (p. 76)

While *The Exile* is an amazingly and genuinely frank and complete picture of a missionary wife, it is not without fault. At times the biography becomes too sentimental.... When Pearl is married and when Caroline's beloved brother Cornelius dies, for example, not only does the thought dwell too much on the emotions involved, but the style life itself becomes a bit too flowery, too tender, too romantic for modern taste. Further, *The Exile* is at times too diffuse and repetitive; on occasion it needs to be tightened, to be fixed more firmly on the main materials. But, with all these obvious weaknesses, the portrait drawn of Caroline Sydenstricker remains imprinted in one's memory; and the character analysis is rendered with persuasive depth. (pp. 80-1)

If *The Exile* is a fine biography, *Fighting Angel* (despite an old-fashioned ring in its title) is an even better one. While *The Exile* is on occasion too wordy and too repetitive, *Fighting Angel* is much more taut and focused. Now and then *The Exile* becomes sentimental because Miss Buck admired her mother deeply and was exceptionally devoted to her. Toward her father, however, she is less sympathetic and more objective; hence, the portrait of Absalom Sydenstricker unfolds in a harsher, rougher fashion. (p. 81)

Besides a vividly realized portrait of a human being, there emerges from *Fighting Angel* a compelling delineation of the nineteenth-century type of crusader—the very essence of rock-ribbed individualism, a fiery zeal which, depending upon the direction in which it was channeled, could produce a General Charles Gordon, a John D. Rockefeller, a David Livingstone. Pearl Buck sees her father as a manifestation of a spirit which especially permeated America at a particular time. (p. 84)

In addition to the individual portrait, Pearl Buck graphically depicts missionary life in China, particularly in a closely knit missionary community.... [The] realism and vividness of the work sear into the mind of the reader.

Aside from the elimination of some repetitiousness of idea here and there, perhaps the only way *Fighting Angel* could have been improved would have been to include more instances of Absalom's experiences on his long missionary journeys. (p. 85)

Thematically, *This Proud Heart* is most interesting. The problem of a woman genius—a woman who has both an excellent mind and natural creative talent—who at the same time is desirous of love, motherhood, and normal family life is posed with feeling and realism. (p. 89)

While treatment of the male genius is not especially uncommon in writing, *This Proud Heart* is one of the few mature attempts in fiction to explain and study a woman genius. . . . [The] author has presented Susan's characteristics on a credible level and . . . the conflict between her artistic drives and her romantic needs is sharply defined. Yet Susan is not a completely satisfying creation, principally because Miss Buck's viewing-on-the-outside method of storytelling does not enable us to get deeply enough inside her mind. . . . [We] do not really become convinced by Susan: she is too often aloof and remote from the reader. While external narration may be effective in saga-like chronicles or in biographies, it does not go far enough or deep enough to help us understand Susan's genius more completely and to render her an unforgettable character. A more mental technique of introspection, such as the stream-of-consciousness method, appears necessary in order to bring the problem of genius to a more thorough visualization. The novel is also not helped by surrounding Susan with a handful of stock and type characters. While they never quite succeed in dragging her down to their level, they do dull her luster and weaken our appreciation of her uniqueness.

While the thematic problem posed in *This Proud Heart* intrigues, and the explanation of the problem carries us to about as satisfactory a solution as possible, the novel loses considerable impact because of its stylistic weaknesses. Coming from a reading of the Chinese novels, from a reading of *The Exile* and *Fighting Angel*, one notices immediately the lack of poetic beauty, the lack of exquisite descriptions, and the pedestrian nature of the writing. Many of the phrases are nothing but clichés. . . . The word choice is exceedingly simple, and Miss Buck's selection of nouns and adjectives lacks both variety and a sense of freshness. Further, the dialogue is frequently stiff, forced, and stilted. So ordinary and flat is the style and mechanics of presentation that the overall effect of the novel is reduced. (pp. 89-90)

What is especially evident in this novel is the hard core of mental activity in Pearl Buck's work which continually helps to elevate it above the superficiality of ordinary bestsellers. In her fiction she usually presents some theme which the reader can wrestle with intellectually. Even if the book does not succeed, one feels that he is in the company of an alert and challenging mind which offers much valuable thought and insight. Stylistically, *This Proud Heart* is a disaster; thematically, it has several rewarding moments. (p. 90)

Too often today, Miss Buck is judged on the basis of her work after receiving the Nobel Prize. While it has become a critical commonplace to remark that a writer's best work is always completed before the Nobel Prize is granted (the reward itself seeming always to mark a decline in the writer's talent), this situation is particularly true of Pearl Buck's efforts. In the 1930's she produced several fine books; after this decade she never again reached the same level of achievement. (p. 92)

That Pearl Buck's decline as a novelist was not immediate and that she still could write novels worth attention and discussion was proved by the publication in 1939 of *The Patriot*. (p. 104)

The Patriot possesses considerable value for its insights and explanations of relatively recent Chinese history, so that it furnishes a historical account of political and social importance. . . .

Part Two of the novel, which deals with I-wan's stay in Japan, is by far the most effective section. It presents one of the most realistic and convincing portraits of the Japanese character found in literature. Japanese attitudes of love of country, duty, and endurance are particularly well delineated; and Japanese qualities of delicacy, mannerliness, and love of beauty contrast sharply with their stoicism, militarism, and cruelty. (p. 106)

In writing *The Patriot* Pearl Buck discarded the poetic, semi-biblical style found in the *House of Earth* trilogy. Simplicity of style is retained, but the prose contains no poetry and no melodic movement. Nevertheless, while the style is characterized only by its utter simplicity and its matter-of-factness, it is perfectly suitable to the story being told and fits harmoniously into the narrative movement. It often helps to add a compelling verisimilitude of setting, especially to the Shanghai scenes and to the Japanese episodes.

The third part of *The Patriot* is the least successful. . . . Much of the story manipulation in this last unit of the novel is too apparent and farfetched. . . . *The Patriot* is a cracking good story. It is such a tale as a village storyteller would relate in order to captivate his listeners, but in its final section it suffers from just such liberties as a storyteller too concerned about suspense and tying up loose ends would seize. (p. 108)

The various aspects of hero worship render [*Other Gods*] extremely satisfying on a problem-probing level. Unfortunately, the style does not achieve the level of the theme and the sensitive analysis of the topic discussed. But what might be called Miss Buck's American style has improved. It is more mature, more elaborate, and more pliable than that of *This Proud Heart*. To be sure, it is still only journeyman prose, and the writing does not delight or scintillate as does Miss Buck's Chinese style. The novel is also weakened by some obvious manipulations geared to keep up suspense. . . . The novel also has a peculiar bloodless quality, due partly to the style, but due also to an attempt to avoid the more realistic aspects of mob worship. It is only the problem studied in its various manifestations, the intellectual hard-core of Pearl Buck's work, which raises the book above mere popular contrivance. (p. 112)

The Mayli episode is the chief factor in the failure of *Dragon Seed* to achieve artistic success. The Mayli material is a disastrous attempt to intrude romantic materials into a context of realism. (p. 119)

Pearl Buck's handling of the Mayli material illustrates a pitfall of the natural storyteller's technique—a pitfall to which Miss Buck succumbs more and more in her post-Nobel Prize work and which comes to blemish most of the later novels at some point or other. . . . Make-believe romance has intruded on basically realistic material and has reduced the impact of authenticity of event and logic of character portrayal.

Another defect displayed in *Dragon Seed* is a conscious attempt to use the novel as a vehicle for patriotic propaganda. This aspect is most obvious in the radio news scenes which bring the Chinese a knowledge that their fight is part of a world-wide struggle against evil. . . . [*Dragon Seed*] was predicated on the need and desirability of more active support for China, and it definitely had been intended to arouse sympathy for the Chinese cause.

While the intrusion of farfetched romance and evident propaganda mar the novel, *Dragon Seed* contains much to make it worth while. Its most attractive feature is its style. Pearl Buck had not used the early semi-biblical, semi-traditional style since *A House Divided*. This prose, particularly effective in *The Good Earth*, is handled with considerable success in *Dragon Seed*. Simple, often poetic, pliable, fitting the material with a picturesqueness, the prose of *Dragon Seed* satisfies both the eye and ear. Many of the passages could, with a few word changes, seem to be the work of Hemingway. . . . In the sustained excellence of its style *Dragon Seed* comes close to *The Good Earth;* its prose does not, however, possess so much poetry and color as Miss Buck's most famous novel.

Other similarities between *Dragon Seed* and *The Good Earth* are apparent. The same deep feeling for the value of the land is present in both books, and the same quiet tone and the chronological approach concentrating on the lives of two generations characterize the two novels. *The Good Earth*, however, rises to several climaxes; *Dragon Seed* tends to move in an even, steady manner without crucial elevations of interest. Both stories contain a realism which, at times, verges on Zola-like Naturalism. . . . The novel renders Japanese behavior vividly and disturbingly. If, in fact, *Dragon Seed* had kept to a more probable story line, divorced romance from realism, and retained the authorial objectivity demonstrated in *The Good Earth*, it could have rivaled Miss Buck's Pulitzer Prize novel in several ways. (pp. 119-21)

The Promise [a sequel to *Dragon Seed*] is very recent history fictionalized. . . . [The book] takes on historical importance because it is a thoughtful, challenging explanation of the disaster which overtook the Chinese in Burma. (p. 122)

The Promise is, in almost every way, out and out propaganda, a patriotic and stirring appeal for the Chinese cause. The prejudice of the white men, their feelings of superiority over Asians, their refusal to treat the Chinese with equality, the harm that these attitudes are causing in the war against Japan—these matters are reiterated throughout the novel. . . .

Since the novel is so dominated by propaganda, it possesses little artistic value.

Only one of the John Sedges books [i.e., those written under Pearl Buck's pseudonym], *The Townsman*, is of especial importance. Unless a person had inside information, he would never guess that Pearl Buck authored *The Townsman* since the settings and characters are totally different from those found in her previous books on American subjects. (pp. 125-26)

The finest feature of the book is its success in presenting the authentic flavor of the early settlements in the West. . . .

In addition to the realism of background details and of some of the basic incidents, the novel's dialogue evinces much credibility. Considerable attention is given to dialectal forms, to picturesque expressions, and to quaint oddities of word choice and sentence construction. The style of the book does not distinguish itself except where the dialectal elements and the picturesque speech give the novel a pleasantly natural coloring. The non-dialogue writing does not consist of the semi-biblical style found in the early novels about China; it is rather an ordinary, commonplace, and undistinguished prose most similar to the style used in *Other Gods*.

While much of *The Townsman* attracts because of its realistic flavor, the book also possesses definite appeal because of its central character—Jonathan Goodliffe. Jonathan is a thoughtful, prudent, upright individual "too ready to think of work instead of play." (p. 126)

Jonathan Goodliffe is well depicted. His motives and feelings make sense; his life, his ideas, and his influence on the life of Median possess the genuine feel of truth. Unfortunately, he is too drab and colorless an individual to make a Dickensian impact on the reader's consciousness. (pp. 127-28)

The Townsman has value as a chronology of an American pioneering family and of the growth of a prairie town; however, it is weakened by several story improbabilities, by several type characters, and by some overly obvious propaganda. . . .

The sermon about racial prejudice in America jars the story line out of logical development and pushes some of the characters to a secondary role since they exist not in or for themselves but simply to help draw a moral. Didactic concerns mar certain parts of the book. (p. 128)

All of the John Sedges books are competently written, but only several sections of *The Townsman* and the vivid portrait of a minor character, Lew Harrow, in *The Long Love* exceed mere journeyman competence. Pearl Buck proves that she can write entertainingly and informatively on a wide variety of American subject matter, but the John Sedges novels display relatively little feeling for depth and for effectively realized characterization. The overemphasis on message and the general feeling of elation that everything will turn out all right give them a Victorian quality which often rests on sentimentalism and is unworthy of the talent behind their conception. (p. 129)

[*Pavilion of Women* has] much to recommend it. First of all, the style is poetic, lush, and colorful. Deliberately romantic in tone, it is most reminiscent of the first part of *East Wind: West Wind*. While the style is often exuberant and exotic, it is in perfect keeping with its subject matter. The setting of an old, rich, and comfortable Chinese family receives an added luster and charm as the style blends perfectly with the scene. Second, Pearl Buck evinces as much knowledge of the customs and activities of a wealthy Chinese family as she does of the peasant groups. The background and details are thorough and convincing; time and place sweep into the mind with genuine verisimilitude. Third, *Pavilion of Women* exists as one of the most vivid demonstrations of Miss Buck's uncanny ability to invent fresh episodes and to entangle her characters in imaginative situations which exemplify never-flagging interest, variety, and considerable narrative pull.

Because of the significance of the theme—the question of personal meaning and immortality—and style excellence, *Pavilion of Women* should be an important and memorable novel. Such is not the case. Its failure stems from an overly evident manipulation of the narrative to support Miss Buck's didactic purpose: to prove the value of selfless love and devotion to others. . . . Seemingly insolvable problems are either resolved easily or simply pacified. Every knot can be untied or loosened if one acts with selfless intent and altruistic consideration, Miss Buck too obviously implies. And, while the reader would like this to be true, he knows from experience that this is simply not true—or at least not in as uncomplicated a way as Miss Buck would have it. An oversimplification and an unfortunate sentimentalism have set in. A sentimentalism, which Miss Buck would have scorned in books such as *The Good Earth* or *The Mother,* has, unfortunately, come to the forefront more and more often in Pearl Buck's post-1939 fiction. (pp. 132-33)

With the important exception of a relatively brief section of *A House Divided* and such novels as *Other Gods* and *China Gold,* Pearl Buck generally kept her work on American and Chinese subject matter separated. Relatively late in her writing career, however, she produced several novels of descriptive value and thematic interest in which the worlds of the West and the East met within the pages of one book. The possibilities for illuminating comparison and contrast between two countries, which Miss Buck had, up to this point, largely subordinated to portraits of one area, are best exemplified in *Kinfolk.* (p. 134)

Although its plot is too plainly contrived, *Kinfolk* is critically interesting because it is an amalgam of the strong and weak points in Miss Buck's later work. The main themes are well conceived and credible. The picture of life in Anming is exceptionally vivid, instructive, and meaningful; the characteristics of the hamlet stand forth with stark boldness. The scenes in America are less persuasive, although the Chinatown impressions furnish novelty. Unfortunately, too many popular touches are mixed into the ingredients. . . .

In short, *Kinfolk* is a potpourri, a distinct example of the effect of trying to blend unsuccessfully ingredients belonging to two different kinds of novels—the "serious" and the "popular." (p. 137)

Closely related to [her didactic novel] *Command the Morning* in its concern with the morality of the atomic bomb's use is Pearl Buck's play *A Desert Incident.* (p. 140)

In order to reinforce the framework of *A Desert Incident* Pearl Buck does, for her, an unusual thing: she uses symbolism. . . .

Miss Buck's venture into symbolism is disastrous, partly because she attempts to cover too many areas of life. As Brooks Atkinson noted in his review of the play, the drama is so "overloaded with points of view that it leaves its main theme as anticlimax." Further, her use of symbolism is alternately grandiose and overly simple so that a jarring incongruity results between what the symbolism intends to do and what it actually says. Her symbolism obfuscates where it should enlighten, and it is thoroughly deficient in both appropriateness and subtlety. (p. 141)

In looking back over the career of Pearl Buck, one may draw some evaluation of her literary status. Although she has been virtually ignored by critics for over twenty years, it may be maintained with much justification that she has written at least three books of undoubted significance: *The*

Good Earth and the biographies of her father and mother. Certainly, *The Good Earth* is a masterpiece that will be remembered by subsequent generations as a work which powerfully and movingly describes a whole way of life. Although it perhaps seemed more immediate during the depression years, its universality of theme and the beauty of its style should render it timeless.

The two Nobel Prize biographies are among the most deeply felt and penetrating analyses in any literature of the missionary caught in an alien climate, the demands of the missionary life, and the concomitant reaction to such demands. While Absalom Sydenstricker exemplifies the very essence of the drive and intensity of the nineteenth-century missionary spirit, his wife Caroline symbolizes the perennial demands of humanity for a more compromising balance between flesh and spirit.

Several of Pearl Buck's other books—particularly, *Sons, The Mother,* and *The Patriot*—possess moments of greatness. Although they do not achieve the heights they sought, they do contain many notable sections, several compelling episodes, and make use of an intrinsically poetic and arresting style.

At about the time of the Nobel Award—actually after the completion of *The Patriot*—Pearl Buck's writing career certainly seemed to be in the ascent, and to promise further important achievement. After this period, however, Pearl Buck's humanitarian preoccupations seemed to increase. These interests, carried into her fiction, immediately weakened the objectivity of her creation. She began to assert didactic considerations to such an excessive degree that novels such as *Dragon Seed* and *The Promise* become propaganda efforts on behalf of China's struggle against Japan. (pp. 150-51)

After 1939 she became more facile at constructing her plots, handling dialogue, and in the technical aspects of her craft; but no subsequent significant growth in the artistic features of novel writing occurred in Pearl Buck's work. No experimentation in technique took place, and she made no attempt to penetrate more deeply into character analysis, showed no willingness to seek subtleties of tone or mood, and indicated no interest in using myth or symbolism or other elements characteristic of the modern novel. On this account alone Miss Buck must be neglected by some of the more recent literary critics because her total disregard of such concerns as myth and archetype, stream-of-consciousness, and symbolism gives critics very little to analyze and explicate. Her novels do not furnish the layers of meaning and the complexity which modern literary criticism demands. (pp. 151-52)

In addition to her refusal to adopt more modern techniques in her handling of the novel and her post-Nobel Prize obsession with didacticism, several other factors are involved in her lack of popularity with the more influential literary critics. For one thing her work has suffered from the inevitable critical reaction against her best-seller status. (p. 153)

Another factor in Pearl Buck's loss of prestige in serious literary circles stems from her optimistic, affirmative point of view. She has not lost her faith in progress, and she exalts a Rousseau-Thomas Paine Transcendental type of belief in the innate goodness of most men. . . . On the other hand, bleak pessimism, subjective studies of anguish, and searing indictments of humanity are very much the fashion at the moment. (p. 154)

[Let us remember] that Miss Buck is following a certain school of novel writing, and in her literary work of the 1930's she adheres to the characteristics of this school rather well. Judged by her standards—"to please and to amuse," to relate a captivating story, and to deal with significant problems—Miss Buck must be granted considerable success. (p. 155)

Even admitting Miss Buck's success with the most pronounced aspects of the old-fashioned Chinese school of storytelling, one comes, in the long run, to feel that this type of writing possesses inherent defects. For example, it tends to lead to farfetched episodes and improbable occurrences; it also usually does not probe the characters as deeply as possible. In these circumstances characterization can easily become somewhat superficial, and the characters can veer toward types rather than toward individualism. The traditional storytelling method has elements which are too limited and too narrow to lead to the highest peaks of art. This ancient form of narration pointed an easy way and, thereby, artistically hampered Miss Buck's possibilities. (pp. 155-56)

> *Paul A. Doyle, in his* Pearl S. Buck *(copyright 1965 by Twayne Publishers, Inc.; reprinted with the permission of Twayne Publishers, A Division of G. K. Hall & Co., Boston), Twayne, 1965.*

*   *   *

BUTOR, Michel   1926-

Butor is a French novelist, essayist, philosopher, translator, editor, and author of children's books. Numbered among the New Novelists, Butor defies true literary classification in his disregard for traditional forms. In an attempt to give his reader new tools for examining reality, Butor combines elements of poetry and philosophy with innovative structural ideas. He experiments with interior monologue, surreal imagery, and a shifting time factor to create a complex and highly original fictive language. The influences of Proust, Kafka, Faulkner, and Joyce can be felt in his work. Butor has also made a number of interdisciplinary artistic contributions, working with serialist composer Henri Pousseur to create the opera *Votre Faust,* supplying a text to the photographs of Ansel Adams and Edward Weston in *Illustrations I,* and working as both writer and illustrator with Gregory Masurovky on a 1976 issue of *Obliques.* He has also collaborated with Maria Grazia Oltolenghi on *Tout d'oeuvre,* and is the author of numerous essays on music and painting. Butor received the Prix Renaudot for *La Modification* in 1957. (See also *CLC*, Vols. 1, 3, 8, and *Contemporary Authors,* Vols. 9-12, rev. ed.)

VIVIAN MERCIER

Michel Butor occupies a paradoxical situation in what we may call the hierarchy of the *nouveau roman.* On the one hand, he has written four novels of unquestionable though uneven merit.... On the other hand, he has published a series of brilliant articles on the theory of the novel, to be found in his volumes of criticism, *Répertoire* and *Répertoire II,* which have made him at least as important an expounder of the newness of the New Novel as Alain Robbe-Grillet or Nathalie Sarraute; yet it can be shown that all his novels except the last break very little new ground and owe much of their success primarily to Butor's mastery of those old-fashioned components, plot and characterization.

Naturally, this mastery appears most strikingly in Butor's

most popular novel, *La Modification (A Change of Heart)* [(1957)]. (p. 215)

The scope of the novel is restricted to one man's reflections, memories, dreams, and perceptions during a railroad journey between Paris and Rome which lasts not quite twenty-four hours (21 hours, 35 minutes, to be exact). Within this larger restriction an even narrower one is imposed, for we are not allowed to share this one man's experience directly except when he is occupying a third-class compartment that seats eight passengers when full.... What he does in these intervals outside the compartment is made known to us only by anticipation or by memory, if he happens to remember.

As a result, the reader shares much of the protagonist's claustrophobic reaction to his confinement.... A rather simple grammatical device intensifies the reader's identification with the protagonist: the whole experience is narrated in the second person. (p. 216)

The basic structural element in *A Change of Heart* is, quite simply, a timetable, a train schedule.... Like every such timetable, it translates time into space and space into time: "This train will stop at Dijon and leave again at 11:18, it will pass through Bourg at 1:20 p.m., leave Aix-les-Bains at 2:41...."... (p. 221)

In each of Butor's three other novels we shall find a schema—usually in some sense a timetable—by which time and place are intimately related. The characteristically punning title of his second novel, *L'Emploi du Temps* (*Passing Time*...), means "timetable" as well as "daily routine" and, most literally, "use of (one's) time."

In every Butor novel, however, alongside this logical, mechanistic, workaday schema, we can trace a totally different type of structural device: intuitive, artistic, nocturnal. Dreams, myths, rituals, works of art (real or imaginary) are used separately or in combination as analogues of the characters' experience in what we may call the objective or materialistic or daylight world.

In *A Change of Heart* this nocturnal element consists mainly of a continuous dream which Léon takes up at the point where he had left off, each time he falls briefly asleep during his uncomfortable and exhausting night on the train. This dream or nightmare contains elements of a *rite de passage* or initiation ritual: Léon is undergoing an ordeal, but more and more he begins to feel that he is on trial; the dream becomes toward the end a vision of judgment. (p. 223)

[There is an] extremely old-fashioned character analysis in *A Change of Heart.* True, Henriette [Léon's wife] is a dim figure and Cécile [his mistress] an over-idealized one, but this is because we see them only through Léon's eyes. His estimate of them is one of the touches which contribute to an extremely lifelike portrait of a man of forty-five whose neck is being chafed by the marriage yoke. Butor works very contentedly within the French classical tradition of character drawing, presenting Léon as at one and the same time an individual and a type. Without intervening to comment in his own person, Butor can still make us aware of the detached irony with which he often views his protagonist. (p. 225)

A Change of Heart, then, has a great deal in common with the traditional novel. What links it and Butor's other novels most closely with *le nouveau roman* as a school is the almost obsessive concern with structure, though this seems unnecessary in a work that is already held tightly together by a logical plot. It is plotless novels that need to be given form by the use of schemas or myths.

Other characteristics of the New Novel to be found in *A Change of Heart* are the readiness to make unheralded shifts from one level of time to another and the interest in ''point of view'' that leads to the experiment of writing an entire novel in the second person. The employment of stream-of-consciousness technique is peculiarly appropriate in a story whose main action is internal, psychological. (p. 226)

Passage de Milan (1954 . . .) compresses into its punning title the *locale,* the catastrophe, and one of the myths with which it deals. 15 Passage de Milan is a seven-story apartment building (with a basement, naturally) in Paris. The little street on which it stands is presumably named after the Italian city, but the French word *milan* . . . can mean ''kite'' in the sense of a bird of prey. . . . (pp. 226-27)

[*Passage de Milan* reveals a] schema, which bulks as large in this novel as in the other three. Briefly, it consists of the multiple levels of the apartment building, the channels of communication between them, and the timetable of the movements of all the occupants and their visitors from floor to floor and in and out of the building. It will help the reader greatly to understand from the beginning that each of the twelve chapters into which the book is divided corresponds to an hour on the clock, from seven in the evening until seven in the morning, the hour which rings out from the clock tower of the neighboring convent in the last sentence of the book. (p. 227)

[Almost] all the inhabitants of the building have been brought into contact with each other through their awareness of the party on the fourth floor. And this party was of a special kind, a festival celebrating the passage from adolescence to adulthood. (p. 231)

[During] a large part of the book, one is not conscious of the presence of a narrator at all. The frequent passages of third-person, past-tense narration presuppose the telling of a story by *someone, after* the events. But this kind of impersonal, omniscient narration is too familiar to attract our attention. Hardly more disturbing is the still more frequent use of present-tense narration in the third person; this of course brings us much closer to the events than the past-tense narration with which it alternates—without, one feels, very compelling reasons for the shifts back and forth. Occasionally, however, we are made very conscious of a narrator who is inviting us to stand by him and observe what is happening. . . . (pp. 232-33)

L'Emploi du Temps (1956), Butor's second novel . . . is a less ambitious, less experimental work than *Passage de Milan.* The events are recounted in the first person and past and present tenses by a single, clearly identified narrator. . . . Because of one's constant, even oppressive awareness of the presence of a narrator, there is never any doubt as to who is speaking or thinking. Paradoxically, however, just because we are limited to a single viewpoint, we can never be sure of the trustworthiness of the narrator's reports of events or his interpretation of them; we have been robbed of the illusion that we are able to see and judge events for ourselves.

Butor has exploited the basic untrustworthiness of all one-sided narration as brilliantly as any novelist before him. One cannot deny that *Passing Time . . .* has a plot, but one is tempted to add that it has two: a subjective one and an objective one. (p. 239)

Once again, in *Passing Time,* we can trace a schema and a myth—two myths, in fact—as well as a plot. And once again the schema involves both time and place.

The time element is the more significant of the two, for the book is in essence a *recherche du temps perdu.* . . . Instead of the past forcing its way into the present, as in Proust, we find the present forcing its way into a narrative concerned with the past. (pp. 242-43)

Usually, when a mythical parallel is used in a modern novel (as in Joyce's *Ulysses*), its existence is only hinted at and the reader is left to work out the parallel himself. By making the parallel explicit but erroneous [as for example in *Passing Time*], Butor creates an ironic flavor unique in such use of myth. (p. 246)

The style which Butor has devised for the neurotic, almost psychotic, Jacques [the novel's protagonist] is obsessive nearly everywhere that it is not apocalyptic. Sentences several paragraphs in length are held together by the repetition of key phrases, often containing a relative pronoun. (p. 247)

Butor uses [a] kind of prose poetry, these paragraph-long clauses, much more sparingly in *La Modification,* but an outstanding characteristic of Butor's prose throughout his novels is [a] reaching after a sustained melody, usually elegiac in tone. The proliferating relative clauses, often strung together in chains, create a feeling of free association—each memory that surges up begets another, which recalls another, which prompts a fourth, which leads to a fifth, which . . . and so on. (p. 249)

[*Degrés* (*Degrees*, 1960) is], for me, his most ambitious and original work in the genre—yet, at the same time, because of its very ambition and originality, an artistic failure. Although it does in fact come to an end in less than four hundred pages, it seems—and in one sense actually is—interminable. . . . The only solution Butor finds to the problem of bringing the machinery to a stop is to kill off his narrator, or rather to have his narrator collapse under the magnitude of his self-imposed task, as Jacques Revel [of *Passing Time*] almost did. This device seems an abdication, on the part of the novelist, of his artistic function. (p. 250)

[By] and large, we find [in *Degrees*] little of the irony that seemed evident in *A Change of Heart.* One feels that Butor, like his narrator, had made up his mind to write this book, and so gritted his teeth and went through with it. (p. 254)

Degrees, like its immediate predecessor, *A Change of Heart,* is written in the second person. But this time the intimate second person singular, *tu,* is used throughout. . . . (p. 255)

The shift in viewpoint from Part I to Part II should permit us to see school life through a student's eyes instead of a teacher's, but since Vernier is really still the narrator and since he has relied on information supplied by his nephew in Part I, we are not conscious of much change of perspective. (p. 256)

In Butor's other novels we could draw a hard-and-fast

boundary line between the schemas and the myths, but in *Degrees* we can no longer do so. [The] notion of a culture that can be transmitted to the next generation, of a standardized education that can be imposed upon the individual, is the underlying myth of *Degrees*. . . . [As] we read passage after passage describing what secondary education actually consists of in the classroom, we feel that we are watching the enactment of inexplicable rites, sanctioned by a body of myth that everybody takes on trust. (p. 259)

Degrees resembles *Passage de Milan* more than it does the two intervening novels. Although not all of the later novel takes place in the school building, we do see parallels between the many-storied *lycée* and the apartment building. In both books, Butor is trying to handle the relationships of a large number of characters in space and time. In both, the portrayal of individual character is subordinated to the achievement of an overall effect and an overall structure, though the characters in the earlier book are considerably more interesting and more successful in arousing our sympathy. In both books there is still a plot, but the catastrophe, which is inadequately prepared for, completely overshadows the other elements of the plot.

In *Degrees* Butor has created a doctrinaire example of the New Novel in which everything else has been subordinated to an essentially arbitrary structure that bears little relation to the rudimentary plot. This structure is, as he has said, a sort of descriptive machine—and furthermore a machine that, like some of Queneau's novelistic structures and some examples of contemporary "sculpture," destroys itself. (pp. 263-64)

In all of Butor's novels we find a determined attempt to adapt form to content. . . . Butor has insisted that new literary techniques make possible the discovery of new subject matter and, conversely, that the discovery of a new subject matter demands the evolution of a new technique to deal with it. Also, his seemingly rigid schemas are instruments of discovery which serve to "provoke inspiration." . . . In a sense, a myth too is a schema, a structure borrowed from the past instead of the present, but it is a less rigid structure than the true schema—open to all sorts of interpretations and containing many ambiguities. The dialectic established between the schemas and the myths, especially in *Passing Time,* is Butor's most original contribution to the practice of the novel and provokes some of his most evocative writing. (p. 264)

> *Vivian Mercier, "Michel Butor: The Schema and the Myth," in his* The New Novel: From Queneau to Pinget *(reprinted with the permission of Farrar, Straus & Giroux, Inc.; copyright © 1966, 1967, 1968, 1971 by Vivian Mercier), Farrar, Straus, 1971, pp. 215-65.*

LUCILLE BECKER

[Butor's] journals stand in the same relationship to other works of this type as do his novels to the traditional novel, for in both he refuses to interpret. Instead, he solicits the participation of the reader whose collaboration becomes an essential part of the book. . . .

Time plays an important part in *Où. Le génie du lieu 2,* as it does in all of the author's work. Past, present and future are mixed. Weather conditions also figure prominently and impressions predominate of mud in Seoul, rain at Angkor, fog at Santa Barbara, and snow in New Mexico. Above all,

the book is governed by an ambivalent love-hate relationship with Paris. There are sections entitled, "I Fled Paris," and "I Hate Paris," but the last words of the journal are grouped together in the form of a love poem to the city to which he is inexorably drawn. "All of the trips I take," he concludes, "are to the beat of your pulse." (p. 443)

> *Lucille Becker, in* Books Abroad *(copyright 1972 by the University of Oklahoma Press), Vol. 46, No. 3, Summer, 1972.*

KATHLEEN O'NEILL

Michel Butor's *Passing Time* is a story in which the detective hunts himself. In this circular, self-contained structure any connection with an external reality is tenuous. Is Bleston really so oppressive, or is Revel extremely paranoid? Did he actually commit any crime? The reader cannot be sure, for he perceives reality only as it is reflected in the narrative of which Revel is both writer and actor. Indeed, the only certain reality is Revel's consciousness where he plays criminal, detective and victim simultaneously and where his fate is determined by the interplay of these internal agents, whose behaviour is spurred, but not designed, by external circumstance. (pp. 29-30)

On the most obvious level, *Passing Time* is written in the first person, the subjective voice of the self. Yet this same voice embodies both second and third person narration. For Revel is not only writer but reader of his own journal, becoming by benefit of both knowledge and time a more objective, third person narrator. Finally, near the end of the novel he disassociates himself from his plot and speaking as if to another, accuses himself of deception. By this tri-partite narration, an all-encompassing consciousness is created, which writes, interprets, acts and reacts in its fictional world. It traverses the range from total subjectivity to apparent objectivity, becoming a world in itself. Still, at base, the world it creates is profoundly subjective, entirely narrated in the divided, yet single, voice of the self. The question, then, is not what bearing this voice has to some external reality, but what its role is in respect to itself. (p. 30)

The concordance of these three persons, the writer, the reader and the detective, in one voice reflects a creative consciousness which simultaneously obscures and elucidates its obsessions. I will resist the temptation to draw an analogy between the three voices and the Freudian superego, ego and id, though Revel's story contains other classically Freudian elements: as sexual trauma, repression, sublimation and the like. Nevertheless, the psychological implications of Revel's narrative are fairly explicit even without a psychoanalytic construct.

Ironically, the first person voice which wants to explain things does the most to obscure them, creating a fantastic causal connection between a chance remark and an automobile accident, or drawing grandiose parallels between Revel and mythical heroes. But this is the voice of the self, which is concerned not with truth but with self-preservation. Beset by loneliness and fears of inadequacy, the first person voice tries to distract itself, to cloak the fact of its impotence, or to vent its frustrations in unthreatening ways. Thus, rather than compete with James Jenkins for Ann's attention, this voice creates a great murder plot in which James is the prime suspect. Revel's fictional world is an attempt to deal with his problems by masking them.

Nevertheless, the truth will out, and Revel, despite his obfuscation discovers the fact of his impotence through his fictionalizing. In fact he takes to writing in horror of the one concrete act he performs in the novel, that trivial act of repudiation in which he burns the map of Bleston. The second and third person voices, more objective, less intimately bound to the self, reveal that Revel has written rather than act, denying the first voice its escape into fiction.

Thus Revel is the victim of his own psyche which reveals that he is in fact guilty of a crime, but not the one which he imagined. "My betrayal of George Burton hurt no one but myself." By his refusal to act on his needs and desires, Revel has betrayed only himself, condemning himself to continued isolation. This discovery gives Revel a new self-understanding, but it seems a poor victory. In coming to understand himself, it appears that he has killed a part of that self, the emotional and creative part, creative though irrational and escapist. . . . He has been reduced to a voice, still filling in gaps, the importance of which neither he nor the reader can any longer believe. . . . (pp. 31-2)

In Jacques Revel, Michel Butor has illustrated the twin dangers of the creative process. The writer runs the risk, first of all, of becoming enmeshed in his own fiction. Having created a pattern to illustrate reality, he may be seduced by the fiction, finding in it justification for his avoidance of that external reality he originally sought to explain. He can work out his fantasies, anxieties and frustrations without fear of consequence. Yet, he will only be "Passing Time" since this denies him any life apart from the solitary pleasure of an imaginative existence, where action becomes unnecessary, if not impossible.

The other possibility is that the writer will construct his fictional world, and upon understanding it will extricate himself from it. This is what the detective, Revel, does when he realizes that the purpose of his narrative was not to elucidate reality but to obscure it. "The pattern is complete and I am left out of it." . . . The problem here is that where Revel was once too involved in his subject, now he is too distant. He seems emotionally barren, neither his earlier neurotic, escapist self, nor a well adjusted participant, but merely an empty shell.

Perhaps it is too much to ask that Jacques Revel grasp the full significance of his own story. Perhaps we are to understand that a narrow path must be trod between comprehending one's life and retaining some subjective attachment. Michel Butor's detached and yet sympathetic creation gives us a model. (pp. 32-3)

Kathleen O'Neill, "On 'Passing Time'," in MOSAIC: A Journal for the Study of Literature and Ideas *(copyright © 1974 by The University of Manitoba Press; acknowledgement of previous publication is herewith made), Vol. VIII, No. 1, (Fall, 1974), pp. 29-37.*

THOMAS D. O'DONNELL

Butor, as a writer and artist, finds himself in a somewhat awkward position. On the one hand, he subscribes to the theory that his ideal reader must be encouraged and/or coerced to participate actively in the work of art: the reader's effort must be commensurate with that of the author, and Butor finds himself open to accusations of literary elitism and hermeticism. On the other hand, Butor does not accept the human condition as it stands, socio-politically or intellectually. Echoing Rimbaud, Butor insists that life be

"changed": "Any literature which does not help us toward this end is eventually, and inevitably, condemned." Ironically, a single theme, that of *alchemy,* suffices to emblematize the contradictory dictates of hermeticism and didacticism.

Butor, like most modern scholars, sees alchemy . . . as a tradition of knowledge into which one must first be initiated in order to become, ultimately, an adept. The transformation of matter is a metaphor for a more arduous and elusive spiritual transformation; the true, and subversive, nature of this ultimate science is hidden from the uninitiated through the use of a system of codes to be deciphered; the keys to aid this decoding are to be found in the *Book,* passed down from the adept to the initiates.

Butor's interpretation of the basic nature of alchemy is admirably suited to becoming the basis of an entire aesthetic theory. If Butor's purpose is no less ambitious than the incredible goal of "changing life," he must begin by changing himself. Butor described his own initiation in a "capriccio" published in 1967, entitled *A Portrait of the Artist as a Young Monkey.* In this very Joycean and vaguely autobiographical work, Butor recounts how several years after World War II, he spent seven weeks in a Bavarian castle, and how he dreamed that he was transformed by a vampire into a monkey, able to reverse the transmutation only after diverse trials and tribulations. (p. 150)

On the narrative level, several physical transformations are involved. On an aesthetic level, the number of transmutations in *Portrait* is greater.

The student Butor himself is first transformed into an artist, or at least into a potential artist, through the imitation (i.e., the aping, as a young monkey) of his predecessors and through a "voyage of initiation." This trip leads him to a "derangement of the senses" and finally to an ability to decipher what Baudelaire would have called the "confused words" which he finds surrounding him. (pp. 150-51)

By writing about the mysteries encountered, the artist transforms reality by transferring it to the plane of fiction.

If he is successful, the artist will ultimately transform reality itself, in its own realm. Butor understands Rimbaud's insistence upon the alteration of life through art in a very literal sense. While not actually a political polemicist, Butor is far from being a pure aesthete, as there is a social lesson to be found in everything he writes.

Finally, after the artist has decoded his reality, he *recodes* it, or rearranges it, in artistic form. One effect of this procedure is to make the Butorian book rather difficult to read. The reader must make the appropriate effort, after all, if he wishes his own way of seeing life to be transformed.

The monkey of Butor's title is not to be interpreted as simply an ironic tribute to Stephen Dedalus. Rather, it serves to link Butor's *Portrait* to the iconography of alchemy. . . . Furthermore, Butor reminds us in *Portrait,* "In Egypt, the god of writing, Thoth, was often depicted as a monkey." . . .

The appearance of Thoth not only provides an additional link between art and the image of the monkey, but also introduces the theme of Egypt. Egypt is thematically appropriate to *Portrait,* because of the possible Egyptian origins of the art of alchemy. . . . More importantly, it is to Egypt that the future writer of *Portrait* will go to be reborn as an artist.

The myth of rebirth goes hand in hand with the myth of the transmutation of metals, and, more generally, with the entire European hermetic tradition. Moreover, this thematic element of *Portrait* determines the very structure of the *capriccio. Portrait* is based on the number seven, and specifically on the seven days of the week.... Playing on the fact that the French week ends on Sunday while the German week ends on Saturday, Butor is able to create a chronological cycle in which endings are identified with beginnings. Thus *Portrait* does not "end"; instead it may serve as an introduction to Butor's other works. (p. 151)

[A set of colors associated with the phases of preparation of the philosopher's stone appears] over one hundred times in *Portrait,* in references to eye coloration and clothing.... [The eye] colors go from flavescent to crimson lake and back again, completing the cycle appropriate to any alchemical work. Clothing colors, on the other hand, are patterned in a fairly straight progression. Thus Butor's seemingly arbitrary choice of colors in *Portrait* reinforces the book's structure, that of a circle superimposed on a straight line.

Portrait of the Artist as a Young Monkey is, among other things, a key which Butor gives his readers to help decipher the works written before (and after) *Portrait*'s publication. Alchemy, in whatever sense we may attribute to it, is primarily concerned with transformation. Each of Butor's novels deals in some way with a very human form of transformation, the *rites de passage*.... In each case, plot follows the same pattern, as ... [in typical] initiation ceremonies. The protagonist, male, undergoes a transformation, usually against his will. He is separated from the comforts of female companionship and is forced to undergo a ritual death and some form of discomfort or hardship. Following his ordeal, he is reborn, or is at least given the promise of possible rebirth. The end result, generally, is a *book*....

Butor's art is an effort to transform the world and simultaneously to transform the self—tasks certainly more arduous than merely changing lead into gold. Thus, although part of the very modern *nouveau roman,* he participates in the tradition of the literature of alchemy. Butor the artist transforms the reader; the reader, having been initiated, must then transform the world. (p. 152)

Thomas D. O'Donnell, "Michel Butor and the Tradition of Alchemy," in The International Fiction Review, *July, 1975, pp. 150-53.*

VALERIE MINOGUE

In his various novels, Butor explores the nature of reality and the part imagination plays in our perception—or creation—of it.

In *L'Emploi du Temps* [*Passing Time*], many different elements of experience come together in Revel's narrative of his experience in Bleston. His affective experience, for instance, is intimately associated with his cultural experience—his response, among other things, to a detective novel, to various films, to the Theseus tapestry seen in Bleston Town Hall, and to Bleston's two cathedrals. Jacques Revel in Bleston is an individual consciousness set at a point of confluence which he uniquely registers and interprets. (p. 42)

Butor's novel is narrated in the first-person, which ... allows the observation of conscious processes in the narrating mind. We are not, as it were, plugged in to an unselfconscious being ..., who unwittingly distorts all he sees, but are introduced instead into the preoccupations of a highly conscious and self-conscious narrator, who reflects on the limitations and distortions involved in his grasp of his experience.... [There] is here a conscious process of examination, comparison, selection and organisation.... When Revel, on the first of May, recounts his arrival in Bleston the previous October, he does so with the full awareness of the time that has elapsed, and with the deliberate determination to achieve lucidity. The rain on the windows of his compartment ... is already a significant image of the myriad mirrors he encounters in the course of his stay in Bleston, from the actual mirrors in the Bailey and Burton households, to the metaphorical mirrors of consciousness in which each image is multiplied and modified.

Jacques Revel is a Theseus who must make his way through the labyrinth of false impressions, and destroy the Minotaur, Bleston: he is a detective of his own experience, who must identify and bring to justice Bleston, the murderer of his consciousness.... The function of the journal for Revel, and of the novel for Butor, is to achieve lucidity, while also reconstructing the poetic and mysterious relationships suggested by experience. *L'Emploi du Temps* is Revel's effort to grasp his experience.... The emphasis lies on the act of construction of the narrative, on the organisation of representations of reality, as they become available to the narrator. And the narrator has problems, for he exists both in a complex associative and emotional world, and in the world of time.

He inhabits a confusing world of mirrors, repetitions and similarities which suggest parallels, but are not identities. Each object and person in the novel has its "reflet" or echo. There are two stations, Bleston New Station and Bleston Hamilton, Hamilton also being the pseudonym under which the writer George Burton publishes his detective fiction. There are three similar Chinese restaurants; a fair moves about the city on eight different sites; Revel has two copies of the detective novel, two maps of Bleston; there are two sisters, two Frenchmen; Theseus is doubled with Oedipus; there are two cathedrals, the old and the new; there are seven different murder systems, reflecting one another. This labyrinth that Revel moves through is not a once-for-all invention; it is not stable. (pp. 42-4)

In this shifting labyrinth of appearances, Revel's perception is weakened by forgetfulness—and is, in any case, always selective. The selection is made according to preoccupation, and new events create new preoccupations. Thus Revel finds serious gaps in his account.... Perception is all too open to error: what we give all our attention to may turn out insignificant, while things scarcely noticed may turn out, in the shifting perspectives of time, to have been capital.... There is the further complication that while we are involved in retrospection, life goes on providing us endlessly with more information and more experience, while we are still sorting out what we have already. There is always hope, however, that lucidity will prevail.... (p. 44)

Apart from the problem of shifting focus, due to the action of time, observation itself, in Butor's novels, ... is far from static; the parallels, reflections, and echoes that abound not only repeat, but also modify, subtly or radically, what went before. We are here in a central area of creative deformation. When Revel looks at the Theseus tapestry in Bleston Town Hall, he at once associates the tapestry figure of Ariadne with Ann Bailey—the only young woman he knows in Bleston. . . . Simultaneously, we have the imposition of Ann on the Ariadne figure, and the recognition that this impostion has little or no objective justification.

It is the characteristic of a labyrinth to offer parallels and similarities which are not identities, and finally to swamp the individual in delusory appearances which obstruct progress. It is by the *récit,* that Ariadne thread to which he clings, that Revel tries to disentangle the web of his experience—to perceive similarities but also observe differences. . . . In [carefully] exploring such distortions of perception, Butor is precisely exploring that vital element of reality—*l'imaginaire.* (pp. 44-5)

Butor seems . . . to accord to [the] element of *déformation* a vast creative power; he sees it as a vital part of our reality. . . . [It] is from such distortions that the novels emerge. Butor points to the labyrinth of the world, criss-crossed by cultural and emotional patterns, and demands that we find our way through it, identifying and exploring those patterns. . . . (p. 45)

> *Valerie Minogue, in* Forum for Modern Language Studies *(copyright © by* Forum for Modern Language Studies *and Valerie Minogue), January, 1976.*

C

CAIN, James M(allahan)   1892-1977

Cain was an American novelist and screenwriter. He is best known for *The Postman Always Rings Twice*, which became a popular film. Considered a precursor of the "hardboiled school" of realistic novelists, Cain frequently used as his fictional milieu the violent world of mobsters and racketeers. (See also *CLC*, Vol. 3, and *Contemporary Authors*, Vols. 17-20, rev. ed.; obituary, Vols. 73-76.)

JAMES T. FARRELL

James M. Cain's novel, *Mildred Pierce,* wantonly squanders what could have been a very good and representative American story; it could even have been a great one. (p. 79)

One of the striking and promising features in the early portions of this novel is that the two main characters are presented with reference to objects and to conventional conceptions. They possess little of the individuality of many merely literary characters. The style of the book is objective, even a little flat in places; it records movements, performances, the handling of things, such as Bert bracing the trees, Mildred cooking, and the ingredients which go into the making of something she will sell. Thus there is presented a life in which things, commodities, have almost become the protagonists. (pp. 80-1)

[*Mildred Pierce*] has been developed in terms of Hollywood simplicities but does not indicate the character of the opportunity Cain has squandered. Cain's stories are swift moving, punctuated by shocks and violence. His novels are written as a kind of literary movie. But since greater latitude is permitted the novelist than the scenarist, novels like *Mildred Pierce* have the appearance of greater reality than do most films. Unrestrained by a production code, a Cain story can follow the patterns of real life more closely than can a motion picture. In *Mildred Pierce*, Cain began with a real problem, one relatively untouched in contemporary writing. *Mildred Pierce* could have been a poignant account of the middle-class housewife. The fictional character, Mildred, could have been representative of hundreds of thousands of such women. At times there are suggestions of this. The opening portions of the book are promising. But then we see where James M. Cain has learned his literary lessons. Story values take the place of Mildred's problems. Plot involvements, relationships based on plot and story, falsify what was begun as a story about people. (p. 83)

Cain writes of people who are cruel, violent, self-centered, and who have a minimum of awareness. In his world there is neither good nor bad and there is little love. The values of these people are very crude, and they are described in such a way that no concept of experience worthy of the name can be implied to the author. People commit adultery and the wicked are not always punished. If the wicked are punished it is purely fortuitous: punishment is the result of the needs of the story and not of the stern hand of Providence or of the pitiless forging of a chain of necessities. This, plus the element of violence, frequently unmotivated, deceives careless readers: they consider Cain to be a serious writer. (p. 84)

Writers like Cain stand between the work of a serious and tragic character which has been fathered in America by such men as Dreiser and the work derived from the more-or-less-forgotten writings of Robert W. Chambers, Gene Stratton-Porter, or Harold Bell Wright. And in this in-between, neither-fish-nor-fowl literary medium, James M. Cain has become the master. He is a literary thrill-producer who profits by the reaction against the sentimentality of other years and, at the same time, gains from the prestige of more serious and exploratory writing. Thus James M. Cain is not an insignificant or unimportant American literary phenomenon. He has helped to perfect a form which can properly be termed movietone realism. (p. 85)

One of the major virtues of serious realism is that it describes the pitiless force of circumstance and the equally pitiless drive of human emotions which often play so central a role in causing the tragic destruction of human beings. But in this pseudorealistic type of novel . . . the pitiless force of circumstance and of human impulse is replaced by the fortuitousness of automobile accidents and the like and by a melodramatically simplified conception of good girls and bad girls. (p. 89)

James T. Farrell, "Cain's Movietone Realism" (originally published in The New International, *1946), in his* Literature and Morality *(copyright © 1947, 1974, by James T. Farrell; reprinted by permission of the publisher, Vanguard Press, Inc.), Vanguard, 1947, pp. 79-89.*

W. M. FROHOCK

Two things may be said about James M. Cain with the greatest assurance. One is that nothing he has ever written has been entirely out of the trash category. The other is that in spite of the cheapness which sooner or later finds its way into his novels, an inordinate number of intelligent and fully literate people have read him. He has been translated in many parts of the world, and writers whose stature makes him look stunted have paid him the compliment of imitating him—as Albert Camus did, for example, in *The Stranger*. (p. 87)

The preface to *Three of a Kind* makes it clear that [Cain] has schooled himself grimly to produce the kind of effect he wants, with every sentence supercharged and a new jolt for the reader on every page. He is one of the few writers now practicing in America who are really sure-handed in the manipulation of their materials. And if he writes what he does, it is because he has had ample proof that it is what the public wants. (pp. 87-8)

The Postman is a distinguished book, certainly not for what is in it, but for the number and kind of people who read it. An analysis of it is bound to teach us a lot about the literary climate in America *circa* 1934.

The Postman is Cain's book, almost in the same sense in which *Don Quixote* is Cervantes' book: nothing he ever writes will break down the association—he can neither live it down nor live up to it. The obvious ingredients of its success have been enumerated many times. . . . The list must always include a large item of just plain trickery. By this I mean things like the strange device at the end of *The Postman*, where we suddenly find that what we have just read has been written down by a man in his death cell. The first-person narrative has carried us along with it because we have been listening to the man talk. The sentences and even the mistakes in grammar are the sentences and the mistakes of a living human voice, and catch the rhythms of vernacular speech with an authenticity which can be achieved only the the special talents of an O'Hara, a Lardner or of Cain himself—talents close to a kind of genius. And during the course of our becoming acquainted with Frank Chambers, the one fact of which we have been the most thoroughly convinced is that he is anything but a creature of superior perception. Discovering that this story which has so long enthralled us is composed of the death-bed jottings of a man who could have made his living any time writing for M-G-M is like being caught by the rising houselights wiping our eyes at an especially corny movie. (pp. 88-9)

It takes very few samples like the above to convince one that Cain works on the assumption—justified by the facts, of course—that he can do with the reader just about what he likes. The reader is a sort of victim, whose weaknesses are there to be exploited. . . . The significant fact about this trickery is that if we did not happen to think twice, Cain would be getting away with it completely.

The scenes in which Cain lays his novels have much to do with the success of such legerdemain. Somehow the phoniness of *The Postman* is less phony because the action takes place in and around a hamburger joint in a part of California which has magnified the tawdriness of such establishments until the neon light and the false front create what is almost a special and separate cosmos. In the first part of *Serenade* you get the less well-known parts of Mexico. The backdrop of *The Butterfly* is the creek-branch country of West Virginia. In every instance, the place is one which naturally collects curious characters, so that the reader does not have to strain at the incredibility of daughters whose one purpose in life seems to be incest, [or] Irish steamer captains with a taste for Mozart. . . . So long as the scene helps trick you into accepting the people, Cain has no worries. The plot will do the rest.

For the essence of the Cain novel, and the second big item on our list of ingredients, is the plot itself. Everyone says so, including Cain. In the preface to *The Butterfly* he explains that what he writes about is not so much sex, or violence; it is Pandora's box. A man wants something terribly badly; he takes the steps necessary to get it; and when he has it the steps cannot be retraced, and the thing turns out to be very harmful indeed to him. (pp. 89-91)

What Pandora's box contains invariably turns out to be sex, experienced with perfect animal intensity, sometimes with a little hint of abnormal or the forbidden about it. And sex, so conceived, is inseparable from violence. Violence is at once associated with the sexual act itself, and made an inevitable accompaniment of anything which tends to frustrate the sexual experience. In addition violence stimulates sexual activity, as in the scene of Nick's murder. For Cain, sex and violence are not so much subjects as necessary accessories of the plot.

The plots themselves are not particularly new. Cain seems content, as a matter of fact, to refurbish the oldest and most nearly infallible ones, giving them new settings and a special twist or two. The plot of *The Butterfly* [for example] is a variation on the *Oedipus*. . . . In other words, while plots are the essential ingredient for Cain, his success comes from the way he handles them.

This handling involves, most especially, his dialogues. They do the work of telling what is on the character's mind, what he feels, what the motives are for what he has just done; they foretell what is going to happen; and by doing all these things and thus eliminating the necessity of analysis and description, they insure the great rapidity of the story's tempo. (pp. 91-2)

The pace of *The Postman* is terrific. . . . [Such] pace can be attained only by the omission of everything except what is most essential. And it is characteristic of Cain's dialogue that it can bridge all the gaps and prepare the next event while you are still watching what has just happened.

The American novel has come in recent years to depend very heavily upon dialogue, and upon a kind of thought-stream handled in an indirect discourse which is couched in the same language the character speaks in his dialogue. . . . But of all our novelists, only Hemingway does as much as Cain with as few words; and Hemingway's dialogue is frequently so profoundly concerned with the revelation of the psychology of his characters that he cannot, as Cain does, entrust to it the job of keeping the story moving without third-person intervention. . . . Cain's dialogue is lifelike only to the extent that it prevents us from saying . . . that people simply do not talk like that. Once we are convinced and the illusion is established, Cain's problem is one of giving us what dialogue the story needs.

Clearly, dialogue like this can be used only for a certain kind of character. If the author utilized complicated people with complex motives, or even people with the ability to think in complex ways about simple motives, it would not work. But the Pandora's box plot takes care of this. The character has only one drive, to open the box. It is very doubtful whether Cain cares about people, as such, at all; what he wants is someone who has to open a box. (pp. 93-4)

The elements of a Cain novel add up to a kind of bogus tragedy, in which ill luck takes the place of fate. Perhaps here is one reason why the illusion of life is so strong in *The Postman.* Luck has no place in tragedy, but it has ample scope in our daily lives. At any rate, the illusion of life is there, so strong that we accept any number of details which, in another book, would thoroughly spoil the reader's pleasure. Go back and read, for example, out of its exciting context, the paragraph after Nick has been killed. He has been screaming out the window of the car in drunken delight at hearing the echo scream back from the hills. The bottle crushes his skull just as a loud cry leaves his throat. And as Frank realizes that what they had to do has now been done, the answer of the echo comes back. Only after a considerable number of readings does one even realize what a piece of ham Cain has persuaded him to swallow at this point!

There is a connection between the realization of Cain's constant hoodwinking of his reader, and the conviction that *The Postman* is a thoroughly immoral book—immoral not so much because of the unpraiseworthy behavior of the characters, as because of the unpraiseworthy behavior of the reader. Everything in Cain's novel is a conspiracy against the reader, to excite him into hoping that somehow Frank Chambers will get away with his murder.... And Frank Chambers does not deserve this sort of sympathy from the reader. We have been tricked into taking the position of potential accomplices. (pp. 97-8)

What we have in *The Postman* is a dose of unattenuated violence, describable in the jargon appropriate to the dignity of the book as possessing "terrific punch." If the book were one of greater dignity and higher seriousness, we would stop talking of punch and begin to discuss "impact" or "concentration of effect." Such suddenly delivered impact is commonly recognized as one of the essentials of tragedy. Cain's books do not strike a tragic note, however, because the violence in them is not endowed with any sort of moral significance. We are aware of his violence not as something which we must accept because it is a part of Man's Fate, but as something for a clever writer to play tricks with. (pp. 98-9)

> *W. M. Frohock, "James M. Cain: Tabloid Tragedy," in his* The Novel of Violence in America: 1920-1950 *(copyright, 1946, 1947, 1948, 1949 by University Press in Dallas; copyright, 1950 by W. M. Frohock; reprinted by permission of Southern Methodist University Press), University Press, 1950, pp. 87-99.*

DAVID MADDEN

In Cain's best fiction, aesthetic distance is achieved and sustained partly because of his obsessively objective, neutral, dispassionate attitude toward the basic elements of his novels. His techniques forcibly, deliberately, and continually turn us back to the pure experience itself. (p. 61)

[In *Serenade*] Cain shows how one man seizes the American dream of success and how it conflicts with his dream of the primitive woman. (p. 63)

In Cain's novels, the amateur hero's relationship is simply with a woman, and they go on what Cain calls a love rack together because one of them wishes for something and the wish comes true. When the American dream comes true, it turns into a nightmare in an everlasting present in which the lovers are isolated from the human community.... Cain's heroes are inside-dopesters with an impulse to self-dramatization who speak in an aggressive voice and who fall from a height they have willfully reached. Jack Sharp boasts superior know-how in every area touched upon in the novel.... [Typically], in *Serenade,* it is sex and violence all the way.... [The] theme is that a man out of touch with himself and his masculinity can learn the wisdom of the body from a woman who is sexually supercharged. (p. 64)

Stripping down to essentials is not a conscious theme in *Serenade,* but Cain, like Hemingway, demonstrates in his technique itself how life, stripped down, feels.... Although Cain operates mainly within the realm of terror, he strives in almost every novel to convey at the height of terror a sense of the beautiful. (pp. 65-6)

Cain's imagination does not process in terms of a conception and thus transform his raw material ... : rather, with basic fictional techniques, Cain expertly manipulates and controls all the elements for calculated effects. So we spoke of Cain's inventive powers, his structuring mind—a mind aware of itself and of the reader's mind....

[Cain's vision] has the impersonal objectivity of the camera eye. Cain doesn't set out with a vision—his concentration on craft obscures the vision that does emerge for the receptive reader.... Cain, the twenty-minute egg of the hard-boiled school is overtly tough in diction and action but inadvertently lapses into sentimentality. (p. 66)

[In Cain], more than in most writers, a study of craft requires an awareness of the fascinating ways in which the author deliberately, and indirectly, creates a special relationship between himself and his ideal reader.

In *Serenade,* Cain makes so many apt assumptions about his readers that we are palpably aware of the author's intimacy with the reader-community he has visualized for his work. Cain is a performer aware of his audience. They want to see him do it again. As he manipulates and reverses stock expectations and responses, his knowledge of what his reader wants is phenomenal. Part of his ability lies in the way he mingles serious and popular fictive elements. Even the serious reader becomes so involved that he is unaware, until after finishing a Cain novel, of ways in which the author's achievement may be examined technically as literature. Sophisticated literary elements operate in Cain, but so "naturally" that they neither tax the popular reader's patience, nor, at first, impress the sophisticated reader. (pp. 66-7)

Cain's style serves the ... function of depicting the action itself. There is a remarkable compatability between Cain's raw material in *Serenade* and his terse diction.... The sense of authority we feel in Cain as he relates action is a triumph of style. Cain is a master of rhetoric in his use of description, dialogue, selectivity and compression. Looking back, we see that Cain has achieved his effects by skillful omission, and suggestion, and condensation. Execution seems the best word for what he does; he executes his moves, cleanly, sharply, "racing ahead like a motorcycle." (p. 68)

Cain's situations, themes, characters, and style are cliché-ridden. . . . [He] consciously sets out to resurrect, control, and transform the cliché for expressive use. Juana is a whore with a heart of gold, but it is also the heart of a killer. . . .

Cain's use of devices, though it sometimes suggests the hack writer, elevates the device to the status of a major literary tool. Even when we catch him employing a device, we experience less a disruption of illusion than a deepening fascination.

One winces at failures of technique in Cain . . . because there is not much more to Cain than skillful execution of technique. . . . But Cain makes the reader feel terror, and every device of the novel that will heighten that experience is made to work. (p. 69)

Cain almost never slows down the showing to tell. What we follow in *Serenade* is the spine of surface narrative action. In the opening of *Serenade,* so much happens so fast, the reader either immediately rejects what happens or willingly suspends his disbelief and finer instincts and submits to Cain's will. . . .

Serenade is neither serious nor popular; it is pure entertainment, an experience in which strong distinctions between one sort of reader and another seem superfluous. But as Edmund Wilson has said, "There is enough of the real poet in Cain—both in writing and in imagination—to make one hope for something better." (p. 70)

> *David Madden, in* Journal of Popular Culture *(copyright © 1974 by Ray B. Browne), Summer, 1974.*

JOHN D. MacDONALD

There is a special debt we owe them, a debt to Chandler, Hammett and Cain. They excised pointless ornamentation, moved their stories forward with a spare, ruthless vigor and so superimposed the realities we already knew with characterizations we could believe, that they achieved a dreadful, and artistic, inevitability. . . .

"The Institute" is a faint and embarrassing echo of the persuasion that used to be [Cain's]. It is not the intent of this reviewer to make a witless and vulgar display of disapproval. . . . The intent is to show where grasp of the methods and materials has faltered and weakened.

The plot is uniquely absent.

It is too easy to isolate the improbabilities. . . .

Instead, it is interesting to isolate Cain's remaining strengths. Pages 64 through 75 concern the use of business muscle to force the acquisition of a company in trouble. A lot of this is tight and fast and believable. (p. 18)

Cain, without a plot, without the fascinating convolutions of chicanery, has to make do with emotional and cultural complications, and here he is too much at the mercy of his own dead horses, which whip back when whipped.

And so, one wanders down these confusing and windy corridors, listening for the distant Hoohaw, a rattle of chains, a distant flavor of tension remembered.

The debt remains, and here in "The Institute" are some gossamer strands of the control which once created that debt. (p. 20)

> *John D. MacDonald, "A Mystery and a Romance," in* The New York Times Book Review *(© 1976 by The New York Times Company; reprinted by permission), August 22, 1976, pp. 18, 20.*

*   *   *

CALVINO, Italo   1923-

Calvino is an Italian novelist, short story writer, essayist, critic, and editor known for his imaginative blendings of reality and fantasy. His stance is humanistic and his tools are wit, elements of science fiction, and a lyrical tone. His involvement with the Italian resistance movement during World War II is reflected in many of his works. (See also *CLC*, Vols. 5, 8.)

NICHOLAS A. DeMARA

Il Sentiero dei nidi di ragno . . . is basically a neo-realistic novel. The work deals specifically with the civil war, yet Calvino did not create it as a piece of polemic literature. He does not appear to glorify the partisan revolt, but simply to present the circumstances of a particular situation. Calvino of *Il Sentiero dei nidi di ragno* is not a resistance writer, but rather a writer of the resistance. He is an author who chose that moment in history as the framework for his narrative. He is a sensitive observer of humanity, whose experience in the partisan movement precipitated specific observations about a period of intense social and political turmoil. . . . *Il Sentiero dei nidi di ragno* reflects many aspects characteristic of the neo-realistic current, while at the same time revealing a fairytale quality peculiar to the poetics of Calvino. (p. 26)

Calvino brings expression to his material through a language and style which are notably neo-realistic in character. Even a quick reading of the novel will evidence a style characterized by a highly descriptive, colorful language, interspersed with regional expressions and songs, and controlled by the mechanics of simple sentence structure. Although stylized, descriptive passages periodically recur in the work, the narrative as a whole proceeds as a reaction against the *bello scrivere*. The simple style suggests that Calvino is unhampered by the thought of writing well. Greater emphasis seems to be placed on the narrative than on the style. The situations he is describing are so familiar to him that they appear to flow without the push of a conscious literary effort.

Clipped sentences and phrases tied together by punctuation dominate Calvino's style in this novel. The effect is that produced by the anonymous narrator. Calvino himself affirms in the preface to the third edition of *Il Sentiero* that the civil war experience had established a directness of communication among men which was extended to the realm of literature. Thus Calvino's fiction in the immediate post-war years often assumed the mood of oral narration. Such a mood finds expression in the rapid flow of sentences in which the syntax is straightforward. (pp. 27-8)

[A clipped, disjointed style such as this] is generally clumsy and anti-literary. But here, as in other instances, Calvino makes such a staccato style serve two purposes. First, the use of short phrases permits him to fuse narrative and psychological reflection in the same paragraph. [For example, the] disjointed statements seem to combine the pattern of Pin's thoughts with the narrative sequence [in the passage describing Pin's reaction to the pistol theft]. The effect is such that Calvino is able to reveal both the action and the young boy's response to the action within the same passage. The reader, finding himself drawn into the mind of the boy, derives a deeper understanding of the sequential nature of his thoughts and sensations. Second, the staccato style serves to create tension within the narrative. . . . Calvino, under the influence of the neo-realistic current, is apparently more concerned with depicting the reality of a situation and the atmosphere under which it develops than in producing an elegant prose style.

Calvino's language is another element which tends to render the novel a neo-realistic work. The passion of neo-realists to reproduce a particular situation often led to the use of dialect and crude expressions. Such anti-literary language is present in varying degrees within *Il Sentiero*. (pp. 29-30)

[In] carefully reproducing the reality of a given situation, [the Italian neo-realists] described the unique characteristics of the particular region in Italy where the action was set. (p. 30)

One of the cardinal principles of neo-realistic artists was to draw material directly from life and to reproduce faithfully real situations through traditional methods. (p. 31)

Calvino renders the historical and physical setting of *Il Sentiero* real by casually presenting incidental data which are highly characteristic of the resistance period in Liguria. . . . The description of the daily activities of the partisans is . . . interspersed with references which pinpoint the action to Liguria. . . . All these references help to define the historical and physical setting of the work, while reinforcing the reality of the situation. (pp. 31-2)

Italian neo-realistic prose . . . was modelled on American literature. The stylistic trends, political ideas, and social morality which appear in Italian neo-realistic prose in the immediate post-war era had already found expression and were delineated in the works of Ernest Hemingway. (p. 32)

It is [Calvino's] opinion that the Italians had gone to Hemingway and other Americans with the direct intent of drawing from them that which was necessary to provide a new impulse to Italian literature. . . . In [Calvino's 1954 essay entitled "Hemingway e noi,"] he discusses the influence of Hemingway on his contemporaries and admits that his early work (i.e., *Il Sentiero*) reveals such an influence. . . .

[Hemingway's curt, factual style and his anti-literary techniques] are deliberate and consciously directed towards the objective presentation of experience and the reproduction of real life situations. Such an effort toward authenticity has been described as one of the cardinal principles of Italian neo-realism. It is therefore not difficult to see a marked relationship between Hemingway and the Italian neo-realists. (p. 34)

It is a sense of vital hope which separates Calvino from Hemingway. Kim [in *Il Sentiero*] and Jordan [in *For Whom the Bell Tolls*] are both lonely heroes, but Hemingway has Jordan belong to a lost generation. . . . Hemingway denies his hero hope for the future and makes him the passive victim of a meaningless determinism. Kim, on the other hand, is free. Calvino has provided him freedom of thought and decision. More important, he has instilled in him a sense of hope which encourages the use of freedom for the possible creation of a better world.

The use of freedom and the question of self-determinism are two ideas which Calvino develops to a greater extent in his trilogy, *I Nostri antenati*. Under the guise of fantastic situations, he comments on problems threatening the freedom and identity of modern man. *Il Visconte dimezzato*, published in 1952, might be seen by some as a turning point in Calvino's early career. Rather than considering *Il Visconte dimezzato* a turning away from neo-realism, it appears more reasonable to view *Il Sentiero* as a preannouncement of Calvino's great success in the realm of fantasy. A careful study of *Il Sentiero* in the light of the trilogy will demonstrate that his first novel reflects many aspects of his poetics which directly contradict neo-realistic principles. (pp. 41-2)

Although [Calvino] remains faithful to the trends of neo-realism by utilizing such techniques, he diverges from that popular current in many instances. An attentive reader will note that Calvino is not consistently anti-literary. Crude language and a staccato prose style are counter-balanced by passages in which descriptive imagination and a unique sense of beauty predominate. . . . (p. 42)

Utilizing vocabulary [in these passages] which is no longer confined by the cultural limitations of his characters, Calvino reflects . . . his own sophistication. . . . Calvino makes use of metaphor and colorful images in his descriptive passages, while he generally avoids such figures of speech in the narrative parts of the work. (p. 43)

Passages such as this hint at Calvino's intense interest in nature. In many of his later novels, such a preoccupation with nature, as well as a highly developed sense of fantasy, come to dominate his poetics. Although *Il Sentiero* exemplifies, for the most part, the principles of neo-realism, it also evidences these two essential characteristics of Calvino's later works. Neo-realistic prose is little concerned with either nature or fantasy, except when such elements are essential to the reproduction of a particular scene. It is significant that Calvino has been able to fuse these elements in his first novel, thereby creating a work characteristic of the immediate post-war era, and yet one which is distinctively his own.

In *Il Sentiero*, Calvino permits nature to assume a strange, almost exotic role. The emphasis he places on the description of plants and animals appears to go beyond that which is necessary for the creation of an authentic situation. He remains faithful to realism in selecting characters who often possess the baser qualities of humanity, yet the environment in which he places them is at times influenced by his personal conception of nature. Calvino never portrays nature as an enemy of man. . . . [For] Calvino nature has Rousseaunian qualities. The ills which beset man are caused by himself or his fellow man. (pp. 43-4)

The interplay of fantasy and reality is one of the most distinctive qualities of Calvino's early prose. . . .

In *Il Sentiero* he manages to balance fantasy with reality and shift easily from one to another by making the boy Pin the fulcrum of his work. Calvino understands that while the child's mind has the ability to see an object in its natural form, it can also fantasize about it. In fact, for many children [including Pin] there exists no sharp distinction between the real world and an imagined one. (p. 44)

In *Il Sentiero* Calvino portrays an essentially realistic

world, but through the use of the adolescent figure he is frequently able to inject into the work a sense of fantasy. Pin is a boy who uses profanity with the vehemence of a corrupted adult. But he is a boy who still possesses some of his childhood innocence. It is this innocence which renders him incapable of understanding the world of adults. (pp. 44-5)

The emphasis Calvino places on nature and fantasy in *Il Sentiero* points out that this novel should not be completely isolated from his trilogy, *I Nostri antenati,* even though it displays elements of realistic trends, as well as characteristics reminiscent of some works of Ernest Hemingway. The complexity of *Il Sentiero* prohibits its being solely classified as neo-realistic. It is in part a response to a particular historical period, but it is also the first manifestation of the great diversity of style and subject matter which have characterized Calvino's production in the past two decades. *Il Sentiero* is pervaded by social comment as is the trilogy, *La Speculazione edilizia,* and *La Giornata d'uno scrutatore.* In it, Calvino already displays an unusual interest in nature which he develops most thoroughly in *Il Barone rampante.* And finally fantasy, usually foreign to neo-realistic prose, finds expression in *Il Sentiero* through the imagination of the adolescent protagonist. Calvino's treatment of Pin's imagination prefigures his extensive development of fantasy in *I Nostri antenati, Formica argentina, Cosmicomiche,* and *Ti con zero.* Fantasy, nature, and social comment are three basic elements of *Il Sentiero* which recur throughout most of Calvino's works. His first novel contains realistic elements popular in the immediate post-war era, yet it reveals the great diversity of Calvino's genius which has made him one of the most successful contemporary Italian novelists. (pp. 46-7)

> *Nicholas A. DeMara, "Pathway to Calvino: Fantasy and Reality in 'Il Sentiero dei nidi di ragno',"* in Italian Quarterly *(copyright © 1971 by* Italian Quarterly*), Winter, 1971, pp. 25-49.*

JOHN GATT-RUTTER

[Calvino in *Il sentiero dei nidi di ragno*] creates two non-communicating levels: the spontaneity of the politically naïve partisans; and the almost cynical calculations of Kim [Calvino's mouthpiece] and of the author himself, who, in their different roles, ordain the ordinary people's destinies for them, impersonating 'History'. The politicized intellectual remains in charge, and the novel remains a picaresque study of 'low life' and adventure seen from above. . . .

Nevertheless, the adventure, the freedom and the comradeship of life in the Resistance stand in qualitative contrast to the constraints of 'normal' social living. This is where *play* becomes Calvino's most positive, even (unintentionally) revolutionary element. But play appears here as a product of his particular artistic sense, and not of his political consciousness, though Calvino discovers play through life with the Resistance.

This spontaneity in his play is both a strength and a weakness. It accounts for the freshness of Calvino's writing, but also for its failure to develop to its full depth and revolutionary potential. Not the hilarious eruptions and libertarian explosions of Aristophanes and Rabelais, but the more composed and 'hermetic' fantasies of Ariosto and R. L. Stevenson are Calvino's avowed literary nurseries. Calvino admires Lewis Carroll, but has not learnt from the *Alice*

books. The play-element in Calvino is poor in critique, and critique is the dialectical complement to play which is indispensable in a world whose economic, social and political structures are so inimical to the unalienated activity of play. (p. 320)

Naturally, play is bound to be an element in any work of art. Without it the aesthetic sense is inexplicable. But in Calvino it appears not only in a general aesthetic sense, but in specific elements of both content and form. In *Il sentiero* these elements tend to remain at a more or less trivial level. . . . But there are hints here and there of greater wealth.

First, Pin's sense of exclusion from the mysterious adult world. This provides at least a germ of critique as a dialectical component in his character. Second, a keen sense of the curiousness of things—mountain and forest landscapes, as well as Pin's spiders and fireflies, the colourful and grotesque variety of human appearance and mannerism. . . . And third, Calvino's tendency (often remarked upon, not least by himself) to reveal an abstract geometry hidden in relationships of motion. . . . (pp. 320-21)

The first of these aspects—the mystery of adulthood—has proved an impasse for Calvino, his chief limitation as a writer. The childlike psychology is characteristic of all his narrators or protagonists, whatever their supposed age. This psychology is effective in presenting the incomprehensible world we live in *as* incomprehensible, and in presenting it both with the crisp and vivid objectivity of an external observer, and with the subjective bewilderment of that same innocent observer. Calvino's 'child' is not, like Alice, a 'wise child' who sees through and corrects adult folly, hypocrisy or bullying. The child's eye in Calvino's stories does not easily detect the all too comprehensible structures that underly the incomprehensible chaos of phenomenal reality, the world of appearances. The omnipotence of money, the property system, the family and female dependence, the dead weight of institutions—these are some of those structures, and Calvino is clearly aware of them not only in his theoretical essays but in his narratives themselves. Yet his stories remain strangely inconsequential, almost indifferent. (p. 321)

From such neutral lines of vision, the wealth of realistic detail which Calvino very skillfully weaves into his narratives remains merely a *spectacle:* at no point is the very real drama developed or internalized, despite some visually powerful scenes. . . .

The limitations of Calvino's 'naturalism' or 'neo-realism' are therefore limitations of *manner,* not of *matter.* The drama is there, but Calvino will not enact it. A far more fruitful probe into a tense reality might have resulted had the author introduced other viewpoints. . . . As it is, Calvino writes sonatas for a solo instrument which is muted throughout. Each novel falls down somewhere between being a half-hearted satire of feckless and irresponsible middle-class intellectuals and a half-hearted inquiry into the apparatus of our dehumanized modern reality. The best that Calvino manages is the sense of something inexorable. . . .

Calvino's narrative viewpoints will always be childlike: not in the manner of Voltaire's Ingénu, but in the negative sense of someone who does not understand. His narrators are Candides who have no Voltaire to make pointed remarks over their heads. This serves to heighten the sense of horror and estrangement . . . ; but it also trivializes the picture: the incoherence of reality is misrepresented, simplified as the surface 'objectivity' of the childlike observer. . . .

The other two elements we have noticed in *Il sentiero*—Calvino's visual curiosity (what critics have called his *voyeurisme*) and the abstract geometry he conjures out of this very same amorphous world of appearances—these two elements can be traced without difficulty throughout Calvino's work, in varying forms and combinations. . . . [As] statements about the world, visual curiosity and abstract geometry continually risk lapsing into the status of well-turned clichés or facile tricks—unless the visual curiosity and abstract geometry are not merely external effects, but instruments to explore an important theme in a way attempted by no other writer before Calvino. The distinction is between play and child's-play; between play as total and free involvement with *experience,* and play as idle toying with surface *appearances.* (p. 322)

[Literary] insights and political insights in Calvino are not, in origin, identical (as they are in Brecht), but forcibly juxtaposed. It is only when Calvino succeeds in deploying the deeper significance of his *literary* play that it reveals its *political* significance, not by an arbitrary application of political themes or intentions, but by capturing new aspects of reality.

Where this happens, Calvino produces some of the best short and long stories in a literature whose strongest genre is *novellistica. Gli amori difficili* (mostly written in the fifties and included in the *Racconti* of 1958, but republished as a separate volume in 1970) are stories about 'lovers' who never meet. The Euclidean possibilities of this—to Calvino—are almost inexhaustible. The descriptive possibilities offered by the love-object (which can be embodied in, or associated with, a harbourful of folk, a photographic studio, a day at the office, a snow-covered ski-run, or a motorway alive with headlights) are likewise inexhaustible. But Calvino uses these formal possibilities to explore a problem that has many dimensions—physical, psychological, literary, social, perhaps metaphysical. The problem is the taboo against reality—the human reality typified as 'eros'. (p. 323)

The taboo against Eros—like all taboos—is ultimately *political:* an atavistic social prohibition, internalized by each individual as unconscious repressions or conventions, but reinforced by the churches and the police. These stories of Calvino's show 13 different ways in which this repressed Eros seeks fulfilment (a meeting of human beings as *persons*) but never meets with more than a fraction of success. . . . These stories—better than perhaps anything else Calvino has written—are rich in signification at all sorts of levels which nearly always perfectly coincide, and equally rich in the corresponding skills of narrative and suspense.

Certainly, Calvino has here perfected an instrument to penetrate the false rationality of the increasingly acute form of alienation characteristic of the latter twentieth century in one of its relatively affluent sectors—the industrial triangle of northern Italy, from Genoa and its Riviera to Turin and Milan. His 'voyeuristic' description here embodies the intensely desired but never truly possessed reality of people and things. His geometry—parallel or divergent lines, circumferences held away from their centres, planes which

never quite coincide, zero turning into infinity and vice versa—expresses, with as much (contained) anguish as elegance, the failure of the subject and object of Eros, of Desire, to meet. And always, what we may call Calvino's 'negative epiphany' is freshly perceived, new and unexpected. He avoids—and here we may see a limitation of the powers of his art—the most blatant instances or instants of human, social, and political breakdown. . . . Yet all these are *implicit* in Calvino's stories, captured in their germinal moments within people's experience and awareness, in the moments when our modern despair is *born,* rather than in the moments when that despair is ready to erupt into tragedy, death or ruthless coercion. These unpretentious stories of Calvino's are thus to my mind among the best products of political literature—or of *any* literature—written in Italy since the war. . . . They are a serious look at our historical 'human condition'.

I would suggest that the central political perception here is the non-existence of evil, or moral 'wrong-doing', the impossibility of moral judgements. 'Evil' turns out to be nothing else than our social repressions and fears, handed down through unnumbered generations, the memory of their origins lost in prehistory; repressions and fears which have been internalized in every one of us and which can only be dissolved by the world-wide application of Reason—not the abstract Reason of the philosophers, nor the false rationality of capitalist or state capitalist production—but *our* Reason, a Reason which is more or less suppressed by social institutions and conventions all over the world, and which is therefore bound to be revolutionary.

Calvino has therefore found a use for literature which is not merely a decorative use: a use which can ultimately be seen as a political use, and which yet does not impair literature as literature, but, on the contrary, enhances it. (pp. 323-25)

[If] stylistic and formal play is more evident at the surface level of the narration (Calvino avoids explicit moralizing), critique is the very heart of these stories. The failure to communicate, especially between the sexes, is shown in a number of highly original ways, through some entirely new perceptions. These perceptions lift *incomunicabilità* out of the mystery of individual psychology . . . and reveal its institutional nature and origins. (p. 326)

Calvino, no doubt, deliberately avoids using his pen as a magic wand to produce a fictional 'solution' or climax [in 'La nuvola di smog']: the impotence of the educated individual, and even of the organized workers, in the face of the omnipotence of capitalism, is Calvino's theme, and on an urgent social and political issue the bare documentary truth is likely to speak more eloquently than a heroic or tragic fiction. Woman appears here in a more unequivocal light than anywhere else in Calvino: reduced to her socially-prescribed role as sex-object foreign to the male world, she does not understand the serious problems which that world creates, and consequently she is not interested in them, but only in her feminine sway over men. Woman, alluring and elusive, is thus largely responsible for the lack of sustained interest on the part of Calvino's intellectual protagonists in the issues that affect society at large. Calvino shows the *femme fatale* as one of the most effective of the unconscious agents of the *status quo.*

The weakness of the story is the same as the one [evident] in Calvino's other quasi-'neo-realist' narratives—*La specu-*

lazione edilizia and *La giornata di uno scrutatore*—namely, the restricted point of view. This tends to dissipate the effect of the author's remarkable observational and narrative skills. It is only in *Il cavaliere inesistente* that Calvino even partly overcomes this limitation in a more synthetic, polycentric form of narration. He seems *deliberately* to avoid writing a narrative work of major dimensions, preferring 'minor' perfection. Yet the imperfection of most of his minor narratives (and they are all minor) is precisely that certain dimensions are missing.

One of the most interesting features of 'La nuvola di smog' is its opening image—that of the fine black industrial dust that covers everything. This is an orthodoxly neo-realistic documentary detail, but it also takes on the symbolic quality of the Chancery fog in Dickens' *Bleak House,* and seems to indicate more than just the pollution of the urban environment—the very quality and condition of life under our anarchic and dehumanizing industrialism. The earlier story 'La formica argentina' lacks the documentary specificity, but has the universality (and also the vagueness, the quasi-metaphysical air) of the symbolism, in a more Kafkaesque manner. . . . (p. 327)

There is a common theme in nearly all the stories—the 'little man's' attempt to recover a direct contact with nature, to discover a 'reality' that belongs to him, and generally to make his life more livable amid the inhuman surroundings of the modern urban labyrinth. Some stories amount to little more than well-told *barzellette,* amusing anecdotes, not very different from some of those in Guareschi's *Zibaldino* and *Il corrierino delle famiglie.* Indeed, *Marcovaldo* looks very much like Calvino's intelligent riposte to this latter idyll-saga of urban family life, which had appeared in 1954. Some stories, however, are memorable, among Calvino's best works. . . . 'Social realism', in these stories, is lifted into the realms of fantasy, without any loss of authenticity (as opposed to dull verisimilitude), on the innocent shoulders of a Chaplinesque victim-hero.

As regards the development of Calvino's narrative technique, these stories clearly show a feature which is barely discernible in the *Antenati* trilogy, and which becomes perhaps too self-conscious in the Qfwfq stories: if the anti-hero is Chaplin, the draughtsman and designer is Disney. The technique—in line with Calvino's earliest tendencies—is that of the animated cartoon or the comic strip. . . . The lines are simple, the colours bright, the details clear, and all is shown in vivid motion. (p. 328)

This technique entails a *political* application for the 'thumbprint' of Calvino's style: the animated cartoon, with its colour and fantasy, is a *popular* form of art and literature. Calvino here is perfecting and transforming his native stylistic bent as a means of breaking through the barrier that separates 'literature' from the mass of ordinary people, even children, and of tempting them to open a book. . . . Calvino has in this achieved something far more tangible than the desperadoes of *sperimentalismo* and the *neo-avanguardia.* He has, to some extent at least, become *popolo* without ceasing to be Calvino. (pp. 328-29)

The trilogy, published in one volume in 1960 under the title of *I nostri antenati,* looks even more like play and less like critique. The component stories are colourful fantasies in a historical setting. . . . Perhaps its greatest importance for an overall understanding of Calvino is that here, well before

his celebrated work of collecting the fairy-tales which he published in the volume *Fiabe italiene* (1956), Calvino's fantasy play has come fully into the open in a highly polished and very 'playful' work which seems full of promise for the future. (p. 329)

[The protagonist's] Cosimo's discovery of the identity of work and play in unalienated human activity is the main achievement—also a political achievement—of *Il barone rampante* [the second part of the trilogy]. Formally, the tale is rather loosely episodic, reflecting Calvino's self-conscious adaptation of Voltaire's adaptation of the picaresque novel of adventure, as in the similarly episodic *Il cavaliere inesistente* he adapts Ariosto's adaptation of the popular medieval adaptations of the epic *Chanson de Roland. Il barone* is a miscellany of eighteenth-century curiosities, perhaps pedagogical in intent. But the formal looseness in Calvino's case may also be due to his ideological looseness, his lack of any clear idea of how to proceed after his break with the Communist Party in 1957, and amid the new and unfamiliar problems of the consumer society which was then developing in northern Italy and that society's seemingly irresistible capacity to absorb dissent, rendering it impotent. (p. 330)

[Calvino] imprisons himself in an elegant, but essentially monodic, style—and what is worse, a style that is mandarin, if disarmingly informal mandarin. And he invariably adopts the closed aesthetic of a self-defining (albeit usually original) genre. He really *is* fascinated by a closed system of signifiers which signify nothing but their relations to one another (though he often refers resolutely outwards). Hence his method . . . of narration as the elaboration of an initial image or situation.

Thus, for all its simple fantasy, for all its effortless allegory, the trilogy remains an anachronism, or rather, an archaism. (pp. 331-32)

Even within his self-imposed limits, in the trilogy, Calvino has extended the range of his play and of his critique. Beyond all his particular felicities, and the almost unfailing and lively inventiveness of his writing, what the trilogy makes possible for Calvino is to break outside the familiar limits of modern narrative literature. In a world where the *totality* of experience is possibly richer than ever, but where the *individual's* social experience is atomized and restricted more than ever before, the realistic novelist is bound by his own atomized understanding. The atomized, incommunicant first person thus dominates the modern novel. (pp. 333-34)

The masterpiece of *Le cosmicomiche* is the last story, 'La spirale'. This points forward to the ambitious but sombre efforts of the final section of *Ti con zero,* but it is also an achievement in its own right. Here the grand underlying theme of Calvino's cosmic fantasies becomes explicit in its grandeur and its pathos: that is, the theme of the essential unity of all life in the universe, from the 'first' atom and the primeval shellfish. . . .

The power of this is unmistakable. And yet there remains something rhetorical about it, something voluntaristic, an 'intentional fallacy' perhaps. Once again, Calvino manages to be affirmative only by avoiding the drama or tragedy of dialectical opposition. He sees the universe as love, but as a love that is sex-based, limited to desire, and therefore essentially procreative. But nature's prolific procreation implies either over-population or predation. The corollary of love is death, usually nasty. This predatory, destructive aspect of the universe (whether physical, organic or human) is something that Calvino prefers not to see in *Le cosmocomiche.* (p. 335)

The second section of *Ti con zero,* entitled 'Priscilla', is the most ambitious thing Calvino has ever written, and in some ways his most powerful. It is the epic of life itself, understood as the genetic code that has been transmitted in increasingly complex form from the original single-cell nucleus to the electronic computer programmes of the imminent future. Death *is* faced this time, only to be summarily dismissed. . . . The dialectical tension is not between life and death. It is a different one, springing from Calvino —Qfwfq's pseudo-scientific fatalism—from his conviction that I cannot choose who I am to be, and that I can never join the one I love. . . . (p. 336)

Has Calvino's intelligence outwitted itself? Or is he playing puzzles with the reader? Certainly, he seems to be indulging in deliberate sophistries here. . . . Calvino seems to be serious: the whole drift of his work has been towards fatalism and determinism, towards a radical unbelief in his own freedom. (p. 337)

In the stories of the third section of *Ti con zero*—the section after which the whole volume is named—Calvino dazes himself with still more elegant and complex sophistries of fatalism, and imitates the gait of Borges. . . . Trivial play seems to prevail here. . . . Calvino's latest works at least amend this glibly optimistic form of fatalism. *Le città invisibili* (1972) presents Marco Polo describing to Kublai Kan 55 imaginary cities with female names. Calvino thus brilliantly marries together hints and pointers he detects in Northrop Frye's *Anatomy of Criticism* and Vittorini's *Città del mondo.* . . . (pp. 337-38)

Perhaps Calvino means to imply the presence of money and power by his very choice of protagonists. If so, the implication is too evanescent, and does not save the book's artistic results. Calvino's hermetic structuralism has taken the 'stilizzazione riduttiva' almost to vanishing-point. The Cities are projected in a void, completely detached from the speakers in a dimension where drama is impossible. A stylized, Beckett-like anti-drama may be intended, but it is not quite achieved. Calvino's opium-dream orientalism is not an accidental choice. (p. 338)

Play and critique in Calvino have all but fallen apart. Calvino's intentions are still superior to his artistic achievement, and *Le città invisibili,* for all its stylistic brilliance, is an exquisite failure. Calvino's resistance to all that we recognise as alien is now desperate and marginal. He has opened up to literature vistas more spacious, and possibilities more numerous, and play more varied and inventive, than all but a very few writers—ranging from Dante to Cyrano de Bergérac—but has made out of them only a fraction of what he could have. Calvino has never really been aware of the power of play. His failure to draw out the political (that is, the *human*) possibilities of play to the full is a counterpart to his 'pessimismo dell'intelligenza', his deep-rooted fatalism and diffidence in the possibility of rational action to better our human world, to satisfy desire—and this despite all his attempts to persuade himself to hope and to strive. (p. 339)

John Gatt-Rutter, "Calvino Ludens: Literary

Play and Its Political Implications," in Journal of European Studies *(copyright © 1975 Seminar Press Limited), December, 1975, pp. 319-40.*

JoANN CANNON

Italo Calvino, long recognized in Italy as one of its most prominent contemporary writers, has been for the most part neglected in the United States by all but Italianists. . . . Calvino's works show a marked progression from the neo-realist mode of his first novel, *The Path to the Nest of Spiders,* to the fantastic mode of *Cosmicomics, t zero,* and *The Invisible Cities.* . . . For the latecomer to Calvino's works, a reading of the realistic novels serves as a reminder that the fantastic in Calvino is not a form of escapism, but is grounded in a persistent sociopolitical concern.

In the 1950's, Calvino wrote two short novels, *Marcovaldo or the Seasons in the City* and *Smog,* which present an image of the city that is perhaps even more valid today than it was twenty years ago. The first novel, *Marcovaldo,* is located somewhere between the two poles of the realistic and the fantastic. It is a series of realistic fables dealing with man's struggle for survival in the modern city. (pp. 83-4)

Like all fables, *Marcovaldo* has no concrete historical or geographical backdrop. Although written in the 1950's, the novel might easily be set in the present day. And while Calvino, in the introduction to the novel, implies that it takes place in Turin, the descriptions of the city contain nothing which would distinguish it from any other large, industrial center. The impression of anonymity thus created has a dual function: not only does it lend universality to the fable, but it also signals the fact that all modern cities are essentially alike. (p. 84)

Calvino's fables not only explode the nineteenth-century myth of technological progress, but also the consolatory myth of the idyllic country life: man can no longer find salvation in nature. (pp. 85-6)

Each story or chapter in *Marcovaldo* is a kind of vignette illustrating the realities of life in our modern urban society. The novel is essentially static; there is no development of plot or character. Each vignette follows the generic pattern of the fable as outlined by Calvino in which "a virtuous man realizes himself in an unjust or pitiless society." But unlike the hero of the typical fable who overcomes the obstacles in his path Marcovaldo is doomed to failure. There is no happy ending, no escape from "the city of cement and asphalt."

Smog, a novel written shortly after *Marcovaldo,* is the story of a man who, like Marcovaldo's children, has lost all contact with his environment. (pp. 87-8)

Smog is the specular opposite of *Marcovaldo.* The novels present essentially the same image of the modern, industrial city, in which man is alienated from nature, from his fellow man, and from himself. But this image is reflected from a radically different perspective in the two novels. Whereas Marcovaldo attempts to escape from the city's grayness, its contamination, its squalor, the first person narrator of *Smog* accepts the city's squalor as inescapable. (p. 88)

The protagonist of *Smog* is the fictional projection of the intellectual and moral resignation which Calvino perceives in our society. . . . Caught in a trap, Calvino's hero convinces himself that he has chosen the trap. This kind of rationalization is, in fact, the final resignation. (p. 89)

JoAnn Cannon, "The Image of the City in the Novels of Italo Calvino," in Modern Fiction Studies (© copyright 1978, by Purdue Research Foundation, West Lafayette, Indiana), Spring, 1978, pp. 83-90.

*　　　*　　　*

CAMUS, Albert　1913-1960

Camus, an Algerian-born novelist, dramatist, and essayist, had a profound influence on modern philosophy, particularly on existential thought. His philosophic and literary concerns revolve around the question of the nature and meaning of existence. Camus's conception of the human condition is predicated upon the constants of evil and death. Rejecting religion for reason, Camus concluded that the universe was itself irrational. It was individual action and the power of the individual will that provided life with a value and purpose for Camus. He received the Nobel Prize for Literature in 1957. (See also *CLC*, Vols. 1, 2, 4, 9.)

SERGE DOUBROVSKY

On the whole, it can be said that Camus is the great writer American literature has waited for and who never came. The generation of Faulkner, Dos Passos, and Hemingway already belongs to the past and to history. Its value is one of example and no longer of witness. It so happens that the succession is vacant. There are a hundred authors not wanting in talent, but there is no writer who attacks the problems of our time in depth. If happy peoples can be said to have no history, perhaps prosperous peoples have no literature. (p. 17)

Through the allegorical turn of his mind, through his effort to confine himself to the universal, through his wish to give meaning solely at the level of the human condition, Camus offered in his novels an image of man bare and free enough of the particularities of nationality or history to be immediately accessible. Sartre, on the other hand, whose intellectual and personal approach is so deeply rooted in one moment of both pre- and postwar French consciousness—or "bad conscience"—intrigues, irritates, or fascinates Americans. In general, he remains fundamentally foreign to them. Camus, however, presents through literature what is for the Anglo-Saxon mind often the essential thing: an ethic. And this ethic finds fruitful soil here in America. I would not say that Americans are always sensitive to what is deepest in Camus's thought: the sense of a tangible, vital participation in life that one might call "the solar joy." What they like most is the *Old Man and the Sea* aspect of Camus, the concern he shares with Hemingway or Melville for man's struggle within the universe and against it. Camus continues and expounds a humanistic ethic that stresses effort more than success, and that unwittingly nourishes the ascetic spirit still alive in America in spite of the cult of success and well-being.

But even more, Camus's sense of the tragic goes to the heart of the American situation. In the polemic debate which separated them, Sartre reproached the author of *The Plague* for making the struggle against Heaven the central theme of human activity, for translating the "ideal" situation of occupied France's fight against Nazism into the Manichaean vision of a Humanity aligned together against absolute Evil. Sartre argued that this was a betrayal of the true conditions of man's struggle to make an ideal of humanity triumph. Now—and this is striking—the allegory of the plague retains all its force within the American context, where it seems to find a natural setting. In American society there are no class conflicts; racial conflicts never for an instant put the social structure in doubt; and nothing basic separates either political parties or spiritual group . In the final analysis, because the collective organism is confronted neither with internal dissidence nor really harrowing problems, men of good will automatically find themselves united in the face of evil.... [It is] the *medical* element in Camus that is most acutely felt [in *The Plague*]; the courage which rises above ultimate and inevitable failure, the day-to-day love for men as they are, and a certain confidence in man, in spite of faults which are never moral defects. Here, in short, is an ethics rigorously separated from politics, or, if you prefer, inseparable from the sort of politics that can be reduced to ethics. Camus's humanism is the spiritual face of American democracy.

It is true that if for Camus the human struggle can only end in provisional victories that will ceaselessly be questioned, American optimism tends rather to envisage a progress that is slow perhaps, but sure—a unilateral advance, in spite of retreats or pauses. At first glance one might see in this remark a conflict between two points of view. This would be to misunderstand the writer's role in America. The best American writers have attempted to give body and a voice precisely to those tragic elements that society officially wishes to ignore, but that survive in the unspoken consciousness of many. Hemingway and Faulkner spoke out for those who keep silent. So does Camus in our own day.... I would venture to say that it is not in *spite* of his atheistic humanism, but *because* of it, that Camus is so popular here. Here at last is someone who has expressed in black and white the secular ethics which is at the heart of this American civilization, where piety is most often merely a pious fraud. (pp. 17-19)

Serge Doubrovsky, "Camus et l'Amérique," in Nouvelle Revue Française *(reprinted by permission of the author and* Nouvelle Revue Française*), February 1, 1961 (translated by Ellen Conroy Kennedy and reprinted as "Camus in America" in* Camus: A Collection of Critical Essays, *edited by Germaine Brée, Prentice-Hall, Inc., 1962, pp. 16-19).*

GERMAINE BRÉE

Camus's rapid rise to celebrity between 1942 and 1945 is unparalleled in the history of French literature: *The Stranger, The Myth of Sisyphus,* the two plays *Caligula* and *The Misunderstanding,* together with Camus's role in the Resistance and the widespread interest in his *Combat* editorials, started his career in meteoric fashion. This sudden fame was not easy for the young writer, and there were many in the clannish and often supercilious world of Paris letters who, as long as he lived, reproached Camus for something he had neither sought nor wanted. (p. 4)

Camus never allowed himself to forget that he had once been a lonely child, defenseless against himself and against a paradoxical and often shockingly brutal world. This early unhappiness was the source of much of his strength and even, sometimes, of his inflexibility.

Another of the motivating forces behind both Camus's actions and his work was a violent and apparently never resolved struggle of opposing character traits. Like his Caligula, Camus had a drive toward self-affirmation, which, unchecked, might have turned into a cruel form of self-indulgence that he seemed to identify with the amorality, indifference, and serenity of the cosmos. But Camus also had a passionate need for self-denial, for a kind of effacement within the "world of poverty" that was his as a child. Each one of these powerful inner forces could have led to forms of self-destruction, which the act of writing seems to have held in check. The climate of Camus's work is inseparable from his struggles to maintain a sane equilibrium. At all times Camus refused the romantic delectation of thinking of himself as an individual apart from all others, marked by fate for a singular career. (p. 5)

[The] silent uncomplaining figure of his deaf mother seems to have created in the child an overwhelming sense of compassion, all the harder to bear because of his helplessness. She was the inspiration for one of the essential figures in many of his later plays and novels and suggested a fundamental symbol: the silent mother, the land of Africa, the earth, death.

The silence that both separated and united the mother and son, born as much of her endless labor as of her deafness, was later to influence the young writer's thought deeply concerning the problems of communication and expression. He was often to define the writer's "commitment" as the obligation to speak for those who are silent, either because, like his mother, they are unused to the manipulation of words, or because they are silenced by various forms of oppression.... A major source of Camus's work, which from the very start carried it beyond the frontiers of social satire or recrimination, is Camus's understanding of and sensitivity to that part of all lives which is spent in solitude and silence. He, too, struggled with that almost intolerable compassion which rings in the words of his youthful Caligula: "Men die and they are not happy." It was from this depth of compassion that Camus drew a sense of solidarity with human beings so profound that he could accept them in their fundamental nudity—an acceptance certain doctors come to experience, such as Camus's Dr. Rieux in *The Plague.*

To this basic experience of sadness, Africa added an experience of joy. No one has spoken of the glory of the Mediterranean landscape better than Camus. As a boy he roamed over its beaches and hills. The landscape of North Africa appears in all his writing, carrying with it the sense of freedom and life through his essential symbols: the sun, the sea, and many different sorts of light. "There is a solitude in poverty" he wrote, "but a solitude which gives its proper rank to all things. At a certain level of wealth the sky itself and a night full of stars seem natural possessions. But at the bottom of the ladder the sky takes on all its meaning: a grace without price."

To lose either the sense of one's human vulnerability and therefore solidarity with others, or the sense of one's participation in the grandeur of the cosmos is in Camus's language to move into the "desert" of exile. One can accept a drastic simplification which Camus himself made when he said that he was born in a country—North Africa—which, unlike Europe, taught no lesson other than that "there is on the one hand man, in his essential poverty and vulnerability; on the other, the glory of the cosmos in which he moves." (pp. 5-6)

Young Camus, rather like his character Meursault in *The Stranger,* seems to have had an infinite capacity for living fully in the sensuous plenitude of each passing minute. If death is the essential discovery and the beginning of lucidity in Camus's first works, this awareness seems to be due partly to his confrontation with a problem he might not otherwise have envisaged in the same way. His reaction was first one of revulsion, then of refusal and of a passionate commitment to fight this personal form of "the plague."

The word "revolt" is not used by Camus in any generally accepted sense, and that is where the arguments and admonishments of some of his more highly abstract commentators have failed to reckon with Camus's meaning. His revolt is not directed against the romantic aspiration to transcend and destroy the limitations of the human being. It is directed against all that conspires to lessen any man's capacity for functioning with the greatest chance for happiness within these limitations. The enemies Camus detected and relentlessly fought were all the forces that stifle human beings—another of his basic symbols—whether these forces be mental, individual, or institutional; stemming from somnolence, insensitivity, or the myriad ideologies and systems, the complacent "godless theologies," of our time.

It is in this very personal context, rather than in abstract intellectual formulas, that one must seek the genesis of Camus's work and its freshness. The full flavor of the personality, sensitivity, and imagination of the man has often been lost in unnecessarily complex analyses. If, as seems likely, *The Stranger* continues to be one of the significant works in twentieth-century literature, it is not merely because of the new qualities of tone and energy in the writing. (pp. 6-7)

He was never hampered by the grinding and obsessive sense of limitation and guilt that Sartre seems to feel as a "petit-bourgeois" in the era of "the Masses." ... Sartre settles with his conscience through speech and writing, whereas Camus took positions and acted directly in the political issues of concern to him, whether with or against the point of view prevalent in his entourage. The football player and lightweight boxing champion of Algiers that he had once been never mistook a battle of words for a real battle with all the physical risks, violence, and dangers it involved. Both what he had to say and the way he said it stood out with startling distinctness against the complex and often nebulous background of a literature richer at that time in literary *savoir-faire* than in authentic literary creativeness. (pp. 7-8)

His natural Mediterranean flair for drama and mystification found an outlet in his passion for the theater—all facets of the theater.... A feeling of the stage, of the voice speaking directly to an audience, of dialogue projected across the footlights to link audience and actor is present everywhere in his work. Camus was immensely sensitive to the quality of the human voice. It is one of his major tools of creation and establishes with the reader a certain carefully calculated rapport. Whatever the work, there is always a dialogue implicit in Camus's fictional universe: between himself and his main characters; between them and the reader; between the reader and the author. He and his characters address themselves to an audience.

Camus's unusual capacity for "dead-pan" impersonation, satire, and hoax is one of the highroads to the understanding of the peculiar, paradoxical form of imagination most obviously at work in *The Stranger, Caligula,* and *The Fall.* . . . [His] playfulness and sometimes grim irony have no small part in the genesis of much of Camus's early work and in his favorite method of fictional creation: impersonation. Of *The Fall* Camus explicitly said, "Here I used techniques of the theater, the dramatic monologue and the implied dialogue, in order to describe a tragic comedian." Perhaps *The Stranger* and *The Fall* prove so disturbing to many readers precisely because they are . . . deliberately intended to disrupt the reader's tranquility. . . . [Few] critics have remarked upon the ferocious humor everywhere evident in *Caligula* and the more apparent but even more devastating humor pervading *The Fall.* Some of the confusion concerning Camus's ideas arises from a tendency to equate them with the points of view of his fictional characters. A dramatic monologue, obviously, is not the same thing as a personal confession. The aesthetic intents in these two forms of writing are basically opposed. Clamence, the Satanic impersonator, is Albert Camus's creation, only ironically his mouthpiece, and never Albert Camus himself. In a sense Clamence is a very modern version of Diderot's *Rameau's Nephew,* although no "philosopher," unless it be the reader himself, is there to maintain the dialogue. Camus asks a great deal of his reader. (pp. 8-9)

> *Germaine Brée, in her introduction to* Camus: A Collection of Critical Essays, *edited by Germaine Brée (copyright © 1962 by Prentice-Hall, Inc.; reprinted by permission of Prentice-Hall, Inc., Englewood Cliffs, New Jersey), Prentice-Hall, 1962, pp. 1-10.*

ALFRED CISMARU and THEODORE KLEIN

It is customary to think of Camus as the great apostle of life in this century, and to view his work as testimony to the acceptability, indeed the worthiness of the human condition. It is equally routine to regard Beckett as an exploiter of nihilism, and to brand his literary output as cadaveric, as one denoting a paralyzed, indeed a corpsed universe. Their concept of suicide, however, . . . precludes such simple conclusions and points instead to an unsuspected rapport between the two writers. . . .

In Camus the persona discovered one of its most subtle and sophisticated advocates. The subtlety of Camus found that it was necessary to insist on the integrity of the absurd experience. The "integration" of the persona resulted from the insistence that "There is thus the will to live without rejecting anything of life, which is the virtue I honor most in this world." . . . Camus worked from the presupposition that life is acceptable, even though in the more cynical mood of *The Fall* he conceded: "But in certain cases carrying on, merely continuing, is superhuman." Nevertheless for Camus suicide constituted the avoidance of the absurd, rather than its confrontation, for which he opted. (p. 105)

In the work of Camus . . . numerous are the instances when his rejection of suicide appears without qualifications. *The Myth of Sisyphus* is in fact a treatise on suicide, the one and only serious philosophical problem, a phrase made famous by the author at the very beginning of his essay. The point which Camus wishes to reveal to us immediately is that, if one becomes conscious of the vanity of the human condition, of the nonsense of life, one is no longer capable of accepting the trap of going on, because of habit, or because of the force of inertia. One is tempted, instead, by that exile without return which death exemplifies. Camus writes: . . .

> Dying voluntarily implies that you have recognized, even instinctively, the ridiculous character of that habit, the absence of any profound reason for living, the insane character of that daily agitation, and the uselessness of suffering.

But then he asks the question: "Does denying that life makes sense imply that it is not worth living?" . . . On the contrary, it becomes obvious to him that the less sense there is in a life which carries its own degenerating factors, and which is temporal, the more it is worth living. A challenging approach, to be sure, but one which, if espoused, leads inevitably to the conclusion: "One must imagine Sisyphus happy." . . .

But can one? Does his intolerable burden, or ours, permit such an optimistic *ergo*? Perhaps the answer depends on the temperament of the one who poses the question and cannot be imposed on him by a philosopher, no matter how seducing, or even decoying his language is. For Camus and his followers, however, there is no doubt about the cathartic quality of confrontation, of staring into the face of the absurd . . . and of experiencing the thrill of combat even if the negative outcome is known in advance. For as he declares in his *Lettres à un ami allemand:* "I continue to believe that this world has no superior meaning. But I know that something in it makes sense, and that is man, because he is the only being to require meaning. This world contains at least the truth of man, and our task is to supply him with reasons against his destiny. And the world has no other reason outside of man, and it is the latter we must save." And if man is saved, or saves himself by rejecting the alternative of suicide, then he may be able to join Camus in the great lyrical outburst: "The world is beautiful, and outside of it there is no salvation."

This is not to say that Camus opts for life in view of a future compensation of some kind. Rather, as is evident throughout *The Rebel,* he opts for life because self-annihilation presents a number of insurmountable problems. To begin with, it tends to be considered a flight, a copout, a cowardly form of escapism, or even a trickery. Secondly, suicide cannot be concordant with absurdist reasoning . . . [for absurdist reasoning accepts, in Camus' words, the "desperate encounter between human inquiry and the silence of the universe"]. (pp. 105-06)

But the most powerful argument evoked by Camus against suicide is the fact that the absolute negation that it appears to be, fails to negate very much at all. Suicide is usually thought to be the ultimate act of destruction. But such an act is always willed, always performed in the name of some value. It is always preceded by a *because* and always followed by a *therefore.* It cannot be otherwise, and it follows that, on the contrary, suicide becomes a most powerful act of affirmation. In fact Camus considers it so idiosyncratic that, in his opinion, when occurring, it can only rehabilitate life by renewing its meaning or adding to it. Such a rehabilitation is, of course, tardy for the deceased. But for those who survive, the reintegration into the kingdom of man is facilitated. Little wonder, then, that although he examines the question of suicide, and for a brief time he gives it the status of an alternative, the entire literary production of Camus can be viewed as an apologia of life. (p. 107)

[Both] Camus and Beckett unequivocally reject suicide, but

whereas Camus' rejection represents a celebration or affirmation of life, no such acceptance of life is implicit in Beckett's resolve to go on living. There is no glorification or exaltation of the state of animation in Beckett, nor does his rejection of suicide represent a synthesis or solution. Camus exorcizes Thanatos, the death urge, with the resolve to abide within the context of the absurd, while in Beckett the ubiquitousness of the absurd causes the distinction between life and death to become blurred, thus removing the *possibility* of suicide. Whereas both consider it often, Camus merely rejects it; Beckett, on the other hand, goes further: he invalidates suicide altogether. (p. 110)

> *Alfred Cismaru and Theodore Klein, in* Renascence *(© copyright, 1976, Marquette University Press), Winter, 1976.*

ALLEN SIMPSON

The movement . . . from unconsciousness to consciousness and despair and back to unconsciousness, has been analysed by Albert Camus in his essay *The Myth of Sisyphus.* (pp. 278-79)

Camus' essay deals exclusively with . . . the question of one's response to the awareness that life has no transcendent meaning. The essay "attempts to resolve the problem of suicide . . . without the aid of eternal values which, temporarily perhaps, arc absent or distorted in contemporary Europe." . . . [It] was written during a major world disaster and . . . was acclaimed as an important contribution to the resolution of the problems raised by that disaster. . . .

Camus views Sisyphus' . . . hopeless struggle as monumental, heroic. . . .

[The] emphasis is placed on the torment of consciousness, because it is consciousness that brings the recognition of ultimate futility and defeat. (p. 279)

Camus, at the end [of his essay], returns his hero to his futile labor, stands back and, on behalf of this hero, celebrates his life; and, . . . Camus . . . makes an assumption—a leap of faith, really—about his hero's feelings about his life: "One must imagine Sisyphus happy." Like all leaps of faith, [the author begs] the question. (p. 280)

Camus' absurd hero does not gradually "return into the chain." . . . The struggle to remain awake, to remain always aware of the absurdity of what one does, and yet to avoid paralyzing, nihilistic despair, continues all his life. . . .

In "The Myth of Sisyphus," Camus insists that modern man's greatest task, and his only chance to completely realize himself, is to acquire the knowledge that Camus possesses, and to preserve this knowledge intact and yet not despair. . . . (p. 281)

> *Allen Simpson, in* Scandinavian Studies, *Summer, 1976.*

IRÈNE FINEL-HONIGMAN

In his notebooks and in his novel *The Plague,* Albert Camus often describes the city of Oran in negative terms. He stresses the qualities or characteristics Oran lacks, seeing in this absence a source of inspiration.

In Camus' universe the cities of North Africa, Oran and Alger, serve an essential function. They are not only the background for his works but they are the embodiment of man's relationship with his environment. The topos of Camus' world revolves around a desert-city dichotomy. (p. 75)

In all of Camus' fiction, the city imposes its own personality and attributes upon its inhabitants. . . .

Camus' initial impressions of cities are visual and organic. He focuses on minutia. . . . Camus mentions the city's spiritual indifference and climatic excesses such as Oran's autumnal "deluges and floods of mud." . . . Oran is not in coordination with nature; it is a city which has denied its natural boundaries with the sea and has, therefore, destroyed an essential communion. (p. 76)

Oran in *The Plague* becomes a living entity. The city dictates the habits and concerns of its population. Oran is an enclosed microcosm of modern urban society where nature is denied and forgotten. . . . He endows the city with the literary form given to people. Oran personified in *The Plague* becomes a collective protagonist in its own right.

Textually and contextually Oran structures the novel. In the first line Oran establishes the novel's geographic boundaries: "The unusual events described in this chronicle occurred in 194- in Oran." . . . The limits of the text and of the city are synchronized. The reader and the narrator are imprisoned within the city limits of Oran, escaping only once in the scene of the sea bath. The last line in the novel transcends the specific context of Oran but emphasizes the city: ". . . it would rouse up its rats again and send them forth to die in a happy city." . . . The last word "city" is translated from "cité." The use of "city" distinguishes it from the "town" ["ville"] of Oran.

The Plague is divided into five parts, each section focusing on the progressive relationship between Oran and the plague. . . .

Rieux, the narrator, does not provide political, socio-economic, or statistical information. The leaders and administrators remain anonymous both in name and function, referred to only as "the authorities," "the municipality," or "the administrators." The city is a living organism which acts collectively; its leaders are only appendages. (p. 77)

The plague gives Oran mythological dimensions. In Camus' works the modern city is a mythic archetype of death, exile, and isolation. . . . The stone, like the other elements in nature, is part of the natural harmony of the desert. In the city these same elements become indifferent or antagonistic. . . .

Before the plague, Oran was a city without a past. Oran personified must wait for the advent of the Plague to realize its myths and history. Rootless, neutral, and indifferent to its surroundings, the plague gives Oran a particular heritage, identifying it with a long line of plagueridden cities throughout history. (p. 78)

In Camus' work, Rieux is among the very first to hear the word, and immediately the word, "Plague," provokes a proliferation of images of cities turned into charnel houses and graveyards:

> Athens, a charnel-house reeking to heaven
> and deserted even by the birds; Chinese
> towns cluttered up with victims silent in
> their agony; the convicts of Marseille piling
> rotting corpses into pits; . . . men and

women copulating in the cemeteries of Milan; cartloads of dead bodies rumbling through London's ghoul-haunted darkness-nights and days filled always, everywhere, with the eternal cry of human pain. . . .

For Rieux the connotations are abstract and literary, yet the text has already made its impact on the reader by this profusion of horrifying flash-images. Through the plague, Oran takes its place among these hellish cities. (p. 79)

The Plague can be read on two superimposed contextual levels, as a literal description of the disease's impact on the city of Oran or as an allegory of the Nazi occupation in a European city. Camus prefaces the novel by a quotation from Daniel Defoe: "It is as reasonable to represent one kind of imprisonment by another, as it is to represent anything that really exists by that which exists not." . . .

Camus wrote this work during the war and published it in 1947, the first major French novel after the war. His introductory quotation calls for an allegorical reading. The allegorical structure of the novel is progressively interwoven into the text by a pattern of historical and sociological analogies. The plague is an emblem of exile, death, and arbitrary evil. The city of Oran is not only a besieged city but contains within its walls two substructures: the bureaucracy of death leading to the creation of crematoriums and the all-male quarantine camp, allegories of the concentration camps and the prisoner-of-war camps. Oran in this interpretation transcends its definition as a city and becomes a microcosm of the war-torn state.

The transformation of Oran from a neutral, indifferent city to a victimized, closed, and occupied city becomes the underlying theme in the narrator's chronicle. Indifference gives way to gradual awareness as the plague invades all neighborhoods and affects all citizens regardless of their position or rank. . . . Like the German troops in French cities, the plague supersedes previous administrative systems. The occupied city must adapt to a new order. (pp. 79-80)

The end of the narrator's chronicle of *The Plague* is a denial of the city. Even liberated Oran remains "stifled, strangled" in contrast to the free natural world around it. As protagonist, myth, or allegory, the city is linked to the plague. It can never be entirely free of this association. (p. 81)

> *Irène Finel-Honigman, "Oran: Protagonist, Myth and Allegory," in* Modern Fiction Studies *(© copyright 1978, by Purdue Research Foundation, West Lafayette, Indiana), Spring, 1978, pp. 75-81.*

*   *   *

CARPENTIER, Alejo   1904-

Carpentier is a Cuban novelist, poet, short story writer, editor, journalist, librettist, and composer. His wide scope of interests, which range from politics and botany to the mythology and music of primitive Indian civilizations, is evident in his highly complex novels. His variety, coupled with his concern for time, has brought critical comparison with Jorge Luis Borges. *Los pasos perdidos (The Lost Steps)* is one of his best known works. (See also *CLC*, Vol. 8, and *Contemporary Authors*, Vols. 65-68.)

HELMY F. GIACOMAN

El Acoso, in addition to its many virtues as a novella, is a rare successful attempt meaningfully and consistently to represent in a literary work the complex structure, tone, and rhythm of a specific musical work (Beethoven's *Eroica*). (p. 103)

Both works of art represent radical creative departures for Beethoven and Carpentier. The *Eroica* is a symphony that revolutionized symphonic structure—the continuous and organic mode of connecting the second subject with the first, the introduction of episodes into the development, the extraordinary importance of the *Coda,* are all complete departures from previous musical tradition. In "El Acoso," also, we have an intensification of a highly technical structure, plot, and presentation of characters. Carpentier's deep knowledge of music seems to have led him to adapt many of Beethoven's musical techniques. He succeeds, as did Beethoven, in creating a work whose emotional impact is enhanced, rather than overwhelmed, by intricate technical complexity. If we were to choose a common characteristic in the structural and thematic elements of both works, we would have to say that both represent great examples of the mystery that is the dialectic of art: the wedding of simplicity and complexity.

Carpentier has succeeded in reproducing the symphony on at least three different structural levels that are ingeniously related through characters and style. On the first level, an orchestra is presenting the *Eroica* itself in a concert hall; this playing of the *Eroica* is the dramatic focus of the story. The two main characters, El Acosado and El Taquillero, listen to it and comment, and the music is described as it is performed. On the second level, the various themes of the symphony are psychological stimuli for the personal associations of El Acosado, who, as he listens to the concert, experiences flashbacks of episodes that occurred to him as he hid in the tower. (pp. 103-04)

Thus El Acosado feels nausea in the concert hall, not purely from fear, but because once when he was on the roof, he drank warm water that made him vomit and at that moment the Taquillero was playing that portion of the symphony. Carpentier has used a Pavlovian notion to help achieve a unique association, by way of music, space, and time.

On the third level we have the structure of the short novel itself, which is organized to correspond to the symphonic movements. Both action and characters seem to follow the motifs and themes of the music. We can see that even the rhythmic patterns of words follow important musical rhythms at appropriate points in the story. (p. 104)

Both works are portraits of heroism, the *Eroica* of Napoleon and "El Acoso" of El Acosado. The first movement of the *Eroica* is certainly a section of grandeur and the beginning is the high point. . . . [The] animating soul of the whole movement is ushered in by two great staccato chords of E flat from the full orchestra. (pp. 104-05)

Carpentier begins his story by equating the appearance of El Acosado with the heroic theme. Just as the symphony is dedicated to the heroism of Napoleon, the story centers around El Acosado as a modern hero on a smaller scale. Both have joined revolutionary movements that seek to change the structure of society, bring justice for all, and create a better world in which to live. In the same way that

Napoleon's very efforts to achieve these ends brought his downfall, El Acosado suffers the same fate as his victims and is finally humbled by defeat. Technically, the author of the story uses two words to correspond to the initial E flat staccato chords, which begin the heroic theme: "One," and "Anywhere". To the triple variation of these chords corresponds the physical presentation of El Acosado and his two pursuers. The strings follow the first heroic motive with the second theme, that of El Taquillero. (p. 106)

As the orchestra plays the heroic theme, El Acosado parallels the same effect by his utterance of the Credo. Just as the orchestra leads us to seek new keys and new subjects, the story also introduces to us several characters. The most important of these is El Taquillero, who appears now in an isolated context. At this point in the story we learn more about his past experiences, his subjective emotions, etc. As the symphony moves through the three subjects that form the transition period and develops the first lyrical motive, El Taquillero, who has been listening, leaves the concert hall and goes to visit Estrella, the young prostitute who has just betrayed El Acosado. El Taquillero senses immediately that Estrella has changed, that she does not welcome him as usual. This corresponds to the sudden change from a tender theme to battle and conflict that occurs in the symphony. El Taquillero desperately attempts to distract Estrella from her concern over the visit from El Acosado's pursuers. The counterplay of chords corresponds to the dissonance in the thoughts of Estrella and El Acosado. (pp. 106-07)

The entire *Coda,* with the "development" section, represents the heroic dream of El Taquillero, who as a young man disappointed in love, hopes to become a great composer. The transition in the form of a fugue is illustrated by the stream of consciousness that takes place when he re-experiences female scorn and half realizes that even now his musical vocation can be overcome by passionate desire. El Taquillero's reverie is suddenly interrupted by Estrella's repetition of the word *inquisition*. This word, spoken four times, corresponds to the notes of the horn that occur at the end of the "development" section of the symphony. The horn symbolizes hunting, and Estrella's mention of Inquisition brings to mind her betrayal of El Acosado.

The funeral march that follows is one of the most perfect in form and variation. It is a huge movement, highly elaborated and extended. And yet each time one says, "Oh no, he cannot do that theme again," Beethoven comes up with the most inventive surprise and turns what might have been a repetitious moment into one of blinding glory. . . . Finally when we hear the march melody [in the *Coda*] instead of a simple restatement, we literally see it break into fragments like the speech of one so overcome by grief that he can speak only in halting, gasping efforts.

As we hear the funeral march, Carpentier introduces the humble attitude of La Vieja. He describes her laments as "weeping breath become words." During the repetitions and restatements of the symphony, El Acosado relives the experiences he had while living in the home of La Vieja, lacking food and water. (pp. 107-08)

Throughout this section, El Acosado tells us about his past and his early plans to study architecture when he arrived in Havana. All of his previous experiences are reproduced by the seeds of the musical development. During the fugue, we learn about the thoughts of El Acosado. Among other things, he remembers the poet Heredia and El Becario, who had recommended Estrella to El Acosado. As the fugue finishes and we are resting, El Acosado arrives at a crucial moment, the feeling that he knows the Truth. This mystical moment is represented in the symphony by the sforzando that we spoke of. As soon as the *Coda* begins, we see El Acosado again, this time suffering from hunger and thirst. Thinking of food as he listens to the concert, his associations lead to the past again. His conscience reproaches him for having eaten the food of La Vieja. The dramatic effects of the *tutti* parallel his frustration. With the death of the Vieja and the betrayal by Estrella, the Funeral March closes.

What follows now is a rather short and driving scherzo. Throughout we hear shocks and tremors as of a deep, subterranean disturbance. All is chained power and pent-up tension. . . . When the explosion [of relief] occurs, we are left with a deep, satisfying feeling. Throughout the Scherzo we are faced with a trio of three horns. . . . The entire scene illustrates a hunt.

There is an actual hunting scene in this section of the story. It is in this section that Carpentier develops the frantic efforts of El Acosado to evade the two men who relentlessly pursue him. . . . In this section of the novella, we witness the activities of the Acosado that led him to his present situation: his initiation into the revolutionary party, his betrayal and torture, his consequent condemnation as an informer. All of this and his remorse for having murdered the party enemy cause the mental anguish and guilt of El Acosado to reach an unbearable point, and the mental tension in the story is tremendous as El Acosado recalls his deed. . . . Just as in the symphony the tense mental introspection alternates with the lively chase. . . . The explosion and relief of the symphony parallel El Acosado's decision to talk to the police about his political activities, ending the excruciating torture to which they have subjected him. After he is released, "It was like the beginning of a convalescence, a return to the world of men." . . . (pp. 108-10)

The final movement of the *Eroica* presents a series of episodes in the form of fragments tied together by a central theme. In fact, it is a series of variations on simple themes. Perhaps the most notable feature of this section is its strong dynamic structure. (p. 110)

In the story a similar thematic structure parallels the symphony. A series of episodes of the past life of El Acosado are presented to us: his search for divine help, his attempt to seek refuge in a church. . . . El Acosado escapes from the church, and the sound of the nearby thunderstorm (presented in the orchestra by the brass section) brings him to a café. Here he finds the two men who were chasing him. . . . They rise to shoot him down, but El Acosado escapes and hides in the concert hall. There he expects to evade his tormentors, and listens to the symphony that he had heard for many days while hidden in the tower in the house of La Vieja. . . . [The] grandeur of the thunder shakes the theater in a fitting Finale. We find that the reliving of El Acosado's heroic suffering has taken place in forty-six minutes, the duration of the *Eroica.* (pp. 110-11)

Helmy F. Giacoman, "The Use of Music in Literature: 'El Acoso' by Alejo Carpentier and 'Symphony No. 3 (Eroica)' by Beethoven," in Studies in Short Fiction *(copyright 1971 by Newberry College), Winter, 1971, pp. 103-11.*

ALEXANDER COLEMAN

From the point of view of strictly revolutionary literary ethics ["Explosion in a Cathedral"] was a curiously evasive achievement, dramatizing as it did the contradictory allegiances between private sensibility and public ideology. The two principal characters found themselves driven either toward a lucid, contemplative humanism or a draconian revolutionary spirit formed under the inevitable shadow and example of Saint-Just. Though it was set in the Antilles of the 18th century, most readers took the setting for what it is—pure Zanuck cum Goldwyn. "Explosion in a Cathedral" was the book of a writer who found himself to be an ambiguous if not anguished witness to the first years of a revolution in the here and now. . . .

["Reasons of State"] is variously set in the Paris of the teens and the twenties, and at the same time in a mythical country of a distinctly Central American stripe called Nueva Córdoba. . . . The declining tyrant (who remains nameless throughout) seems to be modeled on a few of those horrific dictators of the past—the "educated tyrant," as Carpentier calls them. . . .

In the long and not especially interesting history of literature and revolution, one thing can be said—politics and comedy rarely mix. Carpentier's earlier novels and stories were often pretty heavy going, what with their tiresome philosophizing and heavily laid-on historical panoplies. "Reasons of State" is something different—a jocular view of imaginative idealism, repressive power and burgeoning revolution, all done with breezy panache. Once again Carpentier has shown how canny and adept a practitioner he can be in mediating between the many realms which his own life has touched upon. (p. 51)

> *Alexander Coleman, in* The New York Times Book Review *(© 1976 by The New York Times Company; reprinted by permission), May 2, 1976.*

GREGORY RABASSA

Carpentier digs into the past; it almost seems as if he cannot get away from it, even in his novel *The Lost Steps*, which is contemporary in time but is really a search for origins—the origin first of music and then of the whole concept of civilization. Taken together, the elements of the search form a mosaic of the factors that went into the making of Latin America. . . .

Heretofore, the analysis of Latin America, with a few exceptions, has been either superficial or an exercise in patriotics. Carpentier has looked deeper, always keeping a historical perspective. He is particularly attuned to the French influence, which other authors have too often neglected—except as a cliché. Haiti and the French pirates of the Caribbean have been the subjects of two previous Carpentier novels, *Explosion in a Cathedral* and *The Kingdom of the World*. In this new novel, too, although it deals with a Latin American dictator, the French element is important, since the tyrant is an ardent Francophile and the novel begins and ends in Paris. . . .

Carpentier's dictator in *Reasons of State* is a polished man. He is . . . an admirer of things French and the culture of Paris. . . .

As is so often the case with the well-written story of an ogre, the reader will, upon entering the mind and feelings of the dictator, come to sympathize with him and wish him well as he confronts his enemies. It is the actual reading of *Reasons of State* that so clearly shows the dangers of the powerful effects of such intimacy. (p. 36)

Carpentier's pathetic Head of State goes down to defeat and is helped into exile with the connivance of the American ambassador. When he reaches his beloved Paris, he finds [himself out of touch]. . . . There is a "generation gap," which Carpentier shows to be as tedious as ever. The Head of State is, then, a man out of his time, left to decay in a Paris that is no longer his. He dies there and is buried near Porfirio Díaz.

Carpentier has given us another facet to the recent upsurge of interest in tyrants in Latin America. Government is obviously important there: novelists are able to use it as an integral part of their work, in contrast to the rather flat and superficial pictures we often get of governments elsewhere. The recent "boom" has produced a subgenre that has its roots in Homer and Thucydides; it may be that our time-kept literary traditions now have Latin America as their strongest energy source. (pp. 36-7)

> *Gregory Rabassa, "Dictators and Other Mortals," in* Saturday Review *(© 1976 by Saturday Review/World, Inc.; reprinted with permission), May 29, 1976, pp. 36-7.*

PAUL WEST

What a spacious, noble view of fiction [Carpentier] has, proposing not chemisms, the darkling plain, the long arm of coincidence, the involuntary memory, the absurd, . . . , but a vision of the horn of plenty forever exploding, forever settling in bits that belong together more than they don't because there is nothing else for them to do. In Carpentier the All and the One remain unknown, and suspect even, but the aggregate of the Many, gorgeous and higgledy-piggledy, does duty for them, never construable but always lapped up. (p. 5)

Carpentier is a master of both detail and mass, of both fixity and flux. With none of Beckett's reductive extremism, little of Joyce's word-smelting multiplicity, he sometimes seems the only senior novelist today possessed of the view from a long way off: as if, during a sojourn on some noetic planet circling Barnard's star, he had seen mankind plain, and all our thinking, our births and deaths, our myths and structures and dreams, all our bittersweet velleities, rammed up against the anonymous doings of nature. . . . He is one of the few writers of whom you can say: If we didn't exist, he would be able to imagine us (assuming he was the only human). In other words, he can not only describe; he can describe what no-one has seen; and, best, he seems to have the hypothetical gift of suggesting, as he describes, that his description—a text woven from words—is experience newly reified, made more available, more dependable, and more reassuring, than daily bread or daily trash.

How odd, then, to find critical notices of *Reasons of State* which chide Carpentier for anachronism or inaccuracy, or which regard the book simply as an exercise in quasi-historical portraiture, or politicist cops and robbers; yet no odder than the complaint, made against his previous novels, that he engages in heavy pondering and actually dares to hold up "the action" in order to think. The truth is that his fiction is ostensible, and his characters . . . are pretexts. He has something more than narrative, or storytelling, in mind, and he uses it as bait. . . . What keeps on coming is the deluge of phenomena, against and amidst whose Niagara not only sentences and paragraphs, but mind and will themselves, are virtually helpless. And this is not only a theme in Carpentier's work: it is also a procedural mannerism evinced in thousands of exquisitely crafted sentences which, lovely in distension, threaten to distend further just because everything evokes everything else, and therefore all sentences are unsatisfactory surrogates for The Sentence, absolute and final, which unlinearly would render them unnecessary. . . . The agon of an articulateness born incomplete; the flirtation with the ghost of an articulateness born complete: these are his preoccupations, much as Beckett's failure to express, aggravating the need to express, is his. (pp. 5-6)

[*Reasons of State*] is far from exclusively political or didactic: a big buzzing blooming confusion fills it. . . . The Republic of Nueva Cordoba disarranges and disorders itself like Rimbaud's mind, from stink bombs at the opera to a general strike led by a stereotypical energumen called The Student. The comeuppance is fizzy and satirically epitomistic.

But diverting and amusing as all this is, it isn't the novel's main impact or the source of its perceptual zeal. . . . Carpentier, transcending satire even while he creates a near-documentary album, conducts us back—through and past matrices, regimes, credos, formulas, and codes, so familiar as almost to seem natural structures themselves—to an atavistic awe larded with unceremonious intrusions. Mind watches mind evolving, and distraction keeps it at full stretch. . . . (pp. 6-7)

Delving into phenomena, Carpentier finds every sense-datum, every phoneme, a cross-roads, down each fork of which he ponders his way, aware that the time-traveller's very presence modifies the space he's in. That long prose journey from "Now" to "the Looking-glass" exemplifies his way of making something infinitesimal exemplify infinity, something natural counterpoint something manufactured, something almost sacred something vulgar. Yet you can lose the whole thing, responding only to swell's augmentations rather than to swell's meaning, if you don't follow the allusion to Kant which at once undercuts and makes a triumphant finale. The passage is a triumph of style, of course, enacting in its movements—playful, dawdling, side-spill and eddy and full halt—its theme. And this reminds us that style for Carpentier is more than embellishment or panache, but a means of participating anew in the universe through the fixed physical configurations of prose rather than in some unwritten reverie. . . . Carpentier the impresario of metaphors, the keeper of an entire zoo of assorted specificities, weaves and reweaves complex patterns of transcendence which are like light streaming through a pornographic stained-glass window. (pp. 7-8)

Can we, the book implies, know what it is we do not know? There is no knowing that, but one lifetime's opportunity to observe acquaints us with the beguiling insufficiency of what we do know. As Carpentier proves, no matter how skilled we are at speculative hypothesis, our knowledge of our ignorance is mostly retrospective, except for the big, cosmic questions. (p. 8)

Paul West, "Despot-au-feu," in Review *(copyright © 1976 by the Center for Inter-American Relations, Inc.), Fall, 1976, pp. 5-8.*

ALAN CHEUSE

[Some] readers may have . . . decided that indeed the reasons for Carpentier's failure to capture an audience here are those same reasons put forth by the earliest reviewers: that his fiction is too "erudite," that he is more a "cultural historian" than a novelist, . . . or that he is a "tiresome philosophizer." . . .

One may quarrel with some of these negative views, but on the question of the absence of a substantial audience for the novelist's work, one flails about like a ghostfighter, firing at shadows, starting at the slightest sound in the woods. What makes the U.S. reading audience so obligingly ignorant of Cuba's greatest novelist? Perhaps the answer does lie in the books themselves. Certainly *The Lost Steps* for all its superficial affinities with the variety of romantic fiction which North Americans love to indulge in . . . presents an odd and strangely formidable face to the U.S. reader. Despite its emphasis on the estrangement of the main character from the life of the modern city and the lushness of its sequences devoted to jungle landscape and its exotic inhabitants, it remains an inherently ironic novel whose bite and tension seem lost in its English translation. (p. 16)

One would think that a better fate might lie in store for *The Kingdom of This World*. Its focus on the 18th-century insurrection of the Haitian slaves against the French colonial forces in the Caribbean offers fertile reading material for both blacks and whites caught up in the present North American struggle for racial equality and social justice. This fact may explain why this novel is the only Carpentier translation available in an American paperback edition. Its relative brevity may also contribute something to its appeal. These factors, in tandem with its adventurous and exotic subject matter—revolution, magic, the metamorphosis of men into beasts—may yet give it continuing life. Still, in a country whose audiences last century praised Melville for his early sea adventures and dropped him when he published *Moby Dick,* the vagaries of literary taste can hardly be accurately predicted.

An historical novel, *Explosion in a Cathedral* offers the broadest spectrum of any of Carpentier's works in translation. . . . Its style is more vital, catholic, and appealing than the other books, and John Sturrock's translation lends Carpentier's pithy amalgam of European and native metaphors and ideas a lustre and excitement some critics have found more appealing than the original Spanish. Carpentier's wedding of fiction and history in these pages stirs the imagination with great force. As the young Cuban named Esteban wades through rowdy scenes of revolution, piracy, and counter-insurrection, or views the baroque undersea creations which crowd the Caribbean sea bottom in mysterious and awesome profusion, the reader may invoke the names of the 19th-century masters of the genre in flattering comparison. This novel cannot be accused of either opacity or pretentiousness, two charges which, perhaps, *The Lost Steps* might generate. And yet it goes virtually unread in this country. (pp. 16-17)

[*War of Time,* a collection of novellas and stories, offers readers] the opportunity to see Carpentier at his playful best. In quasi-allegorical short works which toy with the themes of temporal sameness and historical mutability, the Cuban writer rivals in power and execution some of Borges' major enigmatic fictions and shows a face other than that of the dour, heavy-handed historical determinist some of his critics have made him out to be. The novella ''The Highroad of St. James,'' translated by Frances Partridge, depicts a 16th-century pilgrimage to a Spanish shrine which leads to a voyage of discovery, offering the scents and textures of the New World of the Americas as well as a whiff of eternity. It remains one of the most brilliant short novels of the century and yet, among North American readers, as unknown as were the Indies themselves in Europe prior to the expedition of Columbus. Or less so, since not even legends exist about it in our part of the world.

Reasons of State should appeal at the very least to admirers of . . . European political and social satire . . . or some of the more recent political fiction from Eastern Europe. Because of the rich, thickly lacquered opera bouffe style, its witty, self-parodying recapitulation of many previous Carpentier themes and rhetorical gestures may not be the best or easiest place for readers new to the style of Carpentier to begin. But this account of the fall of an eponymous Latin American dictator with a taste for French culture and local rum offers a grab-bag of marvellous set-pieces (a rebellion here, a massacre there) unparalleled in Latin American ''political'' novels since the publication of Asturias' masterpiece *El Señor Presidente* in 1949. For all of its allusiveness (and for all the allusions it will stir in its readers), it is a marvellously compact work sustained by an uncharacteristic but vigorous sense of humor.

Intelligence and erudition are certainly present, then, in Carpentier's fiction. But so are sex, violence, political uproar, war, revolution, voyages of exploration, naturalist extravaganzas, settings ranging from ancient Greece to contemporary New York City, and characters running the gamut from the simple Haitian protagonist of *The Kingdom of This World* to the worldly wise, word-weary Head of State, the dictator of the latest novel, all of this comprising a complex but highly variegated and appealing fictional matrix. As many elements of the ''redskin'' writer as ''paleface'' (to use Philip Rahv's useful terms for the writer of feeling as opposed to the writer of intellect) exist in Carpentier's fiction. Selden Rodman's complaint that the hero of *The Lost Steps* is ''so very very much the intellectual'' does not hold when applied to the body of the work as a whole. (p. 17)

> *Alan Cheuse, "The Lost Books," in* Review *(copyright © 1976 by the Center for Inter-American Relations, Inc.), Fall, 1976, pp. 14-19.*

MICHAEL WOOD

Latin America has long worn two conflicting masks. One expresses charm, gaiety, sentiment, a mood of comic opera and a long-running *belle époque*. The other suggests torture, massacres, tyrants, and endlessly trampled constitutions. Are the masks connected? Is the first a consolation for the second? Does the second rely on the frivolous complicity of the first? . . . [A tyrant in Carpentier's *Reasons of State*] thinks of Latin American history as an unreal suspension of time. . . .

[The novel questions how tyrants are] able to make themselves so needed, and more important, how is a country to do without them, and to keep their future avatars from

coming back? They are the malign royalty of a whole culture, clarifiers of countless fears and hopes and hatreds: hence their fascination even for those who detest them. Carpentier [shares] with other Latin American novelists, a strong sense of reality as fiction. . . . Reality is full of fictions in Europe and North America too, but I think we imagine the truth can be found, in most cases, if we really need it. In Latin America the truth is often not only unavailable, it is unimaginable, and unwanted. . . . [A] novel in Latin America, instead of being a fictional imitation of a historical world, or a self-conscious record of the movements of an individual mind, can become an attempt to understand a real world that is all too imaginary by means of imagined continuations of it: the good novels of literature combat the bad novels of life itself.

Even death is a fiction in *Reasons of State*. . . . [The] dictator pretends to die, so that people will come out into the streets and get shot down. The frequent and very funny jokes . . . [are] a way of getting at a reality contaminated with illusion. (p. 57)

Carpentier . . . is interested not in myth but in history, and his method is to plunge us circumstantially into an earlier period, before, during, and after the First World War. His tyrant is a man of culture. But he becomes, with time, a man of the past, and after a lengthy American-supported reign is deposed in an uprising, also supported by the Americans. . . .

At times Carpentier seems to want to force history into speech too quickly, and some of his dialogues—between the tyrant and a militant student, between the tyrant and a jazz-playing American consul—are too plainly set-ups, frames for talking dolls. But the book abounds with sharp images and sequences. . . . [For example,] the dictator asked by the American consul whether he figures in the *Petit Larousse,* and weeping in his downfall ''because a dictionary . . . was unaware of my existence.''

This last scene seems to echo [a] flickering sympathy for his ogre-hero, but Carpentier is actually doing something more complicated. When our feelings may be flowing toward the tyrant in his disgrace and exile, Carpentier informs us, very casually, of the man's admiration for Mussolini, then a figure rising in the world. Carpentier wants to turn his dictator into the opposite of a myth: into a historical and human character, mortal, comprehensible, and morally responsible for what he's done. He asks us therefore to perform an act of understanding which I find highly desirable but very hard to manage. He wants us to hold within a single perspective the careless author of futile massacres and the man who cries because Larousse has left him out. Carpentier himself is clearly able to look at both Latin American masks at once. . . . (p. 58)

> *Michael Wood, in* The New York Review of Books *(reprinted with permission from* The New York Review of Books; *copyright © 1976 Nyrev, Inc.), December 9, 1976.*

ROBERTO GONZÁLEZ ECHEVARRÍA

In Carpentier, as in most modern literature, allegory rests on the possibility of carrying the permutations [of allegory] further, to an idea of transcendence that is itself fictional and changeable. That movement away from each metaphor or conceit (the system of ideas to which allegory refers, and more specifically that movable center on which it rests) occurs at the very moment when the implications of a given philosophy threaten the fictionality of the text, by upsetting the balance of the dialectical play.

The plot in Carpentier's stories always moves from exile and fragmentation toward return and restoration, and the overall movement of each text is away from literature into immediacy, whether by a claim to be integrated within a larger context, Latin American reality or history, or by an invocation of the empirical author. But because of the dialectics just sketched, the voyage always winds up in literature and remains as the reason for yet another journey. (p. 22)

History is the main topic in Carpentier's fiction, and the history he deals with—the history of the Caribbean—is one of beginnings or foundations. (p. 25)

But if this origin-obsessed history is the theme of Carpentier's fiction, its deployment is more the product of Latin America's second beginning—that is to say, the eighteenth and nineteenth centuries—than of its remote origins in colonial times. The eighteenth and nineteenth centuries are also the historical setting of three of Carpentier's major works, *The Kingdom of This World, Explosion in a Cathedral,* and *Concierto barroco,* a fact that is clearly not accidental. The persistence of the structure and thematics of fall and redemption, of exile and return, of individual consciousness and collective conscience, stems from a constant return to the source of modern Latin American self-awareness within the philosophical coordinates of the transition from the Enlightenment to Romanticism. The origins of this concern in Carpentier are to be found in the dissemination of a strand of German philosophy throughout Latin America in the twenties, specifically the works of Hegel and Spengler. (pp. 26-7)

Carpentier's work is inscribed precisely at the point where the desire for immediacy stumbles upon the fiction of Latin America. . . . The itinerary of Carpentier's works includes the invention of an archaic language, as in Larreta, an encyclopedic erudition, as in Borges, and the constant desire to inaugurate Latin American writing, as in Neruda. To come to know Carpentier's trajectory is to come to know the problematics of modern Latin American literature. (p. 29)

In a sense, as in *The Lost Steps,* Carpentier's entire literary enterprise issues from the desire to seize upon that moment of origination from which history and the history of the self begin simultaneously—a moment from which both language and history will start, thus the foundation of a symbolic code devoid of temporal or spatial gaps. (p. 32)

Seen from the perspective of his later work and judged by purely aesthetic criteria, there can be no doubt that *¡Ecue-Yamba-O!,* "Histoire de lunes," "El milagro de Anaquillé," and other pieces of [the thirties] appear as hopelessly immature *Jugendwerken,* callow works in which only the barest outline of the future is discernible. Outside such a temporal chain, however, the works of the twenties and thirties constitute in themselves a fairly coherent nucleus, almost a single text wrought around one all-encompassing metaphor or conceit: the alluring otherness of Afro-Cuban culture, the cohesive religious force of which can become the source for a different writing, freed from the strictures of Western mentality. But whereas in Carpentier's later work that metaphoric center is strong, a dense and resilient structure that tenaciously preserves the illusion of unity,

the nucleus formed by the early work is, overall, a distinct example of the impossibility for a fictional text to become an autonomous, self-enclosed unit. The "failure" of that early nucleus is not its falling short of accomplishing a closure, but the ease with which its openness is revealed. (p. 61)

Carpentier . . . does not write directly against the conventions of the realistic novel, but in response to the crisis created by their crumbling. The failings or successes of his text must be seen within that moment of crisis, when fragmentation and dispersal were the order of the day. (p. 66)

What is striking about the documentary tendency in *¡Ecue-Yamba-O!* is the relative independence of [descriptions, plot, and characters], their unmediated incorporation, as in an anthropological treatise—witness the photographs, the "Anima Sola" prayer, the quotations of ritualistic songs. This bringing together of concrete slices of the real world has more in common with the syncopated rhythm of the collage than with the realistic descriptions of the classical novel, partakes more of the *objet trouvé* than of the integrated texture of a Balzacian or Galdosian description. . . .

[The text of *¡Ecue-Yamba-O!*] seems at times like a series of scenes and tableaux written separately and shuffled at random like a deck of cards. It is not stable even in a diachronic sense, for toward the end of the novel the texture of the prose becomes more even, losing some of the metaphoric impetus found at the beginning. (p. 71)

The most striking feature of "Histoire de lunes" is its careful temporal arrangement. . . . The locus of the narrative is the train station, a place of chronometrically determined passage and repetition, and the story, as the title indicates, hinges on the repetitive cycles of the moon. The vague complicity between the cycles of nature and events in *¡Ecue-Yamba-O!* has become more precise in "Histoire de lunes." But there is more, even in the opposition between the two nouns in the title itself: "history," implying a linear development, and "moons," involving a series of cosmic repetitions. The complex game of times, dates, and the cycles of nature begins to form a system of correspondences in this story that was not present in the other texts of the period. (pp. 90-1)

"Histoire de lunes" does not, of course, provide answers to all the questions arising from the various ideological trends of the avant-garde, the concrete sociopolitical problems of Cuba, and the crisis of the novel. But it is a more organized attempt to answer such questions than Carpentier's essayistic efforts, where Hegel, Marx, Spengler, and Ortega, in addition to the contingencies of Carpentier's own life and the history of Latin America, mingle to produce extremely confused statements. Basically, his answer to the problems posed by the narrative is a theological one, whose basis is mostly Spenglerian. The lack of continuity brought about by the crisis of the novel Carpentier solves with an all-encompassing metaphor of order, where the linear development of the plot is not the sole unifying force; rather, order is created by a complex web of symbolic relations outside the action—a sort of symbolic plenum. It is not an order on an assumed temporal continuity, but an atemporal system of symbolic relationships, akin to Spengler's model of culture where all modes of expression are linked by a central symbol derived from the observation of landscape. This allows Carpentier to integrate description and action in "Histoire de lunes" in a way that he had not been able to do in *¡Ecue-Yamba-O!* and had been able to circumvent in "El milagro de Anaquillé." (pp. 93-4)

If the five stories and *The Kingdom of This World* hold the most interest from a purely literary point of view, the book that defines this period in Carpentier's career and distinguishes it from the years of the avant-garde and Afro-Cubanism is *La música en Cuba,* a book that traces in scholarly detail the historical evolution of Cuban music from the colonial period to the present. The forties also encompass Carpentier's most sustained and significant experiments with fantastic literature—a kind of literature that critics have commonly associated with the concept of "magical realism." (p. 98)

History breaks into Carpenterian fiction as a result of the work done in writing *La música en Cuba. ¡Ecue-Yamba-O!,* "Histoire de lunes," and "El milagro de Anaquillé" reflect, without historical precision, events that are contemporaneous, or nearly so, with their author. The research and the writing of *La música en Cuba* furnish Carpentier with a new working method, which consists of minute historical investigation, and creation from within a tradition that the author remakes himself with the aid of texts of different sorts. More specifically, *La música en Cuba* channels Carpentier's fiction into a new course, a search for those forgotten texts which will allow him to "finish" the incomplete biographies of obscure historical figures with the aid of rigorous documentation and almost verifiable chronology. (pp. 102-03)

Another significant change takes place in Carpentier's writing during the forties, on which his research for *La música en Cuba* had a direct bearing: style. In *¡Ecue-Yamba-O!,* "Histoire de lunes," and even the scenario for "El milagro de Anaquillé," Carpentier's prose is laden with the stylistic tics of the extreme avant-garde: daring metaphors, oxymoronic adjectives, onomatopoeia, syncopated syntax. In the forties, Carpentier's prose begins to rid itself of these (although it will never lose them all) and to become the archaic, textured, and baroque prose for which he is known. (p. 106)

Carpentier's artistic enterprise in the forties became a search for origins, the recovery of history and tradition, the foundation of an autonomous American consciousness serving as the basis for a literature faithful to the New World. Like an American Ulysses, Carpentier sets forth in search of this goal through the winding roads and the turbulent rivers of the continent, but also through the labyrinthine filigrees of worm-eaten texts eroded by time and oblivion. . . . [In] recovering history by in a sense allowing the texts that contain it to repeat themselves in his writing, Carpentier is reaching for that elusive Golden Age when fable and history were one. (p. 107)

Carpentier searches for the marvelous buried beneath the surface of Latin American consciousness, where African drums still beat and Indian amulets rule; in depths where Europe is only a vague memory of a future still to come. . . . Besides his attacks against certain Surrealists, which are echoes of skirmishes in the thirties, Carpentier's [prologue to *The Kingdom of This World*] affirms that the marvelous *still* exists in Latin America, and *reveals* itself to those who believe in it, not to those who would apprehend it by a reflexive, self-conscious act. The appeal to faith and

to history ("still"), cast Carpentier's formulations in a Spenglerian mold. Even Carpentier's attacks on the Surrealists are based on Spengler, and it is only by returning to *The Decline of the West* that we can understand the meaning that Carpentier assigns to the marvelous and his definition of the faith that sustains it. (p. 123)

Spengler posited that cultures were like organisms that underwent homologous evolutions until they disappeared (the world as history). . . . For Spengler, as for Carpentier and other Latin American intellectuals who fell under his spell, the New World found itself in a moment of its historical evolution—a moment of faith—prior to the moment of reflexivity, while Europe felt estranged from the forms of its own culture and searched in laws and codes of universal pretensions, like Surrealism, the mystery of creation irretrievably lost. . . . Spengler is the common ground of Carpentier's works of the thirties and forties; the differences are only a matter of narrative strategy. Whereas in *¡Ecue-Yamba-O!* and "Histoire de lunes" he attempts to situate the narrative focus or source within an unreachable African world of beliefs to which his own consciousness has no access, now he will attempt to clear a space from within which he can lay claim to a more broadly conceived faith. The works of the forties are also grounded on a theological view of history and the narrative process except that such theology has become better refined and its contradictions more skillfully concealed. Magical realism, or "marvelous American reality," is but a new theology of fiction bent on bridging the gap between maker and cosmos. (pp. 124-25)

Carpentier's concept of the marvelous or of magic rests on an onto-theological assumption: the existence of a peculiar Latin American consciousness devoid of self-reflexiveness and inclined to faith; a consciousness that allows Latin Americans to live immersed in culture and to feel history not as a causal process that can be analyzed rationally and intellectually, but as destiny. From the perspective to which that mode of being aspires, fantasy ceases to be incongruous with reality in order for both of them to turn into a closed and spherical world without cracks or ironic detachment. . . . (pp. 125-26)

Carpentier's stories of the forties are distinguishable from his earlier production and from that which immediately follows them by their historical setting; costumes, objects, known incidents, and other aspects serve to designate a past epoch which in most cases is the late eighteenth and early nineteenth centuries. . . . [Static] history characterizes Carpentier's fiction in the forties. It is not simply that Carpentier offers a decentered anti-Hegelian view of history, but that the historical process appears as a dynamic cycle of repetitions that results in a static and permanent image, like the spokes of a turning wheel which project static images of themselves. This is why the historical world presented by Carpentier in his stories is always one of imposing buildings and ruins, a world of palaces and dismantled mansions, the two poles of a universe in constant construction and demolition. (pp. 129-30)

All the devices used by Carpentier to evoke the fantastic during the forties must be seen within the context of [a] baroque magic: fantasies conjured in the name of a faith that is the greatest artifice, the all-encompassing fiction, the liturgical sacramental theater where the irreconcilable poles of the contradictions are exchanged, conjugated, where they interplay. Such a faith is the space of literature that does not satisfy the Carpentier of the prologue, but within which all of his gestures are inscribed. (p. 153)

There are many indications of a new Carpentier in *The Lost Steps*. To begin with, this is the first work of his that he calls a novel since *¡Ecue-Yamba-O!* (the title page of the original reads: *Los pasos perdidos. Novela*). *The Kingdom of This World*, though commonly referred to as a novel, was subtitled *relato* (French, *récit*). The distinction is noteworthy. The stories written during the forties and *The Kingdom of This World* are fragmentary accounts of lives caught up in the swirl of history represented as a series of repetitions and circularities. The emphasis falls on the *telos* of the narrative or on the formal interrelation of the various scenes, not on the characters' lives or the motivation of their actions; the characters are like hieratic figures in a large historical tapestry. (pp. 156-57)

Viewed against Carpentier's previous production, *The Lost Steps* represents an attempt at unification and synthesis, if only because it is centered on a continuous and reflexive narrative presence—a narrator-protagonist who sets before the reader a totality of his life and experience in our times, instead of a series of fragments projected against a background of monumental and dwarfing historical events....

Whereas Carpentier wove his previous fictions around the biography of an obscure historical figure, in *The Lost Steps* he himself is the object of the biography, and the writing of the novel becomes a theme of the narrative.... Furthermore, the ideological framework of earlier works (mainly Spenglerian) is set off against a different and conflicting conception of man and history: Sartrean existentialism. (p. 158)

The clash of Spenglerian and Sartrean concepts in *The Lost Steps* reveals its recollective, stock-taking quality—as does the title itself, a translation of Breton's *Les pas perdus* that might allude to Carpentier's Surrealist past.... [The] novel shows a totalizing desire on both the level of personal and world history; as the protagonist moves through the jungle, he believes he is traveling across all of man's history, as if his voyage were not through landscape but through an imaginary museum or through a compendium of world history read backward. His voyage is also through individual memory, across all the stages of his past life, to childhood and ultimately his own birth. The overall movement is toward the moment of plentitude when the end of these journeys will coincide and merge in a true synthesis of the totality of history and the self. It is because of this search for restoration and integration that *The Lost Steps* assumes such an abstract form. (pp. 159-60)

The autobiographical nature of *The Lost Steps*, in all its complexity, is both cause and effect of the strategic position that this novel occupies in the totality of Carpentier's production. Its recollective synthesizing attempt, at both a biographical and literary level, bear the mark of the conversion. (p. 186)

The fact that ["Manhunt"] reconstructs a history closely related to the author, the fact that both protagonists are artists of sorts, and the fact that commitment to the present-in-history leads them away from their vocations justify considering "Manhunt" in relation to *The Lost Steps*. These and other elements indicate that "Manhunt" is, as it were, a postscript to *The Lost Steps*. If the narrator-protagonist of that novel realizes at the end that he must return to the city,

to present history, the drama lived by the two protagonists of "Manhunt" in the city is the future that their predecessor did not narrate, but acted out by writing the text of the novel. If *The Lost Steps* was generated by the questions about history and the artist raised by *The Kingdom of This World*, "Manhunt" centers on the problems of writing that *The Lost Steps*, in turn, opened. Like an *auto sacramental* in its intense and self-reflexive symbolism, "Manhunt" is Carpentier's allegory of writing. What the novel dramatizes is the generation of the text: a liturgical, primeval drama of its birth and death as well as of its filial relations. ...

The question of the artist in contemporary society is, as in *The Lost Steps*, the manifest theme of "Manhunt," and this Romantic topic of the artist's alienation is couched in terms of a longing for the absolute, for oneness and restoration. This desire involves once more returning to a lost paradise, the world of nature and the mother, and a search for God, the maker of order and giver of meaning in the universe. (p. 191)

The most striking and confusing aspect of "Manhunt" is its Faulknerian multiplicity of narrators, a bewildering technical *tour de force* that makes the novel the most inaccessible of Carpentier's texts. No antecedent can be found in Carpentier's work for this experimentation with narrative voice except in *The Lost Steps*. The plurality-in-the-present realized by the narrator-protagonist at the end of *The Lost Steps* is as it were, blown up in "Manhunt," a text narrated by an omniscient third-person and two first-person narrators, who are themselves pluralized. The displacement of narrative voice between third person in *The Lost Steps* and the subsequent unfolding of the protagonist into several selves that comment upon each other are concretely re-enacted in "Manhunt" in the political activist and the ticket seller, who meet fleetingly but whose lives are intertwined without their knowledge. (pp. 197-98)

The text of the novella is composed mostly of recollections of these two parallel yet separate consciousnesses and by their actions in a brief fictional present that is supposed to comprise the forty-six minutes that it takes to play Beethoven's Third Symphony (chapters 1 and 3, encompassing five subchapters). But the fragmentation of the narrative voice occurs not only through the splitting of the narrator-protagonist but also within the consciousness of the hunted one [the political activist] and in the presence of the third-person narrator. (p. 199)

The drama played out in "Manhunt" is that of the text's attempted escape from its sources, its fear of repeating, like a protagonist, an archetype, an archtext. (p. 209)

The Lost Steps and "Manhunt" take to its limits and subvert the metaphor of nature as logos, of the fusion of creative consciousness and nature as the source of narrativity. (p. 211)

The stories written before 1953 hinged on the metaphor binding history and writing into an uninterrupted continuum, a flow from the same source—nature—lost in the past but subject to recall. The attempt to return to that source shows in *The Lost Steps* that no such unity exists, that writing unveils not the truth, nor the true origins, but a series of repeated gestures and ever renewed beginnings. After 1953, Carpentier's fiction assumes another origin, discarding the metaphor of natural writing and fantastic literature. In "Manhunt" Carpentier offers an alternate origin, political history, delving into the background of today's Cuba. In *Explosion in a Cathedral,* his next novel, Carpentier returns to the eighteenth century in the Caribbean as a means of telescoping into the present and beyond (by means of strategic anachronisms) the historico-political process undergone by the New Continent. . . . The quest for origins in the natural fusion of history and consciousness in a utopian past is abandoned in favor of a political history whose origins are to be found in the dissemination of the texts of the French Revolution throughout the New World. The myth of a past utopia has been replaced by the correlative myth of the future, when all versions of history will at last be one, and all steps will finally be found. (p. 212)

The most revealing contradiction in the essays [published in *Tientos y diferencias* (1964)] revolves around Carpentier's concept of the baroque, which he now puts forth as the distinguishing characteristic of Latin American literature, and which has come to replace the "real marvelous." . . . The contradiction centers on the status of literary language. On the one hand, Carpentier maintains that the baroque nature of Latin American literature stems from the necessity to name for the first time realities that are outside the mainstream of Western culture. On the other, he states that what characterizes Latin American reality is its styleless-ness, which results from its being an amalgam of styles from many cultural traditions and epochs: Indian, African, European, Neoclassical, Modern, etc. With the first statement Carpentier is, of course, resurrecting the Blakean and generally Romantic topos of Adam in the Garden after the fall, having to give names to the things that surround him. But the second claim runs counter to the first insofar as the reality in question, if it is the product of manifold traditions, would have already been "named" several times, and by different peoples. (pp. 222-23)

The baroque as a new metaphor, a new conceit designating that which is particularly Latin American, is quite different, however, from the concept of "marvelous American reality" woven in the forties. To begin with, Carpentier insists now on defining cities, not the jungle or the world of nature. More importantly, though, in the concept of "marvelous American reality" the mediator between that reality and the literary text was the self; the conceit was that of the writer as a spontaneous, unreflexive mediator between the transmutations of nature and those of writing. The new theory of contexts, on the other hand, establishes a new relationship. If there is an inherent tension between the desire to name for the first time and a reality that has already been named several times, the theory of contexts assumes and subsumes that tension: it provides for a writing that purports to *name* for the first time even while it is *conscious of naming for the second time,* of being a *renaming.* The text is a context, which is already inscribed in the hybrid reality issuing from previous conceptions; the text, in other words, is a ruse, an evasive gesture that points to itself as a beginning that never was, but knows that it is instead a future of that beginning, its ultimate end. Latin American writing will then be that *third style* that is the future of all styles; their degradation in heterogeneity, when their codes lose their referentiality. . . . The negative way in which Carpentier describes this third style, as that which has *no style,* provides the clue for the grounding element of the new conceit. If the narrative must go beyond itself to contexts and at the same time constitutes, in a sense, those

contexts, then the text is the empty space opened by the negation; it is the point at which things cease to have a style and the locus where they shift from one level to the other. (pp. 224-25)

At the end of *The Lost Steps,* when the narrator-protagonist decides to abandon his quest for the single point of origin in the jungle and return to the city, he gazes at the sign with the name of the café where he has heard about the fate of Rosario and his other companions of the previous voyage: *Memories of the Future.* This is the last threshold he crosses in memory toward the point from which he has written or rewritten his account of the voyage, the threshold of assumed self-reflexivity and history, of writing in the city, in that third style that is the future of all styles remembered. *Explosion in a Cathedral, Reasons of State,* and *Concierto barroco* will be written, so to speak, in that future perfect where the beginning of history is already history. (p. 225)

[Beneath its traditional] outward appearance *Explosion in a Cathedral* conceals a radical experiment with history and the narrative. Though the voluminous historical research that went into the writing of the novel obviously links it with *The Kingdom of This World,* Carpentier's return to the era of revolutions does not imply a continuation of his experiments of the forties, but a revision. The most salient and deceptive feature that issues from this revision is the detailed attention to historical, social, and geographical particularities; the conventional and gradual development of the characters and the focusing of the action on the destiny of a household. On this level, where the novel appears almost as a nineteenth-century popular historical novel of adventure, *Explosion in a Cathedral* allows for a rather conventional thematic reading. (pp. 226-27)

Carpentier offers in this novel a radical revision of the historical process he portrayed in *The Kingdom of This World.* The difference lies in the breaking of the daemonic circle in which history, moved by natural forces, was entrapped in the earlier novel. The clearest indication of this is found not only in the minute details of the social and ideological evolution of the characters, but also in the absence of circularity and in the characters' ability to return to the fray of history after they have completed a first cycle of their lives. . . . Self-consciousness is now a return from which a new departure may take place. There are repetitions and returns in *Explosion in a Cathedral,* but not historical cycles that mirror each other and create a vertiginous *composition en abîme.* The characters return to what appears to be a previous moment in their lives, as history appears to repeat itself in certain events. But the return is not to the same point; it is rather to one that is merely similar and creates the illusion of sameness but is really far removed from the previous one: instead of identical cycles, history in *Explosion in a Cathedral* follows a spiraling movement. And history is no longer determined by cosmic cycles complicitous with nature, it is man-made. (pp. 232-33)

There can be no question that Carpentier is establishing an analogy between the modernism of the eighteenth century and that of his own time, and the futuristic quality of the novel is put within the future-oriented thought of the eighteenth century, with its desire to abolish the past and its proliferation of cities of the future and the like. (p. 234)

But what is peculiar about the future evoked in *Explosion in a Cathedral* is its quality of being simultaneously a past. . . . [In *Explosion in a Cathedral*] there is no counterpoint between ideal project and historical execution but a constant re-enactment of the gap between project and execution, as well as an affirmation of their indissoluble link. By making the future also past, history becomes the dynamic textual counterpoint between means and ends. In other words, the future that the history narrated in the text implies is, of necessity, nothing but the text—which forecloses any projections beyond its own specificity but allows for linear free play within itself. Contradictions are not bypassed and resolved in the novel, but merely begun again and again within the text's own dialectical free play. (pp. 234-35)

The anachronisms [which occur throughout *Explosion in a Cathedral*] perform the function of pointing at the density of the historical field encompassed by the text, which integrates the past and the future on a single horizontal level. History, the grounding object of narration, and the text, its outcome, are one. (p. 236)

[It] is mostly in the presence of the occult, in sects such as the Masons and the Rosicrucians, that the irrational appears in *Explosion in a Cathedral*, investing the gap between reason and action with a quasi-religious and symbol-producing quality. It is by means of this reference to the occult that the text itself partakes of that symbolic quality, the allegorical configuration that invites a reading that goes beyond the peripety of the action and the development of the characters. The most consistent code to which this reading alludes is the Jewish Kabbala, which had a notable resurgence during the eighteenth century and the presence of which in this text is a clear indication of Carpentier's reconciliation with his Surrealist past. (pp. 237-38)

By appealing to the Kabbala, Carpentier is recasting the pattern of fall and redemption, of exile and return—of all his writing—within a system that centers precisely on these themes. . . . But beyond these thematic considerations, the importance of the Kabbala in *Explosion in a Cathedral*, as in Borges's work, is its concern with the nature of symbolic action, its centering on a hermeneutics whereby writing is accorded a crucial role in the composition of the world—as is well known, for kabbalists the world issues from the letters of the Hebrew alphabet. Thus its presence in the novel is not, like history, an external referential code but one which attempts to explicate the text of the novel itself. The metaphor of light is of primary importance in this connection, for although light emanates from a given source, its dissemination through space is so fast that both source and illumination appear as one. The analogy between this metaphor of light and that of the explosion in the painting "Explosion in a Cathedral" is clear; for an explosion is so sudden that cause and effect coincide and constitute a single experience, a sort of instantaneous movement. . . . (pp. 239-40)

The kabbalistic code in *Explosion in a Cathedral* contains the basic elements of Carpentier's new concept of writing, his new metaphor to link writing and history. If Carpentier's fiction in the forties sought its foundation in a theological, transcendental source from which it received order, his new writing will have a much more dialectical conception of the source. Earlier fiction sought an original source, a single fountainhead of origination from which writing

flowed in a continuum. In *The Lost Steps* the irrevocable absence of that source is made manifest, while "Manhunt" issues from the terror of its presence. In *Explosion in a Cathedral*, for the first time, there is a clear separation between worldly and divine realms. The presence of the Kabbala points precisely at the secondary status of writing and of the world. . . . Writing, in other words, is always the future of a past that does not exist, that is re-created. (pp. 241-42)

It is, appropriately, in Esteban's meditation in the second epigraph of the novel that the connotative range of [the] deferred centerlessness of the text is given through the most prominent emblem in the novel, the guillotine. . . . (p. 251)

In the context of Carpentier's persistent evocation of buildings and ruins, the guillotine appears, then, as a frame left standing after the demolition of a house, or before its construction, as the empty, demarcated space around which the house is built. (p. 252)

The central metaphoric chain in *Explosion in a Cathedral* revolves, then, around these emblems of the constitution of the text itself and of its inner dialectics. Rather than a self-reflexiveness of a thwarted return to the source and to a grounding notion of beginnings, as we found in *The Lost Steps*, *Explosion in a Cathedral* posits a kind of writing that appears as a series of returns to origins that turn with the same movement: revolutionary writing in its etymological sense, in that it revolves around an absent axis that is constituted by the very movement of its periphery. . . .

The elaborate symbolic structure of *Explosion in a Cathedral* attempts to come to grips with the relationship between the movement of history and the fixity of emblems, not only in an abstract sense, but in the very concrete mode in which Carpentier's historical fiction tends, by its allegoric and archetypal quality, to move into an ideal realm of signification. (p. 253)

It is the materiality of the emblem, in this as well as in previous novels by Carpentier, that has the most significance. Carpentier's insistence on the guillotine, on costumes, on buildings, on paintings and statues, obviously related to his use of capital letters, is an attempt to invest a character or event with a solid, materially fixed meaning. (p. 255)

What emerges from Carpentier's experiments in *Explosion in a Cathedral* is parody: parody that results from the confrontation of the future with a source, a pre-text, whose ideal, phantasmatic form is violated to allow for a textual free play. In historical terms, the parody results from the overturning of the core of Western civilization by the popular culture arising at the juncture of the eighteenth and nineteenth centuries. In terms of writing, parody becomes the locus created by the fissure, now assumed, between thought and its signs—a humorous allegory that underlines the hollow materiality of signs and the temporal gap between meaning and its representation. . . . [History] has become parodic repetition, its own end, and the sources of the text are revealed in their deformed, desecrated condition, instead of being concealed and covered to safeguard their originality and that of the text. The most superficial indication of a change is the absence of solemnity; humor was almost completely missing in Carpentier's earlier production (with the exception of "El milagro de Anaquillé"). Stemming from this new element and from the recapitulatory nature of Carpentier's works from *Explosion in a Cathedral* on, which recover themes and topics of his earlier works, there is also an element of self-parody that is obviously related to self-reflexiveness. (pp. 256-57)

Faithful to the implications of [the third style, mentioned earlier, which Carpentier defines as nonstyle], the newest narratives constitute a return to the city—not to the city as the stony labyrinth of architecture (of *arch-texture*) but to the city become a mock-up, a stage for comic opera. (p. 257)

[The] degradation of the architecture reflects a similar process in the texts themselves. Now, more than ever, and with increasing impunity, they are a mixture of styles and sources; historical and fictional characters mingle on the same level. Bits and pieces of other literary texts are brought together in a textual amalgam. . . .

The ponderous titles of Carpentier's two most recent novels, *El recurso del método* and *Concierto barroco*, seem to indicate quite the opposite. But their solemnity, which at first glance makes them evoke weighty erudite treatises, belies their parodic nature, for just as *El siglo de las luces* meant precisely the opposite, so do these titles mock rather than designate their overt referents. (p. 258)

As in *Explosion in a Cathedral* and *Reasons of State*, the temporal disposition of *Concierto barroco* is future-oriented. . . . As in *Explosion in a Cathedral* and *Reasons of State*, the text is the moment where past and future are one, in permanent revolution; it is the locus of infinite contaminations. Carnival and Apocalypse were the two poles of the pendular movement in *The Kingdom of this World*. In *Concierto barroco* Carnival and Apocalypse are one. (pp. 268, 270)

As opposed to his earlier work, Carpentier's work of the sixties and seventies contains the possibility of return. . . . The new beginning results only in the consciousness that [the characters of Carpentier's new fiction] must always begin anew, that the steps to the past are lost and those to the future are already here, ready to begin an ever repeated voyage in time whose anticipation is the text itself and their memory of the future voyage. For if the past is lost, the present is never here, except as future, Carnival and Apocalypse are one, the text is a revolution. Writing will always be that *ailleurs*, that future remembered, where signs will cease to shuffle their meanings and will empty themselves out.

In his latest phase Carpentier traces a return, a recapitulatory journey through his fiction, to erase and reconstitute its point of origin. The new version that emerges is one where the crack at the core of *¡Ecue-Yamba-O!* is covered through recourse to that part of the novel—the urban, mixed underworld of cultural clashes and indiscriminate assimilation—where hybridness reigns and where the text emerges as the self-conscious outcome of manifold traditions. . . . The Spengler-Hegel counterpoint of the 1941 essays on the decline of Europe is resolved, as it were, in favor of Hegel. The textual synthesis of Carpentier's late fiction, however, is not Hegelian but post-Hegelian. It is the chaos after the end of history which is simultaneously a self-conscious beginning of history. The search for reintegration is dissolved in a textual amalgam that is at once emanation and source, separation and union, concert and disharmony—concert in disharmony. Carpentier's new

style issues from that productive negativity of nonstyle, from that void in which the memory of the source is lost, in which the archtext is exploded.

Fiction is now the Carnival assumed as the permanent revolution, a history whose end and beginning are constantly commemorated and celebrated. Fiction celebrates the consecration of spring. (pp. 271-73)

Carpentier's legacy is [a] relentless attempt to synthesize history and the self in a form of Latin American writing. While in this sense Carpentier's work has merely repeated a gesture found in all Romantic and post-Romantic literature, he has given that enterprise a particular Latin American character—not, however, by demonstrating the autonomy of Latin American culture, as he once hoped, or by tracing the precise boundaries of a Latin American context. He has demonstrated, instead, the dialectics of dependence and independence that subtend any effort at cultural definition, and made manifest the pervasive heterogeneity of writing. The total novel is a Hegelian experiment whose failure is the very condition of its existence. By having repeatedly taken it to the limit where its unattainability becomes apparent, Carpentier has made possible the total novel and its ironic counterpart, the antinovel. Both possibilities are already present in *The Lost Steps*, in that "I" that attempts to be one and is at the same time many.

Carpentier once defined his role as "translator," and such it has been, ven if not in the way he had hoped. His work, by its encyclopedic and totalizing nature, is akin to the *summae* and cathedrals that appear in thirteenth-century Europe. It is an iconographic storehouse, a monument—the foundation of Latin America's house of fiction. (pp. 273-74)

> *Roberto González Echevarría, in his* Alejo Carpentier: The Pilgrim at Home *(copyright © 1977 by Cornell University; used by permission of the publisher, Cornell University Press; Chapter 4 was originally published in part in* Diacritics *and is reprinted by permission), Cornell University Press, 1977.*

*   *   *

CAYROL, Jean   1911-

Cayrol, a French novelist, poet, essayist, and screenwriter, was an early proponent of the New Novel. His fiction and poetry are dominated by his experiences in a German prison camp, and his heroes are typically Lazarus figures who must readjust to life after a spiritual death. A Christian perspective of redemptive suffering pervades his work.

DAVID CARROLL

In the novels of Jean Cayrol someone speaks, but as Roland Barthes has already argued it is impossible to say exactly who. The Cayrolian voice hides as much as it reveals its source; it is never transparent. It works against the speaker who desires to affirm his presence by speaking. The Cayrolian figure may attempt, like Gaspard of *Les Corps Etrangers*, to remember his past and relate it accurately and completely in order to claim he is present as an identity at the source of his voice, outside and prior to it; but he is never successful. (p. 789)

The Cayrolian voice is a voice without origin, a voice whose source is in no fully constituted subject and which, therefore, cannot be conclusively identified. It is incorrect, perhaps, even to call it *a* voice because it has no specific origin and is never unique. Each voice is plural, not *a* voice at all but multiple, with multiple origins. The invasion of each voice by other voices indicates that it would be impossible to give any voice *a* sense or direction and it is in this way that the Cayrolian voice constitutes a text (a fundamental characteristic of any text being this absence of a definite source, the absence of any subject *hors texte* governing its sense). A text demands the absence or death of the subject in order to signify—it could be considered precisely as a voice (voices) without origin.

It can be seen already, therefore, that the status of the subject who speaks is similar to and perhaps the same as that of the writer in Cayrol's novels, for since the voice can be considered to be textual, the speaker is always in this sense a writer, even if very often it is in spite of himself. I will concentrate here on two of Cayrol's works, *Le Vent de la Mémoire* and *Je l'Entends Encore*, in which the writer appears directly as a figure in the novels, in order to see just exactly what status the writer has in the novels and what his relation is to the text, keeping in mind that he is a privileged figure only in the sense that all figures who speak are writers and all voices texts to be interpreted, never transparent in themselves. In Cayrol's novels the written (the text) has invaded the spoken (the voice) at its origin.

When the figure of the writer appears in *Le Vent de la Mémoire,* he is a mystified figure, a figure fleeing from the differences of the past and from the others, fleeing from the implications of his text, a figure trying to hide behind a mask and to posit himself as a unified presence, an identity complete in itself. Gérard wants to have no memories and to deny the difference at the heart of the present—he simply wants to *be*. He desires to be the same, identical to himself and, moreover, to make his sameness manifest to others. To realize this desire he takes on a mask, a role or personality (the "writer"), which supposedly defines him completely, which is the manifestation of his inward truth, the same as what he is. (pp. 789-90)

The "writer" from Gérard's mystified point of view writes in order to make manifest his own presence, to present his personal and private view of the world, the truth which he possesses. The "writer" is always present in his text because it says exactly what he wants it to say, because it is simply an extension of him. . . . [In order to continuously grasp this truth without interference,] Gérard constructs his "bureau" to be a wall against the others, a physical closure for the self, a space where he can *be*. (pp. 790-91)

Having made himself secure, the "writer" can now write and so the completion of the "bureau" should be a moment of triumph. Instead, he fears the moment because it is the moment of his physical absence from the world, an indication of his death. In fact, it does not free him from the others and permit him to write but closes him in on himself and imprisons him. (p. 791)

The "writer" feels that he must protect himself from the others because they threaten him by interfering with his desired unity and perfection, with his state of total communion with himself. They are always inessential or accessory to him because his truth is supposedly only in himself. . . . The others only work, according to him, to destroy his identity and his image, and thus his pleasure. Any imperfection in the self must be the fault of the others, never that of the self. They insert their voices in his voice, their words among his. (p. 792)

The presence of the others destroys the "perfection" of [Gérard's] writing, his total grasping of himself. Now there is difference instead of unity, a division in the self, distance between the "writer" and his writing, a loss of the immediate comprehension of himself and his work. The "writer" no longer hears his own voice clearly—it no longer says exactly what he wants it to say.

Gérard fears the completion of his "bureau" because he fears the consequences of his physical absence from the world; but he fears more than this the loss of his identity, the invasion of the self by the others, and his own eventual disappearance over which he has no control, his death. He must complete his work, therefore, before he actually dies, so that his death will be insignificant. A work written in his own unique voice, with *his* words, he believes will insure the eternal continuation of his presence. His seclusion in his "bureau", then, is his only means of avoiding the consequences of death, his permanent disappearance. He writes in order to deny the effects of his death, to negate the presence of the others. . . . (pp. 792-93)

In order to establish himself as an identity he must complete his manuscript, and yet he is unable to. Paradoxically, the "writer" is unable to write. He hides himself away in his "bureau" but he produces nothing. The "writer's" manuscript is fictitious. He is sterile and has nothing to say, unable to find his own words and his own voice in order to speak. (p. 793)

He does not write because the "writer" cannot write and sustain his image and identity, write and remain the same, master of his truth and of his words. To write is to be misunderstood, to lose one's sense and identity, never to be the same. He cannot write because he has no secret to reveal about himself, because the sense of his words and the sense of his life always escape him. . . .

Here is where the basic contradiction in Gérard's project manifests itself explicitly, for writing is never a perfect reflection of the self, never a presentation of an inner truth. It is impossible to eliminate the words of the others from one's own words because it is always "their" language that one is using. The sense of any work is never in the "writer" and never unique; and, moreover, writing destroys rather than assures the identity of the "writer" who desires to be present in his work. To write is to proclaim his death, his absence from his writing rather than his presence in it. . . .

The "writer" cannot write without revealing that the identity he claims for himself, the unified presence he claims exists beneath the mask, is only fictional. He cannot write in conformity with his project because he does not possess the truth of who he is, because his truth itself is only a mask, not the perfect copy of an original, but a mask under which there is only another mask, a copy of a copy. The original Gérard is always missing, and the identity he desires is fictional, because it supposedly has no past, no history, no memories. It supposedly simply *is*, present fully in itself prior to any manifestation or narration. Gérard hides behind the mask of the "writer" in order not to admit this, in order to cling to the myth of his own importance, the existence of the self. (p. 794)

Instead of affirming his identity by being spoken in his unique voice, [Gérard's novel] lets speak the multiple voices of the past—it inserts the differences of the past within the mythical present he is attempting to construct. The novel is the emergence of the past in the present, a past which the "writer" is not able to control, not able to mold in accordance with his image of himself. He considers the novel to be against him because he neither controls its sense nor recognizes himself in it. It does not say what he wants to say about himself; it is not the work of his own voice. Rather than reflect his presence, it destroys his desired unity and multiplies his identity. (p. 795)

Le Vent de la Mémoire indicates the impossibility of totally forgetting the past (total recall being equally impossible), of fleeing the past and clinging to the illusion of an eternal undifferentiated present in order to create an identity for oneself. The "writer" is never present in his work and never able to control its sense. A text is always the work of a double and never of an original, unique self; it has multiple origins and senses and never one. It always works against the "writer" who desires to convey his truth, his presence or identity, by means of it. The text reveals that the "writer" is a fiction, a mask which covers no profundity; its source and its sense, therefore, are never in him. It is never the product of his voice. (p. 796)

In Je l'Entends Encore the figure of the writer appears again. This writer, Jean-Pierre, unlike Gérard, desires to know his past rather than forget it; he acknowledges the fictional status of his text, the work of the double, rather than hiding it. At the same time, however, Jean-Pierre wants to transcend the fiction and rediscover the truth of who he is, present at the origin but now lost. The fiction will be his means of arriving at the truth of the past, a past which is not a text and not a fiction, a past conveyed by the true voice of the father [Julien] speaking to him. . . . This desire to return to the origin is a common theme in Cayrol's novels, and it is usually represented by the desire to return to the home where the origin of the self, that which makes the self what it is, has supposedly been guarded. In Je l'Entends Encore as in the other novels the actual return reveals no truth—the origin and the true father are always missing. In Cayrol the past in itself is never grasped because with each return another version of the past comes forth. There is always another origin to be found in each origin; the return is endless.

There is no unique origin because the father is dead. Jean-Pierre, like many of Cayrol's figures, is an orphan, without a home, at the beginning of whose life there is an absence, an uncertainty, a disruption. The absence of the father determines that the past is uncertain, not simply given in itself once and for all times, but always to be invented. . . . The father's voice, which like all voices in Cayrol can never be his alone, is a carrier of death and not an indication of his living presence. In Cayrol's novels the father, when he speaks, is a fiction, never completely himself, never the living source of truth for the son. Without a unique origin for the self, all sons are orphans. (pp. 796-97)

The narration of Julien's life which comprises the first half of Je l'Entends Encore, a discourse supposedly spoken by the father, is in fact only spoken in the name of the father for it is actually written by Jean-Pierre, the son. Jean-Pierre takes on the mask of the father and speaks for him and in his name, as if he were the father. At a certain moment, the first text gives way to another text, that of the son speaking in his own name, and the first text is acknowledged as a fiction. . . . Jean-Pierre invents a fictional Julien and lets him

speak because he cannot accept the death of his father and his own eventual disappearance implicated in this death. (p. 799)

Jean-Pierre writes in the name of his father in an attempt to keep his voice alive, but at the same time there are certain advantages in the death of the father. Because the father is dead and the son must write his words if he is to speak, the son has the illusion of controlling him, of being the father of his father, of replacing him in order to return to the mother [, the source for which he searches]. The father continues to speak through this fiction but it is with the words that the son gives him that he does. (p. 800)

The father must be both dead and alive at the same time; alive as a guarantee of the son's identity and dead so that the son can possess this truth. The fiction of the living father, the story of the father's life written by the son, seems at first to accomplish this end. The son will possess the truth of the father and his own truth by his mastery of the fictional father, through this father who speaks with his, the son's, words. This mastery turns out to be illusory, however, for the words that the father uses to speak and thus his voice are neither his to possess nor the son's. The fiction speaks with its own words, that is to say, with the words that are not anyone's in particular, with a voice whose source is not in any individual or self but only in another voice. The "truth" of the fiction, the sense and reality of the father's existence, continually escapes the son's attempts to possess it. The real father is continually displaced by a double of the father, a fiction or a phantom that the son cannot control. . . .

The son cannot possess the truth of his father, who he really was, because this truth never existed. His father belongs to no one, neither to himself nor to the son. . . . The father speaks to Jean-Pierre but only as a fiction, when dead. (p. 801)

The impossibility of ever seizing this truth in itself makes it necessary that he compose it (write it), and without the real presence of the father the fiction is the only possibility. Each time that Jean-Pierre seems to be closing in on a particular truth in the life of his father, each time someone is about to reveal to him who his father was or exactly what he did or said, the direct revelation of the truth is replaced by another story, another version of his father, incomplete and inadequate. The living, oral testimony which is supposed to convey the truth of the past is complicated by death—by the death of his father, as we have shown, but also by the death of other witnesses. . . . (p. 802)

There is no faithful memory and there cannot be one. The truth is never said. . . . In Cayrol's novels memory is only approximate, a fiction or a matter of voice in the Cayrolian sense; and this limitation indicates the impossibility of ever capturing the real presence of the father, the truth of the self, or the essence of the past. A faithful and exact memory is the guardian of the identity of the self, and the oubli or rature at the heart of the Cayrolian memory is the indication of the destruction of this identity. (pp. 802-03)

The writer is an orphan because he can only invent his parents, that is to say, write them. . . . It is the writer who affirms that the self is not born once and for all times, that its truth is not at the origin nor in itself, that it is always other and never the same, a fiction rather than an identity. . . . The writer does not suffer . . . from the absence of a father;

but on the contrary, the writer only suffers from his inability to write and construct fictions. He suffers not from the fact that his father, mother, and himself are written rather than real, but only from what he cannot tell, that which he finds impossible to repeat or write. . . . In Cayrol's novels an "experience" that cannot be repeated has "traumatic" effects, for it dominates the writer and closes him in on himself. It is not any more real in itself than another "experience", but because of the paralysing effect it has, it functions the same way the real would.

The goal of the writer in the novels of Cayrol and of Cayrol as writer is not to attempt to uncover the truth of the past or the real father, and not to present the reader some personal view of the world; but rather it is to repeat the "traumatic experience" and all "experiences", to destroy their effect, to multiply that which seems to be one. The "trauma" isolates the writer, closes him in on himself, and separates him from the others. It fixes him there where he is, prevents him from becoming other. Left unchanged, that is, unrepeated, the "trauma" defines him once and for all, destroys the possibility for change, is a limit beyond which he cannot move, a kind of death. (pp. 803-04)

The destruction or transformation of the closure, the repetition of that which seemingly could not be told, is also the destruction of the solitary self. The solitary self, because of the closure around it, is without the possibility of becoming other than what it is. With the destruction of the closure the self refuses the ideal of a fixed identity and accedes to the possible. Opposed to the solitary self, the writer is never the same. He is continually beginning again and continually multiplying his existences, his origins, his stories. To begin again is to affirm the dissolution of the identity of the self and the invasion of the self from the start by the others. To begin again is to produce another story, to repeat what is already repetition and never the same.

Cayrol states that the sea is the exemplary metaphor for his work, the sea which is a limit but not a closure, offering access to the possible, to what is other, and repeating itself continually. . . . The sea is never the same; it infinitely repeats not what is the same but what is different; it continually begins again from the traces or *ratures* of the past. The sea is always at the moment of beginning, at the moment of opening to the other, at the moment of difference. . . . The sea has no profundity; it cannot be given *a* sense nor captured as a whole. The sea is not a mirror because it repeats the differences of the past and distorts the present. . . . (pp. 808-09)

The concept of beginning in the novels of Cayrol is not the same, then, as the concept of source or origin, the first time before which there is nothing else; for the origin in Cayrol's work, as we have shown, is always missing. To begin is always to begin again, to repeat the differences of the past, to become other. There is never *an* origin but always multiple origins, never *a* story or text with *a* sense, but multiple texts with multiple senses, never a unique self but an endless succession of masks.

The repetition and duplicity of the sea (the fact that it is not a mirror of what *is*) destroys the closure, that which confines the self to itself and denies difference. The repetition of the sea precedes the moment of the unique occurrence, the fixture of an identity; the double precedes the one and is not the same as it. It follows, then, that the sea is also a

confrontation with death. . . . The sea not only presents a danger of death and contains death, the corpses it eventually rejects and deposits on the beach, but by its repetitions it is death. The sea is always at the moment of (re) beginning, the moment of repetition and difference, which is also the moment of death. Death is there from the beginning, in each (re) beginning, at each moment.

By his writing, the writer affirms the repetition of the sea, the multiplicity of the self, and, therefore, the dissolution of his identity. He accepts the text which cannot possibly be *his* text, a reflection of his presence, but which is always the text of a double. He affirms the multiple versions of the past, the fictional status of his memories, and the death of the father and his truth. He continually takes on masks because he has no identity to reveal—behind each mask there is only another mask. He speaks in the names of others and with their words because he cannot speak in his own name with his own words. In Cayrol's novels the writer himself is written, a fiction, implicated in his text and not outside it. He is continually beginning again, becoming other than what he is, taking on another mask and speaking with another voice. (pp. 809-10)

David Carroll, "Jean Cayrol or the Fiction of the Writer," in Modern Language Notes *(© copyright 1973 by The Johns Hopkins University Press), Vol. 88, No. 4, 1973, pp. 789-810.*

JAMES WALT

An author of poems, essays and novels sufficient in number and quality to establish him as a man of letters, Cayrol isn't above playing Scheherazade and writing a suspense tale [*Kakemono Hôtel*]. He is a novelist of place, in love with the dank, misty, rainy Normandy coast which Flaubert and De Maupassant also loved, and fascinated by the tragedy of people who stumble from mischance to mischance in following their illusions. . . .

Judged by its plot and its improbabilities, *Kakemono Hôtel* is closer to Poe than to Flaubert or Maupassant. But the atmosphere Cayrol creates is the work of a delicate observer grounded in the methods of the realistic school, and he writes with a simplicity Poe would have rejected. *Kakemono Hôtel* is an altogether "happy" addition to the genre of the suspense novel. (pp. 269-70)

James Walt, in Books Abroad *(copyright 1975 by the University of Oklahoma Press), Vol. 49, No. 2, Spring, 1975.*

SPIRE PITOU

Devotees of Jean Cayrol's poetry and fiction will be surprised to find that his latest novel rejects completely the surrealistic manner he has employed until now with such constant success. For *Histoire d'une maison* might be construed as an effort to demonstrate once and for all that surrealistic writers can and may employ the more traditional forms of composition with ease and competence. The first section of the narrative is presented directly by the author, or anonymous narrator, exactly as Balzac or Zola might have developed a tale of avarice or alcoholism; the second part turns to the epistolary format used by Rousseau in *La nouvelle Héloïse*; the fourth section exploits the diary or journal type of presentation favored by Defoe.

These variations in technique heighten the abruptly changing tempo and the kaleidoscopic effect the author wishes to achieve so that the unsettled nature of his characters' lives may be underlined and made to match the uncertain pre-World War II period in which they live—and even dare to hope. Yet the deft and dreadful irony that Cayrol evolves in his work is still present. . . .

This saga of frustration, betrayal and death offers a plenitude of ludicrous and dreadful scenes, but none of these is as disquieting as the calm conviction with which the novelist relates his story. (p. 825)

Spire Pitou, in Books Abroad *(copyright 1976 by the University of Oklahoma Press), Vol. 50, No. 4, Autumn, 1976.*

* * *

CHAR, René   1907-

Char is a French poet. Early in his career he was connected with the Surrealist school, a friend and collaborator of Paul Éluard and André Breton. However, he broke from this early association and continued to develop as a poet of unique gifts. His poetry has been labelled "hermetic" for its verse that often suggests the poet as prophet and poetry as a kind of religion. Char's poetry of the late thirties and early forties reflects his deep concern for the political and social upheaval of a world at war. This period and its effect on the poet lent to all his poetry its characteristic humanity and deeply-felt moral concern. Char's poetry celebrates the joys of life and love in a verse suffused with imagery drawn from the natural splendor of his native Provence. (See also *CLC*, Vol. 9, and *Contemporary Authors*, Vols. 13-16, rev. ed.)

ROBERT NUGENT

In ["Argument"] Char makes clear what is to him the nature of poetry, that is, those aspects which underlie understanding the poems. These convictions have to do with the poet's vocation—how a poet sees the world about him, and, especially, the kind of statement he makes concerning the human condition of which he is a necessary part. These three concerns are obviously interdependent; the poem can be read, however, as a progressive development from one to another, working always towards a poetic theory.

Char is in the tradition of the poet-seers, poets like Jouve or Rimbaud, for example, who believe that a poet's vocation is to express a moment of apocalyptic vision and to experience a profound spiritual insight. Char is unlike Jouve in that the latter poet works from a condition of darkness, from a traditional consideration of the dark night of the soul, into a state of illumination which endows that darkness with form and which gives a tangible body to forces once perceived as incoherent. Char, though working from our world into another, from the "world before" (*l'avant-monde*) into a present one, begins with light; the forces at work in his poetry function, in the words of one critic, like "fire on fire." Further, the world in which Char operates is similar to that described in *Les Illuminations*, one of a dreadful and hidden catastrophe. . . . For Char, a poet must seek to initiate the reader into such a world that he might understand not so much its history but its incoherence, its constant change, its chaos and diversity; the clarity of vision which results emphasizes, for both reader and poet, discovery and "harvest," a realization of change which is a condition of freedom.

Thus Char amplifies a description of the poet's calling to include a meaning of freedom which a poet teaches a reader. Char protests against any force, even light, which would deprive man of his liberty and against all those who would deny him its validity and presence. The initial statement of "Argument" is that "man flees from asphyxiation." This verse indicates that the poet's role, for Char, is to urge man continually to fight any tyranny which would choke him, any restriction in his choice of action that would enclose his attempt to find meaning in the world, any preconceived notion—even of liberty itself—that would terminate a possibility of his becoming his own self-defined identity. The meaning of freedom does not imply, for Char, a traditional Cartesian view of self-evident self-awareness; the implication in Cartesian freedom where being and existing are in the conscious mind alone would limit a poet, in Char's belief, to a closed world of perception. Nor would Char accept, as against Cartesian argument, a Freudian structure of uninhibited, unconscious thought, with either a resultant fantasy or a deformed view of the "real world." (Here Char's poetic is to be distinguished from the freedom of the Surrealists.) For Char it is impossible to speak of man's awareness of himself and of his search for freedom in terms of the unconscious opposing the conscious. To claim the rights of the former alone or to infer poetic value in such a dichotomy would impose tyranny; the tyranny is one of a closed view of a universe which Char is convinced must be seen, that is, conceived of, as poetically and essentially fluid in character.

In this fluidity of vision, which operates on both a moral level of freedom and on an esthetic one of poetic vocation, Char neither denies nor accepts Cartesian and Freudian statements. Rather he would search for a unity within the complexity of an entire given situation; he would seek a situation where his becoming his own self-defined freedom would be possible. . . . Char seeks an open situation, one where all "given" cases are available, one from which he can derive a unity of convictions concerning the poet's role, the value of poetry and the significance of liberty. As man flees a closed situation (asphyxia) on a moral level of action, so does a poet on an esthetic level of writing verse.

In this search for a fluid, open, situation (where both freedom and poetry are possible), a search which makes up the basis of a poet's calling, Char distinguishes between the poet and the non-poet. The non-poet seeks to sustain the various functions of life based on means which, in themselves, are not dependent on the imagination. . . . The non-poet works within a limited space. In the initial poem of *Le Poème pulvérisé* (also entitled "Argument") . . . , Char describes this non-poet: *Les hommes d'aujourd'hui veulent que le poème soit à l'image faite de si peu d'espace et brûlée d'intolérance.* Char's imagination works always within a limit of the possible terms of the spatial or realistic data; he finds in this spatial situation an inexhaustible source of poetic order. (pp. 789-92)

A fluid situation where a poet can fulfill his vocation of freedom is also one of premonition (*l'homme qui s'épointe dans la prémonition*). This premonition results from a spiritual crisis which leads to an esthetic that proves, as had written Baudelaire, an infallibility of the poetic production. The crisis does not derive from romantic inspiration, a sudden overwhelming, as a flooding of a river, in a disarray of emotions and observations. The crisis is, to be sure, similar to platonic *furor*. This *furor*, however, works precisely in terms of an open, spatial, concept which does not deny a pole of consciousness in favor of a pole of unconsciousness (a choice which romantic inspiration cannot resolve); or, in terms already discussed above, a rejection of a Cartesian world view in favor of a Freudian one. Char writes that a belief in the value of poetry can and must, especially in crisis, allow both positions; by allowing both extremes Char can posit a wider range of poetic production (as the Cubist painters found a wider range by allowing both realism and abstraction). In a more open, fluid, working area than would be available through either realism or through abstraction, a poet can find, first, an infallibility of change. He can then find a meaning to this change because two concepts work simultaneously and open up further possibilities of vision. (pp. 792-93)

In line with the problem of how reality is apprehended and seized and the question whether reality is understood through an extension of mind (*entendement*) or through a description of the role of the subconscious in understanding, Char would still insist upon the idea that to apprehend the world, a poet must see the given moment, the phenomenological moment which lies between conscious and subconscious. The phrase *qui déboise dans son silence intérieur* implies neither an inner act of a Cartesian sort which would seek a complete grasp through reason; nor would it indicate an act dependent upon subconscious past associations. A poet must bring himself into involvement with a visual world. (p. 793)

Therefore to write poetry is a process; a poet must present this process because—if it has value—it must consist (as it does for Char) in an affirmation of the outgoing nature of reality. This reality is one of a total experience wherein each individual can find beauty and freedom. This reality is further more than an act of the mind (as it is for Descartes, where the mind gathers together and intellectualizes experience and gives it truth as it becomes part of the mind). The mind, for Char, is truly poetic, is an over-all totality of metamorphoses: *le répartit en théâtres*. There is little passivity of a purely receptive sort in Char (or in Mallarmé, whom he at times resembles). For both poets it is the progressive nature of the poetic experience which counts, a gradual act of spreading the mind towards the object and a gradual bringing of objects toward the mind. This experience is in a very real way an act of theatre, with the stage as the mind and the audience as a phenomenal world that both gives sense to, and receives meaning from, the 'theatrical' image.

If it is a poet's vocation to understand and solve the problem of reality and to re-define the conditions of reality a poet must set forth, he must also have a belief in poetic vision. For Char, this vision is a redefinition of experience; seeing is thought of as a process of freedom. . . . This opening up is a process because a sensual perception is transferred to the intellectual and an intellectual abstraction is transferred to a sensory achievement available to others. That the perception and the abstraction are not contradictory is made possible by the poet's senses as they are poetically active.

Underlying such a process is a vision of change, the unifying force of life. *Transhumance* means the bringing down of cattle from the Alps in winter and taking them up in the spring. So is the *verbe* according to Char, moved and driven according to needs to conform to the hidden laws of life and the varied aspects of the world about him that are

imposed by the poet's eye according to his unique and individual perceptions. . . . Char does not pose this dilemma of artistic creation; his attention remains in a more open and fluid field of a vision of change and movement. Nor would he seek to find in and through art (the *verbe*), in the words of one critic, "an intimation of immortality," as does Proust; Char does not discover in poetry, as would Valéry in *La Jeune Parque,* a means of awakening from the unconscious into the conscious where both lucidity of consciousness and simple pleasures are in vain (*le néant*). Char's concern with the *verbe* does not consist in posing questions of poetic achievement; of suffering, with its dichotomy of acceptance and rejection that must be resolved; or a view of the world as a becoming one thing and denying another. Char accepts the world of change as such and not, as in Christian belief, because it is a means whereby intentions are tested and motives purified.

Underlying this use of the *verbe* is a notion of light, the light where poetic vision and poetic creation occur. Light does not refute dark; for the stage set is, for Char, an interplay of dark and light in which the poet's voyage of exploration takes place. . . . For Rimbaud light is the *théâtre* or *scène* wherein a procession of disassociation and re-integration of images takes place. Light, for Char, rather than making clear a transformation of an object, holds the object; the light in Char is so intense that it appears dark and obscure. The images of his poetry are held, visibly, in such a flood of intense light that the order (*économie*) of the world is overwhelmed. The reader's eye is not accustomed to see so exclusively an object which constitutes an analogy corresponding to a truth a poet is seeking and therefore knowing.

Further, a vision of light does not change the properties of an object so that it appears to become another; nor does it involve an interchange of poet and object, as in Eluard, who wrote in *Cours naturel:* "Mille images de moi multiplient ma lumière," where it is a question of the metamorphoses of the individual poet through a vision of light. For Char, rather than a succession of possible meanings of an object or of possible meanings of an individual poet, the reader receives an impression of obscurity, so much is he used to an impurity of the visual object; Char uses this intensity of light, whose intensity tends to blind the reader or blur the form of the object, to clarify through breaking down pre-conceived notions of time and space which surround an object. It is the role of vision, and therefore a poetic *devoir,* to shatter these relationships; a poem becomes, through light, pulverized. Rather than a statement, a poem is a state of dialogue between light and dark, a dialogue which permits Char to distinguish the real world from the false. From such acts of distinction, which are in fact deeds (*gestes*), Char can proceed to define values.

Through these deeds flows life (*le sang des gestes*); the poet's mission is to enlarge (*agrandir*) this life. The enlarging of life, though it is accomplished on an esthetic level, does not mean that the outlines of the poet's object-analogy are continually enlarged (in a kind of romantic display of energy one might find in Hugo). It implies a further concern with giving direction to values: it is an operation of both breadth and depth. This operation has a moral intent (*devoir de toute lumière*). It implies a way of existence, or a world, similar to Baudelaire's, where there is an ultimate harmony of disparate elements.

Further, an acceptance of values in a world where we tend frequently to limit our knowledge of it is difficult. For Char this difficulty is one of being. . . . In so far as a poem is concerned, it has, on the one had, a power of song, similar to black magic, a power to cast a spell as does Valéry's *charme*. On the other hand, it has a power, through beauty, to redeem; it is not only *le rossignol diabolique*, it is also *la clé angélique*. This beauty operates in a poem as a kind of secular belief, one similar to the comtemplative mystic's finding a divine will which operates in the universe and testing experience by that operation. To be, similarly, for a poet such as Char, poses a dilemma: to ascertain what is impure in the world as a whole, without refusing to affirm the beauty possible in it. And although both poet and mystic remain aware of union and non-union with the object of contemplation, a poet, and again especially a poet like Char, experiences a necessary commitment to find expression for both aspects involved in contemplation. The situation must remain open.

This is not to deny that change, metamorphosis, transformation and above all freedom can not exist. There is a light which makes clear the presence of an object; so there is a light which makes clear a moral necessity. . . . Char believes in a constant presence of dignity and freedom, in their meaning of renewal and transformation of life. To act on this belief is to reduce evil, to project a future hope and faith, to affirm the presence of love. This belief is also an acknowledgement of a possible fulfillment of beauty through poetry.

The keyword to all of "Argument" is *aoûtement*, what a poet has gathered together of metaphors and images, beliefs and commitments. *Aoûtement* is read on several levels. The first is esthetic, the poem itself. A poem is the result of labor, in the sense of plowing, turning the seed under the soil. There is also a moral implication: a process of becoming through a cycle of growth. Char's thought is close to Gide's, in a concern for birth and death (*Si le grain ne meurt*); yet perhaps Char is more concerned than Gide with the eventual, completed cycle of ripening (*aoûtement* in the dialect sense of harvest). Again, rather than a Gidean alternation of kinds of experience, Char would seek a simultaneous action of deprivation and growth (*aoûtement* is also a technical term for a kind of pruning so that a twig is hardened).

This process acts upon itself, "fire upon fire," in a paradox of search for a substantial order through a recognition of constant change. Here Char follows Heraclitus and is close to a modern understanding of change as in T. S. Eliot. . . . As does Eliot, Char presents poetic or existential experiences which cross each other, stand in opposition to each other, so that not only experience as a whole might come to fruition but also a morale be defined, a morale Char defines in the last stanza of "Argument": *Une dimension franchit le fruit de l'autre*. . . . Again Char's ethic is distinct from a Gidean "either-or." Char might think of himself as "transported" (*déporté*) from the ties that bind (as does Gide at one moment before he accepts them in order to break away again), from work (*attelage*), from a permanent condition of love (*noces*). Char constructs once more (*je bats le fer*) of all things that do bind (*fermoirs invisibles*). Implicit is a profound acceptance of life, a desire to make the world understandable, to illumine the world.

Basically, "Argument" sets forth a purity of poetic vision which makes the world immediately available and a defense of any man who has "guarded and intensified the inner flame in his life" (in the words of Heraclitus), in a constant confrontation with dilemmas of violence and peace, blindness and sight. Char is close to Rilke, when the latter poet wrote, in speaking of one purpose of the *Elegies*, that this purpose was "to keep life open towards death," to show the true meaning of love and other human activities, as well of pain and sorrow, within this extended whole. . . ." Further, as with Rilke's first elegy, Char's "Argument" gives us an "intuition into the unity of life and death and into the complementaries of sorrow and joy." Char, too, attempts a reconciliation of pain and sorrow: for if poetry is to have meaning, then the world from which the poem derives, must have meaning. The world's condition, as perceived by the senses, appears to be one of chaos. Yet the activity of the poetic mind, as set forth in "Argument," is to break and shatter this chaos, so that, from the fragmented perception, intellect and intuition, which partake both of mind and spirit, will make sense. (pp. 793-99)

> *Robert Nugent, "The 'Argument' of René Char's 'L'Avant-Monde'," in* The French Review *(copyright 1972 by the American Association of Teachers of French), March, 1972, pp. 789-99.*

VIRGINIA A. La CHARITÉ

René Char is the rare poet who unhesitatingly acknowledges the artistic sources of his creative vision, teleology, and practice. In *La Conversation souveraine* . . . , he identifies and appraises those poets to whom he is indebted as a poet, and he categorically states that his three major precursors are the philosopher Heraclitus, the painter Georges de La Tour, and the poet Arthur Rimbaud. . . . Rimbaud is quantitatively more prominent than either Heraclitus or La Tour, for among all of Char's *hommage* texts, Rimbaud receives the greatest attention and admiration. . . .

Char's *hommage* to Rimbaud . . . goes beyond mere admiration; it is based on Char's awareness that he is esthetically indebted to Rimbaud. . . .

Char and Rimbaud share a cosmic vision of a universe humanized by poetry. They begin with the intuitive knowledge that the discord, fragmentation, and multiplicity which characterize man's daily existence and his world are contradictory in appearance only, for beneath the flux, chaos, and disorder there is a totality of essence. It is the role of poetry to unify the fragments, reveal the original permanent oneness of the cosmos, discover man's integral position in that harmony, and lead him to beauty, fulfillment, and dignity. For Char and Rimbaud, poetry is man's instrument for the refutation of meaninglessness and misery; both are consistent in their conviction that life is worthwhile. . . . Poetry has the position that religion assigns to God; it is the macrocosm of existence, the common denominator of homogeneity, the principle of truth and action; it is not only a-spatial and a-temporal, but, unlike a divinity, it is also immediately accessible in the present. (p. 57)

Revolt is a key concept, and this spirit of protest and offensive action characterizes both poets in several ways. Char and Rimbaud defy esthetic rules and conventions and proclaim artistic freedom; they are against all literary schools and doctrines, commercial art, organized religion, bourgeois conformity. It is true that this spirit of defiance characterizes the young Char of *Les Cloches sur le cœur* (1928) and *Le Marteau sans maître* (1934; this last title is significant in itself) more dramatically than the mature Char of later volumes, but revolt and its possibilities remain a consistent motif in all of his work, and this was one of the initial concepts that attracted him to Rimbaud's work. . . . Furthermore, Rimbaud and Char refuse to accept human manifestations of mass man and, instead, proclaim the individual. . . . (pp. 57-8)

A second similarity in poetic spirit is that of anguish as a positive characteristic inherent in the poetic condition and conducive to poetic creation. Char and Rimbaud view anguish as obligatory, but where Rimbaud is never able to resign himself to having to accept it ("Angoisse," *Illuminations*), Char utilizes it and converts it into a constructive means for poetic triumph. . . . Char remains aware of his limits as man and poet, while, on the contrary, Rimbaud frequently forgets his limits and is frustrated when he is forced to accept them.

A third important affinity in spirit is their concept of the poet's role. The primary role of the poet is to discover totality and communicate this discovery. For Char and Rimbaud, the poet is the initiator, what Rimbaud calls "le principe" and what Char describes as matinal in *Les Matinaux* (1950). . . . For both Rimbaud and Char, the poet precedes the man of action; the poet is the doer, the one who is first in the experience of the oneness of life. The poet is man's guide, his agent, and he is responsible to man.

The idea of moral responsibility in Rimbaud's work is ignored, neglected, and scorned, and it is true that Rimbaud himself does not accept it; however, Rimbaud does recognize categorically that the poet, and he Rimbaud in particular, has an obligation. . . . In a similar vein, Char rejects all previous traditional concepts of good and evil and envisages liberty as the only moral good; yet, unlike Rimbaud, Char demands, affirms, and accepts poetic responsibility in a moral sense. . . . Fundamentally, Char places his faith in man; he is a humanist who not only defends man as capable and worthy of dignity but also poeticizes man, for in his work he substitutes the term *man* for *poet*. . . . On the contrary, Rimbaud humanizes poetry but does not poeticize man. Despite his revolt against the futility of man's existence, Rimbaud's poetry is not humanistic but supernaturalistic. . . . Rimbaud asserts that life is innocent, but he is never able to believe that man is innocent. With this stance, Rimbaud is forced to place his faith in verbal expression as opposed to human expression. This is one of the basic differences between Char and Rimbaud. (pp. 58-9)

Another area of strong esthetic resemblance between Char and Rimbaud is their teleology. In the works of both poets there are similarities in their representation of poetic activity, action, love, experience, risk, human condition, man, nature. It is interesting that Rimbaud and Char examine the same concepts and exhibit the same concerns with regard to the matter or "fond" of poetry; in many respects, they embark upon identical courses in order to gain access to "la Maison." It is in this area that Char's indebtedness to Rimbaud is explicitly evident.

Char and Rimbaud conceive of the notion of poetic activity as the simultaneous experience of life and art; in Char's poetry, this concept is enlarged to include as artistic any creative act of living, and creative activity becomes the basis for his poetics in both theory and practice. Char did not

formulate and adopt this theory in his earliest works, notably *Les Cloches sur le cœur* (1928), *Arsenal* (1929 and 1930), and *Le Tombeau des secrets* (1930); however, *Le Marteau sans maître* (1934) represents his adoption of this principle as the foundation of his poetry, and after the publication of this volume, his poetry is consistently and faithfully constructed on this principle of creative activity. . . . Toward the end of his poetic production, Rimbaud is beginning to evolve in the selfsame fashion that Char evolves. What is project for Rimbaud becomes practice for Char. It is to be noted that, prior to his Surrealist experience, Char concentrated on the act rather than on the activity of poetry: that is, on the agent of the action, rather than on the nature of the activity itself; in this early stage, Char, like the Rimbaud of *Une Saison en enfer,* attempted to equate experience with expression through the actor, and it is also notable that in this same period of development Char is most tempted by Rimbaud's theory of the "Voyant" and by Rimbaud's faith in verbal expression. When Char moves from reliance on the power of the written word to reliance on the capability of man, he also turns from emphasis on act to activity.

One of Rimbaud's overriding concerns is love as the principle of communal participation in cosmic unity. . . . Love is tangentially a constant theme in Char's work, and, like his predecessor, Char views love as a unifying cosmic factor. Prior to *Le Visage nuptial* (1938) Char tends to limit his evocations of love to its erotic nature and concentrates on the sensual experience itself. In *Le Visage nuptial,* he focuses on the activity produced by the lovers and discovers that the couple represents an equal union that permits man to experience immediately his totality and provides man's first basis for exchange, for communion with another. The role of the couple is a vital notion in Char's subsequent expansion of exchange to the fraternal level and identification with others in a universal sense. On the other hand, Rimbaud does not find totality in the union of the couple; he finds a "drôle de ménage" . . . of slavery and dependence; his duality and alienation are reinforced, not overcome. Rimbaud is unwilling to pay the price for the risk of union; for him, it results in a loss of dignity and in dispersion. Char is willing to assume the risk; in fact, he chooses to expose his own vulnerability and identify with others, and, consequently, he ends dispersion, finds reconciliation, and discovers his dignity. Char analyzes experience and the role of participation, while Rimbaud only feels the need for exchange; indeed, Rimbaud's failure to glimpse the need for group exchange restricts him to the individual level, a source of personal frustration and dissatisfaction. Rimbaud did identify psychologically with "Les Communards," and he applauded the heroism that these revolutionaries attained through the risk of self, yet he never again attempted to experience personally joint action, much less reflect upon its possibilities. Char and Rimbaud share the artistic demand for consummated action in the present, but, of the two, only Char realizes Rimbaud's own theory of woman's possibilities. . . . (pp. 59-60)

The human condition is one of abject misery, and both Char and Rimbaud set out to reverse this situation; they wish to terminate man's contradictions and offer him justification for his being through the tool of poetry, which they believe can make man divine without God. In their examination and assessment of man, Rimbaud and Char discover a "bonheur ancien mêlé à son regret présent." . . . Man retains a nostalgia for harmony with himself and with his world, for an Edenic existence. . . . (p. 60)

Char attains [a] synthesis of misery and hope through the dialectic of being-destruction-being. Like Rimbaud, he has nostalgia for an original oneness and harmony. . . . In fact, all of *Avant-monde* . . . is devoted to this primordial unity. Char blames man for the initial rupture; man has ravaged his world, destroyed it, upset the balance necessary for cyclical regeneration; by guiding man from a destructive role to a constructive one in *Le Soleil des eaux* (1949) and *Les Matinaux* (1950), he overcomes hostility and alienation. Char asks man to preserve nature and rebuild it; this creative activity can reestablish harmony with the world. Rimbaud insists on regaining this lost Edenic situation; he offers no means except a "dérèglement de tous les sens" . . . for the attainment of this unity with the world. It is curious that both Char and Rimbaud accept destruction as a natural part of life and find beauty in the ugly or distorted; moreover, both assign value to active destruction as a way of bringing about a new order. The difference is that Char destroys in order to create, while Rimbaud either destroys or uninhibitedly puts forth a new order without any regard to its possible value. In fact, Rimbaud is unable to construct; even emergence is basically destructive in his poetry. Char demands constructive destruction. . . .

The elements of Char's concept of constructive destruction are a "santé du malheur," pulverization, and crispation. According to Char in "Arthur Rimbaud," the last two aspects are to be credited to Rimbaud. Char believes that security, peace, and the absence of threat would lead to a lack of action; his analysis of the human situation has revealed that man acts only when his vulnerability is menaced. Man's innate contradictions of fear, apprehension, defiance, desire, passion, tenderness, and his inherent situation of mortality and finiteness are to be channeled into a concerted activity directed against the menace; the threat must be maintained by the poet. This is the meaning of Char's work, *À une sérénité crispée* (1951). (p. 61)

Of course, Char is a humanist and Rimbaud is not, but it is to be noted that Char's intimate knowledge of Rimbaud's efforts allows him to evolve a poetics based on life, not one based on theory. In this way, Char succeeds in reintegrating man and nature, while in Rimbaud's work man and nature remain at odds with one another and harmony remains an unrealized ambition.

Nature is of prime importance to both Char and Rimbaud, and Char recognizes this affinity between himself and his precursor. . . . Char and Rimbaud recognize that the world of nature is unified and that each element contributes to the construct of the whole; but only Char grasps the parallels between the cyclical process of nature and that of man, between nature as a synthetic whole composed of multiple elements and the human community at large. Although Char and Rimbaud are aware of the mutual give-and-take that occurs within nature, only Char takes the next step and unifies man with nature in the "commune présence" of creative activity.

To realize their vision of cosmic unity and oneness, Char and Rimbaud are constantly engaged in the artistic struggle to efface appearances and unveil the essence of the real. Although these two poets exhibit other strong teleological likenesses, it is in their practice that actual differences emerge. It is to be noted that both Char and Rimbaud find that all forms of expression and all sources of creativity are valid. Moreover, they endeavor to capture the moment of harmony spontaneously albeit Rimbaud is literally spontaneous while Char concentrates only on the effect of spontaneity. Rimbaud relies on the dictates of his inspiration and intuition, while Char evinces a logical, almost mathematical, intellect at work; his reason is always in control of his feeling. Where Rimbaud is uninhibited, Char is disciplined; this is especially notable in Char's deliberate efforts to delete personal details and references, whereas Rimbaud's personal reactions prevail. Further evidence is found in Char's procedural progression from the particular to the general, while Rimbaud rarely goes beyond the particular. Where Rimbaud is a dreamer, Char is the practitioner who realizes a fusion of desire and verb, which remain antithetical for Rimbaud. The young Char of *Les Cloches sur le cœur* is less personal, less objective, less humanistic, and more fervently confident in the power of the verb or written form; but he matures as a poet, learns to control his sensitivity and reactions, learns to reconcile his inspiration and his reason, and learns not to attempt to go beyond the realm of the human. Rimbaud proposes verbal essence and accord only to find greater dispersion, incompatibility, multiplicity, and disillusionment in his own ability to express his vision. Char demonstrates a lived poetics and discovers reconciliation, harmony, and unity. He overcomes his early fears of illusion and death, but Rimbaud remains tormented by them. Char completes and realizes Rimbaud's vision; he brings the necessary corrective, human expression, to Rimbaud's immature faith in the nonhuman. It is impossible to predict the kind of poetry that a mature Rimbaud would have composed, but it is possible to suggest that his work would be similar to the poetry of René Char. Char is very much the student who profited from the successes and failures of his predecessor, and in fulfilling the vision he has remained loyal to it. The text that Char admires most from the entire body of Rimbaud's work is "Génie," which Char interprets as a means for Rimbaud to announce his "congé" from poetry. However, Char does not lament Rimbaud's farewell because he adheres to Rimbaud's tenet that the poet must be, above all, an initiator, a beginner. For Char, it is not satisfaction that one seeks from a poet's work, but scintillation, titillation, provocation. . . . (pp. 61-2)

Virginia A. La Charité, "The Role of Rimbaud in Char's Poetry," in PMLA, *89 (copyright © 1974 by the Modern Language Association of America; reprinted by permission of the Modern Language Association of America), January, 1974, pp. 57-63.*

MICHAEL J. WORTON

In his preface to *Fureur et mystère* Yves Berger writes: "Of all today's poets, René Char is the greatest matchmaker of words. I am thinking here only of those words which, by their sound or their meaning, are least suited to go together. Words which, by their very nature, were destined never to meet." It is clear, even on first acquaintance with Char's poetry, that he achieves much of his success through the juxtaposition of terms which, while seemingly unsuited, nonetheless "work" together, creating new and unexpected images and presenting a world in which objects have a significance which transcends the purely physical. (p. 373)

Char's is not a generous pen. No word is freely given, each being carefully weighed not merely to verify its suitability but to establish its necessity. . . . [For Char poetry] must be *essential,* not merely a verbal or sonorous artifact existing only in the margin of human knowledge. Poetry is *l'eau pure* and, like spring water, both nourishes and purifies, quenching the human thirst for unity and purity. This, then, is the nature of Char's poetic search: he constantly desires lucidity, an awareness of the inherent unity of the world, searching through his poetry which must itself be pure; there can be no mistakes, no uncontrolled movements of lyricism.

This lucidity will result only from a perception of the opposites and contradictions which constitute the world; the poet must therefore create a verbal world which evokes the coexistence of opposites. Char forces words together, making them work their poetic effect through strife rather than through harmony. The obvious advantage of clash is that it opens up rather than limits the connotational possibilities of the words employed, and it activates the creative processes of the reader who must examine the resonances of each term rather than allow himself to be carried along by unity of sense and beauty of rhythm. The term *juxtaposition* will thus be used here to denote occasions when the close proximity of two or more terms results in the generation of fresh interpretations of these words and of their possible fusion.

While Char used this technique extensively in his surrealist period, there the juxtapositions have the effect of shock tactics, whereas in the postwar poems especially the juxtapositions become more thoughtful, and startling oxymorons become less frequent as direct clash gives way to overlapping connotational circles. (pp. 373-74)

Char opens the text of "Fête des arbres et du chasseur" with the hunter addressing his "enemies," the birds:

> Sédentaires aux ailes stridentes
> Ou voyageurs du ciel profond,
> Oiseaux, nous vous tuons
> Pour que l'arbre nous reste et sa morne patience. . . .

It would seem evident that *ailes stridentes* suggests fast, excited movement, such as when a pigeon, frightened from its perch, flies off with its characteristic clattering of wings. This impression is conveyed not by a direct description of motion but by the adjective of sound, *stridentes,* which through its meaning of unusually sharp or piercing sound implies surprise, and also seems initially in opposition to *ailes,* so often associated in Char's work with freedom and softness. The idea of a frightened flurry of movement is thus created by the juxtaposition of initially surprising terms, but within the same line there is a juxtaposition of directly opposing concepts, that of *sédentaires* and of fast, startled movement. Whether *sédentaires* is taken in a literal or figurative sense, a direct contradiction is established which acts as the very definition (or more precisely, as an alternative definition) of the birds. The poet thus stresses in the opening line of his poem the disruptive influence of the hunter who destroys the natural order of the forest. The poem's final contradiction—that of his setting fire to the forest he wishes to keep for himself—is thus heralded by a contradiction set up by the hunter when he first enters the forest. However, the hunter is no more than a catalyst; he merely fulfills his role of "l'exécutant d'une contradiction conforme à l'exigence de la création." . . .

Of the two contradictory attributes which here define the birds, that of having *ailes stridentes* is the more easily acceptable; yet it is the *sédentaires* element which takes precedence both grammatically and emphatically. In this way the poet precludes any over-rapid assumptions in order to forge a fresh, creative view of the world. The birds are, in effect, "captured" at the instant when their immobility transforms itself into movement. This technique of a surprising juxtaposition is thus used to capture and freeze an essential instant.

For Char, opposition and struggle are essential, and throughout his work there are references to enmity, which is seen as generous and productive:

> Le cheval à la tête étroite
> A condamné son ennemi,
> Le poète aux talons oisifs,
> A de plus sévères zephyrs
> Que ceux qui courent dans sa voix.
> ("Divergence," . . .)

The most interesting phrase for the present purpose is "de plus sévères zephyrs," since the close assonance links together words which would seem to contradict each other: if a breeze blows more strongly, it is no longer a breeze. However, the poet in question is "le poète aux talons oisifs," a producer of froth rather than of *l'eau pure,* and the horse, symbol of vitality, is condemning him to undergo the influence of nature, where breezes are not always pleasant. It is not the strength of the breeze which Char evokes here but its *function:* if one is a true poet, dealing with the world, one must attune one's poetry to the harsh and contradictory melodies of nature. The breezes may therefore function as taskmasters without necessarily being gales. With his juxtaposition and assonance, Char is able to fuse the physical and the spiritual qualities of natural phenomena.

Through the poetry the reader is helped to perceive the world in a fresh perspective where accepted definitions are no longer valid: "Je te découvrirai à ceux que j'aime comme un long éclair de chaleur" ("Anoukis et plus tard Jeanne," . . .). The quintessentially ephemeral lightning flash is "long," since, for Char, time is not purely linear; for in moments of true perception and lucidity a "vertical" time, perpendicular to the "horizontal" time of logical progression, is created. The lightning flash is "long" because it transcends the laws of logic and enables man to live in a world of intense reality. Also the flash is a flash of heat, whereas it is normally perceived as a purely visual phenomenon. The poet thereby opens up the field of possible reactions to the *éclair,* which, while at the center of much of Char's philosophy of life, must always remain multivalent.

If the lightning flash is at the heart of much of Char's philosophy, so also is the image of the stream, which has a similar plurality of significance, frequently symbolizing both life and poetry, as when he writes: "Aux épines du torrent / Ma laine maintient ma souffrance" ("Hermétiques ouvriers," . . .). The image of thorny water, while creating a picture of a mountain stream whose little waves peak and catch the light, opposes the softness of water with hard thorns which may inflict pain. This image is not a true metaphor, however, since the poet seeks to restrict none of the possible connotations of the terms but rather to place them in a setting where they can function creatively against each other; he then "confuses" the image further by introducing the idea of foam (*ma laine*). The waves symbolize the summits of existence which must always exist in an onward-moving life, never static nor in the same position, but always there. . . . [The foam] is creative, a continuation of the eternal suffering which is a necessary part of creative existence. The waves are therefore soft (*laine*) and cruel (*épines*), comforting and wounding, but for Char everything in the universe contains inherent oppositions. For this reason his own use of images and symbols can never be static: if froth at one moment represents frivolity and superfluous prettiness, it can also (even simultaneously) have a creative function. This may appear contradictory, but Char, as poet and man, *must* contradict himself, since his existence is based on the lucid perception of a world in which objects coexist in both harmony and strife.

This coexistence is perhaps most clearly posited in the poet's exhortation, "Enfin, si tu détruis, que ce soit avec des outils nuptiaux." . . . Destruction cannot be merely devastation; it must be effected with the aid of *outils nuptiaux,* which in demolishing will create. And for Char, destruction is allied with creation rather than with *re*-creation; destruction and creation simply coexist, neither being superior to the other. Char would seem not to adhere to the traditional "cyclical" philosophy of nature in which birth comes out of death as the phoenix rises from its ashes. For Char, the very act of destruction will form new life, but this process is continually progressive rather than cyclical.

Char's attitude is based on *disponibilité;* man must constantly be open to the influence of everything around him, since significance is an inherent quality of all phenomena. Thus, in "Le risque et le pendule" . . . , he can affirm: "Une poussière qui tombe sur la main occupée à tracer le poème, les foudroie, poème et main" ("A speck of dust, that falls on the hand busy writing out the poem, blasts them, poem and hand"—"The Risk and the Clock" . . .). The essential opposition is clearly between the fragility, the infinitesimal size of the speck of dust and its devastating effect, an opposition which enables Char to indicate that the apparently least significant of objects may radically affect our lives. The close proximity of *poussière* and *foudroie* is evidently comprehensible on at least one level, but it also creates tensions which can never be fully resolved, which must indeed never be forced into any fully coherent system, since the poet's purpose is to generate an examination of the nature of each of these terms which must spark against each other without ever completely gelling.

If Char uses juxtaposition frequently in his poetry, it is not purely as a poetic technique but because it arises organically from his philosophy of life, which, like that of Heraclitus, is based on the coexistence and interaction of opposites. However, the influence of Heraclitus should not be overemphasized, since Char's beliefs stem from his immersion in his native Provence. . . . The recurrence in the works of both Char and Heraclitus of symbols such as the lightning flash and the stream is perhaps misleading, since the assumption might be made that Char's symbols are identical to those of the pre-Socratic philosopher. However, Heraclitus tends to use his symbols in a purely binary way (for example: "It is not possible to step twice into the same river"; "Those who step into the same river have different waters flowing ever upon them"; "In the same river we both step and do not step, we are and we are not"),

whereas Char insists on a simultaneous plurality of meaning, as when he proclaims, "L'essaim, l'éclair et l'anathème, trois obliques d'un même sommet" . . . , where each of the three terms is equivalent to the others, though never totally autonomous.

Char's predilection for juxtaposition results from his desire to *oppose* images and connotations rather than to *impose* terms and connotations on top of each other, as is the case with metaphor, which necessarily filters the relevant connotations. Char wishes to leave possibilities open, to accord to words their full potential of resonance and to ensure that the multiple interactions of the phenomenal world are mirrored in his poetry. Poetry is life and therefore must be apprehensible, though never fully comprehensible. The world is a juxtaposition; poetry must, then, be based on oppositions of images and, necessarily, of seemingly unsuitable words. (pp. 374-75)

> *Michael J. Worton, "Juxtaposition in the Poetry of René Char," in* World Literature Today *(copyright 1977 by the University of Oklahoma Press), Vol. 51, No. 3, Summer, 1977, pp. 373-75.*

JAMES R. LAWLER

One of the most dramatic periods in Char's career is his rediscovery of nature as the central resource after 1935. Surrealism had taken him into nocturnal obsession from which withdrawal was not easy, but his poetry that postdates *Le marteau sans maître* contains the assertion of a Mediterranean warmth and of a language deliberately renewed. He delights in the multiplicity of plants, animals, landscapes, transforms the vocabulary of his poems; at the same time he is attentive to an implicit wisdom that he seeks to convey. He becomes the fervent hunter of meanings who reinvents the myth of Orion. . . .

In reading Char's finest nature poems we are able to gauge his artistic integrity. He composes most often with assurance, as if his work came ripely to his pen; yet he is also ready to wait long months for a single word and to revise completed writings. He is meticulous in his analyses, in the elaboration of his themes. "La Sorgue" . . . is such a poem: although subtitled "Chanson pour Yvonne," it is at farthest remove from spontaneous lyricism, since—"poésie et vérité, comme nous savons, étant synonymes" ("Partage formel," . . .)—desire here engages conscience, and conscience desire. (p. 376)

It is not surprising that Char once named Claudel among his poetic ancestors . . . for he could not but be sensitive to this breadth and vitality and power. But his stance is not that of a weak poet before a strong one. Even as he singled out Claudel, he called him *irresponsable,* a term by which he indicated his lack of sympathy with a writer who he felt had renounced his human burdens and replaced crucial tension by willful surrender. For Char this was not the answer: he himself invokes no divine ocean of faith but rather the river, whose disciplined suppleness and plurality respond to his ethical concern. His parallelisms are not addressed to God but to waters of actuality. The twenty-one *versets* are built on four rhymes, one of which occurs twelve times as a lyrical frame and melodic consonance. We find, then, phonetic continuity—an uneven flow, however, since it is restrained by end-stopped couplets and by the variations on the basic octosyllabic meter in each hemistich. Indeed, the rhythmic energy is reinforced by its very scruples, like the sharp pebbles (in Latin, *scrupuli*) which the stream carries in its bed.

A trimeter opens the sequence, sets the amplitude:

Rivière trop tôt partie, d'une traite, sans compagnon,
Donne aux enfants de mon pays le visage de ta passion.

(River, hasty starter, at a bound, with no companion,
Give the children of my country the features of your passion.)

There is firmness in the opening prayer to a godhead of visible presence. The importance of the initial word—the song's central sonority, for it occurs thirteen times—is pointed up by the rhythm, which makes a customary disyllable into a tetrasyllable (*ri-vi-è-re*): we hear an invocation without indirections, an urgent plea not for the self but for others. The image is at once the message, the adjectival phrases describing a scene whose sense is sacred. . . . The response to Claudel cannot go unheard, for this liturgy turns to immanence and not transcendence, immediacy and not immortality. All of us are in need of intensity, and it can be found, says the poet, in the Heraclitean river. . . .

Rivière où l'éclair finit et où commence ma maison,
Qui roule aux marches d'oubli la rocaille de ma raison.

(River where the lightning ends and my home rises,
Rolling to the steps of oblivion the rubble of my reason.)

The anaphoric development, the division into rhyming couplets, the rhythms underlined by assonance at the caesura convey a measured voice. The poet speaks from his experience, declares his tributary relationship. For him the river is the locus of beginnings and endings, lightning flash and habitation ("Si nous habitons un éclair, il est le coeur de l'éternel" ["À la santé du serpent" . . .]), forgetfulness and awareness, loose stones and stairs. Its vigorous divinity does not banish but embraces; it draws strength from inclusiveness; it marries reason with reason's contrary. . . . On this one and only occasion the first-person singular is used, whereby Char establishes that his song is founded in dependence: he identifies with the river's space, espouses its time. Richly the word pattern finds a parallel balance of sound as words echo one another (*rivière/éclair*) a back vowel is sensuously prolonged (*où/où/roule/oubli*), plosive and liquid consonants accompany a tense action whose meaning is ceaseless change.

Rivière, en toi terre est frisson, soleil anxiété.
Que chaque pauvre dans sa nuit fasse son pain de ta moisson.

(River, in you earth is shudder, sun unrest,
Let every poor man in his night make his bread of your harvest.)

The river is not quietude but ripple and tremor, restlessness and tumult. Earth and sun are shimmering things, for no element or object may remain innocent when mirrored in the depths. . . . The cycle of growth reveals its sense in the loaf of bread; anxiety finds its complementary nourishment. Thus is articulated a fertile disruption which the rhythm of the first line emphasizes, like the absence of rhyme and assonance at the caesura; but *frisson* recalls the continuity that *moisson* recovers, and the insistent alliteration welds the couplet into a single unit.

Rivière souvent punie, rivière à l'abandon.

(River often punished, river left to drift.) . . .

Abandonment and sacrilege are the river's fate, like that of every god. Laconically the poet recalls rejection and disrespect, defilement and infidelity. His expression needs no amplification, its economy indicating the common paradoxes of ecological wastage—active infliction, passive neglect. . . . The abrupt single line evokes contrasting attitudes in each hemistich, proposing without sentimentality the awareness of a godhead spurned.

Rivière des apprentis à la calleuse condition,
Il n'est vent qui ne fléchisse à la crête de tes sillons.

(River of those apprenticed to the callousing condition,
Not a wind but bends at your furrows' crest.)

The poem now rediscovers rhythmic regularity on its four hemistichs, which have new recourse to the paired diction of caesurae and end-words. A simple opposition contrasts the sores of young workmen who are inexperienced in nature's ways with the balm—gentleness, protection, modification—that the river freely offers. This is the waters' healing which is figured by the inflection of the wind touching the ripples. *Calleuse,* the first strong adjective in the poem, receives force from the preceding verbal austerity and from its pronominal position. But no pathos supervenes, just as there is none in the oblique image of the second line which formulates the resolution of pain in impersonal terms and with the syntactic brevity of a proverb.

Rivière de l'âme vide, de la guenille et du soupçon,
Du vieux malheur qui se dévide, de l'ormeau, de la compassion.

(River of the empty soul, of rags and of suspicion,
Of old trouble unwinding, of the elm, of compassion.)

The ternary division of each line signifies the measure wherein pain is made tolerable, suffering assuaged. The soul can be morally and physically dispossessed, empty in a thousand ways; it can also be full of sorrow, impoverishment, distrust. It finds its familiar compeer, unhappiness, which lengthily spins a tale of self-pity. Such dolor has its accompaniment in the river that pursues a parallel course and a defiant solitude. Yet the waters also contain the reflected freshness of a young elm, a verdant growth, an exultant solace; they channel a restoring succor. The polarities of ennui and rejuvenation are thus present in the manner of a pre-Socratic image, not negating one another but proclaiming a profound sympathy between river and men.

Rivière des farfelus, des fiévreux, des équarrisseurs,
Du soleil lâchant sa charrue pour s'acoquiner au menteur.

(River of the fey, the fevered, the knacker in his yard,
The sun dropping his plough to hobnob with a liar.)

After the preceding three sections that identify an idea of pain, a change of homophones at the caesura and the end-word introduces a new emphasis. The river is like common men who live, work and take their ease by its banks, be they fanciful and free in their manners as the familiar *farfelus* suggests, or else of fevered temperament. On the other hand, there are men like the humble knackers who laboriously dissect a dead animal to make a living. The river recognizes men's diversity as its own, just as it greets the sun, both diligent and casual, which momentarily drops its prescribed task to tarry and chat with a congenial storyteller. In this way the couplet names the extremes of rural amity and earnestness, fantasy and toil—necessary if opposite attributes of the river's spaciousness.

> Rivière des meilleurs que soi, rivière des brouillards éclos,
> De la lampe qui désaltère l'angoisse autour de son chapeau.
>
> (River of men better than oneself, river of fog-blooms,
> Of the lamp quenching dread in a circle round its hat.)

Against egotism the river has powerful remedies. One becomes aware of his own shortcomings in frequenting those that obey the highest callings of strength, benevolence, sensitivity.... [The] river can be as a lamp that dispels the night: Char's image of anguish overcome has no grandiloquence but the homely warmth of *chapeau*.... However paradoxical, the lamp's glow and fog are both the river's own and show the vastness of comprehension to which men can turn.

> Rivière des égards au songe, rivière qui rouille le fer,
> Où les étoiles ont cette ombre qu'elles refusent à la mer.
>
> (River of respect for dreams, river that rusts iron,
> Where the stars have the shadow they refuse to the sea.)

As in the previous couplet, the repetition of *rivière* in the first line establishes a lyrical incantation which is reinforced by alliteration and assonance. Two further virtues of the Sorgue are sung: its complementary toughness and subtlety, its *fureur* and *mystère*. There is a need for perseverance, for the tenacity of water that causes iron to rust, that penetrates by affusion. The waters destroy and espouse at the same moment of action.... But the river also initiates reverie and nourishes it, permits the uniquely discreet reflection of stars that the ocean in its turbulence cannot achieve. The broad scheme of moral polarities is the river's force and sacrament, as it is of love....

> Rivière des pouvoirs transmis et du cri embouquant les eaux,
> De l'ouragan qui mord la vigne et annonce le vin nouveau.
>
> (River of powers transmitted, the cry essaying the waters,
> The autumn gale that bites the vine and announces the new wine.)

In this second to last section Char proposes the notion of communication between elements and men, men and elements.... The river creates for us the image of transmission, the refusal to have and hold, the mutual virtues of receiving and giving. The idea is first expressed in abstract terms, as in the opening hemistich of the preceding couplet, then interpreted concretely. The violent cry is channeled into usefulness: undirected pathos discovers a vehicle, a riverbed, an orientation like the shout that becomes a poem or the emotion that becomes purposeful energy. A second illustration of such efficaciousness is the unruly forces of the hurricane whose rage allows us to look to the vigor of the wine to be. Thus past, present and future participate—like abstract powers, human voice, natural force—in order to compose the fury and the certain tenderness: "And a man who can watch the earth through to its end in fruit—/ Failure does not shake him though he has lost all."...

The tenth section, then, brings the interlude of four couplets ... to a close and completes a pattern of rhymes (*c d e d*). Now Char returns to the initial scheme of assonance at the caesura and the end-word:

> Rivière au cœur jamais détruit dans ce monde fou de prison,
> Garde-nous violent et ami des abeilles de l'horizon.
>
> (River with a heart never destroyed in this world crazy for prison,
> Keep us violent and a friend to the bees of the horizon.)

This phonetic return accompanies a reiteration of praise and at the same time a prayer that is said not only for some, as in the first couplet, but for one and all, including the poet himself. In his eyes the river is a very personal godhead, and he must speak of its heart: *cœur*, this inadequate word —"... nous disons *le cœur* et le disons à regret" ...— states nonetheless the humane values that alone justify existence in the frenzied prison of the world. He does not lose sight of men's continuing folly, their blindness to freedom, but his faith tells him that the river's meaning is immortal. However, it is not enough to revere it, for men must act in its likeness—violent as tumult, unfettered yet fertile as bees. The contraries of turbulence and tenderness conjoin in a way that provides hope in the face of death and the absurd. At this point the river is seen to be the inspiriting word and force and luxuriance inseparate from love. (pp. 376-79)

It becomes apparent that such a poem demands close reading for its course to be traced. Only thus can we apprehend the achieved union of nature and thought, poetic object and project. In the parts as in the whole there is energetic adherence to the scene described, rigorous scrutiny, strict explanation. Obscurity does not come from any deception by the poet but rather from his uncompromising probity that proceeds by ellipsis, shifts from concrete to abstract and back again, ensures its intensity by multiple focusing. To study the text is to become aware of meaning as movement—as the sum total of the furious paradoxes of passion and grace, quickness and stability, anxiety and fulfillment, suffering and abandonment, pain and balm, solitariness and pity, relaxation and toil, anguish and comfort, mystery and toughness, severity and promise, violence and friendship. In each couplet, as in the full development, the poem models itself on the river that is indefinable by any single aspect, for it is complex, multiform, unfailingly alert to contradictions. The rhetoric of antipoles is a properly moral vision which, past ideologies having been set aside, creates a compelling figure of responsible strength. (p. 379)

> *James R. Lawler, "Fealty to the River," in* World Literature Today *(copyright 1977 by the University of Oklahoma Press), Vol. 51, No. 3, Summer, 1977, pp. 376-79.*

*　　　*　　　*

CHEEVER, John　1912-

Cheever is an American short story writer and novelist. His fictional world is that of suburban New York and New England, his typical characters are of the upper middle class. This closed social milieu contrasts sharply with the chaos and despair of life in Cheever's fiction, resulting in confusion and frustration for his characters. Cheever, however, is a humanist, and believing in the rejuvenative power of love, treats his

afflicted protagonists with compassion in prose noted for its wit and verbal splendor. Cheever was awarded the 1978 Pulitzer Prize in Fiction. (See also *CLC*, Vols. 3, 7, 8, and *Contemporary Authors*, Vols. 5-8, rev. ed.)

JOYCE CAROL OATES

In Cheever's imagination the concrete, visual world is transformed into emotion, and emotion into something akin to nostalgia. The senses, alerted to a patch of blue sky or swirling leaves or a sudden shaft of sunlight, are stimulated to a recollection that transcends the present and transcends, when Cheever's writing is at its most powerful, the very instrument of perception that is its vehicle. Hence the peculiar airiness of *Falconer*, the translucent quality of its protagonist Ezekiel Farragut . . . , the insubstantial quality of the narrative itself—though it purports to be located in a very real penitentiary and has been interpreted, by various critics, as a triumph of 'realism.'

The novel is a fable, a kind of fairy tale; near-structureless, it has the feel of an assemblage of short stories, and is consequently most successful in fragments: in patches of emotion. The world we glimpse through Farragut's eyes is as capricious and as alarming as a Chagall painting, and while it is occasionally beautiful it is also rather ugly, and at its worst tawdrily unconvincing—when narrative is forced to serve the demands of theme and Farragut 'escapes' prison by hiding in a dead man's shroud and afterward escapes the shroud by a maneuver that would strike us as embarrassingly awkward in a children's movie. No matter that Cheever cannot make his story probable: perhaps it is enough that it works on the level of myth, as a sort of death-and-resurrection suspense novel enriched with innumerable striking passages. (p. 99)

[Farragut] is a husband and a father, but his wife is a stereotyped villainess who would be most at home in a *New Yorker* cartoon, and his son appears to be non-existent. Cheever works up a few 'memories' of wife and son but they are singularly unconvincing, as if his heart were not in it—as if the labors of conventional novelizing had grown tedious, and poetry of a whimsical, surreal nature had become more attractive. We are told too that Farragut has killed his brother Eben, an unpleasant man whom he has disliked for most of his life, but the killing is presented in a quick, truncated scene; like most physical action in *Falconer* it is hastily glossed over. What clearly appeals to Cheever is the pure action of writing itself and *Falconer* is most successful when there is nothing going on except bodiless reverie. . . . [These] observations, lovely as they are, might belong to anyone; one feels that they are Cheever's and not his protagonist's.

Cheever is by nature a short story writer and while in his finest short stories (like "The Swimmer" and "The Enormous Radio") a single surreal image is vividly developed, and draws that forward-motion called 'plot' irresistibly along with it, his novels flounder under the weight of too many capricious, inspired, zany images. (pp. 99-100)

A certain visionary outrageousness in Cheever's art has often resulted in highly successful short stories, and there are certainly a number of powerful passages in *Falconer*, as in *Bullet Park* and the Wapshot novels; but in general the whimsical impulse undercuts and to some extent damages the more serious intentions of the works. This much-praised novel is finally quite disappointing: its victories are

far too easy, its transcendence of genuine pain and misery is glib, even crude. But one should read Cheever for the richness of his observations, perhaps, rejoicing in his capacity to see and to feel and to value. Smallness and even banality are not to be rejected in the 'prison' of earthly existence. . . . (pp. 100-01)

> Joyce Carol Oates, "An Airy Insubstantial World," in The Ontario Review (copyright © 1977 by The Ontario Review), Fall-Winter, 1977-78, pp. 99-101.

ISA KAPP

For three decades the legato Cheever prose has remained as urbane and tempting as an ad in the *New Yorker,* sharing with the magazine that has published nearly all his stories a zealous attention to surfaces, a scrupulous rendition of speech and, not the least of its attractions, a supercilious tone that separates its uncommon reader from the gaucheness and banality of common experience.

Cheever has been called the American Chekhov, and it is true that both writers have a ruminative manner, dwell wistfully on lost opportunities, and are masters at conjuring up a mood, an excitation of the nerves, a vapor of unstated emotion hanging in the air. But when they undertake their favorite identical subject, the seesaw between tranquility and disturbance in marriage, we see how enormous a role the accident of disposition plays in creating the hierarchy of art. Chekhov's plain and pliant responses make us feel that marital disharmony is only one aspect of life, part of the natural order of things, rather than an occasion for outrage. We sense the Russian writer's intuitive sympathy with all of his characters. Cheever's sympathies spring unaccountably back to the observer, as if he were personally affronted, violated in his finer sensibilities by the shabby tales he relates. His heroes and heroines are usually caught in a spiritual flagrante delicto, a bit awkward and pathetic as they come into view through a light frost of derision. (p. 16)

If Cheever is no analyst of motive, it may be because he regards the battle of the sexes as too ferocious for psychological interpretation, rooted instead in some primal biological antagonism or some malevolent caprice of the universe.

Can the author of all this domestic infelicity really believe, as he says in his Preface [to *The Stories of John Cheever*], that the constants he looks for are "a love of light and a determination to trace some moral chain of being"? We have to suppose that he simply does not recognize his own saturnine bent of mind, his speedy susceptibility to the faintest intimations of discord, and to the sorrows of gin. (pp. 16-17)

Perhaps it is to make amends to himself and us for the disproportion in his focus that so many of Cheever's stories launch into lyrical transports when the human outlook is particularly grim. . . .

Despite the rhapsodic thrill of the language, it seems to me one of the least wholesome elements in Cheever's fiction that he so often juxtaposes the pleasing prospect of nature and the disagreeable one of men and women, and lurches so readily from cynicism to exaltation. He does much better when he comes to terms with the blackness in himself, which may be why *Falconer,* for all the abrasiveness of its cat slaughters and brutalities among prisoners, is a strong and plausible novel. . . .

No unhappy ending can stop Cheever's spirits from soaring, however, once Italy enters the scene.... In 1956 Cheever spent a year in Italy, and what an infusion of red blood and charm the change in setting gives to his writing! In the Italian stories—e.g. "The Bella Lingua" and "The Duchess"—the swimming pools and adulteries of Shady Hill are far behind him and Cheever turns into the most likeable of writers. He leans back, develops perspective, takes a robust interest in other people's lives.....

In Italy Cheever grows more springy, outgoing and natural, and the melancholy fog of "pain and sweetness" lifts from his fiction. His lens to the world seems to be set at a more secure point, midway between triumph and disappointment. What an accomplishment it would have been if he could have added that comfortable frame of mind to the rest of his clear and elegant prose. (p. 17)

> Isa Kapp, "The Cheerless World of John Cheever," in The New Leader (© 1978 by the American Labor Conference on International Affairs, Inc.), September 11, 1978, pp. 16-17.

JOHN IRVING

[Cheever's] sympathy for people is consistently strong. [He] shows a steady affection for even the nastiest of his characters—even at their most degraded moments. In the darkest of his stories [collected in *The Stories of John Cheever*] there shines a light; that light is Cheever's loyalty to human beings— in spite of ourselves. . . .

What makes the affirmation of humanity in Cheever's work so successful is that he never chooses easy subjects for love.... Cheever writes about characters difficult to forgive, but he usually forgives them.... It is all the more astonishing an achievement that he reaches such respect for life *in spite of* the way the world is. (p. 44)

Since I'm a novelist—whose taste lies solidly with the novel—I must add that this awesome collection of craft and feeling *reads* like a novel. There is not only the wonder of finishing one good story after another, there is that cumulative weight, that sense of deepening, that I have formerly associated only with the consecutiveness of a true (and truly narrative) novel. (p. 45)

The variety in these stories and the constancy of Cheever's careful voice give this collection the breadth and wholeness of the biggest of novels. . . .

Without quarreling over the difference in magnitude between the art forms of the novel and the short story, it is simply possible to say that John Cheever is the best story-teller living; he practices what he preaches better than any of us, and we believe him when he writes, "We can cherish nothing less than our random understanding of death and the earth-shaking love that draws us to one another." (p. 46)

> John Irving, "Facts of Living," in Saturday Review (© 1978 by Saturday Review Magazine Corp.; reprinted with permission), September 30, 1978, pp. 44-6.

CHARLES NICOL

Some words by their very nature define not our world but an ideal one, one in which we can believe but not live. It was always John Cheever's achievement to see that the middle class pretends that these words define reality, and then acts according to that faith, so that keeping up appearances is not only a desperate task but a noble stance. . . .

In an imagined world where moral truths fly in the face of facts, Cheever's stories [collected in *The Stories of John Cheever*] set up extreme tensions between what should be believed and what must be seen. (p. 93)

Decorum is a concept not often defended or celebrated these days, and the strain of keeping it up is a frequent theme of Cheever's more recent stories.... Vulgarity does threaten the myths by which Cheever's people live, and their perplexity is genuine enough, but Cheever's decorum begins to sound defensive and to run headlong into simple nostalgia. (p. 94)

[The] best of Cheever's more recent stories reveal the mellow craftsmanship of an old master with an abundance of tales to tell. . . .

Cheever has become a virtuoso of the excursive who loves his shaggy dog and prefers the telling to the tale. (p. 95)

> Charles Nicol, "The Truth, the Impartial Truth," in Harper's (copyright © 1978 by Harper's Magazine; all rights reserved; excerpted from the October, 1978 issue by special permission), October, 1978, pp. 93-5.

ANNE TYLER

John Cheever has been publishing his short stories for over 30 years now, and he has gradually spread before us a landscape so solid and believable that the average American reader could almost draw a map of Shady Hill, Bullet Park, or St. Botolphs. We know intimately the Cheever hero—an unassuming man whose innocence and optimism often give him the appearance of someone much younger. And we know the basis of most Cheever plots: a subtle tension between what Cheever calls the "facts" (the moral ugliness, or at best the irrationality, of the real world) and the "truth," which is the underlying goodness and order in which the hero places an abiding faith.

But we tend to remember only this second, gentler side, when recalling Cheever's stories from a distance.... We have an impression of a sort of tapestry, richly woven, stylized, eerily still—if you can imagine a tapestry that depicts barbecue grills and power lawnmowers, and chlorinated swimming pools. . . .

[The] effect of such a mass of writing [found in *The Stories of John Cheever*] ... is to heighten that tension between the "facts" and the "truth." The darker side of the world seems to stand out more distinctly; the main characters' stubborn hopefulness seems more desperate. (p. 45)

Reading *The Stories of John Cheever* is not the patchwork experience that you might expect; it's more like reading a novel, being tugged along by a gathering sense of suspense. Ultimately, which way will the scales tip?

What determines the way an individual story will tip, at least, is the writing style. Some of these stories are written from outside. They're summarized, really, in a cool, often ironic tone of voice: names, dates, events—facts.....

But the stories written from *inside*—where events sometimes equally bleak are alchemized by the peculiarly sunny vision of the narrator—carry a kind of luminous quality that transcends the plot. Men in these stories have an endearing habit of viewing the commonplace as something mythical, and of endlessly forgiving the world its banality and frustrations. . . .

The fact that there is a comic note in some characters' voices does not lessen their ability to move us. There may be something ridiculous about their positions—they may live in a district where death is against the zoning laws, they may wear rayon pajama tops printed with pictures of the *Pinta*, the *Nina*, and the *Santa Maria*—but that in no way lightens their grief at the passage of time, or their bewilderment in the face of a centrifugal force that seems to be throwing them "further and further away from one's purest memories and ambitions." (p. 46)

In his preface, Cheever remarks upon the fact that these stories, like many of his heroes, have been affected by the passage of time. . . . But in Cheever's stories, as in no others that come to mind, this sense of datedness works to their advantage. It gives an added poignancy to already poignant characters; it makes even more surreal the bewildering scenery of their lives. . . . (pp. 46-7)

John Cheever is a magnificent storyteller, and this is a dazzling and powerful book. (p. 47)

> *Anne Tyler, in* The New Republic *(reprinted by permission of* The New Republic; © *1978 by The New Republic, Inc.), November 4, 1978.*

ROBERT TOWERS

Though Cheever disclaims a documentary purpose and (rightly) resents comparison to a social nit-picker like the later John O'Hara, his stories do have a powerful documentary interest—and why not? Documentation of the way we —or some of us—live now has been historically one of those enriching impurities of fiction that only a mad theorist would wish to filter out. Less grand than Auchincloss, subtler and cleverer than Marquand, infinitely more generous than O'Hara, Cheever has written better than anyone else of that little world which upper-middle-class Protestants have contrived to maintain in their East Side apartments, in certain suburbs, in summer cottages on Nantucket, in Adirondack lodges, on New England farms. . . .

Like so many of his nineteenth-century predecessors, Cheever is authoritative in his portrayal of the shabby genteel, of those who must resort to desperate contrivances to keep up appearances, to say nothing of advancing themselves in the world.

He is also wonderfully sensitive to the rhythms of family life within this class . . . ; to the asperities of fraternal relationships . . . ; to the decorum to be maintained in one's dealing with in-laws and, by extension, with servants, babysitters, hired hands, and local inhabitants of a different class . . . ; and to the behavior of children disillusioned with their parents. . . . He catches not only the chronic irritations and disappointments but also the sudden upwelling of great tenderness and compassion.

Of course, Cheever, for all his fascination with manners, has never been primarily a documentary writer. His response to experience is essentially that of an old-fashioned lyric poet. . . . While one might question Cheever's profundity as a moralist, there can be no doubt about his preoccupation with—and celebration of—the shifting powers of light. His stories are bathed in light, flooded with it; often his characters appear slightly drunk with it, their senses reeling.

Light seems to be associated with a blessing, with a tender maternal smile fleetingly experienced, with all that is clean, tender, and guiltless, with the barely glimpsed immanence of God within His creation. At times Cheever appears to soar like Shelley's skylark toward the source of light, a belated romantic beating his luminous wings in the void.

But while the lyric impulse sometimes leads him into a slight (and often endearing) silliness—"The light was like a blow, and the air smelled as if many wonderful girls had just wandered across the lawn"—he is for the most part a precisionist of the senses. Though his imagery of light has the strongest retinal impact, Cheever's evocation of color and texture and smell is also vivid and persistent. He shares with two very different writers, Lawrence and Faulkner, an extraordinary ability to fix the sensory quality of a particular moment, a particular place, and to make it function not as embellishment but as an essential element in the lives and moods of his characters. (p. 3)

Cheever is a writer whose faults have an unusually close connection to his strengths. The imaginative identification with the upper-middle class which allows him to depict their mores and dilemmas with such vivacity entails a narrowness of social range and a sentimental snobbery which can get the best of him when his guard is down. (pp. 3-4)

The most serious embarrassments occur when he attempts an identification with a really alien figure. . . . His condescension to these characters is well meant, full of good will, and hard to swallow.

The snobbery is fairly innocent as snobberies go, attaching itself mostly to well-bred or even aristocratic ladies and causing little damage beyond a maudlin blurring of Cheever's usually sharp vision. . . .

Cheever's role as narrator is always obtrusive. He has, of course, never had any truck with the notion—once a dogma among certain academic critics—that an author should keep himself as invisible as possible, that he should show rather than tell. Cheever-as-narrator is regularly on stage, rejoicing in his own performance, commenting upon—often chatting about—his characters, dispatching them on missions, granting them reprieves or firmly settling their hash. At his most effective he can tell us things about a character with such authority that we never for a moment doubt that his comprehension is total, final. . . .

Cheever-as-narrator is a personable fellow—debonaire, graceful, observant, and clever. His sympathies are volatile and warm. He is a good host—one who likes to entertain, to amuse, to turn a phrase. He is also a bit of a show-off, an exhibitionist. Beneath the gaiety and charm of his discourse, deep strains of melancholy and disappointment run. He is not, however, a cynic. Nor is he a profound moralist. He has no fundamental quarrel with the family or society as they now exist. For the ills of the flesh and spirit his sovereign remedy is the repeated application of love, love, love. . . .

Cheever's highhanded way as a narrator—at its best a display of confident mastery—can degenerate into whimsicality and arbitrariness, especially in the later stories. . . . Sheer contrivance dominates [pieces like "Percy" or "The Jewels of the Cabots"] and others like them, squeezing the little life they contain into pointless and arbitrary shapes. Cheever's real energies during this recent period seem to have gone into those strange, dark novels, *Bullet Park* and *Falconer,* whose eccentricities—however wild—are not allowed to undermine the powerful and moving stories they have to tell.

Thanks to this volume, the best of Cheever's stories are now spread glitteringly before us. In our renewed pleasure in these, we can let the others—the trivial and the miscalculated—recede to their proper place. Cheever's accomplishment in his exacting art is proportionally large, as solid as it is brilliant, and likely to endure—a solemn thing to say (however true) of a writer who has so often flaunted the banner of devil-may-care. (p. 4)

> *Robert Towers, "Light Touch," in* The New York Review of Books *(reprinted with permission from* The New York Review of Books; *copyright © 1978 Nyrev, Inc.), November 9, 1978, pp. 3-4.*

* * *

CHITTY, Sir Thomas Willes
See HINDE, Thomas

* * *

CORSO, (Nunzio) Gregory   1930-

Corso is an American poet, novelist, and dramatist. Early in his career as a poet he received encouragement from Allen Ginsberg and other Beat poets, and both the style and themes of his work reflect their influence. (See also *CLC*, Vol. 1, and *Contemporary Authors*, Vols. 5-8, rev. ed.)

ALLEN GINSBERG

Open [*Gasoline*] as you would a box of crazy toys, take in your hands a refinement of beauty out of a destructive atmosphere. These combinations are imaginary and pure, in accordance with Corso's individual (therefore universal) DESIRE.

All his own originality! What's his connection, but his own beauty? Such weird haiku-like juxtapositions aren't in the American book. Ah! but the real classic tradition—from Aristotle's description of metaphor to the wildness of his Shelley—and Apollinaire, Lorca, Mayakovsky. Corso is a great word-slinger, first naked sign of a poet, a scientific master of mad mouthfuls of language. He wants a surface hilarious with ellipses, jumps of the strangest phrasing picked off the streets of his mind like "mad children of soda caps." (p. 7)

He gets pure abstract poetry, the inside sound of language alone.

But what is he *saying*? Who cares?! It's said! "Outside by a Halloween fire, wise on a charred log, an old man is dictating to the heir of the Goon."

This heir sometimes transcribes perfect modern lyrics anyone can dig: "Italian Extravaganza," "Birthplace Revisited," "Last Gangster," "Mad Yak," "Furnished Room," "Haarlem," "Last Night I Drove a Car," "Ecce Homo," "Hello."

A rare sad goonish knowledge with reality—a hip piss on reality also—he prefers his dreams. Why not? His Heaven is Poetry. (pp. 7-8)

What a solitary dignitary! He's got the angelic power of making autonomous poems, like god making brooks. (p. 9)

[Corso himself states:] "When Bird Parker or Miles Davis blow a standard piece of music, they break off into other own-self little unstandard sounds—well, that's my way with poetry—X Y & Z, call it automatic—I call it a standard flow (because at the offset words are standard) that is intentionally distracted diversed into my own sound. Of course many will say a poem written on that order is unpolished, etc.—that's just what I want them to be—because I have made them truly my own—which is inevitably something NEW—like all good spontaneous jazz." . . . (pp. 9-10)

The mind has taken a leap in language. He curses like a brook, pure poetry. . . . We're the fabled damned if we put it down. He's probably the greatest poet in America, and he's starving in Europe. (p. 10)

> *Allen Ginsberg, in his introduction to* Gasoline *by Gregory Corso (© 1958 by Gregory Corso; reprinted by permission of City Lights Books), City Lights Books, 1958, pp. 7-10.*

GERARD J. DULLEA

[Corso] has neither the philosophical depth or breadth of Ginsberg, which is considerable, no matter what an individual's reaction to him might be. But in many ways, Corso's poetry is more pleasing than Ginsberg's, perhaps because it is more easily recognized as being within more major traditions, especially in the sense of the poetic line; we have come to expect lines that are shorter than a page is wide. Another more comfortable aspect of Corso's poetry is that he has more "negative capability" than does Ginsberg. Like Ginsberg, and most Romantics, his constant concern is with the Self, but he nearly always manages to distill turbulent emotions so that they "merely" inform the intellectual experience of the poem, instead of comprising the poem as do Ginsberg's in "Howl," for example.

But Corso is not an intellectual poet. Anything but. He is, like Ginsberg, a poet of the senses and of the imagination. . . . Ginsberg frequently seems to deliver immediate sensual experiences; Corso usually refines and alters those experiences through his very vivid imagination.

The exercise of this imagination is one of the most characteristic features of Corso's poems, and it works against some of the more objective features. Usually, it takes the form of an absurd, surreal, or illogical phrase such as Ginsberg's own "reality sandwich." And the effect is frequently one of cleverness, of a poet playing his creative game to the utmost. But frequently he thus turns poetry almost into a game of solitaire, since the reader cannot fully understand or even appreciate the composition of a particular phrase because the connection is individualistic and private, apparently known to Corso alone. The connection between the elements of his phrasing may derive partially from hallucinogenics (as is obviously implied in the title of one poem, "Under Peyote"), as some features of Ginsberg's poetry may, but the source of the characteristic in either case is not so important as is its existence. And this existence presents a very difficult, if not impossible, critical problem.

Even Ginsberg, one of his closest friends and probably his staunchest admirer, is not sure exactly what Corso is doing, or more precisely, *meaning*, in his poems [see excerpt above]. (pp. 23-4)

All this is fine if "a poem should not mean but be." But most readers are apparently not hip enough, and therefore expect and appreciate a semblance of meaning. Corso's work as a whole does have some meaning; his central theme is the celebration of life in the face of death. He does insist, however, as Ginsberg notes, on celebrating life, his life, in a way so personal that the rest of us are never sure just what or how he is celebrating. It seems that usually he celebrates the source of his most important life, that of his imagination. He considers himself to be a poet, and a poet to be a free spirit, unbound by conventions such as making sense when talking (writing) to someone else. Or possibly he is *not* writing to or for anyone but himself. He publishes and reads, to be sure, but always there is a nagging sense that the whole thing is a put-on, that he is willing to make money off the public if they are willing to consume his products. If such is the case, he must take great delight in the whole system. . . . (p. 24)

But this delight is meaningful in itself, whether or not it is at the expense of his public. Usually it demonstrates his tremendous sense of humor; in his most serious poem he is rarely surrealistic. And it shows also his concern for "pure" poetry in the sense that abstract painters seek "pure" visual art. The imagination is the source of the art, which rests primarily in the image. The less the image is encumbered by meaning, the better, because meaning is a function of rationalization, not of perception and/or imagination. Therefore, any meaning other than emotional response derives also from the use of imagination, this time the reader's. Often, the connection between a particular image and its context is clear enough in that half of it relates to what precedes or follows. But such connections are virtually always merely associative and nearly never truly logical. (pp. 24-5)

Once this habit of imagery is seen as a game, either for the poet himself or with his readers, it is easier to reconcile its use in what are apparently more serious poems, such as "Marriage." Here, despite the perfectly logical and probable consideration of marital possibilities, there is a regular occurrence of highly illogical and improbable images, such as "werewolf bathtubs and forked clarinets" and "Flash Gordon soap." These serve primarily to assert the identity of the poet, who can think in extraordinary ways and who lives as much in an internal and private . . . way as he does in the mundane and ordinary manner of his middle-class environment. These images are not only bizarre, but also surreal in that they assert a reality higher than the one perceived by the ordinary person, who is too concerned with meaning, which is a process of compartmentalizing the things of his world. The whole thrust of Croso's use of such images is to shatter these compartments, to unify everything in the cosmos by juxtaposing disparate elements in the melting pot of the poet's imagination.

Thus, the use of these images in "Marriage" keeps it from being like ordinary prose, which makes sense, which means. Usually, analysis can explain only the process of association, if that. For example, once the poet is in the cemetery with his girl friend, thoughts of monsters (werewolves) and devils (suggested by "forked") are not unnatural. But "werewolf bathtubs and forked clarinets" are unnatural and totally improbable and unpredictable. That's why they are there. They are not only funny images, but also *imaginative* ones, in the sense that they are fantastic, that they bear little relationship to the ordinary world. They are images that no ordinary person would conjure up. By their use, Corso manages a laugh from his audience while

he asserts his identity as extraordinary man, poet, and lover. (pp. 25-6)

To be sure, the occasional absence of meaning—or at least its impenetrability—is functional and thematic in the poetry of Ginsberg and Corso. It serves to set them apart from ordinary men and to underline what they feel is the totality of personal experience and private vision. It makes their work sensational, in the double meaning of being titillating and of being sensuous. The technique is highly metaphysical in its yoking of disparate "concepts," here frequently only sense impressions, but it differs from the technique of Donne's school in that analysis does not finally prove the justness of the juxtaposition. Such proof would depend too much on reason for these poets of the senses, the emotions, and the imagaination. They trust "vision," not analysis. (pp. 26-7)

Gerard J. Dullea, in Thoth, *Winter, 1971.*

*   *   *

COZZENS, James Gould   1903-1978

An American novelist, short story writer, and editor, Cozzens is known for his moralistic novels of man in society. He rejected sentimentality and romanticism in favor of a more severe realism, but has been criticized for the haughtiness of his upper-class conservatism. Howard Nemerov has called his style the "work of a mind whose cold temper and grim austerity and firm conviction of despair makes existentialists look somewhat cozy and Rotarian, if not evangelical." Cozzens won the Pulitzer Prize in Fiction for *Guard of Honor,* **and has also received the O. Henry Award. (See also** *CLC,* **Vols. 1, 4, and** *Contemporary Authors,* **Vols. 9-12, rev. ed.; obituary, Vols. 81-84.)**

STANLEY EDGAR HYMAN

[There are a half-dozen themes basic to Cozzens' writing which unite his disparate works.] Perhaps the most important of them is the concept of "earned" morality, the discovery of a moral principle through suffering on its behalf. As early as *Confusion,* Cozzens has one of the characters say:

> Despite all teaching there must come an instance in every person's life when such a truth is proved or disproved in such a way as to be convincing, or it is never honestly believed.
>
> (pp. 480-81)

Cozzens' second theme, and a rather more Christian one that seems at times to run almost directly counter to the Stoicism of the first, is the radical imperfectability of man. This emerges sharply in *The Last Adam,* which celebrates a doctor who is lazy, irresponsible, bigoted, self-indulgent, lecherous, arrogant, and at most points pretty well uncontaminated by the Hippocratic ideal. The book defends him in the only terms possible, that he is human, and concludes in the last paragraph by raising him to a kind of Adamic principle. . . . (p. 481)

Sometimes, as in Colonel Ross's soliloquies in *Guard of Honor,* this doctrine becomes a defense of mediocrity and an acceptance of imperfection, the need to compromise theory to fit facts; sometimes, as in Abner's realizations in *The Just and the Unjust,* it is compromise with the sinful world, politics and even life as "the art of the possible" (a phrase quoted repeatedly in *Guard of Honor).* At one extreme, this acceptance of the old Adam leads to the view of men as simply brutes.... At the other extreme it sees a kind of triumphant Good Life in being human.... (p. 482)

Another theme basic to Cozzens' work is that of power and authority. Many of his characters play God, and manipulate the lives of others with a visible or invisible omnipotence.... [Frequently] this all-powerful authority is a parent.... In opposition to these God-figures, and perhaps equally symbols of the parent, there are Devil-figures in a number of the books.... [Their] powers differ from these of the God-figures in that the latter gain their authority through controlling men; the former through controlling Fate. (pp. 482-83)

A subsidiary theme here is chance and luck, which are very important in Cozzens' cosmology.... Frequently this chance or luck involves heavy irony: the *San Pedro* is lost because the one ship that passes her, an obscure sugar tramp from Cuba ... has no wireless.... (pp. 483-84)

A number of lesser related themes recur throughout Cozzens' work. One of them is the impulse to self-hurt or self-destruction, what Freud implied in "the death-wish."... Many of Cozzens' characters show some of the symptoms. At the same time, in direct opposition to this, Cozzens is concerned with a kind of survival-instinct, what Freud sometimes called "Eros" or "the life-wish."... [The] tragedy in *The Son of Perdition* and *S. S. San Pedro* is that everyone seems to have lost it. Even though this impulse and these survivors are presented as generally admirable, the concurrent old age seems to affect Cozzens with horror. He feels the passage of time almost obsessively, a thing symbolized in at least two books by a sweep-secondhand racing around a watch.... By way of resistance to this [bitterness about age], there is a frenzy of physical action in the books.... (pp. 484-85)

Obviously, not many of these themes have the cheery comfort traditionally associated with best-sellers, and the question of Cozzens' popularity with a mass audience becomes something of a problem. The factor that comes to mind first is that although Cozzens employs a modern sensibility, his works are not modern novels. They remain apparently unaffected by the revolution in fiction that Joyce, Gide, and Kafka inaugurated in the twentieth century, and Stendhal, Melville, and Dostoyevsky anticipated in the nineteenth. (*Castaway,* which is quite possibly influenced by Kafka, is the one exception here.) Cozzens professes to despise his contemporaries, and ... claims that with a few unnamed exceptions none of them can write, and that his models remain Shakespeare, Swift, Steele, Gibbon, Jane Austen, and Hazlitt. His literary aim, he adds, is "to recreate or retell," not to shape and transform experience. He thus ranges himself in the realist or naturalist tradition, with such contemporary writers as Wells, Bennett, and Galsworthy.... And yet here he does not quite fit into any group. His work has an imagination and a brilliance far removed from the plodding dullness of [Virginia] Woolf's butts, and it is distinguished from the work of the American naturalist novelists—the Dreisers, Farrells, and Halpers— by being *written* rather than hacked out of the corpse of language.

One of the ingredients of Cozzens' popularity, and a thing that may suggest more fruitful comparisons, is his work's reliance on technical knowledge, its heavily researched quality. *S. S. San Pedro* displays an astonishing knowledge of the mechanical workings of a ship; ... *Guard of Honor* is stocked with medical and legal lore as well as military detail and airplane technology; and even *Castaway* involves an authentic and carefully detailed department store. Insofar as this suggests comparison with such careful contemporary researchers as Sinclair Lewis and Upton Sinclair, the fact that Cozzens produces a vivid and pulsing sense of reality, not the caricatured or editorialized surface of life, removes him from their company; and even the more accurate comparison with the Steinbeck of *Grapes of Wrath* is unfair to Cozzens' greater honesty and tough-mindedness. The obvious affinities of Cozzens' vast canvases and carefully researched detail are with Balzac and Zola, and, to a lesser extent, with Dickens. His work is realism, not naturalism, and if it lacks the power and depth that our major contemporary American novelists, Hemingway and Faulkner, gain through symbolism, its realism has compensating virtues: at all times a ready comprehensibility, and on occasion a kind of shimmering truth. In choosing in most cases to write from research rather than out of direct experience.... Cozzens has consciously chosen the Balzac-Zola tradition. In taking up one profession after another, he is apparently attempting a social chronicle similar to theirs, if on a smaller scale, a Professional Comedy to match Balzac's Human Comedy. At least he can hardly be charged with lack of ambition.

The fact that Cozzens focuses, not on all of society, like Balzac and Zola, but on sections of the middle class only, on the professions, is of enormous significance, and is a very important factor in his popularity. It is also his least attractive feature. In a sense, Cozzens is the novelist of the American white Protestant middle class, the chronicler of its doing and values, and his work represents those values so thoroughly as to make all of his books, from *The Last Adam* on, exercises in making peace with the world as constituted. (pp. 485-87)

A factor much less visible on the surface, but one probably responsible for Cozzens' wide appeal even more than the books' pattern of prejudice, is the books' appeal to their readers' sexual frustrations and dissatisfactions.... As it is with the middle-class reading public, sex is an obsessive factor in Cozzens' books, but little of it is what used to be called "normal" or could still be called healthy. The principal effect the books give is of general resistance to adult heterosexual relations ranging from mild inhibition to the most extreme revulsion. (p. 490)

Sadism is an equally omnipresent motif in the books. In the early novels it is very violent and very graphically described.... In the later books, the sadism is much milder and less overt ... but it becomes much more markedly erotic.... (pp. 491-92)

This happy gamut of sexuality is naturally accompanied, like the prejudice, by the fitting short nasty words, although unlike his younger rivals, Cozzens does not use any of the forbidden four-letter Anglo-Saxon words ... but makes do with the three-letter varieties. (p. 492)

Cozzens' work seems to divide into three clearly demarcated stages: the first four exotic works; the two short novels, *S. S. San Pedro* and *Castaway,* as a transitional stage symbolically killing off the old machinery and personality;

and then the five mature professional comedies. . . . The first period is stylistically the worst, full of adolescent "poetic" writing, cheap ironic effects, high-flown words like "rescission," "tergant," and "macillant," and plain grammatical error. By the middle period—the two short transitional novels—Cozzens has developed his style to a point of high rhetoric, as effective as it is scarce in contemporary fiction. In *S. S. San Pedro,* the rhetorical style is still somewhat self-conscious. . . . By *Castaway,* the style becomes assured and entirely under control. . . . In Cozzens' final period, this sort of "prose with a heightened consciousness" is largely renounced, and the style attempts to appear entirely artless, a quiet, good, and almost invisible verbal texture.

At the same time, Cozzens' use of other devices altered. In a book like *Michael Scarlett,* the author's voice constantly intruded with editorial comments. . . . This authorial voice soon disappeared, and was replaced as a point of view by the consciousness of the chief character or of several of them, through which the book's events are focused and interpreted. A central symbol for many of the books does something of this job of integration: the cock pit in the book of that name, the octopus figure of the Company in *The Son of Perdition.* . . . In the later books, these key symbols are subtler and less obtrusive: the rattlesnake in *The Last Adam,* the courtroom itself in *The Just and the Unjust.* . . . As a concomitant of this increased symbolic subtlety, the too-easy foreshadowings of the early books slacken off. . . . By the time of *The Last Adam,* these foreshadowings are of the very gentlest sort, one brief mention of the possibility that the construction camp might be polluting the water; and in the later books, the foreshadowings—like the death of Walter in *Ask Me Tomorrow* and of the defendants in *The Just and the Unjust*—are just as apt to prove false. Cozzens' other devices also increase in subtlety, and his use of such cheap radio formulae as a single trick of speech to mark each character, like Aunt Myra's alternating lucidity in *The Last Adam,* dwindles in *Guard of Honor* to as fine a point as the connectiveless speech of the sergeants . . ., and is succeeded by much more effective cinematic devices: counterpointed conversations; and images, like a drink or a light switch, that serve as a transition between scenes.

Cozzens' aesthetic doctrines, too, become better integrated in his work. *Confusion* is full of little essay-speeches on the importance of form and technique . . . but by the time the writer, Edsell, appears in *Guard of Honor* he is seen objectively and even rather patronizingly, and Cozzens' aesthetics are stated only by barest implication. This pattern is paralleled by that of quotations in the books. In the early books, the quotations and literary references, including the Provençal, furnish the sort of phony exoticism that Poe made peculiarly his own. . . . In the later books the quotations and references are almost entirely from Shakespeare and the Bible, and they function organically and even symbolically in the work. . . . (pp. 494-97)

There is no question but that Cozzens' work, except in regard to his larger dramatic frames, shows a steady progress toward greater mastery of his craft, increased consciousness of his effects, and constantly augmented scope. Except for *Castaway,* however, he has given us every ingredient of first-rate novels except the novels themselves. His faults, the prejudices and blockages that make his treatment

of race and sex so unsatisfactory, and his constant dissipating of tragedy into irony and melodrama, seem to be the obverse of his virtues: his enormously representative quality and his uncompromising honesty. When Cozzens can write novels with the breadth and depth of *The Just and the Unjust* or *Guard of Honor* on as taut and satisfactory a dramatic frame as *Castaway* has, when he learns to combine the realism of his later work with the symbolism of his middle period and deepen both in the process, he should be a novelist to rank with the best America has produced. If he never achieves such a combination of elements that he has already shown he can master individually, or develops only along the lines of his recent work, he will nevertheless have given us, in *Castaway* and in fragments of the other novels, an impressive "art of the possible." (p. 497)

Stanley Edgar Hyman, "James Gould Cozzens and the Art of the Possible," in New Mexico Quarterly *(copyright, 1949, by The University of New Mexico), Winter, 1949, pp. 476-98.*

BRENDAN GILL

By Love Possessed . . . is a masterpiece. It is the author's masterpiece, which in the case of Mr. Cozzens is saying a good deal, yet it would be saying too little not to add at once that *By Love Possessed* would be almost anybody's masterpiece. No American novelist of the twentieth century has attempted more than Mr. Cozzens attempts in the course of this long and bold and delicate book, which, despite its length, one reads through at headlong speed and is then angry with oneself for having reached the end of so precipitately. No other American novelist of this century could bring to such a task the resources of intelligence, literary technique, and knowledge of the intricate, more or less sorry ways of the world that Mr. Cozzens commands. If he had failed, the very ruin of his work might have served as the occasion for grateful thanks and—like that beautiful failure *Tender Is the Night.* . . . But Mr. Cozzens is at every point far from failing. He has been superbly ambitious and has superbly realized his ambitions. Rarely seeming to exert himself, only once showing signs of strain, he has performed the sleight of hand that all writers dream of and that few have the discipline and energy, let alone the talent, to accomplish—that of arresting and rendering the surface of life (oh, yes! this is precisely how it looks) and at the same time revealing in undiminished contrariety the flow of things beneath the surface (but this, alas, is how it is). Like all the supremely satisfying novels, *By Love Possessed* contrives to let us recognize the truth not only of what we have experienced as individuals but of what we have not; it radically alters and enlarges us even as it gives delight. An immense achievement, and if Mr. Cozzens isn't practically beside himself with relief and pride at having brought it off, then life in its incessant pursuit of irony has, as usual, gone too far.

Not that Mr. Cozzens's achievement is a surprise. The fact is that he has been a formidable writer for a long time now, quietly—indeed, almost stealthily—extending his range and advancing from strength to strength. . . . Mr. Cozzens is by no means an unrecognized American novelist; nevertheless, he is in some quarters a neglected one. . . . Mr. Cozzens is an especially awkward case for critics, because he is not merely invisible as a man; he does his best to become invisible in his work. The hints of personality that remain unpurged—a presence reticent to the point of aloofness and even, if approached too closely, of truculence—are of little use to them. . . . Mr. Cozzens, in a singularly old-fashioned way, invents his books. He chooses a subject and works it up, and the heroes he creates are not in his image but in images appropriate to the subject being treated. Moreover, he is at pains to see that the treatment never dominates the subject. He is a stern creator, and though there are plenty of lively characters in his assorted worlds, there are no runaway ones. The Cozzens intellect, which is of exceptional breadth and toughness, cooly directs the Cozzens heart, with the result that a Cozzens novel is always perfectly under control; to our pleasure, the god of the machine is in the driver's seat. (pp. 432-34)

By Love Possessed is, as a story, spellbinding from start to finish; it is also, indivisibly, an eloquent summing up of Mr. Cozzens's moral preoccupations. Tolstoyan in size and seriousness, from its beginning pages it gives the impression that the author has gathered all the feeling, all the knowledge, all the wisdom to be found in his earlier books and has here deliberately pushed them to their limits. It is the work of a man at the top of his powers saying (not without sadness; one has so little time at the top, and the view is stupendous), "Here is where I stand. Here is what I make of what I see." The title contains the key word of the novel, which is love, especially with sexual love. (p. 434)

Such is the power of Mr. Cozzens's masterpiece that life may never be the same for us. We will be nursing Arthur Winner's hurt, and ours, for a long while to come. (p. 435)

> Brendan Gill, "Summa cum Laude," in The New Yorker (© 1957 by The New Yorker Magazine, Inc.), August 24, 1957 (and reprinted in Just Representations: A James Gould Cozzens Reader, edited by Matthew J. Bruccoli) Harcourt, 1978, pp. 432-35.

FREDERICK BRACHER

The eight novels published [between 1931 and 1939] include at least four that are of major importance by any set of standards, and taken as a whole the Cozzens novels constitute a record of continuing achievement matched in our time only by Faulkner and Hemingway. (p. 5)

Though full of ideas, the novels present no ideology. At a time when violent social conflicts might seem to force a writer to consider the dynamics and direction of American society and to take a firm stand on one side or another, Cozzens has remained a spectator rather than a partisan. . . . Cozzens' thinking is empirical and eclectic; he follows his sense of experienced reality rather than any abstract pattern of ideas. Accordingly, although he deals with politicians and his books may have political implications, he is not in Irving Howe's sense a political novelist. Instead he belongs to the line of social novelists, headed by Jane Austen, who enjoy "the luxury of being able to take society for granted." Whether any serious novelist can today afford this luxury may be debatable. Cozzens nevertheless does take society for granted, and writes about it as though its gradations were static and permanent. . . . His preference for setting his stories in old, established eastern small towns enables him to utilize the historical dimension in picturing modern man, and his protagonists are not confronted with unique contemporary problems, but are shown struggling with the perennial old ones. (pp. 6-7)

Cozzens' view of human life is limited by his temperament

—"the struck balance of his ruling desires, the worked-out sum of his habitual predispositions"—but he does not further limit it, artificially, by putting on the blinders of ideology.

Nevertheless, by comparison with most of his contemporaries Cozzens is a highly intellectual novelist. One of his special gifts is a talent for subtle, articulate interpretation. . . . (pp. 7-8)

Prominent in the novels is the assumption that duty and accomplishment are more important than enjoyment or happiness. Moreover, Cozzens' doubts of the possibility of progress, his disbelief in human perfectibility, his preference for liberty and diversity rather than equality and conformity, and his respect for traditional values embodied in a settled, stratified social order are conservative traits. Cozzens distrusts the simplistic habit of mind that resolves social complexity into the elementary stereotypes around which liberal and revolutionary enthusiasms concentrate. (p. 9)

All the novels contribute to a formidable indictment of the cheapness and vulgarity that seem inseparable from mass culture. Cozzens protests against a "liberal" church which substitutes personal adjustment for worship and encourages self-satisfaction instead of humility. He attacks the self-indulgence, product of a weakened sense of personal responsibility, which leads to juvenile delinquency and adult infantilism; the moral complacency which protects the genteel from reality; the failures of discrimination and taste exemplified in the "gilded swill" offered by mass media of entertainment; the dwindling of a sense of honor among people only concerned to get their share. Nevertheless, despite his admiration for Swift, Cozzens does not share Swift's misanthropy; his attack is aimed, not at man, but at the things men do. (pp. 10-11)

[The] central figures of Cozzens' novels lead normal workaday lives and are more apt to renounce even those modest satisfactions sometimes available in ordinary life than to try to pluck bright honor from the pale-faced moon. If they are not precisely common men, they are at least conscious representatives of the modes of life in the classes to which they belong; and their solid, tangible reality gives force to Cozzens' analysis of the upper levels of American society.

In a literary sense, too, Cozzens might be called conservative, or even neoclassic. He is interested in situations rather than processes; his plots, limited by the unities of time, place, and action, define a dramatic present instead of tracing an evolutionary development. Cozzens seems to be one of those writers who find limitations, whether self-imposed or traditional, stimulating rather than stultifying. . . . Cozzens' style is precisely articulate, even in those occasional passages that resound with a deliberate Victorian magniloquence. Such rhetorical flourishes are consciously artificial, and along with the quotations and allusions woven into the texture of the later novels, their ironic contrasts provide incidental commentaries on contemporary life. They also serve, at moments of emotional pressure, as a defensive device, holding the reader off at arm's length. (pp. 11-12)

The tone of Cozzens' writing is, in Richard Ellmann's words, "detached, . . . cool, disenchanted, a little superior." . . . What appears in Cozzens, rather, is the mild arrogance of self-respect often observable in men who, like

Julius Penrose and Abner Coates, judge themselves by stricter standards than those they tolerate in other people. The tone is appropriate to the principal characters in the novels, who are usually superior in competence to the masses and intelligent enough to recognize the fact, though too sensible to proclaim it in a society that is largely other-directed. (pp. 12-13)

In the novels the basic magnanimity of the central characters is modified by an increasing humbleness in the face of the contingencies of human existence. One evidence of it is an increasing tolerance in the later novels for contradictory ideas, a practice of balancing alternatives by giving each man's views and values a fair hearing. Cozzens' basically Pyrrhonistic habit of mind appears both in his distrust of absolutes and in his custom of stating both sides of a case without committing himself to a final explicit evaluation. The problems raised in the novels, like those in real life, are usually insoluble if regarded in simple terms of right and wrong. . . . [This] habit of increasing the tension by balancing alternatives is a major source of power in the novels.

It is also the justification for calling Cozzens primarily a moral writer. Intensely American in his distrust of arbitrary authority, he shares the Protestant reliance on the moral judgment of the individual. (pp. 16-17)

Although he analyzes exhaustively the determining causes of critical events, his characters are not shown as the victims of a strict mechanistic determinism. They act as though they had free will, and their choices seem to them, and to the reader, to be morally significant. Unlike the cross section of life depicted by such a naturalist as Dos Passos, Cozzens' picture of society is selective, and by choosing the *aristoi* as his principal subject matter he tends to increase our awareness of the upper ranges of human possibilities. In this respect the novels share the classical aim of establishing an ideal of human behavior, without ignoring contemporary man's falling away from the ideal. (pp. 18-19)

Cozzens' sense of vicissitude and mortality is poignant, but the feeling that dominates his novels is not tragic acceptance, but regretful "compunction . . . for the human predicament." (p. 19)

Cozzens' novels represent a serious effort to understand and recreate an important segment of American society. The tone is at once ironic and sympathetic, the structure is perspicuous, and the writing for the most part is lucid and polished. . . . To the reader interested in life rather than exhibitions of a writer's exotic sensibility, Cozzens offers a scrupulously honest report of American society as seen by a detached, highly perceptive observer. It is somewhat old-fashioned fare, but nourishing. The best of Cozzens' works are evidence that the traditional social novel, with its high seriousness and moral urgency, is still viable in a period of experiment and disorder. (p. 20)

The five major and characteristic novels are *Men and Brethren*, 1933; *Ask Me Tomorrow*, 1940; *The Just and the Unjust*, 1942; *Guard of Honor*, 1948; and *By Love Possessed*, 1957. All five novels are centered on a professional man's working life, presented in accurate detail and with an abundance of good shoptalk. (p. 24)

Underlying all the major novels is a basic moral principle: men must learn to adapt both their desires and their princi-

ples to the irresistible forces of circumstance. The principal conflict in the novels is internal and psychological; the problem is to reconcile the discrepancy between the ideal and the possible. (pp. 24-5)

Although primarily concerned with moral problems, Cozzens is not given to outright moralizing. . . . By unobtrusively directing the reader's sympathy toward some of these characters, Cozzens embodies his moral values in the heroes. The novels thus fill the ancient traditional function of providing models of behavior; and they enrich sensibility by showing men not only how to act, but how to feel.

The heroes who reflect Cozzens' moral sensibility have a good many traits in common. In the later novels they are matured, responsible, decent members of the upper middle class, neither romantic rebels against society nor visionaries who believe they can cure the troubles of our proud and angry dust. . . . But the disciplined man of reason has not always held the center of Cozzens' moral stage. In the early novels the central figures are active rebels, fighting authority in its various forms and protesting against the iniquities of society and the condition of man. (pp. 25-6)

The two earliest, *Confusion* (1924) and *Michael Scarlett* (1926), have similar heroes and a common theme: a glittering, accomplished youth, at odds with society, is finally defeated by a world which does not measure up to the standards he demands. These novels are romantic not only in their glorification of the aristocratic rebel, but in their richly sensuous decor and sympathetic picture of romantic love. Both suggest that a major literary influence on Cozzens when he began to write was the Fitzgerald of *This Side of Paradise*. (p. 27)

Although *Confusion* and *Michael Scarlett* are very immature performances, they foreshadow the later novels in several important ways. Both are vivid, carefully researched and documented pictures of a society at a particular time. (p. 29)

The novels preceding *S.S. San Pedro* are all concerned in some way with attitudes toward a father-image; the important characters either rebel against authority or exemplify the calm, competent assurance of the man in charge. (p. 35)

The Last Adam not only marks the final appearance of the early type of Cozzens hero, but introduces what is to be the principal subject matter of the later novels: American society. The village of New Winton, Connecticut, is an organism, a tight, closed system of interrelated energies. It is presented and analyzed in detail: social structure, mores, economy, government. . . . [The society depicted in *The Last Adam* is one] which, despite the virtues of some of its members, is as a whole narrow, selfish, and complacent. In the later novels society, with all its faults, is pictured as nevertheless providing the stability and order essential to any kind of good life, and the admirable men have learned to adapt to it instead of fighting it.

A transitional book in this progression of attitudes toward society is *Castaway* (1934). In this short novel society does not appear at all, but by a picture of one man's helpless inadequacy in solitude the book demonstrates our dependence on other men. *Castaway* is an experiment in allegorical fantasy unlike anything else Cozzens has written, but it is extraordinarily effective and compelling. An ambiguous, richly imaginative psychological ghost story, it leaves the reader with a haunting sense of significances just over the threshold of consciousness. (pp. 37-8)

[Although] the fertile wealth of implications and the precision of the writing make *Castaway* a richly enigmatic little masterpiece, it is atypical. In writing it Cozzens demonstrated how successfully he could exploit the vein of Kafkaesque fantasy, and having shown it, turned back to the lucidity and fully articulated intention of his later novels. (p. 46)

Cozzens makes fully articulate the flashes of remembrance or intuition that occur in the mind of a principal character during the course of action or talk. The device is used constantly throughout the novels . . .; and if it is unrealistic in the strict sense that thought so fully explicated would take up much more time than a momentary pause in a conversation, the device is obviously intended to be taken with that willing suspension of disbelief which any convention, on the stage or in a novel, requires. (p. 51)

It should . . . be noted that the baroque style of *By Love Possessed* is neither completely representative nor entirely new. The eccentricities are exaggerated, to be sure, but they are exaggerations of tendencies already present, though kept under stricter control, in Cozzens' earlier novels. So far as sentence structure is concerned, Cozzens has two characteristic traits: a fondness for elaborate subordination which results in nests of parenthetical comments within subordinate elements, and a habit of appositival coordination in which one expression (noun, verb, modifier) is followed by others that explain and bear the same grammatical construction as the first. These traits, infrequent in dialogue, are common in meditative or descriptive passages. (pp. 51-2)

Cozzens' style, although sensitive and ornate, is not poetic. The surface is dense and in the later novels often forbidding, but it is clear in the sense that the poetry of Pope is clear—the meaning not always easy to grasp on a first reading, but fully articulated and expressed if a reader makes the effort required by the compression and complication of the structure. . . . The one Cozzens novel that might be called poetic—both in its primary use of image and symbol and in the feeling it gives of being autogenetic, of having been discovered as an organic whole by the writer instead of being deliberately constructed—is *Castaway*. But even here the writing is sharp and precise. (p. 54)

In addition to being complex and ornate in its structure, Cozzens' style is "literary" in the sense that the reflective and descriptive passages use a good many uncommon words, similar to the inkhorn terms of Elizabethan writers, and a wealth of half-quotations and allusions. (pp. 54-5)

Apart from their preciseness of connotation, Cozzens seems often to use exotic words out of an almost Elizabethan exuberance, a simple delight in rich materials. . . . Cozzens writes for an audience literate enough to enjoy deliberate virtuosity and able to look at the literary equivalent of late Victorian gingerbread architecture, not with Puritan outrage, but with amusement and affection.

These devices—the ornate complexity of sentence structure, the use of literary words, the excess of alliteration—give to parts of Cozzens' later novels their stylistic effect of slightly old-fashioned magniloquence. . . . Even at its most rhetorical, Cozzens' style in *By Love Possessed* is rich,

sonorous, and masculine. The sentences are architectual in their feeling for rich materials and their concern for an explicitness of structure which baroque embellishment may cover but does not conceal. If the decoration is occasionally so literary as to approach the grotesque, at least it is determinate and perspicuous, sharp in the sunlight with no blurred, fuzzy edges. (pp. 55-7)

Cozzens' magniloquence is not motivated by the pious reverence of the antiquarian; he uses Victorian mannerisms with a full, ironic awareness of their incongruity in an age which, as Julius Penrose notes, is cheap and maudlin. The ironically artifical speech of some of the characters provides them with a kind of defense against falsity, against too open a revelation of deep feeling. (pp. 57-8)

Another device that serves to establish an exact degree of separation between the author and his characters is the use of full names to designate the principal characters in *By Love Possessed*. . . . The device may sound mannered, but it serves to establish the slightly formal tone that Cozzens seems to intend. (p. 60)

Cozzens' particular temperament may also be indicated in the frequency with which certain words are used. "Compunction" occurs over and over again throughout the novels, and its connotation—a faint suggestion of arrogance and guilt mingled with pity or sympathy—seems to define the author's contradictory combination of habitual feelings: protectively detached, oversensitive almost to the point of being finicky, yet worried and involved. The impression is reinforced, especially in *Ask Me Tomorrow*, by an excessive use of other words suggesting a kind of partial disengagement, or shrinking involvement: *mortifying, harassed, crest-fallen; qualms, chagrin, wounded feelings; quailed, shrank, recoiled*. Like his sentence structure, Cozzens' diction reflects his basically Pyrrhonistic temperament, his apoetic intelligence, and his troubled aloofness.

The intricately qualified observations and judgments of the Cozzens heroes are matched by the complexity and magniloquence of the style in which they think and speak, and a very conspicuous trait of this style is its frequent incorporation of quotations, half-quotations, and allusions. (pp. 60-1)

If Cozzens' style, with its usual lucid precision, its occasional deliberate flights of rhetoric, and its fondness for quoting from the "Ancients," might be described as classical, the same term could be used for another characteristic of his novels: a tight structure, based on the classical unities. The typical Cozzens novel is primarily dramatic; its purpose is the immediate presentation of significant character in action; and an important part of the action is what the characters think. (pp. 65-6)

Cozzens does not trace the slow development of character molded by environment and experience over a long period of years. Instead, he confronts us at once with fully formed characters involved in some complication of critical action. (pp. 66-7)

The novels are as scrupulously organized as they are fully researched and documented, but despite the complicated ordering of events and the heavy load of accurate, detailed information carried, they never seem schematized or mechanical. (p. 68)

All of the Cozzens novels, including *Castaway*, have the traditional virtue of being rich and meaningful on the simplest level of narrative: they tell a story that is realistic, compelling, and representative of universal human experience. They accurately reproduce the speech and behavior of particular individuals; they evoke a vivid sense of place; and through a careful unity of time, they achieve a heightening of a dramatic present. Characters are not merely presented, as on the stage; they are analyzed with shrewd psychological insight by the central consciousness of each novel. Accordingly, instead of the gossamer insights of poetry a reader feels the firm iron of a controlling intelligence. But this traditional framework of the realistic novel is enriched by the devices of a highly literary style, full of allusions and quotations that provide both embellishment and ironic contrasts. Less apparent, but highly important in creating the pervading resonance of this author's writing, are the devices of juxtaposed or echoed incident, which may explain Cozzens' demand for readers with "the wit to see the relation which I could not stop to spell out between this and that." (pp. 114-15)

The picture of society in Cozzens' novels is in a double sense static. For one thing, the writer is more interested in situation than in process; he does not, characteristically, trace in chronological order the slow changes in an individual or family or social group. Instead he presents people as they are at a given dramatic time and place, only incidentally offering, through flashbacks, some explanation of how they got there. In a more important sense, the picture of society is static in its implicit denial that change is equivalent to progress and the implied doubt that progress is possible at all. Although Cozzens does not go to the extreme of the Augustan poet, complacently insisting that whatever is, is right, his attitude toward social inequalities and injustices is not at all reformist. On the whole, Cozzens seems content to limit himself to an examination of things as they are, rather than as they might or should be. (p. 119)

Of the various ranges into which Cozzens fits his characters, a few are nonevaluative, like his treatment of the differences between men and women, but most ranges of difference are treated as though they constitute a hierarchy. . . . He is particularly interested in exploring the extremes of the range of aptitude, in contrasting the intelligently competent with the stupidly shiftless. (p. 121)

The existence of . . . characters, in whom the heart of darkness common to all men is so imperative that no amount of social conditioning can repress and contain it, is one of the circumstances which the Cozzens heroes have to admit and adapt themselves to. Though he shares many of the traditional values of liberalism—the appeal to reason, a high valuation of individual liberty, a tolerant open-mindedness —Cozzens does not share the liberal's belief that education and reform can eliminate the basic evils of society. Rather, he seems to agree with orthodox theologians that a better society is possible only if its architects adapt is to such immovable objects in the social landscape as the succeeding generations of the sons of perdition. (p. 206)

The function of reason in the Cozzens novels is to clarify the limits of the possible, and to warn men not to work outside those limits. Cozzens is often referred to as a pessimist, and in the basic theological sense he undoubtedly is. But what is often mistaken for pessimism is a reflection of his underlying moral belief: man is, in varying degree but always to some extent, limited in his abilities and circumstances; feeling—the "wild, indeterminate, infinite appetite

of man"—is unlimited. If an infinite appetite coexisting with limited powers is not restrained by reason, frustration and unhappiness are bound to result. Man in general, however, is possessed by love, so much at the mercy of his feelings that he rejects reason's sober injunctions in favor of "youth's dear and heady hope that thistles can somehow be made to bear figs." (p. 212)

In regard to most problems of ethics, Cozzens' distrust of oversimple solutions leads him to answers which are ambiguous if not actually equivocal. It is not merely that he makes us aware of the exceptions to every rule; there are a bewildering number of rules, and though each may seem convincing as presented in a particular context of character and action, taken together they lead to contradiction and tension. (p. 222)

Drawing fine moral lines of this sort is the painful, continual responsibility of the Cozzens heroes, and the reader is kept constantly aware of the moral tension by having his sympathy directed toward both alternatives. (pp. 226-27)

That it is later than one thinks occurs frequently enough to men in middle age, and Cozzens' inescapable clocks and sundials keep the reader constantly aware of the inevitability of change, the necessity of ripening into maturity, and the end of the cycle which makes ripeness for action only a prelude to ripeness for death. (p. 231)

The moral landscape of the novels is painted in sober grays and browns. . . . Like the Stoics, Cozzens seems at times to overvalue reason, renunciation, and resignation. (p. 234)

It is nevertheless not accurate to call Cozzens a Stoic; he is too much of an eclectic to be so neatly labeled. Cozzens shares, to be sure, some of the main points of the Stoic moral code: the emphasis on reason, discipline, and self-control; the acute melancholy sense of the universal flux of things, of change and vicissitude, in which he resembled Marcus Aurelius; the definition of freedom as the ability to discriminate things within our power from those not in our power. But while he agrees with the Stoics, and the Christian theologians, as to the necessity of accepting the factual situation, or the will of God, he does not share the Stoic glorification of *ataraxia,* indifference toward the external vicissitudes of life. (pp. 234-35)

Cozzens' sense of what is reasonable and right in human conduct is constantly qualified by observation of how men, possessed by love, actually behave; but the melancholy which runs through the novels does not come from a passive acceptance of man's limitations and mortality. Rather, it is a by-product of the experience of moral tension: Cozzens is acutely aware of the unequal conflict between what inescapably is and a healthy man's refusal to accept it with reasoned resignation.

Against disasters and the steady attrition of time, the Cozzens hero has some supports more positive than the desperate indifference of the Stoic. One of the strongest is a sense of solidarity with the past, and it is probably no accident that the novels are filled with descriptions of monuments and architectural records of another day, which serve as points of relative stability in the stream of change. (pp. 235-36)

Cozzens seems to have a strong feeling for the virtue which in the Renaissance was called "grace," a sense of what is fitting and seemly. It is a virtue requiring the exercise of whatever endowment of discrimination and sensibility a man may have, and it is conspicuous in the magnanimity of the "natural aristocrats" who are Cozzens' heroes. The moral imperatives that motivate the magnanimous man cannot be proved to have value. They can only be asserted, but Cozzens is eloquent in asserting them. (p. 242)

[The] novels in chronological order show a parallel growth of moral warmth and depth in the author. The clinical tone of the early novels reflects an ironic detachment similar to the troubled aloofness of Francis Ellery. In the course of thirty years Cozzens' objectivity, though it remains unsentimentally, realistically alert to men's differences and failings, has been sweetened by the compassion for imperfect man which is the message and the mark of all great literature. (pp. 281-82)

> *Frederick Bracher, in his* The Novels of James Gould Cozzens *(© 1959 by Frederick Bracher; reprinted by permission of Harcourt Brace Jovanovich, Inc.), Harcourt, 1959.*

JOHN CHAMBERLAIN

"Ask Me Tomorrow" is definitely not in the mode of Compton Mackenzie's "Sinister Street" or Fitzgerald's "This Side of Paradise," the two youthful "quest" novels that were so widely imitated in the interwar period. The Cozzens portrait of the writer as a young man is tenderly ironic; the author applies the same objective criteria in looking at himself as he does when looking at others. Incidentally, "Ask Me Tomorrow" is a perfect depiction of the Europe that traveling Americans knew when the dollar was a dollar. . . .

As Cozzens grew older, he "saw the stout, stubborn will . . . gaining impressive victories." He also came at a later age to realize "how temporary are the patterns and the point one can impose on life." In "By Love Possessed," written when Cozzens was 54, the diminished future that must come to all aging dukes who attempt to control life is a matter for cosmic irony. Arthur Winner, the small-town lawyer who turned down the offer of a judgeship in his 50's on the ground that middle age was not a time for new beginnings, has been compelled by a series of shattering experiences to realize that it was an illusion to believe "power really matters." But he fought a good fight, and that is what counts in the making of character.

In his preference for responsible individuals Cozzens was something of an anomaly among the major novelists of his period. Hemingway preferred the character who made his separate peace. Fitzgerald gloried in the romanticism of defeat. Farrell's Studs Lonigan welches on his idea of being strong and tough and the real stuff. One has to go back to Willa Cather's generation to find "ordering characters" to match those of the big Cozzens novels. (p. 11)

> *John Chamberlain, "Writer of Character, "in* The New York Times Book Review *(© 1978 by The New York Times Company; reprinted by permission), August 6, 1978, pp. 10-11.*

MATTHEW J. BRUCCOLI

Though over-written and perhaps pretentious, *Confusion* [Cozzens's first novel] introduced the search for values or standards of conduct that would characterize all of Cozzens's work. . . .

Michael Scarlett showed what would be the mark of Coz-

zens's fiction: his ability to treat a subject with authority, for the novel manifests a knowledge of Elizabethan literature and society remarkable in a twenty-two-year-old Harvard drop-out. (p. xii)

Cozzens's first three novels developed superior young figures who need an occupation worthy of their abilities; however, *Cock Pit* was the first novel in which he used material he knew from experience and observation. It established what became the most notable quality of his major fiction: the authentic presentation of a profession and the society associated with it. This authenticity is something more than accuracy or realism. When Cozzens learned something, he really learned it and was able to use the information without appearing to be writing from research.

After three novels in which rebellious figures were treated sympathetically, Cozzens created a character who embodies disorder and destruction. . . . *The Son of Perdition* marked the end of Cozzens's apprenticeship in terms of his attitudes towards his characters. . . . *Son of Perdition* shows the need to impose at least the effect of stability on society, although Cozzens fully acknowledges the power of chance.

S.S. San Pedro is the first of his books that Cozzens now regards worth claiming. . . . [It] details the unaccountable sinking of a ship; but the real subject of the novelette is the dissolution of authority. (pp. xii-xiii)

Dr. George Bull [of *The Last Adam*] is a transitional figure in the development of the Cozzens hero. An old rebel against conventional behavior and a careless doctor, Bull is nonetheless a necessary member of the community—both an establishment figure and an outsider. *The Last Adam* is not a sentimental country-doctor novel. Indifferent to his patients, contemptuous of his townsmen, and in some ways incompetent, Dr. Bull nonetheless embodies the vitality of life. (p. xiii)

A reversal of *Robinson Crusoe*, *Castaway* shows a man who is unable to survive alone in the abundance of a modern department store. The meanings of *Castaway* are not political. Cozzens's subject is the inadequacy of the modern individual and the deterioration of character. (p. xiv)

Men and Brethren, published in January 1936, is the first full portrait of what can now be recognized as the Cozzens hero—the man of experience, education, and responsibility who serves his community and profession as a matter of duty. Ernest Cudlipp, an Episcopal priest who is vicar of a parish chapel in a New York slum, is the best depiction of a clergyman in American literature. *Men and Brethren* is significant in Cozzens's development toward tightly structured novels in which a multiplicity of events impinge on the central character in a period of two or three days. The controlling point of view is Cudlipp's, and everything in the novel is filtered through his intelligence. (pp. xiv-xv)

Ask Me Tomorrow. . . . interrupted the cycle of professional novels and is uncharacteristically personal, drawing on Cozzens's experiences as a tutor in Europe. This portrait of the writer as a young man is ironic and even satirical, for the tutor himself undergoes an educational process as he recognizes his vanities and learns to temper his pride. . . .

The background [of *The Just and the Unjust*] is a murder trial in a small community in the northeast, during the course of which Abner Coates, an idealistic and naïve lawyer, comes to accept the realities of his profession—which are the realities of his life. The theme of the novel is limitations—a basic Cozzens theme: the limitations of the law as well as the limitations of human nature. *The Just and the Unjust* has been frequently called the most authentic American novel about the legal profession. (p. xv)

Guard of Honor . . . is the best American novel of World War II and is generally regarded as Cozzens's finest achievement. It is a war novel that does not depict battle or heroics. . . . Complexly structured, *Guard of Honor* shows the full development of Cozzens's concern with "the dramatic inner meaning that lies in the simultaneous occurrence of diverse things." (p. xvi)

By Love Possessed is Cozzens's most thorough examination of moral complexity—not moral ambiguity. The epigraph to *The Just and the Unjust*—"Certainty is the Mother of Repose; therefore the Law aims at Certainty"—echoes through Cozzens's later work as it is shown that there are no certainties. At best there are choices in which emotion, experience, and imperfect reason respond to circumstances determined by chance and by what has already happened. Learning to recognize his limitations, the Cozzens hero makes his moral choices and does his best to maintain the stability of his world. (p. xvii)

Less tightly structured than his other major novels, *Morning Noon and Night* is Cozzens's only first-person novel. The narrator, Henry Worthington, ruminates on his career as a highly successful business consultant and admits that luck has been the chief factor in his life. The characteristic Cozzens conclusion in this novel with its clear valedictory note of summation is that while recognizing the over-riding factor of chance, the responsible man acts responsibly. The subject of *Morning Noon and Night* is vocation, which is the dominant subject in Cozzens. Throughout his career Cozzens has been concerned with the interconnections between character and occupation. (p. xviii)

His prose is precise; his meanings are clear; and, before *By Love Possessed,* his style is unembellished. The increasing dignity of style enforces Cozzens's objectivity. The "coldness" that critics have cited in Cozzens's observation of his characters is the stoical detachment of a writer trying to achieve "the stability of truth" in dealing with profound matters of human conduct. The periodic sentences and heavy subordination of *By Love Possessed* and *Morning Noon and Night* can intimidate only those who have not mastered the structure of the English sentence. The by-no-means overwhelming use of uncommon words achieves exactness of statement. Such words are intended to fix the reader's attention and, if necessary, send him to a dictionary. Cozzens's developed style is the natural expression for a highly literate writer with a traditionalist's respect for language. The complexity of sentence structure is appropriate to the complexity of his thinking. His use of open or concealed literary allusion in *Guard of Honor, By Love Possessed,* and *Morning Noon and Night* does not exclude the much-cherished general reader. The allusions are there for readers who recognize them; but the meanings of the books do not depend on that recognition. Cozzens is not a mandarin author; his work is far more accessible than that of many novelists currently in critical favor. He does not, in fact, make extraordinary demands on readers—beyond requiring them to pay attention.

To concept of vocation is central to Cozzens's representations of general nature, but he fully credits the determining factors in human conduct—education, social position, intelligence, training, luck, and what used to be called "character." The mark of Cozzens's people is that their values and behavior are developed in terms of their professions. You are what you do and how well you do it. (p. xix)

[Cozzens] has declined to accommodate temporary concepts of relevance. He has refused to play the game of literary success—"writing only to say as precisely as he can what by standards of his own he judged worth saying." At present his work is disparaged or ignored by custodians of literary reputations. Weighing their standards, Cozzens must assuredly want it no other way. If there is truth in the comforting promise that justice will be done to masterpieces, the novels of James Gould Cozzens have a safe place of proper stature among the sound achievements in American literature. (p. xx)

> *Matthew J. Bruccoli, in his introduction to* Just Representations: A James Gould Cozzens Reader, *edited by Matthew J. Bruccoli (copyright © 1978 by Harcourt Brace Jovanovich, Inc.; reprinted by permission of the publisher), Harcourt, 1978, pp. xi–xxi.*

NOEL PERRIN

The dominant theme in James Gould Cozzen's novels is that of order imposed on a meaningless world—or, rather, that of order being maintained, and even occasionally extended. . . .

It is always a comparative handful of men whom Cozzens shows as holding society together and keeping it orderly: the few adults of his novels, as opposed to the many children.

The best and smartest of these grown-ups operate somewhat the way Shakespeare's dukes do in the late comedies. That is, they are the centers of their societies, and not merely in some social sense, but truly in the middle, so that most information passes through them, and most connections are made by them. (p. 278)

One can trace the growth of the ducal type in Cozzens's earlier work, the hard-won but triumphant mastery of a town or an army base in the great novels, and the final defeat in *Morning Noon and Night.* . . .

The type first appears in *The Last Adam*, not as a duke but a duchess. Mrs. Banning is the upholder of stability and order in New Winton, Connecticut, as her son Guy will be after her. (Though probably not in New Winton. Probably in Hartford or New York.) What is surprising when one looks at the whole sweep of ordering characters in Cozzens is that both Mrs. Banning and Guy are viewed satirically. Or, at least, more satirically than not. Cozzens is far too complex and realistic a writer to deny them their genuine power and worth. . . .

Mrs. Banning *does* have one characteristic that foreshadows the later ducal characters. She is able to hold a good many thoughts in her mind at once, without getting muddled and without losing the power to act. (p. 279)

Cozzens reserves his sympathy in *The Last Adam* for three quite different sorts of characters. The first, exemplified in Mr. Banning, is the person who has simply opted out, who attempts to order nothing more intractable than a flower garden. The reader is invited to feel a certain scorn for Mr. Banning's weakness (he is not a true man—read duke—as his father had been) but a good deal more sympathy for his insight, even when it cripples his power to act. . . .

The second type is represented by three important characters in the book: Mrs. Banning's daughter Virginia; Dr. Bull, the last Adam of the title; and Miss Janet Cardmaker, Dr. Bull's mistress. . . . All three are members of New Winton's small upper class, and all three feel contempt for the orderly and ordering life of that class, as seen in Mrs. Banning and in such minor characters as Matthew Herring. All three are, in fact, centers of disorder. Virginia might be a young Sartoris out of Faulkner. . . .

If Virginia Banning is Cozzens's Sartoris, Dr. Bull is his Gatsby. Symbolically, it is apt enough that Virginia dies at sixteen, and that Dr. Bull and Janet leave no descendants—are each the last of their families. (p. 280)

[May Tupping, an example of the third type], is a very faint sketch of the good dukes who will dominate the later books. Intelligent and responsible, May is literally the center of communication in New Winton; she plugs the town in to itself. (p. 281)

May is, at twenty-two, too naive and too powerless to be more than a sketch of what a full Cozzens ordering character will become. She perhaps also starts from too low a social position. But she is clearly already an adult in Cozzen's terms. . . . It is within her mind that Cozzens first formulates ducal awareness and duty. (pp. 281-82)

In *Men and Brethren*, published three years later, the characteristics that May and Mrs. Banning possess only embryonically or comically appear at close to full force. Ernest Cudlipp is the first of Cozzens's major ordering characters. . . .

Cozzens first uses in *Men and Brethren* what is going to be his favorite and most successful narrative structure. Using his central character as a batter, he throws pitch after pitch, sending them at steadily shorter intervals, until there seem to be a dozen in the air at once. Or to put it more abstractly, he presents the mounting tension, over a brief period, of more and more almost insoluble problems coming at the central character (and the reader) faster and faster until it seems impossible for him to deal with them all. (p. 282)

Just when a character in a Cozzens novel begins to think that he alone can hold the world together, he is likely to discover that not only is he not alone in this ability, but that from time to time there is someone holding *him* together. (p. 284)

Ernest is a stoic who happens also to be a Christian minister. Presumably what led Cozzens to invent him was an interest in the traditions and social dynamics of the Episcopal church and an even greater interest in the natural ordering roles played by ministers, not any new awareness of a transcendental It.

The Just and the Unjust, though published six years later than *Men and Brethren*, is a step backward in the presentation of the ducal character. (The book itself is no step backward.) Ernest Cudlipp long ago accepted his obligation; what we watch is how he fulfills it. But Abner Coates in *The Just and the Unjust*, though he comes of a ducal family, decides only at the very end of the book to accept his.

What we watch is the process by which a nice young man finds himself forced to give up his scruples and his privacy and become an adult. (pp. 284-85)

One way to describe *Guard of Honor* is as the search for a duke. In the context of a novel nearly all of whose characters belong to the U.S. Army Air Force, "duke" means someone worthy to command an Air Force base or a substantial military unit.

For most of the book, there seem to be no such people—at least not among those with sufficient rank to be given command. (p. 286)

The search for a duke is not carried on by any of the characters in the book, but by the reader. The stupider characters are unaware that there needs to be any search, because for them rank and worthiness to command are identical (or almost identical—some of them make a separation in the case of Colonel Woodman). Since General Beal is two ranks higher than anyone else at Ocanara, he is automatically their duke. The smarter characters have already decided before the book begins that the search is useless. No one of ducal caliber is available. (p. 287)

By Love Possessed, among its many richnesses, contains a study of the aging and death of dukes. (p. 289)

[Arthur Winner] is a reigning duke: the most fully drawn, the most admirable, and the most believable that Cozzens created. He is the culmination of the development I have been tracing. But at the same time he is in two ways quite different from any earlier duke. (p. 290)

One is that he sees much less prospect of using his power to reward merit or extend justice than they did. . . .

The other difference is that Arthur Winner neither holds nor aspires to office. He avoids it. In the somewhat loose sense that I am using the term "duke," it is possible to be one as a private citizen. But both in Cozzen's novels and in real American life, office, power, and responsbility are so intimately allied that actually to refuse office comes close to declining the ducal role. (p. 291)

Cozzens leaves no doubt that Arthur Winner is fully worthy of the crown. The whole book is a statement of that. In addition, there are symbolic details at the beginning and end of the book to drive it home. (p. 292)

[*Morning Noon and Night*] completes Cozzens's study of dukes. [It] is a denunciation of ducal characters, by one.

The duke who attacks his class is old Henry Worthington, a man of sixty-five, like his creator. Our Hank, he usually calls himself. He is the central character, the man whose loose and baggy autobiography the book purports to be. He is as ducal as human beings come. (pp. 292-93)

Dukes are especially likely not to be nice people, Henry says, because they have power. Ernest Cudlipp and Norman Ross and the others had power, and used it to do good. Arthur Winner came to doubt that you could do much good with power, and his doubt was strong enough to keep him out of office. The lightning striking the ducal oak out at the lake is a symbol of that doubt. But as a private lawyer in Brocton, he continues endlessly to solve social problems and to work at keeping his society intact. (The oak survives, though damaged.) He sees no other rational option.

Like the Shakespeare of Sonnet 94, Henry Worthington views power primarily as the capacity to injure other people. And, taking issue with the sonnet, he says he has never seen a man with that capacity who didn't use it. "Power (the pleasure of the prince) simply by being in-being unfailingly brings hurt to someone, and never can do none."... (pp. 293-94)

If that is true, there is an end to the heroic figure of the duke; we are left only with the duke-as-bully. In fact, if we follow the strict logic of the sonnet, it is an end of dukes altogether, because there are no more "Lords and owners of their faces," only a race of stewards....

The stout, stubborn will, in short, has abdicated. And the novelist, James Gould Cozzens, has closed his career with a non-novel.

Back in the beginning, it was the lords of disorder—Dr. Bull, Janet Cardmaker, Virginia Banning—who left no heirs, while May Tupping and Guy Banning are sure to. Now it is the last duke whose line runs out. Henry Worthington has one daughter. She had two children, who died pointlessly in a plane crash, and she is not able to bear more children. There will be no more dukes.

But though Cozzens in effect disavows his own earlier novels and their ducal heroes, the reader is not obligated to. *Guard of Honor* and *By Love Possessed* have passed from their creator's control. Norman Ross and Arthur Winner exist in their own right as two of the great ordering characters of twentieth-century literature. (p. 294)

> *Noel Perrin, "The Good Dukes," in* Just Representations: A James Gould Cozzens Reader, *edited by Matthew J. Bruccoli (copyright © 1978 by Harcourt Brace Jovanovich, Inc.; reprinted by permission of Harcourt Brace Jovanovich, Inc. and Southern Illinois University Press), Harcourt and Southern Illinois University Press, 1978, pp. 278-94.*

*   *   *

CREASEY, John   1908-1973

Creasey was a British crime novelist. The most prolific contributor to the genre, Creasey published more than 550 crime novels during his career. He was financially if not critically successful, his novels selling millions of copies in twenty-six languages. Creasey won the Edgar of the Mystery Writers of America in 1962 for *Gideon's Fire*. He published under thirteen pseudonyms throughout his writing career; among these the best known are J. J. Marric, Gordon Ashe, Michael Halliday, Anthony Morton, and Jeremy York. (See also *Contemporary Authors*, Vols. 5-8, rev. ed.; obituary, Vols. 41-44, rev. ed.)

ANTHONY BOUCHER

[Creasey's books about George Gideon of Scotland Yard written under the J. J. Marric pseudonym] are marked by the technically dazzling handling of a large number of plots in small compass—in [the case of "Gideon's Fire"], arson, child-rape, murder, domestic and financial fraud, to name only the most prominent—each of them developed as fully as the average crime writer could do in a single-minded novel.

They are further distinguished by the facts that the crimes involved have a solid real-life plausibility, that Gideon himself is an interesting and believable man, and that the author has a good novelist's acute understanding of the small interplays of character and personality, whether the relationship be between a detective and his superior officer, or a widow and her half-perceptive, half-callous child. All of the Creasey avatars are skilled at telling an exciting story; Marric, in addition, can *write*—and he's never done better than in this splendid new book. (p. 26)

> *Anthony Boucher, in* The New York Times Book Review *(© 1961 by The New York Times Company; reprinted by permission), January 22, 1961.*

A wave of midgets is at present invading the Science Fiction field. In [*The Famine*] Mr. Creasey's well-known Dr. Palfrey of Z5 (an international peacekeeping organization) has to cope with world-wide infestation by a race of rapidly breeding midgets (period of gestation nine days!) with gargantuan appetites, rather mysteriously produced by an accidental nuclear explosion in a South American republic. Dr. Palfrey is hardly impressive in his efforts to save Earth's rapidly devastated food supplies and the ethics of his solution are more than a little dubious. Credibility level low and writing lower still. (p. 292)

> *The Times Literary Supplement (© Times Newspapers Ltd. (London) 1967; reproduced from* The Times Literary Supplement *by permission), April 16, 1967.*

Among the many different kinds of thriller written by "J. J. Marric" under one name or another, [Creasey's] straightforward manly Scotland Yard stories of Commander Gideon are the most efficient and convincing; and [*Gideon's Power*] is another, principally concerned with engineered power failures. (p. 1018)

> *The Times Literary Supplement (© Times Newspapers Ltd. (London) 1969; reproduced from* The Times Literary Supplement *by permission), September 18, 1969.*

JULIAN SYMONS

J. J. Marric is one of the many pseudonyms used by John Creasey.... The early books about Commander George Gideon of Scotland Yard's C.I.D. are the best things in Creasey's large output. A C.I.D. Inspector who once lived next door to Creasey asked, "Why don't you show us as we are? You don't have to put in the dull part." The portrait of Gideon is an attempt to show a fully rounded character—excellent up to a point but marred in the end by excessive hero worship, and lack of humor. Apart from Gideon, the strengths of the books are those of other Creasey work, an apparently inexhaustible flow of ideas and the ability to generate excitement in describing action. The weaknesses are again characteristic, lack of the imagination necessary to vary a formula once it has been established, ... and a level of writing that at its best is no more than flatly realistic. The first Gideon books were pioneering works in the form of the police novel, and they promised more than Marric has been able to perform. (p. 206)

Creasey's Gideon books, written as J. J. Marric, are his best work.... His stories are notable for the ingenuity of the ideas with which he overflows, and also for his very slight attention to sex and his total avoidance of cruelty. Unfortunately the writing of the books is never equal to their often clever conception, and his people think and behave with a schoolboyish naiveté. (p. 212)

Julian Symons, in his Mortal Consequences: A History—From the Detective Story to the Crime Novel *(copyright © 1972 by Julian Symons; reprinted by permission of Harper & Row, Publishers, Inc.),* Harper, 1972.

WILLIAM VIVIAN BUTLER

Fact and fiction remain uneasy bedfellows in *The Masters of Bow Street,* John Creasey's massive . . . family saga about the generations of struggle preceding the creation of the Metropolitan Police Force by Sir Robert Peel. Creasey's normal output was eight to twelve books a year. Having stockpiled novels frantically for three years, he was free to devote the last twelve months of his life entirely to *The Masters of Bow Street.* It was almost as if subconsciously he knew he was dying, and planned this book as a spectacular farewell.

That, surely, is how it should be judged: as a massive, bravura spectacular, a last-minute *bombe surprise* to round-off the incredible forty-year, six-hundred book feast which Creasey has given his fans. Here, in full display, are all the elements that made old Creasey Creasey: the driving narrative, the subtly understated heroics, the simple humanity, the strident small-l liberalism, the all-embracing love of London—and, above all, the dogged vulnerable heroes, outwardly stalwart warriors, inwardly chronic worriers, badly needing (and inevitably finding) ministering-angel heroines to help them through.

I have revelled in this Creasey world far too often in my life to feel anything but misty-eyed at its sudden, marathon final appearance in fancy dress. An excited blurb calls *The Masters of Bow Street* "a great multigenerational masterpiece" and I simply can't bring myself to disagree. Under pressure from a grateful memory of all those years of Creasey fiction, it seems downright churlish not to concede one fact. (p. 344)

William Vivian Butler, in The Spectator *(© 1975 by The Spectator; reprinted by permission of* The Spectator), *March 22, 1975.*

NEWGATE CALLENDAR

The Creasey formula [consists] of a fairly rat-tat-tat style—short sentences, lots of padding, emphasis on plot gimmicks, very little in the way of characterization. "Let's Kill Uncle Lionel" is typical of the species. . . . [It] is a Supt. Folly mystery. Folly is the fat Scotland Yard operative who is only too clearly patterned after John Dickson Carr's Dr. Gideon Fell.

In this book, however, Folly doesn't enter until almost halfway through. There is a great deal of preliminary stuff before the murder occurs. Finally, things get down to a traditional, almost Agatha Christie-like British mystery. . . .

"Let's Kill Uncle Lionel" is not badly written. It is hastily and sloppily written, but at least Creasey has some expertise. (p. 38)

Newgate Callendar, in The New York Times Book Review *(© 1976 by the New York Times Company; reprinted by permission), April 11, 1976.*

*   *   *

CREELEY, Robert   1926-

Creeley is an American poet, short story writer, novelist, es- sayist, and editor. A founder of the Black Mountain movement and a close associate of Charles Olson, he has exerted an important influence on contemporary poetry. His style is spare but intense, with an affinity for the rhythms of natural speech. Like others of his school, he believes that form must reflect content, and often employs a short, breath-determined line. William Carlos Williams found in Creeley's poetry "the subtlest feeling for the measure that I encounter anywhere except in the verses of Ezra Pound." (See also *CLC*, Vols. 1, 2, 4, 8, and *Contemporary Authors*, Vols. 1-4, rev. ed.)

WARREN TALLMAN

Like Henry James' early but decisive 'The Madonna of the Future', [Creeley's 'Three Fate Tales'] are explanatory, illustrative, cautionary, an attempt to reach down to the basis for his stance, with nothing more primary,

> nothing more strange, taken or not, than just
> that, the self, which is single. And I make it
> such, so call it, because it is so. I only call it
> what it is.

The self is single, separate, apart, keeping its own time in its own spaces. Creeley's attempts to explore the implications of this fact dominate his writings in much the same way that Hemingway's work is dominated by the fact of violence or Faulkner's the fact of fear. But just as it isn't Faulkner's desire to murder us, so it isn't Creeley's to use his stories as launching pads to hoist readers out into some incomprehensible blue, leaving us hung up out there, one star to a sky. Beyond the singleness, because of it, is a more important need and desire causing each self to seek some way to become more. (pp. 93-4)

The little city mouse girl scampers forth into life and almost found death [in the first tales, but in the second,] the little country mouse lady totters forth towards death—which is also fate, fated, must be—but finds her life instead. Finds it with such intensity of vitality that even 'when it comes time to bury her, one would not be too surprised should the knotted old hands reach up and, pushing the shovels aside, pull the dirt over all by themselves.' She, whose sentences, whose speech, whose very words 'slide into one another,' carrying her life away, has gone forth from her life to a place where one sentence, 'carefully cut' into stone, will not break down. Able to count on nothing else in all her sliding days, she can *count* on that, and by counting can resume the underlying rhythms and walk the waters. (pp. 98-9)

The city mouse girl and the country mouse lady are replaced in tale three by an actual mouse who becomes caught in an interplay of shadows and substance. It's the moon's fault for coming out full, making the night 'very bright outside, almost like day but still very different.' Under the brightness 'each object in the field that was big enough to have a shadow had its own.' The shadows are easy to see, 'black and distinct,' but easy to mistake, because 'there were no sharp details such as are to be seen when a bright sun is shining.' The show begins with the shadow of a cat 'black and irregular on the snow.' A pause as Creeley goes over to pick her up, then sees she has a mouse, 'no pleasant sight to watch.' Still, it is for this he has her so he starts to walk away but is caught:

by the strange sight of their shadows, the mouse's, though smaller very distinct and the cat's like some horrible shadow trying to erase it.

Unpleasant enough to acquiesce as the cat finishes off the mouse, but unpleasant exceedingly to become caught 'absorbed, completely caught' in the horrible shadow of a cat finishing off the smaller, distinct shadow of a mouse. Particularly when the mouse shadow then disappears and reappears:

> coming towards me uncertainly, jerkily until
> I saw that what it wanted was to hide in my
> own shadow, which I now saw to be there,
> just as their own, long and black on the
> snow.

Here, the transition is from the chill of having become so absorbed in a shadow show that the shadows have become more real than the substances to the deeper, even more unsettling chill of discovering that your own shadow has become part of the show. (p. 99)

[Chances] are that this tragedy of one blinded mouse, far from being a culmination of the unpleasantness, is instead the very incident that helps to 'lessen that first impact of horror.' For chances are that the 'horror' the teller feels has less to do with the end of the mouse under the cat's paw—which is also fate, fated, must be—more to do with that moment when distinct intensities of black shadows on the white snow so caught him up, so absorbed him, that the shadows threatened to become more real than their substances. When the mouse seeks safety in the shadows and blunders into the man it's goodbye mouse. But what a relief for the man to become substance again in the field of shadows.

But what does the man in the moonlight mean when he adds that this interplay of shadow and substance 'has the point of all I believe'? What he means has to do with the 'horror' he feels when he and his shadow become part of the show and he realizes that there is nothing in among the shadows that he can count on. This is method to the moon's madness. By transforming substances into the shadows that are so distinct and 'powerful in themselves' that they cannot be ignored and yet so indefinite that Creeley cannot tell, the moon reminds him that nothing can be counted on unless it can be singled out. The mouse proved it when it disappeared into the shadow and blundered into the man. The little girl proved it when her sound disappeared into a blur of noises. And the old lady proved it when her memory disappeared into a blur of words. Which is where the belief enters in. Because the self is single there is only individual knowledge, and because there is only individual knowledge the artist must count on, count with, count by his own eye and ear and memory, disguisedly the subjects of these tales. These become the means by which he measures the things of this world, nothing so general as Shakespeare's imagination, bodying forth what his eye in fact sees his ear in fact hears his memory in fact retains, moment by moment. . . .

Creeley doesn't believe that he can *give* readers what he sees, hears and remembers any more than he can give us his eye to see with, his ears to hear with or his memory to remember with. But he believes in 'other wisdoms,' believes that we have *corresponding* objects, events and oth-

ers, which we have been able to make our own so that as he singles out his we can understand in light of ours, reader tangent to writer. (p. 100)

[The] tales in *The Gold Diggers* suggest nothing so strongly as they do a photograph album kept through the years with figures of family, relatives and friends recurring in various combinations and places—at the seashore, on picnics, at home during the summer, on outings, vacations. What one looks and listens for among these pictures from Creeley'd hallways are the recurrences. . . . There are many chairs—those formal arrangements of men, frequently occupied by men: in a yard in New Zealand, or tilted against a tree looking out at an open plain that reaches 'for more miles than any man ever knows of,' or tilted against the wall of a room at a party, or stood on in a grove by a man picking olives, or jiggling about during a seance. In 'A Death' children play with sticks and throw stones and the sticks recur as twigs, trees, the chairs mentioned, as boats, as tables, and the stones recur as pebbles, as rocks, boulders, gravestones, chunks of gold.

In one real sense these sticks and stones and their variants are both elementary and elemental in Creeley's world, as elementary as the childhood nursery saw and as elemental to his spaces as rock and wood are to the material world. They stand about in his tales in much the way that Klee's arrows or Chagall's violins stand about in their paintings. Among persons who recur the foremost would seem to be a husband and father who haunts the scene as always missing, absent, elsewhere, yet always also somehow present. But there is so much more than a preliminary study of this kind can even mention that it will obviously want a good many readers to single out a full count of persons, objects and events.

And it will eventually be for each reader to make out from the furnishings mentioned—and many more—such human sense as corresponds to what sense he may have of his own house, spaces and furnishings, 'sticks and stones bottles and bones.' Here let me only suggest that the tales need to be read as a group and that the recurrences go on in part against the background of a childhood and adolescence being recounted from the perspective of 1951, Creeley's 25th year. And let me only suggest that as a group they convey some sense that the recounting is a summing up into a goodbye. The last, title-tale of the volume carries suggestions of finality as though old bones were being broken once for all in order to close some open other doors. For an artist with a marked capacity for directness and intensity of perception, 'The Gold Diggers' tale is exceptional, vibrating with pressures, heavy with the impact of what he has to tell.

However, the impact, pressure and intensity I mention are only part of Creeley's writing behavior. There are some cats in the tales, but one wishes that there was a dog too, the kind Whitman mentions as moving along the street in constant and instinctive rapport with the shifting circumstances which confront him. Such dogs need not debate whether to stand still, sway sideways or skedaddle. Their perceptions shift instantaneously into their responses with a kind of mindless kinetic intelligence. Creeley's writing moves with the same motion through the environment he is counting over. What his eye, ear and memory confront along the streets, walks and halls of his own house and spaces is bodied forth—stand, sway or skedaddle—with instant animal immediacy. Only this dog is a sly one, like a fox, like a serpent, like a man, and so bodies forth a human motion in the midst of human objects, events and others. . . . Time has its own tales to tell and I venture to guess that where fiction is concerned Creeley's tales will figure prominently in the telling, not only for the exceptional care and almost bewildering beauty with which his sentences move as they take measure but also . . . [with] a strong sense that Creeley has managed one of the subtlest and most sensitive accounts extant of what it is like to be a human animal in our time. (pp. 101-03)

The commitment to singleness [of self] removes the all but ingrained temptation to reach out for wisdoms, ideas and masterpieces which carries all too many artists' energies to further and further rooms. Recognizing that he is single, Creeley stays at home and thus attempts to possess the house he actually occupies. His advantage follows from the fact that there never have been wisdoms, ideals and masterpieces located in some elsewhere beyond man. He is himself the wisdom, the ideal and the masterpiece—such as he is. (p. 103)

All writing is thought moving from word to word and when Creeley crosses over into the writing world he continues to move just as in the everyday world, one step, street or party at a time. And no knowing until he gets there which is which or next. The same exceptional concentration continues, only now his conspicuous gift for phrase-making enters in, the art of fielding the objects events and others he encounters on the pathless writing paths he moves along and getting them across to readers with superlative grace, skill, impact. Because the paths are pathless—maybe this way, maybe that—the fielding has to be catch-as-catch-can, in the dark, out of the blue. . . . There must be at least a dozen poems in *For Love* that will always cause readers, particularly other writers, to shake their heads in disbelief. How on earth did he manage that one. And that one. And that one.

Much of the management traces to the concentration mentioned, deep in a dream of the occasions he moves among. But perception is perhaps a better word, meaning 'to take from'. (pp. 103-04)

Creeley moves into the writing world when and as some occasion stirs his interest, starts him thinking. He writes as long as interest continues, driving toward no particular conclusion but instead a cessation, that point of rest which tells us that the day, work, preoccupation or demon is done, at least for the moment. Which means the individual stories or poems can be fully as elusive as would be any one act or event in an individual's life. It is when occasion is linked to occasion that characteristic attitudes and actions emerge making life intelligible. Similarly what is obscure in a given story or poem becomes intelligible as in the other stories and poems certain recurrences, call them rimes, form into a kind of meeting place, call it rime-thought. (p. 107)

Because so many of the lyrics [in *For Love*] are so brief one might wonder how anything as reaching as full rime can find room. Answer is that in any given poem—or story—it doesn't. Any sensible man knows that what happens on a single occasion will scarcely open doors to full revelation of his life. It takes many and many a time. Individual Creeley poems are phases of the one poem he is always writing, just

as, in a larger sense, all the poems and tales ever written are parts and parcels of the one song and story named Man. That Creeley's writing tends toward the microcosmic traces to the individual, perhaps his New England origins, the strict eye, utilitarian instincts and puritan conscience. (pp. 109-10)

It is a measure of Creeley's importance that he is able to single out from our customary speech an elan, spirit or air equivalent to or at least reminiscent of that which informs so many Elizabethan songs. (p. 113)

> *Warren Tallman, "Robert Creeley's Tales and Poems" (1962 and 1965), in* Open Letter *(copyright © 1976 by Warren Tallman), Winter, 1976-77, pp. 93-118.*

TERRY R. BACON

"I begin where I can and end when I see the whole thing returning." These words, from Robert Creeley's preface to *The Gold Diggers* . . . , express his early sense of writing, a sense predicated on the notion of evolving form. Implicit in his statement is the concept of poetic form as a function of an organic condition of structure—framed by an indeterminate point of departure and a somewhat more determinate point of termination, the latter somehow dependent upon the perception of some condition of the evolving process (i.e., "the whole thing returning"). The manner in which Creeley's poems end is an aspect of poetic structure, and when the ending is perceived as intrinsically whole or complete, his poems exhibit what Barbara Herrnstein Smith has termed "poetic closure."

In any consideration of structure in an art form which has language as its mode of expression, there are the inherent restrictions of grammar. Creeley accepts language as a limitation and integrates that medium through which he must express himself. with whatever thought or emotion he wishes to express. . . .

Creeley's poetry is expressed in the perpetual NOW. It is a "real time" rendering, in a very solipsistic sense, of the universe he perceives. The poetry is process; he shapes it "momently" as he writes. (p. 227)

Critical . . . to an understanding of Creeley's poetic structure (and, hence, his poetic closure) is what is implied: the "what's to be said" is an integral and complete statement containing all of the semantic elements necessary for the communication of sense. It is an ordered thought process because it is composed of perceptions which are transferred from poet to reader in what Charles Olson called an "energy-discharge," and the perceptions take the form of a statement which, by its very nature and purpose, is meant to communicate.

But Creeley's impulse to stop in the act of writing is not meant to imply that he seeks to render statements developed or explored to their fullest. The questions and not the answers intrigue him. (p. 228)

Closure is a particularly useful critical tool in the examination of projective verse because a poetry of evolving form seems to preclude the predetermination of a principle of structural development which will lead the poem inexorably to a termination point that appears not only appropriate but integrally essential. (p. 230)

[Most of Creeley's] early poems exhibit some degree of

closure. Most frequently, he uses an associative, sequential, or dialectical thematic structure in which closure is reinforced by one or more formal devices. Closural allusions are occasionally used, but more often the last stanza or the final lines of a poem exhibit what might be called a change of address, tone, or perspective. These changes constitute a shift in point of view, a shift which is clearly a deviation from the poem's thematic structure, and this strengthens closure. These changes are often accompanied by formal deviation (normally a change in the number of lines in the last stanza from the number of lines in earlier stanzas).

One of the most frequent formal devices Creeley uses to insure continuation within the poem and to allow for closure at its termination is "syntactic suspension." This device operates by creating, by the end of each of the internal stanzas, a force for continuation through the omission of punctuation (e.g., a period) which would normally allow for the syntactic termination of the poem at those points. Hence, the poems are syntactically suspended at the end of each internal stanza, and this compels the reader to continue until he reaches the period at the end of the poem.

Syntactic suspension is accomplished by enjambment and by the use of non-terminating punctuation marks (i.e., dashes, commas, semi-colons, and colons) where punctuation at the end of an internal stanza is used. . . . Syntactic suspension, like all closural devices, is not in itself sufficient to attain closure, but it is effective when used in conjunction with others. "And," in *For Love* . . . , demonstrates the operation of most of the formal closural devices Creeley uses:

> A pretty party for people
> to become engaged in, she was
>
> twentythree, he
> was a hundred and twentyseven times
>
> all the times, over and over
> and under and under she went
>
> down stairs, through doorways,
> glass, alabaster, an iron shovel
>
> stood waiting and
> she lifted it to dig
>
> back
> and back to mother,
>
> father and brother,
> grandfather and grandmother—
>
> They are all dead now.

Formal deviation occurs when the seven two-line stanzas are followed by a single last line. And as none of the "couplets" provides an opportunity for syntactic termination, the reader is compelled to proceed to the single last line—which terminates with a period. The dash at the end of the seventh "couplet" operates as a sharp break or change in thought and acts as a "lead-in" to a conclusive statement. The last line is a very strong closural allusion. All of these devices combine to provide strong closural force, and, although most of Creeley's poems do not exhibit closure as strong as this, "And," is an example of the simultaneous operation of the closural devices Creeley employs most often. (pp. 234-36)

Most of the poems in *For Love* (1962) and *Words* (1967) exhibit one or more of the closural devices discussed above, and it is this group of poems that I would classify as his early poetry. At the end of *Words* four short pieces appear under the title "Fragments." These "fragments" have the form of journal entries—the poet's record of isolated thoughts, perceptions, or impressions. With "Fragments," Creeley began the practice of recording these isolated perceptions without developing or extending them into poetic structures. The fragments exhibit an austerity of expression that becomes more and more characteristic of Creeley's later poetry, and their appearance at the end of *Words* signaled the direction in which Creeley's poetry was moving. The extension of this practice into book form came with *Pieces* (1969).

Pieces was written as a journal. Three dots were used to separate entries made on different days, and a single dot to separate individual entries. The published work is composed of poems interspersed with fragments and prose entries. The poet's perceptions in *Pieces* are more dissociated and do not, as a rule, follow the patterns of thematic development evident in the earlier books. . . . The perceptions, which tend more toward metaphysical speculation than the nature of human relationships (the predominant theme of *For Love*), move increasingly to the extremes of either pure abstraction or mundane domestic observations. The entries that are thematically related do not necessarily manifest that relationship in a systematic thematic structure; rather, they take the form of disjunct observations on a single theme. There is little of Creeley's earlier tendency to close the poems with either a stated or implied observation, idea, or pronouncement. (pp. 238-39)

["Kid"] is more indicative of the direction in which Creeley's poetry is currently moving:

> The kid left
> out back waits
> for his mother's
>
> face to
> reappear
> in
>
> a win-
> dow,
> waving.

The poem records a single perception whose irreducible quality is evident in the fact that to restate it one needs to use almost every word in the poem. The only closural force in a poem of this type is that inherent in the emotional-semantic complex that produced it: the closure presumed to exist in any syntactic structure. . . . The structural integrity of a poem like "Kid" is the integrity of the single, unified perception organized according to known syntactic principles. The sense of finality or "clinch" is present to the degree that the reader perceives what is recorded in the poem as an integral perception or experience. (p. 241)

Pieces and *A Day Book* were transitional works, bridges between the more developed poems of Creeley's earlier books and the less developed fragments that are more typical in the later ones. Both of these transitional works contain poems of a length comparable to the longer poems in *Words,* but the isolated fragments and short, undeveloped poems like "Kid" are more common. What precipitated this shift toward conscious artistic constriction was probably Creeley's increasing awareness that in insular perceptions is the intensity of focus (and, hence, energy) that dissipates in protracted effort. His concern is with capturing the NOW of a life situation, with rendering the ever-present moment of experience. That concern has always been an essential part of his poetics, but in the later poetry his focus has narrowed—with the consequent result that the perceptions are more distinctly isolable. (p. 242)

[Some] of the "things" in his latest book [*Thirty Things* (1974)] are so narrowly focused that reader speculation is either meaningless or futile:

                    Alice

                The apple in
                her eye.

"Alice" is one of the extremes that Creeley's poetry has moved toward: the utterance is no longer even a complete sentence. Here is fragmented thought, a syntactically incomplete statement. With this the poet edges toward silence. "Alice" is a statement of non-statement, a poetry (if you will) where closure is a meaningless concept because structural development is (apart from the sequential arrangement of the words) non-existent. (p. 243)

In narrowing his focus, Creeley expands the speculative possibilities of the situations he deals with by refusing to qualify them. By consciously restricting the manner and extent to which he deals with a situation, he increases the number of perceptual associations that follow from what he does say. Paradoxically, he says more by saying less. . . .

Creeley's poetry places a great deal of the burden of empathetic understanding on the reader, thereby creating an epistemological dilemma. . . . Creeley's perceptions are epiphanies: glimpses of moments in the life situation that are brought into sharp focus through the high energy transference that is presumed to occur. The extent of the reader's own experiences will to a large degree determine the extent to which those perceptions are meaningful. In any case, the poems are projective; they are manifestations of that continually speculative situation, that circumstance that, for Creeley [as revealed in an interview], is "constantly provocative." . . . (p. 245)

The closural force present in much of Creeley's poetry, especially in the early work, does not preclude or militate against that speculative situation. . . . Creeley's poetry has as its structural basis a pattern of associated perceptions, not, as is the case with much poetry, an "undercarriage" based on referential logic. The perceptions are necessarily enclosed in a syntactic framework, and the framework is itself a part of the structure of the poem. But the closure of the structure does not necessarily imply the termination of the perceptions, as might be the case if his poetic structures were based on referential logic. (pp. 245-46)

The examination of closure in Robert Creeley's poetry illuminates not only Creeley's development as a poet but the essence of projectivism as well. Throughout Creeley's work there is a prevailing sense that most of the poems are integral, that, even when they are purposefully anti-closural, they are complete. This is as true with the early developed poems as it is with the later undeveloped fragments because the integrity in either case derives from the integrity of the perception—whether it is a single, unified perception . . . or a more complex pattern of associated perceptions. . . . The extreme constriction of some of the later "things" . . . moves his work beyond the realm of closural analysis, but the integrity of the perception remains—and this is a key to the essence of projectivism. (p. 246)

Terry R. Bacon, "Closure in Robert Creeley's Poetry," in Modern Poetry Studies *(copyright 1977, by Jerome Mazzaro), Winter, 1977, pp. 227-47.*

["Hello: A Journal"] takes Creeley hop-skip through nine Oriental countries and brings back for his readers these post-card poems full of enthusiasm, humor, perceptiveness, affection. The form suits his open style—Creeley rises to the occasion of their abbreviation and spontaneity with an uncanny poet's sense for the right word sustained at a very high pitch, traveling faster than sound, not a bit of jet lag in evidence. (p. 128)

Publishers Weekly *(reprinted from the January 30, 1978, issue of* Publishers Weekly, *published by R. R. Bowker Company, a Xerox company; copyright © 1978 by Xerox Corporation), January 30, 1978.*

D

DANNAY, Frederic
See QUEEN, Ellery

   * * *

DOCTOROW, E(dgar) L(aurence) 1931-

Doctorow is an American novelist and editor, best known for the widely popular novel *Ragtime*. Major fictive concerns with Doctorow are the cyclical nature of history and ways of knowing. His four novels have been progressively deeper experiments with history and fiction, culminating with *Ragtime*, which has been controversial for the fictions it presents about historical figures. (See also *CLC*, Vol. 6, and *Contemporary Authors*, Vols. 45-48.)

JOSEPH MOSES

Time defeats us in two ways: it bullies us by pursuit, and it mocks us with evasion. We grow older; we are consumed. Yet, at the same time, the events that practice on our mortality, that "do us in," are themselves disordered, senseless, refusing to cohere. E. L. Doctorow is a remarkable novelist precisely because he confronts the mockery of time directly and attempts to master it with footwork fancier and more playful. . . .

[In] *The Book of Daniel* Doctorow already demonstrated his preoccupation with actual history, with real event. The outstanding achievement of that book was to establish a linearity that threaded among the confusions of three decades. . . . The central metaphor was brilliant. The images spectacularly appropriate. Equally impressive was Doctorow's handling of the tension between the character Daniel —the Daniel Agonistes—and the narrating Daniel, the desperate sardonic intelligence determined to see it all in pattern and in place. . . .

This sense of directly engaging history—"The real-world act" Doctorow calls it in [*Ragtime*]—and of bringing to the contest intelligence and wit, identifies *Ragtime,* unmistakably, as a sequel to *Daniel*. . . . Like so much in the novel, . . . the slicing of time is a many-sided metaphor as well as a reality, a framework for comic distortion as well as a metaphor. . . . The reconstruction and division of history is obviously a tentative, slippery business, impossible as it is humanly inevitable. . . .

In making meaning out of history, ambiguity is a richness that cannot safely be trimmed away. And Doctorow does as little trimming as possible. He merely pushes an ambiguity in one or more directions. (p. 310)

Still, if random history is to be disciplined, it will be put in order only by sacrificing history, by substituting in its stead a human design. In *The Book of Daniel* Doctorow gets out of this dilemma by dramatizing a tension between the "two" Daniels, by dramatizing the balance and the will necessary to cross the distance between event and pattern. In *Ragtime* he executes a more comic and audacious maneuver.

Narrated history either understates or overstates. Therefore, Doctorow does both—and pulls his distortions center stage. He proclaims them. He delights in them. He comments about them. On the more intimate level of personal history, we have the families of Father-Mother-Younger Brother and, eventually revealed, their immigrant counterparts in the family of Tateh-Mameh. Their namelessness and the anonymity of Doctorow's staccato prose emphasizes a presentation as flattened as Tateh's silhouettes. (The ambiguous metaphor strikes again.) They are allegories of American history, of the melting pot, of the middle-class life, of making sacrifices, or making good in technological, democratic U.S.A. Whatever the intricacies of their roles, they follow prescribed allegorical destinies as surely as characters in Hawthorne. Heartbreak or joy may lie just beyond their outlines, but it is only the suggestion that Doctorow wants. Otherwise he controls by refusing them dimension and keeping their very excesses within an obvious comic understatement. Even the black Coalhouse Walker Jr. and his Sarah begin as limited, contained personal histories—though their tragedy is that they become part of a larger, more public history.

On the other hand, in dealing with the public record, Doctorow goes to the opposite extreme and pronounces control, not by diminution but by the most flamboyant augmentation. The facts he uses are crucial to his purpose, for through them he can demonstrate the range of the liberties he is taking, the vigor of his comic sweep. . . .

The outrageous, the hyperbolic, the impossible—these are the elements from which Doctorow fashions a coherence so factitious and arbitrary it no longer distorts, but attains a purity and comic integrity of its own. (p. 311)

For all the differences of tone and manner, public event and private history both exhibit related aspects of Doctorow's showmanship and comic control. (p. 312)

Joseph Moses, "To Impose a Phrasing on History," in The Nation *(copyright 1975 by the Nation Associates, Inc.), October 4, 1975, pp. 310-12.*

JONATHAN RABAN

[As] John Barth pointed out some time ago, the modern, or at least the modernist, novel is in constant danger of petering out into a one-sentence idea whose actual performance over the length of a book is of little consequence. . . . On this level, *Ragtime* is an immense success. When the first rumours of it were filtering out from the advance extracts published in *New American Review,* I heard of it as one might hear a new joke that is going the rounds of the office. Here was this new book that had Freud and Jung riding through the Tunnel of Love at Coney Island together . . . fantastic! What did they do in the Tunnel of Love, I asked. They . . . well . . . they ride through the Tunnel of Love. It's the *idea,* don't you see? Indeed, in the book itself, this memorable occasion takes up exactly as much space as it was allotted in my informant's report. *Freud and Jung took a boat together through the Tunnel of Love.* And *Ragtime* is chock-a-block with glittering, unexamined conceits of that kind—little firecrackers that glow with suggestive, but finally fraudulent brilliance, because they can be pursued no further than the sentence which encapsulates them.

The brightness of *Ragtime*—and it is a consistently bright, thoroughly readable book—tends to be of this variety. It flares up on the page, and as quickly dies. Begged questions are lost in the hiss of the next firework. Doctorow is never less than a stylish writer; but whether he actually has a style is questionable. . . . [His] sharpness and verbal ingenuity are undeniable. But there is an odd dissociation between the writer and his object. . . . It is impossible to deduce a sensibility from behind [his] kind of prose. It is connected neither to the character through whose eyes we are supposed to be looking, nor, in any meaningful sense, to the author. Here is language caught in the act of freeloading—a skillful mode of writing which is indigenous to journalism but which tastes unsatisfyingly bland in a novel. When Doctorow escapes "the little world of personal experience which has bound the novel", he moves into the big world of the smart colour feature—a freedom which is disputable, to say the least.

Whatever its supposed limitations, at least the world of personal experience operates to a system of strenuous internal logic. In most novels, things happen because they are necessary to the narrative, because the situation dictates or requires them. In *Ragtime,* they just happen. . . . [His] *coincidentallys* and *meanwhiles* are no coincidence; they are basic materials in the fabric of *Ragtime* and they betray the essential triviality of its relationship to the public historical world in which Doctorow has invested so much faith. He grasps arbitrarily and wildly at public facts and events like a man trying to hitch lifts on the wings of passing eagles. The first third of the novel (and it is worth mentioning that Doctorow performs most of his tricks early on, and *Ragtime* soon subsides into a quite conventionally-told, moderately exciting story) hops and skips from private to public, from one batch of characters to another, by means of these spurious linkages. Sometimes Doctorow has the air of a frantic amateur stage manager who finds that he has lost half his cast by the middle of Act Two of *H.M.S. Pina-*

fore. "And what of Tateh and his little girl?" he enquires, in the first sentence of Chapter Twelve. To which the reader can only reply, Well, *you* should know. Sometimes the sheer difficulty of trying to keep a whole chunk of American history on the go leads him to try, Busby Berkeley fashion, for set-pieces which will keep the entire cast doing the same thing at the same time.

> All across the continent merchants pressed
> the large round keys of their registers.

And woe betide the unfortunate merchant who happened to be picking his nose at the time.

The idea of mixing public and private, imagined and real, is eloquent in synopsis (as it is eloquent in the many adulatory reviews which *Ragtime* has collected). But in execution, it turns out to be terribly clumsy. The various bits of the novel look as if they had been joined to one another by strips of sticky tape, and Doctorow has made no particular effort to match the bias of the materials. His private characters are fey-sentimental, and the period New York in which they live—a city of heartrending poverty, gaslit colour, etcetera—is by Malamud (in *The Magic Barrel* and *The Assistant*), out of Henry Roth (in *Call It Sleep*) and Abraham Cahan (in what is really the first major descriptive novel of the Lower East Side, *The Rise of David Levinsky*). Passages like [the one] in which the real Evelyn Nesbit visits the tenement where the imaginary Tateh lives with his daughter, are simply *ersatz*-writing. (pp. 72-4)

But it is the public characters who are the least satisfactory. Doctorow has not reinvented or reimagined them. He has bought their crude popular images off the peg, and simply put them, on rows of hangers, into his book. . . . If History was too important to be left to historians, Doctorow has made it over to the most orthodox school of caricaturists. He has stripped his public characters of their individuality, and their only claim to life in *Ragtime* is that their names were once attached to real people. . . .

The point at which the book really settles down is where it starts on the story of Coalhouse Walker. . . . Here Doctorow's prose is as efficiently gripping as, say, Peter Benchley's in *Jaws,* and questions of depth and character are kept at bay by the race of the plot.

That is the trouble with *Ragtime*. The moment one begins to question it on any grounds of serious literary merit, it falls apart—a cunning, fragile house of cards. Its major interest lies in the way in which it suggests a recipe for the contemporary bestseller. It is written to be read fast: too much attention on the reader's part kills it stone-dead. It is a splendid book to talk *about*—a big, party-size idea which is itself stuffed with attractive little ideas. It is designed to titillate the imagination without overstretching it. Its prose will present no difficulties, and will offer numerous small pleasures, to those who prefer reading magazines to reading books. There will be a very large number of people who know little, and care less, about either the novel or history, who will see *Ragtime* as the most dazzlingly sophisticated exploration of both the novel and history that they have ever read. (p. 74)

Jonathan Raban, "Easy Virtue: On Doctorow's 'Ragtime'," in Encounter *(© 1976 by Encounter Ltd.), February, 1976, pp. 71-4.*

PAUL LEVY

Almost all British critics, and by now several thousand

common readers, will have come to the conclusion that Mr Doctorow spent the years between the writing of his last and excellent novel, *The Book of Daniel,* and the birth of *Ragtime* constructing a plot. The plot was not simply that of a novel, but of a sales campaign. The plot succeeded: Doctorow's truly dedicated researches yielded a formula for success, and a style in which to clothe it most gaudily. Reflective readers will forgive me for finding *Ragtime* as meretricious as the bicentennial celebrations themselves. . . .

My reasons for finding *Ragtime* so appalling will be known to those who have read more than one other review of it. There is the too-deft split-level plot, which manages to splatter its pages with a little nostalgia here, a little noble left-wing sentiment there, and lashings of semen wherever the reader's interest threatens to wane. There is the name-dropping. . . . With one exception the fictitious characters at the would-be centre of the book have no proper names: they are called Father, Mother, Mother's Younger Brother, and in the case of the East Side Jewish immigrant contingent, Tateh and Mameh. Doctorow's splendid gift for inventing names is matched by his skill at characterising their bearers. The exception, Coalhouse Walker, an absolutely bourgeois black man who is supposed to be a musical disciple of Scott Joplin, is given a name, presumably because it would be too difficult to manipulate him from respectability to armed rebellion without a handle; and what would one call him—The Black Man? The Negro?—without alienating the book's natural constituency of trendies. . . .

It is widely supposed that *Ragtime* raises certain points of a philosophical nature concerning the relation of history and fiction. A dust-jacket philosopher, George Stade, reviewing *Ragtime* in the *New York Times Book Review* [see *CLC,* Vol. 6], said that 'in this excellent novel, silhouettes and rags not only make fiction out of history but also reveal the fictions out of which history is made'. This bold statement is false on two counts: *Ragtime* is not excellent and it does not 'reveal the fictions out of which history is made', at least, not in any way that actually illuminates the history of America in the period in which it is set, the ten years before the 1914-18 War. On the third count, it is true that *Ragtime* 'makes fiction out of history', that is, it falsifies history. Freud, Jung, Emma Goldman, Henry Ford, Pierpont Morgan, Stanford White and Harry Houdini simply did not perpetrate the grotesqueries they are made to commit in its pages. That is all. There is no problem. The characters in *Ragtime* that bear those famous names are not historical personages; they are merely pawns in Doctorow's particularly dotty and tasteless game of chess. (p. 21)

I rather sympathise with the view of the Oxford don who, discussing Doctorow's pretensions, told me that what *enrages* him is writers of genuine historical novels who get their facts wrong. *Ragtime* he dismissed as beneath consideration. (pp. 21-2)

> Paul Levy, *"Historical Truth v. Fiction,"* in Books and Bookmen (© *copyright Paul Levy 1976; reprinted with permission*), June, 1976, pp. 21-2.

WALTER L. KNORR

[An] unanticipated glow of recognition comes over the [critic of Heinrich von Kleist, a German dramatist and short story writer,] who, reading leisurely as directed through E. L. Doctorow's *Ragtime,* discovers amid the likes of Harry Houdini, J. P. Morgan, and Henry Ford a black couple whose actions take on an increasingly *deja vu* aura. The two produce an illegitimate daughter which the mother, Sarah, buries alive. The protagonist family discovers and resuscitates the child and takes it in to live along with its mother. On the scene at the narrator's home arrives one Sunday the father of the child, one Coalhouse Walker, Jr., a proper and dignified ragtime pianist who, when refused an audience by Sarah, contents himself with genuflection at the cradle of his child and a few Scott Joplin rags at the family piano. The visits become routine, become a courtship of Sarah after the fact.

To the Kleist critic the problematic child is a familiar motif: *Das Erdbeben in Chili, Der Findling;* the name Coalhouse closely resembles the family name of Kleist's greatest fictional protagonist, Michael Kohlhaas; the courtship in reverse is reminiscent of the *Marquise von O—.* Thus, by the time the courtship between Coalhouse and Sarah is under way, Doctorow has signaled to us his familiarity with and, dare one say, indebtedness to the novellas of Heinrich von Kleist. Even the most skeptical must admit that the similarities transcend coincidence. In what follows the tactic becomes transparent: in Coalhouse Walker, Jr., Doctorow is presenting us an updated black version of Michael Kohlhaas, the sixteenth-century Brandenburg horse-trader who becomes the scourge of Saxony after a degenerate Saxon count makes him the victim of a practical joke. (p. 225)

The dominant theme of the Coalhouse episode, outraged innocence seeking to force justice upon an unjust world through terrorism, is likewise the dominant theme, overtones included, of Kleist's novella, not to mention certain public events in our own age. In adopting Kohlhaas as model Doctorow transforms the theme of class discrimination of the Reformation to that of racial discrimination in our era.

Doctorow evokes Kleist in *Ragtime,* not just the giants and freaks of the turn of the century. His strategy is legitimate and has a long tradition. By exploiting foreign literature of the past Doctorow exercises his license to fictionalize— even if it is with real personages; in doing so he also evokes in his readers an "anxiety of critical reception," a fear on our part that we might not be getting all of his signals, as if to balance off his own "anxiety of influence." All of this naturally calls into question the desirability and value of literary scholarship as it presently is practiced, as a dismantling and reconstruction of an individual work within all of the possible modes of allusion: synchronic (contemporary), diachronic (historical), metachronic (archetypal), literary (imaginative variations of the archetypal), and non-literary (documentary). The natural affinities among historical recurrences—to speak in Vico and Joyce's terms—are ultimately part of the rhetoric of fictional and biographical characterization, of a self's justification for its own vectors, of the not-so-unique individual's response to not-so-unique circumstances. We may find it quaint, elegant, or exhilarating to recognize Michael Kohlhaas in Doctorow's Coalhouse rather than Nat Turner, but it is one of Doctorow's Houdini-like elusions that such quivers of familiarity in his reader ultimately mean quite little to his novel's themes. (pp. 226-27)

Even when fiction and social history once again become

distinct genres, *Ragtime* will survive as a sterling example of a work which finds several ways of mixing the two. (p. 227)

> Walter L. Knorr, "Doctorow and Kleist: 'Kohl-haas' in 'Ragtime'," in Modern Fiction Studies (© copyright 1976, by Purdue Research Foundation, West Lafayette, Indiana), Summer, 1976, pp. 224-27.

DAVID EMBLIDGE

Surely the best-known work by E. L. Doctorow is *Ragtime* (1974). . . . But Doctorow's other two novels, *Welcome to Hard Times* (1960) and *The Book of Daniel* (1971), which have been obscured by the commercial hoopla over *Ragtime,* may in some respects be better pieces of fiction. (p. 397)

The novels are rich in texture and themes, actually too rich to discuss comprehensively here. However, there is a central motif in all three which gives both structure to the plots and a tone of irony to the characterizations. This motif is the idea of history as a repetitive process, almost a cyclical one, in which man is an unwilling, unknowing pawn, easily seduced into a belief in "progress." Doctorow pays detailed, loving attention to the external, concrete facts of cultural history, creating a feeling of uniqueness in time and place. Yet in reality these surface details which smack of growth, change, and differentiation are illusory. We find that beneath them certain patterns of belief and action prevail no matter how much the outer world may seem to change. In two of the books, a repetitive form of music is used as a metaphor for this historical principle. Furthermore, the image of repetition emerges through character development; in all three novels we find a tragedy of revenge.

Like most classic American Westerns, *Hard Times* has the feel of allegory in it. In our national mythology of the pastoral Eden waiting for us somewhere out toward the setting sun, there is one emotional constant: hope. . . . *Hard Times* reverses this standardized mythic concept of the West, bringing our view of the pioneering life a bit closer to the reality of the struggle, violence, and frequent failure that actually prevailed. The novel is dystopian, the story of a failed, sterile Eden.

The narrator, Blue, is Adamic in nature, but despite two falls from apparent grace, he never learns the meaning of evil in himself or others. This is his curse. (pp. 397-98)

Blue always had the feeling that [the town] Hard Times was "certified" as a place in the world, and so when the next season brings a small boom in repopulation and prosperity [after a period of destruction], he feels convinced his faith is well founded. Though at the time he thought continued improvement was certain, he later realizes that the hopefulness of this time was really their best moment. On this point rests one of the novel's central themes. Blue says that somewhere in there "there must have been a moment when we reached what perfection was left to our lives." . . . [But he shuddered to think that whatever] "perfection was . . . it maybe was past, silently come and gone, a moment long, just an instant in the shadow of one day, and any fool who was still waiting for it . . . didn't know what life is."

In essence this is Gatsby's problem revisited: Blue also wants to turn back the clock, to rebuild a past dream by projecting it into the future, but, as Fitzgerald said in *The Great Gatsby,* "he did not know that it was already behind him, somewhere back in that vast obscurity beyond the city [the West, the vision of Eden], where the dark fields of the republic rolled on under the night." The rest of Fitzgerald's prose-poem ending is a literal parallel to Blue's situation. Doctorow is nowhere more succinct in stating the illusion of hopefulness as it projects into the future than when he has Blue tell us, "Like The West, like my life: the color dazzles us, but when it's too late we see what a fraud it is, what a poor pinched-out claim."

In fact, one can say that the novel becomes a masochistic crescendo of recollection as Blue finishes the tale. (p. 399)

Like the sparse landscape and cold light of the [novel's setting on the] Dakota plain, the prose style of *Hard Times* is lean and simple. Not so in *The Book of Daniel,* where stylistic complexity is of at least two kinds. One is sheer bulk of information, for whatever the setting may be, whatever the subject of dialogue, we move slowly through a deep snow of words. We feel the very friction in the narrator's own thought process. Another cause of complexity is the shifting of voice between first and third persons, reflecting the narrator's struggle to review experience on both existential and analytic levels, first hand and at some distance.

Why these stylistic choices? Because we have here a political novel told in the voice of a participant in its painful events who wants simultaneously to express his feelings and to understand his experience rationally. The narrator is Daniel Lewin, born Daniel Issacson and born outside the novel as one of the Rosenberg children in the infamous atomic bomb treason case of the McCarthy era. Though the parallels to the facts of this case and the lives of the Rosenberg children are many, they are not perfect, and it would be a mistake to view the novel as "their" story; Doctorow begins with their family situation but imagines in his own way the consequences of such traumas. (pp. 400-01)

Part of the book's moral tension derives from the fact that Daniel is never able to ascertain whether his parents were innocent or guilty. Eventually, though, he becomes if not indifferent to this question then at least ambivalent about the answer. Instead of answering it he arrives at an even more unsettling conclusion: "Of one thing we are sure, everything's elusive." . . . (p. 401)

Because Daniel works on the premise that "everything is elusive," the book can only be a series of doomed attempts to discover an unavailable truth. The story is very much Daniel's lament for himself, and Whitman's logic at the closing of "Song of Myself" seems to apply directly: "Do I contradict myself? / Very well then I contradict myself / (I am large, I contain multitudes.)" and "Failing to fetch me at first keep encouraged, / Missing me one place search another, / I stop somewhere waiting for you." Thus it is evident why Doctorow turns to Whitman for one of his epigraphs, a quotation expressing the poet's cosmic role of music maker not only for "accepted victors" but for "conquer'd and slain persons" as well—as though distinctions don't matter.

The density of the style and the psychological tension in the point of view set the stage for thematic developments much like those of *Hard Times.* History, for instance, is the villain again with its reappearing trends engulfing feeble mankind in delusions of false progress. (pp. 401-02)

The greater part of the entire novel, indeed of all three novels, serves to illustrate [the] antiprogressive idea [exemplified by Artie Sternlicht's wall collage: "Everything that came before is all the same!"]. Daniel studiously travels into one historical subject after another, all somehow at least tangentially related to his parents' case, but he always arrives in the same philosophical port defined for him most precisely by Sternlicht. However, Sternlicht believes that this principle of historical repetition is a consequence of the double-think repression which is seen as inherent in corporate liberalism, the archenemy. (p. 402)

Daniel reviews the sociopolitical background of his parents' execution in a section called "True History of the Cold War: A Raga." He examines from his radical perspective, in line with Sternlicht, the falsehoods, delusions, errors, and vanities of the Cold War, drawing on many scholarly texts such as William A. Williams's *The Tragedy of American Foreign Policy*. Like Blue in *Hard Times* who writes history in order to understand himself, Daniel reads it to explain his family's past. . . .

[The] juxtaposition of dual concern for repetition and logical disjunction in Daniel's private life and in America of the fifties suggests why Doctorow calls the "True History of the Cold War" a *raga*. This Hindu form of devotional music is itself characterized by an emphasis on sequences—of chord progressions, melodic interpolations and rhythmic patterns. *Raga* taken literally means *color* or *mood* and each raga has a definite ethical or emotional significance. The string instrument called *tamboura* sets up a monophonic continuous tonal horizon as a background for the sitar's complex overlay of melodic development. Given this musical structure as metaphor, we can infer that Daniel's "True History" is analogous to one of the many ragas, and therefore it is only one version of cold war history, simply his version at the occasion of this "playing" or telling. Thus the title "True History" is ironic to say the least, and we are brought back again to the thematic idea that "everything is elusive," most of all historical truth. (p. 403)

[When he meets with Selig Mindisch, his parents' betrayer,] Daniel sounds again like Blue in *Hard Times*, also like two important characters in *Ragtime*. The rendezvous with Selig Mindisch takes place at Disneyland, and Doctorow's narrative method here is an essay in the new journalism at its very best, cutting satirically through the elaborate veneer of illusions to the dark heart of latent cultural values.

Daniel explains, for instance, that Disneyland's cartoon mentality is an attenuation of historical reality reinterpreted to preclude individual confrontations with painful facts and ambiguities in the past. The exhibition on pirates ignores the effects on mercantile trade of this kind of professional criminal; instead we see romanticized buccaneers. . . . Disneyland is a fantastic tribute to historical mindlessness, and there couldn't be a better setting for Daniel's final confrontation with his old nemesis: the elusiveness of truth. (pp. 403-04)

In *Ragtime* Doctorow indulges in what earlier writers of "romance" like Twain called "dressing up the tale." Though again we witness an almost encyclopedic survey of descriptive facts about the life of a historical period (1902-1915), this overlay of apparent objectivity is just that: a slick veneer of illusions. Below this glossy surface, however, is another impressively successful narrative technique

treating essentially the same themes. The hallmark of the narrative form here is a fanciful intertwining of "real" historical figures . . . with fictional characters. As in romantic history itself (Bancroft's *Montcalm and Wolf* comes to mind), Doctorow's imagination takes us on a voyeuristic expedition into the private, psychological lives of people we could never really encounter in this way. (p. 404)

Again the point of view, in political terms, is that history, especially the American brand, is far from a progressive evolution toward peace among men. The book is an indictment of the recurrent malignancies of spirit beneath the period's chimerical technological progress and social harmony. . . .

Life in the present in *Ragtime* is a continuous recapitulation of the past. Doctorow says of this period in particular, "The value of the duplicable event was everywhere perceived," and these recurring events become metaphors of history's capacity for redundancy. The "duplicable events" are such small things as ice cream soda fountains in every town, all made of Belgian marble, or advertisements everywhere for "Painless Parker the Dentist." Other larger examples are the predictable patterns of baseball, [and] the stock prejudicial images in the Anglo mind of Negroes and immigrants. . . . (p. 405)

But above all this there is a double apotheosis of the phenomenon, the first half of which is Henry Ford's system of mass-produced Model T automobiles. . . . The other half of the apotheosis is J. P. Morgan's elaborately researched theory: "There are universal patterns of order and repetition that give meaning to the activity of this planet." One of these patterns is reincarnation, and Morgan believes he and Ford "are instrumentation[s] in our modern age of trends in human identity that affirm the oldest wisdom in the world." Morgan has spent millions to prove this theory, but Ford discovered the same idea in a twenty-five-cent booklet bought at the Franklin Novelty Company, so that again we see how irrelevant the surface details can be. Only the underlying forms are important.

Having established this concern for truth and illusion in our historical imagination, Doctorow can proceed to weave a story to demonstrate it in action. A character named Coalhouse Walker appears. . . .

He plays "Wall St. Rag" by Scott Joplin. "Small clear chords hung in the air like flowers. The melodies were like bouquets. There seemed to be no other possibilities for life than those delineated by the music." And what are the characteristics of this music? A left hand ostinato conveying a distinct basis of fundamental repetition and a right handed liveliness allowing for a wide range of improvisation on the melodic line. Thus we can sense that the structure of the music once more becomes symbolic of the historical process: endless recurrence under a distracting facade of individualistic variation. At the very end of the novel, when "the era of Ragtime had run out," Doctorow nails down his point by musing: "as if history were no more than a tune on a player piano." (p. 406)

An interesting possibility of interpretation [of the novel, and especially of Coalhouse's need for revenge] is that the entire Coalhouse story is a cipher for a tragic recurrent pattern in American history. The embattled Negro, drawn into upward mobility through imitation of high white culture, is beaten down for racist fun by white trash; the system of justice, even when used in the Negro's defense by white bourgeois sympathizers, does no good; the Negro turns radical and threatens to destroy white private property representing the social and financial success no longer available to him; everybody except the Negro and his revolutionary colleagues wonders why; the Negro is caught and killed.

We find, then, a background feeling of slow but unstoppable repetition in the way things go, and a foreground of hope and mad determination to make things change. This is almost exactly what appears structurally and thematically in *Hard Times* and *Daniel*. There are other subplots in *Ragtime,* and Doctorow handles them all deftly. One notices that in these subsidiary episodes too the experience of endless recurrence, often in fruitless pursuit of impossible goals, predominates. (p. 407)

In their quests for revenge, Doctorow's main characters seek to make things the way they were, and in so doing reenact a common pattern of fruitless human behavior. A final general inference then is that Doctorow's vision is a dark, almost Melvillean one—not morbid, jaded, or exhausted, but finally pessimistic or at least resigned about hopeless human nature. Paradoxically, in the very attention he gives to describing the tangible stuff of social life in a specific time and place, he finds moments of beauty, passion, and happiness, each with its own inherent value. Nonetheless, behind it all, like muzak no one really hears, like an unfelt but life-sustaining heartbeat, there are the recurrences of history, the unalterable instincts of human behavior, the mandala of self on which we all turn toward a future like the past no one understands. (p. 408)

> *David Emblidge, "Marching Backward into the Future: Progress as Illusion in Doctorow's Novels," in* Southwest Review *(© 1977 by Southern Methodist University Press), Autumn, 1977, pp. 397-409.*

*   *   *

DONOSO, José   1924-

Donoso is a Chilean-born novelist, short story writer, literary critic, and translator now residing in Spain. Central to his work is his refutation of the psychological theory of the autonomous, integrated personality: characterization and plot development are depicted through differing narrative points of view. Donoso creates a fictional world where nothing is stable, nothing sure, where reality and fantasy are intertwined. This fantastic world is presented in highly structured, objective prose, Donoso achieving an ironic effect through the description of the irrational in rational terms. (See also *CLC*, Vols. 4, 8, and *Contemporary Authors*, Vols. 81-84.)

ALEXANDER COLEMAN

It is quite interesting that the work of José Donoso . . . has often been described as traditionalist, traditionalist, that is, in the English sense, admiring as he does James and Austen. There has even been mention of the word *costumbrismo,* referring to the genre very much dear to nineteenth-century Spanish writers generally considered to be minor—except Larra, of course. . . . The stories [in *El veraneo y otros cuentos*] unquestionably give every evidence of a modest and perfectly calculated kind of realistic literary practice. But to see nothing more than this in the stories is to hide their insidious and quite beautifully disguised thematics.

In the title story, for instance, the whole nightmare of marital infidelity is reflected in a perverse and distorted way through the relationships of the various servants of the triangle, and through the way in which the appropriate children manipulate not only each other, but also the servants in turn. The result is a complicated and perfectly executed depiction of intricate human domination, alleviated only when a realm of feeling between the children cuts through the vertical social structures of hate and authority that the adults have created for their children and which they wish to pass on to them.

And so, too, for the language—apparently odd chatter between servants and children and amongst the children themselves, but in reality a linguistic mask for one of Donoso's nuclear fantasies, the alternance and conflict between Life and Authority. (pp. 155-56)

Other stories in the collection, such as "Una señora" and "Fiesta en grande," are superb set pieces that . . . are expressive of Donoso's essentially urban sensibility. The polarities of "civilized" and ordered existence finally break down, and man is confronted with an overwhelming sense of the violence of nature and man and consciously throws himself into a maelstrom of unconscious, inhuman, and murderous void.

Any discussion of Donoso's thematics must also take into consideration the tone—violently Romantic in spite of everything—which characterizes the evolution of his characters from constriction to expression. (p. 156)

In two later novels, *El lugar sin límites* and *Este domingo,* both of 1966, [the] multiple dependence and relationship of class is delineated in a masterful fashion, a portrait of a society in which the etymological meaning of *travesty* is fully explored, a world where all objects are signs to their opposites, a terrifying confusion of doubleness. But in spite of the confusion of identity purposefully practiced by Donoso in his short stories, one is often left with a unique vision of the central character of the story. . . . (p. 157)

Against the rigidities of society, there is an ever-present oceanic sense in Donoso into which his heroes plunge. These pathetic and at times comic figures are pilgrims of their own brand of truth, vague searchers for a freer self and society, constantly at odds with the reality of their own spiritual suffocation. A groping for a sense of transcendence, a whole process that inevitably entails the encounter with the monster that is within them, engendered out of the mathematical rigidities with which societies function in apparent order. . . . [In] a few of the early stories, a good story is robbed of its impact by a too obviously psychological explanation in lieu of an ending. (pp. 157-58)

But certainly our sensibilities are constantly engaged by Donoso's stories—above all, because of the sheer power of the inarticulate that underlies them all. He is always careful to draw for us a miniature portrait of a society, often from the point of view of a childlike narrator who is sensitized to the significance of every detail. What draws us out as readers is the power of the unspoken in him, the deadly attraction of nothingness. It would seem that his work, glanced at in a cursory fashion, does more than its share of the reader's work, because it is so evidently a refraction of a society, but this aspect can only cloud our vision of this wholly contemporaneous literary achievement. The carefully appointed society with which Donoso began to depict in *Co-*

ronación and in the stories is for us a functioning lie possibly pointing to a truth; the words surround rather than express a reality. If they denote anything, one would have to mention a society that is itself inauthentic and false. (p. 158)

Alexander Coleman, "Some Thoughts on José Donoso's Traditionalism," in Studies in Short Fiction (copyright 1971 by Newberry College), Winter, 1971, pp. 155-58.

CHARLES M. TATUM

An important aspect of the prose fiction of the Chilean novelist José Donoso is the child point of view which he uses to portray his characters' loss of innocence and youthful spontaneity. Donoso employs this technique most successfully in the novel *Este domingo* and in the short stories "Paseo," "El hombrecito," and "China." In each work an upper-class adult male protagonist remembers his childhood and adolescent years in his parent's or grandparent's home. A subtle change from the adult point of view to that of the child occurs within the narration as the language, verb tenses, and conception of reality begin to convey the shift in perspective that characterizes each age. Almost unaware of the transformation, we find ourselves viewing the adults (through the narrative filter of the child point of view) as they act out their pretensions and false values and give expression to their anxieties and complexes. (p. 187)

[Donoso uses the child narrator] to portray an uncorrupted, fantasy-filled existence in which the child acts out his normal feelings and instincts unfettered by social constraints. Through the use of the child point of view Donoso often satirizes the [foibles of] the adults but his primary intent is to depict the pathetic transformation that occurs in the individual as he matures. By juxtaposing the two ages directly through point of view he makes us aware of the glaring differences between the child's spontaneous unsocialized behavior and the falseness and sham of the adult's attitudes and rigidly confined self-expression.

Donoso uses this technique effectively in *Este domingo* as he alternates between the child's world and that of the adult. The child point of view serves several functions in this elaborately constructed novel: 1) to make a statement about how, as the individual matures, the innocent and fabulous world of childhood slowly changes and becomes corrupted 2) to give the reader a perspective on the adult world seen through the child-narrator's eyes 3) to reveal the Oedipal relationships perpetrated by the adults on the children and 4) to set a pattern which suggests a kind of cyclical "eterno retorno."

The three sections of *Este domingo* narrated from the point of view of the child present a world set apart, structurally, from that of the adults. The child's life revolves around the weekends spent at the grandparent's home. There is almost a complete absence of the narrator's mother and father except for an occasional negative reference to them. (pp. 187-88)

Through the use of the child point of view Donoso succeeds in creating [a] superficial tranquility and sophisticated exterior that suddenly erupts into irrational and often violent acts. He conveys the apparent calm by means of the child who views his reality through the naturally limited perspective of his naïveté. The full implications of the pent up frustration and repressed sexuality only become appar-

ent to the adult-narrator in retrospect. As an adult he views the events and relationships of his childhood and adolescence with the fear that his own life is following along a pattern similar to that of his parents and grandparents. In Donoso's fiction as the individual matures he becomes increasingly aware of the sham of the superficially comfortable world he inhabited at an early age, and subsequent to this awareness comes the realization his fate will be the same. (pp. 189-90)

In the first and third sections of the novel Donoso describes through the children's improvised games the grandeur and leisure that characterized Chile's aristocracy. But like the dust that covers the old leather trunks, to the reader his world emerges in decline, rescued only by the children's imagination. The decadence and falseness of the adults is reflected in their activities. Their creation of fantastic games in the second section of the novel ("Los juegos legítimos") is a mockery of the antics of their parents and grandparents. They unconsciously satirize by devising a play that mimics the false actions of the adults. (pp. 190-91)

The process of growing aware, the inevitable knowledge of a reality that invades childhood, robs the child [protagonist of "El hombrecito"] of his carefree, innocent conception of things and slowly instills in him the horror of the human condition.... In Donoso's fiction as man grows older he becomes more reluctant to allow emotions and involvement with others to interrupt his well-established routine. He becomes more stratified and rigid which eventually destroys him emotionally and mentally. (pp. 192-93)

Through a deceivingly traditional form and language Donoso evokes for us a child's world. Utilizing a technique that is common to his fiction he draws the unsuspecting reader into an intricately constructed web of suggestion. (p. 193)

[Donoso] suggests the existence in his fictional characters of a cyclical never-ending process of loss of innocence. Unable to regain it, his protagonists become caught in a web of perverted values, aspirations, and attitudes in order to escape the eternal questions of the human condition. (p. 195)

Charles M. Tatum, "The Child Point of View in Donoso's Fiction," in Journal of Spanish Studies: Twentieth Century (copyright © 1973 by the Journal of Spanish Studies: Twentieth Century), Winter, 1973, pp. 187-96.

HARLEY D. OBERHELMAN

El obsceno pájaro de la noche is a complex statement of the metaphysical problems faced by humanity in the twentieth century. Published in 1970 at a time when Chile's political system was turning to state socialism in search of solutions to age-old nagging social and economic injustices, a careful reading of Donoso's text reveals a deep concern for national problems and at the same time marks the author as a major practitioner of the "nueva narrativa" in contemporary Spanish American letters.

Donoso, whose *Coronación* (1958), *Este domingo* (1966), and *El lugar sin límites* (1967) announced his principal theme, the inner world of the collapsing Chilean oligarchy, achieves a masterpiece of major proportions with *El obsceno pájaro*.... It is clearly within the current of the innovative Spanish American novel of today in its cataloguing of the decline of bourgeois systems and values and in its creation of a new realism based on multiple mutations of the author's (and the reader's) creative imagination. There is a double axis on which Donoso's concept of reality is based; the novel moves simultaneously on an exterior and an interior plane, leading eventually to a negation of both levels of action. A new socio-economic system must replace the exterior reality of Chilean life just as the negation of the traditional protagonist points the way toward new novelistic forms. (pp. 107-08)

Action in the novel is fragmented so that the reader must constantly reconstruct the basic thread: a history in retrospect of the wealthy, landed Azcoitía family and especially of the family's charitable asylum for aging women, the Casa de Ejercicios Espirituales de la Encarnación de la Chimba. (p. 108)

If the principal purpose of the contemporary Spanish American novel is to chronicle the profound transformations which are causing a restructuring of a whole society, then this latest novel of Donoso fully measures up to the assignment. (pp. 108-09)

It is through Don Jerónimo's secretary, one Humberto Peñaloza, that the complicated relationship between exterior and interior reality in the novel comes into focus. Peñaloza is one form of a multiple protagonist whose constant metamorphoses create a series of unusual characters.... (p. 110)

Humberto Peñaloza, one of the principal forms of the central multiple protagonist, provides an entrée into the vertiginous inner world of Donoso's novel. The almost endless succession of metamorphic changes results in a variety of narrative points of view, all of which ultimately coalesce into a single undefined "yo." Paralleling these changes is a similar line of development in the multiple character of Inés Santillana de Azcoitía, who throughout her lifetime was so influenced by her mysterious, witch-like nurse, Peta Ponce, that she eventually assumed the personality of the person who ultimately destroyed her mind. (pp. 111-12)

Such a juxtaposition and multiplicity of characters results in a confused, schizophrenic world of inner reality. Inés suffers from advanced schizophrenia as the novel ends, and Boy [the grotesquely deformed offspring of Don Jerónimo and Inés] is clearly the deformed product of a chaotic society in the last stages of decay. In a sense La Rinconada, the artificial world in which Boy is to lead a Segismundo-like existence, is a universe in miniature which should be viewed as a copy of Chilean society. Its staff of carefully chosen monsters duplicates the political and administrative bureaucracy which dominated Chile under the hand of the oligarchy. Donoso meticulously delineates the guidelines which governed the special world enclosed within the walls of La Rinconada.... (pp. 112-13)

Donoso's creation of La Rinconada with its false system of values and goals is a direct attack on a system of government which exploits the unfortunate masses as a foundation for its power. (p. 113)

The national consternation caused by the death of Don Jerónimo is reminiscent of the turmoil which followed the death of Mamá Grande in the celebrated short story by Gabriel García Márquez. His death also represents the end of an era in Chilean politics, and at the same time it heralds the termination of the power of the oligarchy. (pp. 113-14)

Following the death of Don Jerónimo, the announcement of plans to demolish the Casa de Ejercicios Espirituales marks the final negation of the legacy of a decadent aristocracy. Significantly, the occupants of the Casa are to be moved to bright, new quarters made possible by the bequest of one of the late residents in her final will. This monument to the Azcoitía family and to the memory of their ancestor for whom it was first constructed is doomed to die amid the rubble and dust of the Casa itself. Coupled with the symbolic destruction of the physical representation of external reality is a most surprising final scene which negates the multiple "yo," i.e., the narrator of the novel. Abandoned in the vacated Casa, the narrator is placed in a series of sacks, all of which are carefully sewn shut. (p. 114)

Donoso reduces the inner level of reality in the novel, the first person narrator, to the physical limitations of a bundle which a nameless old woman carries from the Casa into the brisk winter night. The final action develops under a bridge where a fire has been built to warm the bodies of a group of impoverished drifters. The old lady offers the contents of her sack to increase the fire: sticks, boxes, stockings, rags, newspapers, trash. Such is the ultimate form of Donoso's protagonist, and the destruction of inner reality is complete in the ashes of a sputtering fire.

In *El obsceno pájaro de la noche* Donoso reaches a new level of achievement within the framework of the "nueva narrativa." His use of fragmented and distorted protagonists parallels his destruction of temporal unity.... The negation of time is an aspect of the more general negation of reality which abounds in the novel. For Donoso the complete rejection of the traditional social and economic order points the way toward a "new" reality; it is suggested that the new home to which the inhabitants of the Casa de Ejercicios Espirituales are to move is symbolic of the new social and economic systems which must replace the decadent past. (p. 115)

As is so often the case with the contemporary Latin American novel, the work itself takes on life and rushes forward spontaneously to ends not originally envisioned by its creator.... Donoso in no instance seeks to present his protagonists as single psychological unities. His statement, "... soy una persona y soy treinta" [I am one person and I am thirty], clarifies the reasoning behind the multiplicity of characters in this work.... (p. 116)

> *Harley D. Oberhelman, "José Donoso and the 'Nueva Narrativa',"* in Revista de Estudios Hispánicos, *January, 1975, pp. 107-17.*

RICHARD J. CALLAN

Two of the finest short stories by the Chilean novelist José Donoso ..., "Paseo" and "Santelices," deal with humdrum characters whose quiet lives are disrupted when they develop a peculiar fascination with animals. There is no direct commentary to interpret the characters' outlandish behavior, however, nor to indicate to what extent it might be realistically credible. (p. 115)

The narrator of "Paseo" tells of the personality change that took place in his aunt, a rigid, orderly spinster, wholly devoted to the well-being of her three brothers, whose housekeeper she was. Suddenly forsaking the domestic ritual of a lifetime, she took to wandering around the streets until one night she disappeared and was never heard from again. No motive is given for this transformation save that a strange little alley dog had intruded into her life and household and then returned to the streets whence it came, taking her along.

Unquestionably, the sight of the dog shivering in a doorway one rainy morning had shaken Matilde, touching some dormant or unsuspected emotion. The wretched animal, wounded, abject, and disfigured by multiple crossbreedings, epitomized everything that she most abhorred and avoided, everything that she was not. . . . It is possible that as she looked into the eyes of the little bitch, Matilde perceived her own face, her inferior, animal face, staring back at her from the other side of consciousness. (pp. 115-16)

[Matilde's] existence, just as her brothers', was limited to the world of Logos, hence her intolerance for weakness, inferiority, uncleanliness. Moved as if by some perverse consistency, she spurned or ignored whatever pertained to the world of Eros: "mysterio" . . . [mystery], "magia" . . . [magic], "lo fortuito" . . . [the unexpected], "desperfectos" . . . [imperfection, the absurd]. All these related words and concepts, with their opposites, are repeated throughout the text, establishing a marked dichotomy between order and chaos, between consciousness and the unconscious, and underscoring the thematic polarity of the story and the archetypal objective it implies: the reconciliation of opposites for a more balanced life. All of which ties in with Donoso's love of symmetry and his refusal to recognize any distinction between opposites in the psychological sense—there being, in his view, no constancy of comportment, no unity of personality. Like Jung, he sees the human psyche as a potential totality, a multifaced whole, whose every mark and attribute includes its contrary. For Jung, this potential wholeness can be realized in proportion as the unknown opposites are brought to consciousness. This is my understanding of Donoso's "obsession" (his word) with demolishing the so-called psychic unity of man—the myth that one is always the same person. In "Paseo," as we shall see, Matilde comes to realize in an instinctive manner the wholly reversed view of herself (what Jung calls the Shadow). Hence the symmetry of the tale. (pp. 116-17)

Equally curious, although seemingly secondary [to the story of Matilde], is the story of the narrator, that is, the nameless adult from whose perspective these childhood memories are recalled. José Donoso finds the question of point of view intriguing: . . . "[point of view is the great element for exploring, and making, and remaking, and unmaking the writing of a novel]."

In "Paseo" we see a boy whose mother had died and who was growing up in a cold and colorless household. The whole world of Eros was out of his reach, although he longed for it. He wished his aunt would show affection for him, but he always felt he was peripheral to her life. . . . [He felt] the pull of the unknown: the night of Matilde's first walk he sat in the library . . . "[listening, anxiously listening to the far off sound of a ship, and to the rumble of the unknown city, terrible yet desired, spread out under the stars]." The sea, the city, night, adventure, the unknown— all of these function here as symbols of the unconscious, which is at once fearsome and desirable because it is the font of life and renewal. The boy stayed on in that constrictive house; and while the upheaval in Matilde's life seemed

horrifying to him, what was really horrifying was the brothers' inability to break out of their shell. If as an adult he thinks it was best that she died after having disappeared, we can surmise that the deadly influence of those three men turned the nephew into a replica of themselves.

But Donoso has given his tale yet another flip and thrown doubt on the fidelity of the narrator's recollections: . . . "[perhaps my imagination and my memory betray me]." As Donoso was saying, point of view makes and remakes and unmakes the text. Nevertheless, if these dramatic events are products of the narrator's imagination, and this story is his, not Matilde's, the end result is still the same because it reveals *his* rejection of the Dionysiac principle: the sclerosis of consciousness is then his own, and all the rest projection.

In "Santelices" the point of view is that of the protagonist (although presented in the third person), but here the protagonist suffers from delusions. Santelices is a timorous filing clerk who lives in a rooming house and collects pictures of wild animals of the cat family. The cruel and menacing beauty of these beasts fills him with excitement. His collection is kept secret, especially from his landlady, Bertita, but on the day the story begins this nosey and tyrannical woman finds it and burns it in a rage. . . . (pp. 119-20)

Meanwhile, from his office window, Santelices has been observing a girl in a patio five flights down. He sees her every day playing with a cat, and later with five or six new kittens. His long-distance friendship with her (wholly one-sided) gives him a sense of security and fortitude. Now he feels able to stand up to Bertita, whose ingratiating ways are wearing thin, and he even taunts her. Finally, he tells her a fib about having found a better place to stay and his intention to leave her, which causes her to break into tears. Later that night, following a premonition, he hurries back to his office, looks out the window, and he sees that the girl is now surrounded by panthers and jaguars and tigers, and that she is waiting for him to save her. Without fear or hesitation, he climbs onto the sill and jumps to her rescue.

The main plot, concerning the nameless girl and her cats, is a clear instance of the archetypal hero's dragon fight: she is the captive princess awaiting deliverance from monsters. Understood psychologically, this myth represents the struggle to liberate consciousness from the domination of the unconscious. The drawback for Santelices is, of course, the disastrous outcome which contradicts and seemingly disproves this interpretation of the myth. (p. 120)

After Bertita's blowup, Santelices sits in his office all day trying to put off the moment when he will have to return to his room and find that he has nothing left. The pathos of his destitution is surprisingly moving at any level. Loss of ego is an archetypal and temporary experience in puberty, but it remains to be seen if Santelices' loss is definitive. A transference has immediately taken place from his destroyed photographs to the cats in the patio. These, too, increase in number and size, and yet this repetition is really of secondary importance, because a precious new ingredient has been introduced: the girl as friend and inspirer (whether or not she is a fantasy) points to a great advance over Santelices' previous state, although there is no basis for this progress (since he has fled without protest from Bertita). It is the girl, the Anima, who moves him to conquer the monster of the unconscious at home (Bertita) and to attempt to duplicate his valiant deed in the patio. But, of course, all the minutiae of the heroic dragon fight, with which the author fondly plies us, lead to naught. Santelices, who presumably could be stabilizing his hold on consciousness by transpersonal means, is in fact the victim of a fatal hallucination. (pp. 121-22)

[The] basic similarity between the two stories is that both protagonists experience an instinctual drive toward fulfillment. Matilde submits to it, having learned to recognize a power beyond her control, and literally abandons her former one-sided way of life. Santelices, weaker and immature, surrenders to the fascination of the unconscious images, but is overwhelmed by them and carried helplessly by their impetus to his destruction. (p. 122)

> *Richard J. Callan, "Animals as Mana Figures in José Donoso's 'Paseo' and 'Santelices'," in* Essays in Literature *(copyright 1975 by Western Illinois University), Spring, 1975, pp. 115-23.*

MARTIN S. STABB

Donoso himself considers the *El obsceno pájaro* "una cosa ya completamente barroca" [a completely baroque thing]. Deeply enmeshed within this narrative *tour de force* and central to the intent of the novel is the erotic motif—or cluster of motifs. As in much of Donoso's work, the force of the theme derives from a kind of kinetic discharge between opposite poles: youth-age, wealth-poverty, power-impotence, etc. Moreover, his concept of literary character . . . transforms the inhabitants of his books into masks, into *personae*, as this term is understood in classical drama. As such they become the vehicles through which the "gods" read elemental forces—express themselves. A special feature of this technique is that the masks are changed with such vertiginous frequency that instead of characters possessing normal identities we have mere nuclei, beings who serve as focal points for the author's thematic concentration. . . . [For] Donoso sex does [in the words of Susan Sontag] "annihilate character," but this is precisely what he wishes to do in a novel such as *El obsceno pájaro*. Similarly time, disease, and the fear of death annihilate character.

The central figure of the work, "Mudito," is clearly a study in annihilation, and much of what destroys him is essentially erotic in nature. . . . [The] violent transformations from infantilism to old age, from *machismo* to femininity demonstrate perfectly Donoso's penchant for the literary mask as opposed to the integrated traditional character of earlier fiction.

The structural symmetries that abound in the *Obsceno pájaro* are well illustrated by a comparison of the Mudito masks with their feminine counterparts. Just as Jerónimo, Humberto, Mudito and the "Giant" are related personae, Inés, Jerónimo's barren (?) wife, Iris, the oversexed vulgar adolescent, Peta Ponce, the witchlike crone and the ever-present "yellow bitch," (perhaps Peta's "familiar"), are symbiotically intertwined. These figures, moreover, further underscore the pervasive sexuality of the novel. (pp. 173-74)

Finally, it appears that all these symmetrically ordered masks can be arranged in the form of a triad; the Humberto-Mudito-Jerónimo personae at one point, the Inés-Iris-Peta Ponce personae at another, and at the third, the product of the two, The Monster, alias "the baby" or

simply "Boy." If one accepts this structural scheme for the novel, then it becomes clear that the emphasis on *lo monstruoso*, which some readers of the work consider to be its central theme, is meaningful only as a synthesis, or focal point of the work's essentially erotic elements. . . .

[In Donoso's case] the degree to which Eros affects characterization, shapes structure, and provides a unifying matrix for the new novel is unprecedented by comparison with earlier Spanish American fiction. (p. 176)

[A] writer such as Donoso fills his novels with a rich assortment of unreal personages who may be mutilated, ambiguous, multi-layered, hyperdeveloped in some respects, and atrophied in others. All aspects of their being, and especially their sexuality, reveal that they exist as purely literary entities, and that the author is not attempting to give us exact portraits of real people. (pp. 176-77)

Donoso neither applauds sex nor views it as nature's remedy to cure mankind of its ills. On the contrary, for him the erotic is a dark force, tinged with the satanic and leading only to obsessive desire and a fruitless quest for pleasure or release. He seems to say that although we may never meet a Mudito or an Iris Mateluna we know that behind the masks of everyday existence there lurks a world of elemental fear, of implacable destructive power, of crippling impotence and of gnawing, unsatisfied lust. In short, the erotic is clearly a defining characteristic of that *obscene* night-bird chattering in the "unsubdued forest" so menacingly described by Henry James Sr. in the novel's epigraph. (p. 177)

> *Martin S. Stabb, "The Erotic Mask: Notes on Donoso and the New Novel," in* Symposium *(copyright © 1976 by Syracuse University Press), Summer, 1976, pp. 170-77.*

JOHN CAVIGLIA

[In Donoso's] early fiction, a limpid style and straightforward narrative technique provide the matrix for the portrayal of complex characters, who are often, and variously, obsessed: a fat man who dances himself to death, a youth whose ambition is to do nothing but sleep, a transvestite who earns his keep by doing flamenco dances in drag, and so on. . . . [Critics] widely proclaimed the largely traditional nature of his narrative. The delirious and intractable complexity of his most recent novel, *El obsceno pájaro de la noche*, is consequently all the more startling, for this is clearly a work intended to confound the reader. The narratorial voice, adrift in time and space, confuses past and present, fuses distinct characters, and proliferates events with a manic inventiveness that utterly disregards verisimilitude. . . .

[A] disjunctive leap from tradition to monstrosity is itself internalized in the themes and structures of *El obsceno pájaro;* in the last analysis this work belongs to that characteristically modern variety of fiction which, in presenting the *Bildung* of its author, defines the preconditions of its own existence as well as the necessities of its nature. By reflecting upon the revolution that engendered it, the novel reflects upon itself. The principal character is a would-be author, Humberto Peñaloza, who begins his career in the attempt to identify with the traditions of his society, only to reject them; eventually he ends in nightmarish isolation as a servant of retired servants in a former convent (la Casa), where he is ultimately sewn into burlap bags and transformed into that physical correlative of solipsism, the Imbunche [a creature invented by Donoso as a nonce symbol for this novel]. It is there, in squalor and confinement, that he deliriously evokes his former life. . . . *El obsceno pájaro* is both process and end product. The process is the tale itself, which presents, in parallel, the *Bildung* of the author and the birth of a monstrous son to the traditionalist Jerónimo Ascoitía. The end product—the recall, representation, and deformation of that process, that is to say, the novel— is analogically as monstrous as that child. Humberto (later called Mudito, the mute one) imagines his past, his prospects as a young man, in a retrospective present whose disillusionment shatters the author's own image as if reflected on broken water. (p. 33)

Humberto's luckless quest for personal existence threads the labyrinth of *El obsceno pájaro;* it has two initial stages, which one might call sociological and psychological. In the first, Humberto considers himself a member of society, existing to the degree that he incarnates its norms and traditions. At this stage his existence *is* his normality, his likeness to others; it follows that, insofar as he is unique, he is both indefinable and ephemeral, a shifting, shadowy thing. In the second stage, after the abandonment of society, Humberto turns to self-reflection and feels that he exists to the degree that his many notions of himself—his selves— are like one another. In consequence, he perceives inner difference as alienation. Donoso's character therefore becomes a kind of interface between an outer (sociological) and an inner (psychological) dimension. In both directions, he confronts dramas of difference and identity that have the same paradoxical structure; in both, the notion of personal existence is assimilated to that of likeness, of identity. We have arrived at the premises that are successively explored in *El obsceno pájaro:* to be is to be like others and to be like oneself. The existential dilemma posed by these assumptions is essentially taxonomic, for it is based on the relationship of concrete singularities to the generalizations that describe their likeness to other members of a class; that is to say, Humberto is like others and like himself only at a relatively high level of abstraction. Consequently, the X equals Y of Donoso's paradox applies to the genus or species and is not a concrete equation; it is made possible only by virtue of ignoring uniqueness. It is, however, precisely the uniqueness of the singular that makes it necessary that X not equal Y. . . . These premises granted, Humberto is indeed in a quandary, for existence, which is likeness, presents itself to him as abstraction, as virtual nonexistence. And his anguished predicament is exacerbated by Donoso, who not only contrives to have him opt between the singular and the norm but further exaggerates these possibilities for existence into the extremes represented by the monster and the mask. Humberto must therefore choose between normality and aberration run rampant. (p. 34)

The dominant obsession of Humberto Peñaloza, like that of his father before him, is ['that impassable barrier that separates us from the possibility of being someone']; as his desires become self-conscious in his youth, they will be structured by a discontinuity, symbolized by a vertical, architectural surface. This first obstacle is a class barrier. . . .

In *El obsceno pájaro* social identity is most often represented by a mask, a persona. In one example of many,

Humberto says to his father: . . . '. . . I swear to you that I shall be someone, that in place of this sad, featureless face of the Peñalozas I'll acquire a magnificent mask, an enormous, luminous, smiling, well-defined face, which everyone will have to admire.' . . . His desire takes on mock-heroic form in the Gigante, an enormous, grotesque pasteboard mask worn by a man who distributes advertisements. This artifact, which towers over the first third of the novel, is both imposing and empty. Any nobody can slip it on to acquire a presence larger than life. Its face can give any nobody definition, but in turn it masks whatever individuality the wearer might have. The containing form, like a dictionary definition, includes every individual it defines, but only by virtue of blotting out singular characteristics. By implication, social visibility entails a renunciation of the self; the visible man is identified with his class. (p. 35)

In *El obsceno pájaro* clothing plays a symbolic role not unlike that of the mask; it also conceals the self with fabric cut to patterns informed by both tradition and norm. . . .

El obsceno pájaro organizes itself about a space: a mask, a wall, a surface that appears both normal and harmonious from the outside, but only by virtue of concealing inner abnormalities. Humberto Peñaloza is privileged not only to penetrate the facade and become a witness to the interior but also in a sense to be its keeper, for he is put in charge of the Rinconada. (p. 36)

Humberto . . . is painfully cognizant of the hollowness of masks, which reduce existence to an exterior surface. From the time of the Gigante's end, Humberto turns with increased and hopeless anguish to the possibilities of identity offered, not by exteriors, but by what is behind faces and facades. From this point in the novel society at large, the phenomenal and normal world, becomes virtually inaccessible to the narrator; and we pass from a reality typified by an interior invisible behind a wall to one that almost hermetically excludes outsides. In Donoso, walls are formidable and nearly perfect barriers between mutually exclusive worlds. (p. 37)

As a normal man who has abandoned the normal world, Humberto is a fitting keeper for the Rinconada. Like Mudito, he is a kind of turnkey controlling access to the outside world. Indeed, he exists at the juncture of two worlds; he looks out, looks in, and belongs neither out nor in. He is the excluded interface. . . . Donoso has executed a clever about-face upon the reader, for as it turns out, both the world without and the world within are void—the former of uniqueness, the latter of normality. The reality upon either side of the walls of the Rinconada defines and contains the absence of the other. Humberto, normal to those outside, monstrous to those inside, can be identified with those walls to which he has the key; he faces upon two realities defined as absences, that is, as excluding each other. Humberto is consequently an interface between voids.

Needless to say, in *El obsceno pájaro* the outside world is not so normal or the Rinconada so monstrous as this presentation would make it seem. They are the abstracted extremes of those modes of being toward which Humberto successively tends. In due course, the second tropism manifests itself in the Rinconada, where he finds that he is slowly and inexorably being invaded by monstrosity. . . . The kind of definition provided by norms is . . . decomposed into an indefinable multiplicity. Characteristically,

Humberto becomes (or imagines that he becomes) not a monster but, rather, many monsters. He loses (or imagines that he loses) his normal identity, without attaining singularity. In other words, the abandonment of the norm, as seen from his obsessive perspective, leads not to unique individuality but to disintegration and chaos. In *El obsceno pájaro* the first alternative to existence as a public figure, a hollow man, is the invasion of the inner man by forces that multiply his image in a nightmare of mutation and metamorphosis. (pp. 37-8)

[His flight from the Rinconada] concludes the second stage of Humberto's search for personal existence. He enters the Casa. His father and Jerónimo, who personifies all the father wished for in Humberto, are abandoned. From the time that the Gigante's head is destroyed, the narrator addresses himself to the Madre Benita. In effect, he abandons the masculine principles of social harmony, normality, and public visibility, as well as monstrosity, its demonic inversion, to adopt new principles altogether, which are associated with the feminine. (p. 38)

[In the Casa, the] chattering crones translate the past as well as the present into language. Their personal memories imperceptibly merge with those of their oral tradition to produce a linguistic world with long perspectives on the past, perspectives that are confused since their recreation is not exact. The imprecisions of memory, the decay of facts in oral transmission, the willful embroidering upon events too tame or too often repeated to be interesting—all conspire to blur the distinction between history and invention. (pp. 39-40)

Unlike the garrulous old women, [Mudito] supposedly does not speak. But he is not kept from generating language in some fashion, for he is the narrator of the novel. And there is a more important difference in Mudito; he is conscious of the relation of language and being. The old women—petty greed and squabbling aside—are satisfied with what they are and are not. They do not reflect on the language that babbles through them. Mudito does not assume, as they do, the unison of words and things. He is all too painfully aware of the fragmentation and elaboration of facts that take place in the Casa. In short, he knows that words are nothing in themselves and that beings who exist in language, as these old women do, are nothing. And it is this knowledge that will take on the reality of fiction, as he becomes weaker and more wizened, progressing toward the culmination of effacement in that demonic womb the Imbunche. (pp. 40-1)

As the cocoon grows and tightens about him, his capacity for creation grows in proportion. Finally, tightly sewn in burlap, an Imbunche, he is absolutely sealed, absolutely a world to himself, tattered rags about a hoard of garbage. And we can imagine him, paradoxically, finally capable of authorship.

The need for this autistic end is rooted deep in the novel. In one sense, the Imbunche is a womb. Mudito recapitulates his life in reverse in order to return to it, growing younger as he ages, and ultimately becoming a newborn. In this return he is living out a lasting fascination with the procreative process embodied in Iris, whom he obsessively sees as little more than an ambulant womb. (p. 41)

What Mudito creates in his version of Iris is a model for a kind of creativity that remains implicit: authorship. And the womb must be rejected as its correlative—even when parthenogenesis is granted—for two important reasons. The womb both creates a being and expels it into the world. The Imbunche, on the other hand, excludes the world and, in including only Mudito, includes nothing. Or rather, the Imbunche includes Mudito become language, for when the Imbunche is opened, it yields only foul rags, tattered paper, castoffs such as the former servants hoard, counterparts of the *idée reçue*. Humberto's *Bildung* (perhaps more suitably an *Untergang*) is a process that, having explored the possibilities of existence in society and the psyche, finally substitutes language for existence itself. As a model for literature, the Imbunche signifies the absence of both world and author from the work; the language that supplants Mudito succeeds him as the interface between voids. And since language must have a source and referent to be language, the novel concludes by figuring forth its own annihilation.

El obsceno pájaro means to deny its source and referent and therefore, as a verbal construct, its own existence. The Imbunche, the symbol of that annihilation, represents a figure exhausted by language, and that language, in turn, is exhausted by the possibilities of retrospect. It is fitting that this creature, whose only powers lie in recall and revision, comes into being at the novel's conclusion, for having no prospects and no contact with the world, he could never provide the substance for narrative. His peculiar mode of consciousness, however, suffuses the novel in attenuated form. From the perspective of *El obsceno pájaro*'s conclusion one discovers that retrospect is much more than a function of the novel's end and that hindsight indeed informs the structure of the work. Embedded in the mutations and permutations of this apparently untidy novel, there is a remarkably precise morphology of memory. . . . We note that, in terms of narrative sequence, the future is prologue to the past and that, in terms of chronology, Mudito provides a perspective on the Rinconada from the Casa. We can conclude that *El obsceno pájaro*, through recall and recreation, carefully jumbles the progression of time in such a way that recall itself is made into a structural, synchronic constant of the novel. Plotting the novel opens a space in the tightly woven surface of the text, across which the work contemplates itself, a space that becomes distinctly visible only from the work's conclusion. The function of such fiction is to lead the reader to the final realization that the end has been present from the beginning, that the distance, the perspective of the end, is the distance and perspective of the narrator from the start. Such a novel conceals the distance, tangling time with time with such diabolic enthusiasm that one could think the knot forever raveled. But ironically, the confusions are themselves a function of the distance and a key to its meaning, for it is the anguished awareness of a disintegration of the self that is the product of the *Bildung*, and it is this awareness that decomposes the chronological simplicities of the narrator's personal history. And the reader, once he is aware of the presence and meaning of the distance, can proceed to take its measure. The perspective of retrospect, which enabled the narrator to encode the significance of his *Bildung* as confusion, enables the reader to decode that message in analysis. (pp. 41-3)

The devolution of being that Humberto experiences passes from a social to a psychological state, from external norms to internal chaos. Mudito makes the process into a precondition for authorship by adding a third stage, in which the distance from the self is memory and ultimately narrative invention. We have arrived at the structure of an author's *Bildung* that equates synchronic and diachronic distance. The coming into awareness of oneself is the diachronic image, and it is reflected upon synchronically by a form of the final stage of consciousness. Such authorship is made possible by the end, which originates and structures the vehicle for the image. The irony of the end, however, is so radical that it must be curbed to enable it to recreate the naïve image of youth, since the alternative to that innocent belief in norms, as we have seen, is chaos. The author, in other words, cannot portray his present self, for he has come to see himself as undefinable. He can no longer be the content of a work, but only its vehicle. (p. 44)

El obsceno pájaro maintains a precarious balance between its desire to come into being (projection of the self as other, as norm) and its desire to undo itself (rejection of the self as other, as norm). In the last analysis the monster is a fitting image for the novel, as a figure of that ambivalence. To the degree that it is normal, a monster is both viable and recognizable; it is always a monstrous something, a product of an order that it does not absolutely violate. But a monster is defined as deviating. Its superficial aberrations are sustained by the deeper constraints of its species, which abnormality threatens but cannot destroy without itself suffering destruction. A novel of this genre proposes to communicate through its familiarity but sabotages that process through its deliberate strangeness. *El obsceno pájaro* is normal only that it may exist. Its aberrations are the relative manifestations of a strangeness that is desired as absolute. With an eye to the etymology of "monster," one could say that the novel is demonstrous: it points out, in the work, the impossible absence of all but the work itself. (p. 45)

> John Caviglia, "Tradition and Monstrosity in 'El obsceno pájaro de la noche'," in *PMLA, 93* (copyright © 1978 by the Modern Language Association of America; reprinted by permission of the Modern Language Association of America), January, 1978, pp. 33-45.

*   *   *

DOS PASSOS, John   1896-1970

An American novelist, essayist, poet, and journalist, Dos Passos is best known for his sociopolitical novels of pre-World War II America. His central concerns are social injustices, the exploitation of the working class, and the injurious emphasis on materialism in American society. Detail and realism are important elements in Dos Passos's work, often emphasized through such innovative means as his "newsreel" and "camera eye" techniques, and the inclusion of bits of biography. Strongly political, Dos Passos moved from his early, left-wing revolutionary philosophy to a later conservatism. The *U.S.A.* trilogy is considered to be his masterpiece. (See also CLC, Vols. 1, 4, 8, and *Contemporary Authors*, Vols. 1-4, rev. ed.; obituary, Vols. 29-32, rev. ed.)

F. R. LEAVIS

After *Manhattan Transfer* (1927) one remembered the name of John Dos Passos. After *The Forty-second Parallel* one looked eagerly forward to the succeeding members of the trilogy (for something of that order seemed to be promised) in the conviction that we had here a work demanding serious attention as no other appearing under the head of the novel during the past two or three years had done. *Nineteen-nineteen* is a challenge to justify the conviction.

The Forty-second Parallel established Mr. Dos Passos as an unusually serious artist—serious with the seriousness that expresses itself in the propagandist spirit. . . . [He] cannot be interested in individuals without consciously relating them to the society and the civilisation that make the individual life possible. (p. 102)

The undertaking involves a peculiar technical problem, one that none of the methods customarily associated with the novel will meet. No amount of enthusiasm for collective humanity will dispose of the fact that it is only in individuals that humanity lives, that only in the individual focus does consciousness function, that only individuals enjoy and suffer; and the problem is to suggest that multitudinous impersonality of the ant-heap through individual cases that, without much development, interest us as such. *Manhattan Transfer* represents a sufficient degree of success. It is of the essence of Mr. Dos Passos' method here—and of his vision of modern life—that of no one of his swirl of "cases" do we feel that it might profitably be developed into a separate novel; and yet we are interested enough. Here we have them in poignant individuality, a representative assortment of average men and women, engaged in the "pursuit of happiness"—a pursuit sanctioned by the Constitution, but, of its very nature, and by the very conditions of the civilisation to which they belong, vain. (p. 103)

Manhattan Transfer ends with Jimmy Herf (the character to whom the author seems closest) walking, with an air of symbolic finality, out of New York. *The Forty-second Parallel* gives us the America into which he walks—a large undertaking, which calls for some modification of technique. The representative lives stand out more and are given less in episode-dialogue and more in consecutive narrative; narrative admirably managed in *tempo*, and varied dramatically in idiom with the chief actor. The "Newsreels" interspersed at intervals are a new device, their function being by means of newspaper-clippings and the like, in ironical medley, to establish the background of the contemporary public world. Moreover, also at intervals, there are lives, admirably compressed and stylised in what might be called prose-poems, of the makers, the heroes, the great men, the public figures, of American civilisation. Thus Mr. Dos Passos seeks to provide something corresponding to the symbolic figures of a national epic or saga. (pp. 103-04)

In the close of *The Forty-second Parallel* we see America welcoming an escape from . . . "getting ahead," a "meaning" with which to exorcise the void, in the War. *Nineteen-nineteen* gives us the War. The second part of the trilogy is decidedly less lively than the first. For one thing, the monotony of this world without religion, morality, art or culture is here, perhaps inevitably, emphasised. And this leads us to the more general question: What is lacking in the work as a whole (so far as we have it)?—why, in spite of its complete and rare seriousness, does it fall so decidedly short of being great? (p. 105)

The artistic shortcomings of Mr. Dos Passos' most ambitious work (which is not, like *Manhattan Transfer*, held together by the topographical limits of the setting) might . . . be, not merely excused as inevitable, but extolled as propagandist virtues: they are necessary to a work that exhibits the decay of capitalistic society. (p. 106)

[The] shortcomings of the work both as art and propaganda are related to a certain insufficiency in it when it is considered as an expression of personality (which on any theory a work of art must in some sense be). It is more than a superficial analogy when the technique is likened to that of the film. The author might be said to conceive his function as selective photography and "montage." That this method does not admit sufficiently of the presence of the artist's personal consciousness the device called "The Camera Eye" seems to recognise—it at any rate seems to do little else. What this judgment amounts to is that the work does not express an adequate realisation of the issues it offers to deal with.

How far the defect is due to the method, and how far it lies in the consciousness behind the method, one cannot presume to determine. But Mr. Dos Passos, though he exhibits so overwhelmingly the results of disintegration and decay, shows nothing like an adequate awareness of—or concern for—what has been lost. (p. 107)

It seems to me the more one sympathises with his propagandist intention, the more should one be concerned to stress what is lacking in his presentment of it. To hope that, if the mechanics of civilisation (so to speak) are perfected, the other problems (those which Mr. Dos Passos is mainly preoccupied with) will solve themselves, is vain: "you know," says someone in *Nineteen-nineteen*, "the kind of feeling when everything you've wanted crumbles in your fingers as you grasp it." Men and women might, of course, find happiness—or release from unhappiness—as perfect accessory machines. But that is hardly a hope for a propagandist to offer. (pp. 109-10)

> *F. R. Leavis, "John Dos Passos (1932)," in his For Continuity, The Minority Press, 1933 (and reprinted by Books for Libraries Press, 1968), pp. 102-10.*

JEAN-PAUL SARTRE

A novel is a mirror. So everyone says. But what is meant by *reading* a novel? It means, I think, jumping into the mirror. You suddenly find yourself on the other side of the glass, among people and objects that have a familiar look. But they merely look familiar. We have never really seen them. The things of our world have, in turn, become outside reflections. You close the book, step over the edge of the mirror and return to this honest-to-goodness world, and you find furniture, gardens and people who have nothing to say to you. The mirror that closed behind you reflects them peacefully, and now you would swear that art is a reflection. There are clever people who go so far as to talk of distorting mirrors.

Dos Passos very consciously uses this absurd and insistent illusion to impel us to revolt. He had done everything possible to make his novel seem a mere reflection. He has even donned the garb of populism. The reason is that his art is not gratuitous; he wants to prove something. But observe what a curious aim he has. He wants to show us this world, our own—to *show* it only, without explanations or comment. . . . We recognize immediately the sad abundance of these untragic lives. They are our own lives, these innumerable, planned, botched, immediately forgotten and constantly renewed adventures that slip by without leaving a trace, without involving anyone, until the time when one of them, no different from any of the others, suddenly, as if

through some clumsy trickery, sickens a man for good and throws a mechanism out of gear.

Now, it is by depicting, as we ourselves might depict, these too familiar appearances with which we all put up that Dos Passos makes them unbearable. (pp. 61-2)

Dos Passos' hate, despair and lofty contempt are real. But that is precisely why his world is not real; it is a created object. I know of none—not even Faulkner's or Kafka's—in which the art is greater or better hidden. I know of none that is more precious, more touching or closer to us. This is because he takes his material from our world. And yet, there is no stranger or more distant world. Dos Passos has invented only one thing, an art of story-telling. But that is enough to create a universe. . . .

Dos Passos' time is his own creation; it is neither fictional nor narrative. It is rather, if you like, historical time. (p. 62)

The fictional event is a nameless presence; there is nothing one can say about it, for it develops. . . . In Dos Passos, the things that happen are named first, and then the dice are cast, as they are in our memories. . . .

The facts are clearly outlined; they are ready for *thinking about*. But Dos Passos never thinks them. Not for an instant does the order of causality betray itself in chronological order. There is no narrative, but rather the jerky unreeling of a rough and uneven memory, which sums up a period of several years in a few words only to dwell languidly over a minute fact. Like our real memories, it is a jumble of miniatures and frescoes. There is relief enough, but it is cunningly scattered at random. One step further would give us the famous idiot's monologue in *The Sound and the Fury*. But that would still involve intellectualizing, suggesting an explanation in terms of the irrational, suggesting a Freudian order beneath this disorder. Dos Passos stops just in time. As a result of this, past things retain a flavour of the present; they still remain, in their exile, what they once were, inexplicable tumults of colour, sound and passion. Each event is irreducible, a gleaming and solitary *thing* that does not flow from anything else, but suddenly arises to join other things. For Dos Passos, narrating means adding. This accounts for the slack air of his style. (p. 63)

Passions and gestures are also things. Proust analysed them, related them to former states and thereby made them inevitable. Dos Passos wants to retain only their factual nature. . . . Dos Passos imposes upon us . . . the unpleasant impression of an indeterminacy of detail. Acts, emotions and ideas suddenly settle within a character, make themselves at home and then disappear without his having much to say in the matter. You cannot say he submits to them. He experiences them. There seems to be no law governing their appearance.

Nevertheless, they once did exist. This lawless past is irremediable. Dos Passos has purposely chosen the perspective of history to tell a story. He wants to make us feel that the stakes are down. In *Man's Hope*, Malraux says, more or less, that "the tragic thing about death is that it transforms life into a destiny." With the opening lines of his book, Dos Passos settles down into death. The lives he tells about are all closed in on themselves. . . . We constantly have the feeling that these vague, human lives are destinies. . . . [Beneath] the violent colours of these beautiful, motley objects that Dos Passos presents there is something petrified. Their significance is fixed. Close your eyes and try to remember your own life, try to remember it *that way;* you will stifle. It is this unrelieved stifling that Dos Passos wanted to express. In capitalist society, men do not have lives, they have only destinies. He never says this, but he makes it felt throughout. He expresses it discreetly, cautiously, until we feel like smashing our destinies. We have become rebels; he has achieved his purpose. (pp. 64-5)

[The] narrator often ceases to coincide completely with the hero. The hero could not quite have said what he does say, but you feel a discreet complicity between them. The narrator relates from the outside what the hero would have wanted him to relate. By means of this complicity, Dos Passos, without warning us, has us make the transition he was after. We suddenly find ourselves inside a horrible memory whose every recollection makes us uneasy, a bewildering memory that is no longer that of either the characters or the author. (pp. 65-6)

Dos Passos reports all his characters' utterances to us in the style of a statement to the Press. Their words are thereby cut off from thought, and become pure utterances, simple reactions that must be registered as such, in the behaviourist style upon which Dos Passos draws when it suits him to do so. But, at the same time, the utterance takes on a social importance; it is inviolable, it becomes a maxim.... Dos Passos makes a pretence of presenting gestures as pure events, as mere exteriors, as free, animal movements. But this is only appearance. Actually, in relating them, he adopts the point of view of the chorus, of public opinion. (pp. 66-7)

In order to understand the words, in order to make sense out of the paragraphs, I first have to adopt his point of view. I have to play the role of the obliging chorus. This consciousness exists only through me; without me there would be nothing but black spots on white paper. But even while I *am* this collective consciousness, I want to wrench away from it, to see it from the judge's point of view, that is, to get free of myself. This is the source of the shame and uneasiness with which Dos Passos knows how to fill the reader. I am a reluctant accomplice (though I am not even sure that I am reluctant), creating and rejecting social taboos. I am, deep in my heart, a revolutionary again, an unwilling one.

In return, how I hate Dos Passos' men! I am given a fleeting glimpse of their minds, just enough to see that they are living animals. Then, they begin to unwind their endless tissue of ritual statements and sacred gestures. For them, there is no break between inside and outside, between body and consciousness, but only between the stammerings of an individual's timid, intermittent, fumbling thinking and the messy world of collective representations. What a simple process this is, and how effective! ... [Dos Passos] can give all his attention to rendering a single life's special character. Each of his characters is unique; what happens to him could happen to no one else. What does it matter, since Society has marked him more deeply than could any special circumstance, since *he is* Society? Thus, we get a glimpse of an order beyond the accidents of fate or the contingency of detail.... (pp. 67-8)

Dos Passos' man is a hybrid creature, an interior-exterior being. We go on living with him and within him, with his vacillating, individual consciousness, when suddenly it

wavers, weakens, and is diluted in the collective consciousness. We follow it up to that point and suddenly, before we notice, we are on the outside. The man behind the looking-glass is a strange, contemptible, fascinating creature. Dos Passos knows how to use this constant shifting to fine effect. . . .

Dos Passos' world—like those of Faulkner, Kafka and Stendhal—is impossible because it is contradictory. But therein lies its beauty. Beauty is a veiled contradiction. I regard Dos Passos as the greatest writer of our time. (p. 69)

> *Jean-Paul Sartre, "John Dos Passos and '1919'" (1947), in his* Literary and Philosophical Essays, *translated by Annette Michelson (copyright © 1955 by Rider & Company; reprinted by permission of Hutchinson Publishing Group Ltd.), Rider, 1955 (and reprinted in* John Dos Passos: A Collection of Critical Essays, *edited by Andrew Hook, Prentice-Hall, Inc., 1974, pp. 61-9).*

HERBERT MARSHALL McLUHAN

The reader of Dos Passos . . . is not required to have much more reading agility than the reader of the daily press. Nor does Dos Passos make many more serious demands than a good movie. And this is said not to belittle an excellent writer who has much to offer, but to draw attention to the extreme simplification to which Dos Passos has submitted the early work of James Joyce. *Three Soldiers* (1921), *Manhattan Transfer* (1925) and *U. S. A.* (1930-36) would not exist in their present form but for the *Portrait of the Artist as a Young Man, Dubliners* and *Ulysses.* It is as a slightly super-realist that Dos Passos has viewed and adapted the work of Joyce in his own work. (pp. 148-49)

From [the imagists Dos Passos] learned much that has continuously affected his practice. Their romantic tapestries and static contemplation of the ornate panorama of existence have always held him in spite of his desire to be a romantic of action. (p. 149)

[In] recent decades the artist has come to be the only critical spectator of society. He demands and confers the heightened significance in ordinary existence which is hostile to any self-extinction in the collective consciousness. So that when the balance is lost between individual responsibility and mass solidarity, the artist automatically moves to the side of the individual. With equal inevitability, the less resourceful man, faced with the perplexities of planned social disorder, walks deeper into the collective sleep that makes that chaos bearable to him. The work of Dos Passos is almost wholly concerned with presenting this situation. His people are, typically, victims of a collective trance from which they do not struggle to escape. And if his work fails, it is to the extent that he clings to an alternative dream which has little power to retract the dreamers from their sleep, and even less power to alert the reader to a sense of tragic waste. (pp. 149-50)

Dos Passos is not a thinker who has imposed a conceptual system on his material. Rather, he accepted the most familiar traditions and attitudes as part of the material which his art brings into the range of the reader's vision. It is by the range of his vision and the intensity of his focus that he must receive criticism. (p. 151)

Looking first at the technical means which he employs as a writer, there is the basic imagistic skill in sharpening perception and defining a state of mind with which *Manhattan Transfer* opens:

Three gulls wheel above the broken boxes,
orangerinds, spoiled cabbage heads that
heave between the splintered plank walls,
the green waves spume under the round bow
as the ferry, skidding on the tide, crashes,
gulps the broken water, slides, settles slowly
into the slip.

Many passages of this wry lyricism counterpoint the episodes of the book. The episodes and characters are also features of a landscape to which these lyric chapter overtures give point and tone. The point is readily seized and the tone extends over a very narrow range of emotions: pathos, anger, disgust. But Dos Passos employs the impressionist landscape monotonously because he has never chosen to refract or analyze its components to zone a wide range of emotions. . . . The author is sensitive to the ugliness and misery as things he can see. But he is never prepared to explore the interior landscape which is the wasteland of the human heart. . . . (pp. 151-52)

Dos Passos too often seems to imply that [human] suffering is sordid and unnecessary or that some modification of the environment might free his characters from the doll-mechanism that is their private and collective trap. Seeing nothing inevitable or meaningful in human suffering, he confronts it neither in its comic, intelligible mode, nor in a tragic way. It angers and annoys him as something extraneous.

The difference from Joyce is instructive. For in *Ulysses* the same discontinuous city landscape is also presented by imagistic devices. The episodes are musically arranged to sound concordantly. But Joyce manipulates a continuous parallel at each moment between naturalism and symbolism to render a total spectrum of outer and inner worlds. The past is present not in order to debunk Dublin but to make Dublin representative of the human condition. . . . The most ordinary gesture linked to some immemorial dramatic mask or situation sets reverberating the whole world of the book and flashes intelligibility into long opaque areas of our own experience.

To match Joyce's epiphanies Dos Passos brings only American know-how. . . . Joyce contemplates things for the being that is theirs. Dos Passos shows how they work or behave. (pp. 152-53)

Joyce constantly has his attention on the analogy of being while Dos Passos is registering a personal reaction to society.

It is not a serious criticism of Dos Passos to say that he is not James Joyce. But Joyce is his art master and the critic is obliged to note that Dos Passos has read Joyce not as a greater Flaubert, Rimbaud or Mallarmé, but as it were through the eyes of Whitman and Sandburg, as a greater Zola or Romains. This is negative definition which does not bring into question the competence of Dos Passos or belittle the quality of positive delight he affords. His *U. S. A.* is quite justly established as a classic which brought into a focus for the first time a range of facts and interests that no American had ever been able to master. But it is in the main an ethical and political synthesis that he provides, with the interest intentionally at one level—the only level that interests Dos Passos.

Manhattan Transfer, which corresponds roughly to Joyce's

Dubliners, cuts a cross-section through a set of adult lives in New York. But the city is not envisaged as providing anything more than a phantasmagoric back-drop for their frustrations and defeats. The city is felt as alien, meaningless. Joyce, on the other hand, accepts the city as an extension of human functions, as having a human shape and eliciting the full range of human response which man cannot achieve in any other situation. Within this analogy Joyce's individuals explore their experience in the modes of action and passion, male and female. The stories are grouped according to the expanding awareness of childhood, adolescence, maturity and middle-age. Man, the wanderer within the labyrinthine ways at once of his psyche and of the world, provides an inexhaustible matter for contemplation. Dos Passos seems to have missed this aspect of *Dubliners.* But in *U. S. A.,* while extending his back-drop from the city to the nation, he did make the attempt to relate the expanding scene to the development of one mind from childhood to maturity. That is the function of "Camera Eye." "News-reel" projects the changing environment which acts upon the various characters and corresponds to riffling the back issues of *Life* magazine. (pp. 154-55)

[In *U. S. A.*] the development of political consciousness of the "Camera Eye" persona is not so much parallel with as in contrast to the unfolding landscape of the nation. And this again is close to the way in which the development of Stephen Dedalus in the *Portrait* as a self-dedicated human being runs counter to the mechanisms of the Dublin scene. The author's political and social sense unfolds without comment in the "Camera Eye" sections, with "News-reel" providing the immediate environmental pressures which are felt in different ways by everybody in the book. Both of these devices are successfully controlled to provide those limited effects which he intends. But the insights which lead to these effects are of a familiar and widely accepted kind.

That, again, in no way invalidates the insights but it does explain the monotony and obviousness which creeps into so many pages. The reader of Dos Passos meets with excellent observation but none of the unending suggestiveness and discovery of the *Sentimental Education* or *Ulysses.* For there is neither historical nor analogical perception in the *U. S. A.,* and so it fails to effect any connections with the rest of human society, past or present. There is a continuous stream of American consciousness and an awareness that there are un-American elements in the world. But as much as in any political orator there is the assumption that iniquity inside or outside the U.S.A. is always a failure to be true to the Jeffersonian dream. The point here is that this kind of single-level awareness is not possible to anybody seriously manipulating the multiple keyboards of Joyce's art. (pp. 156-57)

The failure of Dos Passos' insights to keep pace with the complex techniques at his disposal is what leaves the reader with the sense of looseness and excessive bulk in *U. S. A.* In the equally bulky *Finnegans Wake,* on the other hand, which exploits all the existing techniques of vision and presentation in a consummate orchestration of the arts and sciences, there is not one slack phrase or scene. *U. S. A.,* by comparison, is like a Stephen Foster medley played with one finger on a five keyboard instrument. There is that sort of discrepancy between the equipment and the ensuing concert; but it is not likely to disturb those readers who have only a slight acquaintance with Joyce.

Manhattan Transfer and the *U. S. A.* trilogy are not novels in the usual sense of a selection of characters who influence and define one another by interaction. . . . The novel as it has been concerned with the problems of "character" and environment seems to have emerged as a pastime of the new middle classes who were eager to see themselves and their problems in action. . . . The middle classes found romance and glamour in the commonplace, but they were not prepared for the profound existentialist metaphysic of the commonplace which Joyce revealed.

In such a perspective as this the collective landscapes of *U. S. A.* represent only a modest effort at managing the huge panorama of triviality and frustration which is the urban milieu of industrial man.

But the fact that a technological environment not only induces most people into various stages of automatism but makes the family unit socially non-effective, has certainly got something to do with the collective landscapes of *U. S. A.* Its structure is poetic in having its unity not in an idea but a vision; and it is cubist in presenting multiple simultaneous perspectives like a cycle of medieval mystery plays. It could readily be maintained that this method not only permits comprehensiveness of a kind indispensable to the modern artist, but makes for the intelligible rather than the concupiscible in art. The kind of pleasure that Dos Passos provides in comparison with Hemingway is that of detached intellectual intuition rather than that of sympathetic merging with the narrative and characters. (pp. 158-59)

Although Dos Passos may be held to have failed to provide any adequate intellectual insight or emotion for the vast landscape of his trilogy, his themes and attitudes are always interesting, especially in the numerous biographies of such folk heroes as Edison and the Wright brothers, Debs and La Follette, Steinmetz and Isadora Duncan, Ford and Burbank. These sections are often masterly in their economy and point. The frustration of hopes and intentions in these public figures provides the main clue to the social criticism which underlies the presentation of dozens of nonentities. For it is usually pointed up that the great are as helplessly ensnared in merely behavioristic patterns irrelevant to their own welfare, as the crowd of nobodies who admire them.

The frustration and distortion of life common to the celebrated and the obscure is, in Dos Passos, to be attributed to "the system." No diagnosis as crude as this emerges directly. But over and over again in the contrast between humble humanity and the gormandizing power-gluttony of the stupidly arrogant few, there is implied the preference for a world of simple, unpretentious folk united in their common tasks and experience. It has often been noted that there is never love between the characters of Dos Passos. But there is the pathos of those made incapable of love by their too successful adjustment to a loveless system. Genuine pathos is the predominant and persistent note in Dos Passos, and must be considered as his personal response to the total landscape. Yet it is a pathos free from self-pity because he has objectified it in his analysis of the political and economic situation.

The homelessness of his people is, along with their individual and collective incapacity for self-criticism or detachment, the most obvious feature about them. And home is the positive though unstated and undefined dream of Dos Passos. . . . For those who are critically aware he pre-

scribes the duty of selfless dedication to the improvement of the common civilization. And in three uninteresting, short novels since *U. S. A.* [*Adventures of a Young Man, Number One,* and *The Grand Design*] he has explored the problem of discovering a self worth giving to such a cause. (pp. 159-60)

Dos Passos may have lost his stride as an artist through the very success of those social causes which were the militant theme of *U. S. A.* To have a cause to defend against a blind or indifferent world seemed to give tone and snap to the artist in him who has since been overlaid by the reporter. But if this is the case, nobody would be happier than Dos Passos to have lost his artistry on such excellent terms. (p. 161)

> *Herbert Marshall McLuhan, "John Dos Passos: Technique vs. Sensibility," in* Fifty Years of the American Novel, *edited by Harold C. Gardiner (abridged by permission of Charles Scribner's Sons; copyright © 1951 Charles Scribner's Sons), Scribner's, 1951 (and reprinted in* John Dos Passos: A Collection of Critical Essays, *edited by Andrew Hook, Prentice-Hall, Inc., 1974, pp. 148-61).*

JONATHAN MORSE

[An] attitude of determined omniscience informs all of *U.S.A.,* even the biographical sections. Of the five historical personages who were still alive when Dos Passos wrote about them, none retains any control over his own destiny; that privilege is reserved for the abstract forces of history conceived under the aegis of Marxist-Veblenian determinism. The biography of Thomas Edison is oblique in emphasis; its subject, discussed in the past tense, is unable to free himself from his obsolete and socially dangerous work ethic because "he never worried about mathematics or the social system or generalized historical concepts." Henry Ford waits in seclusion for death, helpless and uncomprehending before the changes he has brought about. Orville Wright, left behind by a historical process gone wrong, lives an authentic life only in other people's memories. . . . Such are the lives of those who are swept up in the dialectic of history. Each suffers a spiritual death as his individuality becomes a part of the workings of historical law; and Dos Passos, the scientific historian, notes the phenomenon and passes on to other things.

In these historical sections of his novel, Dos Passos has consciously limited his powers of observation to those possessed by the Camera Eye: he observes, speculates, and even predicts, but before the abyss of motivation he draws silently back. The lives of the twelve representative Americans in the explicitly "fictitious" sections of *U.S.A.,* however, are more open to analysis. They are subject only to the psychological constraints of verisimilitude, and Dos Passos seizes the opportunity to simplify his history by coming to conclusions. He never ceases to write as a historian, but when the subjects of his history are men and women of his own creation, the history he writes becomes simpler, clearer, and more theoretical. (p. 544)

Although the lives of "real" personages always contain biographical data unnecessary for an understanding of their significance to history, that is not the case with characters whom the historian creates *pur sang* as illustrations of the breadth and power of his thesis. The more diversity there is among these characters, the more impressive will be the demonstration when the lines of force that they ride all converge at the appropriate point in history. It is to this historical convergence that Dos Passos' characters come by diverse routes, and only when they are finally there are all their individualities finally obliterated.

To achieve this convergence of emotional outcome, Dos Passos makes use of a number of quite unrevolutionary novelistic techniques. He delimits his narrative by arranging for most of his twelve characters to cross one another's paths, and he foreshadows and prefigures as assiduously as any disciple of Gustav Freytag. (p. 545)

These devices are old ones, and Dos Passos brings them up to date only in technical ways—by domesticating Freudian psychology in his family biography of Joe and Janey Williams, for instance, and by consciously making his characters' every journey a symbol of change. When he depicts travel, indeed, Dos Passos gladly allows the old and respectable tradition of the picaresque to bear much of the burden of characterization. Here as elsewhere, Dos Passos modifies convention freely as he traces the history that molds his characters' demands. Doc Bingham's disappearance shortly after the beginning of *The 42nd Parallel,* followed by his reappearance shortly before the end of *The Big Money,* is, for instance, from one point of view, simply an old-fashioned way of rounding to a conclusion; but if we consider the change in the way Doc Bingham is depicted—from an entertaining petty scoundrel to a genuinely harmful grotesque—we will see that Dos Passos has used this classic unifying device in a newly paradoxical way. (pp. 545-46)

Dos Passos' chief technical innovation, therefore, is a matter of eclectic flexibility. Insofar as he opens the confines of his novel to linguistic metamorphosis he is a follower of Joyce, but the idea of building a novel around a theory of history is less Joyce's than Tolstoy's. As the great majority of his many novels demonstrate, Dos Passos was solidly at home within the limitations of the nineteenth-century novel; even in *U.S.A.,* his most technically radical book, the verbal unorthodoxies are only a Joycean means to a Tolstoyan end. The Camera Eye's interior monologue could not have been created without the example of *Ulysses,* but its purpose is far different from Joyce's purposes. It exists to convey a single attitude, a Tolstoyan one, toward passivity in the face of historical experience. (p. 546)

We pass beyond the illusion of verisimilitude to the illusion of predictability; we find ourselves believing that we can perceive concrete phenomena simultaneously with their abstract causes. This error of perception arises from our viewing fictions through the eyes of an artist who focuses our attention on the one trait that his fictions share with historical reality: the trait of their having originated in a past. Dos Passos works always with the idea of referring phenomena to their origins; everywhere in the present he seeks to uncover the half-obliterated traces of ideal motive.

He cannot fully succeed in this, of course, but we can at least expect his determinist historicism to resolve all seeming inconsistencies. The biographies of Mac McCreary and Margo Dowling—the only two in *U.S.A.* with "happy" endings—are, therefore, particularly important to the novel, for they demonstrate that Dos Passos' paradigm of history is meant to apply equally to all possible circumstances, without regard to the raw data and random motions of individual humanity. (p. 547)

History, as the distinctively human instinct, lives only in

language. As the narrator of the trilogy says, "mostly U.S.A. is the speech of the people." . . . It is only to be expected, therefore, that those afflicted by ailments of their history will suffer in their language. Mac, at the end of his biography, has abandoned his native language and its links with the revolutionary history into which he was born; they are left behind in depraved Mexico City with the bookstore where he sold "all the American and European papers and magazines . . . especially *The Police Gazette* and *La Vie Parisienne."* . . . But in abandoning the corruptions of the old language he has not gained a new; his Spanish is adequate only to the petty politics of domesticity. It is an ironic outcome, but Mac's whole life has been a process of accommodation to history's sardonic jokes. We may assume that his future, however stultified, will at least be willed into tranquility; individual comfort for Mac has been worth the sacrifice of a language that has worked for Doc Bingham but not for the Goldfield miners. . . . (p. 548)

One of the minor characters in *U.S.A.,* Doc Bingham, changes epiphanically in order to make the change in America more evident to us. In *The 42nd Parallel,* Doc Bingham is a picaro, a mere literary type, but by the time he reaches *The Big Money,* he has taken on the specific flesh and blood of caricature. In this last avatar, Doc Bingham's zaniness is obviously based on the personality of Bernarr Macfadden, the eccentric and highly successful publisher of *True Story, Photoplay,* and several other magazines whose object is to exploit the uneducated; and it is only fitting that Newsreel LIII . . . , which introduces Margo to us, is a collage from Macfadden's tabloid *New York Graphic,* a newspaper that specialized in human-interest titillation. This, after all, is Margo's world. . . . The blocks of prose among the headlines offer . . . effortless involvement with blind contingency; they are all taken from the women's pages, and they progress from advertisements for a dancing school and a male beauty contest through fashion news and a crazy pot-pourri of advertisements for furniture and rejuvenative medicine to the adverb-soaked atmospherics of an interview with Peggy Hopkins Joyce, an actress famous for her lucrative divorces. SKYSCRAPERS BLINK ON EMPTY STREETS, the Newsreel informs us, and in its context this is an image of the American woman's body: bare ruin'd choirs, where late the sweet birds sang. We have been reading in the previous section about Isadora Duncan; now, with the words of a popular song,

> Make my bed and light the light
> I'll arrive late to-night,

the curtain opens and we see little Margie, the future movie star, waiting with a lantern for her drunken father.

On one side of this image of calculated pathos is an image of the almost mythical dancer, whose whole life became the magnificent failure of her art; on the other side are the promises of the advertisements, eternally false, eternally renewed: "He touches every point in the compass of human need. It may look a little foolish in print but he can show you how to grow brains." The operating assumption of such prose is that the reader never will grow brains; that beauty of language always conceals ugliness of motive. Under its surface, reality is always ugly; that is the lesson the *Graphic* teaches people like Margo, for whom it can come only as a truth reconfirmed.

Margo has learned the lesson very early, from a primal disillusion. Like many of Dos Passos' characters, she has been betrayed in infancy by her parents. Her mother has died denying her ("'She gave her life for yours, never forget it'; it made Margie feel dreadful, like she wasn't her own self, when Agnes said that," . . . her father is a feckless alcoholic whose unpredictable moods have made Margo's childhood a nightmare of instability. The good moments occupy only the beginning of Margo's memory; they are related to the increasingly rare occasions when Fred, her father, has managed to get off his train sober. (pp. 550-51)

By any normal psychological standards Margo is a neurotic, suffering from a disordered perception of reality. In the world of *U.S.A.*, however, her immediate, intuitive relationship with Margolies leads to a spectacular success of the classic Horatio Alger kind—the one unequivocal success in the book. The only thing that may harm her in the immediate future is speech, as we have seen; but Margo's world is a world in which the good news of Sacco and Vanzetti's "blood and agony" . . . is drowned in a flood of newsprint by William Randolph Hearst, whose

> power over the dreams
> of the adolescents of the world
> grows and poisons like a cancer. . . .

If true speech ever does come to Margo, it will come too late either to hurt her bank account or to save her soul. Victimized by her own success, Margo remains subject to the control of the psychic forces that have made her what she is. Her sexual power, brought into being by Fred Dowling and Frank Mandeville, now serves Sam Margolies and Rodney Cathcart. Individual psychopathology, once it has acquired economic value, ceases to be individual; its victim becomes a symbol, too valuable to change. (p. 552)

Regeneration of the diseased society through the sufferings of a tragically flawed artist: it is an older answer to the problem than Margo's, and a more respectable one. Its remotest ancestors are Job and Philoctetes, but in the Harvard College of Dos Passos' youth it spoke most persuasively through the voices of Oscar Wilde and the Walter Pater who wrote, "Not the fruit of experience, but experience itself, is the end." By the time he came to Camera Eye 25, however, Dos Passos realized this dictum through a new and sinister image: not Pater's "hard, gemlike flame" but its smothering antithesis: the ethercone, the anesthesia of a life cut off from everything but a train of ephemeral sensations. Pater's vision of the world, like his prose rhythm, has been made obsolete; the capitalist values of *U.S.A.* have little to do with gems. (p. 553)

[As] the voice of the Newsreels reminds us after every biography, life in *U.S.A.* is nothing but a series of random, entropic motions made in darkness and silence. The Camera Eye's silent movie ends as abruptly as a broken film, in the middle of a sentence, the acknowledgement of despair uncompleted: "we have only words against." . . . The next words on the page are the capitalized title of the last biography: POWER SUPERPOWER. Words in action are power, but all possibility of our acting has been taken from us by "the law . . . with the strut of the power of submachineguns sawedoffshotguns teargas and vomitinggas the power that can feed you or leave you to starve." The capture and destruction of our language are now complete. (p. 554)

At the end of the trilogy . . . the silent Vag has nothing to

live in except his aching body. His past has vanished into a silent mass of empty time; only the body turns incurious eyes upward to watch a powerful airplane bearing the corruptors of language passively across space. The ground on which the Vag stands is full of the drama of natural forces at work, all clearly visible from a higher vantage point . . . , but the vomiting businessmen in their airplane "sit pretty," unable to assimilate any of it, aware of the record of time in space only as "the billiondollar speedup." Their collective blindness is a lack of history, an inability to learn from what has been seen. They too suffer from the illusions of memory.

U.S.A. is in fact a novel about how America remembers the Vag's "mother's words telling about longago, . . . his father's telling about when I was a boy. . . ." . . . It is an attempt to re-establish the continuities of history for a nation which, in the upswings of the business cycle, has always tried to drown out the past in the raucous hallucination of an eternal present. In this respect, *U.S.A.* is a conservative book; its object was to explain to the age of Fitzgerald that that age's brightest new beliefs—spontaneous generation of capital, freedom of the individual from accountability to historical laws—were illusions. Dos Passos is most conservative precisely when he is most revolutionary; he tells us then that individual memories are valuable only as they become part of the older, stabler collective memory that is history.

But in the society chronicled in *U.S.A.*, history becomes a record of its own destruction, the 1500-page chronicle of language guttering into silence. Rather than commit himself to the new speech demanded of him by the logic of his self-destroying artifact, Dos Passos retreated, confining himself for the rest of his long career to the safe deadness of nineteenth-century literary language. But *U.S.A.* remains. Under its great cairn of words lies the corpse of the traditional American way of looking at history: Emerson's way, the way that says history is only memory writ large. As a theory of history, *U.S.A.* is no more useful than any other theory; we can value it high or low according to how we are able to use its predictive powers. My plea here is only that we should read *U.S.A.* *as* a theory of history. Such a reading may help us reevaluate not only *U.S.A.* but the entire American literary achievement of the 1930s. (pp. 554-55)

> *Jonathan Morse, "Dos Passos' 'USA' and the Illusions of Memory," in* Modern Fiction Studies *(© copyright 1977, by Purdue Research Foundation, West Lafayette, Indiana), Winter, 1977-78, pp. 543-56.*

*   *   *

DUDEK, Louis   1918-

Dudek is a Canadian poet, essayist, and editor. He was one of the most important contributors to the modern poetry movement in Canada during the 1940s. Critics have noted the prose-like quality of his poetry, which presents a verse that is strongly philosophical in content. Pound's influence is felt throughout Dudek's poetry, especially in his long poem *Atlantis*, in which he explicates the present through the past. Dudek is the founder and former editor of *Delta* magazine. (See also *Contemporary Authors*, Vols. 45-48.)

NORTHROP FRYE

Mr. Dudek is introverted and emotional: what takes fresh

and novel shape in his poetry is a sensuous reaction. In *The Transparent Sea . . .* , a retrospective collection, the best pieces are songs conveying an immediate mood, such as the one beginning ''A bird who sits over my door''; or studies in the movement and sound of words, like ''Tree in a Snowstorm''; or ideas that suddenly twist round into paradoxes, like the admirable opening poem on the pineal gland, or his comparison of the universe to a watch which makes religion a search ''for larger regions of clockwise justice''; or quick vivid sketches like ''Late Winter'' or ''Lines for a Bamboo Stick,'' the latter with an Oriental reference; or a study of swift movement, like his picture of a little girl skipping called ''The Child.''

One of his favourite adjectives is ''wet,'' and some of his best poems have the quality of the wet water-colour that is done quickly and makes its point all at once. Sometimes an image strikes him in a grotesque form, as in the astonishingly successful ''Mouths''; sometimes as a muttering and brooding anxiety, as in the near-prose fantasy ''The Dead.'' One often feels that a poem is inconclusive, but then one often feels too that the inconclusiveness is part of the effect, as it is in a sketch (pp. 305-06)

In short, I feel that when the poet says

> The world I see (this poem)
> I make out of the fragments of my pain
> and out of the pleasures of my trembling senses

he is telling us the exact truth about his poetic process.

It follows that he is working against his best qualities when he writes in a sequence, whether of description or thought. Here he is dependent on habit, and produces the *clichés* of habit. In the ''Provincetown'' sequence there is the same kind of maunderlust that filled so much of *Europe*. Sexual imagery is also a trap for him, for sex is something he feels self-conscious and explanatory about. At other times he is not satisfied with inconclusiveness, and some of the poems sag into platitude in an effort to round off, as in ''On Sudden Death'' and elsewhere. Yet . . . there is much to be grateful for in Mr. Dudek's book, and a great variety of pleasant and melodious writing. (p. 306)

> *Northrop Frye, in* University of Toronto Quarterly *(reprinted by permission of* University of Toronto Quarterly*),* April, 1957.

DOROTHY LIVESAY

[''Functional Poetry: A Proposal''] establishes Dudek as the contemporary Canadian poet most consciously concerned with shape, form and sound: the origins of rhythm. He feels that the widening scope of prose rhythm has set up an impasse for poetry which he would like to break through. . . . His aim apparently is to invade the fortress where prose has taken hold and return it to the rightful owner, poetry. . . . (pp. 26-7)

Before he reached this eighteenth century critical position Dudek as man and poet went through many phases. His earliest poetry in *East of the City* is lyrical and imagist: concerned not with sound effects so much as with pictures in rhythmic arrangement. Already the clouds and the sea he is so fond of observing represent his objective correlative for the world of poetry: a world where recurrent rhythms subject to wind and weather, subject to sun and moon, are expressed through language. . . . In many of these short lyrical pieces the poet's ''eye'' is on the object but in the

background is a subjective, emotional ''I'' responding to these objects. . . . Dudek's search for ''straight language and relevance'' is certainly to be found in these early poems. Nonetheless he is not wholly free from the metrical bonds of the past. (pp. 27-8)

Even twenty years ago . . . Dudek had made his stand known. He was opposed to ''musicality'' à la Keats. He wanted poetry to reveal itself naked, without the props and embellishments of sound. His best poetry is unified, of a piece, and not discursive as is prose. . . .

Dudek's apparent philosophizing, his didacticism, are in reality a consideration of possibilities. His prose content, like his prose syntax, is a kind of disguise. (p. 30)

It would be a mistake to assume that [Dudek's] simple, straight-forward use of languages, which never falls into obscurantism or ellipsis and which is always syntactically complete, is necessarily the language of prose. Dudek's poems are rhythmic wholes. . . . Order and control are the keynotes to this poet's work: as in sculpture, the whole must be visible at a glance, but the detail must be exact, and highlighted where essential. Moreover, none of Dudek's poems can be accused of being too short or too long (for even his ''epic'' poems are a series of short apprehensions). Quite frequently the poems seem to lack drama and dramatic tension, but they are a true rhythmic mirror of the poet's intention. No word or phrase can be taken away; none can be added. There is, further, only the sparest use of adjectives; instead there is strong reliance on nouns, verbs, clauses. (p. 31)

[Proof] that Dudek is more concerned with musical articulation than with onomatopeia—music as ''cry''—is to be found in the texture of his vocabulary. Although he maintains a harmony of vowel sounds there is apparently no effort towards alliteration, assonance or half-rhymes (except in a few of the latest lyrics in *En Mexico*). It is as if the poet had an instinct for the right sounds without consciously working to make them so. (p. 32)

Sound harmonies . . . , together with a beautifully balanced phrasal pattern, enhance the *conceptual* conclusion which is the theme of all Louis Dudek's poetry: that harmony and order in nature towards which mankind strives. All his recent poetry of the fifties and sixties, with the exception of the satirical pieces of *Laughing Stalks*, repeats the same theme. . . . As a sculptor takes a lump of clay and fashions it into varying shapes he retains the essential element that makes it a work of art: rhythm. So in his cool, grave, lucent poems does Louis Dudek create and magnify his world. (p. 35)

> *Dorothy Livesay, ''The Sculpture of Poetry: On Louis Dudek,'' in* Canadian Literature, *Autumn, 1966, pp. 26-35.*

PAUL DENHAM

At first sight, Louis Dudek's long poem *Atlantis* appears to be a re-working of the material of his earlier volume *Europe* (1953), since the imagery and structure of both are drawn from a North American's passionate pilgrimage in various parts of Europe. However, this volume is at once more concrete and more philosophical; he is not just looking for Europe, but for a submerged continent, a vision of a kind of Platonic reality underlying the dizzying multiplicity of human experience. He explains his procedure thus:

Every object a word, language, the
record we make
a literal transcription,
then a translation
into moral, abstract meaning.

The "translations" are the weakest aspect of the poem: too often Mr. Dudek's abstractions become rather ponderous, and the rhythm of the verse, so surely handled throughout much of the poem, tends to go flat.

Perhaps the most satisfactory parts of the poem are those which deal with the arts; here he seems to feel less need to "translate" everything, yet still manages to convey a vigorously realized sense of the importance of the arts to his exploration. The reader may not feel that he has found Atlantis, but the journey is an important and intriguing one in any case. (p. 234)

Paul Denham, in Canadian Forum, *January, 1969.*

DOUGLAS BARBOUR

What struck me . . . as I read through [Dudek's *Collected Poetry*] was the way in which certain approaches to subject matter, certain ways of articulating what can only be called arguments, form a part of his poetic *content* right from the start. Although he doesn't find the proper form for his "statement" right away, he is always striving for an intellectually tough poetry. Even in the early poems, where his control of "voice" is weak, the philosophic tone that marks all his serious poetry is present.

One of Dudek's continuing interests has been the *process* of thought. His poems often provide paradigms of that process, or icons of the results of that process. They move from a formal, traditional metric towards a prose-like, argumentative, "open" metric, which often resolves (in the longer poems, and especially *Atlantis*), into a near-prose of short maxims which remind me of La Rochefoucauld. (pp. 110-11)

"On Poetry" is interesting partly because it is an early poem in which Dudek essays the open form. But he does not stick with it, and many of the poems of the next few years . . . are in traditional forms, like the quatrains of "Flower Bulbs". This very interesting poem, which is a love poem of sorts, is yet very reminiscent of metaphysical poetry in the way it uses an image from nature as a basis for a closely argued and witty proposition. The argument is just as important as the lovely image which informs it, if not more so. (p. 111)

"Line and Form" is one of the most interesting of the pre-*Europe* poems, because it is so obviously an essay in the aesthetics of universal creation. Aesthetics is one of the major areas of philosophy that interest Dudek, and the concerns of this poem will reappear throughout all his later poetry. . . .

Even in such an obviously philosophical poem [as "Line and Form"], however, Dudek makes use of what is an obsessive image in his work, and that is the great Sea itself. Here the line, "an ocean arrested" is both a major link in his argument and a reference to the vast chaos of possibilities that the sea has always represented to man. It is a natural reference for Dudek to make, for he has always been possessed by the sea; it appears in all his work, from the early tone poem, "The Sea", through *Europe* and *En Mex-*

ico, to *Atlantis* and beyond. Although his poetry tends to be intellectual and lacking in obvious emotionalism, the sea always provokes emotional outbursts from him. It is his true muse. (p. 112)

I find few of Dudek's "humorous poems" funny, and I don't think his sense of humour is amenable to poetry. Too often such poems telegraph their punchline and utterly fail to provide the "surprise" of a good joke. Arthur Koestler says that the "unexpected" climax to a good joke must be "both unexpected and perfectly logical—but of a logic not usually applied to this type of situation. It is precisely this "logical unexpectedness" which is missing in Dudek's poems. His parodies of Canadian poets, however, especially those of A. J. M. Smith, A. M. Klein, and Irving Layton, are often dead on, and reveal and acute *critical* wit.

The Fifties are crucial years in Dudek's career, however, because during them he wrote the two long poems, *Europe* (1955), and *En Mexico* (1958). It was in these poems that he came into full command of his voice, and it was there that he truly became a philosophical poet. *Europe* is an extended personal essay, a travelogue by a philosopher with a gifted and far-ranging eye. The branches of philosophy which engage Dudek's mind—philosophy of history, politics, aesthetics (and art-history), and ethics—all appear in *Europe* and in *En Mexico*. All will reappear in *Atlantis*. (p. 113)

I think it is important to note that Dudek is a student of modern poetry and a follower of Ezra Pound. Unlike many of the younger practitioners of the popular poetry of primitivism he lashed out against in "Poetry in English", he is a highly educated student of poetic tradition, especially of twentieth-century modernism. . . . He is the only one of the three *Cerberus* poets [Irving Layton and Raymond Souster are the other two] even to attempt a truly long poem. He has walked the paths of his art alone. If he has not been completely successful in his poetic quest, surely one of the reasons is that he had to do it all by himself: he had no other poets in Canada to share his particular problems and efforts.

Europe is an oddly likeable piece of writing. Although I am not at all sure that it fully succeeds as poetry, I find myself completely won over by the man behind the work. This says a great deal for the poem, for I began the *Collected Poetry* with a definite bias against him, based mostly on my disagreement with many of his criticisms of his fellow poets in "Poetry in English". In *Europe* the poet shows such a genuinely and engagingly interesting mind, uses that mind to deal with such interesting materials, and expresses his opinions with such a refreshing forthrightness, I found it impossible to dislike him. In this he is like Ruskin, another traveller in Europe, to whom he refers occasionally in the poem. As he continues to speak on various subjects during the poem's progress he wins our respect because his intellectual engagement with them is so clear and intelligent. He is also like Ruskin in creating a series of little personal essays, even if they appear to be parts of a poem. Although they contain many richly poetic images and metaphors, the very stuff of poetry, to bolster their various arguments, they are basically essays. . . . (pp. 113-14)

[His style] is witty, and provocative of thought, but, despite its appearance, and the rhythmic control of certain parts, it would strike many readers as very different, at bottom, from what they know as poetry. This reaction may merely reveal their ignorance of certain aspects of modern poetry, as Dudek suggests, but the periodic sentences and the syntax of those grand periods, are surely qualities normally associated with scintillating prose. . . . Dudek has carried Pound's dictum, "that poetry should be written at least as well as prose" to its limit. . . . What one misses in so many of Dudek's poems are the "passionate moments" [which Pound also asks of verse] that would lift us out of ourselves. What we find, however, are qualities of meditative vision and intense ratiocination that are seldom to be found in any other Canadian poet.

In *En Mexico,* Dudek continues to work with the open form, the long discursive, essay-like "canto", and the philosophical voice he had developed in *Europe. En Mexico* displays a new mastery of rhythm, however, in many of its parts. . . . [Dudek's "A Note on Metrics," an obvious development from an early Pound essay,] is his major statement on the uselessness of traditional forms for the contemporary poet. Although he continued to use those forms in the fifties, he has not used them in any of his published work since 1958. It appears that the Note was the final nail in the coffin of traditional verse, as far as Dudek was concerned, for in it he insists that if you write in one of the formal metres, especially iambic, you "thus neglect the essential music, which is that of your sounds, *as they fit the content of your poetry,* and you produce for the most part an empty rattle of sounds." *En Mexico,* and all the poems following it, are written in the light of that statement. . . . *En Mexico* is a more successful whole than *Europe* because of Dudek's new mastery of rhythm, but the centre of interest in the poem remains the philosophizing that the trip to Mexico engenders. (pp. 115-16)

The mixture of the maxims and the images of life in Mexico creates a powerful commentary on contemporary civilization, just as Dudek wants it to. Because the whole poem provides such a resonant context for them, these short aphoristic statements have a power and interest that is entirely lacking in Irving Layton's "Aphs" from *The Whole Bloody Bird.* There is a decorum to Dudek's epigrams which the boring and boorish statements of Layton lack, and that decorum is provided by the unity of tone of the whole poem. (p. 116)

In many ways, *En Mexico* stands as Dudek's most successful poem: an organic, unified whole.

"Lac En Coeur", another fairly long poem of the time, is a quiet meditation full of questions about life. It is a lovely small personal poem, an essay from "the mind and heart of love" of the natural world around the poet. But it is a philosophical meditation, sharing, as do parts of *Atlantis,* the concerns of such poems as Yeats's "Lapis Lazuli" and the later *Cantos,* but without their "passionate intensity." . . . (p. 117)

Atlantis is not the unqualified success that *En Mexico* was. It is Dudek's longest piece of sustained writing, gathering all his themes and ideas into a single massive argument. Yet, in the final analysis, it fails because he is unable to incorporate everything he wants in quite the manner he wants. Had he paid attention to W. C. Williams's *Paterson,* rather than just the *Cantos,* he might have learned an invaluable lesson: that if you do use actual prose, it can mix with your own poetry without much trouble, so long as you juxtapose with care, but if you merely make your own poetry too prosaic in places, the obviously "poetic" parts of your poem will clash with the rest. This is what happens in *Atlantis,* and it is a definite fault in the poem.

The tone of *Atlantis,* from the very beginning, is that discursive tone that presents the personal essayist, once again *en voyage,* once again looking around and noting with great precision and wit what he sees, and then reflecting upon it. The casualness of the speech . . . does not mask, but subtly underlines the wide range of allusions and ideas the speaker commands. This tone, this manner of speaking, allows for a great breadth of material, but not for everything. In fact, it is a curious paradox of this poem that the sections of "pure poetry" are both the most powerful, and the most out-of-place, parts of it. (p. 118)

In the body of the poem, Dudek continues to reflect upon things; he discusses town planning, moral philosophy, aesthetic history, the concept of pity, the reasons for art, and much else. He even goes in for a very esoteric aquarium list, which he then transforms, through some very precise description, into a lyrical celebration of the many varieties of ocean-going life-forms. All these discussions are fascinating as discussions; some of them fall terribly flat as poetry. . . .

The Epilogue to *Atlantis* almost saves the whole poem. This is a poetry like that of the late *Cantos:* pristine, the language pure and magnificent as it apotheosizes "Atlantis", that region of the human/divine soul for which Dudek has quested through all his poems. The first two pages of the Epilogue shine with the very "Light" they celebrate, but the effort of such an ecstatic flight proves too great, and the poet returns to earth, except for a few leaps of a line or two, for the remaining five pages of the poem. Still, it is beautiful, it is a passionate moment, however brief, and yet it does seem somehow out of place in this particular poem. It is not that Dudek is wrong in his approach to poetry; he is following a major modern tradition, one whose value has been proven time and again. It is merely that in *this* poem he has failed to weld all his various elements into a harmonious sculpture of words. (p. 119)

[The groups of longer poems collected in the section, "Reflections After Atlantis"] continue the approach worked out in *Europe, En Mexico,* and *Atlantis.* "The Demolitions", an elegy for destroyed architecture, is essentially a lyrical, autobiographical essay. "Canada: Interim Report" is a bitter, politically oriented, polemic. There are some rather neat juxtapositions, but the tone is too angry, the bitterness too diffuse; it all sounds like a variant on the poems Souster and Layton had in *The New Romans,* and that kind of poetry is something Dudek has always, until this poem, had the good sense to ignore. The philosopher ranting can provide little pleasure or stimulation, for he is using language in a manner, for him, meretricious, "A Circle Tour of the Rockies" is a mistake from start to finish, but not for the same reasons as "Canada: Interim Report", and it is a mistake of major interest, which also differentiates it from that poem. It is another very good essay, and one could imagine Ruskin, or even Dr. Johnson, writing it in prose. But to even *think* that such language would work in a poem about mountains betrays the kind of one-sidedness Dudek's preoccupations have led him to. There is absolutely no sense of a response to the overwhelming (*emotionally* overwhelming!) *grandeur* of the Rockies. . . . Dudek failed to recognize the limitations of his poetic; he did not understand that it was not meant to deal with the kind of grandeur (the Awesomeness that the great Romantics felt in the presence of mountains) the Rocky Mountains are. His refusal to use image or metaphor to any extent in the poem is the measure of that failure of recognition. (pp. 120-21)

I see [Dudek] as a product of the Enlightenment who has been forced to cope with certain aspects of humanity (the "Evil" of the twentieth century which he has written so many pages about) the eighteenth century did not have to face. But he seems somewhat out of place, really, in a world which is still living in the Romantic Age, for Romanticism has touched him only slightly, if at all. Perhaps that is an overstatement, but I think it helps to define him and his art. . . . Dudek pleases us most when he is rational, meditative, the philosopher to be listened to and argued with, but not possessed by. (p. 121)

> *Douglas Barbour, "Poet as Philosopher: Louis Dudek" (originally published in* Canadian Literature, *Summer, 1972; copyright © 1972 by Douglas Barbour), in* Poets and Critics: Essays from "Canadian Literature" 1966-1974, *edited by George Woodcock, Oxford University Press, 1974, pp. 110-22.*

*   *   *

du MAURIER, Daphne   1907-

Du Maurier is an English novelist, short story writer, playwright, editor, biographer, and autobiographer. She is predominantly known for her Gothic novels, which have made her a highly successful popular author. The wild Cornish coast is the setting for most of her novels, notably *Rebecca*, which combines the mystery, romance, and melodrama characteristic of the Gothic novel. Though never a critical success, du Maurier popularized a genre that is imitated to this day. (See also *CLC*, Vol. 6, and *Contemporary Authors*, Vols. 5-8, rev. ed.)

SEAN O'FAOLAIN

Jamaica Inn [makes] one realise how high the standard of entertainment has become in the modern novel. I do not believe R.L.S. [Robert Louis Stevenson] would have been ashamed to have written *Jamaica Inn*, with its smugglers, wreckers, wild moors, storms, its sinister inn, misplaced confidences, pretty and gallant heroine, and romantic love story. . . . There is here all the melodrama that one can desire—and let nobody say "It is an old fashion." The old fashion was good. (p. 144)

> *Sean O'Faolain, in* The Spectator *(© 1936 by The Spectator; reprinted by permission of* The Spectator*), January 24, 1936.*

BASIL DAVENPORT

So Cinderella married the prince, and then her story began. Cinderella was hardly more than a school-girl, and the overworked companion of a snobbish woman of wealth; the prince was Maximilian de Winter, whom she had heard of as the owner of Manderley in Cornwall, one of the most magnificent show places in England, who had come to the Riviera to forget the tragic death of his wife Rebecca. . . . There was some mystery about Rebecca's death . . . ; but the book is skillfully contrived so that it does not depend only on knowledge of it for its thrill; it can afford to give no

hint of it till two-thirds of the way through. But the revelation, when it comes, leads to one of the most prolonged, deadly, and breathless fencing-matches that one can find in fiction, a battle of wits that would by itself make the fortune of a melodrama on the stage.

For this is a melodrama, unashamed, glorying in its own quality, such as we have hardly had since that other dependant, Jane Eyre, found that her house too had a first wife. It has the weaknesses of melodrama; in particular, the heroine is at times quite unbelievably stupid, as when she takes the advice of the housekeeper whom she knows to hate her. But if the second Mrs. de Winter had consulted with any one before trusting the housekeeper, we should miss one of the best scenes in the book. There is also, as is almost inseparable from a melodrama, a forced heightening of the emotional values; the tragedy announced in the opening chapter is out of proportion to the final outcome of the long battle of wits that ends the book. But it is as absorbing a tale as the season is likely to bring.

> *Basil Davenport, "Sinister House," in* Saturday Review *(© 1938 by Saturday Review, Inc.; reprinted with permission), September 24, 1938, p. 5.*

Forty-eight hours after having turned the last page of "Frenchman's Creek" you have some difficulty in remembering what it was all about. What you do remember is the impression of rich, satiny, glass-slippered triumph that Miss du Maurier made in the reading, the conquering Prince Charming atmosphere of the entire performance. Remembering that, the details of an almost preposterously innocent but very smooth, very skilful, very bright-eyed fairy tale come back. This is the story, in a vague Restoration setting, of a gallant French pirate and a beautiful lady of St. James's who loved and parted. By all the rules it should have turned out a tame if decorative trifle. Miss du Maurier, of course, makes rather more of her little effort, but exactly how she achieves her effect of truly romantic sensibleness is something of a mystery. The tale has ease, charm, a certain finish, and yet none of these things seems to matter very much by comparison of her tone of voice. It is this ring of innocent assurance in matters of pure ordinary conviction with the extra-romantic make-believe that does the trick. . . .

What is there not merely to reconcile the reader to this faded tinselly stuff but to draw from him a faint breath of wonder? Analysis does not really help. Miss du Maurier's graces of style are not to be despised, and even her too artificially pointed dialogue, somewhat in the manner of Restoration comedy, has its elegant merit. But it is, above all else, the astonishing self-confidence with which she unfolds so girlishly daydreaming, a history that infects the reader, and in so doing carries him along as far and as fast as Miss du Maurier wills. Like "Rebecca," its predecessor, "Frenchman's Creek" is dope—though of an inferior sort. But an element of dope enters into all fiction, the best included.

> *"Pirates and Lovers," in* The Times Literary Supplement *(© Times Newspapers Ltd. (London) 1941; reproduced from* The Times Literary Supplement *by permission) September 13, 1941, p. 457.*

JOHN RAYMOND

In the thirties, Miss du Maurier was a kind of poor woman's Charlotte Brontë. Her *Rebecca*, whatever one's opinions of its ultimate merits, was a *tour de force*. In its own way and century, it has achieved a position in English Literature comparable to "Monk" Lewis's *The Bleeding Nun* or Mrs. Radcliffe's *Mysteries of Udolpho*. To-day Miss du Maurier the novelist is Miss Blurb's favourite Old Girl whose published appearances are heralded with the brouhaha of a privileged ex-hockey captain come down to give the home team a few hints about attack. This, one imagines her telling newcomers to St. Gollancz's, is how it should be done. Frankly, I cannot help feeling that Miss du Maurier's books have been successfully filmed so often that by now she may be said not so much to write a novel as shoot it. The present scenario [in *My Cousin Rachel*] is a honey for any Hollywood or Wardour Street tycoon. Slick, effective, utterly mechanical, the book is a triumphant and uncanny example of the way in which a piece of writing can be emasculated by unconsciously "having it arranged" for another medium. Close-ups, fade-ins, sequences by candlelight or long shots from the terrace—it has all been taken care of in the script and there is little call for anything in the way of imagination on the part of the director. . . .

Producers, admiring the general effect, will forgive such occasional anachronisms, as "forget it," "slapped my bottom with a hair-brush," and "Why not tell these gossips I'm a recluse and spend all my spare time scribbling Latin verses? That might shake them." Boyish sulks, mares in slather, and a lot of old lace at the throat and wrist, eked out with constant cups of poisoned tisane, complete the formula. A rare and irresistible bit of *kitsch*, whose clichés will soon be jostling and clashing in merry carillons up and down the premier cinema circuits of the English-speaking world. (p. 163)

John Raymond, in New Statesman (© *1951 The Statesman & Nation Publishing Co. Ltd.), August 11, 1951.*

EDWARD WEEKS

Daphne du Maurier has a talent for mystification. In *Rebecca* she wrote of a heroine we never saw in the flesh but whose spell was woven through every page. In *My Cousin Rachel* . . . she tells the story of an Italian widow who captivates two English bachelors, Ambrose Ashley, the elder, whom she married and subdues in Italy, and Philip, his cousin and heir, whom she comes to live with in Cornwall after Ambrose's mysterious death. (pp. 78-9)

Miss du Maurier is a caster of spells, and the first she casts is on Ambrose in Tuscany; the second upon Philip when he is drawn out of his solitary rustic state by the cries for help from abroad. . . .

And then comes the third spell as Rachel begins to wind him around her finger as she had his cousin. . . .

Rachel in her Italian sophistication and Philip in his naïve manhood are a pair to watch. The minor parts—Seecombe, the old steward; Nick Kendall, the guardian; Tamlyn, the gardener; Louise, the girl Philip might have married—are well drawn, and the mists and cold of the Cornish coast with its occasional bright pane of sunlight are beautifully contrasted with the heat and haze of Tuscany in the blaze of August.

The last spell and the hardest to throw off is the plausibility that Philip Ashley, so diffident, so unliterary, and so close-minded, would have been willing to tell this story on himself. In real life neither wild horses nor a psychiatrist could have pulled it out of him. (p. 79)

Edward Weeks, in The Atlantic Monthly *(copyright © 1952 by The Atlantic Monthly Company, Boston, Mass.; reprinted with permission), March, 1952.*

PAT ROGERS

[Francis Bacon] seems an odd choice for Daphne du Maurier, with her fine wayward imagination and her gothic suggestiveness. Few Elizabethans had less of the mantic about them than Bacon; few steered a less infernal course. . . . Bacon was humdrum both in his grandeur and his decadence. He went meekly, if glumly, to his disgrace, arraigned as a Poulson and not as a Trotsky.

Yet some compulsion has drawn the author of *Jamacia Inn*, the biographer of Branwell Brontë, to this unlikely assignment. . . . [In writing *The Winding Stair: Francis Bacon, his Rise and Fall,* her] feeling was that 'the ordinary reader . . . has never been sufficiently interested in, or understood, the extraordinary complexity of Francis Bacon's character and the many facets of his personality. The endeavour to explain him would be a challenge.' It is a challenge boldly taken up, with evidence of energetic reading, an orderly and consecutive narrative, and a warmly personal tone. . . .

But the book remains something of an uphill struggle. Though the story is accurately and sympathetically told, there is not much real penetration into the springs of Bacon's activity. Sensibly, since Bacon was a great writer, Dame Daphne tries to make his works supply some kind of revelation. But they won't afford the kind she wants. The major works on scientific method have a few choice phrases culled from them; Dame Daphne combs the essays for clues to Bacon's personality, and does what she can with speeches in Chancery or pamphlets on diplomacy. We are constantly told, Monty Python-fashion, that Bacon was The Most Brilliant Intellect of the Day, but we are forced to take this on trust. There is nothing wrong with searching out the 'intimate side' of a great man, even if it means itemising some fairly routine household accounts. But the ordinary reader (however patronisingly defined) wants explanation of the greatness besides chitchat about private foibles.

Anxious not to overplay her hand, Dame Daphne studs the biography with reminders about the dearth of evidence. Sometimes she is pawky. . . . At other moments she grows impatient [or quizzical]. . . . Dame Daphne loves to lose herself in a reverie of what might have been; the whole text is replete with 'may well' and 'perhaps' and 'possibly' and 'would have' and 'we have no means of knowing.' Responsible scholarship seldom has need of such a battery of conditionals, for the historical imagination should function not to muse or to guess . . . but to reanimate the known.

When we reach the time of the Shakespearian First Folio, the Baconian heresy naturally provides 'food for speculation'. The biographer disappears briefly behind an intrusive passive voice [which suggests the possibility of collaboration between Bacon and Shakespeare]. . . . Not a shred of evidence is brought to support this half-hearted contention, and indeed it scarcely could be. The true Baconians, with their ciphers, anagrams and hermetic signals behind Shakespeare's back, would find such lukewarm advocacy disappointing. The answer is that Dame Daphne would like to add *Macbeth* and *Twelfth Night* to Bacon's claims as The Most Brilliant Intellect: on the other hand, she is forced to emphasize as always, the poverty of physical evidence. Daphne du Maurier has many literary gifts, but I am not sure that this book has fully enlisted them. Her archaising vein ('But stay, what was this?') is perhaps more suited to Cornish romance, and her cosy relationship with her hero 'Francis' consorts oddly with his fiercely private nature and conscious dignity. Against this must be set a brisk narrative pace, an avoidance of pedantry, and some shrewdness in judging people.... As an all-round character study, I am still inclined to prefer Catherine Drinker Bowen's *The Temper of a Man* of a decade ago. But there is always room for another book on anyone as complex and diversely gifted as Bacon. The man who took all knowledge as his province should not be left to specialists and scholars; he deserves a revival, and if Daphne du Maurier has not taken us to the inmost recesses she has made a good studio portrait of the outer man.

> Pat Rogers, *"Saving Her Bacon,"* in The Spectator (© 1976 by The Spectator; *reprinted by permission of* The Spectator), *July 31, 1976, p. 20.*

E. S. TURNER

Growing Pains is about the delights and irresponsibilities of adolescence, the sowing of mild oats.... Writers of best-selling fiction tend to have peculiar bees in their bonnets, but if Dame Daphne has any she is keeping them for later. She writes with enough warmth and humour to captivate all but those who are allergic to the small stuff of childhood and other people's dogs and boats.

> E. S. Turner, *"Mild Oats,"* in The Listener (© British Broadcasting Corp. 1977; *reprinted by permission of E. S. Turner*), *June 9, 1977, p. 760.*

DORIS GRUMBACH

[Daphne du Maurier] has chosen to use whole portions of her girlhood diaries [in "Myself When Young"], verbatim, to gird her memory. The result is a gently gushing prose, full of exuberant clichés and heedless adverbs ("The tide of adolescence was running at full spate" and "This beauty is too much. It's defeating, utterly bewildering, Beauty most exquisite.... Somehow profoundly unhappy" ...). (p. 18)

If the memoir would have benefited from less wholesale use of diaries, it surely would have gained from the excision of numbers of her early, jejune poetry. There is also much conventional foreshadowing of events ("There were so many stories waiting to be written. Perhaps one day ...").

I suppose what I would have liked is to hear the mature successful novelist remembering her youth in her mature voice, suggesting the sources of her fiction in full detail instead of dropping tantalizing hints about it, and estimating from her present vantage point her contributions to popular fiction.

In one place Daphne du Maurier records that "scrappy but endearing letters came from Carol (a suitor) almost every day." Her own book is often like that, scrappy but, somehow, endearing. (pp. 18, 20)

> Doris Grumbach, *in* The New York Times Book Review (© 1977 by The New York Times Company; *reprinted by permission*), *November 6, 1977.*

In its opening chapters, Daphne du Maurier's slim autobiography of early years, *Myself When Young*, reads like a novel. This is both strength and weakness for thus it provides passages of interest and charm but it also unfolds a life of apparent artificiality. The novel later fades and in its place is a kind of journal. In neither framework, unfortunately, does the author allow the reader to sufficiently know her. Not often enough is one able to fathom why she thinks as she does. And in some instances one wonders if she thinks at all. Except with animals and places, her relationships often seem unreal. Her descriptions of people are, for the most part, clinical and detached rather than warm and loving. Or is this only British understatement? I doubt it. Her sub-title is "The Shaping of a Writer," and one sees this taking place, but it fails to satisfy fully....

Yet the book has a fascination. Daphne du Maurier was a child of privilege, growing up in a world that will never happen again. (p. 81)

> The Critic (© The Critic *1978; reprinted with the permission of The Thomas More Association, Chicago, Illinois), Spring, 1978.*

*   *   *

DURAS, Marguerite   1914-

Duras is a French novelist, screenwriter, and dramatist whose work is often linked with that of the New Novelists. Her fiction is strongly visual and experimental, employing cinematographic techniques to explore themes of time, love, and the difficulty of communication. Critics have praised her talent for dialogue and her poetic evocation of atmosphere. She has collaborated with Alain Resnais, and is perhaps best known in America for *Hiroshima mon amour*. (See also *CLC*, Vols. 3, 6, and *Contemporary Authors*, Vols. 25-28, rev. ed.)

ALFRED CISMARU

As does all her fiction after 1953 (the date of *Les Petits chevaux de Tarquinia*, a transitional work), Madame Duras' first play [*Les Viaducs de la Seine-et-Oise*] falls within the general pattern established by such writers as Samuel Beckett and Eugène Ionesco, to mention only the most famous among contemporary anti-dramatists: generally plotless compositions from which motivation, that stock prop of the traditional theater, is patently absent; completely or partly anonymous characters; banalities expressed by disarming clichés; disregard for psychological verisimilitude; meticulous, precise, and detailed presentation of objects; and obsessive and contradictory fragments of thoughts and souvenirs. But in adopting this pattern ... Marguerite Duras' stage always evokes a psychological atmosphere, suggests a most human situation, seizes and seals the authentic impasses of heroes and heroines dissatisfied with their condition. Hope, weak, evasive, awkward, emerges somehow, even though aspirations hardly materialize, even though reincarnation remains utopian when it does not die in embryo, and even though the essential mediocrity of life becomes ultimately entrenched in the body and soul of most personages. For in spite of everything, the struggle involved in the attempted metempsychosis gives meaning and reason to one's existence and reaffirms the dignity of one's humanity. The total despair of the corpsed universe observable in the plays of Beckett and Ionesco is absent from the dramas of Marguerite Duras. But in order to achieve this delicate balance between the lack of a firmly established, friendly reality and Man's need of it, the author had to construct with the greatest care. The world, such as it is, is unlivable for her characters. But it is their world, and they will not abdicate until they have not made a number of gestures and have not pronounced a number of words for if they did not make those gestures and did not pronounce those words we would wonder what else they could do outside of seeking death by the most expeditious means. (pp. 145-46)

As in most of her recent novels, Marguerite Duras points . . . in her first play . . . to the absolute necessity of never quite giving up, of never capitulating entirely. Man's dignity requires the effort more than the result, as in the case when the action contradicts laws and causes the death of the one who acted. Attempting to give meaning to one's meaningless existence is viewed by her as an eminently worthy deed. And the popularity of *Les Viaducs de la Seine-et-Oise* . . . demonstrates that spectators share, albeit intuitively, the brilliant preoccupations of the author—as it proves, of course, that she is highly capable of capturing knotty, contemporary problems (the play is based, after all, on an actual case) and of reorchestrating them into lucid, literary compositions that shed light on the terrible impasses we are forced to face in our terrestrial existence. (pp. 149-50)

> *Alfred Cismaru, "'Les Viaducs de la Seine-et-Oise': Duras' Dramatic Debut," in* Renascence *(© copyright, 1971, Marquette University Press), Spring, 1971, pp. 145-50.*

ERICA M. EISINGER

The basic theme of Marguerite Duras' novels, plays, and films is the interplay between love and destruction, conflicting drives which are often resolved in the violence of a criminal act. The fascination with the *crime passionnel* or love murder leads Duras naturally to a reliance on the detective story, a genre where murder is central and where the dual structure of crime and investigation offers a model for parallel movements toward violence, then communion. Duras shares the affinity of the authors of the *nouveau roman* for the themes and techniques of the detective story. Like Robbe-Grillet, Claude Ollier, and others, Duras' work adopts the basic detective story format: a mysterious crime followed by an intense effort at understanding. But where the *nouveau roman* focuses on the puzzle element of the detective story, Duras emphasizes the human drama of moral involvement in the mystery of another's criminal act. . . .

Duras turns to the detective story along with the new novelists because she accepts its definition of reality as potentially violent and not immediately knowable. (p. 503)

Violent death, murder or suicide, is a central aspiration of all of Duras' heroines. This unconscious drive toward annihilation becomes unleashed through the dramatic confrontation with the crime of another. Duras' novels recount the transformation of an aimless, self-destructive woman into a purposeful detective. (p. 504)

The fundamental preoccupation is never the murder itself but its repercussions. . . . Duras' concern is with the irrational obsession of her heroine with the crime of another. The forward-going action of the traditional novel, which relates the adventures of an active hero, is replaced in Duras, and in the *nouveau roman* as a whole, with the detective story's reverse chronology which presents the story through the optic of the passive observer, the investigator, quite literally a "private eye" for the reader. (pp. 504-05)

Duras' women readily slide into someone else's drama because their own lives are so empty and devoid of action. . . . Duras' heroines have no existence prior to the crime; like the pure detective, they gain their identity through the investigation.

In the very earliest of Duras' novels, *Les Impudents* (1943) and *La Vie Tranquille* (1944), the pattern is set: the crime which is committed by a male—the brother—provokes the woman to action. . . . The early novels . . . develop the formula: the transformation of the heroine from witness of the murder act, to investigator, to victim in the sexual act. Lovemaking is seen as a kind of investigation, an effort to understand the violence of the criminal act. (p. 505)

The method of detection in *Le Marin de Gibraltar* is the one which Duras' future investigators will employ. All rational explanation of the evidence is discounted. . . . Physical proof yields to intuition; what is sought is not the "airtight case" against a suspect but the spiritual communion between hunter and hunted. Doubt is never entirely dispelled, even at the end of the inquiry. Discovery is a leap of faith, not an assertion of fact. (p. 506)

In Duras' novels, the intense heat, persistent intoxication, excessive sleep, and hypnotic dialogue provide a . . . dampening of consciousness so necessary to the detective enterprise. (p. 507)

The maid [heroine of *Le Square*] exhibits the need of Duras' other women and, indeed, of all criminals in detective literature to share her murderous aspirations. It is not enough to commit a crime in perfect safety; it is necessary for someone (the detective) to know. The criminal can only really exist when he or she is identified as such by the detective: the detective creates the criminal. The detective, too, is dependent on the criminal for he only comes into existence at the inception of an investigation. Thus, the detective/criminal team, as the criminal/victim team, offers a model for the study of the interdependence of the couple, a theme which is explored in the tense relationship between Anne Desbaresdes and Chauvin in *Moderato cantabile*.

Anne Desbaresdes is the archetypical dispossessed Duras heroine. . . . The absence of first-person possessive adjectives reveals her alienation from her surroundings. (p. 508)

The initial scene of the music lesson reveals much of Anne's character and introduces themes that will be reinforced by the contrapuntal episodes between Anne and Chauvin later. The sonatina itself is significant. Diabelli is best known, not through his own work, but through the Beethoven variations. And will not Anne and Chauvin essentially be playing a variation on the theme acted out by the first couple? Anne replays the lesson, this time with Chauvin the teacher and herself the pupil.

The sonata form contains, *en abîme*, the nucleus of the novel's structure with its three major movements of the music lesson, the crime, and the investigation. The sonata's return in the last movement to themes stated in the first is the very model of the detective story plot adopted by Duras whereby the detective reproduces the opening crime in the final confrontation scene. (pp. 508-09)

The men to whom [Duras' heroines] are attracted exercise

the fascination of death. They are murderers, fugitives, outsiders: the representatives of death. Their function is to lead the women through the *rites de passage,* by means of endless conversations, to the point at which they accept the fate of the women who preceded them as victims.

The method of initiation is not the physical act of love, but dialogue, a ritual form of question and answer which resembles a police interrogation. Like a well-briefed inspector, Chauvin already seems to know a great deal about Anne. He seems, in fact, able to see through the walls of her villa and to describe the interior, just as he sees into the inner desires of her soul. Thus, he speaks to her in the God-like voice of the second-person plural. . . . The *vous* is the voice of the detective who relates to the criminal how he performed his act in a triumphant display of knowledge. It is the persistent use of the second person which elicits the confession, forcing the criminal to assume responsibility for his act.

In a similar way, Chauvin gains control over Anne by the sheer duration of the dialogue, by the hypnotic effect of the endless repetitions. His commands, "parlez-moi, continuez," do elicit the capital revelation that has been awaited from the beginning, the confession of identity between witness and victim. Anne and Chauvin must talk until the magic words are said, until they have achieved in words what the other couple accomplished in deed. . . . (pp. 510-11)

Anne and Chauvin adopt the notion of the participation of the victim in the crime with such force that this explanation must clearly be a projection of their own situation. They unravel the mystery gradually, not in a scientific attempt to get at the facts, but through sheer invention. Their investigation is not just a reconstruction but a creation of its own. . . .

The key to a comprehension of the mysterious past is the detective's ritual of reenactment which brings the fusion of identity between one individual and another. To understand the suffering of another, Duras suggests, one must become him. (p. 512)

[*L'Amante anglaise*] is the most police-like of all of Duras' creations. We never see the actual crime take place, only its investigation by an anonymous questioner. The entire novel is built on the question-and-answer form of a police interrogation. (p. 515)

It is, in fact, a reworking of her own play, *Les Viaducs de la Seine-et-Oise* (1960). The change in title reveals Duras' interest—in the novel—in the mystery of Claire [heroine of *L'Amante anglaise*] and her capacity for invention. What intrigued Duras in the play was the fatality of the viaduct. In the novel, Duras shows the murder to have been as inevitable as its detection, yet fundamentally incomprehensible. As the gratuity of the title *L'Amante anglaise* suggests, no investigation will succeed in understanding Claire's private world of madness. . . .

The notion of the viaduct reveals a definite conception of the world, where from disparate pieces of reality it becomes possible to reconstruct the whole. Despite the dismemberment and the geographical dispersion of the separate entities, each part cries out for the whole; an appearance of unity is maintained. The vision of the parts leaving and returning from the viaduct could be diagrammed as a group of

concentric circles which corresponds to the obsessive forms which haunt other *nouveaux romans,* notably the "huit couché" of *Le Voyeur* or "l'as de trèfles" of *La Route de Flandres*. The recurring motif represents the attempt to impose a pattern on the chaos of reality, to seek in repetition a grand design in the universe—an attempt which fails in the *nouveau roman* as the very circularity of the form forces an infinity of interpretations. (p. 516)

The questioner in *L'Amante anglaise* may also be a writer: the novel is his project. Like so many new novels, *L'Amante anglaise* is an "anti-novel." The complete use of the question-and-answer form underscores the tentativeness of the writer's task. Duras has lost confidence in the straight narrative; the dialogue which was always a cornerstone of her work now takes over completely. The role of the author is not to explain, or even relate, but merely to ask questions and to listen. The novel ends without concluding. Duras has sent out various possible versions of Claire Lannes' crime, all going in different directions, much as the parts of the body all left on different trains. If they are to converge at a center, it is for the reader to determine the location. (pp. 518-19)

The anonymous questioner fails in his investigation, because unlike Anne Desbaresdes . . . he does not become the other, which would end the need for all questions. The failure of the questioner to exhaust the enigma of Claire Lannes compels the reader, like a Duras character, to take up the inquiry. . . .

Claire Lannes is typical of Duras' heroines in her capacity for identifying with others. All of Duras' work leads toward this identity, whether it is the fusion of past with present, or the fusion of one individual with another. (p. 519)

The theme of involvement is very close to the notion of responsibility articulated by the authors of existential fiction. Duras may represent a bridge between the moralists of the earlier period and the current group of new novelists. . . . It is no accident that Duras is practically the only experimental novelist to deal with the couple and consequently to envision the possibility of dialogue. . . .

The detective story for Duras opens moral possibilities. The investigations in her novels do not necessarily end in failure. A communion is achieved. The detective's fusion with his victim opens the way toward a wider moral involvement and enhances the opportunities for human understanding. . . . The criminal act is itself a love act, as if murder could transcend the excruciating separateness of the individual and bring one, for that privileged moment, into communion with another. (p. 520)

Erica M. Eisinger, "Crime and Detection in the Novels of Marguerite Duras," in Contempory Literature (© *1974 by The Board of Regents of the University of Wisconsin System), Vol. 15, No. 4, Autumn, 1974, pp. 503-20.*

FRANCIS S. HECK

[The purpose of this study is to reveal a] possible dimension to . . . *Dix heures et demie du soir en été,* namely that of symbolism in the relationship of the heroine, María, to the criminal, Rodrigo Paestra.

On one hand, the María-Rodrigo relationship might be interpreted as a possible "incarnation" of love in order to serve as a counterpoint to the awakened passionate love between María's husband (Pierre) and her friend (Claire). Another possibility exists, however: Rodrigo as the symbol of the creative inspiration, with María as the artist seeking to embody or "incarnate" the idea. The novel thus gains an added dimension as we follow the heroine's oscillation between these two possibilities, that is between the possibility of physical love or a deterrent to the passion of Pierre and Claire, and the more spiritual possibility of an artistic creation. (pp. 249-50)

Hence, a new dimension—the heroine as artist or creator—might be viewed as being superimposed on the usual Durasian formula of human love which fails, that is, utopian incarnation. The end result for María the artist, however, is failure, just as it is for María and Rodrigo as possible lovers. The end result, though, is not what counts. What counts, and what is paramount both for María the artist and for María in love, is that there exists a brief moment of hope and high aspiration which excites and pleases the perceptive reader. (p. 253)

> Francis S. Heck, "'Dix heures et demie du soir en été': The Heroine as Artist, A New Dimension," in Romance Notes, Winter, 1975, pp. 249-53.

ROLAND A. CHAMPAGNE

Diabelli's sonata provides the mood for many encounters in Marguerite Duras' *Moderato Cantabile*. The enchantment of this sonata performs much like the Sirens who provided Ulysses with a magnetic attraction and a need for self-discipline. In *Moderato Cantabile*, the sonata creates a "controlled" (*moderato*) and "lyrical" (*cantabile*) atmosphere for Mlle Giraud and the young Desbaresdes, Anne and her son, as well as Chauvin and Anne. Each of these couples participates in the alternation between the binary themes of reason-madness, possession-dispossession, the explainable-inexplicable, and construction-destruction. The setting of *Moderato Cantabile* is organized according to a perpetual alternation between those poles. At first, the mood of Diabelli's sonata attracts the characters toward a milieu of "hateful contraries." The tune itself becomes an enchantment of the "controlled and lyrical" community of these "hateful contraries." On the one hand, the "controlled" elements are lined to reason, possession, the explainable, and construction. These elements dramatize a world of correspondences which can be articulated, created, and mastered. On the other hand, the "lyrical" elements are linked to the irrational, dispossession, the inexplicable, and destruction. These traits characterize an unchained world which cannot be grasped. Thus, two forces are produced which fascinate and polarize the community of *Moderato Cantabile*. Nietzsche's Apollonian and Dionysian distinctions (*The Birth of Tragedy*) are akin to these two worlds. Indeed, Marguerite Duras' novel develops Nietzsche's study of the ties among music, literature, and culture. These ties in *Moderato Cantabile*, however, are concentrated about the dual forces of the "controlled" and the "lyric."

Diabelli's music . . . introduces the music into the literary world of *Moderato Cantabile*. But this music achieves an ambivalent effect. The very name "Diabelli" implies "diabolic" from which the incantation of Satan's "hateful contraries" develops a pattern of refusal, the supreme diabolic act. . . . [*Moderato Cantabile*] presents a "theater of the spoken word" whereby words become animated in a dia-

logue with silence, gestures, and physical sensations. As the readers of *Moderato Cantabile*, we become spectators of the isomorphic metamorphosis of mere words into a living dialogue.

The sonata provides the atmosphere for other realizations of the dialogue of "hateful contraries." . . . The pounding surf, the clamor of the crowd in the café, the siren at the arsenal, and even the silence among the characters echo (*redoublement*) the musical atmosphere of the sonata. This atmosphere is created by a tension between the two forces of the "controlled" (*moderato*) and the "lyrical" (*cantabile*). (pp. 981-82)

The conversations of the characters portray the ambivalence of these controlled and lyrical forces. The "theater of the spoken word" becomes especially vivid in portraying simple and fragmentary dialogues. These dialogues represent the tensions between reason and the irrational, possession and dispossession, the explicable and the inexplicable, and construction and destruction. (p. 983)

The fascination of the binary forces of the controlled and the lyrical is perpetuated by the themes of intoxication and madness. This atmosphere is a fascination which obliterates the distinct relationships among characters and objects. (p. 984)

The gestures, physical sensations, and spoken words are all set in motion to transform the characters into objects (isomorphs). . . . Indeed, the very structure of *Moderato Cantabile* revolves about the metamorphoses of people into objects. While the characters cannot express themselves through words, the objects, as well as the words themselves, recreate the lives of the people around them by tracing the rapports of the controlled forces. The gestures, perfumes, sounds, conversation, and silence replace the characters from whom they emanate.

Silence itself, as the absence of the spoken word, creates a dialectic of "hateful contraries" which generates the bonds among these physical sensations. While conversation creates a rapport among several characters, it is silence which remains to express the love, death, and madness which had tied together those victims of the café-crime. . . . Indeed, the reader participates in this dramatic portrayal of silence by his own silent reading of the "sous-conversation" but also by his active re-construction of what Nathalie Sarraute calls "the tropisms." Hence, the reader becomes another character "isomorphed" into an object by his silence and his words. (pp. 984-85)

The visions, sounds, and perfumes perceived by the characters also participate in [the dramatic life of the novel]. (p. 985)

The olfactory sensations of Anne and Chauvin especially represent their relationship. The evening of the dinner-party at the Desbaresdes, Chauvin recalls his love for Anne as Anne's magnolia tree emits a unique perfume. The magnolia tree's perfume becomes an "objective correlative" (to use T. S. Eliot's term) for the inexplicable bond between Anne and Chauvin. However, this bond between them excludes the child. . . . The child cannot participate in this physical sensation which is exclusively enjoyed by Anne and Chauvin. (p. 986)

Gestures evoke the human predicament of being trapped by the "hateful contraries" of controlled (*moderato*) and lyrical (*cantabile*) forces. . . . Duras creates a new phenomenology as the gestures in *Moderato Cantabile* indicate the relationship between the characters. The hand becomes increasingly important to dramatize human relationships. (pp. 986-87)

The hands of Chauvin and Anne especially portray their relationship. Their cold and deathly ("mortuaires") hands tremble to dramatize a love which is virtually extinct. Sometimes their hands are joined above the table to indicate an open and expressive friendship. Sometimes their hands are hidden under the table to imply a secretive, shameful liaison. Their hands are joined to express their unity during that gesture which portrays the consummation of their love: the kiss of their deathly cold lips. These gestures thus dramatize the impossibility of their love as their "conversations" explore the possibilities of developing their friendship.

The dramatic presentation of silence, sensations, and objects is only one of the cinematic techniques of Duras. . . . The eclectic techniques of Duras recall three problems with her linking of a literary text with music and film: (1) is it possible to completely reconstitute time with memory? (2) is it possible to escape this new world of literature, music, and the film? and (3) is it possible to speak of "metaphor" or of "symbol" in a phenomenological world of objects? (p. 987)

Moderato Cantabile can be considered to be a study of forgetfulness. Its cyclical structure, indicated by Anne initially ("ça recommence" . . .) and by Chauvin later ("ça recommencera" . . .), destroys the linear understanding of time. . . . The cinematic techniques of Duras seem to be exploring these limits of forgetfulness with a fragmentary narrative that has few formal transitions between the fragments. Thus, the empty spaces preclude the possibility of completely tracing the past or even the present time.

The cinematic presentation also confuses a linear, temporal sequence in the narrative. . . . The effect is the suspended animation, created by Beckett, whereby the movement of time is assigned to a perpetual beginning, always in the act of being completed, but never finished. . . . Thus, an ambivalent world of controlled and lyrical forces is being produced which re-creates the impossibility of drawing a time-line uniting past, present, and future in coherent succession. . . .

We have spoken of the isomorphic transformation of persons into objects. . . . Objects are no longer the signs or metaphors of something else. Objects may exist for themselves, have rapports with other objects, and even predicate human existence. . . . Humanity becomes transformed into neutral objects in this narrative which studies the polar attractions of objects fascinated by "controlled" and "lyrical" forces.

The destruction of the love between Anne and Chauvin is . . . the ultimate result of the "greater realism" of this polar community. In order to perpetuate the circular structure of life itself, death is a prerequisite of a rebirth. (p. 988)

Roland A. Champagne, "An Incantation of the Sirens: The Structure of 'Moderato Cantabile'," in The French Review (*copyright 1975 by the American Association of Teachers of French*), *May, 1975, pp. 981-89.*

DÜRRENMATT, Friedrich   1921-

A Swiss-German dramatist, novelist, short story writer, critic, and essayist, Dürrenmatt views the world as chaos and believes that modern man is no longer master of his own fate. Because of this, pure tragedy is no longer possible: comedy and the grotesque are for Dürrenmatt the theatrical forms of our time. His works reveal his obsession with justice in a world where the complexity of power only reinforces human impotence. His response to this world is not despair, however, but rather courage and unwillingness to surrender in the face of absurdity. Dürrenmatt has explicated his approach to drama in a volume of brilliant essays, *Theaterprobleme*, where he explores the meaning of his own plays, their critical reception, playwriting, and the role of the artist. He has also contributed to the genre of the detective story, which he feels reflects the ambiguity of truth and justice for contemporary society. (See also *CLC*, Vols. 1, 4, 8, and *Contemporary Authors*, Vols. 17-20, rev. ed.)

ADOLF D. KLARMANN

[Two facts stand out about Duerrenmatt's work], even upon a casual examination of his plays. Almost all have been reworked at least once, and almost all bear unusual baroque title and subtitles in which, as may be expected, the term "comedy" predominates in one form or another. *It is Written* (1945-46) and *The Blind Man* (1948) have no subtitles. *Romulus the Great*, "an unhistorical comedy," exists in two versions (1949 and 1957). *The Marriage of Mr. Mississippi*, "a comedy," produced in New York early in 1958 as *Fools are Passing Through* in an adaptation by Maximilian Slater, has two versions (1952 and 1957). *An Angel Comes to Babylon*, "a fragmentary comedy in three acts," has three versions (1948, 1953, and 1957). *The Visit of the Old Lady*, "a tragicomedy in three acts," of 1956 was originally to have the subtitle "a bullish comedy." (p. 79)

In Duerrenmatt's love of the macabre, there is a definite kinship to Kafka and E. Th. A. Hoffmann and a spiritual affinity to the graphic art of Alfred Kubin in the conceptualization of a situation as well as in its *mise en scène*. Duerrenmatt visualizes scenes with the eye of an experienced draftsman before he translates them into the idiom of an imaginative stage. . . . (p. 81)

It is Written [Duerrenmatt's first play], the play about the Anabaptists in Münster, in spite of its immaturity and its lack of economy and discretion, best demonstrates Duerrenmatt's characteristic dramatic devices. In form and subject matter it is a kindred spirit to such divergent plays as Goethe's *Götz von Berlichingen*, Hauptmann's *Florian Geyer*, Sartre's *Le Diable et le bon Dieu*, and Cocteau's *Bacchus*. It also shows Duerrenmatt's love for Nestroy and the Viennese folk theatre. . . . (p. 82)

We note the primacy of the stage and the reintroduction of improvisation as practiced in the commedia dell'arte and in Viennese folk theatre. The "Idea" has a prominent place in the Duerrenmatt design. Here, as in other instances, it sometimes takes over the play and carries the author merrily and recklessly to a burlesque exuberance—he calls it "Übermut"—which he considers an essential condiment of the comedy. Words, he says, are of great but not of exclusive importance. Almost as important are stage "Ideas" (*Übermut*), the rhetorical gesture which he loves so dearly and which according to him was lost for the world of drama when a naturalistic actor with bad memory could not remember his part. Striking also is his varied use of the Tieck-like touch of romantic irony. . . . The device of the monologue is very important here as well as in the next few plays. It serves several purposes: first, it introduces a character in the manner of a *conférencier,* who comments on actions past and future with conscious anachronism. . . . [The] second function of the monologue [is] the time filler, the substitute for a curtain between scenes, and also as the *raconteur,* and the obliterator of time and space. The monologue may also, in an expansiveness of language, grow into something like a couplet or *chanson,* a *Liedeinlage* à la Nestroy. . . . (Sometimes, however, to the boredom of the audience, Duerrenmatt allows himself to be intoxicated by his own eloquence.) (pp. 82-3)

Duerrenmatt comes to grips [in *It is Written*] with man's greatest glory and even greater tragedy: his incomprehension of an impatience with the design of the world order and his foredoomed attempts at correction in the role of the self-appointed savior. This is also the crucial problem of *The Marriage of Mr. Mississippi* and *An Angel Comes to Babylon.* (p. 84)

Summing up Duerrenmatt's first dramatic effort, we see certain tendencies come to the fore which—with greater skill and discretion—remain typical for his drama: The grotesque setting of a tragicomedy with strong emphasis on the bizarre and macabre; ample variations of romantic irony by the *conférencier* method, by parody, by anachronism, and by exaggeration; the yielding to idea and exuberance (*Einfall* and *Übermut*); the broad use of the soliloquy for purposes of persiflage, epic link, curtain, elimination of time and space, and intensification into a *chanson;* the use of choral speaking and similar vaudeville techniques; the preëminence of the stage by every conceivable trick of the trade; and the consistent mixture of the tragic and the comic in the shocking contrasts of sequences. (pp. 85-6)

[*The Blind Man,* a version] of the Job story, set at the time of the Thirty Years' War with the Italian nobleman Negro da Ponte playing the part of Satan, is the story of a faith which is stronger than all efforts to maintain it by deceit, or deny it, or destroy it. By means of its epigraph from Matthew 9:29, "Then touched he their eyes, saying according to your faith be it unto you," Duerrenmatt approaches the ramparts of unprotesting acceptance which our age has lost. (p. 86)

This play blends tragic and grotesque rather than comic elements. The satanic retinue of da Ponte and their make-believe world for the benefit of the Duke is reminiscent of Wedekind's *King Nicolo* with the many scenes of grotesque crudeness. On the whole, the stage is rather tame; the set is the ruin of the Duke's castle throughout, and eerie changes are achieved with lighting.

Though the play is heavy-footed, with its flirtations with *King Lear, Hamlet, King Nicolo* and German Neo-Romanticism, it is still noteworthy for its poetry, Its concern with man's lot in a world without faith places it in the main stream of twentieth-century drama. (p. 87)

If *The Blind Man* is Duerrenmatt's most Shakespearean play, then *Romulus the Great* is his most Shavian. This persiflage of history again follows a pattern important in modern drama, namely the use of classical, Biblical, or historical subjects to reflect contemporary concerns. As far as the bizarre and spectacular are concerned, *Romulus the Great* makes the least demands on the stage and easily falls into its four acts. Purely from the point of view of constructing a viable play, it is probably his most successful. It is clever, witty, graceful, full of fine repartée and irony. There are few if any stage tricks, and Nestroy's impact is felt in the cleverness of the dialogue and in the conception of certain characters. The play, in its travesty of the military in the dying Roman Empire and on the humorless, mission-ridden submissiveness of the future idol of Germanic hero worship is also a good example of Duerrenmatt's characteristic irony. (pp. 87-8)

The next two plays return to the more or less complicated symbolical stage business of *It is Written.* They apply it, however, with much greater skill and discretion. The first, *The Marriage of Mr. Mississippi,* is a *Lehrstück* (Learning Play). It owes something to Wedekind (particularly *The Marquis of Keith*); it shows evidence of linguistic affinity to Sternheim's annihilating satire of the correct bourgeois; and in its quality of "demonstration" it is closely related to Brecht. Yet, in spite of all these associations, it is very much the author's play, and the comparisons are coincidental rather than derivative. (p. 89)

How great a part is played by the stage as symbol and as vehicle of the tragicomedy is evident from the extensive stage directions. It is spiced with such remarks as, "the room smells to high heaven" with it bourgeois lack of taste. There are two windows in the background; their view: confusing. Right, a Nordic city with apple trees and Gothic cathedral: left, a cypress, ruins of a classical temple, a bay, a port. The explanation of this confusion is given in "Problems of the Theatre" where Duerrenmatt speaks of the dematerialization not only of the stage set but even more so of the locus of the drama:

> . . . in *The Marriage of Milord Mississippi* . . . I expressed the indefiniteness of the locale (in order to give its spirit of wit, of comedy) by having the right window of a room look out upon a northern landscape with its Gothic cathedral and apple tree, while the left window of the same room opens on a southern scene with an ancient ruin, a touch of the Mediterranean and a cypress. The really decisive point in all this is that, to quote Max Frisch, the playwright is making poetry with the stage, a possibility which has always entertained and occupied me and which is one of the reasons, if not the main one, why I write plays. But then— and I am thinking of the comedies of Aristophanes and the comic plays of Nestroy—in every age poetry has been written not only *for,* but *with* the stage.
>
> (pp. 89-90)

Some of Duerrenmatt's best writing and most gripping thinking goes into [the character] Übelohe's recitation of his struggle with his author for a different fate and a worthier love than Lilith-Anastasia, but in vain, for the author is infatuated with his fate as if it were his own. (p. 92)

Akki [protagonist of *An Angel Comes to Babylon*] is Duerrenmatt's stroke of genius, with his brusque sentimentality, his wit, his intelligence, his embarrassed charity, his decency and his love of freedom and the world of make-be-lieve.... Vienna somewhere between Raimund and Nestroy could well have evoked that rare atmosphere of fairy tale and irony which Duerrenmatt creates by bringing down to earth a professional angel—an empiricist pedant, utterly confused by the duplicities of the earth and enthralled by its scientific oddities—whose mission is to deliver a creation of Divine whimsy to the poorest of mortals, the last beggar of Babylon. Nestroy's sharp tongue can be heard in the social satire of the good-natured wickedness of the people, the banker, the merchant, the prostitute, the laborer, as well as in the constant allusions to the present. Bureaucracy come in for a ribbing, whether in the form of the typically Central-European policeman or the rank-conscious hangman, nor does the clergy with their petty foppery and greed escape attention. But Duerrenmatt's sharpest satire is reserved for the perfect state, the Mussolini-like, super-welfare state, where happiness is decreed and begging is outlawed as treason and as a disgrace to the fatherland. (pp. 96-7)

When compared to his other works, *The Visit of the Old Lady* is Duerrenmatt's most conservative play. The idea of absolute justice—which was earlier personified in the Old Testament concept of a Mississippi—grows to "classic" proportions in the figure of Claire Zachanassian.... She returns after forty years to exact punishment in kind on the man [Ill] whom she had loved and loves even now, the man who had caused her deepest humiliation and misery; and conversely, her greatest material triumph and retribution: "The world made a whore out of me, now I am making it into a brothel." (pp. 98-9)

Claire Zachanassian symbolically hovers over the play from beginning to end. In the second act she is literally suspended on her balcony over the action below watching the Gülleners change from upright defense of morality to corruption by temptation, patiently observing the progress of the chase until Ill, her black panther, is brought down. She is symbolic of the very corruption which destroys man's moral fiber by letting him first taste the innocent pleasures such as a bit of long-forgotten chocolate or a cigar, whetting his appetite for more, and thus letting him succumb to the corrosive gravity of his own guilt. As Übelohe already knew, man is not wicked, only weak and afraid of the stifled voice within: "Temptation is too great, poverty too bitter." For in the end the now prosperous Gülleners must forever fear the retribution of the Erinyes.

In his "Problems of the Theatre," Duerrenmatt maintains that the old sense of tragic guilt no longer exists—all of us share in it without anyone's being at fault because none of us has willed it, for "it really goes without anybody." But in this play the concept of a community of guilt is broadened so it includes the conscious acceptance of it by all. (p. 99)

Ill, the town grocer, is the only one who knew her well when as a minx of seventeen she left town. He must talk to her; and his reward is to be the office of mayor. Here the genius of Duerrenmatt posits the dramatic irony: the man who had wronged Cliare is expected to be the interlocutor. He accepts in all innocence, for he feels that whatever had happened, could not have been very serious: time and his memory have expunged his wrong. (p. 100)

What in the end is the magic sense of Duerrenmatt's com-edy and who are its heroes, if any? If unmasking is a basic function of comedy, then Duerrenmatt fulfills it in every instance. One basic trait is common to all his characters up to but excluding *The Visit of the Old Lady*, namely immutability. They are what they are, and for better or for worse they remain what they are, unbroken by life or by death. Therein lies also their tragedy, for most of them cannot conceive that their cause may be wrong or selfish or sought in their own image. Their *hubris* is their downfall. They do not pass the "*Bewährungsprobe*" (the test). They do not hesitate, in humility or Promethean vanity, to presume on the will of God or to sit in judgment over their fellow men, be it in the Münster of the Anabaptists, or the Germany of the Thirty Years' War, or dying Rome, or the present age, or Biblical times. They are the self-styled heroes and saviors and martyrs who come back again and again, as the resurrected Saint-Claude and Mississippi sing at the end of their play. As the ancient Bishop in *It is Written* knows, they try to fly before they learn walking, and their very deeds, whatever their motivation, are the traps of a guilt that they are neither aware of nor understand, but which brings about their punishment.

But then there are also the the Jobs of faith like the blind Duke, and the Quixotes like Übelohe. They are not heroes, they are the courageous. And there is Ill, who literally grows as a character as he gradually begins to comprehend his guilt and to accept the necessity of punishment. We witness for the first time in Duerrenmatt's work a tragic transformation from the role of Claire Zachanassian's persuader to a grateful reliance on the incorruptible moral support of his fellow citizens, to his growing suspicion of their betrayal as he realizes that he is the collateral for the new luxuries, including the new church bells, up to a frenzied fear that drives him to attempt an escape by train, only to find himself surrounded by the Gülleners at the station. (pp. 102-03)

Better than the blind Duke or Übelohe [Akki] represents Duerrenmatt's true hero—the nonhero. He is the little fellow, who knows that he cannot win against the mighty and principled. He knows he must survive. For, unless the unheroic Akkis survive, there will be no happiness, no beauty, no poetry, no refuge for Divine grace, only grim pursuit of duty, and sooner or later the great heroes will have finished off each other and the world. This fear of extinction keeps Akki ... and the world, and us, running.... (pp. 103-04)

Adolf D. Klarmann, "Friedrich Duerrenmatt and the Tragic Sense of Comedy," in The Tulane Drama Review *(copyright, © 1960, The Tulane Drama Review), May, 1960, pp. 77-104.*

WILLIAM GILLIS

Friedrich Dürrenmatt has written three detective novels. None of them has that aura of philosophical profundity which surrounds his other works: plays like *Der Besuch der alten Dame,* for instance, or prose works like his "noch mögliche Geschichte," *Die Panne.* But the detective novels do have a reason for being.

In many of his works Dürrenmatt is concerned directly or indirectly with an almost obsessive idea: justice.... In each of the detective novels it is the main idea and in each one it is treated differently. To be more precise, we might say that these novels are variations on a theme.

Dürrenmatt's optimistic philosophical conclusion in *Der Richter und sein Henker, Der Verdacht,* and *Das Versprechen* is this: If man wants justice, he must pursue it, but more often than not, the certain attainment of it is something he must leave to Heaven. What literary form is better suited to that "message" than the detective novel? It *is* the literary form in which the seeker of justice pursues the perpetrator of injustice. Dürrenmatt's only problem is to exalt the form, to make us realize that justice does not lie solely in the hands of the ingenious Scotland Yard man or the private eye. (p. 71)

The dramatic technique of which Dürrenmatt is a master pervades [*Der Richter*]. The prose style has a clarity and simplicity which one does not expect in a philosophically-inclined work (though Dürrenmatt's prose style is another problem in itself because it is of such a variable nature and because it has hidden intricacies). While the author now and then veers from his purpose (at one point becoming a character in his own novel) to engage in good-natured satire, generally speaking he is economical and he makes every sentence count. Every detail of the book, except for these occasional excursions, is a part of the theme that if man strives eternally, Heaven will be on his side; it is a theme which would be juvenile in the hands of a lesser man. (p. 72)

Dürrenmatt exalts the detective genre to express his basic concept of the absolute certainty of justice, of man's relationship to the power which governs it, and of the validity of the human pursuit for a better world. He considers it a part of his philosophical business to reach a mass audience through his novels without diluting that one main idea which permeates much of his writing: justice. (p. 74)

> *William Gillis, "Dürrenmatt and the Detectives,"* in The German Quarterly *(copyright © 1962 by the American Association of Teachers of German), January, 1962, pp. 71-4.*

EDWARD DILLER

Paradox and grotesquerie are more than stylistic devices for Dürrenmatt: they are his reaction to our world, a world which, in contrast to earlier times, has lost all unity, has become chaotic beyond all comprehension, and therefore terrifying. (p. 328)

George Santayana calls the grotesque "... an interesting effect produced by such a transformation of an ideal type as exaggerates one of its elements or combines it with other types." Through this transformation the artist regains his freedom, and, with it, subject material which can no longer be found but must be *invented*, for parody and grotesque presuppose invention. This deliberate distortion of history and this sovereign willfulness in treating historical figures is illustrated in *Es steht geschrieben* (It stands written), in the figure of Nebukadnezar in *Ein Engel Kommt nach Babylon* (An Angel Comes to Babylon) and in practically all characters and events in *Romulus der Grosse.*

Why, then, asks Dürrenmatt, do we always and only use the Greek tragedians as models from which to derive dramatic principles? Why not for once, try to learn something from Aristophanes, the great master of comedy? The tragedians present to us events of a distant, mythical past as if these events were contemporary, they try to overcome distance in order to move us. Aristophanes walks in the opposite direction: his comedies take place in the present, but

we are supposed to laugh about what is close to us and what we care about; and therefore Aristophanes creates distance between the play and us: Dürrenmatt believes that *this distance is essential for comedy,* and that a truly modern play must be a comedy in the Aristophanic sense. . . . (pp. 330-31)

The underlying cause of the grotesque that is traceable in Dürrenmatt's writings is that of monstrous *incongruity or disparity between human idea* (plan, expectation) *and reality.* . . .

Since Dürrenmatt, like his master Aristophanes and like Brecht, believes that the timely play must create distance between stage action and audience, he uses all species of the grotesque to oppose the illusionistic theater. The theater of today, he complains, is really not today's theater at all but a relic of the past. . . .

Dürrenmatt turned to comedy at a time when he despaired of the possibility in our time, and when he denied the existence of a "hero" in the conventional sense. (p. 333)

Dürrenmatt [in his "21 points" to *Die Physiker*] starts with the discovery of an idea, insight, or conceit, and develops it to its worst possible consequence. The worst possible consequence occurs when there is a clash between logic and accident (i.e., between idea and reality, or between human reality and fate). Such a clash can be expressed philosophically by means of the paradox, stylistically by the grotesque. The paradox is then the purpose of the drama; it is the intended goal of Dürrenmatt's drama—a confrontation with the fundamental dichotomy of conceptual life and physical reality. The grotesque leads us into, and forces us to recognize, the paradox—a relationship of ideas to reality, that cannot be comprehended. When man encounters the paradox, his thought processes fail him—an important experience for Dürrenmatt. It is one of the few experiences where man must admit his limitations and must accept his status as a finite human being. This achievement of man is central in Dürrenmatt's writings and its expression is evidenced in his style. Where incidents of the grotesque are found, one finds men in conflict with their proper character, distorted to a point to repugnance or horror. And yet, in this condition is an element of revealed truth and humor—the ridiculous strivings of man attempting to become more than himself. The result, as one of Dürrenmatt's characters cries out in despair, is that the world of man is

> An eternal comedy
> That illuminates His magnificance,
> Nourished through our impotence.
>
> (pp. 334-35)

> *Edward Diller, "Aesthetics and the Grotesque: Friedrich Dürrenmatt,"* in Contemporary Literature *(© 1966 by the Regents of the University of Wisconsin), Vol. 7, No. 3, Autumn, 1966, pp. 328-35.*

EDWARD DILLER

Dürrenmatt's assertions frequently cause a reader to stop precisely at a point where serious analysis of basic assumptions should begin. His statements on the absurdity and chaotic quality of the world, for example, might seem to indicate that Dürrenmatt has resigned himself to the necessity of regarding the world as "chaos" and given up the job of trying to order or formulate his basic ontology in a coherent fashion. . . . [However there is] an overwhelming mass of evidence to indicate that the roots of Dürrenmatt's writings are firmly planted in an orderly personal theology that he uses to measure and judge the perplexing problems of our times. (p. 28)

In one of Dürrenmatt's short stories, *Der Tunnel*, some specific questions are asked about the significance of human existence and its relationship to God. Dürrenmatt paints a terrifying picture, showing the impotency and the complete lack of direction of modern man and the absurdity of his smug and limited undertakings. (p. 29)

Now why should Dürrenmatt, a product of the twentieth century, not assume that man has the power or capacity to improve on the world, or even aid in his own redemption, for that matter? Simply because to do so would assume that man has powers of salvation that could rob God of His power and His glory.

Thus, the great theological question which presses upon Dürrenmatt is: How shall God be glorified in an age which rejects the whole question as ridiculous? (pp. 30-1)

The theologian of *Ein Engle kommt nach Babylon* must burn the theology professors to prove his own theology, and the other numerous ministers and politicans of Dürrenmatt's plays retain or lose their positions on the basis of their ability to propose acceptable "political illusions" to a people or a regime. (p. 32)

The justification for any ideology is that it has meaning, but the final message of this play is that the planned efforts and cultivated schemes of men ultimately turn out to be meaningless. It is in this "meaninglessness" that the real significance of Dürrenmatt's plays is revealed. This play concludes with the words that the conflicts and ideas of men end in absurdity, but whereas absurdity is the conclusion drawn from life by post-war French dramatists, it becomes a significant starting point for Dürrenmatt. . . . In the ridiculous conclusions of man's most sublime undertakings a kind of divine justice is revealed . . . which serves the purpose of illuminating the power and the glory of God and pointing out the impotence of man by comparison. By means of strange accidents, human ignorance, and fumbling ambition, man is returned from his sublime flights of ambitious fancy to his original limited state. (p. 33)

What lies at the heart of Dürrenmatt's soteriology is the exclusion of the human element in the initiation of the saving process through fate so that the pure grace of God may be magnified. Assuming that, Dürrenmatt can express the sense behind man's dependence on the free mercy of a saving God; or extrude the the evil by which, as he clearly sees, God is robbed of His glory and man is encouraged to think that he owes to some power, some act of choice, some initiative of his own, his participation in that salvation which is in reality presented as divine grace. . . . (pp. 33-4)

There is accordingly nothing against which Dürrenmatt sets himself with more firmness than every form of hubris. This includes man's desire to administer justice by playing God and judging what is good and what is evil. Real justice can be administered only by God and in His name only, or justice would illuminate the glory of men rather than of God. . . .

Dürrenmatt bemoans the fact that fate and universal justice have vanished from the modern stage. . . . Dürrenmatt feels it is his obligation to revive fate because of the important role it plays in men's lives. Where fate directs its inescapable and terrible force against the individual, one must confront it stripped of pretensions, aware of one's own finiteness and fraility—certainly an important message for an age in which man insists upon independence from God.

But if Dürrenmatt's God is the Judge, he is also the Redeemer. Crime, punishment, and redemption are bound together. (p. 34)

What may have at first seemed like initial frustration for Dürrenmatt's characters turns into the doctrine of "irresistible grace" or "effectual calling"—the basis of Calvinistic salvation; and it lies much more deeply embedded in Calvin's system, and in Dürrenmatt's, than does the doctrine of predestination itself. (p. 35)

Dürrenmatt's religious conception reflects an overwhelming vision of a God who will not give His glory to another, for He alone is the author, preserver, and governor of all things. And only when this is recognized, only when an attitude of absolute dependence is sustained through all the activities of life, does religion contribute an additional dimension to life. (p. 36)

Dürrenmatt assumes the existence of an ontology in which the whole order of the world is brought into a rational unity with the doctrine of grace. It is only with such a universal conception of God, established in a living way, that one can face, and accept, possibly with some hope, the spiritual dangers and terrors of our time. (p. 37)

The power of man's ultimate salvation is in the hands of God alone. This is the root of the soteriology of both Dürrenmatt and Calvin; this deep sense of human helplessness and this profound consciousness of indebtedness, for all that enter into salvation do so only by the will of God. But the Fall, which was also willed by God, substantially changed human nature so that now all man wills and does is sin. Hence, Dürrenmatt's emphasis on the omnipotence of God makes short shrift of man's concept of justice or freedom. (p. 38)

Dürrenmatt (like his contemporaries, the eminent theologians of Switzerland, Karl Barth and Emil Brunner) has rejuvenated the spirit if not the letter of Calvinism. The great attraction it has for drama, as well as modern dialectical theology, is its dramatic emphasis on the omnipotence of God and the nothingness of man and then having established that principle beyond any reasonable doubt, Dürrenmatt (as Calvin once did) draws systematic inferences about the forces that determine the incomprehensible, paradoxical nature of man's existence, i.e. the contradictions between human and divine justice, the sinful nature of man (his distance, since the Fall, from God), the intrinsic evil of human action, the divine prerogative of election or reprobation of men (both of which, however, work to glorify the greatness of God and reveal the impotence of man), the apparent incongruence of proximate and remote causation, and predestination. Thus, and in no uncertain terms, Dürrenmatt truly becomes the minister's son reminding us through the medium of literature that God, and not man, must rule the world. (pp. 38-9)

Edward Diller, "Friedrich Dürrenmatt's Chaos and Calvinism," in Monatshefte *(copyright © 1971 by the Regents of the University of Wisconsin), Spring, 1971, pp. 28-40.*

STEPHEN TAPSCOTT

"I describe human beings," Friedrich Dürrenmatt writes, "not marionettes; an action and not an allegory. I have presented a world, not pointed a moral." In this composite dramatic world of complex ironic situations, the authentic man of genuinely heroic stature, ultimately, is the self-conscious fool who is so dominated by fortune that even his tragic nobility becomes a source of somersaulting absurdity. Dürrenmatt's is a formless world, anonymous and abstract, but is personalized concretely in individual protagonists, so that the plays avoid the abstract irony of Pirandello or Sartre, for instance, or the deliberate alienation of Brecht. The characteristic perspective for Dürrenmatt's world is distance, a vantage point from which to recognize personal form and social chaos. This distance, the characteristic of comedy, reflects, as Dürrenmatt acknowledges, an attitude toward the universe beyond the stage, as well. . . .

Adopting a surreal landscape from the Expressionism of the early twentieth-century theater, dialogue from the Naturalism of post-Romantic European movements, and mythic themes from ancient drama, Dürrenmatt evolves a dramatic style in which form works ironically against content. With generally "comic" techniques—conceit, double reversals, the clown-figure—Dürrenmatt works to tragic conclusions. The result is layered irony; gay, innocent tragedies and somber comedies combine in a hybrid form which seems to resemble tragi-comedy. Dürrenmatt himself refers to his "comedy with a tragic end." Yet these plays avoid the desperate egocentricity of Existential absurdity and of Black Humor, for the comic absurdity of the modern world, personalized, becomes the modern tragedy generalized: tragic wisdom is made possible through comic means. (p. 352)

The *mise-en-scène* of Dürrenmatt's plays is bizarre and placeless, as poetically simple as Beckett's "country road," and as politically complex as a stylized Genêt landscape. Situation, not personal psychology, dominates the dramatic action in a universalized setting, and the story itself once more becomes important in the theater. (p. 353)

Dürrenmatt in his sympathetically "foolish" heroes offers a personalism that is skeptically optimistic despite the desperate circumstances in which his heroes find themselves: the very folly of the wise-but-not-bitter fool removes Dürrenmatt's heroes from the tragedy of their circumstances. . . . [Dürrenmatt's heroes] are unanimously out of rhythm with their "lunatic" societies. . . . Yet all are men of courage, often voluntary "fools"; they have their apocalyptic hope in the future with respect to the past, and each realizes that "our only control is over the present." The tragic vision is still possible in the disjointed society, though pure tragedy is an anomaly. More than suffering, foolishness is the process of divestiture and self-exhaustion that leads to a final vision. (pp. 354-55)

The man standing outside the world while dealing in it—the fool who distances his vision with moral and historical perspective instead of positioning himself in the hurly-burly horrors of his society—is the anti-hero whose choice is authentically tragic: a choice whether or not to capitulate. . . . Dürrenmatt's heroes essentially create themselves through choices concerning the "riddle of misfortune." (p. 355)

Dürrenmatt's heroes . . . begin by choosing their proper absurdities and conclude by finding in their choices the possibility of integrity. Dürrenmatt's heroes are fools, active within the sphere of human contemporary absurdity, who find significance and hope after double-reversals of fate make them genuine fools of society. Their folly is not feigned and defensive, like Hamlet's, nor organic and magnificent, like Lear's; it is rather a mode of integrity for acting in a genuinely foolish world. (p. 356)

Dürrenmatt, avoiding the comic technique of distancing the fools in their wisdom and the equally potent technique of psychological seriousness about "madness," twists the pattern of "foolishness" by making the fool a tragic hero himself, then an authentic fool, without abandoning the elements of distance and judgment: the fool never ceases to be a fool. As agents of social criticism, Dürrenmatt's heroes enjoy no privileged distance from which to adjudicate. Lear goes mad by seeing the cruelty and isolation of the individual in the world. But Dürrenmatt's heroes merge the two figures of Lear and jester; as ironic counterparts, they are each the central figure of the action, unlike Edmund and Edgar in their assumptions of new identities. Though often denied a final salutary vision, Dürrenmatt's heroes salvage a sliver of grim and grinning optimism, because as authentic fools, each retains his freedom to choose his proper absurdity. "In laughter man's freedom becomes manifest," Dürrenmatt writes, "in crying his necessity. Our task today is to demonstrate freedom."

This principle of ironic double-reversal is particularly evident in Dürrenmatt's play *The Physicists*, an anti-Promethean tragi-comedy. . . . The punishment of [Prometheus] was explation through a scapegoat-figure, purifying all humanity and guaranteeing somehow the continued enjoyment of the gift of knowledge for humankind. In Dürrenmatt's play, however, the physicists have recognized the terrifying danger from the abuse of that gift. By their research and their use of the Promethean gift, the scientists have unwittingly realized the potential for social violence. . . . Trying to protect his reputation as a madman, each scientist kills the nurse who inevitably falls in love with him. Eventually each man realizes, ironically, that he must now remain within the madhouse and that he now deserves to stay; in order to protect his pacific innocence, each has killed. Unlike Brecht's Galileo, Dürrenmatt's scientists cannot disclaim their knowledge. Their ritual purifications have only made them more directly guilty. Now they are truly absurd, fools within the madhouse in a lunatic world. (pp. 356-57)

The tragic fool's view of historical continuity, looking forward into an optimistic free choice of future, also looks ironically backward into archaic forms of myth and history. Especially potent, even in Dürrenmatt's dramas of the modern power system, are the ritual myths of the year-king and the sacrificial victim, the reparation for societal guilt, and the society's hope for a new life through such rituals. Curiously, Dürrenmatt displays a disdain for the academics of the "mythic" school and their exposition of underlying myth in many dramas, claiming that once the rituals are regarded merely as myth, the ritual strength of each myth is effectively emasculated. (pp. 358-59)

As Dürrenmatt explains in "Problems of the Theater," the audience should be an integral part of the dramatic enterprise. But because the myths underlying tragedy have been made impotent—implicitly, the individual no longer signifies—the audience can no longer participate in those shared cultural beliefs, as a Greek audience could. Instead of a religious and emotional alcohol, the myth is now only an intellectual sugarplum; its proper use is now ironic, not tragic. The year-king, the scapegoat, the fool, become tragic heroes in the comic tragedy of today, but without the nobility of tragic vision nor the wisdom of the choice of fate. . . .

Dürrenmatt's heroes . . . are offered only several versions of absurdity, but their choices emphasize the arbitrary freedom which they maintain. . . . The modal convolutions of Dürrenmatt's world make the individual first a voluntary fool, then a tragic fool, and finally a fool again with a comic dimension. (p. 361)

[Dürrenmatt's heroes] are themselves comic or absurd in an antic and absurd world, and their tragedy is that their personal foolishness does not conform to the established folly of their worlds. Generically, "tragi-comedy" seems the most appropriate category for the fate of these comic heroes, who are neither anti-heroic nor heroic, but most characteristically un-heroic. But Dürrenmatt's dramatic ironies reverse the usual process of tragi-comedy. Instead of arriving at a tragic end through a comic device, Dürrenmatt pivots his heroes' fate on the "as if," giving them tragic stature by keeping them comic. (pp. 363-64)

> *Stephen Tapscott, "The Fool as Tragic Hero: A Generic Reading of Friedrich Dürrenmatt," in* Genre (© *copyright 1975 by Donald E. Billar, Edward Henston and Robert Vales; reprinted by permission of the University of Oklahoma), December, 1975, pp. 352-65.*

G. F. BENHAM

On the face of it Dürrenmatt's first essay into [the detective story], *Der Richter und sein Henker,* contains sufficient traditional elements to explain its abiding popularity. . . . Written as it was in installments it enjoys all the sculptured, architechonic advantages of the *Roman Feuilleton.* (p. 147)

On first reading Dürrenmatt's *Der Richter und sein Henker* one is struck by the strangeness, the disconcerting oddity of the overall impression which this novel leaves. Where, one asks, is that feeling of delight, that essentially cathartic, reassuring feeling that things have turned out right? In its place one experiences a disconcerting *je ne sais quoi,* a nagging, worrying feeling that the equation has worked itself out unsatisfactorily. Initially one is inclined to dismiss this reaction, perhaps attributing it to Dürrenmatt's failure to cope with what was, for him at the time, a new form. But this too is unsatisfactory. The reader is left with no alternative but to re-read—and read more closely, paying particular attention to Dürrenmatt's departures from the "classic" tradition.

The figure of Kommissär Bärlach dominates this novel from the earliest stages until the close; small wonder, then, that it is here that we find the causes for the reader's unusual reaction to this novel as a whole. (p. 148)

[The] unreflecting acceptance so characteristic of the usual response to escape literature has no place here. The reader is forced to re-examine, to criticise.

The apparently benign Kommissär is presented in a way which initially makes critical examination rather difficult, for he is clearly the most sympathetic character in the novel. (p. 152)

One feels that his inhumanity, total absence of moral scruple and willingness to involve himself in crime as a matter of whim, without any apparent gain to be drawn from it, marks Gastmann as a very particular kind of criminal. Written only seven years after the end of the war in Europe . . . , [the novel] echoes ominously the gratuitous criminality and the inhuman treatment of the individual during the Nazi period. This particular thematic strand is central to the sequel, *Der Verdacht,* written one year later, 1952, which likewise has Bärlach as its hero. (p. 153)

> *G. F. Benham, "Escape into Inquietude: 'Der Richter und sein Henker'," in* Revue des Langues Vivantes, *Vol. XLII, No. 2, 1976, pp. 147-54.*

E

EBERHART, Richard   1904-

Eberhart, an American poet and playwright, is best known for his antiwar poems. His intense religious and moral convictions inform all his work. (See also *CLC*, Vol. 3, and *Contemporary Authors*, Vols. 1-4, rev. ed.)

DENIS DONOGHUE

The Visionary Farms is a *drame à thèse* which owes a great deal to the expressionist tendencies of the early plays of Eugene O'Neill, Thornton Wilder, and Elmer Rice. It is not in any important sense original; it does not enlarge the range of dramatic art; but it provides an opportunity of examining an interesting alliance between modern dramatic verse and those non-representational procedures which have been developed in the theatre in such plays as *The Hairy Ape*. (p. 223)

The theme of *The Visionary Farms* is not "money" but the larger motive of "Progress," which Professor [Richard M.] Weaver has described as the "god term" of the present age.... It is probably the only term which gives the average American or West European a concept of something larger than himself, which he is socially impelled to accept, and for which he is ready to sacrifice.

The context of *The Visionary Farms* is largely determined by such considerations: its "scene" is a climate of feeling in which Progress is cultivated without restraint from any other values. (pp. 223-24)

If *The Visionary Farms* is a *drame à thèse* it is such with a difference, for Mr. Eberhart has not presented a realistic enactment of the ruin of a commercial empire in 1919. Rather, he has dramatised his impression of the inevitable conclusion of the cult of Progress. The play, technically related to America in 1919, is visionary in the sense in which one applies the word to such works as *R.U.R., The Trial, Brave New World*, and *1984*. (It will be understood that these comparisons are descriptive, not qualitative. Qualitatively, *The Visionary Farms* is nearer to John Hawkes than to Kafka.) ... *The Visionary Farms* does not study anything. Rather it envisages, in fear and solicitude, and enacts this vision.

The technique by which Mr. Eberhart dramatises his conception includes among its most active features these two: distortion and simplification. The two procedures cooperate in the quasi-expressionistic structure of the play. The characteristic form of distortion is a gesture, not toward the baroque, but toward the rudimentary. If one examines the presentation of character, time, and incident in *The Visionary Farms* one finds that in each case the distortion takes the form of cutting away the circumstantial details which the physical laws impose on normal living. For instance, all the characters in the play are one-dimensional. To describe "Hurricane" Ransome as symbol of Progress-mania is not to give special attention to one feature from a fully rounded character; it is to name the only feature, the only dimension, which is *there*. There is nothing more to him. The audience is not encouraged to see him as a whole man, but rather as a bloodless symbol, logical conclusion of a grotesque cult. He is Man, from whom all levels of existence other than the predatory have been cut away by greed. (pp. 224-25)

The treatment of time in *The Visionary Farms* exhibits similar distortion. Taft telephones the State University to send down a chicken surgeon; the surgeon arrives within a few seconds.... Distortion of this kind has, of course, a dual function. In addition to "interpreting" the action it also evokes in the audience responses quite different from those envisaged by a realistic play. It is an indication that the probable is not to be relied on, that we are in a Kafka-like world.

Similarly, in the treatment of the incidents the technique of distortion sets aside plausibility, causes, and expectations, cutting away all indication of the part played by these forces in human decisions. Existence and behaviour as presented in *The Visionary Farms* show hardly more than a nominal connexion with the rational. Man has thrust himself *down* the scale of existence, throwing away his Reason as he approaches the rudimentary or animal level of behaviour. Motives are so attenuated that they are indistinguishable from the movements of a machine.... (p. 226)

Distortion and simplification—but there is no real distinction between the two. Or, rather, in the most significant parts of the play the two merge to cut away all trace of the complex or the circumstantial. The effect is, of course, cumulative; its success is a matter of loosening the audience's instinctive adherence to those factors in the everyday world which (however precariously) operate in terms of cause and effect, circumstance and probability. This adherence is not totally severed. What remains has the effect of supplying, as it were on the margin, a severely critical and "proper" attitude to the events being enacted. If this is the purpose of the procedure it is successful. . . . (p. 227)

The pervading tone of *The Visionary Farms* is satirical, but the satire is based not so much on derision as on solicitude. In this respect Mr. Eberhart is to be associated with Eugene O'Neill and many other modern American dramatists who have, in their plays, composed manifestos repudiating the unrestrained cult of Progress. In a wider context *The Visionary Farms* and *The Emperor Jones* are protests against the excesses, the perversions, of those assumptions which have dominated post-Renaissance civilisation. (pp. 227-28)

The Visionary Farms implies that if ordinary, day-to-day life continues to be based exclusively and fanatically on current "progressive" values it will at some unspecified date look very like the pathetic, monstrous life of the Parkers and the "Hurricane" Ransomes in 1919. Thus the satire and the solicitude.

The rhetorical intent of *The Visionary Farms* . . . seems naïve and oversimplified. It is true that neither *The Visionary Farms* nor *This Music Crept By Me on the Water* attains a "perfect" judgment of its material. *The Visionary Farms* is committed to a strong but simple rhetoric by its use of "planned derangement." (p. 228)

Mr. Eberhart's procedure is deliberate, but it must still be assessed. Here the dramatist has gone astray. The comments of the Everyman group (which may be regarded as, collectively, choric) are designed to "bring on thoughts / To estimate these matters to a standstill." But the last scene, which might possibly stand being "undramatic," fails by being uncreative. The choric comments are forced on a dramatic fable which does not substantiate them. . . . [These comments] are inadequately supported by a play whose very essence was the clarity which arises from distortion and simplification. . . . [Realism] has been set aside, in the Fahnstock story, in favour of one-dimensional expressionism, and with a high degree of short-term success. This success has been achieved primarily by Mr. Eberhart's "simplifying vision." Not content with this modest achievement, the author has tried to insinuate, through the Chorus, ambiguities and complexities which are not *there* in the story of Adam Fahnstock.

For evidence we would point to the form of *The Visionary Farms*. Mr. Eberhart has deliberately withheld from his play the significance of form *as form*; indeed this is the *formal* counterpart of the play's thesis. Professor [Joseph Wood] Krutch has argued, with reference to post-Strindbergian drama, that if one is going to argue that life is meaningless, one cannot make the point in a play where the play itself constitutes meaning. . . . [Such] arguments are the source of Mr. Eberhart's refusal to "tie a neat dramatic package." The story of Adam Fahnstock is presented with minimum emphasis on form *as form* because the mode of living which it represents is so weird and insane as to point away from meaning altogether. At all costs, therefore, Mr. Eberhart has avoided giving it the significance and "shape" implied by classic form.

Mr. Eberhart is a genuine, if remarkably uneven, poet. (pp. 231-32)

[This is evident in *The Fury of Aerial Bombardment*, a poem that] exhibits a unity of tone which is reflective and severe, though not quite "grand." The language of *The Visionary Farms* is a little lower than "mean." Particularly in the play-within-a-play the representation of speaking voices is consistently realistic. (p. 233)

One can hardly profess to hear in this play that "more impersonal voice still than that of either the character or the author" which Eliot posits: the voice which issues only from an entire dramatic universe, such as the universes of Shakespeare or Racine. Mr. Eberhart has not created his universe. (p. 234)

In *The Visionary Farms* the regular end-rhymes of *The Fury of Aerial Bombardment* have gone, but the line of four stresses remains, as in

> Roger, are you capable of such vile trickery?
> Neither you nor I was to blame for Hurricane . . .

By using an identifying vocabulary, syntax, and rhythm, Mr. Eberhart has caused Adam Fahnstock's role to emerge, valid and capacious, from the situations in which he is placed. (pp. 234-35)

> *Denis Donoghue, "Richard Eberhart: 'The Visionary Farms'," in his* The Third Voice: Modern British and American Verse Drama *(copyright © 1959 by Princeton University Press; reprinted by permission of Princeton University Press), Princeton University Press, 1959, pp. 223-35.*

BABETTE DEUTSCH

[Richard Eberhart's] concern has steadily been with the incredibility of the actual. His war poems, lyrical in spite of their fierce concision, speak concretely and eloquently of the incongruousness of the concepts of man and of war. He writes with stunning impact of the mindless butchery, the small cruelties, and the greater horror as

> The Earthquake Opens Abrupt the World,
> Cold Dreadful Mass Destruction.

But in the midst of animal anguish and moral disaster he is alive to the dreamlike vision of anti-aircraft seen from a distance: "a controlled kind of falling stars," and he is not afraid to call attention to "the beautiful disrelation of the spiritual." (pp. 415-16)

> *Babette Deutsch, in her* Poetry in Our Time *(copyright © by Babette Deutsch; 1963 by Doubleday; reprinted by permission of Babette Deutsch), revised edition, Doubleday, 1963, pp. 415-16.*

PHILIP BOOTH

What I first admire about *The Quarry*, reading it whole, is how totally it is Richard Eberhart's. No matter what my response to single poems, I read them all as being demonstrably Eberhart's in rhythm, diction, and risk. However native this integrity, it's more than a negative virtue in the world of programmatic poetry where Eberhart's skilled juniors too often write what read like interchangeable translations of some Imagist Eskimo. It's no wonder that the Programmatic Poets, currently bent on murdering whatever elders are tall enough for parricide, have neglected knifing Eberhart in his always vunerable back. The virtues of Eberhart's poems, like their flaws, are simply too individual to be imitated. The self-defined Beats, by Kenneth Rexroth's example, once flirted with sanctifying Eberhart, but for the wrong reasons: they saw him merely as the single "academic" who seemed handsomely careless of traditional forms. Since the once-New Criticism denies the very possibility of a naive (or non-ironic) poet, Eberhart has been as curiously immune from serious consideration as he has been exempt from attack. Given our existential modes of criticism, and those multitudes of poets so existentially influenced, there's been small room for reading a poet whose primary perceptions are religious. I have no idea as to what church Eberhart may possibly belong, but I am sure beyond doubt that he is fundamentally a religious poet, and that at his best his religion and poetry are one. (p. 63)

Eberhart's poetry implicitly argues, I take it, that "the visible world is part of a more spiritual universe from which it draws its chief significance; that . . . harmonious relation with that higher universe is our true end; that . . . inner communication with the spirit thereof . . . is a process wherein work is really done, and spiritual energy flows in and produces effects, psychological or material, within the phenomenonemal world." That great mouthful is, of course, from those Conclusions which climax *The Varieties of Religious Experience.* [William James'] definitions of religious inclination strike me as precisely defining Eberhart's first concerns. (p. 64)

[I refuse] to review Eberhart in any conventional way; I'm inclined to pursue *The Quarry* with as little "existential judgment" as possible. Such judgments, James says, derive from questioning "what is the nature of it, how did it come about? what is its constitution, origin, history?" The question of the *nature* of a book is impossible to avoid, and such a question will, understandably, underlie most reviews of *The Quarry.* But insofar as *only* this question gets asked, the reviews will merely confirm each other's prejudices, and will do Eberhart only Mississippi justice. It is, for instance, already a cliché of criticism that Eberhart publishes too much, that he is his own worst editor, that his poetry is egocentric, abstract, technically careless, and mindless to such glib rhyming as "finest beliefs" with "mankind's griefs." All this may or may not be true, but it is no more or less true in *The Quarry* than in any number of Eberhart's earlier books. Whenever it might have been when critics could tell Eberhart how to write somebody else's poems, that time has long since passed. Eberhart's long integrity deserves, rather, asking of *The Quarry* James' second set of questions: "What is its importance, meaning, or significance now that it is once here?" The answer to this, James says, is not an existential judgment, but a "proposition of value."

It seems to me that a proposition of value is exactly what Eberhart's best poems repeatedly propose. It's no tautology to say that what they propose *is* their value. Eberhart's intent, within and beyond his best work, is to propose moral possibilities in a universe so complex that even its grandeur is all but incomprehensible. How to live, believing in God, is no small proposition. That such a proposition seems largely dated to most mid-century poets is of no concern to Eberhart; he is that most timeless of rare birds, a religious romantic. When he succumbs to his dramatic temptations, and prints poems like *The Quarry*'s "Father and Daughter" or "Father and Son," the devil has clearly got hold of his coat-tails, and I find myself blindly embarrassed. . . . No matter how historical the meters of these

poems, Eberhart fakes-out his primarily speculative voice when he tries to dramatize it; his diction in such cases strikes me as being absurdly inhuman. When he prints his unmeditated addresses "To Bill Williams," "To Auden on His Fiftieth," and "To a Poet Who Has Had a Heart Attack," I feel of such poetry as I feel about Goergia: I'd like to reform its conventions with a single quick verb. (pp. 64-5)

As befits his romantic tradition, Eberhart is repeatedly most incisive when his poems confront death. This "savage mystery" has been his lifelong concern, and he is most his own poet when, considering mortality, he observes himself as man-in-relation-to-nature. He is most unashamedly religious when he speculates on his own relativity to the cosmos, when he searches to find what Frost would call his "place among the infinities." . . . Particularly when death and youth are juxtaposed in his poems, Eberhart commits himself to a paradox commensurate with his own tensions. Where Ransom is peculiarly fascinated with dying women or mourning girls, Eberhart expends himself in confronting the death of boys or young men. *The Quarry*'s elegy for Bunny Lang and "Death by Drowning" are (for all their Eberhart-virtues) less valuable than "The Groundhog" or "The Fury . . . ", but Eberhart has equalled these poems in a remarkable new sonnet, "Am I My Neighbor's Keeper?" . . . [How] vital to his poetry is Eberhart's seeming innocence. Even as Eberhart is finally innocent in the specific Vermont drama of being his neighbor's keeper, the poem of that murder nowhere refuses guilt. . . . Eberhart's poetry is always tempted toward comparable simplification, but its great virtue lies in refusing as much. Posing moral choices in a world where God is seldom apparent, Eberhart writes a poetry where virtue is nonetheless *possible.* Innocence, in his poems, is not a refusal of guilt, but a healthy counter to it. Eberhart is handsomely unconcerned with how humanity may have fallen with Adam. Minnesota-born, he's resiliently far from the guilt of any New England Primer. Precisely as Adam *chose* his bite of Eve's old apple, Eberhart's poetry makes guilt an open choice. He's not above apples, but not about to transfer his guilt to Eve. In poem after poem, he opts for choice itself; death may be inevitable, but it's less (and other) than a final punishment for guilt. What death *means*, in Eberhart's poetry, is an inexplicable mystery. Eberhart's great honesty is that his poems confront this mystery on its own terms, reserving for themselves only the equal mystery of life's sweet vitality.

Given the mystery his poems uniquely confront, it's small wonder that Eberhart celebrates life with an almost animal-innocence. Against death and guilt (separate though they are) Eberhart counters his own almost infinite human potentials. But *given* death and guilt, as derived from God's inexplicable essence, Eberhart's poems must *deduce* man's place in the universe. Typically identifying himself with a spider "caught in nature," Eberhart (comically) begins a next stanza: "How to expatiate and temporize / This artful brag." This mode of resolution (especially when its tone is serious) is what puts his critics off. Criticism is accustomed to inductive poems, the existential conclusions of which may be carefully tested against the poem's internal evidence. But Eberhart very often (as in "The Fury . . . ") begins with a cosmic assertion, and deduces *in the process of writing* whatever evidence may sustain it. There's a divine madness in this approach that often seems more mad than divine; when it doesn't work it fails miserably. But where it does succeed, its virtues are the virtues of innocence itself: the poems stand, in a world needing redemption, as emblems of the inherent goodness they approach. Even in his lesser poems, Eberhart is too deeply a part of nature to be unnaturally humble about his vital stake in it. Where Eberhart's poetry intellectualizes the mystery of death, his humility is real. . . . [In other places, however, he acts the] poet-as-Prometheus, as his own hero. . . . But Eberhart's self-concern is uncalculated, save as poems and children are his gamble against mortality. His self-concern is, rather, a strong return to that state of incalculable naïveté where animal-ego is its own defense against death, where children are innocent, and where poems may redeem one's guilt before God. (pp. 65-7)

Eberhart has his own North Country sense of the wilderness in which he has long walked lonely. The very title of *The Quarry* suggests both hunting and cutting from hard granite; Eberhart's earlier book titles define comparably solo concerns: *Undercliff* and *Burr Oaks* imply both climbable heights and workaday dangers; each suggests a locus for *Reading the Spirit;* both admit of *Great Praises,* allow *A Bravery of Earth,* and invite *Song and Idea.* As such titles tell, Eberhart's thematic concerns have been remarkably consistent, from his fine undergraduate sonnet, "Burden," to *The Quarry* itself. "A New England View: My Report," "Ways and Means," and "An Evaluation under a Pine Tree, Lying on Pine Needles," are however variously, perhaps "typically Eberhart" in this new book. But what distinguishes *The Quarry* is Eberhart's new ability to flesh his religious spirit, and to meditate wholly as himself.

Richard Eberhart has often been a parabolic poet, but never more so than in "The Kite," that hugely long lyric which introduces *The Quarry.* As in "Sea Burial from the Cruiser *Reve*" (which is actually about the Viking funeral of an old skiff, but might equally seem to be about a dead child), he has often abstracted from his subject its most poetically generalized possibilities. "Sea Burial . . . " is an admirable poem of its kind, but "The Kite" is observed in a depth that the sinking rowboat finally is not. Few people have ever flown a Navy target-kite, and Eberhart (a former gunnery officer) typically confronts his readers with an experience in which few of them have previously shared. . . . [The] poem is a parable of the spirit's possible soaring. The thirteen pages of this poem involve six sections of religious speculation; what's remarkable is how densely that speculation is fleshed by the gear and tackle and trim of kite-flying. (pp. 67-8)

"Four Exposures: Light Meter," is equally new, being at least as resourceful and intellectually inventive as I. A. Richards might have been on the same subject. . . . This difficult long poem is again thick with the specifics of its own experience; it is structured in ways that confound the least charge of formal carelessness. . . . *The Quarry* is distinguished by such synoptic poems as his final two "Meditations," each of which provides an indexed perspective on his oldest concerns. Poetry, in such poems, is demonstrably Eberhart's church; he is most himself where such poems pray for their own resolution. . . .

I find [these poems] humanly sustaining. They are as totally remote from Southern hypocrisy as they are from the literary lynchings which nightly occur in New York, New York. . . . Even where I feel less Christian than Eberhart surely is, I envy him his belief and read his poems with a

new assurance that Santayana was right in arguing that "religion and poetry are identical in essence." (p. 68)

Philip Booth, "The Varieties of Poetic Experience," in Shenandoah *(copyright 1964 by Washington and Lee University; reprinted from* Shenandoah: The Washington and Lee University Review *with the permission of the Editor), Summer, 1964, pp. 62-9.*

M. L. ROSENTHAL

[Young Richard Eberhart] held a number of jobs connected with slaughterhouses and meat-packing, which may well have contributed to the death-obsession in his poetry, though there was a more crucial experience as well. A poem written in his late forties, "Fragment of New York, 1929," is a superb instance of the persistence of these early impressions. Certain reverses arising from a monumental embezzlement by the Hormel treasurer—the subject of Eberhart's play *The Visionary Farms*—all but ruined the family [his father was vice president of that company] when Dick was eighteen. At about the same time his mother died of lung cancer. . . .

Richard seems to have been very close to his mother, and tended her during her terrible illness. The experience became a powerful element in his sensibility. It *forced* the relationship, and left the young man with a surfeit of death-horror, a vision of life's morbid depths against which his instinct for affirmation carried on a recurrent struggle for many years. See, for instance, "The Day-Bed," written several decades later. The images of "a bright shape, a green new dream" with which it ends can never quite overcome the tormenting memory that sets the poem going. . . . (p. 26)

[Joel H. Roache in his biography, *The Progress of an American Poet,*] suggests that Eberhart's career involves a shift from alienation to affirmation, and that it symbolizes, in general, the basic nonalienation of American poets in this century. But Eberhart, like every poet of sufficient distinction, is a unique set of complexities and motives; his poetry, like most poetry, has grown around both his wounds and his healing visions. "Alienation" can be positive—it has a hundred meanings to go with its negations. "The scene is bad, so be of good heart" is one of the lessons we can learn from this poet's inspired and politic career. It is a lesson more encouraging, of course, to survivors than to victims. (p. 27)

M. L. Rosenthal, "Steps to Status on the Literary Ladder," in Saturday Review *(© 1971 by Saturday Review, Inc.; reprinted with permission), March 6, 1971, pp. 25-7.*

CALVIN BEDIENT

[If one] cut away the puffed romantic locks [from *Collected Poems 1930-1976*] . . . , there would be almost nothing left. Too many self-congratulatory poems, in any case, on the superiority of being a poet—the reader feels like a bored voyeur. (p. 363)

The writing is almost never happy. Typically American in this, Eberhart struggled all his life for an individual manner, mixing gaucheness and gracefulness in an unstable, not quite convincing way. Consider again the celebrated last stanza of "Fury of Aerial Bombardment":

Of Van Wettering I speak, and Averill,
Names on a list, whose faces I do not recall
But they are gone to early death, who late in school
Distinguished the belt feed lever from the belt
    holding pawl.

Was his true gift after all for the impersonality of these lines? How Latin, incidentally, their restrained sinuous rhetoric and ammoniac pungency. We might have had a Housman with contemporary grit; instead we have a vague son of Blake. (pp. 364-65)

> *Calvin Bedient, in* Sewanee Review *(reprinted by permission of the editor;* © *1977 by The University of the South), Spring, 1977.*

DAVID PERKINS

Throughout his career Eberhart has written essentially two kinds of poem. One is the lyric that assigns symbolic values to images and explores the implications thus activated. In "New Hampshire, February," for example, two frozen wasps are brought indoors. As the speaker breathes on them, they come to life. They "withdraw to ice" again when he stops. He feels like God. . . . But one wasp blunders onto the kitchen floor and the speaker, equally by accident, steps on it:

> And so the other is still my pet.
> The moral of this is plain.
> But I will shirk it.
> You will not like it. And
> God does not live to explain. . . .

Usually the success of such poems lies more in the imaginative materials than in the performance the poem makes. But at his best Eberhart's imagination freshly expresses the difficult complexity of the human situation in general. In general—for even when his metaphors or symbols are concrete, the object of concern is not. His subject, in other words, is less some particular instance or embodiment of life, agony, death, art, love, joy, God, and so forth, than the abstraction itself. And in many poems, such as "Meditation Two" or "Sanders Theater," even the ghost of a dramatic occasion has vanished, and there is straightforward meditation. To sustain attention in this mode presents an utmost challenge. Since the thing rendered is simply the poet's thoughts, associations, and mental processes, there must be some extraordinary quality of language and rhythm, or maybe some profundity of reflection, to distinguish the poem from the ordinary range and movement of our own thoughts. There must be something to justify and sustain the peculiarly heightened attention we bring to the reading of poetry. Eberhart excites such attention all the more by the naked and passionate sincerity of his concern. Hence the prosy character of his expression seems the more anticlimactic. . . . (pp. 730-31)

> *David Perkins, in* The Southern Review *(copyright, 1977, by David Perkins), Vol. XIII, No. 4, Autumn, 1977.*

*   *   *

ELLISON, Ralph   1914-

Ellison is an American novelist, essayist, short story writer, and editor. His best work, *Invisible Man,* **is generally considered an outstanding contribution to American postwar fiction. Although this work deals specifically with the black**

American's fight to overcome the anonymity caused by social stereotypes, many critics see the novel as a more universal portrayal of the human struggle for identity. Ellison effectively uses a surrealistic and ambiguous narrative to recreate the absurdity and irrationality of black repression. *Invisible Man* won the National Book Award in 1953. (See also *CLC,* Vols. 1, 3, and *Contemporary Authors,* Vols. 9-12, rev. ed.)

DAVID LITTLEJOHN

Ralph (Waldo) Ellison stands at the opposite end of the writer's world from Richard Wright. Although he is as aware of the issues of the race war as anyone else, he is no more a consciously active participant than, say, Gwendolyn Brooks or William Faulkner. "I wasn't, and am not, primarily concerned with injustice, but with art." He achieves his extraordinary power through artistry and control, through objectivity, irony, distance: he works with symbol rather than with act. He is at least as much an artist as a Negro. He accepts both roles so naturally, in fact, that he has made them one. His one novel [*Invisible Man*], the supreme work of art created by an American Negro, is essentially a Negro's novel. It is written entirely out of a Negro's experience, and reveals its full dimension, I am convinced, only to the perfect *Negro* reader. But it is not a "Negro novel." Like Gwendolyn Brooks, like Faulkner, like most serious artists, he has transmuted himself and his experience almost entirely into his art. Only by turning to his essays and interviews can one discover the degree to which his own opinions, on racial issues or any other, are implicit in *Invisible Man.*

Invisible Man (1952) was not, Ellison insists, "an attack upon white society." . . . It is not, really, a race-war novel. But as no Negro's life in America, not even in the symbolic recreation, can be entirely free of racial combat, there are elements in the book that can be legitimately read in a race-war context. (pp. 110-11)

Several instances of direct propaganda occur, although each time in so organically convincing a situation that one does not think of attributing them to Ellison directly. They are simply taken as true, dramatically and substantially. (pp. 111-12)

[This] book is, among other things, a complete story of Negro life in America. By nature something of a pacifist, a quietist, Ellison is much more free than the embattled protestors like Wright to try to tell *all* of the Negro's story. It has been the theme of his entire creative life, in fact, that there is far, far more to the Negro's story in America than oppression, suffering, and hate: "The view from inside the skin," he insists, "is not so dark as it appears to be." (p. 113)

The focus of all [his] propaganda and history and ironic sociology is the nameless hero, the Invisible Man ("invisible," that is, to white men's eyes), the Negroes' Joseph K. It is his story, really, not the race's, not the war's, except insofar as he is of the race and in the war. (His non-naming, through five hundred pages, never becomes obvious or ominous—a testimony to the subtlety of Ellison's art. It is simply never needed.) The creation and loving sustenance of this narrator-hero, with all his follies and limitations, are among the triumphs of the book.

Reaching out from the central artifice of the narrator-hero are other displays of Ellison's art. His style, the "fine texture,'' is exact and acute, the language (usually) at fingertip control. Hear the crisp offhandedness of wicked ironies, the cool black humor; or . . . the needle-sharp evocations of sensation and interior pain. He can manipulate language, as he can character, event, and design, for the optimum effects of irony, of a balanced double vision. Certain devices, tiny tricks, he leaves about like fingerprints: the strange selectivity of detail that leaves characters and objects and events undefinably charged, ''off,'' ever so slightly left of real; the pre-announcement of a thing some lines before it is identified, giving to it an eerie surreality. Ellison has also, to move to items of slightly larger focus, the fullest sense of drama; he knows when to signal and advance a key moment, how to pace and position effects for the fullest build-up of artful tension or comedy or suspense: he can work up cool quiet horror like Harold Pinter, or handle the giant crescendo of effects needed for pageants like Clifton's funeral or the Harlem riots.

His rhetorical skill is prodigious, and he is not reticent about displaying its range. Not only does he indulge himself in perfect mimicry of the tall tale, the emotion-charged address, the Negro sermon; he also allows himself chances for Joycean word display, and makes his hero's hold on history a ''way with words,'' a gift of tongues, an awesome and dangerous eloquence like his own.

Ellison's creative imagination, if such a talent can be singly regarded, is also more prolific than that of his peers. His exotic range of living characters, their vividness and magnitude; the extraordinary sequence of scenes and situations, each rendered with overflowing fullness—rooms, inner states, mob scenes, the fantasia of the hospital, the unforgettable battle royal at the Southern white men's smoker with which the novel opens: such independent creations bear witness to one of the most awesomely fertile living imaginations in American writing. (pp. 114-16)

His proper tradition *is* that of the great American novelists, as he so hoped it would be, and it is among them, rather than among the New Negroes, that he should be judged. Hawthorne and Melville, certainly, are of the family, and Faulkner and Fitzgerald: all the great ironists of the double vision, the half-romantic, half-cynical creators and retailers of the corrupted American dream. They are all symbolic artists, who charged their objects and events and effects with preternatural significance, who designed their fictions into national myths. He is not up *there*, of course; but I see no reason not to assign him a place—even for one unbalanced book—at least in the high second rank, with such other ironic idealists as Sherwood Anderson or Nathanael West. (p. 119)

> *David Littlejohn, in his* Black on White: A Critical Survey of Writing By American Negroes *(copyright © 1966 by David Littlejohn; all rights reserved; reprinted by permission of Viking Penguin Inc.), Viking Penguin, 1966.*

HELEN WEINBERG

Ellison's *Invisible Man* presents the theme of the individual activist quest for spiritual freedom in a [pure,] abstract form. . . . Ellison's narrative does not compromise with its theme: there are no resolutions in love. The invisible man, the Southern Negro narrator, elects to call himself only ''invisible man.'' This anonymous Negro thrusts again and again, in a series of episodes, parallel and repetitive more

than sequential and developing, against the walls of his environment. That he does not prevail against the environment does not lessen the dramatically-perceived nature of his quest: the search for an authentic identity beyond the labels the world would give him. Frustration is everywhere, and he finds the group with which he most identifies, the Negro group, most susceptible to the world's labels for it, most confined, and most self-defeating in its pursuing of group purposes.

In electing to be an invisible man, the narrator elects to be free of all labels, white or Negro, for himself; he elects to lose his group identity and to live alone, alienated and free. The choice of invisibility (by living underground) as freedom is the end-choice, after the above-ground struggles of the novel. . . . The Prologue and the Epilogue of the book deal with the idea of invisibility, giving a surreal context and emphasis to many of the realistically described scenes inside the main narrative. Ironically, anonymous is what the Negro is in a white society: by electing this condition for himself, as a defense against white society's labels for him, which he has found set him and his brothers against one another, he makes the only free choice which remains available to him. Living underground in a hole, full of light from 1,369 lights lit by voltage stolen from the Monopolated Light and Power Company, and full of sound . . . , he feels he truly lives at last. ''I myself, after existing some twenty years did not become alive until I discovered my invisibility,'' he says.

The invisible man is both the victim hero trapped in an absurd world and the activist hero. In the Epilogue to the novel, he says, ''All life seen from the hole of invisibility is absurd,'' and he has experienced throughout his adventures above ground a cruel victimization from the absurdities, black and white, of the world. Yet he has acted; he has sought himself and finally found himself in the ironic recognition of his own invisibility. (pp. 188-89)

In an essay, ''Black Boys and Native Sons,'' Irving Howe has attacked . . . Ellison for having deserted what he considers to be the authentic tradition of Negro writing, the social protest novel best characterized by the work of Richard Wright. One of his complaints against Ellison is his making the narrator-hero of *Invisible Man* speak of his life as one of ''infinite possibilities'' at the time that he is living in a hole in the ground. Ellison, in answering Howe's essay, accuses Howe of having missed the irony in this. Not only does Howe, a social literary critic, miss the irony, it seems to me he also missed the specific evasion of social considerations in the quest for personal and spiritual freedom proposed here by a Negro writer whose concept of his own novel is that

> it's a novel about innocence and human error, a struggle through illusion to reality. . . . Before he could have some voice in his own destiny he had to discard [all his] old identities and illusions; his enlightenment couldn't come until then. . . .

The hole is twofold: the ultimate trap and the freely chosen place where he may burn the old papers and roles behind him before going to his next activist phase above ground.

While the main theme is uncompromisingly one of identity and freedom in *Invisible Man*, Ellison, like [James Baldwin in his *Another Country*], finds it necessary to invoke love.

Ellison, however, does not culminate his hero's quest in the conclusive and resolved terms which love, as the final truth, gives to *Another Country;* he rather sees that the freedom of a Negro person may evaporate in hate, and love becomes necessary to supply a balance that enables progress toward freedom of the self. (pp. 190-91)

> *Helen Weinberg, in her* The New Novel in America: The Kafkan Mode in Contemporary Fiction *(copyright © 1970 by Cornell University; used by permission of the publisher, Cornell University Press),* Cornell University Press, 1970.

JANE GOTTSCHALK

For his novel of the American scene, Ralph Ellison uses American authors to support major ideas, ideas controlled by the dominant image of vision inherent in the title of *Invisible Man* and fully exploited in the fiction. References to American authors are sophisticated jokes, often very funny. As aware as Mark Twain that humor is a weapon, and as aware as T. S. Eliot that juxtaposition of allusions contributes to a total effect, Ellison plays with names of American authors and teases with allusions to American literary works. Flashing briefly here and developed there, the references reveal illuminating and humorous support of themes concerned with identity, with black leadership, and with the state of American society, a contemporary Ellisonian waste land.

Booker T. Washington, Emerson, Whitman, and T. S. Eliot figure prominently in comic handling of names and/or allusions, the tone set in the opening lines of the Prologue. To declare the quality of his invisibility, the naive narrator informs readers that he is "not a spook like those who haunted Edgar Allan Poe."

Names used in serious jests are Booker T. Washington and Emerson, and each allusive shot is like b-b spray hitting in different directions. Washington was an educator and a leader—and a writer because of his leadership—and references to his name, in Ellison's unique handling, serve several purposes. (p. 69)

The bronze statue of the Founder is described by the narrator as a "cold Father symbol" of outstretched hands grasping a veil over the head of a kneeling slave; the problem for the narrator at that moment is interpretive. Is the Founder removing or replacing the veil? . . . More than one reader has called attention to the similarity of this description to the actual statue of Booker T. Washington on the Tuskegee campus. . . . (p. 70)

It is in the recounting of Dr. Homer Barbee's sermon immediately preceding the moonlit view of the statue that another playful dig is taken at the black educator as leader. This time, allusions to a work by Walt Whitman, the poet of democracy, stimulate alert response. In his tribute to the Founder, Barbee also praises Dr. Bledsoe for carrying on after the death of the Founder, suggesting that though there might be a difference in time, there is little difference in the type of educator—translated leader for the purpose of Ellison's theme. . . .

Both the portrait of the "black and mythical Lincoln" and the tribute to Bledsoe are presented by Barbee, an invited guest of Bledsoe. Since Barbee is blind, anything he says should be suspect; again, vision or seeing is the image in control. He cannot see the truth. This passage, therefore, seems to reinforce the theme of black leaders not being leaders of black people. The Whitman symbols are reversed by the blindness of the black Homer; the Founder was not Lincolnesque, and his successor, Dr. Bledsoe, is not the man so elevated by preacher rhetoric, a fact soon to be discovered in the narrative by the invisible man. With a created character type, with an actual name, and with allusions, the black-educator-leader in American society is put down. (p. 71)

Invisible Man is wide-ranging; the narrator is not the only black American with an identity problem. There are the veterans of the episode at the Golden Day. . . .

If the name of Washington suggests at least two different motifs, the name of Emerson, as Ellison toys with it in *Invisible Man,* is certainly no less multileveled. Sometimes it means a private joke referring to the actual nineteenth century writer, sometimes it refers to a created character of that name who has several functions, and sometimes it is used as a kind of type—merged with family characters in the novel.

The name is introduced in the novel by Norton when he asks the narrator if he had studied Emerson. Readers knowing the full Ralph Waldo of Ellison's name, are able to smile as the narrator is embarrassed because he hadn't, and Norton tells him, "You must learn about him, for he was important to your people. He had a hand in your destiny." . . . Later, in his final campus interview with Norton, the narrator announces his intention of reading Emerson. Norton approves. "Very good. Self-reliance is a most worthy virtue." . . . The private joke slips in again when the narrator is at the paint factory, worrying about using "Emerson's name without his permission." . . . (p. 72)

The final use to which Ellison puts the name of Emerson is to have the narrator recognize him as a manipulator like others. "And now I looked around a corner of my mind and saw Jack and Norton and Emerson merge into one single figure. They were very much the same, each attempting to force his picture of reality upon me and neither giving a hoot in hell for how things looked to me. I was simply a material, a natural resource to be used. I had switched from the arrogant absurdity of Norton and Emerson to that of Jack and the Brotherhood, and it all came out the same—." . . . In his confrontation with Ras during the riot in Harlem, the narrator takes another step forward: ". . . I had no longer to run for or from the Jacks and the Emersons and the Bledsoes and Nortons, but only from their confusion, impatience, and refusal to recognize the beautiful absurdity of their American identity and mine." . . . The list of those who had run him gets longer, and in the castration dream, there are "Jack and old Emerson and Bledsoe and Norton and Ras and the school superintendent, and a number of others." . . . Is the Emerson referred to in these passages the character created in the novel or the actual writer? Or both? Ellison riddles a riddle.

Because Ellison has referred to T. S. Eliot as a literary ancestor and has acknowledged several times the impact upon him of "The Waste Land," readers should not be surprised that *Invisible Man* is also a comic waste land in prose. There is no naming of Eliot in the novel, but Ellison quotes Harry's speech from Eliot's *Family Reunion* in his frontispiece with an excerpt from Melville's *Benito Cereno;* Harry's remarks anticipate the general theme of seeing. But an early allusion sets the stage for the Ellisonian waste land, and other imagery and characters develop it. Readers familiar with Eliot's work are brought up sharply as the narrator describes his college campus: "If real, why is it that I can recall in all that inland of greenness no fountain but one that was broken, corroded and dry? And why does no rain fall through my recollections, sound through my memories, soak through the hard dry crust of the still so recent past? Why do I recall, instead of the odor of seed bursting in springtime, only the yellow contents of the cistern spread over the lawn's dead grass?" (pp. 73-4)

The waste land, it becomes clear, is not only the college campus. Eliot's work draws heavily on the fertility myths, in which society is represented by the land, its sterility or barrenness symbolizing lust, its fertility, love. In addition, Eliot's "The Waste Land" is his parallel to Dante's *Inferno* as his "Ash Wednesday" is his parallel to the *Purgatorio;* in "Ash Wednesday" love and women are redemptive. *Invisible Man* suggests all of these elements. After the narrator leaves the college, many of the scenes are set in an underworld, literal or figurative. (p. 74)

With the story of Trueblood, of obviously ironic name, Ellison plies ironies, revels in the tall-tale, and goads readers into laughing response. There is ironic foreshadowing when Norton twice remarks to the narrator that the land had been barren before the Founder came and now it is fertile.... He soon discovers confirmation; incest gives concurrent paternities. Norton rewards Trueblood with a hundred dollars, matching the response of white society as they lapped up his story. The grim humor has a sharp point. Toward the end of the visit, Trueblood mentions his other children. "'Lissen to the younguns,' he said in embarrassment, 'Playin' "London Bridge's Falling Down"'." ... In Part V of "The Waste Land" Eliot had written: "London Bridge is falling down falling down falling down." And, for Ellison, American society is falling down as it envies known incest, as with Norton, and rewards, as with the white citizens near the campus. (p. 75)

[References] to sex extend the range of association, but none of them represent love. The prostitutes at the Golden Day speculate hilariously about Mr. Norton, and Emma, although she is Jack's mistress, has an eye for the narrator. Sex is a joke, and society is sick. Women are used and use others.

Exceptions in the novel in the presentation of women are Miss Susie Gresham of the black college to whom the narrator pays tribute in retrospect ... and Mary Rambo, a mother-figure who takes in the narrator when he needs help after the explosion at the paint factory and to whom he is trying to return during the Harlem riot. Although her suggestive name is not so simply interpreted because of Rambo, Mary is an obvious allusion to Christ's mother, a redemptive figure. Eliot uses Mary in "Ash Wednesday," his *Purgatorio,* as representative of a different role for women, helping to redeem the time. Ellison seems to do the same.

There are other clues in Eliot's work and in Ellison's that all is not completely lost. In the fertility myths, the burial of a princely figure, or a king, can help the land to become fertile again, can help society to become healthy. Tod Clifton (whose first name means death) is the most princely character in *Invisible Man,* his qualities so marked that even Ras,

the Harlem enemy of the Brotherhood, cannot destroy him: "Youth! Intelligence! The mahn's a natural prince." ... Clifton's bolting from the Brotherhood, his being shot on the streets of New York, and his moving funeral planned and executed by the narrator alone are key episodes which prompt the action of the narrator. After Clifton's funeral, there come the rupture with the Brotherhood, the Harlem Riot—and the bursting of the water main which ultimately sends the narrator to the coal cellar to think. Salvation by water is suggested in Eliot's work; water helps to "save" the narrator in Ellison's work. Near the end of "The Waste Land" the protagonist asks, "Shall I at least set my lands in order?" Shall he assume some personal responsibility? At the end of *Invisible Man,* in the Epilogue, the narrator ponders leaving his hibernation "since there's a possibility that even an invisible man has a socially responsible role to play." ... (pp. 76-7)

Jane Gottschalk, "Sophisticated Jokes: The Use of American Authors in 'Invisible Man'," in Renascence (© copyright, 1978, Marquette University Press), Winter, 1978, pp. 69-77.

JOSEPH T. SKERRETT, JR.

"The Birthmark" ... displays, I think, enough of Wright's influence—as well as Hemingway's—to justify some concern on Wright's part that Ellison might be able to steal his thunder, in time. In the story, a black man and his sister have been brought to the scene of an alleged auto accident to identify the body of their brother; they discover, when they attempt to find an identifying birthmark below the navel, that he has been lynched and castrated. Outraged but helpless, they must return home and accept the lie that Willie was hit by a car, because, as the white policeman puts it, "We don't allow no lynching round here no more."

Like a Hemingway story, "The Birthmark" is immediate and dramatic; it begins with Matt and Clara emerging from the police car to approach Willie's body. Its power is developed through the cumulative effect of the dialog, rather than through the sparse interpretive commentary of the narrator. But the dialog is dialectal rather than idiomatic; the particularities of black Southern speech are indicated orthographically. This is, of course, Wright's style and not Hemingway's—or Ellison's as we have become familiar with it in later work.

Like Wright's "Big Boy Leaves Home," Ellison's story draws a strong contrast between the summer calm of nature —"the green stretch of field fringed with pine trees" and "the pine needle covered ground" where Willie's body lies —and the human violence and hatred which brings brother and sister, white man and black man to this place. But Ellison's is a very brief tale, without the extensiveness of one of Wright's long tales. And Ellison's hero is frustrated, entirely stalemated by the cynical insistence of the white police that Willie was not lynched because lynchings don't happen there anymore. (p. 147)

Ellison's insight into the social conditions that block Matt's impulse to wrench the gun from the white man's hand is more cynical than Wright's. In the stories of *Uncle Tom's Children,* as well as in "Silt," white economic power is an important aspect of the characters' sense of frustration. Nature is indifferent. The flood in "Silt" has ruined all the land; it is Tom's economic servitude to Burgess that makes the flood almost "too hard" to bear. But in Ellison's story, as Matt and Clara alight from the police car, nature gives the reader a foresight of its complicity: "two large birds circled slowly, black shapes against the still blue sky." And it is the white policeman who interprets the sign, giving it its proper name: "'Them damned buzzards,' he said." The narrator and the reader are thus let in on the tragic complexity of the experience in store for Matt and Clara. (pp. 147-48)

The rapid development in the direction that has since become characteristic of his work—a style and structural habits closely related to patterns of speech and behavior—can be traced in the three stories which followed these earliest efforts.

["Afternoon"] is almost without formal structure. It follows the two young boys, Buster and Riley, through what seems a typical pre-adolescent day.... The story, for all the effectiveness of its rhetoric, has no dramatic center, nor organizing narrative idea. Its movement is manipulated, rhetorically, by the narrator, who otherwise does not have a presence in the story. Despite the references to Jack Johnson and to other, more general folkloristic elements, Ellison does not shape the narration so as to transcend the typicalness of the boys' daily experience. "Afternoon" is a rhetorically sophisticated "slice-of-life" fiction, and has a lot in common with the pastoral opening of Wright's "Big Boy Leaves Home." But Wright's adolescent's idyll is a contrast to the stark reality of racial violence, while Ellison's seems nostalgic, self-contained, rather pointless.

["Mister Toussan"] is a brilliant exercise in brevity. Buster and Riley demonstrate the uses of the imagination as each tells his creative version of Mr. Toussan—Toussaint L'Ouverture utterly transformed by hearsay, ignorance and projection—and his rejection of Napoleon. The boys quite consciously create Mr. Toussan's dismissal of the oppressive whites, building narrative details in the dialogical manner of formulaic sermonizing or teaching. After Buster has told his version, with Riley chorusing good lines, asking questions and adding details, he begins his version with "Come on, watch me do it now." The imagination in the act of performance is what matters; the boys are left at the end of their flight of fancy wondering why such "good stories" are not "in the books." The story as performance event, which seems to be Ellison's main point here, is structurally underlined by Ellison's virtuosic closure.... Riley closes the story-telling with a formulaic closure to which Buster cannot object, for it is part of the rules of performance events that they not be artificially prolonged. When the rhythm and spirit are exhausted, the story-telling ends.

> "Aw come on man," interrupted Buster.
> "Let's go play in the alley...."
> *And that's the way ...*
> "Maybe we can slip around and get some cherries," Buster went on.
> *... the story ends,* chanted
> Riley.

Thus both the boys' and the author's performances end simultaneously. Ellison structurally reiterates his theme. In this story he found his voice and struck a balance between an expressive narrative presence and a dramatic narrative structure. The narration contains an example of storytelling which is in itself a commentary on the "truth," the validity and usefulness of narration. In affirming the meaning of narration as an act of the imagination in its own right, Ellison took a major step away from Wright's ideological aesthetic.

The third Buster and Riley story, "That I Had the Wings," ... is a more thoroughly developed but more conventional fiction than "Mr. Toussan." Here the boys' imaginative play gets them into trouble while revealing to the reader their real yearning for escape from the confining supervision of the adult world. Riley is scolded by his Aunt Kate for singing a song about being "President of these United States" and swinging on the White House gates, for not only does the boy's song take the Lord's name in vain, it also voices dangerous ambitions.... Though Riley apologizes, he angers Aunt Kate by refusing to sing an alternative song—"That I Had the Wings of a Dove" to satisfy her that the day's dangerously secular vision has been expunged. For it has not. Riley has his eye on the birds, all right, but not with a view toward heaven. Their symbolic value for him is in their freedom to fly.... He and Buster make parachutes for the chicks and toss them off the roof of the barn. Aunt Kate interrupts them, the chicks land hard and are killed. Worse than the failure of the parachute plan is the shame Riley feels at Aunt Kate's scolding. (pp. 150-52)

"That I Had the Wings" is a sensitive and dramatic perception of the emotions of childhood. Like something from the hand of Mark Twain, it reaches out from a firm grounding in the world of the child to comment on the human desire for freedom from limiting discipline, be it loving and protective or not. Riley's desire to see the birds fly is a projection of his own rebellion against "his place" both as a child and as a Negro. Riley is a kind of Bigger Thomas, the black child who has not accepted the rationale of the black community concerning ambition, self-assertion and other aspects of the individualist ethic. But the narrator puts no large interpretations on the action of the story; there is no suggestion that Riley will become a rebel like Bigger. Ellison is satisfied to present the boy facing a boy's version of a universal human problem, the battle with family and authority. (pp. 152-53)

[These] three stories demonstrate not only a broadening of literary models to include more distant—i.e., less proximate—figures like Twain, but also a successful effort to draw upon more personal, more intimate data. The change from the public themes and representative figures of the earlier work to the private and closely observed world of the boys involved a reintroduction of the self and marked the achievement of control over the narrator-effacing techniques of Hemingway and Joyce. Ellison has acknowledged in an interview that the central incident of "That I Had the Wings," the business with the chicks and the toy parachutes, was drawn from memories of his own childhood. "Mister Toussan" and "That I Had the Wings" are, furthermore, finished and polished manipulations of "the simple structural unities of beginning, middle and end" which had eluded Ellison's control in his earliest work. (p. 153)

Joseph T. Skerrett, Jr., "Ralph Ellison and the Example of Richard Wright," in Studies in Short Fiction *(copyright 1978 by Newberry College), Spring, 1978, pp. 145-53.*

RICHARD FINHOLT

Ellison, after Poe, is the American writer most self-consciously committed to the ideas of the mind thinking, of the mind, that is, as the ultimate source of transcendence or salvation. But he is also the inheritor of a wellspring of emotional pain, the collective black experience in America, that has received its traditional artistic expression in the blues beat and lyric. Several critics . . . [as well as] Ellison himself have emphasized the influence of blues forms and themes on the structure of [*Invisible Man*], but some of these critics, perhaps wishing for Ellison to be more black than American, have not given proper emphasis to its intellectual framework.

In fact, the novel amounts to a critique of both the intellectual and the emotional dimensions of the American experience. The Brotherhood (an obvious pseudonym for the Communist Party), which prides itself on its "reasonable point of view" and "scientific approach to society," . . . represents the *head* of the social structure, as do also such characters as Bledsoe, Norton, Emerson, and all who think without feeling; and characters like Trueblood, Emerson Jr., Lucius Brockway, Tarp, Tod Clifton, and Ras, all those who feel without thinking, represent the *heart*. Given the two dimensions, the invisible man's problem . . . is "How to Be!" And . . . salvation is the attainment of a balance, of a unification of mind and body, thought and feeling, idea and action, that forms a pattern of existence with the potential to transcend the "biological morality" . . . imposed from within and the social morality imposed from without. (pp. 98-9)

[It] is Ellison's vision that all men, whether powerful or weak, are puppets controlled by invisible strings . . . , like Clifton's dancing Sambo doll. . . . Ellison's vision is of a complex chattering-monkey society composed of blind, mindless puppets wearing the masks assigned to them, playing the roles demanded of them, striking out blindly at the targets provided for them. A metaphor for this society is the battle royal . . . , in which the young black boys are set plunging and swinging wildly about a boxing ring. Blindfolded, they fight "hysterically," in a "confused" state of "terror" and "hate," while not one blow reaches the southern whites who are the makers of their pain and confusion. . . . (p. 99)

Tatlock and the invisible man use each other as scapegoats, and the invisible man will go on to strike out at a long string of scapegoats, each representing a different social or political affiliation (Bledsoe, Brockway, Ras, Brother Jack), will himself serve as a scapegoat for all these groups, before he is finally driven from society by an ironic amalgamation of black revolutionaries and white reactionaries. The invisible man is accused of treachery by the spokesmen of every group represented in the novel . . . , is haunted by his grandfather's confession to having been a "traitor" to his people . . . , is overcome by the irony that even his grandfather's formula for avoiding treachery ("overcome 'em with yeses") leads him to betray his race. . . . The ultimate question in Ellison is: To what "society of gods" can the "dispossessed" . . . reverse-*pharmakos* give ultimate allegiance?

[Ellison] envisions no unifying force at the center of the cosmos; where . . . others see a pattern of meaning on which to build what Ellison calls a "plan of living," Ellison sees only "chaos." The human problem then becomes how "to give pattern to the chaos which lives within the pat-

tern" of the "certainties" . . . upon which blind men have built their societies. . . . Ellison's philosophy might be called existential transcendentalism. As he told John O'Brien in *Interviews with Black Writers*, "Human life is a move toward the rational. Whatever man must do in order to bring order to the society is what he considers rational. For a moralist, the problem is to point out that such order is not imposed by nature and it is not imposed by God. It's a human thing." In other words, just as man creates his own damnation, he must create his own salvation, just as man has spent his existence imposing pseudorational strings on himself, he must train himself to be true to the truly rational. (pp. 100-01)

Therefore, the invisible man discovers that salvation is ultimately a function of "the *mind*," . . . and his allegiance passes over to an ethereal realm of intellectual principles. (p. 101)

The invisible man discovers, almost too late, that the Brotherhood's ideal of reaching people "through their intelligence" is the mask for a sinister, paternalistic policy of taking advantage of people "in their own best interest." . . . The true principle . . . can be discovered only at the conclusion of an arduous rite of passage through the underworld (expressed metaphorically by ubiquitous images of tunnels, subways, and basement rooms . . .), through the "lower frequencies" . . . of the human psyche where the blues originates, the unconscious world of primitive human emotions and instincts where the thinking man discovers that beneath the social and racial allegiances he is "linked to all the others in the loud, clamoring semi-visible world." . . .

The American black man, Ellison seems to be suggesting, is in a special positon to achieve the balance of thought and feeling, of responsibility and freedom necessary for "transcendence" over society's death grip on the individual unconscious. On the one hand, owing to the "given circumstances" of his "origin," the blues experience, he has had "not much, but some" of the "human greed and smallness" and "fear and superstition," . . . which has corrupted the white mind, burned out of him. On the other hand, to remain isolated from the intellectual patterns that structure history . . . , isolated in an albeit free world of pure feeling, is to remain in "that world seen only as a fertile field for exploitation by Jack and his kind, and with condescension by Norton and his." . . . The blues experience has purified the emotions of the black man, Ellison seems to be saying, but unless his mind can learn to see the meaning underlying the blues form, and to take the responsiblity for his own salvation, he will never be able to transcend the imprisoning social structure.

The theme of the blues is emotional pain, not as triumphed over, but as lived with, endured. (pp. 101-02)

[Ellison] suggests that the blues expression of the southern Negro is the only response possible in his violence-prone world, "the consolation of philosophy" having been denied to him. . . .

Ellison associates the blues and the black experience with the hysteria of "confusion," a motif which recurs again and again in the novel . . . ; it is the confusion that arises, presumably, from suppressing intellectual energy. . . . [For example] the invisible man finds himself echoing the blues refrain of Louis Armstrong, "What did I do / To be so black / And blue?'' . . . after he discovers, but cannot understand, the "joke" played on him by Bledsoe. . . . (p. 103)

Confusion is in turn linked to what Raymond M. Olderman in "Ralph Ellison's Blues and *Invisible Man*" calls the "scapegoat" motif of the blues. Super-Cargo (superego), for example, represents internalized white authority . . . to the mental patients in the Golden Day . . . , and when given the opportunity to express their suppressed intellectual energy physically, they instinctively attack him and not Mr. Norton. . . . Both Super-Cargo and Norton represent some truth beyond the limited roles they play in the social structure, but since the blues mentality of the inmates is not prone to intellectual analysis, a symbolically appropriate scapegoat satisfies the emotional demands of the occasion. . . . (pp. 103-04)

In *Natives Sons* Edward Margolies has described Ellison's hero/narrator as a blues "singer," who sings "a record of past wrongs, pains, and defeats," each episode serving "almost as an extended blues verse." While the novel is certainly an episodic account of painful defeats at the hands of a number of different scapegoat figures, Margolies, who seems to see blues as the sole structuring purpose of the novel, fails to recognize that the invisible man comes to reject the illogic of the blues form when he realizes that he has become a scapegoat for Ras. . . . His mind has developed to the point where, like Powerhouse and unlike the waitress, he can separate the personifications from the principles they represent. But the frightening discovery is that this "confoundingly complex arrangement" of marionette strings has corrupted even the black man's treasured emotional heritage.

Just as Ellison links confusion to the blues, he in turn links the blues to the nature of southern Negro preaching. At the lowest level of his blues reverie in the prologue, the invisible man finds a black preacher perpetuating confusion by patterning the words of his sermon on the emotional response of his congregation rather than on any pattern demanded by the sense of their meaning. . . . But, ironically, it is precisely the invisible man's gift for the sound of words that the Brotherhood will harness to its corrupt purpose. . . . Brother Jack rebukes the invisible man at one point by telling him, "You were not hired to think," . . . which seems an inappropriate thing to say to a lecturer, but of course he was hired to sing the blues. (pp. 104-06)

[Ellison has a] Freudian understanding of mankind's sense of its own insufficiency, a sense that motivates the "simple yet confoundingly complex arrangement of hope and desire, fear and hate." The marionette strings project outward from the collective unconscious to confuse not only the black man's feelings but the society's truest principles.

The "escape" of the hero from the regressive patriarchy of the South . . . to the more egalitarian North is an ontogenetic recapitulation of the phylogenesis of Western society; it mirrors the transformation of the "primal horde," in Freud's formulation, into the "brother horde." The "Brotherhood" (dropping the "r" in horde) represents the new cooperative society (the first act of cooperation being the murder of the father). . . . But the implicit irony of the brother horde is that one cannot transcend the father, and to murder the father is merely to institutionalize murder, and thereby perpetuate the need to murder the father. (pp. 106-07)

Ellison has written in "Richard Wright's Blues," the blues offers "no scapegoat but the self," . . . the self that discovers "on the lower frequencies" that it is "linked to all the others" by a shared heritage of fear and viciousness. That is the "beautiful absurdity" of the "American identity," and that, the invisible man discovers, is the meaning of the blues.

But the brother horde can work only if the shared heritage is denied. So, when a universal desire surfaces somewhere, as in the case of Trueblood's incest, it must be treated as a gross perversion and the offending individual excised brutally from the community, made a symbolic scapegoat. The blues is a danger to the social fabric because of its emphasis on the commonality of human emotions. . . . For this reason Trueblood can bear the "guilt" heaped upon him. By making him feel the universality of his emotions . . . , the blues has led him to face and accept the fear that society is constructed to deny: the fear of individuality. . . . (p. 108)

But there is a danger in emotional freedom. There really is a "chaos" out there on the borders of society; an individual needs "a socially responsible role to play," . . . or he will revert in his "cynicism" . . . to the barbaric condition of anarchy and chaos, where the unconscious rules unrestrained by anything except necessity. This is what the invisible man calls "Rinehartism"; "Rine the runner and Rine the gambler and Rine the briber" seems at first to be the essence of individual "possibility" . . . ; his "possibility" seems to be the antidote to the "social responsibility" . . . preached by society, which turns out to mean nothing more than the "SACRIFICE" . . . of the individual. But Ellison understands that the social morality (the brother horde) is ultimately determined by the biological morality (the primal horde) that enslaves us all and that there cannot be, therefore, any ultimate freedom from, only moderation of, evil and pain.

When the individual submits to society's ideal of responsibility, the *"uncreated features of his face,"* the surface idiosyncrasies that make him different from all other men, remain uncreated. . . . In Aristotelian terms, he is all substance and no form. Since this "formless" . . . man is invisible to both others and himself, he must wear a mask assigned to him, as the invisible man does throughout the novel, merely exchanging one mask for another as his affiliations shift. However, when the individual becomes too free from responsibility, when his possibilities are without limit, he becomes nothing but face, all form and no substance, having denied the common substance that makes him one with all other men. (p. 109)

The invisible man transcends the dangers of the dialectical opposites, collective responsibility and individual possibility, by achieving a synthesis of them. Thus, he drives Brother Jack into a frenzy when he espouses a new, balanced ideal called "personal responsibility." . . . He becomes a whole man, both substance and form, body and mind, emotion and reason when he learns how to balance between . . . his "duty toward others" and his "duty toward himself." (pp. 109-10)

[He] will not accept the scapegoat role society has chosen for him to play, but neither will he overstay his "hibernation" in an underground world of pure possibility. The promise of the invisible man is that he will emerge with enough balance to articulate the feelings that we all have locked in our minds. . . . (p. 110)

Richard Finholt, "Ellison's Chattering-Monkey Blues," in his American Visionary Fiction: Mad Metaphysics as Salvation Psychology (copyright © 1978 by Kennikat Press Corp.; reprinted by permission of Kennikat Press Corp.), Kennikat, 1978, pp. 98-111.

*   *   *

EXLEY, Frederick   1930-

Exley is an American novelist. *A Fan's Notes* **and** *Pages from a Cold Island* **are the first two books of his planned "fictional autobiographical trilogy." (See also** *CLC*, **Vol. 6.)**

DEREK MAHON

[*A Fan's Notes* is] a work of depth and seriousness—a moving, richly humorous record of humiliation and perseverance. Perhaps only in tightrope America, where to trip once is to die more than a little, can one immediately recognise loneliness as a metaphysical condition. This, almost, is what Exley does, with a bitterness, a wild obscenity and a slow undertow of unkillable love that recalls Céline. He is conscious of other American masters (Melville, Scott Fitzgerald), but he is 'literary' only in the sense that anyone who writes is literary now. Exley-the-narrator seeks love and fame; like Gatsby, he believes in the green light of American romanticism; and he finds ashes. Love is blonde Bunny Sue with her butterscotch thighs and sexual expertise, and her mental vacuousness. She lives at Heritage Heights, Chicago. All he can do is look. Fame, too, is for looking at, despite his ambition as a writer. It happens on TV screens: a few have fans, but most are fans of the few. Exley has a dream in which he fights with a younger man, a representative of 'the generation to whom President Johnson has promised his Great Society; the generation which will never know the debilitating shame of poverty, the anguish of defeat, the fateful irony of the unexpected disease'; and as he loses, he sees that the idea of remorse has no place in the young man's dialectic. It's a painful lesson. (p. 155)

Derek Mahon, in The Listener (© *British Broadcasting Corp. 1970; reprinted by permission of Derek Mahon*), *January 29, 1970.*

STANLEY REYNOLDS

As a work of art [*A Fan's Notes*] is rambling, unclear, repetitive, and written in that curious overblown American style exemplified by the now famous remark of the US Ambassador to the Queen about redecorating his house and 'encountering elements of discomfiture in the refurbishing'. The effect here is rather like getting button-holed by a drunk in a bar who grips you by both lapels, breathing whisky and polysyllables into your face, and never uses two words where he can possibly find 10 that'll do. Indeed, one American critic found this pompous, drunken prose pleasing, but then there is no available means of data-computing the elements of individual selectivity processes or, for that matter, no accounting for tastes. The book does tell us something about one neurotic American's corruption and near-destruction in pursuit of fame and success. . . . The dream is so strongly believed in that it is followed into real madness. Jobs, family, friends, everything is sacrificed to the dream of fame, with increasingly destructive drunkenness the only way of sustaining the false faith in one's talent. (p. 158)

Stanley Reynolds, in New Statesman (© *1970 The Statesman & Nation Publishing Co. Ltd.*), *January 30, 1970.*

RICHARD P. BRICKNER

[Exley leads a] trouble-seeking, trouble-rich existence [in *Pages From a Cold Island*]. He is always putting, indeed pushing, his foot in it. Everything with him is more than enough, or less than enough; there is no unqualified enough. But as he describes his embarrassing, often comic, occasionally joyful meetings with the strangers he drags or tickles out of the blue, as he tells of the intimacy with the strangers that seems to constitute most of the intimacy he knows, he reminds us that a large part of the trouble he discovers is trouble we, too, have had, and that much of the rest is trouble we haven't the nerve to seek. Most of us have adversity thrust upon us; Exley achieves it.

He makes the most of this achievement in his books. He is a kind of redeemer, exonerating our mischievous wishes, and less frequent acts, while experiencing them. He operates with a helpless force of Id that carries us, as readers, beyond embarrassment for him and for our own desires and crudities, to a state of amused, relieved acceptance. It is easy to imagine that if everyone behaved like Exley, the world would become unpopulated mud; but the author acting in our place makes it possible to see that our fear is usually greater than it need be. Exley does for us the writer's job. Above all, however, he is obsessed with literary courage and performance in continuing the story about writing his own biography.

Appropriately, the stranger who preoccupies Exley most in *Pages From a Cold Island* is Edmund Wilson, whose death marks the beginning of the book. . . .

Both Wilson and [Gloria] Steinem, in a dreamlike-lifelike relation that only a novelist of genius could make convincing, are involved in the very viability of *Pages From a Cold Island*. When Wilson dies, Exley happens to be reading *Memoirs of Hecate County* in order to decide if he should teach it at Iowa—the Iowa job undertaken because he has been unable to finish writing his own book. And Exley believes Steinem will somehow show him the way out of the unrelieved desolation that has characterized his abandoned first draft. (p. 6)

The eventual interview . . . [with Steinem] is strained. But Exley makes it funny, and metaphoric for a lot of the human intercourse that takes place under far less artificial circumstances. Further on he uses Steinem to help make the point that ultimately unifies his book.

After the Steinem episode, it's back to Wilson. . . . Exley doesn't say so, but it's as if he feels that every moment and every minor fact of Wilson's 77 years had a point, all the points collecting in a magnificent accumulation of coherence—in contrast to the alcoholic blowsiness, assaultiveness, indiscipline, *error* of his own life. Wilson, as he is presented, controlled people as well as all kinds of information; Exley *is* controlled, and most of what controls him is out of control. He has spent three periods in mental institutions. (pp. 6-7)

Unruly, brimming over with more than enough love, self-abasement, envy, Exley is nonetheless admirable. He has the courage of his obsessions. Like Wilson, he is *sui generis*, and he suffers for it. What's more, very few people who behave the way Exley does have his clarifying gift. He exposes, he is the writer. He sets himself apart from public figures like Steinem, by holding "with Emerson . . . that one speaks to public questions only as a result of a weary cowardice that has so debilitated his energies he is no longer able to do his own work or rest easy with the painful prospect of articulating his own demons." Exley has found a purpose for his suffering, and he embraces us with it to our benefit. (p. 7)

Richard P. Brickner, "Redeemer of Mischievous Wishes," in The New Leader *(© 1975 by the American Labor Conference on International Affairs, Inc.), May 26, 1975, pp. 6-7.*

RONALD De FEO

A Fan's Notes is both a funny and a sad book, exploring the American obsession with "making it." It contains some splendid writing, a host of memorable tales and character sketches, and, above all, a sense of a man who has lived and suffered. At times the book tends toward inflated prose and overdrawn scenes and sections (the chapter on "Mr. Blue," for example, is not important enough to warrant such space), and we do occasionally grow weary of the self-deprecating Exley persona, but as a whole, *A Fan's Notes* is an unmistakable achievement.

At one point in *Pages from a Cold Island* Exley tells us that some readers of his first book expressed doubts that he would produce anything more because of the exhaustive nature of that initial performance. Their doubts were not entirely groundless, for although Exley has written a second book, the more we read of it, the more we begin to feel that he has already said all there is to say about himself. . . .

Exley tries too hard to impress us with the significance of the moment. And often, despite his lengthy efforts and his tough, no-holds-barred tone, he fails to convince us that the moment really has such significance. . . .

Since Edmund Wilson is one of Exley's literary heroes, it is not surprising that some of the best passages in the book focus on Exley's visit to Wilson's upstate New York home and his conversations with Wilson's secretary Mary Pcolar. But even in the Wilson sections we feel that Exley is working at too high a pitch. His awe of Wilson inspires him to produce gushing and embarrassing passages noting his sense of loss and despair. He reminds us that Wilson never made the cover of *Time* and that his books never sold as well as those of Harold Robbins and Jackie Susann. I would imagine that Wilson might have found some solace in these facts of literary life. Of Wilson's stature and value there is no question: to read him was both a joy and an education. But we do wonder what it is about Wilson and his work that stimulates Exley. Since he spends so much time mourning him, it is odd that he is never very specific about his passion.

A Fan's Notes was an intense, deeply felt book. By comparison, *Pages from a Cold Island* is slack, gossipy, and often petty. The troubled, defeated, comic narrator of the earlier book has grown coarse and loud. The new book is very readable, but from Exley we expected far more. At one point, he quite rightly accuses Mailer of posing and posturing, but he obviously fails to see these very elements in himself. (p. 1004)

Ronald De Feo, in National Review *(© National Review, Inc., 1975; 150 East 35th St., New York, N.Y. 10016), September 12, 1975, pp. 1003-04.*

C. BARRY CHABOT

While Frederick Exley's *A Fan's Notes* envisions a culture every bit as inhumane as we find elsewhere in contemporary fiction, his novel represents a significant turn. Exley's America may fail and brutalize him, but he comes to momentary recognitions of his own not insignificant failings. Simply, unlike his fellow protagonists, Exley in *A Fan's Notes* carries the burden of guilt; indeed, he at times equates remorse with the very conditions of humanity. . . . Exley cannot always sustain an awareness of his own complicity in the sufferings of this world and often is overwhelmed by his rage at a callously indifferent America. Nonetheless, the significance of Exley's fragmentary and tentative introspective recognitions probably leads beyond *A Fan's Notes* and suggests a bad faith pervasive in much recent fiction.

Exley begins bumptiously enough. He desired "nothing less than to impose [himself] deep into the mentality of [his] countrymen." . . . Watching New York emerge as he stood on the prow of an approaching ferry, the city's "golden shadow on the water was like an arm stretched forth in benediction, promising that it would deny [him] nothing." . . . But the promises prove illusory. Whatever its allure, New York steadily resisted Exley's furious courtship. Rather than being hailed as a true son of the city, Exley found only frustration and his dreams of fame gradually curdled into the waking nightmare of a rage "induced by New York's stony refusal to esteem [him]." . . .

Frank Gifford and the New York Giants provide the only solace in this first assault on New York. Exley locates personal failure as one of the reasons for his passionate attachment to Frank Gifford and the Giants. (pp. 87-8)

One reason Exley does not envy Gifford his remarkable success is that he eventually sees success within America as illusory. The ironic interlude with Bunny Sue, Exley tells us, proved "a time when more than any other I felt at one with my country." . . . In a way, the narrative transforms Bunny Sue, "that American girl" . . . and "most insistent seducer" . . . , into a metaphor of the culture she epitomizes for her hapless admirer. Despite her voluptuous enticements and promises of gratification, which echo those of New York's "golden shadow," Exley cannot couple with her—he is impotent. (pp. 88-9)

Success in Exley's America, then, means not fulfillment but emasculation. This hollows out the tokens of success, rendering them enticements which only entrap their unwary pursuers. The promised freedom imprisons the ardent within the tight circle of the obligations their attainment entails. (p. 89)

In this way, Exley's failure to couple with "that American girl" becomes emblematic of his interactions with all others. Just as he instinctively refuses to mingle with that womb, just as he withdraws from the apparently spurious enticements of America, Exley consciously withholds himself from most humans. (p. 90)

Exley's social vision . . . hardly distinguishes him from his colleagues. His America is as relentlessly superficial and dangerous as Mailer's, Pynchon's, or Vonnegut's. Likewise, his instinctive, self-preservative withdrawal from it replicates theirs. *A Fan's Notes* makes its decisive contribution elsewhere. For all his self-protective gestures, Exley does not, like other protagonists, exempt himself from his critique. By embedding the evolution of his rage at America within his gropings toward personal understanding, Exley seems more alive to the necessary ramifications of his vision and its potentially seamy consequences. As we move away from the social vision and approach the personal level, the special import of *A Fan's Notes* becomes available.

In his initial need to crash the consciousness of New York, Exley feels a paternal inheritance: "I suffered myself the singular notion that fame was an heirloom passed on from my father." . . . Before descending upon New York, he and his USC colleagues cynically concoct a resume embodying an outrageously exalted self-image. While walking down Park Avenue to the first job interview earned by his spurious identity, Exley notices the incongruity of his suit. His discomfort increases quickly, for he recognizes that the interview could involve questions based on the resume:

> That was as close to the interview as I ever got, as close to that or any of the interviews my friends had worked so passionately to get me. For suddenly I saw my father . . . he rose before me as I had seen him last—in his casket. . . .

The image of his dead father haunts Exley and stays for now his courtship of New York.

If the father now slows the quest, he initially generated it. Exley's father was that most pathetic of heroes, the small-town athlete who for one reason or another never leaves the scene of his youthful triumphs. (pp. 90-1)

In Exley's own . . . courtship of New York we can see both an emulation of and competition with the father, an attempt at once to complete the father's project and better it. . . .

A Fan's Notes offers a powerful image of a boy deeply eager for private confirmation from a loved father. (p. 92)

Exley's complex and anguished relationship with his father also prefigures that with America. Exley stands before the United States with the same desires, same ambivalences, and same grievances he had previously directed toward his father. New York stonily turns aside his advances no less consistently than his father seemingly denied him the longed-for recognition. In both instances Exley reacts to a felt humiliation with hot outrage. (pp. 93-4)

In the silence beyond the final word of *A Fan's Notes* the novel itself gets written. With its publication Exley returns to the world of men seeking confirmation of his vocation and his transformation from fan to fledgling star. Exley strives again to wedge for himself some certain place in the consciousness of New York, and if he succeeds, he will not only be transformed, not only assume and complete his father's quest, but also figuratively transcend his own mortality to live on in the consciousnesses of his readers. Therefore, despite his protestations, Exley does not withhold himself once and for all from others. Rather he withdraws from the world and its work only to come back, to offer it a gift he hopes it will prize. Most simply, he absolutely needs something out there; he hungers for recognition—from his father, from New York, from the America he claims to scorn. . . . That fate is not simply anonymity, but utter selflessness. (pp. 96-7)

As *A Fan's Notes* comes to a close . . . Exley shoulders his personal responsibility for the cultural brutishness he has analyzed in such anger. Thus implicating himself in his own critique, Exley accepts sin and remorse, transgression and guilt, as inescapable baggage in human life. Put another way, Exley eventually sees the very capacity for feeling guilt (not guilt itself) as the grounds of our common humanity. Without that capacity culture itself is an impossibility. Exley's more basic recognition—namely, that selfhood is necessarily born in, and only in, relationships, that it exists in-between, not internally—forces his acceptance of liability for and to others. In abandoning essentialist ideas of identity for an interpersonal one, Exley must also recognize that we must all be in some degree responsible to others, hence the radical need for a capacity for guilt.

These intertwined beliefs convert *A Fan's Notes* into a powerful if oblique commentary on much other recent fiction. The novel demystifies the saving distance so many protagonists carefully place between themselves and a malevolent America. If selfhood necessitates relationships, that distance will cruelly become a prison within which they wither. Moreover, in most fiction that distance is at least implicitly moral, for it sets the protagonist apart from the solely external sources of moral corruption. If Exley [reasons] aright, however, in the very attempt to exempt themselves from the sink of American society, these protagonists necessarily pain and diminish those they leave behind, turning hollow any pretentions to moral superiority; their serenity of conscience becomes a construct of monumental bad faith. In almost every way, then, *A Fan's Notes* calls into question the generative assumptions of much contemporary American fiction.

But Exley himself cannot always sustain his difficult, alternative vision. The detachment and need hover unevenly in *A Fan's Notes,* almost as if Exley cannot finally bring himself to face those twin humiliations—his guilt and need for others. Despite his accumulated knowledge, we last see Exley yet again refusing "to be drawn into the world's work." . . . The new vision, however, is not completely repressed, for it returns as a nightmare. Rather than turning his back to others as he does each day, in the nightmare Exley finds himself running toward his tormentors. He preaches to them the necessity of living "the contributive, the passionate life" . . . ; he wants to restore to them the emotional heritage, the ache of remorse, necessary if they are to reclaim their humanity. The nightmare only troubles the conscience of an Exley made uneasy by the repression of his own, hard won, alternative vision, just as *A Fan's Notes* itself subverts the vision of much recent fiction. If only in the negativity of its shining nightmare, then, *A Fan's Notes* inaugurates again the possibility of inserting oneself squarely amidst the reciprocating dependences of this difficult world. (pp. 98-9)

C. Barry Chabot, "The Alternative Vision of Frederick Exley's 'A Fan's Notes'," in Critique: Studies in Modern Fiction *(copyright © by James Dean Young 1977), Vol. XIX, No. 1, 1977, pp. 87-100.*

F

FALLACI, Oriana   1930-

Fallaci is an Italian novelist and journalist. Approaching her work as a socialist and a historian, she is deeply concerned with politics, feminism, and the influence of people in power. Her interviews with numerous leaders and political figures are known for their candor and controversial method of questioning. (See also *Contemporary Authors*, **Vols. 77-80.)**

ISA KAPP

Fallaci enacts each of her assignments [as interviewer] as though it were a boxing match or a love scene. She springs into many different postures in rapid succession to unnerve her opponent, and alternates verbal scratches with relenting pats until her subject releases what she takes to be the essence of himself.

Whether or not these disingenuous tactics are necessary to overcome the self-protectiveness of public figures, they certainly testify to her belief that nothing could be duller than objective fact, and that the pursuit of truth must be peppered with friction. She specializes in the production of a spurious electricity, not so much to switch a clear light on political leaders, as to disclose in them a weakness here, a downright meanness there—those small shocks and sparks that journalism assumes are the surest devices for wakening its somnolent audience.

Fallaci brings the same rousing mixture of tactician and implied crusader to her new book, *Letter to a Child Never Born*, which became something of a *cause celebre* when it was first published in Italy; and if there is a danger that histrionics may subtly alter the substance of a political discourse, they certainly seem out of place here, considering the centrality and seriousness of her subject. Advanced as a novel, the plot proceeds as a monologue-debate on procreation and the right of a woman who has conceived a child to decide whether she should allow it to live. Never inhibited by fine scruples, Fallaci—that is to say, her main character—formulates all sides of the issue herself, and is indeed the heroine of all its emotional reverberations.

From page one, she addresses to her unborn child a disheartening recitation of its prospects, dutifully arraying the diverse shapes of human adversity. War, disease, humiliation, betrayal, slavery—there is no end to her lexicon of oppression. By the time she shares her conviction that "the family is a lie," "work is blackmail," and love "a gigantic hoax," the baby must be not a little discouraged for himself and much concerned with the self-dramatizing disposition of his mother-to-be as well as her indiscriminately scalding rhetoric. (p. G7)

The reader worries about her stability as she fluctuates from assuring the embryo "You looked like a mysterious flower, a transparent orchid," to charging, "you hurl yourself against my body like a vampire." The doctor suggests she is subconsciously resisting the child, and soon everyone's suspicions are confirmed. She leaves her hospital bed and goes on a ten-day car trip to carry out her magazine assignment, and the baby dies.

At an imaginary trial in which the heroine is both accuser and accused (so we may feel confident that she will receive clemency), the spectrum of views on abortion (or, more exactly, deliberately placing the fetus in danger) is rather eloquently presented. Ironically enough, Fallaci is at her best not when she is up in arms, but when she is putting concrete facts in order. . . . [The] unborn child, captive audience until now, makes the most bruising accusation of all: she did not believe in life. But the baby should have known that his mother would have the last word, and that it would be uttered with bravado:

> "But elsewhere a thousand, a hundred thousand children are being born, and mothers of future children: life doesn't need you or me. You're dead. Maybe I'm dying too. But it doesn't matter. Because life doesn't die."

To go one step further and say that life doesn't need vindication of this caliber, and to resist the throbbing, self-vaunting tone of *Letter to a Child Never Born* is not to deny that Fallaci has taken on a stirring complex subject at an opportune moment. . . . A laudable verve has gone into bolstering the biological and doctrinal particulars of the book's argument, and snappy phrasing corsets some of its emotional excesses. But for most women real ambivalence about giving birth to a child does not arise from petty considerations like vanity or missing out on a journalism assignment, but from graver problems of health, poverty or temperamental capacity. The question of abortion (or even childbirth) has had relatively little place in literature until recently. Precisely because its increasingly respectable status has created an immense uncertainty that neither dogma nor common sense, sentiment nor severity are altogether

189

adequate to, we want, in the writers who deal with it, largeness of mind, refinement of spirit and—something we cannot reasonably expect of Oriana Fallaci—a disciplined ego. (p. G10)

Isa Kapp, "Oriana Fallaci and the Facts of Life," in Book World—The Washington Post *(© The Washington Post), February 13, 1977, pp. G7, G10.*

FRANCINE du PLESSIX GRAY

Fallaci's new book ["Letter to a Child Never Born"], which she calls a novel, takes the form of a passionate dialogue with the unborn child she once carried during a three-month pregnancy. Its theme is easy enough to identify with, being central to the lives of most women: the general ambivalence of joy and fear towards the act of giving birth, the more agonizing ambivalence towards giving birth to an illegitimate child. Yet although the book has moments of intense emotional power it too often lapses into a bathos that is as disconcerting as it is unexpected, coming as it does from this rapier-witted debunker of all bourgeois clichés and historical sentimentalism.

"Letter to a Child Never Born" is a profoundly sad work that balances between two sorrows: the primary sorrow of knowing that an illegitimate child exists within her, the more profound sorrow Fallaci experiences when her pregnancy is terminated. . . .

I wept a bit over this book yet felt rather ashamed of my tears, as if I had found myself crying at 3 P.M. over "Guiding Light." Although many feminists would like to transgress this ultimate taboo, the task of writing about our unborn children presents almost insuperable esthetic problems because of the biological luridness of the theme and the inevitable sentimentalism it evokes in us. Fallaci, alas, falls deeply into this double trap. She presents us with romantic fantasies of the growing fetus which might be compatible with a bambino-worshiping Mediterranean culture (her book has sold 400,000 copies in Italy) but which I find as lurid as the bottled fetuses touted by anti-abortion agitators. "There you are at six weeks . . . how cute you've become! No longer a fish, no longer a larva. . . . You've grown wings. What's it like in the egg?"

Like much of the intimate confessional writing presently being explored by women, Fallaci's book is also flawed by the dominance of a passionately engaged narrator over a subsidiary cast of sloppily limned, two-dimensional characters. In this respect, Fallaci's literary problem is further complicated by a strident brand of feminism that makes a cardboard villain of every man with whom she comes in contact during her pregnancy. . . . [They] all offer her the cold judgmental stare that has been the stock in trade of pulp literature dealing with the theme of unwed motherhood. The father of Child—a cowardly sniveler with poor taste in flowers, who sits on her bed to weep more comfortably—is the most stereotyped character of all. At the book's conclusion, only Fallaci's parents, a woman friend and a kind womanly doctor pronounce her innocent of the charges of having murdered Child.

In Jonathan Cott's marvelous interview with Fallaci in "Rolling Stone", she refers to "the solitude that oppresses women intent upon defending their own destinies . . . an internal solitude that comes from being a woman with responsibilities in a world of men." This inevitable solitude of the "emancipated" woman is the real theme of Fallaci's new book. One feels that she is left alone with her own destiny, a woman who considers love "a gigantic hoax invented to keep people quiet and diverted," who sees the family as "a lie constructed the better to control people." Notwithstanding its severe flaws, "Letter to a Child Never Born" is a poignant testament to this new solitude, and also to the older tension between our desire for liberation and our equivalent desire to be shackled to the process of nurturing. In her best moments, Fallaci, as always, strips truth down to its naked bone. She exposes the poignancy of these contradictions and the agony of our new-won freedoms. (p. 3)

Francine du Plessix Gray, in The New York Times Book Review *(© 1977 by The New York Times Company; reprinted by permission), February 13, 1977.*

["Letter to a Child Never Born"] is an attempt at a general consideration of the state of motherhood from the point of view of a successful, single, Italian reporter—a worldly, cynical, independent, globe-trotting iconoclast. It is written in the form of a monologue addressed to the unborn child that the woman suddenly discovers she is carrying. . . . A sad story but a wordy one, full of absurd generalizations, of posturing (the author casts herself alternately as Elektra and Peter Pan), and of bathetic self-ennoblement. (pp. 125-26)

The New Yorker *(© 1977 by The New Yorker Magazine, Inc.), February 21, 1977.*

HOPE HALE DAVIS

Fallaci focuses [the whole of *Letter to a Child Never Born*] on the child's physical presence within the heroine; the fetus as imagined from an article becomes the other main character, and is addressed throughout. . . .

Though her tone tends to be arch, Fallaci makes the process of pregnancy marvelously vivid. . . .

The novel neatly encapsulates the battle between an old longing that may be irresistibly instinctual, and the urge of women toward outer fulfillment, worldly success. (p. 15)

Fallaci is famous for her interviews with celebrities. . . . Her power is such that she could bring to heel the Duchess of Alba, with all her 63 titles, by threatening to choose another Spanish aristocrat as her subject. Fallaci never hesitates to speak freely. Ending long hours with Alfred Hitchcock, for whom, before their meeting, she had felt only a banal admiration, she said, "With all your cordial humor, your nice round face, your nice innocent paunch, you are the most wicked, cruel man I have ever met." After hearing his gleeful boasts about the sickening real-life murders his films had inspired, she overcame her fashionable blindness to what she now could see as "really evil." Give her credit for that.

The price of journalism, though, can be high. When she brought out in America *The Useless Sex* (1964), a survey of the state of women in countries she had visited, *The New Yorker* said that her "quest was not fruitful, her research was not diligent, her observations are not intelligent, her style is not witty, her conclusions are not interesting, and her translator is dreadful."

Carried away as the critic must have been by syntactomania, there is enough truth in the blast to explain Fallaci's obvious difficulty in giving her novel depth and richness. Even its brevity seems less by design than by default. She tries to fill it out with three cautionary "fairy tales" told to the baby as warnings about the world. These tales, involving social inequities and apparently based on her own childhood, grow increasingly bitter. The last one breaks out of its mold to reveal in raw anger what must be the source of Fallaci's prejudice against the United States. It tells of a girl forced, for a few cans of beans, to wash the dirty underpants of soldiers who had been expected to bring the "tomorrow" her father had dared and suffered for all his life. (p. 16)

Hope Hale Davis, in The New Leader *(© 1977 by the American Labor Conference on International Affairs, Inc.), March 14, 1977.*

JOHN BEGLEY

Unlike most modern novels I have read in recent years, [*Letter to a Child Never Born*] will be difficult to forget. In the form of a novel, and I frequently found it necessary to remind myself that it was a novel and not a private journal I was reading, it is an intensely personal reflection upon the purpose and value of human existence. The medium of expression is a tragic monologue in which an unmarried, liberated career woman confronts the question to give life or to deny it. . . .

To the end the mother retains her independence by refusing to agree with the child's decision to die on the grounds that "it is not enough to believe in love if you don't believe in life." For her the meaning of life is to search for meaning. For all its ambiguity, life is its own justification.

The monologue is an extraordinarily difficult literary form to sustain. It requires the disciplined talent which Ms. Fallaci obviously possesses. . . . Few readers may share the vision of life related in this novel. However, all should find this encounter with a gifted novelist very worthwhile. (p. 38)

John Begley, in Best Sellers *(copyright © 1977 Helen Dwight Reid Educational Foundation), May, 1977.*

*   *   *

FARRELL, James T(homas)   1904-

Farrell is an American novelist, short story writer, critic, poet, and editor. Considered a naturalist in the tradition of Dreiser, he paints an angry and powerful picture of lower and middle-class urban life. His literature is often socially oriented, exploring themes of alienation, chaos, and communication. Its realism is enhanced by the language of his characters, an accurate rendering of contemporary urban speech. Farrell is an extremely prolific author, whose work has frequently found critical disfavor. He has also written under the pseudonym of Jonathan Titulescu Fogarty, Esq. (See also *CLC*, **Vols. 1, 4, 8, and** *Contemporary Authors*, **Vols. 5-8, rev. ed.)**

ARTHUR VOSS

The world of most of Farrell's fiction is not a pretty or happy one, since, as he has said, much of his writing has been concerned with portraying "conditions which brutalize human beings and produce spiritual and material poverty." (p. 267)

It must be admitted that a number of Farrell's stories, especially his earlier ones, show the influence of other writers. Farrell has frequently treated everyday characters and the emptiness, vulgarity, or sordidness of their lives in the manner of Chekhov and Joyce; he has written some Sherwood Anderson—like studies of repression and frustration; and he has written still other stories which are reminiscent in various ways of Hemingway, Lardner, and Dreiser. It must also be admitted that Farrell's work in the short story is very uneven, that at times it is overly doctrinaire, and that it is sometimes undistinguished in form and style. But though one does not find the artistry of a Chekhov or Joyce in Farrell, one does find intensity and moral seriousness and, in at least a few of the stories, an ability to powerfully affect the reader. (pp. 267-68)

Arthur Voss, in his The American Short Story: A Critical Survey *(copyright 1973 by the University of Oklahoma Press), University of Oklahoma Press, 1973.*

LEWIS FRIED

Farrell's major fiction ("the story of America as I knew it") is funded so greatly by the struggles of his youth and maturity that we are in danger of reading the Bernard Carr trilogy as mere autobiography. (p. 52)

I want to suggest, however, that the trilogy is an act of, and meditation upon, the historiography of culture. The novels express—and dramatize—the problems besieging a writer who wishes to study the politics of social life. For both Farrell and Carr vivify a method of inquiry that portrays the experience of novelty, of historical emergents, as authentic expressions of change in human endeavor and nature. Breaking the backbone of a deterministic phenomenology, in this case the vulgarized Marxism of the 1930s, Farrell and his fictional *alter ego* wish accurately to study choice and individuality by rescuing them from an inexorable dialectic. Within this large theme, Farrell is concerned with "making of self," the process of individuation that marks the moral and intellectual growth of an American writer. (pp. 52-3)

Farrell's decision to focus on the maturation of a writer during a turbulent decade was a faultless choice; he could portray the difficulties of giving order to a past and present by exploring a consciousness concerned with that precise problem. Moreover, the period itself provided a ready-made setting to examine the obligations of a writer to his solitary craft and the public's difficulties. Finally, the fictional author is a maneuverable character that permits his creator to study social and political life without compromising a sense of probability; such a protagonist's strength lies in his ability both to expose and democratize events and feelings native to particular classes by revealing them to the reading public. (pp. 56-7)

[Carr] cuts through social strata without distinctly belonging to any level. As a result, a picture of the Depression is developed unlike those found in avowedly proletarian novels in which the protagonist does not hope to intellectually appropriate a culture, but is, instead, disinherited from it.

For Carr's working-class origins (his father is a brick-layer), and spiritually impoverished background (the South Side) place him outside a community concerned with the free play of the human imagination. Early in his career, Farrell had begun to crystallize the injustice of this retrogressive heritage: a split between the promise of American life with its potential to share experience through institutions and media and the real tragedy inherent in the education of an average American youth. (p. 57)

[The] point Farrell was making, one that was the concrete center of the heady aesthetic polemics of the thirties—of whom and of what shall one write—was that culture, in this sense man's objectified self-consciousness, develops from the struggles of an historical comity of thinkers privy to experimentation and tradition. (pp. 57-8)

Farrell's individual novels are more than an examination of the aspirations, dreams, and delusions of a given number of South Side Irish-Americans. His fiction is a unified whole; it is a sustained meditation upon the emergents of the past, upon the consequences of choice, deliberation, and action. The times and places of his fiction are symbolic environments that foster platitudes, fables, and conduct that impede rational endeavor and infect the inhabitants of his art with the germ of spiritual poverty. He is arguing that a scientific method of inquiry must be applied to the self and its gregarious nature. The problematic must be confronted and mediated; energy must be directed towards the conceptualization of the unique, and the removal of obstacles in the path of rational social goals. His works, then, have a political dimension; they aid in the reconstruction of our own conduct so that we may effectively participate in the life of the community (p. 65)

> Lewis Fried, *"Bernard Carr and 'His' Trials of the Mind," in* Twentieth Century Literature *(copyright 1976, Hofstra University Press), February, 1976, pp. 52-67.*

JOSEPH W. SLADE

[Farrell's] characters continually pat psychic pockets to assure themselves that their pasts are intact. Such characters rarely strip their personalities bare; they clothe them, instead, with steady if minute accretions of experience. Characterization is Farrell's principal strength as a novelist, and it derives from the poor man's existentialism to which he subscribes. With the possible exception of Eddie Ryan, who figures either centrally or peripherally in most volumes of the cycle, Farrell's people do not leap abysses in dramatic bursts of faith. Although they agonize over choices and despair of meaning, their universe is not absurd to them. . . . Their lives are almost entirely circumscribed by banality—"pitiless banality"—and stereotypical illusion, not because they are comfortable with such conditions but because it is too painful to live without them.

The humans in *A Universe of Time* assimilate experience slowly, usually by converting an event's significance to a cliche that will take its place with the other cliches by which they understand the world. Repeating the cliches gives their lives definition, as if they were tracing the same pattern over and over again in sand, or, as one of Farrell's narrators puts it, as if a stream were cutting its way through earth. The process serves as a holding action for the self, which the passage of time threatens to erode. (pp. 68-9)

[In] *A Universe of Time* characters do not always intersect, let alone interfere with each other. Hell is not so much other people as it is the failure to create any but the most ordinary relationships. More than is the case in any of Farrell's previous works, humans are isolated from one another, washed into *cul de sacs* by the flow of time. The very

structure of the volumes makes this obvious. Although he uses traditional unifying devices such as symbols, parallel scenes, counter-balanced characters, and frequent motifs, Farrell develops his narratives along a strictly linear line with very little chronological experimentation. No major character appears without his biographical luggage, and within five pages of his entrance Farrell inevitably opens the suitcase to reveal the entire history of that character—before the next character comes along. Some people crop up repeatedly, while others never enter the plot a second time, but there is usually little room for them to interact because all those open suitcases are in the way. Numerous chapters are split into still more numerous sections; they are moments of time important in their discreteness only for their incremental value. In short, time marches on, and with it march Farrell's humans.

The nature of time is paradoxical. Its pulse gives life meaning. yet so far as Farrell's characters are concerned, its impervious monotony robs experience of significance. . . . [Love] between humans—where it exists—has the effect of arresting time, nullifying it if only temporarily. (p. 70)

In another sense, love *is* an index of time for characters who measure the ebbing of their lives by reference to a poignant former passion. . . . Love hardly ever flourishes in the present; it blooms in the past toward which husbands and wives yearn, or, less often, in the future toward which they look with eager, illusory anticipation.

Virtually all of the marriages in *A Universe of Time* degenerate into routine or discord. While men turn maudlin remembering fine hopes, the loss of love strikes women hardest. . . .

Women in *A Universe of Time* crave gentle sex in their youth, achieve transfiguration in childbirth, and thereafter enter spiritual decline. To fill the void of their lives they compensate in one or more of three distinct ways, all of them detailed with the thoughtful Freudianism at which Farrell excels. The older, more pessimistic opt for religion, usually Catholicism, in order to spend their leisure in church or in calling down anathema on the men who have abused them. . . . By contrast, younger women flush with what can only be called pornographic fantasies low in explicit erotic content but high in sentimental stereotypes: they dream of being hugged tightly to a tweed shoulder. . . .

A third compensation of Farrell's deprived women, occasionally shared by males, is a faith in their children. If they have been denied fulfillment, they reason, then their progeny can perhaps succeed. (p. 71)

If his women respond to time's ravages in comparatively simple Freudian or romantic tropisms, Farrell's males grapple philosophically with process—with a similar lack of success. Each time a would-be historian thinks he has distilled the laws of history, even that he has discerned patterns, Farrell undercuts him to make it plain that he has grasped illusion. (p. 72)

Older men, of course, are especially prone to [reflections on the past]. In their musings they stumble over the faultlines of historical process and balk at endorsing purposive continuity. Again and again they are drawn to the betrayals of man's aspirations toward controlling the movements of time. . . .

Younger men, although they may also be persuaded of the

meaninglessness of history, usually beat their breasts in defiance. (p. 74)

Eddie Ryan quite early learns what his elders know intimately, that his aspirations toward Destiny can quickly be blunted by apprehensions of death.... Before he leaves the university, Eddie borrows from physics the principle that Henry Adams once applied to history with devastating effect: The Second Law of Thermodynamics. References to entropy abound in *A Universe of Time*. Human institutions decay, culture patterns become chaotic, random motion increases—the universe is running down to final equilibrium and death. (pp. 74-5)

Eddie's faith in the Second Law fluctuates with his moods as he tries to graft it onto a perenially renascent romanticism. *The Silence of History* ends on a heroic note, with Eddie speaking in first person....

[Most] characters in *A Universe of Time* choose, like Eddie, to sidestep the full implications of a meaningless universe. To accept entropy as a principle is to accept a bleak —if objective—view of existence. Farrell's humans prefer illusion. (p. 75)

At first glance, the pervasiveness of the concept of entropy would seem to place Farrell in the company of such postwar American novelists as Mailer, Heller, and Pynchon, but he does not use entropy in any structural sense, does not quite grasp its function as "time's arrow," as physicists fittingly refer to it, does not in fact understand entropy very well, as he has acknowledged. From the standpoint of Farrell's announced intention in *A Universe of Time*, to present "a relativistic panorama of our times," his failure to employ entropy in a sophisticated manner is unfortunate, if only because the Second Law would provide a foundation for a relativistic scheme and also legitimite chance, the chief element in Farrell's mature "naturalism."

By adopting time as an element in his fiction, Farrell has tried to counter the charge that his naturalism is antiquated. Unfortunately, the charge remains justified, if only because time in the cycle does not function as an entropic or dynamic force.... [The] principal difficulty centers on his approach to time and history.... Farrell has said that historical process reflects the operation of "multiple causation." Judged by this standard, the shortcoming of *A Universe of Time*, is that the causes are not sufficiently multiple, particularly for a cycle of so large a scale. Biological accident, Freudian influences, environmental conditioning, and economic injustices are not enough. Left out almost entirely is technology, the major force of our era. (pp. 75-6)

When [Farrell's characters] fulminate against the tyranny of time as fate, they actually are chafing under the oppression of the past. (p. 76)

Confronted with death, such men may rail against the meaninglessness of time, yet they plumb it over and over again. The net result is a stasis of the self that shades into narcissism. Farrell's characters do not lack time to do what they want. Indeed, time weighs heavily as they wait passively for "a brand new life." ...

The present *is* vast, as Farrell's title claims, frighteningly so, and his humans dare not face it without first collecting *all* the bits and pieces of their selves. Besides being vast, the present is thin when measured against the past. Once

good at depicting the density of life in cities, Farrell has focused on urbanness itself in another attempt at modernizing his naturalism.... The drawback is that he has lost the ambience which once served him well, so that his classic naturalism, which emphasizes environmental conditioning, is less and less compelling. Under those circumstances, the supposed alienation of his humans is not so convincing as it might be, for the reader does not always see what they are alienated from, and since epiphanies are of low-wattage in *A Universe of Time*, the characters do not always understand their alienation either. (p. 77)

[His characters'] very generality works against Farrell. So large a canvas requires many characters, yet it does not contain multitudes that well. Principals emerge from common molds in polished detail, but it is also true that there are too many widowed mothers, too many fatherless, rootless wanderers, and too many mongoloid infants. Perhaps humans are very much alike, but similarity does not sustain interest. This lack of discrimination is worsened by Farrell's language. For a writer who in the past specialized in direct, pungent styles, the language of *A Universe of Time* seems careless. Individual words appear to have lost their value; they must be combined, aggregated.... Overburdened by pedestrian dialogue and narrative, the volumes of *A Universe of Time* do not concentrate experience, but diffuse it. This may very well be deliberate on Farrell's part: a banal aesthetic does complement banal subjects. The risk in that method of course is that the technique can cloy, and garrulity can make time creep for the reader as well as for the characters.

These qualifications notwithstanding, *A Universe of Time* represents achievement and new direction for Farrell. The task of his characters is precisely the obverse of his method. Because nothing happens to them that has not happened to other humans, they must try to distill meaning from attenuated, commonplace experience....

Whether Farrell is still a naturalist is almost beside the point. Intended or not, the message of *A Universe of Time* is that the romantic self, which finds its last refuge in narcissism, is bankrupt. In demonstrating its exhaustion, Farrell shows that he understands human isolation, and that he understands what it means to be without significant resources to alleviate isolation. That understanding makes him very modern indeed. (p. 78)

> *Joseph W. Slade, "Bare-Assed and Alone: Time and Banality in Farrell's 'A Universe of Time',"* in Twentieth Century Literature *(copyright 1976, Hofstra University Press), February, 1976, pp. 68-79.*

LEONARD KRIEGEL

What I instinctively knew when I first read Farrell now seems to me his major contribution to American writing: his stubborn insistence on the validity of all lives for the creation of fiction. In this, he followed the lessons of his own masters, Balzac and the 19th-century European realists and Dreiser, writers whom we conveniently pigeonhole but who really have little in common other than their insistence that craft in fiction be matched by situation.... *Studs Lonigan* is certainly among the more memorable realistic fictions ever written in this country, but it would be difficult to cull a single memorable phrase from all of its pages. The work does not really rely on language but rather on the situations language describes and on the relentlessness with which Farrell hunts Studs down for us. So many of the terms critics love to use to praise a work of fiction do not apply to *Studs:* it is neither "lyrical" nor "poetic"; it lacks the broad canvas of Stendhal or Balzac; and few great novels have been less "uplifting." Its power is that it grinds its readers down, insisting on the validity of these lives in their time and place. And it does this more successfully than many other novels labeled its superior. (p. 373)

Like all writers who have written a great deal, Farrell's weaknesses are amply illustrated. And his weaknesses should be recognized, particularly by critics who number themselves among those Leslie Fiedler once called his "few surly defenders." Farrell is certainly not a stylist of distinction. The slang of *Young Lonigan* was already dated when the book first appeared. The same slang appears in *The Dunne Family* [his latest novel] and it is still dead to the touch, even for someone who recognizes that its purpose is to establish the truth of the time about which Farrell is writing: "cripes" and "my eye" and "rats" are undoubtedly verifiable as the language of a time and group, but it is also a slang which appeals, as J. D. Salinger once remarked of psychoanalysis, to "the peership of tin ears." . . . His realism is often too photographic. And there are moments when one suspects his world was frozen in the 1930s and that he has cut himself off from a good deal of what is happening in contemporary American life. . . .

At times, Farrell can be brutal. But his brutality is not contemporary. A city novelist as knowing as any this country has spawned, Farrell avoids exactly those aspects of urban life which are so brutal that the novelist's job is done for him simply by his setting down what there is. The terror of Farrell's Chicago is the terror of aimlessness and drift; violence, when it occurs, is distinctly recognizable, on a small scale. It is Studs beating up Weary Reilley or Red Kelly. Even the scene in which Studs and his team pile on Jewboy Schwartz is not really violent, not, at least, by today's standards. They build up the violence in themselves, make of it something far greater than what it was. What frightens the reader is their vain bragging afterward, their collective fear about the inadequacy of their own quests for manhood. Violence resides in the paucity of their experience, both individually and collectively. (p. 374)

No one has written better of what motivates young men in the city than has Farrell. And it is another of his virtues as a writer that has come to haunt him. He insists that he does not want to be known as a "midwestern facsimile of the Lower East Side of New York," a writer about "slums." He points to how he deliberately made Studs the son of a relatively successful painting contractor and builder who is highly optimistic until his business is destroyed, as his oldest son lies dying, during the depression. And yet, he protests too much. . . . With all of its faults—and it has a goodly number—*Studs Lonigan* is one of the very few American literary works that manage to depict a commonplace life as a tragedy because *it is commonplace.* It reminds me of Benjamin Britten's magnificent opera, *Peter Grimes;* Peter's plebeian dignity is, strangely enough, what Studs would create for himself, if only he could.

The objections usually voiced about Farrell are so much less substantial than the man's achievement. How many other writers have been able to take people on their own terms? He creates individual men and women, unable to

frame the world so that it will be receptive to *their* aspirations. The situations in which they find themselves inherently possess that sense of "quiet desperation" that Thoreau and Henry James noted in American life. They do not wish to be rebels; they value "respectability" too much and they willingly conform to a Protestant work ethic that has given them better lives than their forefathers in Ireland knew. . . . In *The Dunne Family,* the quest is still for "respectability." The novel is not melodramatic, and it is certainly not particularly ironic, as was much of *Studs.* But it is filled with scenes characteristic of a Farrell milieu. The middle-aged Dunne children count the number of visitors to their dead mother's wake as a reflection of their status. Their aspirations are petty, their fears overwhelming, their pride mere self-puffery. Strangely enough, however, the reader feels sympathy for these middle-aged victims, these American failures. (pp. 374-75)

Like Balzac and Dreiser, Farrell has written remarkably well of the task of the modern city in creating those whom it must ultimately destroy. He is overwhelmingly a city writer, both because his own experience has been of the city and because the city is a natural testing ground for modern man. . . . Farrell's city landscapes are tightly structured. Compare, for example, the use to which he puts Chicago with the use Meyer Levin makes of it in *The Old Bunch.* . . . There are certain striking similarities between Farrell's Irish and Levin's Jews, and *The Old Bunch* was published in 1937, two years after Farrell had completed *Studs Lonigan.* In *Studs,* Chicago is a presence, almost a physical presence, the way a major character is; in Levin's novel, it is simply the place where most of the action occurs. Chicago is the frame in which Studs's manhood exists, and it is difficult to conceive of Studs as Studs in any other place. The city is woven into the text, just as it has been woven into the lives of the characters. . . .

Farrell is a stubborn writer. Merely to read his latest novel is to be reminded once again of the price he has paid for his art. The characters in this book commit what must be the single unforgivable sin left in America: they lead drab lives. They lack style, they lack power, and they lack courage. They sense that they have been defeated, but they are not sufficiently aware of the causes of their defeat. Inevitably, they blame others, conceive of the world as plot. How little Farrell is willing to allow for the passage of time. It is the integrity of his vision, his ability to capture what was there, that he demands the reader acknowledge. *The Dunne Family* is an old-fashioned novel, as, for all its headlines and popular songs, the *Studs* trilogy was. The Dunnes are like the vast majority of mankind; they promise they will be better, do better, only to shrivel up into their fear and bitterness and guilt. (p. 375)

I do not mean to use Farrell's realistic method as a weapon to attack other kinds of writing. To do that would be unfair. . . . There is no particular virtue in writing the way Farrell does. Realism is a mode he simply accepts as natural, and he probably cannot handle the kind of material he works with in any other way. . . . What I want to suggest is that Farrell has made good use of what is still the primary literary tradition in the West. He is a remarkably skilled and imaginative writer and his prose reflects the themes he deals with. . . .

[Farrell] understands that man keeps his humanity alive in seemingly small ways. And in this, he is another of the significant literary figures of the 20th century who have been forced by history to acknowledge that since ideology, *any* ideology, is the enemy of truth, it is inevitably also the enemy of art. . . . Farrell's fiction can be seen as part of the major literary struggle of our century, what the brilliant Austrian Marxist, Ernst Fischer, defined as "the struggle of the *practice and recognition of truth* against the domination of ideology." The loss of individual identity has reduced the human both in scope and possibility. The way in which Farrell has fought against this reduction of the human can be seen in the very fiction that has been dismissed as "naturalistic." For most of mankind, identity must be earned; for the writer, it is the manner in which his art, his culture, and he himself merge. And because he knew who James T. Farrell was, the writer was able to create Studs and Danny O'Neill and now Eddie Ryan as reflections of the human predicament. The truth to which he gave voice in *Young Lonigan* can still be seen in *The Dunne Family*. Behind the desperation with which the Dunnes live out their lives, behind their fear and hunger for something better, something more, there exists a sense of possibility. Farrell may be a pessimist, as his critics have charged. But if he is, he is a pessimist who still believes that man is capable of creating himself anew. (p. 376)

> Leonard Kriegel, "Homage to Mr. Farrell," in The Nation *(copyright 1976 by the Nation Associates, Inc.), October 16, 1976, pp. 373-76.*

BARRY WALLENSTEIN

A landmark in American literature has just been achieved with the publication of James T. Farrell's fiftieth book, *The Dunne Family*. Farrell is known as one of the major Chicago novelists, a naturalist, a modern classic. Yet in many people's minds, he has been locked into a dead-issue decade; his work is thought to be synonymous with the reductive struggles and frustrated ideals of the 30's. The irony is that during the 30's Farrell was not only popular and recognized, with his fiction praised in the leading journals, but a member of the avant-garde, and already looked upon with suspicion by the dogmatists of proletarian literature. In his critical writings during the "Red Decade" he considered writers not then in fashion, such as Joyce and Ibsen, and confronted issues, like the social functions of literature, with an independent spirit. Again and again he declared that literature lay beyond the dictates of any political program, however righteous.

The two series he is best known for, the *Studs Lonigan* trilogy and the *Danny O'Neill* pentalogy, books which prompted H. L. Mencken to acclaim Farrell in 1947 as "the best American novelist," are, in a way, works still in progress. His later books merely represent more recent installments in his huge *comédie humaine* of making it or going under in the many strata of the American middle class.

Farrell's predilection is for assessing the flat appearance of his characters as clues to their essential natures. The fact that he is less interested in their existential possibilities has separated him from the dark ironists of contemporary fiction, writers like Burroughs, Barthelme, Heller, and Pynchon. The current taste is for the novel as an exercise of wit that takes place on the edge of human experience, not necessarily congruent with "acceptable" reality, whereas Farrell's fiction rests on a belief that objective truth regarding the social as well as the psychological state of man is available and can be rendered in art. (pp. 82-3)

Though they are called naturalistic, Farrell's books do not present characters who are predetermined animals helplessly at sea among forces they cannot understand. Rather, these characters develop within a framework which encourages a study of their motivations. Farrell's underlying Marxism is another factor here, one which blocks the pessimism endemic to naturalistic fiction.

In the more recent books, the Danny O'Neill role as author's persona has been taken over by Eddie Ryan. Eddie says what Farrell has always believed in, that "his future depended solely on himself." The artist-hero hates moral or intellectual weakness and is a warrior in a moral battle. When Eddie chooses, at a pivotal moment, to go to the library instead of going home, he regards this first as simply a "symbolic gesture," but later calls the decision a "purely personal moral assertion." . . .

The aesthetic pleasures of Farrell's work and its ultimate achievement have specifically to do with the way he portrays characters who appear and reappear within the complex structure of his novels. His artistry lies in the total absence of a straining after effect; all the details, the empty talk, the inflated attitudes are attended to and selected with a sensitivity that knows the truth of "the middle" is a flat truth and one that must be suffered over a long time in order to sink in. Like Faulkner's saga of Yoknapatawpha, the work demands of the reader that he lose himself in it or else fall out of touch with its geographical and moral life. Entry into Farrell's world requires the same kind of suspension of disbelief we normally connect with less direct and less realistic fiction or poetry. To enter this somewhat unattractive world imaginatively is to expend more than reading time. By calling it up for our notice, Farrell demonstrates one of the moral functions of literature, its ability to make us care more than we thought we could for people who seem so far removed from ourselves, whose world seems such a rebuke to our own.

In *The Dunne Family* Farrell shows again how variously he can generate sympathy without condescension for the stark, ordinary, sentimental life that is his subject. (p. 83)

Living barely above the poverty line, each of the three Dunne children gains some satisfaction from fantasy, "an ingrown life in a cluttered one-room apartment." These pipe dreamers are artful dodgers, rationalizers pressed by the need to invent masks and keep up images. The three are obsessed with upward mobility and the need to get free, but the passion of their obsession is flattened out in Farrell's language, which relies on cliché to bring home the pretext and self-deception necessary for even the modest success they do achieve. For instance, Larry is described as "on his way up in the shoe game." He is also a believer in the firm handshake and the power of positive thinking (in this he is a forerunner of Middle America's current infatuation with EST, TA, TM, etc.). . . .

The Dunne family is a symphony of revealing clichés that become developed in Farrell's hands into full-blown metaphors of life in the middle:

> At sixty-one, Dick Dunne was still waiting for his ship to come in. The waters were rough and there was no abatement from the battering of the waves, but he still believed in the safe return of his ship with a cargo of rewards for him.

As these worn phrases float over the plot, they illuminate the condition of stasis in which the life of Farrell's characters is ineffectually lived. (p. 84)

As Farrell's persona, Eddie Ryan, who is a writer himself, functions on the periphery of the plot. . . . Eddie is in the story mainly to bring light and energy into the drab existence of the family. His letters are the only comfort to Grandma Dunne. When his first book arrives (*Studs Lonigan,* here called *Jud Jennings*), the Dunne household is proud and anxious at the same time.

Eddie and the purpose he serves are introduced early in the book when Jenny Dunne, musing over her hard and lonely existence, comes around to the terrible recognition that her life is meaningless and matters very little to anyone. "Who should care?" she asks.

> To Edward Arthur Ryan, it did matter. Edward Arthur Ryan was a young man determined to make it matter to as many people in the world as he could reach. . . . It was not a case of Edward Arthur Ryan merely making the life of his Aunt Jenny matter; he would make as many lives as he could matter.

While this may sound calculating in the mouth of a young writer, it has always been Farrell's idea as a novelist to offer a perspective that encourages and rewards compassion in the midst of all the squabbles and battering, all the grief, misery, and hatred which characterize life in his world. This perspective informs *The Dunne Family* no less than its forty-nine predecessors, and for serving it faithfully Farrell richly deserves the measure of honor that has been coming to him in recent days. (pp. 84-5)

> *Barry Wallenstein, "Artist of the Middle" (reprinted from* Commentary *by permission; copyright © 1976 by the American Jewish Committee), in* Commentary, *December, 1976, pp. 82-5.*

ANN DOUGLAS

Perhaps the central reason for Farrell's neglect is that he has confronted a problem modern America has determined to evade: our sense of history predicates a vision of Anglo-Saxon progress and expansion which our intellect no longer supports. . . .

Farrell's work begins with his admission that our sense of historical mission, our destiny of significant resolvable struggle, is failing, but this admission does not then transmute itself into a richly textured literary sensibility: admission instead becomes a dramatized insistence. (p. 488)

[Farrell's prestige] coincided less with his merits than with a special set of circumstances operative in the 1930s. The Depression gave Americans their first intimation of the complexity and possible termination of their historical purpose, a suspicion that they inhabited a world unyielding to their intentions and conceptions. No twentieth-century author has understood and articulated this American fear better than Farrell. . . .

Farrell dramatized in *Studs* that mass culture was the indispensable agent and analogue of our vanishing historical consciousness and that, in protecting people from the pain of historical awareness, it also deprived them of experience and of history itself. (p. 489)

The logic of *Studs* is almost as destructive . . . to radical programs as to humanist ones. . . . Farrell's city, unlike Dreiser's, never functions as a metropolis; it is a collection of warring provinces, a conglomerate of uncongenial, if similar, suburbs. There is no hope for internationalism or political sophistication in Studs' South Side. Ethnic prejudice comprises the very identity of Studs and his neighbors; because they don't know who they are, they cling to their pride in what they are not. (p. 492)

[Through] its peculiar kind of literary achievement as well as its chosen subject, *Studs* is sympathetic to a radical social critique. Farrell never condescends to his characters. His style, while more powerful and various than many critics have realized, is based on a principle of non-interference with his subject matter; *Studs* is superior to the world it describes precisely because it refuses at any given moment to be demonstrably better than that world. The novel's structure depends on Farrell's determination to reorder but not to omit any aspect of his material. We see Studs' world finally from Farrell's perspective, but we see all of it. Farrell's art is his commitment to integrity. At his worst Farrell is verbose but never distracted. . . . These people's lives don't matter in any traditional sense available to the author or reader. . . . Yet the extraordinary quality of *Studs,* as of much of Farrell's work, derives from his implicit insistence that these people's lives should matter; his characters should have a sense of "history." (p. 493)

No one could deny that sociology—which one might define loosely as the examination of the status, interaction, and environment of social groups partially detached from the full context of circumstance—helped to form Farrell's literary technique. Yet it is less true to say that Farrell wrote sociological fiction than to say that he wrote about people so enmeshed and entrapped in the static stereotypes of their culture that their lives *are* sociology; they are not historical creatures. Sociology, in other words, is less Farrell's technique in *Studs Lonigan* than a kind of operative metaphor for the impoverished quality of middle- and lower-middle class existence in urban America. (pp. 493-94)

Studs, despite its third person voice, is largely a stream-of-consciousness narrative with obvious and acknowledged affinities to James Joyce's work. . . . [However, Studs'] inner life is not a refuge from his outer life, nor even a complex counterpoint to it. In *Studs Lonigan,* consciousness itself has been demythologized, demystified, as it was not in Joyce's work. . . . Studs' mind has no free play at all; it is a collage of accepted clichés which Studs tries to correlate to his stunted psychic needs. Studs' consciousness is the reader's subject, never his or her guide. Studs never forms the material around him into perceptions, much less ideas. In a very real way, Studs has no inner life. His thought patterns could be said to constitute an external stream-of-consciousness. (p. 494)

Studs' monologues throughout *Studs Lonigan* reflect the loss of . . . epistemological mastery. Studs is an individual, and a real one; he is "there" as few characters in literature are "there," as we know our own selves to be "there." Farrell never lets us lose touch with the longing for self-fulfillment which animates Studs and which is our test of a unique human being. Studs' tragedy, hardly an unshared one Farrell implies, is that he is an individual who needs to be and feel himself, yet who has nothing but a cross-section of the mass mind to achieve that goal. (p. 495)

The language, verbal and physical, which the characters of *Studs Lonigan* use reinforces [the] picture of a closed, self-cancelling world. The book is in part a contest between two languages, neither of which expresses its users. (p. 497)

Studs has slipped gradually into total conformity, not because society has given him so much, but because it has given him so little so continuously that he can conceive of no alternative to acquiescence. Throughout the novel, Studs is subjected to a series of rituals which cannot accomplish their ostensible purpose. (p. 502)

Studs had only one thing going for him: his youth, his health, his body. These had inadvertently given him clues to a sense of freedom, buoyancy and pride altogether alien to his world. Farrell is aware that society can take over the mind more swiftly than the body. Studs could be said to have inherited mental conformity; we have seen that he is unable to express himself. Yet, until he is an adult, his physical life functions in part as an interpreter of lost languages. He loses the knowledge his body gives him; his terror at this loss is less the obsession with youth it seems to us, and to Studs, than the traumatized preoccupation with the period when all the odds were not against him. His physical self had provided his only metaphor for hope. (p. 503)

It is no accident that the disease which kills Studs is a heart ailment. His consciousness narrows to a concentration on his heart: he has become a time-bomb. Time is terrifying because it is potentially divorced from experience; the hours and days notch Studs without enriching or even using him. At one point during the early days of the Depression, Studs and Catharine go to watch a dance marathon. Couples with swollen ankles and faces dark with fatigue cling to each other to stay upright, to respond to the prodding of the master of ceremonies. "'I wonder when something is going to happen,'" Studs remarks to Catharine. "'I guess this is what happens,'" she replies. . . . The dance marathon becomes a metaphor for Studs' existence; the m.c. keeps alive that facsimile of hope expressed by stupefied endurance. Studs and Catharine stay for hours, waiting to "see if anything will happen." . . . Time functions as a vigilante on guard against the possibility of significance. (p. 504)

It is rare in the annals of the novel that a controlling consciousness be allowed to die, and to die on stage. Somewhat like Studs and Catharine at the marathon, the reader must confront how much harder it is to face the end of a hopeless enterprise than to witness the demise of a flourishing one. By writing his novel, Farrell has in part redeemed Studs' life, but chiefly as a warning, and one that has no easy juncture with whatever conscious wisdom we use to conduct our lives.

Studs' death testifies to the unwanted, unbearable perception that time passes as surely when experience is repeatedly postponed as when it is possessed. . . . Studs' life was borrowed and it never fit him; his culture maintained rather than sustained him. There are no answers here. . . . *Studs Lonigan* tells its readers what they must not forget, not what they must do; Farrell's objective is to force and discipline perception. He offers nothing to palliate our terror of space and time, of the failure of history, of the potential collapse of significance itself; he simply brings us face to face with our fear. Farrell warns that, while genuine resources may exist, we will not find them until we explore

our induced commitment to the cheapest of palliatives. (pp. 504-05)

Ann Douglas, "'Studs Lonigan' and the Failure of History in Mass Society: A Study in Claustrophobia," in American Quarterly *(copyright © 1977 Trustees of the University of Pennsylvania), Winter, 1977, pp. 487-505.*

* * *

FAULKNER, William   1897-1962

Faulkner, an American novelist, short story writer, and poet, is considered one of the greatest writers America has produced. Although a variety of attitudes and themes are evident in his work, Faulkner is best known as the chronicler of the decadent South. His genius transcends regionalism, however: in his evocation of the mythical Yoknapatawpha, Faulkner's brilliant narrative technique, complexity of characterization, and innovative use of time sequence mark him as a major figure in American letters. Twice the recipient of the National Book Award and the Pulitzer Prize, Faulkner also received the Nobel Prize in 1950. (See also *CLC*, Vols. 1, 3, 6, 8, 9.)

WARREN BECK

Faulkner has not only remained guilty of occasional carelessness, especially in sentence construction, but seems to have persisted in mannerisms. On the other hand, his progress as a stylist has been steady and rapid; his third novel, *Sartoris*, while still experimenting toward a technique, was a notable advance over his first two in style as well as in theme and narrative structure, and in his fourth novel, *The Sound and the Fury*, style is what it has continued to be in all his subsequent work, a significant factor, masterfully controlled. (p. 53)

Repetition of words, for instance, has often seemed an obvious fault. At times, however, Faulkner's repetitions may be a not unjustifiable by-product of his thematic composition. Some of his favorites in *Absalom, Absalom!*—not just Miss Rosa's "demon," which may be charged off to her own mania, nor "indolent" applied to Bon, but such recurrent terms as *effluvium, outrage, grim, indomitable, ruthless, fury, fatality*—seem to intend adumbration of the tale's whole significance and tone. Nor is the reiteration as frequent or as obvious here as in earlier books; perhaps Faulkner has been making an experiment over which he is increasingly gaining control. (pp. 53-4)

[His] word-series, while conspicuous at times, may have a place in a style as minutely analytical as Faulkner's. In their typical form they are not redundant, however elaborate, and sometimes their cumulative effect is undeniable—for example, the "long still hot weary dead September afternoon" when Quentin listens to Miss Rosa's story. . . . [Often] the amplification redounds to the significance of the whole scene. Quite often, too, these series of words, while seemingly extravagant, are a remarkably compressed rendering, as in the phrase "passionate tragic ephemeral loves of adolescence." . . .

In the later books profuseness of language is always knit into the thematic structure. Thus the elaborate lyrical descriptions of the sunrise and of a spring rain in book three of *The Hamlet* furnish by their imagery and mood a sharp, artistically serviceable contrast to the perversion of the idiot Ike Snopes, and as such they deepen the melancholy perspective from which this episode is observed. (p. 54)

There is nothing unique . . . in Faulkner's use of direct and forceful diction or fine figurative image. What is most individual in his style is its persistent lyrical embroidery and coloring, in extended passages, of the narrative theme. In this sense Faulkner is one of the most subjective of writers, his brooding temperament constantly probing and interpreting his subject matter. Thus his full style is comprehensive in its intention. He may often be unfashionably rhapsodic, but he seldom falls into the preciosity that lingers over a passage for its own sweet sake. Definition of his story as a whole and the enhancement of its immediate appeals to the imagination are his constant aims. (p. 55)

[Side] by side with [a] richly interpretative style there exists in almost all of Faulkner's work a realistic colloquialism, expressing lively dialogue that any playwright might envy, and even carrying over into sustained first-person narrative the flavor of regionalism and the idiosyncrasies of character. In the colloquial vein Faulkner's brilliance is unsurpassed in contemporary American fiction. He has fully mastered the central difficulty, to retain verisimilitude while subjecting the prolix and monotonous raw material of most natural speech to an artistic pruning and pointing up. *Sanctuary,* for an example, is full of excellent dialogue, sharply individualized. (p. 58)

Master of colloquialism in dramatic scene though he is, Faulkner sometimes lays aside this power in order to put into a character's mouth the fullest expression of the narrative's meaning. . . . For the most part, however, the transcending of colloquial verisimilitude in the novels is a fairly controlled and consistent technique, the characters Faulkner most often endows with penetration and eloquence being his philosophical spectators. Undoubtedly his chief concern, though, is with a lyric encompassment of his narrative's whole meaning rather than with the reticences of objective dramatic representation.

Thus many of his characters speak with the tongues of themselves and of William Faulkner. . . . The justification of all such practices is empirical; imaginative writing must not be judged by its minute correspondence to fact but by its total effect; and to object against Faulkner's style that men and women don't really talk in such long sentences, with so full a vocabulary so fancifully employed, is as narrowly dogmatic as was Sinclair Lewis, in *Main Street,* insisting that Sir Launcelot didn't actually speak in "honeyed pentameters." (pp. 59-60)

It is interesting to note that Faulkner's full style somewhat resembles older literary uses, such as the dramatic chorus, the prologue and epilogue, and the *dramatis personae* themselves in soliloquy and extended speech. The aim of any such device is not objective realism but revelation of theme, a revelation raised by the unstinted resourcefulness and power of its language to the highest ranges of imaginative outlook. No wonder that with such a purpose Faulkner often comes closer than is common in these times to Shakespeare's imperial and opulent use of words. If unfortunately his ambition has sometimes led Faulkner to perpetrate some rather clotted prose, perhaps these lapses may be judged charitably in the light of the great endeavor they but infrequently flaw. (p. 61)

In his most characteristic writing Faulkner is trying to render the transcendent life of the mind, the crowded composite of associative and analytical consciousness which ex-

pands the vibrant moment into the reaches of all time, simultaneously observing, remembering, interpreting, and modifying the object of its awareness. To this end the sentence as a rhetorical unit (however strained) is made to hold diverse yet related elements in a sort of saturated solution, which is perhaps the nearest that language as the instrument of fiction can come to the instantaneous complexities of consciousness itself. Faulkner really seems to be trying to give narrative prose another dimension.

To speak of Faulkner's fiction as dream-like . . . does not imply that his style is phantasmagoric, deranged, or incoherent. Dreams are not always delirium, and association, sometimes the supplanter of pattern, can also be its agent. The dreaming mind, while envisaging experience strangely, may find in that strangeness a fresh revelation, all the more profound in that the conventional and adventitious are pierced through. Similarly inhibitions and apathies must be transcended in any really imaginative inquiry, and thus do Faulkner's speculative characters ponder over the whole story, and project into cumulative drama its underlying significations. Behind all of them, of course, is their masterdreamer; Faulkner's own dominating temperament, constantly interpreting, is in the air of all these narratives, reverberant. Hence, no matter how psychological the story's material, Faulkner never falls into the mere enumeration which in much stream-of-consciousness writing dissolves all drama and reduces the narrative to a case history without the shaping framework of analysis, or even to an unmapped anachronistic chaos of raw consciousness. Faulkner is always a dynamic storyteller, never just a reporter of unorganized phenomena. His most drastic, most dream-like use of stream of consciousness, for instance, in *The Sound and the Fury,* is not only limited to the first two sections of the book, but it sketches a plot which in the lucid sections that follow gradually emerges clear-cut.

As clear-cut, at least, as Faulkner's stories can be. Here again is illustrated the close relation of his style to his whole point of view. If Faulkner's sentences sometimes soar and circle involved and prolonged, if his scenes become halls of mirrors repeating tableaux in a progressive magnification, if echoes multiply into the dissonance of infinite overtones, it is because the meanings his stories unfold are complex, mysterious, obscure, and incomplete. There is no absolute, no eternal pure white radiance in such presentations, but rather the stain of many colors, refracted and shifting in kaleidoscopic suspension, about the center of man's enigmatic behavior and fate, within the drastic orbit of mortality. Such being Faulkner's view of life, such is his style.

To this view the very rhythm of Faulkner's prose is nicely adjusted. It is not emphatic; rather it is a slow prolonged movement, nothing dashing, even at its fullest flood, but surging with an irresistible momentum. His effects insofar as they depend on prose rhythms are never staccato; they are cumulative rather than abrupt. Such a prose rhythm supplements the contributions of full vocabulary and lengthy sentence toward suspension rather than impact, and consequently toward deep realization rather than quick surprise. And the prolonged, even murmur of Faulkner's voice throughout his pages is an almost hypnotic induction into those detailed and darkly colored visions of life which drift across the horizons of his imagination like clouds— great yet vaporous, changing yet enduring, unearthly yet of common substance. It might be supposed that his occasionally crowded and circumlocutory style would destroy narrative pace and consequence. Actually this hovering of active imagination, while employing the sustained lyricism and solid abstraction which differentiate Faulkner from the objective realist, furnishes the epitome of drama. The whole aim is at perspective, through the multiple dimensions of experience, upon a subject in that suspension which allows reflection. The accomplishment is the gradual, sustained, and enriched revelation of meaning; in Faulkner's novels drama is of that highest form which awaits the unfolding of composite action, characterization, mood, and idea, through the medium of style. (pp. 62-4)

Faulkner's whole narrative method . . . may seem to be a retrogression in technique. Two main tendencies in modern fiction have been toward a more and more material dramatic presentation, depending simply upon the naming of objects and acts and the reporting of speech, and on the other hand, toward an ostensibly complete and unbroken reproduction of the free flow of consciousness. These methods have produced books as radically different as *The Sun Also Rises* and *Ulysses,* yet they have elements in common. In both types the author attempts to conceal himself completely behind his materials, to give them the quality of integral phenomena, and in line with this purpose the style aims at pure reproduction, never allowing definition and interpretation from any detached point of view. These have been honest attempts, a great deal of fine craftsmanship has gone into them, and some of the products have been excellent in their kind. Yet at their most extreme these have been movements in the one direction toward bareness, impoverishment, and in the other toward incoherence. Confronted by the imperfections and confusions of the present scene, and made hyperskeptical by deference to scientific method, the writers who have attempted absolute objectivity (whether dramatic or psychological, whether in overt event or stream of association) have sometimes produced what looks like an anti-intellectual aesthetic of futility and inconsequence. So in another sense Faulkner's narrative technique, particularly as implemented by his full style, instead of being a retrogression may represent one kind of progression through the danger of impasse created by too great submission to vogues of photographic or psychographic reproduction.

Yet Faulkner's is not altogether a return to an older expressiveness, not a complete departure from the modern schools of Hemingway and Joyce. In his colloquial passages he is quite as objectively dramatic as the one, in his rehearsal of the fantasies of acute consciousness he follows the other—and it should be remembered that he is superlatively skillful at both, so that it cannot be said that he puts these objective methods aside because he cannot use them. Furthermore, Faulkner is fond of employing in extended passages one of the favorite modern means of objectivity in fiction, the first-person narrator, using the device toward its most honored modern purpose, the attainment of detached perspective and the creation of realistic illusion concerning large vistas of the story. In short, there is no method in modern fiction which Faulkner does not comprehend and use on occasion. Fundamentally Faulkner's only heterodoxy by present standards of style is his fullness, especially as it takes the form of descriptive eloquence or abstraction and definitiveness. What is stylistically most remarkable in his work is the synthesis he has effected between the sub-

tleties of modern narrative techniques and the resources of language employed in the traditionally poetic or interpretative vein. That such a synthesis is feasible is demonstrated in the dynamic forms of his novels, and it may be prelude to significant new developments in the methods of fiction. (pp. 64-5)

> *Warren Beck, "William Faulkner's Style," in* American Prefaces *(reprinted by permission of Warren Beck), Spring, 1941 (and reprinted in* Faulkner: A Collection of Critical Essays, *edited by Robert Penn Warren, Prentice-Hall, Inc., 1966, pp. 53-65).*

KENNETH G. JOHNSTON

The sound of ticking clocks and watches often provides the accompaniment for William Faulkner's tales of decline and change in the South. A clock strikes the quarter hours in the afternoon quiet of the Sartoris mansion; Miss Emily's "invisible watch" marks the passage of time within the shadowed rooms of the decaying Grierson house; and Quentin Compson's timepiece, once his grandfather's, its hands twisted off, ticks on, adding to the sound and the fury of his final day. The sound is appropriate because, as Robert Penn Warren has observed, "the anguish of time, the tension of change," is Faulkner's basic theme. But in Faulkner's short story "Barn Burning," there is a silent clock. In the wagon of Abner Snopes, "among the sorry residue of the dozen and more movings," there is a clock, "which would not run, stopped at some fourteen minutes past two o'clock of a dead and forgotten day and time." (p. 434)

"Barn Burning" is a chapter in the continuing story of [the South's] stubborn retreat. A generation after the war, the planter-aristocracy is still quite powerful as we see by the fact that Major de Spain is a large landowner and lives in a white mansion, staffed by Negro servants and furnished with imported rugs and glittering chandeliers. But there has been an erosion of his authority. . . . The Justice of the Peace, although finding against the plaintiff Snopes, reduces by half the penalty assessed against him by his landlord. It is thus symbolically appropriate that the broken clock is in the possession of a barn burner who, by means of the law and the torch, is successfully challenging the authority of a standard-bearer of the old tradition. For time is on the side of Abner Snopes. He represents a new emerging force, a new class, in the post-bellum South. When he walks across the "hollow portico" at the Major's mansion, his stiff foot strikes the boards with "clocklike finality." . . . But the glow in the night sky tells us that he has lost this skirmish, too. Meanwhile, "the slow constellations" wheel on. . . . (p. 436)

> *Kenneth G. Johnston, "Time of Decline: Pickett's Charge and the Broken Clock in Faulkner's 'Barn Burning'," in* Studies in Short Fiction *(copyright 1974 by Newberry College), Fall, 1974, pp. 434-36.*

BRENT HAROLD

Although Faulkner never thought of his work as political in the usual sense . . . early in his career he commenced a determined struggle against dehumanization in his social milieu (soulless technology and commercialism, the alienation of human powers and identity) and, more importantly, in the literary milieu itself. By the time he wrote *The Sound and the Fury* he had experimented with versions of at least three of those dominant aesthetic modes of his time which were, according to [George] Lukács, the modernist options. Unlike most of his contemporaries, Faulkner had sensed the denial of human and artistic potential latent in those modes and, at least in his essential method, rejected them. The three modes may be roughly characterized as positivism (detached observation, a transparent medium); art for art's sake (literary solipsism, an opaque medium); and primitivism (deference to states of existence unrealizable in art and unavailable to its audience).

Faulkner's second novel, *Mosquitoes* (1927), may well be his weakest, but it contains, as Michael Millgate and Hyatt Waggoner have shown, a powerful and pertinent literary manifesto. The satire of Dawson Fairchild (usually identified with Sherwood Anderson) as a "bewildered stenographer . . . clinging spiritually to one little spot of the earth's surface," noting "details of dress and habit and speech, . . . trivialities in quantities," implicitly rejects several related versions of the malady of the observer. . . . (pp. 214-15)

Faulkner reacted to his own verbal passivity and conventionality . . . by assuming, in other early works, narrative condescension toward his subjects, achieved in part by outrageously whimsical metaphors such as "the moon had crawled up the sky like a fat spider," or "twilight ran in like a quiet violet dog." (p. 215)

The literary criticism in *Mosquitoes* is accomplished primarily not in satire at the expense of writers but in the portrait of the novel's hero Gordon, a sculptor. . . . Unlike the passive novelist of surfaces and the precious poet, the sculptor actively shapes his materials, penetrating with his chisel to essential form. . . . Sculpture was quite obviously [for Faulkner] . . . a way of announcing, in effect, that he had launched himself on a trajectory that would take him beyond the literary styles of his day. He would write not as writers write but as the potent and fully human Gordon sculpts. . . . He obviously enjoyed employing the diction of shaping and carving to suggest Gordon's consciousness and on quite a few occasions borrowed it for other narrative tasks as well, notably in combatting his own still predominantly romantic feelings about women and nature. . . . (pp. 215-16)

As for primitivism, the third mode offered Faulkner by his milieu and tradition—it may certainly be found in abundance in his third novel, *Sartoris* (1929). The novel centers upon a lost generation character (young Bayard) whose drunken ride on a stallion that "moved beneath him like a tremendous, mad music" becomes, like sculpting, an image of what the author could not yet consistently achieve in literary style, although—because Bayard's dynamism is self-destructive, nihilistic, and obscure—it is a contradictory, unsatisfactory image. Blacks depicted singing in the background in "quavering, wordless chords" and formulaic references to "liquid" birdcalls with which they are associated establish another vague center of value in the novel. (When the blacks are removed from the mystical backdrop and given words and a role in the plot, they become, for the most part, comic shufflers embarrassing to many admirers of Faulkner.) Such primitivism may be encountered occasionally in later work, as in the clairvoyance of the characters of *Light in August;* but it is implicitly criticized in advance by the vision of *Mosquitoes* and, despite what many critics have written, it runs counter to Faulkner's dominant fictional strategy.

Faulkner's verbal appropriation of the sculptural motif in *Mosquitoes* suggests that even when he was to reach beyond a neighboring artistic medium and take his models of psychic health from among ignorant countrypeople, Indians, idiots, even bears, dogs, and cows, he had no intention of deferring to such forms of simple, untainted or wordless existence. . . . Despite Faulkner's tirades against words, which should be read . . . to refer to certain misuses of language, his essential impulse was to create a prose which would actually embody some of the desirable qualities of primitive forms, thus demonstrating their availability to sophisticated audiences.

In Faulkner's conception, sculpture expressed its respect for reality, not in "clinging" fidelity but aggressive embrace, in shaping, in appropriation. In this sense all the experiments for which *The Sound and the Fury* (1929) is famous—especially its shocking violation of conventional arrangements of time and space—move toward the sculptural. Having emancipated himself from the traditional obligation to be a faithful observer of his own materials, Faulkner could create a version of Negro speech to transcend the dichotomy in *Sartoris* between the romantic idea of Negroes' "wordless" unity with nature and the stereotypically "realistic" portrayals of the same people. (This would explain what otherwise appears a startling conversion, during the year 1929 in which the two novels were written, from racism to non-racism.) He had discovered both the creative freedom and the technical means to use a character type as a motif. . . . (pp. 216-17)

Quentin's section is the most painful to read . . . because the section was a deliberate experiment in the language of disintegration and alienation. Quentin's thoughts and impressions are presented as a flow amid which he is passive, often lacking the force to shape it even with punctuation. His compulsive meditations on everything from such basic human functions as sex and eating to such abstractions as Time and Honor become a model of death in life. . . . [Even] Quentin's descriptions of processes in the present often take on a Hemingwayesque linearity and purity of image that in this context, in which one senses the latent powers of Quentin's creator, seem to plod. (pp. 218-19)

From all the languages which together delineate Quentin's mind, the language of certain other characters within this section comes as a relief. A bit of dialog from Shreve—humorous, energetic, imaginative, metaphorical—is the brightest spot in a dozen pages. . . . Major relief comes in conversations with the Negroes Roskus and Uncle Louis Hatcher, both of whom have speech refreshingly simple, colorful, and pleasantly rhythmic. Quentin, weary, it would seem, of the language of his interior monologue, conducts these conversations almost as interviews, saying only enough to keep the interviewee going. . . . (p. 219)

Louis's dialect, heavier than Negro speech Faulkner created in later books, does not dehumanize him, as their dialect does the Negroes in *Sartoris*. On the contrary, Louis's speech is the embodiment of an enviable ease with the self and nature. . . .

The values usually assigned to Benjy are the virtues of his defects: irrationality and passivity. Lacking the human powers possessed by his brothers, he is able, despite his agitations, to live in the world more comfortably and, paradoxically, more humanely than either of them. Yet Benjy's powerlessness and wordlessness are represented in his section by language of considerable poetic power. . . . Faulkner was able to use the motif of mindlessness as an opportunity to experiment with an alternative to Quentin's tortured language. (p. 220)

The prose of Faulkner . . . while innovative in the extreme, seems to derive both strength and sustenance not from a nostalgic attachment to historical events but from an historical orientation. To become immersed in that prose is to experience a valuable alternative to the historical identity problem which [many see] as characterizing modern literature and life.

It is also essential to see, however, that Faulkner's fictional method of providing aid and comfort for the alienated (his bourgeois readership, if not that abstraction of the acceptance speech, "man") presents serious problems. If he had a more creative, dialectical, and historical sense than many modern writers about the artist's role in society, his sense of the dialectic of social change was nevertheless defective. . . . [The] inner logic, even the specific moral virtues of Faulkner's literary method must always have precluded his making an alliance with militants black or white; . . . his very method of overcoming the split between art and popular life required "complete dependence upon himself." For instance, in "The Bear": the linguistic "prop" is Ike's passionate meditation on Southern history. This speech, implicitly compared with that great chronicle of popular life, the Bible, is thematically linked with Ike's powerless initiation into the wilderness in the hunting sections of the story and thematically opposed to what are seen as the instruments of man's simultaneous willful domination of and alienation from the wilderness: the compass, the railroad, the gun. Ike recounts the past in such a way as to indicate the need and inevitability of future change and even insists on the strength in black people which will enable them to prevail in the end. But the Northern black man who "liberates" Sophonsiba from her place on the Edmonds farm—like most of Faulkner's other agents of social change—is given a fatuously abstract language, like that of an out-of-context Declaration of Independence . . . , which in the dichotomous value scheme of the novel the reader experiences as roughly aligned with the other unattractive, willful, abstract elements in the work. Faulkner was right, of course, to criticize this man's idealist revolution by fiat (not to speak of his idealistic farming); but he offers—can offer—no active alternative. The political act consistent with Ike's attractive speech—the rather passive repudiation of ownership as an alienating instrument of domination—is itself dramatized as a kind of alienation: from sexuality, from history itself. Despite his passionate will to aesthetic transformation—but because of the specific aesthetic results—Faulkner could not imagine a will to social or political transformation that would make one not a "detached and heatless" outsider to history but rather a warmly involved creator of it.

Faulkner's equation of verbal strength and health with deprivation and powerlessness de-emphasizes the painful reality which in actuality provides the motivation to social change. (Joe Christmas, perhaps Faulkner's closest approach to that reality, is, as many have remarked, an unsatisfactory wordless figure, one of Faulkner's infrequent lapses into primitivist obscurity.) What Marx and other theorists have seen as the goal of social change, namely the

achievement of a more harmonious, humane existence, is made the precondition. The result is, that while Faulkner inspires his readers with verbal models, he experiences himself, and one experiences him, as without real allies in the form of creative, transforming energies in the social and political realms. The burden of his progressive outlook falls largely on language alone. In this, despite his historical orientation, he may be thought of as having more in common with such solipsistic singers as Joyce, Henry Miller, Nabokov, or Hawkes than with such realists as Shakespeare, Austen, Balzac, or Steinbeck, for all of whom the act of writing was one of many creative roles within or without established society. (pp. 227-29)

> *Brent Harold, "The Value and Limitations of Faulkner's Fictional Method," in* American Literature *(reprinted by permission of the Publisher; copyright 1975 by Duke University Press, Durham, North Carolina), May, 1975, pp. 212-29.*

ROBERT MARTIN ADAMS

There are little touches [in Faulkner's early novel, *Soldier's Pay,*] of narrative pace—crucial incidents withheld . . . , ironic juxtapositions, abrupt yet unmarked transitions within and between scenes which would confirm a sense of Joyce if one approached them with the Joyce parallel already in mind. Yet as a whole, Faulkner's novel is not Joycean in either theme or style. The almost wordless figure of Lieutenant Mahon, a massive, unmovable rock in the stream of time, fills the center of the novel; he can hardly fail to remind us of Benjy, who will occupy a similar position in *The Sound and the Fury,* but for such a figure there is no parallel in Joyce at all. Around his unmoving figure the characters range themselves in response to various motivations and impulses, but not in accord with an underlying pattern, least of all a mythological one. The book fulfills "normal" narrative expectations by moving in time; its structure involves no sense of the cyclical. In all these ways, therefore, *Soldiers' Pay,* even as it confirms Faulkner's early acquaintance with Joyce, makes clear that mannerisms and surfaces were what the young Faulkner chiefly imitated. And much the same argument could be made regarding *Mosquitoes,* which an early reviewer commended, rather condescendingly, on the ground that the writing was occasionally good when it wasn't Joyce. It is a study of ephemerids, with more contempt for its characters and more esthetic lecturing than the author can quite control; and again it is through mannerisms that Joyce's influence makes itself most clearly felt. . . . But the basic tone of the novel, determined by its character as satiric social comedy, is closer to the youthful Aldous Huxley than to Joyce.

Faulkner's two apprentice novels are very different indeed from one another, but alike in showing clear awareness of Joyce and a set of superficial or fragmentary responses to him. *The Sound and the Fury,* which shows fewer traces of direct influence or imitation, is in fact much closer to the techniques and structural energies of a Joycean novel. The book makes much more thorough-going and consistent use of stream-of-consciousness techniques than did any of Faulkner's previous novels; those streams are choked and barricaded in more elaborate ways, and more intricately dappled with thematic repetitions. Under its surface, never quite explicit but increasingly felt as the novel progresses, is a mythical parallel (a parodic crucifixion, descent into hell, and resurrection) which can be treated either as a central narrative pattern in itself or, more interestingly, as a shadowy counter-structure to the contemporary fable. The energies of the reader are completely involved in piecing together fragments which, when assembled, tell a bitter tale of futility and circularity. Like *Ulysses, The Sound and the Fury* is relatively indifferent to the moral note, which is simply a way of saying that good and bad intentions don't count for much in the book's economy. The doom of the Compsons is deeper than any villain can spin out or any savior redeem. (pp. 84-5)

More than anything else, it is the field of centripetal-centrifugal forces in violent self-contained conflict that defines the greatness of *The Sound and the Fury;* the book could be described as a series of private, defeated furies united in a common doom. Having no use for the trappings of epic, and little interest in mimetic tricks or parodic parallels, Faulkner wrote a far tighter and more economical novel than *Ulysses* had been. . . . Quentin Compson, in the complexity of his mental processes and the layered, allusive quality of his mind, is comparable to Stephen Dedalus, but he takes no time out to exercise on the Indian clubs of literary criticism, as in the "Library" scene. His thinking on time is . . . pointed and functional (fictionally speaking). . . . *Ulysses* had made some play with scrambled or undefined identities or different persons passing under the same name; Faulkner, as a man obsessed with temporal repetition, makes his reader discriminate between two Quentins, two Maurys, and no fewer than three Jason Compsons—yet holds these various confusions strictly subordinate to a passionate historical complexity in his own mind, which doesn't allow or require him to say a word of incidental explanation. . . . Faulkner has built from the bottom up and the inside out in turning Joycean techniques to his own purposes. He was not only a less informed but also a less formal artist than his great predecessor; certainly in *The Sound and the Fury,* he worked under a greater head of emotional steam, toward a more shattering, intimate, and personal experience than Joyce in many parts of *Ulysses* was attempting. Faulkner's masterpiece isn't, therefore, in any sense a Joycean imitation, though it's clearly a book which, without the example of Joyce, would not have taken anything like its present form. When Faulkner said that in writing it he had put the entire question of publishers and publication out of his mind, he meant something more than editors and audiences; a whole set of structural devices and narrative conventions went with them, as he stripped his novel down to the basic themes and the techniques essential to bring them living forth. That so much evidence of Joyce's presence remains is surprising; but it simply confirms that the Joycean influence wasn't for Faulkner either a passive or an adventitious thing; it was built, so to speak, into the structure of his fictional vision, into the way he defined consciousness, into the way he wove a web of past circumstance into a tissue of present action.

For example, Benjy is, beyond all question, the central pivot of *The Sound and the Fury,* not just because of his nature but because of his positioning. Around him all the other lives in the book revolve, to him the reader is constantly referring back his later experiences in the novel. His mental arrest, though different in all sorts of ways from the deadly stasis in which Stephen Dedalus is frozen during the first three units of *Ulysses,* functions similarly in the novel. He is the screen through which the reader's mind must penetrate; but, more than that, he is the hopelessly marred

materials out of which full humanity must be built—built by the reader. . . . Benjy's consciousness is in fact less a flowing stream than a crossword, cross-referenced puzzle, a Daedalian maze. Simply by positioning him at the head of the novel, Faulkner converted into instant advantages most of the inherent deficiencies of "stream-of-consciousness" method. But in so doing he imitated, in a way that can't be described as "imitation" simply because its essence is boldness and audacity, the pattern of Joyce's fictional construction. No doubt this is one reason why Faulkner's novel has seemed, like Joyce's, to stand a little apart from other fictions, as involving the reader more radically, to the hazard of his equanimity, in a perilous personal enterprise.

After *The Sound and the Fury,* traces of Joycean structure and verbal device fade gradually from the work of Faulkner. Indeed, there is a pronounced mythical structure underlying *Light in August,* and both *As I Lay Dying* and *Absalom, Absalom* make sustained use of a monologue which, if not fully interiorized, is at least given a heavy coloring of individual manner. But none of these novels reminds us decisively of Joyce; they are a working—eloquent, funny, impassioned—of indigenous materials that Faulkner needed no specially Joycean techniques to handle. Occasionally in later years, when he tried to draw his artistic calculations *very* fine, Faulkner fell back on fictional mechanisms as a substitute for the kind of unitary passion he generated in *The Sound and the Fury.* The solemn machinery of *A Fable* represents his most notable failure of the sort. . . . But the greatest of Faulkner's novels is less an example of Joycean influence or even inspiration than of Joyce's liberating effect on an indigenous and independent inspiration. Even apart from the masterpiece that resulted, it is one of the most interesting examples in literature of influence accepted and converted into the direct opposite of itself. Thus it became a substantial influence in its own right. . . . (pp. 86-8)

Robert Martin Adams, in his AfterJoyce: Studies in Fiction After "Ulysses" *(copyright © 1977 by Robert Martin Adams; reprinted by permission of Oxford University Press, Inc.), Oxford University Press, New York, 1977.*

RICHARD GRAY

How can we be "in" history and "outside" it at one and the same time? The problem that dogged Faulkner throughout his career can be stated as simply as that, but not his answer to it—because, of course, the answer does not lie in this expressed opinion or in that but *in the imaginative discovery of Yoknapatawpha County.* Loving his inheritance and hating it, involved with its mythology and yet well aware of the difference between history and myth, Faulkner was in a sense obliged to create his fictional world—a paradigm of his region existing beyond established categories, where all that he had found in the South and felt about it could be absorbed into a coherent form of knowledge. . . .

[Whenever] in his later years—when he was inclined to be more expansive on such matters—Faulkner was asked to talk about his home and his relationship to it, those two words, "loving" and "hating," came up almost inevitably, closely linked together. (p. 201)

With *Sartoris* . . . began the chronicles of Yoknapatawpha County. They did not, of course, spring full grown from

Faulkner's head: he built them up slowly, adding a character here or altering a detail there, so that they have a repetitive, incremental pattern rather than a strictly chronological or logically consistent one. We need not infer from this, though, that (as some critics have argued) Faulkner was ever unaware of what he was doing *in principle*. Far from it, his aims—if not their detailed consequences—were, I believe, quite clear to him from the first; he was trying, as he knew, to create a microcosm of history. By this I mean he was attempting . . . to capture the essence of his region, its story compounded of legend and fact and the nature of his own involvement with it. Certainly, he may have kept returning to the same episodes while he was writing the series, often changing his interpretation of them as he did so. But this, instead of working against his general aims, actually helped him to fulfill them: because he was thereby adopting the classic procedure of the kind of historian he wanted to be—which is that of continually reenacting and recomposing the past. One reason why the story of Yoknapatawpha is such a convincing imitation of the story of the South, in other words, is precisely this, that it *does not have a predetermined, linear pattern*. Thanks to Faulkner's habit of writing and revising it over a number of years, it is founded—much more clearly than the work of any other Southern writer—on a dialectic between today and yesterday, a sustained engagement of event with memory. (pp. 205-06)

[There] is still a fairly common tendency, among both professional critics and readers in general, to associate Faulkner with the aristocratic strain in Southern thought; and to assume that the part of his fiction that deals with old Southern families and decaying mansions more or less accounts for the whole. Very often, if we were simply to read discussions of Faulkner's work rather than the work itself, we would be left with the impression that his real interest lies with the privileged, the powerful, or those once powerful who have fallen on hard times, and that he is concerned with the lives of the poorer inhabitants of his region only in so far as they are relevant to this.

No impression could, I think, be more misleading. To accept such an interpretation of Faulkner's work it is necessary to ignore a good half of it, and to forget that the barriers that Yoknapatawpha society erects between the privileged and the dispossessed are fairly easily surmountable. There is an extraordinary richness and fluidity about Faulkner's portrait of his environment, even on the simple journalistic level of reporting what he has seen, and that necessarily means an avoidance of the kind of mythologizing that would identify the Sartoris family with tradition first and last, or their homeplace with the entire South. Existing alongside the plantation order the Sartorises represent, sometimes mingling with it but always retaining its separate identity, is another world altogether that has nothing at all to do with vast cotton fields, slaves, or bold cavalry charges against the Yankees. . . . [He also presents] the domain of the small, and usually poor, farmer, with its own dangers and its own sort of heroism—the sort, perhaps we could say, that stubbornly confronts the ordinary instead of attempting to transcend it. Clearly, it lacks the glamour of the old plantation, but, for all that, it—and the values it embodies, the way of life it consecrates—forms as honorable a part of the Southern tradition as the planter's world does. (pp. 210-11)

Faulkner's special achievement, I think, was that . . . his version of the farming community and the Jeffersonian myth was based on a full acknowledgement of their latent contradictions rather than the more usual, and more convenient, attempt to neglect them. Certainly there are people in his work . . . [who] have the same courage and capacity for endurance that those earlier heroes have, and possibly the same general ability to set will above circumstance. But just as many of his characters must remind us of [early] peasant grotesques; even more to the point, there are a few here and there who manage to seem victorious and defeated, heroic and comic, at one and the same time. (p. 211)

Even in his most idealized form, which is rare in the Yoknapatawpha series, Faulkner's yeoman is quite unlike his previous avatars because he is neither as uncomplicated nor as insubstantial as they normally are. . . . What saves [Faulkner from sentimentalism or strained heroics] is his respect for the hard edges of the real—his recognition, among other things, of the commonplace, grim details of his characters' lives. (pp. 211-12)

He uses folk humor, not merely to criticize and place, but to celebrate. What he is after besides historical analysis is some sense of involvement in peasant life—its raw energy and the excitement that can occasionally spill over into violence—and for this his models are the people at the beginning of the humorist tradition rather than those at the end, whose undeclared purpose it was to honor the gusty pleasures of the life they described. They include . . . anonymous balladeers and amateur story tellers. . . . (p. 213)

Faulkner deals with [a favorite folk theme of Southwestern humorists,] the horse-swapping theme, in . . . *The Hamlet*, the first part of the Snopes trilogy and the one most deeply involved in peasant life. . . . [The] bare bones of the story [involve] the familiar idea of the trickster being hoist on his own petard. But what gives these bones life and flesh . . . is Faulkner's choice of narrator. V. K. Ratliff, the itinerant salesman who acts as unofficial reporter and historian to the poor folk of the county, tells us everything that happened. And his voice, which is that of a man speaking to and about friends, colors the entire incident. . . . This, really, is the edge Faulkner has over most of his predecessors here, the other writers who have used the trickster theme. Ratliff, the story teller, is telling us about his own people, with whom he shares a certain idiom and a distinct system of values. . . . Just by speaking he reminds us of the folk community, invokes its traditions. And by speaking *to us,* by drawing us into the special world of his language, he seems to be asking us to become part of that community for a moment. (pp. 215-16)

Again, [in the famous episode of the "spotted horses,"] it is Faulkner's use of language that determines how we respond to these events. Its energy is a verbal equivalent for the energy of peasant life, its raw violence and color such that we are reminded possibly of the paintings of Brueghel. . . . [The] basic story is told to us by a voice that bears the accents of Frenchman's Bend but remains unassigned. It is the voice, in fact, of the community; the tale of the Texas ponies is part of the common history, the collective memory of the folk, and it is as such that we hear about it.

Put like that it may sound as if we are told everything in a strictly impersonal way, as in a ballad. That is not the case, though, and the reason for this is that Faulkner, as he goes along, manages to add other and quite different inflections of speech or dimensions of commentary to his story. At the very beginning of the tale, for instance, he places us firmly within the *ambiance* of Frenchman's Bend by a very simple device: turning from the anonymous narrator for a moment he allows the conversation and comment of a few bystanders to establish a perspective on Flem Snopes's arrival. The result is rather like those moments in Hardy when we are asked to stand back with the locals—people who have never left Wessex and are never likely to—to witness the appearance of an invader; necessarily, we are drawn closer to them, because we share in their reactions and their sense of distance from the man they describe. . . . The comments pass back and forth, question and answer, statement and response, and slowly a portrait is built up—an intimate portrait, seen from the inside, of that community which is equally the admiring witness and the amazed victim of the horse trade. Some of this intimacy then in turn carries over into those moments when the individual vantage point is lost and we are returned to the anonymous narrator. . . . A sense of communion is sustained because the voice, or at least the perspective it establishes, does not necessarily change even when its source does.

Communion there may be, but it is never quite perfect; the feelings of intimacy aroused by the story are always less than complete. Why? Because, really, . . . Faulkner's intention is not to reject all sense of difference between us and his folk characters, but to make us respond with them *even while we are aware of our separateness from them.* We must, he feels, know them for their relevance as cases —representative types of the rural life, and the traditions it fosters—quite as much as for their close connections with ourselves; and his way of ensuring that we do this is to use language occasionally to *draw us back* from the scene. Every now and then another idiom will be employed, quite different from the ones I have mentioned, more elegant and self-consciously sophisticated, which establishes our status as spectators as effectively as a camera moving away from close-up into long shot. . . . We can share in the humor of the folk, Faulkner implies, and consequently learn something about their traditions, but we cannot dissolve our identities, our experience and language, into theirs. Not only cannot but should not, since in order to know these people thoroughly we *must* apparently stand apart from them sometimes; we must participate in their history and also step aside from it occasionally so as to take a larger, more inclusive view. That seems to be the belief implicit in Faulkner's handling of the horse-swapping episodes in *The Hamlet,* and his excursions into folk comedy in general; and it is perhaps one of the reasons for their unique character and success.

The trouble with trying to define anything in Faulkner's novels is that sooner or later the definitions begin to break down under the pressure of the accumulating evidence; for all their apparent accuracy, they have to be qualified as soon as they are invoked. The moment, for example, that we really try to explain what Faulkner wants us to feel about his folk characters, the sort of response he is hoping to elicit, we find that conventional classifications are far too restrictive and we are forced to use apparently self-contradictory phrases like "sympathetic detachment." . . . No distinction can hold still for very long after it is applied to the world of Yoknapatawpha, and this for the simple reason

that Faulkner's work seems to depend for much of its excitement on the actual engagement between the closed world of definitions and the open spaces of raw experience. Any category he uses (and which, subsequently, we may use to understand his work) serves him only in a provisional way; once adopted it is continually being modified or subverted—changed, in fact, by the mass of conflicting particulars that Faulkner feeds into it. To some extent, this could provide us with an explanation for Faulkner's special use of language—that is, if we accept the fairly commonplace notion that language contains within it its own implicit values and categories, a certain way of structuring the world. Faulkner, we could say, stretches words and syntax to the limits for the same reason he stretches categories: so as to squeeze new meanings out of the conflict between the rules and the occasions which those rules are meant to (but do not quite) circumscribe. . . . [This] general principle of Faulkner's—of never letting anything stay undisturbed by its contrary—applies as much to his use of the comic and heroic versions of the folk character as it does to anything else. . . . [The] low note of peasant comedy and the higher note clearly echoing Jefferson . . . is there usually just as every received element in his work is there: to be quickened into life by contact with individual experience—and to acquire form and strength . . . from the counterthrust of its opposite. (pp. 218-19)

Faulkner himself has described this ability of his better, more memorably, than anybody else can. "There's not too fine a distinction between humor and tragedy," he said once in one of his talks at the University of Virginia, "even tragedy is in a way walking a tightrope between the ridiculous—between the bizarre and the terrible." With very little alteration those words could, I think, be used to describe the kind of tension I have been talking about here: "walking a tightrope," achieving a balance between different perspectives, is precisely what Faulkner is doing. . . . They also bring us back, though, to another problem altogether—since clearly they have a larger frame of reference than just the people of Frenchman's Bend—which is, the relevance of all this to Faulkner's *general* criticism of experience. What does his treatment of the folk tradition have to do with that? How do his versions of the poor farmer fit into the total imaginative structure of his work— if, really, they can be said to fit in at all? Obviously, to ask this question is to move beyond consideration of any local, intrinsic interest Faulkner's portrait of the South may possess and to start thinking about its representativeness, the use of Yoknapatawpha society as a model for the study of social and historical relationships in general. To use Allen Tate's valuable distinction, it is to pass from the provincial context to the regional. . . .

The book that, I think, could act best as a paradigm here is *As I Lay Dying.* One of Faulkner's four or five finest novels, it is almost entirely concerned with the Bundrens, a family of poor whites, and the journey they take to Jefferson where they have promised their mother Addie Bundren she will be buried. (p. 221)

As a supreme example of the artist who communicates before he can be understood, Faulkner does not "think" in the sense of having certain ideas, which he then sets about putting into words—that is, in his best work he does not. On the contrary, such ideas as his novels may contain are a product of the words themselves—a specific imaginative language that attacks, and at the very least drastically re-works, established concepts. . . . Faulkner's meaning is discovered in [his] style. . . . Are the Bundrens fools, most people ask when they try to "think about" or explain *As I Lay Dying,* or are they heroes struggling (as Faulkner once put it) "against God in a way"? The proper reply to this . . . is that the question itself is misconceived because it presupposes an either/or situation where none exists. The Bundrens are fools *and* heroes, and any inquiry which is so phrased as to ignore this paradox begins on the wrong foot immediately. . . . The journey that forms the spine of *As I Lay Dying* is a trial, among other things, a way of testing strength and endurance; and the qualities the different members of the family reveal during the course of it seem intended to invite our respect along with our laughter. (pp. 222-23)

[Another] characteristic strategy of Faulkner's that is ex-ploited to the full in the story [is] . . . the device of the mul-tiple narrator. . . . The Bundrens are presented to us in a variety of mirrors, as it were, which are meant to encom-pass them and to reflect eventually the "truth" about them. Voices join to tell us about their lives, to agree, to present evidence, or just to argue. No one voice can be regarded as authoritative but equally no voice can be discounted either; consequently, during the course of the debate, each mem-ber of the Bundren family tends to assume a multidimen-sional personality. He or she becomes as rich, edgy, as pro-tean, and occasionally as baffling as somebody we might know from our own intimate experience. (pp. 223-24)

The entire structure of *As I Lay Dying* is dialectical, in-volving a continual and fructifying movement between in-ner world and outer. . . . (p. 225)

I doubt if it is possible to exaggerate the importance of . . . the almost dreamlike way in which the reader is tumbled down into deeper and deeper levels of a character's mind. Just when we think we have a clear picture of somebody like Dewey Dell, and can place her as an attractive, emo-tionally generous, but rather simple-minded farm girl, our assumptions are suddenly undermined—our snobbish de-tachment shown up for what it is—by the revelation of her inner fears and misgivings. We move in beneath the equable surfaces of her behavior to something else, a terror or sense of disaster by no means simple or simple-minded, that can only be expressed in the sort of language that lies com-pletely beyond her personal reach. . . . In case we should now begin to feel secure, when Dewey Dell's conscious fears have been expressed, Faulkner will occasionally offer us a further jolt. Without any warning, he will take an abrupt step down beyond this toward a more incantatory and imagistic level of expression that is meant, clearly, to recover Dewey's *sub*conscious for us—the secret, sublimi-nal impulses that help make her what she is or prompt her to do what she does. . . . Just as certain aspects of Dewey Dell lie beyond the reach of her own words or the words of her companions so, we must suspect, the full scope of her character developing and changing in time is something that no language can properly contain.

If this sounds at all plausible as a way of explaining the ef-fect Faulkner's narrative technique has on us it is, I think, because the gap between language and experience I am talking about now is something to which the entire novel testifies—in its plot, its assignment of motives, even its stated "message." Really, what words *are* adequate to ex-plain Anse Bundren's reasons for traveling to Jefferson? How, if and when we try, *can* we describe his motives for doing what he does when he gets there? Of course, he goes to Jefferson to honor a promise he made to Addie when she was dying, but he also goes there to buy a new set of false teeth and, with the help of his improved appearance, to acquire a second wife. . . . [Obviously] one of the classic strategies of comedy, which involves raising expectations only to reverse them, often dictates the movement of the book. It is as though the writer were trying actively to lure us into a particular opinion, a certain way of looking at his characters and their behavior, so that the lesson he is bent on giving us can then be carried to us on the backs of our own shattered preconceptions. We learn, partly, by being taught a system and being told afterwards how constricted that system is. . . . One vocabulary is suddenly discarded for another one quite different, and then, almost as soon as we have come to accept *that* as accurate, it too is discarded in favor of something else. (pp. 226-27)

Faulkner's style . . . exists, as one of his critics has put it, at the extreme "edge of order"—exposing the inadequacies of language and grammar by pushing both to their lim-its. . . . [Words] are the ultimate category in *As I Lay Dying,* the prime example of the human need to classify experience. One passage in the novel, in particular, empha-sizes this point: it is given to Addie Bundren, the mother, when she is already dead. . . . Issuing as it does from a cof-fin out of the mouth of a corpse, what she says here seems to have an oracular weight and authority to it—which is appropriate, really, since this is the closest Faulkner ever dares come to stating the "message" of his book.

> . . . I learned that words are no good, that words don't ever fit even what they are trying to say at. When he [Cash] was born I knew that motherhood was invented by someone who had to have a word for it be-cause the ones that had the children didn't care whether there was a word for it or not. . . . I would think how words go up in a thin line, quick and harmless, and how terri-bly doing goes along the earth, clinging to it. . . .

There could hardly ever have been a more devastating as-sault on the harmful effects of language, the way in which it can castrate the personality and reduce experience to a se-ries of rules. We talk, Addie suggests, and as we do so more than likely we impoverish and distort what we are talking about. (pp. 227-28)

As I understand it, neither the author nor his characters is dismissing categories entirely, although admittedly they come pretty near to it. Rather their intention, as expressed in the sum total of their actions, is to make categories as open and provisional as they can; "words" and "doing" are not seen as warring interests really, but as the two sides of a mutually profitable partnership, involved in a process of exchange that must last as long as the possibility of an absolute explanation or terminal vocabulary is excluded—in other words, indefinitely. A continuing transvaluation of values of every kind: that I think is what *As I Lay Dying* is arguing for, with the main emphasis resting on the idea of continuance. And this in turn would explain why the book itself does not seem to finish but merely stops short with the arrival of a new character, the second Mrs. Bundren, trailing a fresh set of possibilities in her wake—because its procedures are meant to be a demonstration of its "message," right down to the very last incident described on the last page. The best books, Faulkner appears to be saying, are like the best men: they do not stay still, ever. Living in a state of constant interchange between categories and raw experience, they must always be on the move, altering by leaving themselves open to strange influences and fresh conditions. Look, he seems to add with a touch of characteristically well-placed arrogance, here is an example of the sort of thing I mean—right here in the book I have just written. (pp. 228-29)

[Faulkner offers] the actual processes of his traditionalism, the way in which he involves the notions of the past with the exigencies of the present, as a design for living. As I have tried to explain, the "words" that Addie Bundren criticises so vehemently in *As I Lay Dying* are used essentially as a synecdoche. They refer us to all the forms, linguistic, moral, and social, which the human intelligence devises for dealing with experience. Behind her monologue lies the belief that there are certain intricate patterns implicit in everything ordained by a particular culture, including its language, which tend to systematize and inhibit its members' thoughts. . . . [Far] from inventing these patterns, Addie suggests, the individual may hardly be aware of their existence. They are inherited, imposed on him perhaps without his conscious knowledge, and since they are largely cultural (rather than biological) they can be included, most of them, under the familiar heading of *tradition*. This brings us back to Faulkner. With Addie's help he argues for a dialectic, a marriage between these "words" and "doing" so that the individual can reap the benefits of his culture without becoming completely enculturated. And it does not take a very great deal of effort. . . . [This] is exactly the sort of contact with tradition on which his own work is based. . . . The medium is the message in more than one sense in Faulkner's best novels, and this because his own relationship to his past (that is—it is worth repeating it—the relationship to inherited forms which makes such novels possible) supplies him with a sort of blueprint, an original basis of judgment. I do not want to make too much of this at the expense of some of Faulkner's other achievements: it should never lead us to forget, for instance, about the sheer historical accuracy of his renderings of folk dialect or the close acquaintance he reveals with the smallest details of country life. But it is still, I think, decisive evidence of the scope and weight of his attachment to his region: that, when all the accounts are in, he can actually use his own "Southern-ness" as a means of assessment. He can make something out of being born in a specific time and place, with a particular set of beliefs and practices to hand; and then afterwards, not content to stop there, he can make something out of this, the nature of his own encounters with the South, as well. (pp. 230-31)

[For] all the fluidity and social mobility of Faulkner's imaginary world and the overall consistency of his techniques, there is a clear distinction to be made between his portraits of farm and plantation. His farm people may fall under the sway of the past, but they rarely succumb completely, and never for very long. Their lives are basically situated in the here and now; and, if there is one thing nearly all of them have in common, it is a firm commitment to activity, sustained purposeful movement. . . . By contrast Faulkner's plantation folk seem pretty goalless and stationary: fixed

quite literally in the past like Bayard Sartoris I or fixated by the past like his great-grandnephew, they have about as few significant connections with the South of the interwar years as they possibly could have. One reason for this difference, I believe, is that Faulkner, like many writers involved in the Southern "renaissance," must have recognized just how anachronistic the strictly practical or programmatic side of the aristocratic ideal had become. (pp. 235-36)

[For] whatever reason or reasons the plantation dream *is* firmly associated with the past in Faulkner's novels; which of course raises real problems for those—like Bayard Sartoris III or his grandfather "Colonel" Bayard Sartoris II—who live in the present. [They are drawn] back continually toward something that, like a half-remembered incident, at once obsesses them and eludes them. . . . Their lives become a sort of dialogue with specters, conducted in a language they hardly know. (pp. 236-37)

Gradually we are coming to something quite central to Faulkner's work, which grows directly out of his preoccupation with the plantation myth and gives it a wider relevance and impact. I mean by this the interest he shares with so many other writers of the Southern "renaissance" in the *idea of history*, the precise nature of the relationship obtaining between past, present, and future. . . . [It] is, I believe, his treatment of the planter families of Yoknapatawpha County that gives it a peculiar relevance and urgency. For people like Bayard Sartoris III and Quentin Compson the past is such a constant, nagging presence that the question of how to cope with it becomes their main preoccupation; so Faulkner can and, in a sense, must deal directly with the entire subject of the historical dimension whenever he describes them. The problems of time and identity are basic to their lives; and thanks to this they can be treated on one level rather like traditional hero figures, confronting dragons or meeting a challenge that (admittedly, in a much less obvious way) all of us must face. (p. 237)

Unlike *The Sound and the Fury* or *Light in August, Absalom, Absalom!* has never been supplied with a satisfactory "key": something that, while not explaining all of its labyrinthine complexities, might at least offer the reader a convenient means of entry into them. The title of the novel is a case in point here. Most of the titles Faulkner gives to his books contain a clue to the larger meaning of the action, whatever personal associations they may contain besides, and to this rule *Absalom, Absalom!* forms no exception. Critics have admitted as much, but they seem unwilling to follow the admission with any close analysis; beyond saying that there is probably a reference intended to the Biblical account of King David. . . . It *is* difficult to determine how far [Faulkner] would wish the reader to take the more detailed parallels between the stories of David and Sutpen: their common preoccupation with the crimes of incest and fratricide, for example, or the sense in which both describe an outsider rising to high station among men. But such difficulties hardly matter, I think, since what is far more important is the feeling of historical recurrence—the sense of the past repeating itself—which the broad rhythm of analogy between the two situations is intended to evoke. For central to *Absalom, Absalom!* is its examination of both this recurrence and, more generally, the tangled web of coinciding and conflicting forces that we call history. The book is, . . . like *Sartoris* and nearly all Faulkner's other ventures into the plantation tradition, a study of the meaning of history; and that is why events and experiences in it are so interrelated that each dimension of time seems to impinge physically on the other two, and each person appears transformed into "an empty hall echoing with sonorous defeated names" that he must try to understand if he ever wants to understand himself. The past, the present, and the future are interwoven and every incident [is] rendered, re-interpreted, and then rendered again. . . . [History] is a continuum out of which the individual person emerges and to which he eventually belongs. A series of intricate and unbreakable "strings" bind him to all other people before and after him, whom he influences and by whom in turn he is influenced. . . . [Any] particular experience, the moment when Thomas Sutpen knocks at a door, for example, may be of enormous bearing subsequently, however trivial it may appear at the time; and it means too that the past may so shape the present or the present the past as to make the one a mirror image of the other.

Like Robert Penn Warren, Faulkner sees man as a kind of spider entangled in the very web of historical circumstance he has helped to create. . . . The point, as Faulkner makes it, is that any perspective must be [inadequate] that does not take cognizance of this extraordinary interrelatedness, and consequent complicatedness, of men and events. The burden of *Absalom, Absalom!*, in other words, is not merely to tell us what history is, but to instruct us also in the way that we, the products and producers of history, should behave.

The importance of history, and its bearing on human behavior, are presented in their clearest and most consecutive form in the biography of Thomas Sutpen—insofar, that is, as there is any incontrovertible thread of facts in his case that can be said to emerge from the welter of countercommentary. . . . Sutpen [seems] to be innocent in the sense that the tragic hero often is, in that he adopts a particular purpose or "design" and then tries to fulfill it without reference to circumstances and other people. He has little capacity for compromise and no especial interest in it, either. (pp. 238-40)

[It] is almost impossible to separate the meaning of the story from its medium of communication, the various narrative and linguistic frames within which it is set. *What* is said in the history of Thomas Sutpen, in short, is more or less determined by *how* it is said; the different perspectives offered by the narrators furnish a means of definition and ultimately the standard of judgment also. . . . [All] those perspectives when taken together, as part of the composite effect of the novel, offer an approach to that sense of the complex simultaneity of every moment—and consequent interrelatedness of human beings—that Faulkner takes to be the prerequisite of the accomplished artist and the properly developed man. The historians may not know the truth as individuals, in other words, but their very contradictoriness pushes the reader toward some awareness of that truth, the multifaceted character of historical experience. (p. 243)

[Within] the "postage stamp" world of *Absalom, Absalom!*, as we have seen, the past [lives] in the present, reflecting it and being reflected by it, and time [becomes] a pattern of dependencies. The private and public levels of experience, also, are interrelated, affecting and to some extent even imitating one another. And experience itself within this psychic continuum is rendered in all its variability, its capacity for change and surprise: Faulkner's use of several, very different narrators and his kaleidoscopic prose style are alone enough to ensure that. The impetus created by the entire fictional technique in effect pushes the reader toward an awareness of the reality that the characters have evaded, and some consequent understanding of the function of history—which function, as [Faulkner] conceives of it, is to stimulate the growth of the consciousness by enlarging and complicating everything with which that consciousness must deal. History, it emerges even as we read *Absalom, Absalom!*, is an energy latent within us rather than a burden that, like Aeneas, we must carry on our backs. (p. 253)

Faulkner wanted to embrace the contradictions latent in his background without forfeiting coherence, to describe the mansion and the country store and his own ambivalent feelings about them in one great variegated portrait; and his stories, or more accurately his gradual invention of Yoknapatawpha County *for* those stories, was his means of achieving this. By developing Yoknapatawpha as a medium he could see the South clearly and yet in extraordinary detail because Yoknapatawpha was, as he liked to put it, an apocryphal county. It was described in the novels and tales but somehow existed separate from them; it was a fiction located, as it were, behind the fictions Faulkner wrote and published—and as such it enabled him to investigate the different aspects of Southern life, to keep them at an aesthetic distance, *and* to metamorphose them into parts of a larger plan. . . . As a place eventually existing complete in the author's mind it stands behind almost everything he says—something greater than the sum of his perceptions, which is nevertheless *there* buttressing them, giving them a substance and congruence they would not otherwise possess. . . . He comes as close as anybody does, and closer than most, to seeing his region steadily and seeing it whole. (pp. 254-55)

Richard Gray, "The Individual Talent: William Faulkner and the Yoknapatawpha Novels," in his The Literature of Memory: Modern Writers of the American South *(copyright © 1977 by Richard Gray), Johns Hopkins University Press, 1977, pp. 197-256.*

*   *   *

FOURNIER, Pierre
    See GASCAR, Pierre

G

GADDA, Carlo Emilio   1893-

Gadda is an Italian novelist and short story writer. His works, noted for their linguistic brilliance, reveal Gadda's love of language and rhetoric in their unique blending of archaisms, dialects, and puns.

ROBERT S. DOMBROSKI

In spite of the profound treatment of the themes of human alienation and insignificance diffused throughout his fiction, Carlo Emilio Gadda's importance is largely verbal. He employs numerous styles and lexical modes with equal success, from the arduous structures of classical Latin to the austere language of modern science and the spontaneous automatism of the surrealists. At times his style appears dry and reflects a desire for order and rational systemization, while at other times it is characterized by violent, uncontrolled expression and hyperbole. This mixture of harmony and disharmony, order and chaos, is the logical extension of the double edged attitude toward reality manifested in Gadda's War Journal and memoirs. However, to infer from this that experience alone dictated his literary technique would be to oversimplify. The First World War, to be sure, left Gadda with an extreme dislike for an external world which he judged incompatible with his nature and thus false and illusory. But in order to transform his alienation into art he needed to establish the theoretical premises that might justify as well as universalize his vision.

Gadda's culture, reflecting as it does vast and diverse readings in every sphere of human knowledge, is composed of many strands of thought and so defies exact classification. Nevertheless, at least two modern thinkers may be said to have aided in providing a philosophical basis for Gadda's style and use of language: Kant and Bergson.

In the post-war period Gadda came under the influence of Kant through the teachings of Piero Martinetti. . . . (p. 210)

According to Kant's epistemology, nature or the external universe is nothing but a construction which the mind imposes on phenomena. The world independent of our knowledge (things in themselves), called by Kant the world of the "noumena", is unknowable through reason. . . . True knowledge [for Martinetti] has for its object a reality that transcends the world of phenomena, and on this reality depend the moral decisions relevant to human life. (pp. 210-11)

Kantian epistemology deals a damaging blow to the conception of art as mimesis. For if nature is but a product of the mind, what we imitate cannot exist beyond ourselves. The artist thus is granted the freedom to create according to his intentions; he is emancipated from all external limitations and the work of art becomes a universe of its own, no longer bound to the representation of empirical or moral truth or to the rules of logical discourse which the traditional concept of mimesis implies. Gadda, like many of his contemporaries, recognizes the arbitrariness of mimesis and the freedom of the artist to convert reality and language to serve his personal ends, with the condition, however—and here Martinetti's teachings are present—that the transformation or re-elaboration of the world be motivated by ethical responsibility. (p. 212)

Rather than to specific objects of representation, ["ethical realities" for Gadda] refer to the state of the writer and his awareness of the truth of his being and the falsity of the external universe. . . . [In] terms of what can be called Gadda's aesthetics, the artist, on the one hand, has freedom to find the forms best suited to his vision; on the other, he should be aware that pure invention or absolute art tends to become "caviled embroidery" which for Gadda is tantamount to falsity. (p. 213)

Kant-Martinetti's influence on Gadda does not go beyond [the] general premises . . . that the writer has a moral imperative to combat falsity and in doing this he may select a form of expression appropriate to his vision. However, although generic, these ideas are important because they establish, more or less, a theoretical basis for Gadda's polylinguism, and because they help shift the focus in the study of Gadda's works from the extravagance of the page to the spiritual reality of the author.

Gadda's belief in ethical commitment is one important aspect of his poetics. Another, which contradicts the metaphysical reality which the former attitude implies, is Gadda's denial of finality, understood as a definitive general law by which the universe is explained. Again, the genesis of this sentiment is to be found in his experience. His prime impulse, dictated by his upbringing and culture, is to verify the existence of a rationally governed universe. He is, however, constantly disillusioned in his inquiry by his perception of the world as chaos. His belief in the existence of "true reality" beyond appearance is weakened by his awareness that in a universe devoid of reason this end is impossible to attain. The only knowledge left for Gadda is the truth of pain ("la cognizione del dolore") acquired through the contemplation of the grotesque in nature, the irrational, disordered universe. . . . Knowledge for Gadda is therefore one and the same with the perception of evil. This explains, accordingly, his constant search for evil and vice to which *Quer pasticciaccio brutto de via Merulana* is an extraordinary monument.

Gadda's denial of *a priori* finality finds in the philosophy of Henri Bergson a suitable basis for justification. . . . For Bergson . . . the evolution of the world is not a development *a priori* along pre-established lines, but rather the unpredictable thrust of life. . . . Although Gadda has never explicitly mentioned his indebtedness to Bergson, the structure of his fiction clearly embodies the philosopher's thoughts, at least those concerning final cause. From his early stories published in *Solaria* to the mature fiction of *Quer pasticciaccio* the character of Gadda's prose is conspicuously fragmentary. There is a perennial disorder in his texts, lack of symmetry, and a notable sense of unfulfillment. The denouements are always absent even in those novellas where the narrative is more sustained, such as in "San Giorgio in casa Brocchi" or "L'incendio in Via Keplero". On the other hand, it is the particular instant, things in themselves and their relationships, that attracts Gadda the most. He sees matter as having its own inherent finality unrelated to any possible, pre-conceived narrative plan. His aim is to exhaust things of their expressive potential and to deform them linguistically. This goal, it should be stressed, is based on his ethical mission to root out the falsity of the external world. The stylistic and linguistic variations in his narrative technique are a means to this end.

Gadda himself has repeatedly specified the ethical function of his fictional style and speech: chiefly, his use of dialect within the framework of literary prose, his occasional recourse to macaronic syntax, and his taste for grotesque caricature and baroque description.

A recurring theme in virtually all of his theoretical works is that there is no one language that possesses artistic preeminence. He rejects as romantic superstition the myth of the absolute efficacy of popular speech and even apologizes for what he calls the punctual and redundant language of the petty bourgeoisie, for it too, he argues, represents a manner of being. The writer must remain open to an infinite possibility of expression. And to do so, he adds, he must discipline himself in both past and present tongues and in the jargon of society's numerous institutions. Rules, traditions, and literary modes, if adhered to religiously, are obstacles to art. (pp. 214-16)

[Dialect] is the author's weapon in his struggle against the false rhetoric of constituted society. It is an expression for the most part devoid of abstractions and generalities, because it has its roots in a dense social environment. The more totalitarian a society becomes the more it resorts to abstract slogans to express its needs. Through the use of dialect we tend to return to reality, however distasteful it might appear. Dialect therefore is one means of defense against political as well as linguistic oppression. (p. 216)

Another means of redeeming language from falsity is the macaronic style. . . .

The function of the macaronic for Gadda is . . . both ethical

and gnosiological; it reveals and destroys every abuse of reason and speech effected by fraudulent words. . . . [The] mixture of styles and languages reflects Gadda's creative impulse in his acceptance of the task to render as expression every shade and highlight of life. It is the interpretation of consciousness and its mechanism as well as the description or distortion of phenomena. (p. 217)

[The] reader is aware that it is Gadda himself who modifies the external world because there is no sense in offering another image of an already existing universe. Gadda's delving into the core of reality, his tendency to push language to its limits and beyond, is typical of expressionistic deformation. For this reason, if the adjective "baroque" is used just to characterize Gadda's stylistic extravagance, it is without doubt misleading. (p. 218)

One way we may arrive at a better understanding of Gadda's "baroque" is to consider how, as a literary critic and especially as a translator, he approaches his preferred texts. Gadda almost always classifies his favorite authors as baroque, or least anti-literary, insofar as they, in his view, have a negative taste for reality. . . . But although Gadda's activity as a critic shows a preference for the baroque attitude, his literary style is far more extreme than even that of the most ingenious and violent of baroque craftsmen. (pp. 218-19)

Gadda's translation of [Quevedo's] "El mundo por de dentro" is important because it serves as an index of his baroque taste and also because he undertook it in the same period as the writing of *La cognizione del dolore*, for which reason Gonzalo's lashing out at appearances may have been influenced by [Quevedo's] example. The translation also marks the limits of the similarities between the two authors, illustrating to what extent Gadda's baroque style may be compared to one of the most, if not the most, extreme writers of the Baroque Age. (p. 219)

Gadda shares in the baroque vision with his belief in the infinite interrelationship of things. But while the traditional baroque writer casts his vision in more or less objective, mimetic forms . . . , Gadda's style is rooted in own personal psychic modulations. (p. 221)

Robert S. Dombroski, "Moral Commitment and Invention in Gadda's Poetics," in Rivista di Letterature Moderne e Comparate, *September, 1972, pp. 210-21.*

ROBERT BONGIORNO

In [*Quer pasticciaccio brutto de via Merulana*], as if to underline by contrast his stylistic intentions, Gadda chooses the plot of a "giallo," a detective novel. This trite formula of murder and robbery with a little sex thrown in has been used countless times by the hacks who grind out cheap novels for consumption in the railroad stations of the world. If we were to abstract the plot . . . , we would have a decidedly second rate product. . . . Gadda takes this cliché structure and raises it to the level of the most profound art. His prose texture is capable of extracting the metaphysical and ethereal from the corporeal and banal. (p. 49)

[There] is a mystical union between Gadda's prose texture and his vision, the former corresponding to the physical, the latter to his metaphysical world, the first being a kind of objective correlative of the second. (p. 50)

To get at the essence of a particular phenomenon Gadda's tactic is often . . . to try to exhaust all descriptive possibilities. Like Faulkner at times, he seems to feel the scattergun technique increases the probability of successfully bracketing the phenomenon under observation. He strings out nouns and adjectives as if each one contained a part of the truth. The more parts he can amass, the closer he will come to a true whole. Like a gestalt psychologist, he believes the whole is more than the sum of its parts. Each word contains a clue in the "case" of reality and it is significant that the Italian word for case, "caso" also means random chance. He believes that all catastrophes have a multiplicity of causes . . . , so that even if all the causes of a catastrophe were known, the guilt would have to be so widely distributed as to be dissipated. Any moral fervor he might work up has to be immediately snuffed out by the realization that it is impossible to pin the blame for anything on any other thing. Every human relationship (internal and external) is suspended in equilibrium in its force field by a polar tension. But the tension varies, or can vary, in intensity, in time. And sometimes it is extinguished altogether. All factors are variable, all causes are multiplex, all relationships are relative. This is the essential vision Gadda wishes to communicate. But his tool of communication is flawed and refractory.

Gadda is a man who loves language too well not to realize its defects and shortcomings. His pessimism regarding the possibility of verbal communication matches that reached by Giuseppe Ungaretti. . . . Ungaretti seems to believe in sympathetic magic, the cabalistic notion that the ability to name a thing brings the power to control it. Control over the world is lost when it becomes too complex for you to be able to name the things in it. Gadda desperately tries to name them anyway.

By count there are fifteen separate languages or dialects (which for Gadda's purposes are distinct languages) in *Quer pasticciaccio* . . . as if by employing every mode of communication available to him, the author hoped to hit on the magic words, by chance. . . . Gadda employs archaic Italian and unsophisticated dialects as if they still maintained, or were closer to, that innocent purity, as if they still could mean. (pp. 50-2)

Any evolution of a language is bound to result in its devaluation. But this depressing situation does not deter Gadda from trying to extract some sense from it by describing it. One advantage to the reigning chaos is its humor. (p. 52)

Gadda uses the juxtaposition of contrasting languages for comic effect and to underline the hopelessness of human dialogue. . . .

[He] takes every opportunity to point out the shady and shaky genealogy of the Italian language by indiscriminately accepting every orthographical variant in existence, plus a few he invents himself. . . . He does this not only to point out the persistence of the past, but also to show that linguistic rules, intended to facilitate communication, restrict it instead by narrowing the speaker's resources. (p. 53)

In his complex criticism of Fascism, Gadda leads the reader lexically and syntactically through the labyrinthine absurdities of the fascist mind. . . . Instead of a reasoned, sequential exposition of the deficiencies of Fascism, Gadda embodies its spirit in the convolutions of his prose. In *La Madonna dei filosofi,* Gadda's booklength explanation of

Fascism's hormonal enchantment of the Italian people, he uses a similar technique, but with the added complication of couching post-Freudian terms and concepts in an archaic Italian. (p. 54)

Gadda continually debunks and punctures flatulence and rhetoric [in *Quer pasticciaccio brutto de via Merulana*]. The judicious insertion of an earthy dialect expression acts as a corrective to a pompous speech. . . . The narrative viewpoint often shifts to the Roman plebes to restrain the excesses of the protagonist. Literary pretensions are checked with ironic references. . . .

Finally, as if to make fun of the neat conclusions of the "gialli" which he has, in a sense, been imitating or parodying, Gadda's ending is inconclusive. . . . The whole thing has been a mistake . . . almost. Or maybe. . . . The vertical black line between the girl's eyebrows paralyzes the protagonist, leading him to reflect on and almost change his entire conclusion. The significance of this small physical detail brings to mind many poems of Montale in which a slight corrugation in the smooth surface of reality presages a cataclysm or is emblematic of a change coming in his theme or outlook. In this same way, every wrinkle in the fabric of Gadda's prose is significant. Each fold and pleat of his language carries a message. (p. 56)

Robert Bongiorno, "Prose Texture as Content in Quer pasticciaccio brutto de via Merulana," in Romance Notes, *Autumn, 1972, pp. 49-56.*

JOAN McCONNELL-MAMMARELLA

After the first few pages of *Quer Pasticciaccio brutto de via Merulana,* the reader is struck by Gadda's skillful and, in certain instances, even unorthodox handling of the Italian language, a fact which immediately distinguishes him from most contemporary Italian authors. Gadda's language is a potpourri of archaic and learned words, dialects, highly specialized terminology and neologisms, all blended together in a framework of standard literary Italian. The result Gadda achieves demonstrates the rich expressive potential of the Italian language in its broadest sense.

It therefore becomes obvious that Gadda's view of language differs from literary Italian. He openly rejects formal linguistic restrictions because such conventions conflict with his definition of language. For Gadda language is a continuum; while, on one hand, it synthesizes human experience from by-gone centuries, it must, on the other, be capable of recording contemporary man's achievements and aspirations. (p. 139)

Gadda's language may thus be defined as eclectic. This eclecticism, far from being an isolated example, represents a continuation of what critics term "plurilinguismo," an anti-purist trend that stands in opposition to the more traditional "unilinguismo" or cult of classical linguistic models. (pp. 139-40)

Gadda's opposition to the "lingua d'uso" represents a protest against the low intellectual level of the petty bourgeoisie. . . . Not only does linguistic standardization strip a language of its wealth but it also restricts an author's creativity. Language instead should enable the author to express his ideas in more than one way. . . . (p. 140)

In the *Pasticciaccio* we find the best examples of Gadda's rich use of language, a characteristic which appears in his earlier works, although to a lesser degree. The loosely constructed plot confirms the lack of importance Gadda attaches to the narrative. As the reader soon discovers, Gadda never has true narrative interests in the situations he chooses for his novels, but rather uses them as a springboard for engaging in peripheral discussions which titillate his linguistic fantasy. Although such a technique creates a fragmentary, often confusing narrative, the linguistic variety of these descriptions compensates for the weak plot.

Gadda's language in the *Pasticciaccio* is much more than a generous sprinkling of dialectal, popular, or learned expressions, thrown in for color or effect. It is correct to state that the author has succeeded in adding a new dimension to the Italian language. He creates a complex interplay of standard Italian, dialects, archaic forms, specialized terminology, foreign borrowings, and, many times, his own neologisms sometimes in the same paragraph and, at times, in the same sentence.... Gadda's skillful mixing of traditionally incongruous words is particularly efficacious when he employs the "style indirect libre." The contrasts between the plebian speech patterns of the majority of the characters in the *Pasticciaccio* and the cultural, often erudite or specialized language of the author add linguistic depths that overshadow the rather flimsy plot.

The vocabulary innovations of the *Pasticciaccio* can be divided into three major categories: archaic and learned words, dialects, and original neologisms. The author's propensity for archaisms and learned expressions confirms his debt to the classical heritage of Italian. (pp. 140-41)

[The] Manzonian inspired style used for a major portion of the prose narrative is another example of the author's homage to literary Italian. (p. 142)

The *Pasticciaccio* is also dotted with words lacking literary tradition. There are copious examples of words from the sciences, specialized fields, and the world of technology....

If Gadda's linguistic experiments were confined to obsolete, foreign, or highly specialized terms, we could define him a reactionary, a conservative, or the like, but this is not the case. In addition to the literary aspect of his vocabulary, we find a second important division: namely, the use of popular, particularly dialectal words. Since the *Pasticciaccio* is set in Rome, the principal dialect is Romanesco with a liberal admixture of Neapolitan ..., Abruzzese ..., and Venetian.... The various dialects help Gadda describe the political and social climate of Fascist Rome in the late 1920's. (pp. 142-43)

By using dialects, Gadda accentuates the social and economic division among his characters in a way that probably would have been impossible had he limited his vocabulary choice to standard Italian. In such cases, Gadda recognizes that the spontaneity and occasionally the vulgarity of many dialectal phrases and expressions produce more forceful effects than literary Italian. (p. 143)

It is important to point out that Gadda's purpose is not that of writing a novel in dialect. Since his use of dialect is primarily literary, he is not concerned with the philological niceties of exact phonetic transcription and the like.... Rather he is concerned with the various linguistic effects to be attained by mixing standard literary Italian with the dialects.

In studying Gadda's vocabulary, we must not forget the third and most original division: that of his own neologisms. As we have seen, Gadda's linguistic versatility enables him to cull new words and expressions from learned, specialized, and popular sources. Failing, however, to find words suited to his particular needs, he does not hesitate to create new ones. (pp. 143-44)

[For Gadda] linguistic taboos do not exist. To satisfy his artistic creativity, he draws on all possible sources, even those considered anti-literary or anti-intellectual.

Another facet of the linguistic richness in the *Pasticciaccio* and Gadda's work in general stems from his tendency to digress. The bulk of his narrative is a series of essays (*I Viaggi la morte*), short stories (*Accoppiamenti giudiziosi*) or sketches (*L'Adalgisa*); both the *Pasticciaccio* and *La Cognizione del dolore* are incomplete. This fragmentism confirms Gadda's involvement with language and style rather than plot. Many times Gadda will elaborate on details to such an extent that the reader will forget the main thread of the narrative and have to turn back to remember what is happening. This preoccupation with language, however, explains why Gadda is omnipresent in every page of his narrative.

The other important aspect of Gadda's artistic creativity—and this perhaps is the fundamental explanation for his linguistic richness—results from his cultural formation not only in the traditional academic definition but also in a more general, modern sense. (p. 146)

It would ... be absurd to define Gadda a traditionalist because of his literary fonts or even a progressive because of his recourse to the dialects, or an eccentric because of his own linguistic creations. Gadda is no one of these but all three combined. His language is vital, sometimes shocking, sometimes abstruse, sometimes bitter, sometimes comical, but always to the point.... No matter what Gadda is discussing, no matter how involved he may be in a certain issue, language remains his primary concern. His linguistic virtuosity offers by far one of the most remarkable contemporary examples of what can be done with the Italian language in all its manifestations from the most literary to the most popular. (p. 147)

> *Joan McConnell-Mammarella, "Gadda's 'Pluri-linguismo' in the 'Pasticciaccio',"* in Studies in Honor of Mario A. Pei, *edited by Joan Fisher and Paul A. Gaeng, University of North Carolina Press, 1972, pp. 139-47.*

GIAN-PAOLO BIASIN

No doubt Gadda's [*Anastomòsi*] is emblematic for the theme of literary diseases. The levels at which we may read it range from the simple and elementary one of technical and medical positivism to the subtler and less obvious one of literary metaphors, where we pass through images and situations that are typically Gadda's and that find a remarkable enrichment and deepening precisely by their being placed in such a meaningful context.

I do not believe it is necessary to insist too much on the first level of reading. The text, even in the original title with which it first appeared in Milan's paper *L'Ambrosiano* ("Ablazione di duodeno per ulcera"), is a technical description made with the rigorous punctilious precision worthy of a handbook for anatomy students. Even the most absent-minded reader will not fail to notice the scientific, anatomical, and technical terms woven into the description. These terms are important because, according to Gadda, they confirm the validity and the vitality of "the contributions of techniques" to literary language in a particular, in fact a specialized, field. His vision is not at all a *regard médical:* there is in it something other and different that, going beyond the scientific status of the words through which it is manifested, posits the text in its literariness.

First of all, the atmosphere of the operation is removed, distanced from the very beginning; it takes place in an almost mythical elsewhere: "I would think I recognize, in a cell or in a strange hypogeum of ancient Egypt's centuries, the unperturbed performers of an embalmment, who on the corpse of King Amenhotep are performing the unusual and unspeakable, yet necessary, acts of a consecrating compassion." . . . The recourse to the rite of embalmment, with the sacred and mysterious quality connected with it, is not without reason if one remembers that, for the ancient Egyptians, Thot, the god in charge of funeral ceremonies, was also the god of medicine, numbers, and writing. Gadda "de-scribes" a surgical operation that is literally performed in the presence of death and in which the modern surgeon "seems to go through a ritual," to fulfill "the necessary acts" . . . , acts not dissimilar from the ancient ones.

Another element, one of a moral character, accompanies these acts, beginning with the preliminary washing of the surgeon's hands—completed with "the serene care of one who has reached the knowledge of the ends and the means," whereby "the gesture of the ancient Roman official loses the ancient meaning" and becomes the function of one "who will exclude the evil from the darkness of the body, and after exact minutes he will reassemble the reasons of life." . . .

A third element, one of an aesthetic-historical character, is added to modify the apparent scientific status of the description: Gadda, the profane, in front of the "shapeless heap of bowels," of the "poor guts" of the patient, remembers "the trash of flabby things that become a scheme in the fantastic anatomical tables of Hundt's *Anthropologium,* in the gratuitous ribbon's knots of Peyligk's *Philosophiae Naturalis Compendium,* rather than the truthful, admirably clear drawings of the painter and anatomist Leonardo da Vinci, who was able to portray the tangle of the bowels's turns with beauty and evidencing lines." . . . Actually Gadda identifies with Leonardo (the subtitle of a famous book of his is *Disegni milanesi*) and joins him "in a sort of gnosiological polemics, which he performs on swelling buboes with straight cuts, with the cold lucidity of a surgeon." . . .

Another element, however, distinguishes Gadda's text: affective participation. It is the author's eyes that, beyond "the margins of a frightful breaking" made by the surgeon, together with him but with a certainly nonscientific attitude, watch "the flabby and slimy secret of creation, . . . the sacred viscidity of that which is the prime *I* and in the second place thought" . . . ; it is a "consecrating compassion" that makes Gadda refer to the patient as a "poor Harlequin" . . . , a "late specimen of the human species" . . . , "a ripped-up, unbaptized puppet." . . . Gadda's affective participation culminates in a beautiful lyrical image that would not be expected in the middle of the description of a surgical operation: "A dismay satiates me: tiredness has muddled my knowledge, has bandaged it with distant, lost desires, which float fatuously on contingency; I would like to walk on the beach, and drink the indigo of the sea again, and recognize the untouched bodies of the living who lose their memories in the sun." . . .

At this point, however, it is necessary to underline what at once likens Gadda to the surgeon and at the very same moment distances him most greatly: the word. Gadda's word almost imperceptibly transforms the surgical operation into a cognitive one, and the latter into a literary operation. A general remark by Olga Ragusa [from her article "Gadda, Pasolini, and Experimentalism: Form or Ideology?"] can be applied with particular effectiveness to *Anastomòsi:* "in Gadda there is an added metaphysical dimension, the work serving not only to depict reality, however apparently deformed, but also to epitomize the process of knowledge."

The ritual and sacral aura of the ancient embalmers and the modern physicians is the aura of the man of every time as he faces the mystery of nature, the body, death—the irrational, in sum. Gadda's pen accompanies the surgeon's scalpel in his search, and that ancient, sacral aura surrounds both men: one thinks again of the "frightful lozenge," of the "unbelieved nakedness, inner to the formal nakedness we know"; but at this precise point a totally literary mechanism is turned on, the analogical word, the metaphor. The surgeon "insinuates the point of his unperturbed knowledge into that heap of flaccid tripes"; "his dialectic is manifested in his silent acts"; "he has read the idea of nature in the heap of the slimy appearances," while "his daring needlefuls" will "enter the thought of nature." Furthermore, the process of literalization makes the electric resector become "almost a new pencil of our times" . . . ; and just at the beginning of the operation, in the culminating moment of the sacral ritual that must lead to the discovery of an equally sacral mystery, here "the master without words has grasped his sharp, shining pen." Here Gadda, master of the word, identifies completely with the surgeon Carpiani, master without words, and has put his sharp, shining pen into the surgeon's hand, or rather has put himself in the latter's place, in order to perform a difficult literary and cognitive operation. The surgeon is Gadda, the scalpel is the pen. Thot, the ancient god of embalmments, recalled from the very beginning, is again, here and now, the god of writing.

Exactly as the surgical operation is "a biological remaking, a rethinking of nature's construction through the needles, a rewilling, a restoring Form," by using "a practice *unrealized* by Being," so the writer's (any writer's) operation is added on to reality, realizes a practice of Being, is in itself a remaking, a rethinking, a rewilling, a restoring *form.* The word, indeed, is both supplement and *pharmakon.* Like the surgical operation, the word restores form to the "tangle" in the "heap of livid appearances" that are searched in the inside of anatomy.

With these remarks we have come to a further level of reading and of critical examination: the level directed to discovering and analyzing the elements that constitute Gadda's literary operation. As they appear in the long passage from *Anastomòsi* quoted at the beginning of the chapter, these elements are the following: (1) the organic "tangle," or life's "mess"; (2) juxtaposed to it, the "prime *I* and in the second place thought," or the "living I, which had been only plasma organized during the years by a differentiating

idea''; (3) the "evil" closed in the "darkness of the body";
(4) the "unperturbed knowledge"; (5) the "whiteness" of
the surgeon, juxtaposed to the "secret" and organic "darkness" and suggesting the idea of the mother or "matrix of
resurrection," which calls to mind a painting of Saint Ann
(done by Leonardo among others) and which points to an
Oedipal complex that is fundamental in Gadda. He recognizes it as such, but apropos another author, of course.

As any attentive reader would expect, these thematic and
structural elements of *Anastomòsi* must be understood in
order to comprehend Gadda's whole work; they perem_pto-
rily point from a text to *the* text, and they form a signifying
chain that supports the entire narrative texture with implacable rigor.

The organic tangle or life's mess is the raw material, but
also the primary origin, the prerequisite of Gadda's cognitive and literary operation, as well as of a very precise
trend in modern art. . . . In *Anastomòsi* we see the best
example of organic tangle in its most elementary, secret,
biological manifestation: life pulsating inside the human
body.

But the notion of tangle is for Gadda much more complex
than that and could perhaps be compared with Borges's
"labyrinth" in its gnosiological implications. . . . The notion of tangle (or mess) appears as a notion of totality underlying all the phenomena; in a literary context, it becomes [in the words of Gian Carlo Roscioni] "either a
mimesis of the real deformation, or the deliberate breaking
down of an apparent order, preparing the creation of a new
reality." The best accomplishment based on Gadda's notion of tangle is perhaps the novel bearing the emblematic
title *Quer pasticciaccio brutto de via Merulana*.

In keeping with his premises, Gadda incorporates the notion of the "I" within the more general and deeper notion
of tangle and realizes a constant reduction of the "differentiating idea" of the individual. In *Anastomòsi* not even the
face of the patient is seen, nor is his name mentioned. . . .
(pp. 129-34)

Gadda's style is thoroughly based on the "spastic usage"
of language in order to obtain "a dissolution-renovation of
value" of each noun, as well as on the contributions of the
various techniques, the literary and the common language,
and the final result is a truly luxuriant vocabulary. This
vocabulary, in itself, is a symptom of a sort of linguistic
alienation, of a mannerism à la Binswanger, that constitutes
both a prologue and a reply to the baroque of the world.
Gadda's style produces . . . a myriad of images and scenes
all seen in the same perspective (and therefore indicating
the meaningless but vital chaos of reality), and a series of
"mirrorlike structures" at the syntactical level. . . .
(pp. 139-40)

Indeed in Gadda one finds all the elements considered by
Auerbach and Lukács as they describe the modern novel:
hostility toward contemporary society, fragmentation of
reality, and escape into the psychopathological.

Therefore it will be necessary to examine how Gadda succeeds in historicizing his *vision du monde;* hints and allusions to a precise historical and social reality, of course, are
not lacking in *La cognizione del dolore, Quer pasticciaccio
brutto de via Merulana, L'Adalgisa,* or *I viaggi la morte.*
But he has also written a novel-treatise that makes these

hints and allusions explicit and that makes them the basis
for a true personal psychoanalysis of history: *Eros e Priapo
(Da furore a cenere)*. Our critical attention will be focused
on this work instead of the others because it is a clarifying
summa of their motifs.

Gadda's intention in writing *Eros e Priapo* is clearly manifested from the very beginning: "Evil must be known and
notified. And when it is announced with trumpets from the
high mountains, then and only then the secret mechanism
of every sequence will be known by us and almost seen
functioning under the fragile crust of surface dialectics and
the sugar of official bulletins." . . . The result is "an erotic
history of human kind" . . . , such as Gaius Suetonius and
Publius Tacitus gave us in antiquity when they described
"Nero's dirty and bloody madness, and Tiberius's dark
psychosis." . . . Like these two historians of ancient times,
Gadda is not a psychiatrist. . . . But Gadda wants to and
knows how to show the "gangrenous" smell he perceives
in the historical and social phenomena of his times using
psychoanalysis as an instrument of "his attack on the
world, of his taking possession of the matter, of his protective aggressions, of his 'concrete fury'." . . . Gadda's language is patterned (in the original, which cannot but be betrayed by the translation) after the high Latin of the ancient
historians and is corrected by the *diminutio* of dialectal and
spoken insertions. It immediately reveals the author with
his neuroses and idiosyncrasies. . . . Though unfinished,
Eros e Priapo is an exceptional enlargement of Gadda's
perspective, of his polemic against the world and society—a
polemic that in the preceding works remained veiled by
metaphor or was accomplished through an allusion or perhaps even a precise but fleeting hint. (pp. 140-42)

But the erotic history of mankind is above all developed as
an erotic history of fascism and especially of the leader
[Mussolini] who embodied it. (p. 144)

If in Mussolini, Eros not guided by Logos becomes Pria-
pus, on the contrary in Gadda, Eros inspired by Logos
becomes the sponsor of a highly civic enterprise, the act of
knowledge and denunciation of evil. But obviously Gadda's
Eros could not be content with this. . . . Gadda's Eros is
actually disguised as Logos; it becomes Logos. After all,
we are talking about a book by Gadda, and in erotic phenomenology a book has a well-defined meaning:

> Generally, exhibition is the fundamental act
> of narcissistic psychosis. The transposition
> of the prime exhibiting act into another ex-
> hibiting act with a sublimated content is de-
> termined by a process that is symbolic and
> analogical. . . .
>
> (p. 148)

[Gadda] carries out the exhibitionistic act of writing and of
publishing in order to be recognized. He writes *Eros e
Priapo* in the first person; then, using brief incidental and
parenthetical insertions (such as "De Madrigal says," or
"De Madrigal continued"), he almost surreptitiously introduces his alter ego, De Madrigal, with his airy and mocking
name, as a mirror of himself and of what he is saying. (p.
149)

But in *Eros e Priapo* De Madrigal is more than Gadda's
spokesman. Let us remember the author's taste for the
phantasmagory of language, verbal manipulations, noun
transformations, and puns. . . . At this point it will not be

surprising to discover that De Madrigal is not as much a character, an alter ego for Gadda as were Gonzalo and Ingravallo, as he is a pretext, a verbal play, a noun transformation, literally an anagram:

ALI' OCO DE MADRIGAL;

if we break it down and then reassemble it letter by letter, it becomes

CARLO EMILIO GADDA.

This is a good example indeed, in the context of the novel-treatise, of Eros become Logos, with a wink to the reader and a scoff to "toothless eternity."

The last quotation refers back to the pole that opposes history, that is, the absolute. Returning to *La cognizione del dolore,* where an understanding of the longing for the absolute is fundamental to an understanding of the protagonist Gonzalo, one notices that, just as evil is not only physical, it is not only in history. . . . Gonzalo pursues his stubborn and exhaustive cognition of or acquaintance with grief exactly as the surgeon in *Anastomòsi* proceeded with the point of his unperturbed knowledge. At all levels, for Gadda it is a cognitive operation.

At any rate, *La cognizione del dolore* has an inner development similar to Svevo's and Michelstaedter's, with a desperate lyricism that harkens back to Leopardi (and therefore to Schopenhauer) and an emphasis on psychopathology that is not an end in itself but rather expresses a precise and compassionate *referto* on the human condition. Furthermore, Gadda is able to deal with the most directly literary aspect of his *vision du monde*. He does so, significantly, by representing Gonzalo speaking to his doctor, who does not understand his outburst of rage directed initially and not by chance against the pronoun "I" ("the foulest of all pronouns"). . . .

> That lousy, incomparable I. . . swaggering. . .
> erect. . . beplumed with attributes of every
> sort. . . purplish, and feathered, and taut, and
> turgid. . . like a turkey. . . in an open fantail
> of engineering diplomas, of noble titles. . . . . .

Gonzalo's outburst is beautiful from a rhetorical standpoint the cogent and panting pauses, the aphorism of lice, the mannerist stratification in the comparison involving the caper (in assonance with monad), and in the Italian original the final rhyme "ingegnereschi/cavallereschi." But the importance of this outburst is in the fact that it is the narrative climax of Gadda's discourse that started with the organic tangle in *Anastomòsi* ("a heap of flaccid tripes"— here "a sack of foul guts" with "miserable" boundaries) and developed in. . . "Como lavoro" and *Eros e Priapo*. This discourse is not so much on metaphysics as it is against metaphysics, and as such it should be considered in a wide cultural context. Taking Nietzsche as a starting point, then psychoanalysis (and particularly Georg Groddeck), one remembers Michelstaedter's considerations on "the words of fog," the subjunctive, the introductory particles of speech; and, along the same interpretive line, one recalls Derrida's contemporary statements that seem to frame Svevo's analogous intuitions philosophically.

Gadda's polemic against the pronouns emerges as a part of a much larger cognitive polemic. His considerations on history and literature are fundamental on this point:

Our words—you'll allow me—are everyone's words, very much published ones, handed down to us by peoples and doctrines. . . . Our phrases, our words are moments-pauses (the waiting landings, so to speak) of a cognitive-expressive flow (or ascent). . . . Their history, which is the crazy history of man, illustrates the meanings of each of them: four, or twelve, or twenty-three; the nuances, the minimal variations in value; in other terms, their semantic difference.

A writer's technique, to a certain extent, grows out of a pre-individual background that is the common adoption of language, that is the semantic stock (bearer of meanings) of a history-experience already realized and consolidated. This stock is formed and articulated through acceptance or antithesis, by enrichment or negation of certain expressive modes. The adoption of a language should be referred to a collective work, historically capitalized in an idiomatic mass, historically consequential in a certain development or more generally in some sort of deformation. In sum, this experience goes beyond the boundaries of a single personality and allows us to think of a history of poetry in a collective sense.

These remarks could be compared with T. S. Eliot's "Tradition and the Individual Talent"; in any case, they illuminate "the expressive contributions of techniques" in Gadda's work. *Anastomòsi* is a particularly meaningful example of the effective use of the terminology of surgical technique, but in Gadda's pages one finds the "idiomatic masses" elaborated "in the different technical milieux" listed by the author as follows: "factories, army, navy, arts and professions, commerce, official bulletins, sciences, fashion, underworld, medicine and clinics and insane asylums, stock-exchange, business, clothing, journalism, police, bureaucracy, law, agriculture, rackets."

Gadda's considerations on words, however, go beyond a purely stylistic problem. On the one hand, they correspond to the latest results of structural linguistics; on the other, they could be appropriated by Raimondi in *Metafora e storia* (metaphor and history, with metaphor incorporating history and in turn being created by the latter).

But another point is worthy of examination. After having politely asserted that there is "some exactness" in his "modest thought" that a writer should be a bit "the Encyclopedia," Gadda fully realizes that the encyclopedic project is impossible. The catalogue of the appearances of reality, the linguistic and stylistic accumulation and variation . . . never exhaust totality. That is why the encyclopedia cannot be completed, the book must remain open, writing does not exhaust the word. "One must actually look at the world, in order to be able to represent it; so, by looking at it, one happens to note that to a certain extent the world has already represented itself: already, before the poet, the soldier has spoken of the battle, and the sailor of the sea, and the woman-in-childbed of her delivery."

Gadda's writing, then, only appears to be representative and is necessarily unfinished; in Jacqueline Risset's words, it continuously searches for "the point that prevents the closing, . . . the indefinite crossing of plans that always sends *forward*, toward the unspeakable point from where it is born in the midst of disorder."

Even in the minimal (but not secondary) example of *Anastomòsi*, in the context of a thematic-symbolic analysis, it is possible to find the unspeakable point from which Gadda's whole writing originated: it is the primordial disorder, the organic tangle, the biological "darkness of the body" to be cut under the light by a "sharp, shining pen." Through the chain surgeon/whiteness/mother, the metaphor of the pen leads to that emblematic image in which it seems that the heuristic germ of Gadda's representation is concentrated: it is precisely that Mother, constituting the term *ad quem*, from which continuously, without ever being able to be concluded, his writing is born. (pp. 152-55)

> *Gian-Paolo Biasin, "The Pen, the Mother," in his* Literary Diseases: Theme and Metaphor in the Italian Novel *(copyright © 1975 by Gian-Paolo Biasin), University of Texas Press, 1975, pp. 127-55. 127-55.*

ROBERT MARTIN ADAMS

[In] his collection of short journalistic travelogues titled *Le Meraviglie d'Italia*, Carlo Emilio Gadda discusses, with a preternatural solemnity verging on heavy irony, the Freudian theory that behind every pattern of adult behavior lies a childhood trauma, buried but capable of resurrection. . . . [He] moves on to describe a veritable cornucopia of his own fixations with their originating traumas. . . . But the most important trauma, which needs no explanation, came when, as a little signorino momentarily neglected by his nursemaid, he was playing at being a tiger. He was busy being a real tiger, prowling on all fours through the "jungle"—the shrubbery of the park—when he happened to put one of his forepaws into a "marmellata," that is, a turd.

The episode, like most of Gadda's, is simple but controlling. All his major writings, though they start bravely in some ostensible direction and make preliminary progress toward it, fall sooner or later into a filthy and disgusting mess. They bog down in excessive details and elaborate irrelevancies, spin off into linguistic gyrations, and finally— as if confessing all delays and subterfuges to be useless in the end—plunge toward a vision of ultimate evil, an intricate and accumulated filth before which the author can only shudder and stop. The author's problem is not to reach that inevitable end, but to delay or avoid it. One has a great sense in reading Gadda, as in reading Beckett, that the story is forcing itself out across obstacles interposed by the reluctant author—that he knows where it's going, and doesn't want it to get there. This is part of a rather distinct though never formally defined Gadda-persona, who is severe, withdrawn, ironic, correct—a literary functionary, of rather narrow and old-fashioned tastes. He is not only erudite, but pedantic, much given to planting allusions and personal recollections in his prose, and then footnoting them at the bottom of the page. He often takes occasion to reassure the reader that this or that detail of his narrative is historically accurate; and this crucial point is often a linguistic one, to the effect that such and such a word was spoken when and where he has used it, and carried the peculiar import he assigns it. Being such a clean-minded man in matters of speech, he is inevitably a man of nasty

ideas, with a deep relish for garbled and distorted dialects, among which his own, especially in moments of deep feeling, is particularly colorful. The normal run of his prose is elevated, polysyllabic, periphrastic, poised, and slightly aloof; but lists seem to excite him, whether they are lists of objects for sale in a flea market, or foods that might be eaten at an assembly of gross and uncontrollable gourmands. He plunges into such lists like a man frenziedly scratching an open sore; and in the course of their pouring forth, the language is grotesquely smeared and distorted, with accumulated diminutives and adjectival suffixes and agglutinated verbal complexes which seem pasted together by the heat of the author's raging disgust. He makes much use of contaminated language—Italian smeared over with layers of Spanish, Latin, Greek, and the special distortions of regional dialect—romano, milanese, veneziano. And beyond these quasi-realistic devices, always pressuring the language and forcing it out of shape like a landscape of Vlaminck, is the overpowering feeling of the author's own tastes and attitudes, his presence just around the corner of the word. (pp. 114-16)

His books have generally appeared in disconnected pieces, at a considerable interval after their composition, and several times over. What seems a light, ironic, journalistic sketch is sometimes reworked—or not even reworked, simply incorporated— as part of a new and generally darker whole. . . . What [, for example,] is the status of the fragments in *Novelle del ducato in fiamme*? Are they first drafts toward *La meccanica* or fragments from an already envisioned novel? . . . [Unless] Gadda wants to, and is able to, clear it up, it remains once more mess surrounding the interpretation of his mind and thought. The fact is, I think it is not a particularly unwelcome mess as far as Gadda is concerned. He gives one the impression of a laminated and labyrinthine personality, whose books are created out of a long personal development, and all of them bear the marks of that development. (pp. 118-19)

A first impression of *Cognizione del dolore*—the first-written though second-published of Gadda's two major unfinished novels—is that its narrator is hopelessly incompetent. In labyrinthine meanders he wanders away from whatever subject he has undertaken, and entangles himself in irrelevant intricacies from which he seems doomed never to escape. (p. 120)

[A sentence which] is typically Gaddaesque in its intricate scheme of inflection (the grammatical involvements are as devious yet tenacious as those of Proust) . . . is notable for its many uncoiling subordinate clauses, its high level of euphemism, the slow distillation of its irony. The style works down from initial elevation toward a compressed vision of disgust, picking its way with deliberate and meticulous care from one puddle of moral filth to another. Elaborate syntax, a finicky and precious vocabulary, false starts and pedantic self-corrections, all serve our sense of a reluctant narrator. Yet under the author's pomposities or alongside them, the truth emerges, slipping out sometimes despite his apparent intention. (p. 122)

Gadda's language is highly textured and many leveled, laced with Spanish, Latin, and pompous scientific erudition both real and fake; it is erratic in syntax, as if out of control, prone to run its sentences into obsessive, interminable lists, but also to break off suddenly and then explode in an exclamatory afterthought. The author is very conscious of textures, of material surfaces, their minglings, and their contrasts: at one point a sweaty peon lumbers across a walk and through a doorway, leaving cakes of compressed dung behind him while a cat slips alongside him, a velvety shadow between the man's feet.... The nervous animism of nature, the constant agitation of objects, their power to stick in the recurrent mind, even to generate themselves by spawning lists which the narrator is powerless to control— all this leads toward and points up the psychic emptiness and sickness of the central character in [*Cognizione*], Don Gonzalo.... [He] is evidently a philosopher by temperament, a distant and ironic contemplator of the human scene. Plato and Kant are his professed interests, but in lieu of them both, it's not hard to sense that another name could be substituted as the guiding spirit of his life, and that is Schopenhauer.

With his usual spirit of mystification, Gadda refers several times to an ancient Inca curse, an illness without a name, described in an early book of colonial times; he also invokes the solemn spirt of genealogy, and describes a lengthy lineage from which Don Gonzalo presumably derived a disposition to his withering psychic disease. But it is a disease which has widened and generalized, under the influence of thought, from a particular *male* (ailment) to a general *male* (evil) afflicting human nature. (pp. 123-24)

Comparisons with Proust have been made on the score of the scene in which Don Gonzalo tramples underfoot the portrait of his father, and smashes a watch of some sort— whether gold or silver or nickel-plated, depending on the malice of the particular scandal-monger reciting the story. But the comparison is superficial at best; the specific act may be similar, but the complex of reasons behind it is very different. Gonzalo is enraged with his father (as nearly as we can discover) for having left the family saddled with a useless and impractical villa; he smashes the watch because it has been given to him as a graduation present at a time when he is in need of a new pair of shoes. (p. 124)

Basically Gonzalo is an outcast from the feast of life. His appetite for affection and reassurance is boundless, inordinate; but that is because his sense of ego, selfhood, is dying within him. The contradiction comes out in the matter of eating. Don Gonzalo is reputed to be a monstrous, uncontrollable gormandizer. That lobster or crab on which he nearly choked to death in Babylon is exaggerated, in popular rumor, to a great, glaring monster, almost as fiendish as its gluttonous devourer. The terrible bottles of wine that he consumes are enumerated as if they were evidence of hideous and inordinate luxury. Yet in "reality," so far as we are given to see that, the hidalgo is an abstemious dyspeptic —so eaten up, himself, by jealousy and frustration as scarcely to be able to swallow a mouthful of soup for the bile that chokes him.

When he figures this great, gross, pragmatical pig of a world—in a long silent fantasy toward the end of the novel —he figures it under the guise of a station restaurant full of stuffed shirts pretending to be individuals, and glutting themselves on food and complacent observances by way of sustaining this illusion. There they sit, waited on by frock-coats as empty as themselves, bloated with the empty dignity of their situations, flattering one another and themselves with empty postures of mutual admiration.... Under the surface of things, it goes without saying, the restaurant is a disaster; the food is a greasy mess, none of

the fruit-knives cut, the waiters curse and kick at each other, and in a final vision slimy spears of asparagus, dripping with butter, spiral off, followed by waterspouts of risotti. And yet . . . :

> All of them, all: and most especially the gentlemen at the tables. All were most distinguished! None of them, ever, had ever thought of suspecting that they themselves might be nincompoops, not to say three-year-olds. . . .
>
> And that was life. . . .

It is life, of course, as seen not by a rigid and disinterested moralist, but by a man who is starving to death, physically and for lack of self-esteem. (pp. 125-26)

The root of this [novel's] deep, unredeemable disorder, this near-abdication of the author before the horror of his own vision, is found in his diatribe against syntax, particularly against the pronouns "I" and "you." They constitute the myths of individuality—not formally "believed," so much as enacted by the strutting, pretentious "I" of the Roman daylight or the slinking, animalesque "I" of the Celtic forests—in either case, an unknown, unacknowledged, uncriticized, unexpressed subject of every proposition.... The very contempt he feels for this railway-station-restaurant called life, and for the wiener-schnitzel selves infesting it, implies a setting of himself apart; physically, spiritually, intellectually, in every possible way, he maintains himself apart—and that implies not only a definition but an emphasis on self as a definable unit. (pp. 127-28)

In fact, he wants and does not want a self, as he really is a glutton on a self-imposed starvation diet, really is a man of profound tenderness self-condemned to bitterness and celibacy. The very form of the novel suggests anguished indecision, radical and immutable disorder, conflicting unresolvable motives. The book moves, not forward to a resolution or a conclusion, but like an ink-stain on a carpet, spreading out and sinking deeper. Intricate contaminations of language and exasperated, difficult syntax express the contaminated life and exasperated spirit toward which the Gaddan universe is inevitably and hopelessly sliding. *Cognizione del dolore* lives by its rhetoric; it is a complaint, an unbeliever's sermon *de vanitate mundi,* all the more despairing because it demonstrates the vanity of the persona delivering the sermon.

At the heart of Gadda's other great novel, *Quer pasticciaccio brutto di via Merulana,* is exactly the same constellation of forces as in *Cognizione;* only the circumstances are slightly altered.... [The] mordant intelligence is a policeman, tracking down the perpetrator of the murder, not a philosopher declaring *a priori* a condition. There is, thus, a little more semblance of forward motion to the plot: though Don Ciccio's investigation, following the stain-in-the-carpet pattern, spreads out and sinks into Roman society, at the same time it moves heavily after the specific criminal.... But in the process of finding him, Don Ciccio finds so much filth, squalor, and hypocrisy—of which the murderer is victim and symptom, far more than cause—that pinning the specific outrage on him comes to seem anticlimactic, if not irrelevant.... What defeats Don Ciccio in the end, producing an impulse which is just about to become repentance when the book breaks off, is the universal human mess of the world, a vision—alas!—of flesh and blood. (pp. 128-30)

For all his elaborate irony and deep cynicism, Gadda seems to me a more humane writer than Joyce—less cold, less distanced in his point of view—at least that point from which he starts. . . . [He] likes to get close up to life, though he never forgets to remind us of how bad it smells. To a much greater extent Joyce tends to stand above his characters, looking at the patterns they make or looking through them. I do not get the sense that for Gadda there is much to be seen by looking "through" a character. His personages do not have much depth of character, and there is nothing much beyond them; yet they are not flattened, one does not get the sense of dealing with stencils. The stupid ones contain no hidden wisdom, they are just stupid, and usually dirty and brutal as well. The thoughtful are helpless in the torment of their own thought. Like Joyce, Gadda celebrates in the end a failure of mind—a failure of accommodation to the mess and inexactness of people and history. Both men alternate between seeing this diaster of the mind on the one hand as hilariously comic and on the other hand in the darker tones of self-pity. The grotesque distorting mirror of other minds gives back to them fantastic, shivering images of themselves, with which they love to play elastic games—they are everywhere present in their fictions but nowhere explicitly.

The strongest influence of Joyce on Gadda has evidently been in the matter of prose style, where one must fight hard to avoid the adjective which is Gadda's pet abomination, *baroque*. . . . His is a highly allusive and literary style, however, full of buried and not-so-buried allusions to literary history, literary analogues, and literary predecessors. . . . Gadda is likely to get snagged at any moment on some of the author's personal history or hangups, he is ponderous with the weight of his erudition, but frequently punctuated with hoots of laughter or mockery of his own pretensions. Every tiger-hunt ends with a hand in a turd; and the anti-phase of this cynicism is a kind of strained emotional writing, more than a little reminiscent of Joyce's addiction to purple patches, which he is prone to enrich with swoons, languors, and other trappings of glimmering passion. One is intensely conscious of both authors as stylists, of the dynamics, contrivances, and contrasts into which the language flowers under their hands. It goes almost without saying that both move with the extraordinary modern fluidity that Joyce and Dostoevsky created from the realm of fantasy to the realm of "reality" and back again. . . . Gadda and Joyce both use inter-lingual punning, but to different effects; for Joyce the device often implies a mythic substructure or connection, for Gadda it is more likely to be a curlicue or roundabout executed either for its own sake or toward an ironic juxtaposition—in any case, an opaque rather than a transparent device.

Gadda, I think, has a deeper, more ingrained sense of vulgarity and its opposite than does Joyce; that is to say, lacking Joyce's powerful sense of original sin, in which all men are involved together, he has fewer democratic instincts, and is more conscious of manners. Joyce's social spectrum doesn't rise much above, or sink much below, the sphere of the ignobly decent: Gadda's grammar alone is aristocratic. (pp. 131-32)

> Robert Martin Adams, "Carlo Emilio Gadda," in his AfterJoyce: Studies in Fiction After "Ulysses" (copyright © 1977 by Robert Martin Adams; reprinted by permission of Oxford University Press, Inc.), Oxford University Press, New York, 1977, pp. 114-33.

GAINES, Ernest J.   1933-

Gaines is a black American novelist and short story writer. His fiction deals with the victimization of the poor, uneducated black, often in settings drawn from Gaines's native southern Louisiana. Character portrayal in Gaines is realistic and convincing, and has been compared to Faulkner's. *The Autobiography of Miss Jane Pittman* is his best known work. (See also *CLC*, Vol. 3, and *Contemporary Authors*, Vols. 9-12, rev. ed.)

WILLIAM PEDEN

Gaines's strength lies in his quietly compassionate depiction of plantation Blacks in his native Louisiana. . . .

"A Long Day in November," the best piece in *Bloodlines* (all five are good), is a masterly novella of a young boy, his father and mother, and their world on a Louisiana plantation. There are no technical pyrotechnics here, no violence, but in their place a steadily seen and beautifully rendered picture of family life, alive with the minutiae of day-to-day existence. . . . The novella is climaxed by two powerful scenes that in less skilled hands would become either ludicrous or melodramatic. . . . Gaines's fine sense of control, his effective use of dialogue, and the quiet resonance of his scene-building [are evident]. . . . (p. 238)

Different as the fictional worlds of Alice Walker and Ernest J. Gaines are, they share one thing in common: they are the work of mature writers who in one manner or other (and quite apart from their concern for their race) have moved from the platform of sociology to the realm of art. "What moves a writer to eloquence is less meaningful than what he makes of it," Ralph Ellison has said. In their best stories, Miss Walker and Mr. Gaines have made that implied transition. And that makes all the difference. (p. 239)

> William Peden, in Studies in Short Fiction (copyright 1975 by Newberry College), Summer, 1975.

LARRY McMURTRY

Ernest Gaines's fiction has been characterized from the first by its quiet force. The characters in his several fine books often raise their voices, but the author declines to raise his. These characters are mainly poor, and mostly black; their lives are seldom far removed from the threat of violence, physical or emotional or both. Sooner or later the violence arrives, and the characters cry out at one another, or to the heavens. Their pain, struggle, bewilderment, joys and agonies are registered with precision and sympathy, but the strong prose that carries their stories is not affected by the fevers or the biases of those it describes.

A swimmer cannot influence the flow of a river, and the characters of Ernest Gaines's fiction—from Catherine Carmier to Miss Jane Pittman, and from Miss Jane to the Rev. Phillip Martin of "In My Father's House"—are propelled by a prose that is serene, considered and unexcited. It is the force of Mr. Gaines's character and intelligence, operating through this deceptively quiet style, that makes his fiction compelling. He is, pre-eminently, a writer who takes his own good time, and in [the case of "In My Father's House"] the result of his taking it is a mature and muscular novel.

The Rev. Phillip Martin is a pillar of the black community in the little town of St. Adrienne, La. . . . He is at the height of his influence as a civil-rights leader. . . . [Then his] past abruptly catches up with him. A stranger arrives in the town: a deeply uncommunicative, desperately lonely young man who calls himself Robert X.

Robert X, as it happens, is Phillip Martin's son, one of three children of a liaison formed in Reverend Martin's wild early years, long before he got the call. He has neither seen nor sought his first family in more than 20 years, during which a combination of poverty, neglect and profound outrage have broken it. . . .

The sudden appearance of this tortured, dying boy forces Phillip Martin to—if one might put it mildly—reassess his life. . . . We have revealed to us an individual, a marriage, a community and a region, but with such an unobtrusive marshaling of detail that we never lose sight of the book's central thematic concern: the profoundly destructive consequences of the breakdown of parentage, of a father's abandonment of his children and the terrible and irrevocable consequences of such an abandonment.

Not the least of the book's virtues is the variety and richness of its minor characters. Phillip Martin's guilty search into his past takes him, internally, down a long road of memory. Externally it brings him into contact with a number of people . . . whose portraits are done with Flaubertian economy but equally Flaubertian vividness. The dialogue is spare, but unerring, and humor will keep slipping in subtly, despite the tragedies behind these lives. The tone of the book is determined by Mr. Gaines's decision—a brilliant one—to set the novel not in the expected context of a sweaty, dripping Louisiana summer, but in the miserable, frigid, sunless Louisiana winter. . . .

There are few blemishes on the book. Now and then a character strays into polemic; once or twice the tone breaks. Perhaps Robert X should not have been allowed to speak at all, for his condemnatory silence is far more eloquent than the little that he eventually says. But these are small blemishes indeed on a book that attempts a large theme, and is fully adequate to it.

> Larry McMurtry, "Reverend Martin's Son," in The New York Times Book Review (© 1978 by The New York Times Company; reprinted by permission), June 11, 1978, p. 13.

JULIAN MOYNAHAN

In My Father's House would make a gripping play with its tight plot and strong scenes of confrontation, its Ibsenite central character . . . , and its central unsettling question, which brings together public and private issues of great moment to the black community in modern America yet which opens historical perspectives reaching from slavery days to the present.

The question relates to a profound cleavage between the male generations, between black fathers and sons. . . .

There's little doubt that the Reverend Martin and his ravaged older son are meant to represent historical generations. Also, the year 1969 [the year of the novel's action], a time when much of the impetus of the civil rights movement had been checked, following the King and Robert Kennedy assassinations, and when the cult of the guerilla warrior and of the gun was spreading among disillusioned younger blacks, is deliberately chosen to heighten the intergenerational tension. Gaines, however, is far too good a writer to let the narrative thin out into mere allegory. The milieu of

St. Adrienne and its rural neighborhoods, where both blacks and whites function within a regional culture amalgamating French Catholic with Southern Baptist influences, is solidly built up.

> Julian Moynahan, "Spectral Visitation," in Book World—The Washington Post (© The Washington Post), June 18, 1978, p. E5.

MEL WATKINS

In ["In My Father's House"] Ernest Gaines returns to the fictional terrain he carved for himself in "The Autobiography of Miss Jane Pittman" and "Of Love and Dust." . . . The characters too are familiar; they are the staunch rural types, like Catharine Carmier and Jane Pitman, who meet life's adversities with stoic heroism and whom Mr. Gaines has portrayed with such authenticity in his previous works. All are familiar—all, that is, except Robert X, who emerges in this tale as a Giacomettilike figure amid a landscape peopled by stalwart, Old South provincials.

In this sense, "In My Father's House" is a striking departure for Mr. Gaines, for during the first half of this novel the mysterious Robert X controls the tempo of the narrative. It is his presence, eerie and initially inexplicable, that dominates the story, and ultimately, precipitates the action. Mr. Gaines has unleashed an alien force in the insulated folk world that has heretofore delineated his fiction. And although Robert X never emerges from the shadowy torpor in which he has been cast, he is the catalyst that shakes the traditional assumptions and tentative equilibrium of the St. Adrienne blacks, the Rev. Phillip Martin, and even the white power structure with which they are in restrained conflict.

"In My Father's House," however—despite the larger social, generational and regional themes that are touched upon in its finely textured narrative—is focussed primarily on a much more primal situation. It is the discovery of the stranger's relationship to the Rev. Mr. Martin, literally the pillar of the black community, that initiates the events that shatter the consanguinity between the clergyman and his congregation. . . .

In dramatising this crisis in [Martin's] life, Mr. Gaines has melded two disparate fictional styles. At the outset, with the stranger's unsettling arrival, "In My Father's House" reads almost like a mystery. . . . The tale intrigues because of [Robert X's] ambiguity and the townspeople's reaction to him.

After Robert X's relation to the Rev. Mr. Martin is unveiled, however, Mr. Gaines shifts gears. The focus moves to the reverend and the struggle with his own demons. . . . Each part functions well in itself, but there are problems with the transition. One wishes that Robert X were not so summarily dispatched, that his character were explored with the same sensitivity the Reverend Martin is accorded. And the shift from an objective, factual rendering at the beginning of the story to a more subjective, nearly stream-of-consciousness narrative is jarring.

Still, this is a powerful, deeply probing novel. Mr. Gaines has taken numerous risks and, for the most part, he is successful. The Rev. Mr. Martin emerges as a complex, memorable character. . . . And through Mr. Martin's agonizing journey, the complicated makeup of St. Adrienne's black community is revealed—from the calm, self-satisfied respectibility of its middle class to the more base, tortured alliances of its nether life.

Although "In My Father's House" is neither as expansive in scope nor as movingly optimistic in tenor as Mr. Gaines's widely acclaimed previous novel, "The Autobiography of Miss Jane Pittman," it is a deeply layered, resonant tale. Its themes of alienation between parents and offspring, and the irrevocable unity of past and present, are certainly large enough to command attention. And Mr. Gaines's ability to portray the rhythm and cadences of Southern mannerisms is unerring. Despite some minor flaws, this is a solid contribution to the impressive oeuvre of one of America's finest Southern writers. (p. C19)

> *Mel Watkins, in* The New York Times *(© 1978 by The New York Times Company; reprinted by permission), July 20, 1978.*

*   *   *

GARRETT, George 1929-

Garrett is an American novelist, short story writer, poet, critic, and editor. He is noted for his technical control of many fictional forms and for his masterful storytelling. (See also *CLC*, Vol. 3, and *Contemporary Authors*, Vols. 1-4, rev. ed.)

WALTER SULLIVAN

George Garrett is a mature writer—*Do, Lord, Remember Me* is his third novel, his fifth book of fiction—and the fruits of his long apprenticeship are apparent here. (p. 160)

It may not be possible to end this kind of book in a manner that is thoroughly satisfactory. . . . [His] conclusion seems a little thin, if only from a technical viewpoint. . . . [But this is a minor complaint when] balanced against Garrett's overall performance. Telling his story largely from a series of first person points of view, he remains totally in control of his material. He uses flashbacks and passages of psychological probing with effective restraint, and his people are Southern and funny sometimes, but they are never caricatures and they are never lugubrious. And even if the handling of [the death of Smalley, the novel's protagonist,] is not technically perfect, the meaning is clear. Evil is redeemed through dissolution and pain. And it is only redeemed. It is not effaced or even assuaged, this side of Paradise. (p. 161)

> *Walter Sullivan, in* Sewanee Review *(reprinted by permission of the editor; © 1964 by The University of the South), Winter, 1964.*

F. H. GRIFFIN TAYLOR

George Garrett would seem to share with Juvenal an appreciation of the virtues of the backwater, an admiration for simple loyalties, and a propensity for what Winston Churchill called the harsh laugh of the soldier. (p. 308)

Mr. Garrett is a Southerner who, after having lived in other places and countries, has decided to live in the South, and has committed himself to his native region in fact as well as in name. . . . He does not, as perhaps he should not, attempt to explicate the principles on which he takes his stand, but he is very clear as to what he does not accept. . . . As a poet Mr. Garrett is committed not to ideas nor abstract concepts, but to a place and its people.

Mr. Garrett has chosen to stand on familiar ground. He is not unconscious of his task to give shape to and if necessary to defend the views of his region as he sees it in the present. Acceptance of the present seems to be central to his position. He does not dwell on the past at all. At the same time he also exemplifies that *prise de conscience* of men of letters signalized by Baudelaire's proclamation of *"ma blessure"*, since which the locus of the struggle has been at least partly in the artist himself. Thus a recurrent theme in these poems is the need to recognize one's own imperfection, one's own disfigurement. . . . The poet also accepts the occasional ignominy and the contumely not infrequently the lot of the artist in our time, not infrequently, he suggests, deserved. Yet Mr. Garrett is not cut off from others; he is not lonely nor isolated . . . , for as a Southerner he is always aware of the society of which he is a part. He perceives the social fabric and his place in it with a sense that never sleeps. (pp. 309-10)

He calls his book *For a Bitter Season,* and with justice. It is singular for its compassion and affection for others. His laughter is sometimes wry, and sometimes reminiscent of François Villon. . . . Man is flawed by his vanity, his inconsistency, his blindness in love, his folly, his death. The poet accepts these things and accepts the place in which he finds himself and has chosen to be, but without abandoning hope —"we have lived too long with fear"—for out of these things and this place grow his poems, his children, and all the things he loves. The place he lives in may sometimes most resemble a compost heap, but he loves it for what grows in it. (p. 310)

Mr. Garrett's interest in all that goes on around him is mirrored in the variety of his poems. He does not disdain the trivial. On the contrary, he seems to have a special affection for, and shows much of his humor and gaiety, in the poems he has deliberately made to be throwaways. They are not properly in the category of light verse, because in them one senses that the poet's intention is to say, "Let's not be so solemn, let's not write every line as though it were imperishable when we know very well that much of our verse, all of it perhaps, will, like ourselves, perish very soon." They serve to remind us that any poet's best efforts owe much to the countless other poems that have been written by him and discarded along the way; owe much to the poems that have been written by others, too. (pp. 310-11)

In ["Egyptian Gold", a] poem about the pickpockets of Rome, and in "Crows at Paestum", Mr. Garrett's gifts show to their best advantage. Both poems move effortlessly from the simple (often for Mr. Garrett at least faintly ridiculous) to the sublime. In both, on the deserted hillside overlooking Paestum and in the crowded Roman piazza, the poet sees himself as part of the teeming present and the speaking past. He yearns for no more perfect state of affairs. He eyes the present with all its imperfections and leaves the reader in no doubt about what he approves and what he does not. It is plain that he has known the loneliness and estrangement men experience in a mechanized society. Knowing the metropolis and its undeniable importance for the artist, he has elected to live in and write out of his own country where men are loved or hated as men and not as fleeting abstractions. (p. 311)

> *F. H. Griffin Taylor, in* Sewanee Review *(reprinted by permission of the editor; © 1969 by The University of the South), Spring, 1969.*

DAVID R. SLAVITT

Death of the Fox is splendid, a magnificent book, and very probably one of the dozen best novels to have been written in my lifetime. Indeed, it is so extraordinary a work that it raises certain questions about the history and the future of the novel itself, about the relation of the novelist to his public, and about the ultimate mysteries of Fame and Fortune which lie not only at the heart of this novel but at the heart of the experience of all of us. (p. 277)

The technical excellence of both [*The Finished Man* and *Which Ones Are The Enemy?*], the wit, the appeal were as irrelevant as the eloquent need of some poor sucker who buys his lottery ticket and sits back to wait for the big money. Each of them was a good book in its way. *The Finished Man* was a more than usually ingratiating first novel about Florida politics and—perhaps—Garrett's father. *Which Ones Are The Enemy?* was a novel about army life in Trieste—where Garrett served—and was more polished, more authoritative in its tone, surer in its technical aspects, richer. . . . Really, a damned good book. In each case, however, the bright pebble of experience that Garrett was weaving into his nest of ironies and clarities was important to *him;* the craft with which he managed the novels was of interest to a few hundred enthusiasts of the novel. (p. 280)

Death of the Fox is a huge book, but its devices are minute and precise. . . . The fictional constraint is very nearly as oppressive as Ralegh's own, in that the possibilities of action are severely limited. There is thought, of course—recollection, analysis, regret, celebration. But thought is a frustrating business unless there is some medium for its expression, some translation into speech and gesture, some resulting action. The great motion of the book, then, is the building of concentration and frustration, and then moments of release as, by the smallest but most satisfactory exercises of choice, Ralegh performs.

These performances, moreover, are frequently the historically reported ones, small pieces of bright fact that have survived in histories and biographies. This is what any historical novelist would try to do, working in as many of these little nuggets as possible. But for Garrett, the strategy is more ambitious. His scheme, so far as I can tell, is to make these little pieces of business the flowering of the garden he has been so carefully tending for hundreds of pages, the embodiment of attitudes, the natural result and necessary crown of all the internal business of intellection and recollection. (pp. 287-88)

Even the most cursory investigation into the details of Ralegh's life and into the history of the period will show how precise Garrett has been in maintaining that balance between imagination and factual correctness, and between Ralegh's limited area of freedom and the web of necessity in which he hung. (p. 290)

[Instead] of cribbing from Garrett and history, I shall cite the concluding sentences of the book: "The ax is bright in the dwindling sunlight. Flashes high before it falls. Higher by far a lone gull banks and circles on the darkening air. Then flies away to vanish over the Thames."

The key words, I think, are "by far" for they are the connecting words. Obviously a gull can fly higher than an ax. The connection establishes, merely by syntax, a point of view below in the crowd, a pair of eyes that looks up to the flash of the ax, and then, at the last moment, deciding not

to look at its fall, averts to a gull higher by far, and by so doing admits to Ralegh the dignity he has earned, indicts the blunder of King James, and, most important, makes those historical judgments in immediate, sensuous terms.

So long as that kind of thing can be managed, there is a place for historical fiction, a very high place, and one that has only rarely been attempted. It is especially in the light of that rarity and the difficulty of which it is symptomatic, that I delight in and admire *Death of the Fox*. (pp. 293-94)

> *David R. Slavitt, "History—Fate and Freedom: A Look at George Garrett's New Novel," in* The Southern Review *(copyright, 1971, by David R. Slavitt), Vol. VII, No. 1, Winter, 1971, pp. 276-94.*

BRUCE B. SOLNICK

[*Death of the Fox*] is called "a novel about Ralegh," and though the author's note explicitly states that it is not a biography, . . . it can and perhaps should be read as a biography written with the literary liberties available to the novelist but not to the formal and traditional biographer.

Garrett, making full use of the freedom available to the novelist—who is not held to the strict limits of accountability of the historian or the biographer—does a fine job of placing Ralegh in the involved intrigue of the Elizabethan world. Though the book is long, the reader's interest is maintained throughout. (p. 36)

> *Bruce B. Solnick, in* Américas *(reprinted by permission from* Américas, *monthly magazine published by the general Secretariat of the Organization of American States in English, Spanish, and Portuguese), January, 1974.*

*   *   *

GASCAR, Pierre (pseudonym of Pierre Fournier) 1916-

Gascar is a French novelist who began his writing career as a journalist. The influence of his experience as a German prisoner of war during the Second World War is felt throughout his work. Gascar's fictional world is one of cruelty and hostility, the tone of his work is pessimistic and despairing.

CHESTER W. OBUCHOWSKI

Inasmuch as war looms large in *Les Bêtes* and lies at the very center of *Le Temps des morts* Gascar impresses one as being of that class of writers, of which Ludwig Renn and Norman Mailer are prominent representatives, who achieve by far their highest literary flights under its crushing impact.

With *Les Bêtes* it is the world of Kafka born anew: strange, somber, mysterious, irrational, eternally menacing. The animals, swarming everywhere, quail helplessly before the onslaughts of their human tormentors, who, in their turn, fail not only to breach the curtain of incomprehension isolating the species but also that which segregates them from their fellow creatures. And in the three most powerful stories, those directly embraced within this study, a Kafkaesque dream-like haze envelops the impotent animals and anguished humans, overlying the world of reality and lending an air of timelessness to their tragic situation.

Not necessarily intended as such, "Les Chevaux," the book's opening selection, can readily be taken to be a strong indictment of war.... Throughout, war is ingeniously painted as epic chaos and a *massacre des innocents*. (pp. 327-28)

The grim face of war again terrorizes men and animals alike in "Les Bêtes," which gives its title to the volume. A masterly contrived piece, it would rate inclusion in any anthology of contemporary short stories.... In a world gone mad, in a concentrationary world, humans thus become dehumanized, being reduced to life on an animal plane.

"Entre chiens et loups" ... has as its setting a military kennel in the French zone of occupation of post-World War II Germany. Here, under simulated conditions of war, human targets, grotesquely clad in not entirely protective clothing, are pitted against dogs whose savagery is as nurtured as it is natural. (pp. 328-29)

On balance, the book's human kind have all the better of it in their relentless strife with their animal relations.... It is with the grim consequences of the brutalization of man that *Le Temps des morts* deals. (pp. 329-30)

Gascar obviously had an initial advantage in writing of a world he experienced in his own person, albeit outside the gates. In addition, perhaps because he avoided even a literary entry therein, he has had to trust in the magic of poetic suggestibility where others have, in large part, relied upon the elaborations of a grim realism. His oblique, insinuating approach, one thinks, served him well. (p. 332)

Gascar's is a highly exceptional gift for generating mood, for evoking atmosphere. He is a master at giving broad resonance to the naked word, to the isolated, seemingly insignificant act. The narrative is stark and the language fittingly laconic, if occasionally disfigured by an imagistic extravagance that savors of surrealism's automatic writing. An air of mystery shrouds the village and the surrounding countryside. The atmosphere is heavy with anxiety.... The author, who continually employs counterpoint in contrasting the Arcadian peacefulness of the cemetery, where men leisurely transplant sod and water flowers, with the madness of the world without, again effectively resorts to it [in depicting the crowded death-trains], simultaneously detailing the appalling suffering of the doomed deportees entombed within the boxcars and the symbols of peace visible to those of them gazing out of the narrow open panels: luminous landscapes, trees, free men standing relaxedly in fields, mechanical harvesters. (pp. 332-33)

Le Temps des morts discreetly eschews needless refinements and graphics, is piously conceived. The macabre, always a dangerous obstructant in works of this sort, does once impose itself, when the cemetery hands accidentally uncover a mass grave. For the most part, however, it has yielded to poetic evocation. These factors, united with the becoming economy of words and simplicity of intrigue, the admirable consonance of mood and expression, the sustained emotion, and the deep, if verbally restrained compassion, serve to make of *Le Temps des morts* the work of power and artistic integrity demanded by the subject. It may well be the most effective fictional portrayal of the concentrationary universe yet to have appeared in any language. Surely its position of preeminence in France cannot be seriously challenged.

The one piece by Gascar related to war and the concentrationary world that cannot by any stretch of the imagination be conceived as having been inspired by a moral intent is the not at all short short story "Le Bonheur de Bolinka" [also published as "Les Femmes"].... A gross, rough-hewn comic element ceaselessly disturbs this atmosphere of tragedy, further debilitating the slack narrative and converting *Le Bonheur de Bolinka* into the only artistic *malheur* amongst the works by the author bearing on the miseries spawned of war.

Looking back upon the war-associated stories of *Les Bêtes* and the elegiac *Le Temps des morts*, one deduces that Gascar could not but have been aiming to shock the reader into a sense of moral outrage, to sound a mighty note of warning. The concentrationary world, he clearly predicates, lives on, if in shrunken proportions. At any moment, anywhere, it is suggested, mass exterminations could again be launched. Alas, he would strike at our conscience while holding out no great hope of regeneration. He seems to see us all as infected with a malignant cancer of the soul, as potential accomplices in murder. And he finds no God to buttress us. Incomparably more than anything else, it is this deep-dyed pessimism that subtracts from his missionary effort. (pp. 334-35)

> *Chester W. Obuchowski, "The Concentrationary World of Pierre Gascar," in* The French Review *(copyright 1961 by the American Association of Teachers of French), February, 1961, pp. 327-35.*

JUDITH J. RADKE

It is in the half-light of limbo that we see the forms of animals and men in Gascar's *Les Bêtes*.... The stories with a war or pre-war setting take place in semi-darkness, an absence of light.... The evening light in which animal forms proliferate and images of fear multiply is both that of a tormented world at war and that of the interior recesses of the minds of individual men.

When one is at that time of day which is "entre chien et loup," it is difficult to distinguish the man from the animal, the animal from the object. The title, "Entre chiens et loups," given to the longest story of this collection, is doubly ironic: it intimates that the conflict of man and dog described in the story is that of the dog with a more savage animal, a wolf, and it describes too that indistinct twilight in which the story is bathed, one in which it cannot be determined if the ambiguous shape seen in the distance is dog or wolf. One form appears to already be, or be about to become, another. The bench on which the butcher kills his animals resembles his victims with outspread legs; trees become "crucifiés" in the winter light.... (p. 85)

There is not just a superficial resemblance of forms in the dimness nor does Gascar stress this similarity solely for the purposes of comparison, in a symbolic or metaphoric fashion. In this dream-like atmosphere one form becomes another; there is a constant metamorphosis. There is the constant possibility of change in man and animal, either in the direction of evolution or that of atavism.... We are threatened by a rapid proliferation of forms, constant transformations....

There is here no line completely separating the animal kingdom from the world of men.... Gaston is an entirely new species.... He is the animal form of a new species of hate or evil which invades and conquers us each time another conquering horde invades our soil. We will return home one day and find this new species installed in our home, waiting for us.

In such an animal-man world, it cannot be assumed that man remains superior to the animal in the hierarchy of species. This superiority in the order of creation is a myth which the commandant in charge of training dogs for attack would like to believe, just as he would insist that man's word "war" denotes an orderly, rational and impersonal science, a civilized skill. (p. 86)

From the very first, [the narrator] senses that it is man, the common soldier, that is being regimented and controlled . . . , and that the dogs are but hiding their violence under a deceiving cloak of obedience. He recognizes their insubordination. Man, the "master," has nurtured the savage force of the dog, but he cannot truly control and discipline that force, which he would set loose against his fellow men.

For it is man who is the hunter as well as the hunted. The commandant is not superior and apart from his dogs. . . . The dogs are the reflection of a savage atavism in man himself. Although the organized, passionless nature of his violence deceives the commandant and makes him see himself as superior, it is really he, not Franz, who is a throwback to a previous form of man. "Man is a wolf to man": the "wolf" of the title of this story—the wolf which might be mistaken for a dog—is indeed man himself, the primitive man of hate and bloody justice from which we have tried to escape since the beginning of the species. (p. 87)

The animal has not always been the image of man's malediction. Gascar finds delight in the variety and beauty of animal forms which abound in the creation and in the imagination of man. . . . There are legendary animals too, those which man creates to express his needs and aspirations. . . . (pp. 87-8)

There is a complicity, one might say an identification, of animal and man in these mythic forms. It is the myth of creation, the ark and the flood, as well as the myths of Pegasus, the centaur and dolphin of antiquity, which Peer and the boy of "La Vie écarlate" dream once again. . . . Peer sees the horses as images of man's flight and need, but the liberating flight which he and the horse make together ends upon awakening. . . . (p. 88)

In a world where man is alienated from man and animal both, the forms of man and animal change. . . . The horses are no longer proud and beautiful, but are described as . . . crouching dogs. They are shades, their rhythm broken as well as their pride. . . . Peer is also like an animal which has been broken. Only his furious attacks upon the horses break the indolence and the kind of "unconsciousness" which help him endure this purposeless, solitary life of war. Both his apathy and the ferocity which results in him as a reaction to it make a different man of him, one in which we do not recognize the form of the "human" being.

The setting of "La Vie écarlate" is not a wartime one, yet one recognizes in the butcher's wild and gratuitous slaughters the carnage of war and the alienation of man and animal. Here the natural order of things has been changed. It is true that man has always killed animals for food, but now the killing has become a personal thing, the butcher is a madman, and the lovely image of the sea-horse with the boy on his back gives way to the grotesque image of the carcass of a "mouton-homme" hung on a hook. (pp. 88-9)

The apathy and loss of effect of this changed form of man are as shockingly cruel as his violence. . . .

Man and animal no longer share together the companionship of the creation and the flood nor the harmonious beauty and freedom of the animal-man world of myth. Now they but resemble one another in the cruel metamorphosis which has transformed them both. (p. 89)

The images of the fugitive, of the hunter and the animals he pursues, recur in Gascar's later novels and stories, and along with them, the persistent theme of the longing to penetrate into a new morning. The hope of enlightenment is constantly repeated even though the means of achieving it is not quite clear. Through Paul, the hero of *Le Fugitif*, like Franz a man with no identity of his own, Gascar expresses this hope. . . . The passive attitude . . . expressed by this man in limbo does not seem typical of the man Gascar himself, a man actively involved in the political struggles of his time, nor is it similar to the passionate cry of Franz, but it does indicate the hoped-for evolutionary direction which the metamorphosis of forms may take.

Although the reader feels keenly the subdued horror and feeling of eternal guilt evoked in *Les Bêtes*, the oppressive half-light of these early war-time stories is not definitive. (To be sure, the possibility of rebirth "dans la lumière révélée," in a luminous state of pure mind, is as yet extremely remote, only an elusive dream.) Like Franz's witness, these stories are warnings of a danger already upon us. Gascar exhorts the individual man not to regress further from the human condition he once attained. He calls attention to the menace hidden from us by a comforting protective myth. He asks at least recognition of the struggle which must be made against the "animals" of man's malediction so that man may arrest his atavistic return to the primitive forms from which he has come. (pp. 90-1)

> *Judith J. Radke, "The Metamorphoses of Animals and Men in Gascar's 'Les Bêtes',"* in The French Review *(copyright 1965 by the American Association of Teachers of French), October, 1965, pp. 85-91.*

NANCY WILLARD

If Heraclitus had written fiction, it would have resembled the novels and stories of Pierre Gascar, where earth, air, fire, and water, and the vivid creation which they support are no less alive than man himself. Gascar's tales are like those enormous medieval tapestries, where princes and violets are set down with equal clarity, and the prince must share the stage with water, owl's ears, and the webbing of frog's feet. . . . [In] his stories simplest acts become ancient rites: he sees his own life blessed with the permanence of a myth.

In his collections of stories, *Les bêtes, Les femmes, soleils,* and his autobiographical writings, *La graine* and *Le meilleur de la vie,* good and evil have the taste of water and sun, guilt and hate have the sting of blood and salt. They cannot be separated, for more than an act of language keeps them together. The elements participate directly in the lives of his characters, fuse with their values and surround them with an ethical landscape of their own making. Transformed to a wasteland or a garden, nature mirrors their acts of hate or acts of love, just as an internal conflict, says Gascar, may be triggered or reinforced by a symbol. (pp. 104-05)

With symbols Gascar makes a new language. He never writes of ideas but fuses them with the material world where they were born. . . . Like Bergson, Gascar believes that when you try to describe your feelings, spreading out in space what occurred in time, you lose the very nuances you want to seize. . . . Symbols allow Gascar both to order his experience and to avoid the generalities that destroy its vitality. (p. 105)

The syntax of Gascar's experience is concrete things. *Le meilleur de la vie* contains a curious defense of that syntax. A harnessmaker and a wheelwright engage in a verbal dual to see who can invent the most fantastic images. The result is a strange yoking of things and properties: trumpets of sunshine, snails' boot, and woolen pistols, an inventory from a world of dreams. Each utterance seems to transfigure the dim workshops where they are announced. (p. 106)

Language always buckles when you have to deal with the anarchy of nature. . . .

Threatened with anarchy, man tries to impose his will on nature, by naming it, denying it, possessing it, and killing it. Hunting, says Gascar, is an attempt to arrive at a world where animals have names. (p. 107)

Confronting nature, man confronts his fate as well. Fate is the final power, the man who comes to arrest you, the trapdoor at the end, the stone hat of death. Yet it is also a power carried in ourselves, a power we hardly know until we commit the crime of which we thought we were incapable, so that we look to the gods for an explanation. Gascar's favorite image for fate is the blind man. (p. 109)

Gascar shows man hunting beasts and man hunting man as if he were a beast. In both cases, the possibility of love is destroyed. Fate shines brightest in the lives of the poor or the outcast, and Gascar allies himself with both. (pp. 109-10)

What astonishes the reader in *La graine* is Gascar's apparent lack of involvement in the deaths he causes and the deaths he witnesses. "Incense, worms, holy water, blood . . ., never once did I find my hands suspect." Though not admitted, the guilt is there, however. . . . Over and over, Gascar raises the question: how shall a man free himself of the past events which hold him trapped? "Freedom bears our own name, our own face," he writes, "and . . . all our attempts to escape the world that oppresses us bring[s] us back to ourselves, to the scrutiny of our own past."

And because the past is always present, every relationship of victim and master conceals an older quarrel, which Gascar describes in "Entre chien et loups." A Polish refugee named Franz has the job of playing victim to dogs being trained for tracking by the military. . . . Behind the game lies the real issue: authority tries to order and destroy what is irrational and indestructible. When it wears a human face, it is sometimes called anarchy, nihilism, mass individualism. (pp. 110-11)

The heroes of Gascar's novels are victims, for whom exile or war has disrupted the habitual ways of organizing their lives. Their world consists of what their senses tell them is true. Gascar knows the danger of this position from his childhood when a simple change of perspective, a new view of his own landscape could show him suddenly, underlying the familiar, a nameless void. Not surprisingly, his heroes escape from the tedium of ordinary life into a great loneliness. Standing in the abyss that opens when they cease to

believe in the value of that life, it seems to them they have always loved strangers. It is like finding yourself in a boat, says Gascar in *Le meilleur de la vie* under which you feel the whale sigh as you sweep away from the old moorings towards the horizons of nausea. (p. 111)

Gascar's heroes, unwilling to live with questions, too often reach for traditional answers which will free them from the past by imposing a meaning on it. Nothing, says Franz in "Entre chien et loups" is easier for man than to believe.

Perhaps *Le fugitif*, a novel set at the end of World War II, shows best the range of answers which a man may seize in the name of his own freedom. . . .

The truth Paul seeks is an absolute justice that will give meaning to his suffering. He wants all Germany to be guilty down to the smallest tree, for guilt implies the existence of laws which have been broken. Yet he knows the trees are not guilty, they are part of an order of things that is timeless. . . . The war has only disturbed the surface of the forest where he hid. . . . (p. 112)

What Paul asks of the new truth is that it shall come like an apocalypse bringing a value to life quite apart from the ordinary flux of human existence: a new reality, risen out of the fire and death of war. . . .

Though his characters occasionally take death for an answer, Gascar does not. The narrator in "Le temps de mort" discovers the true revelation of death when, digging a grave in a prison camp, he discovers several corpses hideously decayed: death is man's surrender at the end of a blind alley. . . .

If Gascar envies the dead anything, it is their freedom. After the accident in which Paul is presumed to have died, he loses his legal and social identity and becomes no one. Now he has the freedom of a dead man who returns to the earth desiring only to watch the spectacle of life and to understand it. (p. 113)

By losing his life, Paul finds it. For the past is not something we carry after us, though its existence depends on ours. "Those who leave us and those who die are joined to us by a steadfast though invisible flame, a reminder that reveals a presence." . . .

When a man is at home in the living flux which cares nothing for him, then the elements reveal themselves as symbols through his most insignificant experiences. As a child, sitting in the wine cellar of his neighbor's house, Gascar celebrates mass with the earth. . . . The tasks of harvesting become the worship of corn, whose shape recalls the secret power it serves. . . . Gascar's truth can be touched and eaten. It is the spiritual bread of a communion that springs from his joyous affirmation of the material world where everything passes and nothing is forgotten. (p. 114)

Nancy Willard, "The Grammar of Water, The Syntax of Fire," in Chicago Review *(reprinted by permission of* Chicago Review; *copyright © 1971 by Chicago Review), Vol. 22, Nos. 2 and 3, 1971, pp. 104-18.*

*   *   *

GASS, William H(oward)   1924-

An American novelist, short story writer, essayist, critic, and philosopher, Gass considers his work to continue the tradi-

tion of the Symbolist poets. **His is an intense and experimental fiction, which gives close attention to novelistic style and structure as well as to the words themselves. The use of typographical devices and inventive metaphors together with an often philosophical tone colors Gass's work with a marked poetic quality. (See also *CLC*, Vols. 1, 2, 8, and *Contemporary Authors*, Vols. 17-20, rev. ed.)**

GORE VIDAL

Gass's essays are often eerily good. At his best, he can inhabit a subject in a way that no other critic now writing can do (see, in particular, his commentaries on Gertrude Stein). (p. 108)

Like many good books, *Omensetter's Luck* is not easy to describe. What one comes away with is the agreeable memory of a flow of language that ranges from demotic Midwest . . . to incantatory. . . . (p. 109)

The stories in *In the Heart of the Heart of the Country* seem to me to be more adventurous and often more successful than the novel. "The Pedersen Kid" is beautiful work. In a curious way the look of those short sentences on pages uncluttered with quotation marks gives the text a visual purity and coldness that perfectly complements the subject of the story, and compels the reader to know the icy winter at the country's heart. In most of these stories the prevailing image is winter. . . . At actual zero degree, Gass, perversely, blazes with energy.

The title story is the most interesting of the collection. Despite a sign or two that the French virus may have struck: "as I write this page, it is eleven days since I have seen the sun," the whole of the story (told in fragments) is a satisfying description of the world the narrator finds himself in, and he makes art of the quotidian. . . . (p. 110)

Gass's problem as an artist is not so much his inability to come up with some brand-new Henry Ford-type invention that will prove to be a breakthrough in world fiction (this is never going to happen) as what he calls his weak point—a lack of dramatic gift—which is nothing more than low or rather intermittent energy. He can write a dozen passages in which the words pile up without effect. Then, suddenly, the current, as it were, turns on again and the text comes to beautiful life (in a manner of speaking of course . . . who does not like a living novel? particularly one that is literate). (pp. 110-11)

> *Gore Vidal, in* The New York Review of Books *(reprinted with permission from* The New York Review of Books; *copyright © 1974 Nyrev, Inc.), July 15, 1974 (and reprinted in his* Matters of Fact and of Fiction: Essays 1973-1976, *Random House, 1977).*

JEFFREY MAITLAND

In [*On Being Blue*] poetics and philosophy pull apart, emerge from, and re-enter each other in eros—primordial blueness. Poetry at its best, at its bluest, does not paint images of sexual acts, but with reverential attentiveness to the being of language, makes language present as lovers make themselves present to each other. Philosophical thinking at its best, blue reason, attains concepts in the same way. The erotic logos of lived-through-thought reaches its conclusions and insights not through the constipated step-by-step-premise-to-conclusion-thinking represented by academic philosophy but with the multifaceted and multi-directional vitality of life lived to its fullest.

Blue is not simply a word or symbol that designates the color blue or some interior mental state; it is a mode of being in and of that which is. It is a mode of being around which Gass hopes "to wind my Quink-stained mouth" thereby aiming at making flesh word. The site of *On Being Blue* is primordial blueness. *On Being Blue* is at once the poetic performance and display of the very site into which it inquires philosophically. To be read at all, this book calls for our return to its site, that we become blue readers. This return provides for reaching deeper than a sexual response to sexual imagery and for a thinking that doesn't lose but yet goes further than a mere philosophical critique of a theory of color. *On Being Blue* asks us to yield ourselves in loving attentiveness to the being of language, poetic word, and concept, as it unfolds and speaks through us. As blue readers, we participate in the very performance of that which this work seeks to articulate.

The attempt to perform primordial blueness is the attempt to touch and be touched, not merely by sexuality, but by eros. *On Being Blue* is a witty, brilliant, and finely wrought work which ought to be read by all lovers of language. And yet for all its cleverness, beauty, and brilliance, it forgets to touch the heart. (pp. 709-10)

> *Jeffrey Maitland, in* Modern Fiction Studies *(© copyright 1977, by Purdue Research Foundation, West Lafayette, Indiana), Winter, 1977-78.*

PAUL WEST

[Gass's] brow is high, his taste learned and eclectic; his responses to books and their authors are both delicate and earthy, and sometimes orchestrated in their own right as complex fugues of unapologetic, wry inventiveness. This professor of philosophy and novelist (*Omensetter's Luck*) is as far from your run-of-the-mill reviewer as Cockaigne from Kalamazoo. . . .

Who . . . is Gass? And what? The Phantom of the Opus? The Satrap of Succulence? He is the poetic essayist doubling as critic, but also, through some agile feats of mnemonic possession, being Proust, Valery, Colette, Malcolm Lowry and Gertrude Stein (as all of whom he is superb), and Freud, Sartre, Henry Miller and Faulkner (as all of whom he is very good). As if hypnotized. As if ravished. As if, thanks to a book-review editor who gives him lots of space, driven to disgorge an ectoplasm that, while being superprose, is also one form of interference with the soul, the belly, the very chemicals that transmit thought. Uncanny stuff, out of Walter Pater by American Gothic, his essays are a series of autos-da-fe staged in the central nervous systems of the writers he likes, He tells how it feels to be Proust, and the others, and how it feels to be them in the act of being creative. If a tag be needed, [*The World within the Word*] is biotic criticism. . . .

Every essay he writes has a tonic undertow of backsides and blatant vulgarities, not to titillate or be raw but to evince the All—the flux, the heterogeneous plenty—in which, for Gass and others like him, all elements are equal, grist for the stylist's mill. As in this bristling collage from a lecture-essay, "The Ontology of the Sentence, or How to Make a World of Words," in which Gass the professional philosopher and analyst of language gets Gass the verbal Daedalus to do his stuff. . . .

He reaches a point of voluptuous crisis, at which there is nothing that doesn't belong in the next sentence. No categories prevail except that of what gets into his words and what does not. And this isn't "mere" panache, impasto, purple patch, it's *vision*, fleshed out with jackdaws, snowmen, cascara ("a purge with a name like a river"), his own mother's "miscolored toes," and such a recognition as "There is no o'clock in a cantina." His world *is* words, *his* way of being. No wonder he likes images of hurdlers, waterskiers, and that of Cyrano led by the nose. Gass sings the flux, under this or that commercial pretext, and in the end renders what he calls "the interplay of genres . . . skids of tone and decorum" into cantatas of appreciative excess. A rare gift that yields startling art.

> Paul West, "Wizard of Words," in Book World— The Washington Post (© The Washington Post), July 9, 1978, p. E8.

DENIS DONOGHUE

In "Fiction and the Figures of Life" Mr. Gass said that "the esthetic aim of any fiction is the creation of a verbal world, or a significant part of such a world, alive through every order of its Being." The only difference I can find between this and the argument of "The World Within the Word" is that the autonomy of that world within the word is declared more insistently than before. . . .

If you say that a poem is a world, or makes a world, you merely ascribe to the poet the powers of God or the ambition of Absolute Idealism. There is little harm in talking about a poem as a well-wrought urn, because you're not claiming that the whole world has been consigned to the urn, without remainder. . . .

My only quarrel with Mr. Gass is that he hasn't really examined the problems raised by referring to the world within the word. If he wanted to go the whole way, into Pure Poetry or even Absolute Fiction, that would be fine, though impossible in practice. It would be clear, charming, touching, especially when its program would find itself refuted by Language itself. But he doesn't want to go the whole way, he still wants to cry "Purity and Purification" while enjoying the fleshpots.

He speaks of "creating and defending a connection between what William James called the buzzing, blooming confusion of normal consciousness—of daily life with its unstimulating bumps, its ceaseless, enervating grinds—and the clear and orderly silences of mathematics," and says that this is what our science, art, law, love and magic "are principally about." But his theory makes it impossible for him to show how the buzz and the silence could be connected. (p. 7)

I don't think his theory of fiction, strictly considered, amounts to much. Nothing is solved by saying that in a novel the word "revolver" never killed anyone, or that "in the story of Mary, if Mary dies, the novelist killed her, her broken heart did not." Yes, yes, we know that, Mr. Gass, but keep going, now tackle all the problems raised by your Mary, Mary.

Still, I have at least two good reasons for rejoicing in Mr. Gass's book. One: It is by Mr. Gass, and, like his fiction— "Omensetter's Luck," "In the Heart of the Heart of the Country," etc.—it is written with verve and a high spirit. Two: It raises by its practice a possibility raised in theory by Roland Barthes in "The Pleasure of the Text," that knowledge itself may be *delicious*. . . . Mr. Gass will not

thank me for suggesting that his book is best read as a sensuous experience, but the fact is (embarrassing to a sobersides like me) that his sentences, true or false, are pleasures. Reading them, I find myself caring about their truth or error to begin with, but ending up not caring as much as I suppose I ought, and taking them like delicacies of the palate. (pp. 7, 39)

I don't believe that the things which constitute life are as transparent or as easily spiritualized as Mr. Gass's theory says they are. I am of Walter Benjamin's party in this argument, especially when he said that "consciousness, and more particularly 'pure' consciousness, is the illusory synthesis in which the genuine synthesis, that of life, is imitated." But when Mr. Gass's cry is provoked by a particular writer (Lowry, Sartre, whom he doesn't care for, Colette, for whom he is all care), I listen. (p. 39)

> Denis Donoghue, "Counterstatements," in The New York Times Book Review (© 1978 by The New York Times Company; reprinted by permission), July 9, 1978, pp. 7, 39.

ROSS FELD

[Employing in *The World Within the Word*] a prose style equivalent to the Slinky toy, Gass lands always on this: that writers have only language, language has them—and though the domestic relation may at times chafe and bite, it remains irrefutably monogamous. To slight the sentence— launched with a capital letter, tied off at the end with a period's pip—is to commit a basic error. Sentences make reality, not vice versa. . . .

As readers, we're conned, is Gass's basic and delighted message; and the illusion, the misunderstanding, is the very crux of the game. . . .

Gass has remarkable metamorphic talents when dealing with a writer he likes—Malcolm Lowry, Colette, Valéry: he seems to wrap his own very much alive grip around their ghostly pencils—but no one more engages his brilliance, and to greater effect, than Stein. Succumbing happily to her famous opacity—"intricacy no objection, patience a demand, unreadable plans a pleasure"—Gass proceeds, inch by inch, to lift Miss Stein's formidable skirts, then with scrupulous care reset them exactly. And what's revealed is not only the subtle racket her thing-language makes—the sharp breaks, caroms, and kisses—but also a very convincing thesis: that out of her hard-shelled and formally beautiful paragraphs emerges a courageous and absolutely sexual story—lesbian self-sufficiency objectified into art. Stein didn't merely provide aliases for the love that dare not speak its name: she *condensed* it in language, where it was safe from clarity while secure in candor. Gass's detective work is splendid, his analysis keen, his attention breathtaking; at these temperatures, literary criticism turns into gold. (p. 90)

> Ross Feld, in Harper's (copyright © 1978 by Ross Feld; all rights reserved; excerpted from the October, 1978 issue by special permission), October, 1978.

*　　*　　*

GHELDERODE, Michel de   1898-1962

A Flemish dramatist, poet, short story writer, and essayist, Ghelderode was born Ademar Martens, but legally changed his name in 1929. His characters live in a world that is gro-

tesque and fantastic—the world of Peter Breughel and Hieronymous Bosch. They portray themes drawn from history and from the Bible, but shrouded in death, evil, and decay. He has created works to be performed by marionettes, and often gives puppet-like qualities to his human characters. Ghelderode's work shows the influence of Poe, with whom he shares a love of the mystical. His masterful command of language evokes a supernatural atmosphere that is reinforced by striking visual and aural effects. (See also *CLC*, Vol. 6.)

JACQUES GUICHARNAUD with JUNE GUICHARNAUD

The surface characteristics of Ghelderode's universe are dazzling. In many of his plays masqueraders, grotesque figures, living corpses, gluttonous and lustful men and women frantically move about in a decor of purple shadows, full of strong smells, and throw violent, foul, or mysterious phrases at each other in highly colored language filled with Belgian idioms, archaisms, and shrieks. Even in the plays where the language is closest to modern French, the dialogue and long speeches are profuse and frenetic. There is no rest in Ghelderode's theatre; the shock is permanent. Everything is pushed toward a paroxysm of language and spectacle—a flamboyant theatre, based on Flemish culture, its legends, its humor, its puppets, and its painters, from Brueghel the elder to James Ensor. But in overstressing Ghelderode's Flemish background, so obvious in itself, one is in danger of losing sight of his works' deeper value and of seeing them only as an overwhelming display of folklore. A joyful or macabre kermis, his theatre uses the village fair, the mountebank's stage, overcrowded cabarets, and the swarming streets of the red-light districts as an image of man's condition. Thus the picturesque quality of this tumultuous world becomes more than just a curiosity: rather than set up a barrier of exoticism, it heightens the colors of man's everyday world.

Ghelderode was aware of the reciprocal relations between life and the masquerade of carnival. . . . Often a character and his theatrical image are opposed or juxtaposed. . . . Although these effects, midway between Pirandello's and Genet's, may sometimes be somewhat oversimple or, on the contrary, rather obscure, they do help to make Ghelderode's works a kind of theatre of theatre. Using clowns, mimes, jesters, and masqueraders, Ghelderode opposes more charitable images of Creation with his vision of life as a parody of Creation, as a painful Farce. (pp. 165-66)

One substance of this enormous Farce is felt in all its frankness and weight—the flesh. It may sometimes have its charms, as in *Hop Signor!*, with the executioner Larose, the "handsome blond athlete" who chews roses. But usually it is deformed, obscene, stinking, and always demanding. Brought into play by every possible means, it nails the characters to earth. Even in suffering it is the object of baroque acceptance, not of negative distress, as in Beckett's theatre.

More generally, Ghelderode's theatre is made up of matter, a stuff that is forced on all the senses. Flesh, crimson velvet, gold, and excrement are an essential part of both the spectacle and the language. Ghelderode's poetry consists in constantly harking back to that bath of matter. Lavishly handled, it leads to nothing other than itself and to the appetites of which it is the object: avarice, gluttony, or sexual desire. Constantly present to all the senses, matter is the stuff of the characters' actions and excitement.

Ghelderode used the device of baroque amplification to create a burlesque of man's condition. Most of his characters are kept in a state of indignity by the weight of their bodies, their physical deformations, their sensual relations with other matter. Any objects that would ordinarily be accepted as signs of grandeur are shown in decay or given monstrous forms. . . . (pp. 166-67)

All this would be no more than a savage masquerade and pure farce, colored by a theatrical awareness of life, if every play did not have a more or less explicit higher appeal. (p. 167)

The actual evidence of the flesh is what gives rise to the mystery of death. And the very fact of inevitable death . . . gives Ghelderode's theatre its tragic aspect. On the whole, the plays are constructed according to two different patterns: either they are similar to certain types of baroque and classical comedies of intrigue, although the artificial happy endings of traditional comedy are replaced by a necessary death—a negation of the life of the flesh and the senses, of indeed the very motivation of the plot (*Hop Signor!, Magie rouge*)—or both levels are constantly juxtaposed, so that an awareness of their permanent relationship creates the play's tension (*La Ballade du Grand Macabre, Mademoiselle Jaïre, Fastes d'enfer*). Fundamentally an annihilator of the characters' universe of intrigue and sensual pleasure, death is also the bearer of meanings that give tragedy its transcendency and always more or less transform the play into a mystery. (pp. 167-68)

Since the conflict is, above all, one between death and the flesh, it is only natural that Ghelderode often allude to the mystery that best expresses it: the raising of Lazarus. It is also natural that within that mystery he choose and develop the theme of *jam putet* in all its horror. . . . Ghelderode's force lies precisely in the skillful mixture of the greatest horror and the most knockabout farce. . . . Neither element can exist without the other; each issues from the other. When the farce is not vigorous enough, as in *Sire Halewyn*, the play is reduced to a pompous Romantic-symbolist melodrama; for the mystery of death is so grandiose that it must be enveloped in rites, in ceremonies, which of themselves turn to buffoonery.

Ghelderode's theatre indicates a way toward the realization of a primordial drama in which tragic horror and the frankest guffaws are indissolubly mixed. His use of local tradition carried to its extreme possibilities is not far removed from the method of the Elizabethans and the Spanish dramatists. He touches on the primitive joys of the body, its appetites and their satisfaction, which are inseparable from the ambiguous fear of individual or collective death. Antiphilosophical and even anti-intellectual, his works are the long and instinctive cry of a soul in misery, imprisoned in matter that is both sumptuous and rotting. (pp. 168-69)

> *Jacques Guicharnaud with June Guicharnaud, in their* Modern French Theatre *(copyright © 1967 by Yale University), Yale University Press, 1967.*

PAUL M. LEVITT

The two principal reasons for Ghelderode's attraction to puppet theatre are his dissatisfaction with living actors and his inclination toward caricature. (p. 973)

A devout Pauline Catholic, Ghelderode sees man as the puppet and God as the puppet master. By employing the world-as-stage metaphor, Ghelderode is able vividly and dramatically to place man in the religious scheme of things: namely, at the end of a string drawn by the hand of God. In the diction of puppetry, Ghelderode finds a vehicle to describe his own search for God and for personal meaning. . . .

However, there is a more practical reason for Ghelderode to promote the use of puppets in place of actors: marionette theatre offers an inexpensive forum for young or unproven playwrights. . . . Marionette theatre provides a means of breaking away from stale dramatic conventions and of encouraging improvisation. (p. 974)

Like Pirandello, Ghelderode believes that flesh and blood actors, popular opinion to the contrary, are the ones who destroy a playwright's creation through their inept, stumbling attempts to recreate the dramatist's conception of his characters. The problem is that the actors' own personalities, gestures, faces, voices, and histories are glaring reminders to the audience that what they are seeing is not an embodiment of the playwright's character, but only an imperfect look-alike, a feeble attempt by a man to be someone he is not. Ghelderode treats this problem of the actor's inherent duality of character in *Trois Acteurs, un drame*. In this play three actors virtually destroy a play in which they are acting because they cannot prevent their own personal complications from becoming inextricably involved with their acting. (pp. 974-75)

Ghelderode's characters are never "human" in the modern sense of psychological realism. . . . His characters are reminiscent of those found in Medieval *mystère* plays. He sees man, according to Leonard Pronko, "in Manichaean terms of dark and light, good and evil, flesh and spirit." . . . Is it any wonder, then, that his characters are anti-realistic, stylized figures, fashioned, as it were, out of wood? . . . Ghelderode has been criticized for failing to differentiate character by means of dialogue. He gives, as Auréliu Weiss remarks, "the same language to all his characters. Whatever their education or social class, they all express themselves in the same stylized language." The practical result of creating one dimensional characters who speak alike is that virtually any play of Ghelderode's may be performed by marionettes. (p. 975)

Ghelderode also admires marionettes because they are *made* for their roles from non-living material, which gives them a magical quality. A marionette's very *raison d'être* is the play and in an important sense the marionette *is* the character and no one else. There can never be a problem of duality; once the play is over so is the marionette's life. . . .

A logical retort to this argument might be that a marionette is, after all, controlled physically and vocally by an imperfect human being. But Ghelderode responds that the person pulling the strings is of minimal or no importance to the people in the audience as they perceive the play. The people see the marionette; they never stop to ask who is pulling the strings and is doing the speaking. The dramatic illusion is complete. (p. 976)

Traditionally, marionettes—and this is also true of Ghelderode's characters—are caricatures of human beings, not replicas. Their faces are painted and carved into one relentless expression. They represent essentially one unchanged aspect of human personality. (pp. 976-77)

Ghelderode's dramatic world [is one] of archetypes, monsters, and personified sins. In all of Ghelderode's plays, whether written specifically for marionettes or not, his characters are grotesquely exaggerated to represent, both physically and mentally, single aspects of human nature. . . .

[*Pantagleize*, a Ghelderode play] with marionette-like characters, cannot be fully appreciated unless the hero, Pantagleize, is perceived as a dangling, jerky puppet. Oblivious to the revolution going on around him, Pantagleize is concerned only with telling everyone what a lovely day it is. Thus, the most convincing productions present him as Chaplinesque: happily bouncing around on the ends of strings, with a simple and innocent expression fixed on his face. (p. 977)

The severity of Ghelderode's caricatures forces one to realize how close his characters are to puppets—and to clichés. (p. 978)

> Paul M. Levitt, "Ghelderode and Puppet Theater," in The French Review (copyright 1975 by the American Association of Teachers of French), May, 1975, pp. 973-80.

* * *

GINZBURG, Natalia 1916-

Ginzburg is an Italian novelist, short story writer, essayist, dramatist, and translator. In work that is characterized by simple vocabulary and unadorned prose style, Ginzburg creates powerful and deeply moving fiction, deceptive in its simplicity and subtlety. (See also *CLC*, Vol. 5.)

DONALD HEINEY

Because of her immature urge to be a Russian or some kind of foreign writer, [Natalia Ginzburg's] early work is curiously abstract; the setting is placeless and timeless and the characters have no surnames. As it develops her fiction becomes gradually more specific and personal and the same time less fictitious; she moves from imitations of Chekhov to a fiction that is indistinguishable from autobiography. Yet from the beginning all her narrative is recounted by the same voice. The voice is feminine and fundamentally that of the author, even though it is attributed in the early fiction to narrators very different from Natalia Ginzburg and simultaneously expressive of these characters. The voice plays over and defines the surface of the narrative, and breaking through to this surface, interwoven with it, are the voices of other characters who are soon perceived as recurring from one story to the next, in a kind of modal counterpoint. Almost without exception her writing is about families. There is a recurrent note of ending; families are fragile things, dispersed by war and deteriorating of their own accord through death, through marriage, through the desire of the children for freedom. . . . She is particularly a specialist on relations between parents and children, on the affections that hold them together and are at the same time balanced by the antagonisms and struggles that hold them apart, and on the complicated, ambivalent, quasi-sexual and yet chaste relations between brother and sister. In her narrative the family is neither a happy nor an unhappy institution. It simply is, and the people in it are sometimes happy and sometimes unhappy. When the narrating voice is happy it is frequently humorous, and when it is unhappy it regards the situation with irony. In place of Italian lamenting or Jewish lamenting there is a kind of French and existentialist pessimism of acceptance. (pp. 87-8)

[A] perky and slightly rebellious stoicism is the ethical thread of all of Natalia Ginzburg's work.... The tribal toughness is assertive and cranky in the male, resilient, intuitive, and conceding in the female. The family is presented totally without sentimentalism. Like a pride of lions they are held together by powerful biological forces, yet each is wary and self-contained, skeptical of the others, ironic of the father's claim to dominance but conceding to power after the first ritual scratches. The family forms through marriage and birth, consolidates, then gradually disintegrates. Commonly the narrator is a semi-spectator in this process; particularly in *Valentino, Sagittario,* and *Lessico familiare* she takes only a peripheral part in the drama and her primary function is to record the voices of others. Natalia Ginzburg only reluctantly writes about herself, even in the book that purports to be a kind of autobiography.... Ginzburg has no pretensions to ... [Flaubertian] objectivity; with a quite cheerful humility she confines herself to the small scale of her own knowledge and observation. She is a kind of compassionate tape-recorder, and one that filters language so as to allow only a subtly chosen pattern of assonances to arrive at the ear of the listener.

The voices of the family resemble each other and yet are distinctive. (pp. 88-9)

È Stato cosí, an early short novel, begins with a pistol-shot in the manner of Simenon. Natalia Ginzburg gropes for a manner and tentatively takes up the *roman-policier,* but soon falls into the voice that threads its way through her work from its earliest stories.... Her work is full of ... insignificant details that are [significant because they contribute to the mood]. The story-telling consciousness is easily distracted; when its eye falls on something of a curious shape, or even the most ordinary of objects, it often loses the thread or seems to. (p. 90)

The naivete of the story-telling voice in [*È stato cosí*] and in *La strada che va in città,* dating from 1946-47 and 1941 respectively, develops into a kind of sibylline and oblique simplicity in *Tutti i nostri ieri* (1952) and *Lessico familiare* (1963), without losing either its freshness of diction or its fundamental innocence. One of the more intricate aspects of her work is the relation of this voice to the sub-voices of the secondary characters.... At other times and particularly in *Le voci della sera* (1961) a kind of *dixit* device is used, borrowed with a perceptible suggestion of tongue-in-cheek from the epic. Characteristic remarks, made not at any particular time but simply typical of the character and embedded in the family consciousness, are presented in a kind of litany punctuated with *dice* [he says] or *diceva* [she says].... (pp. 90-1)

A somewhat more intricate dialogue form is a kind of *erlebte Rede* in which the primary narrating voice, while retaining its own timbre and its particular irony towards events and characters, descends to assume at least partially the rhythm and speech-pattern of the character whose remarks are reported.... The whole narrative oeuvre of Natalia Ginzburg, seemingly so rich in character, actually resides in the consciousness of [a] single narrator, the possessor not only of a keen auditory memory but of an extraordinary and flexible talent for mimicry.

The *dixit* device is not the only Homeric borrowing in Natalia Ginzburg. There is a suggestion of the epic manner as well in [the] way of dipping downward into the voice of a character and then rising again to regard the flow of narrative with detachment.... The world of her body of narrative is a feminine world. It is a world in which tea-pots and the making of babies are important but politics, business, and war are not; or, more precisely, in which politics, business, and war are recognized as affecting the destinies of all, but not susceptible of feminine control, and therefore viewed with a combination of indifference and irony that rescues the narrating ego from total impotence. To be ironic about a power over one's destiny is no longer to be totally in the control of that power. The narrating consciousness takes refuge in a world of trivia, but the trivia are in some way elevated to the archetypal. Furniture, family quarrels, broken engagements, bicycles, the way of washing windows: the tiny details, massed together and linking one by one, begin finally to form vague metaphysical shapes. The dominant shape that emerges, subsuming and strengthening the others, is a recognition of the tragic sense of life, a pessimism relieved by good humor.... The obscure force that holds together brother and sister, part jealousy and part affection, a hatred at its roots, is a persistence that transcends politics. (pp. 91-3)

Donald Heiney, "Natalia Ginzburg: The Fabric of Voices," in The Iowa Review *(copyright © 1970, by The University of Iowa), Vol. 1, No. 4 (Fall, 1970), pp. 87-93.*

CLOTILDE SOAVE BOWE

In essay after essay of *Mai devi domandarmi,* we have a celebrated novelist stripping down her own intellect in the characteristic succession of flat, functional sentences which caused Pavese to call her style a 'lagna' and invite the reader to feel superior and at the same time unaccountably ignored.... [Regarding her article on old age], we finish reading a plot dealing with an unfortunate love affair between a grey, unstriking woman and a grey, unsuccessful man, and the book may then remain in our memory as ill-defined and unsatisfying because it has depicted the twilight world of fractured relationships and unheroic encounters only too exactly: it has borrowed the language and atmosphere of the effect which it aimed to produce. Ginzburg sets out, like Flaubert in *Madame Bovary,* to reproduce the colour grey and will always run the risk of being accounted a failure because she succeeds in depicting greyness absolutely. (pp. 788-89)

There is an initial soporific effect in all Ginzburg's fiction: its delimitation of the fictional territory to the family. The plots of her main novels and stories all involve one or more family units into which the reverberations of political and historical events in the exterior world are filtered through by *reportage* of its members as they return centripetally from outside. The reader is thus at once presented with a context that is familiar and undisturbing. No surprise or alarm is elicited by the fictional setting; what is required from the reader is a genteel curiosity. In order to accentuate this impression of routine reality staged inside the walls of a family domicile, Ginzburg adopts the strategy of inserting a first-person narrator into the household so that every event in the novel is related from the limited emotional viewpoint and intellectual involvement of the particular family member conducting the story. The narrator who is providing this *io interno* is not necessarily the most impressive or attractive member of the household, so that the spectator-reader often faces an entirely plausible but defective or even neurotic interpretation of the events which he is witnessing. This further contributes to the illusion that it is the author herself who is expressing a limited and partial view of the world. . . .

Already [in her second published story, *Casa al mare*], the writer is uncompromisingly entangled in the emotional stance of the protagonist who has the internal vantage point on events and is simultaneously but not retrospectively conducting the narrative. In Ginzburg's next story, *Mio marito* (1941), the first-person narrative is shifted for the first time to a female figure emotionally involved in the events described, and this, with one or two exceptions, will remain Ginzburg's standard procedure in the remainder of her published work, except, of course, the plays. The canonical subject matter with its disintegrating marriages, infidelity by one or both partners and concluding suicide is also established by *Mio marito*, and developed along set lines which will recur with varying degrees of expansion and ornamentation in Ginzburg's subsequent novels. (p. 789)

[In the preface to *Cinque romanzi brevi*] Ginzburg declares that she had such a horror of surnames that she could never use them fluently until her last novel *Le voci della sera*, but it is also noticeable that a character's Christian name is usually held back until it is necessary as a device for labelling the speaker or distinguishing between the four or five children in a family who form Ginzburg's average narrative cast. Her characters' names are never fully integrated emotional components of their personality; they are functional tickets for recognition. . . . In fact, as one moves on to Ginzburg's longer fiction, one can see that there is no qualitative difference between short story and novel as such. The novels seem to differ from the short stories, which have a standard cast of three characters, merely by being longer and expanding this cast to between twelve and twenty, each involved in their own variation on [her recurrent themes of] unhappy love . . . or disintegrating marriage. . . . [With her first novel] there was a general impression that the writer had already produced a definitive style: precise, compact and moving along with a rhythm closely matching daily life. She seemed never to indulge in expressions that were superfluous to the plot. (pp. 790-91)

[Ginzburg's second novel *È stato cosí*] consists of a long monologue which is almost completely bereft of commas (Ginzburg later explained that commas are like steps, and steps cost effort, and she was so depressed at the time of composition that she wanted to eliminate all sense of physical effort). . . . The manner of the novel is lax, off-hand and grey, a formal orchestration of monotony and hopelessness. . . . (p. 791)

[The resolution of the plot of *Valentino*] by a suicide and two parallel domestic arrangements in isolation is the most artificial of Ginzburg's negative statements on life in a closed fictional circuit. All the characters return to a position inferior to the point from which they started out. Each is shifted through an emotional crisis for which he has insufficient strength of will, and the 'greyness' of their final predicament is too explicitly stated. . . . The tone of [the] final tableau . . . is close to a pulp *fotoromanzo*, and indeed it is hard to avoid the impression that the writer has dismissed this particular plot with a somewhat facile conclusion.

Tutti i nostri ieri (. . . 1952), is the longest of Ginzburg's novels. The book has a maturity and fluency which makes it, together with *Lessico famigliare* (. . . 1963), one of the writer's greatest achievements. Its success seems in part a function of its unusual length, which offers the writer scope for a fuller deployment of the intricate inter-relationships of two separately defined family units. The division of the book into two main parts (town/North, country/South) gives it, a much improved structural balance when compared to her previous fiction, where the narrative leaps between urban sophistication and rough countryside can seem sudden and arbitrary. The first part shows the vicissitudes of two quintessentially bourgeois families who live on opposite sides of the same street in an unnamed Northern town. Although for once events are not narrated in the first person, the key character is a younger sister in the less wealthy of the two families, Anna, and the movement of the narrative has the same rhythm as her own adolescent awakening and involvement in the situation which surrounds her. In the early pages of the first part we find a kind of childish filter applied to everyday occurrences, and this distorted perspective by the internal narrator can again be seen as Ginzburg's most sensitive narrative device. . . . Clearly the device places a kind of natural limit on the collective insight which is permissible in a given situation. . . . Yet the girl/woman's privileged view of her elder sister Concettina allows the author to present a masterly refinement of the characteristic female, vain and mediocre, which has so far dominated her fiction without being given a fixative portrait. In relation to Concettina, Anna is in a position to hear half-understood gossip at table or the crying behind a locked bedroom door; she witnesses Concettina's gloom in front of a new dress or a bathroom mirror and the continuous politics of *fidanzamento* as played out by a selfish elder sister. Hence the cumulative picture becomes irresistibly credible. . . . (pp. 792-93)

[Cenzo Rena] is an inspired fictional creation for Ginzburg: here is the character who can swing the novel's setting to the country and the South. . . . In fact, Cenzo Rena is a village intellectual and rich man somewhere in Puglia, takes a positive attitude to social problems, and shows a real understanding of political issues in their context. . . . Thus he provides Ginzburg's fiction with an authentic left-wing *engagé* figure, and his decision to take the blame for a German soldier accidentally killed in his house—tantamount to an act of suicide—rounds off the second part of the novel with a politically motivated sacrifice which is all the more plausible by being the exact counterpart to the depressive suicide that resolves Ginzburg's story line elsewhere.

This is the only novel, in fact, which ends on a positive note, creating a rift in the otherwise uniformly grey curtain which falls over the Ginzburgian family. The style is misleadingly flat and placid for a story ending in violence and war. Ginzburg is not so much banishing horror or macabre tones from her account as naturalizing them to the point where they lose their power to shock or surprise the reader, who is under the general narcotic of the casual juxtaposition of chatty inconsequentiality and family disaster. The elemental moments of birth or death are thus cut down to the status of a visit or a meal or a new hat. . . . Still, in *Tutti nostri ieri*, Ginzburg cannot resist her functional motif of a character's death in isolation. . . . The novel, in fact, is constructed to include the whole range of Ginsburg's recurring motifs: Giuma's seduction of Anna, Anna's marriage to Cenzo Rena, at first one of convenience, later developing into love, Ippolito's suicide, the nanny's lonely death in a *pensione*, and the obsessive preoccupation with holidays, clothes and motor car of a prosperous bourgeoisie. But the strength of *Tutti i nostri ieri* lies both in the working out of Ginzburg's central themes and a sustained combinative interest in the infinite possible permutations of the siblings in two large households. Her attention is focused not on why people do things, but on how they act. New women or girl characters are invariably described by the clothes they wear (colour, fashion, cut, material), and several men in Ginzburg's fiction are presented with a *ciuffo* or *piumacchio* of hair, which in subsequent scenes they straighten or throw back from the forehead. This perfunctory characterization, deliberately close to caricature, throws an unusually large part of the reader's attention on to the transactions of the cast, the old unfashionable plot line. (pp. 793-94)

Sagittario is a short, static study in petit-bourgeois femininity.... The resolution of the story is the same pointless solitude that awaits the main characters in *Valentino*....

[*Le voci della sera*] is a return to the extended family saga of *Tutti i nostri ieri*. (p. 794)

[The plot] seems loose and tenuous, and the strength of the novel lies entirely in the texture of shifting fragments of conversation, sketches of past events, reports, juxtaposed blocks of dialogue which recall the particular timbre of a person's voice or the favourite phrases in their everyday vocabulary....

[The ingredients of *Lessico famigliare*] are those of a *journal intime*, coolly exhibited to the public, unadorned autobiography where there is no narrative re-invention of the well-known figures or historical events which occur in the text. Her previous narrative family settings finally merge into the author's own family when she was a child, and the internal first-person narrator becomes, as seemed increasingly likely, none other than the author herself. But the self-portrait of a clumsy girl with inferiority complexes is partly the projection of a retrospective literary *persona* for herself. It strengthens the image of a writer who with perverse humility wishes to appear shocked and surprised at her own success.

Ginzburg, therefore, passes herself off as a product of chance and culture rather than art. (p. 795)

> Clotilde Soave Bowe, "*The Narrative Strategy of Natalia Ginzburg*," *in* The Modern Language Review (© Modern Humanities Research Association 1973), October, 1973, pp. 788-95.

ISABEL QUIGLY

There is little point in saying what happens to Natalia Ginzburg's characters, so haphazard does it appear. Everything happens, and nothing—or nearly nothing. So it has been in all her writing over the past thirty years, memoirs as well as fiction. The style never varies, nor do the characters; nor does the treatment she gives them (though the social world they move in has changed drastically). Birth and death, love, relationships, separations, the large matters of personal life, are given the same amount of space on the page, the same weight in the telling, as the supposed trifles....

Is she a comic writer? Well, *Lessico famigliare* is one of the most memorably funny books about family life in Italy

or anywhere else. Yet sad, too, her characters ... doomed to an everlasting melancholy that has little to do with circumstances or even, in a sense, with unhappiness; a sort of low-spiritedness, a sense of fatality, a weather of greyness lit by very occasional moments of tender remembrance and longing, as relationships, mostly unsatisfactory, are lit by impulses of warmth, affection and loyalty directed towards the unlikeliest people. Flicked rather than buffeted not so much by fate as by their own limitations, these people centrally set in a shifting society—always bourgeois, always familiar to their creator, who never strays from the world she knows so well—take on an emblematic character; if only as symbols of the inconsistency of their world and its eternal, eternally altering relationships.

Famiglia consists of two novelle, one called "Famiglia", the other "Borghesia" (the two main Ginzburg themes). Both end with the main character's death through illness in hospital, both reflect the changing attitudes in Italy to things like marital breakups and illegitimacy, and both have a roundabout action in which people behave with a sort of consistent unpredictability, an illogicality with no central thread except something like selfhood; not selfishness but a stolid integrity (of sorts) which is hard to classify but brilliantly portrayed. They don't communicate much with one another except in flashes of sympathy, moments of calm and sudden awareness of affection, need, even sweetness. They live from moment to moment, perched precariously on mood.

They are not described very closely, yet the flat phrases used about them take on an extraordinary vividness: an anorak, a hairstyle, a way of walking, why are they memorable, and seemingly familiar? Signora Ginzburg goes beyond social realism, realistic though, in a baffling sort of way, her characters are. They are what Forster envisaged as umbrella-owners, and behind them is the bourgeois certainty of never quite being lost or totally poor....

> Isabel Quigly, "*The Low in Spirit*," *in* The Times Literary Supplement (© Time Newspapers Ltd. (London) 1978; reproduced from The Times Literary Supplement by permission), June 2, 1978, p. 607.

*   *   *

GIONO, Jean   1895-1970

Giono was a French novelist, poet, essayist, playwright, short story writer, editor, and screenwriter. His work centers around the peasant culture of his native Provence, showing the interdependence of man and nature, and the importance of the individual. Strongly influenced by the Greek tragedies, he endeavored to translate into provincial form the complexities of the ancient classics. His early work is characterized by its rich, pastoral lyricism, his later style becoming more psychologically oriented, if slightly less poetic. Three of his novels have become films directed by Marcel Pagnol. (See also CLC, Vol. 4, and *Contemporary Authors*, Vols. 45-48; obituary, Vols. 29-32, rev. ed.)

NORMA L. GOODRICH

[*Le Grand Théâtre*] falls neither into the category of literary criticism, nor into that of prose fiction. Although it purports ostensibly to be a 'conversation' between the boy Jean Giono and his father ..., its first section is largely the latter's monologue.... *Le Grand Théâtre* is both theology and that branch of philosophy termed eschatology [doctrines concerned with finality of the world, life, or matter]. . . . [The second section] serves primarily to illustrate apocalypse in our century. Giono here, then, has not only re-written the most famous of all apocalyptic texts [from the Bible], but has furthermore modified and re-stated it. (pp. 116-17)

As we approach this complicated work—and when has Jean Giono regaled us with simplicity?—it will be less crucial to list the author's recollections of his best-known predecessor than to discuss his variations and his additions to the text attributed to John of Patmos. They are modern additions, which stem largely from two specialized areas: mathematics and astronomy. Giono's artistic method, always distinctive and unpredictable, consists here of a sliding from well-known apocalyptic to his own illustration thereof. It may also be of some interest to note in passing how Giono's approach here differs from that of D. H. Lawrence, for example, since he is a novelist to whom Jean Giono is often compared. . . . (p. 117)

Like *Revelation*, the father, or the author in his stead, to be sure, conjures deftly with numbers, and like the authors of the Bible, he proffers what he terms "grandiose commonplaces," in what we may all agree is unlike Giono's own colorful and highly metaphorical style. Like John of Patmos, Giono's father looks as a matter of course towards cosmic cataclysms, universal catastrophes, all announcing the approaching end of the world. . . .

Once having anchored an unsuspecting reader to familiar imagery, Giono proceeds to re-interpret suavely and calmly to refute several major points of apocalyptic. Soon after having added his own prophecies, he rejects the future prophetic, declaring that the present tense must be rigorously employed since apocalypse is upon us all. . . . The predictions are thus modified to corroborate the end of the world in the sense that the end of our personal worlds is close, is here, is now, ergo that apocalypse is present. The human history which here interests Giono "becomes not merely a series of happenings but the disclosure and consummation of . . . human destiny . . ." Even were the world to end, however, "the end-situation within history" need not be "construed as the ultimately valid end," since the father-prophet does not confuse apocalypse with death. (p. 119)

In short, as evidenced in many illustrations, which it doubtless amused Giono to detail, as it amuses the reader to recognize, we would thoroughly enjoy apocalypse. There is a dearth of pure joy in the universe. . . . We would therefore stay to the last curtain, for apocalypse as previously defined does not necessarily destroy our lives. . . .

What is *Apocalypse*? To Giono's father, who loved the sweet shadows under the centaurs, the golden locusts with lion's teeth, and all such splendors, it is also literature in the line from Vergil to Ariosto's *Orlando Furioso*. What else? With its patent allusions to Rome, it is political writing, its author pouncing upon and utilizing events like foundlings. But most of all, it constitutes a timely warning to beware of super-civilizations which would forbid to man the sovereign remedy for all holocausts: death itself,—that final triumph, as Giono would characteristically believe.

In addition to these refutations of *Revelation*, Giono's modern apocalyptic contains two blocks of material . . . relating to astronomy [and] . . . mathematical thinking. (p. 120)

Giono introduces new material, which marks his apocalypse as being of the twentieth century, while by its use he repudiates science, as he did in *Le Hussard sur le toit*, preferring poetry or art on whose grounds he himself is probably to be preferred.

His own terrain, where he commands our instant respect . . . is human nature, which he can reliably observe and from whose case he can posit conclusions later generalized to apply to all humanity, then to our planet, and finally to the universe. Very wisely the novelist finds apocalypse verifiable in one person whom he takes . . . for his illustration. (pp. 121-22)

The reader is introduced to him via the father's discursions upon apocalyptic, but the method used, or the author's technique in this parallel material, which serves as concrete illustration of apocalypse, contains the chief interest of the piece. . . . The reader is introduced to Oncle Eugène . . . who is becoming blind [and deaf in his old age]. . . . This feeble and unintelligent septuagenarian is himself a world, a universe even, in whom apocalypse unfolds; he typifies the only verifiable illustration *within our grasp* of man succumbing to a series of awful calamities. . . . There is much apocalypse in this old man's frail body.

Apocalypse is apprehended, not intellectually, but by our senses. . . . (p. 122)

The abyss of ten thousand years is the past into which all present plunges, then, faster than the speed of light. In this abyss of space Uncle Eugène floats with thousands of years to go, perhaps, before touching bottom, on his way towards a new universe, of which there are thousands. When we contemplate the heavens, we also gaze into this abyss in the description of which all our numbers are inadequate. Uncle Eugène arrives at the end of a world, which has perhaps also ended. (p. 123)

The Giono text is itself a work of art and an apocalypse, rather than a criticism thereof, as in the case of D. H. Lawrence. Giono proceeds throughout more subtly even where he may agree with Lawrence; while the latter had demonstrated by argument that apocalyptic thinking represents a popular or mass reaction, Giono allows his father, a man of the poor, to speak the text. While Lawrence brilliantly analyzes the symbolism of the text, Giono-the-apocalypticist points out a philosophical error inconsistent with his knowledge of man: that apocalypse excludes death. Where Lawrence feels a grudging admiration mixed with contempt and scorn for John's *Apocalypse*, and while he concentrates upon the mythological interpretations of the text, Giono goes behind the text to put himself in the author's place and thus, allying himself with John of Patmos. . . . [While] Lawrence treats various aspects of *Revelation* in chapters, Giono re-constructs the whole, making it apply to our own times. Lawrence is interested in *Revelation* as a past fact; Giono is interested in it as a present, living entity, a power still in the world.

Jean Giono's apocalypse text, *Le Grand Théâtre*, is, like all his writings, anthropocentric. Man, he says, is here on earth like a spectator in a vast theatre, a privileged viewer before whom and to whom revelations occur. . . . Dangers to man . . . threaten him only because of his past, asserts Jean Giono, diverted from diurnal fiction for the nonce to become an apophatic theologian as he re-composed a Book of the Bible. (pp. 124-25)

Norma L. Goodrich, "Jean Giono's New Apocalypse Text: 'Le Grand Théâtre'" (1964), in The French Review (copyright 1970 by the American Association of Teachers of French), Winter, 1970, pp. 116-25.

FELIX RYSTEN

While Giono [in *Naissance de l'Odyssée*] tells what "really" happened in legendary Ithaca, he cajoles the reader into a suspension of disbelief, a tongue-in-cheek reminder of the ancient epic, which creates the comic element in this modern companion piece to the *Odyssey*. (p. 378)

In this world of deception all existence runs its course free of convenient aid from Olympus. Ulysses must struggle for himself and with himself in a universe devoid of conventional godheads, be they anthropomorphic or transcendent. Giono has preferred to create a world where the presence of the supernatural is manifested in all creation, rather than in a traditional being or man-chosen object. (p. 379)

It hardly need be reiterated that in Homer's account Ulysses often comes to the fore as a schemer, the power of which is only matched by his physical prowess.... The *leitmotiv* of Giono's narrative finds its origin in [Athena's observation that she and Ulysses "are both adept at Chicane"], while it is also at this point in the *Odyssey*—Ulysses having returned to Ithaca—that Giono begins the novel proper. (p. 380)

As Homer tells us, there was disharmony upon Olympus which prevented Ulysses from reaching his home in blessed safety. As a parallel, Part I of Giono's novel ends on a note of doubt and fear. Walking along, Ulysses senses an "inquiétude" walking alongside him as a reminder that he has deliberately distorted the truth.... A fabulous hero has thus been born in the stories of a man who furtively tries to hide his identity.... (p. 381)

Nearing its conclusion, *Naissance de l'Odyssée* moves back to its beginning. Giono skillfully suggests with the last word of the novel the one that began it, *aplati*. The hero glimpses behind the dense foliage that protects the pond his angry and spiteful son. Telemachus, with wet hair matted like a helmet, is—so ends the final sentence—sharpening "un épieu en bois de platane."... With the word *platane* Giono has recalled *aplati,* and in so doing has once more "flattened" his hero. Although the menacing intrusion upon an idyllic scene of a grown child at play is unexpected, it may convey Giono's view that the perpetual bliss of an enchanted world can too readily be destroyed by hate and resentment. However, in order to provide a point of stability for Ulysses, Giono has created a Penelope so affectionately that it is difficult to miss his preference for the woman of the narrative.

In the *Odyssey* it is said of Penelope that she has an excellent brain and a genius for getting her way.... It is this combination of qualities, together with a casual negligence, which Giono has selected to portray an idle, but not unsympathetic woman. For Homer she bore a resemblance to the spider-that-was-Arachne, endlessly weaving and thus repeating the truth of death; for Giono she is a latter-day Ariadne who provides more than one thread in the maze of her husband's doubts to lead him astray in his search for the monster of *inquiétude*. (pp. 382-83)

In a real sense it can ... be said of Ulysses that he has

become the healer of minds grown apart from nature, a healer of the spirit in man dulled with labor and monotony. His success has depended, as Giono implies, upon the mythological enlargement of his human personality which has never lost touch with the natural world of the senses. With enchanted disrespect Giono has spoofed a hallowed epic without turning his vagabond hero into a subject of ridicule. The mockery never obscures Giono's love for his principal character who set out to seize the world and who, in intense cosmic communion, gathered each day for better or for worse. With imagination victorious, but never so triumphant that the reality of the natural sense impression is shut out, Giono concludes with Ulysses that the secret of their happiness lies in communion with sand and water, with flower and tree, with the land which partakes of the Woman, with the earth which has become Penelope.... She has the russet color of the pond, Ulysses' microcosmic world which, in ultimate transfiguration, is about to become the perilous sea that brought him home to Ithaca. (pp. 386-87)

Felix Rysten, "Jean Giono's 'Naissance de l'Odyssée'," in The French Review (copyright 1971 by the American Association of Teachers of French), December, 1971, pp. 378-87.

MALCOLM SCOTT

Throughout the period from the publication of *Colline* in 1929 to that of *L'Eau vive* in 1943, there are constant references in Giono's writings to the power of language and its role in the world. Often these references develop into a major theme within particular works; even where they do not, they still help to form a *leitmotiv* that recurs persistently during some fifteen years of Giono's career, and which throws light in a hitherto unexplained way on his view of the role and significance of language....

[Giono's] fascination with speech is manifested, throughout the 'peasant' writings, by a constant stress on the physical utterance of words, even on the workings of the speech-organs themselves. In *L'Eau vive,* Giono recruits one of his favourite images—the snake—to describe the writhing of the tongue in the darkness of the mouth.... (p. 289)

This stress on the spoken word can be seen as appropriate to the settings and characters of Giono's pre-war writings. If he wanted to write of language at all, then, in these novels of peasant life, it had to be of the spoken tongue and not of the written language.... Yet this in itself clearly does not account for the emphasis laid on speech. For one thing, Giono's first fictional work, *Naissance de l'Odyssée*, written before he embarked on the *cycle paysan*, although published later than the early books of that series, already shows the same fixation. Giono retells the Ulysses myth in such a way as to bring his obsession with speech into the forefront of the action. His Ulysses is no longer Homer's conquering hero, but rather 'courageux par les seuls exploits de la langue' [courageous through the lone exploits of language] ..., compensating for his frustrated and neurotic character by creating in speech an image of himself that men will admire.... It is, in fact, difficult to read for more than five or six pages without encountering some reference to the force of speech. Giono's insistence on the theme causes him to flood his first book with countless allusions to it, indiscriminately perhaps, until the impact is lost. It is not until the opening novels of the *cycle paysan* that we see him controlling his material fully, assigning a definite structural role to the theme of spoken language and gaining increased effect by doing so.

In *Colline,* extraordinary verbal powers are the property of only one character, Janet, and are brought into relief by the paucity of speech of the other inhabitants of the village. Janet's earthy eloquence and metaphor-packed delirium is crucial to his role in the novel. He is the first of a string of characters in Giono's fiction who enjoy, or are thought by other characters to enjoy, a special insight into Nature. . . . [Janet's] malice is in accordance with Giono's intention in *Colline,* namely to present the harsh and vindictive side of Nature rather than the benevolently smiling face of Mother Earth seen in many of the later books; Janet, as Nature's suspected accomplice, must thus use his knowledge against Man. In this, his weapon, and also the symbol of his malice, is his tongue. (pp. 290-91)

Just as Janet misuses his knowledge, so too does he misuse, in a sense, his power of speech. Very few of Giono's characters are guilty of this; and when they are, it is usually to achieve a contrast with the good effects of the speech of other, more important characters. This is seen in the second novel of the Pan Trilogy, *Un de Baumugnes.* Here, Louis misuses his glib tongue to seduce Angèle . . . , while the life-denying gloom of the inhabitants of La Douloire is expressed in their non-speaking. . . .

Contrasted to this is the marvellous rustic eloquence of the narrator Amédée, and also the semi-magical appeal of the voice of Albin. . . . [The] final comparison of Albin's voice to the voice of Nature is obviously the highest compliment that the Nature-worshipping Giono can pay to its beauty. But the comparison has a further and more vital function. It serves to integrate the theme of speech with another of Giono's obsessively repeated themes: that of *le mélange,* in which the diverse elements of creation, animate and inanimate, human and non-human, take their place on an equal footing. Albin's echoing of the sounds of Nature in his voice symbolizes his assumption of his rightful place within *le mélange,* unlike the proud peasants of *Colline* who bring disaster down on themselves by wishing to remain outside and above the non-human world. (p. 292)

Again and again, the human voice is compared by Giono to natural phenomena. (p. 293)

Many . . . images may appear insignificant and commonplace unless they are seen in the overall pattern of Giono's work, in which case they assume a meaning that is crucial to his ideology. Those characters whose voices 'contain' Nature are those who are at one with it, and who represent Giono's positive standpoint in the pre-war period; while the description of natural sounds in terms of the human voice, like the other forms of personification of Nature in Giono's work, serves to reduce the gulf between Man and Nature by suggesting unsuspected similarities, and thus underlines the theme of *le mélange.* . . .

In *Jean le Bleu,* Giono's fictionalized autobiography, it is finally affirmed, through the mouth of the poet Odripano, that Man can reintegrate himself with the rest of the animal kingdom through vocalization, by being absorbed into Nature's pattern of ritual calling. . . .

It is noticeable that in ranging the human voice alongside the other sounds of the universe, Giono often envisages the voice merely as sound, and not as a verbal agent at all; or

rather, words are seen as a later embellishment, a sophisticated human development, moulding precise meanings from the original instinctive utterance. Man's voice always retains the vestiges of this original animalic sound, which manifest themselves at moments when instinct speaks louder than intellect. . . . (p. 294)

This insistence on Man-produced sound, as Man's contribution to the sounds of the world, finds another extension in the theme of music. . . . Throughout Giono's pre-war work, in fact, the effect of music on a listener is described in the same terms as that of speech. . . . Also, analogies between music and the world of Nature are created through Giono's imagery the many musical instruments described by Giono, some real, some invented, and which assume something of the mythological importance of Pan's pipes, have as their primeval ancestor 'cet instrument premier d'où tout rejaillit, d'où toute musique a coulé, la libre, chanteuse terre qui est là tout autour avec son poids de bêtes . . . [this primeval instrument from which everything did spring, from which all music has flowed, the free, singing earth that is everywhere with its animal weight . . .]' . . . .

'La libre, chanteuse terre', 'le chant du monde'—such images recur constantly in Giono's writings, and remind us that for him song, which occupies so large a place in his work, and where lies the fusion of speech and music, has its roots, like these two elements separately, in the melodious sounds of Nature. This is stressed time and again by his imagery, which accords the gift of song to so many diverse natural phenomena. (p. 295)

The use of imagery by certain carefully selected characters in Giono's novels is noticeable . . . as early as *Colline.* When Janet sees a whip lying on the floor and describes it as a snake . . . this is partly due to his delirium, and partly to his gift of metaphorical vision. Janet sees the whip as a snake; Gondran sees it as a whip. This is the difference between the sick mind and the healthy mind, but is is also the difference between the poet and the ordinary man. (p. 297)

[The] initial inspiration of [the theme of language] is probably the same as that which helped to create Giono's first fictional work, *Naissance de l'Odyssée,* namely Homer. The original *Odyssey,* read and loved by Giono since childhood, bristles with references to speech and song, both human and divine. The vocal accomplishments of Giono's characters are prefigured by those of Homer's Odysseus, a master of 'the graceful art of speech', as well as by other characters in the *Odyssey.* . . . (p. 298)

When Giono turned from his direct rewriting of Homer to his peasant novels, he simply transferred to the new context the same intense interest in speech, incorporating it into his new themes and characters. The voices of the gods become, in gradual stages, the voices of Nature, and hence the 'song of the world'. . . . The fusion of Giono's love of classical literature and his adoration of the Provençal countryside—the two dynamic impulses behind his work—is nowhere more interestingly achieved than within this theme of speech.

Like Homer, too, Giono was not afraid to celebrate in his works his own gifts as a story-teller. (pp. 298-99)

In addition to this element of self-celebration in Giono's

work, there is also the romantic elevation to mythic status of the often pithy and picturesque speech of the peasant. . . .

Furthermore, the insistence on spoken language that this article has traced does not prevent Giono's work from being also a celebration of his medium and his powers as a writer. In his unique stylistic world, where the colloquial and the poetic are fused, the borderline between the spoken and the written language is blurred. . . . [For] Giono, the healing powers and world-role ascribed by him to spoken poetry are, or should be, the properties of literature also. (p. 299)

There is a strong suggestion here that Giono's own ambition, in the pre-war days before his flight into historical fiction, was to be a healer through words. This helps to explain his position in inter-war literature: his re-affirmation, along with those otherwise vastly different writers Bernanos and Malraux, of the spiritually renovating values of heroism and stoicism; and, above all, his constantly reiterated stress on the world's natural beauty and its promise of a cure for modern ills.

Thus Giono's writings refer frequently, albeit indirectly, to his own ambitions as a writer. In writing books about language and, obliquely, literature, he is contributing to that mass of self-reflective writing that looms large in the twentieth century. And in claiming for the poet a special role as a bringer of enlightenment to men, he allies himself to both the romantic and symbolist traditions of the nineteenth century. (p. 300)

Giono seeks . . . to refer us to the material world, to make us rediscover through his words the physical beauties of Nature. . . .

Co-operation with Nature, its re-creation through words, and especially its rejuvenation through imagery—which unearths new aspects and encourages new angles of vision —this is the mission of Giono. . . .

Que ma joie demeure, . . . is Giono's most important treatment of the impact of poetry, including the image, on men's lives. With great honesty, productive in part of the novel's pessimism, he describes Bobi's difficulties in communicating his message to the peasants of the plateau. The problem is primarily linguistic. (p. 301)

Poetry is seen here as something less than the universal panacea that Bobi hopes it will be—not because of any inherent limitations in poetry itself, but because of the lack of comprehension and misuse of poetry displayed by the peasants. . . . The poet can provide the first imaginative insight on a problem; but the true advancement of society demands that the poet must stand aside and be replaced by the more practical man. (p. 302)

The failure of Bobi's poetry may well reflect a feeling on Giono's part that he had failed, or would fail, to communicate his healing joy through the medium of his books. . . .

Que ma joie demeure is in fact the last novel to present so romantic a vision of the peasant's world. The next novel, *Batailles dans la montagne,* stresses instead the hardships of a peasant community struggling against a hostile nature. Soon, too, Giono was to abandon his *cycle paysan* and embark on his *chroniques* and historical novels. He was largely to abandon also the rich imagery of his pre-war

books, which seems to have been a conscious attempt on the part of this underrated artist to carry the reader with him into a joyful appreciation of Nature's vitality. His failure, or self-supposed failure, to convey his own joy in Nature, leading to a conscious under-playing of the poetry that had been the intended vehicle of that joy, may lie at the heart of Giono's switch to his post-war 'second manner'. (p. 303)

Malcolm Scott, "Giono's Song of the World: The Theme of Language and Its Associations in Giono's Pre-war Writings," in French Studies, *July, 1972, pp. 289-303.*

*   *   *

GIRONELLA, José María   1917-

A Spanish novelist, poet, short story writer, essayist, and travel writer, Gironella creates a fiction that bears the influence of the cinematic technique employed by many contemporary Spanish writers. Although his novels often have a political content, Gironella does not write from an established political point of view. Rather, he seeks to present the various sides of an issue and explores the political and social motivations of his characters.

RONALD SCHWARTZ

Gironella revived the Spanish tradition of nineteenth-century Realism. His novels represent a break from the introspective, aesthetic and intellectualized pre-Civil War novel. The trauma of his Civil War experiences caused his return to Realism and to the exterior world with its imperative political and social problems. Gironella is a serious writer . . . who reflects both his personal traumatic experiences of the war and the realities of postwar Spain in his work. (p. 18)

At first glance of the author's career, Gironella's virtuosity in a multiplicity of genres is indicative of his refusal to submit to Spain's literary paralysis. In fact, the brilliance of Gironella's literary career which already spans two "literary generations [both the "Generation of 1939" and the "Generation of 1950"] and may possibly help to engender a third, may be revealed either as a commentary upon modern man or upon Gironella, the writer constantly in search of himself. (p. 19)

Whatever the stylistic defects of his first two novels, [*Where the Soul Was Shallow* and *The Tide*], both works are written with extraordinary vigor; their feeling of exhilaration and their vitality of prose may be partly explained by the novelist's anxiety for success and popularity. His first two novels probably fall into the category of popular literature. (p. 27)

[Gironella's] insistence on writing in [*The Cypresses Believe in God*] about things Spanish, combined with the prolonged and voluminous character of the novel and its inventory of human types and the Spanish spirit, is an accurate implementation of the goals partially described in [*Novelist Before the World,* Gironella's treatise on literature] and subsequently attained in *The Cypresses.* Although Gironella did not rely upon *Novelist Before the World* entirely for the creation of *The Cypresses* since his ideas about the novel and his career were constantly changing, he was convinced that in *Novelist* he had laid the cornerstone of his literary career and had found a formula for continued success. His early novels, however amateurish they were, display certain aspects of Gironella's aesthetic doctrines which matured with later literary successes such as *The Cypresses Believe in God*. *Novelist Before the World*, then, is not only an index to his early works but probably plays a formative role in the writer's subsequent career. *Novelist* should be considered as a list of partially fulfilled concepts deriving from a glowing, youthful idealism and pertaining particularly to the author's first two published novels. (p. 28)

The most important theme in Gironella's early novels is his description of man—man in search of himself in the labyrinth of society. His first novel, *Un hombre (Where the Soil Was Shallow)*, is an autobiographical and romantic work. (p. 38)

The plot of *Where the Soil Was Shallow* is surprisingly simple for it only traces the activities, growth and education of a young man.

A basic problem with the novel is that the reader knows from the outset, Miguel will not triumph, for his search for ideal values is hopeless from the very beginning. (p. 39)

The delineation of Miguel's character loses in intensity when the author inserts a multitude of episodic incidents that detract from his protagonist's development. However, the sections in which Gironella explores Miguel's relationship with his mother are the most significant in the entire novel for they reflect the writer's attempt to reveal personal experience.... Although skeletal autobiographical facts are partially adhered to, the chief difficulty with *Where the Soil Was Shallow* is its falsification of the worlds in which the author did *not* live. Despite autobiographical similarities, Gironella is detached from what he describes. Consequently, the novel suffers from artificiality whose episodic incident replaces badly needed sections explaining motivations and inner feelings. (p. 40)

Historically, Miguel's spiritual search is the author's own quest for a new life after the shattering experiences of the Civil War. Although Gironella carefully avoids presenting this motivation as the chief impetus, he substitutes Miguel's mother's death as the principal reason for his spiritual quest. Her death symbolizes the end of a matriarchy—Spain cast into upheaval because of civil war....

What *Where the Soil Was Shallow* lacked in organization and balance because of a young writer's inexperience and exuberance, *The Tide* made up for in professional skill. Gironella had learned from past errors. *The Tide* presents a cohesive plot in a highly realistic historical setting. Events themselves help to determine the fictional lives of the personages. However, its plot is melodramatic rather than imaginative although *The Tide* extends Gironella's search further into man and his problems. (p. 41)

The greatest asset of this novel is its depiction of an entire world, unified and integrated in the historical period it describes with personages and problems well developed in a realm of possibility.... The novel's action moves at a rapid, nervous pace to its conclusion and its emotional rhythm is like the long sweep of a giant wave that gains impetus, crashes on the shore, and recedes slowly back to sea. In contrast to *Where the Soil Was Shallow*, *The Tide* is a tense, highly organized, and far better written novel. Its unity results from its surprising economy and deftness. For all of these good qualities, *The Tide* fails because of Giro-

nella's limited perspective. No matter how logically conceived or easily visualized, his personages are stereotypes and colorless creatures representing a concept rather than vital incarnations of reality. Despite excellent delineation, they are used as props. (p. 43)

The salient feature that redeems these early novels is their portrayal of the "romantic life" of their protagonists. In fact, Romantic elements pervade subsequent novels as well. His early novels, in particular, show the gradual transformation of his Romantic protagonists into complex modern figures typical of the twentieth century. (p. 44)

The cycle of Civil War novels opening with *Los cipreses creen en Dios (The Cypresses Believe in God)* in 1953 is one of José María Gironella's best achievements. Facing new responsibilities as a social writer, Gironella retains certain romantic ideas of his first two novels but controls them for a greater social purpose—the explanation of Spain's Civil War....

The Cypresses is Gironella's most ambitious work, as it is his largest novel in scope, breadth, and depth up to that time. (p. 51)

The life-death struggle is of primary thematic concern in *The Cypresses*. It is presented symbolically—burning of forests, poisoning of rivers, droughts, and realistically—the death of the spirit. Death as a negative stimulus forces Gironella's protagonists to react more vitally to life. (p. 62)

Gironella not only stresses the complexity of Spanish politics and the inevitability of Civil War, he also explains the rebellion in less than adequately documented conclusions.... The strong convictions of his characters, nevertheless, give strength to their opinions and establish the author's persuasive power as a novelist rather than as an historian. (pp. 63-4)

Gironella's rigid adherence to a preconceived stylistic pattern allows for very little prose variation. Apparently Gironella has schematized his personages purposely, making them symbolic of all individuals and their struggles in Spain. An alternation of three points of view for a total panorama of Spanish life is difficult since some incidents may not serve Gironella's original fictional purpose. In *The Cypresses* much historical documentation could be excised easily, thus reducing the size of the work and giving it cohesion. Although the novel provides enough accurate historical and economic information for an historical document, *The Cypresses* is too broad. Gironella might have concentrated on fewer events and characters. As it is, a growing list of characters with those of the sequels, *One Million Dead* and *The Peace Has Broken Out* makes it probable that Gironella prefers breadth to depth in the recreation of a social climate. (p. 65)

Despite its melodrama, extensive descriptions of political ideologies, stereotyped minor characters and unimportant family episodes, *The Cypresses Believe in God* is one of the best novels to come out of Spain in the past fifteen years. Gironella has attempted to impose not only a cosmos on the chaos of the Civil War years but adds an epic tone for historic events in the tradition of the great generation novels of Balzac and Galdós. An excellent observer, he can photographically recreate an entire world, typically Spanish and authentic in his description of Spain's bourgeoisie. (pp. 66-7)

The Cypresses also displays Gironella's sense for unified composition and an integrated whole. His earlier novels demonstrate his ability to describe but with little discipline to select detail or theme. In *The Cypresses* he limits himself sensibly . . . , avoiding sententious and repetitious passages. The fusion of his characters is another improvement. . . . Gironella's care in tracing lives and deeds and their movements through the whirlwind of historical and political events creates the grandiose, epic quality of the novel. (p. 67)

José María Gironella's sequel, *Un millón de muertos (One Million Dead),* continues and amplifies the vicissitudes of the Alvear family of *The Cypresses Believe in God,* alternating like its predecessor fiction with condensed resumés of historical data. It suffers equally from Gironella's attempt to include all phases of the war. It is excellent in almost photographic narrative and in dramatic dialogue. (p. 70)

Even more ambitious than its predecessor, *One Million Dead* has potent reasons for success because it so broadens the base upon which rests *The Cypresses Believe in God.* It expands upon each of the Alvears; it extends the geographical focus of *The Cypresses* beyond Gerona to all Spain; it relates from a panoramic perspective, sociological, political, religious, and military conflicts of Communists and Falange simultaneously, and it unfolds the drama of a nation in the throes of civil strife as impartially as political conditions permit. Still, Gironella was successful on the historical level but not necessarily on the fictional one since his *a priori* judgments of Communist personages . . . as sadists, gangsters of a villainous cause, are unrealistic in contrast to the heroics of the Falangists. (p. 82)

The attempt to capture provincial flavor is a failure as is differentiation of characters. Each in its own way is weakened by what Gironella defines as "the inevitable truth," so that autobiographical experiences and characters inspired by real people never achieve a true objective existence. Gironella's war novels, thus, show little psychological perspicacity. It is this interest in laying bare the significance of the Civil War that causes this "sameness" in settings and personages. (p. 84)

One Million Dead abounds in excellent exterior descriptions. The battle scenes are masterful in details of strategy and combat. The novel is less successful in the portrayal of interior life. Gironella prefers that interior monologue and dialogue alone reveal characters who are often pale types, colorless and without individuality. His predilection for the external did not allow him to adjust his perspective to grasp individual idiosyncrasies and dimensions of feeling and understanding. His impersonality and neutrality of spirit disallow empathy and, consequently, penetration of an interior world. Although Gironella believed the major flaw of *One Million Dead* was "tone" and "synchronization" of events with action, his isolation from interiority is far more serious.

The Cypresses Believe in God is certainly more poetic and artfully written. *One Million Dead,* on the other hand, is the more systematically organized and analytical. *The Cypresses* may be considered as a fictional work with historical pretensions, but *One Million Dead* is essentially an historical study overlaid with fiction. *One Million Dead* is hardly what Gironella desired. Its lack of vitality prevents

it from being a commemoration, an evocation for Spain of the unforgettable past, a voice eloquently speaking to generations still to come. (pp. 84-5)

After *One Million Dead,* José María Gironella suffered a nervous breakdown which he called *la extraña enfermedad* ("a strange illness"), and described graphically as *el túnel negro* ("the black tunnel"). Because of his inability to concentrate on writing the conclusion of *One Million Dead,* he turned to description of the symptoms of his breakdown and the universality of his preoccupations. He wrote some eight thousand pages about the specters which inhabited his psyche, the best of which appear in *Los fantasmas de mi cerebro (Phantoms of My Brain).* (p. 86)

In perspective, the transitional *Phantoms of My Brain* is artistic raw material whose energy of execution shows Gironella's direction for the future. His *Phantoms* indicates the variety of themes for future works (travel, science, history). It is a serious, heterogeneous, autobiographical study, as it is an experiment in writing styles (realistic, surrealistic) and genres (the essay, the short story). *Phantoms* establishes the fertility of his mind, his enormous vitality, and his growing ability to control themes unified and sustained in execution. His task is to develop a personal style and aesthetic based upon descriptive analysis of his own psychological reactions. (p. 97)

Through his fantasies [as revealed in the short stories that comprise *Todos somos fugitivos (We Are All Fugitives)*], Gironella establishes that all men are fugitives from loneliness, disease, time, reality, heredity, death, and from each other. Each clearly written fantasy is dramatically sustained by highly original perception, and these stories, written after recovery from a nervous breakdown, indirectly indicate how the author's fantastic world of hallucinations touches upon profundity. His new-found aesthetic sense effectively creates, in the realm of the short story, a private cosmos that is undeniably Gironella's own. (p. 105)

Mujer, levántate y anda (Woman, Arise and Walk) is José María Gironella's first novel after his illness. After the hallucinatory worlds of *Phantoms of My Brain* and his exploration of the improbable in *We Are All Fugitives,* Gironella turned to the physical, emotional, and spiritual realities of contemporary Spain. He is chiefly interested in his rediscovery of Spain and its people.

Woman, then, is the author's first fictional response to psychological disturbance after recovery from his nervous breakdown. It is a poorly written and unimaginative reworking of the Faustus theme of sin and redemption. (p. 106)

[In it he] offers a pseudo-religious moral novel of contemporary morals and manners that says very little of any consequence although it does seem to indicate a greater recognition of mental illness in contemporary Spanish society. (p. 109)

Gironella is effective when he evaluates himself and his nation for a broadening of the intellectual horizons of Spain. Spain's insularity is the essential problem that creates dogmatic thought and behavior. Therefore, Gironella resolved to enlarge his own perspectives through travel. To gain keener insights into his own nation and its problems and counteract his own mental inertia, he embarked on a European tour with his wife. Essays under the collective titles

"Temas italianos" ("Italian Themes"), "Temas france-ses" ("French Themes"), and "Temas anglosajones" ("English Themes") published in *Phantoms* reveal in his experiences abroad his perspicacity and intelligence. (p. 112)

Although *Japan and Her Ghosts* [one of Gironella's travel books] appears more scholarly and contains much information about the Japanese, it usually lacks the vitality of the personal approach and dialogues of *Persons, Ideas and Seas*. Neither work is completely unified. Still, Gironella's *Japan and Her Ghosts* blends perspicacity of observation with greater selectivity in experience. Excision of trivia, freedom from bondage to chronology, and selectivity in the choice of thoughts and impressions, all contribute to a new standard of objectivity and artistic creation.

Gironella has gained immeasurably in his analysis and evaluation of political factors. The emergence of this quality and its dominance over these travel books promises new strength to his continuing career. *Persons, Ideas and Seas* initiated his interest and *Japan and Her Ghosts* sustained this interest with more serious historical foundations. The latter shows that a new transitional Gironella is becoming not only an essayist, but social critic and historian as well. His next work may have significance beyond Spain. (p. 130)

Gironella as critic is stronger in setting forth autobiographical details than he is in any other aspect of the art of criticism. He is admirably specific when he treats of himself and these essays add measurably to an understanding of the workings of his personality. Any criticism of his revelations of himself is that his remarks are usually superficial rather than indicative of a deep understanding either of himself or of his art. (p. 149)

Upon the Alvears focuses all primary action in *The Peace Has Broken Out*. The revelation of their story gives this novel what interest it possesses. Unfortunately, the Alvears are not so interesting in themselves as in the earlier volumes. All too often their reactions are predictable. Gironella had failed to utilize to advantage his "fusion" of history and fiction. (p. 154)

Since Gironella gives to his characters little new insight into themselves, it is reasonable to assume further continuations will be as verbose and episodic. Although *Peace* lies well in the tradition of the generation novel, it lacks the sweep and vitality of Gironella's earlier war novels, nor does it compare with its great predecessors of the nineteenth century. (p. 155)

In [Gironella's] best novels his sympathy with the average man shows in leading characters typical of their society and era. The essential nature of the Spaniard for Gironella appears ingenuous without artificiality. He shares with his fellow Spaniards his interest in explaining the complexity of the Civil War and although he does not consider himself superficial, he does intend Spain, with the Alvear family as his creative focus, to be the omnipresent if silent heroine. Such a conception hardly can be confined to the limits of the war novels.

On the other hand, Gironella's career is more than a dedication to *vox populi*. He has produced some complex and stylized works in diverse genres that demand artistic concentration. The short story of Gironella illustrates this

point admirably. Gironella is a Catalan of great vital energy and capacity for recuperation and experimentation. His popularity rests on his utilization of personal and universally Spanish experiences to establish, in a slowly developing but real talent, the validity of the singular complex event which dominated his life—the Civil War. His talent is still, even now, in its formative stages.

Although his career is always in a state of flux, Gironella's current literary position is his commitment and his struggles with success and artistic endeavor. (p. 174)

It may be that his development, as well as sometimes abrupt changes in style and subject matter result from flexibility and individual susceptibility to influence from a dynamic world of ideas. Nevertheless, and although his conscientious artistry and search for improvement in himself and his work cannot be denied, his literary success seems largely due to his revival of the generation novel of the nineteenth century in Spain. (p. 175)

Gironella is transitional, still a promise, a question, and Spanish letters must await his evaluation; for Gironella's personal cosmos is continually changing under the dynamic impulses of his talent. (p. 177)

Ronald Schwartz, in his José María Gironella *(copyright 1972 by Twayne Publishers, Inc.; reprinted with the permission of Twayne Publishers, A Division of G. K. Hall & Co., Boston), Twayne, 1972.*

JOHN E. DIAL

The publication in 1971 of José María Gironella's *Condenados a vivir* marks, in a sense, the completion of a statement, a statement that is at once tenuous and compelling. The work does not belong to the series begun in 1953 with *Los cipreses creen en Dios* [*The Cypresses Believe in God*]; it exists as a work apart. Its setting is Barcelona and not Gerona, and its author has fashioned a new gallery of characters; but Gironella's procedure and style remain the same. His vision of Spain from the Republic to the present is now open to scrutiny. If the clarity of his vision has at times been suspect, no one has denied the energy with which Gironella transferred that vision to paper. It is hardly legitimate to speak of the Spain of Gironella as one speaks of the Spain of Galdós and Baroja; their strengths are not Gironella's nor his weaknesses theirs. But in this century of ambitious novels, Gironella's project has few parallels, and none in Spain.

There exists a lingering suspicion that Gironella is not really a novelist at all, that his major work is as close to journalism as it is to fiction. . . . His penchant, in recent years, for writing travel books has not lessened the notion that Gironella's forte is reportage. His narrative style is simple, direct, and, some feel, singularly undistinguished. Even critics . . . who treat Gironella relatively kindly, often carp at his stylistic conservatism.

The uncertainty of Gironella's place in modern Spanish letters stems also from the conviction in some quarters that his success is primarily commercial. One cannot help but think that the undercurrent of resentment that pervades much Gironellan criticism is related to the novelist's singular popularity. Juan Luis Alborg's statement that *Los cipreses creen en Dios* made Gironella the most widely read Spanish novelist in Spain and abroad is difficult to dispute. Not really a member of any generation or school, Gironella practices his craft with the assurance of one who reaches a large public. [He] has declared that he does not write for critics; he writes for the man in the street.

Of course, not all criticism of Gironella has been adverse. (pp. 98-9)

Often when Gironella is discussed, criticism varies in temper and tone according to the political sympathies of the commentators. (p. 100)

As one ponders *Los cipreses creen en Dios, Un millón de muertos* [*One Million Dead*], and *Ha estallado la paz* [*The Peace Has Broken Out*] (along with *Condenados a vivir*), it becomes apparent that the author has attempted to give every ideology its day in court. Communists, Anarchists, Falangists, Republicans, and, in the fourth work, hippies, present their views, as do Catholics of every stripe. For some readers these novels must be a sort of guessing game. When is the novelist being the devil's advocate, and when is he being Gironella? Furthermore, one suspects that the author experiences some pleasure in knowing that there are leftists who consider him fascist and rightists who consider him communist. (pp. 100-01)

Seldom has a novelist felt such a continual need to make clear his intent. This recurrent preoccupation is reflected in the fact that all his novels have explanatory forewords of some kind. . . . What emerges from these prologues and articles is not simply the picture of a man who approaches his work with a clear sense of vocation but of a writer whose principal work is a response to a single impulse. . . .

[No] one who reads Gironella's first novel, *Un hombre* [*Where the Soil Was Shallow*], can doubt that the spirit which hovered over the author as he wrote it was that of Pío Baroja, and indeed Gironella has indicated as much. (p. 101)

La marea is predictably cliché-ridden, his Germany, despite his hope to the contrary, as manifestly unauthentic as was the Europe of *Un hombre*. Nevertheless *La marea*, with its stereotypes and its melodrama, represents the completion of a young author's apprenticeship—or, expressed in other terms, the second world war is a dress rehearsal for Gironella's Spanish Civil War. (pp. 102-03)

[*Los cipreses creen en Dios*] was for many Spanish readers the first general account of life under the Republic, just as *Un millón de muertos* would be their first contact with a general treatment of the civil war. . . . Gironella was determined that the book would be "completo." "If this book attempts to demonstrate anything," he says in a note to the American edition, "it is this: that there are in this land thousands of possible ways of life." In his travel books he is perpetually standing in awe of the world's diversity, of its contradictions and paradoxes. Proceeding with his chronicles, he has never veered from his determination to have his own country's complexity reflected in his work. (p. 103)

[His] decision to center his novel in Gerona, the city he knew best, is generally applauded. The question as to whether that city was really a microcosm, as Gironella suspected it was, is really immaterial. A modern history of Gerona was never projected. . . . Gerona is simply a stage, decorated minimally. Events which happened elsewhere are transferred to this city that reflects Spain's predicament. This device of the microcosm is reasonably successful, but

in placing a large number of actors on such a small stage, Gironella has, perhaps, strained his readers' credulity. He fills the city with wonderfully articulate priests, Monarchists, Falangists, Communists, Anarchists. Usually avoiding allusions to the "mood" of the town, he focuses on its citizens, their joys, their hates, their prejudices.

Los cipreses creen en Dios is thus essentially a novel of vociferous confrontation. Ideologies meet head on in the streets, in the cafes, in the barbershops of Gerona. The small city's streets seem to be jammed with political activists, most of them intense and, like Jules Romains's characters, talkative. They are given robust personalities, and many are interesting, but they never develop significantly; one simply gets to know them better. They meander in and out of the novel's pages arguing, gossiping, stating and restating their positions. Gironella has created a world of ideological "types," a practice he has never considered unartistic. (pp. 103-04)

The conflicts of the divided Spains are symbolized by the Alvear family. Around this middle-class family, modeled after the author's own, *Los cipreses creen en Dios* is constructed. The anticlerical Matías and his conservative wife, Carmen Elgazu, live simply. . . . Except for the extraordinary saintliness of César, their second son, there is nothing exceptional about their children. Whatever mild ideological tensions exist have been swept away by a combination of sensible compromise and love. The daily routine of this family, recorded in rich detail, is the real core of the novel.

Ignacio, the eldest son, is the central figure. . . . Gironella, without employing any innovative narrative techniques, is able to present two sometimes converging, sometimes conflicting points of view: a stricken nation is shown drifting toward war as a sensitive young man (Ignacio-Gironella) saw it; at the same time a complicated period of modern history is viewed from the vantage point of a mature novelist whose omniscience is limited perhaps only by defective research. In the prologue, which Gironella calls an *Aclaración indispensable,* the author declares that he felt it necessary for his protagonist to carry within himself the Civil War. He ends the note to the American edition by saying that Ignacio Alvear "is a type of young man who abounds in present-day Spain." The two Spains exist, then, not only within families but also within individuals, even within Gironella himself. (p. 105)

A problem persists [in *Un millón de muertos*] in that these characters seem to have been specifically designed for the first novel in the series rather than for its sequel. In *Los cipreses creen en Dios,* where they were meant to exemplify attitudes, ideological positions, and sectors of society, they are, in the main, credible, or at least eloquent, witnesses to the events transpiring in Spain on the eve of war. Asking them to function as actors on a larger stage is perhaps expecting too much of them. Some characters thus seem blurred. But Gironella professes that he knew that he would have to submerge the individuality of his people in what he calls the "vorágine colectivo"; and in the third volume of the series they would, he said, recover their intrinsic importance. (pp. 106-07)

Un millón de muertos is, among other things, a reply to several books written outside Spain; Gironella refers specifically to the efforts of Malraux, Hemingway, Koestler, Bernanos, and Barea. "Apart from their literary value," he says, "these works cannot stand careful analysis. They set forth the drama of our country to suit themselves; they abound in folklore, and whenever they face up to the subject in all its magnitude, they are obliged to turn tail. They often sin through unfairness, through arbitrariness, and they arouse a remarkable feeling of discomfort in the informed reader." (p. 107)

From the beginning Gironella was determined to show in his chronicles what the war meant to both sides. At the end of *Un millón de muertos,* the dramatic exodus through Catalonia into France of half a million "fugitives" is feelingly described. The odyssey of these exiles, who would scatter throughout the world, figured prominently in Gironella's plans; and in *Ha estallado la paz,* the third volume in the series, the reader is furnished with vivid glimpses of Spaniards in Russia (Cosme Vila is there) and France. *Ha estallado la paz* is, however, mainly a novel about the victors, about the immediate postwar period in Franco's Spain. . . . Gone, indeed, or at least blunted, are the tensions which formed the basis of the previous volumes. But it is history as much as anything that has created an artistic problem for the author; for, while his formula is essentially the same, history has changed the material with which he must deal. (pp. 108-09)

If in *Los cipreses creen en Dios* Gironella seems at times to dwell on the thematically insignificant, on the daily routine of a small Spanish city, it is against a backdrop of intense drama. Every event discussed in the café is crucial or seems to be. In *Ha estallado la paz,* however, nothing seems momentous. This is not to say that the time right after the war (1939-41, the period embraced by the novel) was unimportant or uninteresting; a new regime was taking shape, and the resultant uncertainty produced a new kind of tension. Gironella's unfailingly accurate portrayal of life in those years is perhaps unexcelled. (p. 109)

Because of the limited period covered in *Ha estallado la paz,* there are many unanswered questions, many unresolved conflicts; given Gironella's intention to extend his project, this air of inconclusiveness is probably inevitable. It is to be supposed that the leisurely pace which characterizes *Ha estallado la paz* will continue in subsequent *episodios.* Had Gironella chosen to close the cycle with one long book, the result might have been something like *Condenados a vivir.* . . . Covering the period from the end of the Civil War in 1939 to 1967, the work might be looked upon as something of a preview of future *episodios.* Politics is deemphasized. At the same time, there are new preoccupations, new tensions. Spaniards have had to respond in recent years to new issues, and Gironella seems to feel that he has a mission to record accurately that response. *Condenados a vivir* is largely a novel about a nation emerging from its isolation, about that nation's coming to grips with problems that are international in scope. Gironella approaches such subjects as *el abismo generacional,* drugs, and alternate life-styles with the kind of excitement and determination that one has come to expect from him.

The possibilities, then, appear to be limitless. Gironella has travelled extensively in recent years, and his curiosity is boundless. He wants to get everything down on paper; there is no indication that he has abandoned his intention to make his story *completo.* (p. 110)

> John E. Dial, "Gironella's Chronicles Revisited: A Panorama of Fratricide," in Papers on Lan-

guage and Literature *(copyright © 1974 by the Board of Trustees, Southern Illinois University at Edwardsville), Winter, 1974, pp. 98-110.*

*   *   *

GOMBROWICZ, Witold   1904-1969

A Polish-born novelist, playwright, and short story writer, Gombrowicz lived in Argentina from 1939 to 1963, and then settled in France. He viewed man as a social animal, needing the affection and stability of personal relationships, but needing at the same time to express independence and individuality. His works, with their modern existentialist themes and brilliant satire, have been noted for their important and innovative contribution to European letters. (See also *CLC*, Vols. 4, 7, and *Contemporary Authors*, Vols. 19-20; obituary, Vols. 25-28, rev. ed.; *Contemporary Authors Permanent Series,* Vol. 2.)

LUCIEN GOLDMANN

[Gombrowicz' plays *Ivona, Princess of Burgundia* and *The Marriage*] are compelling satires of society. . . .

The two plays deal with two different societies. In *Ivona, Princess of Burgundia* it is pre-World War II European society (the play was written in 1935) or, more precisely, the ruling classes of that society. *The Marriage* (1946) is about the new society which resulted from the war and from the seizure of power by the communist parties, with emphasis on the events leading up to that seizure. But Gombrowicz goes beyond the localized framework which he attacks and which inspires him to describe an essence which, if not universal (something difficult to imagine in a social satire), is at least much more general. *Ivona, Princess of Burgundia* describes the dominant strata of any more or less bourgeois society; *The Marriage,* the essential schema of a revolutionary seizure of power by the masses and its consequent transformation into dictatorship, as in Russia, Poland, and most other "people's democracies." All of this is presented, of course, from Gombrowicz' aristocratic point of view and in the light of his Christian values.

To some extent *Ivona, Princess of Burgundia,* written in the *entre-deux-guerres,* reflects the ideas of that period's dominant philosophy, existentialism—specifically, *Christian* existentialism. (p. 102)

The play's structure is simple and precise. The court (King Ignatius, Queen Margaret, Prince Philip, and courtiers) of an imaginary country encounters *essence* and finds it intolerable since essence reveals truth in a society where everyone is frantically trying to hide it, both from themselves and others. The situation persists until there is a unanimous decision to see to it that the intruder be killed, "from above"—Gombrowicz emphasizes this term—and to reestablish the original state of affairs.

Were it not for the line where Ivona affirms her faith, with a "contemptuous" expression for the others, she could be defined . . . as akin to "nothingness." Ivona is without admirable qualities. Stupid, ugly, practically wordless (she has eight lines in the play), she is an object of everyone's hostility and ridicule. In her few lines she tells us only that she lives in a circle which offers no way out. (pp. 102-03)

The Prince, bored by the routine of daily life, blasé, unable to find any further interest in his existence, decides to scandalize his entourage with a great joke: he announces he is going to marry Ivona. . . . The Prince tires of his joke and wants to leave Ivona, but finds this no longer possible. Ivona has taken possession of him; he is part of her, she of him. He must now take his joke seriously.

Ivona awakens in the King repressed memories of his past crimes. She makes him want to be himself, to go on killing. The Queen feels that her most intimate secret—that she loves and writes poetry—has been pried from her and is in danger of being made public. And this, society would never accept. In short, the society cannot continue to function unless Ivona is eliminated. (p. 103)

But even after Ivona's death, the King, Queen, Prince, and dignitaries still feel disoriented. How should they behave now that normalcy has been restored? How should they react to this sudden, radical transformation? By respecting the formalities. . . . Unanimity restored, "normal" life can continue.

The structure of *Ivona, Princess of Burgundia* is relatively simple because various modalities of inauthentic existence within a specific social group are made visible in an encounter with a single character. The universe presented in *The Marriage* incorporates a further dimension of reality: time and becoming. The play is a grotesque but homologous transposition of events which occurred in several Central European countries as well as in Russia, all viewed from Gombrowicz' aristocratic and Christian perspective. The grotesque is present in both plays, but in *The Marriage* it assumes a distinctly oneiric form, for reasons which seem clearly sociological. In 1935 Gombrowicz was depicting a society in which he was still living and in which he continued to participate. In 1946 he stood at a distance to re-create a historical development which, in his view, had led to the suppression of history. By the phrase "at a distance" I [mean] . . . that the social class (the aristocracy) from whose perspective Gombrowicz wrote, had disappeared and no longer played any role in the society born of the events transposed by Gombrowicz.

The oneiric is emphasized from the beginning. We seem to be in the north of France. Two soldiers stand before a ruined church; a few moments later the church is transformed into the childhood home, in Podolia, of one of the soldiers. We are in both France and Podolia, both here and there. The plot is a nightmare based on past events, and like all nightmares, a memory relived in the present. But it is also a concrete, present reality since those past events led to the current situation: i.e., the ruined church and the disappearance of values in the name of which the events are related and judged. (pp. 103-04)

The link between this imaginative creation and contemporary social realities (or the transposition of certain concrete political elements in which the creation had its origin) seems plain. The end of the war—whether that of 1914 or 1930—brings about a serious social crisis wherein a rebellious population (represented by the drunkard) endangers the values that provide the basis for the traditional social order. Since the drunkard cannot overthrow this order by himself, a precarious equilibrium results. Before the old order is shattered in favor of either restoration or revolution, the two hostile social forces confront one another. The representatives of the old regime and legitimacy and the dissatisfied, rebellious masses face each other, afraid of each other, both unable to decide to take the offensive. The outcome depends in large measure on the position taken by the combatants who are returning from the front. Most of all—although the play does not explicitly state this—it depends on the position espoused by the intellectual and managerial levels of society. (Gombrowicz' text nowhere defines Henry's and Johnny's social rank. It only indicates that they stand between the dethroned and degraded political forces of the old regime, and the threatening population.) (pp. 107-08)

In the crisis following the First World War and, in some countries, the Second, the situation was exactly analogous to the one described in *The Marriage*. The definitive factor in determining which way the scales would tip was whether the intelligentsia rallied to the forces of conservatism and restoration or to those of revolution. In any event, it seems that this is what Gombrowicz felt, and that the three decisive elements in the play (the king, the drunkard, and, standing together between these two, Henry and Johnny) correspond exactly to that historic situation.

One thing is clear: in the play, the course of events and the outcome of the confrontation between king and drunkard depend on the attitude of Henry and Johnny. In the second act, they line up on the side of tradition; the result is instantaneous: order is restored, the drunk is in prison, the marriage will take place.

Moreover, the events in the first act correspond to what happened after the crisis that shook society in all countries of the West at the end of World War I.

But the play is not a transposition of the experience of these countries. The play's importance is linked to the twist of events which occurs later in the play, which corresponds to what actually took place first in Russia and eventually in the other countries of Central Europe. The first act does not end with the drunkard's being thrown in jail. The conflict continues. It will flare again in the second act. (p. 108)

According to the play, a legitimate monarchy can exist only insofar as it is based on a transcendent faith. Without that faith Henry's adhesion to legitimacy could only be superficial. (p. 109)

[Regarding the second act of *The Marriage*,] it is rather easy to elucidate the transposition of events and the point of view from which the play was written. Atheism prevents the intelligentsia from having any effective, basic commitment to re-establishing the old values rooted in Christian faith. Since their knowledge goes no further than man, the defense of these values is merely a problem of ethics and utility. It can easily be undermined by anyone who speaks in the name of man and makes him the center of a new religion that is "human and terrestrial, dark and bestial." Thus the intelligentsia allies itself with the brutal, rebellious masses to overthrow the old regime and bring about the triumph of the revolution. But this alliance is not grounded in a new legitimacy, a new order at once valid and humane. It springs solely from dictatorship and executive omnipotence.

In the union of Johnny and the fiancée, again it appears that Gombrowicz' aristocratic point of view enables him to see things that would have been difficult to locate by anyone more involved in the new society. The fact is, Henry and Johnny (or—and I do not think that the play's perspective is distorted by this comparison—Stalin and Trotsky, the new rulers and those who remained their political adversaries) are not simply two antagonistic forces. They start out as comrades, equals, friends, two sides of a single entity, namely, the group of revolutionary intellectuals. Their subsequent evolution and, in particular, their coming to power leads some to imprison the masses, seize the executive power for themselves, forget their former ideals, and become dictators. The others remain loyal to their past. It is a past they share with the people who made the revolution possible. They continue to hope for a new legitimacy. (p. 110)

Once again [in the third act] there is a homology with political events. There is the external threat of war, the withdrawal into self, the harassment of the opposing forces—who are asked to participate in a ceremony supposedly necessary to the unity of the country—though this participation is, in effect, suicide. As Gombrowicz sees it, these events result in an omnipotent executive power which has historically suppressed history: the funeral march that sweeps away the play's universe by the operation of an obscure force, incomprehensible to the very people who set it in motion. This force comes "from below"; the drunk is as much its priest as the dictator. Finally, there is the affirmation that these events may make sense at some time in the distant future when they will be seen from "on high." For the moment, however, no one can understand what they mean or even what they are. (p. 111)

Lucien Goldmann, "The Theatre of Gombrowicz," in The Drama Review *(© 1970 by The Drama Review; reprinted by permission; all rights reserved), No. 3, 1970, pp. 102-12.*

ROBERT BOYERS

The project of *Ferdydurke* is an existential quest for a solution to the problem of form, a problem which is characterized from a variety of perspectives, but which refuses to yield anything but further problems, more intricate questions. While it is pleasant enough, in studying Gombrowicz, to recall Chekhov's famous distinction between "the solution of a question and the correct putting of a question," and his conclusion that "Only the last is required of the artist," Gombrowicz puts so many questions, and with such incredible abandon, that one is hard put to take consolation in the recollection of precedents. (pp. 284-85)

Gombrowicz's handling of the problem of form is in an older tradition, ultimately, I think, more satisfying than many more recent experimentalists want to concede.... Where one has every reason to suspect a writer like Robbe-Grillet of deliberately concealing meanings which even he would be unable to identify, concealing them in the interests of sheer surface play and display, Gombrowicz's fiction more closely resembles the Kafkan parable—pregnant with meanings too painful to liberate from the contexts of fiction. Where in Beckett we have, in Frank Kermode's terms, not much more than "a form commenting upon itself, an autistic stir of language," a fiction which at its climax "virtually disclaims its own authenticity," Gombrowicz juxtaposes the grim and the farcical in such a way that neither can operate without reference to the other, and to our lives. Gombrowicz's fictions stand in analogy to our lives, rather than as digressions from human experience, and his allegorical creations never threaten to disappear into thin air.

The problem of form, as Gombrowicz treats it, then, is basically an existential, rather than merely an artistic, problem, and requires an approach that can account for its terrible consequences in human lives. Gombrowicz's method in *Ferdydurke* involves an examination of three standard milieus, each of which is founded upon a rigid structure and imposes upon the individual a series of forms that stand between him and others. Thus, we are taken for relatively extended visits to a secondary school, an ostensibly typical middle-class home, and the country mansion of provincial aristocrats. Each milieu is described in a detail that can only be called enigmatic, and is organized around recurrent motifs that appear in numerous guises but do not develop. Nor can it be said that Gombrowicz's vision of modern culture, including its intersection with older traditions that have as yet to be completely displaced, is arranged in patterns of increasing intensity—the emotional level of the novel is relatively constant, and while conflicts can assume the form of genuine encounters, there is never any possibility of resolutions in time. In fact, time has no function in this novel—the reader can never be disposed to consider events in terms of probabilities or historical necessities, nor is there any question as to the propriety of simultaneities established by the novel's structure. What Gombrowicz posits is a hypothetical present flexible enough to embrace any number of anachronisms. Obviously, in Gombrowicz's view, the problem of form transcends historical considerations, and the novelist's meanings cut across superficial social structures. Thus, each of the novel's three main sections ends on a note of anarchic destruction signifying an abolition of social distinctions and symmetries which had been carefully constructed, but no permanent strategies of evasion are available to the protagonist.

The problem of form in *Ferdydurke* is further complicated by the fact that the protagonist does not really know who or what he is, as we do not know him. Though he addresses us in the first person, he assigns several names to himself in the course of the novel, and he is hardly what one would call a stable personality. At the beginning of the novel he tells us that he is thirty years old, and that he is writing the present work in order to explain himself and gain entrance to an adult world which had seemed to deny him admission ever since he could remember. Thus we have a variant of a literary phenomenon that has become so familiar in our time: the work in the act of creating its creator. Only, of course, what *Ferdydurke* enforces ultimately is an existentialist view of man as perpetually in the act of becoming, perpetually insecure and filled with that neurotic dread of extinction that is a visible component of works by Sartre, Beckett and others. That is to say, no stable, focused personality is emergent in *Ferdydurke*.... What astonishes Gombrowicz's protagonist, as it must astonish us, is the degree to which we are bound by forms and conventions the fragility of which we are thoroughly aware, and towards which we direct a devastating cynicism. Stranger still is our inability to sustain a stable identity as a result of this commitment to forms. Gombrowicz's is a radical vision of the human personality precisely in this sense, that while he does not claim to know what constitutes a satisfying psychological maturity, he counsels against acceptance of conventions that provide most of us with a measure of security and hope.

Gombrowicz's fiction, then, is nourished by his understanding of art as insurrection, and is characterized by a strenuous effort to indict what passes for sanity in the twentieth century. His novel stands as a kind of symbolic attempt to be reborn through suicide, involving the cutting away of human possibilities as they are ordinarily conceived, leaving the subject at once exposed and isolated. There is no suggestion that Gombrowicz's protagonist will prove to be either brave or strong, that he will find the strength to fashion himself in the image of his desire. All he knows, like his creator, is that he must cease to live for others, that he cannot forever continue to be a projection of the needs of others. If that is to be his only sanity, his only security, then he will better destroy himself. The conclusion of *Ferdydurke* suggests there may be no viable prospect for rebirth, and there is nothing ennobling in the suffering and confusion to which Gombrowicz's protagonist is subject, to which he in fact subjects himself by his inability to reside comfortably within the confines of conventional milieux. His insurrection, then, is largely defensive in nature—he mocks and imaginatively destroys what he cannot tolerate, what threatens to enlist him in procedures that seem to him insane, but his responses to experience are basically bizarre and compulsive—he is a very sick man, not at all suited to make the existential, conscious choices that a Sartre might commend. Obviously, Gombrowicz's exposition refuses to adhere to therapeutic imperatives—he can proclaim nothing more than the necessary destruction of inhibiting forms. (pp. 285-88)

[The analogy between a philosophical conflict and the contest between the features of adolescence and senility] are precisely the terms of Gombrowicz's fictional explorations, both in the novel *Pornographia* and in *Ferdydurke.* The dynamic is set in motion on the very first page of *Ferdydurke,* with the protagonist's reference to earlier dreams of regression to adolescence, dreams which so absorb him in his present moment that he surrenders to them, the dreamer succumbing finally to the identity of fifteen-year-old ward of the philologist Pimko. The process whereby such a startling conversion is effected is not really novel at all: the protagonist's acquiescence is never really threatened, despite his occasional calls upon police . . . to dispel the nightmare. . . . Once he consents to hear himself addressed as "Johnnie," we cannot but assent to that manipulation of reality which is Gombrowicz's revenge upon us and upon the world we share. What he will make us see, whether we wish so to be taken into his confidence or not, is the perversity with which we customarily relate to reality, and the way that relation affects human potential. The perversity lies in our gravitation towards the vulgar and infantile in experience, despite the necessary revulsion from these elements, and the intellectual detachment which we affect to maintain from what is gross and petty and ignorant. In Gombrowicz's words: "What a curse it is that there is no permanent, stable order of things in our life on this planet, that everything in it is in perpetual motion, continual flux, that it is a necessity for everyone to be understood and appreciated by his neighbor, and that what fools and simpletons and oafs think of us is as important as the opinion of the wise, the subtle, the acute! For at heart man depends on the picture of himself formed in the minds of others, even if the others are half-wits . . . the more inept and petty criticism is, the more constricting it is, like a tight shoe." (pp. 289-90)

[Our] cultural institutions are empowered, in Gombrowicz's view, to impose upon their constituents an unreality so bewildering, so oppressive and so pervasive that they tend to think of reality as a kind of dream from which it is impossible ever to awaken, or escape. So dulled are they, and by extension all of us, by exposure to meaningless disciplines and empty conventions that they are unable to conceive of an alternative experience. . . . The official dreams of sanity to which we consign our waking lives and the private dreams of self-possession and maturity dissolve in one another, and the subjective consciousness struggles to objectify itself, so as to validate its own existence. Ultimately we acquiesce in those forms that others recognize as valid identities, and no longer need to think about conventions and authorities external to ourselves. The problem ceases to concern "the other," for we have ourselves become that "other" we had feared and courted. As Gombrowicz's protagonist says, "how can one escape from what one is, where is the leverage to come from?" (p. 290)

Gombrowicz's universe [is] an arena of disproportion and formal absurdity. His purpose is to drive a familiar situation into a depth of intensity in which it illuminates a universal form that cannot but be our concern. . . . [The] parody of a particular structured situation becomes a paradigm of structured relationships and structured responses in general, and we respond as much to an idea of experience as to constituent events themselves. . . . Clearly, too, we are impressed by the controlled oscillation between what is simply ludicrous and what is patently absurd. We note how even in revolt Kotecki betrays that exasperation before the inscrutable that may easily turn into acquiescence, perhaps even awe. (p. 292)

[What] Gombrowicz shows us is that we need forms, even as we reject them, or some of them, that there lives within us the perpetual child, jealous of his freedom, his *form-less-ness,* yet anxious to grow up into forms. Our generations are shaped and molded and deformed by the institutions we make for ourselves, and those who would escape them, the spontaneous, natural types, are after all types, as subject to forms as the rest of us, in their own ways perhaps even uniquely slavish.

There is, in the course of *Ferdydurke,* a search for the perfect youth, the stable boy par excellence, or the archetypal modern girl, but as the perspective of the entire novel indicates, it is not a meaningful search, so permeated by childishness is everything, and so tainted by consideration of forms is youth. (pp. 293-94)

Gombrowicz's rejection of the modern girl is considerably more ambiguous, yet in a distinctly more recent tradition. He rejects her finally because she does *not* threaten established order, because he sees that in her, formlessness has been elevated to a kind of behavioral imperative, and has grown into a style as deforming of spontaneity as any more conventional rigidity. (p. 295)

Confronted by the perverse hungers of the human animal, by mundane experience in its crudest manifestations, the girl reverts to a pattern of response that betrays her inadequacies as a model of the liberated personality. She is as unable to deal with experience in terms of genuine sentiments as anyone else. (pp. 295-96)

[Gombrowicz's] humor operates on cultural boundaries where normative ideas of decency are overstepped and the fall to "obscene" recognition is as pleasant for readers as it is shattering to the dupes who flit in and out of Gombrowicz's pages. . . . Bergson speaks of comedy as involved in a "slight revolt on the surface of social life," but this is hardly adequate to account for the savage and bitter irony we find in Gombrowicz. The humor of *Ferdydurke* cuts beneath the surfaces of social life much as it does in comedy of manners, or more recent fictions associated with that dramatic tradition. (pp. 298-99)

[Subliminal and gestural communication] is, as we have often been told by therapists as well as by novelists, frequently more meaningful and sincere than spoken communications, language being inadequate to convey meaning in many cases. There is no reason, however, to assume that gestures of one sort or another, as part of the repertoire of subliminal communications which are not codified, will be more genuine as expressions of sincere feeling than any other mode of interpersonal relationship. What we see is that even in the absence of strict denotational signification for communications other than linguistic utterance, conventions are at work all the time to effectively obstruct authentic relationship. Indeed, the conventions most often assume a value in themselves, and the pleasures of working through such conventions are cultivated wholly apart from the content of the communication they are designed to facilitate. (p. 299)

The object of such situations is not knowledge but higher and higher levels of competition, and to lose is to be humanly diminished only in the sense that one's assurance of invention and potency is shaken. Roles do not so much change under the pressure of such competitions as they are played with less enthusiasm for a time, until players can somehow be refreshed. . . . If the playing of roles is a consolation, it is meager compensation for the conviction that is regularly enforced by the protagonist's experience: that our relevance for others depends upon our participation, or refusal to participate, in the communal myths which are all the sustenance we shall ever share.

The morbid fantasies to which Gombrowicz's protagonist is heir, and their extension into extreme forms of rejection, are functions of an individualism that is consistently thwarted in attempts to locate an appropriate context for its exertions. The problem is familiar to readers of Dostoevski, many of whose characters find themselves locked into postures of hysterical rejection, in search of forms to shape and give direction to their revolt. . . . The available forms and conventions will not do, and as no relationship is conceivable without some mediating agency, isolation becomes the norm for such men.

Trapped by an individualism that is as pathetic as it is defiant, Gombrowicz's protagonist regresses first to the condition of childhood, and finally to the communal past, stretching his arms toward the sunken islands of innocence, where forms are not of a day, but expressions of an age, the inheritance of generations not harried quite as ours has been. (pp. 301-02)

A passion for humiliation marks Gombrowicz's protagonist, and it would seem that in order successfully to wallow in his unnaturalness he must find it necessary to posit the existence of a contrary condition. . . . What is clear is that Gombrowicz does not indulge in mere atmospheric writing for its own sake, though he works within a framework of recurrent enchantment and disenchantment, and manages to evoke a ghostly music from the oppressive permutations

he contrives for his characters. The major dimension of this section of *Ferdydurke* is disenchantment—the contagion of the dream cannot, finally, be separated from the element of unnaturalness and guilt that early plays at its edges, and inexorably invades its center. (pp. 303-04)

For almost at the outset of our excursion into Gombrowicz's aristocratic cuckoo-land we are beset by specters of the monstrous, by eccentric deformations that express an embattled conformity to unnatural and stifling conventions. Thus, the yokels of the rural countryside greet Johnnie and his companion with frantic barking, and refuse to accept protestations of good intentions. . . . (p. 304)

Johnnie and Mientus, as representatives of civilization, come to the countryside for their own peculiar purposes, with no consideration of the needs of those to whom they profess their good intentions. The political relations between advanced industrial societies and what is euphemistically referred to as the third world need hardly be invoked here to establish the veracity of Gombrowicz's account, and its continuing relevance. What is so terrible in Gombrowicz's vision, though, is not simply the fact of rapacity deluding itself beneath a cloak of good intentions, but the internal acquiescence of the eternal victims, their reversion to the status of dogs not only for the sake of others, but within the confines of their own hearts. . . . The conventions and forms that operate without remission in the urban universe to which Johnnie, and most of us, are accustomed, have extended their dominion everywhere, and we can no longer legitimately speak of a state of nature pristine in its innocence and isolation. Nor, probably, were we willing to tell ourselves the truth, could we have done so at an earlier time, for Gombrowicz's view does indeed cut across historical divisions, and the problem, we see, is as much man as it is the civilizations he has built.

The problem of form is manifested throughout the novel in an increasingly bizarre treatment of the expressive functions inherent in individual parts of the body, analytically detached from the whole. . . . He manages by turning his characters into caricatures of themselves at crucial moments, so that we can know them, as they can know themselves, only by the gross distortions to which their physiognomies are subject. It is not, however, a matter of simple manipulation, as of soulless puppets, for Gombrowicz provides ample justification for the systematic reduction of his characters. . . . [The] body nowhere reminds us of a machine, an organism with neither vitality nor soul, so much as when we are made to focus on a single element of that body, a nose in detachment from a face, a finger viewed without relation to its hand, an idiotic, toothy grin that seems to abolish from the facial surface all other features. Gombrowicz gives us all of these, and others, and always he reminds us of their sources in the external forms and introjected rigidities of our experience. (pp. 304-07)

For Gombrowicz is not primarily concerned with character, but with a broader, speculative problem, and he employs a peculiar convention not because he is constrained to do so by the mores and political exigencies of his culture. (p. 307)

Gombrowicz's universe . . . is surely enough to make anyone despair of forms in general as they function in human experience. . . . For what we have seen is that things which draw their identity from the forms they embody are very rarely themselves, that what they and we are in truth cannot be embodied in static forms, even when we are able from time to time to divest ourselves of superficial trappings and modulate our expression. In Gombrowicz, forms take on all the assumptions of self-perpetuating mythologies, and they wait as traps for those who would evade predictions of necessity. Thus, in the countryside, it is a baronial myth that presides, and defections from the normal are as predictable within the contexts of this myth as altogether conventional behavior. . . . For to call attention to forms which are traditionally established in a culture is to introduce a level of rationality and skepticism that severely undercuts social stability. We see that even violations of form work from the established conventions of a culture, rather than seeking to get beyond them to a set of assumptions that are fundamentally different. (pp. 310-11)

Ferdydurke contains a good deal of that monologous philosophizing we find in the novels of Günter Grass. . . . Both writers undercut the occasional ponderousness of their pronouncements on aesthetic imperatives by a skillful employment of irony and of hyperbolic excess. Moreover, both surround the more abstract and theoretical passages of their respective fictions with especially bizarre digressions that work unlikely variations on their central concerns. It is in these digressions that both Gombrowicz and Grass confront the brutality of the contemporary experience more directly than at any other point in their work, and what is so striking is their capacity to call terror by its proper names without evoking very strong feelings about it one way or the other. . . . Concomitant with this tendency is an adherence to ideas which is at most conditional, always on the verge of retreat or qualification. The only certainty in Gombrowicz is the condition of perpetual immaturity or becoming which we are all to embrace, consciously, and not entirely without hope, though we must know as well how we long for completion, for forms that inhibit growth, change, life itself.

The pity of it all, and this is not the least of Gombrowicz's triumphs in *Ferdydurke,* is that he betrays in the very composition of his fiction, in the novel's structural progression, his own bewilderment in the face of a tyranny he cannot dispel. For in the midst of his wildest digressions, we see that the principle of organic wholeness binds Gombrowicz, and though he tells us that experimentation is all, arbitrariness the only certain rule of composition, and that finally "the poet will repudiate his song," he cannot refrain from suggesting the structural significance of the most minor detail. What we shall never cast off, it would seem, is "the burden of being created inside ourselves by others," or by the ideas of others. (pp. 311-12)

Robert Boyers, "Gombrowicz and 'Ferdydurke': The Tyranny of Form," in The Centennial Review *(© 1970 by* The Centennial Review*), Vol. XIV, No. 3, 1970, pp. 284-312.*

* * *

GORENKO, Anna Andreyevna
See AKHMATOVA, Anna

* * *

GRACQ, Julien (pseudonym of Louis Poirier) 1910-

Gracq is a French novelist and critic. He combines in his

work the surrealist's use of myth and dream with a meticulous, almost classical, prose style.

EUGENIA V. OSGOOD

In *Au Château d'Argol,* as elsewhere in his writings, the approach of Julien Gracq to history is basically that of a Surrealist. History, which is for him mainly culture and civilization, is only a thin crust above what he calls "le tuf paléolithique" of our primitive drives. . . . [By] and large, Gracq sees the movement towards historicity as something limiting and deadening. . . . The *deep* history of humanity or of the human "soul" (a word Gracq very much likes) is to be seen primarily in a spacial perspective, as it erupts here and there on the surface of the planet. (p. 319)

Yet Gracq, the history professor, does not entirely turn his back on historical fact. On the contrary, from certain real events he selects materials to illuminate and intensify his narrative, while always taking care to remove them from their setting in time. . . . Myth—that "counter-history" of the Surrealists, a crystalization of human dreams where (in the words of Aragon) the "visage de l'infini" [aspect of infinity] lurks behind concrete forms—is always present in Gracq's work. There is no sharp cleavage between history, myth and nature, but rather an interpenetration, a working-together toward a gradual disengagement from the historic and toward a *dénouement* which is also a liberation.

Argol [the castle of *Au Château d'Argol*] is the archetypal castle of Celtic legends and Gothic novels, so dear to the Surrealists. However, it has been shaped by history, and through its architecture and furnishings history continues to exercise an indirect influence on the human beings who are within it. . . . The architecture of the building is a jumble of styles, designed to cause uneasiness and a feeling of *dépaysement*. A mixture of medieval and barbaric elements, its irregularity attacks the very idea of completeness. . . . (pp. 319-20)

The juxtaposition of contraries and the emphasis on the unusual create a tension which can be both exciting and ominous. . . . [The] material details, especially the architectural ones, are almost the equivalent of historic determinism, conveying the idea of predestination, of an ineluctable fate regulating the actions of the characters. The whole castle appears like a cage constructed by a sorcerer to coerce the inhabitants and to mold them to his own perverse whims. To counteract the spell cast by history, barbaric elements are introduced, both in the castle and in its surroundings. The wild and the untamed are suggested by the many animal pelts, by the "savage" horizon, by the virgin forest, and by the brilliance of the sun. (pp. 321-22)

The castle/forest relationship is a live and dynamic one: the castle is obviously a "lieu privilégié" [privileged place] which, in spite of all its historic shortcomings, allows man to enter into a pact with nature. On the other hand, the cemetery, also laid out by man, is only an assemblage of old stones, gradually sinking into the sand. The contrast between the permanence of the natural universe and the transitoriness of all that is human is graphically represented in the chapter's final passage where a "navire céleste"—a majestic cloud—slowly passes through the sky above the graveyard. . . . (p. 322)

Superior to anything wrought by the historic process, the forest, the sea, the earth, the seasons constantly influence man. . . .

There is a romantic concordance between human feelings and nature which holds true for all the protagonists in the novel. Their meditations follow the obsessive uniformity of raindrops and become powerfully and monotonously penetrating. (p. 323)

Although the action of the novel is almost completely internalized and consists of a cluster of mental states, linear time—inextricably bound with the traditional view of history—has not been entirely excluded from Argol. At least part of the real (hidden) history of the protagonists evolves diachronically, and the mechanical time of the clock measures human duration, felt and valorized subjectively by man. (p. 325)

But myth itself is not all-powerful: created by man, it is bound by historic and human limits and will disappear when the human race dies out. Mythic cycles are the time of the human imagination, but the seasonal rhythm of nature is more fundamental and owes nothing at all to man. Though undoubtedly indebted to German romantics, Gracq has evolved his own special geo-physical perception of time; it is experienced as an "état second" when man actually senses the pulse of the planet and becomes part of the cosmic cycle. (p. 326)

The imprisonment of modern Man, prepared by the historic process, is a fundamental element in the works of Malraux, Sartre, and Camus, and Gracq sees the point of convergence of their thought and his in the basic question: How can one exist in prison? However he finds the answers to these other writers unsatisfactory because they are couched mainly in ethical terms. In their novels—which Gracq brands as "défaitiste"—man emerges as a "grand malade," either the victim of anguish, trying to exercise a useless freedom, or a prey to the absurd, separated from himself and hopelessly alienated.... Gracq looks to surrealism for the hope, optimism and belief in the potential of the human mind which our epoch so badly needs. The Surrealists' concern with recovering man's primitive powers of communication, synonymous with a greater openness toward the "coeur du monde" and toward the intimate essence of other consciences, is also a major issue for Gracq. He feels that man should leave his individual seclusion and merge into "something else," where he can be traversed and bathed by the unifying and reconciliatory Dionysian flux.... (p. 327)

Au Château d'Argol, published almost simultaneously with Sartre's *La Nausée*, has been described as the latter's opposite, and as an antidote and a cure for nausea, offering a Surrealist solution to an existential problem. Interestingly enough, this solution is a quasi-religious one: it is accomplished through salvation and regeneration of man's psyche.... Gracq believes that the "spiritual" problem warrants reexamination from a Surrealist point of view, and he proceeds to do so in *Au Château d'Argol*. The result is a new variant of that part of the Grail legend in which the free circulation of the "blood of the world" is said to bring youth and integrity back to man and his universe. (pp. 327-28)

The emphasis on the moments of fulfillment, on "moments privilégiés," brings Gracq's conception of history close to the mythology with which his work is saturated.... The Hegelian version of the myth of man's fall, the demonic version of the Grail legend, the mythology of the forest, the myth of the "self," the Faust myth, the myth of the night, all contribute to the structuring of *Au Château d'Argol* and Gracq's subsequent *récits*. (p. 328)

In spite of his interest in a solution to man's historic dilemma, Gracq likes unresolved conflicts and hypotheses, and all his stories are *open* stories. There is a series of "opening" actions in Argol. Mostly pilgrimages without a definite goal, they start from a narrow historic situation and then move into mythical space where dreams are made concrete, a deeper level of communication established, and a new vista unfolded. (p. 329)

What attracts Gracq to history is its *magic* rather than its logic, its mysticism rather than its materialism (even if the latter is dialectic). He denounces the opacity of much historico-critical reconstruction and its distortion of our vision of the past. On the other hand, the great hours of "magical politics" and of the "grand jeu" are said to be the luminous moments with which human becoming is interspersed. While André Breton wrote *L'Art magique*, choosing from the wealth of the world's artistic creations those which were animated by the surrealist spark, Gracq could probably write a comparable *Histoire magique* centering on some of the neglected instants of history which contained a very special kind of magic. (p. 331)

Eugenia V. Osgood, "A Surrealist Synthesis of History: 'Au Château d'Argol'," in L'Esprit Créateur (copyright © 1975 by L'Esprit Créateur), Fall, 1975, pp. 319-31.

SHEILA GAUDON

What differentiates *Un Balcon en forêt* from the preceding three novels of Julien Gracq [*Au château d'Argol, Un beau ténébreaux*, and *Le rivage des Syrtes*], which are based on imaginary situations, is that it is apparently concerned with historical events, namely the first seven months of the second world war in the Ardennes forest, in the district where the decisive German offensive was to take place. The events, however, provide only a broad framework in which other forces are at play. This is clearly brought home to us by the presence of an intricate intertextual network, consisting of oblique or direct references to Shakespeare, Swedenborg, Gide, Jules Verne, André Breton, Saint-John Perse, Rimbaud, Lewis Carroll and probably many others, and by an equally powerful thematic structure giving the work a type of coherence that is not dependent upon the actual historical content of the "story".

Among the numerous literary references, there are two that are very different from the others in their scope since they play an important part in establishing the specific tonality of the book: the Wagnerian epigraph and the allusion to E. A. Poe's *Domain of Arnheim*....

On the most literal level, the epigraph reflects the situation of Grange and his men who are indeed "guardians of the forest," but beyond this fact, the very name of Parsifal conjures up all sorts of connotations that tend to make us forget the contemporary setting. (p. 132)

Medieval allusions are present throughout the book, together with a certain evocation of the enchanted woods of fairy tales.... This vaguely evocatory magic provides the setting in which images of enchanted sleep find their place —the deep enchanted sleep that in Wagner's *Parsifal* envelops the castle and forest of the wounded Amfortas.... It is the strange heavy slumber of the guardians of the Grail, pervading Gracq's own interpretation of the legend in *Le Roi Pêcheur*, that dominates "cette armée au bois dormant." ... Sleep, the enchanted sleep of the Sleeping Beauty, figures in its very essence *waiting*.... The dawn which the guardians of Amfortas' castle are waiting for is neither a positive nor a negative signal. It points neither to success nor catastrophe. It says only that something will eventually happen.

The early allusion to Edgar Allan Poe's *Domain of Arnheim*, an account of a symbolic boat journey to a domain where the traveller may find bliss is in itself more clearly valorized. The journey related by Poe is preceded by an exposition explaining that the individual, under certain fortuitous and unusual circumstances may be happy.... Poe's hero travels by boat to the castle of Arnheim, the ideal place he has found to seek happiness. The seemingly normal boat carrying him into the maze of enchanted streams becomes a fairy bark gliding magically into still waters in the middle of which is the splendid castle of Arnheim. (pp. 132-34)

The beginning of Grange's journey from Charleville to Moriarmé follows a similar pattern. As the author establishes firmly the geographical reality, with the train following the meanders of the river between the hills, through pastures as neat as an English lawn, through ever-deepening gorges, he is also marking a fairly specific parallel with Poe's symbolical journey.... Grange's rêverie before he sleeps at the end of the first day is the departure point for a passage to a different world.... The ugliness is being left behind to be replaced by the starry night. Is this, as in Poe's tale, progressive discovery of bliss? In any event it is clear that Grange's journey up to the "Balcony in the forest", although it is presented as a real physical journey by train and army truck, is more of a movement into self, into solitude. Movement is thus replaced by immobility. What is a reality at the beginning of the book becomes symbolical, an image of movement in the stillness, which is not without its threatening aspects.

The Poe signal takes on an added significance in the light of Gaston Bachelard's reading of the *Domain of Arnheim* in *L'Eau et les rêves*.... Poe's *rêverie* is that of death, and the principle vehicle of his *rêverie* is "heavy" water.... (pp. 134-35)

When, at the end of the winter on his return from leave in Chinon Grange takes up the Parsifal theme, and asks himself what they are waiting for ("Qu'est-ce qu'on attend ici?") the question is accompanied by images of total liquefaction.... This in itself is an answer: death is already present in the sluggish oily waters—heavy waters not yet stagnant.... Although in the war context the wait for the enemy attack intensifies as spring approaches, the water imagery clearly indicates that the real action is taking place on the personal level. This is confirmed almost immediately by the complete interiorization of the landscape.... Grange is increasingly aware of something about his own personal quest. In the limbo in which he waits he has a need for and a sense of freedom....

[As the wait for the enemy attack intensifies, the] Parsifal theme (waiting), is no longer a mere impression.... [It] is clearly woven into the texture of the "récit". (p. 135)

In the pattern of a "quest", death is an accident, a possibility that may forever separate the erring knight from the object of the quest. An "adventure" in which death and truth (or meaning) are both at the end of the road, can be read more efficiently in terms of initiation than in Arthurian terms, and *Un Balcon en forêt* easily lends itself to this reading....

Initiation, involving originally a body of rites "to produce a decisive alteration in the religious and social status of the person to be initiated," comprising ordeals centered upon ritual death followed by rebirth to a new condition, is a spiritual preparation for the understanding of the world of the society in which it takes place. It is based on the sacrality of the cosmos, and man undergoing the experience gains access, through his initiation, to the values of the spirit. Grange undergoes a personal form of initiation.... (p. 136)

In *Un Balcon en forêt* the first "initiation signal" appears in the first sentence of the book. Grange's military rank is that of "aspirant". Thus the candidate for initiation, the novice, doubles from the outset the officer-candidate. He is also travelling away from his normal environment without knowing where he is being taken, a recurrent feature of initiation patterns, where the novice may even be blindfolded....

The very setting "A Balcony in the forest", high above the Meuse evokes another essential feature of initiatory rites: in many primitive religions the candidate is led up into a forest to undergo the ordeals—he will be as near as possible to the heavens in order to reach out to the cosmos, and to be able to receive more easily the consecration sought. (p. 137)

The rupture in continuity, Grange's break with his normal life, is stressed by the total absence at the beginning of the *récit* to his past life and by the new rhythm assumed once the first conditions of the initiation have been established. Life in the military setting vegetates. The monotony, the semi-paralysis of the French military is englobed almost exclusively in a descriptive mode: all actions, the regular descents to Moriarmé, all conversations—even if they could be presumed to have taken place only once,—are related in the imperfect tense, thus integrating them into a background, removing from them all contours, and excluding any precision from this first season in the forest. (p. 138)

Grange does not sleep at night, and his extreme sensitivity to the night sounds echoes another characteristic of the novice's period of ordeals. He remains conscious, present in the world, receptive, while others sleep: darkness is menacing, but this is part of the trial.... Grange is semi-aware of the cosmos but is unable to reach its true meaning because like Parsifal, he does not know what question to ask. His journey through the ordeals will prove whether he has the spiritual capacities necessary to make the required ontological change.

However, no change of this kind is possible without a mediator, an initiator, and it is as he is returning one Sunday afternoon from Moriarmé through the misty cloistered forest, daydreaming, that the "aspirant" encounters his initiator: Mona. Although women cannot themselves undergo the initiatory trials, they are frequently the initiators—the taking of the neophyte to a woman's hut symbolizing once more a return to the cosmic womb, and often comprising what Eliade describes as an "ambivalent sexual pantomime" involving a risk of death. (pp. 138-39)

Mona is under the sign of water, poetically symbolical of transiency.... [The] omnipresence of water imagery ... gives the novel a perfect coherence on the thematic level and reinforces the link between initiation and death. (p. 139)

[When] Grange, wounded, is himself facing physical death, it is entirely on the individual level that he meets it. He experiences the release, the freedom sought, the terminal calm of a person free from all bonds. The return to the personal level is complete. One sign of this is the absence of the pronoun "on" from the final pages. (p. 144)

The final page contains both the poetic image of Grange letting himself sink into the sweet silence, the peace of a field of asphodels, and that of a weary man pulling the blanket over his head and going to sleep. To sleep, to die. To sleep, perchance to dream? (p. 145)

To see in Grange a second Parsifal, or a passenger for the Domain of Arnheim, would require, in my opinion, a serious distortion of the [structure of *Un Balcon en forêt*]: there is no grail to be found, no ultimate bliss to be attained. The adventure is pure movement and there is no answer to the questions asked.... His is purely a secular world, in which initiation patterns lead *nowhere*. This critical interpretation of the "magical" framework is ... prominent in the book.... One could perhaps characterize Gracq's art in *Un Balcon en forêt* by this ability to convey meaning through images which break the surface of the narrative.... (p. 146)

> Sheila Gaudon, "Julien Gracq's 'Un Balcon en forêt': The Ambiguities of Initiation," in Romanic Review (copyright © by the Trustees of Columbia University in the City of New York; reprinted by permission), March, 1976, pp. 132-46.

*   *   *

GRASS, Günter   1927-

A German novelist, poet, playwright, and artist, Grass has also been active in the German Socialist Democratic Party. As a representative of the generation of Germans who grew to maturity during the Second World War and a former member of the Hitler Youth, Grass in his work is never far from the problems confronting contemporary Germany. He is a brilliant stylist, displaying a genius for handling a variety of narrative styles. Woven into his work are elements of the fantastic, the grotesque, and the absurd, presented in Grass's exuberant linguistic style, with its flare for puns and word play. He received the Georg Büchner Prize, Germany's most prestigious literary award, in 1965. Grass once trained to be a painter and sculptor, and now illustrates his own works. (See also CLC, Vols. 1, 2, 4, 6, and Contemporary Authors, Vols. 13-16, rev. ed.)

ANN L. MASON

Grass has repeatedly expressed his scepticism about the use of symbols, associating this mode with Nazi propaganda and with ideological thought in general.... (p. 69)

For Grass, the symbolic mode is tied to the German idealistic tradition. As a result, he constantly devalues fixed symbolic patterns in his works and discovers symbolic equivalents for ideas, traditions, or historical conditions that exhibit simultaneously their relevance and their absurd arbitrariness. Grass both uses and parodies his use of this mode. He makes connections playfully and too profusely, as with the dog in *Hundejahre*; he makes clear the grotesque discrepancy between symbolic equivalents and the occasions of brute reality, thus emphasizing the inadequacy of the whole symbolizing process. In *Hundejahre*, the scarecrows, which have so often been identified with the Nazis, are revealed as insubstantial and insufficient to express the reality they represent; in the scene in which Amsel is beaten by the Nazis, his artistic constructions are juxtaposed ironically with the more terrifying image of the assailants.... (p. 70)

> Ann L. Mason, in Contemporary Literature (© 1976 by the Board of Regents of the University of Wisconsin System), Vol. 17, No. 1, Winter, 1976.

THOMAS Di NAPOLI

[Grass's works] deal with the question of guilt, specifically Germany's guilt, but more importantly, universal existential guilt.

The picture he paints, to use his own words, is gray, perhaps depressing to some of his readers, but the reason for the gray is because this color is mid-way between black and white, and therefore closer to the reality which Grass knows is somewhere between evil and good. (p. 436)

"Where's the witch, black as pitch?" sing the unknowing children of Grass. A chorus too aware of this figure's significance chants a response whose mocking echo—Ha, Ha, Ha!—lingers long after the reader has put aside the work in which this character is found, Although she appears in this form only in *The Tin Drum*, this enigmatic figure does not confine her activity to this one novel, but rather casts a menacing shadow over all of her creator's work....

Those of Grass' heroes who feel pursued by the wicked witch react in a manner typical of fugitives. Now they turn back to face an accusing past, now forward to face the future with all its uncertainty. Such a fear of the past, coupled with an apprehension of the future, cannot help but effect one's present. For Grass, it does so specifically by strengthening the need for confession: "What would Catholicism be without the Witch who blackens every confessional with her shadow?"

In Oskar Matzerath, the author of these lines as well as of his own life's story, Grass has concentrated the multifariousness of guilt, from the guilt forced upon a person by one's peers or elders to that self-imposed guilt whose tracks lie too far in the past for even an omniscient gnome like Oskar to retrace. (p. 437)

Grass' characters ... are aware enough of guilt yet ignorant of its origins; hence they are destined to chase an illusory phantom with a multitude of names. On this relentless chase the best one can expect are infinitesimal pauses during which one can forget for a moment one's sense of guilt. There is a danger, however, in this line of thought, namely the danger of confusing such stops along the way with one's destination. In Grass' unique language this would be tantamount to mistaking the "local anaesthetic" for the genuine cure.... (p. 438)

"And he's always running off to pray." The words are spoken of Joachim Mahlke, the reluctant hero of the second part of "the Danzig Trilogy," *Cat and Mouse*; though they might seem insignificant at first glance, these words nonetheless contain the theme of eternal flight sustained by hope, which is central to Grass' work. The idea expressed here spells the difference between the genuine religious writer and the nihilist. . . . Awareness of [the relationship of fear and hope] by the reader is essential to an understanding of Grass; and it is basic for an understanding of all the bizarre surrogates which charlatan redeemers would peddle to Grass' characters or which their fantasies devise for them.

The most dynamically sustained image Grass has used in his portrayal of man's running search for absolution is that of the locomotive coursing its way back and forth in an almost timeless journey. Grass has taken a common theme in postwar German literature and has grafted onto it the idea that religion is not the final destination of one's journey, but rather a vehicle to help one along the way. In his works, both themes come to complement each other, yet retain their own identity. In doing so, a certain tension is established between the train as a purely nihilistic image—which it would tend to become without the balancing effect of the religious allusions—and religion as the end point of one's search—which *it* would become in turn had Grass not associated it with the train motif. (pp. 438-39)

[In] transferring certain properties from the religious realm to an object essentially alien to that sphere, Grass has not only added an important note to a traditional theme—even cliché—in German literature, but has at the same time cast doubt on the efficacy of religious institutions to effectively comfort a guilt-ridden individual. That is why such imaginative alternatives to the traditional confessional are found in Grass' work. . . .

[Plagued] by guilt, Grass' characters are forced by what they feel to be the irrelevance of traditional means of absolution to resort to more viable alternatives.

The surrogates chosen by Grass' disenchanted heroes are of two fairly distinct types. The first variations comprise a group whose alternatives are external in origin, each unique in itself, yet similar in that they have but a superficial, ephemeral effect. The last variation, on the other hand, originates within the person seeking absolution and so is a genuine, if at times futile, alternative.

Within the first group are three pairs of "compensatory aids": alcohol and novocain, which are found in the novel *Local Anaesthetic* and the play *Max*; tears and laughter, found in *Dog Years*; and the television screen and the so-called "miracle glasses," present in *Local Anaesthetic* and *Dog Years* respectively. (p. 440)

Recognizing the inefficacy of the aforementioned alternatives, some of Grass' characters are not content with such superficial "solutions." This leads to a final option available, one originating within each of them as individuals: writing as a means of self-realization, self-confession.

Oskar Matzerath, who in *The Tin Drum* narrates his autobiography, Heini Pilenz, who relates the strange story of his friend Joachim Mahlke in *Cat and Mouse*, and the authorial triad of Brauxel-Liebenau-Matern, which is "collectively responsible" for the writing of *Dog Years'* three parts, are the principal proponents of this method.

Before Oskar, who is in a mental hospital when the novel opens, can record his life-story, he has to send his attendant for paper. The type he requests is white, which Oskar equates with innocence, since no one has yet recorded his

life—i.e., his guilt—upon it. At the end of the novel Oskar is about to be released from the asylum where he had voluntarily sought refuge from the reality of the outside world. Thus from the opening lines he is as aware of the wicked witch, from whom he has been fleeing, as he is at the end of the work, when narrated time and narrative time merge. The purpose of his narrative, then, is to retrace his steps in order to discover exactly when this figure first pointed her accusing finger at him and, of course, why she did so. (pp. 442-43)

> *Thomas Di Napoli, "Guilt and Absolution: The Contrary World of Günter Grass," in* Cross Currents *(copyright 1977 by Convergence, Inc.), Winter, 1977, pp. 435-46.*

H. WAYNE SCHOW

[*The Tin Drum* has] an epic range in its temporal and cultural matter [and] a largeness of vision which, in its own way, comprehends the tragicomic implications of personal existence and historical development. (p. 5)

In confronting the structural variety and ambiguous richness of *The Tin Drum*, we find that they . . . derive from an extraordinary cornerstone—the functional complexity of the protagonist-narrator, Oskar Matzerath, whose creation is an achievement of imaginative and technical brilliance. As a result of Oskar's bizarre stance and strange capabilities, Grass manages to combine features of the most disparate novelistic forms as well as provide multiple perspectives on his social and historical materials.

Grass's most obvious departure from convention was to make Oskar a dwarf and a highly unusual one at that. (p. 6)

Though *The Tin Drum* is not a historical novel in the strictest sense, it is firmly embedded in a recent, particularized (and for these reasons highly convincing) historical matrix. Oskar's family history through three generations unfolds between 1899 and 1945 in the highly charged political and cultural tensions of Danzig and from 1945 to 1953 amid the post-war contradictions of West Germany. . . . Such "placing" inclines us to regard him (with certain reservations) primarily as a real person in an immediately real world and, therefore, capable of being influenced by that world. Thus, even though Oskar outrages us frequently, we have some encouragement to sympathize and identify humanly with him. (Perhaps he is so upsetting to us at times, because he seems potentially "one of us". . . .) (pp. 7-8)

[But Oskar's characterization is not] wholly consistent with the limitations implicit in the surface realism of the novel. Grass has endowed him with several powers of a kind ordinarily encountered only in fantasy, including precocious adult awareness from birth, and the ability to arrest arbitrarily his normal physical growth at the age of three and to commence it again, ostensibly by choice, some years later. (p. 8)

[These capabilities make Oskar] doubly an outsider. Not merely is he a freakish "exceptional child" freed from conforming to conventional patterns of development; almost as if by virtue of his supernatural awareness, unique abilities, and shrewd willfulness he stands above adults in the normal world, marching to his own drumming, exploiting the climate of license in which he moves.

This relationship to society suggests in some obvious ways the stance of the picaresque hero, as critics have frequently noted. Like the Spanish picaro, Oskar stands socially, morally, and to an often surprising extent, emotionally removed from the events around him. He makes his way through the world largely on his own terms, confident in his ability to manipulate and survive. Where the picaro moves up and down the social-class structure, usually in the role of a resourceful servant, Oskar by virtue of his small size and seeming insignificance enjoys considerable mobility and can turn up in the most improbable places. As an observer he enjoys an additional advantage: people around him assume unthinkingly that his arrested growth extends to his mental development as well, an impression he deliberately cultivates. Accordingly, no one pays any serious attention to him, and he comes and goes freely, witness to the most private acts of family, neighbors, and even public figures.

Characteristically, picaresque fiction lends itself to satire because the picaro's mobility provides a wide range of material for satiric attack and an appropriately detached viewpoint. If in *The Tin Drum* Grass is an eclectic novelist incorporating a surprising number of fictional modes, he is not least of all a satirist. His targets range from the quixotism of Polish patriotism to the morally bankrupt aestheticism of the Nazis; from the petty pleasures of the *petite bourgeoisie* between the wars to the indulgence of post-war Germans in excesses of guilt; from the shallowness of post-war German materialism to the special lunacies of modern art. For all such subjects, Oskar is a remarkably effective satiristic medium, an advantageously placed reflector of what is outside himself. (pp. 8-9)

Grass himself acknowledged that his novel was indebted to the form of the picaresque novel, in the same breath observing that it was similarly descended from the *Bildungsroman*. . . . To see how Grass has spanned these genres is to grasp in part Oskar's psychological complexity. (p. 9)

From his early years . . . Oskar has been searching for self-understanding in the way of a *Bildungsroman* protagonist. He is involved in a quest for identity which has intensified to the point of crisis as he lies in the mental institution writing his autobiography. Unquestionably, writing his story is his attempt to clarify and resolve that crisis. (p. 11)

One of the most persistent means by which Grass discloses Oskar's identity-quest—thereby emphasizing the inward focus characteristic of *Bildungs*-fiction—is the series of symbolic polarities in relation to which Oskar compulsively attempts to project and understand himself. . . . Grass's protagonist returns repeatedly to the opposition of Dionysus-Apollo—especially as exemplified in Rasputin and Goethe, those heroes of his idiosyncratic early education and figures of his own ambivalance ("my two souls," he calls them, echoing Faust). . . . Similarly, Oskar persistently sees himself in relation to both Jesus and Satan. In the former comparison he seeks a bit desperately to realize a transcendental identity and mission, seeing himself as the offspring of a holy triangle (however comically ironic). . . . [Disappointed] in his pleas for a miracle to build faith on, he responds with a psychologically predictable perversity, blasphemes Christ by setting himself up as the sacrilegious Jesus of the teenage-hoodlum Dusters. . . . (pp. 11-12)

[Women] are used to clarify symbolically the protagonist's spiritual struggle. Oskar's mother epitomizes certain paradoxes which lame Oskar in his quest for self-identity. . . . As Oskar's education in life continues, the contradictions of the feminine increasingly contribute to his spiritual and psychological ambivalence, in particular the tension between woman as spiritual ideal and woman as destructive force. (p. 12)

[Oskar's] conscious decision to grow . . . [is] a metaphor for acceptance of personal and social responsibility in the *Bildungsroman* sense. His physical growth is appropriately a painful ordeal (he becomes eventually an undersized hunchback rather than a dwarf), symbolizing the difficult and half-fearful reluctance he experiences now that he can (and must) pursue his identity independent of the deceased parental generation. . . .

Oskar's inconclusive posture at the end of his narrative can hardly be called a triumph. His reluctance to leave the psychological shelter of the mental institution and face the challenges of the world outside is the obverse of the conventional pattern of development in the *Bildungsroman*. (p. 13)

Oskar's failures are not entirely due to his own shortcoming. If he is morally and psychically lamed, as symbolized by his grotesque hump, he is so (Grass seems to imply) because that is the inevitable effect of a barbaric and bored world on one of Oskar's sensibilities. Oskar cannot escape the moral imperative to accept human responsibility. . . . His difficulty to find some adequate basis and direction as he is impelled from within to come to terms with his life. Quite clearly to Oskar's credit, he ultimately finds the life of materialistic superficiality in post-war Germany ("the bourgeois smug" he had denoted prophetically in a satiric poem during the war) attractive to neither of the two souls in him. . . . [His] retreat to the mental institution and ambivalence about leaving suggest that such exploitation is out of harmony with the humanly significant direction his growth is seeking. . . . Grass surrounds his protagonist with a corrupting cultural environment, implying that in such a world the traditionally positive outcome of the *Bildungsroman* is no longer possible. (p. 14)

Viewing Oskar with some sympathy is not meant to oversimplify his character nor to deny that at times he is offensively amoral and spiritually impotent. Emphasizing the intensity of his human involvement should correct a view which sees him as exclusively responsible for such failures, regarding him primarily as picaro, more an influence than influenced. . . . [Grass managed to make Oskar so convincingly complex] by making him a dwarf and exploiting the natural and symbolic ambiguity of that position, by making him an uneven participant in the life around him by virtue of his limitations and relative disinclinations, but by allowing him some partial emergence from his purely dwarfish, ahuman position. . . .

As if this were not enough, Oskar is given a drum on his third birthday. . . . On the psychological level . . . the drum can be seen as a crutch for Oskar's insecurities: "for without my drum I am always exposed and helpless," he says. . . . Clearly, reliance on the drum implies a stance inimical to normal adjustment, an aesthetic detachment opposed to social conformity. If the drum signifies an idiosyncratic limitation in Oskar, it is also paradoxically the symbol and means of his superiority, for his virtuoso mastery of it clearly marks him as an artist.

Through Oskar as drummer (. . . and *litterateur*, since he has created an extraordinary autobiography), Grass explores . . . the unique, lonely, demanding, powerful, and at times dehumanizing role of the artist. . . . Grass's inquiry seems to epitomize in Oskar several artistic stances simultaneously, including some which are ostensibly contradictory. What kind of artist is Oskar? In one simple way he is a drummer whose art is romantic self-expression, a means of celebrating his triumphs, of venting his sorrows. (pp. 15-16)

In another romantic perspective, Oskar is a drummer whose art mystically clarifies reality and truth. His drum is a medium of both memory and imagination through which he is able to reconstruct the past. . . . (p. 16)

The ramifications of Oskar's art do not end with these imaginative forays and mystical revelations, for the possession of such unusual powers presents opportunities for manipulation, whether for good or ill, and Oskar quickly discovers these exploitive possibilities. In his provocative exploration of these multiple tensions, Grass raises the central questions of the artist's relations to life and society, including the moral implications of his position. (pp. 16-17)

In Grass's treatment Oskar's stance as artist repeatedly yields ambiguity and paradox. (p. 17)

The implications of Oskar's artistic ambiguity are "both/and" rather than "either/or." Oskar's art can express the conscience of grieving humanity, as in the lyrical concluding chapter to Book One when he is contrasted with the artist-musician, Meyn, who sells out to the Nazis; but it is (in the perversity of its pied-piper musical magic) an analogue of Hitler's aesthetic entrancement of the German people. . . .

In this sphere Grass's criticism of modern culture and of German culture, in particular, is relevant. While the artist may attempt to influence his age, his stance is at least as likely to be influenced by the culture in which he lives. Historically, as in the later nineteenth century, aestheticism wins adherents among the sensitive in proportion to the disillusioning conditions and values prevailing in a culture or an age. Oskar is not alone in being driven into the arms of aestheticism. (p. 18)

In his loosely rambling but probing analysis of the uses of art and the implications of the artist's role, Grass does not provide a single view or simple answers but rather paradox after paradox. The ambiguities central to Oskar's developmental problem reflect the challenges, anguish, and failures experienced by twentieth-century German artists and intellectuals and, finally, have their universal applications. Oskar's psychological and situational flexibility, more than anything else, allows Grass so many explorative opportunities.

The hero as detached picaro, the hero as involved apprentice to life, the hero as artist, the hero as existential man; the novel as social history, the novel as satire, the novel as philosophical inquiry, the novel as psychological study, the novel as tragicomedy, the novel as realism *and* the novel as symbolic imagination; offensive yet satisfying, amoral yet profoundly moral, pessimistic yet paradoxically affirmative: what a remarkable combination to be found in a single work, what a complex vision. And Oskar unifies it all. (p. 19)

H. Wayne Schow, "Functional Complexity of Grass's Oskar," in Critique: Studies in Modern

Fiction *(copyright © by James Dean Young 1978), Vol. XIX, No. 3, 1978, pp. 5-20.*

MICHAEL HOLLINGTON

[Günter Grass's] novel *Der Butt (The Flounder)* . . . seems to have put paid to the view that his recent work exhibits a continuous decline from the standard of his first novels. . . .

Despite its characteristic baroque complexity of form the book has many immediately attractive features that make it fairly easy to understand why it has been so successful. It is probably the funniest book Grass has written; it contains some agreeable sensations, titillations, and provocations; and its subject is women's rights.

But it is a great deal more than an opportunistic exploitation of popular contemporary issues. It is at once an original contribution to the form of the novel, a more achieved success than *The Diary of A Snail,* and a serious contribution to discussion of the meaning of contemporary history. It brings to the subject of women in history an astonishing range and complexity of perspectives. (p. 35)

[The fisherman's wife] conceives, and so the novel begins with a transparently obvious and commodious symbol of fertilization (*Tristram Shandy* is a model for several of its features). Immediate large draughts are taken on this idea: copying the epic boasts of Arthurian literature, the narrator claims eternal life for himself and his wife. The story of the speaking fish is an archetype recurring throughout history, its characters constantly reborn. The narrator, like Oskar Matzerath in *The Tin Drum,* is given supranormal powers of memory—though in this novel they stretch back as far as the stone age. (p. 36)

[I wish to emphasize] how witty and sophisticated the handling of the Grimm story ["The Fisherman and His Wife"] is in this novel. Essential to its purposes is the idea and practice of an inexhaustible and promiscuous artistic imagination. And so the history of women which the novel writes is an outrageous and hilarious travesty of traditional 'male' scholarship. The tone is set by a colourful account in the first month of everyday life in stone age Danzig, in which pastiche of Levi-Strauss supplies information for the gaps that orthodox history and anthropology cannot fill. (pp. 37-8)

The treatment of recorded history is equally preposterous. The proposition that male historians have neglected to give an adequate account of women's role in history draws forth an elaborate fictional pseudo-history of women. Its categories are deliberate sterotypes . . . which alternate in an absurdly stylized dialectic designed to mock the Hegelian *Weltgeist* riding its way through history. The fictional biographies are sustained in large measure by their function as parodies, each section creating its own stylistic milieu in the manner of Joyce, perhaps, and each of the women offering excruciating evidence of the continuity of female artistic productivity in the form of bad medieval carols or worse baroque hymns. (p. 38)

But I think it would be mistaken to see parody as an end in itself in *Der Butt.* In and through the playfulness a deeply thoughtful exploration of the importance of art as calculated fabrication is mounted. . . . As in the earlier novels, Grass is here committed to the moral necessity of [the past's] recovery; injustices against women, like the realities of Nazi Germany, would sink into oblivion without the effort of constructing their history. But history, unless it confine itself to the collection of fragmentary ephemera, must narrate, and so falsify. Narration is essentially artificial—it selects, combines, arranges details, shapes events and patterns them against each other in order to create a coherent structure. History, for Grass, is vitally dependent on the techniques of fiction; but fictions are catalysts of further fictions, with the potentiality of a dialectical transformation of continuity into progress.

In exploring the roles of men and women the novel takes as a premise the existence of antithetical truths about the matter. From one perspective it gives unequivocal endorsement to the feminist hypothesis of a deep psychic disorder underlying the masculine role in history. History itself, such an argument runs, is essentially neurotic, the expression of a search for substitute satisfactions to assuage a deeprooted malaise. The basic male trauma is the ejection from the womb. . . . (pp. 39-40)

Grass's characteristic womb images recur *en masse* in this novel. . . . [The] psychic life of men is obsessed with the image of a lost paradise. The idea of a small, contained world not subject to the process of temporal change . . . is polarized against a frightened apprehension of the real world of change and differentiation as something open and unstructured and therefore dangerous. Sexuality becomes a perpetually unsatisfied search for the womb, violence the expression of frustrated rage at its failure. . . .

But the novel gives this set of propositions no more than conditional assent. For one thing, if it is to apply at all, it must apply to women as well as men. Right from the start, when the fish's offer of support involves the consulting of a ridiculous and cumbersome bureaucracy, the behaviour of the feminist radicals is frequently no more than a parodic imitation of masculine styles. (p. 40)

The novel cannot find, in the attitudes of the radical feminists, a convincing alternative to the male-dominated past. They are imprisoned in a sterile, undialectical polarization of roles which corrodes their conception of liberation. The official, discredited version of the Grimm story with its satiric caricature of the female shrew has its applicability to the novel after all.

Perhaps the most important thing to stress about *Der Butt* is that it is not finally concerned to establish any external or abstract description of the problem of the sexes at all. Its ambition is rather, I think, to convert the negative, destructive conflicts resulting from the polarization of male and female roles into a positive dialectic of men and women by embodying within itself a model of how such a dialectic might operate. The structure of *Der Butt* embodies a principle central to Grass's thinking about art—the idea of the resistance of the material to the process of artistic shaping. Following the aesthetic stated classically by Brecht, its form is discontinuous: no style and no narrative logic is allowed to attain authoritative status. Poems punctuate and comment on the separate scenes of the novel, isolating them from each other. Styles alternate and undermine each other, the characteristic baroque sentences of Grass challenged by a spare, terse diary style. Above all, the material of the present, public and private, constantly intrudes: the narrative must digest into itself the contingent, unfinished experience of daily living.

It is Ilsebill who, within the novel, sustains this resistance.

The biographies of the women are narrated against her refusal to fill the role of 'das ewig Weibliche', her constant critical skepsis and insistence upon the concerns of the present. It is she who prevents those women becoming mere parodies, and so referential merely in terms of other art: her determination (and that of the other contemporary feminists) to interpret those stories in terms of their meaning here and now gives them the capacity to move us. Humorously and indirectly, as the dedication and conclusion imply, the novel is a celebration of Ilsebill's obstinacy.

The function of the narrative 'I' can be approached in a similar way. Its immediately established protean exuberance is a provocation—put crudely, it is designed to come across at one level as a giant male chauvinist ego. Inevitably it elicits multiple feminist challenges: it masks a fundamental insecurity, it proclaims a desire to dominate. Again these objections are seen as the path to psychic freedom. Once more it is an existentialist novel, in which Grass 'puts himself in question' as he attempts to reply to the feminists.

I am describing a model rather than proclaiming an unqualified success. In *Der Butt* the novel, as a historical form, is very far from being dead; it may not be at ease with its continuing existence but its state of unrest is self-evidently a creative one. (pp. 41-2)

Michael Hollington, "Back to the Pisspot," in London Magazine (© London Magazine *1978), October, 1978, pp. 35-42.*

ANTHONY BURGESS

Günter Grass's primary function, from *The Tin Drum* on, has been to be good for the German people. The Nazis had both etiolated and inflated the German language. Grass restored blood and particularity to it and hurled whole dictionaries at his readers. He did not and still does not write what Thomas Mann would call novels, since naturalistic fictional technique would have imposed on him the duty of depicting with gloomy accuracy the shameful *ante* and *post* and *bellum* times, the alternative being to produce escapist fiction. He has looked at a diseased and convalescent and over-affluent Germany with the eyes of fantasy, that kind termed Rabelaisian, which admits monstrous exaggeration, word-play, mad catalogues, intestinal jokes and noises, allegory, magic, the setting of the historically embarrassing in a context of laughter. Grass and Rabelais meet in a generalized devotion to eating. *The Flounder* is not a wine and garlic book but a beer and dill one. On one level it may be described as a history of the Baltic lands in terms of food. Grass rightly says that nutrition is the most important thing in the world and that the professional historians ignore it. On another level we can call it a neo-mythical fantasy of the age-old struggle for dominance, now at its height in free Germany as elsewhere, between men and women. . . .

It is perhaps best to take this fantasy . . . as a celebration of life in all its gross particularity, with Grass still telling the German people to beware of the abstractions that have too often made them flounder in a nordic mist and to consult the needs of the stomach. . . . Grass makes all his points early and then keeps piling more of the same mash on our plates. I felt full about a third of the way through.

He is not a novelist. He is a fantasist in a venerable European tradition, and he is also a kind of poet.

Anthony Burgess, "A Fish among Feminists," in

The Times Literary Supplement (© *Times News-papers Ltd.* (London) 1978; *reproduced from* The Times Literary Supplement *by permission*), October 13, 1978, p. 1141.

WILLIAM McPHERSON

In *The Flounder* [Günter Grass] dishes up the history of the German branch of the human race from the end of the Stone Age to the present as seen from the perspective of the digestive tract. Flavored with dill, stuffed with prunes, and awash in beer, *The Flounder* is a kind of Germanic *One Hundred Years of Solitude*, a Baltic *Ulysses* (at least in scale), and fantastic in any language. . . . (p. G1)

The Flounder is a very European novel, one in the tradition of Rabelais and Beckett, not that of Thomas Mann. It is full of jokes and bawdy stories, allegory and mystery, exaggeration and learning. It has all the trappings of what is described—self-described, in fact—as a "major novel." . . . Fortunately, it is a bravura performance—it had better be because to fail in an endeavor of such vaulting ambition is to fall flat as . . . well, as a flounder—by a brilliant virtuoso, a vastly intelligent, sensitive and humane writer with a zany eye for the preposterous. Above all, it is a novel of ideas. . . . [While] I admire Günter Grass's novel, I found its brilliance more dazzling than radiant; it flashes rather than glows. After finishing it, I felt stuffed, rather like the man in the old Alka-Selzer commercial who exclaims. "I can't believe I ate the whole thing." (p. G4)

William McPherson, "A Fish Story," in Book World—The Washington Post (© The Washington Post), *November 5, 1978, pp. G1, G4.*

JOHN SIMON

The Flounder is even more epic in conception, if not in scale, than Günter Grass's previous big novels. (p. 57)

[All] major historical periods and sociopolitical phenomena enter into this tale of food and sex and power struggle through the ages. Significantly, no matter how repressed women are in any given time, they manage—usually through cookery—to control their men. . . .

There are nine principal women in [the narrator's] historical past, as well as two more, for good measure, in the near past and present. Those figures, nine and 11, recur throughout the three levels of the work. . . . (p. 58)

What is this? Is Grass trying simply to outdo Dante's use of the Christian mystical number nine in the *Vità nuova* and *The Divine Comedy*? Or is he just playing games? I think it is actually part of his basic technique, which relies both on flashbacks and flashforwards, and even more on a method of simultaneity and correspondences, to demonstrate that all time is of a piece, and that various periods are only like so many transparent spheres within other spheres revolving and interacting. (pp. 58-9)

The concept of *The Flounder* is both gigantic and detailed; it is to the execution's credit that, in so many ways, it comes up to the concept. There are, to be sure, interpolated poems that do not seem to me to live up to, and thus advance the cause of, the prose; and even the prose occasionally falls off. The complex structure and episodic nature of the work might militate against total emotional involvement on the reader's part, yet such is Grass's imaginative power and stylistic variety and verve that even episodicity ceases to be a serious drawback. One must

admire the author's voracity—only a man who adores food could acquire such lexical knowledge of cookery and put it to such eloquent use; and be awed by his omnivorousness, for countless other subjects are absorbed and put to imaginative work with like gusto.

A whole spectrum of languages—from Gothic doggerel to the latest megalopolitan slang—is handled by Grass with equal assurance. . . .

The Flounder is the first major satirical feminist novel; it is also the first major satirical anti-feminist novel. For in it Grass scrupulously makes both men and women equally ridiculous in their more fanatical isms. Yet in the end Grass gracefully accepts the future as he sees it: the coming of a new age of female hegemony. (p. 59)

John Simon, "What's Cooking?" in Saturday Review (© 1978 by Saturday Review Magazine Corp.; reprinted with permission), November 11, 1978, pp. 57-9.

MORRIS DICKSTEIN

"The Flounder" is one of those monstrous miscellanies like Rabelais's "Gargantua and Pantagruel," Burton's "Anatomy of Melancholy," Sterne's "Tristram Shandy," Melville's "Moby Dick" (a Grass favorite), Flaubert's "Bouvard and Pecuchet," and (in our century) Joyce's "Ulysses," that can take on the guise of narrative fictions but whose wilder energies lie elsewhere—as inflatable vessels of bizarre information, vehicles for all kinds of encyclopedic, mythological, and historical lore. . . .

Frequently these are scabrous and scandalous books, more blatantly obscene than other kinds of fiction—Mr. Grass is no exception here—yet they're also the work of intensely bookish men, anal types, collectors and compilers, shy but lecherous antiquarians. One of the things they collect is words, language; they have a passion for lists as well as facts, for epic catalogues and literary parodies. Where many novelists use language as a transparent medium for picturing the familiar world, these novels are more directly entranced with language itself and are written in a spectrum of styles as wide-ranging as their subject matter. . . .

A comic epic stuffed with maniacal research and ingenious analogies, "The Flounder" is by far the most audacious product of [Mr. Grass's] historical imagination. Not in its feminist theme however: by temperament Mr. Grass seems attached to his masculine prerogatives though depressed at the havoc they have wrought in the world. But the challenge of feminism does not possess his imagination the way the spectacle of the Nazis once did. The sardonic ferocity of "The Tin Drum" turns more pensive and playful here.

What stands up as vividly authentic in "The Flounder" is its original conception, the use of culinary history and sexual history as a vehicle for history. As in Joyce, Mr. Grass's sweeping panoramas of human life are more effective for being concretely localized. But Mr. Grass is an exile, an orphan. Like the shtetl that haunts the Yiddish writer, German Danzig [Mr. Grass's birthplace], has come to exist exclusively in his work. "Men survive only in the written word," saith the Flounder. In this novel Mr. Grass undertakes to record and preserve not only the lost world of his childhood, as in "The Tin Drum," but all of Danzig's history back to the Stone Age. . . .

Mr. Grass is an earthy writer with a coarse sense of humor,

a bubbling sensual gusto, and an infectious appetite for life. Not a conventional realist, he diffracts history through symbols and parables, using distortion and exaggeration to limn essential reality all the more sharply. He revels in the traditional German affinity for the grotesque, but he has eschewed the solemnity of Gothic painters and expressionist playwrights; instead, with a special mixture of comedy and horror . . . he became one of the tutelary spirits of the comic apocalyptic mode of the 1960's.

But where American black humorists sometimes settle for a casual nihilism, a send-up of history as an absurdist joke, Mr. Grass, despite his comic extravagance, remains a serious socialist obsessed with what history means and where it is going. This impels him to his political work, though it damages him as a writer. He has Chile on his mind, Watergate, the Yom Kippur War, the slums of Calcutta, and this can easily dilute his writing into topical discursiveness. Mr. Grass's cooks save him, for they give body to his politics and unite them with his gustatory temperament. Though comic creations, Mr. Grass's cooks, like Oskar, are all unyielding obsessional types, hedonists, ascetics, patriots, all mute but enduring witnesses to the special horrors of their age. Cooking tripe, boiling potatoes, hunting for mushrooms or ladling out soup at every stage of Europe's history, the cooks bring together Grass the novelist and Grass the socialist, for they make it possible for this burly Falstaffian imagination to write "history from below." Under the sign of the animal appetites, which no social coercion has ever managed to stifle, Mr. Grass recovers the point of view of the anonymous masses and rooted impulses usually left out of official history. In other words, he has written a real novel. (p. 66)

Morris Dickstein, "An Epic, Ribald Miscellany," in The New York Times Book Review (© *1978 by The New York Times Company; reprinted by permission), November 12, 1978, pp. 12, 66.*

NIGEL DENNIS

Grass has said that he wrote [*The Flounder*] as a fiftieth-birthday present to himself, and a birthday present need be pleasing only to the recipient. Much of *The Flounder* seems to have been pleasing to Grass—a nice change, probably, from all his political involvements of previous years. . . . It may have been fun fiddling with the number nine and finding other notions to apply it to, such as providing the book with nine sub-heroines who are also nine cooks. But what if none of the nine is interesting to read about? Even the greatest rambling novelists—those who work by whim and self-indulgence—run the risk of being bores; even Rabelais and Sterne, the greatest of the ramblers, are most decidedly bores from time to time. Grass is a much smaller man, and a much greater bore. He becomes interesting only when he is interested himself. (p. 22)

The open message that runs through the book is that he adores women when they are what they rarely are—compliant, unaggressive, kitchen-hearted, and chubby. To suggest that they are as mean and domineering as we are only when they are perverted by the masculine principle may enable a man to get on with his books; but I think the intelligent woman-reader will see through his pretense very easily and become fond of Grass—if she ever does—because he is a baby. The coarse, permissive words that overwhelm the sentences . . . do nothing to revitalize a language struck dumb by the Nazis, and less than nothing to inject reality into a dream. The more one is titted and twatted and cocked and cunted, the more sentimental and scatty the work appears to be at heart, and I think it is very probable that the soft and flaccid element is what has pleased the Germans . . . A loving neolithic mistress-and-mother with six tits provides a crude sort of humor, a warm sense of bed and *Schmalz,* and the illusion that the writer is gifted with a rich imagination. This is all very unfortunate. (pp. 22, 24)

The high quality of the cookery does not improve the quality of the fiction; it only means that this bad novel has something of a good book in it. Of three other short sections of the work, the same may be said. Two of these, puzzling as this may seem, are little items of autobiography which are far more imaginative than the parts of the book that are supposed to be imaginative. . . .

The first of these sections shows Grass in his native Danzig, which has been razed to the ground by RAF pattern bombing and is now in process of being rebuilt. . . . Great vaults that were once buried far below their Gothic or baroque superstructures have now become the surface of the city; the dead of hundreds of years ago are yielded up in the fragments of their coffins to share the world of the living. . . . This little bit is beautifully done: it is what imagination *is*. One can ignore the novelese that is mixed up with it and carry away the tiny, memorable pictures.

The second inspired section is a visit to Calcutta. . . . [Here] again Grass provides the perfect imaginative touch —the neat, well-dressed little schoolgirl from a well-to-do home walking quietly to school with her satchel of books, and picking her way in the most natural manner through the hordes of the half-naked and the diseased. Here, indeed, are a few "fully considered" pages.

The third impressive section confirms D. J. Enright's adaptation to Grass of Cyril Connolly's well-known aphorism: in every fat novel by Grass, Enright remarks . . . , there is a slim masterpiece struggling to get out. In *The Flounder* it is a hideous story of four lesbians going for a picnic and three of them "raping" the fourth. . . .

This story would make a fine short novel—in the hands of another writer. For Enright has also observed that there is a flabbiness in Grass that takes the edge off his best efforts, and that the old-fashioned elegance of, say, Thomas Mann can cut much deeper. Such is the present case. . . .

I hope that as time passes these three extracts will grow stronger than ever and reach the maturity that memory bestows on good things; the process will be helped by the fact that the bulk of the work will fade away to nothing. The cookery, of course, should belong to the residue, but unless one is to the kitchen born, as Grass obviously is, there is the difficulty of remembering so many recipes. I would like to think that one of those rich foundations that devote their wealth to the advancement of the arts will see to it that these many small works of devotion are removed from the general muddle of *The Flounder* and given to the world in a decent, orderly manner. (p. 24)

Nigel Dennis, "The One That Got Away," in The New York Review of Books (*reprinted with permission from* The New York Review of Books; *copyright © 1978 Nyrev, Inc.), November 23, 1978, pp. 22, 24.*

PAUL ZWEIG

Like much American fiction of the 1960s, *The Flounder* represents a variety of what I would like to call kitchen-sink modernism: form and control are out the window; anything goes, including the kitchen sink, or, in this case, the kitchen stove. Into his enormous stew of a narrative, Grass stirs large chunks of social history, some fanciful anthropology, travelogues, fairy tales, a virtual cookbook of succulent recipes, mock-romantic pastoral, including some of the great mushroom-hunting passages in recent literature (maybe the only such passages), autobiography, contemporary politics, the whole seasoned with a liberal sprinkling of poems about which the best I can say is that they don't survive translation. The book is so loaded with invention that it lumbers—I was going to say flounders—from "Month" to "Month," under the weight of its exuberance, as if Grass were determined that the feast will not let up, even for a minute. After all, the narrator has a few thousand years of lively memories to draw on, and he swerves back and forth among them in a weave of lyrical repetitions that provide a unity of sorts to this sprawling under-history of Baltic Prussia, where, incidentally, Grass was born.

The Flounder is also a more or less good-natured spoof of the women's liberation movement, at least of its earlier, tight-lipped phase, when it looked as if open war had been declared between the sexes. . . .

All this is good fun: an *Iliad* written by S. J. Perelman; a modernist potpourri owing more to Rabelais than to James Joyce; a joking version of the conspiratorial fantasies of, say, Thomas Pynchon. The amount of sheer information in the book is simply staggering. The passages on cooking, and the history of nutrition in particular, are unique. Yet, perhaps because of the ballooning extravagance of all this fun and history, Grass seems often to be struggling to keep his Rube Goldberg machine of a book from jingling to a halt. Only a thousand-armed juggler could succeed, and Grass never seems to have quite enough arms. The sheer bulk of the historical detail, the leaping about among dimly evoked characters and scenes, the overall blandness of the narrator's voice and character, make it difficult for the reader to keep up his narrative headway, and I found myself wading forward in places as if through glue. Only at times do Grass's "Cooks" and their men come alive as more than counters in a vast thematic chess game. Of them all, Dorothea of Montau, a beautiful but thin-minded medieval masochist, and Fat Gret, the sixteenth-century mountain of flesh and fornication, make a durable impression. The rest remain names. . . . But the book's creaky progress swallows up such scenes in the weariness of too many details, too much clotted history, and not enough of the Rabelaisian celebration to which Grass aspires; not enough strong characters to carry the flow of the book and make us care about its heaped, often magnificent rhetoric. (p. 81)

> Paul Zweig, "Too Many Cooks," in Harper's (copyright © 1978 by Paul Zweig; reprinted by permission of George Borchardt, Inc.), December, 1978, pp. 80-1.

*   *   *

GRAVES, Robert   1895-

Graves is an English poet, novelist, critic, translator, and editor. Stylistically traditional in many ways, his verse is both technically complex and artful. He is a romantic whose work takes classical lines and clarity, whose poetry revolves around themes of love, childhood, and the spirit world. These ideas are also visible in his prose, perhaps most importantly in *The White Goddess*, an exploration of the poet's muse and mythology. Graves is also recognized for his historical novels and his wide-ranging criticism. (See also *CLC*, Vols. 1, 2, 6, and *Contemporary Authors*, Vols. 5-8, rev. ed.)

MONROE K. SPEARS

Oxford Addresses on Poetry discusses "the hard core of our English poetic inheritance, namely poems inspired by the Muse rather than commissioned by Apollo, God of Reason," to quote Graves's foreword. "A good many of the younger University members agreed with me that such poems are alone likely to survive concentrated pressures from commercialized or politically slanted literature and entertainment," Graves observes, and continues: "The ornate academic Victorian tradition and the more recent but no less artificial Franco-American modernism, seemed to them equally bankrupt. . . ." As his Muse-worship hardens into dogma, Graves seems to envision it here as the basis of a literary program. But such programs are, of course, Apollonian; and furthermore Graves does not really believe any living poets are worth reading. His thesis is, therefore, as applied to contemporary poetry, completely negative. (Curiously, however, he reminds his readers on occasion that he and Laura Riding wrote *A Survey of Modernist Poetry*, one of the first books to recognize and defend the poetry that he now holds to be worthless.)

Graves's case against Modernism is threefold. The first argument is based on pure xenophobic prejudice: modernist poetry is un-English. He calls it Franco-American, and observes that "Anglo-American poetry of, say, 1911-1929" was "based on Continental models and psychological theory." Often mixed with this argument is the second, a "traditionalist" complaint that Modernism is based on a confusion of the arts and that it doesn't make sense. In *Food for Centaurs* he said, "All I know is that a Modernism based on a confessedly impossible attempt at adapting English poetic practice to the aesthetic principles of French painting makes no sense; and has never made any sense." . . . His third and most fundamental objection is that modernist poetry is in motive "critical, rather than creative," and is thus a form of Apollonian poetry, which is always "composed in the forepart of the mind," on a preconceived plan, and based on a "close knowledge of rhetoric, prosody, classical example, and contemporary fashion." . . . In contrast, Muse poetry, the kind Graves writes and approves of, he describes as "composed at the back of the mind; an unaccountable product of a trance in which the emotions of love, fear, anger, or grief are profoundly engaged, though at the same time powerfully disciplined. . . . The effect on readers of Muse poetry . . . is what the French call a *frisson*, and the Scots call a *grue*—meaning the shudder provoked by fearful or supernatural experiences."

This sounds like the same distinction that Matthew Arnold once made, in the course of explaining why the 18th century was an age of prose, between poetry conceived in the wits and poetry conceived in the soul. After Eliot's devastating commentary on the relation of this crude dichotomy to Arnold's own poetry, conceived in "the soul of a mid-century Oxford graduate," and his patient exposure of the falsity of any such assumption that the creative and critical faculties are necessarily opposed to each other, one would hardly expect Graves to restate it in cold blood. But Graves has no respect for Eliot; either he never read the passage or he would brush it aside.

Graves's theory of poetry—if it can be dignified by the name of theory—is essentially a perfectly conventional late Romantic notion of poetry as emotional and magical; it is remarkable only in its crude simplicity and vulnerability. Thus he believes quite literally in inspiration, as we have seen; true poetry is composed in a trance, without design by the conscious mind. (pp. 661-62)

During the last twenty years or so, however, Graves has embodied this notion of poetry in a private mythology, which he has elaborated with increasing explicitness. The central belief is that all true poetry is both inspired by and a celebration of the White Goddess. The White Goddess is both the Muse and the archetypal Woman, from bride to matriarch.... (pp. 662-63)

Graves's private myth is in itself intriguing and often delightful; it has given him, in Yeats's phrase, "metaphors for poetry," with some excellent results. But as a criterion for the judgment of poetry in general, it seems to me too preposterous to discuss seriously. As Graves uses it in the *Oxford Addresses,* it involves judging the poem by its content or subject-matter and by its relation to the poet's biography, and specifically to his love-life. These are old-fashioned heresies, popular in the last century, but now fortunately rare. In this volume, too, Graves dedicates himself even more single-mindedly than in the past to one purpose: the attempt to demonstrate that the kind of poetry he has written and wants to write is the only true poetry, and that poetry of any other sort is worthless. His criticism is, therefore, of little interest aside from the light it throws on Graves's own poetry. (p. 663)

Graves's scholarly and miscellaneous writings are more intimately related to his poetry than is his criticism. Nor can the criticism be meaningfully separated from these writings, for they are crucial to the question of Graves's beliefs—a question that must be confronted in evaluating the criticism. (pp. 663-64)

But, as [J. M. Cohen] has observed, Graves's approach to history is essentially that of the detective: he expects to find a solution that no one has discovered before—both in his historical novels and in his scholarly works—by deciphering and interpreting the concealed clues. Thus, as a kind of historical Sherlock Holmes, he finds the true and simple solution which previous investigators have been too stupid to see.... In this role he has propounded a whole series of reductive solutions: that Jesus of Nazareth was merely another Essene, absolutely faithful to the Jewish religion; that Milton was merely a trichomaniac; that the *Iliad* is merely an anti-war piece, suitably to be translated in prose with interspersed ballads and illustrated by Ronald Searle. But *The White Goddess* is the most astounding of them all, since it provides, directly or by implication, simple answers to all the mysteries of poetry and religion, from tree-alphabets to the meaning of the Trinity.

When he is not playing Private Eye among the historians, Graves likes to play Houdini among the spiritualists: he provides physical explanations for presumed supernatural phenomena, or makes magic natural. (pp. 665-66)

I have never understood why literary critics and classical scholars did not utter louder cries of outrage at the definition of myth Graves inflicted on a large and inadequately defended public in his Penguin *Greek Myths.* "True myth may be defined as the reduction to narrative shorthand of ritual mime performed on public festivals," he said pontifically. Graves seemed to regard the myths as having no psychological or archetypal significance whatever; his procedure in interpreting them was to "pay careful attention to the names, tribal origin, and fates of the characters concerned; and then restore it to the form of dramatic ritual, whereupon its incidental elements will sometimes suggest an analogy with another myth which has been given a wholly different anecdotal twist and shed light on both." Obviously, this kind of interpretation allows enormous scope for purely speculative reconstruction, since most of the "historical" events with which the myths are to be correlated are lost in the mists of pre-history. (p. 666)

Though he is anti-Modern, Graves is thus emphatically not a traditionalist. He has no reverence for the past and he is not interested in learning from it; instead, he re-shapes it in his own image. Truth, as he conceives of it, is private and individual. Here again, one is reminded of the Private Investigator of the tough detective story. Like these heroes, Graves has an admirable independence and a genuine integrity, but also an arrogant belief that he alone is intelligent and honest. Like theirs, his investigations tend to justify a low view of the rest of humanity and especially of his rivals. Like them, he displays much ingenuity and learning in his interpretations of events and characters, but also a certain coarseness of perception and a tendency to oversimplify. The most striking manifestation of this cast of mind in Graves is his inclination to reductionism—that is, to reduce large and complex matters to one single aspect and insist that there is nothing more to them. (pp. 667-68)

Similarly, Graves is addicted to crude dichotomies.... Graves is a fanatical etymologist, convinced that the true meaning of a word is the etymological, but given to concocting his own etymologies, with scant respect for the judgment of linguistic scholars. (p. 668)

In the *Oxford Addresses* Graves ..., like a true Romantic, equates religious and poetic truth.... (p. 669)

Graves thinks of religion as closely related to magic, an art of propitiating the external powers, and he rejects the accepted etymology which relates the word to *binding* beliefs. Finally, since poetry is the primary homage to be paid to the Muse and her chief invocation and worship, it is hard to see what men who are not poets, or not good poets, are to do. It would seem to be a highly exclusive religion: essentially an aesthetic religion for poets only. (p. 670)

[As] a religion, it will not stand serious inspection. It remains, finally, a protest, not standing alone but meaningful only in the context of the religion against which it rebels....

[*The Oxford Addresses on Poetry*] must have been very successful lectures, but they are hardly worth preserving. (p. 671)

[In *Food for Centaurs,* Graves described his poetic ideal:] "I said that a clear, personal voice was better than all the technical skill and daring experimentation in the world— really good poetry always makes plain, immediate, personal sense, is never dull, and goes on making better sense the oftener one reads it. 'Poems are like people,' I said, 'there are not many authentic ones around.'" As criterion for poetry in general, this is so arrogantly exclusive as to be preposterous; as description of Graves's own practice, it is excellent. Certainly Graves has succeeded in writing the kind of poetry he here defines—or perhaps one should say that he here defines the kind of poetry he has succeeded in writing.

The writing of poetry to a prescription this specific as to both form and content has certain obvious dangers. The chief is monotony. . . . [It] has also the great disadvantage of being esoteric. . . . Many of the poems are therefore didactic and Apollonian, even while expounding a doctrine that opposes these qualities. As to style, there is, in addition to the danger of writing to formula, that of reacting from Modernism into an excessive simplicity—into a conventionally late-Romantic "poetic" style. (pp. 671-72)

[In] the foreword to *Man Does, Woman Is,* he reveals that this volume "closes a three-book sequence dramatizing the vicissitudes of poetic love." Since the Muse can be known only as she is incarnate in a particular woman, clearly this is the story of a love affair with a real woman; but equally clearly it is both the record and the product of a love affair with the Muse. The poems themselves are testimony and fruit of an encounter with the Muse, and the story they tell is that of the poet's love for her latest mortal incarnation. In a sense, this is, like so much Romantic poetry, reflexive: that is, its ultimate subject is the writing of poetry. But Graves differs from other modern Romantics such as Wallace Stevens . . . in rendering vividly and convincingly the specific human aspect of both the Poet and the Muse.

This ambiguity of subject is sustained throughout the three volumes and preserved in careful balance. To resolve it would reduce most of the poems to either conventional celebrations of romantic love or conventional difficulties of the poet with his muse; what keeps them interesting is the constant analogy and interplay between the two subjects. (pp. 672-73)

"Dance of Words" deals with the nature of meter and the role of inspiration, arguing for traditional forms given an individual rhythm. . . . The pattern is basically iambic pentameter, yet highly varied, and with a recognizably Gravesian rhythm. There is a regular stanza pattern, but not so regular as to seem archaic. The language is natural, unstrained, personal, in accord with Graves's definition of his ideal. These observations hold true of most of the poems in the volume. When Graves goes wrong, the trouble is usually in an incomplete fusion of the two subjects, together with the liability to occasional unconscious absurdity that is inherent in so emotional and romantic a style. (p. 674)

[Grave's perfected style at its best is] easy, natural, colloquial, but rising effectively to the taut dramatic climax and then modulating away in the last line. The restraint everywhere else makes the penultimate line very moving. . . . The poem ["The Undead"] is sardonically amusing, and there is something pleasantly outrageous in Graves's brutal way of addressing us, his zombie readers—though if we are old readers of Graves we are not surprised by this treatment. After rereading and reflection, however, one ceases to be amused and becomes increasingly conscious of the monstrous arrogance that lies behind the

poem. For the poem is, in fact, a belated example of nineteenth-century special pleading for the Artist, the Genius, as superior to the ordinary human being and therefore not subject to the same rules, laws, moral codes. Its only new twist is that it admits Muses on equal terms with Poets to this very exclusive order. The metaphors of the poem tie in with those of others to suggest that only Poets and Muses are alive: everyone else is in an underworld, a Hades, a living death. . . . Although Graves would wince at the comparison, he resembles his *bête noire,* Ezra Pound, in that his Hell, too, is only for the others. (pp. 676-77)

Graves calls for poetry to "make sense." . . . There is a certain irony in the fact that so bitter an opponent of Modernism should write poetry that can be said to make sense only insofar as it is ambiguous. . . .

Graves has shown an increasing tendency to write Apollonian poetry in the course of expounding and illustrating his Muse doctrine. For poetry based on any dogma or formula will be didactic, even if the dogma is anarchic. (p. 677)

It seems to me, then, that Graves will not do as the latest version of the Poet as Hero. His stance as Romantic Lover is, in spite of superficial modernizations, essentially archaic. His arrogantly personal and eccentric interpretation of the past has made him unable to learn from it, and his doctrinaire attitude toward Modernism, with his absolute lack of generosity toward possible rivals, has led him to refuse to learn from his betters among the moderns. He is a genuine and highly accomplished poet, but a limited and dubious exemplar. In prose, he is a first-rate autobiographer and informal essayist, an interesting scholar-detective for those sophisticated enough to supply the necessary context for his revelations, and a deplorable literary critic. (p. 678)

> *Monroe K. Spears, "The Latest Graves: Poet and Private Eye," in* Sewanee Review *(reprinted by permission of the editor; © 1965 by The University of the South), Fall, 1965, pp. 660-78.*

ROBERT H. CANARY

[The framework of *Watch the North Wind Rise*] exhibits a duality characteristic of the genre of the "fantastic," [and] it provides an example of the way in which similar dualities may be found in utopian works. . . . (pp. 248-49)

Although set in a future alternative world, *Watch the North Wind Rise* maintains a certain tension between natural and supernatural explanations for what Venn-Thomas sees in New Crete, as well as for the dream-journey which takes him there. The poet-magicians who have summoned him believe implicitly in their own magic powers, but the magic which Venn-Thomas actually observes is explainable in terms of psychological suggestion and common sense. . . . (p. 249)

New Crete shares with many other utopias a caste system, and *Watch the North Wind Rise* includes both implicit and explicit satire on this feature of utopias. (p. 250)

The world of the utopia may thus be seen as existing in opposition to the author's own society, to other utopias, and (again) to an implicit notion of human possibilities. New Crete may also be seen as both a reproduction and an idealization of Late Bronze Age Crete, a Golden Age or lost Eden—though Graves's destruction of his own utopia at the end suggests that he believes in the Fortunate

Fall.... Societies which aspire to be perfect, as utopias do, are almost inevitably static, and New Crete seems to have been created as an escape from the consequences of man's history. But to be human is to change, and change is coming to New Crete at the end of the novel....

At some level, *Watch the North Wind Rise* is a projection of the conscious concerns and latent impulses of the poet Venn-Thomas-Graves. To begin with, it is obviously concerned not only with the kind of society implied by Graves's poetic values but also with the kind of society ideal for poets. The two are not identical, for the poetry of New Crete—and its music as well—is insipid and academic. (p. 251)

The failure of New Crete is the failure of the utopian ideal itself. The soft, good life which it provides its inhabitants does not arouse the strong emotions which Graves thinks necessary for true poetry. Poetry is to act as a mediator between innocence and experience, good and evil, but here is only innocence and good. (pp. 251-52)

Watch the North Wind Rise has many of the characteristics of the "fantastic" genre, which is to be located in an area of tension between the natural and the supernatural. As a utopian fiction, it also presents oppositions between notions of the possible, between social ideals, and between the idealizing and satiric impulse. Such formal dualities make it a particularly appropriate vehicle for the reflections of a poet who has always seen poetry as the result of mastering conflicting impulses. The congruence of the formal structure of the novel with the internal dynamic of its plot gives *Watch the North Wind Rise* an organic unity unusual in Graves's fiction.... (p. 253)

> Robert H. Canary, "Utopian and Fantastic Dualities in Robert Graves's 'Watch the North Wind Rise'," in Science-Fiction Studies (copyright © 1974 by R. D. Mullen and Darko Suvin), Fall, 1974, pp. 248-55.

PATRICK GRANT

In a brief but sharp review of Graves' *The Greek Myths*, ... [H. J. Rose complains] that Graves includes "sentimentalities of his own devising, legitimate enough in a work of the imagination, but quite out of place in a handbook of mythology, where a story should be told as the authorities tell it, or epitomized from their account." (p. 145)

The predicament can be summarized simply: the contemporary mythographer inherits a formidable equipment of technology and scholarship, and can no more ignore it than he can ignore the modern prose in which he expresses himself and which is no less a fruit of the same soil. To treat myth, in this light, as object for study is to provide a useful service of one sort, but it robs the story of its affective and noumenous dimension without which it does not remain mythic. On the other hand, to treat it without the context of historical analysis is to run the risk of divorcing the story from the lived and incarnate actuality which engendered it. The problem of reconciling these contraries is formidable, and although the theorists have made presentations of great sophistication, the proponents of ritualism, of euhemerism, and of psychology have found reconciliation extremely difficult. The analytic mind, its force bound by its own strength, simply finds in mythology the infuriating paradox (and rebuke) of a whole meaning which existed prior to the divisions of speech by which the very sophistication of

analysis is achieved. In such a predicament, claims Graves, the artistic imagination is singularly powerful, and by its means we can focus afresh on the old stories to experience them new and whole—as poetry undivided, not as prose analysed into sober familiarities. Consequently, though he will adapt the modern skills and sciences, Graves does not aim to reproduce their results: to criticize him for not doing so is to fall into a trap, as he scornfully expects we will.

I do not claim that Graves provides an answer to the problems of modern mythography, as will soon enough become clear, but I do believe he perceives the problems with clarity, and enjoys unusual gifts of imagination and scholarly talents of a higher order by means of which he affects a distinctive and original solution, however wrongheaded he seems to many serious scholars of the subject. (pp. 145-46)

As is now commonplace, the complementary opposite to the spirit of the prosaic, or Apollonian which Graves deplores, is the lunar White Goddess, the muse of poetry, representing the female in her three roles as mother, lover, and layer-out, who assures that the enskied imaginations of mankind aspiring to spiritual autonomy stay rooted in the mysteriously cyclical and passionately grounded conditions of human nature. She reminds us that language is but a remote declension of the flights of cranes and the beauties of trees. She tells us that science is not the only means of describing phenomena, and warns that "as soon as Apollo the Organizer, God of Science, usurps the power of his Mother the Goddess of inspired truth, wisdom and poetry," then, inevitably, "negatively ethical" ... behaviour follows.

In one way, the White Goddess is a very complex and highly syncretic figure (such as only a sophisticated Apollonian mind could conceive), but she is also, in more conventional terms, the Muse, for "poetry began in the matriarchal age, and derives its magic from the moon, not the sun." ... (p. 148)

[Graves], as a mythographer, insists that he is not to be understood by the analytic means of the literary critics. They "can be counted upon to make merry with what they can only view as my preposterous group of mares' nests," ... and Graves claims instead that his presentation of the single variable theme of poetry and myth rather "commits you to a confession." ... He insists, moreover, that at the centre of poetry (and ultimately of language, and of the alphabets in which the insights of poetry were first recorded), lies a secret. The poets are essentially preservers of the ancient knowledge from which civilization increasingly departs as its powers of articulation develop. Much of the eccentricity and monomania of modern poets is simply their "concealing their unhappy lack of a secret," and Graves laments that "there are no poetic secrets now," ... as there were among the ancient bardic colleges of pre-Christian Britain or among the early Christians, though the Athanasian creed has since made them disastrously explicit.... (p. 151)

Graves insists also that the origins of myth are in religious ritual—in "ritual mime performed on public festivals" ... which celebrate the birth, fruition and death of the year. The modern rift between poet and priest has therefore become a particular bane for literature. Especially since the Puritan revolution "It has become impossible to combine the once identical functions of priest and poet without doing violence to one calling or the other." . . . Graves claims that true poetry, whether modern or ancient, remains an inspired initiation to the "secret." . . . Graves has consistently argued for this primacy of inspiration, but he insists . . . that a true poem must be cast in meter, and must preserve the full meaning of every word. (pp. 151-52)

The series of equivalences between certain of Graves' attitudes as a mythographer, and the mainstream of European mythography until the seventeenth century can now be summarized. There is a common conviction that (1) myth is the fountainhead of inspired poetry; (2) myth, like true poetry, contains the profoundest cultural secrets; (3) by inspiration and formulation in stirring meters these secrets find most valid expression; (4) the poet's task is priestlike; (5) great learning and love of nature are indispensible poetic tools; (6) etymology reveals the full and original meaning of words to be "polysemous," and prior to reductive conceptualization that distinguishes historical fact from imaginative fancy; (7) such conventions find expression in an almost perversely disorganized and digressive style. In all this, Graves appears "old European" rather than modern.

Where, then, does Graves depart from this model? Mainly, as is well enough known, in an obdurate and consistent refusal to acknowledge God the Father as the source of any true poetic inspiration. The mystery for Graves resides with the mother, and in all his study of mythology Graves reverts to the hypothesis that patriarchy, and the patriarchal gods, were regrettable results of schism from a prior matriarchal order wherein woman, as mother, lover, and crone, was worshipped as the Great Triple Goddess, the power of the waxing, full, and waning moon, and of the three-season year of spring, summer, and winter. . . . The single theme of all poetry and living mythology is the identification by the poet of himself with the waxing year, and his inevitable fate is that of the king whom the Goddess Queen of the ancient matriarchy took to herself and ritually sacrificed to ensure fertility: "every Muse-poet, in a sense, dies for the Goddess whom he adores, just as the King died." . . . (p. 154)

Graves runs risks in . . . taking on so boldly the world of specialized scholarship and daring to show it up while also interpreting it accurately. . . . [The key lies in] Graves' perception that the facts can not be misrepresented, only refocussed, if the ground is truly intuited and imagined. And organized scholarship has been less than convinced that Graves has indeed honoured the facts. *The White Goddess* is, in particular, problematic. It is without footnotes or bibliography, which has almost compelled more recent scholars, even when directly concerned with matriarchal mythologies, to ignore it. . . . The omissions also render almost impossible the confirmation, and sometimes even the application, of particular arguments and suggestions which Graves makes. . . . And how can Graves be expected to decipher complex etymological riddles without a scholarly knowledge of the languages? Where is the archaeological evidence to be found for the imagined "iconotropic" reconstructions of familiar mythological materials? (pp. 159-60)

With *The Greek Myths* the issue is even more vivid, for the confrontation is more direct. For a start, Graves' ordering of the materials seems as random as the argument in *The White Goddess*. The freely indulged exercises in etymology have been classed as "Howlers," and he seems to ignore

important modern efforts similar to his own, for instance the work of Rose, Kerenyi, and the *Oxford Classical Dictionary*. His preference for late commentators, such as Dictys, leads him, furthermore, to syncretistic interpretations in which conflations of such late sources are made without due regard for tradition or authority. Moreover, he often omits earlier sources while citing the late ones, and the claim to "assemble . . . all the scattered elements of each myth" . . . can hardly be upheld. . . . Add to this his postulating unidentified but imagined icons to demonstrate that the stories, for instance of Paris and Heracles, are misinterpretations of original graphic representations of the Goddess, and the credibility of most readers is strained. (pp. 160-61)

[Although] Graves abjures the failures of Christianity, he has remained nonetheless faithful to Western thought and tradition in probing the roots of those failures. I believe he belongs, in consequence, more readily among the mythographers of the mainstream of Western tradition prior to the Puritan revolution which inaugurates the modern era of technology and scientific nominalism. . . . Graves is himself a product of a highly articulate and "prosaic" post-Renaissance culture, and his perspectives and techniques are highly self-conscious and sophisticated. Certainly he realizes the dimensions of experience he desires to uncover and revitalize cannot simply or prosaically be demonstrated: he appreciates the importance on the one hand of not turning myths into objects for study, and also of avoiding purely subjective interpretations. The facts of history themselves must yield the secret, as the earlier mythographers knew, and Graves undertakes to show how they may. His technique is ironic, his method proleptic, and his focus the White Goddess. (pp. 162-63)

> *Patrick Grant, "The Dark Side of the Moon: Robert Graves as Mythographer," in* The Malahat Review (© The Malahat Review, 1975), July, 1975, pp. 143-65.

*   *   *

GREEN, Julien   1900-

Green, a French novelist and playwright, has also published his journals and diaries. Born in France of American parents, Green resides in France while retaining his American citizenship. His works reflect his metaphysical struggle with the questions of evil, alienation, and mortality which confront contemporary man. (See also *CLC*, Vol. 3, and *Contemporary Authors*, Vols. 21-24, rev. ed.)

WALLACE FOWLIE

[Julien Green's *Sud* represents] one of the few really successful attempts in recent years at creating the pure tone of tragedy: all the ambiguities of the characters; the richness of their inner life which is communicated; the vigor, simplicity, and directness of the writing. (pp. 191-92)

The play is a tragedy on the theme of homosexuality, but it is also on a far more universal subject, and the public might well fail to recognize the immediate subject. Ian suddenly and hopelessly falls in love with Eric on meeting him, but he never confesses his love. The beauty and power of the play are precisely in this silence of Ian. It is quite possible that Ian had not been aware, or fully aware, of his nature. His meeting with Eric is a moment of illumination. (p. 192)

In his dramaturgy, as in his novels, [Julien Green] passes

easily from the real world to the surreal world. A supernaturally evil atmosphere surrounds many of the scenes, and yet there is intense drama in the effort of the characters to resist their fate. Especially in *Sud,* Julien Green calls attention to one of the most tragic aspects of physical love in the modern world. The human problem is never described or analyzed, and yet it is seen in its religious context. For Ian, love is forbidden in that irremediable way that the French associate with the tragedies of Racine. (p. 194)

> *Wallace Fowlie, "Green," in his* Dionysus in Paris: A Guide to Contemporary French Theater *(copyright © 1960 by Wallace Fowlie; reprinted by arrangement with The New American Library, Inc.), Meridian Books, 1960, pp. 191-94.*

NICHOLAS KOSTIS

Julien Green's novels aim and unfold towards sign, which becomes identifiable as symbol. I do not wish to imply that Green is a Symbolist novelist in the same formal or historical sense as the nineteenth-century Symbolists. I do maintain that his particular style, his manner of creating a world, his process of characterization, and his own relationship to his books lead to the creation of an extremely private, perhaps hermetic work of art, which, while it has the conventional form and characteristics of a novel, is nonetheless a system of signs which represent forces and states of mind that one feels are directly affecting, even torturing the author.

On the surface, the reader meets in Green's novels what one might reasonably call characters. They are recognizable as human beings. There is a strong evocation of the three-dimensional material world; there is conventional dialogue; intensely visual descriptive passages; and the elements of psychology in characterization. On the formal level there is also a highly refined and conscious structure and style. But all this representative and recognizable reality, all these conventions, all this ordinary experience are given, through repetition and juxtaposition, 'meta-meaning', that is, meaning behind and beyond the definition and value of their phenomenal presence, a secret sense in which human figures, gestures, shadows, objects, emotions, and characteristics, in which rooms and atmosphere, all translate, like hieroglyphs, the unspecified pressures at work within the author. More simply, the symbolism I speak of is that quality of suggestiveness found in all serious novels but here carried much farther. Green evokes certain experiences and works them into a highly personal system of associations, which grow more and more rigidly defined, specific, and predictable as they recur obsessively and relentlessly. At a certain point, the phenomenon—whether it be a human being or a stream of light—becomes so strongly sign that it loses its autonomy as phenomenon. It is because this suggestiveness is so formal and dominant that I call it by a different term: *symbolism.* Thus all of Green's work becomes uncommonly symbolic. This is the most remarkable aspect, I think, of Green's novels taken as a whole, and consequently it lies at the heart of his vision. (p. 11)

One observes no attempt [in Green's work], stylistically or otherwise, to crystalize a past or independent reality (except in the grossest sense that all artistic creation springs partly from the sum total of a novelist's experience). Rather, each situation, image, description, stylistic fact is assigned a specific value or role as the novel progresses, until the novel becomes a highly complex and self-contained system of signs which have little value or meaning in themselves but which, as they are repeated over and over in innumerable combinations, become the author's private set of hieroglyphs and ritual symbols. . . .

[These] symbols do not exist to evoke a world or a concrete vision of ordinary experience of reality. Rather, the concrete world exists to provide symbols which will evoke less concrete but nonetheless terrifying, unseen, and undefined forces. (p. 12)

Green's novels are not primarily psychological, and the sense of *crise* in them can hardly be explained in psychological terms. Rather, the author uses psychology stylistically to evoke an atmosphere suggestive of a darker metaphysical reality, and to translate the force of that reality. Similarly, dreams do not represent a psychological aspect of Green's characterization, nor do they signify the subconscious explanation of a conscious situation. For Green, dreaming is a process of selection: of including and excluding elements and placing them in relationship to each other in order to arrive at a symbolic reality more real than life. . . . There is no illumination in the dream state, for it is merely a more abstract configuration of concrete reality, both reality and dreams being configurations of the same inscrutable and indefinable forces. Green's constant use of the dream within a dream reinforces the sense that 'objective' reality is only one more dream within the series of concentric circles, a dream world dominated by enigma. The memory of what has gone on in the subconscious mind while one has been asleep is frequently vague after one has awakened, even if it remains at all, and Green's characters rarely remember their dreams.

This is characteristically the Green vision and the Green manner. The human condition is, above all, presented as enigma. There are no possible formulas or truths, no conclusions or wisdom, pragmatic or moral. There is only the enigma and its implications, which are intuitively grasped from the rite of the novel. It is thus that one must talk in terms of symbols rather than simply in terms of plot, imagery, description, style, psychology, and characterization. Green borrows figures from nature and builds up his own special world which conjures up and signifies the demoniacal forces and the dilemmas which underlie, he feels, both nature or being. His novels are less representations of reality, mirrors of nature, *mimesis,* or visions of fantasy than they are exorcisms. (pp. 13-14)

The force which defines reality in Green's world is death. The only certainty, it constitutes the foundation of being and reality. It makes his world a disquieting one of unresolved tensions, conflicts, and contradictions. A precarious metaphysical truce rarely endures. The ultimate source of every antithesis is the life-death antithesis. Instead of *cogito ergo sum* Green implies *morior ergo sum.* . . . Not only must any symbolic interpretation of the novels written before *Le Visionnaire* take into account this obsession with death, but this very fascination and fear of death is the key which unlocks the mystery of the symbols.

The novels written up through *Minuit* (composed when Green was beginning to return to Christianity) all deal with death, and in each there builds up a haunting obsession with death. Each of the characters in these novels is to be understood by his reactions to this total threat, whether it be the elderly M. Mesurat or the young hero of *L'Autre Sommeil*.... Many of Green's characters seek release in their obsessions, and in manias, and sadism. Others construct an artificial bourgeois world of order, symmetry, and material comfort, with their concomitant tyranny of habit. Some turn to eroticism. Still others seek release in the act of dreaming. Finally, there are those who wage a more successful metaphysical battle in which the individual overcomes this terror-ridden finite existence and its finite end, death. This precarious equilibrium between anguish and forgetfulness is full of potential disturbance, and invariably some crisis is precipitated.

Death is the force that dominates each character's consciousness. It can be called a 'force', because it is felt as power and because it translates itself into intense fear, terror, and longing to escape. It cannot be analyzed or localized. Concrete forms such as a dead man or even a dying man are inadequate to translate and express its nature, which penetrates to the very heart of an individual's being, dominating all that he sees and dictating his actions. It is more like a demi-urge or universal demon that holds the strings of being. In this sense, an entire gamut of phenomena—the art or science of psychology, the material and visual world, and the familiarity of gestures and acts—is necessary to communicate the force. Green's novel limits itself to such a communication; it goes no farther. Thus one must talk of incantation. He does not—cannot—analyze the force or draw 'wisdom' from it. The force remains the 'raison d'être' of the novel. The novel is neither salvation nor insight, and all characters and situations are subservient to the incantation.... [Death's] terror drives the human forms to passion as an escape, but the very passion drives its victims back to death. This is the structure of Green's world.

Death has never ceased to plague Green, and it pervades his entire work with varying intensity.... After his reconversion, however, death harasses him primarily as the threat of damnation.... If Green's reconversion freed him somewhat from being terrorized by death, it did not free him from anguish.... After *Le Visionnaire* pervasive fear of death is transposed into fear of life. The character's consciousness ceases to struggle with unknown, undefined forces and struggles instead with consciousness. This struggle takes on general metaphysical guises of sin versus Christianity, damnation versus salvation, flesh versus spirit. The body as an obstacle to the salvation of the soul now becomes the theme around which the symbols of his novels are organized. (pp. 14-16)

Two visual images in particular are indispensable to the symbolic structure of Green's novels: the room and chiaroscuro. The author integrates these two images into the structure of each novel, expanding them to meet the demands of an expanding vision. The first of these, the room, may be found in all his novels.... Closely related to the image of the room as a prison is that of the window, which stands for liberation.... It may be said, nevertheless, that the early novels, centered around Green's obsession with death, are structurally dependent on the image of the room as a prison. Chiaroscuro, on the other hand, is vital to the aesthetic structure and moral implications of Green's later novels, which are affected by his preoccupation with dualism, the conflict pitting the soul against the flesh. (pp. 16-17)

Nicholas Kostis, in his introduction to his The Exorcism of Sex and Death in Julien Green's Novels *(© copyright 1973 Mouton & Co. N.V., Publishers), Mouton, 1973, pp. 11-17.*

BYRON R. LIBHART

My own contention is that the works set in America are, in fact, exceptionally significant in revealing the true Julien Green through his fiction. This belief is based in large part upon the author's stressing the age twenty in his life—the age he reached during his first stay in America from 1919 to 1922—as that point at which he attained his definitive character....

There are two general areas in which the frustrations of Green's American characters are primarily a reflection of problems in his own life: the matter of "belonging," particularly in the sense of nationality, and that of personal morality. Each of these has its complexities in Green's life. Not only does he feel somewhat divided between France and America, but as far as the "American" side of him is concerned, there is the additional problem of political loyalties within that country—that is, to the South or the North. And the matter of personal morality is, not too surprisingly, closely allied to the problem of religious commitment and to an understanding of his abnormal sexual nature.... (p. 345)

In a more general and perhaps more important way, America represents an intrusion in Julien Green's life, a threat to his early acceptance of France as his true homeland, so that the very word became almost synonymous with *unhappiness* for him.... (p. 346)

Green's religious faith in general was severely shaken during that sojourn because of the deep moral crisis he experienced in America, which must have caused him henceforth to consider that country the setting par excellence for frustration. For Julien Green, morality and sexuality are very closely related matters. In fact, moral decency and sexual restraint seem almost synonymous in much of his writing—an attitude resulting largely from an early exposure to his mother's American puritanism.... (p. 347)

Though one may argue that nearly all of Green's characters suffer from some kind of *dépaysement* in the broadest sense—being out of their element, so to speak—Green sees this problem for the most part as the natural heritage of the American. The North-South dilemma is most clear-cut in the case of Ian Wiczewski in *Sud:* though his personal problems certainly outweigh all political considerations, his feeling particularly alone and despondent upon the sudden discovery of his sexual abnormality is definitely intensified by his being at the same time a Northern officer among Southern aristocrats on the very eve of the Civil War—truly a stranger in a strange land, in more than one respect. In *Le Voyageur sur la terre*, there is a definite connection between Daniel O'Donovan's schizophrenia and the conflicting influences of a Southern aunt and a Northern uncle. As for the Civil War itself, certainly Green's exaggerated notion of its lasting effects is responsible for its prominence in *Sud,* where it serves as more than the historical background, providing really a secondary plot.... What is extraordinary is not the *degree* of Green's interest in the Civil War, but the *character* of that interest, a rather archaic rallying to the South's cause, as if to please a long-deceased mother who had deeply impressed upon her little boy the injustice of the North's position. For him, as for her, to be Southern means to have suffered, and to have suffered unjustly.

But there is in Green's America another type of displacement even more profound: that of the characters who suffer, as the author himself had suffered, from feeling trapped in an environment that runs counter to and creates conflicts with their personal values. . . . (pp. 348-49)

We must not look to Julien Green's American works in the expectation of discovering any significant new insight into the problem of what ails America today; for the setting of these tales is a land that in a sense never existed—a curious place made up partly of the reality he knew there, partly of the distorted concepts bequeathed to him by his mother or created by his own troubled mind; and the character we behold on that bleak landscape is for the most part a tormented individual who does not belong there—an unhappy *voyageur sur la terre*—Julien Green himself. (pp. 351-52)

> Byron R. Libhart, "Julien Green's Troubled American: A Fictionalized Self-Portrait" (copyright © 1974 by the Modern Language Association of America; reprinted by permission of the Modern Language Association of America), in PMLA, 89 (March, 1974), pp. 341-52.

TREVOR FIELD

It is a temptation not always easily avoided to discuss the work of Julien Green by way of thematic or atmospheric generalizations, as opposed to an appreciation of precise narrative and artistic qualities. Gloomy, sultry, ominous; the epithets are by now very familiar—too familiar, perhaps, for they tend to deflect critical attention from Green's concern with problems of literary form and style. . . .

In complete contrast to [the] earlier novels, which were set either in the United States or in an anonymous French province, . . . *Épaves* (1932) based on madness and death, is a restrained and muted account of a crisis in the life of a mediocre Parisian bourgeois, Philippe Cléry. (p. 103)

Although the novel is full of obsessions, imaginings and dreams, its structure is noticeably different from that of the preceding ones; and it is this static, in many ways circular plot which underlies much of the argument that follows. . . .

One of the simplest uses to which mirror imagery is put in this novel is a reinforcement of Green's criticism of the lack of frankness that pervades bourgeois life, stifling individual development and human happiness. (p. 104)

Apart from representing an indirect method of watching the actions of other people, the mirror obviously provides the characters with a chance to look at themselves. In fact, they regularly do so, and we can distinguish here between two sets of circumstances: on the one hand, they may find in the mirror a direct way of seeing the truth about themselves; on the other, the mirror is used to check personal appearance, and in this context external features have the effect of hiding a more or less unpleasant inner truth. (p. 105)

[The] mirror is not only a familiar object that reintegrates Philippe into his past life, but also a vital tool in his attempt to spot a physical difference that might correspond to the inner truth so unpleasantly revealed. . . .

[After] capitulating weakly to a demand for money from a worthless sponger, Philippe checks his appearance in a mirror, in a darkened room. . . . Never has he appeared so handsome, and his childish reaction is to stand to attention like a soldier. But the magic effect is short-lived, for he immediately remembers that his physical strength is a useless illusion, and the imagery which accompanies his turning away in horror from the mirror is significant: "il se fit l'effet d'un personnage de comédie qui eût compris et joué son rôle comme un rôle tragique" [he gave the impression of a character from comedy who had understood and played his role as a tragic role]. . . . This idea of theatrical characters is another recurring theme in the novel, and parallels the theme of trying to hide the truth from oneself by means of a mirror image: external appearances in both cases represent a deliberate attempt to disguise the nature of an underlying personality. (pp. 107-08)

Just as the desire to hide personal truth, perceived in front of a mirror, is matched by the partial disguise involved in Philippe's seeing himself as an actor, so the unwelcome realisation of this truth is paralleled by an uncomfortably objective viewing of his own situation half-way through the novel. . . . [Philippe] goes into a cinema to pass another hour or two. The mediocre film that is showing startles Philippe and holds his attention because of the position of the deceived husband, and for a few seconds his own real life and the fictional story on the screen overlap so much that he is left straddling the two worlds, and unsure of his footing. The film goes on, a comedy for the rest of the audience but a tragedy for Philippe, until at last, as if from a position outside himself, he sees the image coinciding with truth, so that he is faced with a picture of himself. . . . (p. 108)

The use of mirror imagery, as illustrated hitherto, has revealed a more or less subtle, but quite conventional use of a particular device in order to reinforce certain narrative episodes or psychological observations. To emphasize fully the thematic relevance of this basic image, we should note the way in which the creation of an inner world, symbolized by the mirror, is connected with the theme of reading and writing in the novel. (p. 110)

[The] difficulties of both writing and painting have always stopped [Philippe] from settling down to any serious artistic work. The result . . . is that he tidies some books on his shelves and blows the dust off them. . . . Green is clearly taking advantage here of the age-old idea that books in general and novels in particular are analogous to mirrors, which in the context of *Épaves* are often used by people who are searching for or concealing the truth; while a second, more specific point is that Philippe's complacency in tidying his books instead of creating a new one of his own is another refusal to come to terms with himself and an attempt to be satisfied with the tidy appearance of the external and most meaningless aspect of a potential means of self-examination.

Mirror imagery, it is clear, dominates this novel. It symbolizes the indirect and false relationships shared by members of a bourgeois household torn apart by jealousy, suspicion and shame; it represents, both in literal terms and in the device of the cinema film, a direct apprehension of the characters' true positions and natures; equally, it serves to illustrate in a number of ways their desire to conceal either their whole bodies or their true characters from themselves; and it shows how people are tempted to escape from the realities of life and art by withdrawing into a world of personal fantasy. (p. 111)

Art and life coincide in the experience of a fictional character, but—most important of all—of a character who is herself pictured writing a novel, and it is possible to see *Épaves* as a vital step on the way from Green's early, unreflective tales of horror to this essentially modern fascination with the position of the novelist as a character in his own fiction. (p. 113)

Trevor Field, "Reflections of a Novelist: Mirror Imagery in Julien Green's 'Épaves'," in Symposium *(copyright © 1975 by Syracuse University Press), Spring-Summer, 1975, pp. 103-16.*

* * *

GRIEVE, Christopher Murray
See MacDIARMID, Hugh

* * *

GUILLÉN, Jorge   1893-

A Spanish poet, critic, and translator, Guillén celebrates life in a poetry that is pure, complex, and highly disciplined. Although his life was touched by the violence of the Spanish War, he has retained his optimism and spirituality. Showing the influence of Valéry and Juan Ramón Jiménez, his work transcends the local to achieve an artistry that is of universal proportions. He is considered by many to be Spain's greatest living poet.

ROBERT G. HAVARD

What Guillén's early poems indicate, above all, is a scrupulous care on the part of the poet, an ideal of perfection that is apparent both in a thematic context and in the business of making poems. (p. 111)

[The basic idea of the theory of pure poetry] is that of *elimination,* which in turn contains implicitly the notion of a compression or synthesis: elimination of the non-poetic. . . . The stringencies of this theory, which must have influenced (though not riveted) Guillén's sensibility, help to explain his special affection for the short poem where strict confines allow for a more densely worked piece, and from which, hopefully, flaws may be cast out.

Outstanding amongst the short poetic forms employed in the first *Cántico* is the *décima.* The seventeen *décimas* of this volume are most representative of Guillén's inclination towards a concision coupled with a disciplined roundness of form. The *décimas* also express, in one image or another, Guillén's most characteristic theme: that of man's fundamentally positive relationship with reality. . . . [The] essential property of the *décima,* which is its concision, makes this poetic form most appropriate for correlating the poet's dynamic concept of reality. It is more accurate to speak in terms of poetic tension than in terms of theme: the *décima*'s tendency to concentrate itself into stark image form, as opposed to the more discursive tone of the sonnet, for example, is a key factor in its accommodation of Guillén's uncomplicated positivism in the first *Cántico.* (p. 112)

[Guillén has a] predilection for an unusual rhyme-scheme constructed out of two quatrains and a central couplet in lines five and six [patterned as ababccdeed]. (p. 114)

[This] pattern affects not only the words that rhyme but also the rhythmic structure of the poem as a whole. The couplet has the function of concentrating and even partially arresting the poem's rhythm at its centre. In the [traditional rhyming pattern of the *décima,* called the] *espinela* . . . a

pause inevitably occurs at the end of the fourth line; and lines five and six, with their distinctive overlapping rhymes, have the function of relating the poem's separate parts and of re-charging its momentum. It is likely that Guillén objected to this somewhat rigid system and wanted more variation in his rhythm; indeed, even in his *espinelas* he prefers to abandon the traditional pause at line four, often using enjambement instead. Both types of *décimas* show that Guillén wished to complicate the rather fluent or andante rhythm which had been a feature of this form; but his achievement is more apparent in the new couplet *décima,* with its additional rhyme and central compression. . . . [Its] centralized couplet has the effect of organizing the poem in a symmetrical fashion (4-2-4). Now this is no incidental distribution, for the notion of symmetry or, more specifically, of concentricity, is a key motif in Guillén's early work and is inextricably related to his concept of perfection. A correspondence between the poem's form and theme may be found in the majority of these early *décimas.* (pp. 115-16)

[In the poem 'Panorama' for example, the poet stands at the top of a tower and views the patterned placement of streets in the town, all radiating from the foot of the tower.] The impression which the poem makes, then, is one of symmetry and concentricity; and this is clearly enhanced by the poem's own structure. In relation to the dominant motif of form, we may also appreciate what may be termed the poem's psychological properties; which is to say that, ultimately, the form is no more than an image of a mood or a psychic condition which the poet had experienced. Guillén has informed us that the concrete origin of the poem was the cathedral tower at Murcia; and we may easily imagine how the character of that townscape inspired a vision which is essentially tranquil, one of timeless harmony. The antithesis of this poem, both in mood and form values, is 'Rascacielos' of *Clamor.* This later *décima,* which, logically, does not have the centralized rhyme pattern, is a vision of a modern city in the United States. Though it is again constructed out of geometric form values there is little suggestion here of balance and symmetry. There is only one movement in the poem, and it is that which traces the upward thrust of the towering skyscrapers. This movement, in 'Rascacielos', comes to image the notion of a propulsion towards an uncertain future, which is itself in keeping with the disenchanted theme of *Clamor* and in opposition to that search for an experience of permanent beauty which characterizes *Cántico.*

The point I hope to have made about 'Panorama', however, is that the poem's formal and compositional qualities contribute in a positive way to what the poem has to say. Indeed, I should go further and suggest that the poem really *says* nothing; rather, it constructs itself into a total and complex image, and this image owes as much to the poem's formal qualities as it does to anything else. By *formal* I mean both the internal geometric vocabulary of the poem and the structure of the poem as such, which may be considered external but is nonetheless inseparable in terms of its contribution to the total image. (pp. 116-17)

As so often is the case in Guillén's poetry, the sudden intuition, the momentary experience of beauty, of harmony, or of plenitude, becomes the permanent value which the poem immobilizes. (p. 122)

Guillén's fundamental theme [in *Cántico* is] that, while the experience of harmony is available to everyone, it is not easily obtained; what is needed, in fact, is a forceful and determined drive to secure that permanent experience. . . .

Clearly, in longer poems the narrative element allows for a more explicit development of the theme, whereas in the emblematic *décima* it has to be perceived in terms of the values of distilled images. This is . . . the theme which runs consistently throughout Guillén's work. . . . (p. 125)

[One] of the remarkable features of the original *Cántico* is its uniformity of tone and consistency of technique. This is not to imply a limitation, for the primary objective of this volume was to correlate, in distilled, emblematic poems, an impression of the central concept of 'plenitud'. It is in the sense of this total concentration into image form that the poetry of this volume is most properly described as *pure poetry*. Furthermore, the formal virtues of this volume should not be considered as cold or academic incidentals, for they constitute a significant contribution towards the relation of a very human experience. (pp. 126-27)

Robert G. Havard, "The Early 'Décimas' of Jorge Guillén," in Bulletin of Hispanic Studies (© copyright 1971 Liverpool University Press), January, 1971, pp. 111-27.

K. M. SIBBALD

[Although] Guillén did indeed write, at some point in his career, poetry which might well be described as dehumanized, pure, classicist or Gongoristic, by the time [*Cántico (1919-1928)*] was ready for publication he had freed himself from these categories. . . .

His poems [before 1925] were often occasional pieces, lacking substance and almost always without the polished sophistication which distinguishes every edition of *Cántico*. (p. 24)

[Guillén] revised his early work [for *Cántico*] . . . in order to present a book of poems which had organic unity. (p. 25)

[Desiring to translate poetic experiences as faithfully as possible, Guillén] rejected sentimentality and realism. Such an attitude need not imply the dehumanization of poetry. Indeed, by this very rejection, Guillén focussed attention upon those things he considered to be at the very centre of human experience. . . . The very symbol of transitory beauty, the rose, which is often used by Guillén, defies oblivion. The axe bites into the pine but, in so doing, takes part in the pattern of creation and recreation. There is a certain mystery in creation and the poet's task is not to explain away the mystery but, first, ensure that the mystery holds no terrors, and secondly, to recreate the wonderful mystery of 'creation' in his own poetry. This can only be done if that mystery is approached in a controlled and reasoned manner. Thus, Guillén enlists the help of geometrical shapes and symbols. The one he uses most consistently is the circle. . . . The figure of the circle is the symbol of perfection. . . . Guillén follows tradition and uses this perfect figure to describe the progress from birth to death. In such harmony, therefore, death . . . cannot impose disruption upon life. . . . In [*Cántico*] the complete circle becomes the symbol of the universe. In such a universe involvement is always total. Death is no more and no less a

part of the cosmic unity than any of the human activities. . . . (pp. 32-4)

The main concern, then of [*Cántico*] is with life. Guillén uses vital physical forces to defy historical time and reaffirm the unity of creation. (p. 34)

As Guillén explained . . .: 'Past and future lie latent as ideas. Only the present is real, although the unreflecting person is not conscious of its palpitation and regards as without time any act taking place *now*. All roads lead one to the universe at its pinnacle of abundance, of consistency, of health'. (p. 36)

The poet is powerless to prevent time passing. He can, however, perceive order in the motion of time. Consequently, all the seasons and also day and night appear in [*Cántico*]. When that order is disturbed the poet is threatened; reality becomes unreal. The poet depends on the things he sees. If they are blurred or indistinct, chaos, the antithesis of order and form, results. By creating his own time outside historical time, therefore, Guillén minimizes disruption. (p. 38)

K. M. Sibbald, "Some Early Versions of the Poems of 'Cántico (1919-1928)': Progress Towards 'Claridad'," in Bulletin of Hispanic Studies (© copyright 1973 Liverpool University Press), January, 1973, pp. 23-44.

EDMUND L. KING

Poetry, it might be argued, has always inclined to Platonism or at least to Platonizing, and [Guillén's collection] *Cántico* acknowledges the proposition by opposing it, by affirming the value of living in the real world, by celebrating the experience of consciousness, that consciousness which, without experience, would not know that it existed. (p. 697)

Between the beginning of the book and the end are, in the complete Spanish original, 332 poems that celebrate the ordinary experiences of life, experiences that thus become extraordinary, experiences by definition—and faith—good —all the "normal" things that can be encountered in a day (and of course as long as one is awake, in a night). And since reality is what is, not what was or what may be, we have a rhetoric of the present, things in space more than actions in time, more nouns—far more—than verbs. Only the consummation of love generates verbs of action rather than of state. . . . (p. 698)

It's a daring trick to try, and Guillén brings it off in Spanish without a bobble: no doubt there are smiles of assent in the audience, but there's no snickering, no tittering. I cannot imagine such a performance in modern English. . . . [The] "normal" experiences represented by Guillén, of "dawns, mornings, noons, evenings, sunsets, nights, springs, summers, falls, winters, heat and cold, light and shade, earth and sky, the sun, the moon, the stars," through the fanatical purity of Guillén's spatialization transcend the dazzlingly representational and inevitably become representative. (p. 699)

Edmund L. King, in The Hudson Review (copyright © 1978 by The Hudson Review, Inc.; reprinted by permission), Vol. XXXI, No. 4, Winter, 1978-79.

H

HEIFNER, Jack 1946(?)-

Heifner is an American playwright.

CLIVE BARNES

["Vanities"] probably owes something to the Mary McCarthy novel . . . "The Group," for [the] tracing of women's careers from the aspiration of youth to the seeming eternity of maturity is indeed very incisive. Yet the play, with its softly bitchy dialogue, its overlays of sentiment and wit, and its clear, sometimes obvious, development of character, constantly holds the interest. These people never quite come alive as people, but they do have a perfectly valid dramatic life on the stage. They are one degree removed from reality, but it is Mr. Heifner's skill to keep that one degree totally consistent. . . .

There are few surprises, but at least there are a few. Mr. Heifner corrals his ladies with some accuracy, and even his clichés have the tinkle of truth and a giggle of merriment. He makes much of the shrill cries of femininity and powder-room gossip translated through the absent ears of man. (p. 23)

> Clive Barnes, in The New York Times (© 1976 by The New York Times Company; reprinted by permission), March 23, 1976.

MARGO JEFFERSON

Watching ["Vanities"], a play that begins in high-school days of the early 1960s, is unnervingly funny—like flipping through an old yearbook. Visions of teased hairstyles, pep rallies, the intricate maneuvers of back-seat sex unreel; individuality yields right of way to the necessities of being Cute, Neat and Popular. But then the decade moves on, into assassinations and political demonstrations, and suddenly it's 1974 and the characters have pushed, shoved or stumbled into lives of their own. And yet the old styles and selves never disappear entirely; they lurk below the surface, popping up from time to time—to show that we haven't changed as much as we feared or hoped. . . .

"Vanities" is an astute, snapshot-sharp chronicle of this process in the lives of three Texas girls. In 1963, Joanne, Kathy and Mary are aggressively vivacious cheerleaders; five years later, in their college sorority house, they are confronting their futures with nervous jauntiness; in 1974, they reunite, briefly, in New York. Their lives have diverged; their friendship, which once thrived on assumptions as well-coordinated as sweater sets, is strained and ambiguous. Old-time banter rings false, like cue cards flashed too quickly, too late. Their attempts at honest conversation only show that they can no longer afford to have very much in common.

Heifner's fast-moving, sneakily stinging dialogue and economical staging—the women sit at vanities between the acts, meticulously changing their hairstyles, costumes and attitudes—ingeniously balance caricature and realism.

> Margo Jefferson, "The '60s Generation," in Newsweek (copyright 1976 by Newsweek, Inc.; all rights reserved; reprinted by permission), April 5, 1976, p. 78.

JULES AARON

[Vanities is] a penetrating examination of contemporary mores. . . . The script is a hilarious and fascinating study of the emptiness of the "successful" American woman, developed through a series of conversations rather than actions. A disturbing yet appropriate timelessness permeates the script. Even the details seem ambiguous; we never know the psychological and emotional states of the three women. The play deals with the façades of the American Dream and asks if it is enough to be "popular" and "accepted." (p. 264)

The play transcends the clichés of its subjects; the script and production suggest an irony beyond even the most knowing of the women. It is appropriate that the final toast is not to "remembering" but to "forgetting." (p. 265)

> Jules Aaron, in Educational Theatre Journal (© 1977 University College Theatre Association of the American Theatre Association), May, 1977.

* * *

HELLER, Joseph 1923-

Heller is an American novelist, playwright, and short story writer. He masterfully employs black humor and satire, effective for their recognizable groundings in contemporary culture. Since his best-selling *Catch-22*, Heller has suffered something of a creative lull, punctuated by a play and two novels. None of these subsequent works has received the critical acclaim given his early masterpiece. (See also *CLC*, Vols. 1, 3, 5, 8, and *Contemporary Authors*, Vols. 5-8, rev. ed.)

JOHN SIMON

No salute is due Joseph Heller's rather self-indulgent anti-war and anti-universal indifference play, *We Bombed in New Haven,* a belated foray into Pirandellism covering ideological and technical ground that is already flyspecked with footprints. Actually, the play has flunked out of every school it attended. At the Pirandello Academy it failed to master the basic precept that there can be no easy answers: here, when Sergeant Henderson unmistakably dies before our eyes and Captain Starkey sends his own son (however expressionistically depicted) to perish as the logical consequence of having sent all the other young men entrusted to him to their deaths, all the suggestive ambiguity evaporates and we are left with simple, tearful preachment. At the Absurdist Institute it did not learn the first lesson: to create figures that transcend reality (usually downward); here, at best, we have bitterly funny naturalistic types who fall on their fannies when the rug of reality is pulled out from under them. At the Brecht Cram School it never absorbed that racy deviousness that makes all characters tangily complex. At the Pinterian Mysteries, it was never initiated into the power of the unspoken. *We Bombed in New Haven* is a well-intentioned universal dropout. (p. 164)

> John Simon, "'We Bombed in New Haven'" *(1968-69), in his* Uneasy Stages: A Chronicle of the New York Theater, 1963-1973 *(copyright © 1975 by John Simon; reprinted by permission of Random House, Inc.), Random House, 1976, pp. 164-65.*

ALFRED KAZIN

[The essence of *Catch-22* is that though it is ostensibly about the 1941-1945 war, in which Heller served, it is] really about The Next War, and thus about a war which will be without limits and without meaning, a war that will end only when no one is alive to fight it. The theme of *Catch-22* . . . is the total craziness of war, the craziness of all those who submit to it, and the struggle to survive by one man, Yossarian, who knows the difference between his sanity and the insanity of the system. But how can one construct fictional meaning, narrative progression, out of a system in which virtually everyone but the hero assents to madness, willingly falls into the role of the madman-who-pretends-to-be-sane? The answer is that *Catch-22* is about the hypothesis of a totally rejectable world, a difficult subject, perhaps impossible so long as the "world" is undifferentiated, confused with man's angry heart itself—but expressive of the political uselessness many Americans have felt about themselves since World War II. So Heller, who combines the virtuousness of a total pacifist with the mocking pseudo-rationality of traditional Jewish humor, has to fetch up one sight gag after another. . . . The book moves by Yossarian's asking sensible, human, logical questions about war to which the answers are madly inconsequent. Heller himself is the straight man on this lunatic stage, Yossarian the one human being in this farcically antihuman setup. The jokes are variations on the classic Yiddish story of the totally innocent recruit who pokes his head over the trench, discovers that everyone is firing away, and cries out in wonder—"One can get killed here!"

Yet the impressive emotion in *Catch-22* is not "black humor," the "totally absurd," those current articles of liberal politics, but horror. Whenever the book veers back to its primal scene, a bombardier's evisceration in a plane being smashed by flak, a scene given us directly and piteously, we recognize what makes *Catch-22* disturbing. The gags are a strained effort to articulate the imminence of *anyone's* death now by violence, and it is just this that makes it impossible to "describe war" in traditional literary ways. Despite the running gags, the telltale quality of *Catch-22* is that it doesn't move, it can't. The buried-alive feeling of being caught in a plane under attack, of seeing one's partner eviscerated, produces the total impotence of being unable to move, to escape. And this horror-cold immobility is reproduced not in the static, self-conscious distortion of the gags but in the violence of the straight, "serious" passages. (pp. 82-4)

The urgent emotion in Heller's book is thus every individual's sense today of being directly in the line of fire, of being trapped, of war not as an affair of groups in which *we* may escape, but as my and your nemesis. The psychology in *Catch-22* is that of a man being led to execution, of a gallows humor in which the rope around one's neck feels all too real (and is plainly stamped General Issue). (p. 85)

> *Alfred Kazin, in his* Bright Book of Life: American Novelists and Storytellers from Hemingway to Mailer *(copyright © 1971, 1973 by Alfred Kazin; reprinted by permission of Little, Brown and Co. in association with the Atlantic Monthly Press), Atlantic-Little, Brown, 1973.*

CAROL PEARSON

Catch-22 is a linguistic construct that requires people to do whatever their superiors wish. The novel is an examination of the destructive power of language when language is used for manipulation rather than communication. It is based on the existential premise that although the universe is irrational, people create rational systems. The linguistic expressions of these rational systems are cultural myths. People live by these myths whether or not they describe reality. . . . *Catch-22,* accordingly, points out the discrepancy between our myths and our realities and suggests that we would do better to stop creating rational systems and to start living in tune with an irrational universe. In doing so, it rejects abstract, rational language in favor of nonrational, metaphoric language.

To understand the causes and consequences of the debasement of American language, it is useful to see why Heller's characters accept myths as true which are in violent contradiction to their experience and to see who benefits from the acceptance of such myths. The characters in *Catch-22* court comforting lies rather than [face] unpleasant truths. When Snowden's insides slither onto the floor, Yossarian realizes that "Man was matter, that was Snowden's secret." . . . (pp. 30-1)

But Yossarian can find no transcendental comfort to explain suffering and to make life meaningful. As Vance Ramsey explains, people react to meaninglessness by renouncing their humanity, becoming cogs in the machine.

With no logical explanation to make suffering and death meaningful and acceptable, people renounce their power to think and retreat to a simple-minded respect for law and accepted "truth." In Rome the M.P.'s exemplify the overly law-abiding person who obeys law with no regard for humanity. They arrest Yossarian who is AWOL, but ignore the murdered girl on the street. By acting with pure rationality, like computers programmed only to enforce army regulations, they have become mechanical men. . . .

In the society which results when men fear thought so much that they merely accept what others tell them, the law becomes merely a facade covering humanity's basest instincts. Society becomes only an institution to perpetuate these instincts and to help the victims adapt to the order of Darwinian nature. The victims share responsibility with their tormentors for their debasement and suffering because they do not reject their tormentors or the system that perpetuates suffering. This conspiracy of suffering is demonstrated most effectively in the "Eternal City" episodes.... This picture of humankind preying upon one another with the blessings of every institution of society is consistently maintained in the novel. (p. 31)

That people should accept such a world depends upon their inability to question it and upon a fundamental despair which makes change seem impossible. People need insight and hope in order to revolt, but the desire to escape the horror of accepting responsibility in a meaningless and seemingly cruel universe has made them psychological cripples. In order to shelter its citizens from fear, society enfeebles language, for it is through language that we understand and share our understanding of reality. (pp. 31-2)

Ordinarily, people remain completely sheltered from terror, never questioning the assumptions of society.... A blanket of idealistic language so successfully shelters the characters that they are as unable to comprehend death or fear as they are to value human dignity or worth. Hence, language is made into an object of deception rather than of expression, examination, or communication, and the dominant occupation of men and of society becomes "protective rationalization."...

Most of the characters in the novel, however, acknowledge the power and authenticity of language as a closed nonreferential system. Language becomes so important that Wintergreen can effectively control generals and their men because he runs the mimeograph machine....

Language is powerful because it is equated with reality: Captain Black believes, for example, "The more loyalty oaths a person signed, the more loyal he was."... When experience conflicts with linguistic reality, the characters disregard experience....

In a world in which language is equated with reality, words, such as patriotism, duty, honor, courage, and loyalty, are employed to dupe them men into risking their lives for a tighter bomb pattern. The logical provisions of Catch-22 parody this use of language. In the most notable example of Catch-22, the men are forced to keep killing others and risking their own deaths by its provisions. (p. 32)

Other provisions of Catch-22 are equally absurd, contradictory, and mechanical, and each is a rationalization for brute power, which entraps and victimizes those without power. (p. 33)

However, Catch-22 only works when the victim believes in the power and authenticity of language and fears reality too much to question what he is told. Yossarian finally discovers that "Catch-22 did not exist . . . but it made no difference. What did matter was that everyone thought it existed, and that was much worse, for there was no object or text to ridicule or refute, to accuse, criticize, attack, amend, hate, revile, spit at, rip to shreds, trample upon or burn up."... Even though Catch-22 does not exist as a law, the charac-

ters of the novel believe it does. Language, therefore, does not describe their actions, it prescribes them.

By the end of the novel, Yossarian rejects abstract language because it invariably cloaks self-interest.... [But] even from the beginning of the novel, Yossarian is conscious that his experience clashes with the myths of his society. Therefore, his views seem insane to those around him.... The hospital psychiatrist declares Yossarian insane, but Yossarian concludes that his whole society is crazy, since "all over the world" "men went mad and were rewarded with medals."... (pp. 33-4)

Finally, the question of Yossarian's sanity reduces to the discrepancy between the world of abstract language epitomized by Catch-22 and the sensory world of the brothel. Nately's discussions with the old man in the brothel cogently reflect this disparity.... Although the old man's hedonistic morality is limited, Heller presents him as more "sane" than those who willingly die for Colonel Cathcart or for a tighter bomb pattern. To be crazy enough to refuse to die for a "principle" that is merely a rationale for another's gain, is moral. Dr. Stubbs summarizes the judgment of the novel when he responds to the news of Yossarian's refusal to fly by commenting: "That crazy bastard [Yossarian] may be the only sane one left."... To be insane is to be in tune with a universe that is fundamentally irrational and chaotic. (p. 34)

The positive irrationality of Dunbar, Orr and Nately's whore parallels the irrationality of many countercultural groups of the 1960's. For example, the YIPPIE's idea of political action was to run a pig for president. The popularity of Catch-22 in the sixties and seventies may partially result from Heller's rejection of the rationalist tradition. Critics who complain that the ending of Catch-22 is impossible and irrational—that Orr could not literally row to Sweden in a life raft, for example—miss this point. Catch-22 rejects reason and abstract, rationalist language as tools that an oppressive culture uses to deceive us. A discussion of Catch-22, therefore, while helping students identify the causes and consequences of the debasement of language in our culture, can also lead to thought-provoking debates on the future of rationality and language in our culture and on the possible consequences and dangers of asserting irrationality as a value. Since Heller uses language effectively to convince us of the failure of language, he causes us to reexamine the language of literature as a means of discovery and communication, suggesting that we should look to the artist rather than the politician to teach us about ourselves and our reality. (p. 35)

> *Carol Pearson, "'Catch-22' and the Debasement of Language," in* The CEA Critic *(copyright © 1974 by the College English Association, Inc.), November, 1974, pp. 30-5.*

MIKE FRANK

Heller makes it clear that the real enemy, the source of the true danger, is that principle which can allow Milo so glibly to overlook Nazi crimes against human life. And that principle, as the text makes abundantly clear, is an economic one. For Milo contract, and the entire economic structure and ethical system that it embodies and represents, is more sacred than human life. (pp. 77-8)

The most important manifestation of this thanatotic American morality, important because it extends the responsibility from particular individuals or groups to American society at large, is Milo's bombing of his own troops as part of a deal with the Germans. . . . In Heller's America war is merely another way of making money and getting ahead. . . . It is an America in which the Protestant ethic has run wild, so it is hardly surprising that Yossarian, who believes in the paramount importance of the individual human life, must rebel.

The enemy within then—the villain of the piece—is not any of the individual characters, all of whom are more foolish than evil, but the Protestant ethic itself with its disregard for human life and its deification of the profit motive. (p. 78)

Like the puritan ethic from which it derives, the American ethic Heller portrays conceives of life as a means to an end, and therefore as expendable. Corollary to that conception is a distrust of, even a disdain for, those aspects of human existence which are most pleasurable and generative of life. Foremost among these, for Heller's puritans of capitalism, is, of course, sex. Although the sacrifice of human life on the altar of free enterprise is the most dramatic example and image of thanatos in *Catch-22*, the pervasiveness and profundity of the thanatotic impulse is nowhere so evident as in the repeated denial of the life force, eros. Examples of this denial are abundant. A group of officers resort to sadism in their treatment of a prostitute because it is the only way they know of getting a reaction, for them the act of sex is meaningful only when destructive, and the infliction of pain becomes the means of human contact. Similarly Aarfy, whose fraternity manners enshrine one of our pervasive myths of noble virility, cannot avoid thinking of sex as dirty and reprehensible. . . . Implicit in Aarfy's value system is the absolute incompatibility of money and sex, an incompatibility very much in keeping with the puritan view of the matter. Since Aarfy's world—which Heller presents as very much like ours—takes wealth as its highest good it must necessarily reject any healthy sexuality. In view of this it is outrageous but not surprising that Aarfy later rapes a servant girl and then murders her, because, as he says, "I couldn't very well let her go around saying bad things about us, could I?" (pp. 78-9)

This pervasive unwillingness to accept sex, and the erotic impulse, as healthy has its effects even on those whose sexual impulse is less corrupt. . . . Unashamed of sex and yet convinced that men marry only virgins, [Luciana] is caught in the double bind of a ruthless puritanism.

As if to suggest that a moral standard based on the denial of love cannot sustain life in particular, Heller allows only one of his characters—the chaplain—a successful marriage; and the chaplain is one of the novel's two moral protagonists who reject the accepted norms and attempt to discover new ones. (p. 79)

[Critics] have objected to the novel's emphasis on sex. . . . But Yossarian's sexuality is much more than mere indulgence in superficial sensuality. The significance of Yossarian's sexual urges is made very clear when Heller tells us that, haunted by the ominous presence of death and unable to forget his dead friends, Yossarian "thirsted for life and reached out ravenously to grasp and hold Nurse Duckett's flesh." . . . For Heller, as for Yossarian, sex is an affirmation of life which, beyond its biologically reproductive function, works to unite people. In a society so given to separa-

tion and destruction healthy sexual communion becomes one of the few moral acts possible. (p. 80)

[When] a doctor tells him that to convince the authorities that his liver is infected—and thereby remain safely in the hospital—he will have to give up sex, Yossarian replies, "That's a hell of a price to pay just to keep alive." . . . His insistence on these sexual prerogatives parallels his ultimate refusal of the chance to return home offered by Cathcart and Korn. In either case he is given the opportunity to save his own life only by sacrificing one of the things that makes life worth saving. By rejecting both offers Yossarian shows that, some critics notwithstanding, he is not a coward intent on saving his own skin, but rather someone devoted to preserving the principle of life, the principle that Freud called eros.

It is fitting that in the world of *Catch-22* the most eloquent spokesman for life should be the resident patron of a whore house. The old man who argues with the ingenuous Nately in the brothel has no use for ideologies, all of which he sees as excuses for the imposition of one's will on another. To Nately's argument that "anything worth living for is worth dying for," he responds, "Anything worth dying for . . . is certainly worth living for." Beneath the clever word play is the realization, central to *Catch-22*, that life itself is the one indispensable requirement for any set of values, and that to sacrifice life for those values is in effect to save something by destroying it. But beyond any ideological questions the old man is an expression of the way an indulgence in eros can eliminate the neurotic compulsion to win, a compulsion consistent with the puritan ethic's emphasis on success and deriving from the systematic repression of healthier impulses. In accepting those impulses the old man commits himself to life rather than to a factitious honor, is freed from the megalomania that afflicts almost all the book's American officers, and can feel comfortable with the realization that "we will certainly come out on top again if we succeed in being defeated." . . . (pp. 80-1)

Certainly it is noteworthy that the brothel presents us with the book's only scenes of interpersonal warmth. This house is very much a home, both for its residents who are insulated by it from the raging destruction outside, and for Yossarian and his friends who, in fact, seem to enjoy its warmth far more than its services. And indeed one soon notices that for all its overtly sexual references the novel is remarkably free of any salaciousness; but this ceases to surprise when one recognizes that in *Catch-22* sex is not so much a specifically physical and genital activity as it is a recognition and embracing of libido in general, the protean creative and regenerative impulse. (p. 81)

While the puritan impulse is manifest in almost every character in the book it is, of course, clearest in the person of Milo Minderbinder, a virtual allegory of protestant capitalism. . . . Heller makes it clear that, even apart from whatever moral judgements we as readers may wish to make of such unscrupulously self-serving behavior, the puritan ethic has a dark underside. Milo's very name, Minderbinder, suggests the limitations imposed by the principles he chooses to follow: the profit motive binds the mind and thus deprives Milo of a fundamental moral freedom, the freedom to choose, since his options are severely limited by his ethic. . . . In this he is the exact opposite of Orr who, if not the book's moral protagonist, is certainly its morally paradigmatic figure. As his name indicates Orr embodies the principle of alternatives and thus freedom and choice. Orr is the only character in the work who succeeds in escaping from the thanatotic system. All the rest, except for Yossarian, lack the freedom to choose and are caught, perhaps permanently, on that little thanatotic puritan island.

There is something very—although, no doubt, inadvertently—fitting about the choice of an island to epitomize one of the dominant characteristics of American civilization; for another fiction set on an island provides the myth on which *Catch-22* plays variations. The myth is that of Robinson Crusoe who, in his drive for individual achievement and personal salvation, is prepared to relinquish all claim to human contact. (pp. 81-2)

Catch-22 may be considered a *bildungsroman* to the extent that it chronicles Yossarian's growing awareness of the thanatotic nature of the system in which he is caught, as well as his consequent decision to react against it in the interest of eros. (p. 85)

[Finally] Yossarian leaves Pianosa on an odyssey that, he hopes, will eventually lead to Sweden. The Sweden he aims for is located, perhaps, not so much in the real world as in the geography of the moral imagination. It is, nevertheless, a country noted for its freedom from war—thanatos—and its liberalism in sexual matters—eros. (p. 86)

> Mike Frank, *"Eros and Thanatos in 'Catch 22',"* in Canadian Review of American Studies, *Spring, 1976, pp. 77-87.*

RICHARD LOCKE

"Catch-22" is probably the finest novel published since World War II. "Catch-22" is the great representative document of our era, linking high and low culture, with its extraordinary double-helix form, its all-American G.I.-comedy characters, its echoes of Twain, Faulkner, Hemingway, Miller and Céline. Its only rival is Pynchon's gargantuan "Gravity's Rainbow"—much larger, more learned and intelligent, but top-heavy, and a colder, deadly work of art. (I should add that if "Catch-22" recalls Dickens in its comic fertility and complex form, then Heller's second novel, "Something Happened," seems an impressive if tortuous attempt to rewrite Henry James—to provide a counterpart to "The Portrait of a Lady," to chart the postwar civilian hell of narcissism.) (p. 37)

> Richard Locke, in The New York Times Book Review (© 1977 by The New York Times Company; reprinted by permission), May 15, 1977.

ELIOT FREMONT-SMITH

[*Good as Gold*] is being touted by its publisher as doing for the White House what *Catch-22* did for the military of World War II—that is, a demolition job on our more positive illusions. The method is certainly the same: Every cliched absurdity is played straight and at length; a lot of little jokes illumine the big joke, which is that everything is a bad joke. But the timing is off. . . .

This inevitably blunts the effect of Heller's tardy absurdities and makes the bad joke seem merely old. To be shocking today, *Good as Gold* would have to accomplish the opposite of what it intends: It would have to offend our current cynicism by revealing the deep integrity, selfless dedication, and nobility of democratic spirit that guide our government. It might not sell, but it would be new.

Not that *Good as Gold* is without offensiveness. It does bore. It is also anti-Semitic. If Heller believes (and I'm willing to think he thinks he does) that everything is base and mean and rotten to the core, this goes double for the Jews. . . .

The protagonist is Brooklyn-born, Columbia-graduated Bruce Gold. Now 48, Gold teaches college English . . . and writes reviews and articles for unread intellectual journals. . . .

Gold is a schlub, a manipulator, a self-conscious hypocrite. His failing is in not making enough money. It's vaguely for this, and his general dullness—not his dishonesty—that his family despises him. His family consists of a nasty, senile father, an older brother, four older sisters, and their various spouses, each of whom is more self-centered and envious and unpleasant than the next—the Snopeses of Coney Island. Their reunions take up many pages and move the plot along about an inch. The lust for money moves it more. . . .

The Jews in *Good as Gold* are uniformly portrayed as snivelling, deceitful, self-aggrandizing, and ambitious beyond their worth. . . . (p. 74)

Ah, one says correctly, but the Wasps are just as bad. I had several dialogues with myself during the course of *Good as Gold*. For example: Yes, but to a Wasp anti-Waspism is a tiresome irritant only, while to a Jew anti-Semitism has to be something different. And technical stuff: Heller allows no empathy, no identification with Gold, and therefore no possibility of tension in the reader's mind—and *that's* where he goes wrong (in contrast to his second novel, and the one that moved me most, *Something Happened*). If all is hokey-jokey and intended to be distasteful, it's going to be distasteful. Especially because it seems a political polemic but has no discernible point other than everything is shit. Questions to myself: Must a work of imagination have a point? Isn't the point that everything is shit okay? Answers: Yes, it must; and No, not interesting enough. Side remark: Am I getting old?

And more to the heart of it, the embarrassments: For when I say I'm bored with *Good as Gold*, that's true, but not entirely true. I am suspicious that boredom is a cover for being offended—a sophisticate's way of dealing with something he would like to call "in bad taste" except that the phrase has such a dumb ring. And except that the "bad taste" has to do with anti-Semitism. (pp. 74-5)

Also this: it is conceivable that Heller is somehow saying that we are all one, that neither Jews nor gentiles have a corner on viciousness. If so, a sentimental and denigrating corollary is apparent—that the former learned from the latter's example. . . .

But if Heller can be said to breathe conviction into any character, it's Conover. His rhetoric—"kike" and the rest—carries more force of sneering feeling than anything else in the book. And not even this is power-packed. It's nostalgic, as if Heller *missed* rougher, more explicitly dangerous times. *Good as Gold* doesn't deal with evil, it merely gets off on it. (p. 75)

> Eliot Fremont-Smith, *"Kvetch-22,"* in The Village Voice *(reprinted by permission of* The Village Voice; *copyright © The Village Voice, Inc., 1979), March 5, 1979, pp. 74-5.*

LEONARD MICHAELS

In his diary Kafka asks, "What have I in common with Jews?" Immediately he answers, "I have hardly anything in common with myself and should stand very quietly in a corner, content that I can breathe." Thus, failure to identify with his people inspires a joke about failure to identify with himself. The same failure, and the same joke extremely elaborated, describes much of Joseph Heller's third novel, "Good as Gold."

As the title boasts, "Good as Gold" is a dazzling commodity. It is in fact another big book about Jews—literally about a Jewish professor, Bruce Gold, who has an idea for a book about the Jewish experience in America. He sells the idea to friends of his in publishing, two sleazy, conniving opportunists.... Both see the Jewish book as potentially lucrative, but while Lieberman wants it to be sensational, containing such things as what it feels like for a Jewish man to have sexual intercourse with "gentile girls," Pomoroy wants Gold to write a book "useful to colleges and libraries." In any case, Gold's idea for the Jewish book, which occupies him through the first chapter, is never realized because he does too many other things....

Though Gold never writes his book, we finally have the book he lives, "Good as Gold." It is indeed about Jews and a lot more, and it satisfies the requests of vulgar Lieberman and grimly serious Pomoroy, for it is both high and low in comic spirit. It contains much truth as well as gross, slapstick lunacy.

While the title speaks ironically about Bruce Gold's intention to make money on the Jewish experience, it also mocks him with paradox, suggesting in his very name problems of identity and value. How good is Gold? Is Gold good? (As for Bruce, a Gaelic name, what is a Jew doing with it?) Beyond all this doubleness, the novel has a double plot that reflects its deepest subject, alienation—being what you are not, feeling what you don't feel, thinking what you don't think, living a life that is not yours. Essentially, then, "Good as Gold" is about some American Jews, their bastardized existence, their sense of congenital inauthenticity. Kafka's agonies of personal identity are brought up to date by Heller and remade American—bold and commercial.

Virtually everything about his hero is ambivalent or inconsistent. (p. 1)

Most important to the description of Gold is his oppressive family. Much of the time in the novel is spent with them, mainly at the dinner table in scenes that are delightfully theatrical and funny; they probably could be staged with little change. The family characters tend to be hilariously obnoxious.... (pp. 1, 24)

Along with Lieberman, Pomoroy and other amusing, revolting Jewish friends from his youth in Coney Island, the family determines one plot of the novel that is exquisitely realistic—that is, grotesque, witty, lugubriously banal. Its Jewish characters are comically limited, but they suffer, they have pasts, they have interior lives, and they constitute the roots, trunk and branches of Gold's inescapable, basic identity....

The Protestant characters in the novel, in contrast to the Jews, are essentially unproblematic and mechanical. They determine most of the other plot, which is mainly fantastic but includes an astounding vision of our leaders in Washington. Astounding because, while fantastic, it doesn't seem incorrect....

In contrast to Gold's ambivalent character, there is at least one figure in the novel who is absolutely who he is, a man of ultimate authenticity: Hugh Biddle Conover, an old dying Protestant of infinite wealth, father of the woman Gold wants to marry. Father and daughter, Gold imagines, can be instrumental in getting him a job in Washington, in the President's inner circle. The realistic-Jewish-plot and the fantastic-Protestant-plot, as separate from each other as Gold is from himself, come together with concentrated ferocity when Gold visits Conover's immense estate ... to ask for the hand of his immensely tall blonde daughter....

Conover's speeches are too flatly punishing to be terribly funny. Long, detailed, precise, full of venomous hatred, they are not only impossible in reality, but the hatred seems finally to exceed the comic situation. This happens again in an extended comment Gold makes on the career of Henry Kissinger. In both cases the satirical animus is focused on loathsome qualities of Jews, but the book is essentially about Jews, especially those like Gold, who wants to escape his identity while exploiting it, particularly by making a lot of money on a big book about Jews. Heller himself is implicated, but only insofar as "Good as Gold" is about such books and the people who write them. He exploits the exploiters. He has his cake and eats it, too. Indeed, the novel self-consciously comments on itself in the title and in other places, and thus seems literally to feed on itself....

Father and daughter, comic Protestants of Gold's imagination, play the same role Jews once played in the Protestant imagination. The reversal is much apparent in contemporary movies and novels, but Jewish artists can be trusted to balance attacks on Protestants with lots of anti-Semitism. For these satirists the truth of our American life lies between ugly and funny. In Lenny Bruce, Woody Allen and others, a powerful satirical convention has been established, and it is just what Heller says, ironically: good as gold. His novel comments on itself constantly, and the merciless denunciation of his scapegoat hero is the price Heller pays for his artistic conscience. (p. 24)

[The] self-conscious complexities of the novel make it inconsistently funny and sometimes tiresome.

However Protestants are conceived and treated, it is one of the themes of "Good as Gold" that Jews violate themselves in their relations with such unreal creatures of their own minds, especially when Jews yearn for tall blondes and jobs in Washington, where successful Jews are "slaves." The chief example, for Gold, is Kissinger....

According to Gold's father, it is possible Kissinger isn't a Jew. This is relevant to the novel's paradoxical, ironical character, because it gives the final twist to the relations between Bruce Gold, an imaginary hero, and the real living Kissinger, a non-Jewish Jew married in fact to a tall blonde. In brief: Bruce Gold yearns to escape what he is so that he can become what he isn't, which is precisely what he hates....

The way Heller plays with this psycho-physical transmogrification of his hero is remarkably impressive, and I suspect that Bruce Gold is a uniquely original hero. Has there ever been one who is the self-despising alter ego of a world-famous person? A hero who exists, in his very essence, relatively? At the core of its satirical vision, "Good as Gold" seems to have combined Einstein's theory of relativity with Kafka's agonies. (p. 25)

Leonard Michaels, "Bruce Gold's American Experience," in The New York Times Book Review (© 1979 by The New York Times Company; reprinted by permission), March 11, 1979, pp. 1, 24-5.

*   *   *

HESSE, Hermann   1887-1962

A German novelist, poet, and essayist, Hesse became a Swiss citizen in 1923. His prose and poetry are often drawn from autobiographical sources and possess a lyricism sharing more with the German romantics of the late eighteenth and early nineteenth century than anything found in modern literature. Thematically he is concerned with the plight of the artist in society as well as the psychological motivations of human behavior. Hesse became rather a cult figure in the 1960s for works like *Siddhartha*, which center on his romantic conception of the young alienated hero and reflect his unique blending of western and oriental philosophy. Hesse also wrote under the pseudonym of Emil Sinclair. He received the Nobel Prize in 1946. (See also *CLC*, Vols. 1, 2, 3, 6, and *Contemporary Authors*, Vols. 17-18; *Contemporary Authors Permanent Series*, Vol. 2.)

THOMAS MANN

[Even] as a poet [Hesse] likes the role of editor and archivist, the game of masquerade behind the guise of one who "brings to light" other people's papers. The greatest example of this is the sublime work of his old age, *The Glass Bead Game*. . . . In reading it I very strongly felt . . . how much the element of parody, the fiction and persiflage of a biography based upon learned conjectures, in short the verbal playfulness, help keep within limits this late work, with its dangerously advanced intellectuality, and contribute to its dramatic effectiveness. (p. 17)

This chaste and daring work, full of fantasy and at the same time highly intellectual, is full of tradition, loyalty, memory, secrecy—without being in the least derivative. It raises the intimate and familiar to a new intellectual, yes, revolutionary level—revolutionary in no direct political or social sense but rather in a psychic, poetical one: in genuine and honest fashion it is prophetic of the future, sensitive to the future. I do not know how else to describe the special, ambiguous, and unique charm it holds for me. It possesses the romantic timbre, the tenuousness, the complex, hypochondriacal humor of the German soul—organically and personally bound up with elements of a very different and far less emotional nature, elements of European criticism and of psychoanalysis. The relationship of this Swabian writer of lyrics and idyls to the erotological "depth psychology" of Vienna, as for example it is expressed in *Narcissus and Goldmund*, a poetic novel unique in its purity and fascination, is a spiritual paradox of the most appealing kind. (pp. 17-18)

The electrifying influence exercised on a whole generation just after the First World War by *Demian* . . . is unforgettable. With uncanny accuracy this poetic work struck the nerve of the times and called forth grateful rapture from a whole youthful generation who believed that an interpreter of their innermost life had risen from their own midst—whereas it was a man already forty-two years old who gave them what they sought. And need it be stated that, as an experimental novel, *Steppenwolf* is no less daring than *Ulysses* and *The Counterfeiters*?

For me his lifework, with its roots in native German romanticism, for all its occasional strange individualism, its now humorously petulant and now mystically yearning estrangement from the world and the times, belongs to the highest and purest spiritual aspirations and labors of our epoch. Of the literary generation to which I belong I early chose him . . . as the one nearest and dearest to me and I have followed his growth with a sympathy that sprang as much from our differences as from our similarities. . . . He has written things—why should I not avow it?—such as *A Guest at the Spa* and indeed much in *The Glass Bead Game*, especially the great introduction, which I read and feel "as though 'twere part of me." (p. 18)

Thomas Mann, in his Reden und Aufsätze II, Hermann Hesse zum siebzigsten Geburtstag and Nachträge, Dem sechzigjährigen Hermann Hesse (© 1960, 1974 S. Fischer Verlag GmbH, Frankfurt am Main; © 1974 S. Fischer Verlag GmbH, Frankfurt am Main), S. Fischer Verlag, 1960, 1974 (translated as the introduction to Demian: The Story of Emil Sinclair's Youth by Hermann Hesse, Holt, 1948 and reprinted in Hermann Hesse: A Collection of Critical Essays, edited by Theodore Ziolkowski, Prentice-Hall, Inc., 1973. pp. 15-20).

ANDRÉ GIDE

With Hesse the expression alone is restrained, not the feeling or the thought; and what tempers the expression of these is the exquisite feeling of fitness, reserve and harmony, and, with relationship to cosmos, the interdependence of things; it is also a certain latent irony, of which few Germans seem to me capable, and whose total absence so often spoils so many works by so many of their authors, who take themselves terribly seriously. (p. 22)

Hesse's [ironies], so charming in quality, seems to me to depend on the faculty of leaving himself behind, of seeing himself without looking, of judging himself without complacency; it is a form of modesty that becomes all the more attractive because more gifts and virtues accompany it. . . .

However diverse (in subject matter if not in tendency) may be Hesse's books that I have read, I recognize in each of them the same pagan love of Nature: a sort of devotion. The open air circulates through their pages that quiver with panicky breaths, like the leaves of forest trees. In each of them, too, I refind the same indecision of soul; its contours are illusive and its aspirations, infinite; it is infatuated with vague sympathies, ready for the reception of any chance *imperative;* little determined by the past to find in submission itself an aim, a reason for living, an anchor for his floating impulses. (p. 23)

[Hesse has said] that all creatures under the sun live and develop as they wish and according to their own laws; man alone allows himself to be fashioned and bent by the laws that others have made. The entire work of Hesse is a poetic effort for emancipation with a view to escaping imitation and reassuming the genuineness compromised. Before teaching it to others, it is necessary to preserve it in oneself. Hesse arrives at it through culture. Although profoundly and fundamentally German, it is only by turning his back on Germany that he succeeds. Those in his country who were able to remain loyal to themselves, and not to allow themselves to be deflected are rare: it is to them he addresses himself and says: however few you may be, it is in you, and you alone, that the virtue of Germany has taken refuge and it is on you that her future depends. (p. 24)

André Gide, "Preface to 'The Journey to the East'," in his Autumn Leaves, translated by Elsie Pell (reprinted by permission of the Philosophical Library, Inc.), Philosophical Library, 1950 (and reprinted in Hermann Hesse: A Collection of Critical Essays, edited by Theodore Ziolkowski, Prentice-Hall, Inc., 1973, pp. 21-4).

JEFFREY L. SAMMONS

For the Germanist of my own age, over thirty but not yet too far over, the great enthusiasm for Hermann Hesse among younger people poses a vexing dilemma. For the fact is that many of us, with important exceptions, do not think that Hesse is a writer of the first rank. . . . (p. 112)

Hesse's stylistic mediocrity directs attention to other problems. First of all, his characteristic stylistic posture is certainly willed. There is a certain amount of vivid writing in *Steppenwolf,* here and there in *Narcissus and Goldmund,* and elsewhere, while *Siddhartha* is, of course, exceptionally mannered, as is, to a lesser extent, *The Glass Bead Game.* . . . (p. 113)

The inner way and the search for wholeness [, Hesse's themes,] are aspects of a criticism of modern society with sources in the resistance to the developing phenomena of the modern world in German Classicism and Romanticism around the turn of the nineteenth century. As Hesse came out of his adolescent crisis in the mid-1890s, he began a lonely and isolated time during which he read deeply in this tradition. This reading was the formative cultural experience of his life, and indeed one that was not very different from what he would have acquired had he gone through a normal course of university education, for Goethe, Schiller, and the Romantics were the axis of German *Bildung*—although, to be sure, Hesse's point was the opposite, that he could learn as much by himself as at the university. For all that he protested against the vulgarization of *Bildung,* especially in *Steppenwolf,* he shared its assumptions: that in this unparalleled flowering of German culture, along with its assimilation of Classical antiquity, Renaissance art, and Indic studies, were to be found the guidelines for responding to and evaluating the experience of the present.

The transplantation of the effort of German Classical-Romanticism to find an alternative for society into the crises of the early twentieth century is the key to neo-Romanticism, of which Hesse is one of the major exemplars. It may be seen most clearly in *Steppenwolf,* for despite the change Harry Haller undergoes in his way of dealing with the strains between the ideal and the real, nothing has been altered in his secularized and aesthticized scheme of redemption. Salvation and truth lie in exactly the same place at the end as at the beginning. . . . Except for Dostoevsky and Nietzsche, there is scarcely an artist or thinker to whom Hesse alludes who lived later than the 1830s. These spirits are in a profound sense all alike, insofar as they are in touch with the one and all, that timeless realm where the poles of opposites touch and spark ethereal comets. This fraternity hovers above life and history, and it is only with infrequent intermittence in touch with the feeble and shabby emanation that is our environment. Harry Haller believes this at the beginning, and the truth of it is demonstrated to him at the end. (pp. 118-19)

[To Hesse], pitiable and disreputable turmoil is the life of man in society, that part of human existence that is beneath the concern of the wise man. The inner way escapes and withdraws from it; the search for wholeness transcends it and discovers the cosmic unities that ultimately govern the world.

This search for wholeness, to which every one of Hesse's major works bears testimony, probably does not arouse active uneasiness in the ordinary American reader. . . . But to anyone sensitive to such matters in the German tradition, the theme is acutely troubling. For it is one thing to seek after unity in the world or in our perception of it; it is another to postulate ultimate unity and to regard all disharmonies as regrettable excrescences or ignorable and trivial aspects of an unimportant "reality." It is not wholly clear just where Hesse stands in this matter. (p. 122)

[The] use made of the organic metaphor through the nineteenth century and up until the advent of Fascism made it a dubious legacy indeed. The chief mischief it caused was to make the Germans incapable of dealing with the class conflict and of constructing a society that would accommodate it. Class conflict was simply impermissible, for society was to be a harmonious, organic whole. Although Nazism can hardly be called either harmonious or organic, many Germans thought it would be. Hesse never saw the connection between totalitarianism and the organic metaphor. . . . (p. 124)

Furthermore, unike such contemporaries as Musil, Thomas Mann, or Hermann Broch, Hesse appears to have made little effort to understand the modern civilization and society he so deplored, and consequently any assent to his cultural critique will share a striking lack of precision. Hesse's characteristic stance before his environment and civilization is one of uncomprehending bafflement, which does not prevent him from firm denunciation. Examples abound in *Steppenwolf.* What Harry Haller calls "jazz" is the very substance of the horrid vulgarity of the modern environment, when compared with the high idealism of classical music, but what he here abominates is not really jazz, but popular big-band dance music. It is true that this distinction was not very sharply made in the twenties, except by connoisseurs; nevertheless, Hesse was so appalled by modern culture that his alter ego flails away at an enemy of which he has a very superficial understanding. (pp. 125-26)

The vision [in Hesse's work] is not only conservative, it is blindered; it fails to focus upon the true shape of the problem. Hesse's lack of comprehension of the world whose rejection he insists upon could be demonstrated at length upon the inept account of the "feuilletonistic age" that is given at the outset of *The Glass Bead Game.* (p. 126)

[Hesse] did possess an instinctive sense for the worst excesses of pernicious nonsense. Sometimes he mounted a fairly coherent attack on the nonsense, such as in the often-quoted and somewhat unexpected passage in *Steppenwolf* in which the spirit of German music as a surrogate for reason is subjected to a sharp critique. Unfortunately, he is often a cliché-ridden writer, and it is the provenance of these clichés that is a cause for concern. Two examples are prominent enough in his writing to deserve some remarks.

One of these is the *Führer* principle. . . . [Its] permutations are widespread in neo-Romanticism, which developed . . . the theme of the great, creative personality who stands above common morality and moves the world by the force of his elite genius. The ideological purpose of this theory is to counteract the analysis of the dynamics of class in the course of history. Hesse puts a pure example of this into the mouth of Demian: "If Bismarck had understood the Social Democrats and made an arrangement with them, he would have been a clever ruler, but not a man of destiny. So it was with Napoleon, with Caesar, with Loyola, with all of them." Indeed, *Demian* ends with the word *Führer*, and the novel celebrates the amorality of the elite man with the mark of Cain for whom the rest of mankind is trash. . . . The theme reappears in the Tractate of *Steppenwolf:* "We are not here talking about man . . . such as those running around on the streets by the millions and who are no more to be regarded than sand in the sea or the drops of the surf; a couple of million more or less do not matter, they are material, nothing more." It is in the light of such careless use of an inhumane cliché that Hesse's critique of the bourgeoisie must be seen, for the Tractate continues shortly afterward: "A human being who is capable of comprehending Buddha, a human being who has a sense for the heavens and the depths of humanity, should not live in a world ruled by common sense, democracy, and bourgeois culture."

There is a continuous pattern in Hesse of subordination to a superior, wiser authority. The will to rebel is, to be sure, always present: Siddhartha and Goldmund insist on finding their own route through the world; Sinclair is so uncertain within that he has difficulty in following Demian; Haller resists for a long time the primitive, elemental authority of Pablo; and Knecht, when he breaks out of the Castalian order, is accused of wishing to choose his own master. Hesse apparently could not see how parochial this dilemma of individualism was. (pp. 129-30)

[The] hunger for wholeness did not generate in Hesse the thirst for holocaust, a loud insistence that only a cleansing bloodbath could clean the trash out of bourgeois society and restore heroism and purity. This tone is, however, deposited in Hesse's writings. Again *Demian* is the most offensive text. . . . I confess that I have difficulty distinguishing [*Demian's*] rhetoric from that of the early years of the S.S. into which the spirit of apocalyptic, elitist heroism eventually flowed. . . . If a writer is indeed obligated to the spirit, as Hesse so endlessly preached, then his first duty should be a sensitivity to language and its humane employment, not simply to be an indiscriminate blotter that absorbs uncritically all the hysteria and nonsense that may be in the air at the time. (pp. 131-32)

The sound of the apocalypse is heard in *Steppenwolf* also, although there it is all part of the experiment of the inner man, and consequently one does not know where to draw the line between the inner phantasmagoria and real existential choice. . . . *Steppenwolf* is the only book in which Hesse experiments with the ecstasy of violence and slaughter, although there are slight premonitions in a smaller compass in *Narcissus and Goldmund.* The destructiveness belongs, of course, to a psychodrama that takes place within the confines of Harry Haller's own skull, which is why *Steppenwolf* is Hesse's most comic book. But one may fairly ask if it is responsible or intelligent for an author of such profound pacifist convictions to give tongue, even as part of an aesthetic game, to bloodthirsty imaginings that were meant by others in dead earnest and were soon to be realized in a very concrete way.

Hesse is, by any severe artistic or intellectual standards, a minor writer, although a not uninteresting one if regarded with proper skepticism and sufficient knowledge of his context. For all his high-mindedness and humaneness, his consciousness unwittingly reflects ideological positions that have had catastrophic consequences. The substance of his writing is not mainly artistic, but priestly and homiletic, and he was not intelligent enough to wrestle effectively with the issues he raised. There is always a kind of shrinkage in Hesse from the consequences of the doctrines he is experimenting with; they are blunted by crossing them with incompatible doctrines, or they are made ultimately inconsequential by being placed in a play of the imagination that is intransitive because it is hermetically sealed from the detested world outside. His effect is to sugar-coat the dynamite of the German irrational tradition, and there is plenty of evidence that when that tradition is turned into pablum, those who overindulge in it are likely to wake up with a cosmic stomach ache. (p. 133)

Jeffrey L. Sammons, "Hermann Hesse and the Over-Thirty Germanist," in Hermann Hesse: A Collection of Critical Essays, *edited by Theodore Ziolkowski (copyright © 1973 by Jeffrey L. Sammons; reprinted by permission of Jeffrey L. Sammons), Prentice-Hall, Inc., 1973, pp. 112-33.*

TERRY EAGLETON

Hesse is, of course, one of the most significant of 20th century novelists, and his poetry . . . is for the most part engaging enough; but it has little of the potency of his fiction. In a familiar modern way, poetry is content to be, self-consciously, a "minor" mode; Hesse is a skilfully lyrical, sometimes poignant poet, but in what one must confess is a fairly conventional manner. . . . [Intellectually] speaking, Hesse is rather second-rate; and whatever one might think of this as a judgement on his novels, it certainly seems an apt characterisation of his delicate, but somehow dreamy and depthless poetry. . . . (p. 74)

Terry Eagleton, in Stand *(copyright © by* Stand*), Vol. 19, No. 3 (1978).*

MARK BOULBY

Apart from their astonishing success in America, [Hesse's] works seem to be surviving in Germany despite the adamant hostility of many worthy critics, and his reputation there is probably on the rise. . . .

Das Glasperlenspiel is quite properly seen by Hesse himself as a work of contemporary relevance. . . . There is in the early versions some revulsion against art and learning, against "bourgeois" prejudices. His outlook, in 1936, is however clearly revealed in the figure of Dasa ("Indischer Lebenslauf") who is unmoved finally by the demands of society and refuses to have recourse to violence. . . .

One finds, if one looks for it, much that is a pointer to the later Hesse in his early writings. . . .

A dissatisfaction with stereotyped everyday life and with immobility shows itself early. What is called (by [Volker] Michels) "die Aktualität der Alternative" is offered as a new path.

It was in the pauses between his major works that Hesse wrote much of what appears in *Kleine Freuden* (as also in *Die Kunst des Müssiggangs*). As time goes by, so one finds him more willing to be explicit and in certain directions uncompromising. By the early 1930s, in fact, he has become an adamant pacifist. . . . [He] is convinced that the world is sick above all else from a lack of brotherly love. . . .

Hesse's path, he felt, was an inevitable choice, even if it might appear "der Weg eines Don Quichote". . . . From 1933 we have the "mature" Hesse before us, still given at times to shrill moments of depression, but fundamentally unchanging in his conception of the world, which is pacifistic, rationalistic, and full of hortatory idealism.

> Mark Boulby, "The Quixotic Emigrant," in The Times Literary Supplement (© Times Newspapers Ltd. (London) 1978; reproduced from The Times Literary Supplement by permission), October 20, 1978, p. 1230.

* * *

HINDE, Thomas (pseudonym of Sir Thomas Willes Chitty) 1926-

Hinde is a British novelist whose subtle satires are usually concerned with the effect of social change and progress on the individual. His well-plotted novels are most successful when examining the tangled motives and delusions of his characters and their ineffectuality before some implacable truth. (See also CLC, Vol. 6, and Contemporary Authors, Vols. 5-8, rev. ed.)

PETER PRINCE

[Agent,] ostensibly anyway, follows the tortuous trail of a spy who has been parachuted into enemy territory to carry out secret demolition work. Almost certainly Mr Hinde means us to understand that in reality this mission is a fantasy, invented in the mind of the 'spy', and that the 'enemy territory' is, in fact, the man's own environment which he is now seeing afresh through the new, possibly improved, vision his insanity has given him. Interestingly, even knowing one is watching a man in the grip of a delusion doesn't detract from the story's poignancy and tension. The man's plotting may be quite pointless, his fears of discovery groundless, the crimes he commits in chasing his mad goal horrifyingly unnecessary—all the same he is somehow still a rather impressive figure in his lonely tenacity and courage. But a very anonymous one. We know little about this man or his past; not much either about the environment he's working in. Since finishing the book I've been trying to decide whether I'd have liked more details: to have known just a bit more about the man and his setting might have helped over some of the novel's especially baffling passages. (p. 894)

> Peter Prince, in New Statesman (© 1974 The Statesman & Nation Publishing Co. Ltd.), June 21, 1974.

[Agent, which follows the efforts of a] nervous, faceless figure to gain control of his surroundings and initiate his mission of infiltration, at every point cunningly and bewilderingly inverts the logic of the spy story. Graham Greene has made spy fiction into an allegory of guilt and evil, but the imagination of Mr Hinde, who is right to object to the inevitable comparisons with Greene, works in an opposite direction, away from the apportionment of responsibility towards questioning, disorientation, dislocation. This agent is not a hound of heaven but rather a self-reliant Conrad character whose profession is an existential one, demanding that he confront his own exposure and redundancy. . . .

The spy novel generally ends in the avowal of certainties, the winning of the ideological war; this one, however, opens out into a darkling plain of endless scepticism: the agent realizes he will never escape from secrecy and fear, and accepts the mission of danger and certain death as a gift. . . .

[The narrative] is elliptical and inexplicit, refusing to clarify the nature of the mission, scattering clues we are as anxious and as powerless to interpret as the agent himself. The spy story normally delights in technical information, but such tactical certainty is not allowed here: Mr Hinde indeed seems to parody it when the agent relapses into the appreciative language of the technical manual. . . .

The reticence of the style is cinematic: it will not explain or connect, but simply offers images; . . . and there is a cinematic detachment to the character's bland observation of his own actions, frozen and impotent, gaping at things rather than dealing with them. . . . His memories are cool and detached . . . at once an object and a subject, as in a film.

The action develops through a series of images, which are superficially Greenean—or rather suggest the nausea of Sartre. . . .

But Mr Hinde's nausea is not spiritual, like Greene's, the exploration of a waste of accidie, or existential like Sartre's, the monstrous assertiveness of objects: it is sociological—the world in which the agent sustains his life of risk and daring is soiled and dreary. . . . The heroism of the agent's occupation is now an anachronism; Mr Hinde has written a sour elegy for this fictional form.

> "The Post-Heroic Style," in The Times Literary Supplement (© Times Newspapers Ltd. (London) 1974; reproduced from The Times Literary Supplement by permission), June 21, 1974, p. 656.

RUSSELL DAVIES

[Our Father] is an awkward, squalid, hurrying affair, but then so is the society in which, about which and presumably for which it has been written. How good an excuse this can be held to be is a large question, and Thomas Hinde's is not the only case in which it arises; but Mr Hinde does pose the problem in a particularly acute form, since he seems more intent than most novelists on flinging society in its own face. Moreover, the search for a moral authenticity which, on the whole, he does not find in English behaviour gives his work an enragé air that is particularly strong in Our Father. Many parts of the novel manifest a nervous anger that goes beyond the requirements of energetic narrative, and whose true source and purpose are never quite revealed.

The central difficulty is the figure of Hugh Burkett, one of those "impossible" characters it is so tricky to bring to life. . . . [It] is difficult to keep step with a figure who consists so entirely of reactions and resentments as Hugh Burkett does, and whose intransigent peevishness so dominates the author's chosen style. . . .

One could say that Hugh tore through the book shaking [the other characters] out of their complacency, except that they have none to speak of. What makes them even more infuriating to Hugh (it's a fury he sometimes exercises by putting on bogus voices over the phone, a very British-fiction thing to do) is that they are not really worthy of his majestic paranoia. Neither are they worthy, which is more to the point from the reader's angle, to stand for the society to which Hugh feels himself so superior. Society, and London society in particular, can do better than this in the line of humbug and viciousness, as Mr Hinde seems to recognize every time he lets himself go on the subject of the capital.

The story is propped between two bookends; an introduction and epilogue. . . . Like a good deal else in the book, it requires dismantling, a job which only mechanically-minded readers are likely to take on.

Russell Davies, "Thy Will Be Undone," in The Times Literary Supplement (© *Times Newspapers Ltd. (London) 1975; reproduced from* The Times Literary Supplement *by permission), October 10, 1975, p. 1173.*

ROBERT EAGLE

[Hinde] is the most painstaking, perceptive and inventive living novelist whose work I have read in months. . . . [His] strength is characterisation. . . . Joyless grating well describes the way Hinde's characters get on with each other. Always rubbing each other up the wrong way and longing that someone is going to rub them up the right way. Ranging from the grossly exhibitionist to the abjectly timid they uniformly push themselves along their particular treadmill of frustration, sexual, ideological or material. (p. 31)

The author's feelings for his creations are hard to guess. There is an Old Testament savour to the [*Our Father*]: the tyrannical old Father, the Cain and Abel brothers, the harsh justice meted out to the weak. But Mr Hinde is inscrutable; he records the grotesque and futile with grim impartiality. (p. 32)

Robert Eagle, in Books and Bookmen (© *copyright Robert Eagle 1978; reprinted with permission), January, 1978.*

* * *

HOCHHUTH, Rolf 1931-

Hochhuth is a German dramatist and essayist now residing in Switzerland. His first play, *The Deputy*, was an immediate and controversial success. In this drama Hochhuth explores the possible complicity of Pope Pius XII in the deaths of European Jews during World War II. This play set the tone for Hochhuth's subsequent dramatic output. He desires to revive the theatrical conventions of the great German playwright Schiller, and to this end employs a traditional dramatic context for plays that voice his moral concern for contemporary political and social problems. Although he has been criticized for the strongly polemical character of his plays, he is generally credited as being the founder of the documentary theater. (See also *CLC*, Vol. 4, and *Contemporary Authors*, Vols. 5-8, rev. ed.)

RICHARD GILMAN

[*The Deputy*] manages to survive its own deficiencies and even its incorporeality, persisting in the memory as an instigation, a catalyst and an obduracy. The play as adapted and performed is very much less than the printed text, that text is in turn less than the truth of history, yet something remains that cannot be appeased, neutralized or overthrown. (p. 163)

[The] play sets going a moral energy outside the framework of history and independent of its details. This is the high, or soul-supporting, interpretation. On lower levels *The Deputy* is regarded as a strict historical assertion which can only be established or disproved, or alternatively, as a no less strictly intended work of art obliging us to canonize it or deflate its pretensions. But what is so significant about Hochhuth's work is that it cuts through categories, being neither art nor history nor pure moral gesture nor autonomous call to arms. If it is anything at all it is an act of frustration in the face of categories and complexity, an attempt to give definition and location to an overwhelmingly diffuse and imprecise moral anguish. (pp. 163-64)

As Eichmann was, for the people who tried him, the active principle, upon whom was heaped all the rage and frustration that stemmed from the fact that there was no other agent at hand and, even more, from the intolerable pressure of historical complexity, so Pope Pius, in Hochhuth's sortie against the past, is the negative principle personified, the fixed point of silence who is made to account for and bear the responsibility of silence everywhere. (p. 164)

Two things go wrong, however, in Hochhuth's drama, if not in his moral vision, or at least his moral impulse. The first is contained in the enormous blunder of ascribing to the Pope's personality and human deficiencies more of the responsibility for the Church's failure to speak than rests upon the institutional nature of the Church herself. As Michael Harrington and Guenter Lewy have pointed out, by failing to take into account the nature of German Catholicism, with its pervasive anti-Semitism, and, beyond that, of the nature of the organized Church itself, perpetually risking shame by its considerations of physical survival, Hochhuth has reduced the issues to an intolerable degree.

It is true that he inserts some explanations from the realm of policy—the Vatican's desire for an independent, mediating role, its fear of Russia—but his portrait of Pius as a narrow, tight-lipped, terrifyingly abstract and unfeeling man is so unrelenting and is made so central to his thesis that the effect is to abase history to the level of personality. But what is essential to keep in mind here is that exaggerated and unfair as this portrait undoubtedly is, the real crime is not against Pius but against moral complexity, just as the real failure of imagination rests not in an ignorance of what Pius was but in an ignorance of what we all are in our relations to fact, evil, necessity and transcendence.

This imaginative deficiency is perhaps even more sharply revealed in the figure of the Jesuit, Fontana, who might have been the locus for a true examination of conscience, an arena for moral debate and illumination. But Hochhuth is unable to make more of him than a narrow agency of opposition and indictment, an emblem of revulsion from moral failure and an unchanging container for the corrective act. Dramatically, there is no growth on the part of this character; once he has learned the facts about the extermination of the Jews he simply swings into predictable motion, approaching every so often a pseudo-Dostoevskian confrontation with the anguish of faith besieged by social horror but sinking continually back into mere functionalism, a rod of indignation with which to beat Pius and a weight to throw into the scales.

All this having been said (there has been no space to describe the play's technical and structural weaknesses—its wobbly stance between a Brechtian epic mode and a portentous lyricism . . .) there remains the truth that *The Deputy* cannot be measured by its own dimensions. It survives in part by its very inadequacy, which is to say that its attempt to locate guilt instructs us in the supreme difficulty of the task. (pp. 165-66)

The real value of Hochhuth's play is precisely that it can force us back into history, into the intricacies of the relationship between spirit and aggrieved body, between personal responsibility and institutional indifference. If it does this inadvertently, through a passion ill-matched with its instruments, it does it in any case. *The Deputy* can be described as an accident which rides the weight of necessity, an error which can lead to truth, a failure which makes most of our successes strangely unsatisfying. (p. 166)

> *Richard Gilman, "The Deputy Arrives" (1964), in his* Common and Uncommon Masks: Writings on Theatre 1961-1970 *(copyright © 1971 by Richard Gilman; reprinted by permission of Random House, Inc.), Random House, 1971, pp. 163-66.*

JOHN SIMON

[Among Hochhuth's artistic forebears, two great German historical dramatists figure] prominently: Kleist and Hebbel. It is Kleist's Romantic passion that largely informs *The Deputy;* its idealistic young Jesuit hero owes something to the Prince of Homburg and even to Michael Kohlhaas, figures whose noble passion makes them politically or socially culpable, but who are more troubled and complex than, say, the hero of Schiller's *The Robbers.* And it is Hebbel's notion of historical drama, based on Hegel rather than Kant, in which protagonists become symbols of their society, their age and the workings of history, that importantly affects Hochhuths's dramaturgy. (pp. 167-68)

[Historic] drama can emphasize either half of its name: it can make history subserve the ideas and effects of drama, or it can use the drama as a vehicle for momentous historical truths. Though either approach is valid, the former is more likely to produce a work of art, the latter a tract in dramatic form. (p. 168)

[A] major stumbling block is the question of contemporaneity. It is all right to be fiercely critical or freely inventive, or both, where a figure of the distant past is concerned—where our own world and memories are not incriminated and the plea of insufficient evidence can be advanced. Thus *Becket* may grossly caricature a twelfth-century pope and elicit no more than the arching of an isolated eyebrow, whereas *The Deputy* may make a twentieth-century pope less unsympathetic than its author personally considers him and yet provoke outcries of "Caricature!" from critics all over, regardless of race, creed or competence.

Let us consider the main artistic charges (as opposed to political ones) that have been leveled against Hochhuth's Piux XII. We are told that this Pius is not a worthy antagonist for the idealistic hero—in other words, the "caricature" argument in more sophisticated form; and that *The Deputy,* asserting as it does its historical authenticity, has no business imputing motives of a damaging yet unprovable sort to the Pope. Now, if you believe in a categorical imperative to do right, as Hochhuth does, Pius can no longer be an equally convincing defender of an antithetical position, as Kleist's Elector or Antony in *Julius Caesar* can be. Absolute morality compels a pope to speak up in behalf of six

million human beings, dead, dying or yet to die—even if the consequences, to himself and all Catholics, were more manifestly dangerous than they may have appeared to be. By keeping the Pope as close to absolute silence as dramatically feasible, Hochhuth is actually lending the greatest possible dignity to a position he considers untenable. (pp. 168-69)

Hochhuth has indeed put forward all conceivable reasons for the Pope's silence: the safety of Catholics, business and financial considerations, ecclesiastical politics (danger of schism), European politics (Hitler as bulwark against Stalin and Communism), a kind of aristocratic hauteur and lack of human warmth, failure of nerve. Hochhuth does not insist on the equal relevance of all—indeed, he allows directors, actors, audiences and readers to consider some of them irrelevant. If, however, it is objected that the particular juxtapositions are misleading, I reply that the need for compression makes them inevitable. (p. 169)

If Hochhuth had written a play about Pius XII and only about him, it is entirely probable that the play would have been, by accepted standards, more dense although not necessarily more substantial: much polemical material that is relegated to the "Historical Sidelights" of the play's appendix could have been set forth in greater detail in the play itself. Hochhuth, however—and here lies what is both the glory and the foredoom of his undertaking—is after something bigger: a historical fresco of the entire complex of events that begat and tolerated Auschwitz. No matter how important the Pope may be to the play, other elements are of equal importance: the Germans, the Nazi Party, big business and science gone mad, the Catholic Church, other churches, individuals everywhere, and the metaphysics of evil as embodied in the play's one predominantly mythical character, the Doctor. What ultimately drags the play down to some extent is the very opposite of insufficient historical data: the excess of usable, and used, documentation.

We should note, then, that the Catholic Church, for example, is seen in the play not only as the Pope, but also as the Apostolic Nuncio to Berlin (who is a historic figure), the Cardinal (who, I suspect, also has a historic basis), the Abbot, three quite different monks, an important lay adviser to the Holy See, and above all, as the young Jesuit, Riccardo Fontana, who stands for not only the two priests to whom the play is dedicated, but also, in Hochhuth's words, "for those priests, mostly nameless, who instantly set love for their neighbor above all utilitarian considerations—ultimately at the price of their lives." It is thus that the entire spectrum of clerical reaction to the plight of the Jews is represented.

So the deputy—or vicar, or representative—of the title is not the Pope, who shirks his duty, but Riccardo, who takes on the Pope's burden and dies for it. Riccardo is a profoundly religious figure, and it is largely because of him that the play can justly call itself "a Christian tragedy." Indeed, it is the only major religious play written since the last war that I know of, and it is perhaps a fitting piece of worldly irony which would brand this one, of all plays, as irreligious. What makes Riccardo into a Christian tragic hero is not only the fact that he assumes the guilt of his Church and unsolicitedly becomes the vicar's vicar. It is also the fact that Riccardo's magnanimous desperation forces him toward two of the gravest sins a priest can commit: insubordination to his spiritual superiors, climaxing in the contemplated political assassination of the Pope; and an attempt to murder the villainous Doctor of Auschwitz. (pp. 169-70)

Riccardo's counterpart is Gerstein, who represents the secular hero and the lay sacrifice: the man of moral action who must, in a time of assassins, besmirch himself by ostensibly joining with evil in order to undermine it, and who presumably dies a death which is as anonymous as, but less expiatory than, the priest's. As opposed to these two, there are the two poles of culpability: the scientist whose evil knows no bounds, and the Pontiff whose goodness, unfortunately, does; or to put it more abstractly, the sado-satanist doctor whom metaphysical silence drives to unconscionable crimes, and the high-minded trimmer whom unconscionable crimes leave physically silent. . . .

But if *The Deputy* is too multifariously ambitious to be a complete success, it does not flinch from attempting to pursue a theme into most of its terrible ramifications. In fact, the construction of the play is by no means unskillful in the way it manipulates characters through various scenes— dropping them and picking them up again—toward a final, perhaps somewhat disappointing showdown. The suspense leading up to the Pope scene is ably handled, and there is also an effective contrapuntal construction: scenes involving individuals alternate with scenes involving larger groups or their typical representatives. (p. 171)

What makes *The Deputy* . . . important, however, is not so much the political revelation it may have made. Nor technical devices such as having the same actors enact several contradictory parts, to convey that in our age it is merely a matter of "military conscription . . . whether one stands on the side of the victims or the executioners." Nor the elaborate stage directions which bitterly project certain characters into the future—describing, for example, such and such a Nazi as a solid citizen of postwar Germany. What *is* momentous is that in an age that has progressively convinced itself that its significant dramatic form is dark comedy—that, to quote Dürrenmatt, "our world has led to the Grotesque as to the atom bomb, just as the apocalyptic pictures of Hieronymus Bosch are grotesque, too"—that in this era when "the death of tragedy" has become a literary commonplace, *The Deputy* stands as a valid tragedy: not great, but good, and anything but commonplace. (p. 175)

> *John Simon, "'The Deputy' and Its Metamorphoses" (1964), in his* Singularities: Essays on the Theater 1964-1973 *(copyright © 1975 by John Simon; reprinted by permission of Random House, Inc.), Random House, 1976, pp. 169-75.*

R. C. PERRY

Hochhuth's aim in writing *Der Stellvertreter* [*The Deputy*] was clearly a polemic one. His study of historical documents confirmed him in his conviction that Pope Pius XII could and should have protested against the Nazis' treatment of the Jews during the Second World War. The play is a passionate accusation, and the author has used all the skill at his command in his attempt to transmit his sense of moral outrage to the public. He has chosen to write his play in the form which is best suited to the task of generating emotion in the audience—that of the conventional 'theatre of illusion'. The main action consists of Riccardo's vain efforts to get the Church to condemn the deportations. He goes from one dignitary to the next, until finally he forces his way into the presence of the Pope himself. When he,

too, refuses to act, Riccardo becomes convinced that the only course of action remaining open to him is to go to Auschwitz to share the Jews' suffering. The play ends with his death in Auschwitz. . . .

Hochhuth claims to have respected history in writing his play, but since most of the characters—including Riccardo —and all the dialogues are fictitious, there can obviously be no question of historical authenticity in the strict sense of the term. It is clear, however, that the play does have an authentic basis. (p. 828)

The key scene of the play—Riccardo's confrontation with the Pope—is, of course, unauthentic. There was never any confrontation of this kind as far as we know. But there is an underlying basis of fact which makes it possible to justify this invention within the terms of the play. It is clear that the Pope knew of the deportation of the Jews, and in the appendix Hochhuth demonstrates that several appeals were made by various bodies in the hope that the Pope would publicly condemn the atrocities and rescind the concordat with Germany. Pius's attitude is symbolized in the handwashing incident, which forms the climax of the scene. (p. 829)

The effectiveness of Hochhuth's accusation depends on his being able to demonstrate that the main actions and dialogues of the play do have this solid basis in history, and to a large extent he succeeds. . . . [In] Act V the author tries to express in dramatic form the horrors of Auschwitz, a task which he realizes is virtually impossible. . . . The final scene is meant to drive home the author's message by showing us the logical consequence of the Pope's refusal to act: the triumph of evil. It is debatable whether this scene is a fitting conclusion to the play—the impression it makes on the reader is one of crude melodrama and excessive sentimentality, and in most stage productions it has been cut. However, whatever one's opinion of the final act, it does not affect the validity of the argument contained in the main body of the work.

Der Stellvertreter is written in free verse. It has a basic iambic quality, and most lines have either four or five stresses, but, in fact, the verse is so irregular both in rhythm and length of line that many people who saw the play but did not read it did not realize it was in verse at all. Hochhuth himself has said that he chose verse because it enabled him to concentrate the mass of material he had studied into a form which was performable on the stage. . . . (pp. 829-30)

On the one hand . . . the author felt the need for a medium which would raise the play from the sphere of the document, but on the other, it was important that the language should have an aura of authenticity and be a suitable medium for conveying historical information and factual argument if the work was to have the desired effect. Critics differ as to how far Hochhuth has achieved this combination. (p. 830)

Hochhuth's verse is, in fact, a very free and flexible medium which allows him to include in his play a wide variety of vocabulary and types of language. In Act IV, for example, he has reproduced an official pronouncement which was made by Pius in October 1943. . . . The text of this pronouncement is the only passage in the play which could claim to be literally authentic. It provides a certain amount of evidence as to the Pope's reaction to the deportation of the Jews from Rome, but Hochhuth has incorporated it in such a way that it ceases to be an historical document and becomes further fuel for his fire.

In different parts of the play, the author reproduces dialects, military language, Nazi and ecclesiastical jargon, and, in some cases, notably that of the Cardinal, characterizes individuals through their language. This differentiation of language would appear to constitute a step towards Naturalism, but, as we know, Hochhuth is not primarily interested in the characters for their own sakes, or in their environment as a conditioning factor—their functions are variously to explain and demonstrate the facts of the historical situation and the contemporary reaction to them of certain circles, and at the same time to act, either directly or indirectly, as vehicles for the author's accusation. In order to arouse our empathy, Hochhuth shows us several individual fates in naturalistic detail, but this is only a means to an end, not an end in itself. The various different types of speech are intended to add to the dramatic effectiveness of the play and also to create an authentic atmosphere; the jargons are distillations of real jargons which reveal attitudes that certainly existed, and the dialects are meant to show the wide range of people who were responsible to a greater or lesser extent for Auschwitz. (pp. 832-33)

> *R. C. Perry, in* The Modern Language Review (© *Modern Humanities Research Association 1969), October, 1969.*

*   *   *

HOUSEHOLD, Geoffrey   1900-

Household is a British novelist, short story writer, and author of children's books. Best known for his suspense novels, he pays close attention to plot development, and somewhat less to character portrayal. His work deals with themes of danger, human endurance, and personal honor. Household considers Daniel Defoe, Robert Louis Stevenson, and Joseph Conrad to be his principal influences. (See also *Contemporary Authors*, Vols. 77-80.)

REGINA BARNES

The picaresque novel has a long tradition in English literature from Daniel Defoe to John Buchan, and on to its present active exponent, Geoffrey Household. He has written almost a dozen such books of suspense or adventure, among which *Rogue Male* (1939) achieved the greatest distinction.

As in many of his other novels of action, *The Lives and Times of Bernardo Brown* is thick with incident, thin on characterization. . . .

Household re-creates his familiar world in this novel. One is aware of his intimate knowledge of geography: the British west countryside, the Mediterranean, Hungary and Roumania. His reiterated themes of courage, loyalty, personal honor and endurance ring with customary geniality. As in other novels . . . the beset protagonist measures his skills against unknown adversaries and accusations with sometimes unexpected, but always unfailing, expertise. Nor does he falter as an upholder of traditional virtues even though his travails may temporarily involve him in cuckoldry or pimping. One can always, figuratively, detect the scent of obliging hawthorn, briar pipe and good tweeds.

Unfortunately however, *The Lives and Times of Bernardo*

Brown creaks. The Arabian Nights have entered the shadows; one hopes that Mr. Household will employ his genial and deft style in a new novel of greater staying power. (p. 28)

> *Regina Barnes, in* The New Republic (*reprinted by permission of* The New Republic; © *1974 by* The New Republic, Inc.*), March 16, 1974.*

PETER S. PRESCOTT

Among writers of elegant suspense stories perhaps none has been as erratic in the quality of his performances as Geoffrey Household. A reader might, with some confidence, slap grades on them—an A for this, but no more than C-minus for that—though the disparities are difficult to detect in early chapters. In one specialized subspecies of thriller, however, Household remains pre-eminent: the manhunt novel. No one has written a better chase story than "Rogue Male," though many have imitated it, including Household himself in "Watcher in the Shadows"—certainly the next best of its kind—and in other stories.

Manhunt novels are exceedingly difficult to write well. In addition to the usual suspense paraphernalia of plot, pace and minimal stabs at characterization, a good chase story provides a contrast between the terror of what is happening and the cozy familiarity of the landscape within which it happens. Whether the setting is urban or rural makes no difference, but it must be precisely realized through lovingly informed detail—and I think that only a writer who is more than ordinarily fond of, and knowledgeable about, his city or his part of the countryside can bring it off. . . . Household, in ["Red Anger"] uses this effect to heighten suspense. . . . (p. 81)

[His] new device—a double quarry pursued by two teams of villains—works pretty well (give the book a B-plus), though this kind of story is more effective when a classic simplicity of plot and motive prevails. I wish Household had kept us guessing about the good faith of Alwyn and his family; were he an ironist like Len Deighton he might have twisted his tale at the end to show that Alwyn was indeed a villain, Adrian a dupe, and the foreign agents stout good fellows.

But Household has never been an ironist; he is instead a romantic, a deeply conservative writer for whom it is an article of faith that an honorable man in danger in his own land will prevail. (p. 84)

> *Peter S. Prescott, "Son of 'Rogue Male'," in* Newsweek (*copyright 1975 by Newsweek, Inc.; all rights reserved; reprinted by permission*), *September 22, 1975, pp. 81, 84.*

Julian Despard, alias Gil, alias Herbert Johnson, once a university lecturer, now, ostensibly, a publisher's representative, heads a cell of Magma [in *Hostage*], a secret international organization dedicated to the overthrow of society and the establishment of the New Revolution. By accident he comes across various items of information which convince him that the upper echelons of Magma have planted a nuclear device somewhere in London and plan to explode it. . . . The plot is not unlike that of Geoffrey Household's fine earlier novel, *Rogue Male,* but Despard is a cooler, more self-possessed character than the unnamed hero of that book. In his diary he analyses his thoughts and emotions with clinical, even inhuman objectivity; nevertheless, it is one of the author's triumphs to have made him a completely credible, even sympathetic figure. Despard's style sets the tone for the whole book: terse, with not a redundant word or episode, highly intelligent, and absolutely compelling. (p. 911)

The Times Literary Supplement (© *Times Newspapers Ltd., 1977; reproduced from* The Times Literary Supplement *by permission), July 29, 1977.*

*   *   *

HUGHES, Richard   1900-1976

Hughes was an Anglo-Welsh novelist, dramatist, poet, short story writer, and author of children's books. His prose is noted for its lack of stylistic complexity, a technique that allows Hughes to present an honest and credible depiction of the psychology and motivation of his characters, notably the children characterized in *A High Wind in Jamaica*, his best known work. (See also *CLC*, Vol. 1, and *Contemporary Authors*, Vols. 5-8, rev. ed.; obituary, Vols. 65-68.)

GORONWY REES

The Wooden Shepherdess is the second instalment of Richard Hughes's long historical novel, *The Human Predicament*, of which the first volume, *The Fox in the Attic*, was published in 1961. So long a gap in publication presents the reader with its own difficulties, particularly as *The Human Predicament* is designed, Mr Hughes tells us, as a single continuous novel, and not as a trilogy or a quartet. . . . The most a reviewer can do, therefore, in considering the present volume, is to report progress, rather than pass any final judgment. For Mr Hughes is a very conscious and deliberate artist, and if there are certain episodes in the present volume whose significance we do not entirely grasp, we can be confident that it will not be concealed by the time the novel is completed.

The first thing to say, perhaps, is that Mr Hughes triumphantly surmounts the difficulties he has imposed on himself by his method of publication. He is . . . a very slow writer. . . . But slowness has its rewards as well as its penalties, and in Mr Hughes's case one of them is that the novel's long process of gestation has given birth to certain scenes of almost hallucinatory vividness and power. It is as if the writer had sunk into some profound slumber in which, as in a dream, the imagination was set free to conjure up visions and images unaffected by the passage of time. Such a gift makes Mr Hughes almost unique among contemporary novelists, but like so many precious gifts, it also has its dangers, of which one is that certain scenes stand out so sharply in our minds that we are not always able—as yet—to see how they are related to what comes before and after. . . .

Mr Hughes surrounds his hero [Augustine] with the historical personages of his period; . . . he has as deep a passion for history as he has for literature, and he records it with . . . accuracy and respect for truth. . . .

In Augustine's case, the sinister spirit who presides over his destiny, as of the other characters in the novel, is . . . Hitler; in one sense indeed one might say that Hitler rather than Augustine is the true hero of *The Human Predicament*. . . . In *The Fox in the Attic* Augustine stood on the fringe of the events which culminated in Hitler's abortive *putsch* of 1923, and Mr Hughes's account of the *putsch* itself was a remarkable feat of historical imagination. (p. 504)

Mr Hughes practises something akin to the arts of the magician and the necromancer. Behind the veil of an unobtrusively natural style he traffics with unseen spirits and the powers of darkness; who knows, perhaps they speak with the voice of history herself, the owl which only flies by night? Throughout *The Wooden Shepherdess* there recur incidents of harsh and unexpected violence, which convey the feeling that something has gone wrong at the very heart of things. But the evil which pervades them only reveals itself in the concluding section of the novel, which is a quite brilliant reconstruction of Hitler's Night of the Long Knives.

Mr Hughes himself, in a note to *The Wooden Shepherdess*, points out that whereas, in his account of Hitler's Munich *putsch*, he was able to depend on good historical sources, there are no reliable witnesses to the events of 30 June 1934, because all those most closely concerned were liars. Thus he has felt free to exercise a greater degree of choice and selection, in effect a greater degree of imagination, in his narrative of what happened on that appalling night and the subsequent days. His account is wholly convincing, and his picture of Hitler, stirred out of indecision into abrupt and bloodthirsty action by the prospect of direct confrontation with the Reichswehr, is an unforgettable one. (p. 505)

Goronwy Rees, "Night Owl," in New Statesman (© *1973 The Statesman & Nation Publishing Co. Ltd.), April 6, 1973, pp. 504-05.*

RONALD DE FEO

[Upon publication of the first volume of *The Human Predicament*, titled *The Fox in the Attic*, Richard Hughes] was called a genius, compared to Tolstoy and generally treated as a great modern novelist who had set out to produce the great English novel of the decade. There are many things in the world I will never understand; this response is one of them. . . . The book maddeningly jumped from one scene, character, country to another, trying to appear big and vast; moved, despite the constant shifting, at a snail's pace; and was so mannered that the reader was nearly suffocated by style. *The Wooden Shepherdess* is the perfect sequel: it is as impossible as its predecessor. . . . Hughes has the strange notion . . . that by recording one disconnected scene after another, thinly sketching a host of wooden characters and tossing in references to historical events, . . . he is producing some statement about our century. What he is actually producing is one incredibly rambling and pointless novel. . . . Hughes has been an impressive stylist, but here style does him in for he composes scene after scene in the same lapidary manner, with the result that all scenes seem equally important, whether they be major or minor, and the novel grows hopelessly static. Some critics have decided to reserve judgment on Hughes's series until it is completed, but I fail to find any significant pattern emerging and also fail to understand how a volume three or four will alter the hodgepodge effect of the first two books. (pp. 779-80)

Ronald De Feo, in The Hudson Review (*copyright © 1973 by The Hudson Review, Inc.; reprinted by permission), Vol. XXVI, No. 4, Winter, 1973-74.*

WALTER SULLIVAN

[Richard Hughes] is anything but a flashy writer, and I must confess that I am mildly put off by his style. This, however, is only a matter of taste, and whatever polish his prose may lack is vastly compensated for by the certainty of his vision. (pp. 142-43)

Readers of *The Fox in the Attic*, the first novel in Hughes's projected trilogy, will encounter many of the characters they met there in *The Wooden Shepherdess*. The early sequences of this novel occur in the United States in the 1920s. . . . Hughes develops, subtly and in a low key, a reversal of the old clash of cultures theme that was so dear to the heart of Henry James. In a way Hughes's Americans are not convincing. The obvious surface details seem wrong from time to time, though the speech patterns are right and Hughes knows a great deal about the clothes and the cars and the houses. What seems wrong is something about the spirit of the time: the looseness, the irresponsibility are not quite the same that we have seen in Fitzgerald and Hemingway and Faulkner and Cowley. But this is finally of little consequence. Augustine is an Englishman, and it is largely through his eyes and according to his point of view that the vagaries of the New World are conveyed to us. (p. 143)

Writing about historical figures and hewing the line of historical fact are not easy. The novelist is bound by the dimensions of what was: his imagination is strictly circumscribed by reality. The case of Nazi Germany is a special problem; good writers, such as Katherine Anne Porter, have failed in trying to write about it out of an excess of feeling against the material they seek to employ. Hughes succeeds. His dramatization of the Night of the Long Knives is masterful—cleanly written, balanced, totally convincing, and moving in a way that no adjective can describe. (p. 144)

The joining of the public and private themes is [in the final scene] extrapolated, enlarged, transfigured into a melding of the metaphysical and the mundane. All of our realities are encompassed in a scene that is absolutely successful. We could not legitimately ask for more. (pp. 144-45)

> *Walter Sullivan, in* Sewanee Review *(reprinted by permission of the editor; © 1974 by The University of the South), Winter, 1974.*

*   *   *

HUNTER, Evan (also Ed McBain)   1926-

Hunter is a prolific writer whose work includes novels, detective fiction, a science fiction novel for children, and a play. He is perhaps best known for an early novel, *The Blackboard Jungle*, which was adapted into a popular film. (See also *Contemporary Authors*, Vols. 5-8, rev. ed.)

JULIAN SYMONS

The most consistently skillful writer of police novels is undoubtedly Ed McBain. Under his real name of Evan Hunter . . . he has written some highly successful novels, and he has used other pseudonyms, but the formula of the police novel suits his talent particularly well. He began with Steve Carella, a detective working for an unnamed big-city police force, and equipped him with a wife named Teddy, who is beautiful but both deaf and dumb. As the series developed, Carella's fellow detectives—like Cotton Hawes, who was named after Cotton Mather, and Meyer Meyer, whose father thought it would be an excellent joke to duplicate surname and first name—were introduced. Sometimes half a dozen detectives appear in a book, sometimes only one or two. The cases vary from the macabre to the comic, and the stories are told largely in crisp believable dialogue

between detectives and suspects, or between the detectives themselves. Often the dialogue has a nice note of deadpan comedy. (p. 205)

> *Julian Symons, in his* Mortal Consequences: A History—From the Detective Story to the Crime Novel *(copyright © 1972 by Julian Symons; reprinted by permission of Harper & Row, Publishers, Inc.), Harper, 1972.*

NEWGATE CALLENDAR

It's hard to see why the Ed McBain books about the 87th Precinct have been so popular through the years. He turns them out by formula, and his 26th title, "Let's Hear It from the Deaf Man," . . . is no exception. The best that can be said is that the prose moves fast, even if it is of the rough-hewn-features-and-flinty-blue-eyes department. Otherwise, this novel about police routine has nothing to recommend it. . . . (p. 34)

> *Newgate Callendar, in* The New York Times Book Review *(© 1973 by The New York Times Company; reprinted by permission), April 1, 1973.*

[*Last Summer*] was mildly convincing on the surface . . . but oddly superficial at the core. Deep down, as the saying goes, it was shallow, the stuff perhaps of a modish, middle-brow, box-office film. . . .

The scene is set [in *Come Winter*] for a repeat—and a development—of the activities of the earlier book. . . . Will Mr Hunter write the mature study of people drifting casually, almost insensately, into evil which *Last Summer* promised but did not achieve? Will he make the concept of evil plausible in what they do, show that he has something to tell us about it? A sequel to a previous book like *Last Summer* inevitably sets such questions, and hopes, stirring in the reader's mind.

The hopes are not fulfilled. *Come Winter* is a repeat, and little more, . . . with the same characters—almost. . . .

Resource has gone into the making of the tale; it has pace, and conviction about its detail. But Mr Hunter poses questions he does not answer, hints at depths which he does not explore. It would be pleasant to hope that subtle and imaginative treatment could give a film of the novel the dimension it lacks, expanding what are no more than hints and suggestions to serious and interesting themes.

> *"The Slippery Slopes," in* The Times Literary Supplement *(© Times Newspapers Ltd. (London) 1973; reproduced from* The Times Literary Supplement *by permission), July 13, 1973, p. 797.*

NEWGATE CALLENDAR

[Ed McBain] has, in some ways, broken his usual format [in "Hail to the Chief"].

Gang war is the substance of the book. There is no mystery. McBain, early along, introduces us to the strange mind of the guiding genius of one of the teen-age groups, the young man responsible for all the trouble. His name turns out to be Randall M. Nesbitt. He has dark hair, dark brooding eyes, a sloping, bulbous nose and heavy jowls. He looks as though he always needs a shave. And he has his own kind of logic. . . .

It's a bleak, curiously convincing character McBain presents. You'd almost think he patterned him after a living model. Could the title of the book offer a clue? (p. 49)

Newgate Callendar, in The New York Times Book Review (© *1973 by The New York Times Company; reprinted by permission), October 21, 1973.*

["Streets of Gold" is a] pop epic that takes the form of a family history and autobiography by Iggie Di Palermo—in later years known as Dwight Jamison—a blind jazz pianist who rises from a New York slum and attains stardom briefly in the fifties and sixties. . . . The scenes of tenement life are warm, witty, and accurate-sounding, yet tend toward coarseness and violence, and it's an open question whether the truthfulness of, say, the homosexual-rape scene (reminiscent of the teen-age rape that climaxes Mr. Hunter's "Last Summer") can redeem its squalor and familiarity. When we come to Iggie's decline, which hinges on a bit of standard adultery, the familiarity of his story becomes really depressing. Yet much of the book has a definite personal stamp, and its evocations of jazz—of a "jump into water that's icy cold and deep"—are pleasant. (pp. 90, 93)

The New Yorker (© *1975 by The New Yorker Magazine, Inc.), January 13, 1975.*

NEWGATE CALLENDAR

[McBain's hero in "Where There's Smoke"] is a retired detective lieutenant named Benjamin Smoke, and McBain labors greatly to make him believable.

But he doesn't really succeed. . . . Smoke is a bored man; he has left the force because he is bored. Crime is predictable, criminals are stupid. . . . He has always solved anything that came his way; he *wants* to fail in a case, to come across a mind smarter than his.

All this is, of course, is an authorial gimmick: McBain has seized upon it as a means of attempting to infuse his character with something a bit different. But Smoke is an ordinary man, basically, who in this book has an ordinary case with ordinary criminals and an ordinary solution. "Where There's Smoke" (even the title is a gimmick) is competent, but there is not a shred of originality in its plotting or characterization, much less its writing. (p. 47)

Newgate Callendar, in The New York Times Book Review (© *1975 by The New York Times Company; reprinted by permission), October 12, 1975.*

JAMES R. FRAKES

The country may not be exactly drooling with hunger for another novel about "Westering," but Evan Hunter, in ["The Chisholms"] evokes some freshness from the tritest materials and focuses our concern on complex, often perverse, human beings rather than on the vacuous panoramic vista that too often dominates this genre. When the Chisholm family pull out of barren Virginia in 1844 and head doggedly for the promised land, they do not automatically become archetypes, rendered featureless by the author's grim determination to make some Big Statement about the pioneering spirit of our hardy forefathers or how Noble Women Helped to Win the West. (p. 42)

This family may be the center of the action, but the action itself is familiar if not hackneyed by now. "The Chisholms" contains just about every standard ingredient of frontier narrative. . . .But Mr. Hunter still plays fair by judicious proportioning: the buffalo gallop for only a few

paragraphs, the gang rape occupies only four sentences, the saloon whores are only local color bits. The stripped narrative line is one of Hunter's prime virtues, so that when he decides *not* to cut short an action—the harrowing Indian raid on the isolated family, the tonal mixture of comedy and horror when the rather charming horse thief is hanged—he has truly earned his license.

Perhaps it was wise to make this novel back away from the larger issues raised by the graphic events; perhaps it was nothing more than a failure of nerve. At Fort Laramie, Will, the eldest Chisholm son, lying in a tipi between two Indian women (well, one's a white woman from Boston who has gone native), starts to brood about his experiences. And he *almost* has a revelation about such issues as law vs. justice, the eye-for-an-eye absurdity of capital punishment, human predatoriness, limited natural resources, racism, but, "Trembling in the night, troubled, he moved closer to the squaw for warmth, and finally fell asleep. By morning, he'd forgotten what he'd almost understood." Because he forgets—and because the author stays on the surface of the prairie—we can only nod complacently and wearily when, on the last page, the whole crew turn into frieze figures: "'See?' Bonnie Sue said, pointing vaguely west. 'That's California there.'" (p. 43)

James R. Frakes, in The New York Times Book Review (© *1976 by The New York Times Company; reprinted by permission), September 19, 1976.*

NEWGATE CALLENDAR

[In "Goldilocks", Ed McBain] leaves his famous 87th Precinct to write a novel about murder and adultery in Florida. A man coming home finds his wife and children murdered. His story has a few holes in it, and he comes under suspicion. . . . There is considerable soul searching before things get straightened out. McBain goes through all this in his usual professional manner. But there is one little mistake in the book. A suspect says she was listening to the radio. "They were playing a Stravinsky piano quartet, I don't know which one." Sorry, Ed. There is no such thing as a Stravinsky piano quartet. (p. 34)

Newgate Callendar, in The New York Times Book Review (© *1978 by the New York Times Company; reprinted by permission), February 18, 1978.*

*   *   *

HUXLEY, Aldous   1894-1963

Huxley was a British-American novelist, essayist, short story writer, poet, critic, and playwright. His novels are generally considered novels of ideas: Huxley was interested in many fields of knowledge and his ideas on science, philosophy, religion, and other topics are woven throughout his fiction. His concentration on the philosophical content of a work led critics to find his fiction overly didactic and artistically unsatisfying. This tendency was adumbrated in his later works when, drawn to the philosophy of mysticism and discarding the more objective and satiric tone of his early novels, Huxley created characters that served as little more than mouthpieces for his ideas. Continually searching for an escape from the ambivalence of modern life, Huxley sought a sense of spiritual renewal and a clarification of his artistic vision in hallucinogenic drugs, an experience explored in one of his

best known later works, *The Doors of Perception*. (See also *CLC*, Vols. 1, 3, 4, 5, 8.)

FREDERICK J. HOFFMAN

Huxley has often demonstrated in his novels the fact that ideas may possess qualities which are comparable with those which animate persons—and this particularly in a period of time when ideas are not fixed, calculated, or limited by canons of strict acceptance or rejection. Ideas, as they are used in Huxley, possess, in other words, *dramatic* qualities. Dominating as they very often do the full sweep of his novels, they appropriate the fortunes and careers which ordinarily belong to persons. (p. 190)

The best examples of the novel of ideas are Huxley's novels of the 1920's. To be sure, he did not always use this form; nor is any of his novels purely a novel of ideas. In his shorter pieces, most notably in "Uncle Spencer," "Two or Three Graces," and "Young Archimedes," Huxley writes charmingly and sympathetically of persons and reveals a remarkable talent for a complete delineation of characters who are interesting almost exclusively as persons. But the works which mark the development of Huxley as a novelist —*Chrome Yellow, Antic Hay, Those Barren Leaves,* and *Point Counter Point*—are, each in its own way, novels of ideas. Rarely does a Huxley character give himself away directly; rarely if ever does Huxley fail to give him away. The position, the point of view, of the Huxley character is usually revealed in the course of Huxley's discussion of his tastes, his intellectual preferences, his manner of behaving himself in the society of his fellows. Thus the *idea* which each is to demonstrate becomes in the novel the point of view he adopts—or, actually, *is.* (pp. 194-95)

[In] the case of Huxley, there is a close interaction of the essayist with the novelist. They parallel each other for a time; they frequently supplement each other. The essayist is a sort of "supply station," to which the novelist has recourse. He is the "port of call" at which the novelist stops, to take on necessary and staple goods. The reputation of Huxley is chiefly that of the novelist. In another sense, however, he is the essayist-commentator upon twentieth-century morals and ideas. Just as his characters are often subordinate as persons to the ideas or points of view they express, so his novels as a whole are often mere carriers for the cargo of ideas which their author must retail.

The essayist's attempt to give animation to his ideas leads to the novel of ideas. In the course of Huxley's development as novelist, the characters of his creation stumble, swagger, or are carried through his novels, supported almost always by the essayist. (p. 197)

In the novels of the 1920's, the essayist in Huxley strode along with the novelist. . . . Beginning, perhaps, with *Eyeless in Gaza*, the essayist far exceeds the novelist. . . . [In Huxley's later novels, he] is alternately a caricaturist and an essayist; he is no longer a novelist of ideas, but a philosopher who knows not how gracefully to leave the house in which he has lived so graciously all his life. (p. 199)

Huxley is no longer a novelist. His recent novels are lengthy essays, to which are added entertainments. But his novels of the 1920's *are* novels of ideas—ideas clothed, ideas given flesh and bone and sent out into a world in which they may test themselves. (pp. 199-200)

Huxley's novels of ideas are an expression of the tremen-

dous vitality which ideas had in the 1920's; they are also a testimony of the intellectual confusion of that period. . . . Most important of all, these novels are a brilliant portrait of the age, or at least of its intellectual interests and habits. Whatever defects of manner the novels of Huxley suffer, his vital interest in the intellectual concerns of his time has resulted in several dramatic portraits of contemporary life and thought. (p. 200)

> *Frederick J. Hoffman, "Aldous Huxley and the Novel of Ideas," in* College English *(copyright © 1946 by The National Council of Teachers of English), December, 1946 (and reprinted in* Forms of Modern Fiction, *edited by William Van O'Connor, Indiana University Press, 1948, pp. 189-200).*

EVELYN WAUGH

[The setting of *Antic Hay*] is Henry James's London possessed by carnival. A chain of brilliant young people linked and interlaced winds past the burnished front-doors in pursuit of happiness. Happiness is growing wild for anyone to pick, only the perverse miss it. There has been the single unpredictable, inexplicable, unrepeatable calamity of "the Great War." It has left broken hearts—Mrs. Viveash's among them—but the other characters are newly liberated from their comfortable refuges of Conscientious Objection, to run wild through the streets.

The central theme of the book is the study of two falterers "more or less in" their "great task of happiness," Mrs. Viveash and Theodore Gumbril. Everyone else, if young, has a good time. (p. 19)

The story is told richly and elegantly with few of the interruptions which, despite their intrinsic interest, mar so much of Mr. Huxley's story-telling. The disquisition on Wren's London should be in a book of essays but the parody of the night-club play is so funny that one welcomes its intrusion. The "novel of ideas" raises its ugly head twice only, in the scenes with the tailor and the financier, crashing bores both of them but mere spectators at the dance. They do not hold up the fun for long.

And there is another delicious quality. The city is not always James's London. Sometimes it becomes Mediterranean, central to the live tradition. The dance winds through piazzas and alleys, under arches, round fountains and everywhere are the embellishments of the old religion. An ancient pagan feast, long christianized in name, is being celebrated in a christian city. The story begins in a school chapel, Domenichino's *Jerome* hangs by Rosie's bed, Coleman quotes the Fathers. There is an insistent undertone, audible through the carnival music, saying all the time, not in Mrs. Viveash's "expiring" voice, that happiness is a reality.

Since 1923 Mr. Huxley has travelled far. He has done more than change climate and diet. I miss that undertone in his later work. It was because he was then so near the essentials of the human condition that he could write a book that is frivolous and sentimental and perennially delightful. (p. 20)

> *Evelyn Waugh, "Youth at the Helm and Pleasure at the Prow: 'Antic Hay'," in* London Magazine *(© London Magazine 1955), August, 1955 (and reprinted in* Aldous Huxley: A Collection of Critical Essays, *edited by Robert E. Kuehn, Prentice-Hall, Inc., 1974, pp. 23-5).*

CHARLES M. HOLMES

[Huxley's] early poetry is a record of the highly complicated inner struggle which influenced, even determined the theme and the shape of his much more popular, much more successful fiction. After *The Burning Wheel* he quickly produced *Jonah* (. . . 1917), *The Defeat of Youth* (. . . 1918) and *Leda* (. . . 1920), and he appeared several times in the annuals *Oxford Poetry* and *Wheels*. Although this work shows some development in technique, some improvement in quality, it illustrates more clearly Huxley's shifting and ambivalent attitude toward the very practice of literary art. Like his fiction, Huxley's verse embodies his need to express himself entangled inextricably with the problem of how to do so. From the earliest poems the crucial inner conflict appears; Huxley tries various styles to express it; the need to choose a style then intensifies the conflict as Huxley is forced to choose between sincere expression and effective poetry. It is this dilemma I have attempted to follow, up to the point where Huxley virtually abandoned verse for fiction.

The first sign of inner conflict is a startling inconsistency between poems expressing a rebellious desire to shock and other poems voicing merely conventional sentiment. Huxley's first published poem, "Home-Sickness . . . From the Town," is as obviously anti-Victorian as anything he ever was to write. . . . As in so many of the novels, a deliberately shocking frankness about sex is combined with the makings of a new poetic style forged of knowing allusions and esoteric words. Yet in *The Burning Wheel* a few months later we find verses in the very manner Huxley seemed to have attacked, poems almost shockingly banal and stale where conventional phrases and worn-out notions abound. "Escape" begins like inferior Tennyson. . . . "Philoclea in the Forest," an even staler poem, is set amidst Arcadian wood-moths, flowers, and lutes. "Sentimental Summer" is a maudlin poem of love. . . . (pp. 64-5)

Although there is something typically youthful in this inconsistency, in Huxley's case it was a most important symptom, not just the sign of an inevitable but temporary stage. His inconsistency in poetic attitude and style was rooted in deep and lasting inner conflict, a conflict destined to increase, to plague him for years, to become and remain the most important force in all his work. "Home-Sickness . . ." is an exaggerated recognition of the real, "Escape" and "Sentimental Summer" a sincere gesture toward the ideal. Like Shelley and other romantics of the century before, Huxley saw a clash between the two. He presented the ideal as beauty, as love, or as spirit, and the real as the disappearance or transcience of beauty, the loss of love, sometimes replaced by lust, or the ugly facts of the surrounding material world. Most important, not only is his own soul affected by this clash; it is also both a part and an illustration of it. . . . [Huxley] finds both the ideal and the real within himself. Only occasionally could he project a vision of the ideal untarnished by unpleasant actuality, seen residing outside, in others, or within. Though he has been called a "frustrated romantic," he was inwardly split as most of the romantics never were. He visualized a purer love, a permanent beauty, a world deserving nothing but our devotion and his praise. But he recognized his own tendency toward such romantic flights of fancy, and he also understood the frequent sordidness of actuality, in the world, in others, but—most disturbingly—in himself. (p. 66)

But more surprising than these contradictions is his own reaction to them. His inconsistencies apparently leave him unperturbed. He can be disturbed, of course, by what he finds in the world and himself, but not by the pattern of contradictions in his response. Yeats, who was at least as sharply split as Huxley, began to search for "Unity of Being" and regularly found his art a way to resolve his inner tensions. Huxley was not so much trying to dissolve his inner conflict as attempting to express or project it in his verse. Though he may have been searching for inner harmony, he seems to have been more interested in something theoretically external—a usable, original, aesthetically pleasing style. *The Burning Wheel* not only shows that inner conflict exists, it shows Huxley trying several different poetic styles, several different ways of putting the conflict into words.

In the title poem, "The Burning Wheel," an obviously symbolist style is used. The wheel of life, "Wearied of its own turning," painfully spinning "dizzy with speed," agonizingly yearns to rest. . . . The real-ideal conflict is seen here not through the specific emotions of the poet, but rather as symbolically generalized and abstract, as the opposition of life and death, the tension between activity and calm. The theme will find new symbols in the novels: the crystal of quiet described with such intensity in *Antic Hay*, and the connected pair of cones in *Eyeless in Gaza*, symbolizing the same quiet along with the flux of tortured lives. But Huxley immediately abandoned this kind of symbolism in his verse. Three other styles dominate the early poems.

"Escape," "Sentimental Summer," and their ilk are written in a "romantic" style, a diluted version of the manner perfected a century before, now superannuated though still so frequently used. It is easily recognized, in Huxley's early poems, by the direct, unguarded expression of emotion, by supposedly "poetic" phrases and words, by imprecise and worn-out metaphors. We find it, of course, when Huxley can believe in his ideal—when, for example, he can see love as untarnished by lust. . . . But just as frequently it expresses his disillusionment; his sense of the real, the unpleasant, the actual, victorious over the imagined, the ideal. . . . Most of the poetry in this romantic style is buncombe, soon to be parodied by Huxley himself in *Crome Yellow* when Denis Stone idealizes the older Anne in the lyric he calls "The Woman who was a Tree." Yet Huxley never abandoned either the romantic attitude or the corresponding style. They are important in almost all of his novels, from *Antic Hay* and its visions of young Gumbril to the synthesized utopia of Huxley's final statement, *Island*.

Huxley also tried a simple dialectic, a style embodying versified argument or discussion. Yeats had already begun to use it for expressing inner conflict, for presenting artistically his battles with himself. But Huxley was attracted by a curious potential unappealing to Yeats—the fact that two sides of his conflict could be expressed in dialectic with no demand that the conflict be resolved. . . . He frequently seems to be nurturing his conflict, almost preserving it as a subject for his poems.

Huxley was to transform his dialectic style into the sparkling conversations of the novels, the house party discussions of *Crome Yellow* and *Those Barren Leaves*. But his fourth, "ironic" style was an even more congenial voice, destined to be the one his public wanted to hear and most frequently heard. It became the characteristic trademark of his fiction, the tone of *Point Counter Point,* the very conception of *Brave New World.* Suggested as early as "Home-Sickness . . . From the Town," with its "debile" women and allusions to Rousseau and Keats, the style depends on the ironic contrast provided by the unexpected, in the form of such learned allusions and esoteric words. Its irony also involves another favorite Huxley strategy, setting the real against the ideal by putting human beings into a zoo. (pp. 67-9)

When Huxley shifts in a single volume from one style to another, juxtaposing "treasured things" and "golden memories" with turd-kicking children and souls as elephants' snouts, he is obviously unsettled, perhaps thoroughly confused. Yet his experiments, his vacillations in style seem to have made his conflict even more severe. Faced with the dilemma, the conflict posed by the real and the ideal, Huxley had tried four different styles in attempts to express himself, to put the conflict into words. He found that sincerity asked for the use of one of his styles but poetic effectiveness called for the use of another. To be candid about his state of mind, dialectic was the obvious choice, and it dominates his contributions, a year after *The Burning Wheel,* to the 1917 volume of *Wheels.* (p. 70)

Huxley seems gradually to have realized that his dialectic style, burdened by such complexities and awkwardnesses as these, could never be as effective as his ironic style and its amusing human zoo. But the greater aesthetic discipline the ironic style imposed either inhibited or made impossible sincere and frank expression. As a result a new element of inner conflict appeared; the clash between sincerity and the desire to develop effective style became another dominant motif of his career. In a later essay, "Sincerity and Art," Huxley tried to escape from the dilemma. Being sincere, he claimed, is not "a moral choice between honesty and dishonesty," but rather "mainly an affair of talent." . . . The writer does not have to expose his feelings, to explore his deeper self, to heed the cries of his truest inner voice. He merely needs to use his talent, to compose the most skillful, the most carefully polished poems.

The slim, rare volume *Jonah* (1917) seems to demonstrate this conclusion in the craft so evident in the dozen poems it includes. The idealistic Huxley of the romantic style, the split Huxley of dialectic have all but disappeared. Instead of the self-conscious involutions of "Retrospect," we find Huxley's ironic style prevailing again, this time reinforced by the influence of other poets. "The Oxford Volunteers" reflects the bitter manner of Wilfred Owen, but more frequently the poems echo the work of Arthur Rimbaud, whose startling imagination helped Huxley to fill his weird, ironical zoo. "Behemoth," for example, is a Rimbaldien kind of fantasy. . . . Even more Rimbaldien is "Zoo Celeste," one of the four *Jonah* poems actually composed in French. . . . The world of Rimbaud's famous "Après le Déluge" . . . is larger, more dazzling, more varied than Huxley's zoo, and his poem a more remarkable imaginative achievement. But "Zoo Celeste" is hardly less fantastic and less odd.

Rimbaud suggested motifs and subjects, and ways of rendering ironically the imagined and the ideal. Another Frenchman, Jules Laforgue, helped Huxley to find a congenial tone and to apply his ironic style to himself. Temperamentally and stylistically the converse of the older symbolist, Laforgue developed a bored, self-deprecating irony

as evident in *Jonah* as the fantastic imagery so clearly drawn from Rimbaud. . . . ["Jonah" itself is a] remarkable example of this peculiar, efficient, distinctive style, as Laforgue's ironic use of scientific and medical words is merged with the spirit of fantasy of Rimbaud. (pp. 71-3)

These unusual poems were produced by subjugating at least a degree of sincerity to talent. They do not represent, as Huxley's romanticism proves, the attitude he consistently really felt, nor do they even hint at the struggle raging within. But they involved or suggested a kind of compromise procedure, a strategy allowing Huxley to write effectively without completely stifling the voice of inner conflict. He could use his clever, ironical, exaggerated style as an inverse kind of "sincere" poetic mask. The poet, to a degree, is there for all to see. But his deeper concerns, his sensitivities are hidden; he is protected even in self-expression by the masking effect of his style. . . . *Jonah* shows Huxley grappling with the sincerity-art dilemma by developing a style that would serve him as a mask. Wearing it, he could make gestures toward the sincere while composing his best ironic poems.

Huxley never transformed his need for a mask into a theory, as Yeats was soon to do as part of his system in *A Vision.* His problem was too personal for such objective treatment, too elusive and complex for any highly organized plan. He preferred presenting himself in verses like "The Contemplative Soul" as a weird, deeply submerged, ship-inhabiting fish:

> Fathoms from sight and hearing,
> Where seas are blind and deaf,
> My soul like a fish goes steering
> Her fabulous gargoyle nef. . . .

Since a danger awaits if the soul-fish comes to the surface, it decides to remain far down below. . . . Perhaps Huxley is already aware of his future: the final images [of this poem] hint at the mysticism he will eventually pursue. But the secret, whatever it is, is only barely suggested beneath the comical, self-deprecating mask.

Though Huxley had formed a style useful for deceptively partial self-expression, he did not employ even it with any consistency. It was a limited, temporary resolution of his dilemma, even though it produced the best of his early poems. The style of his next group, for the 1918 cycle of *Wheels,* is merely the purest, clearest expression of the impact on him of Rimbaud. . . . Unlike the *Wheels,* 1917, selections they are not in dialectic, nor are they in any other previous Huxley style; they are prose poems in the manner of *Illuminations,* with something of the energy of Rimbaud's imagination. (pp. 73-5)

Rimbaud the visionary, who saw beyond sordid actuality to an ideal, inspired the most important of these poems. "Beauty" is a glowing, lyrical disquisition, and—for Huxley—a surprising autobiographical admission. The search narrated in the poem is not really for beauty itself but for a way of living in the world with minimum conflict, and at the same time for a posture that will help him to create. Like the Rimbaud of "Being Beauteous," Huxley sees a dazzling female image, a "perpetual miracle, beauty endlessly born." But whereas Rimbaud will fall "à traverse la mêlée." Huxley's much longer poetic search continues. . . . The only true poets are centaurs, he concludes [after his long search]; their bellies travel close to the ground but their heads are in the air.

As this final image hints, though "Beauty" is an idealistic, visionary poem, it is the vision of an idealism severely challenged by actuality—so severely that it may corrode away. No mask, no ironical pose appears in the poem. The poet instead suggests that he is tempted to be a cynic—not to hide his idealism underneath a comic mask, but to flaunt his discovery that the ideal is mocked by the real. (pp. 75-6)

The idealist-turned-cynic accounts for Huxley's next book title, the volume he called *The Defeat of Youth and Other Poems.* The title refers to the volume's opening sonnet sequence, a group of poems directly avowing the cynical view. They redescribe Huxley's earlier idyllic view of love; reaffirm his idealized vision of true beauty; trace the change of love to lust in consummation; and leave the weary poet disillusioned, now in sight of a very different truth. The quest for the ideal, it appears, has been forsaken; the strategy of hiding conflict behind a mask has been abandoned; the poet has no choice but the cynical, tired view, and his earliest and least effective style, the romantic.

Yet the poems which follow "The Defeat of Youth" [in this volume] demonstrate that nothing could be farther from the truth. Cynicism is another alternative, another temporary phase. (pp. 76-7)

The Defeat of Youth is a more bewildering set of contradictions, of contrasts in attitude and of the various Huxley styles, even than those in Huxley's first book, *The Burning Wheel.* Yet this great variety apparently served as a kind of creative catharsis, a test which isolated the worst and the best and helped the vacillating poet to make his ultimate choice. In *Leda,* Huxley's last collection of early verse, and in the handful of poems for the last three collections of *Wheels,* the ironic style becomes once and for all Huxley's most frequent, most characteristic voice, and he regularly appears exposed and hidden with his mask. . . . [The] best and most typical are the four "Philosopher's Songs," the self-deprecating lyrics of a bard who continues to find the ridiculous or the grotesque in life and love. (pp. 77-8)

The conflict masked in the grotesquerie of poems such as these, Huxley's increasingly obsessive concern for love and lust, is a little more obvious in "Morning Scene" and "From the Pillar." In the first the poet sees, poised above Goya's image of scattered hair and tempting bosom, "a red face / Fixed in the imbecile earnestness of lust." In the other he seems to project an exaggerated version of himself [split by a mixture of hatred and envy]. . . . Huxley's desire both to accept and reject the flesh may account for yet another experiment, the final one before he virtually abandoned writing poems. All his poems before *Leda* had been short ones. He needed a more flexible, more extended mode of expression, especially to explore the continuing problem of the flesh. The temporary answer appears in the two poems which begin and end the volume, poetry in the form of narrative.

"Leda," which has found many critical admirers, is a long, elaborate treatment of the myth so powerfully compressed in Yeats' sonnet "Leda and the Swan." . . . [Though expansively and elegantly composed of blank verse, the] poem is not only a polished handling of the myth, it is also an allegory of Huxley's plaguing concern. Leda is the ideal, another vision of "perfect loveliness." Jove, embodying superhuman, transcendent power, is driven like mere mortals by restlessness and an irresistible sensual itch. His pos-session of Leda is the rape of "almost spiritual grace." Like the parade of women who soon will people Huxley's novels, Leda is unable, unwilling to resist. . . . Even centuries ago, the implication is, the gross forces of life destroyed the virginal ideal.

"Soles Occidere et Redire Possunt" (Suns are able to set and to return) is a narrative in a less traditional, more flexible medium. In loosely rhymed stanzas with a line of varying length, Huxley traces a day in the life of a friend killed in the War. Yet just as the friend sounds very much like Huxley, the style combines the elements Huxley had already used before. John Ridley, the supposed subject of the poem, lies in bed engaging in dialectic with himself, an idealized dream battling with an approaching "quotidian" task. . . . Through Ridley, Huxley seems to project his own life once again, but at greater length than in any earlier poem.

"Soles" and "Leda" both were abortive efforts, however; neither was a final answer, a proper mode for self-projection. Blank verse, however well he could employ it, was obviously a style wedded to a remote past. The contrasting jerky, cacophonous rhythms of "Soles" were the work of a poet really out of his element, who seems to be writing for the first time all over again. Earlier, his work in dialectic had allowed him the freest self-expression, yet his self was often what he most deeply wanted to mask. The ironic style had provided the mask and produced his most effective poems, yet its very indirectness, with the brevity it encouraged, inhibited full expression of his themes. The long narrative poems had at least helped to suggest an answer. If no style of poetry would work, perhaps the combination of prose and narrative would. Huxley was not quite yet ready to publish his first novel, but he was more than ready to try to master the short story. Before 1920, the year of *Leda,* was over, he had in the stories of *Limbo* most auspiciously begun. (pp. 78-80)

Charles M. Holmes, "The Early Poetry of Aldous Huxley," in Texas Studies in Literature and Language *(copyright © 1966 by the University of Texas Press), Vol. VIII, No. 3, Fall, 1966 (and reprinted in* Aldous Huxley: A Collection of Critical Essays, *edited by Robert E. Kuehn, Prentice-Hall, Inc., 1974, pp. 64-80).*

ROBERT E. KUEHN

Aldous Huxley's career resembles that of several other eminent twentieth-century writers: he began as an *enfant terrible* and ended as a sage. . . . Each of his novels, from *Crome Yellow* through *Island,* is indisputably modern, even though the later books differ so radically from the earlier ones. Huxley seems to have been born mistrustful of received attitudes and disdainful of those creeds that provided his forebears with a sense of order, continuity, and spiritual composure. His intellectual temperament, if one may call it that, was skeptical, restless, experimental. In his youth he was a debunker of moribund truths; in middle age he became an ardent seeker of new truths or of fresh combinations of old truths. His zestful assault on the old order of things in *Crome Yellow, Antic Hay, Those Barren Leaves,* and pre-eminently in *Point Counter Point* gave way in time to a strenuous and eclectic attempt to find a new order, to fashion a "perennial philosophy" from disparate fragments of the human past. The transition was not quite as abrupt as it is sometimes made to seem: the road to mysticism is as clearly implied in *Those Barren Leaves* as is the road to orthodoxy in *The Waste Land*.

Huxley has always been a hero to the young, for his interests have consistently matched those of the generation just coming forward. Men fifteen years younger than Huxley have testified to the "liberating" effect of his early stories and novels; ... he was an advocate of pacifism long before pacifism became an unarguable mark of sanity; his loathing of technology when it is allowed to develop without ethical imperatives and his fear of the terrible consequences of over-population and the despoliation of nature were subjects of his fiction and essays years before they became subjects for the popular press.... And yet Huxley never courted the good will of the young or of any other group. His mind was free and adventurous, and his books were unfailingly of their time and place.

Huxley's novels are original in the sense that no one else could have written them: each is stamped with Huxley's peculiar mode of invention and with that witty inflexion that is his alone. We find in the novels an odd array of characteristics that constitute the Huxley vision and the Huxley style: an impressive and sometimes showy awareness of culture in all its multiplicity; enviable clarity of argument and facility of expression; the ironist's relentless tendency to demonstrate the differences between appearance and reality in things great and small; a love of unlikely, learned, and sometimes gruesome comparisons; and that "foible" that Peter Quennell describes as "his love of following up an irrelevant train of ideas, regardless of literary consequences." The novels are the very antithesis of the revered Jamesian model. They are quirky, full of ideas and lively debate, richly reflective. Better novelists have not succeeded in describing the age—roughly 1920 through 1960—with anything like the massive and significant detail that we find in Huxley's fiction.... *Point Counter Point* [for example] is 1928 London, and part of its value for us lies in its brilliant, dense, and authentic evocation of life at just *that* moment in English civilization.

I would suggest that the proper way of viewing Huxley is as a *moraliste*, a writer who has more in common with Montaigne and Pascal than with, say, Hardy or Conrad. Huxley's well-developed interests in philosophy, biology, sociology, economics, religion, anthropology often intrude upon the design of his novels because these interests were, for him, more important than design. Huxley is a cerebral rather than a poetic novelist. He is a satirist and a proselytizer of humane values who used the novel form because he found it sufficiently congenial to his purposes. He was a writer more passionately interested in truth as fact than in truth as myth, a writer who had the courage always to do as he pleased and who consequently displeased many, especially those whose definition of the novel was more rigid than his own. (pp. 1-3)

Contemporary reviewers of his early novels were charmed by their freshness, their sprightly erudition and casual impieties. But the praise faded as Huxley, the "amused Pyrrhonic aesthete" of those early years, became increasingly obsessed with the problems of modern life. His somewhat presumptuous attempt to dramatize these problems in his fiction met with disapproval, and the disapproval persisted. His colleagues in the arts—Eliot, Maugham, Virginia Woolf, to name only three—found his books unsatisfactory, and many subsequent critics have concurred: David Daich-

es, Arnold Kettle, D. S. Savage, Sean O'Faolain, William York Tindall. (p. 3)

[For Huxley] mere art was never enough, and hence his novels are maddeningly encyclopedic. Few writers have imposed upon fiction quite the weight of exposition which Huxley would have it bear, and perhaps only Tolstoy, in *War and Peace*, has done this successfully. Huxley's contrivances—his "long diaries or autobiographical documents"—may bore or disappoint the reader whose expectations have been shaped by long and exclusive familiarity with the novel of sensibility. But Huxley's novels are a deliberate departure from this tradition and we are misguided in blaming him for failure to conform to the canons of that tradition. ...

Huxley is no Fielding—he was never quite able to combine the instincts of the novelist with the habits of the essayist in the happy fashion of Fielding in *Tom Jones*. But Huxley's unsentimental view of man, his moral passion, his dependence upon humoural characters to convey his meaning are comparable to Fielding's; and like Fielding, he made his novels the carriers of diverse accumulations of experience and learning.... Few British novels of the twentieth century, aside from *Point Counter Point*, are comparable to *Tom Jones* in their intellectual energy, diversity, and thoroughness. (p. 5)

Huxley's reputation is of course problematical. Most readers prefer the early, Peacockian satires; others—Christopher Isherwood, for example—prefer the wisdom and gravity of the later works. But even the most hostile of Huxley's critics would probably admit that our literature would be greatly diminished without him. The man we meet in the books is arresting, for we see Huxley struggling heroically with those very problems that have made our century so turbulent and imploring us again and again to reason patiently, to view life clearly, and to be better. His moral seriousness and intellectual honesty are awesome. (p. 6)

> *Robert E. Kuehn, in his introduction to* Aldous Huxley: A Collection of Critical Essays, *edited by Robert E. Kuehn (copyright © 1974 by Prentice-Hall, Inc.; reprinted by permission of Prentice-Hall, Inc., Englewood Cliffs, New Jersey), Prentice-Hall, 1974, pp. 1-7.*

JEROME MECKIER

[*Island*] embodies a collection of the right responses to problems that the brave new world handled badly. But there is even more to the novel than that. Unlike *News from Nowhere, Looking Backward*, and other positive views of the future, *Island* can be defended as a reasonably complex novel in which a would-be utopian's attempt at optimism is challenged by the possibility that his characters inhabit a Manichean universe.... Unlike most utopians, Huxley tries to confront several inescapably negative factors in his perfect society, and these ultimately convince him that utopia is not of this world.... I do not wish to discredit the novel's many positive aspects. However, these have been the exclusive focus of all the discussions of the novel to date, while Huxley's insistence that the novel is really about "the precariousness of happiness, the perilous position of any Utopian island in the context of the modern world" has been consistently ignored. One cannot overlook the presence and power of evil in Huxley's last complete novel, nor can one eliminate the author's suspicion that no temporal society can overcome them forever.

Although *Island* is Huxley's conception of a model society, it also serves as the testing ground for some final questions: is utopia really possible? Will the rest of the world tolerate an ideal society, or is the nature of man and the universe too contaminated to leave such perfection alone?

Two misleading assertions generally accompany any discussion of Huxley's utopia. One is that *Island* is not a novel at all but an extended essay for which Huxley devised only the thinnest of plots. More so than in any other Huxley novel, the plot in *Island* is supposedly the simple vehicle for the novelist's thoughts. The other insits that *Island* is both synthesis and palinode. As synthesis it allegedly resolves the philosophical dualisms—real versus ideal, religion versus science, body against mind—that pervade Huxley's previous fiction. By dissolving the opposing elements heretofore at the heart of the ironist's vision, the novel deprives the ironist of his irony. Huxley's triumph as thinker and synthesizer, this argument implies, thus meant defeat for Huxley the creative artist. *Island* achieves philosophical significance at the cost of aesthetic value. As palinode the novel reportedly abandons Huxley's customary scepticism in favor of optimistic prophecy, thus making utopian speculation feasible once more.

Read more imaginatively, *Island* emerges as a moderately sophisticated exercise in counterpoint, less successful than the technical experiments in *Point Counter Point* and *Eyeless in Gaza* but never as dull or as 'talky' as some have claimed.... The growth of the reader's comprehension and the acceleration toward [Pala's] dissolution become the novel's contrapuntal melodies. Worst of all, the prevalence of cancer in Huxley's utopia precludes optimism. Literal instances of this disease contribute to Huxley's metaphoric sense of a cancerous temporal world and of Pala as an ideal society insufficiently antiseptic. The history of Pala begins and ends with an emphasis on cancer.... Far from being a dull moral tract or a one-sided hymn to the future, *Island* is a relatively suspenseful novel that grants the possibility of individual salvation while growing increasingly sceptical about the world's desire for a perfect society. (pp. 619-21)

The need to make the novel do more than tell a story—a need he often discussed much too apologetically—set Huxley off from the so-called congenital novelist who seldom raised the fundamental questions about man's Final End and the purpose of life. *Island* is not merely a series of fascinating ideas held together by the minimum of plot. Huxley devised a story that would accentuate the novel's moral implications.... By learning to admire Pala while contributing to its destruction, Will reveals himself as a true Manichean. The Manichean and the contrapuntalist both share a frame of mind that sees life in terms of opposites. To some extent the Huxley who builds a perfect society only to disband it comes dangerously close to a Manichean world view in which there is a negative reaction to every positive force. (pp. 621-22)

Before Pala, Will's attitudes are similar to the early Huxley's. During his sojourn on the island, he begins to resemble the Huxley of the later novels and essays.... [By] helping to ruin Pala, he provides one of the novel's major ironies: he is spiritually cured, yet partly due to him Pala succumbs.... Farnaby becomes a sort of perverse Everyman who unwittingly illustrates what Huxley considers a depressingly cyclical historical process: man is able to recognize and love the good only after he has helped to destroy it. The two overlapping plots—Will as a student in utopia and Will as a conspirator—emphasize the Manichean nature of man, his ability to know the best and choose the worst.

Most utopias bog down under the weight of "the necessary exposition", the extensive Baedeker the author must supply so that the reader comprehends the *modus vivendi* of the ideal society. Utopias almost invariably become essays about the future.... *Island* never quite bogs down in this way.... Huxley manages to include his ideas about the educational methods a perfect society might employ and the ideal family structure. He comments on the societal use of drugs, such as the *moksha* medicine (the truth-and-beauty pill), which opens the minds of the young to life's higher mysteries. But exposition in *Island,* extensive though it is, is more dramatic than the essay-like lectures in previous utopias because Huxley's exposition is Will's therapy. Pala tries to cure Will of the infection he represents, an infection compounded of cynicism and Western materialism. The lectures in the novel are tied to Will's lengthy convalescence, on which the safety of Pala also depends.... [The] Palanese must genuinely heal Farnaby if their society is to convince the reader of its merit. (pp. 622-23)

[*Island*] is as dualistic as Huxley's earlier fiction, for Will is exposed to the conflicting demands of East and West, Pala and Joe Aldehyde, heaven and hell. Although the Palanese are mentally and physically sound, living proof of the hypothetical validity of Huxley's formula for utopia, Will must choose between cynicism and belief, sickness and health.

Throughout the novel Huxley assembles what he considers the components for a model society. He fashions into a synthetic whole his favorite ideas from his own reading and writing of the past twenty-five years. *Ends and Means, The Olive Tree,* and *The Perennial Philosophy,* to name only three, contained suggestions for many of the positive elements found in *Island*. Oriental mysticism, Sheldonian classifications of individuals by temperament and physique, genuinely progressive education, decentralization of government, and *coitus reservatus* as a means of birth control —these and many other ideas become parts of the master plan for the perfect society. Throughout it all, Huxley remains a curious utopian who undermines as he builds. In addition to such grotesques as the Rani and Colonel Dipa, who are as reprehensible as any character from Huxley's earlier, more cynical fiction, there is the presence of cancer, a negative element no amount of social planning or mystical enlightenment can eradicate. That this disease survives in utopia raises the possibility that contamination may be inherent in the nature of temporal things. If so, utopian perfection is an illusion.... (pp. 624-25)

The power of cancer in Huxley's final novel is unmistakable.... Huxley himself was suffering from cancer as he wrote. In addition to functioning as an actual disease in *Island,* cancer also becomes Huxley's metaphor for an ineradicable sickness in temporal man and his world, a sickness too essential an element of life for any society, no matter how perfect, to withstand indefinitely. Despite his utopian synthesis of ideas developed over a quarter of a century, Huxley cannot overcome his sense of life as a dualistic process in which there is a counter for every point. The best somehow contains the seeds of its own demise: Pala is contaminated by the oil beneath its surface. This substance brings out all the non-utopian elements in human nature. (p. 625)

Throughout the novel Dr. MacPhail's wife is dying of cancer, "slowly wasting to extinction". Symbolically, Lakshmi is at the center of the novel. Huxley parallels her deterioration and the island's. Pala is both a utopia and the story of the vulnerability of any ideal. The novel exposes the fragility, perhaps even the futility, of utopia at the same time that it describes the society its author would establish were such an endeavor possible within the temporal order. (p. 626)

Will asks the child, Mary Sarojini, if she knows "what cancer is?" She replies that "it's what happens when part of you forgets all about the rest of you and carries on the way people do when they're crazy—just goes on blowing itself up and blowing itself up as if there was nothing else in the whole world." Cancer thus reveals itself as a malicious variant of Huxley's perennial target: the self-centered ego, the preoccupation with the temporal, physical self that permits the individual person—or a single cell in a larger body—to conduct itself as if the part were the whole. Mary's definition of cancer makes this disease the perfect metaphor for any nation practising self-aggrandisement. Rendang, as it puffs itself up to swallow Pala, represents the cancerous spread of war and annexation characteristic of world history. (p. 627)

In depicting heaven, *Island* never forgets hell.... [Will] broadens his conception of perfection to include the presence of negative factors. Unfortunately, no society seems capable of reconciling yes and no. Huxley's conviction that evil is ubiquitous does not condemn the individual to a Manichean existence, but it rules out any chance for utopia in this world. In transcending his Manichean outlook by learning to accept both halves of himself, Will no longer allows his unattractive aspects to undermine belief in his capacity for good. But a society's unattractive elements can, and in *Island* do, undermine its ability to function. *Island* therefore offers salvation primarily on the personal level. Surely this is a curious conclusion for a utopia. The individual need not function as a Manichee but the world appears to remain irreparably split. (p. 629)

Perfection for Huxley involves making beauty one with horror, a perception of life's inescapable unity, in which, for the individual, the horrible cannot eclipse the beautiful. The latter is the stronger because it can accept the former. Such a perception, however, cannot carry over into the social and political sphere.... Politically speaking, horror consumes beauty. In the temporal order, no fusion of them seems possible outside the consciousness of the enlightened individual. (p. 630)

Island is Huxley's most successful synthesis. It is also a contrapuntal novel. While Will learns to reconcile the good and evil within himself and in the surrounding world, the novel is pulled in the opposite direction by Pala's failure to survive, by Huxley's unwillingness to falsify what he considered the basic fact in the temporal, historical process: the succumbing of the ideal to the real, the noble to the ignoble, Pala to Rendang. Will transcends the historical process; Pala can do so only temporarily. The novel's two plots capture this essential dichotomy as the exposition plot leads to personal salvation and the action plot terminates with societal collapse. That Will contributes to the collapse while on his way to enlightenment further emphasizes the Manicheanism that constantly challenges and finally modifies the novel's utopian mood. (pp. 631-32)

No matter what the ultimate force in the universe may be, no matter what one contends is man's Final End, the temporal order remains bound by the second law of thermodynamics, of which cancer, whether in the individual body or the body politic, is a graphic illustration. Ironically, Huxley has finally found the ideal recipe but he is still sceptical about the world's ability to take 'yes' for an answer. *Island* shows what a perfect society could be like under impossibly ideal circumstances. The novel also demonstrates why utopia must always mean "nowhere". (pp. 632-33)

Jerome Meckier, "Cancer in Utopia: Positive and Negative Elements in Huxley's 'Island'," in The Dalhousie Review, *Winter, 1974-75, pp. 619-33.*

CHARLOTTE LEGATES

[The] paintings of Pieter Brueghel the Elder had a profound influence on the writing of Aldous Huxley. Huxley seems to have been attracted to Brueghel's attitude toward life. Both artists saw individuals as isolated, yet forming a pattern of existence. Both saw a juxtaposition of tragedy and comedy as the nature of both life and art. Both were fascinated recorders of social customs and events. Both celebrated life above art, seeing art as a tool to record reality rather than an ideal to shape reality. And because of their similar attitudes, Huxley used a number of Brueghel's painting techniques in prose.

The key to understanding the Huxley-Brueghel relationship lies in Huxley's 1925 essay on the artist, which appeared in *Along the Road....*

[Here] Huxley analyzes a number of Brueghel's paintings on the bases of both formal construction and literary meaning. (p. 365)

But the real importance of Brueghel to Huxley does not lie in the relative originality or merit of Huxley's comments on the painter. A more interesting question to the literary critic is the relationship between works of art in two media which are joined by a common attitude toward life. In this case, both artists have used the same basic methods of situational presentation; and Huxley seems to have gained technical insight and reinforcement from his examination of Brueghel's works.

Huxley was strongly attracted to Brueghel's method of artistic construction.... For Huxley, the inclusion in the works of art of vast numbers of figures which are, individually, dissociated, but which together make up a vast and striking pattern was an exact imitation of life itself.

This sort of visual arrangement expressing realism is essentially the same arrangement Huxley used in the novels of the twenties. *Point Counter Point* is probably Huxley's best example of the revelation of the lives of dissociated groups and individuals which, when juxtaposed, form an overall pattern with implications which go far beyond the novel itself. Spandrell, Quarles, and Rampion in isolation—as they essentially are within the bounds of the novel—seem individuals whose ideas are taking them nowhere and whose lives have meaning only to themselves. But taken together, the characters form a complex view of the battling forces of life which will go on eternally. (pp. 366-67)

A second reason for Huxley's admiration of Brueghel is the artist's multiple vision of life. On the one hand, as Huxley observes, "Breughel's anthropology is as delightful as his nature poetry. He knew his Flemings and knew them intimately." . . . On the other hand, Brueghel was "a man profoundly convinced of the reality of evil and of the horrors which this mortal life, not to mention eternity, hold in store for suffering humanity. The world is a horrible place; but in spite of this, or precisely because of this, men and women eat, drink and dance." . . . (p. 367)

Huxley's multiple vision of life is most evident in his earliest novels, such as *Antic Hay*. Like Brueghel, Huxley shows his characters at moments of orgiastic gaiety. . . . But again, like Brueghel, Huxley was convinced of the horror and evil of the world. The trauma of World War I hangs over *Antic Hay* like smoke. Characters like Gumbril, generally sympathetic, are capable of senseless cruelty. . . . (pp. 367-68)

Both Huxley and Brueghel create characters who hide from the tragic side of life in the comic. The London of *Antic Hay* is hell, as Coleman suggests; but to hide from the facts of outer social and inner personal crumbling, the main characters in the novel must indulge in hilarious, witty, and loud drinking parties, culminating in rides such as the final wild one through London which closes the novel. . . . Both Huxley and Brueghel were well aware of the dark side of life, but both felt the need to respond to it in a partially comic way rather than to accept a black, existential despair as their philosophy of life.

Huxley was particularly struck by Brueghel's multiple point of view in the religious paintings. . . . Again, Huxley adopted this method as his own. He rarely used the single point of view or the transforming consciousness in his novels, but instead looked at events from several different points of view, thus preventing any sense of tragedy. When little Phil dies from meningitis in *Point Counter Point*, we do not see the event from the single point of view of his mother, who certainly has a tragic sense of the event. Instead we see it also from his father's point of view, a father who cannot get wholly involved in the event, as he has been unable to get really involved in anything else that has happened in his life. (p. 368)

By seeing events from the points of view of both the chief participants and the casual observer, both Brueghel and Huxley create a sardonic atmosphere around pivotal events in their works. . . . In the all-over flux of life, is one point of view really more important than the other simply because we want it to be? Both Huxley and Brueghel answer no. (p. 369)

Many of Huxley's short stories hinge on a particular social or historical event. . . . It is through careful use of contemporary detail that Huxley is able to create for the reader the

feeling for time and place for which his fiction is noted. In the same way, there can be no doubt of the location and time of Brueghel's pictures, for they are such close recordings of his time and place.

A final point on which Brueghel and Huxley are quite similar is their view of the relative positions of life and art. . . . Unlike many artists of his time, Brueghel did not pursue classic beauty, nor was he interested in perfecting techniques of other artists. Instead, his primary interest lay in recording life around him, both openly, in his straightforward views of peasant life, and covertly, as in the political protest of his religious paintings. One art critic describes Brueghel as "interested in the study and description of all aspects of life. . . . He is barely interested in showing man as he ought to be; on the contrary, he represents him as he really is, with a kind of humourous violence, with his defects, his passions and his prejudices, leaving to the spectator the task of drawing a moral from what he paints."

By changing "paints" to "writes," the same passage could apply equally well to the Huxley of the 1920's, whose characters too are full of flaws and foibles, and whose satire is presented without a contrasting "golden mean." Huxley wanted to record life exactly as it was lived, without a shaping sense of beauty or purpose. Consequently novels such as *Crome Yellow* and *Antic Hay* are often accused of shapelessness and diffusion. That is exactly the effect Huxley wanted, for it is the shapelessness and diffusion of life which he is attempting to recreate. . . . Huxley stands in contrast to other British novelists at the beginning of the twentieth century who were far more concerned with art than with an exact recording of life. . . . Huxley, like Brueghel, is more interested in making a record of life as it is going on around him, without losing control and therefore the reader's interest, but at the same time without forcing the experience toward a unified, "artistic" conclusion.

Huxley's view that life should dominate art did not change during his lifetime, although he did change from a recorder of life to a teacher. *Island*'s purpose is to teach us a valuable lesson about life's possibilities; its primary purpose is not to entertain or astound us with its art. Brueghel also at times seems to attempt to teach a lesson about life, especially in his illustrations of various proverbs. Again, for both artists, life is the dominating force, art simply its tool, although it is a tool used remarkably skilfully by both. (pp. 369-71)

Charlotte Legates, "Huxley and Brueghel," in Western Humanities Review (copyright, 1975, University of Utah), Autumn, 1975, pp. 365-71.

I

IONESCO, Eugène 1912-

Ionesco is a French dramatist and major exponent of the theater of the absurd. He creates a darkly comic portrait of the human condition, exposing man's tragic alienation, his obsession with violence and power, and the impossibility of true communication. In this world, the grotesque is exaggerated, the ordinary made surreal. To Ionesco, "theater is the projection on the stage of the world within." Though personal and dreamlike, this vision assumes universal proportions. An experimentalist, he has also written short stories, a novel, and a screenplay. (See also *CLC*, Vols. 1, 4, 6, 9, and *Contemporary Authors*, Vols. 9-12, rev. ed.)

HORST S. DAEMMRICH

In the play *Rhinocéros* (1959) Eugène Ionesco creates a dynamic pattern by juxtaposing the archetypal motif with its infernal inversion. The audience, while watching society's spiritual decline and hopeless loss of identity, witnesses the rebirth of a slovenly drunk, unable to cope with life, who becomes a staunch, defiant defender of humanity. The first act opens with a picture of society in which everyone follows his narrow interests. And though people (an alcoholic, a grocer, a café owner, a logician, a housewife) live side by side, they fail to establish a truly human relationship—in the sense of Schiller, Buber, Camus, or Heidegger—because they lack the courage for existential encounter with each other. When their mode of life is threatened by the sudden appearance of a rhinoceros they are momentarily united by a common feeling of loathing and terror.

But as soon as they relate the strange phenomenon to their experience, each individual's perception, reflecting his isolation, becomes a divisive factor.... [As] the beasts increase in number and form a herd, united by savage instinct, the people begin to respond to the essence of "rhinoceritis." And while some still argue the necessity of a policy toward the phenomenon, others have begun to embrace the menace. The atavistic relapse into a primitive, instinctive, and pre-human condition holds the promise of salvation for all who are unwilling to develop their spiritual potential and commit themselves to a life which requires respect and love for others. As the action progresses and the metamorphoses spread, the audience becomes painfully aware of the complete renunciation of human values.... (p. 94)

While Bérenger, the lone alcoholic, sees person after person . . . transformed and absorbed in the indistinguishable herd, he experiences a true spiritual rebirth. Initially unable to face life, he scarcely notices the appearance of the first rhinoceros. But as society changes around him, he becomes deeply concerned for others, offers help and compassion, and finally defends humanity: "Come on, think, you'll realize that we have a philosophy that these animals don't have, an irreplaceable system of values. Centuries of human civilization have built it." . . . [He] begins to contemplate the riddle of human existence and . . . becomes fully conscious of the challenge confronting man: "I am the last man. I will remain so to the end! I will not capitulate!" To interpret these last lines of the play as optimistic would express a humanistic view but do injustice to the nature of the archetypal motif. Bérenger, though he understands the essence of the existential commitment, cannot turn toward others and live in the world, because he is left alone. He transcends himself, represents the view of an ennobled man, but stands in total, tragic isolation. (pp. 94-5)

Horst S. Daemmrich, in MOSAIC: A Journal for the Study of Literature and Ideas *(copyright © 1972 by the University of Manitoba Press; acknowledgment of previous publication is herewith made), Vol. 5, No. 3 (Spring, 1972).*

DOROTHY KNOWLES

When speaking of his dramatic writings, Ionesco has always insisted on their obsessional nature and . . . before the first performance of *Rhinocéros* in Paris, he described as his starting-point a particularly haunting obsession, the mutation of people into dangerous monsters once they have succumbed to some new fanaticism or ideology. Had not the preceding 25 years proved that they not only looked like rhinoceroses, but had really been turned into these ferocious beasts? That was as far as Ionesco was prepared to go at that moment in explaining his play. In February 1961, in a private conversation, that is to say after he had read the various interpretations offered of his play, Ionesco said that *Rhinocéros* was not a play against Nazism but against any fanaticism which makes of men killer-animals, and in *his* personal experience this fanaticism was Nazism. Throughout the play Ionesco insists on the thickening and greening skin of those undergoing the metamorphosis. For the French, during the last war, green was the symbol of the German soldier and thus of the Nazi brute. (p. 296)

Strangely enough, to turn a 'herd' into a 'society' used to be the preoccupation of political philosophers, whereas Ionesco now seemed to be suggesting that the 'herd' is already *over*-socialized. It was not socialization that made the Nazis so terrible, but their dehumanization. By replacing 'nazification' by 'massification' Ionesco was either underlining a subsidiary theme, or else he was deliberately side-stepping the main issue. There is a further subsidiary theme which accounts for the universal success of [*Rhinocéros*], that is to say the theme of depersonalization. Ionesco has claimed that by treating this theme he had put his finger more or less subconsciously on a burning problem of the day, common to all countries whether in the East or in the West. It is, of course, one of his favourite themes, witness *La Cantatrice chauve* and *Jacques ou la soumission,* in which people are presented as empty shells. (pp. 303-04)

Time and time again in his writings since 1961, [Ionesco] has returned to his obsessive idea that every new system of expression, once generally adopted, becomes another convention, another ideology and thereby loses its essential truth, that every revolution when successful becomes in its turn just another established régime—Ionesco conveniently passes over the matter of the character of the revolution or régime. Such an attitude is clearly apolitical. . . . Yet the fact remains that with *Tueur sans gages,* his first Bérenger play, and *Rhinocéros,* Ionesco, yielding apparently to the Brechtian vogue, had ventured outside the four walls in which the actions of the personal dramas of his earlier plays had been confined, into the political and social arena. His withdrawal therefrom was, however, immediate, and is made clear by Bérenger's final speech which gives no lead as to how to combat the rhinoceritic disease, but is turned instead inward on the self. . . . Indeed any form of commitment in art is anathema to him, as he believes that no political system can 'free man from the pain of living'. Shall we, on the other hand, look for an aesthetic explanation of this opposition? Political commitment in writing is incompatible with his particular notion of art, which he sees as the transcription of a sudden and intuitive experience, a direct vision of the world divorced from conceptual thought. (p. 305)

Ionesco's dramatic work as a whole is expressive of his defence against the world, against the invasion of his personality by the common language and ordinary customs. Ionesco is always 'Jacques' striving desperately to avoid *soumission.* Ionesco-Bérenger is incapable of uniting with others in active resistance; only a passive, isolated resistance is implied in *Rhinocéros.* It is here that the real ambiguity of the inspiration—rather than the 'meaning'—of *Rhinocéros* is to be found. It may be argued that a play has no 'meaning' outside itself, even a play of ideas, but it has an intention and a direction. On the one hand the play expresses a precise political experience; on the other it expresses a timid man's retreat into himself and final stand against a frightening outside world, referred to by Ionesco's own expression 'naturellement allergique à la contagion'. . . . Neither the personal nor the political experience produced a positive response in the dramatist, whose work depends for its artistic unity, which is very real, on a negation. (p. 306)

> *Dorothy Knowles, "Eugène Ionesco's Rhinoceroses: Their Romanian Origins and Western For-*

tunes," in French Studies, *July, 1974, pp. 294-307.*

EDMUND WHITE

Ionesco has always been such a master of the banal that he has run the risk of seeming either trivial or merely satirical. In his early absurdist plays "The Bald Soprano," "The Lesson" or "The Chairs," he pushed the polite conventionalities of middle-class life to the point of madness—mad refusals to deal with failure, danger, old age, suffering or anything else that good manners are compelled to ignore. The object of his contempt appeared to be the smug bourgeoisie, and since ridiculing the bourgeoisie is a venerable national sport, as insipid and familiar a French pastime as one could hope to find, after a while Ionesco came off as a bit of a bore himself.

In recent years, however, he has revealed himself to be far more complex and anguished, and his first novel, "The Hermit" . . . forces us to revise our old impression of Ionesco's work altogether. Quite simply, Ionesco is afraid to die. His fear is not a fashionable intellectual posture, but rather an abiding visceral pain, an agony that he dramatized brilliantly in his play, "Exit the King," that he described with childlike sincerity in "Fragments of a Journal," and that now he has elaborated with great skill in his novel. . . .

Ionesco has not been lampooning middle-class pieties; rather, he has been watching with horrified fascination a cocktail party in a tumbrel inching toward the scaffold. How can they laugh like that? How can they talk, flirt? How can they do anything but shiver in solitude?

The hero of "The Hermit" does withdraw and shiver. . . .

Am I being gullible in assuming that the hermit speaks for Ionesco? Perhaps Ionesco has invented a foolish little man who, like Bouvard or Pécuchet, receives an inheritance and sets out to solve the world's problems—not the problems of horticulture or metallurgy that Flaubert's buffoons essayed, but rather modern philosophical problems (alienation, the nature of the infinite, existential dread, determinism and so on). Perhaps the entire book is a witty spoof and I've been taken in.

I think not. That the hermit is a clerk, neither young nor old, handsome nor ugly, intelligent nor stupid, simply makes him representative. He is as pathetic and as solemn, as pedantic and as touching as Gogol's clerks, as we all are. And he is as suspicious of patriotism, ideology, ambition as Ionesco himself. Indeed, the hermit's voice is indistinguishable from Ionesco's own in his autobiographical "Scattered Images of Childhood.". . . (p. 6)

> *Edmund White, in* The New York Times Book Review (© *1974 by The New York Times Company; reprinted by permission), October 27, 1974.*

CHARLES I. GLICKSBERG

Like Beckett, [Ionesco] does not take literature seriously, though he keeps on writing plays. He acknowledges his indebtedness to Kafka, who shared his obsessions. His plays, like the fiction of Kafka, are not intended to convey a message, a rationally defined meaning. He composed *The Bald Soprano* in order "to prove that nothing had any real importance." . . . He finds existence "sometimes unbearable, painful, heavy and stultifying, and sometimes it seems to be the manifestation of God himself, all light." . . .

It must take a great deal of courage for a dramatist of the absurd to write at all. He must fight his own battle of the mind against the enervating feeling of futility. He is caught in the meshes of the destructive logic that supports his aesthetic of the absurd. If life, insofar as he can make out, is without meaning or purpose, then why take the trouble to repeat the lugubrious theme that life is without meaning or purpose? If, however, he is not bothered by the need to justify his creative venture, he is brought up short by the difficulty of embodying his vision of a reality that cannot be framed in words. How, as he practices the art of the absurd, can he name the unnameable? How give flesh and form to the ineffable experience of nada? (p. 223)

In order to capture the elusive features of the Absurd, Ionesco focuses on the elements of the comic, the grotesque, and the contingent in the life of man. Death for Ionesco represents the upsurge of the uncanny, the threat of nothingness, the quintessence of the Absurd. He protests against the fate of death, though he realizes that his protest is but an ineffectual gesture, an empty outburst of rhetoric. The finality of death reveals the distinctive character of the Absurd. The tragic and the comic interpenetrate. The drama of the Absurd is born of the dismaying insight that modern man, despite all his technological conquests, cannot escape his mortal lot. . . . The absurdist hero struggles fiercely against annihilation, but in the end, as in Ionesco's *The Killer,* he is overcome.

The type of drama called forth by this numinous encounter with the Absurd eliminates the possibility of tragic affirmation in the manner of the ancient Greeks. The absurd is simply there, a *tremendum mysterium* that is neither to be worshiped as divine nor assailed as diabolical; it is a haunting consciousness of the nothingness that waits for man. The tragedy of the absurd, like the nihilistic tragedy, seems to be a contradiction in terms. There is nothing the dramatist of the Absurd can affirm. Born of paradox and culminating in paradox, his plays abandon all illusion, though he is aware that these illusions constitute the essential humanity of man, his never-ceasing search for transcendence. The intimations of the Absurd emerge from this conflict between these all-too-human illusions and the adamantine indifference of the universe. The absurdist hero is defeated and dragged under, but he never pretends that the outcome will be other than it turns out to be. A dauntless truthseeker, he prefers, like Bérenger, the protagonist of *The Killer,* to know the worst that will befall him rather than to remain deluded. He is able to endure the wounds that existence can inflict upon him and laugh at his mortal predicament. (pp. 224-25)

The humor Ionesco employs is at bottom a method for ordering the inchoate mass of material that the world places at the disposal of his imagination. (p. 225)

[Ionesco] is the visionary poet who can never get used to the strangeness of existence. He can make no sense of this phantasmagoric universe, these phantom presences that represent people, these moving lights and shadows and the all-enveloping curtain of darkness. He looks on the world as a rare spectacle, an incomprehensible and yet amusing show and he reacts to it with a sense of wonder, but it also induces anxiety and dread. He is caught in a series of irreconcilable contradictions. "Nothing is atrocious, everything is atrocious. Nothing is comic. Everything is tragic. Nothing is tragic, everything is comic, everything is real,

unreal, possible, impossible, conceivable, inconceivable." His work, despite its exploitation of the comic vein, gives expression to an obsessive pessimism. Death is the epitome of the Absurd. . . . Death overtakes all men, regardless of their merit, and if that is so, then what is the purpose of living? Ionesco remarks: "We are made to be immortal, and yet we die. It's horrible, it can't be taken seriously." He cannot forget himself because he cannot forget that he must die, those he loves will die, and the world will ultimately come to an end.

Death is the supreme humiliation man is made to suffer, the outrage he is powerless to prevent. Death is meted out to all; and it is this knowledge that leads Ionesco to stress the vanity of life. All his reading, all the works of art he has studied, emphasize the implacable truth he perceived early in life: the inevitability of death. Why should he concern himself with the social, economic, and political problems of the hour when he knows that we are slated to die and that no revolution can save us from death. (p. 227)

Though Ionesco's obsession is fixed on death, it is not, like the work of Edward Young and Thomas L. Beddoes, morbid in content. It voices a universal theme. It is a source of anguish, and it is this metaphysical anguish, which never lets up, that incites him to creativity. By writing he keeps the issue of mortality alive even though this intensifies the anguish he feels, anguish born of the "fear of nothingness." . . . It is this accursed knowledge that we are doomed to die that turns us into killers. Death is the tormenting question mark for which we can find no answer. Though this perpetual "Why" that we ask gets us nowhere in the end, we continue to interrogate the world of being. Why for millennia should the sons of Adam resign themselves to the intolerable imposition of death? If they begin to love life, they are soon overcome by the certainty that it will shortly be taken away from them. "This is the incredible thing: to love a life that has been thrust upon me and that is snatched away from me just when I have accepted it." . . . He is afraid that in dwelling repeatedly on this archetypal theme he may yield to the vice of self-pity or indulge in sentimentality. He writes: "I have been, I still am tormented at once by the dread of death, the horror of the void, and by an eager, impatient desire to live. Why does one long to live, what does living mean?" . . . He does not know the answer. It is the thought of death that makes living an impossible burden to bear. Like Camus, Ionesco rejects suicide as "unforgivable failure; and we must not fail." . . .

Ionesco comes to grips with the theme of death in *The Killer* and, later, in *Exit the King.* (p. 228)

Offhand no theme seems less promising than the one Ionesco has chosen to deal with in [*Exit the King.*] What dramatically fruitful results can be derived from the thanatopsian motif? The agonizing struggle to cling to life of a king who is dying and knows he is dying—what, after all, can the most gifted and original playwright do with such refractory material? The words of the Preacher in *Ecclesiastes,* the poignant cry of *memento mori,* the Dance of Death, the sermons and sonnets of John Donne, the lucubrations of the Graveyard School of poets—the potentialities of such an essentially static and sterile theme have already been exhausted. Nothing new can be added; no genuine conflict can possibly arise. The battle the condemned person wages is cruelly unjust. As in Andreyev's play *The Life of Man,* Death is always the winner. There is never a moment of doubt as to the final outcome. However desperate his resistance, the chosen victim must give in. It is only a matter of time. Here is the grim drama each man acts out at the end of his life: a drama that lacks the element of suspense. The plot must, of necessity, follow a preestablished pattern. Why did Ionesco revert to this theme that he had already sounded in *The Killer*?

Because it sums up the distinctive aesthetic of the Absurd. Because ... death is Ionesco's constant obsession, the primary source of his inspiration. In *Exit the King* he is writing a twentieth-century version of *Everyman*, in which the theological and moral gloss is left out. There is no God to pass judgment on life or to intercede for the dying man. Heaven and hell no longer exist. After death, there is—nothing.

Ionesco invests the theme with universal overtones. Each man is the virtual ruler of a kingdom, his body, which he is forced to surrender after a comparatively brief reign. The outlying provinces renounce their allegiance; the parts of the internal kingdom refuse to obey their sovereign. Or they break down, one by one, and are no longer capable of responding to his commands. He ceases to be in control of his subjects; he lacks the strength to support his crown and scepter. (pp. 229-30)

> *Charles I. Glicksberg, "Ionesco and the Comedy of the Absurd," in his* The Literature of Nihilism *(© 1975 by Associated University Presses, Inc.), Bucknell University Press, 1975, pp. 222-33.*

JUDITH D. SUTHER

The generic difference between [*Le Solitaire,* a novel, and *Ce Formidable Bordel!,* a play,] is actually slight, beyond obvious and superficial differences in form. Whether or not the generic question be judged a fruitful subject for debate again matters little. The novel is full of "dramatic" techniques and over half the play is built on "non-dramatic" chunks of prose appropriate to a novel.... What I find compelling about this symbiotic pair, however, is not the havoc they play with generic labels, but the images they project of our struggle with the demons of existence. The demons have not changed appreciably since the plays of the '50s, indeed since long before that. What *has* changed in *Le Solitaire* and *Ce Formidable Bordel!* is the intensity, I would even say the authenticity, of the struggle. Le Solitaire and Le Personnage, Ionesco's unnamed protagonists, try very hard to understand what is happening to them as the hated but protective routine of daily life dissolves into an amorphous *disponibilité,* time passes, revolutions come and go, and still the awaited event, the ordering agent, does not make itself known. (p. 689)

With some minor divergences and a major one at the end, [the two works] follow the same narrative line, include most of the same characters portrayed similarly, and even share numerous phrases, snatches of dialogue, and techniques of sceneic development. Without presenting my remarks as an "argument" or a "case," I will simply record some reasons why *Le Solitaire* and *Ce Formidable Bordel!* speak to me of a solid, increasingly convincing artistry in Ionesco.

These reasons derive in one way or another from the obsessional presence of death in the novel and the play. Death, or the awareness of death, is not the only interest in either work, but it is the driving force behind their structure, im-

agery patterns, and minimal plot line. In this sense, Ionesco is offering a kind of extension of *Le Roi se meurt* (1962).... Others among Ionesco's more recent plays show this preoccupation with death: *Le Piéton de l'air* (1963), in which Bérenger, believing in nothing, flies off into space, leaving his daughter behind to recite a litany of dim hope whose key word is "peut-être"; *La Soif et la faim* (1966), whose setting is progressively swallowed up in mud, the viscous mire of existence and the sign of encroaching death; *Jeux de massacre* (1970), whose epidemic and famine are presided over by a funereal black monk; *Macbett* (1972), with its perverse victor Macol who will create a kingdom where evil reigns and death will overtake the inhabitants before their natural term. It is obvious from these plays that Ionesco has tried over a period of years to come to grips with the demon of death. Though it does not dominate the plays of the '50s so insistently as it does those just mentioned, the fact of death is never absent from Ionesco's theatre.... (pp. 690-91)

In *Le Solitaire* and *Ce Formidable Bordel!* death is not personified; it does not nakedly stalk the streets, nor is it embodied in any one character or event or object (as it was, for example, in [earlier plays] ...). The awareness of eventual death is the impetus for the very movements of Le Solitaire and Le Personnage. I say "movements" rather than action, since these nameless protagonists, operating in a mode now conventional to post-modern art, displace themselves in space without incurring any of the involvements or repercussions that an act would entail. The sharp and aching knowledge of their own imminent non-being provides a trunk onto which Ionesco grafts the bizarre plants of his imagination, those intertwining growths that reach out through twenty-five years of his plays. These projections, [consistent components of Ionesco's work,] which converge in *Le Solitaire* and *Ce Formidable Bordel!* are (1) the repetitious banality of everyday conversations; (2) the proliferation of objects and the related motif of the sameness of people; (3) the passage of time; and (4) the fact of solitude. Underlying them and eventually crowding them out is the spector, occasionally the vision, of death. (p. 691)

However empty [the parrot-like] utterances may be, they help develop the dominant theme of death in both works. They underscore the desperate search of Le Solitaire and Le Personnage for that elusive something, that message from the unknown which will somehow infuse meaning into life before the life itself is swallowed up into the ontological void. (The phrase "vide ontologique" is Ionesco's own, which he uses to describe the sense of non-being that permeates the consciousness of his heroes who are surrounded by objects and propelled by time, but who are unable to establish their own place in either space or time ...). (p. 693)

That the banality of these conversations and monologues is intimately tied to the theme of death can be seen clearly in the old woman who sells Le Personnage his new apartment.... [A short, typically Ionescan series of nonsense statements] sets the old woman off on a revery. It is a beautiful revery, telling of the death of the woman's husband and her own awakening to the reality of death.... The wonder of this passage is that it avoids the trap of bathos and balances finely between the ordinary details of this ordinary woman's life, and the sudden lyricism of her confession. Though probably not on a conscious level, the conceit of the oxymoron is at work here apparent opposites, every-day trivia and a personal intimacy with death, become so interrelated as to suggest a new reality of their own. This fusion is effected throughout *Le Solitaire* and *Ce Formidable Bordel!* The terror of death's nearness is increased by the vacuity of life, by the very fact that no advances are ever made toward an understanding of life itself, which soon will end. (p. 694)

The last scene of *Ce Formidable Bordel!* presents a neat complement to the overstuffing at the end of *Le Solitaire.* Whereas Le Solitaire is caged by objects, Le Personnage finds himself surrounded by nothing. . . . His furniture quietly disappears until he is alone in his armchair on a deserted stage. This reversal of the proliferation process was used to great effect in *Le Roi se meurt.* . . . In *Ce Formidable Bordel!*, it functions like the overstuffing in *Le Solitaire:* in one case, the protagonist is figuratively hemmed in; in the other, he is literally so. The effect is the same. The obsession is also the same, this fertile mania for eschatological images which pervades *Le Solitaire* and *Ce Formidable Bordel!*

Le Solitaire and Le Personnage see the people in their lives as scarcely more compelling than the objects. . . . The people are interchangeable, the names are interchangeable, they multiply or disappear like objects. . . . The soldiers who swarm the streets in *Le Solitaire* and *Ce Formidable Bordel!* owe an obvious debt to an earlier herd of pachyderms. These techniques are, of course, nothing new with Ionesco. . . . [Interchangeable] and protean creatures have [always] inhabited Ionesco's plays. (pp. 695-96)

Le Solitaire, in particular, tries beyond human bounds to identify one jot of sense in the chaos around and inside him, before his time is up. His effort perhaps comes across more amply than that of Le Personnage because the protagnoist of the play is generally silent, while the first-person narrator of *Le Solitaire* documents his struggle from its meanest detail to its grandest hallucination. It is the very oversupply of people in the long history of the earth that most puzzles Le Solitaire. . . . Could they all, he wonders, have been as bewildered, as unanchored, as he is? Could they have died without enlightenment? This sense of exile within the timeless continuity of human life underlies the third major theme of *Le Solitarie* and *Ce Formidable Bordel!*—the passage of time.

Although it rather lurks below the surface until the '60s with *Le Roi se meurt,* the passage of time has haunted Ionesco's plays of the last fifteen years. . . . This ancient theme, usually dignified by the name *tempus fugit* when poetry is under discussion, reaches a paroxysm in *Le Solitaire* and *Ce Formidable Bordel!* In the pathological sense, the term paroxysm indicates a crisis or recurrent intensification of a disease; this is precisely what occurs in the novel and the play. In approximately the last third of both . . . , careening time and violence combine to paint a nightmarish picture of death as it overtakes its victims. (p. 696)

The only antidotes to total disorientation in *Le Solitaire* and *Ce Formidable Bordel!* are drink, sleep, and sex (an occasional and unsuccessful antidote). All three of these induce a temporary oblivion which both imitates and delays the final oblivion. . . .

Once Le Solitaire and Le Personnage reach the depth of alienation at which all temporal reality loses its meaning,

the end is in sight. We might expect either of them to stop eating and simply die, or walk outside and be shot by a stray bullet left over from the revolution, or succumb to some random agent of destruction. But they survive, and here the two works diverge; the titles are explained by the final scene. In *Le Solitaire,* a miraculous tree sprouts from the mound of refuse in the inner courtyard (a figure of the protagonist's inner life). . . . The tree is bathed in bright light and accompanied by other trees. A silver ladder leads into the clear blue sky. As this vision comes closer to Le Solitaire, it fades and disappears altogether. But, he says, "Quelque chose de cette lumière qui m'avait pénétré resta." . . . In *Ce Formidable Bordel!* a similar vision—the same tree, the same light, but no ladder—elicits a fit of wild rage from Le Personnage, who laughs maniacally, repeats "quelle bonne blague," and shouts directly at the spectators, "Quel bordel! Oh la la, quel formidable bordel!" . . . (p. 698)

From the novel to the play, either Ionesco had a change of heart or he decided to indulge in paradox once again. Le Solitaire . . . sees a sign of something beyond the present agony; Le Personnage sees more of what he has already seen, which is nothing. . . . [The] quiet watchfulness at the end of *Le Solitaire* is more satisfying than the gigantic joke which closes *Ce Formidable Bordel!* In each case, the passage of time has catapulted the protagonist into the judgment seat; the judgments passed by Le Solitaire and Le Personnage are, on the face of it, worlds apart. Yet they may be heads and tails of the same coin, of the ancient fact that the nature of death is unknowable.

There remains the chief structuring element in the two works, solitude itself, [which is], . . . one of Ionesco's major preoccupations. This claim is verifiable in almost all his plays, indeed in the very principle of metaphysical isolation which he illustrates at such harrowing lengths. A lesser known side of Ionesco's view of solitude, however, is revealed in his diaries, interviews, and occasional writings. It is this side of solitude, the "luminous" side, that informs *Le Solitaire* and *Ce Formidable Bordel!* and helps explain the sudden visitation of light at the end.

Like Le Solitaire and Le Personnage, the varying personas who speak with the mouth of Eugène Ionesco seek solitude. They seek it as a means of combatting the pressures of collectivism, bureaucracy, social necessities, and noise. They seek it also as an asylum where they can study their own terminal illness and prepare themselves to die. . . . Is solitude the complement of non-communication? [No, for Ionesco maintains that solitude is essential, and that modern man suffers from lack of it.] (pp. 698-99)

In *Le Solitaire* and *Ce Formidable Bordel!* are concentrated Ionesco's best efforts to date at sustaining a hero who does know how to be solitary, or at least one who is learning the art. (p. 700)

The divergent endings, and . . . the titles of the novel and the play, probably give us the clearest sign we may expect of whether or not Ionesco has made peace with his demon. The answer, of course, is first yes and then no. . . . *Le Solitaire* and *Ce Formidable Bordel!* come closer than any of his previous works to dealing effectively with the obsessional subject of death; to my taste, the novel comes closest. A gathering of references to conversion of manners and transcendence in these sibling creatures would extend to some length and might suggest a pattern in Ionesco's conception of eschatology. . . .

[In the closing scenes of both works,] the scene is theatrical in the extreme . . . , the reaction of the protagonist is clearly stated, if ambiguous in meaning. This ambiguity, or ambivalence, is true to what we know of Ionesco's [negative] way of seeing the world. (p. 701)

[The] configuration derived from light is a fascination of long standing with Ionesco. It returns to serve as a matrix for *Le Solitaire* and *Ce Formidable Bordel!* Whether its positive or negative aspect prevails in the end will probably remain a moot point. For Le Solitaire, it is the positive, for Le Personnage, the negative. For Ionesco, the constant maintenance of the paradox is becoming a conclusion in itself. The dance with death executed by these lone figures traces, if not a conclusion, then a moving statement on life and death. (p. 702)

> Judith D. Suther, "Ionesco's Symbiotic Pair: 'Le Solitaire' and 'Ce Formidable Bordel!'," in The French Review, (copyright 1976 by the American Association of Teachers of French), April, 1976, pp. 689-702.

Since Eugène Ionesco moved on from his first, more purely Absurdist phase to what might be called the Absurdist Symbolism of *Tueur sans gages* and *Rhinocéros*, he has tended to produce works which follow the same pattern. There is a central character—often called Bérenger—who is in some respects a projection of the playwright himself, and who undergoes a series of public and private experiences, either because they simply happen to him while he himself remains more or less passive (*Le Roi se meurt*), or because he bumps into them as he proceeds on a quest for truth, happiness or the transcendent (*La Soif et la faim*). These plays are Absurdist in that they present a beleaguered consciousness, on the verge of paranoia or even in the grip of paranoiac hysteria, struggling with unreliable and incomprehensible events; and they are symbolist in that they not only make use of overt symbols but also exploit the traditional symbolic polarities of religious sensibility; the light and the dark, the high and the low, the frightening and the reassuring.

The world and Ionesco's temperament being what they are, the conclusion is invariably sombre. In *Rhinocéros*, all the humans are animalized except Bérenger himself; in *Le Roi se meurt*, King Bérenger dies as his kingdom collapses about his ears; in *La Soif et la faim*, Jean Bérenger ends up as the frantic slave of sadistic monks. It is as if these plays were predominantly nightmares, interspersed with brief and inexplicable phases of euphoria, similar to the rare moments of relief that the author himself experiences in his general awareness of the pain of living. . . .

These two latest plays [*L'homme auxvalises* and *Ce formidable bordel!*] run true to form in being examples of ambulatory and stationary paranoia, depending on nightmare effects. In *L'homme aux valises*, the anonymous hero, referred to simply as "le premier homme" and encumbered with two suitcases, is engaged on an unexplained journey, which is a sort of Absurdist pilgrim's progress. Railway stations turn into harbours. Paris does not seem to be where it should be, the members of the hero's family appear and disappear in a bewildering confusion of ages, civil war is apparently raging in various places and, above all, the trav-

eller has to run the gauntlet of different oppressive authorities, such as policemen, doctors and consuls. In the end, "le premier homme" and a large cast of representative characters perform a circular ballet, symbolic no doubt of the meaningless repetitiveness of life's disturbing round.

The hero of *Ce formidable bordel!*, referred to simply as "le personnage", is a recessive, alienated character to whom things happen. He inherits a fortune, and this prompts his fellow office-workers to show various degrees of envy and spite. He has his meals every day in the same restaurant, and is taken over by an enterprising waitress who becomes his mistress. He buys a flat in a block, where various curious characters display their absurdity in lengthy monologues. An incomprehensible war breaks out, as if society beyond the end of the street were always seething with unreliability. The mistress of "le personnage" leaves him, and he experiences a sort of panoramic vision of life, in which generations of concierges and people he has known appear and disappear. In the last scene, breaking the silence that he has maintained throughout, he cries that nothing is comprehensible and laughs uproariously at the thought that life is "une bonne blague", a great joke, or "un formidable bordel", a colossal mess or mix-up. This is the Absurdist laughter which can alternate with tears of anguish as the fundamental response to existence.

It is interesting to see how Ionesco can ring the changes on the Absurdist/Symbolist obsession, but the admirer of his earlier works cannot help feeling that these later plays are perhaps rather fluid and shapeless in their development; they could be shorter or longer without their essential nature being changed. If the raw dream or nightmare is being used as material, perhaps it needs to be processed more rigorously into an aesthetic form for the waking state.

> "Dreams of Absurdity," in The Times Literary Supplement (© Times Newspapers Ltd., 1976; reproduced from The Times Literary Supplement by permission), July 16, 1976, p. 867.

*   *   *

ISHERWOOD, Christopher   1904-

Isherwood is an English-born novelist, playwright, poet, essayist, filmwriter, translator, and editor. Like other members of the "Auden group," he was influenced in the 1920s by the philosophies of Marx and Freud. He is generally considered to be at his best when writing detached social satires, depicting a tragic view of life that is outlined with humor. Describing himself as "a born film fan," he has experimented with cinematic and episodic techniques in his fiction. Much of his work is autobiographically oriented. Isherwood collaborated with Auden on three plays, works of fantasy which combine verse with prose. He has also explored an interest in Hindu mysticism, translating and editing several books of Indian philosophy. (See also CLC, Vols. 1, 9, and Contemporary Authors, Vols. 13-16, rev. ed.)

ANGUS WILSON

"'I'll even forgive myself. As a matter of fact, I just have. Do you know something, Jane,' I said, as I emptied my glass, 'I really do forgive myself, from the bottom of my heart.'" So speaks Stephen, the central character of . . . *The World in the Evening*, and on these words the book ends. Forgiveness of oneself is, of course, a spiritual state highly to be desired; but for those who accept the idea of personal guilt—and Mr. Isherwood belongs firmly to the generation of the guilt-acceptors—the deliberate statement of self-forgiving is an act of high seriousness. The slightest hint of triviality either in the conviction of sin or in the belief in its atonement is liable to produce an inelegant impression upon those who are asked to witness the confession.... It is exactly some such chasm between high intention and inadequate capacity that will, I am afraid, disturb Mr. Isherwood's admirers who have waited so long for this novel, and will, no doubt, delight his critics who have waited equally long to say ''I told you so.''

This failure in central purpose is particularly sad because *The World in the Evening* shows no decline in Mr. Isherwood's powers; indeed, in the understanding of certain human relationships and, above all, in technical control both of range and of organisation, it shows, I think, a very considerable advance. (p. 62)

[Isherwood's] new hero Stephen is the creature of his own imagination, not a convenient cover name for autobiographical reporting. To the extent that his new novel has, I imagine, drawn more deeply upon his invention than his earlier work, this is true. Nevertheless it is impossible not to equate his hero's spiritual odyssey with his own.... A great deal of the novel is highly entertaining, much of it is percipient, some of it very moving, but it is not important at the level to which it aspires.... Nothing in Mr. Isherwood's earlier work suggested that either his intellectual powers or his emotional strength would sustain a novel of the kind that could satisfy Dr. Leavis' criteria. To succeed in the portrayal of a man's progress from an undeveloped state of emotional parasitism to the inner conviction of a total and satisfying meaning in life that allows him to forgive even himself would require, surely, either the tornado of Dostoevsky's emotions sweeping good and evil alike before it, or the enveloping calm of Tolstoy.... Stephen is a peculiarly feeble vehicle for the expression of spiritual truth. There is, of course, nothing unacceptable in presenting the spiritual progress of a feeble personality, even if it be only from minus six to minus four, but the author must be fully aware of the smallness of his compass.

Mr. Isherwood is, I suspect, only a very little conscious of the triviality of Stephen's story. He is afraid on occasion, I think, that he may seem to have lost his sense of proportion.... Whatever happens it must not seem that grace has robbed him of his sense of humour, finding God must at all costs be shown to be tremendous fun. Of course, Mr. Isherwood is too perceptive, too sophisticated not to see how unbecoming this archness is in other godly folk. We are given many examples of the irritating little jokes which the Pennsylvania Quakers employ to humanise their rectitude. Nevertheless, when he is ill at ease with his own theme, he uses exactly the same tactic, though the archness and charm are more worldly, more *New Yorker* than those of his Quaker characters. The most distressing example of this comes with his hero's final confession of self-forgiveness.... This episode is either the crux of the whole theme or it is nothing; yet the author is careful to present it at the end of a conversation between Stephen and his wife when both are ''high'' after a few cocktails. It is true that all we have learnt of Stephen tell us that he might not be able to say such a thing unless he were drunk, but Mr. Isherwood somehow contrives to present this circumstance as charmingly excusing the confession, when clearly it either needs no excuse or it should not have been made at all.

The truth is that Mr. Isherwood is not much at ease with ''goodness'' and ''good people.'' In his earliest novel, *All the Conspirators*, the conventionally ''good'' were the targets of [irony].... They were the ununderstanding, the blundering, the philistine, the deadening forces in life. Conventional morality in the hands of the hero's mother and her elderly City friend was simply a weapon to deny the young self-expression and to treat themselves to the pleasures of self-inflicted martyrdom. This deadly, selfish, conventional goodness which Isherwood understood very well and ridiculed most entertainingly is continued in the character of Lily in *The Memorial*—once again the hero's mother. But in that novel ... we get his first presentation of a less conventional goodness which we are meant to respect [in the character of Mary].... [Mary's most striking feature] is the self-consciously jolly, leg-pulling sort of way in which she protects her emotions, her ''goodness'' from the world.... [Mary] is really the last ''good'' character in Mr. Isherwood's work until *The World in the Evening*. She is an Understander, an Acceptor.... In all the Berlin stories that followed, the Understanding and Accepting were done by Mr. Isherwood himself, and very brilliantly, if a little self-consciously, he did them. With [*The World in the Evening*], ''good'' characters appear again and once more they hide their emotions in the same rather embarrassing ''chaffing'' way. It is as though the author had communicated his own unease at the spectacle of ''goodness'' to his characters. There has always been a certain preoccupation with the ethics of his public school days about Mr. Isherwood's work.... [Its last imprint is left] in this sort of self-deprecating facetiousness in which his ''good'' characters talk. It is a version of the traditional ''chaffing'' and ''rotting'' with which the cricket-captain hero of the school disguises—and ... all too often advertises—his merits. I do not think that Mr. Isherwood has ever quite lost his idolatry of that school hero. (pp. 62-4)

[Isherwood has a] general disregard for intellectual competence. The intellect plays almost no part in his scheme. There is an awful passage in the book when the doctor, Charles, tells Stephen his philosophy of life. It revolves around the idea of a high sort of ''camp'' which is the mark of true artistic greatness.... This sort of arrant nonsense should never be treated seriously, but I fear it is not only Charles and Stephen who do so, but Isherwood himself. It is a nice, cosy substitute for thought.

The element of cosiness is very important in Mr. Isherwood's work. It is a somewhat smug emotion.... [Reading the Berlin stories we] are left with the feeling, not that these characters have been sentimentalised, but that somehow, because Herr Isseyvoo is so understanding a man, we have been privileged to get on to cosy terms with people whom we would otherwise have found worthless. There is nothing against liking bad people as I am sure Isherwood does. Still less against finding the inevitable elements of good in them. But there is something a bit disturbingly smug about doing so in a cosy, happy family way. It is this cosiness which throws out the balance of *The World in the Evening*. It is at its worst in the character of Sarah, who is the true vessel of spiritual light in the book.... The note of cosiness, of the homely vessel of spiritual depths is overdone. It is, in fact, in the two principal characters chosen to expound the theme that *The World in the Evening* breaks down. Sarah, the true saint, may be as homely as you like; Stephen, the saint in travail, may be feeble and ineffectual; but we must be convinced that beneath the deceptive outward symbols there lies an inward grace of wisdom and strength, and we are not. (pp. 64-6)

If the author pretends to too much spiritually, he is admirably aware of his experiential limitations. This, I am sure, is a great strength in a writer. For Isherwood the important experiences happened before 1939 and he uses that period to illustrate his present position. . . .

[With *The World in the Evening* Isherwood has made advances in] the understanding of personal relationships and the extension of technical range. . . . The growth of his understanding of people has demanded a corresponding growth of technique. . . .

Mr. Isherwood has always had a powerful sense of place and time, of exact situation and the unspoken implications of such a situation. . . . Ultimately, however, Mr. Isherwood is even more a novelist of character than of place. In *The World in the Evening* [Elizabeth and Jane seem] more deeply felt and more truly realised than anything he has done previously. . . . The relation between Stephen and these two women is the first serious attempt of Mr. Isherwood to explore the complex patterns of emotional love. (p. 66)

Elizabeth is beautifully done. The intense egoistic preoccupation with life's meaning to *her,* the clinging to life combined with the neurotic and hypochondriac preoccupation with death, the awful paradox of a tired, ageing woman genuinely committed to a world of high, sensual values—all this is entirely convincingly presented. . . .

Jane is an improvement on an old theme. She is, in great degree, Sally Bowles seen again, but in *The World in the Evening* Mr. Isherwood has lost that satisfaction in standing apart, and that equal satisfaction with being cosy with the disreputable, which tinged so much of his earlier work with a sort of ironic sentimentalism. Jane is at once less of a bitch than Sally Bowles and also less sentimentalised. In Jane, I think, Mr. Isherwood, without altogether realising it, has drawn a very human, pleasant young woman who stands out above all his cosy saints. (p. 67)

Mr. Isherwood's previous novels have made few demands on his technical skill. . . . [In] *The World in the Evening,* he uses the Woolfian technique of change of time and place, of memory, journals, and letters with a logicality of sequence and a unification of purpose. . . . (pp. 67-8)

> Angus Wilson, "*The New and the Old Isherwood,*" in Encounter (© *1954 by Encounter Ltd.*), *August, 1954, pp. 62-8.*

STUART HAMPSHIRE

Mr. Isherwood is an experimental writer who has invented a form of his own. Like most experimental writers, he is sometimes estimated unjustly, and interpreted anxiously and angrily, because the critic, or reader, is not always sure how he ought to be read and what his intentions are. He shocks, because he is truthful in an unfamiliar way. Also he evidently uses fiction for an oblique moral purpose. But he is a subtle moralist; there are no reassuring hammer-blows, as in Orwell, which tell the reader quite unmistakably which side he ought to be on, leaving him complacent among the angels. There is doubt, insinuation of opposing points of view, and therefore discomfort. It is as if the author, through the narrator, is still making up his mind what

he believes, or where he stands, as he writes: at least he successfully creates the illusion of a tentative development within the stories that he tells.

Mr. Isherwood's novels . . . constitute a peculiar kind of contemporary history. Their peculiarity is the combination of an intensely private private life recounted against the background of public events: first, Fascism and [then] the war that emerged from it. . . . [He] has sustained the story of a hero who is obstinately loyal to the values of private life and of personal relations . . . of friendship and truthfulness. (p. 86)

The centre of Mr. Isherwood's experiment is the use of his hero, Christopher. The sequence of the novels constitutes a very peculiar kind of *Bildungsroman,* in which a hero of our times undergoes formative experiences. The peculiarity is that he is not too profoundly changed by his experiences: he protects himself by observing, and keeping a record of his observations. The purpose of the record is to establish his own identity. . . . There is another kind of novel which is an inquiry into the protagonist's identity, and which starts from the question "Who (or what kind of person) am I?" . . . Literary egoism of this kind is the expression of a fluid personality, of an uncentred "I." The memoirs of an egoist help to provide him with a centre. The fluid ego flows into a succession of situations, modifies each of them a little, and is temporarily shaped by them; but each time it resumes its way along other channels. Any shape that can be discerned is discernible only in the succession of incidents; these are the situations in which, to his surprise, and, as it seems, through no purposes of his own, the unidentified hero successively found himself. So the literary egoist, using the ambiguous first person singular, can represent the hero also as a tracer element, which will mark the diseased organs of the social body as it passes. Mr. Isherwood has used the device subtly for many years. He contrives to suggest some doubt about what kind of truthfulness to expect: the truthfulness of fact or that of imaginative reconstruction. The reader's uncertainty is more sharply provoked in [*Down There On a Visit*] than in the Berlin stories. For these are stories of distorted private lives, and the distortion is intrinsic to them and cannot be so closely associated with known historical events.

All four of the episodes [in *Down There On a Visit*] seemed to me like visits to hell; but they are lightly and humorously described by the narrator, who, exercising his professional powers as observer, evidently enjoyed himself. And it is typical of him that he should. His reflections on war and peace are ghastly in their banality and smugness, and his reflections on love only slightly less so. . . .

The reader who, hot for moral certainties in the contemporary manner, tries to disentangle Mr. Isherwood's attitudes and opinions from the narrator's will fail. . . . (p. 88)

> Stuart Hampshire, "*Isherwood's Hell,*" in Encounter (© *1962 by Encounter Ltd.*), *November, 1962, pp. 86, 88.*

FRANK KERMODE

Few writers have been more persistently anxious about themselves, their contemporaries, or the times they lived in [than Isherwood], and those who have seemed not to have wanted to state their anxiety so obliquely. He is a little like St. Augustine deploring in conceited Latin the depravity of another evening world. He studies our amusing, apparently self-willed deformities almost as if what mattered was their intrinsic comic value, almost as if he did not know that the pressures that create them are beyond the control of the individual will; yet his whole way of looking at them is ultimately conditioned by the political and psychological preoccupations of his contemporaries, and that to a degree most unusual in English intellectuals. On the face of it nothing could be more dispiriting than an *œuvre* of which the main theme is escape from Mother, enacted against sketches of a decaying continent. But Mr. Isherwood is not serious, and so the Berlin stories [become] conceited variations on a desperate theme. . . . (p. 121)

Being farcical about desperate matters is a trick associated with cabaret, especially German cabaret. . . . It has never been naturalized here, except momentarily by Isherwood himself. . . . [Jocular desperation is a highbrow solution] to the big problem of how to achieve specifically literary effects without shutting out life and politics. For the Freudian artist it is a problem complicated by his own alienation from society. Without it he wouldn't be an artist, but it complicates his way of looking at public events, especially at a time when . . . 'the destiny of man presents its meaning in political terms'. (p. 122)

[The problem of treating public events in a work of art] is presented in an apparently relaxed fashion in *The World in the Evening* (1954). Gerda, the refugee help, stands for total acceptance of our condition as good—internment camps, bedpans, love, everything understood and included. Stephen, the hero, is cut off from precisely this, and his relationship with Gerda is one of those sex-free affairs between tormented men and life-accepting women that recur throughout Isherwood's work. Stephen's dead wife Elizabeth was a highbrow novelist whose work Gerda dislikes. (pp. 122-23)

Elizabeth, in this strange, tense book—for the appearance of relaxation is entirely superficial—is representative not merely of a style to be escaped from, but also of a mother to be defeated; and the whole work is really a literary battlefield upon which the political and the psychological interests fight it out. The result is not always happy. . . . Yet the opening chapter is a superb beginning to a book in which sexual failure and irresponsibility are indices of a general collapse of communication between persons. (p. 123)

People found [*The World in the Evening*] disappointing because it was as unlike the Berlin books—and *Prater Violet*—as it could well be, coming out of the same skull. Yet it is by no means so unlike *The Memorial* (1932). . . . Here also Isherwood, with a different diagnostic method, explains the time's deformity. Such aetiological inquiries impose upon the novelist, as upon the physician, a technique of flashbacks, confrontations of cause and symptom. This necessity happens to have made *The Memorial* a more difficult book than *The World in the Evening*, but the two books are as it were linked behind the backs of the Berlin stories. . . . [*The World in the Evening*] is less ambitious and more expository in method, certainly; it came after the flight from art, from the Elizabeth kind of novel, in the Berlin books. *The Memorial* is altogether more serious, and equally desperate. The best way to put this is in terms of Isherwood's theory of High Camp, as expounded by the doctor, Charles, in *The World in the Evening*.

True High Camp always has an underlying seriousness. You can't camp about something you don't take seriously. You're not making fun of it; you're making fun out of it. You're expressing what's basically serious to you in terms of fun and artifice and elegance. Baroque art is largely camp about religion. The Ballet is camp about love. . . .

The Berlin stories are High Camp about civilization; *The World in the Evening* is decadent Camp; *The Memorial* was written while the idea was germinating, and is pre- or proto-Camp. (pp. 124-25)

The Memorial is certainly a work of art. The central event is the erection in 1920 of a war memorial in a small town deep in Manchester's Cheshire fringe. . . . Some of the people who come to the ceremony we have met before, though eight years later, in the first section of the book, which has a somewhat Conradian time-scheme. (p. 125)

It is difficult to give much idea of *The Memorial*, of the careful structuring and the compulsive stresses. It is, however, a book of enormous skill, heavy but without redundancy. 'It was to be about war,' wrote Isherwood, 'not the War itself but the effect of the idea of "War" on my generation. . . . I was out to write an epic; a potted epic; an epic disguised as a drawing-room comedy.' The determination, epic though it may be, to drape everything round a few central episodes involves having people remember rather than act; this becomes noticeable and irritating. And there is a tendency to slide over the sill of irony into identification with the manner criticized: 'Anne was plunging into a simple but very smart frock,' or, 'Oh, it was cruelly unjust, it was fiendish that she should have so many sorrows to bear'. Yet *The Memorial* is the best completed novel of a most distinguished writer: a genuine interpretation of the times. (p. 126)

> *Frank Kermode, in his* Puzzles and Epiphanies: Essays and Reviews 1958-1961 (© *Frank Kermode 1962*), *Routledge & Kegan Paul, 1962.*

COLIN WILSON

[Auden, Isherwood, Spender, and Upward] set themselves up as the Next Generation (after Joyce, Huxley and Eliot) and achieved literary eminence by a kind of *coup d'état*. . . .

Yet of the group, Isherwood seemed to be the odd man out. Auden and Spender were starting where Eliot left off, writing about the world of aeroplanes and pylons and guerrilla warfare. Upward's prose in *Railway Accident* and *Journey to the Border* was as complex and allusive as you would expect from someone who knew his *Ulysses* by heart. By comparison, Isherwood seemed deliberately naive. There was no evidence that he'd ever read anybody—except possibly the early novels of Knut Hamsun, which have the same artless directness. How could he reconcile being The Novelist—one of the company of Balzac and Dickens and Tolstoy—with this deliberately low-key approach? (p. 313)

[Isherwood's detached, observant first-person narrative is reminiscent of] Henry James; the James of *The Aspern Papers* and *The Sacred Fount*. Not that Isherwood's narrator 'Chris' is ever as complicated or analytical as James's mouthpiece. Yet, as I now suddenly realised, the basic spirit behind Isherwood's enterprise is Jamesian. Professor Sampson once compared James to a man who looks at life through a magic mirror, like the Lady of Shalott, always the observer, never the participant. What is the difference between James's mirror and Isherwood's camera? (p. 314)

[In James, a] problem seems to arise because the novelist is untrue to his original conception: of being a camera. For the moment he attempts to exclude himself from the scene, to photograph a group of people who exist only in his own mind, he is only pretending to be a camera. . . .

But why *should* the novelist want to be a camera? Is not the whole enterprise dishonest—or at least, muddled—from the beginning?

The answer to this question can be seen by referring to any of the early camera novels, from Knut Hamsun's *Hunger* or Rilke's *Malte* to *Ulysses* and Olyesha's *Envy*. . . . The 'camera' novel is essentially the 'outsider' novel. It is about a man 'outside' everyday life—what Husserl called the communal life-world—looking in. There is a tremendous gain in intensity and subjectivity. And that word reminds us that one of the earliest 'camera novels' was Kierkegaard's *Either/Or*—not, perhaps, strictly a novel, but certainly achieving a kind of philosophical detachment, combined with subjective intensity, which is typically Jamesian.

So it becomes possible to understand how Isherwood could see himself as The Novelist—even, perhaps, as the Great Novelist—without abandoning his humanistic creed of truth, attention to detail, and refusal to get overblown. The philosophy—such as it is—may have come from Forster, but the essential idea came from Kierkegaard, via Rilke, James, Joyce and Aldous Huxley. (I am not suggesting that Isherwood was influenced by any of these—except possibly Huxley—but that this is where we should look for literary parallels.) The ideal is a peculiar kind of honesty—an honesty that becomes almost a monkish vocation. The aim is to tell the truth—about oneself and other people—with a precision and honesty and thoroughness that would have alarmed Rousseau. (p. 316)

Readers of Isherwood's first novel *All the Conspirators*—started when he was twenty-one and published two years later—might be forgiven for feeling that the results of the method are hardly spectacular. But then, most first novels are at least partly autobiographical—designed to allow the writer to get some of his pet obsessions off his chest—and this is no exception. . . . The main impression it makes on the unprepared reader is of triviality. . . . Its main interest is that it gives us a very clear picture of what Isherwood had to fight against, the suffocatingly dull and respectable middle-class background. (p. 317)

Anyone who has been exasperated by *All the Conspirators* would hardly be reassured by the next novel *The Memorial* (1932). The technique is reminiscent of Aldous Huxley's *Point Counterpoint* of four years earlier; modern readers will be reminded of Angus Wilson. It is about a group of middle-class, rather cultured people in the 1920s, and again we are aware of how oppressive Isherwood found the whole milieu. 'Eric turned away from the window, deeply sighed. He was weary—weary to the bone.' Yet the book is finally far less oppressive than *Point Counterpoint* or [Upward's] *In the Thirties;* the reason being that Isherwood so obviously *likes* people. He writes of them with the same kind of keen observation and sympathy as E. M. Forster—Carolyn Heilbrun has commented on the 'roundness' of Isherwood's characters. This gives the novel an inner glow that saves it from negativeness.

From the first words of *Mr. Norris Changes Trains* (1935), you can see that Isherwood has achieved his freedom. He has still not quite achieved the confidence to speak of himself as Christopher Isherwood, but in all the essentials, William Bradshaw *is* 'Chris'. (Even the names are his own middle ones.) Isherwood's 'British' characteristics—his detachment, his good manners, even his shyness—have now ceased to be a disadvantage and have become his strength. For he is no longer trapped in a mood of self-disgust. (p. 318)

In *Kathleen and Frank* [Isherwood's tribute to his parents], Isherwood comments about his mother: 'She can't have cared much for his *Mr. Norris*—its humour was too sour, it was too preoccupied with drinking and dirty rooms and lowlife types to suit her taste . . .'. In measuring the distance from the impotent rebel of *All the Conspirators,* one becomes aware of how far Isherwood has come in five years. And how far the impetus that has driven him towards freedom has been his mother. He has found a subject as remote as possible from Kensington—so remote that it has even freed him from the need to cock a snook at Kensington. So the negative element that made the first two novels rather oppressive has vanished. The surprising thing about *Mr. Norris,* in spite of the brothels catering for perverts and the brooding shadow of Nazism, is that it is such a sunny and open-hearted book. Berlin has given Isherwood his freedom just as certainly as Paris and Zurich gave Joyce his; but this Artist as a Young Man has no need for silence, exile and cunning, and apparently no resentment about the things he has fought so hard to escape.

I re-read the book after reading *Kathleen and Frank,* and was surprised to discover that one of its most remarkable qualities is its honesty. In the last pages of *Kathleen and Frank,* Isherwood speaks openly of his homosexuality. . . . It does not matter that 'Chris' [of *Goodbye to Berlin*] allows us to assume that he is a perfectly heterosexual young man, and that in the dramatised version, he even gets Sally Bowles pregnant. The pruderies of the thirties were such that it was still not possible to admit openly to homosexuality, if only for legal reasons. . . . But what is absolutely clear is that this thoroughly irks Isherwood. Part of his hard-earned freedom was the right to be defiantly honest; so he steers as close as he possibly can to admitting it in the Berlin novels, and seems to try to make up for the suppression by an additonal honesty about himself and his motivations. It is this feeling that Isherwood is a totally honest man that gives all his novels—but particularly the four 'Chris' novels—their durable quality. (pp. 318-19)

Of all Isherwood's books, *Goodbye to Berlin* is the most stunningly successful. The method, the subject and the style have all come together to produce one of those oddly 'perfect' books. I put 'perfect' in quotes because in the Jamesian sense, it is far from perfect; it is all over the place: three bits of diary and three long-short stories. In spite of which, it has that air of never putting a foot wrong. It is not necessarily the best of Isherwood's books; both *The World in the Evening* and *Down There On a Visit* are in many ways more substantial and impressive products of the novelist's craft. . . . Yet it has the curious perfection of a healthy child.

This is due to an interesting combination of ingredients. To begin with, as 'Chris' himself recognises, this is because he has cast himself in the role of a camera, the Jamesian observer. But he has gone one step further than James. The narrator of *The Turn of the Screw, The Aspern Papers* and *The Sacred Fount* is basically a lay figure, an excuse for getting the story told. Now Isherwood is too good mannered to take refuge in this kind of objectivity; like a well-bred Englishman, he is anxious to hide his superiority. So he enters the story as a real character, apparently revealing himself as well as Sally and Otto and Bernhard. 'Chris' is not, of course, Isherwood; he is also a lay figure; but Isherwood pulls the strings so convincingly that we hardly notice. And this lay figure of *Mr. Norris, Goodbye to Berlin* and *Prater Violet* is perhaps Isherwood's most skilful creation. . . .

All the Conspirators and *The Memorial* have the same feeling of fidelity as the Berlin novels; but *what* they are reflecting lacks urgency; you admire the precision of the writing without getting very involved with the characters. . . . Isherwood happened to find his ideal subject in the Berlin of the early thirties. His own slightly ambiguous attitude towards his subject gives the whole thing an additional sharpness and clarity. He does not take up a violently moralistic attitude towards his pro-Nazi landladies, and his attitude towards Otto—who is what would nowadays be called a 'yob'—seems oddly compassionate. So the human values remain; the violence is understated—and therefore all the more shocking. The story of the Nowaks, with its poverty and muted tragedy, might have been written a generation earlier by one of the 'socially conscious' writers like Hauptmann or Sudermann; but the fact that it takes place in this brutal, disintegrating society gives it added force. (p. 320)

Prater Violet is, in my opinion, one of Isherwood's most successful works, and this is largely because he again makes use of the brooding, menacing atmosphere of the thirties and the rise of Nazism. The story is ostensibly about his involvement in a preposterous 'escapist' musical film; Bergmann, its German director, feels the full irony of the contrast between this cachou-scented nonsense and the Reichstag Fire Trial, which is at present taking place in Germany.

From the point of view of Isherwood's development, the most interesting thing about the book is the sense of 'Chris's' involvement with Bergmann and the tragedy of Germany. He is no longer cold and detached, and rather enjoying the superiority his detachment gives him. (p. 322)

At the same time, *Prater Violet* makes us more intensely aware than ever before of the limitations of this interesting method that Isherwood has chosen for himself—trying to be a 'pure' novelist in some super-Jamesian sense. By the rules he has laid down for himself, he is not allowed to keep voluminous notebooks of observations, which can then be elaborated into ideas for stories or novels, fleshed out with invention and technical know-how. I have already commented on the resemblance between the basic ideal of Isherwood and Hemingway—to *tell the truth* as it had never been told before. The trouble is basically that a novel is a pack of lies. If a novelist really wanted to tell the truth, he'd write history or autobiography. He doesn't; he wants to *create*, and to make his creation *seem* as truthful as possible. (pp. 322-23)

Yet *Prater Violet* seems to be a dead end. Isherwood's 'mirror' had been so effective because the monstrous figure of Hitler dominated the background; his fundamental sub-

ject had been the contrast between public and private life. (It was a formula that Solzhenitsyn would later use so effectively.) (p. 323)

When his next novel, *The World in the Evening,* appeared in 1954, it was clear that he was making an extraordinary, almost a heroic effort, to deal with these new circumstances. And this is also characteristic of the three novels that followed—his total output to date. Creatively speaking, each one of them has involved a far greater effort than any of the Berlin novels. None is a complete success, and one comes close to failure. Yet it seems to me that this is due to the nature of the problem rather than to Isherwood's response to it. (pp. 323-24)

Novelists could be conveniently divided into two groups: the subjectivists and the objectivists. . . . [The subjectivists] write about inner conflicts and problems, and their success depends on persuading you to 'identify' with the hero or heroine. The objectivists are observers, recorders and story tellers—Jane Austen, Scott, Balzac, Tolstoy, Henry James. . . .

From the beginning, Isherwood took his stand with the major practitioners of the objective novel—James, Hemingway, Joyce (of *Ulysses*) and Forster. Each one tried determinedly to be a camera.

At which point, the problem arises. A camera is all very well for special purposes—recording a war, or some definite epoch of the past. But if nothing in particular is going on around you, it becomes rather useless.

There are two possible solutions for a novelist. One is to forget the camera and invent, as James did. The other is to point the camera inside yourself, as Proust did. Joyce, who could not see any way out of the problem—having moved from subjectivism to objectivism—found 'extra-literary' solutions and played linguistic games. Hemingway wandered around the world with his camera on his back, looking for wars. (p. 324)

In *The World in the Evening,* Isherwood chose a mixture of the two main solutions: he 'invented', and he turned the camera inward. He also decided to avoid Forster's *cul de sac* by bringing the problem of homosexuality into the open. For this is what Forster wanted to write about but never could: the problem of 'the homosexual outsider'—the homosexual as outsider.

All 'subjective' novels are, in their very essence, *Bildungsromans*—that is to say, the hero's problem is to 'find himself'. *The World in the Evening* makes a radical break with all Isherwood's previous novels in that it is about a man trying to find himself—and more-or-less succeeding. Stephen Monk's natural tendency is to be passive and selfish. (p. 325)

The recreation of the marriage between Stephen and the novelist Elizabeth Rydal is superbly done. Yet the whole novel leaves one with an over-all sense of a tremendous effort that has not quite achieved its object. Moreover—and rather surprisingly—there is an air of unreality, of wishful-thinking—about the homosexual seduction scene. Certainly this, in a way, is the core of the book. One suspects that Isherwood even considered making Michael Drummond the legally adopted son of Stephen and Elizabeth, instead of simply a young man they take under their wing; it would add an element of shock, and also emphasize the problem of the divided loyalties of a homosexual. *This* is basically the problem of the novel. Stephen is a passive character, rather feminine, a bit of a gigolo. 'Chris' seems to be fascinated by such characters—Arthur Norris, Otto Nowak, Sally Bowles, 'fabulous Paul' (*of Down There On A Visit*). So now he is writing his first 'true novel' since *The Memorial,* it is to be expected that his hero should be of the same type. The trouble is that most readers do not enjoy identifying with self-proclaimed weaklings (the American word 'fuck-ups' would probably be more precise here); it was the passages of gloom and futility that made the first two novels so claustrophobic. ('He was weary—weary to the bone.') Moreover, we tend to feel that a real-life Stephen would not be married to a nympho like Jane, and would probably never have got married to Elizabeth Rydal earlier.

In short, while the 'subjective' part of the solution works, the 'inventive' part doesn't ring true. We never believe in Stephen as we believed in Chris. Perhaps this is because we accepted Chris's claims that he was a camera—because he was so careful to maintain the conventions of objectivity —and we can't grant similar credence to a man who seems awash with self-pity.

The World in the Evening is by no means a failure; judged as a totality, it is probably Isherwood's best novel. Its weakness may lie in an attempt to adapt the methods of Aldous Huxley. It is a serious attempt to talk about spiritual renewal, to make fictional use of the lessons he had learned from Vedantism; but Huxley himself never solved that problem, and most of the later novels have an analogous problem with 'focus'. The reader doesn't quite *believe* in them as he believed in *Crome Yellow* and *Antic Hay*. So it is with *The World in the Evening* compared to the Berlin novels.

Down There On A Visit (1962) demonstrates clearly that Isherwood had recognised what went wrong with the previous novel: that there was a faint, but nevertheless detectable, air of *mauvais foi*. He appears to retrace his steps— but this is only an appearance. Only the first part, *Mr. Lancaster,* is a genuine throw-back to the old days. It is less successful than some of 'Chris's' other portraits for a reason that the author recognises: 'When I tried to describe him to my friends, I found I could make very little of him as a significant or even a farcical character. I just did not have the key to him, it seemed.' Lancaster is a 'hollow man', a pompous bore who only becomes interesting for a moment when he tries to convince Chris that he composed one of Wilfred Owen's best known lines. If, as one suspects, Mr. Lancaster has created some new and extraordinary form of *mauvais foi* bordering on madness, Chris fails to put his finger on it.

The writing has again the wit and precision of the other 'Chris' books—there were times in *The World in the Evening* when it had become slack. (pp. 325-26)

Technically speaking, the innovation of *Down There On A Visit* is caught symbolically on Don Bachardy's dust-jacket, showing the middle-aged Isherwood looking at a mirror that reflects back his younger self. That is to say, Isherwood has tried an interesting way out of the camera problem by introducing a form of double-exposure. Instead of 'Chris'—

the mirror—we have the action mirrored in a young Chris who is in turn mirrored in the older and wiser Chris. This gives it a greater depth than the earlier Chris novels—and also makes it the ideal conclusion to the series, as Isherwood himself realised at the time.

Yet this in itself means that Isherwood had reached another dead-end. When one looks more closely at *Down There On A Visit*, one can see why. As in *Sally Bowles* and *The Nowaks,* you feel that an essential part of the 'camera' method is to observe people who are either failures or freaks. . . . 'Mr. Lancaster' needs more malice. I am not now speaking of gloating malice, of the kind one finds in the novels of Baron Corvo, but simply of the essential elements of malice—cool superiority. The whole point of *Mr. Norris* and *Goodbye to Berlin* is 'Chris's' superiority to everything that happens to him—rather like Stephen's in *Ulysses*. This is not intended as a criticism of Isherwood's method; a camera is by nature 'superior', since it remains detached from the things it records. 'Paul' is such an interesting exercise because of its ambiguity; 'Chris' *is* superior to Paul, observing him rather pityingly from above, yet is also fond of him, loves him as a fellow human being. (pp. 327-28)

Now the most significant thing about Isherwood as a novelist is that the driving force behind his work is a genuine craving for truth; there is nothing static or passive about his integrity. The honesty shows on the surface in the 'Chris' books, where he is, if anything, a little too self-analytical. But it runs under the surface in everything he has done; it is the basic recurrent theme of all his work.

It is this honesty that enables him to retreat from another dead-end, and produce one of his most successful novels, *A Single Man* (1964). The remarkable thing about this book is that it starts off by looking like his most resounding failure so far, then gradually gets the reader involved until he is laughing, slapping his thigh, and experiencing the sensation described by Holden Caulfield—the desire to snatch up a pen and write the novelist a letter. (p. 328)

Perhaps the most important thing to be learned from *A Single Man* is that the 'problem of the modern novel' is not purely a technical problem; on a much more fundamental level, it is a *personal* problem. If Isherwood had been negative and sour and defeated, the novel would have provided one more piece of evidence that the modern novel has landed itself in a *cul de sac*—or on the strand, like Yeats's post-romantic fish. What is important is that Isherwood has evolved as a human being since he wrote *All the Conspirators;* his odyssey has been long and at times dangerous; *A Single Man* is like a rocket sent up to announce that he has arrived home safely. (p. 329)

[Isherwood] is not suggesting that the answer to human misery and stupidity lies in sainthood or mysticism—only in decency and common sense, and also a certain optimism. For this is the thing that comes over most clearly from *A Single Man* and *A Meeting by the River*: that Isherwood's integrity is born of optimism, of hope. (p. 331)

Colin Wilson, "'An Integrity Born of Hope': Notes on Christopher Isherwood," in Twentieth Century Literature (*copyright 1976, Hofstra University Press*), October, 1976, pp. 312-31.

J

JACKSON, Shirley   1919-1965

Jackson was an American novelist and short story writer. She is best known for her stories which blend supernatural elements with ordinary domestic settings. (See also *Contemporary Authors*, Vols. 1-4, rev. ed.; obituary, Vols. 25-28, rev. ed.)

STUART C. WOODRUFF

No doubt many readers who helped to put Miss Jackson's novel on the bestseller lists for a long time read the book . . . as a mystery or whodunit lacking only a detective to solve the crime. . . .

There is, however, considerably more to *We Have Always Lived in the Castle* than [this] . . . ; Miss Jackson's novel is, in fact, a finely patterned work whose thematic concern is not really mystery or horror at all. To be sure, there is a conventional mystery of sorts—the identity of the poisoner —but unraveling it could hardly be said to strain our powers of deduction. And there is an element of horror as well, although, strangely enough, it is not caused by our discovery that a twelve-year-old girl has dispatched no fewer than four members of her family . . . , and has left an uncle crippled for life from the aftereffects of arsenic poisoning. Parricide on such a scale is certainly regrettable, but the real horror in Miss Jackson's novel originates elsewhere. (p. 152)

In Merricat's opening description of one of her weekly trips to the village we begin to sense the kind of world the castle is a defense against. So mean and small is that world, so lacking in love and understanding, that we soon come to share Merricat's distaste and to approve of the castle-dwellers' self-imposed isolation. The village, representative of the normal outside world, is initially characterized by its dirt and ugliness. . . . More important than the physical squalor and ugliness is the moral dry rot of its inhabitants. The village is a loveless, predatory place, filled with "flat grey faces with . . . hating eyes," with "rotting hearts" "coveting our heaps of golden coins." (pp. 153-54)

In radical opposition to the grubby village and its equally grubby inhabitants stands the castle, guarded by Constance, and in the polar contrasts between the so-called "normal" world of the village and the "abnormal" world of the castle we discover the novel's underlying pattern or design. Whereas the villager is grey and grimy, the castle appears to bask in perpetual warmth and sunshine. . . .

Constance—her name, of course, is emblematic—epitomizes the regenerative power of love and selfless devotion; she is the kind of person the sentimentalist would describe as "too fine" for this world. If she seems not quite believable as a character, like Esther Summerson of *Bleak House,* it is only because she is too good to be true. (p. 154)

Protected by Constance's love and concern, Merricat finds further refuge in her rich fantasy life, particularly in her dream of a "house on the moon." . . . Merricat's imagination insulates her against the world's lovelessness and greed, just as Constance has created a way of life which comes close to matching her sister's lunar fantasy. Since Merricat is the novel's narrator, we see through her eyes only, and soon become accustomed to her point of view. Gradually we find ourselves *sharing* that point of view. In our growing preference for life at the castle, we discover the moral of Miss Jackson's persuasive fable. For it is Miss Jackson's purpose to convert us, to make us feel the moral superiority of life "on the moon" to a drab and mean existence in the village. . . . If life at the castle is demented and "unrealistic," Miss Jackson implies, then by all means let us have more of it.

In fact, as sympathetic moon-dwellers we find the concepts of normal and abnormal behavior highly ambiguous, if not actually reversed, not because Merricat is unable to distinguish between them, but because the novel's angle of vision forces us to find all that is good and meaningful in the lives of three recluses scorned by the community at large. . . . As we pick up clues as to what happened that night at dinner, as we gain insight into the motive behind the parricide, we even come close to feeling that Merricat herself did the right thing. . . . The purpose of the novel is not to shock us with Merricat's bizarre crime, but to define the quality of new life that is its aftermath.

Because we share so fully Merricat's small but brightly illuminated world, we share as well—or at least sympathetically comprehehend—her one great fear; that Constance may return to the normal world as represented by the village. (pp. 155-56)

Just how real that subject is becomes apparent through Cousin Charles Blackwood's visit to the castle, for it is in

301

the antagonism that immediately springs up between Merri-cat and her cousin that the conflict between two worlds—two value systems—is most fully dramatized. (p. 156)

Paradoxically, what Jim Donell and the others do [in their destructive rampage at] the Blackwood house makes less sense to us than Merricat's poisoning of her family, and perhaps this is Miss Jackson's point. She is not trying to justify *what* Merricat did, but to make us understand *why* she did it. And somehow we do understand, and we do for-give, just as Constance has understood and forgiven, and just as the villagers cannot understand and cannot forgive. In the final violent clash between the village and the castle, Miss Jackson makes it clear that the true source of life's horror and madness is to be found in the so-called "nor-mal" world of ordinary people. (pp. 159-60)

In this moment of crisis, Constance is shown to be as de-pendent upon Merricat as Merricat has been upon her; to-gether they exemplify the reciprocity of love and devoted concern. (p. 160)

If we regard Miss Jackson's novel as asking us to love young girls who poison their parents, and older sisters who cover up for them, and to despise as louts ordinary people denied such exotic experiences, then the author is perhaps guilty of some rather special pleading. But the novel has no such palpable designs upon us and involves no more special pleading than any fictional world which asks us to submit for a time to given conditions and premises. In *We Have Always Lived in the Castle,* the conditions and premises are certainly persuasive enough. Through the figure of Con-stance we are shown qualities of human concern and sacri-ficial love rare enough to be either missed or misunderstood by the common run of mankind, rare enough to require withdrawal from the quotidian world for their preservation. In contrast, the everyday world is shown to be an often unlovely place in which to pass our existence, an insight that should hardly surprise most readers. . . . [The] differ-ence [between the villagers and the castle-dwellers] be-comes a vehicle for exposing man's scarcely latent capaci-ties for violence and cruelty. By crowding warmth and love and devotion into the habitable remains of a burned-out mansion, Miss Jackson shows how fragile and precious such values are, and worthy of being preserved at any cost. (p. 161)

In a way Miss Jackson's own avowed interest in [the world of the bizarre] is unfortunate, for she is apt to be labeled as a writer of supernatural fiction. This would be somewhat misleading; even in *The Haunting of Hill House* she goes considerably beyond the mere mechanism of terror by ex-ploring psychological dilemmas that work upon her protag-onists from within. And in her final novel, *We Have Al-ways Lived in the Castle,* she achieves a significantly new dimension in both theme and technique. (pp. 161-62)

> *Stuart C. Woodruff, "The Real Horror Else-where: Shirley Jackson's Last Novel," in South-west Review (© 1967 by Southern Methodist University Press), Spring, 1967, pp. 152-62.*

HELEN E. NEBEKER

Numerous critics have carefully discussed Shirley Jack-son's "The Lottery" in terms of the scapegoat traditions of anthropology and literature, pointing out its obvious com-ment on the innate savagery of man lurking beneath his civ-ilized trappings. Most acknowledge the power of the story,

admitting that the psychological shock of the ritual murder in an atmosphere of modern, small-town normality cannot be easily forgotten. Nevertheless, beneath the praise of these critics frequently runs a current of uneasiness, a sense of having been defrauded in some way by the devel-opment of the story as a whole. (pp. 100-01)

Perhaps the critical ambivalence . . . stems from failure to perceive that "The Lottery" really fuses two stories and themes into one fictional vehicle. The overt, easily discov-ered story appears in the literal facts, wherein members of a small rural town meet to determine by lot who will be the victim of the yearly savagery. At this level one . . . recoils in horror. This narrative level produces immediate emo-tional impact. Only after that initial shock do disturbing questions and nuances begin to assert themselves.

It is at this secondary point that the reader begins to sus-pect that a second story lies beneath the first and that Miss Jackson's "symbolic intentions" are not "incidental" but, indeed, paramount. Then one discovers that the author's careful structure and consistent symbolism work to present not only a symbolic summary of man's past but a prognosis for his future which is far more devastating than the mere reminder that man has savage potential. Ultimately one finds that the ritual of the lottery, beyond providing a chan-nel to release repressed cruelties, actually serves to *gener-ate* a cruelty not rooted in man's inherent emotional needs at all. Man is not at the mercy of a murky, savage id; he is the victim of unexamined and unchanging traditions which he could easily change if he only realized their implications. Herein is horror. (pp. 101-02)

Jackson does not, however, attack ritual in and of itself. She implies that, as any anthropologist knows, ritual in its origin is integral to man's concept of his universe, that it is rooted in his need to explain, even to control the forces around him. Thus, at one time the ritual, the chant, the dance were executed precisely, with deep symbolic mean-ing. Those chosen for sacrifice were not victims but saviors who would propitiate the gods, enticing them to bring re-birth, renewal, and thanking them with their blood. (p. 104)

Shirley Jackson has raised . . . lesser themes to one encom-passing a comprehensive, compassionate, and fearful un-derstanding of man trapped in the web spun from his own need to explain and control the incomprehensible universe around him, a need no longer answered by the web of old traditions.

Man, she says, is a victim of his unexamined and hence unchanged traditions which engender in him flames other-wise banked, subdued. Until enough men are touched strongly enough by the horror of their ritualistic, irrational actions to reject the long-perverted ritual, to destroy the box completely—or to make, if necessary, a new one re-flective of their own conditions and needs of life—man will never free himself from his primitive nature and is ulti-mately doomed. Miss Jackson does not offer us much hope —they only talk of giving up the lottery in the north vil-lage. . . . (p. 107)

> *Helen E. Nebeker, "'The Lottery': Symbolic Tour de Force," in* American Literature *(re-printed by permission of the Publisher; copyright 1974 by Duke University Press, Durham, North Carolina), March, 1974, pp. 100-07.*

JOHN G. PARK

Showing her ability to find pity and terror in the ludicrous and the ludicrous in the terror, Jackson creates a fantasy of the end of the world [in *The Sundial*], which parodies the apocalyptic imagination while portraying it. (pp. 74-5)

The novel is concerned with the nature of belief, with the way desperate people grasp a belief and make it their truth, with how belief and madness combine and lead to desperate behavior, with how belief is a form of madness itself, making people into grotesques. (p. 75)

Mrs. Halloran's *hubris* blinds her to her own limitations, causing her to miscalculate, to gamble for the highest stakes in a situation she could not control.... Mrs. Halloran sought control over the future the way she tried to control the present and failed at both. (p. 78)

Mrs. Halloran sees quite clearly the ridiculousness of the True Believers but cannot see that her own belief is lunacy also. Perhaps to the eyes of the non-believer all belief contains madness. (p. 79)

Waiting for the end with Mrs. Halloran, her invalid husband, Richard, and the apocalyptic Aunt Fanny are nine of the strangest people ever expected to be gathered in one place.... Most of these people share several important qualities. They fear and hate the world and are unable to function independently within it. They have no clear sense of their future and grasp eagerly at Aunt Fanny's apocalyptic visions, for which they willingly bet their lives. Not only weak, they are also utterly selfish, self-centered, and greedy.... Because they are in the twilight zone of waiting, neither the present nor the future world is quite real to them, and they do not know what to do. (pp. 79-80)

Much of Aunt Fanny's madness . . . stems from her experience of childhood loss and betrayal, when she was abandoned and neglected, causing her to create a world of fantasy within. (p. 82)

Evocative of the tone of some of Hawthorne's tales, such as "The Ambitious Guest" and "Ethan Brand," is Essex's confession to Arabella, whose density protects her from any comprehension, that he is filled "with a kind of unholy, unspeakable longing." Essex has looked inward and is sickened by what he has found—a heart of longing beyond appeasement. He speaks of it as a form of original sin: "It is abominable to need something so badly." . . . All within the Halloran house feel such longing in varying degrees, the very basis for their belief in Aunt Fanny's visions. It continues to animate the contagion which gives cohesion to a disparate group, creating a "they-versus-us" syndrome. It reinforces Mrs. Halloran's power of coercion when various members of the group begin to doubt and desire to leave.... The longing of the group reinforces Aunt Fanny's belief in her own revelations as well. (pp. 82-3)

House imagery, a common feature of the gothic tradition, in the form of doll houses, little houses in the forest (as in Mrs. Halloran's dream), houses within houses, and the mansion itself, recurs throughout the novel and generally serves to indicate the presence of a deadly narcissism. (p. 84)

We can see in *The Sundial* several features of what Irving Malin calls the new American gothic. First, a microcosm serves as the arena where universal forces collide. The gothic house functions as an image of authoritarianism, of imprisonment, of "confining narcissism," as well as a receptacle of lost values. The voyage—as when Julia at-tempts to flee to the city—is an attempt to escape the cloying authoritarianism of the house. The journey is also dangerous and terrifying, as Julia finds out. Nearly all of the characters of new American gothic are narcissistic, in one form or another, weaklings who try to read their own preoccupations into reality, as do the followers of Aunt Fanny's vision. Thus, for them "reality becomes a distorted mirror." Especially apropos of Mrs. Halloran, "new American gothic uses grotesques who love themselves so much that they cannot enter the social world except to dominate their neighbors." In new American gothic the family is frequently used as a microcosm and is the source of the members' disfiguring love. The family tends to stunt the full development of its members, who become arrested in narcissism and are unable to grow up, as we see in Aunt Fanny. The reflection, another convention of the gothic, occurs frequently in *The Sundial*. Essex hates mirrors because of his awareness of duplicity. Gloria's many visions in the mirror reflect the narcissism of the whole community that it has been chosen to survive the holocaust and inherit a new world. Most of the characters of new American gothic, Malin argues, are isolates who are unable to belong to the world outside their family or home. While they would like to be a part of the big world, they are too afraid to leave the little world, as is certainly the case of the Halloran group. (p. 85)

The Sundial is a nicely woven novel, where imagery and technique work together well. Through the use of various motifs, such as the house imagery, references to time, Jackson is able to juxtapose character, theme, and incident in startling and ironic ways. One such motif is the reading of *Robinson Crusoe* to the senile Mr. Halloran by his nurse. The passages often contrast ironically with the increasing madness of the characters in the novel. As in her other work, Jackson employs a deft kind of cinematic focusing, creating a simultaneity of effect and capturing well a roomful of conversation. The novel satirizes a human condition where gullibility, cupidity, and culpability reign virtually unrestrained by moral principle and create a community of the survival of the worst. The satire is not without rich humor. (p. 86)

In *The Sundial* Shirley Jackson portrays the elitism of the apocalyptic mind that sees only itself as being worthy of survival and salvation. Such an imagination is essentially nihilistic because it forsakes positive reformatory action for a passive waiting that can easily move into despair, and it accepts powerlessness and surrenders human responsibility to what it regards as an overpowering destiny, in the name of which all crime is possible. To the Halloran household the world will end and begin again with itself as the inheritor, an example of the "presumptive eschatology" of a secular imagination which sees a simple continuation of history after the cataclysm. Here, we have no sense of judgment and renewal in connection with the cataclysm as in traditional apocalypse. A new world is expected, but no personal renewal is promised or demanded, which, as Fancy suspects, will mean no change at all in the human condition. The people gathered in the Halloran mansion have indeed experienced the loss of world and suffer the debilitating effects of anomie.

Apocalypse, properly conceived, is a message of hope for a people in stress and crisis, for it provides a context for the faithful to understand themselves and to act. Such understanding of apocalypse, essentially theological and biblical, contrasts sharply with the apocalyptic pretensions of the Halloran party. They long for a revelation without theology, a revelation without judgment and thus without renewal as well. Because they lacked courage to live responsibly in the present world and because they lacked hope for the future, they abdicated their humanness for the apocalyptic visions of a mad woman and chose to live appearances for reality, a dangerous fiction for life. (pp. 87-8)

> *John G. Park, "Waiting for the End: Shirley Jackson's 'The Sundial'," in* Critique: Studies in Modern Fiction *(copyright © by James Dean Young 1978), Vol. XIX, No. 3, 1978, pp. 74-88.*

*   *   *

JEFFERS, Robinson   1887-1962

Jeffers was an American poet and playwright whose fatalistic philosophy extols the savage beauty of nature over the inadequacies of man. Drawing his themes from the Greek classics as well as from the philosophies of Nietzsche and Freud, he often set his poems against the backdrop of the California coast. His is a grim poetry of violence, incest, and revenge, placing value upon what Jeffers called "permanent things," and upon freedom. The early response to Jeffers's work was highly enthusiastic. Praise came from such critics as Babette Deutsch and Mark Van Doren, and something of a cult following developed. Since the mid-1930s, however, his work has come under critical attack, and his reputation has steadily deteriorated. (See also *CLC,* **Vols. 2, 3.)**

MARK VAN DOREN

The most rousing volume of verse I have seen in a long time [is Robinson Jeffers's "Tamar and Other Poems."] ... Few recent volumes of any sort have struck me with such force as this one has; few are as rich with the beauty and strength which belong to genius alone. ...

[Two] long narrative pieces are its real contribution. ... [The title-poem, "Tamar"], seems to me to point a new path for narrative verse in America. The rhythms, for one thing, are variable and free; now crabbed and nervous, now copious and sweeping, they get their story told as few are told—with style. And their story, though it is anything on earth but pleasant, was magnificently worth telling. Tamar, the heroine, begins by being like the Tamar who figures in the thirteenth chapter of II Samuel, but she develops in an ampler strain. It is obvious that Mr. Jeffers's inspiration has been Greek rather than Hebrew; the House of Cauldwell is the House of Atreus, and the deeds done there are such as have rarely been attempted in song since Aeschylus petrified an audience with his Clytemnestra and his Furies.

> *Mark Van Doren, "First Glance," in* The Nation *(copyright 1925 by the Nation Associates, Inc.), March 11, 1925, p. 268.*

DELMORE SCHWARTZ

[*The Selected Poetry of Robinson Jeffers*] presents a sufficient span of writing ... to give any reader a just conception of what Jeffers has done. Above all, this selection invites a brief consideration and judgment of Jeffers' work as a whole, especially with regard to its sources.

At least one source is the scientific picture of the universe which was popular and "advanced" thought until a few short years ago. (p. 30)

When Jeffers says in his foreword and in a number of his poems that he wishes to avoid lies, what he means by lies are all beliefs which would somehow deny or ameliorate this world-view. When he speaks repeatedly of stars, atoms, energy, rocks, science, and the power of Nature, it is the Nature of 19th-century science which he has in mind and which obsesses him. ... [For Jeffers, Nature] has become merely a huge background which proffers only one delight, annihilation, and which makes human beings seem to him puny and disgusting beasts whose history is the tiniest cosmic incident. (p. 31)

The world-picture of 19th-century science, the World War and Jeffers' portion of the Pacific Coast are not, however, merely sources of his work, but actually, with little disguise, the substance of his poems. (p. 32)

Human beings are often brutal, Nature is sometimes violent, and life is indeed a mystery, but to respond as Jeffers does by rejecting humanity and saluting the peace of death is to come to a conclusion which is not only barren, a result which pleases Jeffers, but also false, and thus in the end without interest and without value. (p. 33)

[What] cannot be adequately defended are the consequences in the poetry itself, both in the lyrics where we are presumably to get a representation of emotions and in the narrative poems where we ought to be getting a representation of human action.

The narrative poems constitute the major part of Jeffers' work and it is upon them that the weight of untruth is most unfortunate. In *The Tower Beyond Tragedy,* for example, the alternatives presented to the hero are: either incest or a complete rupture with humanity. One needs no knowledge of the Agamemnon story to know that this is not a genuine tragic dilemma, either for Orestes or for any other human being. ... [What happens] throughout the narrative writing is not only not true of human life even at its most monstrous—such untruth might conceivably be justified as an extreme use of symbols—but the untruth is essentially a matter of the contexts provided by the poet, the situations which he has furnished for his characters. ... [Characters are] compelled to their acts by nothing but the emotion of the poet, an emotion utterly removed from their lives and differently motivated.

The same lack is present in the lyrics, and as in the narrative it was a narrative lack, so in the lyrics what is absent betrays itself in lyrical terms. ... What is to be noted [in the poem *Science,* for example,] is the number of shifts the poet finds necessary in order to state the observation which concerns him. The machines of science which man cannot manage are named as giants, hybrids, knives. The knowledge of science which makes possible these machines is successively compared to a vision of Diana, a pebble, and a drop of water. ... There is no rule or law which makes it impossible for a poet to go from one metaphor to another even in a very short poem, but such a transit can only be justified if it accomplishes some expressive purpose. Here the shifts, however, weaken each metaphor, preventing the reader from getting a clear picture of a thing, process or condition, by means of which to grasp the notion and the emotion in question. (pp. 33-5)

[In] general, most great poetry does not depend upon the truth of its philosophical beliefs, although it requires them as a structure and a framework. But in Jeffers the beliefs about the world and the consequent emotions are the substance of the poetry, and the observations of land and sea and the narrative characters are merely the means, which reverses the relationship. In the *Inferno,* the Christian system helps to make possible a vision of human beings; in Jeffers, the human beings are there to make possible a vision of Jeffers' ideas of the world. . . . The substance of the poetry is his emotion about humanity and the wide world. The poet's business is to *see,* by means of words, and we can only judge him by what he presents as seen. (p. 37)

When one attempts to write narrative poems about human beings, the obligation of a sufficient knowledge of human beings, the necessity of a definite measure of rhythm intervenes upon one, and literature as an organic tradition enters upon the scene. Jeffers undoubtedly has a keen sense for the landscape and seascape he writes about and he is by no means without a knowledge of human beings. But on the basis of detesting humanity, the natural tendency is to turn away from a strict view of human beings as they actually are and to regard a concern with literature, *technically,* as being at best unnecessary, at worst a hindrance. The result is that the characters Jeffers writes about tend to become repetitive abstractions, and the long line of Jeffers' verse is corrupted repeatedly by the most gauche inconsistencies of rhythm. The causal sequence seems indubitable. The poet has decided that the emotion he feels is strong enough to justify any manipulation of characters. . . . [The] poet is breaking away from literature as well as humanity in his poems, which we are asked to accept as literature, and in which we are presumably presented with humanity. (p. 38)

> *Delmore Schwartz, "The Enigma of Robinson Jeffers," in* Poetry *(© 1939 by The Modern Poetry Association; reprinted by permission of the editor of* Poetry*), October, 1939, pp. 30-8.*

RADCLIFFE SQUIRES

Jeffers' poetry presents some difficulties, but it is in the main poetry of direct statement. Yet even if Jeffers were serving up a pastiche of metaphysical conceits and French symbolism, it seems unlikely that the "esthetic" critics [who have objected to his style] would feel moved to enthusiasm for his sprawling, often careless narratives. The poems need critical re-examination, but the need centers in their philosophical texture, in the relationship of idea to idea rather than the relationship of word to word, nuance to nuance. (p. 8)

In retrospect Jeffers' present reputation is contained within the beautiful symmetry of a completed irony. The virtues which the earlier reception proclaimed were his sense of restrained tragedy, his form and metrical accomplishment. The faults which later criticism has found are those of hysteria, formlessness and dubious metrics. Still, most critics have permitted him to retain one virtue, that of "power." (pp. 9-10)

[Jeffers] came to write violent "stories" about two heroes: Nature as permanence opposed to man as the perverse, ephemeral consciousness. But Jeffers' violence is not so much nostalgia for Thermopylae as it is scorn of modern man's playing the old fool: modern man with his bloody and mysterious myths gone and with his theory of ethics firmly established, yet behaving like a barbarian—like the child, instead of the adult of the age. War appears again and again

in the backgrounds of the narratives as the secret, muted embodiment of a fate which, terrible as it is, may ultimately be the means of humbling the one hero (man) so as to bring him into unity with the other hero (Nature). (p. 18)

Because *Californians* contains stylistic and ideological particles from *Flagons and Apples* while suggesting the emphasis of the mature work, it has usually been thought a "transitional" book. (p. 21)

Considered as a whole, the early efforts are closer to the achievement of *Californians* than is *Flagons and Apples.* They are also cleaner and solider poems than the celebrations of "Helen." If they contain, as I believe they do, the kernel of Jeffers' mature work, and if *Flagons and Apples* (except very rarely) does not, then one must give up the idea that *Californians* is a "transitional" work and recognize instead that it continues the mood that Jeffers has courted with only one deviation since adolescence. That one deviation is *Flagons and Apples.* (pp. 21-2)

Jeffers has loved annihilation no more nor less than creation, death no more nor less than life. But loving both, he could reconcile them only in a mystical experience. If we read his poetry wisely, we gain insight into the severity, the humility, and discipline of a noble and great man's mystical solutions to problems which universally confront all men. (p. 26)

Yet Jeffers' mysticism, like all true mysticism, seeks to objectify as well as to discover the personality. His inner world is not the labyrinth of subjective emotions. It is rather the divine and terrible minotaur who waits in the final cavern of the labyrinth. The formative storm and stress in Jeffers' inner world between the years 1910 and 1918 is recorded in "The Truce and the Peace," and I judge that the important and catastrophic signification of his experience was the decision to destroy his own dandyism, the pastel romanticism of *Flagons and Apples.* (pp. 26-7)

The effect of Jeffers' reaction against dandyism appears in *Californians,* but it emerges full-fledged only in *Tamar* (1924) and *Roan Stallion* (1925). The change between these and *Californians* is far reaching. The regionalism has grown into an allegiance to place, but the Carmel coast of which he writes is a created world where the gothic splendors correspond less to any geography than to conditions of the imagination. The intricate verse forms have, except in a few poems which antedate *Tamar,* yielded to the long sweep of his verse paragraphs. (p. 29)

Taken together, *Tamar* and *Roan Stallion* reveal the double potential in Jeffers, the saga formula and the classical, the diffuse and the unified. All his later work is conceived in relationship to this artistic polarity. But he was never again to achieve the same kind of classical expression as in *Roan Stallion.* He was to write more simply than in *Tamar,* to be sure, but the crowded and episodic nature of *Tamar* is characteristic of even as remarkable a poem as *Cawdor* or as *The Loving Shepherdess,* Yet, if he could not wholeheartedly turn again to the classical control of *Roan Stallion,* he was able to hybridize his classical side with his undisciplined side in the narrative which achieves the greatest success, *The Double Axe* (1948). Part I of *The Double Axe* is as unified as *Roan Stallion,* whereas Part II is as diffuse and formless as *Tamar* or *The Women at Point Sur.* But Part II stands as a commentary on Part I and it takes the form of a strained, interior argument behind which the lurid lights of *Tamar* flash without dispersing the purity and intensity of the argument. Toward *The Double Axe* all of Jeffers' verse moved inexorably, and it is the result of his having been able, after years of dross, to hold the two poles of his artistic nature together. His dramas, it may be noted, display the same pattern. If one discounts his *Medea*, which is contained by the architecture of Euripides, one finds that *The Tower Beyond Tragedy* and *At the Fall of an Age* correspond in their unity to *Roan Stallion*, while *Dear Judas* and *The Bowl of Blood* correspond in their disunity to *Tamar*. Also, his best drama (as poetic drama) is *At the Birth of an Age* which, like *The Double Axe*, divides into two parts: the first, an orderly, lean set of actions; the second, a purposeful disunity spun out into the searching self-analysis of the hanged God. These hybrid creations, combining his two opposed powers, along with *Roan Stallion* and his recent supernatural allegory *Hungerfield* (1952), seem to me to be Jeffers' only long works that have a chance for permanency. (pp. 30-1)

The Women at Point Sur is even more tangled than *Tamar*, ... [and] the lines of the action are twisted into an almost hopeless snarl. (p. 33)

Whatever rhetorical success the poem has, it fails to realize the manifold hopes that Jeffers entertained. Even as a study in abnormal psychology it is not successful, for the psychology with its excessive Freudian stratagems has merely the effect of mechanizing and defeating the characters. As for the poem's advocacy of "old-fashioned morality," it seems closer to what D. H. Lawrence would have called a "phallic" drama. ... [An] orgasm of death is the final impression of the poem, and as such it seems more nearly a summons to a witches' sabbath than an invitation to morality. The primary trouble is, of course, as Jeffers admitted, the number of intentions. On the other hand it is these intentions which make *The Women at Point Sur* important to a study of Jeffers. It is the very matrix of his subsequent narratives. (pp. 34-5)

Jeffers has wanted the world to rehearse his own phases of maturation. His attack on man is a continuation of his attack on himself, for the faults he attacks in his heroes are fickleness, sexual athleticism, and jealousy, and these are more nearly the faults of the adolescent hero than of the mature hero.... Because one repudiates the passions, however, does not mean that one is not fascinated by them; it may mean quite the opposite. And this seems to be the constant and nourishing tension in Jeffers' verse. As a philosopher he negates what as a human being he cannot do without. (p. 40)

Jeffers attempts a grand, although awkward, synthesis of Idealism and pragmatism. The effort to compose these ideologies is documented in the poem "Love the Wild Swan." ... Two quarreling conceptions direct the sonnet: the ordered program of Nature which relegates man to insignificance; and the subjective reality captured by the eye and the mind, which receive the impressions of order and beauty.... In part, of course, the mien of the experience is mystical, but the structure of the experience is founded on an idealistic metaphysics. This aspect of Jeffers' poetry has been strangely overlooked. I do not wish, however, to give the impression that criticism has ignored a German romanticism in Jeffers. The contrary is true. Yet the emphasis has centered in a Nietzschean influence, and that emphasis is not completely justified in a parallel reading of Jeffers and Nietzsche. (pp. 42-3)

Jeffers has made confessions of indebtedness to Nietzsche, and some critics have constructed unilateral hypotheses from his words.... My own reading leads me to minimize the Nietzschean elements although not to discount them, for in the broadest terms Jeffers' poetry mirrors the intellectual power and austerity which we may sympathetically attribute to Nietzsche. (pp. 43-4)

Although it is clear from the youthful poetry that [Flinders] Petrie and [Oswald] Spengler did not create Jeffers' endemic fatalism, I think it likely that they confirmed him in a set of dualisms intellectually related to that fatalism: a dualism between Nature and history, a dualism between Nature and man, a dualism between culture and civilization. (p. 57)

Jeffers' poetry has contemplated a society which he feels is about to enter its period of "finishedness." Like Spengler, he sees the present as the last evolution of the period of "Culture," the sunset glow of the final greatness of the age.... But the final collapse he tells us in "I Shall Laugh Purely" is centuries away.... Meanwhile he sees Western man in love with luxury and machines, inclining toward subjective passions—love, hate, jealousy—and dissipating his energies in minute, if painful, quarrels. The subjectivity mirrors the subjectivity of the declining civilization. (pp. 59-60)

The acceptance of a Spenglerian doom is obviously commensurate with the polarity of death and resurrection in the structure of Jeffers' temperament. But to this *primum mobile* we must add Jeffers' Schopenhauerian tendency to regard the species rather than the individual and to relate all human matters to a historical basis. To this tendency he has sacrificed certain elements of psychological realism in his narratives.... Jeffers is not claimed by the ordinary time-dimension of art. His narratives lean back upon the past and stretch forward into a future—a future complicated, neurotic. This intent explains what must otherwise seem a contradiction too absurd to merit serious investigation: the contradiction between "primitive" characters and their decadent behavior. To understand the characters at all, one must understand that they reflect past, present, and future historicity. They represent Western man in three aspects. One may logically observe, of course, that characters who belong to no absolute time cannot be "real." Often they are not. Sometimes they seem only Jeffers' phantoms created to save himself from the "wolves" of "pain and terror, the insanities of desire" over which he broods in "Apology for Bad Dreams." ... (pp. 63, 65)

Like many of his contemporaries, Jeffers has used sexual symbolism too often, too bluntly, too easily, and there is no point in making a long list of the Freudian images. (p. 74)

The narratives after *The Women at Point Sur* [, however,] are less clinical, as may be observed in the treatment of lesbianism in *Thurso's Landing*.... Although male homosexuality is central to *The Cretan Woman* (1954), after *Thurso's Landing* (1932) Jeffers' interest is not detained by lesbianism. Incest as a symbol for "racial introversion," however, has endured. (p. 78)

The fascination with incest in "The Three Avilas" seems to me more distasteful than in *Tamar* for the reason that it is *not* turned to symbolical account. Even in *Tamar* the symbol is tentative, and it does not become formal until 1927 with the appearance of *The Women at Point Sur*, although *The Tower Beyond Tragedy* (1925) had moved in this direction. The theme does not appear again until *Such Counsels You Gave to Me* and *The Double Axe*. In these it is clear that the use is symbolical, but in each the motivation for incest is different.... In the contrast between *Such Counsels You Gave to Me* and *The Double Axe* lies one of the unnoticed growths in Jeffers' poetry. It is a growth away from Freud, away from the clinical and toward the mystical. (pp. 79-80)

Jeffers' narratives between *Tamar* (1924) and *Mara* (1941) are characterized by a Freudian scheme, with the result that the behavior of the characters is largely pseudo-naturalistic. They yearn toward incest; they revert to infantile dreams. This is not the case with Bruce Ferguson [in *Mara*]. His struggle is not with a hidden impurity entombed in childhood; he struggles with the projections of his own personality.

The volume *Such Counsels You Gave to Me,* which precedes *Mara,* may in this respect be considered a transitional work, illustrating Jeffers' movement toward a Jungian formulation. (pp. 84-5)

The observable trend in both *Such Counsels You Gave to Me* and *Mara* is toward the mystical rather than the naturalistic, toward the Oriental rather than the Western, toward an identification of man with cryptic, divine archetypes rather than disconsolate mechanisms. The momentum of this trend seems to have impelled Jeffers beyond both Freud and Jung in *The Double Axe* and *Hungerfield* (1952), for while neurosis and violence recur, they appear in a framework of supernatural allegory which no recognizable psychology, no behavioristic philosophy conditions. (p. 85)

The single most impressive characteristic of Jeffers' mature work is his preoccupation with all manner of violent action. The origins are not simple, but one can make inroads toward an understanding by considering the perplexing split between Jeffers' didacticism and its formulation. He arranges his characters so that they torture each other unbearably and then moralizes that if this is the human condition, it would be well to "break out" of it. He tries thus to solve the problem of passion through logic, but the effort augments his difficulties if only because it is man's irrational passions which most readily capture Jeffers' artistic allegiance.

This peculiar dichotomy ... between the dictates of intellect and the pleas of passionate imagination gives us the portrait of a man who carefully gathers up dinner crumbs to scatter for the birds but who writes a sadistic poem about a mutilated hawk. (pp. 86-7)

The influence of the war is complicating. No violence appears in Jeffers' verse until after 1918. And more significantly, much of the violence in the poems can be taken as a symbol for war, even though the expression is often sexual. The identification, or at least the blurring in his work, of violence, war, and the passions is not superficial: For if Jeffers despises the brutality of war, he sometimes envisions war as an agency which, by humbling and upheaving, may create benefit. Likewise, if he seeks to deprecate the passions, he nevertheless envisions regeneration as the task of a primitive sexuality.

From his inability either to compose or ignore these conflicts, Jeffers has, I think, been forced to express them in an exaggerated form.... He does not, I suggest, turn to violence because his temperament longs for violence but because it longs to be rid of it. He seeks to destroy his own passions, along with the racial "passion" of war, by deliberately exaggerating them. (pp. 87-8)

Since for Jeffers there is no eternal life, no heaven nor hell, the perseverance of some sort of religious emotion demanding punishment for the original sin has had a profound effect upon his poetry.... Jeffers' characters, riddled with guilt, [cannot] expect punishment for their crimes in an afterlife. Aware, then, of their guilt, they cry out for a fiery cleansing.... (pp. 89-90)

[The] tortured animal plays a symbolic role [in Jeffers' later work]. This is made most clear in *Cawdor* where Michal keeps as a pet a caged eagle which her brother Hood has winged.... When the bird is finally put out of its misery Jeffers describes the flight of its "phantom" in one of his most successful pieces of writing, an elegy where death becomes an affirmation of life.... Not only does this passage articulate a meaning of life, but it also suggests that the eagle and his squalid cage are intended to symbolize the state of man, trapped in pain and filth, but yet performing a "necessary" task in the universal scheme. (pp. 92-3)

The tortured animal, then, is a symbol of man's plight. But often the symbol is dropped, and man himself is tortured, principally in two patterns—castration and crucifixion. (p. 93)

It is noteworthy that in [*Give Your Heart to the Hawks* and *Mara*], where the disease of life becomes especially painful, self-crucifixion is the forerunner of insanity and suicide. In this way the Christ-figure is related to the insanely self-tortured man. And Jeffers takes the relationship one step further by relating the Christ-figure to war. (p. 94)

During the course of Jeffers' career his God has changed from the wild god of Nature incarnate in the roan stallion that shakes "the red-roan mane for a flag on the bare hills," to a more nearly intelligent God in *The Double Axe*. The later figuration is that of Heautontimoroumenos, the self-tormentor, first hinted at in "Apology for Bad Dreams." In the image of the self-tormenting God, Jeffers cautiously narrows the gap between man and Nature. But he does not close it entirely.... [There is a] disparity between divine and human intention. God's torment is not "cruel," it is necessary to knowledge. Human perpetration of cruelty, however, is a different matter. Jeffers would have man suffer the pangs of tragic discovery but he would have him eschew the perversion of a pointless sadism.... (p. 99)

[The] important difference [is] to suffer "like a God, not a tortured animal," for this illumines the whole of Jeffers' scheme, revealing why the tortured animals are an elemental necessity to his negative didacticism. Man may suffer like God, but since man cannot become God, the tragedies of life are only a reflection of celestial tragedy; man's tortures are a dream in Nature, while God's tortures are "in earnest," meaningful, infinite. Within these relationships Jeffers reconciles his simultaneous love and hatred of violence: the "love" on the grounds that violence is a divine activity, the "hate" on the grounds that it is too often a human perversion. (p. 100)

By a devious path Christ comes to his traditional office; He interprets and evaluates pain and experience; He connects man and God. (p. 102)

From the opening of any of the narratives it is clear that Jeffers is deeply interested in the behavior of people whose passions are hasty and clumsy and whose experience is limited to rather elemental discoveries. I have somewhat arbitrarily assigned the term "primitivism" to this predilection. (p. 103)

In the work following *Californians* Jeffers set himself the task of creating characters as primitive as the country which his imagination urged his eyes to see.... Jeffers wanted his poetry to be of this age, while aimed at no age.... [He] told himself that his characters had to partake both of the permanent world of Nature and of the transient world of man.... Jeffers tried to [achieve this] by splitting most of his characters into dual symbols for the antitheses which preoccupied him: impotence and fecundity; decay and growth; decadence and primitivism. His characters behave *symbolically* like primeval savages but they fall *symbolically* into the snares of civilization. As bifocal symbols the inhabitants of his narratives achieve what he wanted them to, but all too often, lacking simple, human reality, they fail to convince the reader that they are characters. This is not so serious a flaw in poetry as it would be in prose but it is nevertheless a fault. (pp. 104-05)

Jeffers' adaptation [of Euripides' *Medea*] allows major shifts of emphasis. Medea, for whom Euripides apologized by saying that she behaves as no Greek woman would, in Jeffers' treatment becomes the primitive par excellence.... [The] tragedy develops from the contrast between her warmth, [Jason's] coldness; her naturalness, his opportunistic realism; her primitive spirit and his civilized urbanity. Where Euripides apologizes, Jeffers reveres. And so the play unfolds as the triumph of the primitive spirit over civilization.... (p. 115)

It is noteworthy that Jeffers' primitive characters seldom, however, triumph over *modern* civilization.... For, indeed, Jeffers, though a faithful primitivist in the long view, does not want primitivism to conquer civilization, but civilization to conquer itself. (p. 116)

Jeffers in an unusually compassionate mood told a world that was faltering toward war:

 I wish you could find the secure value,
 The all-heal I found when a former time hurt me to the
   heart,
 The splendor of inhuman things. . . .

The "all-heal" Jeffers came eventually to call "Inhumanism." . . . His expressed "hatred" derives from and is inseparable from his unexpressed "love" of man. . . . [This] is the touchstone to Inhumanism. (pp. 118-19)

Jeffers recommended . . . that man turn from himself to Nature, where he would find evidence of God. The idea and its peculiarly hard-hearted phrasing had clarified and set by 1927, when he published *The Women at Point Sur*. . . . (p. 120)

The doctrine has not manifested any essential change since 1927, although Jeffers has added density and widened the scope of its application. The doctrine, however, had an immediate effect on Jeffers' literary method. Beginning with *The Women at Point Sur,* he fashioned narratives to illustrate what happens to those who refuse to uncenter their minds from humanity. His masochistic religious intensity and his scientific materialism were pressed into

service so as to place man in the most alarming neurotic light. Incest became his particular symbol for man's self-consciousness.... The great wonder is that these narratives come off as well as they do. Yet they rise above vulgarity partly because the natural descriptions possess such somber beauty that a balance of sanity remains, and partly because the pathologic characters at times achieve such intensity that one is constrained to admire insanity itself. More pertinently, however, the narratives manage to acquire some dignity because Jeffers relates the violence of his characters and the failures of mankind to a plan of God. But "pattern" is a better word than "plan," for it is in the interplay of recurrent decay and resurgence that Jeffers observes divinity. (pp. 121-22)

The net for Jeffers is the symbol which permits man to correspond with all other manifestations of the universe. It is his *multum in parvo*. When he describes the involuntary nervous system (as in *Cawdor* and *Such Counsels You Gave to Me*) in such a way as to suggest that he is describing a solar system in a condition of vast, half-conscious somnolence, he is describing what he conceives as a quiddity common to both organic and inorganic existence. The reticulated nerves of the body, the passions, are the net which man is most aware of.... To allow oneself to surrender absolutely to the net of the nerves is, however, to lose touch with the corresponding net of stars. This is to love humanity rather than God.... (pp. 122-23)

Jeffers offers an escape to the individual, the rare individual presumably. He tells him to find the beauty of life by considering the universe wholly.... Nature, Jeffers suggests, can show the way to the Inhumanist's inner salvation by indicating the mutuality between man and the universe.... (pp. 125-26)

Most of Jeffers' work has focused on man's inability to abide by reason, but not the least rewarding of his poetry is that which portrays the potential nobility of life. The decent life is scarcely free from pain, but the pain is married to peace. And the peace derives from an awareness of belonging to a dignified order of things. (p. 129)

In these poems one is engaged by how different the tone is from that of the "bitter" poems. They celebrate a natural life characterized by perils and sadness but also by tenacity and purpose. And when one reconsiders the principle of reason in Inhumanism, one begins to sense that the whole construct is a thoroughly conventional one. (p. 130)

[In] considering what Jeffers recommends as the desirable life for modern man—the combination of reason and a proximity to Nature—one detects that Jeffers combines elements which are not ordinarily, and probably not easily, cohesive. He asks modern man to be both primitive and profoundly civilized at the same time. He asks him to denature his primitive instincts with civilized reasoning while he insists that he charge his civilization with primitive sensuousness. (p. 132)

To direct man toward a moral self by means of the wise, the solemn lessons of Nature: that has been Jeffers' life work. He has chosen to work with acid and a needlepointed stylus; he has beset his lines with crude, angry ornament, has disguised his message and been willing to squander hundreds of lines in febrile hyperbole in order to justify the admonitory lines. It has not been his nature to write in the convention of the humanist any more than it has been the nature of his times to encourage the convention. Nevertheless, beyond his fatalism, beyond his materialism, the God which Jeffers defines is the God who enhances and propagates life, human life. . . . (pp. 134-35)

Those who object to Jeffers' technique insist that his clambering lines result from an inability to achieve anything else. No doubt he has come to be pretty much committed to an informality. One should, however, remember that as a young man Jeffers achieved a certain metrical virtuosity. *Californians* contains examples of *terza rima,* Spenserian stanzas, and very regular iambic pentameter. And if some of his later conventional efforts are as uncomfortable as farm hands dressed in their Sunday best, there are also some fine sonnets and, upon rare occasions, a beautiful variation of the ballad form. . . . (p. 140)

Jeffers has not assumed a laxity in his mature work solely because of an inability to conform to the demands of regular meter and rhyme, but that as his artistic temperament set in the mold, precision of form became alien to much that he wished to say. We may observe the transition between the traditional prosody of *Californians* and the unconventional prosody of the later work in the poem *The Coast-Range Christ.* . . . [It] is in the emphasis of a prosody based on stress rather than on regular feet, and in the long line, that the nature of the transition lies. (p. 141)

There are lapses, to be sure, where no pattern seems to exist. When these occur at transitional points, such as shifting from one setting to another in the longer poems, I think the reader will find them, at worst, unimportant. But sometimes the lapses are unfortunate, for they leave the poetry embarrassingly suspended between passages of stridulous prose. This is to speak of Jeffers' metrical technique at its worst. To consider it at its best is to recognize that the heavy, sullen rhythm is a dimension of the dark, humorless tales. (pp. 141-42)

[Jeffers' enthusiasm] for the classics reveals itself not only in his adaptations of Greek themes but also in some of the elements of his style. In the middle work from *Cawdor* to *Such Counsels You Gave to Me* he experimented with a few of the devices which are the stock of classical epic: apostrophe, heroic simile, and a deliberately anacoluthic flexibility of syntax which encourages the impression that the poet is simultaneously involved in, and analytical of, a situation, or that a situation possesses a past value that is coeval with a present one. . . . But one suspects that most of Jeffers' classical mannerisms are accretions. They display his admiration for traditional artistry, but they do not always seem to belong in the verse. The least happy examples occur in the volumes between *The Women at Point Sur* (1927) and *Be Angry at the Sun* (1941), the period when Jeffers appears to have striven to capture the high seriousness of traditional tragedy. (pp. 142-43)

The power of Jeffers' language depends partly upon the immediacy of his direct description but in greater measure upon his faith in images. Like the Anglo-Saxon poets, with whom he shares this faith, Jeffers has produced some of the best metaphors and some of the worst. The worst derive from his wish to describe people in terms of vast geographies or to describe impersonal objects in animate terms. . . . His best images reflect his desire to freeze to a standstill the running beauty of natural things; they are embedded sparingly in the matrix of simple language. (p. 145)

[To] arrive at a full appreciation of Jeffers' style, it is necessary to educe his faith in "permanency." This faith relates to the primitivism in his philosophic Inhumanism; in his poetry it is expressed in the repeated symbol of stone. And it comes to the surface as a formal literary creed [in which Jeffers states that poetry must concern itself with permanent things]. . . . I think that this signifies that Jeffers elected to write in the pastoral tradition. If his characters are not purely primitive, they nevertheless inhabit a scene which is purely natural. (pp. 148-49)

By the time he had written *The Women at Point Sur* (1927), Robinson Jeffers had consolidated his experience and he ceased to receive any essentially new insights; what was factually new he tended to file away with what was imaginatively established. For better or worse he had forged a fictive attitude which, though it was in part the result of experience, has since tyrannized his subsequent experience. The attitude, by no means simple, may be described in a general way as a simultaneously sardonic and elegiac melancholy. (pp. 153-54)

It seems evident that the restrictions of Jeffers' elegiac mood are too severe to foster a broad understanding of character such as narrative or dramatic poetry requires. And this indeed is the primary restriction upon Jeffers' ability as a storyteller. Because he himself tends to see things in a light of resigned sadness, he thinks also that this is the way his characters ought to come to see them. One can put up with a single Hamlet in a play—three or four are troublesome. . . . There is a greater difficulty: Jeffers' omnipresent doctrine of Inhumanism which, as an injunction to avoid those very passions which underlie tragedy, is hostile to spontaneity in character. It is true that of all his "tragic" characters only Orestes and Lazarus are absolutely Inhumanists; nevertheless, the doctrine itself haunts the narratives; if the characters do not assail their own "human" natures, Jeffers by interpolation does it for them. (pp. 154-55)

Jeffers' sometimes clumsy, sometimes felicitous acknowledgment of Renaissance drama and his efforts to rework Greek drama suggest that in his own mind he wished to acknowledge both traditions by blending the Greek conception of an abstract fate with the Renaissance conception of a psychological fate. Either of these is potentially rich in dramatic situations, but together they are burdensome. . . . [In] being so exorbitant, the determinism gravely weakens dramatic possibilities. When to this inordinate determinism is added Jeffers' doctrine of Inhumanism, the dramatic possibilities at the level of character all but vanish. (pp. 157-58)

Jeffers' narratives are the diary of disparate phantoms who constitute a sensibility at war with itself. Excepting *Roan Stallion,* they all take on the lineaments of an inner debate which derives its puissance from the discernment of a discrepancy between the laws of God and the laws of man. (pp. 165-66)

[Only] his adaptation of the *Medea* realizes Jeffers' own aim in tragedy as "poetry . . . beautiful shapes . . . violence." And this only because of the organic simplicity that Euripides imposes on Jeffers' restive imagination—an imagination which, when free to follow its own bent, is hardly capable of producing a stageable drama. Almost everywhere else in Jeffers' poetry the contentions grind against each other, reducing human character to dust, destroying those very structures and relationships which recommend themselves as essential to narrative and dramatic success. . . . Yet even after such a large loss, something large remains, and if we do not minimize this remainder, we see that it is poetry. (pp. 166-67)

Although the ultimate psychological effect of Jeffers' narratives is that of the insular soul warring within itself, it is also true that there is a public aspect to the poetry. The poetry is engaged with society to the extent that it takes up an isolated position which assaults society; it is not engaged to the extent that it enters society in order to criticize it. (p. 170)

Intense, almost anarchistic personal freedom; the loose structure, the vigor and audacity of the frontier republic: these are meaningful political conditions to Jeffers. But he believes we have passed beyond the period which produces these as the accidents of growth. (pp. 172-73)

Because Robinson Jeffers has consistently rejected the idea of an infinitely progressing America, he has generally been considered the reversal of Whitman's "dream." (p. 173)

As his interest in, and knowledge of, science grew, science itself became one of his instruments for attacking the humanistic tradition. It is not therefore very astonishing that his use of science has been attacked by humanists. (p. 178)

[One] need only consider the injunction of Jeffers' Inhumanism, the injunction to turn voluntarily from passion, to realize that whatever claims matter has upon man, his will, according to Jeffers, remains free. . . . Jeffers' narratives proceed on the grounds of an emancipated will, and while he may essay to describe the biochemical storms which surround, let us say, the emotions of love or anger, these storms do not of necessity supersede the will. (p. 185)

[God "comes and goes" in Jeffers' work], renewing himself infinitely, but if he "is not to be found in death," then Jeffers' conception of God is separate from his view of Nature; then Jeffers' conception of God is not finally pantheistic, even though for most purposes it is convenient and proper so to describe it. In the pinches, his God retreats from Nature, from death, and becomes a "spirit," hidden in the interstellar, or perhaps interatomic, spaces where the Epicurean gods reposed. This conception might underlie the symbolical implications of Jeffers' use of the word "desert." The desert in verse of the romantic tradition often symbolizes spiritual drought or the absence of God. . . . Jeffers' symbolic use of the desert runs counter to this tendency, and one is tempted to believe that if his God escapes the limitations of matter, which constrain all else, by dwelling in emptiness, it is appropriate that the desert should emerge as the symbol not of spiritual drought but of spiritual fullness. (pp. 189-90)

The "soul's desert" is the password to peace, but by reason of the idealist dilution of his materialism Jeffers has never been able to achieve [a] profoundly sane and dignified peace. . . . Only after burning and humiliation can Jeffers find God in the desert. But what the reader of poetry, or the reader who is interested in the destiny of man, can discover is that in Jeffers' work the first major poetic attempt to bring the split of the modern world together in a primarily materialistic vision has been made. (p. 190)

Radcliffe Squires, in his The Loyalties of Robinson Jeffers *(copyright © by the University of Michigan, 1956), University of Michigan Press, 1956.*

RUBY COHN

A contemporary of Stevens and Frost, Jeffers differs from them in his long free lines and his unrelieved solemnity. Though he turned to dialogue more often than they did, it was originally with no thought of theatrical performance. Only his *Medea* (1946) was specifically intended for the stage. . . . Besides *Medea,* Jeffers wrote five poems in dialogue form, all of them subsequently performed.

The Tower Beyond Tragedy is Jeffers' version of the *Oresteia.* Divided into three parts, the dramatic poem is faithful only to the surface events of Aeschylus. (p. 231)

In [his] conclusion, images are confusing, but Jeffers' approbation for Orestes is unmistakable. Jeffers himself explained his intention: "Orestes, in the poem, identifies himself with the whole divine nature of things; earth, man, and stars, the mountain forest and the running streams; they are all one existence, one organism. He perceives this, and that himself is included in it, identical with it. This perception is his tower beyond the reach of tragedy; because, whatever may happen, the great organism will remain forever immortal and immortally beautiful. Orestes has 'fallen in love outward,' not with a human creature, nor a limited cause, but with the universal God."

Though Jeffers was to write more speakable dialogue, he was not to modify the long, image-strewn lines, spoken by towering characters. . . . Cassandra's prophecies are tedious in their generalizations of doom . . . ; Electra and Orestes regurgitate Freud. The determined loftiness of *The Tower Beyond Tragedy* robs its dialogue of humanity, but then Inhumanism came to be Jeffers' creed.

Nevertheless, Jeffers' next dramatic poem, *Dear Judas* (1929), exhibits his most sustained concern for mere human beings, even though Jesus, Mary, and Judas are hardly typical human beings. Jeffers himself thought that his play imitated the Japanese Noh form, in which ghosts at a haunted place re-enact their lives and deaths. However, Jeffers' re-enactment is heavily verbal, lacking the grace of the Noh's culminating dance. . . .

Since Jesus uses many biblical phrases, and Mary sounds like an unusually self-effacing Jewish mother, Judas carries the burden of Jeffers' rhetoric and imagery, in his usual long uneven lines. . . . (p. 232)

Neither quite Christian in theme nor quite Noh in form, *Dear Judas* is exceptional in Jeffers' canon because of the sympathy for small human emotions—particularly those of Judas and Mary. In spite of Jeffers' rhetorical monologues, gratuitous images, and final didacticism, individual moments achieve a dramatic interplay which reappears nowhere in Jeffers' work.

The very titles *At the Fall of an Age* (1931) and *At the Birth of an Age* (1935) indicate the complementary nature of Jeffers' next two dramatic poems. . . . Both poems are steps along Jeffers' Inhumanist way—a kind of latter-day Stoicism in which man redeems himself by objectifying his experience and viewing it in the light of inhuman durability.

In *At the Fall of an Age*, this Inhumanist view is espoused by the dead Achilles and his Myrmidons. (pp. 233-34)

Jeffers proceeded to express the oppressive symbolism of

rocks, sun, stars, and wild animals in non-dramatic poems which can accommodate them better.... [His next play was an adaptation of Euripedes' *Medea*.] Predictably, Jeffers viewed the Greek tragic heroine as a woman of elemental passions whose violence should teach us to rise above mere human emotion.

Since Euripides' Medea is already a creature of large passions, Jeffers emphasizes this through imagery which derives from fire, water, minerals, and above all animals. (pp. 234-35)

In the context of Jeffers' work, we suspect that he admires his psychopathic heroine, who knows none of the womanly weakness of the Euripidean character. And yet the lush lines root her strength in the psychopathology of sadism. Hell hath no fury like a woman scorned, and Jeffers savors that fury, rewarding her finally with stars that do not scorn her. (p. 236)

Jeffers uses myth to illustrate his Inhumanism—his view that man's grandeur lies in his stubborn and Stoic resistance to the petty ills and delights that flesh is heir to. Man achieves greatness only if he can view himself in the light of the inhuman—mountains and oceans, redwoods and boulders, hawks and lions. Though this rather puerile philosophy furnishes Jeffers with his rhythms and images, it is not only antipathetic to the modern temperament which tends to focus on the human, but it is antipathetic to dramatic form, whose imagery must be integrated into theater, whose rhythm must be spoken by actors. A nostalgia for poetic drama and thirst for operatic acting may explain the awe that greeted production of *Medea*, but today Jeffers' dramatic and undramatic poetry is most instructive as negative example.... (pp. 236-37)

> *Ruby Cohn, "Robinson Jeffers," in her* Dialogue in American Drama *(copyright © by Indiana University Press), Indiana University Press, 1971, pp. 231-37.*

FREDERIC I. CARPENTER

On March 3, 1941, Robinson Jeffers read from his poetry to a large audience in Emerson Hall, Harvard University. The room seated four hundred, but many more crowded the halls outside. The next day I drove Jeffers to visit Emerson's Concord and Walden Pond, and in conversation inquired the title of his next book. "Beyond Good and Evil," he replied; and when I did not hear well, he added: "Nietzsche." Nine months later his new book bore the title, *Be Angry at the Sun;* and on December 7 Pearl Harbor exploded.

At that time the incident did not seem very important. The title poem of the new volume translated the Nietzschean idea into poetic language, while it recalled the German of Spengler (mentioned in another poem), whose *Untergang des Abendlandes* announced the setting sun of all Western civilization. But after Pearl Harbor the new volume seemed almost treasonous: one poem coupled Roosevelt with Hitler as equal instigators of the new world war.... (p. 86)

Now more than a generation later, 1941 looms as a watershed in American history. But it also marks a watershed in the history of Jeffers's reputation. In March, 1941, his popularity had reached its highest point (although some critics had been denouncing him since the publication of *The Women at Point Sur* in 1927). But after Pearl Harbor

his attempts to argue that "The cause is far beyond good and evil,/ Men fight and their cause is not the cause," effectively destroyed his reputation. At the very moment when Americans most needed to believe in the absolute goodness of their cause, Jeffers denied them. And when he refused to describe their arch-enemy Hitler as absolutely evil, they called him fascist.

From 1941 until his death in 1962, Jeffers's reputation suffered eclipse.... But beginning with the poet's death in 1962, a gradual reversal set in, causing his reputation to increase. Now in 1977 a new publisher ... has reissued three of his least popular volumes (*The Women at Point Sur, Dear Judas,* and *The Double Axe*).... (pp. 86-7)

[The worst of the volumes, *The Double Axe*,] certainly deserves reprinting, because the second of its narrative poems, "The Inhumanist," has always been recognized as a thoughtful and original philosophic poem. But "The Love and the Hate," which introduces the volume, has been condemned from the beginning.

"The Love and the Hate," on rereading, seems almost as bad as when first published. The story of the young soldier who returns from the dead to confront and kill the father who had sent him out to die in World War II remains both unbelievable and repulsive. But after rereading, the emotions of alienation and hatred which the poem projected seem to have been realized in the experiences of veterans of the Vietnam War. Recent novels and plays dealing with prisoners of that war who have returned verify the emotions which Jeffers had imagined a generation before. Although sometimes a bad poet, Jeffers was usually a good prophet.

The second volume of poetry now reprinted, *Dear Judas*, seems to me the best. The conflicts are always believable, and the poetry sometimes achieves magnificence. (p. 92)

The Women at Point Sur is the last of the volumes now reprinted, and the most controversial. It is the most complex, and in many ways the most interesting. Antoninus calls it "the most difficult and forbidding of all his poems," yet believes it to be his best. When first published in 1927, its extremes of plot and emotion so shocked many readers that they rejected it, while some turned against the poet entirely. Fifty years later we may confront the problems which it created.

The plot is simple and stark: a Christian minister renounces his faith and proclaims that "what was wrong's right, the old laws are abolished/ ... there is nothing wicked. What the heart desires, or any part of the body / That is the law." To symbolize his apostasy he commits incest with his daughter, April. Then in the second half of the poem he leads his demented followers through episodes of mounting violence and perversion, until at the end he lies down "in the mouth of the black pit." The plot illustrates the total destruction which results from the total denial of moral law. And the first part of the narrative develops this plot logically, with passages of magnificent poetry. (p. 93)

In the second half of *The Women*, Jeffers "suspends what Freud called the censor"—and I, for one, cannot follow him. But others may. And certainly there exists a strange kind of illogic in madness.... The point is that the archetypal plot-patterns of *Tamar* and *The Women at Point Sur* follow a different logic from that of Aristotelian tragedy or of narrative realism. They go beyond the human laws of good and evil to imagine the timeless patterns of inhuman nature. And in so doing they enter the realm of myth. (p. 94)

In all his mature poetry Jeffers sought to explore the realm beyond good and evil. In *The Women at Point Sur* his Barclay specifically announced this purpose. But in this realm there are no roads or reasons, and half-way through this poem Jeffers proclaimed that "these here have gone mad." In their belief that they could live beyond evil, these characters became alienated from the world of reason and law. And this is the fate of all who believe that to go beyond evil means to deny the reality of evil. Barclay proclaimed that there is no evil. . . . (p. 95)

Obviously this extremism is absurd. . . . In *The Women* he put this extreme statement in the mouth of his Barclay, then emphasized that it resulted in madness, and finally dramatized the destruction that it produced. But the emotional intensity with which he realized his characters, and the poetic eloquence with which he described their actions, have tended to make the absurd seem almost reasonable and the evil seem almost acceptable. After *The Women*, therefore, he wrote his "Apology for Bad Dreams" in a conscious attempt to make his own nightmares make sense.

The problem, I would suggest, is one of perspective. These poems literally describe bad dreams—but so vividly that the dreams seem to become realities. By suspending what Freud called the censor, these poems force the reader to realize that the impulses which civilization has repressed remain powerful. They still lurk below the level of consciousness, and if acted upon, result in evil. But his "Apology" warns that "it is not good to forget. . . ."

The world which Jeffers's poetry explores is not beyond evil, but beneath (or before) evil. . . . All his poems, in Santayana's phrase, "stir the sub-human depths of the spirit." They recall those impulses which primitive myth once celebrated, and which early civilization sometimes practiced (the early Pharaohs practiced royal incest), but which modern civilization has put down. Buried beneath the level of modern consciousness, these impulses still exist beneath evil, "at the muddy root of things." Only if the author fails to distinguish between the two realms do problems develop. Jeffers's early poetry had distinguished clearly: "for goodness and evil are two things and still variant, but the quality of life as of death and of light / As of darkness is one, one beauty . . ." ("Point Pinos and Point Lobos"). But his later poetry concerned itself more with the "one." (pp. 95-6)

Frederic I. Carpenter, "Robinson Jeffers Today: Beyond Good and Beneath Evil," in American Literature *(reprinted by permission of the Publisher; copyright 1977 by Duke University Press, Durham, North Carolina), March, 1977, pp. 86-96.*

\+   *   *

JORDAN, June   1936-

Jordan is an American poet, essayist, editor, and writer of children's books. She explores the black experience in Amer-ica in poetry noted for its ironic presentation of emotions ranging from rage to love, and from political to personal concerns. (See also *CLC*, Vol. 5, and *Contemporary Authors*, Vols. 33-36, rev. ed.)

JANET HARRIS

There's so much right about "Dry Victories"—the two characters, who are alive, funny, bitter, cool; the magnificent selection of photographs: slaves and cotton pickers, Congressmen and civil rights leaders, police clubs and hoses at Birmingham and a bombed church, a smiling Southern President and the casket of a Northern one, the whole pictorial history of three decades of hope, anguish, despair—that it's a shame the book isn't completely successful.

The fault here is that while the problems are stated clearly, the conclusions are hazy. Miss Jordan says voting isn't "where it's at"—that civil rights are meaningless without the "economic bases of freedom." Yet nowhere does she deal with the forces that have served to maintain, or at least permit poverty.

"Dry Victories" ends with the boys hoping that "parents and them other folk" will . . . "do something." But what has obstructed that "something," or what it should or could be, is never spelled out.

Janet Harris, "Dry Victories," in The New York Times Book Review *(© 1973 by The New York Times Company; reprinted by permission), February 11, 1973, p. 8.*

HAYDEN CARRUTH

June Jordan's selected poems ["Things That I Do in the Dark: Selected Poetry"] . . . fall into three classifications: political, personal and experimental. (p. 15)

Jordan's experimental impulses fall . . . into two varieties. One is technical, arty, formalistic, *avant-gardiste*, in the manner of the New York poets of the 1950's (of whom she was one). I don't mean her work isn't her own or sounds anything like Ashbery or even LeRoi Jones. . . . But the same self-conscious poeticizing is observable. One section of her book is called, for instance, "Towards a Personal Semantics," and it contains many poems of this sort. . . . They are full of polysyllabic abstractions, images pulled out of nowhere, themes that appear and disappear and never quite define themselves. Maybe these poems would be comprehensible if one heard the poet read them. . . . They do possess a cadential vigor, reinforced by excited, onrushing word associations, that might be effective if chanted in the manner of a black sermon, with antiphonal responses from the auditors. Perhaps then they would be lively and if not rationally then intuitively intelligible. But on the page they are the opposite—flat and murky.

Jordan's other variety of experimentalism may not be experimental at all, narrowly speaking. It is much less self-conscious, almost unconscious—spontaneous and natural [as in "Sunflower Sonnet Number Two"]. . . .

Supposing we could just go on and on as two
voracious in the days apart as well as when
we side by side (the many ways we do
that) well! I would consider then
perfection possible, or else worthwhile
to think about. Which is to say
I guess the costs of long term tend to pile
up, block and complicate, erase away
the accidental, temporary, near
thing/pulsebeat promises one makes
because the chance, the easy new, is there
in front of you. But still, perfection takes some sacrifice
　　of falling stars for rare.
　　And there are stars, but none of you, to spare.

[This is] a sonnet as surely as anything from Petrarch to
Cummings, with that unmistakable movement, that lyric
play. Yet it is changed. Notice the interpermeation of black
idiom, her own voice and literary English. What it produces
is not merely verbal effect but an augmentation of poetic
(human) feeling. (pp. 15, 35)

Even in free poems Jordan is best when she retains this hint
of tradition, working creatively, newly, with the span of
poetry. . . . Just as black musicians have changed, augmented and reformed Western music, making it functionally
their own without quite abandoning it, so Jordan and other
black poets are taking to themselves, rightly, the formal
impulse that was Shakespeare's, Wordsworth's, Browning's. But *taking* it, *commanding* it; not imitating it. (p. 35)

Hayden Carruth, "Politics and Love," in The
New York Times Book Review *(© 1977 by The
New York Times Company; reprinted by permis-
sion), October 9, 1977, pp. 15, 35.*

The proliferation of significant women poets is a fact, and
June Jordan is in the front ranks with such poets as Muriel
Rukeyser, Adrienne Rich, Ai, Alice Walker, and Diane
Wakoski, making major contributions. *Things That I Do in
the Dark* is Jordan's tenth book, a generous and representative selection of new and old poems. Many of the poems
are political, yet Jordan is too talented a writer to confuse
propaganda with art. Her work is informed by a vision that
is intensely original, and we can learn much about community and humanity from this book. (p. 10)

Virginia Quarterly Review *(copyright, 1978, by
the* Virginia Quarterly Review, The University of
Virginia), *Vol. 54, No. 1 (Winter, 1978).*

K

KESEY, Ken 1935-

Kesey, an American novelist and essayist, is best known for the novel *One Flew over the Cuckoo's Nest*. His narratives generally center around the conflict of a strong individual pitted against a society he finds limiting and dehumanizing. Kesey's counter-culture life style has been chronicled in Tom Wolfe's *The Electric Kool-Aid Acid Test*. Both *Sometimes a Great Notion* and *One Flew over the Cuckoo's Nest* have been adapted for film. (See also *CLC*, Vols. 1, 3, 6, and *Contemporary Authors*, Vols. 1-4, rev. ed.)

TERENCE MARTIN

When Randle Patrick McMurphy swaggers into the cuckoo's nest, brash, boisterous, with heels ringing off the floor "like horseshoes," he commands the full attention of a world held crazily together in the name of adjustment by weakness, fear, and emasculating authority.... When, six weeks later, he hitches up his Moby Dick shorts for the final assault on the Big Nurse and walks across the floor so that "you could hear the iron in his bare heels ring sparks out of the tile," ... he dominates a world coming apart at the seams because of strength, courage, and emerging manhood. As Chief Bromden says (repeatedly)—he has made others big.

The early McMurphy has a primitive energy, the natural expression of his individualism. And in the manner of the solitary hero his freedom and expansiveness come from being unencumbered. He has "no wife wanting new linoleum. No relatives pulling at him with watery old eyes. No one to *care* about, which is what makes him free enough to be a good con man." ... The later McMurphy, however, is thoroughly encumbered with the shrunken men on the ward, committed to a desperate struggle for *their* manhood.... (p. 43)

Women in the novel, one comes to see quickly, are powerful forces of control. They represent a sinister contemporary version of a feminist tradition in American literature that goes back, at least, to Dame Van Winkle and that percolates through the popular fiction of the nineteenth-century in the form of domestic tyranny.... Given the highly charged vision of *One Flew Over the Cuckoo's Nest,* female authority becomes non-domestic, hard, insistently emasculating.

Not all of the women are cast in the mould of the Big Nurse. Harding's wife, for example, is a bitch of the first order, whose visit to the hospital shows us all that Harding must overcome in himself as a prerequisite to overcoming something in her. Her remarks are guaranteed to make Harding fall back on defenses whose very existence she scorns.... If her visit suggests how Harding came to be in the hospital, it spells out even more clearly why he is afraid to leave.

In a different way Billy Bibbit's mother denies him the chance to become a man.... Billy, on a comfortable day, talks about looking for a wife and going to college. His mother tickles his ear with dandelion fluff and tells him he has "scads of time" left for such things. When Billy reminds her that he is thirty-one years old, she replies, "*Sweet*heart, do I look like the mother of a middle-aged man?" (pp. 44-5)

Chief Bromden, too, knows of female dominance. His Indian father took his white wife's name when they married and suffered a diminishment of self ever after.... The female reduced the male—the white reduced the Indian. The Chief has only to think of his parents to know the legacy of his people.

Only McMurphy stands outside such woman-power. His name, with its patronymic, identifies him as the son of Murphy, not of Mrs. Murphy.... His latter day companions, Candy and Sandy, function both to emphasize his manhood and to measure the progress of the patients toward regaining (or finding) theirs. Drawn from the stock pattern of the fun-loving, "good" whore, Candy and Sandy evoke attitudes of freedom and openness rather than of restraint and confinement. Whereas the Big Nurse would make men little, they would make men big.

Matriarchy in *One Flew Over the Cuckoo's Nest* comes ... to be expressed in various forms of female tyranny.... But its primary force and motive is to make men be little boys, to make them (want to) adjust to a role wherein lies safety.... [For example, when Big Nurse] finds Billy Bibbit with Candy, she shatters his new-found sense of manhood by wondering how Billy's mother will take the news. Billy wilts immediately; stuttering once again, he disavows affection and friendship, and the Big Nurse leads him into the office, "stroking his bowed head and saying 'Poor little boy, poor little boy'." ... After which Billy commits suicide, unable to become a man and be jerked back to boyhood all in the space of a few hours.

At Miss Ratched's disposal are the three black orderlies (hired for their hatred), the Shock Shop, and the final measure of lobotomy. With their thermometer, their giant jar of vaseline, and their blood knowledge of rape and injustice, the orderlies make women out of men, just as the Shock Therapy machine turns men docile and lobotomy converts even the most unruly into Fully Adjusted Products. These are weapons of terror, dedicated to the proposition that the best man is a good boy. It is small wonder that the patients on the ward seek the relative safety of boyhood and allow themselves to be ruled by stern or selfish non-mothers who, like cuckoo-birds, have no instinct for building nests of their own. (pp. 45-6)

In such a world McMurphy, the epitome of raw, unvarnished maleness, represents all the Big Nurse needs to control. As the contours of the narrative take form, the bigger-than-life McMurphy and the bigger-than-life Miss Ratched come to be opposed in every way. He is the stud, she the "ball-cutter"; he is the brawler, she the manufacturer of docility; he is the gambler, she the representative of the house—where chance has no meaning.

The opposition between McMurphy and the Big Nurse goes to the very center of the novel, to the perception of Chief Bromden. Whenever the Big Nurse seems in indisputable control, the fog machine churns out its mist, scary, safe, and scary again. When McMurphy wins a skirmish, the fog disappears and the Chief sees clearly. (p. 46)

As part of the Chief's mode of perception, the fog machine is a metaphor for tyranny, fear, and hiding which becomes literalized in his narrative. (p. 47)

Machinery, made by the Combine for the benefit of people who choose to live under the Combine, drove Chief Bromden's people away from nature into a world not their own. . . . Machinery, associated with authority, with the ward, with Miss Ratched, represents all that brings people into line. . . . The sound of *Ratched* is virtually indistinguishable from that of *ratchet,* with its associations of machinery and distaff. And *combine,* as Raymond M. Olderman points out, carries with it the idea of "a mechanism, a machine that threshes and levels." The experience in the cotton mill mediates between the Chief's early days with his people and his paranoid existence on the ward; his life, cut into pieces by machinery, has a frightening coherence. (pp. 47-8)

The strategy of literalizing metaphors . . . lends force and credence to the world the Chief sees and presents to us. . . . And the Chief, as we know, has become literally deaf and dumb to the world because the world has treated him *as if* he could not speak and could not hear.

The words *big* and *little* likewise take on special meaning because of the Chief's literalizing vision. When McMurphy first shakes hands with Chief Bromden "the fingers were thick and strong closing over my own, and my hand commenced to feel peculiar and went to swelling up out there on my stick of an arm, like he was transmitting his own blood into it. It rang with blood and power. It blowed up near as big as his, I remember." . . . And so at the beginning—at a time when the Chief is helpless and little in a chair—we have an anticipation of the end: McMurphy's

vital power will flow into Chief Bromden and make him big, at a cost terribly high and terribly necessary. (p. 48)

[McMurphy's] name not only proclaims his paternity but suggests the brawling Irishman of fiction and fact. Moreover, the *sounds* of McMurphy pervade Kesey's novel. . . . [The] Chief hears McMurphy before he sees him, and he "sounds big." He comes into the ward laughing—"free and loud"; it is the first laugh the Chief has heard "in years." (pp. 48-9)

McMurphy's laughter and singing, his tall biographical tales, and the authentic ring of his idiom at once dominate the ward and define him to the other patients. His example, of course, evokes the choked off manhood of the men on the ward and a sense of freedom they have forgotten, or not known. (p. 49)

[McMurphy inspires community] laughter . . . , comic, aware, the signature of a deep experience, the expression of freedom—earned and shared. The fishing expedition, brilliantly handled by Kesey, accentuates the growing sense of community among the patients. (pp. 49-50)

[McMurphy] has much to learn about his new situation beyond the fact of matriarchal authority. He is, at first, what he has always been, the con man, the gambler in search of new territory; and he has managed to get himself committed to avoid the regimen of the work farm. Characteristically, he seizes the opportunity to bet on his ability to outmaneuver the Big Nurse. . . .

McMurphy goes through two other stages in the course of the novel, both the result of increasing awareness. From the lifeguard at the swimming pool he learns the difference between being *sentenced* and being *committed.* He realizes for the first time that he will be released only when the Big Nurse approves a release for him. (p. 50)

[Immediately he begins] playing the game, playing it safe—"getting cagey," the way "Papa finally did." At one time the Chief's father used to poke fun at the government men, speaking to them dead-pan like a stage Indian addressing tourists—to the great amusement of his Council. Like McMurphy, Chief Bromden's father learned to play it smart. The other patients on the ward understand about McMurphy; they are not angry or even disappointed. But there is a fearful cost to McMurphy's decision to think of Number One: Cheswick, who has achieved a certain momentum toward manhood, gets caught in the drain the next time they are at the swimming pool and drowns well before McMurphy, the lifeguard, and the orderlies can bring him to the surface.

McMurphy has one staggering fact left to learn. It astonishes him into meditative silence, then catapults him into his final role of savior. He hears from Harding that only a few of the patients on the ward, indeed, in the whole hospital, are committed. The great majority are there voluntarily, because, as Billy Bibbit says sobbingly, they don't have the guts to be Outside. . . .

Direct violations of the Big Nurse's private office, symbolic sexual assaults, are only the beginning. McMurphy, aware now of what *committed* means, aware, too, that the frightened men on the ward are there voluntarily, and aware, further, that he cannot defeat the Big Nurse and all that is behind her—even as he could not lift the control panel—begins to act for the others rather than for himself.

Before McMurphy arrived, the patients were set against each other in the name of therapy and adjustment. . . . McMurphy once says . . . "All I know is this: nobody's very big in the first place, and it looks to me like everybody spends their whole life tearing everybody else down." . . . It is a central insight for the unsophisticated McMurphy— and one of the truest and most generally applicable statements in the novel. (p. 51)

Kesey, in masterful control of the fully activated materials in his novel, takes his madhouse men one last inevitable step, to an achieved sense of community. (pp. 51-2)

The men on the fishing trip and at the party are a far cry from the little boys who spied on each other and tattled in the Big Nurse's log book. No longer do they *tear* each other down. . . . The language of the novel virtually insists that we see McMurphy as a kind of Christ figure . . . : "Do I get a crown of thorns?" . . ., doling out his life so that others may live. The action of the novel dramatizes the manner in which he makes his sacrifices, amid doubts and rejoicings on the part of his followers. . . . [McMurphy's legacy is] manhood, friendship suffused with affection, and, finally, love. (p. 52)

The specific make-up of the Combine remains vague, as indeed it must, since the word *combine* is not simply a synonym for *organization,* since it is the Chief's protean metaphor for all that mechanizes, threshes, and levels—for all that packages human beings into "products." In this sense, the idea of a Combine contributes powerfully to the dramatic coherence of the novel. (p. 53)

[The Combine is also] recognizably, the world of our suburbs and sub-divisions, standardized, mechanized, virtually anesthetized. . . . Again the Chief faces a world of threshed out sameness; but he brings to it [after McMurphy's influence] . . . a sense of possibility which enlarges the dimensions of his spirit. The Combine, of course, continues to adjust things. But things may be increasingly adjusted . . . because they are increasingly adjustable—which means . . . that the Combine's power to control may exist in ratio to our willingness to forfeit manhood.

One Flew Over the Cuckoo's Nest directs our attention to such a point: we have surrendered a sense of self, which, for Kesey, is involved with a sense of space—and thus possibility. . . . To lose the *sense* of space is to be confined . . . to contribute to the encroaching power of the Combine.

And so Kesey gives us McMurphy, the advocate of our manhood who brings a sense of space, freedom, and largeness onto the ward as something co-existent with his life. (pp. 53-4)

The men on the Big Nurse's ward become stronger once they recognize their inter-dependence. . . . *One Flew Over the Cuckoo's Nest* is an intense statement about the high cost of living—which we must be *big* enough to afford. (p. 55)

Terence Martin, "'One Flew Over the Cuckoo's Nest' and the High Cost of Living," in* Modern Fiction Studies *(© copyright 1973 by Purdue Research Foundation, West Lafayette, Indiana), Spring, 1973, pp. 43-55.

ROBERT FORREY

[There] seems to me to be part of an unfortunate trend among male critics to overpraise [*One Flew Over the Cuckoo's Nest,*] a novel which may be conservative, if not reactionary, politically; sexist, if not psychopathological, psychologically; and very low, if not downright lowbrow, in terms of the level of sensibility it reflects, a sensibility which has been influenced most strongly not by the Bible or a particular literary tradition as much as by comic books, particularly the Captain Marvel variety. (pp. 222-23)

Despite the fact that it became a favorite of the counter culture in the sixties, Kesey's *One Flew Over the Cuckoo's Nest* may actually be much more representative of the older, alcoholic, he-man, rather than the newer, drug, hippie culture. . . . Like Hemingway and Steinbeck before him, Kesey presents as ideals in his first novel the arrogantly masculine ones of drinking, whoring, hunting, and gambling. Kesey is also in the tradition of Hemingway and Steinbeck in depicting his hero as a masculine Christ whom the conspiring world of weak-kneed men and bitchy women try to emasculate. In Hemingway and Steinbeck the Christ analogy is handled with a degree of restraint, but in Kesey it is unabashedly spelled out. Randall Patrick McMurphy's initials are not J. C., as with some of Steinbeck's feisty Christ figures, but he wears a crown of thorns and is crucified for his *machismo* far more explicitly than even Jim Casy or the fisherman Santiago.

The apparent menace to manhood in *One Flew Over* is the Combine, a vague and insidious ruling power which conspires against all who oppose it. The major symbol of the Combine is the machine and Kesey draws on two of the meanings of the noun "combine." A "combine" is, in informal usage, a group of people united for some monopolistic purpose; and also, of course, it is a harvesting machine. In choosing the machine as the central metaphor of oppression, Kesey follows a major literary tradition. . . . Almost always, however, the machine has been viewed as masculine in character. This makes sense because industrial society has been created by men. It is a man's world. But in his novel Kesey identifies the machine with the female. "Big Nurse," the villainess of *One Flew Over,* is a machine-like, castrating female. Her name, Ratched, means a toothed gear wheel in a threshing machine—i.e., a combine. McMurphy understands that the Big Nurse is not the solicitous mother figure she pretends to be but is "'a ball-cutter,'" "'tough as knife metal.'" . . .

Almost all the men in Kesey's imaginary mental hospital have been done in, if not actually committed by, women. (pp. 223-24)

Women have robbed the men in the novel of their masculinity so that they are nothing more than an impotent brotherhood. "'There isn't a man here that isn't afraid he is losing or has already lost his whambam,'" Harding says, referring to their impotency. . . . *One Flew Over* was written from the point of view that man's problems are caused by woman who refuses to allow him to play the domineering role which nature intended him to play. The premise of the novel is that women ensnare, emasculate, and, in some cases, crucify men. The only good women in the novel are two whores who good-naturedly accept their role as sex objects and a Japanese nurse who is powerless to oppose the domineering bitches who control the men.

The Big Nurse is the biggest bitch. She pretends to be interested only in the welfare of the patients, but her real purposes are rather sinister. She refuses to allow the male patients to do anything which might remind them that they are still men. Not only does she forbid them to drink, whore, and gamble; she also rations their cigarettes and denies them the opportunity to watch the world series on television. All of these activities, as much as we may joke about them, have a sacramental value to males, or at least to red-blooded males, and no one understands their importance better than the randy hero of the novel, Randall Patrick McMurphy. By denying these sacraments of masculinity to the men, the Big Nurse succeeds in keeping them in line (at least until McMurphy arrives on the ward). Even the male doctor, who tends to sympathize with the male patients, is afraid of her because he is a drug addict who lives in fear of losing his job. The woman in charge of hiring and firing at the hospital is a good friend of the Big Nurse. Consequently, all the males on the hospital ward are under the Big Nurse's thumb, except perhaps for the black attendants who enjoy a special status. They work hand in glove with the Big Nurse against the white patients.

Since in the sixties the two major challenges to the rule of white American males came from blacks and women, it may be significant that the Big Nurse's closest allies are three black attendants. Specially picked and trained by her for their tasks, they are as cruel and sinister as those dark-skinned harpooners Ahab enlisted as accomplices to help kill the white whale, symbol of God and the phallus, according to some critics. The white whales on McMurphy's colorful underwear crudely underscore his identification with leviathan. (pp. 224-25)

Only when McMurphy arrives on the ward do the Big Nurse and her black attendants meet any opposition. A swashbuckling male, the Marlboro-smoking McMurphy challenges her because he has not yet been emasculated by women nor sexually intimidated by blacks. A bachelor and an ex-Marine who had fought in Korea, he has a devil with an M-1 rifle tatooed on one of his muscular shoulders and a poker hand tatooed on the other. Defying the tyranny of the Big Nurse as he had once defied his communist captors in a prison camp, McMurphy promotes gambling on the ward, organizes a basketball team among the patients, and undermines the authority of the Big Nurse in every way he can. Adapting Christian symbols and myths to his own novelistic purposes, Kesey characterizes McMurphy as a swaggering savior, a messiah of masculinity, erect and profane, shaking the matriarchal power structure. (p. 226)

Only gradually does McMurphy become aware of the dangers involved in standing up for the other patients, but with a martyr's zeal he refuses to back down or give up his struggle, even after he knows the worst.

As part of his crusade to make the male patients men again, McMurphy plans a fishing trip for them, getting special permission for the excursion from hospital authorities. Of course McMurphy also plans to do some drinking and whoring with two prostitutes he has invited along, thus making it all a quintessentially masculine experience. . . . The fishing trip itself is a huge success, with anything a real man, as Kesey defines manhood, could want—fishing, drinking, smoking, swearing, and whoring. If these are the important sacraments of the sexist tradition, McMurphy is the sexist savior, for Kesey obviously cast his story in terms of the life of Christ. "'Be a fisher of men,'" someone told McMurphy before he led his twelve patient-disciples to the sea. (pp. 226-27)

[Angrily ripping open the Big Nurse's uniform] is possibly McMurphy's most important act in the novel, for in exposing her breasts, he is also exposing her womanhood which she had been so careful to keep hidden. She cannot expect to dominate the men unless she can make them forget she is a woman, and her large breasts were a constant reminder to them that she was. By exposing her breasts to the patients, McMurphy destroys her authority.

The patients now know that she is just a woman—McMurphy had established that fact—and they begin to stand up for themselves. . . . Bromden's escape from the clutches of the Big Nurse is meant to carry great symbolic weight, for he represents the primitive male, the "Vanishing American," who was becoming a rare species. Ripping a machine up from the floor of the ward and tossing it out the window, Bromden makes his way to freedom and so, by extension, does the masculine spirit. The castrating Combine and the Big Nurses who run it have not been overthrown, but the eleven patients who escape will presumably keep McMurphy's lusty spirit alive, preaching the message that their oppressors are after all only women. (p. 228)

As Freud emphasized, feelings of paranoia and megalomania often stem from repressed homosexual impulses. *One Flew Over the Cuckoo's Nest* tries to suggest that this kind of psychoanalyzing is nonsense, that the problem is simply that men want to be men but women won't let them. Perhaps this is the case, but the thought persists that no psychologically informed reading of Kesey's novel can ignore the repressed homosexuality that seems to pervade it. Kesey himself was not unaware of this possibility, particularly in the relationship between McMurphy and Bromden which is presumably why the Indian at one point in the novel insists that his strong desire to touch McMurphy is not homosexually motivated. Perhaps Bromden is not latently homosexual. But if he and McMurphy and the other patients are, then what we have in Kesey's novel is yet another group of American males trying desperately to unite into a quasi-religious cult or brotherhood which will enable them to sublimate their homosexuality in violent athletic contests, gambling, or other forms of psychopathological horseplay. . . . Christ had warned that false prophets would come after him. We might add, so would psychopathic saviors. (pp. 229-30)

Robert Forrey, "Ken Kesey's Psychopathic Savior: A Rejoinder," in Modern Fiction Studies (© *copyright 1975, by Purdue Research Foundation, West Lafayette, Indiana), Summer, 1975, pp. 222-230.*

JAMES F. KNAPP

Literary critics have always found ways to contradict each other. . . . Consider two statements concerning Ken Kesey's *One Flew Over the Cuckoo's Nest:* according to Terrence Martin, "The men on the Big Nurse's ward become stronger once they recognize their interdependence. . . ." [see excerpt above], but W. D. Sherman says that "The kind of affirmation which arises from Kesey's novels is an anarchic 'yes' to life, which, despite its joyousness, leaves a man prey to unbearable isolation." Both observations ring true, and yet surely Kesey cannot be affirming a vital individualism, whose price is personal isolation, at the same time that he offers a vision of the necessity of inter-dependence and mutual brotherhood. (p. 398)

So we could attempt to decide whether Kesey's writing preach independence or inter-dependence, just as, presumably, he struggled to reconcile those two poles in his own mind. . . . [The counter-culture to which Kesey belonged felt that if] traditional images socialize traditionally, then *new* images might be found which would have the power to shape minds in *new* directions. Social change could be brought about through the simple, non-violent agency of "creative mythology": initiate a cultural revolution, and the rest will follow. (pp. 399-400)

One Flew Over the Cuckoo's Nest . . . depends heavily on the sort of critique of society which was being made throughout the serious media during the nineteen-fifties. America has become a lonely crowd of organization men, offering its alluence only to those who are willing to pay the price of strict conformity. (p. 400)

By choosing a mental hospital for his setting, Kesey was able to picture society's pressure to adjust at its most coldly, and explicitly, coercive. Identifying social evil with institutional constraints which hinder individuality, he proceeded to set a microcosmic revolution in motion by introducing a powerfully individual character. Randle McMurphy succeeds in destroying the order of the ward, and in liberating some of its patients, not through any kind of direct attack on the system, but simply by refusing to speak the language which sustains it. His most telling weapons are jokes, games, obscenity, make-believe, verbal disrespect. The patients have seen physical violence before, and been left unchanged by it. But when McMurphy violates that language which had marked out, invisibly, the social space of the ward, they begin to be freed of its power, begin to see that other patterns of relationship, other values might be possible. McMurphy's singing in the shower is disturbing and exciting precisely because it challenges that web of indirect, symbolic control through which the *voluntarily* committed patients have been made to choose their own oppression. Like a bawdy William Blake, McMurphy is a cultural revolutionary whose function it is to smash the "mind-forg'd manacles" of his time. (pp. 400-01)

In his second novel, *Sometimes A Great Notion*, Kesey had defined a similar set of oppositions. Setting a hero whose unpredictable independence passes all bounds of reason against a loggers' union whose members are plodding fools at best, Kesey affirms his opposition to institutional conformity—among workers no less than owners. His hero, Hank Stamper, sets out to undermine the strikers' position by supplying their mill with logs almost single-handedly, because he will not bow to group pressure—justified or not. In a gesture which becomes the central image for his defiance, he runs his father's severed arm up a flagpole, all its fingers but the middle one tied down. That act, which, paradoxically, destroys the dignity and authority of the union leader in the eyes of his men, is essentially an audacious, macabre *prank*. The point I would stress, however, is that in each of these cases, we are asked to identify with characters who set themselves in opposition to a world of stultifying, institutional conformity—whether Combine and hospital, or company suburb, or manipulative union. It was institutions such as these which came to be grouped together, during the sixties, under the label Establishment. From this point of view, Kesey is a decidedly "anti-Establishment" figure whose works, in life as well as in art, encouraged social change. (p. 402)

At this point, we might frame an argument something like this: though the counter-culture offered a fearsome appearance of change, it was in fact powerless, because a society cannot be changed simply by the symbolic magic of altering its myths. That is to say, cultural revolution is bunk. (p. 403)

Kesey himself was adept at drawing on the most traditional of images. . . . When he created a hero to break up the order of Big Nurse's ward, he made him in the mold of a thousand dime novels. . . . Nor is Hank Stamper, muscles rippling like steel cables, any exception to Kesey's image of the proper Western hero.

As Kesey conceived it, these frontier heroes must engage in acts which reveal their gritty, solitary fortitude. (pp. 404-05)

By adopting traditional metaphors such as these, Kesey invests his new experiments with the authority of a national history full of exploring. He can be traditional and revolutionary at the same time. In embracing the image of the pioneer, however, he invokes a body of tradition which has helped to sustain a deep continuity within the American experience. (p. 405)

For Kesey, nature was an alien presence that must be transformed by the arts of civilization before it could serve a human purpose. His aim was not to build the mines and mills and cities of the earlier dreamers, but his starting point, like theirs, was the assumption that nature must be mastered by human technology. One consequence of such an attitude has been the enormous physical transformation of the continent, but the full implications of the myth must be understood. When a part of the world was marked as alien territory, that label sanctioned the mastery of everything beyond the frontier—including the people. (pp. 406-07)

In *Cuckoo's Nest*, for instance, the service station attendant only exists to be badgered into submission, the charter boat captain to be outwitted, the psychiatrist to be used, Big Nurse to be defeated by any means possible. Nor are we allowed to feel any real sympathy for the self-pitying, blustering, diarrhetic, athlete's-foot-ridden union men of *Sometimes A Great Notion*. Against such backgrounds, the Kesey hero (himself or his fictions) stands out all the more clearly as dynamic entrepreneur. . . . Kesey's work actually conveys the most traditional of messages: it is the right and the destiny of strong individuals to shape the world to their wills. . . .

But this essay began with the paradox that Kesey has been seen to affirm both independence and interdependence, and I am not quite ready to resolve that contradiction on the side of unqualified individualism. . . . There is a clear concern in each of these books for the problems of forging some kind of community in the face of a cold, alienating world. . . . [We] must set off into the heathen darkness, and build our holy city with ax and gun—or strobe light. But that is only part of the myth. Salvation cannot in fact be complete until Christ, as Second Adam, makes his sacrifice and offers a new pattern for human life. (pp. 408-09)

In *Cuckoo's Nest* [Kesey] creates a character who quite simply learns to be Christ. As McMurphy begins to feel a bond of sympathy for his fellow patients he comes to their aid at increasing cost to himself. Publicly failing to lift a heavy control panel he seems to say: I am mortal like you, but I am not afraid to commit myself. Smashing Big Nurse's window, he cuts himself badly, but restores the spirit of the ward. And when he forgoes his self-interested good behavior to defend another man, and so faces the punishment of shock treatment, he consciously identifies himself with Christ: "They put the graphite salve on his temples. 'What is it?' he says. 'Conductant,' the technician says. 'Anointest my head with conductant. Do I get a crown of thorns?'"... Ultimately, McMurphy sacrifices his mind and then his life so that his brothers may be reborn out of the living death in which he had found them. (p. 410)

Setting himself against the cold impersonality of modern society, Kesey would create a new community based on self-sacrifice and mutual dependency. And yet his community would include only the elect, and, set in opposition to a world of outsiders he regards as unenlightened or downright evil, it would offer no vision of the larger, inclusive society. There was a kind of siege mentality about much of the counter-culture, and perhaps that had something to do with Kesey's attraction to this beleaguered warrior-Christ. But whatever the cause, he seems to embrace aggressive individualism one moment and self-sacrificing brotherhood the next, and the contradiction cannot be resolved because it is rooted in the only words he knew. Society's myths are always open to the movement of history.... But to consciously master so complex a process, to understand all the social messages being transmitted by any body of tradition, and to try to bend them to your own ambition—is to fly awfully close to the sun. Ken Kesey was a cultural revolutionary, all right, but the beast he sought to control had a mind subtler, and more willful, than he ever guessed. (pp. 411-12)

> *James F. Knapp, "Tangled in the Language of the Past: Ken Kesey and Cultural Revolution," in* The Midwest Quarterly *(copyright, 1978, by The Midwest Quarterly, Kansas State College of Pittsburg), Summer, 1978, pp. 398-412.*

*   *   *

KUNITZ, Stanley   1905-

An American poet, editor, essayist, translator, and journalist, Kunitz has been a critically neglected but important voice in contemporary poetry. His work is skillfully crafted, incorporating the rhythms of natural speech, and evidencing a fine ear for the musical cadence of phrases. Often considered metaphysical, his is an intensely personal poetry, exploring the mystery of self and the intricacies of time. Kunitz won a Pulitzer Prize in 1959 for *Selected Poems, 1928-1958.* **(See also** *CLC***, Vol. 6, and** *Contemporary Authors***, Vols. 41-44.)**

BABETTE DEUTSCH

[That sophisticated craftsman, Stanley Kunitz] can commence a lyric with a couplet that might have been composed by one of the metaphysicals: "Lovers relentlessly contend to be / Superior in their identity:". Elsewhere he manipulates a parenthesis with the skill of Cummings, introduces the subliminal imagery of Roethke, sets down public ignominy in a witty shorthand similar to Auden's. But his poems would not be mistaken for theirs. In one, written "for money, rage, and love", on the theft of his wallet in a Roman tram, he speaks of wearing his heart "less Roman than baroque", and indeed, he does not shrink from a grand extravagance of language. He is con-

cerned with the perennial themes of sexual love, death, and the self, and he is also alert to the shames of the century in which he explores these themes. There is a wide range in his work.... Like other inquisitors of the soul, Kunitz sometimes deals in obliquities and opacities. They are redeemed by the energy, by the anguished and pitiless honesty with which he confronts his life and whatever we share of it. (pp. 238-39)

> *Babette Deutsch, in her* Poetry in Our Time *(copyright by Babette Deutsch; 1963 by Doubleday; reprinted by permission of Babette Deutsch), revised edition, Doubleday, 1963.*

WILLIAM F. CLAIRE

[*A Kind of Order, A Kind of Folly*] represents the varied interests of a poet who first came to public attention with the traditionally thin volume of verse, *Intellectual Things*, in the 1920s. It has a freshness and a "kind of order, kind of folly" treatment of many contemporary events that is rarely found in a collection of previously published essays, random speeches, and remarks made for "occasional" situations. As a principal participant in the development of American verse since the twenties, [Kunitz] is obviously very knowledgeable about all significant trends since that time, and is also *au courant* with new poetic activities here and abroad....

Kunitz "keeps" himself contemporary in a way few older poets do, by reading and following younger writers.... Kunitz may be the only poet of his generation who truly knows what is going on among young poets, and his choices are worth considering....

All the Kunitz explorations, whether describing visits back to his roots in Worcester, Massachusetts, or discussing his views of contemporary painters (he has extremely close ties to the world of visual arts), seem interconnected in the "manifold tissue" of his deep humanistic understanding. In "Sister Arts," for example, he demonstrates the possibilities and the actual relationships that have existed between poets and painters through the years. He has no fear in dealing with a subject difficult to generalize about, and often, in the process, transforms his subject matter with brilliant insights and discoveries.

Taken together, this most readable collection represents a testament to one of our best poets, who realizes that "in the midst of this random and absurd universe, one must begin by affirming the value of one's own existence; but that the affirmation must not be too glib or too cheaply won; it must rise out of the wrestling with all that denies it, to the very point of negation." In his ability to affirm the value of his own existence and to share his views in a solidly organized volume of prose, Kunitz has amply demonstrated that he continues to move, as he stated recently, "toward a more expansive universe" and that he proposes to "take more risks" than ever before. (p. 598)

> *William F. Claire, in* The American Scholar *(copyright © 1976 by the United Chapters of Phi Beta Kappa; reprinted by permission of the publishers), Vol. 45, No. 4, Autumn, 1976.*

RICHARD VINE

For nearly half a century Mr. Kunitz has been giving us poems remarkable for their compactness and force. Now, in his seventieth year, he presents us with [*A Kind of Or-*

der, A Kind of Folly,] a collection of prose pieces which—being drawn from many times and many publications—might seem superficially to be too disparate to cohere an an organic whole, constituting one more bibliographically useful but experientially unsatisfying potpourri. But Mr. Kunitz is not a superficial writer, and he deserves more than a superficial response. "All the arts join in testifying that the order that interests the modern imagination is not a sequential order," he writes in his study of Keats. That is true, and it is another way of saying what many of his contemporaries have forgotten: that the invalidation of chronology is not the invalidation of order itself. Mr. Kunitz has many of the old fashioned virtues, one of which (increasingly uncommon in an age infatuated with fragmentation) is consistency. Through all the particulars of this volume, a uniform quality of mind pervades—a quality marked by reasonableness, sensitivity, lucidity, and balance. One thinks inevitably of Aristotle's Magnanimous Man, of Camus' *homme du midi.* His materials he has arranged into associative groups which, like the stanzas of a poem, proceed processionally from one to the next. Just as in a poem we almost invariably have favorite passages, favorite isolatable lines, individual readers will no doubt find their sympathies unequally distributed among the components of this book.... Yet the volume, for all its diversity, is one. It is made so by Mr. Kunitz's persistent conceptualization of the nature of art, and by the tough and unfailing elegance of his style.

I have chosen for the title of this piece a phrase from one of Mr. Kunitz's own poems ("Sotto Voce") because it seems to me to express the essence both of the unity of this particular volume, and of the author's aesthetic in general. Beneath the surface variety, the subject and substance of Mr. Kunitz's work (probably of all poets) is the grace of language itself—grace in every sense of the term. Both the order and the folly are the word.

The book begins with a collection of observations on the nature and state of our knowledge about the physical universe, and ends with a collection of observations on the nature and state of art. The bracketing is by no means gratuitous. Between our objective situation (or what we perceive our objective situation to be) and our ability to make order out of it, subsists all that we do and think, all, finally, that we are. (p. 120)

Mr. Kunitz's aesthetic-ethical judgments ... are myriad. Their most fundamental common factor is the indissolubility of artistic being and moral being, as manifested jointly in style.... Mr. Kunitz's judgments are like a researcher's measurements: careful and concise, candid without malice, infused with sympathy and concern but resolutely disinterested. He does not seek to awe us with esoteric interpretations or idiosyncratic opinions. He wishes only to be succinct and correct—an undertaking more rare and more difficult than we like to admit. A poet is, first and last, one who sees more finely than his fellows. In his criticism as in his verse, Stanley Kunitz is a genuine poet.

Only in some of his more bardic theoretical remarks, when too far removed from a concrete and immediate subject, does Mr. Kunitz occasionally sin in the direction of mellifluous but vacuous grace.... Conversely, when writing of his craft as he knows it and practices it, Mr. Kunitz never errs. It is no doubt a judgment of our age that we find good sense astounding. Mr. Kunitz has it, and to an astonishing degree. He says a great many things which, in this late frantic hour of our art, need desperately once again to be said—which is to say of course that they need desperately once again to be heard.... The spirit by which Kunitz's book is informed—the spirit of simple truthfulness, lucidity, and compassion—will survive to perpetually generate new works and new voices out of its ache. (pp. 121-23)

Richard Vine, "The Language That Saves", in Salmagundi *(copyright © 1977 by Skidmore College), Winter, 1977, pp. 117-23.*

L

LANDOLFI, Tommaso   1908-

Landolfi is an Italian short story writer, essayist, dramatist, poet, and translator. An ingenious fantasist, Landolfi has been linked with writers such as Gogol, Kafka, Poe, Nabokov, and Borges. Because his writing contrasts so sharply with the neorealism of his contemporaries Moravia, Vittorini, and Pratolini, Landolfi stands apart from the mainstream of Italian literature.

PATRICIA M. GATHERCOLE

Though Landolfi's stories [in *Cancerqueen and Other Stories*] may be considered amusing and entertaining, he is not an easy author to understand. The reader must put forth a genuine creative effort to comprehend the subject matter. The author's analytical ability reveals in limited detail the conflict between the sensual and the reflective mind. Long interested in Russian literature, Landolfi at times portrays an anguished mentality analogous to that of a certain Slavic tradition. In his story "The Mute," for instance, we live in the terrified mind of a child murderer who recalls Dostoyevsky's Stavrogin. In the story "Hands" we learn of the man Federico who is haunted by the idea of having killed a mouse one night in the courtyard.

The author in several tales appears to share the Existentialist's notions concerning the absurdity of the world. In "Night Must Fall" a young poet expresses bitter thoughts about the banality of the world. Absurd, disconnected dialogues are found in "Autumn"; for example, the question: "Have you ever noticed how much Vittoria resembles the button on a shoe?" . . . No answer is given but an equally nonsensical remark follows. Fate plays an unwelcome role in a card game ("Misdeal"). Foolish Destiny forces Renato to kill the girl he loves ("The Sword"). . . . (p. 113)

Fantasy plays an extensive role in Landolfi's work. In "Week of Sun" we inhabit the imagination of a madman who tells us of the pain and misery of insanity. We witness the birth of a monster in "Stefano's Two Sons," one with its fingers and toes joined together. All in all, one may say that this collection of stories shows marked originality, though one may term the content weird. (p. 114)

> *Patricia M. Gathercole, in* Studies in Short Fiction *(copyright 1973 by Newberry College), Winter, 1973.*

CLAUDE C. BREW

Though Landolfi titles his story [in *Gogol's Wife and Other Stories*] "Wedding Night," the groom is absent. Taking his place in the focus of the story, and in the young bride's imagination, is a chimney sweep. The story is traditionally structured. In the first section the scene and mood are set and an emotional conflict within the young bride is suggested. The second section, beginning with the chimney sweep disrobing and preparing to ascend and clean the kitchen chimney, presents the central action of the story—and the young bride's imaginative interpretation of it. The last section, after the bride flees the kitchen for the third time, presents a cluster of images and cryptic statements by the narrator which collectively suggest the resolution of the young bride's conflict. (p. 111)

The shyness and awkwardness of the first encounter between the bride and the chimney sweep evokes the traditional confrontation of a bride and groom on their wedding night. . . . The phallic suggestiveness of [the descriptions of the chimney sweep are] even more apparent as the story progresses, and, to the extent that the chimney sweep replaces the groom in the story, the young bride's apprehension that there is something dirty about him that cannot be washed away may be suggestive of her feeling about sexuality.

In seven of the nine stories in *Gogol's Wife and Other Stories* Landolfi employs either a first person character-narrator or a rather obtrusive first person observer-narrator. In the other two, "Wedding Night" and "Sunstroke," he employs a contrastingly unobtrusive third person observer-narrator. In each of these two stories the narrator uses dialogue and the direct thought of the characters very sparingly, telling most of the story in his own voice; yet at the same time he conveys the feeling that we are seeing much of the story as if from the point of view of the main character. In "Sunstroke" the central character is an owl, and most of the story simply describes the rising of the sun. What is interesting, however, is how powerfully the story conveys the attitudes, values, and responses that might be expected of an owl, rather than a human being. In a similar way, "Wedding Night" is not so concerned with the literal events that underlie the story, as it is with how the young bride perceives those events and how her imaginative projection of herself into them effects her emotionally. (p. 112)

From about the time the bride flees the scene for the third and last time a number of images are presented, the cumulative effect of which is to suggest the nature of her emotional reaction to this imaginative projection of her "wedding night." Generally they suggest fear and repulsion. . . .

The bride has surrendered to her fear and guilt-ridden conception about sex before she ever encounters it in reality, and by the end of the story she seems ready to join a gallery of corpses, made insensitive by fear and guilt to one of the central expressions of life—the innocent enjoyment of her healthy and natural sexual desire. (p. 114)

In "Wedding Night" the bride's imagined experience of her wedding night, with its suggestions of pain, revulsion, and fear, leaves her dead to this particular aspect of joy. Far from avoiding "life's consequential issues," Landolfi here treats the perennial human problem of how our imagined anticipation of future events affects our emotional adjustment to those events. Rather than "malicious mystification," his narrative and descriptive techniques are functional and effective. "Wedding Night," like all good stories, intrigues us to return. (p. 115)

> *Claude C. Brew, "The 'Caterpillar Nature' of Imaginative Experience: A Reading of Tommaso Landolfi's 'Wedding Night'," in* Modern Language Notes *(© copyright 1974 by The Johns Hopkins University Press), Vol. 89, No. 1, 1974, pp. 110-15.*

*   *   *

LEBOWITZ, Fran   1951(?)-

Lebowitz is an American essayist. Her first book, *Metropolitan Life*, is both a popular and a critical success. (See also *Contemporary Authors*, Vols. 81-84.)

JILL ROBINSON

Astringent, meticulous with language, Miss Lebowitz is a sort of Edwin Newman for the chic urban-decay set. [In "Metropolitan Life", she] discriminates, takes authority and makes rules, "Large, naked, raw carrots are acceptable as food only to those who live in hutches eagerly awaiting Easter." This is refreshing if you're tired of everyone jogging up and telling you to wear life like a loose garment. . . . Fran Lebowitz wears life like an itchy muffler. She braids its fringes, flings it over her shoulder and savors its discomforts. . . .

"Metropolitan Life" is not simply consistently cross, swift and sly, as if that would not be enough. It introduces an important humorist in the classic tradition. The satire is principled, the taste impeccable—there is character here as well as personality.

You must read about Chicken Little, the bar for the desperate unadopted children who try to pick up parents, and "Writers on Strike," wherein not-writing is done in public instead of at home. Miss Lebowitz has been doing a lot of writing. I want more.

> *Jill Robinson, "Swift and Cranky," in* The New York Times Book Review *(© 1978 by The New York Times Company; reprinted by permission), March 26, 1978, p. 9.*

ANNE FADIMAN

[In *Metropolitan Life*] Fran Lebowitz does for New York what W. C. Fields did for children and dogs. She's a professional fad puncturer. . . .

Lebowitz is funniest when she's genuinely astonished—as when she hears that broken fingernails can be replaced by nails from a nail bank. . . . (p. 82)

When she and her victims are unevenly matched, Lebowitz is less successful. It's no fun to watch her pick on est or CB radios or leisure suits: They've already been bullied to death. Conversely, she can be overly offensive when she takes on topics too large for her, such as homosexuality and race. And sometimes she's just plain confusing—a cardinal sin in this brand of humor. . . .

The major problem with *Metropolitan Life* is that it is a book instead of a magazine article. Lebowitz is strong stuff and should be taken in small doses. (p. 84)

> *Anne Fadiman, in* Saturday Review *(© 1978 by Saturday Review Magazine Corp.; reprinted with permission), April 15, 1978.*

EDMUND WHITE

Like all satirists [Lebowitz] is a moralist, and like most moralists she is conservative. . . .

Lebowitz is clear-eyed. She knows, "There is no such thing as inner peace. There is only nervousness and death." Hence her contempt for the false comfort of self-help books. . . .

Her vigilance against hip new words is tireless. That is, she objects to CB slang because it is "on the one hand too colorful and on the other hand lacking a counterpart for the words pearl gray." . . .

There are few writers who, in the course of registering opinions, do not fail to render, however unwittingly, a portrait of themselves. Fran emerges as urbane . . . , as independent, snobbish and, dare we say it, just a tad lazy.

Urbane—or rather, urban. . . .

Fran's snobbishness should be studied by psychiatrists since it is the perfect ego defense; she looks down on absolutely *everyone*. Perhaps this alienation arises from the plight of the modern artist in contemporary society. In Fran's words, "The servant problem being what it is, one would think it apparent that a society that provides a Helper for tuna but compels a writer to pack her own suitcases desperately needs to reorder its priorities." (p. 1)

It is as a purist, however, that Fran will be remembered. She pleads with the general public to "refrain from starting trends, overcoming inhibitions, or developing hidden talents." (p. 6)

> *Edmund White, "Boston Ferns Don't Make Fettucine," in* Book World—The Washington Post *(© The Washington Post), April 30, 1978, pp. 1, 6.*

*   *   *

LEE, Manfred B(ennington)
See QUEEN, Ellery
*   *   *

LEET, Judith   1935-

Leet is an American poet. Her first book, *Pleasure Seeker's Guide*, evidences a poetic style that is sophisticated, detached, and often prosaic.

LUCILLE IVERSON

In *Pleasure Seeker's Guide,* Judith Leet describes a personality which is absurdly caught between the rigors of a deadly and intellectualized self-discipline and unconscious raging passions. This conflict paralyzes the will to action. Leet places the characters in her poems in a ridiculous and destructive universe; but they are one with it—contain its conflicts, are drowning in it, dying in it. They are unable to acknowledge the feelings of others, or their own, and hysterically preserve their hypocrisy. But this reality, this universe (fortunately), is counterpoised with a fillip of a brilliant, sometimes macabre humor, like Charles Addams' cartoons which, mixing the horrible with the commonplace, make us laugh while telling us about ourselves trapped in self-illusion and folly. (pp. 28-9)

["Vision," from the poem "Death in Dreams (The Interpretation of Nightmares),"] clearly expresses her vision: the nightmare of existence, of human beings repressing their gut reactions, their passions, in order to survive in an insane world, and yet caught, paralyzed, as they slowly self-destruct. (p. 29)

[The] whole poem balances on the razor edge between the unconscious drives of feelings and the placid "reasonable" universe. . . . In the poem, also, is the fear of death, of the unknown, which is equated with feelings, also unknown and repressed, and only erupting in dreams. The dreamer fears that the waves may be a threat instead of a vision and that the water may drown him. . . .

Leet's style of writing, the formal prose line, which arrests and possesses the reader while bursting with a contained energy, exactly mimics her perception of humankind caught between passion and order. We are presented with a cautious, over-intellectualized character wrapped in the formal disciplines and fraught with fears of oblivion and of his own feelings. And all our human foibles are displayed as a riotous joke—much like Evelyn Waugh, perhaps, and his macabre vision. (p. 30)

[Leet's poetry] not only reveals an astonishing power and perception, but also a skill and precision of thought seldom found in a first publication. For Leet . . . brings to her poetry an experience of living and the intelligence and wit of a mature personality. (p. 31)

> *Lucille Iverson, in* Moons and Lion Tailes *(copyright © 1976 by The Permanent Press), Vol. 2, No. 1, 1976.*

KATHLEEN WIEGNER

In her poem, "The Enthusiast," Judith Leet describes a man whose enthusiasm for a lady he has seen leads him to throw himself under the wheels of her car. She does not stop. In many respects the characters in Leet's book, *Pleasure Seeker's Guide* . . . have this same need for the extravagant, the need to break through the confines of expected behavior. And their rewards are equally disappointing. . . .

"The Pleasure Seekers" are . . . people who know what they want and will not give in gracefully. . . .

Leet presents her stories (and they really are stories in the tradition of Chaucer and Browning) in a marvelously detached, and often humorous manner. Even the characters who address us directly have a kind of detached resignation

to their fate which is echoed by the woman who tells her sad story in "The White Tower" (fittingly subtitled, "A Novel in the Form of a Poem"): "In a sense, I am above disaster." The voices sound genuine, I suspect, because we have heard them before in the voices of our friends who have lived through a particularly awful experience and now can tell it as if it had happened to someone else. There is even a certain pleasure in their voices which comes from having lived through something extraordinary while the rest of us were mucking around in our ordinary lives. In this sense Leet's characters are admirable in their foolishness because they appear to find pleasure in it or perhaps because Leet's own perspective is one of bemusement. (p. 42)

> *Kathleen Wiegner, in* The American Poetry Review *(copyright © 1976 by World Poetry, Inc.; reprinted by permission of Kathleen Wiegner), September-October, 1976.*

JOHN R. REED

[*Pleasure Seeker's Guide*] is narrative and only narrative. I honestly do not feel that there is any good reason why these compositions need to be called poems at all. There usually isn't much for prosody to seize upon (rhythm, rhyme, assonance, consonance, figurative language, syntactic structure), and there are no memorable lines. However, Ms. Leet is an excellent story-teller, and she knows it. She even titles one piece "The White Tower (A Novel in the Form of a Poem)." But the form is a disguise, not a true identity. Behind the poetic form, it is still prose. Similarly, "Overlooking the Pile of Bodies at One's Feet" is a monologue that might have worked more effectively as a personal essay, a short story, or even a stand-up comic's routine. . . . So far as I am concerned, it is prose. . . . There is a good deal of wry humor in Ms. Leet's writing, but it is so dominated by simple story-telling—to the injury of any poetic development—that I can feel only that she would be far happier working in some other medium. Perhaps she is writing a novel. (p. 87)

> *John R. Reed, in* The Ontario Review *(copyright © 1976 by The Ontario Review), Fall-Winter, 1976-77.*

* * *

LÉGER, Alexis Saint-Léger
See PERSE, St.-John

* * *

LOWELL, Robert   1917-1977

Winner of two Pulitzer Prizes and a National Book Award, Lowell is generally considered the premier American poet of his generation. Though not allied with any school or movement, he frequently gave voice to his social concerns, which also led many to consider him to be the prototypical liberal intellectual writer of his time. In his work he explored the contradictions in American life and the failure of Puritan ethics. A traditional stylist, he used complicated formal patterns and rhyme schemes while examining very personal topics, in contrast to the free form style of the Beats. This concern with traditional forms culminated in his book-length sonnet sequence, *The Dolphin.* Lowell was also a widely acclaimed translator and playwright as well as critic and editor. (See also *CLC,* Vols. 1, 2, 3, 4, 5, 8, 9, and *Contemporary Authors,* Vols. 9-12, rev. ed.; obituary, Vols. 73-76.)

JOHN SIMON

[In *The Old Glory*] Lowell is trying to capture the ironies, cruelties and inconclusiveness on which America was built: in *Endecott,* the ambiguities are chiefly religious; in *Molineux,* political; in *Cereno,* racial. Beyond that, though, he is concerned with essential human nature, which he sees as paradoxical, untrustworthy, and above all, tenebrose. But, regrettably, there are three obstacles he cannot quite negotiate: the limitations of the one-acter, the demands of dramatic form, the problem of stage poetry.

Endecott, for example, is an interesting figure who manages to arouse our sympathetic curiosity, but only at the expense of swallowing up most of the playlet: his psyche exacts much more attention from us than do the perfunctory characters and negligible events of the play. In *Cereno,* attempts at writing some sequences in the manner of Genet, Beckett or Kafka rub uneasily against patches of realism and even a Hollywood, shoot-'em-up finale. In *Molineux,* the absurdist mode is fairly consistent (though not so witty as in Beckett or Ionesco), but it clashes with stabs at mythologizing—Charon is introduced as ferryman to Boston, "the City of the Dead"!—and throughout one feels a certain confusion between symbol and rigmarole. (p. 182)

Now, this sort of thing is all very well in lyric poetry, but it just does not register in performed drama. And it is true of all three plays that, though they are aware of the things that make a play a play—not merely action and conflict, as commonly held, but also diversified verbal texture, humor, pathos, variety of tempo, absorbing talk and so on—Lowell is unable either to provide enough of them or to marshal them properly. Thus, action tends to bunch up in one place, humor to sound forced, and the language to become static or inconsistent. (p. 183)

Yet the final problem is the poetry itself. Though written in free verse, *The Old Glory* attains to poetry only in Captain Delano's speech beginning "I see an ocean undulating in long scoops and swells . . ." But this passage is only a slight reworking of Melville's third paragraph [in *Benito Cereno*]. . . . Verse that is not really verse can add only pretentiousness to a play, confuse the actors and throw dust in the ears of the audience. It may even deflect the playwright's attention from his primary task.

But could one not write truly poetic plays today? The answer, apparently, is no. . . . Poetry today has, unfortunately, become a minority art, no longer an integral part of the culture, as it was in the heyday of verse drama. Reluctantly we must accept its divorce from the theater, which must at least *seem* to speak the language of the land. The poet, as writer, may still have a place in the theater; poetry, barring a miracle, does not. What history hath put asunder, no man is likely to join together. (pp. 183-84)

> *John Simon, "Strange Devices on the Banner"*
> *(1966), in his* Singularities: Essays on the Theater
> *1964-1973 (copyright © 1975 by John Simon; reprinted by permission of Random House, Inc.),*
> *Random House, 1976, pp. 181-84.*

RUBY COHN

Lowell is the most gifted poet of his generation to turn to the stage. Like Schevill, he came to drama through translation, but the way was prepared by the dramatic turn of his lyrics after 1957, with their loosened rhythms and simplified syntax. (p. 280)

[*Prometheus Unbound* is] syntactically varied, inventive in sound play, and lush in imagery. As Lowell's Phaedra was rendered through Freud, his Prometheus has a contemporary existential consciousness. His language has invigorated two classical tragedies for speakers of English, but his most significant dramatic achievement is the three plays grouped as *The Old Glory*. . . .

Ostensibly dealing with early American history, Lowell's three plays examine that history through the fiction of Hawthorne and Melville, and he focuses on the image of a flag. Lowell has dramatized stories whose cumulative significance equates Old Glory with its rhyme-word "gory." . . .

Conceived as a whole, the three plays of *The Old Glory* comment on contemporary America in contemporary language. All three dramas contain a single act of mounting tension. All three dramas close on violence whose reverberations still ring loudly in our ears. Far from a patriotic celebration, these three plays accommodate the ambiguities of revolutionary action, and they do so in the most controlled verse of American drama. (p. 281)

[The] Indian subplot blurs the central conflict of Endecott versus Morton, and it slows the play's dramatic drive. The most discursive play of the trilogy, *Endecott and the Red Cross* is even talkier in the revised version. Thus the thematic balance of *Endecott* against *Benito Cereno* is achieved at the cost of the former's dramatic focus. . . .

[Mercantile words] punctuate the ethical conflict of the drama—money, pay, cash, trade, profit. Above the commercial undercurrent, however, principle shines in Lowell's play; patriotism is never a simple matter of pounds and pence, as in Brecht's plays. Not money but a flag is the most insistent image of Lowell's three plays, and the flag is first mentioned in conjunction with Endecott. (p. 282)

[Endecott's dream] is relevant to the twentieth as to the seventeenth century, for it is a dream of men who commit cruel deeds in the name of stern religions; it is a dream of countering cruelty with cruelty. (p. 284)

Assonance, alliteration, and irony serve the rebellious demagogue [Endecott]. His picture of men in power casts a shadow upon his own power, and predicts the violence and corruption of power throughout Lowell's trilogy. (p. 285)

To bind the disjunctive short scenes [of *My Kinsman, Major Molineux*], Lowell abandons the free verse of *Endecott* for loose tetrameters, but he uses the same sonic effects—rhyme, alliteration, assonance, repetition. Again Lowell makes the flag his central image; the Union Jack is emblematic of British authority, and the Rattlesnake of the Boston rebellion.

As Endecott is linked and opposed to the Red Cross of England in Lowell's first play, Major Molineux is linked to the Union Jack and opposed to the Rattlesnake flag of rebellion. . . . As the Red Cross of England had to be cut down to prepare the way for The Old Glory, the Boston Rattlesnake had to be subsumed in it. Elegant Molineux and sensuous Morton had to be destroyed for the Old Glory to be realized. (p. 286)

In Lowell's play, Hell is a *donnée*. Before a word is spoken, the Ferryman appears, "*his dress . . . half suggest [ing] that he is Charon.*" Though this may be difficult to suggest on stage, his remark to Robin recalls Dante: "Legs go round in circles here. / This is the city of the dead." But Lowell's Dante has no Virgil; the Boy exclaims: "We've lost our guide." And *we* seem to lose *our* guide as the characters crowd on scene in swift succession.... (p. 287)

[After the Major is killed, and for] the first and only time in the play, Robin and his brother are alone on stage; their lack of self-recognition is meant to trigger ours—we are accomplices in the death of our kinsman.

In *Benito Cereno,* Lowell again uses the past to appeal to our present conscience. Following the events of the Melville novella, his play subverts its intention.... [Lowell] converts Melville's fiction into an ironic commentary upon the symbiosis of oppressor and oppressed, observer and observed. And he does this by joining verbal to theatrical imagery, in an extremely concentrated drama. (p. 288)

Melville's Delano is a man of good will with severely limited perceptions. Lowell's Delano is a man whose good will is eroded by his severely limited perceptions. With characteristic irony, Lowell uses imagery of vision to emphasize the Captain's lack of vision. (p. 290)

In Gerald Weales' acute and succinct summary: "*The Old Glory* is about revolution—Endecott initiates one, Robin joins one, Delano puts one down.... The movement in time from play to play, with its suggestion that there is always a revolution in process, underlines the basic theme of the play—that, under whatever flag, power demands action and that the action is inevitably violent and tyrannical." Lowell's dramatic examination of revolution is less subtle than his lyric poetry, and the plays are less subtle than the fiction at their base. But subtlety may be undramatic, and Lowell's plays are intended for the theater. Without pandering to easy popularity, he has accommodated his elusive imagery to the exigencies of spoken dialogue. Highly rhythmed, it is eminently speakable. The language varies with the play—alternately discursive and abrupt in *Endecott,* conversational but vivid in *Molineux,* and in *Benito Cereno* a counterpoint of lush Latinisms or African phrasings against Yankee cliché. Within each play, however, the dialogue style is consistent. And though each play contains a conflict—Endecott versus Morton, Robin versus Molineux, Delano versus Babu—the dialogue enriches polarity with poetic nuance. Themes are realized in imagery as much as in characters, who share a nervous intensity rather than a credible roundness. (pp. 291-92)

> Ruby Cohn, "Robert Lowell," in her Dialogue in
> American Drama (copyright © by Indiana Uni-
> versity Press), Indiana University Press, 1971, pp.
> 280-92.

ROBERT FITZGERALD

In Lowell's work I have always felt a giant pressure exerted on language and experience, not only in dense and highly wrought poems but in relatively conversational and casual ones as well. In the wide range of poetry that this force has given us, I continue to distinguish two kinds that I noted years ago in "Exile's Return," the opening poem in *Lord Weary's Castle:* the first unverifiable, so to speak, being chiefly dreamwork and earwork ("The search-guns click and spit and split up timber"), the second verifiable, public, and powerful ("A rough cathedral lifts its eye."). His new poem, "Ulysses And Circe," contains both these types of imagination. It is a realization of myth and at the

same time a mythification of reality. Lowell has made his own fiction out of experience including that of the Circe episode of *The Odyssey.* He "translates" the three central persons (including Penelope) into immediate beings in the mind and senses of one, who is Ulysses and the poet, or Ulysses for the poet. Present experience provides much of the detail, but the fiction is mainly "timeless" and only here and there pinned necessarily to this century. The odd life of the poem is given with an odd plainness that rises without effort or inconsistency to rich lines of which as a whole it is careless, being concerned to be a whole, as it is. "Penelope" strikes me as the least immediate figure, section 5 as the blurriest and most pervaded by dreamwork; I am not so nearly satisfied, as I am with the other sections, that it had to be thus and not otherwise. This is a large poem and, I surmise, an important one.... (p. 25)

> Robert Fitzgerald, "Aiaia and Ithaca: Notes on a
> New Lowell Poem," in Salmagundi (copyright ©
> 1977 by Skidmore College), Spring, 1977, pp. 25-
> 31.

G. S. FRASER

Life Studies, [Lowell's] famous transitional volume, was welcomed by myself among other reviewers, for a new kind of direct ease: not, of course, as an ancestor of 'confessional' poetry—if your verses can achieve fame only through hysterical self-exposure and an extra-poetic act like suicide, so much the worse for your verses—but for the skill with which Lowell keyed down his rhetoric and managed to use items of domestic reportage to replace rather worn religious or historical or literary symbols by domestic memorialising. Of course, in doing so Lowell had the advantage through his ancestry and his personal history of being himself a distinctly symbolic personage. The aristocrat without power or wealth except in so far as he embodies the history and the lost hopes of his country is a very poetic figure: especially when the lost dream of the colonial governors, the Founding Fathers, the oldest and the grandest families, was of a sparse republican virtue. Not all American poets were in Lowell's position of being able to give the extremely and intimately particular a general relevance. This was even in wry withdrawal and celebration of polite defeat no mean accomplishment. (pp. 73-4)

For the Union Dead was an even more distinguished book than *Life Studies,* the title poem a masterpiece. Here the particularities of American history and contemporary civilization, ... the bold and dashing and yet intricately patterned contrast between a puritanically heroic, self-immolating past and a predatory, greasy, vulgar present were beautifully done: from being a deliberately difficult *concettisto,* an almost Gongoristic poet (difficult thought *and* difficult language), through a universalising of the personal (or the familiar material of the school history primer) in simple and easy diction, Lowell has become a public poet, a voice of the critical American social conscience ..., more, since he was not a "committed" public poet (a party man of any sort, a Marxist, for instance, but merely an honest observer of the surrounding scene and a scholarly reader of history), he became a public poet whose voice rang with convincing honesty.... (p. 75)

In *Near the Ocean,* ... we have for the first time Lowell using the lyrical mode (not all through the volume, but often). The lyrical mode expresses not merely "all joy" or "this sweet": it is more essentially, as in Keats on Melancholy, an intense fusion of joyous and painful feelings transcending both. . . . ["Near the Ocean"] can be connected with Keats's lyrical-dramatic mode (the ancestor of Browning's and Tennyson's dramatic monologues and of Pound and Eliot's use of the *persona*): but it works the other way round from Keats. What Keats likes to do in "St. Agnes' Eve" and in a different sort of poem, "Ode to a Nightingale", is to begin quiet and sad, work up to richness and exultation, and then modulate down to a more calm and accepting quietness and sadness at the end. Lowell is never quiet: nor, though he varies his scene startlingly in "Near the Ocean", does he modulate—he is repeating in this poem instance after instance of the same theme, sex as murder (physical or spiritual). He starts in this poem on a very high and terrifying note, a sort of controlled scream, and his business is to sustain it—to sustain, if one likes, a kind of monotonous sublime—but the continuing wail of rancour has to be turned, by a kind of undertow of feeling, into a final triumph or exulting. (p. 77)

G. S. Fraser, in Salmagundi *(copyright © 1977 by Skidmore College), Spring, 1977.*

DAVID KALSTONE

Historical judgment and public distance—the tone realized, for example, in "For the Union Dead"—are entangled with [Robert Lowell's] own partly victimized awareness that he is a Lowell and a New Englander. . . . In his best poetry there is an unspoken and often intended plot: the ambition to write resonant public poetry is corroded again and again by private nightmare, by a failure to escape ghosts of the past. . . .

Lowell said that at the time he wrote *Life Studies* he didn't know whether it was a death-rope or a lifeline. His handling of autobiographical material since then suggests that he is still not ready—and perhaps need never be—to answer that question. The tone of *Life Studies,* flat and unadorned, was indeed a breakthrough. But his changes of manner since then, his likening *Life Studies* to still photographs, suggests that those poems did not solve the problem of authenticity, of a style adequate to the facts of his biography or his poetic ambitions. *Life Studies* poses questions about personal poetry and provides only one kind of answer, a solution to which Lowell did not remain committed. (p. 45)

Something in him resists the casual "I" of autobiography. Often, in his most interesting poems, counter-currents draw him away from any mere *present* he is trying to inhabit. In a poem like "Rebellion," and more successfully in "Children of Light," he tends to identify his personal anger with protests against hypocritical and prosperous New England Puritanism, as if satire could dispose of or resolve the quarrel with his personal past. The Catholicism he adopted at that time, as many critics have pointed out, was a peculiarly Calvinistic one, a platform from which he could denounce Boston and the mercantile life he made it stand for; all histories, personal and public, were instances of the Fall. Many of the poems of *Lord Weary's Castle* allow him to hold the past at a distance, as Boston hangs in the pans of judgment in "Where the Rainbow Ends." In the early poems he identifies himself with the finality of apocalyptic religious energy, as if this distancing were the only means he had to breathe and survive. This is a poetry of resonant judgments and memorable closing lines: "The blue kingfisher dives on you in fire"; "The Lord survives the rainbow of His will."

The force with which the younger Lowell saw the world and the past destroyed—poem after poem performed this gesture—was a reflex of their hold on him. No poetic mode was to be congenial unless he could, as Irvin Ehrenpreis puts it, "not only . . . treat himself as part of history but . . . treat history as part of himself." (pp. 48-9)

Lowell's accomplishment in "Skunk Hour" is to have found a tone which at once gestures toward larger meanings and yet allows for the speaker's own crippling private nightmare. The opening stanzas permit him his "fascinated disgust" with the world; the later stanzas counter any impression of self-righteousness, of easy world-weariness which the reader may be tempted to attribute to him. How much he takes to himself the skunks, the crude defiant survivors, is a difficult question. The casual half-rhymes and feminine endings do give way to more resolute and emphatic stresses at the close. The tone is partly one of amused relief and identification, though . . . it also encourages absurd contrasts between the bold skunks and the human who admits his own terror: "I will. I *do* 'scare!'" It is, at any rate, clear that in this poem Lowell moves toward a more exposed autobiographical style, one that does not mask his anger or disabilities behind apocalyptic rhetoric and social critique.

But, to see the nature of this exposure, it would help to look at a poem typical of the barer "life studies." "Memories of West Street and Lepke" shuttles back and forth between the comfortable Lowell living in Boston in the 1950s and his recall of the year he spent in a New York jail as a conscientious objector. (p. 52)

[In the poem] things bristle with an accusatory significance, all too relevant to the speaker, and "I" not at all relaxed or random in his self-presentation. So much of his experience is already second-hand, as in his self-conscious reference to what Henry James had long since identified as "hardly passionate Marlborough Street," as etiolated gesture toward an etiolated frame. Experiences seem preempted by rhetoric of the Eisenhower period ("agonizing reappraisal") or by advertising ("Like the sun she rises in her flame-flamingo infants' wear").

He talks about himself in implied ironic quotation marks. You imagine them around "fire-breathing" and "manic" in the lines "I was a fire-breathing Catholic C.O., / and made my manic statement." Line endings have a similar dry effect: "Given a year, / I walked on the roof of the West Street Jail . . ." The break forces a wry question; a momentary stepping back, "*given,*" indeed. This is the language of a man on trial, who hears words as if they belonged to someone else. "Fire-breathing" and "manic" are overheard characterizations, expressions he cannot adopt completely as his own. Prepared reactions of the "tranquillized Fifties" encrust his responses, make it hard to break through to feeling.

The distance between the speaker and his experience gives "Memories of West Street and Lepke" its special tension, the air that something is being withheld rather than yielded. So, for example, the mind seems to be making some flickering connection between the daughter's "flame-flamingo infants' wear" and the "seedtime" of the "fire-breathing Catholic C.O." It is a linguistic tease, not fully worked out. We are being asked to think about the "dragon" of a father, and the roseate daughter young enough to be his granddaughter, about a passage of vitality. Something is being suggested about failed ideology and the lapse into slogan-encapsulated domesticity of the 1950s and of middle age. (pp. 53-4)

In "Memories of West Street and Lepke," Lowell seems to take very little primary pleasure in the objects named and remembered. The "pajamas fresh from the washer each morning" seem there not so much for themselves as to prepare our curiosity for a later detail, Czar Lepke, "piling towels on a rack." It is one of several parallels, teasing us into wondering what links the speaker in his laundered world to the boss of Murder Incorporated. (p. 54)

Both Lowell and Lepke belong to privileged worlds. The poet, hogging a whole house, remembers Lepke in "a segregated cell full / of things forbidden the common man." Outside, like the scavenger on Lowell's Marlborough Street, is the anarchic variety of the prison of which the younger Lowell was a part: "a Negro boy with curlicues / of marijuana in his hair"; Abramowitz, another pacifist. "Bioff and Brown, the Hollywood pimps," beat Abramowitz black and blue; it sounds like an energetic alliterative game to accompany Lowell from the tranquillized present to a busy, untidy past.

Linked to the outlaw vividness, the young man glimpsed at its forbidden center Lepke. "Flabby, bald, lobotomized, / he drifted in a sheepish calm." A *doppelgänger* for the middle-aged speaker in his tranquilized forties, Lepke is an object of fastidious envy, if only for his pure preoccupation with death. Lepke, at least, is

> where no agonizing reappraisal
> jarred his concentration on the electric chair—
> hanging like an oasis in his air
> of lost connections. . . .

"Agonizing reappraisals" are the thieves of experience in the poet's world; Lepke's "lost connections" open to an oasis not visible on Marlborough Street.

Or so the parallels and the patterns of the poem suggest. The arrangement of details and scenes invites us to make comparisons and contrasts upon which the poem itself deliberately makes no comment (not even to say, as Williams did, "The pure products of America go crazy"). Finally the poet's baffled failure to generalize becomes one of the subjects of the poem. The figures in the frieze have the air of being deliberately chosen and placed, deliberately recalled for the skilled analyst like key figures in a dream. Lost as the connections are between the criminal past and the respectable drugged present, the poem bristles with the challenge to recapture and unite them. Its selective organization teases us toward meaning, even if it is only in the form of a conundrum, a puzzle whose pieces we must match ourselves. (pp. 55-6)

Life Studies has taught its readers how to interpret such poems as "Memories of West Street and Lepke," poems once characterized as random and flat. The short lines, the deliberately low-key vocabulary are ways of focusing our attention. Against such plainness a repeated gesture or word or color can take on unexpected resonance and can suggest obsessive connections between otherwise unlikely figures. "My Last Afternoon with Uncle Devereux Winslow" depends on a network of small details to reveal the fearful links between the five-and-a-half-year-old Lowell

and his uncle, dying of Hodgkin's disease at twenty-nine. The child's wish to escape to imperishable death, his revulsion against his life full of relatives failing and dying—these feelings emerge slowly and by implication. . . . The connections are latent, bristle with significance as in dreams, but as in dreams leave interpretation for afterward.

What happens within single poems happens in *Life Studies* as a whole. Poems in the opening sections throw up muted parallels and resonant images which prepare us for the Lowell autobiography in Part Four. (p. 56)

The critical reader, at some more or less conscious level, associates through memory these disparate experiences and images. It is important that the poet in his poems appears not to. Having recognized the glinting clues for what they are, he does not choose to let them come together directly in his poems. . . . [We] always have to return to the poet's professed state of mind, the dispersal of clues as in a dream, the patient's report only just on the verge of interpretation. . . . It is Lowell's way of posing questions about his life without having, directly, to answer them.

Having tried to bring memories forward in *Life Studies,* Lowell often steps back to consider memory as a problem in his next book, *For the Union Dead* (1964). Writing autobiography brought with it glimpses of chaos and nightmare: Lepke's inner eye fixed on the electric chair; the crazed night cruiser of "Skunk Hour"; the infantile bravado of the mental hospital of "Waking in the Blue." It is no wonder that Lowell so often casts himself in a distanced role, as a baffled spectator, sometimes as a voyeur. . . . The postures —and the poem itself—become a screen between the poet and certain ungovernable experiences, public and private. (pp. 57-8)

For the Union Dead includes a network of observers and observed, one or the other behind glass. "The state / is a diver under a glass bell" ("Fall 1961"). The poems stand by themselves, but they also accumulate, in waves of concentration and dispersal, a series of associations with eyesight and vision. At the center of the book are accounts of nightmares and dreams which have to do with the eyeglasses put aside at night, with eye injuries and the memories they recall. (p. 58)

Memories of childhood are seldom innocent for Lowell. [As in "Eye and Tooth," they] almost always [suggest] twin complicity (here, a boy's erotic games) and powerlessness (here, before the fantasy punishment). "No ease," the poem keeps saying. The adult present is described in past tenses. It is a shift to the present tense that brings back boyhood memories and threatens to overwhelm. "Eye and Tooth," like "Myopia," is a haunted poem, an extreme version of the baffled eye through which Lowell sees most experience in this volume. At some points flawed vision seems a punishment for opening ungovernable ranges of feeling. It can also be his protection. In "Eye and Tooth," "I saw things darkly, / as through an unwashed goldfish globe." What keeps "Eye and Tooth" together is that frail self-assertion, a tainted prophet who sets himself against the almost invincible Mosaic prophecies of his family which fill the rest of the poem. At the outset he is jaunty and self-deprecating, a neglected minnow in his unwashed bowl, or perhaps the ghost of a touring gypsy with a makeshift crystal ball. At the close he is wearied and wearying.

"Eye and Tooth" is a gloss on a pitiful and precarious situation. The book of which it is a part lifts often toward an optative mood, a wish to be transported back to immune pleasures of childhood. (p. 60)

Memory, however much he craves it, never has a nourishing or regenerative force for Lowell, never the reviving power it has, classically, for Proust. There are no madeleines in this world, only a past which has already been consumed. It is for this reason that many of the poems turn toward elegy. "Always inside me is the child who died, / always inside me is his will to die."

The lines are from "Night Sweat" and are followed by the powerful, mysterious, idiosyncratic metaphor that Lowell develops for the passage of memory into art: "one universe, one body . . . in this urn / the animal night sweats of the spirit burn." A resonant couplet, the emphatic close of the first two sonnets that make up this poem, the lines force together grim contradictory feelings. The "urn" contains the spent ashes of a dead childhood and, at the same time, the fevers of creation and nightmare. As the shell of the body, it is devoured by what it burns; as the urn of memory or verse, it preserves what is destroyed. If the lines are about transformation, the stress falls on what is consumed. What he captures is a fascinated repugnance. These are "the animal night sweats of the *spirit*," as if the Latin meanings ("spirit," "breath") behind the English *animal* were just barely still alive. (pp. 61-2)

These "night sweats" are partly the product of seeing ghosts. Memory of and by itself does not animate the present for him, as it does for writers like Wordsworth and Proust. On the contrary, it threatens to overwhelm him, to cut him off from the present and from his living wife and daughter. What are for other writers revitalizing links to childhood are not for Lowell one of the keys to an acknowledged and shared humanity. To redeem himself from monstrousness and isolation is to recognize the decaying mind and body as his links to humankind. The skull in "The Neo-Classical Urn" is the cerebral skull which at once consumes the animal spirits and is itself a death's head. In the tenderer, more human version of "Night Sweat" the urn of writing is also the body, self-consuming, self-embalming.

What I am getting at is that autobiography for Lowell is a problematic form. He probes the reasons unflinchingly in these exposed dream poems at the center of *For the Union Dead*. Involuntary memory won't do. It is more congenial for him to write autobiography from the point of view of the elegist—experiencing himself and others almost entirely as members of Yeats's "dying generations." . . . Lowell gets a tainted joy from the notion that he is "reborn" in his writing. That discovery is repeated again and again in his work. . . . (p. 64)

Lowell spoke of poems like "Myopia: a Night" and "Night Sweat" as writing "surrealism about my life." Five years later, in *Notebook,* he was to call surrealism his "method" —a way to accommodate tumultuous and threatening impulses, to drop his guard and visit the world where vision was as unclear as when he suffered his eye injury in "Eye and Tooth" or removed his glasses in "Myopia: a Night." The emerging poetry of *Notebook* went through several stages. Its publishing history re-enacts the struggles apparent in Lowell's poems all along. The *Notebook* of 1969 begins in a craving for immediacy: "Accident threw up sub-

jects, and the plot swallowed them—famished for human chances." The *Notebook* fattened toward a revised edition in 1970; by 1973 it had become *History.* (p. 65)

What is interesting about *History* is not the distinction between plotted and plotless sequences so much as the plot which Lowell finally chose, the main view of his experience which Lowell was encouraged to take after mulling it over for almost five years. The image is from sculpture: "I have cut the waste marble from the figure." Stone jaws seem to close—as if after all the emotional untidiness of life in *Notebook,* a new protective and self-assertive posture were needed, placing the poet among the ruins of time.

The conversion of *Notebook* into *History* and its two attendant volumes was a bold, willful, utterly exposed gesture. Perhaps no poet since Whitman has made such continuous public revisions of his life. Yet Whitman accumulated everything he wrote into *Leaves of Grass,* as a way of making his book coterminous with his life; it would end only when he did. Lowell, on the contrary, performed a series of amputations and separations. Many of the events and sensations which prompted the Notebooks—his broken marriage, his taking a new wife—are themselves set apart in *For Lizzie and Harriet* and in some of the new poems of *The Dolphin. History* becomes much more his, the poet's, book, a codification of the elegist's position.

Still, it is hard to talk about *History* as if it were a book apart, since earlier versions of these poems are so much a matter of public record. With a career as ample as Lowell's the strenuous efforts at revising and re-ordering seem themselves to belong to the "complete works." Feelings experienced and developed in one context in *Notebook* are encountered in new and surprising guises in *History.* (pp. 66-7)

[His] remorseless crystallization of once intimate experience makes *History* the controlled nightmare it is. (p. 69)

What is remarkable in [the] opening poems [of *History*] are the glimpses of salvage, psychologically aligned with the drift from sleep into dawn. Randall Jarrell said long before that Lowell "seems to be condemned both to read history and to repeat it." Once again on the brink of that experience, he reaches out at the opening of *History* for exotic escape, unavailable but imagined—attempts to be free of the *clutching* and *fumbling* which "history has to live with" and which we have to live with in history. . . . In earlier versions, the dream was told in the present tense. Here it occurs in the irrevocable past, and . . . it envisions waste and dispersal—tantalizing, botched renewal.

Yet, as we move irrevocably into the daylight world after the fall, there is a sense in which the opening dreamlike poems have established Lowell's independent presence. This is to be His-Story, the facts of the past to serve like a medieval mirror poem for private scares and edifications. He "performs" history, appropriates its figures and events for self-confrontation, dream and nightmare. As the historical pageant unfolds, he also takes his place in it, among the perishable thousands this spectacle takes up and discards. (pp. 70-1)

Lowell's sequence always returns us to history and its erosions. The world of this book feels surprisingly like the world of *Lord Weary's Castle*—more so than in any of Lowell's intermediate works. But in this later panorama of decline and fall, the doomed world of *History*, he is much more a participant, much less a witness. The perspectives are as stern and bleak as they were for the Bostonian "Children of Light" in Lowell's first book. But now the alternatives are different. The fallen world of *History* is ringed by signs of a primitive vitality outlasting the willful tyrants, statesmen and artists who emerge and vanish, as well as the poet who has summoned up their ghosts. The bright ungovernable forces were there at the start of the sequence, glimpsed but lost at the poet's awakening—flashing outside human history, like the fierce creature whose crest he cannot snatch in "Bird?" Creatures like these turn up, mocking humans with an unavailable brute power of endurance. In "Sounds in the Night," the insomniac poet can hear "the grass-conservative cry of the cat in heat." "Cats will be here when man is prehistory." Or speaking to "Our Dead Poets," the poets whose memories litter these pages:

> Sometimes for days I only hear your voices,
> the sun of summer will not adorn you again
> with her garment of new leaves and flowers . . .
> her *nostalgie de la boue* that shelters ape
> and protozoa from the rights of man.

Elegy modulates into bitterness and fear. In this context the "rights of man" (and the "writings" as well, with which this sonnet begins) may sound downright murderous.

The alternative to senseless survival, to the "ape and protozoa," is the panorama of human arrangements which are the core of *History*, all of them to some degree seen as destructive and denatured: politics, the family, marriage, art. In the harshest light all these activities have a common denominator, and Lowell, visiting his gallery of tyrants, heroes, lovers and artists, finds refractions of his own thwarted and eroding powers. The old conqueror, Tamburlaine, senile, gives a clue to their common ambitions:

> Timur . . . his pyramid half a million heads,
> one skull and then one brick and then one skull,
> live art that makes the Arc de Triomphe pale.
> Even a modernist must be new at times,
> not a parasite on his own tradition,
> its too healthy sleep that foreshadows death.
> A thing well done, even a pile of heads
> modestly planned to wilt before the builder,
> is art, if art is anything won from nature. . . .

The ambiguous "before"—wilting heads before the builder's eyes? or before the builder wilts?—cements a lurid identity between the tyrant's power and the consuming ambitions of a "modernist's" art. Lowell takes a sardonic and desperate view of what it costs a modernist—or at least one modernist—to win art from nature and build "his pyramid." (pp. 71-3)

"In Genesis" was originally titled "Out of the Picture," one of the last poems in *Notebook*. Now it stands almost as a headpiece to *History*, a way of entering from the natural and primitive dawn into a poet's awareness of history. It places him, as most of the book does, among the consuming and consumed, downplaying at every turn any myth of the nourishing power of art.

What Lowell has finally put on display is a universe as severe as that of his early religious poems, but stripped of their theology and carved out of his own literary experi-

ence. . . . Lowell's identifications with literary and historical figures have been gathering for years—sometimes directly through his historical poems and literary imitations. At other times, writing autobiography has allowed him to discover historical parallels to his own experience. The crystallization of *History* out of *Notebook* is only the latest stage in a steady dialogue, an attempt to place unruly and threatening experience into an understandable pattern. Now the parallels are marched out in chronological order, fraught with his own reflected meanings, a framework in which he can judge himself in turn as husband, lover, son and poet. (pp. 73-4)

Lowell has made *History* the elegiac autobiography he seems to have been searching for so long. . . . History, as Lowell sees it, is made up of the monuments men build to escape their inhuman selves, the mocking order men make from human fear and will. Being part of it is the only way Lowell finds to authenticate his life—an ultimate arrogance, but one in which he is as remorseless to himself as he is to others. (p. 76)

David Kalstone, "Robert Lowell: The Uses of History," in his Five Temperaments: Elizabeth Bishop, Robert Lowell, James Merrill, Adrienne Rich, John Ashbery *(copyright © 1977 by David Kalstone; reprinted by permission of Oxford University Press, Inc.), Oxford University Press, New York, 1977, pp. 41-76.*

DESMOND GRAHAM

All [Lowell's] intelligence, his understanding of shifting levels of experience and of language, led him to complexity but not to a reduction of scale or a restriction of feeling. Certainly he lives with bathos, the ironies of mundanity, but when this comes it comes with a bang:

> In the grandiloquent lettering on Mother's coffin,
> *Lowell* had been misspelled *LOVEL*.
> The corpse
> was wrapped like *panetone* in Italian tinfoil. . . .

The grandeur of Lowell's style reveals that triviality is simply no danger to him. His life-work has been pitched at a point most others dare not envisage. But the lines . . . do carry in them an antithetical problem to that of reduction, and even if they master it, it is not one Lowell always defeated. The lines are in themselves 'grandiloquent'.

Throughout his career, Lowell possessed and knew he possessed a seemingly incurable gift for words: a capacity to transform anything to rhetoric, to elevate and give resonance to whatever came under his hand; a capacity which he increasingly saw as the dangerous ability of art's order and resolution to triumph over the mess of life. And in his later writing . . . he sought to hold at least partly true to this mess by checking art's triumph. The title of his collection *Notebook* . . . is indicative of the extremity of his measures against art. There each unrhymed sonnet is a note, transitional and expedient: the collection as a whole a series of entries based neither on the thorough selectiveness nor the final ordering customary in art. His design is to retain something of the randomness and disorder of life. (p. 67)

Alongside this to-and-fro struggle with the power of art to shape experience, Lowell simultaneously attempted to diminish the potentially hermetic nature of art by offering experience which remained part of a distinct individual's private life. The troubles of marriage or mental breakdown, ruthlessly personal portraits of named relatives or friends dislodged the reader from the security of an understood relationship between the artist and his art: his responses were invited by Lowell to include those normally reserved for the autobiography, the memoir or the diary. To attempt such disturbance was of course not unique to Lowell's work, and most readers shift pretty flexibly between different modes: but that Lowell's methods were struggles with a problem at his work's heart was made abundantly clear in *The Dolphin* (1973). (pp. 67-8)

Lowell tries in *The Dolphin* to bring poem after poem back to its private source: 'fiction should serve us with a slice of life;/but you and I actually lived what I have written' ('Artist's Model 1'). We are given wonderful glimpses of intimate feeling, the texture of emotions in intimate relationships, but Lowell continually draws up back into the same dilemma; and when he does so, he bumps us up against the old problem—the power of his rhetoric. (p. 68)

[*Day by Day*] is the culmination and triumphant solution to this life-long problem; and part of the solution is simple. By using the sonnet sequence as form in the preceding volumes from *Notebook* on, Lowell had forced on his meditations a fixed duration which in the nature of the chosen form encouraged the line of thought to lead to a final thump at the sonnet's end. At least one moment in every fourteen was a sure temptation to his power of resolving conclusively, tying things up. *Day by Day* relaxes these formal demands (or in Lowell's case, temptations) by being written as a series of free-flowing Odes: the poem can range and continue as its momentum directs. The range, however, has one valuable limitation: politics is excluded.... As a result the volume can concentrate on its chosen area: an area wider than that of *The Dolphin,* for once again Lowell writes of his family, fellow-writers, friends, he even writes of 'Ulysses and Circe', as well as writing a sustained account of his life through the new marriage. Thus Lowell has stepped back to allow more room between his art and his life than he had desired in *The Dolphin*'s narrative of marriage.

The rest of the solution is more complex to explain but equally simple in effect. Still thinking of the relations between art and life, Lowell now shifts his attention away from the question of whether his poems are honest in relation to their source experience. (pp. 68-9)

When Lowell does take up the theme of the relations between art and life in this volume his questions are different. Either he asks about the responsibility of the artist towards his life:

> Did the musician, Gesualdo,
> murder his wife to inherit
> her voice of a nightingale? ...

Or he enquires about the responsibility of art in being able to enter experience which in life is intolerable:

> Can poetry get away with murder,
> its terror a seizure of the imagination
> foreign to our stubborn common health? ...

Lowell finds his solutions by side-stepping the problem: his triumph lies in a wholly positive direction. The whole focus of the volume is upon the theme of our capacity to live intensely, to respond as Vermeer's eye responded even if we cannot paint, to feel a sense of significance, to live what Lowell calls 'moments', points of time at which we are es-

pecially aware. This theme he declares in 'Notice': 'we must notice—/we are designed for the moment'. It is the theme of the Romantic artist but the experience is open to us all. In our responsive feelings we live poems. This is a fact of life and the sixty-odd poems of this collection identify it with the heart of life. (p. 69)

The moments which Lowell offers us range widely: from a momentary discovery, 'just the other day', of exactly how he and Berryman differed ('For John Berryman'); to a sudden awareness of the play of light on a tree.... Each moment of perception acutely brings to the feelings the presentness of things, and because this is felt so strongly the moments have their counterpart in time's passage, brought poignantly by approaching old age: 'I miss more things now,/am more consciously mistaken' ('Since 1939'); addressing a child: 'How unretentive we become,/yet weirdly naked like you' ('Sheridan').

Besides the threat from aging there are two further prices to be paid for this embracing of the moment: first, responsiveness can lapse.... Second, a worse pain: that of feeling too intensely. If joy can simply descend on us, as Lowell so directly portrays here—'Joy of standing up my dentist ... Joy to idle through Boston' ('Bright Day in Boston')—so too can suffering ...

As Lowell travels through the wide sphere of his own immediate and recalled experience, making connections, discoveries, he makes from his life ... 'a continual allegory'. It is one which Keats would have understood, for it is an allegory of feeling. Perceptions of loneliness, fear, self-disgust, happiness, gratitude, longing, nightmare, radiance, transform the events and people of his life into elements of a biography of feeling. Lowell as ever, allows his intelligence full play on what he feels, seeking to comprehend the complexity of experience. But this collection is content to rest poems on unresolved, even undramatised conflicts. Awareness is placed beside awareness, happiness darkens into nightmare and breakdown, returns with recovery and the knowledge which is the source for the volume's pervasive tone, that he has survived something he will not finally escape.

Lowell has brought his poetry back to poetry's source.... (p. 70)

> *Desmond Graham, "The Significance of Feeling: Robert Lowell's 'Day by Day'," in* Stand *(copyright © by* Stand*), Vol. 19, No. 3 (1978), pp. 66-70.*

JOHN HAFFENDEN

Robert Lowell's career as a poet moderated or wavered between his natural inclination towards symbolic formalism and his courtship of confessional free verse.... He would not have smarted at being called the heir of the French Symbolists, or more exactly of the Parnassians.... The Parnassians are neglected in favour of the Symbolists, but their standards of formal beauty and objective, often descriptive, verse found for a while a remarkable inheritor in Lowell. Just as the Parnassians both developed and reacted against the extravagances of the great Romantics ... [so] Lowell seemed to stand out for an impersonal rhetoric and conventional forms against the free verse utterances that the age had licensed.

My comparison is validated by the belief that when Lowell

came to revise *Notebook* (1969) for *History* (1973), he gave it what he regarded as a "noble ordonnance", a chronological arrangement, in the gratifying awareness that [José María de] Heredia had set him an example in *Les Trophées*, a sequence of 118 (mostly historical) sonnets published in 1893 and favourably greeted by adherents of diverse schools. . . . For Lowell the epic which he quarried out of *Notebook*, consisting of serried blank-verse sonnets, looked for sanction to his Parnassian forebear. . . . Before trying his hand at historical vignettes, in fact, Lowell had written many fourteen-line poems in free verse, and only then in blank verse. After the spritely, ironic personalism of *Life Studies* and *Near the Ocean*, he must have found the period from 1967 to 1972, during which he seems to have written nothing but unrhymed sonnets, a time of happy reversion to his ideal of "formal, difficult" poetry.

The Dolphin (1973) seems to me to represent the happiest marriage possible between the studied, hermetic, evasive mode that he had indulged for too long in *Notebook* and *History* and a treatment of personal experience which cast back to his fashion of the Fifties. Exploring a symbol of succour, lovingness and constancy, *The Dolphin* makes available the best devices that may be recovered from the Symbolists, raising personal emotion to a level of suggestiveness and immutability. The basic themes of that volume are, I think, those of self-consciousness and self-presentation, Art and the nature of perception, existential consolation and love, the debate between free-will and pre-ordination, and the possibilities of transcendence, all treated with a dignity that approaches inscrutability. The personal is transfigured and given an air of the timeless; at worst, the manner can edge dangerously near that extreme of Mallarmé's, an almost incomprehensible privacy. (pp. 40-1)

Kicking the addiction to the fourteen-line unit, *Day by Day* . . . represents a wilful regression to the type of free-verse expression for which he first won most praise, but which—as he confesses here in "Logan Airport, Boston"—is "a way of writing I once thought heartless". The consummate success is no longer there. Although these last verses continue Lowell's serial autobiography, their sentiments seem just adequate, wry, and unchallenging. Gone are the fierce rhetoric and syntax, and the bitter assaults, of his earlier decades. He makes gestures that are serviceable and unstriving: not cries but murmurs, not rage but renunciation. The prevailing mood is elegiac, rehearsing old friendships and mismanaged love, and indeed the rue and melancholy of certain poems about lost relationships often have an intense poignancy. All too many poems, however, can lapse into a slackness of diction or paragraphing, occasional vapid observations, or a sentimentality which is only evaded by leery ironies. . . . Even allowing for a measure of jokiness in some poems, Lowell's sententiousness or ponderousness can take the edge off irony. (pp. 41-2)

In earlier volumes Lowell gave himself to locutions which are as clumsy as some in this collection, and has often shown a weakness for being heavy-handed with metaphor. (p. 42)

What is new to [*Day by Day*] is the incidence of unambiguously negative remarks about himself, registering obsolescence and incapacity—"I do not enjoy / polemic with my old students . . ." ("Death of a Critic"), "I cannot bring back youth with a snap of my belt, / I cannot touch you—" ("Logan Airport, Boston"), "I cannot sleep solo"

("Wellesley Free"). . . . He registers many occasions of soullessness, but few moments for spiriteness. His posture and tone in general seem passive: his reflexes are sufficient to rumination. . . . In his earlier poems, self-disparagement did give assurance of actual capability. He could expend a little shame in order to imply the resilience of his talent and stature: his brilliance could bear it. (pp. 43-4)

The finest poems [of *Day by Day*]—among them "This Golden Summer", "Milgate", "Ear of Corn", and "Burial"—illustrate Lowell's porcelain sensitivity and are so well made that extrapolation would not serve. Delicate to the seasons, his curious eye is startled by a detail of the natural scene and distils and ramifies a sense of time and place into a large image of life. (p. 45)

Lowell clearly regretted leaving behind the virtuosity of the grand formal manner: he described the conversational idiom of these poems to me in deprecating terms—as "fray" and "shamble". The poems have a premature age in them, but without a quality we could call ripe wisdom. They demonstrate contemplation and achieved art, though the evidence of fresh insight is disconcertingly weak. There remains the authentic feeling, however, true to a tiredness of soul. Time, in Henry James's words, had breathed upon his heart—but not in appeasement. Tender-hearted, enduring without demanding, Lowell's last works everywhere touch magic moments, whimsies, a sense of transience, and the pathos and incorrigibility of his own life. In the final, moving poem called "Epilogue", he states his faith in a poetry of the imagination, a vision which "trembles to caress the light" as against what he regards as the regrettable limitations of his own "threadbare art",

> heightened from life,
> yet paralyzed by fact.

(pp. 45-6)

John Haffenden, "The Last Parnassian: Robert Lowell," in Agenda, *Summer, 1978, pp. 40-6.*

FLEUR ADCOCK

Much of [*Day by Day*] is occupied by the title sequence, dedicated to [Lowell's] wife and tracing a period of their lives in separate but interrelated lyrics; but most of the other poems in the volume are also personal in that they dwell on the poet's past, his friends, and his regular preoccupations (marriage, family history, and, of course, death). However, they do not have the smothering effect of naked autobiography. True, there is some discreet gossip-fodder, and some stimulation of our curiosity. (Which critic is he describing? Whose name is concealed by a dash?) But he looks in many directions—outward, forward, over his shoulder, as well as into his own psyche and surroundings —with generosity, gentleness and wit. "Domesday Book" is about all country houses, not just the one in which he lives; "Marriage" is about the couple in the Arnolfini painting as well as about the poet and his family. He is in fact so universal in places that there is a distracting temptation to quote his aphorisms: "Age is the bilge / we cannot shake from the mop." "Being old in good times is worse / than being young in bad."

Above all, he wrote so well. Released from the fourteen-line stanza of *Notebook* and its successors (which could be monotonous in bulk), he continued his movement away from strict forms and used for the most part a relaxed, supple, free verse which can take in almost anything without pretentiousness and without grating of gears. . . . (p. 85)

There are sagging lines and prosy rhythms here and there; and the collection could have been shorter. But there is so much in it to admire (including the often underestimated virtue of readability) that I find my criticisms giving way to simple relief that we have these poems at all. (p. 86)

> *Fleur Adcock, in* Encounter *(© 1978 by Encounter Ltd.), August, 1978.*

M

MacDIARMID, Hugh (pseudonym of Christopher Murray Grieve)   1892-

MacDiarmid is a Scottish poet, essayist, editor, translator, short story writer, biographer, and autobiographer. Although he has written in English, it is primarily as a writer of Scots verse that MacDiarmid is known. His acknowledged purpose as a poet has been to "revive the independent Scottish tradition of poetry," and to this end MacDiarmid has employed the form of traditional Scots ballads in his verse. The content of his poems is highly political, attributable to MacDiarmid's nationalist and Communist sentiments. (See also *CLC*, Vols. 2, 4, and *Contemporary Authors*, Vols. 5-8, rev. ed.)

JOHN MONTAGUE

MacDiarmid . . . never recognised [a] kind of absentee landlordism of the spirit: one of the aspects of his achievement worth stressing is the way he has got most of himself onto the page. . . . The contemplative centre we value so much in Eliot and Edwin Muir is there, but also the coarser activity, the sparks from the rim of the wheel. Pride, humour, contrariness; patriotism, hatred, nostalgia; love, lust, longing: there is no contemporary poem more varied in mood than *The Drunk Man Looks at the Thistle*. And since there is no achievement without an accompanying technique, the poem is a showpiece of MacDiarmid's early virtuosity, like *Hugh Selwyn Mauberley*, another poem in which a poet examines the civilisation he is involved with. . . .

[It] is clearly from medieval Scottish poetry that MacDiarmid inherits his ability to move from lyric to flyting, as well as his grasp of physical reality. (p. 27)

[The] best of his middle poetry often springs from his fascination with the maimed Celtic tradition, I am thinking of poems like "Island Funeral", "Direadh" and above all, "Lament for the Great Music". . . .

MacDiarmid transposes [the Celtic lines] so that they become a lament, not over a boy, but the civilisation to which he belonged, the original tradition, may it be said, of these islands. And the whole movement of the lines is changed to match the theme so that an almost naive cry of tenderness is keyed to a Whitmanian skirl. (p. 28)

MacDiarmid, with only a smattering of the language, has made the best translations from Scots Gaelic. . . . How much of the tradition does he manage to recreate in his own work? In the shorter poems of place, the deserted glens and cliffs whose names are the only Gaelic words current in daily speech, he can echo Duncan Ban MacIntyre's "in Praise of Ben Dorain", but with a savager note that testifies to his sense of distance from the older poetry's ease with nature (a common note, indeed, in all the Celtic literatures, except perhaps Welsh: early Irish poetry being so full of it that it cannot be compared with anything in English but with Chinese or Japanese poetry, with the quatrain to match the *haiku*).

> The North Face of Liathach
> Lives in the mind like a vision.
> From the deeps of Coire ne Caime
> Sheer cliffs go up
> To spurs and pinnacles and jagged teeth.
> Its grandeur draws back the heart.

It is this sense of isolation, loss, loneliness, that dominates . . . the longer poems: "Lost world of Gaeldom, further and further away from me / How can I follow, Albannach, how reachieve / the unsearchable masterpiece?" There are passages in "Lament for the Great Music" which reach the keening intensity of "MacCrimmon's Lament" . . . or that other death-cry of a civilisation, Gruffudd ab yr Ynad Coch's mourning of Llywelyn, the last independent Welsh prince. (pp. 28-9)

But the current of sympathy fails, and MacDiarmid's imaginative strength is overcome by the triviality of contemporary life in Scotland, "the ultimate Incoherence." And why not, when most of the things he speaks of . . . must seem outlandish to even most poetry readers? One of the troubles here is that the Celtic literatures are still the preserve of scholars . . . , compensating incongruity of poets being more familiar with the culture of the Pueblo Indians and the poetry of Basho and Li-Po than with that which most resembles them in their own countries. (pp. 29-30)

[This is] the central question of MacDiarmid's career: any attempt to concentrate on an aspect of his work tends to be dissipated by "the seamless garment" of his vision, especially in the later poems. Thus *A Drunk Man* sweeps up all the lyrics and doric-ised reading of a particular period, but the first section of *In Memoriam James Joyce* leans back to incorporate stanzas from "In a Caledonian Forest" (*Stony*

Limits) and "In the Shetland Islands" (*The Islands of Scotland*), 1934 and 1937 respectively.

This is the kind of thing which annoys critics bloodhounding for development, though it may well be the clue they are looking for. The primary reason for the change, acknowledged by the poet himself, seems to have been a mystical intuition of the universe as a unity of energies. This was always latent in MacDiarmid, whose early books combine poems of marvellously coarse farmyard detail, like "In Mysie's Bed", with glimpses of interstellar space.... (p. 30)

But when he attempts an explicit statement, as in "Moment of Eternity", which actually *opens* the *Collected Poems,* the language is too conventional to convince us that he has experienced Ygdrasil rather than a Shelleyan dream.... Nor does he come closer in *The Drunk Man* where the visions of eternity are so locally tethered that he can use "the mighty thistle in wha's boonds I rove" to mock the ending of the *Divina Commedia*, the one real failure of taste in MacDiarmid's masterpiece.

It was at some point afterwards, probably during his lonely sojourn in the Shetlands, that his sense of the endless pattern of the universe became overpowering. It can be expressed in political terms ... as well as in the geological accumulation which is the recurrent symbol in *Stony Limits*.... [It can even] take over The Celtic muse.... (p. 31)

Seamless garment or water of life, there is a force in MacDiarmid's later work which often dissipates the contrast and detail upon which, line by line, poetry must depend. And here perhaps one should enter the dangerous but necessary ground of poetic psychology; for the Universe of Light, the poetic equivalent of the Burning Bush seen by Moses in the Old Testament, is only one of the two primary poetic experiences. There is also the Muse, who, even through the medium of someone else's translation doctored into doric, dominates the variety of *A Drunk Man*.... (p. 32)

But the Muse is entitled to her revenge, and she refuses to wear a seamless garment, or else she loses her female shape; the reference to the great Irish poet Aodhagan O Rathaille's Aisling or vision poem "Gile na Gile" in *In Memoriam James Joyce* is tepid, compared to the original.... The combination of grotesquerie and tenderness which marks a poem like "The Tragic Tryst" ... or the comic extravagance which sees the Thistle louping out, "rootless and radiant" into the infinite, like a Doric spacecraft (both from *The Drunk Man*), seem gone from *In Memoriam James Joyce,* to be replaced by, at its best, a cerebral intensity, at its worst, a cataloguing insistence which recalls neither Gaelic nor Scots, but the tradition of compulsive Scottish pedantry. Then, abruptly, the rollcall stops, and we have one of these arias which, as in *The Pisan Cantos,* restore one's faith in the whole enterprise.

> So I think of you, Joyce, and of Yeats and others
>   who are dead
> As I walk this Autumn and observe

The birch tremulously pendulous in jewels of
   cairngorm,
The sauch, the osier, and the crack-willow
Of the beaten gold of Australia;
The sycamore in rich straw-gold;
The elm bowered in saffron;
The oak in flecks of salmon gold:
The beeches huge torches of living orange.

(p. 33)

Superficially [Pound] and MacDiarmid are ambitious and obsessed in the same polyglot way, with the difference that while it is a measure of Pound's commitment that (except for the translations) he has not written any shorter poems since beginning "that great forty year epic", *The Cantos,* MacDiarmid's procedure tends to be the reverse; everything he writes after a certain point in his career can be assembled into larger units like *In Memoriam James Joyce* but may first exist as a separate poem.

Certainly he has been for many years the most interesting of what John Berryman once described to me as "the outriders" in contemporary poetry, the only one who has sought to reconcile defiant adoption of a local or special tradition with the international claims of modern poetry.... [Although] MacDiarmid's later poetry might be more successful if he had learnt ... to break the line for emphasis, his *Collected Poems* makes most contemporary work seem thin-blooded. His aggressive masculine pose may seem inimical to sincerity, but it is close to the concept of *duende* in Lorca's essay or to Wyndham Lewis's famous prescription for modern poetry: one knows that it is a man singing, and not a bird. (p. 34)

> *John Montague, "The Seamless Garment and the Muse," in* Agenda, *Autumn-Winter, 1967-68, pp. 27-34.*

MATTHEW P. McDIARMID

The early MacDiarmid writes pure poetry. Later he will wish, unfairly, to say poor poetry. So much misleading talk has been heard about *Sangschaw* and *Pennywheep* restoring ideas to Scots poetry. Ideas were precisely at this stage, what it avoided. One can only say that he successfully brought it into line with a European fashion of sensibility that was luckily sympathetic to its traditional genius.

But if MacDiarmid's early poetry is not quite so significant of revolution as has been claimed, it has at least, in the lyrics, freed the Scots poet from his folk *persona*. And in his next volume, *A Drunk Man Looks At The Thistle*, a further degree of freedom is achieved, in his discursive writing. I say 'degree', because the manner of pure poetry is continued in much of it, and a style that un-self-consciously presents his individual, modern, intellectual personality is never fully developed. The traditional class character of modern Scots poetry is never wholly forgotten.

It is still "soun, no sense" that seeks to "faddom the herts o' men" in the version of the Russian of Alexander Blok that he calls *Poet's Pub:* "a silken leddy darkly moves" with no more specific motive than to put a dream in the poet's drink. And in a very important respect the moonlit Thistle symbolises Valéry's doctrine of aspiration to pure spirit, pure mind; symbolises it in its despair of realising itself. Valéry's theme and much of his indirect, suggestive, technique are easily identified in the most haunting of its lyrics, *O Wha's The Bride*. The 'gudeman' of this lyric demands an impossible perfection or purity of experience, and is told that he must content himself with the limited, impure but kindly knowledge of the senses, the flesh. (p. 76)

MacDairmid, in his most ambitious poem, may write a more overtly poetical poetry than the Burnsian and post-Burnsian school attempted, and even when exploiting folk connotations free himself from the folk-image of the poet, but his technique and style offer no serious contradiction to the eighteenth century opinion that modern Scots poetry must be, in the main, a colloquial poetry.

That this became his own conscious conclusion is nowhere stated but the fact is patent that after *A Drunk Man* Scots is a dwindling element in MacDiarmid's work. And it seems significant that its decline coincides with his rejection of the ideals of 'pure poetry', and with his pursuit of a "poetry of thought and fact" opposed to what he now called his "irresponsible lyricism". For his new kind of poetry English became increasingly his medium. One would have supposed that there was enough thought in *A Drunk Man,* but it is admittedly thought of a kind that does not require exact statement and develops no argument; it explores impressions, aspirations, not doctrines; it gives no clear pictures.

Where Scots recurs, for the last time considerably, in the Hymns to Lenin, the tone is again colloquial, but now only matter-of-factly colloquial—as in *The Seamless Garment,* where he brilliantly suggests the genius of Lenin's dialectic and Rilke's philosophic verse by images that his cousin in the Langholm weaving shop might be supposed able to grasp.

The vogue for a Communist poetry had again seemed to give his colloquial medium a congenial task, but it was at the expense of that freedom from class context that his earlier poetry had won for the image of the poet himself. There is no vital difference, in that respect, between this Scots verse and Burn's conversational epistles to other peasant-poets. MacDiarmid is indeed unique among West European poets in trying to write a genuinely working-class poetry. . . . (p. 77)

> *Matthew P. McDiarmid, "Hugh MacDiarmid and the Colloquial Category," in* Agenda, *Autumn-Winter 1967-68, pp. 72-7.*

JOHN C. WESTON

[The] mindless, sentimental poetry in Scots explains not only the vehemence of [MacDiarmid's] satire on St. Andrew's societies and Burns clubs in [*A Drunk Man Looks at the Thistle*] but the manner and matter of the poem, highbrow in the extreme, as far removed as possible from the kailyard, or often popular in form and images but applied ironically and unexpectedly to sacred or intellectual topics. (p. 86)

[*A Drunk Man*] forms more of a unity than most non-narrative long poems, like Pound's *The Pisan Cantos*. This sense of unity is all the more impressive in an undivided poem (undivided except for rows of periods and changes of type face and verse form), to which the poet refused to provide handrails, as he defiantly asserts to philistines in his Author's Note. Its unity derives most obviously from its form, an interior monologue in which the Drunk Man speaks, somewhat as does Prufrock in his 'Love Song', sometimes to himself, sometimes to the reader, sometimes in fantasy to others, like Jean (his wife), Burns, Dostoevsky, the people of Glasgow, but always, unlike Prufrock, from a physical situation of which the reader is repeatedly reminded by a pattern of returnings. . . . We keep coming back to the physical, dramatic situation, the *Drunk Man actually looking at the thistle,* as it changes in his mind to all the sublime or grotesque visions and hallucinations of similitudes, yoked by wonderful violence to the thistle, which constitute a good part of the poem. The title is dryly downright in its accurately describing what the poem is about on its most obvious formal level.

But the Drunk Man not only looks at the thistle and sees it metamorphose endlessly; he 'graipples' . . . with it. The poem is about the Drunk Man's struggle with the thistle, and this symbolic conflict provides a thematic unity to correspond to the dramatic unity given by the moonlit, thistle-observing situation. For the thistle represents, not only the traditional Scotland or Scotsmen, but in MacDiarmid's private symbolism, the divided nature of himself, the Scot, and of all mankind, a division which must be exploited, engaged, harmonised. The blossoms represent, like the moon toward which they extend, our spiritual, idealist, romantic aspirations; the roots, our animal and fleshly ties; the disorderly growth of foliage and thorns between represents the contradictory elements of life which must be possessed or integrated without conflict all at the same time. . . . (pp. 88-90)

The simplest practical lesson of the poem, to put it in isolation too simply, is *to be oneself,* a phrase with variations which is repeated for emphasis, but perhaps too much. . . . [The] Drunk Man's general view of history can be taken as a Romantic alternative offered, point for point, to the views of Oswald Spengler's *The Decline of the West*, published a few years before and explicitly condemned in this poem . . . : Spengler presents history, in a view quite antithetical to the Drunk Man's, as deterministic cycles of large cultures, a view in general opposed to progress of all mankind and to the historical efficacy of individual endeavour; and in regard to twentieth-century Western civilisation, opposed to art, philosophy, psychology, and religion as out of harmony with the tendency of the age. (pp. 90-1)

[The] poem results from a unique, imaginative synthesis of diverse literary elements, to speak only of the considerable bookish aspect of the poem, of course. The main unifying and most original idea is MacDiarmid's quite individual interpretation of Gregory Smith's Caledonian Antisyzygy, . . . or as he put it later, in a definition of the term inevitably too simple . . . 'a capacity to entertain at one and the same time without conflict two or more opposite and irreconcilable opinions'.

This struggle with the thistle in which the Drunk Man attempts to entertain opposites and irreconcilables as necessary in the economy of the world has two stages, one in which he develops its implications as to his own history and the other as to the history of mankind. Consequently there are two central sections in the poem, one, after the introduction . . . , about the Drunk Man's individual predicament . . . and the other, after a brief sequence on men and women . . . , about the process of mankind's development. . . . Near the end of this long section on progress comes the ideological climax of the poem, when the Drunk Man affirms his belief in man's past and future progress in quite explicit and pointed terms: 'The thistle rises and forever will'. . . . But this leaves Scotland and the personal problem of the Drunk Man unprovided for. What is Scotland's role and Scotland's drunken poet's role in the cosmic economy? (p. 92)

The Drunk Man is depressed enough by the slow general progress in an indifferent world toward this goal . . . , but when he sees the lack of independent movement at all in the lesser wheel of Scotland, with its crazy and embarrassing cast of characters, he protests . . . , in one of the funniest but bitterest passages of the poem, that he cannot abide his company. Then ensues the tragi-comic discussion with another part of himself, who tells him that Scots have always hated change and new ideas but that he must either die to break their living tomb—as many Scots poets have done before—or renounce his Scottishness. This is the dramatic climax of the poem. . . . The thematic climax came before when the Drunk Man affirmed his faith in mankind in general. Now he must choose whether or not to put that general faith into action by dying for the ineducable Scots. The Drunk Man after a pause, in some confusion, marked by the shattering of the neat triplets and whole lines, refuses to make a choice, and then with an ambiguous attitude toward the weary but glorious progress of mankind, cuts off his agony of decision by calling out like a child for Jean, who will he knows comfort him. Here there appears a row of asterisks, the only such structural signal in the poem. (pp. 92-3)

In the last line and a half, MacDiarmid causes Jean's retort to turn it all into a joke, to bring the whole poem back to earth, away from the heavens and the prophetic future to the hillside in Montrose. This ending to a great Scottish poem is appropriate to Scotland, whose literature, it has often been noted, abounds in flashing shifts of sensibility, in grotesque combinations of lofty idealism and low realism, of delicate fantasy and coarse earthiness. And the sudden shift at the end is only the last instance of an important formal method of the poem, the unexpected juxtaposing of opposite viewpoints and tones without transition. And this method, of course, is an instance of the form echoing the sense, for the most important idea in the poem also relates to bringing together opposites, of struggle toward spirit through flesh, of uniting the roots and the blossoms of the thistle by the counterdirected foliage in between. (p. 93)

> *John C. Weston, "A Critical Note on 'A Drunk Man Looks at the Thistle'," in* Hugh MacDiarmid: A Critical Survey, *edited by Duncan Glen (© 1972 Scottish Academic Press; reprinted by permission), Scottish Academic Press Ltd., 1972, pp. 85-93.*

IAIN CRICHTON SMITH

When one discusses the poetry of Hugh MacDiarmid one is forced to make an evaluation of the importance of ideas in poetry or to put it another way to discuss how ideas are related if at all to poetry. (p. 124)

MacDiarmid's favourite method seems to be a dialectic one. He may have learned this from a study of Communism but he was talking about Hegel before Communism came into his poetry. In this method he veers from one idea to its opposite. And very often he comes down on neither side. (p. 126)

Now clearly the dialectical movement in poetry is not uncommon and can be very exciting. However if the poem remains on *the level of the idea* no final result can ever be arrived at. And often one feels with MacDiarmid that in fact he does not resolve his poems as poetry. The ideas are built up in a staggering profusion, like an insane stair, and no resolution seems to be possible. (p. 127)

[The poem 'Easter Rising'] does not convince us by its ideas. It convinces by its language, its pathos and its music, by the feeling that the whole of Yeats is concerned in this poem and not just his mind. One feels that for Yeats this event was a human event. It has not only changed these men: it has changed Yeats. It will possibly change us. But it will not change us simply because of the ideas. . . . One feels with MacDiarmid's poem and with much else of his poetry of ideas that in fact he himself is not changed humanly. He has only seen with his mind, not felt with his heart. . . .

Now the course of MacDiarmid's progress can be charted fairly clearly. The first two or three books are books of lyrics mainly. Then there is the long poem *A Drunk Man,* on the whole successful because the dialectic there is freshly felt and at the same time the dialectic suits the drunk man. . . . (p. 128)

MacDiarmid did take a wrong turning when he began on his poetry of ideas. . . .

I believe that after the creation of his lyrics MacDiarmid, with that curious distrust that poets have about the value of something simply because of its smallness, felt that he ought to move on to more 'serious' work. . . . I believe that 'The Watergaw' is in every way far more serious than anything he produced on the basis of ideas alone. These long poems may be intellectually exciting but they are not serious. They do not confront us with serious things. They do not, I think, react on us as whole human beings. Their explorations are not deep enough. (p. 129)

I think [*A Drunk Man*] is a major work on many levels though MacDiarmid finds difficulty with the ending. . . . [On] balance the image of the thistle and the moonlight does in fact hold the poem together and holds it at the same time in a real physical world. The later poems seem to me not to be able to get hold of a symbol which will be a unifying thread. Here too in this poem a lot of what he says later on is said for the first time and said freshly. I often wonder whether in fact some of *To Circumjack Cencrastus* may not be passages rejected from the previous poem.

In a sense the dialectic seems to work for this poem partly because the symbolism helps it to. The basic groundwork of the poem which in effect is the struggle towards consciousness of a man and of a nation and of humanity is represented lucidly by the thistle and the moonlight. The thistle can be seen to stand for the man distorted by morality and the pressures of existence. The moonlight can be seen to stand for the Platonic idea, complete, unflawed and often deadly.

The fact too that the thistle is the Scottish symbol allows MacDiarmid to pass from the personal to the national very easily. It is clear also that to a certain extent he does allow the main character to be different from himself. (p. 134)

The change in mood and thought (which in others of the poems may seem arbitrary) does not seem so in this poem because the protagonist is after all a drunk man. It is a very gay poem, a very witty poem, the poem of a writer who has not allowed himself to be overwhelmed by the world. One senses in *Cencrastus* a kind of bitterness of which there is little sign in the *Drunk Man*. MacDiarmid in this poem is still able to objectify his insights without rancour. (pp. 134-35)

The poem does not seem to me to reach any conclusion but it does not seem to matter very much for it is redeemed by so many other qualities, wit, humour, snatches of strange balladic verses, and in general a healthy tone.

Nevertheless in spite of all this and, in spite of the fact that in variety, interest in humanity, glitterings of wit, and sustained rhetoric this poem must undoubtedly be considered major and in spite of the brilliant use to which MacDiarmid puts his symbolism—externalising and internalising the thistle from one moment to another and doing the same with the moonlight (it is perhaps this he learnt from Rilke if he learnt anything)—in spite of the fact that there is a great richness in the poem, one still comes back to the earliest poems of all and one or two lyrics here and there among the later poems.

Essentially MacDiarmid is at his greatest in his lyric poems. Even the *Drunk Man* is itself a collection of lyrics to a great extent. . . . In general he hasn't quite the architectural power necessary for the true long poem and it may be that this is no longer possible anyway.

It is a part of my argument therefore to say that in many of these long poems what he is in effect doing is setting up arguments and then knocking them down with others. Also they lack (these later ones) that which we look for in the greatest poetry, insights into human beings. I believe that it is in the early poems that MacDiarmid is concerned with people and their feelings and that later this disappears even when paradoxically he is claiming to be a Communist. But this is not the whole of my argument. I believe it goes deeper than this.

I believe that what happened to MacDiarmid is as follows. He began as a poet with both a masculine and feminine sensibility and eventually allowed the masculine elements in himself to dominate his work, therefore to a great extent becoming less human than he once was.

For what we find in the early MacDiarmid and miss later is a real tenderness, a real feminine love. . . . It is for this tenderness and for a kind of hallucinatory quality which owes little to logic or reason that I above all value MacDiarmid. (pp. 135-36)

Whatever the imagination is, there is no doubt that it is what we require in poetry at the highest level. How it operates is incomprehensible. What it creates is, strictly speaking, incapable of being managed by the mind. This is true on a very slightly lesser level of 'The Bonnie Broukit Bairn'.

In this poem there are combined in a short space many of the elements which make MacDiarmid's poems distinctive —the concern with the universe and images of it, the intellectual wit, the class-distinction if one cares to call it that. (pp. 138-39)

Along with 'The Watergaw' the 'Empty Vessel' seems to me to be on the highest level of the imagination. One points

to the use of the word 'swing'—a word which one associates with children—but the mind is again defeated by this most moving poem. I have already said that in these poems there is a tenderness which the later MacDiarmid seems to have lost, surrendering himself instead to the masculine principle of reason. All these poems which I have mentioned illustrate this tenderness in some degree or another, this concern with humanity in an almost feminine way. . . . These lyrics are imaginatively in love with the universe. Whatever achievements MacDiarmid later made nothing comes near to the authority of these lyrics, an authority which rests only on themselves. They demand no proof and ask no questions or, if they do, they do not expect an answer. The poems themselves are answers on the imaginative level. The poems answer by music and language and the answer is love, the love which comes from tenderness and care. I know for instance of no poem like 'The Bonnie Broukit Bairn'. Here there is applied to the universe a parochial language, which seems to make it familiar and loved. (p. 139)

When the ideas in the poem are detachable they can be contradicted and often are. MacDiarmid can be contradicted when one discusses his *In Memoriam James Joyce*. He cannot be attacked at all on the level of these lyrics. They are the real proof of his genius. (pp. 139-40)

> *Iain Crichton Smith, "The Golden Lyric," in* Hugh MacDiarmid: A Critical Survey, *edited by Duncan Glen (© 1972 Scottish Academic Press; reprinted by permission), Scottish Academic Press Ltd., 1972, pp. 124-40.*

G. S. FRASER

This essay is a kind of appendage to Iain Crichton Smith's *The Golden Lyric* . . . [see excerpt above], which was at once a wonderful appreciation of Hugh MacDiarmid's early poems, and a wonderful polemic against his later development. (p. 211)

I agree with Crichton Smith that MacDiarmid's later poetry is extraordinarily uneven, and also that the unevenness comes partly from a demand for submission, for practical assent, upon the part of the reader, that is not a properly poetic demand. But I think one can make a much better case for much of MacDiarmid's later poetry, if one thinks of the argument in the poems as being directed not against a reader who is being bullied but against MacDiarmid himself. . . . The element of greatness in MacDiarmid's later poetry lies in an inwardness, an unending inner struggle, in a strenuously lonely man, whose loneliness can, for the reader, be an emblem of his own. . . . The rhetoric of MacDiarmid's best poetry is not the argument with others but the argument with oneself.

The 'ideas', which to Crichton Smith seem so peremptory and cantankerous (so much the ideas of an aggressively self-educated man) are in the end elements in a total composition: like Yeats's 'images'. The pose of wanting to change the reader and the world radically and immediately is part of a properly poetic strategy; the building up of a *persona*, which is something like Hobbes's Leviathan, or the giant figures in Blake, a kind of composite emblematic Man. MacDiarmid is a poet of the 'egotistical Sublime': one who tries to include everything (including long passages lifted from other writers) in himself, rather than, like Yeats, to lose himself in everything. (pp. 212-13)

It seems to me that on looking over . . . 'On A Raised Beach' and still more on looking through one of the much longer later poems like *In Memoriam James Joyce,* one has an impression not dissimilar to that which Wölflinn [art historian and an author of *The Renaissance and the Baroque*] describes: 'enormous weight and massiveness', a distinct lack of 'formal discipline and thorough-going articulation'—though they can be scanned, these long poems are not in any particular metre, and though they are argumentative, they have not, quite unlike *Religio Laici* or *An Essay on Criticism,* or even the *Prelude,* a ground-plan of structure, a reason in themselves why, and where, they should begin and end—and on the other hand there is, in the more striking passages, 'the animation, the restlessness, the violent agitation' of which Wölflinn speaks. In writing these long poems, MacDiarmid too [as Wölflinn sees Michelangelo's men and women] appears to be the 'unresisting victim of an inner compulsion, so that some [passages] are expressive to the utmost while others are totally lifeless and inert . . . Vitality is unevenly distributed . . . some parts are superhuman in their strength, others are all weight.'

The move from the Renaissance to the Baroque is a move from a love of details and particulars for their own sakes (such as we get, for instance, in MacDiarmid's *A Drunk Man Looks at the Thistle*) to something more monotonous but by intention at least grander. . . . (p. 226)

The best of MacDiarmid's early poems, whether lyrical, satirical, comical, or a mixture of all three things, have the qualities that Wölflinn assigns to Renaissance poetry . . . : a sense of the variety of things, a quickness and gaiety, an untroubled acceptance of life within its limitations, what we call humanism. MacDiarmid was the leader of the Scottish Renaissance. In his later work, he is anti-humanistic: he seeks transcendence, he tortures himself and strains: he can no longer represent, nor does he desire, the rhythms, the harmonies, the humours of ordinary human happiness. He has a sense of oppressive weight incumbent on him, he sometimes collapses under this inertly, he sometimes struggles against it with titanic energy. Like Michelangelo, he has a certain *terribilità*. There is much less perception, detailed perception, in his late poems, but a much more unified and grandiose atmosphere. He has moved from the humanistic to the religious; he takes on, deliberately, more burdens than he can well bear. He does nothing that can be done easily and gracefully. He is the lone representative of a Scottish . . . new Baroque. The repetitions, the vagueness, the grandeurs, the movement and stress and the impatience with the limitations of the human condition itself are all there.

The late poems oppress us or impress us or bore us, sometimes, these abrupt alternations of the strenuous and the inert, but they do not offer us, anyway, any more than Michelangelo does, the ordinary kind of artistic pleasure. They are struggling beyond the limits of art. They are not what I turn to, when I am turning to poetry for pleasure. But let us admire the lonely effort that has gone into them, and let us admire the strong old man, stonily intransigent, implacable, struggling always for transcendence. (p. 227)

> *G. S. Fraser, "Hugh MacDiarmid: The Later Poetry," in* Hugh MacDiarmid: A Critical Survey, *edited by Duncan Glen (© 1972 Scottish Academic Press; reprinted by permission), Scottish Academic Press Ltd., 1972, pp. 211-27.*

EDWIN MORGAN

The first poetry [MacDiarmid] wrote was in English, and was not particularly distinguished. Gradually and deviously, between 1921 and 1923, he began to move towards the position of believing that Scots might be revived, and carried out his own experiments in Scottish poetry. What was clear to him—and it is his great historical importance to have seen this—was that the moment had come for an exploration of Scottish vocabulary and idiom quite different from the debased, sentimental, jocose, moralizing tradition of nineteenth-century Scottish verse: in other words, Scots could be placed, and worked in, against the background of European symbolism and modernism. . . . The poems in *Sangschaw* (1925) and *Penny Wheep* (1926), mostly short lyrics, are the first fruits of that enthusiasm, and the former volume is one of the landmarks of modern Scottish poetry. (pp. 6-7)

For those who believe that lyrics are not enough (and MacDiarmid is certainly one of them), *A Drunk Man Looks at the Thistle* (1926) is his most potent testing-ground for a more extended and ambitious use of the imagination. . . . The poem is not tightly knit as argument or narrative, yet it does hold together, because the method of composition perfectly suits the main conception of the work. A drunk man is lying sprawled in the moonlight, looking at a huge thistle which seems to him in his befuddled state to be constantly changing its shape and being transformed into other things. So both the whisky he has been drinking and the moonlight which makes everything strange and mysterious combine to produce a dreamlike atmosphere. (pp. 12-13)

The theme of Scotland is fairly pervasive in the poem, as one would expect from the title. Although the thistle becomes or is likened to many other things, it is basically the Scottish national emblem, and the drunk man looking at it is MacDiarmid's device for commenting, in a great variety of tones, on his own country. (p. 13)

The poem as a whole has remarkable power, and more cohesion than one might expect from the somewhat hectic method of its composition, with passages being put in and taken out right up to the last moment. There are sections that could be clearer, and some that just don't quite come off . . . ; there are problems, here and there, of vocabulary and syntax. But it remains a highly original poem, meaty, visionary, comic, endlessly surprising. (p. 17)

Most observers of MacDiarmid's work are struck by its curious mixing of desire to bring poetry and science together, on the one hand, and on the other hand the recurring element of metaphysical speculation. The former seems to be aligned with his love of the multitudinousness of things, the latter with his equally deep interest in the desolate, the barren, the remote, and the solitary. . . . MacDiarmid comes to us swathed in the Many yet yearning towards the One. If many of his poems are cascades of particularities, others are in praise of an almost mystical emptiness, deprivation, withdrawal, silence, and stillness. (p. 26)

In prose as in verse, it is a kind of irrepressible energy that strikes us most in MacDiarmid's work, an energy which at times outruns the reader's patience or the demands of the subject but which always recovers unexpectedly, pauses, and strikes like a cobra. His methods are his own, and he is a model for no one, but he is one of the great twentieth-century writers, and a writer whose individuality it will take the next century to sift and define. (p. 33)

Edwin Morgan, in his Hugh MacDiarmid (©
*Edwin Morgan; Longman Group Ltd., for the
British Council), British Council, 1976.*

*   *   *

MAILER, Norman   1923-

**Mailer, a novelist, essayist, social critic, and filmmaker, is
one of the most prominent contemporary American writers.**
The Naked and the Dead **is considered one of the major novels
to be written about the Second World War, but his fiction
since has been of uneven quality. He has shown a much more
consistently capable hand in his nonfiction, most of which is
written in the style of New Journalism. Foremost among
these works are** *Armies of the Night* **and** *Of a Fire on the
Moon.* **A writer of powerful prose, he is at his best when attacking the materialism and spiritual malaise of contemporary American society. (See also** *CLC*, **Vols. 1, 2, 3, 4, 5, 8,
and** *Contemporary Authors*, **Vols. 9-12, rev. ed.)**

F. W. DUPEE

Advertisements for Myself is chaotic; its tone is uncertainly
pitched between defiance and apology. So much is this the
case that anyone can easily lay hands on its jugular, and
many reviewers have done so and thought they severed it.
But the condition of Norman Mailer's life and art is that his
jugular remains exposed. With all its faults in view, *Advertisements for Myself* is a confessional document of considerable interest and an engrossing chronicle of the postwar
literary life. It is also an extremely funny book, for Mailer's
gifts as a humorist are among his most reliable gifts. The
one thing that his candor and wit leave unmolested is his
own heavy dependence on the literary past, on *what has
been done.* (pp. 97-8)

[The] attraction of *Moby Dick* to Mailer [who once described a projected thousand-page novel as "a descendant
of *Moby Dick*"], seems to consist largely in its bulk, profundity, and prestige. It is to him, I should imagine, an
image of literary power rather than a work to be admired,
learned from perhaps, and then returned to its place of
honor. And to judge by *Advertisements,* the literary past is
all the weightier for him because it includes the achievements of Hemingway, Faulkner, Dos Passos, Fitzgerald,
and others of their vintage, all of them together representing to him a massed accumulation of potency. How did he
come to write his first published book, *The Naked and the
Dead,* a novel of army life in the late war? ". . . I may as
well confess I had gone into the army with the idea that
when I came out I would write the war novel of World War
II." With this idea in mind he did serve in the army (proud-
ly, as a rifleman) and he did produce, punctually, efficiently, and as if on demand, *The Naked and the Dead.* But
what an idea, and what a phrase, "the war novel of World
War II"! *The* war novel? To be sure, Hemingway, Dos
Passos, and others of their time had used their varied experiences of World War I in the writing of a lot of enormously varied books. Not they, but later journalists and
sociologists, lumped those books together in the misleading, the unreal, category of "war novels." And when the
second war arrived, the same crowd created that demand
for "the novel of World War II" which Mailer determined
to meet.

Advertisements for Myself testifies to his constant preoccupation with those 20's writers, in their capacity not merely

as war novelists but as symbols of literary prestige in general. (pp. 98-9)

No Olympians can ever have looked more Olympian to an
outsider than Hemingway and the others have looked to
Mailer. . . . His genuine appreciation of their work was
laced with a strong sense of their material stature—their
reputation, influence, position in the literary market place.
One sees, too, that his disposition to regard them, and the
literary past in general, in this light, arose not only from the
fact of his coming of age at this formidable phase of their
careers. He also came of age at a moment of rapidly growing prosperity and expanding culture in America, when similar rewards seemed to be within reach of himself and other
aspiring young writers.

Hence, probably, the dreams of worldly power which, in
the pages of *Advertisements,* give unmistakable signs of
being conjoined to his legitimate literary ambitions. Unmistakable? He has been "running for President for years," he
says, and applies the same phrase to James Jones. Such
truculent admissions are evidently supposed to induce in
the reader a state of amused shock. To me they represent a
rather depressing confusion of purposes. Why, with a
thousand-page novel to finish, does anyone *want* to be
President, unless he fears that he will never finish the
novel? (pp. 99-100)

Advertisements may, as Alfred Kazin affirms, resemble
Fitzgerald's *The Crackup* in showing "how exciting, yet
tragic, America can be for a gifted writer." But Mailer's
battleground has at least these resemblances to a city play-
ground: it is strenuous, competitive, gang-conscious, cruel,
sporting, amusing. And though America is unquestionably
exciting to Mailer, it is wonderful how little he ever allows
it to become tragic. Indeed, his response to the excitement
of it is intense enough to preclude his feeling "deeply" any
tragedy in it. One of the advantages of *Advertisements* over
his novels is that the sense of excitement and the laughter
get full play here, unembarrassed by any need to write, or
rewrite, the Great American Novel. America represents
wonderful sport and adventure to Mailer; and they get better as America itself seems to him to grow more corrupt
and menacing. (p. 100)

The various forms of enlightenment which the older writers
brought to bear on their experience seem to have crystallized, for Mailer, into a vague, self-conscious sort of wisdom. This has sought to express itself in appropriate ideas,
Marxist or Nietzschean . . . or Freudian. Of these the
Freudian is Mailer's most pervasive source of ideas and
images. It is astonishing how often in his novels an authoritative older person is engaged in trying to assist some
younger, more amorphous person to maturity. . . . But the
Freudian ideas, like those of other derivation, often operate
not to reinforce and clarify his experience but to embarrass
and devitalize it. The author himself seems frequently to
approach his material as the learner, the disciple, the patient, eager to grow up.

The result in his novels is . . . a sort of tug of war between
his passion for experience and his felt need of enlightening
ideas. And it is in *The Deer Park,* that survivor of what
was to be his eight-part colossus, that Mailer's contradictions reach their maximum intensity. When Alfred Kazin
calls *The Deer Park* a "somehow sick book," "peculiarly
airless and closed," I feel obliged to assent even while re-

belling against the J. Donald Adams-like adjectives. (*The Deer Park* brings out the old Adams in us all.) For this novel about the sex life, the political, social, and business problems of Hollywood personages gathered in a resort resembling (I gather) Palm Springs, is frequently paralyzed by its opposing intentions. The manners prevailing in this unpleasant pleasure resort are superbly observed. The conversation of Hollywood magnates is admirably comic. The routines of the call-girls form a weird dance-like pattern within the slowly moving narrative. In the rendering of such things Mailer's passion for experience is matched by his expert knowledge of what he writes about. How does it happen, then, that this panorama of iniquity is constantly threatening to turn into a waxworks display? For one thing, Mailer's trio of heroes, Eitel, Faye, and O'Shaugnessy, are too sententious and loquacious and self-conscious. In their frequent colloquies they constitute a sort of committee interminably "chewing on" (in committee jargon) the agenda of the day. And with much help from the author, by way of his often intrusive comments on the action, they just about chew the hell out of it. Literally, they all but convert the experience of modern corruption into something inert, dry, and abstract. (pp. 101-02)

With his essential humor, sanity, and (yes!) humility, Mailer seems to . . . give promise of reconciling his appetite for life with his appetite for ideas. But a novel in perhaps a thousand pages? *Raintree County* approached that length, I believe, but *Moby Dick,* in my edition, runs to only 822. (p. 103)

> F. W. Dupee, "The American Norman Mailer" (*reprinted from* Commentary *by permission; copyright © 1960 by the American Jewish Committee*), *in* Commentary, *February, 1960 (and reprinted in* Norman Mailer: A Collection of Critical Essays, *edited by Leo Braudy, Prentice-Hall, Inc., 1972, pp. 96-103*).

LAURA ADAMS

Through the years Mailer has acquired notoriety through incidents ranging from the stabbing of his second wife to his New York mayoralty campaign, and his facility for antagonizing his audiences is well known. Whatever the circumstances of his exposure to the public, Mailer rarely fails to be "good copy" and consequently has been fair game for the media newsmakers. Because of the difficulty of reconciling this notorious Mailer with the much-admired author of *The Naked and the Dead* and *The Armies of the Night,* critics have commonly, at their most charitable, dismissed Mailer's public acts as irrelevant to his written work, or, at their least, considered them damaging to his reputation as a writer. (p. 3)

Ironically, with the awarding of the 1968 Pulitzer Prize and National Book Award to *The Armies of the Night,* Mailer was admitted to the American literary establishment despite his continued violations of its decorum, which, indeed, since that time are more often received as the eccentricities of a literary genius than as the self-indulgences of a publicity-seeking minor novelist.

Far from being antipathetic to his writing, however, as *The Armies of the Night* demonstrates, Mailer's public acts are the tests of the efficacy of his theories without which he could grow neither as a man nor as a writer. To attempt to separate Mailer's art from his life is to invite the question, "What is his art if not the creation of himself?" Part of the

problem we have had in accepting this relationship in Mailer (although not in his Romantic predecessors) stems from his huge ambition and his usurpation of the critic's role with respect to his own work. At a time when he had only one popular and critical success to his name, his fine 1948 war novel, *The Naked and the Dead,* and three comparative failures, his ambitions seemed presumptuous. . . . [In *Advertisements for Myself*] he planned to outdo all other American writers, past and present, by trying to hit "the longest ball ever to go up into the accelerated hurricane air of our American letters." Were these not presumptions enough, the book itself was a rejection of conventional criticism, conventional themes, conventional forms. (p. 4)

Committed . . . to altering the contemporary consciousness, Mailer continually changed and refined his methods in his search for the most effective means to this end. The years between *Advertisements for Myself* (1959) and *The Armies of the Night* (1968) were rich in explorations into both subject matter and style, always aimed at pushing back their existing limits. Much of the difficulty readers had with *An American Dream* and *Why Are We in Vietnam?,* for example, was caused by the unconventional subject matter of the former and the difficult style of the latter. . . . While of uneven quality, the quantity of work produced during this period is prodigious.

Mailer resolved his thematic and stylistic concerns in the work which may be considered the end product of this experimental period, *The Armies of the Night.* That *Armies* is further the culmination of twenty years of writing may be seen through the perspective I have termed Mailer's aesthetics of growth. Since the late 1950's Mailer has had a vision of forces at war for possession of the universe, metaphors for our moral directions which he calls God and the Devil, whose victories or defeats are seen as ultimately productive either of life or death for the human race. The forces of evil, or totalitarians, have been winning for too long, he believes, so that "God is in danger of dying." The machine technology and those who would extend its power have characteristically been Mailer's villains and the human spirit their victim. In order for man's consciousness to grow once more toward the vitality and creativity it had enjoyed during the Renaissance and in frontier America, when the limits of human possibility were explored, each individual must wage his own war against the totalitarian systems which would control and segment him. The battleground is anywhere, the opponent anyone or anything that would prevent human growth, the moment of battle "existential," for in summoning the courage to confront an adversary one pushes himself out onto the end of a limb where "he does not go necessarily to his death, but he must dare it." The reward for victory is growth through renewed courage and self-confidence and the remission of old sins.

To be defeated, on the other hand, is to permit the life-sapping forces to take hold in oneself (cancer is Mailer's metaphor), making future victories more difficult. Our only defenses are our knowledge of the danger and our capacity for courageous action against the enemy. The progress of a human life, then, in Mailer's design, is charted as a series of moments of synthesis resulting from the interaction of opposing forces and aimed ultimately at embracing all contradictions.

To seek victory over what one considers evil and productive of death is to strive toward the heroic condition. Convinced of the need for a heroic leader, a man capable of embodying the ambiguities and contradictions of this discordant age, Mailer began to develop him through the contours of style. That style has always been heavily metaphorical, and attempts to take him literally have often obscured his meaning. The initial reception of *An American Dream* is a case in point. Read as realism, the book seems to justify murder and sexual perversion. However, as a metaphor for America's need to rid itself of its corruption and to seek a new and better self truer to the old American Dream, the novel is one of the finest contemporary visions of America's possibility through a courageous and radical heroism.

Over the years Mailer moved through a series of possible heroes including the amoral hipster of the "The White Negro" and President John F. Kennedy, as well as Stephen Rojack of *An American Dream,* before concluding that the viable hero for our time must be a man in whom the schizophrenic halves of the American psyche, the dream of the extraordinary and the mundane reality, can come together. And so Mailer settled upon a man whom he created as much as discovered for the role: himself.

It is in the combination of the actual and the metaphorical functions of the hero known as "Mailer" in *The Armies of the Night* that Mailer's life and art grow together most significantly. Because we live in an anti-heroic, deflating age, the hero for our time must be comic, capable of ludicrous self-debasement on the one hand and courageous action on the other. Such is Mailer's portrayal of himself. . . . Clearly the Mailer hero is no Superman but a very human being who on occasion summons up the courage to rise above the beast in himself, to outweigh and redeem his failures, although because he is human he will fail again. This knowledge is what makes him a whole man and can make America a whole nation.

Having established himself as the representative American hero, Mailer is obliged to confront those events which are capable of influencing our national destiny, as his works since *The Armies of the Night* demonstrate. . . . [It is] the "detached ego," the persona generally known as "Aquarius" whose confrontations with and experiences of current events provide Mailer the writer with material. The use of himself as an objective observer in these books, rather than as a literary character, represents a shift in emphasis since *The Armies of the Night* from the method to the material. Mailer has overcome the historian's traditional difficulty, determining the reliability of his sources of information, through his own presence at and participation in the making of history. (pp. 5-8)

The progress from the Norman Mailer who wrote a fine war novel in the best American tradition a quarter-century ago to the Norman Mailer of *The Armies of the Night* who created a new literary form to encompass his expanding vision of American life is the result of Mailer's uncompromising adherence to his goals. While it may surely be argued that much of Mailer's work has been ineffective for his purpose, it must also be granted that the nonliterary portions of the work, which have seemed so various, so ill-conceived, so egocentric to some are part of a progressive whole. After all, it is the process itself and the aesthetics that move it rather than his separate performances which constitute Mailer's greatest contribution to his age. (p. 8)

Laura Adams, in her introduction to Will the Real Norman Mailer Please Stand Up? *edited by Laura Adams (copyright © 1974 by Kennikat Press, Inc.; reprinted by permission of Kennikat Press Corp.), Kennikat, 1974, pp. 3-9.*

JOYCE CAROL OATES

Mailer is shameless in his passion for women, and one is led to believe anything he says because he says it so well. He is so puritanical, so easily and deeply shocked, like any hero, that his arguments, which approach the fluidity and senselessness of music, have the effect of making the dehumanized aspects of womanhood appear attractive. (p. 216)

[To] Norman Mailer, "the prime responsibility of a woman is probably to be on earth long enough to find the best mate possible for herself, and conceive children who will improve the species."

But we don't know what the *species* is. A post-Darwinist name for "God"? A scientific concept? A mystical concept? A word? An identity? An essence? Do we locate ourselves in it, or does it push through us, blindly, with the affection of a stampeding crowd? And how long is "long enough"? Should we remain on earth for twenty years, or forty, or dare we hope for an extravagant eighty years, though our last several decades will be unproductive and therefore unjustified? . . . The "power to conceive or not to conceive" is, after all [according to Mailer], the "deepest expression of [a woman's] character. . . ." Not one kind of expression, not even the most pragmatic expression, but the deepest expression! One sees why the mystic is the most dangerous of human beings. (pp. 217-18)

The mechanical fact of possessing a certain body must no longer determine the role of the spirit, the personality. If Women's Liberation accomplishes no more than this it will have accomplished nearly everything.

But there are further problems, further areas of masculine uneasiness. Mailer criticizes Kate Millett for believing in "the liberal use of technology for any solution to human pain." Yes, that sounds like heretical belief so long as human pain is valued as sacred, or important as an expression of personality, or helpful for salvation . . . or even conversation. But it isn't. It is nothing, it is a waste, a handicap, a mistake. . . . Mailer, like all heroic spirits, places a primitive value on suffering. And one feels that he would not shy away from suffering, even the suffering of childbirth, if that were a possibility for him. Yes, to suffer, to feel, to be changed—it is a way of realizing that we live. But it is also a way of becoming dehumanized, mechanized. In fact, a way of dying. (pp. 219-20)

At the start of *The Prisoner of Sex,* Mailer speaks of having taken care of his large family for several weeks during the summer, cooking, cleaning, turning into a kind of housewife, so exhausted with domestic chores that he had no time to write, to think, to contemplate his ego. *No time to contemplate his ego!* (p. 221)

There will be a place in our society for Mailer's heroic mysticism, at the point in history at which women can afford the same mysticism. (p. 223)

Joyce Carol Oates, "Male Chauvinist?" in Will the Real Norman Mailer Please Stand Up? *edited by Laura Adams (copyright © 1974 by Kennikat Press, Inc.; reprinted by permission of Kennikat Press Corp.), Kennikat, 1974, pp. 216-223.*

ROBERT ALTER

Norman Mailer, ... in his shifting and for the moment truncated career as a novelist, illustrates precisely how American writing has tended to move into a new, problematic relationship with history. His first book, *The Naked and the Dead* (1948)—in many respects still his most adequate novel—draws on techniques of Dos Passos, Farrell, Steinbeck, and other American social realists of the 30's in order to present a panoramic view of American society in the crucible of war, the writer using his medium to grapple strenuously with the complex ideological forces that were exposed in the war, and struggling to imagine some way to a livable human future beyond this or other wars. Mailer's two novels of the 50's, *Barbary Shore* and *The Deer Park*, try to explore technical possibilities and human situations beyond the purview of *The Naked and the Dead,* but he remains in both of them an essentially political novelist, keenly attentive to how power is exerted in a particular time and place, how ideology and the moral imagination respond to the felt pressures of power. In Mailer's two novels of the next decade, however, *An American Dream* (1964) and *Why Are We in Vietnam?* (1967), a radical shift occurred, a shift that may explain why Mailer has written no novels since. The very titles, of course, emphasize a programmatic concentration on issues of national destiny, but both novels in fact are largely devoted to the playing out of private fantasies. Frequently articulated with stylistic brilliance, the fantasies do on occasion illuminate certain aspects of the larger American context, but too often their self-indulgence only leads us down some primrose path in Mailer's own teeming mental garden. After such fiction, this abundantly talented writer, losing purchase on both form and subject, seems to have concluded that he had little choice but to become a self-dramatizing journalist. (p. 45)

> *Robert Alter (reprinted from* Commentary *by permission; copyright © 1975 by the American Jewish Committee), in* Commentary, *November, 1975.*

PHILIP H. BUFITHIS

Over the perspective of both officers and enlisted men [in *The Naked and the Dead*] prevails the narrative voice of Mailer, who, Olympian-like, remains a detached, omniscient observer. He conveys the tribulations of war with almost scathing objectivity. (p. 18)

Clearly, Mailer's perspective in this novel seems noninnovational for it is derived from naturalism, the prevailing point of view of the American masters of the 1930s—Steinbeck, Dos Passos, Farrell, and Hemingway—who inspired him. Naturalism's most frequent metaphor, the lawless jungle, is the literal setting of *The Naked and the Dead.* (p. 19)

What makes this novel so disturbing is not the actual horror of war, but Mailer's unrelenting vision of the void—of the lack of love, justice, and mercy. Nothing human is sacred, and the only constant is change. The unpredictable oscillations of nature and man's emotions charge every scene. To be human is to be a mass of uncorrelated impulses. (p. 24)

The mythic heroism of [the three main characters] and the naturalistic universe they oppose is the primary dramatic conflict in *The Naked and the Dead.* In artistic terms, the conflict is between romance and realism. The interplay between these two elements gives this novel its identifying form as a work of art. (p. 26)

The Naked and the Dead is the finest novel in English to come out of World War II. More than any particular philosophy or social theory it may advance, its claim to greatness lies in the fact that Mailer defines war on the raw, sensate level and thereby makes us understand it in a palpable way. (p. 28)

It would be simplistic to say that Lovett [the narrator of *Barbary Shore*] is not real for us because he is not real to himself. The problem, really, lies with the book's artistry. Mailer has set himself a difficult task—to make a pallid character engaging. *Barbary Shore* represents Mailer's first first-person narration, and he has not quite mastered the form. The prose is articulate, but flat. Lovett's vapidity is essentially a function of his characterization, not of his character. (p. 33)

The characters of *Barbary Shore* seem to be less full-bodied creations of humanity than personifications of certain sociological tenets. Lovett alone escapes categorization, and this only because his identity is so vague. (p. 35)

Yet if the characterization of Lovett does not always satisfy, the book as a whole can be enjoyed. It gains in dimension if one thinks of the literary heritage from which it grew. The rooming house brings to mind the cave-like basement in Maxim Gorky's *The Lower Depths* and the squalid tavern in O'Neill's *The Iceman Cometh.* The last third of the novel, like Gorky's play, is a socialist call to action, and Hickey's confessional monologue in O'Neill's play forms an interesting parallel to McLeod's.

Generally, though, the inhabitants of Mailer's purgatorial rooming house remind one of Eliot's people existing, as they do in "The Dry Salvages," "among the breakage," each a separate "sphere of existence." (p. 36)

In conclusion, *Barbary Shore* is a book born of much polemical thought. Thus its final effect on the reader is of life argued rather than life lived. (p. 37)

[Both Faye and Sergius in *The Deer Park*] are unconvincing, each for opposite reasons. Faye is developed beyond any dramatic justification, and Sergius is not developed enough. Though Mailer makes clear the moral urgency of Sergius's situation—the conflicting claims of the "imaginary world" and the "real world"—he seldom presents him reacting dramatically to it, and so the reader does not have a felt sense of involvement with Sergius. . . . (p. 49)

Happily, what more than compensates for the flaws in the characterization of Sergius is the brilliant delineation of the affair between Eitel and Elena. With scrupulous honesty Mailer renders an intensive, intimate portrayal of a relationship—its dynamic of sensual rapture and love, its attendant disillusionment, its deterioration, its final stale disablement. . . . As a novel about the journey of love, *The Deer Park* has a justifiable claim to greatness.

Reinforcing the doomed, airless quality of the Eitel-Elena affair is the novel's setting, Desert D'Or. It is the unifying center of the entire book, a persistent atmospheric presence that gives palpable form to the "prisons of pain, the wading pools of pleasure, and the public and professional voices of our sentimental land." This for Mailer constitutes American culture at large. (pp. 50-1)

Mailer's purgatorial—indeed, Dantean—vision of Desert D'Or imbues his realistic story with an epical gravity and intensifies its moral theme enunciated by Eitel: "'One cannot look for a good time, Sergius, for pleasure must end as love or cruelty'—and almost as an afterthought, he added 'or obligation.'" *The Deer Park* is an ironic prose elegy about people seeking after pleasure as though it were happiness. (p. 51)

[It appears, from *Advertisements for Myself,* that] Mailer may rather enjoy being embittered; he certainly must have got satisfaction from his "Advertisements" because they are written with a freedom and a brio never before found in his work. Gone is the dispassionate, workmanlike prose so characteristic of his previous novels and his early Farrelles que stories of social realism. Now we get a prose of propulsive vigor, of pungently sensuous flourishes grounded upon a brooding earnestness. Together these "Advertisements" form a self-inventory; they show us Mailer grimly taking stock of himself amid a waste of broken resolves to write a novel that would have brought to fruition the early promise he showed at the age of twenty-five in *The Naked and the Dead.* (p. 55)

Advertisements for Myself is an amalgam of the three themes that have always been and still are basic to Mailer's work: the individual in conflict with society, the role of the artist in the modern world, and the nature of the sexual experience. As Mailer treats them, these three themes have the same intention: to delineate the conditions of our social, psychological, and natural existence, and to show in what ways they are at odds.

It is, however, the theme of the artist in the modern world that is central to *Advertisements for Myself.* For essentially what one comes away with after reading this book is an experiential sense of what it was to be a writer in America at midcentury and, by extension, what it is to be a man. For Mailer intends us to conclude that the artist's plight is an intensification or clarification of the plight of every thinking man. (pp. 61-2)

Mailer intends [*An American Dream*] to be a fiery chisel working its way into all the dull lairs of American guilt and malaise. His method is to present a narrator whose senses are unsheathed, who looks at the world—indeed, smells it, feels it, hears it, tastes it—with an accelerated consciousness. . . . Rojack is a man operating on an edge between life and death, for at the dramatic heart of the novel is the conflict between creative and destructive power.

The principal theme of the novel argues, however, for intimacy with destruction, not separation from it. (p. 66)

[Always] the suggestive thrust of his writings has been that insanity is unavoidable in contemporary America. That which social tradition deems sanity, he argues, is actually sickness: the military (*The Naked and the Dead*); political parties (*Barbary Shore*); and show business (*The Deer Park*). . . . The theme of *An American Dream* is the clarification and intensification of the subconscious self. It is about exhuming one's primeval being so that it can invigorate and inform the conscious mind and be brought to bear upon the social and institutional arenas of contemporary America. (pp. 69-70)

To give form to this struggle for unencumbered selfhood, Mailer has fashioned a large-motioned, polyphonic prose of remarkable metaphoric richness. His language is at once energetic, convolute, and lush. It is an orchestration of gusts and magniloquent musings, exhibiting always a quivering awareness of the tangible world. (p. 72)

An American Dream signifies a radical departure from Mailer's earlier novels that were written in the realistic mode. The role of literature for him now becomes one of mystic release and revelation. He found in this book a way to give the immediacy of direct sensation to the morbid or sensuous dream. Areas of our nature usually left unexplored—Mailer would say untapped—are revealed. (p. 73)

[Mailer explodes] the whole Adamic tradition of American literature. *Why Are We in Vietnam?* is a deliberate rebuttal of the revered notion that if man removes himself from the corruptness of civilization and enters the realm of unspoiled nature, he can revive within himself something of the purity of heart and nobility of spirit that Adam must have felt in that first world that God set specially before him. While Mailer believes that man does indeed divorce himself from the mystical harmonies of nature, greedily ravage it, build war machines, decimate his own kind, and seem generally to sing a ghastly paean to death, he clearly suggests, by way of D. J.'s and Tex's Arctic experience, that the origin of man's barbarity is nature itself. Evil was in nature before it was in man. Such is Mailer's premise, and he shares it with William Burroughs, whose novel, *Naked Lunch,* inspired this one. (pp. 81-2)

[The] real achievement of [*Why Are We in Vietnam?*] has more to do with the *re-creation* of cultural contradictions than with *escape* from them; for the greater part of D. J.'s narrative is a verbal prism of the dire divisions within American society. (pp. 82-3)

The novel is a digest of verbal parodies. Nowhere else in postwar American fiction do we see the contradictions of American culture so richly and variously voiced. We can read this novel as an oratorio for many voices, each one of which infuriates, stupefies, or fills us with dark laughter. By re-creating the duplicities and tensions that infect the American character, Mailer enables us to understand, perhaps more clearly than heretofore, why we were in Vietnam. (p. 83)

By mimicking the languages of the land, he helps us to better see through them and thereby resist their beguilements and coercions. Verbal play is restorative, a spiritual tonic. Mailer suggests it is the last physical liberty. (p. 84)

[*The Armies of the Night: History as a Novel, the Novel as History*] is novelistic because it sensitively describes the *effects* of the march on a participant-protagonist, Norman Mailer, and historical because it scrupulously describes the *facts* of the march. (p. 86)

The book's unity of time and its strict enclosure within the limits of a particular event and place give it a classical sharpness of design. There is a precision of vision here that we do not find in Mailer's previous two novels, *An American Dream* and *Why Are We in Vietnam?* Compelled into compliance with what he sees before him, he must now record reality rather than invent it. His previous novels shaped events; now events shape the book—events, moreover, that people know about and can therefore in some fashion relate to. (p. 87)

Mailer's personality in this book can be accurately described with a motley of adjectives: foolish, vain, inspired, deluded, imaginative, energetic, generous, quixotic. Interestingly, America itself can be accurately described with the very same adjectives. This is a recognition that Mailer expects us to arrive at, for he imagines himself as a microcosm of the nation. (p. 88)

We may find Mailer as self-styled Jeremiah rather tiresome. But when he goes about the business of "studying" every "lineament" and exploring human behavior with the old-fashioned tools of the novelist, his writing wholly engages us. For sheer force of social observation and astuteness of character delineation *The Armies of the Night* is a considerable achievement. Most significantly, nowhere else in modern American literature do we see a writer conceiving of his life with such an abundance of drama, energy, and wit. We have to go back to Benjamin Franklin, extraordinary as the association may seem, to find a parallel. (p. 94)

The Armies of the Night seemed a crescendo; the action gradually mounted toward an explosive climax, the clash between demonstrators and soldiers. The book is one large wavelike movement. We remember *Miami and the Siege of Chicago,* on the other hand, as a slide show, a series of arresting images. (p. 95)

[In *Of a Fire on the Moon* Mailer] becomes the technocrat to beat all technocrats, exhaustively detailing the intricate mechanical grandeur of the Apollo-Saturn rocket. He does so, however, in the service of art, not in the service of science. I am an epical poet, he seems to be saying, and therefore take all human experience as my province. (p. 101)

Yet, despite the vibrancy of Mailer's descriptions, the impression one gets is of a vision sought rather than found. Apollo 11's flight, as momentous as Mailer admits it is, does not finally bring him any closer, as he so ardently hoped it would, to a clarifying conception of man's role in the universe. (pp. 101-02)

It is necessary [after attacks on him by Kate Millett and other feminists], Mailer thinks, to reexplore his relationship with women by examining the nature of his love for them and to once and for all set forth in writing his own ideas about the sex game and his own sexuality. *The Prisoner of Sex,* then, is an act of self-clarification. (p. 108)

Mailer is at his comic and mischievous best defending his crony in eroticism [Henry Miller] and lampooning Millett for what he deems her dogged, tractarian approach, her insensitivity to Miller's humor and metaphoric power—in short, her lack of literary-critical skill. (p. 111)

[For] Mailer, every honor, every hope and virtue, makes itself manifest in sex. He believes in this book, as he always has, that to a great extent what you are is how you copulate, that the sex act is the barometer of personality. We might interpret *The Prisoner of Sex,* then, as Mailer's wily toast to the new feminists for making possible an opportunity to ruminate, by way of an attack on them, on the deepest reaches of his self.

A question remains. Do Mailer's ideas about women in this book correspond to implicit ideas articulated in his novels or has Mailer the middle-aged man changed his views? Actually, his views have not altered. He still sees women as adversaries, as biological shamans, as being capable of bequeathing to man godlike powers and of utterly mortifying him. But Mailer's work depends on them, and he knows it. Many of his books could hardly have been written had

he not been loving or hating a woman at the time of writing. (p. 114)

Issues aside, however, what seems most unfortunate about this book is its style. Although *The Prisoner of Sex* comprises Mailer's most energetic expository prose since "The White Negro" fourteen years earlier, too often he and the reader lose the flow of argument in a rip tide of endless sentences swirling with the debris of subpoints and elaborate qualifiers. The reader needs a blue pencil.

Nonetheless, when Mailer is propelling home a point with hard imagery, as he does in his discussion of Miller and Lawrence and in his description of the subterranean drama of the sperm and the ovum, his language sharpens. It becomes trenchant and self-delighting. (pp. 114-15)

[Even] if we do grant Mailer his purpose in *Marilyn*—to set an artist to catch an artist and write a novel-biography—we have to question whether he has really evoked for us the originality of her character. As Mailer treats her, she seems less a character in her own unique right than a composite portrait of his former female creations. . . .

Still there are passages in which Mailer allows authenticated biographical material to firmly prescribe his themes. Such passages are the only effective parts of the book. (p. 118)

[Muhammad Ali] seems a version of Mailer himself, which may explain Mailer's fascination with him for fifteen years. If Mailer were less subtle and more loud, he would resemble Ali more than a little. And if we recall Mailer's other living hero, Henry Miller, the three personalities suggest an unmistakable unity. Each man is embodiment of loquacious defiance. They are romantic individualists in an age of growing collectivism, and they both have an inflammable sense of personal honor. It may not be at all wrong to see them as sympathetic to the values of the past. How agreeable for Mailer, then, that [*The Fight*] takes him to the living past, to Africa, where, if technology and trade are to succeed at all, they must be wedded to tribal tradition. (p. 122)

[Throughout *The Fight* Mailer] harmonizes disparate modes of discourse into one original voice. He chronicles, poeticizes, observes, and analyzes. He works his combinations, much like Ali himself. *The Fight* is the perfect marriage of style and subject. The literature of sport has never seen a better book. (p. 125)

In 1956 with his columns for *The Village Voice,* Mailer transformed his style, cutting free from the influence of Hemingway, from those direct sentences of studied dispassion, and shifted his allegiance to the stylistic tradition of Miller. His prose became gusty, dense, exhortative, eloquently cadenced; it purposively flew in the face of "literature." . . . When Mailer rhapsodizes over Miller, he is idealizing himself.

Genius and Lust can be read not only as its subtitle states, as "a journey through the major writings of Henry Miller," but as an overview of Norman Mailer the writer, for Mailer shares practically the same strengths and defects as Miller. Yet it should be established at the outset that in some significant respects these two men can hardly be called literary brothers or, as a proper regard for time would dictate, father and son. . . . Miller is the last of the buoyant anarchists, a novelist of hearty diabolisms who has always written as he pleased, remaining all but deaf to the world's censure. Trophies, adversative or admiring critics, and fat royalties have been to him very much beside the point. Mailer, on the other hand, has been working since the mid 1950s at the impossible task of disturbing people and then coaxing them to adore him. He is a creature of topicalities, consistently choosing as his subject matter the events, the celebrities, the issues that the nation itself, for reasons he is always trying to divine, has chosen. It is hard to imagine Miller, an unregenerate bohemian sequestered from the clamorous world in his hermitage at Big Sur, appearing on TV, negotiating for movie rights, making big-time deals with publishers, and meeting deadlines. (pp. 125-26)

[Mailer's] early fiction asks: what is the world that man may understand it? But when the mixed reception of *The Deer Park* turned Mailer into an impassioned outlaw, his fiction underwent a radical change. The emphasis shifted. A new question was asked: what is man that the world may understand him? In the early fiction, reality acted upon consciousness. In later fiction, consciousness acts upon reality, or rather transforms it through the egocentric imagination. The direction of Mailer's fiction, then, has been from the mimetic to the expressive, from a world described to a world envisioned. (p. 131)

History chastened Mailer and provided occasion for him to make of his art the perfect fusion of abstraction and objectification, romance and realism. Expressiveness and mimesis became reconciled at last. . . .

The real moral power of Mailer's writing derives from his depiction of human will and human imagination battling against the forces of constraint. The only thing that operates for good in Mailer's world is the individual fighting alone against the institutional powers that be. (p. 132)

But the struggle often turns out to be not as valiant as all that. In Mailer's world, to test oneself against any implacable power is to be caught visibly in contradictions: to attempt seriousness and fall into clownishness; to become doctrinaire in defying the doctrinal; to skirt a ledge between heroism and absurdity; to shift precariously between clarity and turgidity, reason and dream, generosity and self-obsession, libertarianism and autocracy; to be Prometheus with the compulsions of Icarus.

Yet Mailer does not try to neutralize any of these polarities in himself. He refuses to put together a harmonious personality because he suspects that consistency is only another name for inertia. (pp. 132-33)

He insists on believing that man is supernatural, not natural. His struggle, then, has been mythic, epical. . . . [The] magnitude of Mailer's imagination and his extraordinary powers of expressiveness have restored to English literature the fertile, energetic grandeur it has seldom known since the seventeenth century. (p. 133)

> *Philip H. Bufithis, in his* Norman Mailer *(copyright © 1978 by Frederick Ungar Publishing Co., Inc.), Frederick Ungar, 1978.*

*   *   *

MALAMUD, Bernard   1914-

Malamud is an American novelist and short story writer. Thematically, his fiction centers around the concerns of the Jew in modern America. Malamud's work is distinguished by a spare prose style and dialogue flavored with traditional Yiddish humor and dialect. Through his suffering heroes, who are drawn with compassion, Malamud explores the process of redemption through suffering, reaffirming the triumph of the human spirit. (See also *CLC*, Vols. 1, 2, 3, 5, 8, 9, and *Contemporary Authors*, Vols. 5-8, rev. ed.)

GRANVILLE HICKS

To understand Malamud, one must read closely his short stories. . . . Most of them portray poverty-stricken people living in New York or Brooklyn, and Malamud writes of misery with calm poignancy. (p. 218)

What Malamud is always asking himself is how people live with great misery. Some of his people are crushed by it, but most survive, through hope or pride or sheer fortitude. The best, moreover, learn to be compassionate, and compassion is, for Malamud, the first of the virtues. (p. 219)

As almost always with a novel based on a myth or a legend, the reader [of *The Natural*] is distracted by the effort he has to make to follow the author's intentions, but if the book is not completely successful, there is much to be said for it.

There is no difficulty in evaluating Malamud's second novel, *The Assistant* (1957); it is one of the strongest and finest novels of recent years. The method is not at all that of *The Natural;* Malamud relies wholly on a solid, highly selective realism. In his first chapter he makes us see Morris Bober, a poor Jewish grocer, sixty years of age, who watches his business dwindle to the vanishing point. Yet he is not crushed by his sufferings, and he is capable of compassion towards those poorer than himself. He is, we see, a good man, but an unlucky one. . . . (p. 220)

Frank Alpine, when he becomes a Jew, is not only accepting suffering but also finding hope. Suffering, Malamud is saying, is the human lot, but we need not surrender to despair. To escape suffering is impossible; to live a good life in spite of it is not. . . .

Malamud handles the tools of his craft with the greatest skill, selecting his details with rigorous economy, making every scene count heavily. He lets us into the mind of each of his characters, yet tells us only what we need to know. His dialogue has both verisimilitude and flavor, and his narrative is lean and supple. The novel makes an unforgettable impact.

Malamud's [next] novel, *A New Life* (1961) is in a sense a further development of the theme of *The Assistant*. Its hero, thirty years of age, "formerly a drunkard," as Malamud tells us in the first line, arrives at Cascadia College in the Far West to become an instructor of English. Out of New York City for the first time, about to teach in a college for the first time, he is beginning a new life. What his old life has been we are not immediately told, but readers of *The Magic Barrel* and *The Assistant* know a good deal about it. (p. 222)

When Levin's past is revealed to us, it turns out to have been even grimmer than we had supposed. Not only did he grow up in poverty; his father was a criminal and his mother committed suicide. In sodden despair he took to drink, living, as he says, in self-hatred. "I drank, I stank. I was filthy, skin on bone." But then there was a moment of revelation: "I came to believe what I had hoped to, that life is holy. I then became a man of principle." (p. 223)

The Assistant ends with Frank's conversion, but it is with Levin's conversion that, properly speaking, *A New Life* begins. The pursuit of goodness, Malamud is showing us, is endlessly difficult, for the past can never be decisively outdistanced. Indeed, all reason seems to say that a new life is impossible, and yet the Levins of this world go on trying.

Levin is a clown, a blunderer—as Stanley Edgar Hyman says, a *schlemihl*. Uncouth in appearance, inept with women, ridiculous in the classroom, he is to outward appearances a joke. Like Frank Alpine, he is not even consistently honest. And yet, ridiculous as he is, he is a hero of our times. That the reader feels this to the bottom of his being is the measure of Malamud's achievement.

A New Life is more flexible in style than *The Assistant,* and there is greater variety of tone and incident. Malamud lets himself range from lyric descriptions of the landscape to quietly savage accounts of the Cascadia faculty. There is comedy, too, and even farce. It is also true that here Malamud deals more fully and more warmly with love than he has before. On the other hand, he does not drive so intensely to the point as in *The Assistant,* and the impact of the book is less dramatic.

Perhaps it is worth noting that the hero of each of Malamud's three novels is an orphan. They have been thrust alone into a world they could not conceive of making. Roy in *The Natural* has extravagant ambitions, and goes down to defeat. Frank in *The Assistant* expects nothing, but he does learn to come to terms with suffering. Levin seeks virtue, and though he finds the way rocky, he persists.

Writing of the three novels, Hyman has said in the *New Leader:* "In a sense, Malamud has moved from the story of Samson, punished for the misuse of his powers, to Job, suffering because chosen to suffer, to Jesus, suffering voluntarily to redeem." [See CLC, Vol. 2.] This is flying a little high, but the comment nevertheless suggests the seriousness of Malamud's themes and his steady development as a writer. (pp. 223-24)

> *Granville Hicks, in* The Creative Present: Notes on Contemporary American Fiction, *edited by Nona Balakian and Charles Simmons (copyright © 1963 by Nona Balakian and Charles Simmons; reprinted by permission of Doubleday & Co., Inc.), Doubleday & Company, Inc., 1963 (and reprinted by Gordian Press, Inc., 1973).*

CYNTHIA OZICK

In 1958, in his celebrated collection *The Magic Barrel,* Malamud published a short story about a Negro and a Jew. It was called "Angel Levine," and it contrived for Manischevitz, a Job-like figure who has "suffered many reverses and indignities," the promise of redemption through a magical black man [the angel, Levine]. (p. 80)

[The] narrative is altogether offhand about the question of the angel's identity: Levine is perfectly matter-of-fact about it, there is nothing at all miraculous in the idea that a black man can also be a Jew. In a tale about the supernatural, this is what emerges as the "natural" element—as natural-feeling as Manischevitz's misfortunes and his poverty. Black misfortune and poverty have a different resonance—Manischevitz's wanderings through Harlem explain the differences—but, like the Jews' lot, the blacks' has an everyday closeness, for Manischevitz the smell of a familiar

fate. To him—and to Malamud at the end of the fifties—that Black and Jew are one is no miracle.

A little more than a decade later, with the publication of *The Tenants,* the proposition seems hollow. Again Malamud offers a parable of black and Jew culminating in fantasy, but now the fantasy has Jew slashing with ax, black with saber, destroying one another in a passionate bloodletting. The novel's last paragraph is eerily liturgical—the word "mercy" repeated one hundred and fifty times, and once in Hebrew. Nevertheless *The Tenants* is a merciless book. (p. 81)

How was the transmutation from magical brotherhood to ax-murder wrought? Is it merely that society has changed so much since the late 1950's, or is it that the author of "Angel Levine" was, even then, obtuse? If the difference in Malamud's imaginative perception lies only in our own commonplace perception that the social atmosphere has since altered in the extreme—from Selma to Forest Hills—then "Angel Levine," far from being a mythically representative tale about suffering brothers, is now no more than a dated magazine story. One test of the durability of fiction is whether it still tells even a partial truth ten years after publication. The conclusion of *The Tenants* seems "true" now —i.e., it fits the current moment outside fiction. But a change in social atmosphere is not enough to account for the evanescence or lastingness of a piece of fiction. There are other kinds of truth than sociological truth. There is the truth that matches real events in the world—in *The Tenants,* it is the black man and the Jew turning on one another —and there is the truth which accurately describes what can only be called aspiration. Even in the world of aspiration, it is a question whether "Angel Levine" remains true. And on the last page of *The Tenants,* when Jew and black cut sex and brains from each other, Malamud writes: "Each, thought the writer, feels the anguish of the other." This is the truth of invisible faith, and it is a question whether this too can survive.

"The anguish of the other" is a Malamudic assumption, endemic in his fiction. The interior of many of Malamud's fables resounds with the injunction that for the sake of moral aspiration one must *undergo*.... Malamud's world often proposes a kind of hard-won, eked-out saintliness: suffering and spiritual goodness are somehow linked. The real world of humanity—which means also the real world of the Jews—is not like this. "Bad" Jews went up in smoke at Auschwitz too—surely embezzlers as well as babies, not only *tsadikim* but misers too, poets as well as kleptomaniacs. Not one single Jew ever deserved his martyrdom, but not every martyr is a holy man. For Malamud all good men are Job.

Nevertheless there remains a thin strand of connection between Malamud's visionary "Angel Levine" and a commonplace of Jewish temperament, between the messianic insistence on the anguish of the other and the common sense of ordinary, "bad," Jews. The sociological—the "real"—counterpart of Malamud's holy fables is almost always taken for granted by Jews: it is, simply put, that Jews have always known hard times, and are therefore naturally sympathetic to others who are having, or once had, hard times. The "naturally" is what is important. It is a feeling so normal as to be unrelated to spiritual striving, self-purification, moral accountability, prophecy, Waskowian "witness," anything at all theoretical or lofty. This plain observation about particularized suffering requires no special sensitiveness; *naturally* there are Jews everywhere, and some of them are black.

But what has surprised some Jews, perhaps many, is that this Jewish assumption—this quiet tenet, to use a firmer word, that wounds recognize wounds—is not only *not* taken for granted by everyone else, especially by blacks, but is given no credibility whatever. Worse, to articulate the assumption is to earn the accusation of impudence. . . . To its critics, accusers, "Angel Levine" must seem not just dated, obsolete, a sentimental excrescence of that remote era when Jews were as concerned with CORE as they were with UJA—but *wrong*. And many young blacks writing today would regard its premise not only as not a moral hope, but as a hurtful lie. Or else would see Manischevitz's salvation as simply another instance of Jewish exploitation, this time of black benevolence. (pp. 81-3)

[What] was radiant, if illusioned, hope at the time "Angel Levine" was conceived has disintegrated into a kind of surrealism, an arbitrary act of art, set apart from any sources of life. Literature (even in the form of fantasy) cannot survive on illusion.

This is perhaps why Malamud went forward from the failed dream of "Angel Levine" to the warlike actualities of *The Tenants*. (p. 89)

[In] my first reading of *The Tenants,* I was, like many readers, rabidly discontent with Malamud's conception of his black character, Willie Spearmint, later called Spear. Willie Spear is a black writer who has the flavor of an Eldridge Cleaver rather than an Ellison; and this seemed to matter. Malamud, it appeared, had deliberately chosen—for novelistic bite and drama—an unruly spear-carrier, when he might have chosen a poised aristocrat of prose. And up against Spear he set the Jewish writer Harry Lesser, a man almost too fastidious in his craft. The balance was unequal, the protagonists unfairly matched, the Jew too hesitant and disciplined, the black too spontaneous and unschooled.

That the protagonists *have* to be a match for each other at first strikes one as important, because *The Tenants* is partly, despite its directness of language and gesture, a theater-piece designed as stately discourse. Though I admit the comparison is inflated, nevertheless one is put in mind of the eye-to-eye feud of Elizabeth and Mary Queen of Scots in Schiller's *Maria Stuart;* or of Shaw's Joan at her trial, another example of an elevated contest of societal interpretation. *The Tenants* is obviously barer and coarser than these—airless and arid, a flat plain pitting philosopher-king against philosopher-king. Except, for these two figures—the Jew and the black—the book is, by and large, unpeopled. (pp. 89-90)

Willie is a straw man. Why not a black writer who is not only fully literate, but *accomplished*? Suppose Malamud had given us Ellison instead of Willie—then what? Lesser, like Ellison, believes first of all in the primacy, the loveliness, of the sentence; for him literature is the personal courage by which the language is seized. Beyond that lies propaganda. Granted that two-literary-intellectuals-talking-to-each-other does not make a novel (Mann and the Russians excepted), or, at least, would not make *this* novel, Malamud seems to be asking for the sort of resentment that would soon come to surround his formulation: Jewish Intellectual vs. Tough Black Militant. Unequal warfare in the Republic of Letters. Could it not—for fairness—somehow have been contrived as Jewish Intellectual vs. Black Intellectual?

There were, of course, good novelistic reasons why it could not. For instance, the conflict that eventually interposes itself between Lesser and Willie is not intellectual but rawly sexual. Willie has a Jewish girl friend, Irene, whom Lesser covets and ultimately wins. Irene is unfortunately a fiction-device and lives only intermittently. Her narrative task is to convert the two writers into enemies through sexual jealousy. Lesser's importuning landlord, Levenspiel, is also a fiction-device—he is there to give us the novel's pivotal "problem," to put time-pressure on a stubborn Lesser—but Levenspiel, by contrast, manages to live vividly. . . . Levenspiel and Irene and Willie's black friends who slide in and out from the wings are all interruptions in the dialogue between Lesser and Willie; they are pretexts for necessary "action," for novelistic progress. They are not what the book fundamentally intends.

If *The Tenants* progresses, it is not through plot but through revelation. The revelation is one-sided: it happens inside Lesser. We do not really know what happens inside Willie. And what happens inside Lesser is this: the clear realization that the black writer who shares his quarters and also his literary hopes is, more than he is writer, more than he is lover, more even than he is fleshly human being, a ferocious, a mythic, anti-Semite. (pp. 91-2)

As for "being human," not only does Willie reject the term "universal," but he sees himself as almost physiologically different ("Our feelin chemistry is different than yours"), and he goes further yet—he freezes himself into the image of a totem, a *"black man."* The statement "My form is *myself"* is beyond humanity, beyond even art. It stands for something more abstract than either: a political position taken at its most absolute. For a totem *is* an absolute politics: an object, an artifact, a *form* representing an entire people, together with its interests, its cult, its power, its history and fate. The totem has no fluidity, its being is its meaning. Willie has turned the politics of a group into an object—himself, *black man*. In Willie Art is Politics, Politics is Art.

This is why it would not have served Malamud's deepest intention if he had chosen not Willie, but a more "realistic," pragmatic, literate, humane, relatively political, less symbolic black for the novel. In *not* choosing an Ellison, of course, Malamud took on himself both a risk and a certainty. The certainty was the charge of "stereotype" and "blacklash," to which *The Tenants* has already been preëminently subject. The risk—a "stereotype" having indeed been chosen—was the failure of the novel as art. To a degree this *has* happened—to the very degree Willie's stereotyped expectations lead to banalities masking as passions. Something was necessary to stimulate Willie's active vengeance, so we are given a plot-fulcrum, Willie's girl Irene. In return for Lesser's stealing his girl, Willie destroys Lesser's work of ten years; the war is on. But Irene exists to accommodate neither Willie nor Lesser, but the exigencies of a made fiction. All this is too obviously and distractingly schematic—even the lineaments of "parable" cannot contain it—and if I seem to be bringing it up again now, it is only to contrast it with the novel's authentic passions. These are in the mimicry of Willie's writing. (p. 93)

Willie is unabashedly "prefabricated."

But the real question is: who cast this die, who prefabricated Willie? Not Malamud. The source of a stereotype is everything. (p. 94)

Malamud did not make Willie. He borrowed him—he mimicked him—from the literature and the politics of the black movement. Willie is the black dream that is current in our world. Blacks made him. Few blacks disavow him. The black middle class, which is ambivalent about Willie, nevertheless does not disavow him—not simply out of loyalty to the underclass (the loyalty is what is in doubt), but out of covert gratitude. Almost no black writer has disavowed Willie. . . . Surely Baldwin does not disavow Willie; he has become him.

In short, Willie is what he intends himself to be (which is also what he is intended to be by those blacks who do not deny him): a totem, emblem of a community unified in and through Willie's spirit, what he calls his "form"—not man, as Ellison would have it, but *black man.*

What is the meaning of Willie in his self-declared "form"? Willie's form takes up not freedom and fluidity, but unmovable hatred and slavish vengeance. . . . For him literature serves politics—not as propaganda consciously does, as an "arm" or partner or extension or tool of politics—but intrinsically, below the level of rational motivation. Willie's only politics is co-extensive with nearly the whole of his literary imagination; it is the politics and the imagination of anti-Semitism. (pp. 95-6)

"Angel Levine" is not merely out of date, it is illusion; at the close of *The Tenants* Malamud explicitly acknowledges that it is illusion. Lesser's ax—it is the final vision of the novel—sinks into Willie. . . . It is curious, horrible, and terrifying to take in what Malamud in *The Tenants* openly posits: that the Jew in America, beginning . . . with a cry of identification with black suffering, is self-astonished to find himself responding now in the almost-forgotten mood of *zelbshuts*—the *shtetl's* term for weaponry stored against the fear of pogroms. Lesser, a hesitant intellectual, is driven to hauling an ax. But *The Tenants* insists on more than this. Like much of Malamud's work, and specifically like *The Assistant* and *The Fixer,* it offers the metaphoric incarnation of a Malamudic text: whoever wants to kill the Jew has already killed the human being in himself. It is not only no failing, it is the best achievement of the novel that Willie, its black militant, is a stereotype devoid of any easy humanity. The clichés appropriate for a political strategy are unsuitable for describing the soul of a living person. Given the extra-literary truth that black militancy, in and out of print, has now come to define itself if not largely then centrally through classical anti-Semitism, to bestow on a fictional Willie a life beyond his bloody fantasies would have been a savagery akin to Willie's own. To put it another way: to have ascribed to Willie the full and continuing aspects of a decent breathing human being *but for his hatred of Jews* would have been to subvert the meaning of human.

The Tenants is a claustrophobic fable: its theme is pogrom. It remarks the minutiae of a single-handed pogrom so closely that the outer world is shut out. There is almost no city beyond Lesser's tenement, and there are no white Gentiles in the novel. . . . In *The Tenants* the Jew has no allies. Jew and black fight alone in an indifferent world.

There is no means, at this juncture, of determining whether its current worldly truths will one day seep out of *The Ten-*

ants, as the moral radiance of "Angel Levine" had ultimately, through subversion by history, to ebb into falsehood. But—for the moment—Malamud has abandoned the hopefulness of "Angel Levine" and drawn a parable of political anxiety. "Each, thought the writer, feels the anguish of the other" is the last flicker of that hopefulness but does not convince. Willie is Lesser's doom—Lesser, dreaming of love, rigorously apolitical, isolated in his esthetics, becomes the inescapable victim of an artist whose art is inseparable from butchery. (p. 97)

Malamud, in plucking Willie out of the black writing that made him, has not invented the politicization of fiction. And in inventing *The Tenants,* Malamud ironically follows Willie—he has written a tragic fiction soaked in the still mainly unshed blood of the urban body politic. (p. 98)

> *Cynthia Ozick, "Literary Blacks and Jews," in* Midstream *(copyright © 1972 by The Theodor Herzl Foundation, Inc.; reprinted by permission of the author and her agents, Raines and Raines, and the publisher), June/July, 1972 (and reprinted in* Bernard Malamud: A Collection of Critical Essays, *edited by Leslie and Joyce Field, Prentice-Hall, Inc., 1975, pp. 80-98).*

SHELDON NORMAN GREBSTEIN

Malamud best represents the phenomenon of the Jewish Movement; not only is he one of its founders and major practitioners, he is probably its best single exemplar. In Malamud's work we most clearly perceive just those characteristics which define the entire Movement.

First and foremost, there is the theme of meaningful suffering, which in Malamud also implies the quest for moral resolution and self-realization. But the theme of suffering cannot alone sustain either a movement or a writer's career. We can take just so much bad news. Malamud's writing, like that of the Movement at large, is also richly comic. Paradoxically, the comedy is at once a mode of expression of the suffering and a way of easing it. With the Jew humor is an escape valve for dangerous pressures, a manner of letting out things too painful to be kept in. (Could it be that one of the reasons we have able black writers like Ellison and Baldwin but not a Black Movement, is the prevailing solemnity of these writers?) Finally, the Jewish writer speaks in a distinctive literary voice. With Bellow and at about the same time, Malamud invented and perfected a fresh literary idiom, a "Jewish style." This style consists of much more than the importation of Yiddish words and phrases into English, or a mere broken Yiddish-English dialect, long the staple of popular works presenting lovably silly Jewish stereotypes (*Abie's Irish Rose*). Rather, it is a significant development and expansion of the American colloquial style, established as a vital literary medium by Mark Twain. The Jewish style is for the first time in our literary history a voice that conveys ethnic characteristics, a special sort of sensibility, and the quality of a foreign language, yet remains familiar and eloquent to non-Jews. Although dialects and dialect styles tend to be reductive, rendering their speakers either funny or absurd, Malamud's style can evoke either tragic dignity or comic foolishness, or, miraculously, both at once. (pp. 20-1)

His heroes all suffer deeply, but they are also secular men whose suffering is not always voluntary, undertaken wholly for exalted reasons, or blessed by great rewards. Malamud's real concern is for the social and moral aspects of suffering as they impinge upon personality. If his characters expect some recompense for their misery, they would like it in the here and now. In sum, although we have no conclusive biographical evidence to assess Malamud's personal religious commitment, the testimony of his work suggests him to be an agnostic humanist. Some of his own remarks support that deduction: "My premise is that we will not destroy each other. My premise is that we will live on. We will seek a better life. We may not become better, but at least we will seek betterment."

This is Malamud's real toughness, the factor that prevents his treatment of suffering from deteriorating into drippy melodrama or comfortable piety. He has a view of man which perceives the property of conscience, the seeking to be better, not as a divine mystery but as natural to humans as skin, hair, voice. Yet this basically optimistic concept of human nature is checked by an almost equally persistent view of man as greedy, treacherous, lustful, and often vicious. Cheerful idealist and hard-eyed realist peer out through the same bifocals.

Consequently, Malamud's depiction of suffering is ambivalent; in each of his major characters altruism and materialism combine as motives for self-sacrifice. (pp. 21-2)

[Although Malamud draws upon all the Yiddish] varieties of humor, I find the mode of fantastic comedy particularly interesting and successful. In this mode Malamud implies the immanence of a spiritual dimension or realm of human experience without committing himself to a specific faith, doctrine, or theology. In short, the fantastic and the metaphysical enter into Malamud's world as though they were fact, and he solidifies them and ties them to earth by depicting them in the same voice and with the same solidity of specification that he uses for grocery stores and Czarist prisons. One might say that this is Malamud's version of the quasi-religious folklore and superstition permeating *shtetl* life, and as much a fact of that life as its food and drink. . . . Malamud is thus the heir to rich Jewish traditions, and worthy heir that he is, he remakes them his way and reinvigorates them. (pp. 26-7)

Malamud's first novel *The Natural* is largely a work of fantastic comedy, and though a flawed book, there is such verve in it and such an abundance of talent, one might have predicted that this was to be Malamud's *métier*. In brief, Malamud transforms the national game of baseball, familiar to all and in which all are experts, into a contest among demigods and conducted as though it were a sacred ritual in a cosmic arena. This placing together of unlike pairs, baseball and the universe, already inspires a comic response. For the literary reader Malamud provides an extra dimension of incongruity by juxtaposing a sports story, rendered with the appropriate data and terminology, against a mythic context which draws upon the myths of the Quest Hero, the Fisher King, and, to some degree, the White Goddess. (pp. 27-8)

The pervasive dreariness of *The Assistant,* with its central locale of the dark store, is relieved and modulated by occasional but effective comic moments, notably one brief yet vivid episode of fantasy in which Morris Bober receives a visit from the devil and succumbs to his temptation. However, in keeping with the general method of the book, the agent of evil appears not in a spectacular scene but in a muted little encounter so close to credibility it can almost be taken as actual. . . . Malamud blends the fantastic with the realistic, for in such a novel as *The Assistant* the wholly bizarre and surrealistic would be an intrusion. (pp. 28-9)

The fantastic component in *The Fixer,* to some degree anticipated by the characters' dreams and visions in *The Assistant,* consists entirely of Yakov's dreams, fevers, and hallucinations during his long and dreadful confinement. But these, however farfetched, are often too painful to be comic. . . . Indeed, the bitterness of Jewish humor is nowhere better exemplified than in *The Fixer*. A prevailing source of comedy comprises examples of the incredible misconceptions and superstitions about the Jews held by the Russians, misconceptions for which the Jews, not the Russians, suffer. I doubt if a more horrendous humor exists in any culture than this sort, frequent in *The Fixer*. . . . (p. 30)

The comedy of *A New Life* and *Pictures of Fidelman* abandons fantasy almost entirely. Rather, these novels depend upon zany and often bawdy situations and employ the earthy humor, burlesque, and slapstick which derive from human lusts, mistakes, and misconduct. (p. 31)

Quite aside from the burlesque sexuality of *A New Life,* a matter which Malamud treats with decreasing emphasis and increased seriousness as the novel proceeds—and sex becomes love, and love becomes commitment—*A New Life* demands comment as the only instance to date of Malamud as satirist. Although the satire finally collapses under the weight of too much academic detail and too much debate, for a time Malamud's fantastic gift exhilarates his depiction of Cascadia College and its English department. In this respect the novel's scene temporarily partakes in the great tradition of satire as fable: Gulliver's Lilliput, Martin Chuzzlewit's America, Sinclair Lewis's Zenith, all of them peopled not by *homo sapiens* but by goblins in human costume. The problem in *A New Life* is that the satire turns too grittily truthful, too near the quality of a *roman à clef,* and Levin, lovable and interesting as *shlemiel*-cum-lover, becomes something of a bore as academic crusader. Consequently, the novel is too playful to persuade entirely as realism and not playful enough to persuade as satire.

Pictures of Fidelman avoids that mistake. Although hardly Malamud's largest achievement, it is surely his most accomplished as a comic work. The humor arises from the antic misadventures in Italy of a world-be art student and painter. (pp. 31-2)

But as hilarious as such scenes are, Malamud grounds them upon certain hard actualities which keep the book from dissipating into mere ribald spoofing. There is the authentic context of the Italian locale: of cold, poverty, venality, a people scrabbling for the next meal, including Fidelman himself. Simultaneously, there is the presence of great art, part of the air breathed in Italy, and the irresistible appeal to attempt it oneself. Thus Fidelman's wild sexual encounters are played off against his increasingly desperate and futile attempts to become an artist. The incongruous juxtaposition in *Pictures of Fidelman* is, then, that between the coarsely sexual and the sublimely aesthetic.

Too, the novel may be viewed as a kind of comic *bildungsroman,* intermixed with the International Theme and structured as a picaresque story cycle. Fidelman arrives in Italy respectably dressed and with the worthy ambition to become an art critic. Then, just as in the first episode he is robbed of his attaché case containing the initial chapter of his projected book, and swindled out of his extra suit of clothes, the layers of his superficial identity are stripped away episode by episode in a series of comic but also bitter encounters, until he is no longer definable as a middle-class American Jew. Instead, he gains a more basic identity: craftsman and lover. Furthermore, he has travelled there the hard way, through privation, failure, humiliation, abuse, crime, and fakery—an experience which brings him in the book's surrealistic penultimate episode face to face with the devil. In Fidelman Malamud has created his own version of an enduring Jewish comic prototype, the *luftmensch* with feet of clay. We have known worse people. (pp. 32-3)

Malamud's chief distinction as an artist is his command of a particular literary idiom. This idiom not only bears Malamud's own signature, it has so permeated Jewish-American writing that the Movement itself is in some measure distinguished by it. Furthermore, the style is integral to [his] very themes and motifs. . . . In a fundamental sense the suffering and the comedy are embedded in the language, and their peculiar simultaneity or proximity, the sweetly tragic and the bitterly comic, must to a significant degree be attributed to the style. In his own way Malamud captures in English what has been called an untranslatable quality of Yiddish, the admixture of the jocular and the solemn, "the fusion of the sacred and the profane." (p. 33)

First, he avails himself of what is perhaps the most versatile and fluent of narrative modes, selective omniscience. In this mode the writer retains the objectivity, the freedom to move through time and space, and the power to know all, which are the great advantages of the traditional third-person outside narrator; yet by refraining from editorial intrusions and maintaining the focus on a single character or a few characters, the writer can shift into interior monologue or take a stance which allows him to perceive as through the character's eyes without any obvious break in the narrative seam or detection by the reader. This is, of course, a modern technique, and one at the service of many resourceful writers. It is the narrative perspective Malamud has employed in all his novels and, with rare exceptions, his stories as well. (pp. 33-4)

Malamud's best work is realistic, though it should be clear from the frequent and important presence of fantastic comedy that it breaks through strict categories. Indeed, although Malamud is a realist, as demonstrated in *The Assistant, The Fixer,* and the major part of *A New Life,* he is of the best sort: a symbolic realist. The Jewish sense of the Transcendent merged with the Actual expresses itself in Malamud's technique in a hard-rock verisimilitude, in which we smell garbage and know exactly how much money lies in the cash register or what a sadistic prison official does with his fingers when he searches a prisoner. At the same time, we are ever aware of the play of the human imagination upon experience and the inexhaustible intimations of the protean natural world. Symbols and emblems recur everywhere in Malamud's fiction, obtrusive only in the case of his first book, *The Natural,* and even there not inappropriate to a work with a frame of myth. Elsewhere they are wholly integrated.

[So, for example, in] *The Assistant,* the characters' movements in that work—quite normal in a building containing a cellar, a first-floor store, and living quarters above—assume symbolic purport. As already implied, these movements

constitute a dramatic metaphor for the characters' moral conditions. Frank comes up from the cellar where he has been hiding, to the store, and then to a room on the floor above. This parallels his climb from bummery to decency. Conversely, Morris goes upstairs to sleep and dream, his only escape from his prison—the store. In his one concession to evil, he goes downstairs to set fire to his business but is saved from this by Frank, who has already experienced what things are like in the cellar. (pp. 35-6)

[Malamud utilizes] heat and cold, light and dark, fragrance and stench, the indoors and the outdoors. . . . Too, throughout his work he consistently uses weather, season, climate, as corollary and symbolic context for his characters' actions and moral conditions. He also skillfully employs emblems: mirrors, books, articles of clothing, for example. Thus . . . there is always much more to see in Malamud's stories than what will happen next. (p. 36)

[Malamud's style is] three styles, or a confluence of styles.

First there is a "straight" or standard belletristic style; that is, a style composed of the same linguistic materials used by other modern writers, with a syntax familiar to all speakers of American English, and a diction drawn from the common vocabulary of standard-informal usage. . . . Lucid and vigorous, [this style] contains nothing intrinsically alien or exotic and little identifying it as specifically Malamudian if it were taken out of context and seen in isolation. (pp. 36-7)

A second Malamud style, that most unlike the standard belletristic, is a dialect style which deliberately evokes the sound of Yiddish. It demonstrates Malamud's familiarity with the old mother tongue. . . . It also demonstrates Malamud's skill at transliterating that tongue into a kind of English. However, Malamud can hardly be credited with inventing the dialect style or being the first to use Yiddish dialect as a literary medium. . . . In the twentieth century Yiddish dialect has been a staple of comedy and of comedians for decades, although very rare in serious writing. (pp. 37-8)

The third style, the most complex and resonant and that which Malamud has impressed with his own signature, is a mixed or fused style which combines both the belletristic and dialect styles yet is wholly neither. Malamud can be named the co-inventor of this style; he and Bellow began to use it at about the same time, in the early 1950's, though apparently without the conscious indebtedness of either one to the other. The fused style gathers additional force from the juxtaposition or combination of lyric, eloquent, soaring phrases (the belletristic) and homely idiom and vulgate (the dialect). The belletristic exalts the vulgate, infusing it with dignity and seriousness; the vulgate pulls down the belletristic from its literary eminence and makes it speak for ordinary men and coarse experience. The juxtaposition of the two also makes possible that remarkable bitter comedy we observe in Malamud, Bellow, and Roth. (pp. 38-9)

In *The Assistant,* to continue our concern with that novel a moment longer, each of the three styles appears in a variety of uses and combinations. The dialect style, for example, functions appropriately in the conversations of those characters for whom Yiddish was the language of their youth. . . . We also hear this style in certain interior monologues. Perhaps its most consistent use in the novel is to depict Ida, I suspect as a way to fix her into a kind of narrowness or limitation of vision. Of all the important characters, hers is the meanest worldview. (p. 40)

But what is so artistic about using a dialect style for a dialect character? We have the answer to that in Malamud's treatment of Morris, because, in contrast, Malamud shrewdly avoids the dialect style and renders him, whether by omniscient narration or interior monologue, either in the standard belletristic style or the fused style. This "straight" treatment of Morris reiterates his identity as an Everyman figure and comprises the stylistic equivalent to the novel's thesis that all men are, potentially, Jews. To depict him in the dialect style would be to insist upon his ethnic identity and thus to weaken the characterization. Morris's character gains depth, too, in that Malamud shows him as capable of different levels of speech, depending on the situation. To Ida he speaks strictly in Yiddish dialect, as to Karp and others; to Helen and Frank his speech remains homely but closer to standard and almost purged of its Yiddishisms; to Detective Minogue he speaks in a stilted but "correct" manner which reflects the strain he feels dealing with this man within a formal, official context.

On the other hand, Helen and Frank can be rendered in a style which at times borders on dialect in its loose colloquialism, yet without risk of stereotyping. As Helen's style is slightly more literary because of her aspirations and her education, so Frank's tends to be slangy, appropriate to his background as drifter. However, we perceive a subtle but progressive heightening of Frank's speech and interior monologue, as well as of the omniscient narration describing him, on those occasions when he delves into serious subjects either with Morris or Helen, and as his moral ascension continues. He achieves, in his best moments, a striking combination of literary eloquence and lowdown bluntness. (p. 41)

The Natural totally lacks Yiddish flavor, rightly so, yet the style is breezy and slangy—accurate to a world of baseball players. At the same time the earthy colloquialism sets up an artistically desirable tension against the novel's heavy mythic and allegorical machinery, with two beneficial effects: it provides an illusion of actuality; it produces a keen humor. *A New Life* is written largely in the fused style, again seemly to the subject and to the novel's hero, an urban Eastern Jew with an M.A. However, just as Levin's Jewishness overtly plays only a small role in the novel, the "Jewish" elements in his thought and speech are suppressed.... In this novel, too, the mixture of colloquial and belletristic materials generates a comic undercurrent.

The same comic potentiality, inherent in any style which employs idiom, helps to enliven *The Fixer* and prevent it from unbearable morbidity. (pp. 41-2)

First, [Malamud] establishes a continual contrast between the language of all the official proceedings, innately formal and bombastic, and the spontaneous simplicity and pungency of Yakov's own speech. Accordingly, there is posed the repeated incongruity between what is uttered by the various magistrates and functionaries, and the pithy, unaffected quality of what Yakov is saying inside his own head. The incongruity becomes even more absurd in that when Yakov replies to his persecutors, he usually does so in the same stilted manner they use. The result is a kind of chorus of voices. Second, the contrast of voices, of what is said and what is thought, communicates an authentic difference

of tongues.... At the same time Malamud's voice, employing the fused style of an omniscient narrator outside the hero but never very far away, merges with Yakov's. Narrator and hero often become one in that both express themselves in the same way: lucidly, candidly, sometimes earthily, sometimes in short lyric flights. In sum, what Malamud does, linguistically, is to pit the good Jews (Malamud and Yakov) against the bad Russians. You can usually tell the bad guys by their bombast, if they have rank, or if lower class by their nasty, vulgar mouths. (p. 42)

Although the narrative [of *Pictures of Fidelman*] is largely rendered in the fused style, Malamud flies higher with the belletristic and dives lower with the vulgate than in any of his other work. He also takes greater chances with narrative perspective, shifting from objective to subjective narration more frequently and swiftly than ever before. He makes other rapid and varied shifts as well: from the conventional narrative past tense to the immediate present, from exposition to dialogue, from interior monologue or selective omniscience to direct impression. Technically the book is as wild and unpredictable as its hero's adventures. Indeed, chapter five is a technical *tour de force*, a packed and dazzling virtuoso demonstration of Malamud's range, a stylistic splurge. One can only describe it as a neo-Joycean, comitragic, surrealistic, stream-of-consciousness, visionary sequence, perhaps a burst of true madness in poor Fidelman but also containing a portion of almost coherent narrative which advances the story line. There is nothing remotely like it in Malamud's earlier writing. (p. 43)

Although for all its virtuosity and comic gusto *Pictures of Fidelman* is a much less estimable work than such solid accomplishments as *The Assistant* and *The Fixer*, this novel does make a number of important affirmations. For one thing, it affirms that despite Malamud's association with the Jewish Movement and his importance to it, his material is not restricted to the themes and prototypes characteristic to that Movement. It affirms that he retains the capacity to surprise us, a capacity always beyond the scope of a minor writer. It affirms, moreover, that Malamud continues to be devoted to the subject he believes the writer must treat as his mission: the richness of the development of human personality. Finally, it affirms that whether his treatment be somber or comic, his possibilities as a craftsman are far from exhausted. (pp. 43-4)

The Tenants appeared after this essay had been written, and too late to be included in it. However, from my first reading of the book I would amend my conclusions here in only one important respect: it seems to indicate that Malamud is capable of unmitigated pessimism, gloomier even than that in *The Fixer*. Or, we could take a little comfort from the ending of *The Tenants* by interpreting it as warning and object lesson to both Jew and Black: learn to get along, *or else*. In any case the novel confirms my belief that Malamud is still growing. (p. 44)

Sheldon Norman Grebstein, "Bernard Malamud and the Jewish Movement," in Contemporary American-Jewish Literature, *edited by Irving Malin (copyright © 1973 by Indiana University Press; reprinted by permission of the author and publisher), Indiana University Press, 1973 (and reprinted in* Bernard Malamud: A Collection of Critical Essays, *edited by Leslie and Joyce Field, Prentice-Hall, Inc., 1975, pp. 18-44).*

PAUL WITHERINGTON

A New Life deserves to survive on its own terms, its climate of nineteenth-century American myth and its rambling but thematically integrated nineteenth-century structure. Malamud's central archetype here is not, as some critics have insisted, the imported Fisher King of wasteland literature, but that native hybrid, the American Adam. Malamud's allusions to Thoreau, Hawthorne, and Melville establish Seymore Levin's basic transcendental ideal and its qualifications and revisions. Levin's own allusions in most cases, for Levin abuses literary contexts and adopts literary roles to rationalize his failures, allowing himself to be trapped in his own comfortable analogies. But these analogies also point the way to Levin's liberation through action as he learns to control his own fate throughout the novel's two major movements, the purification of impure academics and the legitimacy of illegitimate love. (p. 115)

When Levin first arrives at Cascadia College in Easchester as a new instructor in English, he is naive about geography, assuming as the founders of America often assumed that his new Western surroundings will initiate a new life. Like Roy Hobbs in Malamud's first novel, *The Natural,* Levin believes there is magic in the crossing of space. Dr. Fabrikant, Levin's first idol on campus, tells of the hardships of early explorers searching for the "mythical Northwest Passage," and Levin, missing Fabrikant's irony, responds extravagantly. "Marvellous," he says.

But Levin finds out empirically what Thoreau seemed to know intuitively (and Roy Hobbs never even suspects), that faith in movement and space without an inner conversion leads to a dead end, and that inner conversion makes movement and space irrelevant. (p. 116)

At first, Levin bathes in nature. He takes long walks, plays naturalist, and goes into ecstasy over the harvest of his landlady's walnuts. But the fertility of fall is prolonged by the rain of Cascadia's winter, unlike traditional winters Levin is used to, and he is shocked to see "bread growing in the harvested field" when he is in the mood for decay. . . . Neither the academic year nor Levin's emotional cycle seems in tune with the natural year. The affair with Pauline, Gerald Gilley's wife, does come largely in the spring, but Cascadia's spring, like its winter, is ambiguous, and no simple fertility parallels are possible. (pp. 116-17)

[After] the dramatic events at the novel's center . . . , Levin begins to internalize the seasons, thus to control them. He learns that the real marvel is the marvel of inner space: "Space plus whatever you feel equals more whatever you feel, marvelous for happiness." . . . Near the end, preparing to leave Cascadia with Pauline, Levin remarks, "Beautiful country," and she answers, for both of them, "If beauty isn't all that happens." Like Thoreau's woodsmen who carry summer about with them in a pail, Levin and Pauline carry paradise out of Paradise, her body itself having become "fresh-baked bread, the bread of flowers." . . .

Early Levin realizes intellectually Thoreau's solution, that is, to bathe nature in one's self. Of Levin, Malamud says, "He did not mind the smallness of the town. Had not Concord been for Thoreau a sufficient miniature of the universe?" . . . But not until late in the novel can Levin say, in answer to Gilley's question of how he can teach Thoreau without having been to the wilderness, "I've been to Walden Pond." . . . The change from "Concord" to "Walden"

signifies Levin's own development, paralleling Thoreau's journey to confirm by experience what he had known intuitively.

In the midst of Thoreau, however, Levin's conversion drama thickens. As the transcendental geography of Emerson and Thoreau was crossed by Hawthorne's memory-darkened landscapes, so Levin's situation is complicated and enriched as his basic ideal sprouts horns. Malamud's medium is love, transformed by principle and ultimately transforming principle. (p. 117)

Levin becomes the fallen American Adam, whose nineteenth-century design has been fully analyzed by R.W.B. Lewis. Of Hawthorne's particular version, Lewis says: "The characteristic situation in his fiction is that of the Emersonian figure, the man of hope, who by some frightful mischance has stumbled into the time-burdened world of Jonathan Edwards." Beginning in disguise and cliché, with an emphasis on appearances, Levin's affair with Pauline matures in Hawthorne fashion to an inner drama of the ambiguities of paradise. (p. 118)

As Levin internalizes space, he understands that real magic is an inner transformation, an inner pose that becomes an outer reality. Disguise, like the literal West, is limited, a sign that offers only false freedom a freeway rather than a free way. (pp. 118-19)

When Levin slips into the Puritan pattern that trapped Hawthorne's characters and the ideal of love turns into an ideal of guilt, the allusions become very explicit and very conscious. Seated conspicuously at a basketball game, he imagines himself "Arthur Dimmesdale Levin, locked in stocks on a platform in the town square, a red A stapled on his chest." . . . (p. 119)

The Levin-Gilley relationship here repeats thematically an earlier episode of student cheating, paralleling academic and love plots. A weak student has written an impossibly good paper. On principle, Levin investigates, but both he and the student become ill with guilt. Levin calls off the search when he finds himself the victim of his victim, but that irony (central also in *The Assistant* and *The Tenants*) forces him to reevaluate the issue of who is cheating whom. . . . "A good teacher is a liberator," he learns . . . , thinking of higher laws and preparing himself to dissolve his own reservations about cheating in marriage when love has, in Hester Prynne's forest words, "a consecration of its own."

Hester's later denial of that consecration is almost Levin's fate as he temporarily gives up Pauline and sets out, as compensation, to write the great American essay on—predictably—*Moby Dick*. "The whale on his head, relief through balancing the weight on the heart, a disguise and punishment in perpetuity, a means of keeping his poor ego from shattering into bits." . . . The Melville allusions, though brief, are altogether appropriate at this critical point, interrupting Levin's Hawthorne analogies as they in turn interrupted references to Thoreau, Levin fleeing from myth to myth. They characterize Levin's severe conflict and prepare for its solution. The separation of "head" and "heart" he speaks of at this moment is precisely Captain Ahab's flaw (and that of numerous Hawthorne characters). And in his feelings of inevitability, Levin shares Ahab's mistaking of myth as fate (the horrible death implicit in Ahab's Biblical name) for myth as possibility. (pp. 120-21)

The *Moby Dick* allusions lead into Levin's identification with Duffy, his predecessor and double. At first Levin follows Duffy's career somewhat knowingly as department gadfly, and unknowingly as lover of Pauline. Then like Jay Gatsby who is also a nineteenth-century hero caught in a time-space warp (Easchester in the West, like Gatsby's West Egg in the East, is an ironic misnomer), Levin finds footsteps beside the love bower. He is crushed. But after great pain the humanity he has been studying surfaces, and he understands that Duffy's existence does not subtract from his. All experience is double, archetypal, cumulative. Significantly it is at this stage that he speaks of himself as an explorer in a new sense, not of geographical space, or of bodies in bed, but of the mysteries of ideal love undiminished by repetition.

When Levin accepts the mirror image, he is released from it, learning in two directions. Time, one's personal or racial past, cannot be avoided and must not be used regressively. Freedom too is unavoidable, and must not be feared. Levin learns that Duffy is dead, his suicide note reading: "The time is out of joint. I'm leaving the joint." . . . Duffy's final fling at space and escape from time frees Levin from the parallel, and for leaving Cascadia with dignity, with some choice, as if Hester and Dimmesdale had carried out their plan and stepped through the looking glass, or Ahab had relinquished his "iron way." Not, of course, without pain and qualification.

The early Levin is obsessed with order, naming it first to Pauline in his list of values. "What I can, I plan," he says. . . . Unlike Duffy who simply leaves the dislocated, the "out of joint," Levin takes it on. "Why?" Gilley asks. "Because I can, you son of a bitch," Levin answers . . . , baring an inner order.

This inner order began to take shape earlier during a department crisis paralleling the love crisis. In both, principled action becomes the culmination of awareness and provides the way through the labyrinth of myth. Gilley, the leader without a thought, and Fabrikant, the thinker who cannot act, are the only choices for election to the position left vacant by the chairman's sudden death. Since Levin cannot accept either, he runs against them both. The contest is mainly with Gilley, bringing together again love and academic affairs because Levin's new life must be earned in both areas through insight and, as the transcendentalists would put it, wisdom in action. (pp. 121-22)

In the last scene of the book, Levin and Pauline drive past Humanities Hall where a maple tree is being cut down, "limb by leafy limb, to make room for a heat tunnel." . . . As they drive by, Gilley snaps their picture as he snapped the picture earlier of Duffy and Pauline emerging naked from the ocean. But that emergence was from a play Paradise without commitment, one that neither Hawthorne nor Melville·nor Thoreau believed in. Real paradise is not the prelapsarian Eden, but the fully clothed, fully public exit from the now treeless garden of the humanities, a fortunate fall. Real paradise is the ambiguity that Levin commits himself to, that is, moral freedom.

Three sets of allusions, then, two major and one minor, give Levin's experience depth and illustrate his progession through ideal, testing of ideal, and reforming of ideal in action. Malamud's freewheeling characterization of the foolish and wise English teacher leaves little doubt that most of the allusions are Levin's and that he uses them at first to oversimplify experience or to reinforce his own behavior, exchanging them for other categories when his defenses fail or freedom becomes too imminent. But when he wakes to the potentials of doubleness, he transcends his own sources, making analogy his servant. Late in the novel, in an outrageous dream of himself bringing culture to Cascadia, Levin sees himself as "Levin, benefactor, Culture Hero, Seymore J. P. Bunyanseed." . . . The authentic folk hero (Johnny Appleseed, Paul Bunyan) crossed with the seventeenth-century custodian of Christian myth (John Bunyan), but more: a compromise Thoreau would not have made entirely with the old world of time, nor Hawthorne with the new world of space.

Allusions overlap and interact, as of course they must in Levin's mind, yet their movement here toward complexity and the inner harnessing of myth is clear, and I believe they must be taken seriously. I am not denying entirely Malamud's satire on academics, or the operation of mock heroic or mock pastoral patterns outlined by other critics. But the explanation of Levin's strange character is not to be found only in contemporary examples of ironic anti-heroes or existential rebel-saviors. Looking for literary parallels, we must go back in time to Charles Brockden Brown's Arthur Mervyn, Hawthorne's Robin of "My Kinsman, Major Molineux," Melville's Pierre, or even Twain's Pudd'nhead Wilson, those nineteenth-century clowns who are continually undercut, lovingly, by their creators, but whose ultimate victory within an ideological framework is never denied. (pp. 122-23)

Paul Witherington, "Malamud's Allusive Design in 'A New Life'," in Western American Literature *(copyright, 1975, by the Western Literature Association), August, 1975, pp. 115-23.*

DAVID R. MESHER

In Bernard Malamud's writing, . . . Jewishness is more of a literary device than it is a religious, historical, or sociological representation. Malamud's use of Jewish characters and subjects is metaphorical and idiosyncratic, and it must be understood within the context of his fiction without recourse to external sources and familiar assumptions; further, Malamud's metaphor of Jewishness has changed considerably since his first stories were published, and being Jewish in a recent novel like *The Tenants* no longer means what it did in an earlier work like *The Assistant*. . . . [The] theme of Jewishness is of central importance in many of Malamud's stories and in all of his novels after the first, *The Natural* (1952). . . .

Many of Malamud's early works are predicated upon the protagonist's necessary acceptance of his Jewish identity. This is perhaps most readily seen in *A New Life* (1961), a novel otherwise devoid of Jewish content, where the acceptance by S. Levin, who ignores his origins throughout the work, is only ironically suggested. (p. 18)

Jewishness, in *A New Life* and "The Lady of the Lake," is a matter of identity; it forms an integral part of the individual's personality, and its denial, which is a type of self-denial, is either futile or disastrous. In *The Assistant* (1957), the novel which preceded *A New Life*, the theme of Jewishness is similar but more developed and complex. The story concerns Morris Bober, a poor grocer, his daughter Helen, and their relations with Frank Alpine, who first robs the grocery and then returns and tries to rectify the crime by working in the store. Though Frank likes Morris and falls in love with his daughter, his old habits die hard: he begins to steal from the till and later rapes Helen. Afterwards, Frank is truly repentant; by the time of Morris' death, Frank has become the grocer's double, accepting the burden not only of his impoverished life but of Morris' philosophy of humility and humanity as well. In Malamud's metaphor, Frank becomes a Jew. (p. 20)

Malamud seems to subscribe to the commonplace that the Jews, if a "chosen people," were chosen to suffer. His early work concentrates primarily on Jewish characters, or on other immigrants and minorities co-existing with Jews in the squalid ghetto of the author's imagination. Surely Malamud acknowledges that all people suffer, not just Jews. Though he exploits the Jews' history to create a symbol for suffering mankind in his early fiction, Jews are more than symbols in Malamud's work; they are also the guardians and preservers of a cultural tradition based largely on this history of suffering which no Malamudian character successfully repudiates or rejects. (pp. 21-2)

There are, of course, ... negative characterizations of Jews in Malamud's fiction, like those of the Karps, father and son, the rich and obnoxious opposites of the Bobers in *The Assistant*. The two families represent the two types of Jews found throughout Malamud's early work. The Karps are Jews by virtue of their birth, the Bobers by virtue of their sensitivity and humanity. The latter constitute the more significant category for Malamud, though they may be Jews in metaphor only. The concept of metaphoric Jewishness is perhaps best illustrated by the conversion of Frank Alpine. The final line of *The Assistant* relates simply that after the Passover Frank "became a Jew." ... Malamud does not present this as a religious conversion, though the phrase is vague enough to allow for such a literal reading. Frank has more likely become a metaphoric Jew only, and this is accomplished not suddenly in the last line, but gradually as documented in the novel. Under the tutelage of Morris Bober, Frank slowly learns the significance of suffering, and as a sufferer he evolves, according to Malamud's metaphor, into a Jew. (p. 22)

Sociological changes have altered New York City since *The Assistant*—at least in Malamud's perception—and the Jew [in *The Tenants*] is no longer credible as a symbol of suffering in a contemporary urban American novel. Lesser's suffering, for example, is mostly artistic. ... (pp. 24-5)

Willie, a ghetto black, is a more likely example of suffering. He has the same problems as Lesser in achieving artistic expression, and is financially impoverished as well. But Willie fails to bear his destitution with pride. ...

Only Levenspiel, with his pregnant teen-age daughter, sick wife, and crazy mother, seems to be affiliated with the type of sufferers that characterize Malamud's early writing. But as with Willie and Lesser, changing times have altered the conception of suffering for the landlord, too. ... Indeed, Levenspiel's self-pitying complaints and attempts to move Lesser by sympathy for his family make the landlord a very unattractive, opportunistic figure. The Jew, represented by Lesser and Levenspiel, is only an ethnic identity in *The Tenants;* though still of particular interest to the author, the Jew no longer personifies suffering. The black, however, is

not the new heir to this position in the world's pity, either, as Willie seems to believe. Instead, blacks and Jews in *The Tenants* are Ishmael and Israel, two similar groups attempting, as the rabbi says in one of Lesser's dreams, "to live as one people." ... The failure of the main doubles, Willie and Lesser, who share love, hate, art, and even personality traits, to achieve this simple co-existence suggests the author's bleak view of the future of mankind.

As the conflict between the writers becomes more intense, they regress from individual personalities to racial stereotypes. The violent conclusion of the novel is a graphic demonstration of these stereotypes: though once sensitive and intelligent artists, when Lesser and Willie meet for the final time they have degenerated into superstitious savages. Neither attempts to be a complete man, but only defends the false, stereotyped identity which he has assumed. (p. 25)

Malamud's Jewish characters and concerns in *The Tenants* have obviously changed from those found in *The Assistant*. In his early novels and stories, the Jew was both an individual with human foibles and strengths, and—like Morris Bober—a symbol of humanity's inevitable suffering and possible redemption. By the time of *The Fixer*, however, the Jew has become Yakov Bok: still a sufferer, still humanity's representative, but now aware of the futility and injustice of that suffering. "What suffering has taught me," Bok concludes, "is the uselessness of suffering." ... Yet the Jew is still singled out in *The Fixer*, not just as a victim but, also, as the agent of possible social change, because "there's no such thing as an unpolitical man, especially a Jew." ... Thus, the first change in Malamud's metaphor of Jewishness reflects an altered perception of the world: in *The Assistant* suffering itself is beneficial, while in *The Fixer* it is a condition that should, and can, be corrected. The Jew, because of his history, remains central in each case, first as the sufferer and then as one who must work for human betterment. *The Tenants* exhibits a more fundamental change. Suffering is no more valuable than it is in *The Fixer*, but the sufferers are no longer given sympathetic treatment. They are responsible for their own situations, and hope for some alteration in the human condition is minimized by this very pessimistic portrayal. The guarded optimism and affirmation of life so characteristic of Malamud's earlier works has practically vanished from *The Tenants*.

Still, the Jew remains central in Malamud's fiction because, like the black, his history should provide him with a sense of compassion. The failure of Lesser and Willie to "feel the anguish of the other" until the moment of their mutual destruction ..., shows that the humanity which they illustrate has learned nothing from the lessons of the past. It is humanity, then, that has degenerated in the author's view, and if Malamud's fictive Jew has deteriorated from saint to murderer, he has done so as a reflection of that humanity which he consistently represents. (p. 26)

David R. Mesher, "Malamud's Jewish Metaphors," in Judaism (copyright © 1977 by the American Jewish Congress), Winter, 1977, pp. 18-26.

* * *

MALLET-JORIS, Françoise 1930-

Mallet-Joris is a Belgian-born novelist, poet, short story writ-

er, and editor now residing in France. Her first novel, *Le Rempart des béguines*, drew critical comparisons to the work of Françoise Sagan, largely because of its theme of lesbianism. Mallet-Joris's conversion to Catholicism is considered a major influence on her work. (See also *Contemporary Authors*, Vols. 65-68.)

RIMA DRELL RECK

With the appearance of [*Le Rempart des Béguines* and *La Chambre rouge*] Françoise Mallet-Joris . . . was hailed as a modern successor to the Marquis de Sade and Laclos. Combining a striking command of novelistic technique with scandalous subject matter, Mme Mallet-Joris revealed a preoccupation with the politics of conflicting wills which could not fail to recall these masters of the eighteenth century. The publication of [*Cordélia, Les Mensonges*, and *L'Empire Céleste*], however, has seen the eroticism of constraint take second place to an elaboration of the anatomy of will. Closer to the classical seventeenth century in its analysis of motives and illusions, this inquiry into the will is almost geometrical in form and moralistic in intent.

The exercise of will takes on varying forms in Mme Mallet-Joris' novels. It is expressed primarily by contempt and an effort at isolation. . . . (p. 74)

[Hélène of *La Chambre rouge*] makes a discovery common to the elite in Mme Mallet-Joris' gallery of willful spirits: they are all capable of the degradation they so despise. (pp. 74-75)

Alongside the more disciplined practitioners of will, Mme Mallet-Joris ranges those who devote their lives to elaborating a lie or an illusion which makes existence bearable for them. The original illusion is an ingenuous creation, a harmless fiction, a day-dream voiced once too often. These illusions involve clashes of will only when the existence of one illusion demands the annihilation of another. (p. 76)

A third form of exercise of the will is depicted in Mme Mallet-Joris' novels. This form is simple defiance by those who will not sacrifice themselves to the delicate structure of hypocrisy. Such defiance in no way intends to impose a substitute lie or illusion. It merely demands an independent existence. (p. 77)

However, from the loving care with which Mme Mallet-Joris elaborates a complex anatomy of will in its diverse forms, it would be false to infer that only the simple-minded triumph. They escape the complexities, and also never participate in the clash of wills which exalts more complex persons. . . . For most persons a life without some measure of fiction would be impossible, and for a few a life without a dangerous exercise of will would not be worth living. (p. 78)

> *Rima Drell Reck, "Françoise Mallet-Joris and the Anatomy of the Will," in* Yale French Studies *(copyright © Yale French Studies 1959), No. 24, 1959, pp. 74-9.*

GENEVIEVE DELATTRE

["The look", a term used to describe Françoise Mallet-Joris' predominantly visual, highly objective temperament,] is a look which first of all catches objects, observes them with curiosity, details them with love, perceives their harmony; a look without which the descriptive talent of the author would not succeed. . . . (p. 121)

If this look, objective and creative as well, only embraced

things, it would be but a source of joy. It turns, however, towards human beings and scans them with the same eagerness. At this point, from a well delineated world of gleaming objects . . . we pass into a world of mist and uncertainty, the realm of the lie. Why this transformation? Precisely because objectivity becomes impossible where human beings are involved. The reality of a landscape, of an object, coincides with their appearance. The eye can know them and fix them, at least at a given moment. When we look at Françoise Mallet-Joris' characters, on the contrary, our eyes are met by their appearance only, that is by what they are willing to let us see. Their truth hides behind the fortress of lies which they have erected, in a secret realm where they are overcome by fear when faced with their nudity and vulnerability, with what the novelist sometimes calls their soul.

She is the first one to encounter this opacity of beings. She cannot see more than their external aspects, their physical features, their attitudes—in short, their masks. To surmount this obstacle, she has but a single means: to carry her objectivity to the extreme, that is, renounce all personal intervention and judgment. The author's objectivity then becomes the character's subjectivity. The two possible techniques for such a reversal are narration in the first person, used by Françoise Mallet-Joris in her first two novels (*Le Rempart des béguines* and *La Chambre rouge*), or the interior monologue, of which she makes more and more use in the next two novels (*Les Mensonges* and *L'empire céleste*).

Whatever the technique, the look remains for all—reader, author, and character—the sole means of knowledge, and hence it acquires a frightful power. Although each novel involves a very different set of events, we feel an underlying unity in the world of Françoise Mallet-Joris because it rests upon a fear that is intrinsic to each human being. . . . We see them all engaged in a veiled war with each other, armed only with their look, spying upon one another, ready to seize the minute of weakness which will permit them to freeze the enemy into an attitude forever repulsive to himself. (pp. 121-22)

Since they feel no pity for others, either because of a natural hardness of heart or because of a repulsion for any kind of weakness, the characters of Françoise Mallet-Joris expect none in return. They feel compelled to defend themselves against the possible annexation of their inner self by others. Total indifference is a form of defense granted to only a privileged few. Against the merciless look which seeks to judge, and which will succeed in judging, often unjustly and without appeal, if one allows it to, a secure shelter is to be found in lies. Each one, then, chooses a mask for himself, a flattering attitude, and strives to play his part in an effort to see at last in the eyes of those who watch him the reflection of an image he has chosen. Thus we witness throughout the novels a tragic masquerade, for, instead of the awaited liberation, each person brings about his total enslavement by others. He needs them constantly, he needs their eyes in which to seek reassurance that his mask fits, that his comedy is accepted. (p. 123)

What could be more objective than a mirror? But mirrors lie in the world of Françoise Mallet-Joris. The author places them everywhere. Repeatedly we see a face seeking in them the reflection of its real self and finding only the reflection of what it is in the eyes of others, truth and reality remaining invisible. . . .

Can the lie, then, become a kind of second truth? No. Because deep within every person there remains a realm lighted by the consciousness of a struggle between what he is and what he appears to be. It is surprising to find so little self-analysis in novels where the narration in the first person, or interior monologue, plays such an important part. Introspection is foreign to these characters because they are afraid of it. The look they give themselves strives to remain directed outward toward their reflection. (p. 124)

The dream of what one pretends to be, the reality of what one is: nearly all Françoise Mallet-Joris' characters are torn by this conflict between lucidity and complacency, between a longing for and a fear of authenticity. Each one has condemned himself to live with his double, which he loves or hates but must have in order to escape his own identity, until he no longer recognizes himself. . . . (p. 125)

> *Genevieve Delattre, "Mirrors and Masks in the World of Françoise Mallet-Joris," in* Yale French Studies *(copyright © Yale French Studies 1961), No. 27, 1961, pp. 121-26.*

MARIAN ENGEL

["The Underground Game"] is a story of some complexity, amusing to recall. Guibal [the protagonist], it seems to me, is one of the few warm characters in French fiction in recent years, and as a literary man he is both a study and a warning. He can't please anyone but is himself so easily pleased that he is constantly confused. . . .

This is the work of a mature and knowing talent. Mallet-Joris has always been good, but it is a pleasure to see her swimming in long easy strokes against the tide of intellectuality. She handles scenes and characters with great authority, neatly sectioning her narrative so as to take advantage of every point of view. Her unpretentious hero is a man much sinned against, but he is not resentful, and Mallet-Joris handles developments and changes in his relationships with a light hand. A varied and shifting canvas is more difficult to bring to life than a single, intense subject. (p. 20)

> *Marian Engel, in* The New York Times Book Review *(© 1975 by The New York Times Company; reprinted by permission), August 24, 1975.*

*   *   *

MASEFIELD, John   1878-1967

Masefield was an English poet, novelist, playwright, short story writer, critic, and children's book author. He was often drawn to the sea as a theme for his poetry, and it is perhaps for the poem "Sea Fever" that he is best remembered. Masefield was awarded the Order of Merit in 1935 and was named Poet Laureate of England in 1930. (See also *Contemporary Authors*, Vols. 19-20; obituary, Vols. 25-28, rev. ed.; *Contemporary Authors Permanent Series*, Vol. 2.)

L. A. G. STRONG

John Masefield was a copious writer, and one of the most uneven whom our time can show. His official position as Poet Laureate stimulated him to produce, conscientiously and dutifully, a number of *morceaux*, the poetic equivalent of journalism, works of which the chief interest was the occasion that evoked them. (p. 5)

The more closely one comes to consider any aspect of Masefield's work, the more deeply does one realize that the man is, essentially and all the time, a poet. Even at their

flattest and most dutiful, the worst of the occasional pieces have style and technical polish. They are well groomed. (p. 6)

Love and knowledge of the English countryside were innate. The sea and seafaring folk had been stamped upon the impressionable years of his adolescence. He had learned to fend for himself, and to observe people who worked hard for their living by earning his own amongst them: and, at the right time, the right reading had come his way in a book store, and the future Laureate had drunk of a pure English spring of inspiration, in a country which isolated him, and so increased its power. Strongest of all, his youth gave him a life-long and passionate sympathy with the under-dog, the unprivileged, the victim, the man or woman or child (or animal) who is ''ard done by'. (p. 7)

[Masefield's] masterpiece, *Reynard the Fox*, [is] the finest English narrative poem of the century, and one of the finest in our language. Here was what the poet had been born to achieve. Here was a subject and a setting which gave him full scope for all his powers. Here was a conflict, inevitable, rising from the very nature of things, with a deferred happy ending which satisfied both sides alike, the weary hunted fox escaping the hunters whose urge to destroy him was sublimated in admiration for the gallant dance he led them. In this poem every characteristic, every mannerism is subdued to a single aim. The inspiration flames throughout. (p. 21)

Reynard the Fox is a magical poem, the more magical because the poet's eyes are all the time fixed upon the earth and upon its creatures. Masefield's note of mysticism has never been more strongly and deeply sounded than in this extroverted poem of a typical English activity in a typically English countryside. (p. 25)

It will come as no surprise to the reader that Masefield has written magnificently for children. His peculiar blend of zest and gravity, of relish and intense concentration, together with his love of the technicalities of any craft, make an ideal equipment for a children's writer. *The Midnight Folk*, and its sequel, *The Box of Delights, or, When the Wolves were Running*, are among the most sure-footed and robust books for children ever written. Above all their other qualities, they have magic. (pp. 29-30)

The score, then, for John Masefield, his contribution to the life and literature of his time, is one supreme long narrative poem, wholly English, which no one but he could have written: two or three other long poems, original in matter and manner, which brought violent gusts of energy to the polite, faintly countrified air of poetry in their day: a handful of short pieces which have passed into current thought: a just, spare, and impassioned commentary upon England's greatest writer: two chronicles of high achievement which match their theme: and other books, poems and plays lit with flashes of intense but intermittent light. He has never written meanly, coldly, or carelessly. He has sided always with the weak against the strong. The right things have moved him, whether to anger or joy. Sensitive, gentle, and brave, he has found his mainspring in love of life and compassion for all that live it. (pp. 34-5)

> *L.A.G. Strong, in his* John Masefield *(© L.A.G. Strong, 1964; Longman Group Ltd., for The British Council), British Council, 1964.*

FRASER DREW

[Masefield's] chief dedication is to what he feels is the English spirit and to the interpretation to the world of that spirit, the land and the heritage from which it springs, and the men and words and deeds that it inspires. (p. 15)

From *Salt-Water Ballads* (1902) to *Grace Before Ploughing* (1966), there is frequent evidence of [Masefield's] interest in the early years of Britain. In several poems he combines historical reminiscence with his favorite theme of the persistence of human influence in those places where human existence has been especially violent or tragic or beautiful. (p. 22)

In his retelling of the tales of Tristan and of Arthur, Masefield does not follow Malory or any other Arthurian storyteller completely. He even adds new details, new motives, new characterizations of his own, borrowing and inventing freely in the medieval tradition. (p. 27)

Although he shows corruption in medieval government in a manner that constantly suggests modern parallels, Masefield's picture of Arthurian Britain and its people is generally a stirring and attractive one. (p. 30)

Much of Masefield's work, particularly the two early collections of short stories and several later books of verse, shows evidence of his interest in folklore as well as in his nation's history and her heroic legends. (p. 34)

In the second part of [the poem] "August, 1914," Masefield turns to a theme that has a particular fascination for him, a theme that recurs frequently in his poetry and his prose, the concept of immortality "near the men and things we love," of the persistence of the beautiful and the good near the original scene of that beauty and that goodness, a place "inestimably dear." (p. 51)

[The] interest in the old English past, which led eventually to the novel, *Badon Parchments* (1947), and to the many Arthurian poems, runs through the *Lollingdon Downs* volume (1917) with the concomitant themes of mutability and the persistent influence of the human spirit upon the land. (p. 52)

Masefield's knowledge of the landscape and the land is intimate and reveals itself over and over again in his poetry and in the descriptive passages of his novels and essays. One need look only at the last pages of *The Everlasting Mercy* (1911) or at *Reynard the Fox* (1919) or *The Country Scene* (1937) to find striking evidence of this detailed and sympathetic knowledge. (p. 56)

In [the novel] *The Street of Today,* the countryside near Pudsey and Drowcester creates an idyllic background for the courtship of Lionel and Rhoda and initiates some philosophical digressions on the part of the novelist. Masefield writes much more convincingly about the English April than about the love affair of the chief characters, who are stilted, unreal figures with strange conversations and marionette-like behavior. Often only the descriptive passages redeem the book from dullness. (p. 59)

[It is evident that Masefield] makes little use of the English landscape in his prose narratives. His most successful attempts at fiction, *Sard Harker* and *The Bird of Dawning,* have employed either the sea or a foreign locale.

An examination of the narrative poetry of Masefield yields a far different conclusion. Of the major narrative poems, only *Enslaved* (1920) and *Rosas* (1918) have exotic backgrounds, one African, one Argentine, while *Dauber,* a sea poem, has one long English episode in flashback. The other six are completely English, except for one Argentine sequence in *The Daffodil Fields,* and many of the shorter narratives have English settings. (p. 60)

[The role of the English landscape] never assumes the proportions of that of Egdon Heath and the Wessex country of Thomas Hardy, but it is often more than a pleasant backdrop for the action of the narrative. At times the land, its weather, and its plant and animal life reflect and intensify the moods of the characters in the poems; . . . the landscape is often in contrast to the action, as Masefield employs his favorite device of the juxtaposition of ugliness and beauty, or of the contrast of peace in nature, tumult in man. (p. 61)

["The Love Gift" and "Tristan's Singing"] do not have the reality of the descriptions in the earlier narrative poems. They have a tapestry-like quality, like the pictures in a Chaucerian dream-vision, and the figures of Nature and her attendant creatures have beauty and color, but not life. (p. 72)

Of the long verse narratives by Masefield, the quietest and most serene is *King Cole* (1921). It is as free from the rush and excitement of *Reynard the Fox* and *Right Royal* as it is from the danger and violence of *Rosas* and *Enslaved,* the pathos of *Dauber* and *The Widow in the Bye Street,* and the mixture of beauty and brutality that characterizes *The Everlasting Mercy* and *The Daffodil Fields.* The realism of *King Cole* is softened and sweetened by an extraordinary atmosphere of fairyland, which pervades the whole poem. . . .

The English countryside is here, but it is touched with the supernatural and shines with the spirit. This is no photograph in black and white or in colors, nor yet is it the tapestry of landscape to be found in some of the minor narratives; this is water color, painted by a versatile artist who may be at his very best in this medium. . . .

Among the most appealing lines in the poem are those which catalogue the English flowers and list the birds and butterflies and creatures of the forest that follow the piping of the spirit-King. Masefield's poetry is thronged with descriptions of animals and flowers and with similes that employ them, attesting to his love for all life. (p. 73)

Masefield is aware of English weather and season and is sensitive to every change and token. He praises midsummer nights, autumn, and winter snow, but most of all he loves April. A concordance to Masefield's poetry would reveal April as one of his favorite words. Not only does he describe springtime beauty and joy, but he uses April as a symbol for all that is fresh and lovely and bright. (p. 75)

At times [Masefield's] characters fail miserably, as individuals and even as types, and he is particularly inept in his portrayal of women. He does show great skill at other times in his presentation of the men he knows best—the English sailor and the English countryman.

A survey of Masefield's fiction and narrative poetry reveals that his favorite characters are countrymen, sailors, and sportsmen. (p. 78)

In the first poem of *Salt-Water Ballads* (1902), Masefield pledges himself to the common man, the man "with too weighty a burden, too weary a load." . . .

Many writers have issued credos and manifestos early in their careers and have lived to abandon their beliefs. Masefield is true throughout his life to the men he promises to serve in "A Consecration." Though he writes about the man with "too weary a load" and "the scorned—the rejected," he does not belong to "the literary school which has sprung up from our awakened social conscience." Like Chaucer, he describes and narrates, but, still like Chaucer, he does not moralize or preach. (p. 96)

Often the Masefield hero is the man who achieves spiritual triumph even in physical defeat. . . . The theme of defeat and failure haunts much of Masefield's work from *The Tragedy of Pompey the Great* (1910) through the early narrative poems, *Good Friday* (1916), and *Gallipoli* (1916), and recurs in *ODTAA* (1926) and other later work. . . . The great Masefield quest is for Beauty, Understanding, Truth, and it exacts from the artist the ultimate in courage and sacrifice. (pp. 97-8)

One of Masefield's most notable achievements is the book *Gallipoli,* prose epic of the heroic and ill-fated Dardanelles campaign of World War I. It is a detailed picture of the campaign, an explanation of the reasons for its failure, and a supreme tribute to the courage of the English soldier and his Anzac ally. It is a beautifully written and moving account of a great victory cloaked in outward failure, and it is perhaps the poet's finest study of Englishmen who become "a story for ever." In *Gallipoli,* as in "August, 1914," Masefield's love for his countrymen reaches its most eloquent expression. (pp. 98-9)

It is a commonplace to refer to John Masefield as the sea poet or the sailor's laureate; yet only the reader familiar with the great body of Masefield's poetry and prose can realize the extent to which the sea, the ship, and the sailor have dominated Masefield's life and his work. (p. 135)

Throughout Masefield's poetry the sea, the ship, and the sailor appear and reappear. In the most landlocked of poems, a simile or metaphor of the sea will suddenly light up and make vivid an inland scene or an inland thought, for the poet always turns, whenever in search of a clarifying or life-giving image, to the world which he knows and loves best. (p. 156)

When the reader of Masefield leaves the English ship and turns to the sea itself, he will find treatments of the subject varying from the very romantic to the very realistic. It will not surprise him to learn that one of the three earliest extant Masefield poems is called "Sonnet—To the Ocean." The poem is ponderous and grandiose, with none of the grace of the first published poems like "Sea Fever," but it is Masefield's first recorded tribute to "the thunder of the never-silent sea."

Masefield's best-known poem, "Sea Fever," stamped him early as a romanticist. In "Sea Fever," as in "A Wanderer's Song," "Roadways," and other poems from the 1902 and 1903 collections, the picture is clean, clear, bracing, and glorious, with white clouds flying and the wild Atlantic shouting on the sand. . . . There is a wide range in these early ballads, from the pure beauty of "Sea Fever" to the rough-and-tumble "Bill," "Fever-Chills," and "Burial Party," with their dialect, occasional "bloody's." (pp. 160-61)

With the exception, perhaps, of "Land Workers," Masefield's laureate verse offers little that will enhance his reputation. (p. 212)

These occasional verses are often nobly conceived and gracefully executed, but like most occasional verse they generally bear the unmistakable stamp of the duty done and the deadline met. (p. 214)

Masefield's place among the Poets Laureate is that of a poet well qualified, by practice and by temperament, for his post. His celebration of England, as has been shown above, began long before his appointment to an official post. He fulfilled the obligations of the Laureateship as conscientiously as Tennyson, more ably than Austin, and more generously than Bridges. Masefield's activities in behalf of the theater, the speaking of verse, and other arts were many; in his person the Poet Laureate changed from the incumbent of a nominal office to "a living symbol of the power and authority" of poetry. (p. 230)

The Englishness of Masefield's work is the heart of it. If the prose and poetry that are characteristically and openly English are separated from the rest of his work, little of major importance remains. The greater body of Masefield's work, and the finest part of it, is that in which he dedicates himself to the portrayal and the interpretation of English landscape and life. In this England of Masefield, John Bull sometimes makes an appearance, but always he is countered by St. George. And the spirit of St. George shines brightest in those longer poems and tales which are most likely to live—*The Everlasting Mercy, Dauber,* "August, 1914," *Gallipoli, Reynard the Fox, King Cole,* and the *Midsummer Night* stories.

There is no inconsistency in Masefield's apparent shift from a consecration to the common man to a consecration to England. His England is the England of the common man; and the beauties of that England of the future for which he calls repeatedly in his later work are dedicated to the refreshment and the recreation of the common man in England and throughout the world. The new English theater for which he hopes in one of his later essays is but one of the agents Masefield invokes for the moving of "the world with the glory of the English spirit that is now the one thing left to us." (pp. 230-31)

> *Fraser Drew, in his* John Masefield's England: A Study of the National Themes in His Work *(© 1973 by Associated University Presses, Inc.), Fairleigh Dickinson University Press, 1973.*

*   *   *

MATTHIESSEN, Peter   1927-

Matthiessen is an American novelist, naturalist, short story writer, essayist, and editor. He is deeply concerned with man's dangerous violation of the natural world, and strives, in his words, to "identify a sense of man's fate on earth and instill it in both fiction and non-fiction." His experience as explorer and anthropologist is evident in his work. (See also *CLC,* **Vols. 5, 7, and** *Contemporary Authors,* **Vols. 9-12, rev. ed.)**

PAUL ZWEIG

Peter Matthiessen is one of the important wilderness writers of our time. His *The Tree Where Man Was Born* . . . is a masterpiece of understated prose and exacting description. Matthiessen has clearly trained himself to see as a naturalist. . . .

The Snow Leopard is based on the journal Matthiessen

kept during his trek with the field biologist George Schaller to the Crystal Mountain, in upper Nepal, in 1973. . . . The purpose: to observe the November rut of the Himalayan blue sheep in order to determine whether this little-known species is related to the extinct common ancestor of the goat and the sheep. They also hoped to glimpse another animal, so rarely seen that it is almost a myth: the snow leopard, which comes to stand in Matthiessen's mind for a grail of fulfillment.

For Matthiessen's journey out of time is not only a naturalist's venture into one last wilderness but also an attempt to come to terms with a spiritual longing that had taken possession of him several years earlier . . . and reached a climax when his wife, Deborah, became ill with cancer and suffered for several terrible months before dying. . . . By using the journal form, Matthiessen keeps his reader anchored in this weave of impressions and events; the Himalayas, and Matthiessen's way through them, unfold not as a story but as a filled space of perceptions.

Yet Matthiessen is not content to observe. Repeatedly he strains to see through the high mountain scenes into a place of illumination, outside time and death. He quotes traditional Tibetan religious texts and prefaces each section of his book with mystical epigraphs. He interprets every happy moment as a glimpse of the freedom he seeks and every angry, depressed moment as a failure of his spiritual apprenticeship. At times, this gives his writing a driven, almost hallucinatory quality that I found moving. . . . (p. 44)

All too often, in the midst of intense personal descriptions, Matthiessen lapses into clichés of Zen psychology, which read like footnotes attached to real experiences that didn't need to be explained so neatly. For example, one day he sees a feather lying on a path and is transfixed by this emblem of flight strewn among the stones. One understands such moments of splendid concentration, when the world appears in a grain of sand and eternity, in an hour, as William Blake once wrote. But for Matthiessen, the experience itself—gripping, transient, paradoxical—isn't enough; he must transform it into evidence that he has learned a lesson. . . . This didactic thread ties Matthiessen's journal together, making it predictable and finally impersonal. . . .

In his anxious search for evidence that he is "on the path" of the snow leopard and the freedom the animal represents for him, Matthiessen becomes fascinated by one of his Sherpa guides, Tukten, who he decides is a bodhisattva, a hidden Buddhist master. It is a troubling fantasy, a moving one, but it doesn't serve to make Tukten more present in the book. Rather, it burdens him with accretions of speculation. What happens to Tukten happens to Matthiessen himself. And this is a shame, for when Matthiessen allows his experience to speak for itself, his journey tingles with power. . . .

The Snow Leopard contains . . . passages in which the naturalist, the spiritual apprentice, and the writer converge simply and dramatically. For all the difficulty Matthiessen encountered in working out his "journey of the heart," these passages save the book, making it a truly vivid account of Himalayan travel. (p. 45)

> Paul Zweig, "Eastern Mountain Time," in Satur-
> day Review (© 1978 by Paul Zweig; reprinted
> with permission), August, 1978, pp. 44-5.

EDWARD HOAGLAND

Peter Matthiessen has made [in "The Snow Leopard"] another of his epic trips for us—epic in the sense that he writes about them so much better than anybody else who has been undertaking journeys such as his in recent years. (p. 1)

Usually Mr. Matthiessen's companions have been a scruffy collection of shabby hirelings and rich macho playboys who were footing the bill. So—with his friend and with the noble Sherpas—there is a lightness to this walk for him. What is confusing from time to time is that, as well as this worthy company, he feels the presence of Buddha—the Awakened One—here in high Buddhist country, having lately, in America, become a committed convert himself. Also, his wife has died of cancer, and so memories of her are interjected throughout this radiant but rather fragile, flickering book. (p. 20)

[Twenty] years' experience at note-taking on the trail, of bird study and anthropological reading is at work here. Yet, still, the blue sheep, gentle leopards, wolves, yaks, foxes, ponies and "exalted," "berserk" village mastiffs that threaten to rip him limb from limb are more exact and vivid as natural history for all of this adjoining mysticism. And most of us know, really, that in their airiness, the best of the holy men of the great world religions are probably right, even if we don't choose to invest enough of our time in readying ourselves for enlightenment of that type. So, Mr. Matthiessen's paeans and sutras, his plum-pit amulets and "oms" are not without justification, especially in this huge skyscape where the most awesome sequences of cliff and peak and snow and ice are juxtaposed one upon another. . . .

Largely gone are the dry summaries, the highflown and impersonal plural nouns that have deadened many chapters of Mr. Matthiessen's previous books. A shard of rose quartz, the spores of a cinnamon fern, a companionable mound of pony dung, a dog barking at his pale tent in the moonlight, all may excite him as if this were his first—or at least last—day on earth. On the other hand, except for two or three poignant references toward the end, the interpolations concerning his wife seem not so much insincere as jimmied unnaturally into his diary. Though he must indeed have thought of her with grief and guilt under the circumstances, from falsity of placement and carelessness they do not fit.

Like other diarists, he was at the mercy of his original mood and jottings in preparing his book; and so on the fearful days, the slower, earlier stages of the trip, and scary, lunatic interludes when he was assailed by traveler's depression, we are served a lot of Buddhist theology and history whose accuracy or inaccuracy I cannot attest to. But it is much too telescoped for a layman. . . . Furthermore—and this can be irritating—he often proselytizes, even if only to convince himself. And because five years have passed since the actual walk, the writer, as he neared 50, appears to have jammed in a casual, nostalgic but unsettling entire catalogue of his past trips—to Umbria, Paris, Galway, as well as more apposite "primitive" regions. . . .

Mr. Matthiessen has been getting better. My favorite of his novels is his most previous, "Far Tortuga" (1975), which is a daring feat of dialect and dramatic symmetry, about turtle fishermen in the Caribbean. Fitfully, this "Snow Leopard" seems to me his best book of nonfiction. Otherwise—again—his last would be. "The Tree Where Man Was Born" (1972) is not only a search through Africa for the birthplace of man, but somehow for Mr. Matthiessen's own birth, as if he wished to *start over*.... But what makes the search more interesting is that his focus has shifted from birth to death and transfiguration. (p. 21)

Edward Hoagland, "Walking the Himalayas," in The New York Times Book Review (© 1978 by The New York Times Company; reprinted by permission), August 13, 1978, pp. 1, 20-1.

TERRENCE DES PRES

The best places are not on any map, or so Melville once remarked, and Peter Matthiessen would surely agree.... Most of his work has grown from first-hand experience in distant places.... To judge from references in his work, there seems no place on earth Matthiessen has not at least passed through.

From journeying of this kind have come marvelous books, *Under the Mountain Wall* and *The Cloud Forest* for example, but so too have come the "worlds" of his fiction, *At Play in the Fields of the Lord* and *Far Tortuga* in particular, novels which more than deserve the praise they have received (the latter is an outright masterpiece), but which could not have been written without Matthiessen's uncanny talent for at-homeness in cultures other than his own, and his rare ability to command what anthropologist Clifford Geertz has called "thick description," meaning the dense texturing of detail, the build-up of a world's essential presence through masses of particulars, which can come only from living *in* what one might then hope to record.

Given these credentials, it is important to keep in mind that Matthiessen is not an adventurer, nor have his voyages been impelled by some silly man-against-the-elements ideal. His central thrust has been to celebrate the virtues of lost cultures, to praise the excellence of life apart from human life, to bear witness to creation vanishing. And in this pursuit he has been quietly obsessed with one of the uglier truths of our age: that nothing lasts, that no place, culture, bird or beast can survive in the path of Western—and now Eastern—greed. (p. E1)

The Snow Leopard is Matthiessen's attempt to stand altogether beyond modern time, and the extreme beauty of this radiant book lies in the fact that he fails. (pp. E1, E4)

Simply as a step by step account of daily events—villages entered, peaks crossed, the enormously elating business of survival—*The Snow Leopard* is stunning; and unlike most books about Tibet, which read like inflated cartoons, this one stubbornly refuses to romanticize. Matthiessen is a visionary but he is very hardminded as well, and his attention is wholly with abrupt detail. This allows him to render strangeness familiar, and much that is menial becomes strange, lustrous, otherworldly....

I have never read a book so filled with physical light. The high cold air, the sun's unblotted strength, the bright barrenness of snow provoke in Mathiessen a lyrical lucidity as tight and pointed as a clinical report. Partly this is the result of journal notation, but partly too, Matthiessen achieves this effect of heightened foreground by setting immediate observation against the infinite backdrop of mystical meditation....

The Snow Leopard is much more than a travelogue. It is the resolute record of a spiritual quest, informed by Matthiessen's hope of enlightenment, and by his adherence to a wonderfully poetic version of Zen in which, as he says, the universe itself is the Scripture. His overt goal—to personally sight the leopard—becomes the symbol of his inward aim: to be struck still by a vision of eternal oneness and come away able to sustain "the unsentimental embrace of all of life, *without discrimination*." But while there are true moments of insight, and genuine collapses of time and space into infinity, there is no transfiguration, no vision ultimate and lasting....

There are many other good things in *The Snow Leopard* such as the incisive portraits of the mountain people, of George Schaller [Matthiessen's traveling companion], whose pleasure is to leave civilization as far behind as possible and who, like Matthiessen, loves "to travel light." And oddly, for one so down to earth, there is Matthiessen's belief in the "man-thing of the snows," which we Westerners call "abominable." How fine, he seems to say, if this creature, which we have pronounced nonexistent, manages nevertheless to survive and outwit our efforts to track, bracket and no doubt destroy.

Perhaps, then, the snow leopard is better left unseen. Whatever men possess, no matter how sterling their intentions, they seem finally to spoil. And if Matthiessen had arrived at nirvana, what desire or need would have remained to record his search? Instead he has expressed, with uncommon candor and no prospect of relief, a longing which keeps the soul striving and alert in us all. That is the profound humanity of *The Snow Leopard*, a book fiercely felt and magnificently written, in which timelessness and "modern time" are made to touch and join. (p. E4)

Terrence Des Pres, "Soul Searching in the Himalayas," in Book World—The Washington Post (© The Washington Post), August 20, 1978, pp. E1, E4.

JIM HARRISON

The Snow Leopard is an heraldic book, full of ghosts, demons and unfamiliar mythologies; a well-veiled, lower-case buddhist text set in the virtual top of the world, the Himalayas.... Like all good books it is about death, and the imminence of death is fresh and lively, if you will, because we are drawn hypnotically along into a landscape where neither the beasts nor men are familiar....

Peter Matthiessen must be our most eccentric major writer; his eccentricities are those of thought, not language. His style is not exotic and owns a studied Brahmin grace and wit, though the wit is rather more discomfiting than funny. He writes cleanly and beautifully....

Running concurrent to the outward journey in *The Snow Leopard* is an equally torturous inward journey, and the two are balanced to the extent that neither overwhelms the other. Matthiessen for the first time becomes utterly candid about his life without being "confessional." (p. 250)

In *The Snow Leopard* Matthiessen makes the best run I've ever read at explicating Buddhist and Tantric terminology and hagiography. He has a curious talent for clarifying and dismissing the aura of the secretive and arcane....

Beyond my own clumsy and tentatively stated framework Matthiessen has written a magnificent book: a kind of lunar paradigm and map of the sacred for any man's journey, where the snow leopard itself sits grail-like at the edge of consciousness, an infinitely stubborn koan in beast's clothing. (p. 251)

> *Jim Harrison, "Ten Thousand Octobers," in* The Nation *(copyright 1978 by the Nation Associates, Inc.), September 16, 1978, pp. 250-51.*

LEONARD MICHAELS

Most impressively dramatic [in *The Snow Leopard*] is Matthiessen's account of [his] passage through the Himalayas. In images that are intensely kinesthetic as well as visual, he recreates its magnificent vistas and terrors, its unspeakable otherness and sublimity. Finally, *The Snow Leopard* is such a mixture of various things as to make it difficult to name its literary kind. However, there is no doubt that it is profoundly unified in the day-to-day tribulations and wonders of the expedition and in Matthiessen's sensibility—the poetry of voice, his intelligent simplicity, and his obsessions.

In regard to the obsessions, *The Snow Leopard* is reminiscent of *Walden* and *The Pilgrim's Progress* where the oppressive complexities of intimate human connections are also violently repudiated in a determination to see snow leopards. For this, Matthiessen risked his life and subjected himself to enormous discomfort and pain. (p. 33)

It is then our good luck that he fails to see his snow leopard, that he isn't "ready" to see it, and that his expedition is finally a metaphoric death trip, for now we have the product of his failure, a fascinating and beautiful book, as haunted by funeral resonance as it is by life—the very thing he records, pristine, undefiled by human presence—and also by life, the other thing he records, a vile infection, carried by the human beast, that destroys and pollutes the original manifest goodness of creation. . . .

[Something in] Matthiessen is less good, and therefore better, than Bunyan and Thoreau. In his spiritual ambition, he did gamble with his life and he confesses to not having lost it. (p. 34)

> *Leonard Michaels, in* The New Republic *(reprinted by permission of* The New Republic; © *1978 by The New Republic, Inc.), September 23, 1978.*

ROBERT M. ADAMS

[*The Snow Leopard* is a kind of book] with which we are becoming familiar lately; it is part travelogue, part autobiography, part historical discourse, and predominantly lay sermon, in the shape of a quest narrative. . . . [The] bias of the lay sermon is toward Zen Buddhism; and to the eye of a layman, the exposition of Buddhism seems straightforward, nicely written, but not very new. One certainly need not have slogged through the snows of Nepal to discover it. There is of course no reason to anticipate novelty in the explanation of an essentially quietist philosophy which is, by now, at least a thousand years old; but the curious reader might understandably ask whether, if he'd been in full possession of his own philosophical premises, Mr. Matthiessen would have embarked in the first place on such a strenuous and dangerous expedition. . . .

The portion of [*The Snow Leopard*] describing the expedition itself, it should be said at once, is brilliantly and vividly written. The author has dealt frequently and knowingly

with natural scenery and wild life; he can sketch a landscape in a few vivid, unsentimental words, capture the sensations of entering a wild, windy Nepalese mountain village, and convey richly the strange, whinnying behavior of a herd of wild sheep. His prose is crisp, yet strongly appealing to the senses; it combines instinct with the feeling of adventure. . . . The Zen reflections and discourses on the history of the philosophy are more watery; they often seem to resolve themselves into Sanskrit abstractions like *samadhi, sunvata, kensho, satori,* and *prajna*—terms for which evidently no adequate English equivalents exist, though what precisely their special meaning and intensity amount to, the reader must try to guess. The combination of these elements leaves all the more mysterious the explanation of why Matthiessen was present on this expedition at all. People asked him this question, it seems: he always had trouble telling them. . . . He sought, evidently, some sort of illumination or purification, and seems to have got it momentarily, though it is hard to express. (p. 8)

Because he was seeking, and apparently found, some satisfying spiritual illumination which can best be expressed as ecstatic delight in the rightness of the Now—even, or perhaps especially, when that rightness doesn't correspond with what one thought were one's wishes—Matthiessen takes the snow leopard, which he never saw, as the title of his book and the emblem of his experience. . . . One can't really describe Matthiessen's moral state after his journey without oversimplifying it, because, as a skilled craftsman, he doesn't try to represent himself as permanently enlightened beyond the limits of everyday humanity. The final phase of his journey included some perfectly understandable surliness and even more understandable nostalgia for the departure of a trusted sherpa companion. But the more an authentically ordinary life asserts its ordinary values (concern over distant kids, desire to be home for Christmas), the more one is puzzled by the status of that Zen philosophy which ought to render one oblivious—or at least eager to achieve oblivion—of such entangling involvements. (p. 9)

> *Robert M. Adams, in* The New York Review of Books *(reprinted with permission from* The New York Review of Books; *copyright* © *1978 Nyrev, Inc.), September 28, 1978.*

DONALD HALL

For a long time, [Matthiessen's] writing has been vigorous, metaphoric, exact, luminous, coherent, and resolved. If one sensed that something was lacking, one did not know what to call it. In *The Snow Leopard*, Matthiessen's newest and best book, he tells us: "Not so long ago I could say truthfully that I had not shed a tear in twenty years." When I read this sentence, I suddenly knew: his older books—for all their elegance, for all their correct passion for land and wilderness, for all their steady intelligence—lacked the tribute of Matthiessen's tears. . . .

The Snow Leopard is a serious book, as few books are serious, because it arises from a death, and returns to death itself and all our deaths, without morbidity and without nervous levity; with a clear, level, unavoiding gaze. It is a religious book, a book which tells us how to live. (p. 1294)

There is little overt grief in this book; it is not flown like a flag; but the glimpse we catch of it permits the rest of the book its profundity. Experience of the natural world becomes one with Buddhist understanding, with experience of loss, with acceptance of loss. Religious feeling leads to one state in particular—on its way it implies and necessitates certain behavior—which is a condition of blessedness in which time is canceled and death is known and fully accepted. . . .

Peter Matthiessen never does see the snow leopard. Or perhaps he does; there is a glimpsed shape which *could* have been a snow leopard. But it doesn't matter, for the whole book is the snow leopard. (p. 1295)

> Donald Hall, "*From Death unto Death*," *in* National Review (© *National Review, Inc., 1978; 150 East 35th St., New York, N.Y. 10016*), October 13, 1978, pp. 1294-95.

*   *   *

MATUTE, Ana María   1926-

Matute is a Spanish novelist and short story writer. The Spanish civil war is generally considered the most important formative influence on her career. The fear, the horror, and the injustice of war impelled Matute to write, and the subject of her novels is often the war itself. Her fiction is often peopled with sad, alienated adolescents, growing into adulthood in a world divided by the hate and despair of war. Her prose is noted for its sensitivity and delicacy.

MARGARET W. JONES

Analyses of Matute's works reveal a surprising diversity of techniques. Even within a single novel, this variation in style [is evident]. . . . (p. 5)

A glance at the works themselves will establish this astounding variety of styles. Lush and poetic in one passage, harsh and realistically detailed in another, grotesque and fantastic in still another, these apparently tentative stabs at literary experimentation are, in fact, an intentional effort to fuse the manner of expression with the development of the material.

One of the most original results of the author's stylistic preoccupation is a marked emphasis on descriptions of nature, and specifically, the deliberate deformation of certain elements of nature to harmonize with the emotional reactions of the protagonist. Matute's modern use of pathetic fallacy has not escaped [notice.] . . . (p. 6)

The majority of Matute's references to nature fall naturally into two distinct groups. The first of these is the background against which the action is to unfold. All of nature—trees, sky, land, etc.—forms a stylized whole which, although often harsh and cruel, is nonetheless believable. This type of "realistic," though stylized, treatment of nature will not be considered. The dramatic distortion of natural elements to which I am referring is entirely separate from the comprehensive description of the background and functions specifically in accordance with the point of view of the main character. The general elements of nature which will be examined here are all inanimate phenomena: flora, manifestations of weather, and references to the land and sea.

Although a large portion of this author's writing does offer the above-mentioned distortion in varying degrees, the three major works in which this technique is most advantageously presented are *Fiesta al noroeste*, *Los hijos muertos*, and *Primera memoria*. These prize-winning novels are thematically connected by the attention given to the unhappiness and solitude of the main characters; they sketch as well a strange picture of nature which reinforces the bitterness and desolation of these people.

Fiesta al noroeste deals with the anguished psychological struggle of the main character, Juan Medinao. . . . The tremendous tensions suffered by Juan are reflected in the grotesque imagery scattered throughout the novel. (pp. 6-7)

The use of nature to suggest and enhance . . . pessimistic vision is a common technique throughout Ana Maria Matute's novels. A note of fatalism is introduced as the reader perceives that the characters function in accord with the background, which is by no means static, but a living, threatening participant in the action of the story itself. The impression of man's solitude is reinforced by a hostile nature, which is not only indifferent to his suffering, but also deformed to harmonize with the violence of emotions or events which take place in the work. (p. 8)

[The] descriptive passages in *Fiesta al noroeste* do not consist exclusively by nature symbols; the distorted vision of the protagonist is enhanced by equally grotesque phrases, many of which are particularly rich in living-nature images. . . .

Although the stylization of inanimate nature in this book is not as outstanding as in the later novels . . . , it is clear that an effort has been made to coordinate the feelings of Juan Medinao with his own deformity and his physical surroundings. The equation of flowers-blood and sun-blood . . . suggests a violence which these elements will symbolize to a much greater degree in both *Los hijos muertos* and *Primera memoria*. . . .

With [*Los hijos muertos*], the author has achieved her most ambitious undertaking. . . . The novel is a panorama of several generations of one family, united by the same blood, yet irrevocably separated by different ideas and values.

The problems of the divergent generations are . . . personified in Isabel, the symbol of unchanging tradition, and her cousin Daniel, an idealistic youth. (p. 9)

By juxtaposing events which are presented in no arranged chronological order, the author acquaints her readers with the past life of the characters. Thus past and present are fused and systematically confused, although the evocation of the past is usually connected to some event or key word in the present which suddenly awakens a memory-flashback in the mind of the protagonist.

Presented with material so rich in psychological suggestion and emotional connotation, the reader is placed on an empathic level with the characters. Although the events are seen from a multiple point of view, the bulk of the novel is presented through the impressions of Daniel, a disillusioned man with an extremely pessimistic view of life. It is, therefore, from his disenchanted standpoint that the nature images are distorted and stylized, and it is from this narrow scope that the reader is forced to interpret the narration.

References to a tree of white flowers, symbol of the Corvo family, appear within the first pages of the novel. Allusions to this white flower form a leitmotif throughout the work, a technique used for evocative and, at times, poetic purposes. It often bridges the gap in the counterpoint exposition of time in the alternation of past-present. The significance given to this tree is the first in a series of literary stylizations which change a natural but somewhat static element into a meaningful symbol. (p. 10)

The sun is presented here with a significance symbolically more important than in any previous work, and it is to play an important role both in this novel and in *Primera memoria*. It is most indicative of the manner in which nature is deformed to mark the fatalistic elements in these works, for it is invariably associated with blind violence, hostility, or hatred. An attendant suggestion of horror is introduced by endowing the sun with human characteristics of a malevolent quality. . . .

[The] very insistence on the ominous character of the sun makes a great impact. . . . The apprehensiveness of the men as to their fate and the probable tragic outcome are reflected in the fatalistic *momentos decisivos*. . . . (p. 11)

[Matute's descriptive phrases carefully avoid] any of the natural associations which are usually connected with nature. Each imparts a negative allusion to life, for they are either the expressionistic results of the character's interpretation of his surroundings or portents of impending misfortune. . . .

The stylistic deformation [concerning the distortion of nature] serves the same purpose as in *Fiesta al noroeste*. There is a mutual compenetration of nature and emotion: by allowing the characters to distort a nature that the reader knows is neither good nor bad, the author subtly reveals their reactions to a world which they generally consider hostile. The personification of these elements and the endowment of them with negative characteristics reinforce the feeling of dismay experienced by the protagonists as they unwillingly face a world from which they would prefer to escape.

[*Primera memoria*] continues to use the technique of distortion of nature for the purpose of reinforcing the point of view of the protagonist. The underlying theme of this work is the unhappiness caused by difficulties of the transitional period between childhood and adulthood. (p. 12)

As in Matute's other works, the plot itself is subordinate to the psychological climate of *angustia*, bitterness, and melancholy . . . , for this is a fictional autobiography, making use of the *memoria*, a device not uncommon in Matute's works.

Matia [the protagonist of *Primera memoria*] is undoubtedly one of the most effective character studies of this author's literary career. The sense of nostalgia for the adolescent's lost childhood, the anguish at irrevocably having to become part of a sordid adult world . . . are presented with tender yet powerful expression. (pp. 12–13)

One of the most notable devices used by the novelist in *Primera memoria* is the deliberate effort to oblige the reader to adopt Matia's point of view. Through the exclusive use of the first person, the *memoria*, and the parenthetical interior monologue, the reader is forced to relinquish his omniscient and detached relationship with the character, for this single viewpoint necessarily compels him to see and accept the events only from the standpoint of the adolescent protagonist. Since Matia observes and comments solely in relation to her own troubled state of mind, one must accept her reality, which is so stylized that the whole novelesque world becomes deformed.

It is within this expressionistic technique that the strange presentation of nature becomes most evident. No longer are natural reactions to elements of nature valid, for Matute is using a special device for reinforcing the psychological tension of the novel: the deliberate inversion of commonly accepted elements of nature into symbols of the grotesque disharmony of the protagonist and her world. The inclusion of the reader does not stop at his involvement with the main character; he is made to feel the jarring effect of this antithetical expression. Thus tension is provided not only by the plot and the description of Matia's own emotional reactions, but also by the analogy of these emotions with unexpected and grotesque descriptions of nature. (p. 13)

As in *Los hijos muertos*, the sun is [again] a deliberate symbol of violence. The calculated persistence with which this element is mentioned transforms it into an omnipresent being with definitely evil characteristics. . . .

[Descriptive] passages are used to enhance the special role which the sun plays in this novel. Startling adjectives are applied to it in this work, adding to the note of horror which reflects both the atmosphere of the island and the feelings of Matia. . . . (p. 14)

The very amount of nature symbolism and the progressively increased attention given to this strange interpretation of nature suggest a deliberate effort on the part of Matute to give these elements a functional value. Pathetic fallacy has become trite through its constant use, but this author has employed it in an original way which suitably conveys her vision of life. (p. 15)

> *Margaret W. Jones, "Antipathetic Fallacy: The Hostile World of Ana María Matute's Novels," in Kentucky Foreign Language Quarterly (© University of Kentucky; reprinted by permission of Kentucky Romance Quarterly), Supplement to Vol. 13, 1967, pp. 5–16.*

JANET WINECOFF DÍAZ

[Matute's serious illnesses as a child seem] to have caused her to withdraw deeper into the childhood world of fantasy and imagination, which (combined with the necessary inactivity) may have stimulated her precocious literary and artistic inclinations. . . . The childhood illnesses are perhaps unconsciously reflected in [her] not infrequent use of the sick child, and the still more frequent mention of children who die. And the large element of fantasy in her works may well originate with these same experiences. (p. 140)

[Matute's] illness at the age of eight was particularly important for her interest in, and understanding of, the Castilian landscape, for she was sent to live with her grandparents during an extended convalescence, thus becoming acquainted with a countryside different from that of her summers, with new aspects of life, with the misery, poverty, and struggle for existence. . . . These elements appear in the sullen, resentful villagers of *Los Abel* and *Fiesta al noroeste*, and in the tensions between landowners and those who work the soil in the above-mentioned books, as well as in *Historias de la Artámila* and *Los hijos muertos*. The novelist's first vivid encounter with injustice belongs to this same stay in the country, and is recalled in "Los chicos," one of the tales of *Historias de la Artámila*. (pp. 140–41)

Except for the months in the village school when she was eight, Ana María until the age of ten studied alternately in Madrid and Barcelona in *colegios* run by French nuns. The experience seems to have been largely unpleasant: she has confessed that she considered the *colegio* a torture and went most unwillingly. This attitude is reflected in the character of Soledad (protagonist of *En esta tierra*) and her relationship with the nuns of her *colegio*. Without being thoroughly autobiographical, this character shares with the novelist a similar age, family background, and education prior to the war, and Soledad's sentiments of alienation and rebelliousness were probably common to both. The Matute family's frequent shifts between Madrid and Barcelona caused Ana María to have the feeling of always being an outsider, of belonging somewhere else. . . . The constant sensation of solitude in her works, the numerous lonely, estranged and misunderstood children, may originate in these experiences. If so, the *colegio* years acquire additional importance because of the overwhelming number of solitary and alienated characters in her works, and the preponderance of such themes as loneliness, incommunication, and the most extreme solitude. (p. 142)

An autobiographical element dating from early years is the theme of dolls, puppets, the marionette theater and related motifs (the *titiritero*, the *cómicos ambulantes*, even gypsies and the circus). One of Ana María's favorite pastimes as a child was her marionnette theater. . . . This became an even more important distraction during the war years. It is evidently more than a mere coincidence that *Pequeño teatro*, her first novel in order of composition, is in its entirety a complex symbol based on the analogy between theater and life, reality and farce, human beings and puppets. The marionnette theater also appears in *Fiesta al noroeste*, *Primera memoria*, *Tres y un sueño*, and other works, including some of the juvenile fiction.

Despite the importance of autobiographical settings, of rural and agrarian themes, of the themes of solitude and alienation, and of the world of marionnettes, the greatest input of autobiographical elements in Matute's work may come from another source. The importance of the Spanish Civil War, both for the novelist personally, and for her writing, cannot be overestimated. (p. 143)

While she lost no family or close relatives during the war, one of Ana María's professors was killed attempting to escape to France. But the constant sensation of loss in her works is the result of a loss much more fundamental and irreplaceable: the loss of childhood, of innocence, of beliefs, of a whole world and the values on which it was based. . . . That moral ambiguity, to which some critics have objected in Matute's works, is evidently a result of the Civil War. . . .

Although she has some novels which deal directly with the war as such (*En esta tierra*, and parts of *Los hijos muertos*), Matute from her earliest published works associates the Civil War with the symbol of Cain and Abel, the conflict between brothers. The very title of *Los Abel* indicates this preoccupation, and the symbolic strife is carried to the limit of murder. (p. 144)

The theme of hate and love between members of the same family, a constant in Matute's work, is found . . . in *Los hijos muertos*, reaching its maximum expression in the Civil War, when Daniel and César Corvo fight on opposing sides. (p. 145)

The dominating concern with the Civil War is definitely of autobiographical origin, and where descriptions of the war are offered, they often have an autobiographical basis, as the novelist experienced bombings, witnessed shootings and burnings and other horrors of war. The Cain and Abel theme is not autobiographical in the most literal sense (of reflecting personal experiences or the family life of the writer), but insofar as it represents Matute's personal interpretation of the war which she experienced, it also is of autobiographical origin.

The most important of the remaining themes in Matute's work are the social theme, and those of the child and adolescent. Here, her interests are the result of personal experiences, but the themes themselves cannot properly be considered autobiographical. The social preoccupations are, on the one hand, common to a majority of writers of this generation, and on the other hand, a logical outgrowth of the combination of her interest in the *campesino*, her sensitivity to injustice, and her experiences during the war. Much of Matute's insight into the world of the child and adolescent, her ability to reproduce the world of fantasy and imagination, her understanding of the things by which children are wounded, undoubtedly must have an autobiographical basis. But at the same time, the presence of a good deal of invention is obvious.

When Matute herself was questioned about the autobiographical elements in her work, she first stated that, in her opinion, there were none. . . . She is aware, however, that her writing is extremely personal and subjective, which may contribute to produce the impression of being autobiographical. (pp. 145-46)

An interesting aspect of the question of Matute's utilization of autobiographical material is her apparent concentration on the early part of her life. The autobiographical elements mentioned heretofore . . . come from the period ending with the close of the Civil War, and are thus taken from only the first thirteen years of the novelist's life. From this point on, she uses almost no autobiographical materials. The one important exception is "La Oveja Negra," third story in the volume *Tres y un sueño*, whose protagonist undoubtedly represents Matute herself. Although so transformed by fantasy, imagination, and the surrealistic atmosphere as to seem on the surface to have little or no basis in reality, the events in effect constitute a lyric and symbolic autobiography of the novelist up to the moment of that writing. This is the only case where she has referred in print to any aspects of her adult personal life, most of which she would prefer to forget. . . . These feelings explain, at least in part, why Matute does not recreate the later period of her life, its settings, people and events, as she does those of her childhood.

Drawing, then, almost exclusively on her childhood years, Matute uses frankly autobiographical settings in a majority of her works, and her slim volume of memoirs, *El río*, can be considered autobiographical in its entirety. . . . [With] the exception of the work of fantasy, "La Oveja Negra," her plots and major characters are taken from imagination and not from life. It is noticeable . . . that the utilization of autobiographical elements decreases in her more recent works. In the trilogy, "Los mercaderes" . . . the autobiographical content and the degree of the author's involvement or "presence" in the works are considerably lessened. The two strongest autobiographical elements are those things which the novelist herself has recognized as the most important influences for her writing: the *campo castellano* and the Civil War, both experienced before her adolescence. (pp. 147-48)

Janet Winecoff Díaz, "The Autobiographical Element in the Works of Ana María Matute," in Kentucky Romance Quarterly (© University of Kentucky; reprinted by permission of Kentucky Romance Quarterly), Vol. XV, No. 2, 1968, pp. 139-48.

MARGARET E. W. JONES

Ana María Matute, one of Spain's most important novelists, recently observed that each author actually rewrites the same work through the continual elaboration of a few favorite subjects. This statement is particularly applicable to her own literature, with its limited number of themes and attitudes within a relatively large body of work. Time is one of these themes, and she explores it as a means of subtly transmitting her consistent literary philosophy.

Time is significant even as a simple plot element. The author endows her characters with an almost desperate awareness of the fleeting quality of the moment. The feeling appears most poignantly in the face of death, carrying with it an affirmation of life's values. (p. 282)

As if to emphasize the importance of the subject, Ana María Matute entitled her first collection of short stories *El tiempo*. The thematic basis of this book—the passage of time which implies destruction, the loss of affection or disillusionment—is echoed throughout her literary production. The most extensive novel, *Los hijos muertos*, spans three generations of the same family. Each character can see the ravages time has wrought in his older relatives, yet stands defenseless before the similar fate which awaits him. (pp. 282-83)

[Time] fits into the total picture as one of the key motifs correlative to other major themes, such as death, the question of one's existence, or the justification of man's place on earth. Yet time assumes another prominent place in these works, entering into the very interpretation of reality.

Ana María Matute's foremost concern is man and human nature, to which she attributes unchanging characteristics conveyed to the reader by fixed literary patterns. The interpretation of the eternal condition of mankind moves from a study of individual situations to a view of history, and both specific characters and the wider perspective of history—and this is history in the sense of private history, not great events—derive from an original notion of time. Time patterns hint at a dark side of life and emphasize man's unhappiness, loneliness and the difference between the reality of life and ideal possibilities. (p. 283)

Autoanalysis and retrospection, common devices in most of Matute's works, justify the complex counterpoint of past and present. Yet as the past surges up into the present, parallel episodes eerily meet, fused by the repetition of an action in the present that had already occurred in the past. . . . Such ironic repetition reminds the protagonist of the futility of his struggles and foreshadows a more complex interpretation of time.

[Certain] works move from the linear conception of history into the spiralling succession of events. For these investigations, the novelist turns to archetypes well known in Biblical history: the Cain and Abel pair. No less than seven works elaborate this theme, lifting the brothers out of the

Biblical setting to deal with an unchanging action which fits contemporary behavior as easily as it does Old Testament literature. . . . The reiteration of the same attitude in these characters suggests a spiral conception of history, in which man's own nature traps him into committing the same actions. Ancient conflicts are thus brought up to date and differ only in their modern dress.

This idea is developed in *Primera memoria*. With a technique considerably more sophisticated than anything up to this point, Ana María Matute systematically confuses the past and present of the subject and the narrator, who are actually the same person. (pp. 283-84)

Primera memoria is the first novel of the trilogy *Los mercaderes*, a term also bearing on Matute's theory of human constants. It refers to the selfish side of man's nature; today's *mercaderes* (kin to those whom Christ drove from the temple) take advantage of others or even traffic in their own ideals. . . .

The broadest significance of time patterns in the trilogy falls into place in the final novel, *La trampa*. . . .

The time sequence in *La trampa* is inverted and fragmented through flashback, but here chronological time is secondary to a continuum which reveals the same *mercaderes*, the same heroes, and the same sacrifice, with very slight variations. As in the Cain-Abel story, the betrayal and sacrifice of Christ recurs enough to connect disparate incidents into a widening spiral of repetition within the eternal flow of time. (p. 285)

Temporal patterns emphasize generalizations on human nature; time also enters into the conception of character types in these works. The author's idea of her protagonists conforms to a curious set of time values which do not always agree with normal chronology. There is nothing unusual about her marked division between the periods of childhood, adolescence and adulthood, but the transition between these stages is occasioned by a strange timetable. Children grow suddenly when forced to abandon a world of fantasy and accept the harshness of reality. If they cannot adjust to the adult world or refuse to do so, they must die, and the mortality rate for children in these works is exceedingly high. (p. 286)

Adolescents incorporate an awareness of linear time in their lives; their past often appears in a nostalgia for their lost childhood; they attempt to define themselves in the present and look toward the future with hope. This period is an age of faith, but once his ideals are shattered, the youth moves into adulthood. (pp. 286-87)

The adult, on the other hand, returns to the child's position. He purposely creates his place in the eternal present. Disillusionment with life makes him apprehensive about the future; the past is a wound continually opened to torture him. (p. 287)

The success that Ana María Matute enjoys today is due in great part to the subjective nature of her literature, in which certain themes, ideas and archetypes appear with regularity. Also noteworthy are the strong impression of sincerity and the rich variety of style which conveys her ideas so adequately. By the synthesis of form and idea she constructs a novelistic world which deals with problems of man and human nature. One means of commentary on these problems is through time patterns. Human time contrasted with conceptual time; linear action as opposed to the spiral or circular notion of history are only a few of the aspects of her work which have intrigued her readers and helped to earn her the place as one of the most promising writers in Spain today. (pp. 287-88)

Margaret E. W. Jones, "Temporal Patterns in the Works of Ana María Matute," in Romance Notes, *Spring, 1971, pp. 282-89.*

ELIZABETH ORDÓÑEZ

The world of *La trampa* . . .—the last novel in the trilogy *Los mercaderes* . . .—is characterized by an isolation between the self and others; between the self and itself; pervasive solitude; separation caused by death, divorce and faulty communication. The universal separation symptomatic of alienation is communicated and reinforced in this work of fiction by a form and structure which corresponds to and discovers the thematic content. . . . In addition to the interrelationship between the characters and the outer world in which they move, there exists a correspondence and interdependence between the past and present. The theme of alienation emerges in the novel through each character's delving into the storehouse of memory, as well as acting in the present. However, external action for its own sake is underplayed, the novel concentrating instead upon static internal action as a means of portraying fragmented, alienated characters.

Matia, the protagonist who reappears in this installment now mature, cynical and disillusioned, returns to Spain with her grown son, Bear. . . . [Bear] is unable to find any meaning for his existence in that world of his maternal ancestors until he becomes involved with Mario, the would-be revolutionary, and he accepts the role of Mario's avenger against a man who, decades before, had betrayed Mario's father.

Interwoven around the planning and execution of the murder, is a reunion of Matia's corrupt family and flashbacks which flesh out the life experiences of Matia, Bear, Mario and Isabel. The flashback is a medium for our acquaintance with Beverly, Matia's American mother-in-law, who counsels the alienating solution of divorce and alimony for Matia and David's ailing marriage. This, as well as other amorous relationships in *La trampa*, exhibit primitive, destructive urges between male and female, struggles no doubt influenced, perhaps even determined by a particular set of social circumstances, but nonetheless divisive and destructive of all authentic bonds between the sexes. Not only does division or cleavage exist between lovers, but between mother and child as well. Matia laments the distance between herself and her son; love between mother and child is defined as a depriving force to be rationed out like morphine lest it destroy its victims. This alienating vision of the mother-son relationship originates in part from a peculiarily female form of alienation: Matia's feelings of guilt over the abdication of her maternal role after the dissolution of her marriage.

Let us explore the outer world of the novel and work toward the fictional fabric into which the external reality is woven. The title of the novel is not without significance. The title of the trilogy of which *La trampa* forms a part, *Los mercaderes,* is derived from the Biblical passage in John II:13-15, which tells of Jesus driving the moneychangers and merchants out of the temple. George Wythe sees the concept of "mercaderes" as applying in a general way to all those whose ideals are corrupted by money. (pp. 180-82)

The universe of *La trampa* is created by individual, fragmentary perspectives which share strikingly similar points of view. It is often ironic that isolation can be so intense when all the characters share a common socio-economic superstructure. But precisely because this is so, the potential common bond also functions as the common alienating agent. (p. 182)

Mario, the social activist presumably schooled in the language of alienation, describes himself as a reified being split off from himself. Marx's definition of alienation as universal "saleability" and the conversion of human beings into "things" and commodities provides the theory underlying Mario's self-description. (p. 183)

With Faulknerian-Buñuelesque imagery, Matute describes (in the words of José Domingo) "una familia en ruinas, . . . una sociedad en descomposición." The "trap" and the "trick" implied in the title are . . . the burden of past sins and corruption which must be born by the present generation. Both Matia and Bear describe the old grandmother, who is celebrating her ninety-ninth birthday, as a symbol of a decayed and ruined class which continues to exert power over its descendants. (pp. 183-84)

As the novel draws near to a close with the dreaded birthday celebration of the ancient matriarch, Bear describes the departure of the guests in powerful and strangely fascinating surrealist imagery which extends the unreal, dead, grotesque, and nightmarish setting from the degenerating family mansion into a wider social context. . . . Although the perspective of these decadent, masked monstruosities is Bear's, it is only indirectly his: behind his vision lies an authorial voice which is assembling the fragments of an embracing alienated vision of the world. This haunting, symbolic description of the forces of decay in society is part of a composite representation of a superstructure which indiscriminately exerts control over all the separate and isolated bits of consciousness. (p. 184)

An alienation of the self from the self is made obsessively clear in the description of Isa's workday with its typical activities. . . . The repetition of the adjective "ajenos" ["foreign" or "strange"] insistently connotes the chasm between this dehumanized worker and the fruits of her labor. The typewriter, files and telephone calls define the nature or specific attributes of an alienation confined more or less to the female worker, one who usually does the more menial, mechanical tasks within an already alienated work structure. Isa forms only an infinitesimal part of a giant system which she can never hope to understand. . . . It is ironic that Isa should be a participant in the production of objects designed to increase communication between people, and yet she, herself, is totally alienated from the ultimate function of the final products. (p. 186)

The work world is merely a part of a total conglomeration of urban alienation, of a larger world in which a woman must defend herself from attack, in which communication degenerates into meaningless sounds of rage, and the spirit resigns itself to tedium and indifference.

In this kind of social context both men and women suffer fragmentation from themselves and from their fellow persons. . . . [Each] character seems to be isolated within his own private world. Any of the rather sparse dialogue which does occur is encased within the recollections of each character.

The island, a recurrent image symbolizing existential isolation, functions analogously to the overall contrapuntal structure of the novel. . . . The archipelago image is equally as descriptive of the isolation of the characters to one another, as of the fragmentation of the novel's structure into a chain of separate, seemingly integral units which appear even more so because of their contrapuntal, nonconsecutive disposition.

The scarce dialogue of the external structure is analogous to the recurring theme of silence and noncommunication. Matia maintains that her personal history begins with silence. . . . The loss of the child's voice is associated with the existentialist belief that the loss of the innocence of childhood and the loss of Paradise mark the beginning of the great and inexorable solitude and silence characteristic of the alienated, adult condition. (pp. 187-88)

Matute has been critized . . . for her use of non-functional language in *La trampa*. At times, though, linguistic nonfunctionality seems to be both medium and metaphor for the breakdown in communication plaguing modern society. . . . We are witnesses to a modern despair and distrust of the powers and faculties of languages and its ability to effect communication. Isa's aunts employ a private "semilanguage" of unintelligible monosyllables and gutteral sounds. Repeatedly language, like the culture in which it exists, is dehumanized. It is transformed into hollow sounds which have ceased to signal meaning and serve only as constant reminders of the impossibility of authentic communication. So the very use of a specific kind of language or non-language underscores the fatal isolation and separation of the characters from one another.

Although the principal plot of *La trampa* is rather simple, it is contained within a complex labyrinthine structure of flashbacks and musings which at once parallels and reconfirms the characters' alienation from their world and from each other. The use of a baroque-like, involuted style and structure, probably inspired by the works of Faulkner, is able to portray and to be strongly analogous to a disturbingly alienated outside world. This world view is expressed through imagery and action, as well as conceptualized through structure in *La trampa*. Dialectical analysis reveals the indissoluble interrelationship between an alienated literary and nonliterary culture, between this world of fiction and the real or external world outside it. (pp. 188-89)

> Elizabeth Ordóñez, "Forms of Alienation in Matute's 'La Trampa'," in Journal of Spanish Studies: Twentieth Century (copyright © 1976 by the Journal of Spanish Studies: Twentieth Century), Winter, 1976, pp. 179-89.

*   *   *

MAUGHAM, W(illiam) Somerset   1874-1965

A British playwright, short story writer, and novelist, Maugham was born in Paris and educated in England. He qualified as a doctor in London before he published his first work in 1897. Maugham's style was always rather Edwardian in its elegance. A skilled satirist, "his effectiveness as a critic of life," according to A. C. Ward, "is in inverse proportion

to his solemnity." Best known for his autobiographical novel, *Of Human Bondage*, Maugham also achieved popular success with such plays as *Caesar's Wife*, *The Breadwinner*, and *Our Betters*. (See also *CLC*, Vol. 1, and *Contemporary Authors*, Vols. 5-8, rev. ed.; obituary, Vols. 25-28, rev. ed.)

GRAHAM SUTTON

The immense success of Mr Somerset Maugham is not too hard to analyse. Any good journalist can give the reason of it, any good playgoer recognise the reason at sight. He knows his time. (p. 95)

[To be abreast of his time in such a way that he is a hair's-breadth ahead of it] is the safe place for the playwright to be; and that is Maugham's normal position. He has the right journalistic *flair* in playmaking; he is as up-to-date as you please, but never "advanced"; he takes the world as he will find it to-morrow morning, not as he may find it next year. . . . He succeeds by manner rather than by matter. What he says lies lightly enough upon the playgoer's mind. There have been, I think, no Maugham-controversies, as there have been Shaw-controversies. No one ever lost a night's sleep, nor lived a new life next day, for seeing one of his plays. His strength is in technique, and it is as technician that I would chiefly consider him.

No dramatist is more worth reading for craftsmanship than Somerset Maugham. He is the playwright's playwright, a very fountainhead of technical wisdom for the aspiring writer; but the latter should take him as a whole, whether for his craftsmanship or for his intrinsic interest. To take a playwright thus has several advantages; his philosophy and his technical method (the two things that count) emerge more clearly than from individual plays; contrariwise, the peculiar strength and weakness of each piece are more apparent. Mass-reading also brings out the plays' acting qualities. (pp. 96-7)

Mr Maugham stands the test. At the same time, one feels his touch less sure at some points than at others. He is pre-eminently the playwright of one class—witty, well-bred folk such as one meets in Wilde and Congreve, used by later melodramatists as mere villain-material and revolver-fodder, but restored by Mr Maugham to the light-comedy sphere to which they belong. On the threshold of his career, I should imagine, Mr Maugham grasped the important fact that while wit is essential to light-comedy, in real life it flourishes best at opposite ends of the social scale—among top-dogs and bottom-dogs, the Wilde-Congreve type and the pert gaminage of the music-hall. (p. 97)

Mr Maugham follows Wilde, to whom he owes a good deal. "My dear," says Lady Wanley in *Jack Straw*, "do you never say anything against anyone? It must make conversation very difficult." That is precisely the Maugham note. His plays are full of cultured, witty people, leisured enough to cultivate wit as an art, sure enough of themselves to practise it frankly, witty enough to be funny on the riskiest themes. But their frankness is much more than a witty convention; in the women especially, it is an ingrained quality rising at times to a virtue—a rather terrifying honesty which makes them criticise not even their enemy's case more frankly than their own. (p. 98)

Maugham's women particularly are handicapped by this stubborn honesty; the men have less of it, or do not let it dominate them so much. Perhaps the female sex is by nature less prone to self-deception; but these ladies push honesty to an almost Gallic excess. . . . The men's strength lies rather in a horse-sense, a firm hold on expediency which is essentially British. Maugham-heroes have that quality of doggedness, of blind inability to know when they are beaten, for which the Britisher time out of mind has been both praised and derided. Apart from this (and from the salt of wit with which their creator flavours either sex) they are quite ordinary people; and they are sometimes no more than types, whereas his women are always both types and individuals. His men are less searchingly observed than Mr Shaw's, less epigrammatic than Wilde's, less solid than Mr Galsworthy's. But they all have this quintessential Britishness: they are of the soil, both in their virtues and their limitations.

This class, this upper crust of cultured witty society, is Maugham's happy hunting-ground. He does his best work there, and you might read half a dozen of his plays without suspecting him interested in any other. Nevertheless he avoids it successfully a number of times. (pp. 99-100)

The Land of Promise is an exceptional play, from which the more usual Maugham type is almost excluded. Its hero Frank Taylor, the Canadian farmer, is much more of a bottom- than a top-dog—though he would be dangerously indignant if you told him so. Mr Maugham had tried his hand before on the noble savage—Tom Freeman in *Smith*, a fairly early play; and it is noticeable that in *The Land of Promise* his stage-sense has developed. (p. 101)

These contrasts to the Maugham type are all good dramatic characters, genuinely conceived; when he attempts to caricature the type in *Landed Gentry* he is less successful. His Insoley family is as overdrawn as the parvenu Parker-Jenningses in *Jack Straw*. *Jack Straw* is farce, and demands caricature; *Landed Gentry* is a comedy (very nearly "a play," as your modern dramatist likes to label his comedies when he wants you to take them a shade more seriously), and the caricature comes near to wrecking it. There is dramatic warrant for it, no doubt; the play is a study in contrasts. . . . [However,] *Landed Gentry* ought to *be* a farce; and one cannot help feeling that if Tom Freeman had not whispered in his creator's ear that "the prospect of a young girl having an illegitimate child was no matter for hilarity," farce it must have been.

There is nothing farcical, nothing even unconsciously farcical about *The Unknown*—another "exceptional" play, which surprises the Maugham type in very un-Maughamon circumstances. It is all very solemn and sometimes a little dull. John Wharton, trained in a family deeply (not narrowly) religious and supplied with a *fiancée* to match, goes to the war and returns minus his faith. . . . The play's weakness lies in Mr Maugham's having mistaken a topical subject for a dramatic one; as a stage-piece it suffers from a certain stodginess, which overflows from the professional stodge-mongers to characters who would have been alive and witty in any other Maugham play. . . . I find *The Unknown* a stodgy play to read; and I cannot but believe that it was stodgier still in action—or rather in repose, for there is little action in it. As John admits, faith is a matter of conviction. There is no profitable argument possible. The play argues in a circle; and although, as one of James Agate's characters truly says, many excellent arguments have been so conducted, they are not excellent on the stage; and not all their fidelity to real life can make them so.

Thus both *The Unknown* and *Landed Gentry*, Mr Maugham's least convincing plays, suffer less from lack of interest in their themes than from mistakes in their craftsmanship—*Landed Gentry* because it is cast in the wrong form, *The Unknown* because it is not easily dramatisable in any: misjudgments which are the more curious when one considers the excellence of his technique elsewhere. A stage sense is quite his strongest asset. You need only read the openings of his plays to see how construction has progressed since Tom Robertson's day, when no playwright could set his plot in motion without either two comic servants or endless vociferated asides. Take his first piece, *A Man of Honour;* here is no tedious exposition by minor characters (Mr Maugham has no minor characters, save a few footmen and perhaps Osman Pasha in *Caesar's Wife*). Basil Kent, the man of honour, is going to be married; he expects one lady to tea, two arrive, and he is at first embarrassed; but although the ladies are both married and appear to have called unexpectedly, you soon find Kent treating one of them with marked cordiality; when he retires upstage with her, and you learn that she is a widow, the trend of events seems obvious until, their private conversation ended, they make it clear by their conduct that you are wrong again—and so on, till by a fascinating process of elimination the bride's identity emerges. This is not the shortest method of exposition; but it is interesting from curtain-rise, and as an instance of the art that conceals art, leaves the old methods nowhere. As his craft ripens, Mr Maugham cuts expositions shorter. *Caesar's Wife* gets under way by means of two visitors to Cairo, old friends who must be put *au fait* with the story before they pass by. *The Circle* begins more tersely still; there are certain disreputable facts, which you must know, in Arnold's family history; so in a moment of ill-temper the string of his tongue is loosed, and he speaks plain.

Perhaps these are tricks which all self-respecting modern dramatists practise. More characteristic of Mr Maugham is his fierce economy. You feel him tending towards it in the progressive shortening of those expositions; but he has always been economical, and in various ways. His restraint in presenting a situation is well illustrated in the second act of *The Tenth Man*. . . . George Winter's wife is faced with smashing her lover's career if she insists on divorcing her husband. She will also smash George Winter's, a prospect which weighs with her no more than the lover's ruin does with Winter himself. What she does not suspect is this, that whereas the lover's smash means no more than his retirement from public life, Winter's means penal servitude for himself, his accomplice, and her own foolish father. Hence, when she has to make her choice before these three, the issue is desperately bigger than she knows. Your melodramatist would have made Mrs Winter choose with all the cards on the table; the problem then would have been more difficult, and so more dramatic—for her. But the whole situation would have been less tense than Mr Maugham's, where you see three men's fates decided by a choice in the dark. (pp. 101-07)

Mr Maugham's economy is still more evident in his treatment of individual facts and characters—the separate bricks of which his plays are built up. Dealing with an individual character, he goes straight for the human nature of it, suppressing its attributes. When Mr Galsworthy draws landed gentry he fills in these attributes—their love of dogs and horses for instance, which is expressed in so many of his plays. Mr Maugham's architecture is too severe to admit even such permissible flourishes. His plays are shorn of nearly all accessories: you could produce a whole cycle of them with no other properties than a pack of cards and a box of expensive cigarettes. Such details as he does admit he treats as a ruthless taskmaster his slaves: he makes them work double shifts to justify their existence. Thus, in *The Land of Promise* the yellow mustard-flower betrays the blight which is about to ruin Frank Taylor's crop; Mrs Taylor's innocence chooses it for a table ornament, so that it serves also as peg for a piece of genuine pathos. (p. 108)

Here and there, this economy brings its limitations. Two factors are notably absent from his situations—children and lack of money: the two prime difficulties of come-and-go matrimonial reshuffles such as he depicts. He is not altogether burking the question, however; he draws his characters from a class where it is quite common for neither of these difficulties to arise. No doubt that is one reason why he selects that particular class. Wilde did the same.

East of Suez was another "exceptional" play—one of those surprises which (as when he wrote *The Unknown*) Mr Maugham has always been liable to spring upon his critical analysts. Its brilliant predecessor, *The Circle,* implied that he might soon fulfil his natural function as a comedy-of-manners writer. *East of Suez,* however, did not follow from *The Circle,* being in some respects a return to Maugham's earlier melodramatic manner. Repartee and cynicism were dropped, and the story kept uppermost. It was in actor's parlance a "strong" play, whereas other recent work of his had been less remarkable for that kind of strength than for mental agility. It was more sensuous in tone, more lavish in setting—I speak here of the play in general, not of the prologue, which had nothing to do with the play and might be regarded as a mere bowing of the dramatic knee in the house of Spectacle. Lastly, it was, I think, the first play in which Maugham had drawn a downright wicked woman.... Does the phrase sound melodramatic? Daisy Anderson is not easily defined in a phrase; besides which, she is rather a melodramatic character. But she is convincing, more so than some of her more virtuous sisters. (pp. 109-10)

Mr Maugham's has been called a comedy of manners. It is some way from being that.... The truth is that comedy of manners is an exotic plant which we have cultivated now and then to perfection, but never acclimatised to our soil. We lack the necessary detachment; as a public, we are unable to digest the idea that art need not mathematically tally with life. Lamb's complaint still holds good of us— "We must live our toilsome lives twice over, as it was the mournful privilege of Ulysses to descend twice to the shades . . . we would indict our very dreams." Two recent Maugham plays, *The Circle* and *Our Betters,* are our nearest contemporary approach to comedy of manners; yet they are definitely outside the type which Lamb described as "an airing beyond the diocese of the strict conscience," and there is little doubt that Congreve would have regarded them as comedy of manners spoiled. "Had he introduced a good character," Lamb explains, "a single gush of moral feeling, a revulsion of the judgment to actual life and actual duties," . . . then Congreve might easily have been a little disgusting. But this is precisely what Maugham does. In *The Circle* there is young Elizabeth (youth is unknown to Congreve, by the way) like a wildflower in a hothouse; in

Our Betters, Bessie and her American boy.... To me the baffling question about Mr Maugham is, how far does he approve of these? Are they put in as sops to our moral rectitude, or because Mr Maugham personally desires their company? No doubt they are the elixir of commercial life to the plays concerned; but would Mr Maugham have included them, had he been aiming no farther than at a Phoenix audience? . . . In *Our Betters* at least, these characters create something of an artistic embarrassment. Let me protest, I raise no prudish objection (from the prude's point of view I was completely demoralised by this play, which I enjoyed shamelessly). But Bessie and Fleming Harvey don't "belong." Aesthetically, there is something about the proximity of Bessie to Lady George which brings, shall I say, the faint memory of a capacity for blushing to the most hardened playgoer's cheek. And young Harvey is dreadfully disquieting; one is continually on pins lest he shall spoil good wickedness by a moral outburst, or, worse still, upset the exquisite poise of affectation by administering corporal chastisement to its professors—a horrid *gaucherie* which only his admirable self-control, one feels, prevents him committing.

The same sort of criticism applies to *The Circle:* but in a less degree, for here virtue is less self-conscious. Scene for scene, *Our Betters* contains more authentic Congreve; but there is no doubt which is the finer play. *The Circle* is Mr Maugham at his very best; and like all first-rate work, it is signed unmistakably—in its economy, its brilliant dialogue, its centralised interest, its truth to character and its essentially British flavour. Moreover, it opens a new gambit which adds the last touch to its piquancy.... Here are three people playing the game of odd-man-out, as Maugham's people have so often played it. Like Kent, or Grace Insoley, or Violet Little, or Emily Chapman, Elizabeth Champion-Cheney finds herself involved in a postnuptial attachment. As with both Kent and Violet, the dramatic issue lies between her honest acceptance of the situation and her equally honest reluctance to wrong her husband, Arnold. Like Kate Winter, again, she is warned of the personal penalty of going off the rails. Kate, indeed, had only Perigal's word-picture by way of warning, whereas Elizabeth has a dire object-lesson in her own mother-in-law and Lord Porteous, who have carried out just such an elopement as she contemplates, thirty years before (hence the name of the play). Warned of her intention, Arnold seeks out the father-cuckold's advice; and old Champion-Cheney (who has read his Maugham to some purpose) persuades his son to play upon Elizabeth's feelings by sounding the pathetic note—to let her elope unhindered, to arrange for her to divorce him at whatever cost to himself, and thus to appeal to that incorrigible and self-sacrificing sense of honour which has always distinguished the heroines of Mr Maugham. By all known laws of the Maugham game she should resist temptation—and almost does. She plays that game no less straitly than her predecessors, with a forlorn, desperate courage that makes you love her. And then at the bitter end, quite suddenly and with a frankness you cannot choose but admire, she capitulates.... This is the new twist in Mr Maugham's old method which makes *The Circle* a light-comedy *Wild Duck,* laughing deliberately at the philosophy of previous plays much as Ibsen once laughed at the folk who took his gospel too seriously. (pp. 113-16)

Graham Sutton, "W. Somerset Maugham," in

his Some Contemporary Dramatists, *L. Parsons, 1925 (and reprinted by Kennikat Press, Inc., 1967), pp. 95-117.*

JOHN LEHMANN

Maugham's reputation, in intellectual circles, went up and down like the fever chart of a malarial patient, at one moment the awe-struck enthusiasts appearing to gain the upper hand, at another those who dismissed him as unworthy of serious study. What never varied, ever since the publication of his novel, *Of Human Bondage,* in 1915 (by which time he had become a successful and fashionable playwright), was an enormous public eager to gobble up his books and add to his fortune. . . . (p. 229)

Maugham has frequently been admired for his suprise dénouements. And yet, though they administer an effective dramatic shock, they never disturb on any profounder level. His originality, his power of holding the reader's attention, consists largely in putting conventional stories in exotic settings. The basic plots of the stories in *The Casuarina Tree* are really magazine clichés. They are saved from being nothing more than that by their Eastern colonial trappings, by the cunning twists of their unfolding, and by the remorseless cold irony of the story-teller's eye. And when Maugham allows a slight twinkle to creep into that cold eye, it is nearly always cruel. . . . (pp. 231-32)

> *John Lehmann, "Somerset Maugham" (1966; copyright © 1966 by Harrison-Blaine, Inc.), in* The Critic as Artist: Essays on Books 1920-1970, *edited by Gilbert A. Harrison, Liveright, 1972, pp. 228-32.*

CECIL ROBERTS

All his life Maugham would ask what sort of thing is this soul. He put the question at length in *The Razor's Edge,* and gave an answer he did not really believe but which captured the approbation of the crowd, hence its tremendous success. . . .

Maugham kept his large audience for five decades because of an acute contemporary sense. He timed *The Razors Edge* when a desire for religious comfort was arising from the sorrows of World War II. His hero seeks out the gurus, turns to Yoga and Buddhism. The novel evoked an immediate response in the reading world. . . . (p. 21)

All his life Maugham could never resist putting people he knew into his books under the faintest disguise. He was often faced with threats of libel actions, and some parts of the world seethed with indignant victims who had entertained him. He professed always to be surprised, and often stoutly refused to admit he had used living persons, some of them friends. . . .

Maugham had made great fun of the Grand Old Man of Letters cult in *Cakes and Ale.* [At 80,] he was one himself. All his life the critics had ignored or sneered at him. How could a man who sold millions of his books be any good? A petulant critic, Edmund Wilson, outraged by 'his swelling reputation in America' had asserted that he was 'a half-trashy novelist, who writes badly, but is patronised by half-serious readers who do not care much about writing'. Not a word of this was true. Maugham never wrote a clumsy sentence, his themes were never trashy, he was read by all classes, including those who knew something about writing, such as Desmond McCarthy, Frank Swinnerton, Cyril

Connolly, Theodore Dreiser and St John Ervine. Dr Calder has no doubt about him. 'He has produced much more of lasting value than Wells, Bennett, Galsworthy, McKenzie and Waugh,' he proclaims.

With age, and world-wide fame, his pen still active, Maugham had become The Master. The Establishment that had ignored him for 80 years had to take notice, however grudgingly. . . . (pp. 22-3)

Three years before his death he published an appalling series of autobiographical articles, *Looking Backward.* They expressed the rage of an old man lapsing into senility, a vengeful, disgusting exhibition that shook his friends and scandalised his public. Instead of a serene sunset, like the rose of evening that fell around the Villa Mauresque, the black clouds of an old man's venom darkened the scene. (p. 23)

> *Cecil Roberts, "Maugham Dissected," in* Books and Bookmen *(© copyright Cecil Roberts 1973; reprinted with permission of The Society of Authors, literary representative of the Estate of Cecil Roberts), January, 1973, pp. 19-23.*

MARTIN KNELMAN

The Circle is certainly a reliable old chestnut. The play is set in a very proper London drawing room, in which all the period furniture is arranged just so, and it seems to belong to the Victorian age, though actually the play came out in the 1920s. At first you recoil in some embarrassment from a snobbish mentality which seems more quaint than offensive by now, but in spite of that, . . . the thing really does play.

The Circle is part social comedy, part problem play. The question it poses is this: Should a well-bred English wife, who seems to be set up with every social advantage, throw it all over and run away with another man just because her husband is an insufferable prig and life has become so boring that one could scream? Well, *The Circle* chews on this question as long as it seems dramatically interesting, and then spits out, in its wisdom, an answer: No, if she's really smart, she'll stick it out. . . .

Implicitly, this play is a caution to reckless women: Even if your husband is a drag, you have all the trimmings to console you; but if you run away to live in sin with a man, then you're really stuck with him because you'll have given up everything else. In its day *The Circle's* anti-romantic attitude was considered shockingly cynical, but today it seems conventional—a play that could have been commissioned by Ann Landers as a rebuttal to Ibsen's *A Doll's House.* Its refrain is: "I told her, 'Nora, don't go!'" (p. 58)

> *Martin Knelman, in* Saturday Night *(copyright © 1978 by Saturday Night), March, 1978.*

*   *   *

McBAIN, Ed
See HUNTER, Evan

*   *   *

McMURTRY, Larry   1936-

McMurtry is an American novelist and essayist. His fiction is imbued with images of death and emotional emptiness: the bleakness of modern life in the West is compared to the barren, dry plains of McMurtry's native Texas. His novel *The Last Picture Show* was made into a highly successful film. (See also *CLC*, Vols. 2, 3, 7, and *Contemporary Authors,* Vols. 5-8, rev. ed.)

DOROTHY RABINOWITZ

[As *Terms of Endearment* proves, Larry McMurtry] is possessed of gifts that seem to be growing ever more rare among American novelists, chief among these being a true and literate wit. There are others: a feeling for place, an abundance of energy, and an absolute commitment to the depths and lines of character. This is not to say that his saga of a Houston family is without flaws, for there are a number here, among the more serious of which is Mr. McMurtry's tendency to nudge the reader overmuch and to tell him what to feel. That aside, one is quickly absorbed in the world of his novel, a small but intense universe made vivid by the character of Aurora. . . . [Aurora] is a testament not alone to Mr. McMurtry's talent for characterization but also to the delights of those two classical virtues of the novel, surprise and civilized discourse. (p. 57)

> *Dorothy Rabinowitz, in* Saturday Review *(© 1976 by Saturday Review/World, Inc.; reprinted with permission), January 10, 1976.*

DAVID BARTHOLOMEW

McMurtry's point of view [in *Somebody's Darling*], in detailing dozens of brightly drawn, often scary characters, ranges from acerbic satire to bitter horror; the weakest section, the middle one, by the producer, is as coarse, shallow, and foul-mouthed as its narrator. McMurtry really tells us nothing new about Hollywood—that the purveyors of fantasies are mostly low-spirited, corrupt, and earthbound—but the novel is engrossing, if never as moving as it is knowingly shocking. (p. 2134)

> *David Bartholomew, in* Library Journal *(reprinted from* Library Journal, *published by R. R. Bowker Company, a Xerox company; copyright © 1978 by Xerox Corporation), October 15, 1978.*

[In *Somebody's Darling*, McMurtry] has perhaps attempted the impossible: he's portraying today's Hollywood, from the inside, in all its glossy ugliness, while at the same time trying to coax from that milieu some tenderness, some equivalent for the dead nostalgia of old-time Hollywood. And in the first third of this novel, it seems that he's truly succeeding. . . . [The] scenes in N.Y. may become cartoony . . . , but the texture of Jill and Joe's prickly fondness against the vacant crassness of the film biz is a tragicomic triumph. Then, however, the narration is picked up by Owen Oarson. . . . [The] fight-and-make-up affair between faithful Jill and promiscuous Owen—most of the rest of the book—never quite clicks, not even when Jill herself becomes the narrator. Happily, the focus does finally return to Jill and Joe. . . . If, however, McMurtry can't quite illuminate Jill's romantic waywardness, he zeroes in acutely on each character's romance with the film industry: Jill's doomed passion for it, Joe's surly affection for it, Owen's rape of it and *by* it. On location in Rome, at Hollywood parties . . . , at business lunches—the details and dropped names ring true, the dialogue crackles, and the characters glow. And, perhaps most remarkably of all, McMurtry has adopted the relentless four-letter-worded vocabulary and groinal preoccupations of Hollywood without surrendering some intangible thread of clean-hearted decency—just one of the elusive charms that make this imperfect but lovable book the closest thing to *the* New Hollywood novel to come along so far. (pp. 966-67)

> Kirkus Reviews *(copyright © 1978 The Kirkus Service, Inc.), September 1, 1978.*

JILL ROBINSON

[In *Somebody's Darling*, an] arresting, kindly and wry novel about love, hope and fame, Larry McMurtry manages to be funny as he slouches through Hollywood without ever becoming cruel, cynical or mean-spirited. There is something about everyone here—and something for everyone who has ever felt longing. . . .

McMurtry is a writer's writer, and most of the real readers in America have read one or more of his books, *Horseman, Pass By; All My Friends Are Going To Be Strangers; The Last Picture Show*, among others. I had some wrongheaded idea he was sort of the Clint Eastwood of serious writers—his books would be, I was sure, lean tough books about cowboys being sad in bars. I have some catching up to do. To be sure, there are cowboys here in *Somebody's Darling*—the craggy, footloose romantics, the workers of Hollywood who regard productions as cattle drives and then raise hell in the canyons, take off in their big old convertibles—or sit around talking about the big, bad, good old days.

The main character, the "Darling" of the title is Jill Peel, a director on the verge of fame. . . .

She is a completely refreshing, new person, and like Joe Percy, the old screenwriter through whose eyes we first see Jill, we love her and fear for her all the while having complete confidence in this competent, industrious, maybe dangerously considerate survivor that she is. (p. E5)

McMurtry has taken a risk, and I think, succeeded—sailed through it, in fact—in the way he has chosen to reveal a love story that does not go the way they did in pictures. Instead, this one goes very much like they do nowadays, except for the tenderness and perception which you find in good fiction and real life but never in the pop-psych books which pretend to tell us how we are to love.

Jill Peel resists longing, as one does if one is to survive, through industriousness and friendship, but she is too wise to be chilly. . . . She loves, but without the madness of monks, and such a pleasure it is to know an adult as well as we get to know her. She can cry under an overcoat in a pink Cadillac with three old cowboys from Hollywood and still corner a star and steal her very own movie, just as she steals this book from a platoon of vivid, original characters and takes your heart right away too. (p. E8)

> *Jill Robinson, "Hollywood in the Age of Longing," in* Book World—The Washington Post *(© The Washington Post) November 12, 1978, pp. E5, E8.*

*   *   *

MERTON, Thomas   1915-1968

Merton was a French-born American poet, philosopher, essayist, playwright, editor, and translator. Converting to Catholicism in the late 1930s, he entered the Trappist monastery and took the name of Father M. Louis. Here he led the austere but scholarly life of contemplation that is at the basis of his writings, which often mingle the principles of Christianity with the teachings of Zen. Merton is known for his stern social criticism as well as for his religious works. *The Seven Storey Mountain*, an autobiographical best seller, brought him wide critical acclaim. (See also *CLC*, Vols. 1, 3, and *Contemporary Authors*, Vols. 5-8, rev. ed.; obituary, vols. 25-28, rev. ed.)

JAMES YORK GLIMM

[Merton's] last poem, *The Geography of Lograire,* is, in his own words, a "wide angle mosaic" on the violence, intolerance and alienation of Western man.

In scope and form *The Geography of Lograire* owes much to the attempt at a modern American epic. Like Crane's *The Bridge,* it is structured on a compass motif, ranging from South to North, East to West, through past and present, mixing history with personal experience. Like Pound's *Cantos, Lograire* employs fantastic erudition, and incorporates many sources through quotations and editing. The reader is asked to enter the myths of other cultures—Mayan, Sioux, Moslem, Melanesian. As in Williams' *Patterson,* the reader must make the connections, must see and follow the broad implied themes which sustain and unify the swirling, shifting flow of the long poem. The fragmented form, fractured syntax, and multiple allusions make *Lograire* rough going, but the poem greatly increases Merton's importance as a contemporary poet. (p. 95)

In *The Geography of Lograire* Merton uses his outsider's perspective to analyze and attack the cancer within the Western myth. He gained aesthetic-moral distance on Western consciousness by immersing himself in what he called the "myth-dreams" of other cultures. The myth-dream of a people is their total grasp of reality: their myths, superstitions, knowledge, behavior—in short—their reality construct. Merton tried to see Western man through the eyes of the Sioux Indian, the Mayan, the Kanaka tribesman. His strategy in *Lograire* is to let the Sioux, Mayans and Melanesians describe the coming of the white man in their own terms. By quoting and rearranging primary sources Merton allows us to see ourselves as others have seen us, especially in crisis situations. He also leads us into the myth-dreams of other cultures forcing us to see how rich and full their reality can be. We are made to see Western man both as self and as other as we witness, this time from the side of the defeated, the conquest of the Mayan, the Sioux and the Pacific Islander. Merton achieves this effect by implying that the conquistador *is* the marine, the cavalry officer *is* the National Guardsman and the plantation owner *is* the modern capitalist. (p. 96)

To dramatize the intolerance of the Western world as well as the severity of the clash between world views, Merton often juxtaposes quotations from two cultures. (p. 97)

The North section of the poem presents Merton's own past, his personal myth dream. Called "Queens Tunnel," this section is a surrealistic meditation on Eros and Thanatos set in Queens, Long Island—symbolic to Merton of the final achievement of Western civilization—an enormous junk heap. Scenes from the poet's boyhood become corridors in Hades patrolled by Mafioso-Minotaurs. (p. 98)

The East section of *Lograire* offers a view of medieval Moslem life seen through the eyes of the Moslem Herodotus, Ibn Battuta (A.D. 1304-1369). . . . Merton intends to make the reader enter a society ordered around numinous, rather than material concerns. The Moslem myth-dream, with its prayer, ritual, mysticism and deep integration with the environment, stands in sharp contrast with the stark aggression of Kane and the Puritans [in the North section]. By placing us in another myth-dream the poet attempts to jar us into seeing how arbitrary our own myth-dream is. The Moslems admit that their reality is a construct of be-

lief, superstition and myth, but the European myth teaches that we have no myth, that our belief in our own objectivity is not in itself mythic. (pp. 99-100)

Our unfortunate relations with the non-white cultures of the world arise from our myth-dream which tells us we are "superior" because we have command over the goods of the earth. We take this attitude to the poor nations of the world and, because of our technology, they partially believe it. But the Indians, blacks and orientals of the world have their own myth-dreams (reality-constructs) which they cannot suddenly detach from their consciousness without severe psychic shock. Still, they do not receive the material goods they so desperately need until they abandon their way of looking at the world. We thus demand, however unconsciously, their reality in exchange for the goods of a technological society. (p. 101)

As an intellectual and artist [Merton] understood the Western myth and technology; as a prophet he explained what the myth and the machines are doing to us and what we are doing to the poor nations of the world. Through the ingenious use of historical facts and allusions to current events, *The Geography of Lograire* shows us that we are the victims of our myth to the extent that we do not understand it. (p. 103)

James York Glimm, "Thomas Merton's Last Poem: 'The Geography of Lograire'," in Renascence *(© copyright, 1974, Marquette University Press), Winter, 1974, pp. 95-104.*

PETER KOUNTZ

The writing in *The Seven Storey Mountain* seems to be multi-level. From the very first page, Merton is not merely writing about past events, persons, places and things, historically. Though very much a part of the narrative of the autobiography, this "natural" level is only one level. There is also the very important interpretive level of his writing which, for Merton, is essentially "spiritual." Merton writes the autobiography from his monastic perspective, from his new position as a monk. Thus, the past and its "naturalness" are interpreted "spiritually." And yet, neither level of writing can stand alone.

One result of this two-dimensional writing is that the reader of *The Seven Storey Mountain* may sense a peculiar incompleteness about the book: a lack of development, a kind of emptiness as if something is missing. So, for example, in the matter of Merton's writing vocation and his artistry, the reader is left in the dark. Because of Merton's spiritual interpretation, one does not really know how these qualities developed nor how important they were to Merton except on the spiritual level: gifts of God, and so forth. On the natural level, the day-to-day progression of the purely human dimensions of being a writer and being an artist is not fully developed.

On the other hand, however, this two-dimensional style allows the reader to see that Merton's odyssey was a spiritual one and that day-to-day "natural" existence involving people, places, things and events became increasingly unimportant and clearly secondary to his spiritual life. (p. 233)

[Predominant] is the craft of Merton the writer: the harsh adjectives, the many conjunctions, the repetition, the imagery, yet the starkness and the simplicity of the language. This is the language of a writer-turned-Catholic-turned-

Trappist in the midst of a deep and intense process of re-evaluation, conversion and re-adjustment. (p. 256)

Peter Kountz, "'The Seven Storey Mountain' of Thomas Merton," in Thought (copyright © 1974 by Fordham University Press; reprinted by permission of the publisher), Vol. 49, No. 194 (September, 1974), pp. 250-67.

DANIEL BERRIGAN

[Merton] came closest to being a buddhist poet, in the Chinese manner. The aura was the man; that is why, I think, his translations of Chuang are the best to be found. (p. 386)

The apocalyptic note is there in the poetry. By that I mean something more ... than the terrified squeak of Chicken Little. Something more than powerlessness under the Bomb. It was an old notion—first, taking it all into account (this was a simple demand of truthfulness); then, the resolution, which in the final analysis was out of our hands (indeed, out of the hands of the bombers and bomb makers). But still, the outcome was not out of our hands; it also depended, if we could trust the bible, on the conviction, enterprise, courage of those who could speak up, stand somewhere. ...

Before most of us, poets or otherwise, realized what hung over us, he faced the scientific apocalypse in his *Original Child Bomb* (1962). It is a poem only in the most generous sense of the word, a kind of code, rather, an incantation, a pastiche of quotes, with here and there a cunningly dovetailed underplayed editorial. It concludes on a note of irony, prose flattened to earth, out of shape. (p. 389)

Daniel Berrigan, "The Seventy Times Seventy Seven Storey Mountain," in Cross Currents (copyright 1978 by Convergence, Inc.), Winter, 1977-78, pp. 385-93.

ROSS LABRIE

A problem with [*My Argument With the Gestapo*] is its static and unresolved quality, a problem which no one appears to have been more aware of than Merton himself. He admitted that there was in fact "no action" in the book. ... There is surface movement throughout ... , from the periphery of the war to its vortex, and from the present to the past—but the characters and the underlying situation remain essentially the same, whatever the superficial changes in nationality and locale. The purpose of this was apparently to underscore the moral similarity among the participants in the war, but the narrative effect is to create monotony. The complexity of the design, though, with its interweaving of not only past and present but real and unreal, dreamed and experienced, is stimulating. (p. 116)

[In the respect that the narrator accepts responsibility for the war,] the moral design strongly resembles that of *The Waste Land*.

The burden of such thoughts gives the narrator a taste for moral pronouncements which makes the novel rather sanctimonious at times. ... At these points the novel tends to sink like a stone.

The deep thoughts tend to be more effective when they surface in the reader and when they emerge from the enactment of events than when they are infused into the novel by the narrator. ...

The narrator is effective ... when, instead of moralizing, he attempts to come to terms with the whirlwind generated by the war. This is especially true of his impressions of London. His impressions are inevitably filled with the sense of his own awkward isolation, which is Byronic, wistful, and intractable, giving rise to some of the novel's most evocative moments. ... (p. 117)

The dramatic pressure of the book arises from the fact that the war presents the narrator with the need to race against time. He plunges into the theater of the war in order to see the remnants of his youth before all of the evidence of his past is annihilated. (p. 118)

The unbridled Gothic atmosphere of *My Argument With the Gestapo* is one of the more successful aspects of the novel. London houses have the expression of "patients in a hospital, tired, wondering about themselves, and fearing to be roused from the uneasiness of their secret obsession with disease, by some new, objective alarm, some fresh pain." ... (p. 120)

As in Eliot, the conflagration, which enacts a moral and religious as well as a political and historical process, is likened to Dante's *Inferno*, a poem that was very much on Merton's mind in 1941. ...

Rooms are inhabited by "cold-blooded women with small eyes and metal teeth" ... and by "frightened looking men," all sustaining the air of menace which fills Merton's inferno; through it all there is the sound of the "nightmare-talking" of all London. ... (p. 121)

The air of menace, hallucination, and self-doubt is not always handled with gravity by Merton who uses parody to keep the novel from becoming any starker than it already is. Balanced against the harsh surrealism and suspense of war is an obverse world, a theater of the absurd in which the narrator is a fumbling spy and in which the prevailing standards of reality are those of the popular cinema of the 1920's and 1930's. Though light in texture, some of the allusions to the films go deep, as in the reference to Charlie Chaplin in *City Lights* who is befriended by a drunken millionaire, only to be thrown out and arrested when the tycoon sobers up, a contrast in behaviour which is repeated throughout the film and which touches on the novel's dream/waking motif as well as on the theme of the shared humanity of all. (p. 122)

The influence of films recalls Merton's belief that if people are not given the best art they will fight fiercely for the bad art they are given. The film motif is used to symbolize an ordered world in which meanings are possible, a world which is analogous to the narrator's feelings about the superior intelligibility of the war of Troy in comparison with the war in Europe. ...

The novel's dourness is balanced by the crackle of satiric dialogue and by the absurdity of the macaronic language. Although there are moments of puerile dialogue, there is successful satire—as in the characterization of the quixotic Frobisher family, an example of old guard Yorkshire gentility which recalls much of the cast of Shaw's *Heartbreak House*. (p. 123)

The macaronic language is a kind of Esperanto which contains most of the languages of Western Europe—those of the combatants in the war in other words—without being identified with any one of them. In this sense, it symbolizes the path of unity, cutting across narrow cultural and political borders. This is why it is called the language of Casa. The narrator uses this oblique idiom to express his alienation from the current state of the world and to uphold values which the world is no longer interested in hearing about.... Merton combines it with a Joycean double-talk which brings the novel close to slapstick at times, as in the long digressive burlesque of literary criticism in which is, among other things, a suffocating lecture on the Great Epic.

The use of macaronic was Merton's answer to the bureaucratic minds which got the world into war in the first place.... (p. 124)

All of this expresses itself satirically in the mystified and suspicious reaction of the bureaucracy to the narrator's journal, with its medley of poetry, satire, and macaronic anti-language. Initially regarded as subversive, the journal is finally written off as a collection of smutty souvenirs. Used to manipulating language so that it means what he wants it to—usually as little as possible—the bureaucrat has a strong distrust of any language which, through its unorthodox form, may after all, mean something—which is why the narrator is kept so tirelessly under suspicion....

My Argument With the Gestapo offers an impressive display of atmospheric and linguistic effects which are tied to a coherent and intellectually satisfying thematic design. There are scenes and phrases which are obviously leftovers from Merton's undergraduate days at Columbia, but on the whole he rises above this sort of thing and creates a memorable novel. (p. 125)

> Ross Labrie, "Thomas Merton's War Novel," in Renascence (© copyright, 1978, Marquette University Press), Spring, 1978, pp. 115-25.

ROBERT McDOWELL

It is difficult ... to examine adequately the exceptional qualities of Thomas Merton—because they are so many. If you tried to come up with the components that go into the making of a first-rate poet, your prototype might bear an uncanny resemblance to him. Put simply, Merton is one of our great poetic talents of this century. If anybody has doubts, the *Collected Poems* should quickly dispel them. Reading the work entire is like entering a unique world created just for the occasion. It is no hasty construction, but a self-sustaining environment in which the landscape has been filled out, in which the living and the dead are real. It is as if the poet had tasted and understood every essence that makes up the world we live in, and out of the banquet proceeded to remake it and shape his own. Isn't this the ultimate aim of poetry?

Merton's life was strangely suited to the attainment of this end. Though he lived his last twenty-seven years in the Monastery of Our Lady of Gethsemane where he enjoyed the rare and constant solitude so many poets dream of, Merton never withdrew from Man in a spiritual sense. It is true that he felt revulsion from the world outside—sometimes with compassion, and sometimes without it—but he always somehow *saw* the world.... If what he saw was profound, he was a reluctant prophet. He never exaggerated his individual worth, though his vision was uncompromising and often tinged with an almost late Yeatsean rage. (pp. 381-82)

Also, Merton resembles Yeats in that he continued to grow as a writer. From his formal early poems to his late experiments in Surrealism, the voice remains vital and believable. It is seldom too religious, too metaphysical, too much the social critic; it is a combination of all of these, a large voice emerging to embody a large country. If the voice is not wholly American (it sometimes has the international flavor of Howes) it is, first and last, erudite and convincing....

Merton's language never sacrifices beauty for shock value nor truth for the secure and unimaginative ring of an opinion that is either too personal or too popular. No matter how odd the style, or how tentative the subject, he always *makes sense* in the poem. (p. 382)

> Robert McDowell, in The Hudson Review (copyright © 1978 by The Hudson Review, Inc.; reprinted by permission), Vol. XXXI, No. 2, Summer, 1978.

*   *   *

MICHENER, James A(lbert)   1907-

Michener is an American novelist, short story writer, essayist, art historian, and editor. Although best known as a novelist, he has also been a prolific writer of nonfiction, publishing works on the social sciences, American politics, and travel. *Hawaii*, considered by many to be his finest work, reveals Michener's masterful handling of vast amounts of historical and descriptive detail, offered in a spare prose style that is characterized by its clarity. However, many of his other novels, although always exhaustively researched, tend to overpower the reader with their wealth of minutiae. Michener was awarded the Pulitzer Prize in 1948. (See also *CLC*, Vols. 1, 5, and *Contemporary Authors*, Vols. 5-8, rev. ed.)

BOYD GIBBONS

[*Chesapeake*] is, at times, impressive, for Michener is a tireless researcher; he always has the story—if not the reader—by the throat, and some of his passages of action and violence are vividly written. On the whole, however, I found [it] exasperating to read.

When the moment calls for humor, subtlety, or even silence, Michener too often either leaps onstage to lecture on the obvious, or he reaches for *Pomp and Circumstance* and proceeds to play it on an atomic pipe organ.... Characters in this book tend to make timpanic pronouncements in empty places. Edmund Steed, after finding his wilderness island "a fascinating place," announces, apparently to the grackles and squirrels: "This is the island of Devon, proprietary of the Steeds, and so it shall remain forever." (pp. E1, E4)

Chesapeake is full of ... flat superlatives and cliches, of saucy little slatterns, pert little princesses, rollicking rascals, rapscallions, naughty plans, women who shout like fishwives or who resemble goddesses, madonnas or Hebrew maidens in the Old Testament, hostile Indians, sly and clever foxes, rude trails, rude huts, rude landings, rude warehouses, rude boats, and Canada geese incessantly characterized as great. There are also three "litanies" which are not litanies. The blacks are often heroic, always admirable....

In these days of the docu-drama, or whatever it is lately that passes fiction off as fact, writers are putting words in the mouths of people and events on the blank pages of history. Some of this may be entertaining, but the whole business gives me the willies, and while I was not entirely uncomfortable with the cameo appearances in *Chesapeake* of Clay or Calhoun, by the time Woolman Paxmore visits Berchtesgaden to plead with Hitler for the release of 50,000 Jews, I am not only wondering what in blazes such a chapter is doing in this novel, but am preparing for a Steed to be among the first astronauts on the moon. . . .

Chesapeake is an interesting and ambitious quilt of history, with some nice touches here and there, and the telling never lags. But overall there is a shallowness about this book and the people in it. An experienced writer has become careless with the craft of good writing, and it shows. (p. E4)

> Boyd Gibbons, "James Michener Bridges the Bay," in Book World—The Washington Post (© The Washington Post), *July 9, 1978, pp. E1, E4.*

JONATHAN YARDLEY

It's easy enough to be condescending toward James Michener, and over the years many reviewers have been exactly that. His long, plodding novels are high on sincerity, low on literary merit. The history he serves in such massive helpings tends to arrive at the table half-baked. . . .

Yet Mr. Michener deserves more respect than he usually gets. Granted that he is not a stylist and that he smothers his stories under layers of historical and ecological trivia, nonetheless he has earned his enormous popularity honorably. Unlike many other authors whose books automatically rise to the upper reaches of the best-seller lists, he does not get there by exploiting the lives of the famous or the notorious; he does not treat sex cynically or pruriently; he does not write trash. His purposes are entirely serious: he wants to instruct, to take his readers through history in an entertaining fashion, to introduce them to lands and peoples they do not know.

Hence "Sayonara," "Hawaii," "The Source," "Centennial" and now "Chesapeake." It is in every sense a typical Michener production, with all the weaknesses—and the strengths—of its predecessors. It covers four centuries in the life of the Chesapeake Bay and the Eastern Shore of Maryland. Principally through four fictitious families, three white and one black, it moves from early settlement to Revolution to Civil War to World War to Watergate. . . .

So many characters are rushed in and out of the action that one never works up an emotional interest in any of them. The barrage of historical tidbits is incessant and frequently simplistic. Mr. Michener's homilies tend to the obvious: ". . . a family rises or falls primarily because of the way it marshals its genetic inheritance and puts it to constructive use." "The quality of any human life is determined by the differential experiences which impinge upon it."

Mr. Michener's yearning to involve his characters in as many important historical events as possible leads him down some pretty crooked paths. In the final pages of the book, the involvement of two characters in Watergate is a strained contrivance, a way of ending on an up-to-date note and giving Mr. Michener a forum for some rather tedious moralizing.

Notwithstanding all these considerable weaknesses, "Chesapeake" has the strengths of conviction and decency. Beginning with his first book, "Tales of the South Pacific,"

Mr. Michener has been a passionate and outspoken advocate of racial and religious tolerance; the theme is a central one in "Chesapeake." Although all of his characters are wooden, he does assign important roles to women, taking them well beyond bread- and baby-making—and he was doing this long before feminism became fashionable. He has a sharp sense of the complexities of moral and political issues, and he presents all sides with admirable dispassion before resolving them in, to my mind at least, a right-minded way.

Perhaps his most attractive characteristic is what can only be called old-fashioned patriotism. Liberal on most political and social matters, he is conservative on the old values and the old verities. The America he depicts is a nation making grievous errors throughout its history, yet always striving to fulfill the hopes and promises of its birth. As much as anything else, that may explain his popularity, for in the "Middle America" where he is so widely read there persists a faith in the American vision and a belief that it can be attained.

> Jonathan Yardley, "An American Vision," in The New York Times Book Review (© 1978 by The New York Times Company; reprinted by permission), *July 23, 1978, p. 11.*

GARRY WILLS

[The title *Chesapeake*] is misleading. Michener does not write about the whole Bay but about its quirkiest (in some ways most interesting) part, the Eastern Shore. Nor is the distortion restricted to the title. Michener wants to make broad types of narrow exceptions. His book belongs to that genre of multi-generational Hollywood epic that is advertised as a triumph of the human spirit. We have all seen, many times, the movie this book will become. . . .

The later episodes show how thin Michener finds his Eastern Shore material. He must range all over the world to supplement it. . . . Over and over Michener achieves his Eastern Shore "epic" by leaving the Eastern Shore. At one point, he includes the decisive sea battle of the French navy with the British before Yorktown by the simple expedient of having an Eastern Shore boat nearby to watch it. What we get is a mini-history of the United States seen from the vantage of the Eastern Shore.

The only trouble is that real Eastern Shore people do not watch much of anything but the Bay itself. They were Tory out of sheer orneriness in the Revolution; their boats were a nuisance when not a menace to the patriot cause. Their isolation brewed in them a bitter mix of revivalism and racism that Mencken was still excoriating in the twentieth century. They were more rabid than most Southerners in the Civil War. Their racism and xenophobia remains notorious. . . .

With such rich material to draw on, why did Michener take his characters from central casting? I suppose he meant to suggest the watermen's merger/struggle with fish and fowl by giving us Kiplingesque tales about a "family" of geese and one of crabs. The results are embarrassing. Papa Goose is called Onk-or, apparently because he overheard an Indian's term for his whole family. The Papa Crab is called Jimmy—he, too, seems to have overheard what watermen call all male crabs. The affecting death of the crab under a sudden storm's silt is not only mawkish; it makes me wonder why the slower death of capture, struggle, and boiling delights Michener so when Jimmy goes down *his* gullet instead of the Bay's.

A fatal uncertainty of tone haunts all these attempts at the primitive—as when a seventeenth-century Indian is described as yearning for birds as a "food resource." In one of the churning adultery sequences (which just bind the Steed family together again, as in any good soap opera) Susan Steed undergoes sexual seizures every time she looks at a ship's mast. (p. 31)

> Garry Wills, "Typhoon on the Bay," in The New York Review of Books (reprinted with permission from The New York Review of Books; copyright © 1978 Nyrev, Inc.), August 17, 1978, pp. 31-2.

D. KEITH MANO

They call *Chesapeake*—guess what?—"a sweeping historical novel." I think "whisking" is more apt. The sweepwhisk genre will take a pseudohistorical place or family and trace its/their progress from ice age to Tuesday last. (Michener has saved his ice age description for page 405—a risky and imaginative departure.) Sweep-whisk novels are usually written by people who haven't talent or idea enough to write a short book. The standard *Chesapeake* character, for instance, won't develop, he'll just change costume from century to century. Besides, Michener is more interested in hardware than people: ships particularly: *Chesapeake* has all that mizzen abaft poop to windward hard off the port centerboard and furl your bosun chair gibberish, which doesn't mean a Q-tip to any but 15 readers in America. (p. 1153)

The present-day sections of *Chesapeake* are tedious, idiotic, disjunct, pointless, phony, and offensive. Michener has written a lunch-box-sized, condescending children's book. And he is cheeky enough to end with sonorous admonitions re keeping nature natural: this man who has made a thousand forests tumble down so that his trivial glut might be read.

Michener is a long joke, of course: but a dangerous one. He has been too often and easily read. We inhabit a neglectful time: history-the-discipline is not honored in school curricula now: more and more, "historical knowledge" comes from fiction. This need not be a bad thing: provided that research is meticulous: provided that writers don't recast known truth to accommodate their weak and fantastical brainchildren. . . . No man has done more to corrupt the historical perspective of Americans than Michener, with his unctuous, naïve, sentimental, and downright fraudulent plot-maneuvering. It's ironic: he would not be rich and popular today if readers didn't assume they were getting reliable fact with fancy: that has been his attraction. If Michener wrote honest fiction, took a novelist's chance, he'd be just another unremarkable hack. But he will pretend to retail fact, and that makes him some kind of liar. (p. 1154)

> D. Keith Mano, "Poop Poop!" in National Review (© National Review Inc., 1978; 150 East 35th St., New York, N.Y. 10016), September 15, 1978, pp. 1153-54.

* * *

MIŁOSZ, Czesław   1911-

Born in Lithuania, Miłosz is a poet and essayist now residing in the United States. An early preoccupation with the history

and landscape of his native country matured into a philosophy of poetry which Miłosz explains as the "consciousness of an epoch." His verse is noted for its blending of classical and modern elements. (See also *CLC*, Vol. 5, and *Contemporary Authors*, Vols. 81-84.)

VICTOR CONTOSKI

[Miłosz's] study of the relationship between the creative writer and the oppressive state, *The Captive Mind*, has become something of a classic and achieved a popularity in the West which his essays and poetry can hardly hope to attain. Yet many who know the Polish language consider poetry to be his greatest achievement.

Because of his double vision (Eastern and Western) and his double role (politician and poet) Miłosz is especially sensitive to the delicate balance a critic must maintain. . . .

[Miłosz has attempted] to find a middle ground between the extremes of the public and private person, between the journalist or propagandist and the practicer of Ketman. . . . [In] his sociological essays, his fiction and in particular his poetry this search for a critical perspective is a constant theme. (p. 36)

[This question]—can one ultimately find the proper perspective from which to criticize his age?—has not been answered directly in Miłosz's work, though the constant movement he portrays would seem to indicate a negative response. But for Miłosz the value is not in attaining such a perspective (which may well be humanly impossible) but in seeking it, for the critic of his age is made more sympathetic, more human, by the very uncertainty in which he finds himself. (p. 41)

> Victor Contoski, "Czesław Miłosz and the Quest for Critical Perspective," in Books Abroad (copyright 1973 by the University of Oklahoma Press), Vol. 47, No. 1, Winter, 1973, pp. 35-41.

JOSEPH BRODSKY

I have no hesitation whatsoever in stating that Czesław Miłosz is one of the greatest poets of our time, perhaps the greatest. Even if one strips his poems of the stylistic magnificence of his native Polish (which is what translation inevitably does) and reduces them to the naked subject matter, we still find ourselves confronting a severe and relentless mind of such intensity that the only parallel one is able to think of is that of the biblical characters—most likely Job. But the scope of the loss experienced by Miłosz was—not only from purely geographical considerations—somewhat larger.

Miłosz received what one might call a standard East European education, which included, among other things, what's known as the Holocaust, which he predicted in his poems of the late thirties. The wasteland he describes in his wartime (and some postwar) poetry is fairly literal: it is not the unresurrected Adonis that is missing there, but concrete millions of his countrymen. What toppled the whole enterprise was that his land, after being devastated physically, was also stolen from him and, proportionately, ruined spiritually. Out of these ashes emerged poetry which did not so much sing of outrage and grief as whisper of the guilt of the survivor. The core of the major themes of Miłosz's poetry is the unbearable realization that a human being is not able to grasp his experience, and the more that time separates him from this experience, the less become his chances to comprehend it. This realization alone extends—to say the least—our notion of the human psyche and casts quite a remorseless light on the proverbial interplay of cause and effect.

It wouldn't be fair, however, to reduce the significance of Miłosz's poetry to this theme. His, after all, is a metaphysical poetry which regards the things of this world (including language itself) as manifestations of a certain superior realm, miniaturized or magnified for the sake of our perception. The existential process for this poet is neither enigma nor explanation, but rather is symbolized by the test tube: the only thing which is unclear is what is being tested— whether it is the endurance of man in terms of applied pain, or the durability of pain itself.

Czesław Miłosz is perfectly aware that language is not a tool of cognition but rather a tool of assimilation in what appears to be a quite hostile world—unless it is employed by poetry, which alone tries to beat language at its own game and thus to bring it as close as possible to real cognizance. Short-cutting or, rather, short-circuiting the analytical process, Miłosz's poetry releases the reader from many psychological and purely linguistic traps, for it answers not the question "how to live" but "for the sake of what" to live. In a way, what this poet preaches is an awfully sober version of stoicism which does not ignore reality, however absurd and horrendous, but accepts it as a new norm which a human being has to absorb without giving up any of his fairly compromised values.

> *Joseph Brodsky, "Presentation of Czesław Miłosz to the Jury," in* World Literature Today: Czesław Miłosz Number *(copyright 1978 by the University of Oklahoma Press), Vol. 52, No. 3, Summer, 1978, p. 364.*

JAN BŁOŃSKI

Czesław Miłosz's seemingly accessible poetry has not revealed even a fraction of its riddles. The more intensely one reads "Three Winters" (1936), "Rescue" (1945), not to mention "Treatise on Poetry" (1956) and "From Where the Sun Rises" (1974), the richer and more enigmatic they seem. Surely the emigration of the poet . . . was not favorable to critical reflection. But even the earlier work is filled with contradictions and intimations that eloquently testify to the resistance which Miłosz's poetry presents to interpretation. . . . Homogeneous yet multiform, Miłosz's poetry puts a stop to tendencies whose sense eludes even the most sympathetic of readers. The writer worked against the principle which was gaining ascendancy in Poland at the beginning of this century: the principle of autonomous poetic language.

Hence the abundance of contradictory labels attached to Miłosz. Romantic magus? Lover of classical harmony? Prophet of destruction? Ironic skeptic? Only recently, rather late and ashamed, do we understand, and not without the help of the poet himself, the cohesion of intentions which he probably had right from the beginning, even if unconsciously. In other words, we grasp the concept of poetic language that he has elaborated. It is this which gives us the rules of a given reading and through this we get at his esthetic tastes, philosophical convictions and religious inspirations. And it is for this reason that everything that was once written about Miłosz is not very helpful to us today. It is better to treat the circumstances of the debut, the literary polemics and the political experiences parenthetically. (p. 387)

From its inception Miłosz's lyric is characterized by a preference for dialogue, or at least for polyphonic utterance. It reveals doubt, division; the motive behind the dialogue is the pressing search for an ever-retreating truth. In other words, the polyphony indicates a cognitive understanding of the function of poetry. What, after all, do words like *cognizance, knowledge* or *rescue* mean, words which in Miłosz are similar in meaning? Poetry for him is not a symbolic reaching into the essence of things; nor does he rely on the rational relationships of logical conclusions. It is understood instead as an unending discussion, a relentless and haughty (because it is not accessible to everyone) search which is at the same time full of anxiety because the truth is grim. Equal partners in this discussion seem to be the mind and the body, individual experiences and the recurrent patterns of history, fleeting occurrences and the reflections of philosophers.

In order to articulate his feelings and aspirations, the poet must express himself with many voices and call doubles into momentary being, doubles with whom he nonetheless does not entirely identify. Practically every statement, whether an entire poem or a part of it, is presented as if it were being quoted and is thereby supplied with a certain amount of credibility. Its meaning is rarely given outright. It is instead revealed in relationship to other statements: in order to understand what a given voice is really saying, we must remember its partners. But the personae themselves are not immutable, because each dialogue changes and shapes those taking part in it. Sometimes the same motifs appear in various guises, tinged with pathos or irony. One cannot penetrate this poetry by relying on symbols, topoi or key words. Their significance is always relative, as in a musical quartet where one cannot listen more carefully to the first violin than to the second, nor more to the cello than to the viola. But that is exactly how Miłosz is read— which, after all, should not surprise us. The Polish, Slavic and even continental lyric of those years was dominated by homophony, and the innovation of Miłosz's technique was not even apparent to him in the beginning. (p. 388)

Miłosz has moments of revelation and intoxication with nature, but not more frequently than moments of dread and insatiety. Is he not, in fact, amazed by civilization's every effort and by the difficulty of erecting a culture which is, as he claims, the actual content and motor of history?

The split that is doubt—and its accompaniment, the polyphony of expression—[runs] . . . *within* the idea of nature, the concept of history, and also *within* the concept of the poet. Proof of this is the fact that Miłosz's penchant for dialogue becomes stronger during and after the war, beginning with the lyric (where the poet yields to the voice of a clearly delineated protagonist), continuing with montages of quasi-dramatic monologues ("Voices of Poor People," 1943; "City Without a Name," 1969), lyrico-didactic tracts ("Treatise on Poetry," 1956) and finally, in a multi-voiced symphony ("From Where the Sun Rises," 1974). In the last of these the poet makes use of various forms from aphorism to ode, from lyrical *carmen* to genre scene. He weaves fragments of old chronicles or modern encyclopedias into the verse and incorporates several languages: Polish, Old Russian, Lithuanian, Latin. Miłosz often gives himself the role of a director who manipulates the speakers:

the reader becomes the viewer, who is invited to draw his own independent conclusions. But Miłosz can, if need be, speak directly "from himself," or at any rate so direct the reading that the reader himself reconstructs the genuine or desired hierarchy of the polyphonic pronouncements.

Unlike his Polish contemporaries—and there were many outstanding ones—Miłosz rarely seeks to compress the meaning of his poem into the individual sentence. On the contrary, the basic components of the poem usually remain very clear, firmly fixed in tradition and easy to grasp. . . . The effect, or illusion, of neutrality [achieved in Miłosz's poetry] stems from the precedence which is accorded to the eye. Certain sequences of images occur that are . . . reminiscent of a movie, which relates events in a supposedly "objective" fashion—that is, as they appear to everyone. Many, and sometimes the majority, of Miłosz's loose pronouncements seem not to be poetically characterized at all: we might find them in any novel without expressing surprise or maybe even hear them from the mouth of a relatively educated person. The linguistic counterpart to cinematic "objectivity," therefore, is utilization of "methods used in prose writing," something which the young Miłosz awkwardly recommended to other poets. (pp. 388-89)

[Like "Voices of Poor People," "The Songs of Adrian Zielinski"] represent various responses—skeptical, cynical, esthetic—to the challenge of the Occupation's triumphant nihilism. The poet endorses none of these voices, he simply presents them, usually undercut by irony and somewhat distorted by a limitation (fear, self-interest, resignation) in the persona or in the circumstances. That is why an interpretation of "The Songs"—praise or condemnation of the internal freedom of the individual who will not accept the news of culture's doom—depends on one's understanding of "Voices" in its entirety: each "voice" makes the other relative by referring back to the poet's entire work, or at least to the full context of the dialogue. . . .

[In the early poem, "Tranquil River,"] is a deep intimacy with nature, perhaps erotically colored . . . and it awakens not only a feeling of youth, strength and participation in life's great procession, but also the discovery of one's otherness, individuality, difference. . . . This is also a recognition of evil, for only man, because of his uniqueness, can evaluate the neutral processes of nature ethically. . . . In greeting the day of maturity, the hero will then see himself as being different from his own corporality—i.e., from all of nature. That is the sole message of the autobiographical novel "The Valley of Issa": "Thomas kept noticing that he himself was not only himself. There was one him inside that felt and another him on the outside, a bodily one, the one he was born into, and here nothing was his."

In this way is born the possibility—and necessity—of inner dialogue. At first it will take on the form of a dispute as to the calling of the artist. The alter ego of the protagonist, whose turn it is . . . , speaks distinctly about the semi-mythical prototypes of the Poet. (p. 389)

If one recalls the date of the poem, the combination of lyric and prophetic powers is chilling. Who in 1936 thought about white crags of crematoria? But ambivalent reflections on civilization can be traced throughout all of Miłosz's work up to the present day, and this alone steers one away from interpreting his catastrophism as the mere expression of fear in the face of impending war. (p. 390)

"Tranquil River" is, of course, the river of time, life, destiny. It allows us not so much to examine as to indicate themes in Miłosz's lyric: his understanding of nature, of his calling and, finally, of history itself. Visible everywhere is the Manichean split which cannot be mended with the poetico-religious expectation of the revelation of truth and eschatological epiphany. But it is this very split which makes possible the wealth of polyphonic statement, the creative originality of the poet.

Its deep sources are undoubtedly romantic. From romanticism comes the belief in the imagination, in the prophetic capabilities of the poet raised above the blind, unseeing masses, who are often treated with pitying scorn. But it is that scorn which, in turn, unsettles the conscience, because poetry was assigned the task (again, in the romantic tradition) of spiritual leadership, of having the "dark masses." What is also striking right from the very beginning in Miłosz's poetry is the perception of one's own fate and that of society in terms that are, if not always religious, then surely eschatological and metaphysical. Rarely in modern poetry were the awe of existence, fear and fascination with the unknown and, lastly, guilt and moral responsibility (more generally, the feeling of *sacrum*) more powerfully expressed.

In this light one could say that Miłosz's early lyric was the unexpected revenge of a century-old tradition on the esthetic optimism of the constructivist vanguard which dominated the young Polish poetry of the twenties. The *Żagary* poets saw in the work of the artist, and especially in the revival of the language, the fullest embodiment of productive work by means of which man could encompass and control the world. In contrast to this monolithic utopia, the inspirations of Miłosz and his contemporaries deeply diverged. The temptation of traditionalism on one side and political didacticism on the other could only be overcome by devising a poetic idiom that could creatively use these conflicts to its own advantage. This took place slowly in Miłosz's work, the turning point probably being 1943. From this point on, his word was not aiming for the characteristic autonomy of the avant-garde but for "integrity"—in other words, to achieve autonomy by absorbing so many idioms (as well as experiences) that, by contrast and comparison, one gained independence from everyday speech.

According to Miłosz, the poet is someone who knows how to speak in all tongues—not only the one with which he creates his own idiom. Hence the demand for roots in the past, in history, but also openness to the most various and sundry modern idioms, popular and scientific included. Hence the enormous significance assigned to irony and dramatic forms in poetry, which allow the poet to illuminate problems that normally escape the competence of a lyric poet. And hence the intellectualization of the statement as well as the war declared on the "new Latin," which too often has become the language of a poetry capable only of polishing the specific features of feelings and emotions; and, in addition, the overt identification of poetry with knowledge, the erasing of boundaries between the lyric, the essay and the treatise. Miłosz is, in fact, a much more difficult poet than avant-garde poets such as Przyboś, who for years has been reproached with unintelligibility. Miłosz requires efforts of interpretation on greater significant wholes. The power of the imagination is also, if not above all, a requisite of wisdom for Miłosz, and he wants to effect a renewal in the reader through a combination of reflection and emotion. (pp. 390-91)

Jan Błonski, *"Poetry and Knowledge," in* World Literature Today: Czesław Miłosz Number *(copyright 1978 by the University of Oklahoma Press), Vol. 52, No. 3, Summer, 1978, pp. 387-91.*

ALEKSANDER FIUT

A basic problem in all Czesław Miłosz's poetry is the philosophical and artistic subdual of change, not only as observed on the surface of phenomena—in the ephemerality of human existence, in the succession of historical epochs or in the eternal cycle of nature—but also in the deep structure of culture, in the continual reassessment of signs, meanings and values. The poet doggedly labors to construct a dam of poetry on the Heraclitan river, a dam which is constantly undermined by the rapid currents of change. It is in this way that he also attempts to save himself from his own disintegration into oblivion and nothingness. Images of biological disintegration assault his imagination with too much insistence to treat them lightly. Tormented by the foreboding of the unavoidable catastrophe that threatens the world, Miłosz stands alone in the face of an indifferent cosmos and cruel history, which move across human fate with a destructive force akin to that of nature. . . . Miłosz is incessantly tormented by the hunger for values, the desire for affirmation, the need for support. Yet the only thing left him is a great insatiability, accompanied by the consciousness that it will never and in no way be sated. Nevertheless, he is not a poet who is insensitive to the beauty of nature or who denies the need for civilization's development: enraptured descriptions of the landscape of his native Lithuania and a respect for all remnants of the cultural past are eloquent testimony to this. In everything, however, he sees the germ of annihilation. Overpowered by the thought of passing, with nothing but emptiness in his heart, he experiences the acute absurdity of existence. Because how does one protect oneself from nature if her law is death, and how does one survive in history which blindly annihilates all individual and collective values?

This complex of problems and questions, formulated in Miłosz's prewar poetry but returning in all his work, is usually explained away as a manifestation of his catastrophic world view, which was born in the atmosphere of dread that preceded World War II and nourished by the economic crisis of those unsettling years that still resounded with the echoes of World War I. This, at least, is how Miłosz was read by the poets of occupied Warsaw: Krzysztof Kamil Baczyński, Tadeusz Gajcy, Andrzej Trzebiński. From the perspective of the war . . . he was the one who foresaw, whose prophecy, unfortunately, was fulfilled. (p. 420)

[In] current criticism "catastrophism" has become a broad term encompassing various meanings. This term is most often used to designate the conviction that contemporary civilization is in a critical state. . . . The latest studies of the writings of Stanislaw Ignacy Witkiewicz (or Witkacy) allow us to define this term more precisely. Catastrophism, then, is a conviction voicing the inevitable annihilation of the highest values, especially the values essential to a given cultural system or those having an elitist character. . . .

Generally, one can say that catastrophism is a kind of historiosophic diagnosis postulated for contemporaneity which inevitably leads to a pessimistic conclusion. But it proclaims—and this is important—only the annihilation of certain values, not values in general, and the destruction of a certain historical formation, but not of all mankind. One civilization gives way to another, and the dying culture becomes fertilizer for the new one because projected historical changes are governed by a cyclical conception of time. The fundamental assumption at the basis of the catastrophic world view is the incompatibility of two mutually exclusive value systems. (p. 421)

In the light of the above remarks it is difficult to consider Miłosz a catastrophist. In spite of the fact that he transfers the laws of nature to history, his thinking lacks evolutionary change; he gives meaning to only one part of the evolutionary chain, exposing only its declining phase. In other words, the life of an individual or that of the species becomes the matrix of entire histories because they, like individual existences, are headed for inevitable annihilation. The poet of course detects the social conflicts of his times and shares his contemporaries' fear of war. But he expresses himself in a language of visions and symbols that have universal and timeless meaning. . . . The impending horrors of war are like those of all the preceding wars, they are only one of the components of timeless evil. . . . Old empires crumble, new ones arise, conflicting ideologies battle, cultures change, but the price is always the same: human suffering and the loss of peace and safety. The poet looks at history from a timeless perspective, an almost divine one. He voices the destruction of all values and all mankind, not just one of its historical or social formations.

It is probably for this reason that the values appearing in Miłosz's poetry cannot be broken down into two opposing systems. It is enough to compare his juxtapositions to those in Witkacy's work. On one side are life, youth, goodness, truth, ideal love, humility and beauty. On the other are death, old age, evil, lies, sensual love and pride. Miłosz's axiomatic system is therefore a monistic one. There is only one set of values, universal and eternal, and the opposite values represent their degradation or oppose them with anti-values. The poet does not assume, as the catastrophists do, that these values will be replaced by others, but rather that their lost power will be restored to them. And because their Christian provenance is unquestionable, one is amazed that vital, ethical and esthetic values are all placed in the same rank. It is very characteristic that Miłosz does not juxtapose heaven and earth, mystical flights of the soul and sinful temptations of the flesh. He believes, of course, in absolute beauty, goodness and truth, but this does not mean that the temporal is insignificant and that it is only a springboard to the transcendental. Nor does this mean that art is only a form of contact with the Absolute. It has a mediatory function: it should protect against change by proclaiming the beauty of the world and praising life, while at the same time unveiling the metaphysical underpinning of being. It's a little as if the poet in Miłosz were trying to reconcile the man with the moralist. . . . [The future Miłosz foresees], played out on a cosmic scale, will be the end of the world. Final and complete. History will reach its end. . . . In other words, eschatology replaces catastrophism. (pp. 421-22)

According to Christian eschatology, the history of mankind and of the world can be presented in the following way: chaos/paradise/gradual fall and return to chaos/Last Judgment/paradise restored. Although this cycle is clearly parallel to the abovementioned catastrophic cycle, there are some very sharp differences. The metaphysical perspective, the monistic system of values, the linear concept of time and the projection of a future positive utopia—these are all elements which are lacking in catastrophism. Their presence in Miłosz's poetry has been sufficiently proven, with the exception of the last element. (p. 422)

The poet says the least about the lost paradise of innocence. Its presence, or rather absence, is expressed in the nostalgia for simple and constant values, a nostalgia which is visible in the idealization of the poet's homeland. . . . This paradise is not a land of laziness and abundance, but one of joyous work, which eases harmonious coexistence with nature. This is true happiness of existence joined with rapture at the beauty of the world and a trusting faith in Providence. In other words, paradise is a collection and realization of all the values whose lack the poet constantly feels.

The second stage, the one shown most willingly, is expressed in condemnation of contemporary times as surrendered to the reign of Evil, in distress at the disintegration of ethics and in infernal visions. The presence of the third stage is announced by references to biblical images of the end of the world, especially the destruction of cosmic order. . . . In creating his artistic vision, Miłosz makes use of primal images, those that are most deeply imbedded in the collective subconscious. It is worth noting that fire, a frequent motif in Miłosz's poems, has so completely dominated the poet's imagination that the destruction of the cosmos is shown in the form of a gigantic conflagration. As Mircea Eliade writes, the motif of purification by fire is Iranian in origin and appears only once in the New Testament. It plays an important role, however, in the Sybil's forecasts, in stoicism and in later Christian literature. (pp. 422-23)

Allusions to the Bible were popular at the time [of the *Żagary* poets], indeed quite fashionable. Some poets, however, treated the Holy Book in a totally secular way, without any respect for its sacred character. In Julian Tuwim's "Ball at the Opera" or in K. I. Gałczyński's "The End of the World" apocalyptic motifs serve the ends of satire or entertainment. Not in Miłosz. He never deprives biblical themes of their religious functions. He is of the deep belief that after the catastrophe we will enter the last stage of world history, and then "the real will suddenly appear denuded." . . .

The Kingdom of God, which follows the Last Judgment, will be the unveiling of a new, unforeseen dimension of reality. It will be, as described in "The Gate of Morning," a full realization of values vital, moral and esthetic in complete harmony with nature and other people. Paradise will be one unceasing banquet of beauty, truth and love, of intoxication and awe at the restoration of man's place in the cosmos—a little as if those values had regained their lost, ideal form. This conviction will be expressed outright much later in the volume "From Where the Sun Rises," where the poet proclaims his belief in *apokatastasis:* that is, in the restoration of timeless duration to being. . . .

The collection of images and beliefs connected with Christian eschatology constantly recurs in Miłosz's poetry and becomes an essential element of the poet's thought about

the meaning and aim of all existence. The atmosphere of prewar trepidation, as well as feelings of at first indefinable and later completely obvious danger, influenced the genesis of Miłosz's poetic vision without a doubt. But one cannot reduce it to that alone, because the war, with all of its inhuman cruelty, introduced an additional factor into the composition of ancient religious images, supplementing them with a useful but not indispensable element. Some of the components of the catastrophic vision were only steps leading the poet to metaphysical generalizations. Formulating this paradoxically, I would say that even if the war had not broken out, Miłosz's poetry could still be decipherable in the light of the Apocalypse. (p. 423)

[Miłosz's vision of paradise appears as] a component of a deep desire, wish or even artistic creation deprived of the power and reassuring obviousness of a religious truth. This paradise, which is often an idealized Lithuanian landscape, is always eluding the grasp of the poet, fading in his memory, losing its contours. It is rather an expression of longing for a superior metaphysical order of being, for a just and final settling of the accounts of human destinies. But too enormous is the pressure of direct experience, too acute is the sensation of existential pain and historical irrationality for the longing to be merely longing. There is no certainty. The beautiful dream remains, a hypothesis worthy of attention and approval, a tempting illusion with which the poet would gladly identify but cannot accept to the end. He wanders continually and stubbornly seeks the radiant vision of the Garden of Eden. In other words, wanting to overcome his alienation and disapproval of contemporary times and to allay the need for absolute values, Miłosz translated his spiritual biography into a language of basic Christian concepts. But this translation was only partially successful, because it was lined with a modern skepticism and doubt in his own mission as a poet.

In all the criticism written up until today the main reference point, for polemical reasons, was Miłosz's prewar poetry, because it was to be proof positive that he espoused a catastrophic world view. However, the eschatological theme returns in his later poetry. It is worth noting that the image of paradise is superseded by images of Arcadia and blissful isles. These motifs, as old as Mediterranean culture . . . , appear in the "Shepherd's Song" written during the war. . . . After the horror of the Occupation, it would be sheer naïveté to think that one could sail out to blissful isles. Would it still be possible to think about paradise? The poet rejects the ancient idyll but, remarkably, cannot reject the belief in Ultimate Fulfillment. . . . The memory of paradise brings us to the reflection on the destruction of primal nature by contemporary civilization. . . . [But] Miłosz is far from repeating, after Rousseau, the naïve slogans about a return to nature's womb and its effect on reviving certain noble emotions. He knows well that force and cruelty reign in nature, albeit unconsciously. They would not have existed only in the biblical Eden, because there the laws of violence and death were in abeyance. (pp. 423-24)

Contemporary man rejects [paradise] scornfully as somewhat charming but unreal daydreaming. The sacred sphere loses its meaning or is reduced to a dimension of pitiable caricature. This belief is illustrated in the poem "How It Was" . . . , where Miłosz represents the earth as "the mighty power of counter-fulfillment" . . . where all hope in redemption is rejected and where one escapes the problems of existence by turning to the magic of narcotic stupor.... In spite of the fact that the myth is being more and more ridiculed and degraded, the poet cannot and will not deny it. He is still called "to an unattainable dell for ever shaded with words, where naked the two kneel and are cleansed by an unreal spring."

Miłosz thinks incessantly about the Judgment which awaits us. A poem written during the Occupation, "A Song on the End of the World" ..., was recognized as an ironic summing up of his catastrophic poetic past.... But this poem has another, deeper meaning. The "Song" begins with words which create the illusion that nothing is in any way disturbing the daily rhythm. The Apocalypse, the poet notes, is not a moment preceded by signs on earth and in the firmament.... The end of the world is happening continually, because it is always possible and always present in another, sacred dimension of human history. Through being which is solid only on the surface glimmers death and final destruction. That is why "there will be no other end of the world." (p. 424)

[In "Oeconomic Divina," the] Last Judgment ceases to horrify the poet, because he sees in it a chance to rescue the meaning of existence. Denying the Judgment sinks reality into nothingness and the absurd.

From his diagnosis of contemporaneity the poet draws a conclusion similar to the one he makes in "The World (Naïve Poems)" ..., where he refers to Thomist thought (as he admits): namely, that there is a supernatural order that exists in all of being, a homology of macro- and microcosm as well as a hierarchy of all existences, who find their only certain support and aim in God. In conclusion, it is possible to say that the reference to Christian eschatology in Miłosz's poetry has three functions: first of all, it makes existence meaningful even in change; secondly, it is an attempt to apotheosize modern history; and lastly, it returns poetry to its proper position. This, of course, does not mean that Miłosz has solved his existential problems once and for all. It is difficult to accuse him of naïveté or cheap metaphysics. Inwardly restless, constantly divided and doubting, he seeks without respite the answers to questions which, as he well knows, have no answers. It is for this reason that ... "From Where the Sun Rises," as well as the entire volume of *Utwory poetyckie—Poems,* ends with the tragic admission: "I was judged for my despair because I was unable to understand this." (p. 425)

> Aleksander Fiut, "Facing the End of the World," in World Literature Today: Czesław Miłosz Number (copyright 1978 by the University of Oklahoma Press), Vol. 52, No. 3, Summer, 1978, pp. 420-25.

* * *

MORAVIA, Alberto (pseudonym of Alberto Pincherle) 1907-

Moravia is an Italian novelist, short story writer, dramatist, essayist, and film critic. In his fiction Moravia depicts a world of bourgeois decadence, peopled with characters whose response to life is alienation and indifference. His work is noted for its unsentimental depiction of sexual relationships, stressing the unfeeling, amoral qualities of man in the modern world. Considered to be the leader of the neorealist school of writing in Italy, Moravia produces prose that is spare and colloquial. (See also *CLC*, Vols. 2, 7, and *Contemporary Authors*, Vols. 25-28, rev. ed.)

DOUGLAS RADCLIFF-UMSTEAD

[The theater of the Italian futurists and Pirandello, in which] man is at the best a machine or at the least an impassive block of wood, ... influenced the youthful Alberto Moravia in writing his first novel *The Indifferent Ones....* The plot was consciously structured into two days, like two acts of a drama. The cast of characters was restricted to five figures. Indeed, as in a stage work, the author maintained a strict economy of words and gestures for the characters. There is an obvious theatricality about the novel. The characters move from a living-room to a dining-room as if the stage sets were shifted. Some of the characters hide behind a curtain to spy on others. Just as a crucial moment is about to be reached, a door opens and a maid enters to hinder an extreme solution. Although the scene is Rome, the city is but a backdrop for the theatrical action of the novel....

Of the main characters Cavalier Leo Merumeci is the most dynamic and resolute, crass but concrete. He holds a position with the Ministry of Justice and Mercy; the irony is transparent here as Leo is neither merciful nor just toward others but predatory. He is a petty capitalist, not a grandscale entrepreneur but a manipulator of property and a cautious stock exchange speculator. With his business affairs Leo is enthusiastically involved in the false relationships of the world. (p. 45)

Unlike the other characters Leo has no tormenting secret desire, and thus his activities are limited to an animal level. He never investigates his life as does his hesitant adversary Michele. The nonintellectual dynamism of a self-satisfied character like Leo can transform a man into a puppet. He turns on emotions like a machine.... (pp. 45-6)

[Mariagrazia is also puppet-like,] a walking grotesque mask.... The thickly powdered face, with all the vain efforts to conceal age, is both silly and indecisive. The widow never understands what is going on about her. Her behavior is childish. She struts about with a wounded sense of dignity which is ridiculous in a person of her licentious character.... Her movements are like those of a jerkily operated marionette.... It is as if Mariagrazia has no mind.

But the widow does have her value standards, those of a snob who has always led a life of ease and fears poverty.... Her children are at the most for her an extension of the widow's ego. Mariagrazia is a materialist in the low economic sense of the word. (p. 47)

Lisa's interest in Michele is born of a genuine desire to love and be loved. But it is a story-book or motion-picture type of love that she is seeking. Consequently her actions are artificial and excessively sentimental, like blowing a kiss to the young man as he leaves. (p. 48)

Lisa has fashioned a papier-mâché lover, a creature born of false illusions....

Carla looks like a badly made doll. Her room in the villa is full of ragged, left-over dolls as the widow has not had the funds to refurnish the house. Carla's development seems stunted like her room with its furniture for a little girl.... Unlike her mother, Carla is eager to change the mechanistic rhythm of her life.... She does not wish to remain false and ridiculous. In order to escape the familiar objects of her room—symbols of the old life—she feels that she must commit a sordid act which will ruin the old pattern of existence. (p. 49)

At the same time Carla is giving up part of her humanity to take on a puppet's nonexistence. . . .

By giving herself to Leo, Carla proved she was capable of acting, if only in a negative manner. Her brother Michele, however, can neither adapt himself to the corrupted environment nor transform it. Michele's impotency is at the opposite pole from Leo's dynamism. This apathetic, indolent youth is frustrated every time he tries to break out of his lethargy. He is the most desperate member of the family since he suffers from a lack of feeling. Michele considers himself superfluous and useless. . . .

[In] his introduction Michele is portrayed as an empty-headed puppet. . . .

Michele's whole relationship with Leo is a series of attempts at increasingly violent acts of revenge. But the youth's vengeance is not motivated by genuine indignation at offended honor but by a cerebral desire to conform to accepted standards of behavior. He does not want to remain a spectator of the drama about him. Michele hopes feeling will follow upon action. (p. 50)

This youth can be only a jack-in-the-box or a buffoon. At one early moment in the novel Michele insults Leo before the other members of the family. But his manner of arguing is studied and dispassionate. Finally he apologizes and retreats, as the text indicates, like a marionette. . . .

Michele has been called the first existentialistic anti-hero. Critics have spoken of his ennui or nausea. But his true state is one of torpor which prevents him from transforming his arid intellectual revolt into an active negation like his sister's. He considers himself caught in a puppet's passivity. (p. 51)

Moravia's *The Indifferent Ones* is a novel of defeat. No character completely achieves his aims. The author at first had a tragic conception of his character. But he was not able to write a tragic work as he confesses in the essay concerning the novel: "It became clear to me that tragedy was impossible in a world where non-material values no longer seemed justified and where the moral conscience had grown callous to the point that men—motivated merely by appetite —tend more and more to resemble automata." Paralyzed in the nonexistence of puppets, the Moravian characters attempt to bring themselves to life. These characters are not deformed puppets; rather it is as human beings that Moravia's characters are malformed, for consciously or unconsciously they become immobile blocks of wood. (pp. 52-3)

> Douglas Radcliff-Umstead, "Moravia's Indifferent Puppets," in Symposium (copyright © 1970 by Syracuse University Press), Spring, 1970, pp. 44-54.

LOUIS KIBLER

[Moravia] considers himself a realist writer: . . . he has steadfastly defended realism against all other artistic currents. His defense is founded on humanism, on the idea of man as an end and not as a means; and among the arts, realism alone is humanistic. . . . (p. 4)

When Moravia speaks of reality, he is often referring to objective reality, that reality which exists independently of human consciousness and which would still have intrinsic value even if there were no men. In the novels of Moravia objective reality is most commonly evident in things, in the object experienced by Moravia's characters as a physical presence. It is simply there, contingent (in that there is no apparent reason for it to be there) and autonomous, for it exists in a dimension different from that of human beings, lending itself to neither definition nor explanation nor possession by men. The object can have meaning but it does not have a meaning. This is the conclusion at which Dino, the protagonist of *La noia*, finally arrives. . . . Recognition of the existence of things "outside" is the first step toward creating a rapport with objective reality, which in *La noia* is analogous to Dino's relation with Cecilia, his enigmatic mistress whom he has tried in the past to possess completely. By renouncing possession of her . . . , Dino affirms the autonomous existence of Cecilia and of objective reality. . . . (pp. 4-5)

What a thing is cannot be explained; one can only say *how* it is, and even that unsatisfactorily: a thing is . . . a thing. . . . Ever since Leo in *Gli indifferenti* said: "La vita non è né nuova né vecchia, è quello che è" [Life is neither new nor old, it is what it is] . . . , Moravia has consistently and with increasing frequency used the tautology. Since the publication of *La noia* in 1960, it has become the proposition around which revolves his expression of objective reality. The tautology is congruous to Moravia's predilection for word games and paradoxes. It says nothing—and everything; it turns back on itself reflecting the autonomy and contingency of the object. Certainly the tautology is not a satisfactory definition of objective reality; yet it is the only proposition conceivable because, as Ludwig Wittgenstein pointed out, it is undeniably true, and it does not limit reality whose limits, if any, are not known. (pp. 5-6)

[Objects] in Moravia often possess a curious vital force . . . . This mysterious life force is . . . present in the objects that appear in the story "Invischiato." . . . (p. 6)

The life force or Eros or, as Moravia usually calls it, nature, is also evident in less concrete phenomena such as intuition, a quality that in the Moravian scheme of nature is antithetic to reason and will. Intuition has its origin in nature; reason and will, which seek to dominate nature, are potentially anti-life forces in the service of Thanatos, the force of death and chaos. Despite its contradictions, variety, caprices, and freedom, nature is not chaotic; it possesses an unfathomable but nonetheless certain coherence manifested in the continuity of life. Among Moravia's characters, those most closely attuned to nature are women like Cesira in *La ciociara* . . . and, especially, Adriana, in *La romana*. . . . The Roman prostitute has no illusions about her life: she has a clear and apparently innate sense of what life is and of what she is, and she accepts both. For Adriana life is not abstract but concrete, neither the dream of a future paradise nor the memory of Eden lost; it is not what will be or was or ought to be but what is, here and now, in the present. . . . Mino is just the opposite. Having founded his life on reason and will, he can accept neither life nor himself; his destiny is controlled by the forces of death, and he ends a suicide. Adriana is Eros incarnate and, like nature, she guarantees the continuity of life; she ends her story bearing within her womb a child. Of all Moravia's characters, Adriana is the most deeply infused with the life force; in harmony with things and nature, she has achieved a total rapport with physical and non-physical objective reality.

The very form of the phrase "rapport with reality" implies a second term, that which is in rapport with objective reality. This second term is subjective reality: man's consciousness of himself as something other than and different from an object. Subjective reality is not limited by objective reality: it encompasses thought, will, emotion, memory, dreams, imagination. The central problem of Carla and Michele Ardengo in *Gli indifferenti* is that they cannot find outside themselves a reality that is more concrete than the amorphous and uncertain quality of their subjective realities. Theirs is the tragedy of twentieth-century man's loss of faith in an objective reality. . . . (pp. 6-8)

When objective reality is limited to objects which are neither possessable nor analyzable, it is not surprising that some of Moravia's fictional characters maintain that subjective reality is the more "real" and meaningful of the two. Such is the conclusion of the narrator in *L'attenzione*. . . . (pp. 8-9)

Reality in the Moravian sense—and it is in this sense that the term will henceforth be used—is a synthesis of subjective and objective reality, a blending of the worlds of man and nature. In primitive and unsophisticated peoples the link between subjective and objective reality is intuition. . . . Intuition, however, has become vestigial in many contemporary men, particularly in intellectuals and those living in highly industrialized societies. The former have traditionally affirmed the supremacy of reason over intuition, even to the point of denying its existence. Considering everything from the rational point of view, most of Moravia's intellectuals have apparently lost their innate conception of man as participant in nature: they live in an abstract sphere alienated from concrete and objective reality.

The industrialized man, on the contrary, has been reduced to a mere object. . . . The refrigerators in [Moravia's story] "Sette figli" are more alive than the workers, who, deprived of any concept of themselves as human beings, are no longer ends but means, objects lacking the vital force of nature. Like the intellectual, they, too, have lost their rapport with reality.

The rapport with reality springs from an accord between the affirmation of subjective reality and the recognition of objective reality. It is a just appreciation of man's capacities and his limits. Moravian man is suspended—or rooted —in a kind of Pascalian balance that can easily lead to, perhaps is found in, the sentiments of religion and mysticism. Man's image of himself as a human being, life itself depends on his sense of this balance. The drama of mankind originates in the disturbance of this natural and vital equilibrium; its tragedy has its source in the denial of either subjective or objective reality, or in the separation of the one from the other. Such an act against humanity or nature leads inevitably to alienation. . . . (pp. 9-11)

[Death] is the consequence of alienation, and at the same time the only means by which alienated man can re-establish a rapport with reality. Life depends on an accurate perception of reality and an acceptance of that reality as it is: an acceptance of objective reality as outside ourselves and unpossessable; an acceptance of others as they are and not as we would have them be; an acceptance of oneself as a subject living in a world of people and objects. An accurate view of reality opens out onto the possibility that, among men, man can be an end, for humanism depends on an awareness of one's possibilities and of one's limitations, a knowledge of what a man is and of what he is not. Contemporary men are alienated because their view of reality is unsound and because they have assumed that an action or actions will lead to a rapport with reality. Ironically and tragically, the alienated man in his despair resorts ever more frequently and obstinately to action, which in turn creates greater alienation and deeper despair ("Uomo" . . .). The cycle, Moravia believes, must be broken.

The Moravian view of reality—or, as he calls it, his ideology—leads not to action but to contemplation, which is direct and hermetic communication with objective reality. In contemplation one discovers the authentic rapport with reality, as Dino does when he contemplates the tree. . . . (pp. 12-13)

In contemplation are realized and integrated the experiences of religion, mysticism, art, and reality; contemplation is the most authentic act possible within the limits of Moravian ideology. (p. 14)

In defining Moravian realism, certain popular conceptions of the term must be modified. First, realist art need not deal with "average" men in "normal" situations. The realism of Moravia is neither restricted to nor linked with any social or economic class. . . . Secondly, Moravian realism is not "objective." The visualism of the *nouveau roman* as practiced by Alain Robbe-Grillet is, in Moravia's view, antirealist: since objective reality is beyond cognition, any objective point of view is at the very least uncertain. Similarly, the novel written from an omniscient point of view is inherently false, for it implies that reality is objective and knowable. . . . Finally, as Francesco in *L'attenzione* comes to realize, the "authentic" novel—that which *expresses* reality—is not possible. Reality is here and now; art is memory. . . . (pp. 14-15)

[Moravia believes that the] perspective of realist art must be subjective. If objective reality cannot be known, its very existence is uncertain; and it cannot therefore fix the point of view of the novel. As Francesco discovers, however, some aspects of subjective reality cannot be doubted; here, if anywhere within human consciousness, is a reality that is certain. It follows then that the realist novel will be narrated from the point of view of a subject and, most likely, in the first person. (p. 15)

The structure of a Moravian novel is determined by his ideology, in which the various elements of subjective and objective reality exist and function in relation to each other. . . . Realist art, then, is a metaphor of contingent reality made coherent and meaningful to men through human intentionality and consciousness. . . . Moravia, as he judges from the standpoint of his own concept of reality, can thus maintain that visualism is not realist, for it attempts to exclude subjectivity. Nor is abstraction, which denies objective reality. (pp. 17-18)

Moravia's fiction is full of characters who have set misconceptions, abstractions, and absurdities as their goals and values. Michele in *Gli indifferenti* believes in the concrete existence of abstractions such as sincerity; Marcello (*Il conformista*, 1951) seeks to conform to society's idea of normality; the narrator of *La noia* tries to possess reality. Some mistake people for objects, and still others humanize objects by attributing to them their own feelings. The most significant ethical contribution of Moravia is his investigation of what is necessary and of what is superfluous to the human condition; in other words, he has attempted to determine what is normal in man, normal not with reference to a society or a culture but in relation to reality and human nature. (p. 20)

Even in his "surrealistic" tales, the situations which Moravia depicts are always recognizable as extensions of the present world: the stories are satirical rather than visionary or prophetic. (p. 21)

> *Louis Kibler, "The Reality and Realism of Alberto Moravia," in* Italian Quarterly *(copyright © 1973 by* Italian Quarterly*), Summer, 1973, pp. 3-25.*

ZAHIR JAMAL

A finely attentive and judging engagement with the female predicament has always disinguished Alberto Moravia's work from that of conventional male well-wishers. The speaking subjects of the 30 self-portraits voiced in [*The Voice of The Sea and Other Stories*] make up an alertly differentiated chorus of ever more recognisable and unsettling identity. In brief, lucid accounts of harmonising or counterpointed theme, Moravia's women interpret, with ominous detachment, their estrangement in contexts where they figure chiefly as commodities. (pp. 219-20)

Moravia's watchful prose alertly notices the bewildered, involuntary nature of these self-assertions; the puzzled, distant challenge to themselves of women who confront, behind their 'enigmatic' narrations, the strangers of their consciousness. (p. 220)

> *Zahir Jamal, in* New Statesman *(© 1978 The Statesman & Nation Publishing Co. Ltd.), August 18, 1978.*

PAUL BAILEY

The Voice of the Sea is a collection of thirty stories—all written in the first person, and all narrated by women. Moravia's Roman ladies are a predatory bunch, maintaining a firm metaphorical grip on the balls of the men they choose to make contact with. What is interesting about them is the fact that they are curiously insubstantial, in spite of the numerous references to their bodies: those carefully described breasts and pudenda could just as well belong to some other species. Their various states of mind are set down rather clinically, so that one seems to be reading a series of case-histories. The psychological dossier is no substitute for the achieved work of the imagination.

With one exception, the monologues in *The Voice of the Sea* are mercifully short—the screams fade away after three or four pages. Some of the trick endings would make O. Henry's ghost blush; the contrived conclusion of the story called "Thunder and Lightning" for example, is signalled as early as the third paragraph. . . .

Of Moravia's concern for the plight of women in present-day Italy I am not in doubt; I am convinced, too, by his contempt for the men who run his country. His message is always clear. *The Voice of the Sea* is a tract for the times. I expect more than tub-thumping, though, from a novelist hailed as "foremost". I expect from him those insights that Bassani so agonizingly, and with such effortless artistry, conveys in *The Smell of Hay;* I expect fantasy that comes without contrivance, as it does in the novels of Calvino; I expect to find the atmosphere of a city suggested with the

minimum of scene-setting: Moravia's Rome could be anywhere, unlike Sciascia's Palermo, which is its unique and awful self. *The Voice of the Sea* is a shrill book; shrill with Message, and oddly lacking any sense of the individual life.

> *Paul Bailey, "Ladies of Prey," in* The Times Literary Supplement *(© Times Newspapers Ltd. (London) 1978; reproduced from* The Times Literary Supplement *by permission), August 18, 1978, p. 924.*

* * *

MURDOCH, (Jean) Iris   1919-

Murdoch is a British novelist and playwright. Her training in philosophy plays an important part in her novels which have as a central concern the ethics and moral alternatives of the English middle class. A frequent theme is that love is rare and only possible when a person realizes that someone besides himself truly exists. Some critics complain, however, that the philosopher sometimes triumphs over the novelist, reducing her characters to puppets thrown into situations to make a point. Her novels are intricately plotted and often treat complex and fantastic situations in a melodramatic way. Critical reaction to her work is generally divided; some critics see her as a major contemporary novelist, others as a middle-brow romancer. (See also *CLC*, Vols. 1, 2, 3, 4, 6, 8, and *Contemporary Authors*, Vols. 13-16, rev. ed.)

LORNA SAGE

It is difficult to chart Iris Murdoch's progress, if only because she has a gift for making the variety of possible plots and characters seem inexhaustible. The result of such plenty is that no new novel of hers is going to retain its air of finality for long: it joins the *oeuvre,* it confirms the appetite (in author and readers alike) for yet more novels. She herself would perhaps think this response appropriate, given her stress on art's capacity to strengthen our moral curiosity ('Virtue', she once wrote, 'is concerned with really apprehending that other people exist') but it has its problematic aspect, since it produces a nice confusion between quality and quantity. More does seem to mean better for her; imagination and curiosity are near akin, and curiosity can only be fed with particulars fresh-invented each time. Three years and three novels ago in *The Black Prince* she mocked her own reputation for prolixity in the person of popular novelist Arnold Baffin ('He lives in a sort of rosy haze with Jesus and Mary and Buddha and Shiva and the Fisher King all chasing round and round dressed up as people in Chelsea'), but for all that she gave him eloquent things to say in his defence—'the years pass and one has only one life. If one has a thing at all one must do it and keep on and on trying to do it better. And an aspect of this is that any artist has to *decide* how fast to work. I do not believe that I would improve if I wrote less. The only result of that would be that there would be less of whatever there is.' Arnold's besetting sin, of course, was curiosity.

So *Henry and Cato* offers a lot that's titillatingly different, and at the same time nothing exactly new. It doesn't have the self-consciousness about language of her last, *A Word Child,* but that doesn't imply that she has somehow moved on. For her such formal questions (even self-questionings) are merely local matters—connected with the tone of the particular novel—not the permanent 'issues' that they're assumed to be by many novel critics. . . . *Henry and Cato* is a visual book, dominated by pictures (Henry is an art historian of sorts) and concentrates on the problem of making people *see* (a word that often gets italicised with frustration). It's the work of a robust allegoriser—bold, confident and unfastidious. Which means that it displays equally frankly the richness of illusion Miss Murdoch has achieved and the imperfections she has settled for.

The plot extracts sharp moral humour from the multiple contrasts and overlaps of its two heroes' careers—a technique at which Miss Murdoch has become so carelessly expert that one soon loses sight of its crude binary origins. Here, the book's beginning finds the characters at very different phases: the great decision and battle of Cato's life—his conversion, his priesthood in the face of his rationalist father's blank loathing—has already taken place offstage; whereas Henry has only just (by virtue of a car accident, also offstage) become heir to the family estate. . . . The idea is that Cato seems to be losing his certainties as Henry acquires his. . . . (pp. 61-2)

The descriptive strength of *Henry and Cato* reaffirms the importance for [Miss Murdoch] of *picturing* the variousness of people's lives and landscapes. Lives that cannot be pictured hardly exist. . . . [In] *Henry and Cato* the most telling instance of a life-style is Cato's—he believes himself to have given up the world, but the descriptions of his condemned 'Mission' off the seedy end of Ladbroke Grove are just as suggestive of the tug of things as the tapestry-texture of Henry's estate:

> He took off his macintosh and propped his streaming umbrella in a corner, whence a rivulet proceeded across the floor making pools in the cracked tiles and disturbing a gathering of the semi-transparent beetles who were now shameless inhabitants of the kitchen.
>
> The dim light showed, immediately outside the door, the steep stairs which Cato now mounted to the room above where he once more checked the window which had been partially boarded up and more recently covered by a blanket hung from two nails. . . . There was a chest of drawers with the drawers standing open and empty, a divan bed with a dirty flimsy green coverlet drawn up over disorderly bedclothes, and a small metal crucifix nailed to the wall above. . . . There were two upright chairs and a number of overflowing ashtrays. The room smelt of damp and tobacco and the lavatory next door.

This loving inventory brings out just how cumbered you can be when you have, in theory, nothing; decorum reigns here too, with 'semi-transparent beetles' instead of larks, and 'overflowing ashtrays' instead of 'big Italian vases'. The scene has a pictorial quiet and stasis that places Cato and articulates his identity, especially his unfreedom.

Not surprisingly for a book so visually conceived, *Henry and Cato* imagines hell as sensory deprivation. Conned by Joe into thinking he has been kidnapped by a gang, Cato finds himself locked in total darkness in what turns out to be an old air-raid shelter, and there, truly stripped of possessions, he falls apart—'it was not exactly like going mad, it was more like a gentle disintegration of a tentacular

thought stuff . . . which now floated quietly away into the dark'. . . . Moral existence is a matter of detailed images, without those illusory points of reference people die. *The Nice and the Good,* another novel full of pictorial detail, also used deep shelters under London (and a tide-filled cave) to demonstrate the fragility of mental space unsupported by the colours and perspectives of the art of material life. In Iris Murdoch's world it is spiritual arrogance of the most dangerous kind to suppose that you can become cultureless; she is not much troubled by the snobbish imperative of placing the quality of one kind of life over another, but she refuses to imagine a life that is 'free' of cultural patterns.

Which brings one back to the question of the peculiar kind of illusion her novels are after. She has, at least since *The Nice and the Good* in 1968, settled into a confident formula which stresses both the richness of detail and its disposability ('metaphors . . . used briefly and then thrown away'). Presumably it works so well because it feeds the moral curiosity about 'otherness' without subjecting any one set of characters to the kind of intense scrutiny that might merge them with the author. She no longer seems (if she ever did) interested in building a symbolic system or making a myth: her basic procedure is a loose form of allegory (or allegorising, to emphasise that it's a continuous process) and her mythological figures are deliberately attached to particular pieces of canvas, as though she is insisting on their being human creations. She has depth, but like the depth of her favourite paintings it is limited, and illusory (in the sense that you're meant to accept it as an approximation). Her treatment of minor characters—those not directly necessary to the action, who by their gratuitous presence seem especially to show 'that other people exist'—is interestingly similar to the arrangements of perspective in painting:

> Henry . . . was in the National Gallery, examining the most important acquisition made during his absence, Titian's great *Diana and Actaeon.* The immortal goddess, with curving apple cheek, her bow uplifted, bounds with graceful ruthless indifference across the foreground, while further back, in an underworld of brooding light, the doll-like figure of Actaeon falls stiffly to the onslaught of the dogs. A stream flashes. A mysterious horseman passes. The woods, the air, are of a russet brown so intense and frightening as to persuade one that the tragedy is taking place in total silence.

Henry takes it rather smugly as a reminder of the dangerous forces that toy with human destinies, but his own happy ending will prove him wrong. The forces at work in his world, while no less mysterious, are thoroughly human. What he should have paid attention to was the eerie mutual ignorance of the figures in the painting—Diana in the foreground, Actaeon dying in his underworld, the horseman in the distance. It's this ignorance, this living in separate worlds, that seems to Iris Murdoch to pose the central problems in both art and morality. And while a painting, or a novel, can seem to face and overcome our blindness, they share in it too. The 'mysterious horseman'—the minor character—on the skyline has to stand in for the endless variety of other lives and possibilities that lie beyond. One way of taking an allegory is to see in it a universal image, on which individual dilemmas converge; Miss Murdoch seems to see it rather differently, as a way of expressing the provisional nature of one's world picture. Her minor characters are, in their stylised 'realism', a measure of the scepticism she permits herself about her fictional world. (pp. 64-6)

Lorna Sage, "The Pursuit of Imperfection," in *Critical Quarterly* (© *Manchester University Press 1977), Summer, 1977, pp. 61-8.*

ZOHREH T. SULLIVAN

Iris Murdoch's waifs, orphans, refugees, demons, and saints, all share a common isolation, a loss of community, and the absence of close relationship to "a rich and complicated" group from which as moral beings they should have much to learn. As a philosopher, Murdoch connects this loss of community to the inadequacies of existentialist and empirical thought that rely on self-centered standards of individual consciousness and sincerity, rather than on other-centered values of virtue, love, and imagination. As a novelist, she dramatizes her ethical concerns by increasingly demonizing the existentialist, solipsistic hero who rejects the "messy reality" of involvement with others in order to pursue what he perversely sees as freedom, abstraction, and romance. . . . By failing to see reality as worthy of loving exploration, Murdoch's benighted protagonist is compelled to rely exclusively on personal values as his sole guide to morality. The resulting psychological distortions to which such solipsism is liable cuts a man off completely from others and from society. . . . Murdoch's characters cannot see because they are enclosed in "a fantasy world of our own into which we try to draw things from the outside, not grasping their reality and independence, making them into dream objects of our own.". . . Her protagonists, therefore, can redeem themselves only by discovering new ways of seeing reality and by resisting the false consolations of form and of fantasy which Murdoch defines as "the enemy" of that true imagination which is "Love, an exercise of the imagination.". . . (pp. 557-58)

The response of Murdoch's characters to community is complicated by the paradox of their personalities: although her isolated characters long to be part of a familial, social, or national group, they are at the same time solipsists who rely chiefly on will, ego, and power in order to manipulate the behavior of others according to their own systems and beliefs. Where there is power, there can be no community. Murdoch's concept of community . . . is realized, therefore, only within a nexus of morality, imagination, selflessness, and love. (p. 558)

Murdoch's repudiation of the retreat from disorder has led to her creation of various images of man-made order as alternatives for isolation and as versions of community. Among these, the more important are such social patterns as work, erotic involvements, family entanglements, and the restricted inner spaces of houses within which relationships are explored and confined. . . . In the first instance, work substitutes for community in three ways that serve to illuminate both character and theme. First, the vocation to which an individual is drawn in some cases reflects his psychological inadequacy or reveals an abortive effort to give order and meaning to an otherwise vacuous life. Anna's work with the Miming Theater in *Under the Net,* for instance, suggests her need to fit herself into the theoretical world of Hugo Belfounder in order to win his approval and

love. . . . Second, work might reflect a character's demonic need to control and exert power over others. Such an elusive and magical character as Mischa Fox, the newspaper magnate in [*The Flight from the Enchanter*], is supposed to have "at his disposal dozens of enslaved beings of all kinds whom he controlled at his convenience.". . . Third, work can also serve as a means for a protagonist to redeem himself and to work his way towards self-discovery: the changes in Rosa's jobs in *Flight* from factory worker to journalist and in Jake's jobs in *Under the Net* from hackwriter to hospital orderly to creative artist measure their movement towards selflessness, towards exorcism of their minds from the spells of fantasy and delusion, and towards becoming creative artists in their own right.

Not only work, but rooms and houses in [Murdoch's] novels function metaphorically to define and be defined by the relationships within them. The L-shaped room with its presiding blind and deaf mother, with its empty bed frame within which the Polish brothers make love to and enchant Rosa (*Flight*), Mischa's labyrinthian palazzo (*Flight*), Hannah's multi-mirrored rooms where she is imprisoned by the misperceptions and expectations of herself and others (*The Unicorn*) . . . [are] enclosures that reflect ailments of interiority as manifested in the character of their occupants and in the nature of their spell-bound, erotic, and frequently incestuous relationships.

[Although each of Murdoch's] novels experiments with a variety of communities, I have chosen to focus on . . . three Gothic novels, *The Flight from the Enchanter, The Unicorn,* and *The Time of the Angels,* because of their curious demonic inversions of community, in spite of which they also contain the recurring Murdochian theme of the struggle of love against the many guises of evil in everyday life. The elements of community in these works are Gothic extensions of similar concerns in her other novels. Here, the nets of fantasy are tighter, more difficult to escape, more terrifying, and cause more tragedy (disappearances, suicides, murders) than in her other novels. (pp. 559-60)

The fictional technique by which Murdoch pursues her ideas in these novels reveals a movement from an open to a closed structure. The already limited mental and physical spaces inhabited by narcissistic and Faustian characters in *Flight* and *The Unicorn* contract still further into the final confines of madness and death in *The Time of the Angels.* While *Flight* focuses on several different levels of society and a variety of erotic relationships, *The Unicorn* focuses more narrowly on a few philosophical attitudes and relationships confined within two houses, and *The Time of the Angels* concentrates even more narrowly on the mostly incestuous relationships within only one isolated ingrown household—that of an atheist priest who lives in a bombed-out rectory. These novels, therefore, are dramatizing the consequences of solipsism: the psychological and sexual enslavement of oneself and others through fantasy, delusion, self-abnegation, and power. . . .

Murdoch's society in these novels resembles Northrop Frye's description of a demonic human world, a society dichotomized between the ruthless, inscrutable tyrant on one hand and the sacrificed victim or *pharmakos* on the other, a community held together by "a kind of molecular tension of egos, a loyalty to the group or the leader which diminishes the individual." The setting in each novel also conforms to the requirements of both the demonic and

Gothic traditions: the straight path and rich topography of what Frye calls the apocalyptic is contrasted in Murdoch against the labyrinth or wasteland of the demonic. (p. 561)

The Flight from the Enchanter may be read as an allegory of power, power willingly conferred by psychologically enslaved individuals upon those who seek to control them by force of their personal magnetism and ego. The plot centers on Mischa Fox's attempts to gain control of a small independent magazine, the *Artemis,* its owner's sister Rosa, and various other independent people he can't bear to see free from his control. . . .

Each of the major characters in *Flight* is an orphan, an alien, or a refugee who attempts to compensate for his isolation by creating and controlling his own world, free from the accidents and threats of real life. Mischa Fox, the supreme enchanter of the novel, is both ruthless controller and passive innocent. His own self-image as melancholy lover of the world emerges in confessional talks with Peter Saward when he weepingly recalls incidents from his childhood in an East European village. But this strange region of sensibility within him contrasts drastically with his life as a sophisticated power-magnate who rescues refugees such as Nina, only to trap them into his deathly web, and who manipulates his alter-ego, henchman, and "minotaur" Calvin to carry out his evil designs. (p. 562)

In the Murdochian credo, love is incompatible with power; it never involves the need to change another individual, but consists instead of "the non-violent apprehension of difference" and the delightful perception of the inexhaustible otherness of the other. In this novel, Peter Saward, historian of pre-Babylonian empires, is the only person capable of Murdochian selfless love, "the lover who nothing himself, lets other things be through him." Unlike Mischa, who needs to "place" people in order to control them, and Rosa, who fears intimacy as a threat to her independence, Peter is seen to be totally vulnerable to others, "a personality without frontiers" who never needs to defend himself against the powers of others. (p. 563)

The Unicorn (1963) represents a significant development in Murdoch's handling of the closed Gothic novel—the novel of form, myth, and socio-religious philosophy rather than that of character. Reminiscent of *Wuthering Heights,* "The Lady of Shallot," and Mme. de LaFayette's *La Princesse de Cleves,* this story is about the self-imposed exile and imprisonment of a group of people at Gaze Castle who weave themselves into a web of enchantment designed in part by Hannah Crean-Smith and by Gerald Scottow, her demonic master-caretaker. . . . Part of the ambiguity of the novel lies in the nature of the bonds that imprison Hannah —ambiguous bonds that are variously interpreted by others as superstitious, pagan, Christian, spiritual, evil, or sexual. Hannah is believed to be either under a seven-year spell or undergoing a seven-year period of spiritual suffering as expiation for her adultery and her attempted murder of her husband Peter. (p. 564)

The communities in the novel . . . are composed not of singularly independent centers of significance, but of actors who find safety in a looking-glass world, whose eyes project on to Hannah their image of her, and who see in her the reflections of spiritual, platonic, or courtly ideals. She dies when their faith in her wanes along with their existence as mirror images of her reality. . . . Hannah's mirror is finally

a metaphor for her dependence on the introspective, self-contemplative code of conduct that gradually leads her to utterly disregard all others as independent and complex beings to be known, understood, or loved.

If the ability of a community to create its demonic controllers is seen in *Flight* and *The Unicorn,* Murdoch's *The Time of the Angels* is about the power of the demon to contaminate himself and others. In all three novels the enchanter manipulates the fantasies of victims who need a dominating figure to provide metaphysical meaning and dynamic tension to their otherwise vague drifting lives. In *Time* the need for some reconstructed value system directs this enchanter figure towards mad Nietzschean fantasies of the self as a potential Deity in a nihilistic world. Particularly in her central figure, Carel Fisher, we understand Murdoch's perception of the demonic as the inevitable result of conceptual and imaginative inadequacy in an age that venerates power and solipsism. (pp. 565–66)

Carel is Murdoch's modern representation of a Faust, who like Thomas Mann's Leverkühn, signals the end of a humane intellectual and ethical tradition. The parallels between Leverkühn and Carel (their similar philosophical backgrounds, their pacts with the inhuman, their sexual enslavement of others) emphasize their author's concern with those nihilistic and irrational elements in modern existentialist thought that Mann had earlier seen as responsible for the inhumanity of the Germans during the Second World War. . . .

If the central image of interiority in *The Unicorn* was the mirror, here it is the cocoon. Carel's effect on others takes the form of a kind of spell that imposes on them his special brand of immobility and dehumanization. . . . (p. 566)

Murdoch's choral use of Blake's "Introduction" to "The Songs of Experience" as part of Pattie's musings is intended to suggest a healthy Romantic norm, a positive Romanticism that emphasizes the regenerative power of wonder that accompanies the discovery of the external sensory world through goodness, love, and imagination. Murdoch's pursuit of true imagination as man's key to the discovery and love of others also recalls what Alfred Kazin calls the great theme of Blake's work—the search for imagination "that has been lost and will be found again through human vision." Seen within a framework of Romantic theories of perception, her sudden recognition scenes (such as Muriel's chilling keyhole vision of her father's naked body entwined with Elizabeth's) may be understood as devices intended to startle the self-deceptive mind into seeing the truth of others, and occasionally understanding, as Pattie does, the "face of evil as a human face." Carel's evil then is the result of man's intellectual errors that are created by his inadequate imagination—what Blake would call lost imagination, and Murdoch fantasy. (p. 568)

Her three Gothic novels are crucial to an understanding of her treatment of evil, the dangers of fantasy, and the problem of the discovery of others which is the only means to achieve human community. Within the Gothic form Murdoch has also found powerful images and a "new vocabulary of experience" that capture her sense of the moral and emotional failures of this age: the ruined church as an emblem of the failure of conventional religion to cure the sickness of the age, the incestuous family as a demonic extension of egoism and solipsism, and the enchanter or Faustian priest as a manifestation of modern existential man who defines his own values in a world bereft of the community of men and of God. The retreat of her characters into mental and spatial enclosures that admit neither contingency, humanity, nor love is most perfectly embodied in the progressively inward movements and the enclosed structure of Iris Murdoch's Gothic house of fiction. (pp. 568-69)

Zohreh T. Sullivan, "The Contracting Universe of Iris Murdoch's Gothic Novels" (a revision of a speech originally delivered to the Fourth Annual Conference on Twentieth Century Literature at the University of Louisville in February, 1976), in Modern Fiction Studies *(© copyright 1977, by Purdue Research Foundation, West Lafayette, Indiana), Winter, 1977-78, pp. 557-69.*

GABRIELE ANNAN

Like most of Iris Murdoch's novels, [*The Sea, The Sea*] is a thriller and whodunit on two levels: factual and philosophical. It is not too difficult to do an exegesis of the philosophical content because she leaves so many clues around, not to speak of overt explanations in dialogues and interior monologues. But that does not make it any less exciting. It is action-packed, and the action is handled with her usual virtuosity: there seems to be nothing she cannot get her words round, and she treats the reader to several virtuoso set-pieces.... There are long, marvellously evocative descriptions of the landscape, seascape and weather—weather indoors, too, where a bead curtain clicks in the sea breeze, or else chill damp covers everything like a sinister slime, the perfect atmosphere for breeding demons. She has a spooky way with entrances and exits: characters materialise and disappear with hallucinatory suddenness. As for the characters themselves, they are mostly theatre people, so it is not unsuitable if some of them seem two-dimensional and overact a bit.... [The agonies of the main characters] are almost too much to bear—until Miss Murdoch redeploys their loves and attachments; and one begins to realise that what seemed to be a tragic novel with interludes of comic relief is really a comedy with portholes for looking out at the cosmos.

Gabriele Annan, "Murdoch Magic," in The Listener *(© British Broadcasting Corp. 1978; reprinted by permission of Gabriele Annan), August 24, 1978, p. 250.*

MALCOLM BRADBURY

The Sea, The Sea is clearly one of [Miss Murdoch's] 'mature' books—one of her longest, her richest, her most carefully paced. Love, again, is the kingdom in which everything occurs; it is past love projected and repeated in a mysterious and thoughtful present. This is one of her more magical novels, set in an economical landscape and seascape: somewhere in the north, in and around a gaunt Edwardian house, with a view across the sea, that 'image of an inaccessible freedom'.... (p. 246)

The Sea, The Sea is about the dark chill in loving, the conflict of sacrifice and egoism. It is, in fact, a merciless and painful book.

It is also an elegant one—a comic dance in the Murdoch manner. There is much contrivance. Miss Murdoch is an elaborate but also a very thrifty plotter, and the world she at first makes contingently she then goes on to spend as a pattern. This is part of the magic of invention.... [The]

magic is there partly for its flamboyance, partly to take us beyond reality into a world of dream and re-shaped identities.... Miss Murdoch has written before of the late time in life when we pass between love and death, when old desires become present contemplations, and the 'secret vital busy inwardness' that drives our lives is forced to find meaning. Thus, from the patterns of the love game, and also the pattern of fiction, a kind of truth might emerge. That has always been Miss Murdoch's interest; but ... because of the careful pace and balance of this book, it all comes out with a special exactness. She lets her novel slowly accumulate its form, acquire its mysteries, its magic, its pattern. Then she lets it dissolve again, slowly, into chatter and ordinariness. Magic does not shrink reality, and *The Sea, The Sea* is a kind of *Tempest* on its own account, a book that explores the art of the novel and of magic, and also the need to elicit from life's facts and fantasies a meaning, a sense of the things that matter. (p. 247)

Malcolm Bradbury, "The Semi-Isle," in New Statesman *(© 1978 The Statesman & Nation Publishing Co. Ltd.), August 25, 1978, pp. 246-47.*

FRANCIS KING

Magic and the supernatural run, two lurid threads, throughout a loosely woven book [*The Sea, The Sea*]. Miss Murdoch has always presented love as though it were some kind of spell unaccountable in its mysterious waxing and waning.... Her people are infected with love or infect others in the same way that colds are caught and given....

By one of those coincidences more common in novels than real life, Charles finds that living in the same village is the girl, Hartley, whom he loved in his adolescence and whom he has gone on loving ever since. Now middle-aged, frumpish and déclassée, she lives with her retired husband, a former commercial traveller, in a ghastly little bungalow....

Charles at once begins to plot to get Hartley back, deceiving himself that she must still love him, when in fact all she feels is guilt for the abruptness of her former abandonment of him far back in the past. Guilt is one of the two major themes of the book....

[Magic] is the other theme of the novel. By summoning up good demons to his aid, Charles also summons up the bad ones that cause misunderstanding, unhappiness and a series of deaths, most of them violent.

The narrator, Charles, describes his story as 'a novelistic memoir' and later declares 'I am writing my life as a novel'. The result is a book that has all the waywardness, the inconsequence and the untidiness of autobiography, rather than of fiction. There are some splendid digressions—for example, a tirade against Ireland and the Irish—and some no less splendid descriptions of the sea, of the sky at night and of the appearances of even peripheral characters of no importance whatever. (p. 16)

As always, Miss Murdoch produces passages that simply take the breath away; no other living English writer is capable of them. But they are not as numerous as in the best of her novels. For the last eighty pages or so one is too conscious of the novelist as a marathon runner, flagging and increasingly breathless, who is determined to reach the tape at the 500-page mark ahead of her, even though all the opposition has long since dropped out.

Those who are irritated by Miss Murdoch's faults will find ample cause for irritation here. One of her characters says 'Anyone can love anyone' and he might have added 'Anyone can do anything'. Motives are either, like stowaways, found too late or not found at all. There is far too much melodramatic dialogue in the manner of 'Vilify her, put the blame on her! How splendidly you give yourself away!' There is also some extremely clumsy plotting, with the hero at one point eavesdropping on Hartley and her husband under a window of their house and, miraculously, hearing every word.

But such defects, common in all her novels, always seem to me a price to be paid willingly for such richness of imagination and such grandeur of intellect. (pp. 16-17)

> Francis King, "Love's Spell and Black Magic,"
> in The Spectator (© 1978 by The Spectator; re-
> printed by permission of The Spectator), August
> 26, 1978, pp. 15-17.

JOYCE CAROL OATES

Though Iris Murdoch has defined the highest art as that which reveals and honors the minute, "random" detail of the world, and reveals it together with a sense of its integrity, its unity and form, her own ambitious, disturbing, and eerily eccentric novels are stichomythic structures in which ideas, not things, and certainly not human beings, flourish. (p. 27)

There is a dizzying profusion . . . of characters, incidents, settings, "endings," so much so that even admirers of Murdoch's fiction often complain that they cannot remember a novel only a few days after having read it. . . .

Despite this multiplicity, this richness however, the novels are not really difficult, so long as one reads them as structures in which ideas compete, as in a debate, or, when they are most successful, as in Greek tragedy, in which near-symmetrical, balanced forces war with one another. . . .

Murdoch's philosophical position is austere, classical, rigorously unromantic, and pessimistic. Not that pessimism precludes comedy: on the contrary, it is probably the basis of the comic spirit. . . . [There are] amusing Murdoch characters who realize that they are doomed to happiness and to the mediocrity that seems to imply, since the circumstances of their lives prevent them from continuing the quest for the nature of truth. . . . But suffering itself, in the context of pitiless self-examination, can masquerade as purification, and we are back where we've begun—no more enlightened than before. . . .

There is something noble about a philosopher's quixotic assumption that he or she is the person to protect others from despair; or, indeed, that others require protection from despair. But Murdoch's sense of her mission *is* noble, and in an era when some of our most articulate spokesmen routinely denigrate their own efforts it is good to be told, I think plausibly, that literature provides an education in how to picture and comprehend the human situation. . . .

To a Platonist ideas are real. Iris Murdoch is, perhaps, not a Platonist—not quite. And yet in her novels ideas are far more "real" than they are in other contemporary novels; there are not very many of them, and they are clearly, almost too clearly, set forth. The basic idea seems to be that centuries of humanism have nourished an unrealistic conception of the powers of the will: we have gradually lost the

vision of a reality separate from ourselves, and we have no adequate conception of original sin. (p. 28)

Murdoch believes that the "inner" world is, in a sense, parasitic upon the "outer" world, and that love, far from being this redemptive, all-consuming force that sentimentalists consider it, is in fact the most dangerous of all delusions. It is bound up helplessly with egoism and personal fantasy, the "tissue of self-aggrandizing and consoling wishes and dreams which prevent one from seeing what there is outside one.". . . Mankind is not free. There are few choices, few options, though daydreams and fantasies urge us to believe that there are many, and that the small, distorting window through which we view the world is not a fiction. It has been charged that Murdoch's characters are puppets and that they are jerked about from one improbable crisis to another, and perhaps in response to this Murdoch has had one of her most important spokesmen, Brendan, Cato's mentor in *Henry and Cato*, say that people *are* puppets—puppets in the hands of God. And what is God? . . . Perhaps God is simply another fiction, however, and the various metaphysical substitutes—Reason, Science, History, Society, "Progress"—are false deities. One is left, then, with . . .

One is left with silly inconsequential but deeply absorbing plots. Emotions that feel "genuine" and "existential" enough but are, of course, illusions, sheer phantasmagoria. One is left with other people who are, whether they acknowledge it or not, involved in the same fruitless, albeit highly engrossing, quest. Their "ideas" make war upon one another: their "visions" are always in conflict. (pp. 29-30)

The Sea, The Sea is intermittently brilliant, given life by those off-hand, gnomic, always provocative remarks—essays in miniature, really—that characterize Murdoch's novels, and give them their intelligence, their gravity, while the machinations of the plot threaten to dissipate all seriousness. . . . Scene follows scene, the movement is maddeningly sluggish, one comes to feel that Murdoch is not going to *budge*, and that the strategy of a first-person narrator (so effective in *A Word Child*) was simply an error in *The Sea, The Sea*. Curiously, the novel is not very dramatic. There are a few awkward gestures toward gothic melodrama—Charles is terrified when a mirror is broken in his house, and a vase smashed; he believes he has seen a sea-serpent, and a dim "ghost"—but the "supernatural" is set aside for hundreds of pages, and some of the acts rather perfunctorily explained, so that Charles can concentrate upon his quixotic, doomed "love" for poor Hartley. . . . But much of the novel is static, and Charles becomes unforgivably garrulous. He *is* a vain, self-important fool, and yet one resents being trapped inside his consciousness, however authentic it seems. And it is difficult not to think that the novel's conclusion . . . is not part of another novel, another extended vision.

There are too many sketchy characters in *The Sea, The Sea*, the "fable" is not adequately linked to the "theme," and Murdoch is coming to depend upon a certain category of personage . . . far too often, too glibly, in order to make her primary ideas explicit.

The employment of highly articulate characters is of course not an inevitable sign of a novel's failure; but in Murdoch these characters are used repeatedly; they are self-conscious gods-from-the-machine who "resolve" the protagonist's doubts by uttering certain gnomic observations, and then withdrawing. Murdoch makes an attempt to give them weight, to give some background—usually a "tragic" memory—but their essence is illusive and finally unreal because they are no more than the embodiment of ideas, and constitute, in a sense, the novelist's failure to communicate her theme on a deeper, less self-consciously verbal level; or perhaps it is an impatience with the formality of the novel itself. One has the typically dense Murdochian plot with its cast of highly idiosyncratic, colorful characters, and one has a kind of ongoing choral commentary on the plot and characters. When the story, the people, are convincingly imagined—as in *Henry and Cato,* surely one of the major achievements in fiction . . .—one is not distracted by the commentary; when the story and its people are sketchily imagined, too obviously clownish to be worthy of our serious attention, the thematic statements, the Olympian utterances, fail to work entirely. . . .

Where ideas float about, inadequately embodied in narrative, they are often fascinating in themselves—and surely Murdoch is one of our most consistently intelligent, and rewarding, writers—but the danger is, of course, that they will come to seem increasingly perfunctory. (p. 30)

We are offered unanticipated moments of terrible, even tragic lucidity; we *are* purified by suffering; but our powerful revelations fade, our insights dissolve, and we are back in the world of appearances, of strife and desire and illusion. Given the opportunity to experience freedom we prefer to be, in the end, puppets of God. The work that is central to an understanding of Murdoch's oeuvre is Plato's allegory of the cave: I suggest that all of Murdoch's novels are commentaries on it. (p. 31)

Joyce Carol Oates, in The New Republic *(reprinted by permission of* The New Republic; © *1978 by The New Republic, Inc.), November 18, 1978.*

N

NABOKOV, Vladimir   1899-1977

Born in Russia, Nabokov emigrated to England in 1919, became an American citizen in 1945, and resided in Switzerland during the last years of his life. He was a prolific contributor to many literary fields, producing work in both Russian and English and distinguishing himself as a novelist, poet, short story writer, essayist, playwright, critic, translator, biographer, and autobiographer. Nabokov was fascinated with all aspects of the creative life: in his works he explored the origins of creativity, the relationships of the artist to his work, and the nature of invented reality. A brilliant prose stylist, Nabokov entertained and sometimes exasperated his readers with his love of intellectual and verbal games. His technical genius as well as the exuberance of his creative imagination mark him as a major twentieth-century author. Nabokov also wrote under the pseudonym of V. Sirin. (See also *CLC*, Vols. 1, 2, 3, 6, 8, and *Contemporary Authors*, Vols. 5-8, rev. ed.; obituary, Vols. 69-72.)

R. M. KEILS

The best of [Nabokov's] humor is not inflicted upon us. It appears thinly, a condensate, like something in our breath. It is humor that points at something unseen and unfunny. "Speaking of old men . . . an eccentric librarian called Porlock . . . in the last years of his dusty life had been engaged in examining old books for miraculous misprints such as the substitution of 'l' for the second 'h' in the word 'hither.' . . . all he sought was the freak itself, the chance that mimics choice . . ." (from "The Vane Sisters").

Out of the comic practice of individuals arises the tragic condition of man. Accepting this as a premise of Nabokov's art, the reader finds no surprises in [*Tyrants Destroyed And Other Stories*]. Politicans pursued (perhaps), lovers missed at railroad stops because of the chance shunting of a car, a child's prank. Finally, death. These are some of the colors of the thirteen stories in *Tyrants Destroyed*. (p. 384)

> *R. M. Keils, in* Studies in Short Fiction *(copyright 1976 by Newberry College), Summer, 1976.*

JAMES ROTHER

Can anyone doubt that rather than duplicate the parturitional feat whereby a mountain spews forth a mouse, Nabokov opts for the reverse maternal drama in which a mouse risks conception to bring forth a mountain? Ostensibly in *Ada,* the authorial quest involves the pursuit of Time by Memory, the two being courtly lovers of the mind whose Proustian infidelities often leave us wondering whether in our romance with the past we haven't somehow confused the fictional swain with the autobiographical cuckold. But the real obsession of the book (and of all Nabokov's works since his first "American" novel, *Lolita*) is with facts, and having grasped this, we should have no difficulty making sense of a style whose passion for instructing the reader (mostly in things he never dreamt he was ignorant of) is discernible on every page.

Instruction, of course, suggests the deploying of facts, and the discreet observer of "transparent things," like his fellow peripheralists, never tires of telling us that our night-sea journey is through an ocean of data as much as through a vortex of words—data, it may be pointed out, which have in themselves as meager a rationale as do the varieties of supposition which led their formulators to discover them. And they are everywhere in Nabokov, fastidiously avoiding verification and one another, since, from the parafictional point of view, any collusion of facts within the grand cabal of a novel or story sows suspicion regarding the identical-ness of fiction and reality. Thus, from *Lolita* to the present, Nabokov's *oeuvre* is seamless and of a piece, which is why grave problems arise whenever we try to distinguish his parafictional "fiction" from his parafictional "non-fiction." . . . (p. 40)

Of course, it is nearly impossible to do so. . . . For one thing, the acts of creation which brought both *Ada* and the autobiographical work *Speak, Memory* . . . into being, though disjunct in time, are not in Nabokov's mind really separable at all. The universe which includes these utterances among its paraphernalia also contains not one Russian emigré named Vladimir Nabokov, but thousands of them, each capable of recalling in the leisure of his mind some memorable time when some other Nabokov, with either the same or a different name, remembered having imagined an author imagining him. Such frame-tales are the very stuff of life, not of novels; that we tend to forget this fact and ignore its implications speaks well of our empiricism but not of our perspicacity. Exhibit: a parafictionist (let us for lack of a better name call him Nabokov) undertakes in the year 1969 to publish an account of how a Her or a She (named Ada) was pursued within the confines of some 445 pages of manuscript. (In all fairness to my terminological competitors, it must be admitted that figures in parafiction [not the parafictionists themselves] do frequently quest after some meta-fictional object which, like Barth's Her or She, remains chronically inaccessible.) He envisions a narrator who in turn posits an author having several tomes to his credit. . . . This same author claims to be fifty-two years old at a present moment in mid-July, 1922, and is beginning yet another masterwork, *The Texture of Time*. Not without a certain gourmet's complacency does this man of letters ponder the delicacies of Time and the pleasures of recollection. . . . (p. 41)

In 1922, the original parafictionist, already identified as Nabokov, was in the process of graduating from Cambridge University, having to his credit a number of publications. . . . Having himself always been fascinated with "the texture of time," he undertook to revise in 1966 (a mere three years before the appearance of *Ada*) a memoir which had originally been titled *Conclusive Evidence,* and which had described a "genius of total recall" recapturing from some lost and phantasmagorical past such minutiae as the vague remembrance of "the memory of 'memory's sting.'" . . . Of course, one of the major literary events of 1922 was a book called *Ulysses* about a particular day in 1904—June 16, to be exact—which day begins its odyssey in a Martello tower strangely similar to the "crenelated, cream-colored tower" where, according to the reminiscences of [Nabokov's] *Speak, Memory,* the parafictionist, aged five, spent the summer of that same year. (p. 42)

Nabokov's canon invokes monumental indeterminacy to suggest that to use one's memory is not to remember what has happened, but rather to remember what *is happening.* To demand that memory speak beyond earshot of the present is to make of memory a ventriloquist's dummy which, being unable to speak for itself, must be spoken for just as characters in novels are spoken for. And what this dummy inevitably articulates are facts—facts delivered in the wooden prose of history and which, by their rich profusion in text after text, disguise the ongoing impersonation of truth, deny that what is being said yields no recapturable past. The parafictionist, regardless of whom he is *not* being from moment to moment, can only speak in the language shared by his created selves—those autobiodegradable doubles who, by some magic of dissimulation, give his world resonance within the voice-box of a book. Which is, of course, mute—as mute as everything must be beyond catastrophe, beyond finale's outer rim. (pp. 42-3)

James Rother, in boundary 2 *(copyright © boundary 2, 1976), Fall, 1976.*

W. WALKARPUT

Andrew Field does not exist. The book recently published under his name, *Nabokov: His Life in Part,* is in fact a novel written by Vladimir Nabokov. It is the final and most triumphantly ironic work of one of the most important authors of this century. Such, at any rate, is the impression created upon a reader of Nabokov's fiction by Mr. Field's new book.

I do not actually *know* whether Andrew Field exists, and I would prefer not to find out. Unfortunately, so as to protect this publication and myself from possible legal action, I must appear to assume that Mr. Field *does* exist. But I shall continue to read and think of *Nabokov: His Life in Part* not as if it were some stranger's strange job of biography, but rather as one of Nabokov's own delightful blends of fact and fiction. For there is no other way to make sense of this book.

"I have no desire to twist and batter an unambiguous *apparatus criticus* into the monstrous semblance of a novel," as Charles Kinbote puts it in Nabokov's novel *Pale Fire* (1962). But like Kinbote's "Commentary" on John Shade's poem, *Nabokov: His Life in Part* is not nearly so unambiguous as it seems. Vladimir Nabokov may as conceivably be the author behind Andrew Field's work as he is of the series of Russian novels published under the name of V. Sirin. It would be far from the first time that the author had fooled us for, as his readers well know, Vladimir Nabokov is nothing if not a master of disguise. (p. 72)

More than a few of Nabokov's acknowledged novels are properly read as intellectual comedies in which more or less persistent biographers struggle to pin down their more or less unwilling subjects. The centerpiece of his most ambitious Russian novel, *The Gift* (written in 1937), is the biography of a real writer (Nikolai Chernyshevsky) as composed by Nabokov's imaginary narrator. In *Conclusive Evidence* (1951, later *Speak, Memory,* "An Autobiography Revisited"), Nabokov fashioned his own memoir into a durable work of art. And in *Pnin* (1957) a distinguished Russian émigré, teaching, like Nabokov himself, at an American university, is ridiculed and belittled by a mean-spirited narrator who only succeeds in making his subject more lovable than ever. I submit (as 'Andrew Field' would say) that *Nabokov: His Life in Part* inherits its themes from all of these books; and that, as a deft and complex intellectual comedy, it deserves its place on the shelf of Nabokov's best fiction.

The comedy in this book is easily overlooked and yet, for that very reason, all the more satisfying once it is perceived. It derives from the exaggerated obtuseness of the character named 'Field' as he persists in tormenting the character named 'Nabokov.' 'Field' plays Kinbote to 'Nabokov''s John Shade. 'Field' appropriates 'Nabokov,' he belittles him, he ridicules him, he makes his life miserable—and makes himself ludicrous in the process. . . . 'Nabokov,' meanwhile, performs as the classic comic butt (falling fully dressed into ponds, committing impossible blunders of syntax) and yet somehow—here is the magic—he manages to transcend his "biografiend." It is an astonishing performance. (p. 73)

Nabokov: His Life in Part is not only the comedy of 'Field' versus 'Nabokov'—it is also the sequel to Nabokov's first memoir *Speak, Memory,* and therefore contains the author's long-promised account of his American period. Nabokov's success in co-ordinating these two fundamentally different genres—the autonomous comedy and the personal memoir—marks the true mastery for which this book must be valued. (p. 74)

Those of any sensitivity who try to read *Nabokov: His Life in Part* as a serious biography can only be pained by 'Field's' disrespect for his subject, in much the same way that the naive reader of *Pale Fire* resents Kinbote's distortion of John Shade's poem. In fact, the kinship of these two responses is one of the surest clues to the 'Field' book's true nature. (p. 75)

In his discussions of Nabokov's novels, 'Field' seems at

times to exemplify literary biography's very worst tendency, a denial of the possibility of artistic creativity: "*Glory* is a direct telling of many details of Nabokov's life in slightly altered form." After such statements as this, no reader who has any acquaintance with Nabokov should be able to take 'Andrew Field' seriously. (p. 76)

The paradoxical effort of two characters writing about each other to produce a single book informs the basic structure of at least three other Nabokov novels: *The Real Life of Sebastian Knight, Pale Fire,* and *Ada.* In the last line of *Sebastian Knight,* the famous author and his biographer reveal themselves to be one and the same person, an invisible but strongly implied Vladimir Nabokov. . . . The debate in the *Life in Part* over whether John Shade or Charles Kinbote is the real author of *Pale Fire* is protracted to such an absurd degree that the reader cannot fail to recognize that true responsibility for that novel lies with neither but behind them both in Nabokov's own implied authorship. The issue is neatly displayed in a splendid diagram of the situation of *Pale Fire* in the *Life in Art*—no more of Shade than his legs or of Kinbote than his head can be made out, suggesting that they may indeed be one creature, and the entire scene is illuminated by a radiant sun labelled NABOKOV—but of course 'Andrew Field' takes no note of these things in his accompanying text. The same struggle for control of the implied authorship takes place in the *Life in Part* as in *Pale Fire,* but in the 'Field-Nabokov' contest the stakes are much higher. The names of both contenders appear on the cover of the book. (p. 80)

Vladimir Nabokov's death so soon after the publication of *Nabokov: His Life in Part* is impossible to discuss at this point without pain. But it must be asserted that such patterns do lie at the very center of the master's work. In *Pale Fire,* John Shade dies *into* the last line of his poem when an assassin mistakes the poet for his critic. At the end of *The Defense* (1930), Luzhin perishes *into* the eternity of his chessboard, finally at one with the patterns of his art. Nabokov wrote of Ada and Van,

> One can even surmise that if our time-racked, flat-lying couple ever intended to die, they would die, as it were, *into* the finished book, into Eden or Hades, into the prose of the book or the poetry of its blurb.

Nabokov's final, most oblique and most personal novel concludes as follows:

> —*Done and done then. A portrait of Vladimir Nabokov, Russian-American writer of our time and of his own reality.*

The End. Oh. The End. (p. 81)

.　　　.　　　.　　　.　　　.

[The Editors of *Chicago Review* add the following disclaimer]: The Editors of *Chicago Review* accept no responsibility for the views expressed in the preceding article. Andrew Field is a well-known critic who has published widely, and not only on Nabokov; he teaches at Griffith University in Brisbane, Australia. We offer "NABOKOV: His Life *Is* Art" to our readers as a curiosity merely; the reality of Mr. Walkarput is itself in some doubt. (p. 82)

W. Walkarput [*pseudonym of Brian Stonehill*], "Nabokov: His Life 'Is' Art" (*reprinted by permission of the author; copyright © 1979 by Brian Stonehill), in* Chicago Review, *Vol. 29, No. 2, 1977, pp. 72-82.*

ROBERT MARTIN ADAMS

Sometimes Nabokov in his authorial person mocks the passive or careless reader with his inattention; more often he silently challenges the alert reader by hiding significant clues in insignificant places, covering a real gesture with flashy indirections, hinting through what seem to be accidental correspondences at what seem to be significant significances. The novels click and glitter like sewing machines; they are so active and provoking on their corrugated and baroque surfaces, that one is apt to overlook their retention, at the center, of a touch of romantic sentiment, a shy and well-protected element of human feeling. Beneath even that level, there is occasionally to be found another layer of thought or feeling, perhaps only half-serious but perhaps more than that—persistent enough, in any case, to merit comment—a teasing, tantalizing fascination with the occult and the notion of life after death. (p. 146)

[At the end of *Lolita,*] Humbert undergoes a kind of transformation. He is said to reach through his sickness, rise out of his selfishness, and recognize in himself nothing less than True Love: . . .

> I insist the world know how much I loved my Lolita, *this* Lolita, pale and polluted and big with another's child, but . . . still mine. . . .

Perhaps the rhetoric carries the reader along; Humbert clearly intends it to, and the fact that she is no longer a radiant child tempts us to think that he has perhaps transcended his hangup, is declaring (as forcibly as the long-debauched idiom of romantic passion will allow) an authentic adoration. Yet the last phrase of the passage all but overtly declares itself a self-deception. "Still mine," indeed!—except as a beast in a cage belongs to its keeper, she had never been "his." To possess a nymphet was a selfish fantasy; perhaps the idea of "possessing" any fellow creature is bound to be a selfish fantasy. Humbert's notion that he ever had "possessed" Lolita is as false as his notion that he can or will possess her again. But I don't think these are the feelings with which we read, or are supposed to read, the passage. (Literary moralists, an extremely offensive subspecies of an offensive breed, are always tugging us by the elbow and telling us we shouldn't react as an author has in fact made us react; as a critical procedure, it simply raises taking-out-of-context to the level of a first principle.) At least on the wings of his own imagination and his own undeniable eloquence, Humbert has risen from the state of a loathsome creep to the simulation—at least—of a grand, heroic passion. And if there is, inevitably, enough egoism in every grand passion to suggest the possibility of the lover being a loathsome creep, that may be because grand passions themselves are pretty anachronistic.

Such being the case, we are bound to feel that the very presence of a grand passion in Nabokov's fiction (however ambiguous, however qualified) is more Proustian than Joycean. . . . Humbert is a descendant of Tristan; his story is a *Liebestod. Lolita* as classic romance is qualified chiefly by the uncrucial circumstance that the knight is himself half-dragon, but it culminates, just as securely as any medieval *chanson de geste,* with the hero standing triumphantly over the decapitated monster. (pp. 149-50)

Nabokov's theme of the pure, sustained, difficult, and ultimately fatal passion can be traced from the quite early Russian fictions (*Glory,* for example) through *Ada* at least; though a recurrent theme, it peeps forth only guardedly and intermittently from under the carapace of the hard-shelled, trick-playing, exhibitionistic fictions. One may feel that without this strain many of them would be only glistening mechanical contraptions; yet it undeniably marks Nabokov as of an older and more ample generation than our own. He himself has said something to this effect in *Ada,* by declaring that affairs in Anti-terra (which I take to be the world of his imagination) lag about fifty years behind those on Terra —the real, that is, the imaginary world common to his readers.

Of all these later novels, *Pale Fire* is surely the most oddly shaped, the most heavily laden with verbal and representational tricks; it has received the most loving attention from those readers who delight in the gamesman side of Nabokov's art. Yet within it too there can be found a kernel of something softer and more inward, the germ of a thwarted and difficult romance triumphing over impossibilities. At first glance, *Pale Fire* seems to be a novel in spite of itself. Divided into four parts, it would consist of a bumbling poem by bumbling John Shade, a predatory, paranoid commentary on the poem by Charles Kinbote, and within that commentary a tale of Ruritanian romance (intrigue, escape, ruthless long-range revenge), plus a wildly comic and very informative index. Telling a pair of converging stories across these several obstacles and through incongruous angles of consciousness is a tour de force in itself. As usual in Nabokov, we must take account of distorted consciousness and several varieties of contrived reticence in order to get anywhere near the heart of the matter. Kinbote is the most obviously disturbed of our narrators. . . . [He] is a botched and incompetent artist, vain, self-conscious, self-absorbed, and utterly insensitive to the feelings of others. Apart from his persistent fantasies of humiliation, Nabokov's thought was surely shaped here by an impulse to parody his own parasitic relation, as editor, to Pushkin as poet. The success of his parody is shown by the fact that most readers have been more intrigued by Kinbote and his melodramatic tale of Gradus and Charles-Xavier the Beloved than by the poem of John Shade which provides the pretext for the commentary that provides the pretext for the tale.

Shade's poem is an ungainly and uncouth piece of verse which, from the literary point of view, deserves no better reading than the one it gets from Kinbote. But he is wholly wrong about it in two ways; he thinks it a marvelous piece of writing, and ignores precisely and brutally those passages which do achieve an awkward kind of pathos. (pp. 150-52)

[An] important new element in *Pale Fire* is surely the sustained contrast between Shade, the provincial at ease in his own New Wye environment—interpenetrated as it is with intimations and correspondences of another existence . . . —and the haunted, haunting outsider Kinbote, who is in so many respects Shade's mirror image, moon to Shade's sun. In another analogy, Shade is very like transparent glass, Kinbote a mirror; the one (like Bloom) is the vehicle of intuitions to which he offers no obstacle and so hardly perceives, the other (like Stephen) carries his own story with him, always and everywhere the same. But both characters,

and in this respect they carry forward strikingly a feature of late Joycean technique, are penetrated and infused with messages and images, intimations and intuitions, from outside reality. Some effort has been put into the thesis that Kinbote's Zembla and the entire story woven about it are nothing but a private hallucination. . . . [However], we are not dealing here with an essay in ontology. It's precisely the struggle between two different (and rather awful) modes of reality that creates the interest of the fiction; and to make one of them (however Ruritanian) wholly fictitious is to throw oneself into the arms of the other, however drab. Like others of Nabokov's artist-criminals (Humbert of *Lolita,* Hermann of *Despair*), Kinbote winds up in a mountain refuge, writing the story of his crimes and applauding his own insane ingenuity. Precisely because he's so unchecked, so unreliable, we are not supposed to believe or disbelieve whole-heartedly what he says; we must guess, grope, blunder among the probabilities. And so with the novel of which he forms a part. *Pale Fire* no more affirms or denies anything, including the potentiality of its own cosmos, than does [*Finnegans Wake*]—it is simply an achieved book. Its theme is the invasion of a haunted ordinary by an obsessed fantasy, a zombie in bondage to a spellbound ghost. The inevitably inconclusive conclusion of such an encounter throws us back on the tricks of language, synchrony, mirror-imagery, and recondite reference interwoven with fancy, that make up the detailed texture of *Pale Fire.*

Gamesmanship in this book is more ostentatious than in Nabokov's other novels because it consists, not just of little knots in the narrative lines, but of direct and massive opposition between one theme and another. Kinbote of course is determined that Shade's poem shall not be itself, but rather the poem he would have imposed upon (inspired in) Shade; in addition, the basic structure of footnotes and index imposes on the narrative abrupt leaps backward and forward in time, as well as sidelong motions from theme to theme. There are as many false leads along synchronic lines as there are significant ones. . . . [Whether coincidental data] do or don't have tangential significance is up to the reader to guess; but hardly a fragment of Zemblan is cited that can't be heard as a variety of deformed English, anagrams and backward spellings are everywhere, and playful fantasies like the garden containing all the trees mentioned by Shakespeare entice one into further reflections than they can possibly reward. (pp. 155-57)

Not only the language but the landscapes of *Ada* deliberately conflate spheres of existence—and these are more than the spheres of two very different minds, as in *Pale Fire;* they are two entirely different nations and cultures and even two mirror-images of the cosmos, Terra (our world, which occupies the same ambiguous status as heaven or the afterlife) and the world of the fiction, Demonia or Anti-terra, which all the characters accept as the "real" world. . . . Nabokov distances this imaginary "real" world not only in time (the entire action of *Ada* takes place after the Revelation, also known as the L-disaster), but in a cosmos of incalculable, though peripheral, strangeness. The law of gravity is now and then suspended through the operation of flying carpets, and there is a permanent ban on the use, or even the mention (except covertly) of electricity— which seems to have taken the place of sex as a taboo topic. People speak a mongrel mixture of Russian, French, German, English slang, and erudite English from the small-print section at the bottom of the page of Webster's Second International. Trans-lingual puns abound, along with bastardized place names (Akapulkovo) and a rich array of verbal off-rhymes and almostings (Kaluga, Raduga, Ladoga, Luga, Laguna, Lugano, Lumbago, Ladore, Ladorah, Radugalet); the effect is to blur and diffuse one's sense of Anti-terra by dissolving it into a set of unsteady and constantly shifting overlays. In the large sense, Anti-terra is haunted by fitful glimpses and unreliable intimations of life on Terra.

I don't doubt that Nabokov is particularly delighted with some of the proofs invented by modern physics for establishing the existence of life or anti-life on other planets— proofs which levitate giddily on the laws of bare probability and the total absence of factual evidence. Just so the Anti-terrans can neither accept nor dismiss the existence of Terra.... Anti-terra is a blur of fantasies. Czarist Russia, Hollywood, Canadian frontier-life, and international high society blend together in a froth of cinematic collages. Literature spills over into life repeatedly; we find Chateaubriand's oak in botany textbooks, Chateaubriand's mosquito biting bare legs, John Shade's poem being translated by Ada into Russian, Maupassant meandering through the watery labyrinths of Mlle. Lariviere's mind. Van, as ostensible author, intervenes from time to time; Nabokov as real author does the same; Ada interjects, and so (discreetly) does an unidentified Ed.

Set in this layercake of contrasting contexts, the romance of Van and Ada Veen contains too many elements of derring-do and pre-fab fictional claptrap not to be seen, at least in some measure, as parody or self-parody. (There's an awful possibility that parodic intent may *not* underlie Van Veen's vacant meditations on time, which occupy so much of Section 4; but that's an alternative to be avoided for as long as possible.) In the other direction, the romance is qualified by the inhuman egotism of this marvelously self-satisfied couple and a frank recognition, even on their part, of their own hideous brutality toward others—like a gang of birds setting on a weak member of the flock, they have literally pecked Lucette to death. But at root the romance is to be accepted romantically—one sign of which is the sardonic little review that Nabokov has appended to his own fiction. It is, of course, a silly, sentimental, and superficial review—as if Nabokov were trying to ward off, by parodying, a view of his novel that in fact it invites. Amid the phantoms, demons, delusions, and echoes in which his novels delight to play, amid all the skepticisms and sterilities with which he must surround it and ridicule it, Nabokov retains a core of feeling whose intensity we sense for the most part only reflexively, through the *cheval de frise* of verbal fortifications with which he protects it.

Of all Joyce's influences on Nabokov, probably the most important though the least easy to document is in the matter of imitative prose. The influence is hard to document, not for lack of examples, but because a master of prose style will find the special rhythms and images of his subject, regardless of predecessors or authorities. Prose style in fiction is, after all, not a thing in itself, so much as a matter of fluidity and flexibility in intimating both a scene and a set of feelings surrounding it. Like Joyce, Nabokov writes a wonderfully adaptable and various prose which at its best freezes a bundle of widespread particulars into an instant of suddenly stopped unity.... [He can write] a sentence as

swift and sinuous as the complex of actions that it embraces. On the other hand, when the narrative disappears into the strange sick minds of Aqua or Lucette, though it maintains a difference between them, the language moves with a quick and frightened vivacity, as if disordered and out of control but drawn irresistibly forward by a power outside itself. In moments of stress, when the mind of some character is darting back and forth, seeking some way out, the prose follows it down its different narrative pockets, shaping out the future into a dozen different forms all more convenient than the present. It is an old trick with Nabokov to move uninterruptedly from straightforward third-person exposition into the fantasy of a character, leading the reader unsuspectingly along until "reality" catches up with him, he blinks, and looks back to find the spot where a private fantasy-trail branched off a public one.... [In] the later books, it is used less as a trick for its own sake than as a way of weaving into and out of the minds of characters, sometimes only for a fleeting adjective or the intimation of a point of view. And again, there are moments when Nabokov takes great pains to keep out of the minds of his characters; how determined and appropriate is the superficiality and impressionistic allusiveness of the scene in which Ada and Lucette combine briefly to entertain Van in the large bed of a New York apartment. It is a scene painted entirely in colors, lights, darks, dimly perceived shapes, as if the observing eye were high and distant—a wonderfully poised and discreet piece of pornography, as if seen through Seurat's distracting vision.

This mobility of Nabokov's prose distinguishes him, it seems to me, even from such great admirations of his as Proust and Chateaubriand—indeed, from most of the past masters of "fine style." ... In a twentieth century of insubstantial, phantom persons who nonetheless manage to write wooden and obtuse prose, it is Nabokov's peculiar accomplishment to have inverted the process. His characters may be agitated outlines, but they inhabit a glittering and slippery element of prose that is always capable of, and sometimes achieves, genuine events. (pp. 157-61)

Robert Martin Adams, "Vladimir Nabokov," in his AfterJoyce: Studies in Fiction After "Ulysses" *(copyright © 1977 by Robert Martin Adams; reprinted by permission of Oxford University Press, Inc.), Oxford University Press, New York, 1977, pp. 146-61.*

JOHN UPDIKE

Faithful Nabokovians have met Mary before; she sat for her portrait as Tamara in *Speak, Memory*, lurks near the heart of *Lolita*, and was deified in *Ada*. [In *Mary*], artistically as well as chronologically young, she is the first love of the autobiographical hero, Ganin, for whom her wanton yet delicate Tartar beauty condenses into pure perfume the idyll of rural Russia and the enchantment of privileged youth. But Ganin remembers her from afar, when he is in a Berlin boarding house surrounded by other émigrés, comic and pathetic types of exile from reality.... Ganin wakes from the shadows, from dreaming of Mary, at the end, and slopes off to his future as, it may be, an internationally renowned poet/scholar/novelist. *Mary* not only adumbrates the future of a master, it shines by its own light. From the start, Nabokov had his sharp peripheral vision, an intent deftness at netting the gaudy phrase, and the knack (crucial to novelists and chess players) of setting up combinations. Though his materials are tender, his treatment shows the good-natured toughness that gives an artist long life. Wisely, and nicely, he has spared this venerable text the—he admits—"high-handed revampments" to which his elder self is prone, and has supervised an exact, deferential translation. (pp. 193-94)

> *John Updike, "Mary Unrevamped," in his* Picked-Up Pieces *(copyright © 1975 by John Updike; reprinted by permission of Alfred A. Knopf, Inc.),* Knopf, 1977, pp. 193-94.

JUNE PERRY LEVINE

The structure of *Pale Fire* provides its meaning and delight. . . . [Most critics] have used it as a way of unraveling the "plot"—what happens among the three principal characters, John Shade, Charles Kinbote, and Jakob Gradus—and, therefore, have approached the poem and commentary which comprise *Pale Fire* as separate entities to be studied as two units and then connected, usually by having either poet Shade or commentator Kinbote assigned the authorship of the whole. (p. 103)

In *Pale Fire*, the form itself—a poem and a commentary on the poem—creates the tension of the whole and should be approached like a character: how are we meant to apprehend it? If Nabokov's method of composition is the hero, the reader's method of perusal determines how the hero will be perceived. . . . For the first reading, merely alternating between the poem and the commentary provides sufficient involvement in Nabokov's scheme while, at the same time, keeping the movement of both dimensions clear; on second reading . . . one can start raveling the web.

The web is the controlling metaphor of *Pale Fire*. Sometimes conceived as a plex or grid, the visual pattern and the metaphysical formulation remain the same. (pp. 103-04)

The dimensions that the axes on Nabokov's grid represent are time and space because events occur at the intersection of their relationships. In *Pale Fire*, the poem exists as the spatial dimension and the commentary as the temporal. Within the reality of each of these parts, naturally, time and space operate, but within the created structure of the whole novel, Shade and Kinbote each serve as a single dimension. Shade's poem is essentially self-contained and unalterable, a work of art outside of time. . . . I speculate that Nabokov composed the poem in heroic couplets to emphasize its crafted quality and that he attempted to make it a very good poem. (p. 104)

Throughout *Pale Fire*, Nabokov makes "ornaments of accidents and possibilities." . . . This device is not merely decorative; it is the philosophic substance of the work. Long before Marshall McLuhan informed the world, Nabokov knew that the medium is the message. The major difference between Nabokov and other writers who conceive of life as governed by accident is that Nabokov does not espouse despair, apathy, or anarchy. Like a modern physicist, he is a pattern-hunter in a universe of chance. (p. 105)

Objects and events are plotted, using the axes of poem and commentary for the dimensions of space and time, to create a model of chance occurrence in the Universe. The novelist's dilemma is that he must persuade the reader that chance is operating in a deliberately contrived medium. Two factors work in behalf of his illusion: the reader's experiential acceptance of coincidence in the real world, and Nabokov's skill in choosing the absurdly ill-matched poem and commentary as vehicle. (p. 107)

Yes, complains the disgruntled reader, the novel is clever enough, but learning how the web is spun by spinning it oneself is not enough; I want to know the meaning of the pattern: Nabokov never turns to the real provenance of the great artist—moral questions. It is true that Nabokov as novelist, as well as Lepidopterist, works descriptively. It is also true that pattern in fiction, like pattern in music, has no *intrinsic* value. But a particular pattern can emblemize a particular ethical conception of the universe. The chief feature of the grid, web, or plex is that no axis, no thread, no line is paramount in the entity. Significance is achieved through interconnection. . . . The principal idea of *Pale Fire*, emerging from its structure, is not the ascendancy either of Shade or Kinbote; it is that the random interplay of their lives exemplifies non-deterministic interdependency in the universe. (p. 108)

> *June Perry Levine, "Vladimir Nabokov's 'Pale Fire': 'The Method of Composition' as Hero," in* The International Fiction Review *(© copyright International Fiction Association), July, 1978, pp. 103-08.*

      *   *   *

NIN, Anaïs   1903-1977

Nin, an American novelist, short story writer, and critic, is best known for her diaries. Living in Paris in the 1930s, she became part of several artistic and intellectual circles, where she became acquainted with Antonin Artaud, Henry Miller, and Otto Rank. Her study with Rank, a prominent psychoanalyst, is reflected in both her fiction and her diary, where she explores the power of the subconscious in imagery drawn from dream and myth. (See also *CLC*, Vols. 1, 4, 8, and *Contemporary Authors*, Vols. 13-16, rev. ed.; obituary, Vols. 69-72.)

DUANE SCHNEIDER

The intriguing and engaging narrator of Anaïs Nin's *Diary* has surely earned for herself a place among the great literary creations to appear in this century. Purporting to reveal aspects of her life (and the growth of her sensibilities) in selections from an autobiographical journal, the narrator knows and relates the truth about herself. . . . The creation and development of this narrator unquestionably attest to the power and skill of Nin, the author, and it is therefore unfortunate that many readers have failed to appreciate the difference between the two. (p. 9)

[The] values and techniques [Nin] employed in her fiction are finely honed for use in the *Diary*. Psychological authenticity, which lies at the heart of all of Nin's work, is effected in the *Diary* as in the fiction through the manipulation of symbolism, dreams, and other dramatic devices which generate a sense of immediacy. Similarly, the *Diary* reveals a fine sense of timing, character development and selection, which Nin initiated and Gunther Stuhlmann aided; as in her fiction, but frequently with sustained concreteness, characters appear and reappear in multiple contexts, while typical of both the fiction and the *Diary* is the presence of a chief female character who is omnipresent—as a participant or as an observer—and whose development is presented through multiple exposures in a variety of contexts, through her own self-analysis, or through the responses she evokes from the satellite characters around her.

There is, however, one important difference between the material as it is presented in the fiction and as it is presented in the *Diary;* namely, the presence within the latter of a central consciousness—that of the persona—through whose mind all the characters and incidents are filtered, interpreted, and colored. Every detail she affords us tells us perhaps as much about herself as it does about the person or incident described. In contrast to the situation in Nin's fiction, therefore, narration in the *Diary* becomes simultaneously self-characterization. Under the appearance of a journal that records real-life situations and individuals, there have, in fact, been gathered a set of compelling "actors" in accordance with the literary principle of point of view. The result is neither fiction in the traditional sense nor diary in the conventional sense but rather something of a new art form—the journal-novel.

It is not difficult to describe the characteristics of the persona in each volume of the *Diary;* accounting for the narrator's development and the changes in her characterization, however, may be more problematic. . . . The thematic truth that lies at the heart of the *Diary* . . . is inextricably connected with Nin's conception of the narrator who is compelled to tell her tale, and who in so doing becomes both the subject (teller) and the object (told about). (pp. 10-11)

[One] of the great irritations to some is that the *Diary* leaves out, it seems, as much as it contains. As in some of Nin's novels, a portion of the context is missing or is deleted. But the enjoyment, the wonder, the pleasure, and the surprize of the persona all seem to be present, and the richness of life is felt even if it is not described in detail. The scenes between the narrator and June [from Volume 1 (1931-1934)] are masterpieces of literary control; Nin's sensitivity to diction here is at its most delicate and discerning. None of Nin's works of fiction has a greater unity than this progress of the *Diary*'s heroine in her first public appearance. . . . The persona is depicted as a questor who moves steadily toward levels of self-realization, and in Volume I it is as though each character she encounters somehow contributes to this quest.

However, the strength of Volume I is also its weakness. The character of the persona seems incomplete, unrounded—perhaps unreal. Certainly the narrator is relatively flawless. We soon realize, in fact, that she is depicted as the one who is needed, a kind of savior, and not merely one who needs. . . . This motif, which is developed even more clearly in Volume II, begins to emerge when the diarist observes that she always loses her "guide halfway up the mountain, and he becomes [her] child.". . . (p. 12)

Many motifs, themes and characters reappear in [Volume II] which covers the years 1934-1939. But because the advent of war dominates the scene here, this volume has both a political and social context that is lacking in Volume I. During these years the narrator develops significantly as a writer and forms close and important literary associations. . . . (pp. 12-13)

Simultaneously, the narrator cultivates her image as nurturer and protectress—a pattern of self-characterization that echoes Volume I. She continues to be introspective. . . .

And yet, the narrator herself seems more incomplete than ever, and Anaïs Nin, the author, is not unmasked, nor we feel, was meant to be. The persona is busily engaged with the rites of more self-analysis. (p. 13)

The narrator's vision of the artist transforming the world constructively is a view that she clings to. On the personal level as well as on the cosmic scale, the function of the artist is a beneficial one, and above all, the persona is characterized as one who maintains these values in her personal relationships as well as in her own ideology, which she is forced to create. It may seem like a role that attracts too much self-aggrandizement, and some find it obnoxious because of the unreal consistent nobility with which the narrator characterizes herself or allows others to do for her. . . .

With an agreeable symmetry, not unlike its predecessors, Volume III begins with difficulty and dislocation (also true of Volumes I and II), but ends with success and acceptance —true in Volume I, but only generally so in Volume II. . . . The persona progresses in a logical fashion: the literary initiate of the first volume, who chooses art in the second, becomes the maverick and determined devotee of her own vision in the third volume. (p. 14)

Volume III, however, lacks a continuity that the first two volumes contain. Most of the characters introduced in this volume hold interest for the reader, but some seem superfluous. The narration seems for the first time broken at times, slightly desperate if not shrill. The narrator's problems and friendships are not always so engaging as the nature of her literary achievement. (p. 15)

Although the details and emphases have changed, basically Anaïs Nin's depiction of the persona does not shift significantly in the first three volumes: generous, industrious, ambitious, respected by a core of admirers, the narrator pursues her vision of the feminine perception in her own unique kind of fiction. She does not reject psychoanalysis, but subordinates it to her art and vision. But the fully developed, human narrator, portrayed in her weaknesses and vulnerability, has yet to appear. The narrator in Volume III remains a literary creation, not a live human being. The author's defenses, it would seem, are still up.

The fourth volume, covering the years 1944-1947, represents to some degree the legacy earned from the years of the early 1940's. More fragmented than any earlier volume, it is not, however, weak or uninteresting, and contains some of Nin's finest and most poignant observations about life and literature. A number of familiar themes appear: the narrator continues to be concerned about her own artistic and psychological development, conscious of the restrictions imposed by guilt and neurosis, sensitive to those aspects of her existence which seem healthy and life-giving. Her literary life—printing, writing fiction—receives some fascinating attention here; her gravitation toward the young and her disappointment in the "mature" is dealt with in some detail. A strong sense of humanism emerges in this volume, a clear articulation—through the persona—of a vision of how life may be lived in an integrated fashion.

The sense or need of a persona—shall we say the author's? —also seems less urgent in Volume IV. For the first time the narrator does not have to succeed: she has succeeded. She is not fully rounded yet, but the heroics lie further in the background than ever before. . . . The authenticity and deep sincerity of key passages are impressive, and signify the increased development of a persona who seems human and alive.

It thus seems that the further Nin carried her open-ended *Diary,* the more comfortable she became in allowing for a free and open narrator, in place of the narrower persona who seemed to be created with specific roles and images in mind. Expansion, fulfillment and evolution become a manifestation of the narrator's success and acceptance as a fiction writer and lecturer; the dream has become reality. For Nin, the dream, if lived out, provided for more abundant life; but the dream could also become a tragic trap, for to live within the dream and not to bring it into reality could lead to disaster. (pp. 15-16)

The fifth volume, which covers the years 1947-1955, is far different from the first four, and is more fragmented and less sustained even than Volume IV. Although familiar themes reappear—sympathy, analysis, fiction writing, travel—no clear focus emerges and no clear theme is developed. It contrasts most strikingly with a work like Volume I, with its dramatic and engaging characterizations that are developed in great detail. The incoherence of Volume V in fact mirrors the incoherence of the narrator's life at this time; more than in any other volume, the persona here is less stylized and artificial. . . . In all its fragmentation, it may well be that Volume V, edited carefully, stands as a masterpiece of organic form, imaging in its structure (with short, undeveloped passages) the disconnected nature of the narrator's life. It may have been at this time that Nin chose to redirect her characterization of the persona toward something less glamorous, less dramatic than she appeared in earlier volumes. (p. 17)

The sixth volume of the *Diary,* covering the years 1955-1966, contains more pages, deals with more years, and has far more balance and structure than earlier volumes. Some will say that it cannot rival the first two contributions to the series, which detail Nin's relationship with her literary associates in Paris; and yet Volume VI brings to the reader a narrator who is more open and relaxed than before. "I have decided to retire as the major character of this diary.". . . The openness of the disclosure . . . is characteristic of the tone of the volume; the persona retires quietly in the background and the mood is at times relaxed. The narrator does not have to center the attention on herself, and when she speaks she seems to be candid and confident. . . . It might be said, in fact, that the diary itself now acquires the centrality and focus which the narrator is willing to abdicate. (p. 18)

[The *Diary*], in all its six volumes, details the movement of its narrator, from her first entrances into serious literary composition, through various successes and failures (of virtually every variety), until she finds the true voice that a readership in the United States wants to hear. The persona, created in many ways as a conventional literary heroine, increases in human qualities approximately midway through the narrative and in the final volume is most humanely realized and most fully human of all; narcissism and self-aggrandizement give way to a more balanced self-portrait, one that admits weaknesses along with strengths. As a character in this drama, the narrator becomes more and more unmasked; but we are never certain whether in the process the author also does or not, and we must not assume that the narrator is ever identical with Nin or an accurate representation of her, were such a representation possible.

The legendary *Diary* has, of course, become famous partly because—ironically as the result of the excellence of Nin's art—the narrator seems so "real": she develops; the complexities and nuances of her feelings are explored, and she

finally succeeds in her attempt to arrive at a point in her life where she is both accepted and accepting. But the protagonist of the *Diary* is a literary creation, and our awareness of this fact, far from detracting from the quality, value, and interest of the *Diary,* should serve only to enhance our appreciation of Nin's—the author's—humanism and her powers of articulation. (p. 19)

Duane Schneider, "Anaïs Nin in the Diary: The Creation and Development of a Persona," in MOSAIC: A Journal for the Study of Literature and Ideas *(copyright © 1978 by the University of Manitoba Press; acknowledgement of previous publication is herewith made), Vol. XI, No. 2 (Winter, 1978), pp. 9-19.*

J. S. ATHERTON

A maternal figure at times, [Nin] encouraged, for example, both Lawrence Durrell and Henry Miller; especially Miller, whom she supported financially for some time as well as encouraging his writing. Many other young writers were helped by her in various ways at various times. Although a wealthy woman by Parisian left-bank standards, she sometimes found herself committed to spending more than she had available. It was on such an occasion that the stories in *Delta of Venus* were written.

The request was made by a wealthy old man to Henry Miller for some stories which "cut out the poetry and concentrated on sex". Telling Anaïs Nin about this, Miller explained that writing such stories would be against his integrity and asked her to write them for him. What about her own integrity, she asked; but Miller did not appear to think that this mattered, so—as the money was urgently needed to pay the rents of her various pensioners—she did so. The style of the stories is so different from that of Nin's normal work that I suspect Miller to have taken a large share in the actual writing, but no one else has ever suggested anything of the kind. . . .

Although most of the stories [in *Delta of Venus*] are just frankly aimed at sexual titillation, there is occasionally a seasoning of dry humour evident. The first story contains an account of a beautifully made rubber woman, with each aperture serviceable, which some sailors found the perfect mistress but which gave them all syphilis. But even the unnamed person who paid for the stories in the first place only read one at a time at intervals; read continuously, as they must be by a reviewer, they become boring.

J. S. Atherton, "The Maternal Instinct," in The Times Literary Supplement *(© Times Newspapers Ltd. (London), 1978; reproduced from* The Times Literary Supplement *by permission), July 7, 1978, p. 756.*

WALLACE FOWLIE

"Linotte" is the name [Anaïs Nin] gives herself as she signs letters to her father, Joaquin Nin, the Spanish composer and pianist. It is an old-world term for "finch" or linnet, and traditionally in French it means "scatterbrain," a girl with foolish ideas. Often at the end of a passage, especially one full of conflicts, contradictions and impossible dreams, Anaïs characterizes herself in that way. If she is writing directly to her father, she habitually ends by apologizing for her ideas of a "linotte."

The diary is almost a continuous letter to her father. . . . The purpose in writing these daily episodes in the letters is to reconvert the distant father to his family, to urge him to rejoin them in New York, and to stress her own longing for him. . . .

This early diary anticipates the reconciliation later in France (told in Volume I of the "Diary"), and the passionate love she established at that time with her father. It will be obvious to most readers that this paternal relationship is the basis of Anaïs Nin's attitude toward men and toward love. . . .

Young Anaïs herself is fascinated by the role of the diary in her life, as she feels herself torn between two worlds: the one in which she lives day by day, and that same world as it is transmuted into her diary sentences. Already she is aware of what the act of writing means for her. This act she will call in the first volume of the "Diary" her "drug," and her dreams she will call her "real life.". . .

Her personal development is discussed in her relationship with her childhood diary as much as in her relationship with family and friends. The writing in the diary propels her into what later in her life she will call her inner truth, that truth she learns about herself and about others.

This diary will be a document useful to Anaïs Nin's ever-growing public of readers . . . eager to study her art as novelist as well as her art as diarist. The notebooks, as they accumulated one after the other, became a symbol of the girl's isolation and withdrawal as she moved out of psychic puberty into the initial stage of adulthood.

The psychoanalyst-critic will be struck by the doubts she expresses, more and more frequently, of her sexual attractiveness. She tends toward an identification with her mother, Rosa Culmell-Nin, whose energy, courage and constancy Anaïs celebrates uninterruptedly. Behind this celebration, and usually unexpressed, is the father's abandonment of her mother and the sexual implication of that act. The more purely literary critic will notice the absence of the roster of characters that we have seen in Volume I of the "Diary": Artaud, Dr. Allendy, Otto Rank, Henry Miller, June Miller. He will be impressed, however, by the large number of portraits, characters young and old, that fill so many of the pages of the childhood diary, and above all, the portrait of the girl Anaïs, omnipresent throughout as participant and observer.

> Wallace Fowlie, "The Girlhood of Anaïs Nin," in The New York Times Book Review (© 1978 by The New York Times Company; reprinted by permission), August 13, 1978, p. 11.

NANCY PEPPER

Anaïs Nin's diary served as her mirror, her confidant, the only place where she was truly herself and scrupulously honest about even unpleasant truths. For those who are fascinated by every word of this ultimate diarist, [*Linotte: The Early Diary of Anaïs Nin, 1914-1920*] will no doubt prove an invaluable addition to the adult works, but for those less enamored, it can make uncomfortable reading. Perhaps it should have been left a mirror to oblivion, for its pages read like an unwitting exposure of a young girl's infatuation with extremes of feeling and with her own self-image as a suffering "dreamer". . . .

The mature writer's control and power are rarely in evidence; here the emphasis is on the intensity of her feelings rather than on the intensity with which the reader experiences what she describes. . . .

It is interesting to compare the extreme subjectivity of this early diary with the relish for concrete detail apparent in the later ones but *Linotte* is worth reading more for its interest as an apprentice work than for its intrinsic value. (p. E6)

> Nancy Pepper, in Book World—The Washington Post (© The Washington Post), October 29, 1978.

CARLA WALDEMAR

By nature sensitive, introspective, and emotional, this intense and gifted young girl pours out [in *Linotte: The Early Diary of Anaïs Nin 1914-1920*] the manic-depressive roller-coastering of adolescence in her daily tryst with her one friend, her diary. Arriving in an unfamiliar country, abandoned by the father whose love she craves, she tosses her crystalline, childlike impressions into a whirlpool of blossoming adulthood. . . .

This amazingly precocious diary offers clearsighted evaluations of herself, already the analyst of dreams and feelings we encounter in her adult journals. . . .

It's also a portrait of the developing young writer. She justifies the attraction her journal has: it's not only "unbounded egotism," she remarks perceptively, but a strainer, serving her love of truth and "a way of acting as my own teacher.". . .

[The volume's] special charm lies in the heartfelt outpourings of the girl-to-woman experiences of this sensitive soul. On the threshold of adulthood, she bids a wry farewell to this, her best friend, ". . . it looks as though nothing 'thrilling' is going to happen. I shall nickname you simply the Preface to the wonderful contents of another volume." And it is!

> Carla Waldemar, "Nin's Preface to a Life's Work," in The Christian Science Monitor (reprinted by permission from The Christian Science Monitor; © 1978 by The Christian Science Publishing Society; all rights reserved), November 1, 1978, p. 17.

O

OATES, Joyce Carol   1938-

Oates is an American novelist, short story writer, poet, playwright, critic, and editor now living in Canada. She is an extremely prolific writer, contributing both fiction and nonfiction in books as well as popular and scholarly journals. Her short stories reveal the full range of her artistry, for in that genre Oates seems to be in the greatest control of her material. Her fictional world is violent and tragic, her characters, disturbed and unhappy, are often victims of their social milieu and emotional weaknesses. Oates was the recipient of the National Book Award in 1970 for *them* and has twice received the O. Henry award. (See also *CLC*, Vol. 1, 2, 3, 6, 9, and *Contemporary Authors*, Vols. 5-8, rev. ed.)

JOHN SIMON

I have been an early fancier of Joyce Carol Oates's fiction, which struck me as that always admirable thing: writing possessed of feminine sensitivity that in no way harps on such sensitivity but simply and hardheadedly puts it to work. And surrounds it with other good, solid virtues, neither feminine nor unfeminine, such as looking at the world steadily and long, and blinking only when absolutely necessary. (p. 284)

[It] is with mixed pleasure and apprehension that I watch Miss Oates wildly sowing her gifts in all directions: essays, reviews, poetry, plays, film criticism, and probably a few other genres that slipped by me on the pages of every known and several unknown magazines. It is so much the variousness as the sheer bulk of these outpourings that worries me: I respect a polymath but not a polygrapher. And I wonder whether this material, as uneven as a fever chart in quality, is the product of a steamily teaming brain, or of a bureau full of assorted literary productions that has dogged Miss Oates since college and has finally been unleashed on the world. (pp. 284-85)

[*Sunday Dinner*] is an attempt at an absurdist play, without, I am afraid, the grim lucidity that lurks at the core of good theater of the absurd. . . . The creepy Midwestern family that returns from a visit to Mother's grave and settles down to the usual gripes, bickerings and pontifications to be consumed with the Sunday dinner, is a bunch of tolerable Oatesian grotesques, with one foot in Babbittry, the other in Grant-Woodsy gothic. But when a possibly blind census taker, who is possibly not a census taker and possibly the

long-absconded Father, arrives, joins in the dinner, asks bizarre questions and obtains even queerer answers—not to mention confessions of sins as inscrutably symbolic as they are extravagantly purple, and the whole thing erupts into violence. . . . I tell you, I don't know what I'm telling you, or what I have been told.

Miss Oates provides some funny and well-written lines, but they prove merely that she knows about words, not necessarily about theater. (p. 285)

> *John Simon, "'Sunday Dinner'" (1970), in his* Uneasy Stages: A Chronicle of the New York Theater, 1963-1973 *(copyright © 1975 by John Simon; reprinted by permission of Random House, Inc.), Random House, 1976, pp. 284-85.*

SUE SIMPSON PARK

The title [of "How I Contemplated the World from the Detroit House of Correction and Began My Life over Again"], with its seventeen words, suggests a departure from the conventional practice of relatively short titles. The headnote for the story provides a further hint as to the experimental quality of what is to follow: "Notes for an essay for an English class at Baldwin Country Day School; poking around in debris; disgust and curiosity; a revelation of the meaning of life; a happy ending. . . ." A prefiguration of the contrapuntal nature of the story is evident in these preliminaries: on the one hand, the abstractions of contemplation, revelation, the meaning of life, beginning life over again; on the other, the tangibility of the Detroit House of Correction and an English class at Baldwin Country Day School. (pp. 213-14)

The "notes for an essay" are presented in twelve divisions marked with Roman numerals. At first glance, one surmises from the form that this is the work of a careful student, arranging material in an orderly fashion . . . for the purpose of organizing experience into a coherent system. Such an assumption, however, is erroneous, for the divisions do not constitute a topical outline; neither are they chronological. Instead, they are repetitive, disjointed, and dispersive—in other words, indicative of the state of mind of the sixteen-year-old protagonist, confused, questioning, attempting to make sense of the senseless, to impose order upon chaos. (p. 214)

Three divisions are labeled "Events"—the first, the seventh, and the twelfth. Hence the story begins, centers, and ends in recollected action; and action at least is relatively unequivocal, however ambiguous the motives behind the action. . . .

Events, Characters, and Places are the focal points of her outline, but there is no intrinsic order to the arrangement of points; it is random, apparently unpurposeful. What knits the scraps of information together into a movingly effective totality is not the protagonist's pathetic effort to establish meaningful continuity, but the artist's skillful interweaving of motifs and verbal echoes.

Basic to the ultimate unity of the story is a pattern of contrasts. The title and the headnote suggest this contrapuntal interplay; the story elaborates upon the suggestion. Bloomfield Hills is contrasted with inner-city Detroit, the girl's mother with the prostitute Clarita, the girl's father with the procurer-addict Simon. The differences are vast—and yet in each case the contrast is intensified by a curious and significant identity. But most important is the duality of the girl herself.

The pattern of contrasts is established by unlike settings. Bloomfield Hills is an exclusive suburb with "monumental houses." . . . Detroit, on the other hand, is a world that is "falling out the bottom." . . . (p. 215)

Bloomfield Hills and Detroit, different as they are, are really two sides of one coin, a coin of insecurity and potential violence.

The mother-Clarita contrast also fits this pattern. Whereas the mother is a "lady [with] hair like blown up gold . . . hair and fingers and body of inestimable grace," Clarita is a "woman" with "hair long and falling into strands, not recently washed." . . . The expensive clothing which the girl's mother wears—coat, boots, gloves, a fur hat—provides protection against the cold of the Michigan winter and, symbolically, against the encroachment of the ugly in life. Clarita, in contrast, wears jeans, a sweater, "unwashed underclothes, or no underclothes," . . . and there is no protection for this woman whose face is exhausted, over-wrought, from her experiences as a prostitute since the age of thirteen. (p. 217)

Despite their differences, however, the mother and the prostitute are akin. Both are puzzled by the girl. . . . Neither woman appreciates the younger girl's frustration; neither can answer the questions raised by her actions. And if Clarita is like the mother in her inability to understand the girl, the two are also similar in the inadequacy of what they do offer to her. (p. 218)

Of particular significance is the likelihood that the girl subconsciously considers both her mother and Clarita to be her rivals. . . . In this context the squirrel [killed by her mother's car] may be representative of the girl (note the rhyme) since the girl on more than one occasion mentions the *chattering* of her teeth and describes herself as wearing a close-fitted coat with a fur collar; thus she may see herself as being destroyed in the rivalry with the more powerful older woman. The girl, therefore, wants to hurt her mother. . . . Clarita, too, must be a kind of rival to the girl, though a less formidable one. When the prostitute takes the girl into her apartment above a restaurant, Simon is the older woman's lover, but in a short time Simon has become the girl's lover —whether *also* or *instead* is not made clear. The girl sup-

poses that it is Simon who turned her in to the police when he grew tired of her; she makes no conscious connection between her arrest and Clarita's saying "mournfully to me *Honey somebody is going to turn you out let me give you warning.*" . . . Perhaps there *is* no connection; perhaps, however, her never knowing for sure that her arrest was Simon's doing is suggestive of a refusal on her part to admit another defeat at the hands of a competitor. (pp. 218-19)

Simon is a drifter, a parasite who lives off women. He sleeps mornings and afternoons, coming alive at night and only then with the stimulation of a pill or a cigarette. . . . The betrayal [of Clarita] is instigated by Simon, but the girl shares in it; her ambivalent feelings of guilt and desire are indicative of her sense of having betrayed Clarita, the mother who saved her from the street, and her sense of having achieved some sort of victory in capturing Simon-father, however briefly, for herself.

So Simon is a surrogate father whose whole attention the girl has managed to attain. (pp. 219-20)

The contrapuntal pattern, omnipresent in the story, is ultimately traceable to the dichotomy within the girl herself. She has a desperate need for love, security, self-approbation. Her insecurity is revealed, for example, in the variety of substantives she uses to refer to herself. She never mentions her name. . . .

Moreover, she frequently insists that she makes her own decisions, and yet she knows she does not. . . . (p. 221)

Typical of nearly every division of the notes is an ambivalence, revealed partially through the device of interrogatives. Of herself she has little certain knowledge, only that which can be measured empirically—her age; her height. . . . But value judgments she cannot make. . . . (p. 222)

Pink is used to characterize the culture of Bloomfield Hills. . . . Pink, a color traditionally associated with an innocent baby girl, is also a tainted white and a diluted red, neither pure nor passionate; it is an appropriate color for the "innocently experienced" protagonist and her habitat.

The girl's association of herself and the squirrel, discussed above in another context, is an example of her use of animal imagery in descriptions of characters, suggestive of inability to perceive herself or anyone else as distinctly human. (pp. 222-23)

Religious imagery, too, colors the story, but without evidence of serious commitment on the girl's part. The title and the headnote suggest contemplation, revelation, and rebirth. . . . (p. 223)

The story has made clear that Sioux Drive has not in the past provided a sense of security and self-worth for the girl, and it seems unlikely that it will begin to do so now. The "beginning again" of the title, as well as the "happy ending" of the headnote, is really a return to a place that before had failed her miserably. . . . [For] the present, though, it offers at least a pretense of safety. Repeatedly the girl acknowledges her retreat into security, however tenuous it may prove. . . .

This incredibly concentrated story is developed in such a way that structure, imagery, motifs, verbal echoes work together to create for the reader the actual experience of the experiencing mind of the protagonist. (p. 224)

Sue Simpson Park, "A Study In Counterpoint: Joyce Carol Oates's 'How I Contemplated the World from the Detroit House of Correction and Began My Life Over Again'," in Modern Fiction Studies (© copyright 1976, by Purdue Research Foundation, West Lafayette, Indiana), Summer, 1976, pp. 213-24.

SANFORD PINSKER

Miss Oates' third novel—*Expensive People* (1968)—was a radical departure from the social milieu and gritty realities of her first books. By that I mean, the world of Richard Everett [the narrator] is as much a "fiction" as the fiction he self-consciously tries to write. The result is a parody of the reflexive mode, a book about the making of such books. It is also a Nabokovian romp in the art-and-craft of confessional narration. . . . As in all novels built upon the structural principle of Chinese boxes, the inter-locking frames are apparently endless. Richard Everett's highly personal reading of "The Molesters" (a story Miss Oates originally published in *The Quarterly Review of Literature*) reduces it to the level of biographical allegory; Miss Oates' comments about *Expensive People* are an exercise in a similar brand of impressionism. Both imply partial truths, but when "authors" multiply dizzyingly, readers quickly learn the virtues of skepticism. (p. 89)

Ironies generate from the considerable gaps between [Richard Everett's] narrative intention and its fictive result. Put another way: Richard's account of suburban malaise is an exercise in simultaneously calling tensions into existence and then declaring them inoperative. (p. 90)

Expensive People is more a study in comic nihilism, in suburban emptiness, than it is a seriously rendered psychodrama. . . . Imitation is, indeed, the sincerest form of flattery; parodic echoes—and particularly those which raise the zany to another power—are a very different matter. Like the Ambrose of John Barth's *Lost in the Funhouse*, Richard wears his writer's block on his sleeve. Classical models, earnest advice from how-to-do-it pulps like *Amateur Penman*, Franklinesque lists about what lies in store, all serve to take readers behind the memoir's "plot line" to the comic agonies of its creation.

Yet the gulf between fiction and Reality, between the illusion that is Art and the felt pain that is Life, has its darker, more serious, side. The mobility made possible by affluence becomes as suspect as the itch to exchange one version of suburban life for another. Moreover, Oates is not totally convinced that romantic fulfillments lie just over the next concrete horizon. If Thomas Wolfe could wax lyrical in attempting to prove that *You Can't Go Home Again*, Oates seems just as determined to suggest (albeit, playfully) that in contemporary America one can never *leave*. . . . (pp. 92-3)

[Illusion] and reality are so ineluctably intertwined, the world of *Expensive People* so reflexively absurd, that confusion threatens to emerge as the only norm possible. . . . The generalization spreads across Miss Oates' canon. *All* her children are cut from the same bolt of lava-like cloth; Richard Everett is simply more articulate than those who seethe in a befuddled silence. But, ironically enough, the compulsive attempts to tell his story (however representative it might be as archetype) are diminished by the painstaking—and darkly comic—attention to its own self-consciousness. The result is a fiction which "tells," rather

than *shows*, its intensity. Which is to say, a playful wit keeps poking through the fabric of Richard's confessional memoir. Genuine turmoil is seldom this calculated. (pp. 95-6)

Much of the literary humor in *Expensive People* consists of allusions wrinkled, almost unnoticed, through the novel's surface. . . . [The] "expensive people" share a passion for with-it intellectuality. Their children wrestle with admissions tests, IQ scores and the competitive, cut-throat style of the Johns Behemoth School; their parents sit through droning lectures. (p. 97)

[The] dream maketh villains of us all. Child-molesters (like child *murderers*) surround themselves with high-brow rhetoric and the freighting of twice-told ideas. Richard's existential act [his mother's murder] . . . brings matricide and his memoir into bold, symmetrical relief. . . . As Nadia's notebook knew all along:

> . . . the climax will be the death of X, but one must get past. The trouble is getting there . . . and getting past. As in any first-person narrative there can be a lot of freedom. . . .

Expensive People "got there" all right; getting *past*, however, would happen later, in novels which played Oatesian emotions closer to the non-reflexive bone. (pp. 102-03)

Sanford Pinsker, "Suburban Molesters: Joyce Carol Oates' 'Expensive People'," in The Midwest Quarterly (copyright, 1977, by The Midwest Quarterly, Kansas State College of Pittsburg), Autumn, 1977, pp. 89-103.

MARIE MITCHELL OLESEN URBANSKI

Fifteen-year-old Connie's acquiescence to Arnold Friend's threat-ridden seduction is an appropriate finale to Joyce Carol Oates's "Where Are You Going, Where Have You Been?" in a narrative which, upon careful analysis, suggests existential allegory. Many critics have classified Oates's work as realistic or naturalistic, whereas Samuel J. Pickering categorizes her short stories as subjective romanticism to a fault [see *CLC*, Vol. 6]. Most, however, agree she is writing in the tradition of Dreiser, Faulkner, and O'Connor, but few have acknowledged the allegorical nature of her work. Veiling the intent of "Where Are You Going . . ." in realistic detail, Oates sets up the framework of a religious allegory—the seduction of Eve—and with it renders a contemporary existential initiation theme—that of a young person coming to grips with externally determined fate. (p. 200)

From the outset of the narrative, members of Connie's family recognize their powerlessness and thus their difference from her. Her mother and sister are not attractive, so they do not really count; and her father, who spends most of his time at work, is weak. . . . Thus, in refusing to attend a family picnic, Connie is rejecting not only her family's company, but the settled order of their existence—in which recognition of "excluded alternatives" is tantamount to acceptance of their lives.

The popular music which permeates "Where Are You Going . . ." is at the same time the narrative's *zeitgeist* and *leitmotiv*, serving as the former in order to maintain plausible realism, and the latter to establish allegorical significance. The recurring music then, while ostensibly innocuous realistic detail, is in fact, the vehicle of Connie's seduction and because of its intangibility, not immediately recognizable as such. Attesting to the significance of the *zeitgeist* in this narrative, "Where Are You Going . . ." is dedicated to Bob Dylan, who contributed to making music almost religious in dimension among the youth. It is music—instead of an apple—which lures Connie, quickens her heartbeat; and popular lyrics which constitute Friend's conversation and cadence—his promises, threats, and the careless confidence with which he seduces her. (pp. 200-01)

Oates employs musical metaphor in her description of Friend. "He spoke in a simple lilting voice, exactly as if he were reciting the words to a song." . . . Intrinsic to Friend's function is the fact that he himself is a record. While waiting for Connie to accept his ride offer, "he began to mark time with the music from Ellie's radio." . . . Even their union is presaged by the sexually pointed observation of Connie listening "to the music from her radio and the boy's blend together." . . .

The images which overtly suggest religious allegory while more subtly supporting the existential theme, are interspersed throughout the work. When Connie and her girl friend first enter the local "hang-out" where the girls and boys meet, they feel "as if they were entering a sacred building" where background music seems like that of a "church service." . . . The day of the cook-out, which is significant both because it is the day of her defiance of her parents and the day of her capitulation to Friend, is a Sunday. (p. 201)

Friend is a strange syncretism of O'Connor's Bible-pedaling Manley Pointer in manner, and Satan in appearance. When Connie first observes Friend, she notices his "shaggy black hair," his "jalopy painted gold," and his broad grin. As the narrative progresses, his features appear more ominous, his hair like a wig, his slitted eyes "like chips of broken glass" with "thick black tarlike" lashes when not covered by mirrored, but masking sunglasses; and he looks older. Like Milton's Satan "crested aloft and Carbuncle his Eyes with burnished Neck of verdant Gold, erect," Friend posited atop his golden jalopy, has a muscular neck which suggests the reptilian, as does the fact that he "slid" rather than stepped out of the car. His feet resemble the devil's cloven hooves: "One of his boots was at a strange angle, as if his foot wasn't in it." . . . (pp. 201-02)

Friend's mesmeric influence on Connie further supports my contention that he represents a superhuman force. "Don't you know who I am?" . . . he asks in an eery fashion, as if she had encountered him before, as one does evil. She is unable to make a telephone call for help because he is watching her; she bumps against a piece of furniture in a familiar room; and when he commands her to do what would otherwise seem an irrational act, to place her hand on her heart to understand its flaccidity, she readily obeys. His directives culminate when he convinces her, "What else is there for a girl like you but to be sweet and pretty and give in." . . .

The recurring use of a twentieth-century symbol of irony—the false smile—further veils the existential meaning in realistic narrative. Over the student drive-in hangs a "revolving figure of a grinning boy holding a hamburger aloft." . . . And Friend intersperses smiles with threats." . . .

In the end, Oates makes it clear that Connie, in capitulating

to Friend, is not simply surrendering her virginal innocence, but bowing to absolute forces which her youthful coquetry cannot direct—absolute forces over which she has no control. At this point she thinks for the first time in her life that her heart "was nothing that was hers . . . but just a pounding, living thing inside this body that wasn't really hers either." . . .

In the seduction which Friend engineers, Connie is merely the personification of the female he wishes to dominate, to be taller than, to despoil. The phrases he delivers from his musical repertoire are not even tailored to Connie: "'My sweet little blue-eyed girl' he said in a half-sung sigh that had nothing to do with her brown eyes." . . . (p. 202)

In the presentation of this complex narrative, the major characters represent two distinct personifications in the dual levels of the allegory. It is apparent that Friend represents the devil who tempts the chaste yet morally vacuous girl-victim. Yet upon closer analysis, it appears that Connie takes the active part as *Everyman* experiencing the inevitable realization of her insignificance and powerlessness while Friend, who personifies the Erinyes, is merely the catalyst.

Although Oates uses the trappings of a realist to craft plausible characters—a dreamy teenaged girl, a hypnotic Manson-like man—and renders a facsimile of awkward adolescent behavior and speech, with contemporary youth's devotion to popular music as a convincing *zeitgeist*, this must not obscure her design. She presents an allegory which applies existential initiation rites to the Biblical seduction myth to represent *Everyman's* transition from the illusion of free will to the realization of externally determined fate. (pp. 202-03)

> *Marie Mitchell Olesen Urbanski, "Existential Allegory: Joyce Carol Oates 'Where Are You Going, Where Have You Been?'" in* Studies in Short Fiction *(copyright 1978 by Newberry College), Spring, 1978, pp. 200-03.*

JEREMY TREGLOWN

The solemn domestic absorption of many of Joyce Carol Oates's stories seems narcissistic, . . . though this prolific and highly acclaimed author often writes well and, of course, her concerns are . . . obviously up-to-date: the imposition and effects of sex-roles, especially in marriage; the plight of the educated, jobless wife; adultry-drift; and so on. Half of the 15 stories in [*Crossing the Border*] form a fragmented novel about a couple who have left the States for Canada, so that Evan, a research scientist, can escape doing morally repugnant work in 'defence biology'. His wife Renée is increasingly restless, and her characteristically frantic moves towards and away from an affair with a horrifically self-satisfied married poet are closely described.

Several of the stories are effectively bizarre—one about a mental defective who haunts Renée, for example (though I couldn't help thinking how much more Ian McEwan, say, would have made of this). . . . To often, though, the writing is slackly uncommunicative. Take, for example, this corny piece of literary self-reference of Renée's:

> Our lives are narrative; they are experienced
> in the flesh . . . but they are recollected as
> poems, lyrics, condensed, illuminated by a
> few precise images. It would be dramatic of

me to say that our relationship with Blaine ended at that moment . . .

Well, does she *mean* narratives, or does she mean lyrics? Or does she—as 'dramatic' suggests—mean plays? She couldn't care less, of course: the metaphors are so tired that there's nothing to choose between them. And this tendency to let a group of random shots do service for one on target is symptomatic. (p. 27)

Jeremy Treglown, in New Statesman *(© 1978 the Statesman & Nation Publishing Co. Ltd.), July 7, 1978.*

HAROLD BEAVER

[In *Crossing the Border*] Joyce Carol Oates has produced another fine set of tales—witty, wily and variegated. The theme yet again is one of "marriages and infidelities"; the scene that of her home town (Windsor, Ontario) on the United States-Canada Border. . . . At this political junction (between Windsor and Detroit, Lake Erie and Lake Huron) she plots a series of emotional junctures that also evoke "natural borders". At all such borders travellers, she insists, must confront the abrupt and unexpected challenge of alien "customs".

The stories are linked not only by theme and setting, though, but by the marital rift of an American couple. . . . The woof of their commonplace marital disaffection, adultery and disillusion, threading in and out of alternate stories, binds and packages the volume. . . .

For her central object of concern is the domestic male within marriage. Can the male of the species survive marriage? Can his boyish, exuberant, insecure and romantic self harden sufficiently to bolster and prop the marriage or must it inevitably shatter and dissipate itself in endless impotent and shallow flirtations? Must the female always be so triumphantly and passionately unhappy? Must the men, in dreary self-preservation, always end by begging for forgiveness and support from a woman's strength? In middle age must they turn so scathingly bitter? Are they ever truly capable of loving anyone? . . .

It is a terrible indictment. The heroic task, then, is to preserve the frail compact of marriage. The borders of that compact are defined by several outsiders—an importunate homosexual, a friendly simpleton, a potential lover—who intrude on the married nest. The need is to obviate the danger, to deflect it, to decamp if necessary, to isolate the marriage itself. "All marriages", the lover's voice concludes (amid a buzz of conflicting ironies), are "workable in ways that can't be described". But should the marriage fail, it is the males, exiled from domesticity, who are lost in a limbo: of common rooms, if lucky; if not so lucky, in the stale air of post offices with ex-lawyers, ex-graduates, ex-executives, ex-citizens (black and white), sorting out "acres of mail, mountains of mail, from one shadow to another", in that final haven of peace and communal silence.

Harold Beaver, "Heroes of Marriage," in The Times Literary Supplement *(© Times Newspapers Ltd. (London) 1978; reproduced from* The Times Literary Supplement *by permission), July 14, 1978, p. 789.*

VICTORIA GLENDINNING

["*Son of the Morning*"] is a hugely ambitious novel. Clearly well-researched, it could serve as a basis for the sociological study of the theory and practice of Pentecostal religion. It explores the phenomenon of "revelation" and mystical experience with an extraordinary imaginative thrust. It poses, without answering, questions about the nature of Christ, the church as an institution, and whether there is God or only the desire for God, leading to madness; and whether He is a God of Salvation or a vast metaphysical appetite for souls, a destroyer. . . .

[The] author enters into the heightened feelings and experiences of nearly every character in the large cast—except God's. But the girl's memories of the rape, Nathan's relationship with God, his grandmother's supernatural adoration of him as a child, his grandfather's desperate stoicism, the hysterical fervor of the prayer meetings, the physical hardware of everyone's ordinary life, are all felt and described with a sustained virtuosity. The language, fittingly enough, is biblical, apocalyptic, intense. For me the book is a little too long: Compression is not high on the author's list of priorities.

The sharp edge of irony, however, tempers the intensity when the venality or hypocrisy of the "normally" religious is revealed, without comment. . . .

Echoing Nathan's hunger for God, and God's for him, there is throughout the novel a harping on the huge, crude hungriness of nature, the vicious circle of hunter and hunted. . . .

There is a hungriness in the writing of Joyce Carol Oates, too: an appetite for huge themes and violent emotions, in seeming tension with her analytical, academic side. It makes for great vitality; it also breeds a slight resistance in the reader, as does her extraordinary fluency and productivity. Can so regular a flow of novels, stories, poetry and criticism all be in the first class? Of course they can. Costiveness is not necessarily a literary virtue. The problem for the contemporary reader, however, is that it is hard to see the trees for the forest. We cannot know whether it is her whole oeuvre that will seem the sum of her achievement in the eyes of our grandchildren, or whether one novel, say, will survive as a classic, a Great American Novel, and the rest be unread except by thesis writers. It doesn't matter; "Son of the Morning" is a rich dish that will be devoured by the hungry faithful.

Victoria Glendinning, "In Touch with God," in The New York Times Book Review *(© 1978 by The New York Times Company; reprinted by permission), August 13, 1978, p. 10.*

ROBERT PHILLIPS

Ms. Oates's [*Night Side*] is . . . more than a grab-bag. All 18 tales are concerned with borderline reality, what the author has called "that mysterious realm of the paranormal." [It] differs considerably from her early novels in that almost all the violence is mental rather than actual. . . . [These] are interior tales—stories of individuals haunted by their own uneasinesses and anxieties. What is striking is how Ms. Oates manages to reconstruct the dreams and nightmares which afflict us all. . . . (p. 601)

Robert Phillips, in Commonweal *(copyright © 1978 Commonweal Publishing Co., Inc.; reprinted by permission of Commonweal Publishing Co., Inc.), September 15, 1978.*

O'BRIEN, Darcy 1939-

O'Brien is an American critic and novelist. *A Way of Life, Like Any Other* **is his first novel. (See also** *Contemporary Authors,* **Vols. 21-24, rev. ed.)**

ANTHONY THWAITE

'A Way of Life, Like Any Other' is broadly in the line of 'The Catcher in the Rye': American teenager (in the 1950s here) negotiating parents, other adults, girls, with moods shifting from wonder to indifference, from hot innocence to blasé cynicism. Like Salinger, Darcy O'Brien does this with a humour which doesn't preclude seriousness; unlike Salinger, he stands back and looks at the boy from an unjudging but amused distance.

The success of the book, though, lies not so much in the boy, Salty, but in the portrayal of his parents: father a pathetic remnant of a once-famous Hollywood cowboy star, mother a self-dramatising hysteric, who would be a monster if it weren't for her extravagant ludicrousness.

Mr O'Brien's language is elegantly facetious, distancing through dandifying. Occasionally the references passed me by. . . . But this is a confident, entertaining, funny first novel, with a stylishness that could lead to something more. (p. 29)

> *Anthony Thwaite, in* The London Observer *(reprinted by permission of The Observer Limited), August 21, 1977.*

JOHN LAHR

Darcy O'Brien's first novel [*A Way of Life, Like Any Other*] . . . is a story of growing up in Hollywood among the famous and the faded. As his title implies, Mr O'Brien treats the fools and the fatuity of Hollywood in a matter of fact, throwaway manner. The result is to turn a potential feast into a famine. . . .

Each chapter is a set-piece of self-deception played out against legendary locales which Mr O'Brien conspicuously refrains from describing.

Only the daffy affluence of Beverly Hills comes alive. . . .

The narrator is supposed to grow up in the course of the novel which ends with him at eighteen about to go to college. But the narrative tone is uneven, breaking the fictional convention by jumping ahead of the character in sophistication and losing the dramatic irony. The twelve-year-old narrator, observing his mother's face puffed from drink, describes it as "reticulated with frantic capillaries". Still, the book is an honourable enough first effort. . . .

> *John Lahr, "High Living," in* The Times Literary Supplement *(© Times Newspapers Ltd. (London) 1977; reproduced from The Times Literary Supplement by permission), October 21, 1977, p. 1249.*

["A Way of Life, Like Any Other" is an] eccentric, cynical, and sometimes exceedingly funny first novel about the coming of age of the son of two aging, divorced Hollywood has-beens. . . . The story . . . conveys a great deal of feeling beneath a deceptively deadpan surface. The book has its oddities—such as a bewildering scene in which the boy and his father pay a long afternoon visit to the director John Ford, and a tendency to snatch the reader away from the characters just when they seem most interesting—but it is

certainly the most literate "Hollywood novel" to have appeared in years. (p. 110)

> The New Yorker *(© 1978 by The New Yorker Magazine, Inc.), February 6, 1978.*

NORA JOHNSON

["A Way of Life, Like Any Other"] probably isn't any worse than anywhere else, though the scenery along the way is more surrealistic. . . .

Mr. O'Brien can be very funny, deft and fast and Perelman-like. . . . The first half of the book is farcical, but the tone changes somewhat unsettlingly to something more serious when Salty [the narrator] goes to live with his father. The primal tale of the son pulling away from the mother to identify with the father is not comedy's arena, and the old fraud of a father is drawn with sympathy. . . .

But when mother turns up again to start another new life, Salty insults her . . . ; and when a boiling plum pudding explodes in her face . . . one gets the feeling that Mr. O'Brien blew it up on purpose. Though this mother is right out of Arthur Kopit or Bruce Jay Friedman, previously we have been made to laugh at her awfulness, her daffy Auntie Mame chatter; now Mr. O'Brien's anger boils over where it doesn't belong. . . .

Atmosphere is evoked by the appearance of some real personalities—Frank Sinatra and John Ford (that obligatory tenant of film folklore)—and both are uncharacteristically pleasant. . . . In spite of a certain lack of dramatic pull, "A Way of Life, Like Any Other" is a funny and interesting book.

> *Nora Johnson, "Live from Hollywood," in* The New York Times Book Review *(© 1978 by The New York Times Company; reprinted by permission), April 9, 1978, p. 14.*

*　　*　　*

O'CASEY, Sean 1880-1964

O'Casey, an Irish dramatist and essayist, began his career writing ballads and short fiction. The political struggles of modern Ireland are central to his early work, which is essentially naturalistic in character. His later works blend elements of naturalism with expressionism and are concerned with the more universal problem of individuality in an age of conformity. O'Casey used dialect in his plays to add verisimilitude to setting and character and to establish mood. (See also *CLC,* **Vols. 1, 5, 9.)**

SAMUEL BECKETT

This is the interest of *Windfalls*—that by its juxtaposition of what is distinguished and what is not, the essential O'Casey and the incidental, it facilitates a definition of the former. (p. 167)

Mr. O'Casey is a master of knockabout in this very serious and honourable sense—that he discerns the principle of disintegration in even the most complacent solidities, and activates it to their explosion. This is the energy of his theatre, the triumph of the principle of knockabout in situation, in all its elements and on all its planes, from the furniture to the higher centres. . . . This impulse of material to escape and be consummate in its own knockabout is admirably expressed in the two "sketches" that conclude this volume, and especially in "The End of the Beginning," where the entire set comes to pieces and the chief character, in a final spasm of dislocation, leaves the scene by the chimney.

Beside this the poems are like the model palace of a dynamiter's lesiure moments. "Walk with Eros," through the seasons complete with accredited poetic phenomena and emotions to match, is the *nec plus ultra* of inertia, a Walt Disney inspected shot after shot on the celluloid. The influences of nature are great, but they do not enable the disruptive intelligence, exacting the tumult from unity, to invert its function. A man's mind is not a claw-hammer.

The short stories have more jizz, notably (characteristically) that on the dissolution of Mollser, the consumptive girl who had such a good curtain in *The Plough and the Stars*. Mr. O'Casey's admirers will give him the credit of allegorical intention in "I Wanna Woman."

But the main business, when at last it is reached, obliterates these preliminaries. And no reader so gentle but must be exalted to forgiveness, even of the prose poems in "Second Fall," by the passage in "The End of the Beginning," presenting Messrs. Darry Berrill and Barry Derrill supine on the stage, "expediting matters" in an agony of calisthenics, surrounded by the doomed furniture. (pp. 167-68)

> Samuel Beckett, "The Essential and the Incidental" (reprinted by permission of Samuel Beckett), in The Bookman, Vol. LXXXVI, 1934 (and reprinted in Sean O'Casey: A Collection of Critical Essays, edited by Thomas Kilroy, Prentice-Hall, Inc., 1975, pp. 167-68).

G. WILSON KNIGHT

In most of the plays written after *Within the Gates* we are aware of a certain weakening. The reiterated attacks on the Irish priesthood lack balance; attempts to build youthful sexuality into a saving force pall; and the author's proclaimed communism is never, not even in *The Star Turns Red* where the communist leader Red Jim is little more than a figure of accepted morality, loaded with human fire. O'Casey is a visionary; his various conflicts are always part of some patterned whole suffused with melody and colour; but technical patterning is not enough and it is far from easy to establish any more exact relation of contemporary energies and ideologies to the harmony. Neither communism nor sex-love can bridge the gap. But he fights on, always striving for solutions in human and dramatic terms; striving to relate man to his vision. (p. 133)

[In *The Drums of Father Ned* we] find the usual repudiation of spoil-sport old fogeys and a restrictive Irish priest, Father Fillifogue, set against young people standing for youth, love and freedom. (p. 134)

[There are] two dominating symbolic persons. One is "Father Ned," who does not appear but is continually referred to as their leader and authority by those who stand for advance.... Father Ned is conceived, on the analogy of an Irish parish priest, as an ultimate local authority. Dramatically he exists through oblique reference and the sound of his drums as a summoning, potent and beneficent deity. In close association is the mysterious Echo, heard from time to time, recalling Webster's echo in *The Duchess of Malfi*.

Our second personification is Angus the Young, depicted emblematically as a symbol of youth and enlightenment.... [In] Greek terms we may regard him as a composite of Eros and Apollo. (pp. 134-35)

The symbolic persons here house rich meanings. Father Ned constitutes an obvious admission that the aim of O'Casey's dramatic world cannot be defined in social terms.

Nor, despite his advanced counsels, can we call Father Ned unorthodox. The title he goes by is Catholic or Anglo-Catholic and his authority is recognised just as an Irish community today recognises the authority of its local priest. O'Casey's attacks have always been against particular examples of the priesthood falsifying, as he sees it, their great office, not against Christianity itself nor against the Church. (pp. 135-36)

That Father Ned does not appear constitutes an admission that he cannot as yet be defined in visual terms, and for those we must turn to our second symbolic person, Angus the Young.

Angus might at first be supposed to add little to O'Casey's prepossession with youthful life-joy, but he is far more than a symbol of this alone.... The sexual problem is not solved, and still less does it solve *us*, by showing two young people in love. The emblematical Angus, however, does not incur such criticisms. He is the Platonic Eros, with all its multi-directional potentialities; he is also Apollo, god of art, with his harp; and a bird, for aspiration to higher spheres. He includes O'Casey's poet-dreamers as well as his youthful lovers. What the emblem asserts is what O'Casey has always been meaning: that is, that within the *essence* of youth-beauty there is a pointer of appalling importance. It is the inward and universal essence that is being honoured, independent of particular forms; and since it has this especial independence, this essence must be posited as an external myth-person in his own right. (p. 136)

And if we know this, we shall know too that Eros may encompass the whole of life. Angus' Bird has the colours of the various *aspirations* handled in O'Casey's dramas: black for the priesthood; red for Communism; green for Eire; gold, perhaps for Ulster, but for more too, since gold is O'Casey's highest colour. Elsewhere in the play colours are used purposefully, though without any exact consistency, and this purpose, and it is a purpose driven home by speech on speech, is generously inclusive, with the will to a harmony of all the forces contained.

And yet why do we need two symbolic persons? Because, as the central opposition of *Within the Gates* showed, there are still two positive rival powers in our western culture: Christ and Eros, Hebraic and Hellenic. Until we recognise and establish their identity, both are needed. (p. 137)

> G. Wilson Knight, "Ever a Fighter: 'The Drums of Father Ned'," in his The Christian Renaissance (reprinted by permission of Curtis Brown Ltd., London acting on behalf of the author), Methuen Co. Ltd., 1962 (and reprinted in Sean O'Casey: A Collection of Critical Essays, edited by Thomas Kilroy, Prentice-Hall, Inc., 1975, pp. 133-37).

JOAN TEMPLETON

Though [O'Casey] is the only major British dramatist to have used Expressionism to any extent throughout his work, and though it is often mentioned that he was influenced by the German movement, he has been generally treated as an "experimenter." It is the thesis of this study that the techniques of Expressionist Drama established by

Strindberg and the German writers who followed him are found throughout O'Casey's plays, and more importantly, that his early attempts at Expressionism became a kind of proving ground for his last plays. One finds the techniques of Expressionism in every full-length play from *The Plough and the Stars* in 1926 to *The Drums of Father Ned* in 1958, and they figure significantly in the success of the late comedies. (p. 47)

In contrast to *Journey's End*, which he considered a "piece of false effrontery" both in sentiment and in form, he would go "into the heart of war" [with *The Silver Tassie*]. It is the attempt to create the total effect of an experience, to dramatize the "essence" of a subject, which marks O'Casey's intent here as thoroughly Expressionist. (p. 48)

When O'Casey decided to fling a stone at patriotic militarism in *The Silver Tassie*, he turned directly to the methods of Ernst Toller and Strindberg, two playwrights he especially admired, and wrote a thoroughly Expressionist second act. It is this act which carries the weight of the play's theme, and in O'Casey's exposure of the "heart of war." Act II uses Strindberg's dream structure which became in the plays of Toller, Georg Kaiser, and scores of other writers one of Expressionism's basic departures from realistic theater.... The dream structure was a method by which Toller could present his view of modern society as confused, frightening, and warped.

It served O'Casey in precisely the same way. The curtain rises [in *The Silver Tassie*] on a terrifying vista. The setting is a grotesque blending of the symbols of war and religion: a ruined monastery in the war zone. "Lean, dead hands are protruding" from the rubble of houses beyond the monastery walls.... [The scene intones] a Biblical passage of destruction. (p. 49)

The characters who inhabit this place of death are caricatures in the manner of Strindberg and Frank Wedekind; they do not represent a "type" of person, but an attitude, or a way of looking at the world. The Visitor, the most distorted of these, is a ludicrous representation of militant patriotism.... The soldiers themselves constitute a kind of "group" caricature. (pp. 49-50)

Act II of *The Silver Tassie* qualifies as thoroughly Expressionist because it possesses the dream structure, a deliberately distorted setting, exaggerated caricatures, and at its close, highly symbolic stage action resembling pantomime and usually referred to by the term "stylized." It also has the special qualities of freneticism and grotesqueness found in many of the German plays. The presence of a skeletal figure and the use of many stage properties suggesting death are frequently found in German Expressionism at the height of the movement when the "graveyard scene" became stock. Act II is an Expressionist theme statement: man may cling to the belief that he worships a Christian God, but the real object of his worship is the power of wrath and destruction.

O'Casey's next play, *Within the Gates*, subtitled "A Morality In Four Scenes," bears many resemblances to the "station drama," a favorite form of German Expressionist Drama, in which, through a sequence of "stationen" or stages, the protagonist becomes progressively enlightened. The model for the German plays was Strindberg's *To Damascus*, but this kind of plot structure, of course, is basically that of the morality play and *Faust*, both of which influenced Strindberg. (pp. 50-1)

O'Casey's morality play [however] reverses the themes of the traditional ones, and contains the message that he was to return to over and over again in later plays: merriment and joy are the primary virtues in a world that has denounced them too long.

The Expressionist set is a symbolic garden with giant, formalized flowers. The events which take place in the microcosmic garden world advocate an ironic reversal of Christian myth; man must reject the notion of his "fall" and transform himself into a joyful creature who can delight in his physical nature. *Within the Gates*, like many of the German station dramas, maintains that to find the right way is to undergo a transformation which violates the existing codes of morality.

Within the Gates possesses interesting resemblances to Strindberg's station drama *A Dream Play*. The device of the "Dreamer" is very close to that in Strindberg's play, in which the "Officer," the "Lawyer," and the "Poet" are all meant to be aspects of one "Dreamer."... In *Within the Gates* it is the Dreamer's view of life that the Young Woman accepts before she dies. Like the Poet-Dreamer of *A Dream Play*, the Dreamer in *Within the Gates* is the character who is used to give the author's derogatory pronouncements on the representatives of the established order. And in both plays, the Dreamer characters give similar answers to young women protagonists as they die.

O'Casey next turned directly to the problems of the proletariat with *The Star Turns Red*, a realistic play with isolated Expressionist techniques used to stress particular events and to emphasize some features of the setting. (pp. 51-2)

O'Casey's desire to present in *The Star Turns Red* the real nature of two opposed ideologies [fascism and communism] led him to use the kind of caricature of the Visitor in *The Silver Tassie*. Yet at the same time, the characters are supposed to be particular people with proper names and personal traits. When the fascist Kian, the communist Jack, and the workers' leader Jim begin to speak like pamphlets and chant slogans, O'Casey has deliberately suspended their identity as people in order to use them as Expressionist ideological symbols. The result is a strange and conflicting blend of two dramatic styles. One has to make a distinction between this type of character and those of a playwright like Wedekind, who employed more skillfully the same method. Wedekind's characters are given personal traits, but these traits are distorted in a way that causes us to accept the characters at the outset as representatives of an attitude or an idea. But O'Casey's use of exaggeration is sudden. We are not prepared for the difference between the symbolic function and the previous three-dimensional personality of a normal human being.

As though he had sensed that his experiment in *The Star Turns Red* was a failure, in *Red Roses For Me* O'Casey returned to the structure of *The Silver Tassie*. The Expressionist Act II is a dream sequence which dramatizes the goals of the protagonist Ayamonn and his fellow workers. (pp. 52-3)

Like Act II of *The Silver Tassie*, Act III of *Red Roses For Me* is the thematic center of the play. It is O'Casey's dream of obliterating the gulf between rich and poor in the modern world. The crescendo to transformation through the use of lighting and lyric dialogue immediately recalls scenes in Toller's *Masse Mensch (Masses and Man)* and *Die Wandlung (The Transformation)*. It is interesting that not only are the same techniques employed, but exactly the same hopes are expressed through them. Like Toller, O'Casey hoped desperately for a workers' revolution to free his country from the stranglehold of oppressing institutions. (pp. 53-4)

The plays which I have considered so far demonstrate a basic attitude toward the techniques of Expressionism which can only be labeled "self-conscious." In *Within the Gates*, O'Casey deliberately constructed a modern "morality play" in which he used the structure of the station drama. In *The Star Turns Red*, he used Expressionism to place particular emphasis upon a character's speech or upon a symbolic event, basically the same method, though enlarged, of *The Plough and the Stars*. In both *The Silver Tassie* and *Red Roses For Me*, he included Expressionist acts which are sharply divided from the realistic ones. Although he had used Expressionism successfully in *The Silver Tassie* and *Red Roses For Me*, his use of the new methods demonstrates that for the most part he regarded them as useful largely when they are isolated from a traditional structure. When O'Casey abandoned the separate use of two different styles and merged the techniques of Expressionism with those of his old forte, comedy, he succeeded in creating a unified structure and a sustained atmosphere.

In *Purple Dust* we find the beginnings of this structure. O'Casey is moving toward the creation of a particular kind of comic world in which all notions of realistic "probability" are suspended.... [Unlike] the offstage figure of *The Plough and the Stars*, the speaker [in *Purple Dust*] joins the "real" characters of the play. He is not a shadowy silhouette, but he is explicitly described.... The contrast points to O'Casey's changed attitude toward dramatic structure. No longer is he isolating his Expressionist character from the action of the others; here, the figure is actually an agent of the action in his role as revenging spirit of the flood.... The Figure of *Purple Dust* makes only one speech, and then disappears, but O'Casey's blending of styles here anticipates the much fuller use in later comedies.

Oak Leaves and Lavender looks forward more clearly than *Purple Dust* to the method of O'Casey's last three plays. Here, for the first time, O'Casey relies heavily on blending the methods of Expressionism with other forms. The play begins with a "prelude of the shadows," in which figures out of England's past dance a minuet and lament the passing of the glories of old England. The voice of a lavender seller is heard offstage as the dancers exit.... The central idea of the play is that England's aristocratic past must fade before the coming of a new kind of community of men. Dame Hatherleigh [the protagonist] joins the dancers because she is the last representative of the old order.... O'Casey merges the present representative of the past and the past itself through the merging of the non-realistic and realistic characters.

The result is that Dame Hatherleigh and the dancers lose their identity in time, and become representative of an attitude. *Oak Leaves and Lavender* is always referred to as a "fantasy," but O'Casey's method here is purely Expressionist. It is the method of *The Ghost Sonata*, where Strindberg has characters out of Hummel's "past" join those in his "present"; it is the deliberate fusion of the "dream world" with the "real world" that one finds in *To Damascus, A Dream Play, Masses and Man, The Transformation*, and Kaiser's *Gas*. (pp. 54-5)

Oak Leaves and Lavender is the most extreme example of O'Casey's method of emphasizing theme through set design.... Just before the dancers re-enter at the end of the play [for example], the room comes alive, and the old manor house is now a factory, producing materials to win the war. The manor house's change from oak to steel must occur, for the past is lovely, but it is useless in the war against fascism. Metaphor and idea have become dramatized through stage properties, and the mechanization of the manor house is an Expressionist dramatization of the play's message: England must transform itself into a useful social order for modern man.

O'Casey's use of Expressionism in *Oak Leaves and Lavender* points both backward and forward in the O'Casey canon. The prologue and epilogue of the dancers form a kind of "frame story" that is structurally, though not thematically, divided from the play proper. Yet the merging of Dame Hatherleigh's world with that of the dancers, and the use of the Expressionist set design throughout the play show that O'Casey was attempting here to arrive at an integrated use of the techniques of Expressionism with other methods. *Oak Leaves and Lavender* is thus a transitional play; it displays an indication of the earlier plays' demarcation between Expressionism and Realism, and yet it strongly anticipates O'Casey's final synthesis of method.

The play which marks this achievement is the brilliant *Cock-A-Doodle Dandy*. The use of various modes of comedy—music-hall techniques, satire, farce—is reminiscent of *Purple Dust*. But in *Cock-A-Doodle Dandy* O'Casey has enveloped the whole play in an atmosphere so fantastic that anything is probable. No longer do the techniques of Expressionism seem in any way separate from a realistic primary structure, but rather they are part of the structure from the beginning. (pp. 56-7)

[The presiding spirit] is the Cock, a fabulous representation of a vast *joie de vivre*. Before anyone else appears, the creature enters to dance round the garden, immediately establishing a non-realistic structure. (p. 57)

To dramatize the forces which are responsible for Marthraun and Mahan's suspicious natures, O'Casey uses two fully Expressionist caricatures, Shanaar and Father Domineer.... Shanaar is the embodiment of the view that sees evil in everything. He is a grotesque caricature of the religious dirty mind. (pp. 57-8)

It has been argued that Father Domineer is "too much of a straight 'villain' to be an entirely satisfactory symbol," and that it would have been more appropriate to have him a more comic villain like Shanaar.... To make him more amusing and less a raving representative of horrifying principles would be to lessen his impact. And in the fantastic atmosphere of the play, his character cannot be condemned on the grounds that while the "nonhuman Cock is credible as a mythic creature ... the inhuman priest is too obvious a sign-post to be convincing either as a symbol or a man." It is not the function of an Expressionist caricature to be a man; the problem lies in accepting the character as purely the representative of an attitude. *Cock-A-Doodle Dandy* is a parable in fancy dress. It cannot be judged on the basis of "obvious" versus "believable" characters because it is simply not of the realistic theater.

One reason for the success of *Cock-A-Doodle Dandy* is its integration of form. By wrapping the play in the sustained atmosphere of a super-realistic world, O'Casey is able to use fantastic devices and exaggerated characters without restraint. The merging of the "real world" and the "symbolic world" that we find at the end of *Purple Dust* and *Oak Leaves and Lavender* exists throughout *Cock-A-Doodle Dandy*. . . . It is essentially the total repudiation of the fourth wall and the presentation of an Expressionist version of reality, a heightened and exaggerated vision which can show the "thing behind the thing" rather than merely the thing itself.

In his next play, *The Bishop's Bonfire*, O'Casey again attempted fantastic comedy with a serious message, but the attempt is not wholly successful. (pp. 58-9)

The secondary plot of the play is its weakest point. . . . O'Casey ends the play in a melodramatic resolution of part of his secondary plot. Foorawn's disappointed lover steals the Church money and when she surprises him in the act, he shoots her. She quickly writes a suicide note absolving him from responsibility, and dies. There is too great a difference between this kind of melodrama and the rich comedy of the main plot. And there is no unifying element to bring them together. David Krause has suggested that "symbol, myth, and fantasy" are "catalytic agents" in *Cock-A-Doodle Dandy*, and that one of the difficulties with *The Bishop's Bonfire* is that "there is no symbolic or mythic equivalent" of the Cock to unite the comic and the serious elements. The play lacks the governing atmosphere of *Cock-A-Doodle Dandy*.

The Drums of Father Ned, like *Cock-A-Doodle Dandy*, depends heavily on the Expressionist's removal of realistic criteria. The play begins with a "prerumble," in which the street is "outlined only in a dream-like way." . . . There is an "Echo" which adds ironic emphasis to some of the dialogue, a device which O'Casey uses throughout the play. When the soldiers are forced to leave quickly, they abandon their prisoners, who crawl off the stage in opposite directions, calling each other names. The grim humor is particularly effective. (pp. 59-60)

Father Ned never appears, yet his presence is felt in every scene, and his drums are heard at intervals throughout the play. It is established very clearly that he is the main influence on the young people, O'Casey's heroes, and at first we expect him to appear. But it becomes evident that the reason we do not see him is that he is an idea. (p. 60)

Like the Cock, Father Ned is a force which performs "miracles" and scourges the rascals who would defeat his spirit. The Tostal is a great celebration and Father Ned becomes a kind of presiding God. The fact that we never see him, but only hear about his powers from the other characters, lends an aura of legend and magic to his name. Like *Cock-A-Doodle Dandy*, *The Drums of Father Ned* succeeds largely because of its title "character." If Expressionism is primarily concerned with portraying symbols which can represent the "essences" of things, then surely both the Cock and Father Ned must be considered Expressionist creations. The mythic Cock and the omnipresent priest both embody the essentials of joy and celebration which rule the two plays.

In surveying Expressionism in the O'Casey canon, one is struck by the number of attitudes O'Casey shared with the German playwrights. His opinion that Realism was dead, and that a new experimentalism was necessary to revitalize the theater is basic to Expressionism. His continual denunciation of established political and religious institutions and traditional ways of thinking is one of the distinguishing characteristics of the movement. His political sympathies were those of the "Activist" branch of Expressionism, the writers who during and immediately after the war hoped for a successful workers' revolution. Like the German playwrights, O'Casey was in deliberate revolt against the existing order of things, and he used the new and exaggerated methods to emphasize and to dramatize this revolt.

In terms of specific Expressionist techniques, one finds a general principle emerging from the plays. *The Silver Tassie* contains an Expressionist act sharply divided from its primarily realistic structure. In *Within the Gates*, O'Casey employed the station drama within a four-act morality play. In *The Star Turns Red* he used Expressionism to place symbolic emphasis on particular events, and in *Red Roses For Me* he returned to the separate Expressionist act of *The Silver Tassie*. But in *Purple Dust* and *Oak Leaves and Lavender* O'Casey began to merge with his traditional structure a significant new technique, the dream structure of Expressionism. It is this method which led to the form of *Cock-A-Doodle Dandy*. In 1934 O'Casey wrote that a "new form in drama" was emerging which "will take qualities found in classical, romantic, and expressionistic plays, will blend them together, breathe the breath of life into the new form and create a new drama." When O'Casey succeeded in his attempt to "blend" Expressionism with other styles, he achieved a unique form. He himself realized what he had learned about the use of Expressionism when he wrote in 1958 that he "broke away from realism into the chant of the second act of *The Silver Tassie*. But one scene in as a chant or a work of musical action and dialogue was not enough, so I set about trying to do this in an entire play, and brought forth *Cock-A-Doodle Dandy*." When O'Casey saw that it "was not enough" to isolate Expressionism, but rather that he could better use its dream structure as governing form, then it helped him to achieve triumphant comedies. (pp. 61-2)

Joan Templeton, "Sean O'Casey and Expressionism," in Modern Drama *(copyright © 1971, University of Toronto, Graduate Centre for Study of Drama; with the permission of* Modern Drama*), May, 1971, pp. 47-62.*

RONALD AYLING

It is in many ways rewarding to approach *Juno and the Paycock* together with *The Plough and the Stars* and *The Shadow of a Gunman* as a cycle of political and social plays conceived on an epic scale and deeply tinged by an overall tragic vision; a trilogy similar in some respects to Shakespeare's cycle comprising *Richard II*, *Henry IV* (two parts), and *Richard III*. In each series individual plays, though self-contained and complete in themselves, are more meaningful in conjunction with the other plays relating to their particular cycle, and, together with them, add up to a panoramic view of a country in a state of crisis. Of course Shakespeare's plays are more consciously shaped as chronicles of an age, a particular period of history, than are O'Casey's. . . . O'Casey wrote of the lives and struggles of ordinary men and women at a particular time of social upheaval, and in the process gave the drama something of an epic compass, realising a social and political content that is far wider and deeper than is apparent at first sight.

In chronological order of the subject-matter, *The Plough and the Stars* (1915-1916), *The Shadow of a Gunman* (1920), and *Juno and the Paycock* (1922) cover the most momentous events in recent Irish history, not from the point of view of the political or military leaders, but from that of the ordinary people unwillingly caught up in the indiscriminate savagery and recrimination of civil war and revolution. It is as though Ralph Mouldy, Peter Bullcalf, Francis Feeble and their families were at the centre of the dramatic action (with Bardolph, Nym, and Doll Tearsheet as minor characters) instead of Prince Hal and Hotspur. (pp. 77-8)

In O'Casey, as in Shakespeare's history plays, certain recurrent themes are uppermost: the inter-action of public and private drama, the horror of civil strife and anarchy in the state, and, likewise in both, a continuing debate on the ambiguous demands of justice and order in society.

[Writing] in close proximity to the events he chronicled, [O'Casey] naturally lacked so elaborate or consistent a narrative framework [as Shakespeare in his plays] and the consequent opportunities for cross-reference within plays and from one play to another, yet even so he does succeed in imposing a sense of unity on the Dublin trilogy. This cohesion is maintained by a grim ironic vision of the destructive forces in society, a compassionate concern for the resultant human suffering, a highly idiosyncratic comic technique, and purposeful thematic patterning common to each of these dramas. (p. 78)

Throughout his life O'Casey enriched the surface texture of his writings with a diverse selection of quotations, references, and clichés drawn from both popular and learned sources, using them for a variety of effects, though most often for satire or irony. In *Juno and the Paycock* the quotations—usually given by Joxer—are deliberately commonplace examples culled from Burns, Macaulay, Scott, Thomas Moore's *Melodies,* popular proverbs and Irish songs and ballads. (p. 79)

Indeed, the use of allusion on such an extensive, if mostly unobtrusive scale is comparable—though in the Dublin trilogy at a consistently popular, vernacular level—to the poetic practice of Ezra Pound, T. S. Eliot, and other modern writers. (pp. 80-1)

Though O'Casey's method developed quite independently, it served similar purposes to those [of Pound and Eliot]. Indeed, the irony works both ways in his case, for certain values of the past are criticised at the same time that their contemporary relevance is questioned. This is particularly true of conventional (that is, chivalric) notions of heroism, of martial glory and chauvinism. Legendary heroes and heroines are introduced at various times but always in a context that undermines the usually accepted valuation of them (always, that is, in the Dublin trilogy, for in later plays like *Purple Dust, Red Roses for Me* and *The Drums of Father Ned* the playwright also uses Irish myth in a more straightforward way to symbolise and endorse particular heroic attitudes and spiritual values). (p. 81)

The anti-heroic attitude is buttressed by a formidable assortment of weapons. In *Juno,* for example, the despicable toady Joxer Daly is one of the author's main agents for

working this effect. He is always ready with a made-to-measure, custom-worn quotation to fit any occasion, whether it be a celebration of military bravery (Boyle's imaginary deeds in Easter Week), or of martial valour, or of life at sea. The satire works on various levels: for one thing, there is the credibility gap between what is said and the speaker himself; there is the frequent inappropriateness between what is said and the situation to which it refers; and there is the contrast, too, between what is resolved by the characters being satirised, and what in fact they do. (pp. 81-2)

O'Casey [, however,] is never wholly anti-heroic even in his most pessimistic moments: there is always someone worthy of esteem, always a hint that, despite all appearances to the contrary, there is in unlikely places and people much genuine bravery and self-sacrifice. His writings imply that a good deal of traditional literature, largely concerned with noble heroes and martial feats, has often celebrated courage and self-sacrifice in the wrong people and circumstances; at the same time we are left in no doubt that there is a good deal of positive human endeavour (generally ignored in pre-Modernist literature) that is really worthy of poetic celebration. Juno Boyle is, after all, aptly named: she does assume universal significance by the end of the play and can rightly be regarded as the "goddess" or symbol of womankind and marriage. (p. 83)

He also had the advantage—so often denied to modern writers—that not only did he use material that was common knowledge, nationally, but he also wrote with specific audience attitudes and prejudices in mind, and these could be exploited for his own purposes, too. He could rely upon particular songs and quotations, for instance, having predictable emotive associations for Irish people, and this allowed him to exploit such responses for his own purposes. As a more obvious example one might instance the songs sung by Tommy Owens and Adolphus Grigson in *The Shadow of a Gunman.* Both have strong emotional overtones either of love or hate for Irish people: "High upon the gallows-tree" used to be sung as a sort of national anthem in patriotic assemblies before "A Soldier's Song" was adopted as the official anthem of the Irish Republic, while "Erin's Orange Lily O!" might be regarded as a sectarian hymn for Northern Irish Protestant extremists. The use of these two antithetical "battle-cries" is carefully plotted by the playwright. By having each sung by drunken and irresponsible hypocrites at particularly "awkward" moments in the dramatic action—one in each of the two acts of the play—the dramatist enhances the overall impression that, for all the sectarian hatred between the two contending political movements, they have much in common in discreditable essentials. . . . Taken within the full contexts in which they appear, therefore, the ballads reinforce O'Casey's message—a plague on both kinds of extreme chauvinism—without the necessity of him resorting to overtly didactic means. Owens and Grigson condemn themselves out of their own mouths. Both overdo their attempts to ingratiate themselves with Davoren and to impress him with their importance and devotion to particular sectarian "principles." Understandably, the louder their protestations, the less credible are their claims. Because they are shown to be, in the course of the action, only too representative of extreme public opinion (that is, green and orange attitudes) on both sides of "the border," the dramatist's criticisms are therefore general in application. (pp. 83-4)

This is only one of many aggressive methods employed by O'Casey. Other audacious shock tactics include grotesque and disconcerting juxtapositions of incident and verbal response. Moreover, by choosing generally acceptable patriotic and religious sentiments and having them expressed by characters unacceptable to Irish audiences, and by encouraging stock reactions from the latter at what prove to be wholly inappropriate moments in the dramatic action, O'Casey set in motion a series of emotional and intellectual collisions with which to disturb the minds of the spectators. By these and many other conscious devices the playwright attempted to challenge and sometimes subvert the conventional moral and social attitudes of native audiences. He wanted to startle, shock, even scandalize Irish audiences into questioning inherited political and religious beliefs. . . . (p. 84)

Irish critics especially have refused to see the dramatist as anything other than a slice-of-life realist and, as we might expect with such an approach, many of O'Casey's more obvious satiric effects as well as some subtler touches have been attributed to accidental or historical factors by such critics. (p. 88)

The facts are quite otherwise. Each play for long periods bombards the audience with a wide range of conflicting thoughts and ethical attitudes—seemingly in an objective manner, it is true—putting forward certain basic values which the writer thinks paramount in the particular circumstances, while realising contrary values in ways which are carefully calculated to alienate them from the spectators. The dramatist's deep moral commitment inspires the audacious theatrical experimentation which characterises his Dublin trilogy. The formal daring exhibited in these plays, the liveliness of characters and their vivid idiomatic speech ought not to obscure the fact that such means are used for specific ends. That the plays are rarely as *overtly* didactic as some of his later works does not mean that they serve no propaganda purpose. . . . (p. 89)

> *Ronald Ayling, "Popular Tradition and Individual Talent in Sean O'Casey's Dublin Trilogy" (reprinted by permission of Ronald Ayling and the editor), in* Journal of Modern Literature, *November, 1972 (and reprinted as "Sean O'Casey's Dublin Trilogy" in* Sean O'Casey: A Collection of Critical Essays, *edited by Thomas Kilroy, Prentice-Hall, Inc., 1975, pp. 77-89).*

JULIUS NOVICK

[*The Plough and the Stars* is] about a war fought at home, with shells exploding in the streets and women shot as they stand at the windows. The war in question, the Easter Rebellion, Dublin, 1916, was less squalid than most: a revolution, a struggle for freedom. Out of it, said Yeats, "a terrible beauty is born."

O'Casey had a somewhat different view. In the first two acts of *The Plough* he gives us plenty of revolutionary rhetoric and shows it to us as heady stuff, better than beer—and popular for the same reason. The other two acts are devoted to revolutionary reality, including some unexpected heroism and some (highly comic) behavior that is distinctly less than heroic. But for O'Casey the essential reality of war, revolutionary or otherwise, no matter how splendid the principle for which it is fought, is pain, and pain dominates the last half of *The Plough and the Stars*: fear, madness, miscarriage, and death. No wonder the Irish

Nationalists rioted when the play was new; they did not want to see the seamy side of their glorious struggle. O'Casey had been the first secretary of the Irish Citizen Army, but *The Plough and the Stars* is nothing if not a pacifist play.

> *Julius Novick, "Take a Member of the IRA," in* The Village Voice *(reprinted by permission of* The Village Voice; *copyright © The Village Voice, Inc., 1976), November 29, 1976, p. 97.*

BERNICE SCHRANK

Recurring patterns of destructive disorder underlie and link all the elements of [*The Shadow of a Gunman*] from the sloppiness of Seumas's room to the political messiness of the Irish "troubles." In *Shadow*, O'Casey creates a universe in which God is dead, the religious professions of his characters are full of violence and cant, the ship of state is going down in a blood-dimmed tide, slum poverty is destroying the privacy and threatening the sanity of its inhabitants, and personal relationships are characterized by selfishness and exploitation.

Since the entire play takes place in Seumas's room, its description ought to help establish a pervasive sense of chaos. Predictably it does. O'Casey's stage directions are explicit and relevant. . . . The room is a mess and that messiness has far-reaching implications. O'Casey makes the connection between the room's confusion and Donal's and Seumas's psychological states directly. But the room is also a microcosm of the larger world. The confusion outside is mirrored in the jumble of props which litter the room—religious icons, pots and pans, a typewriter, books and flowers. From the start then, the setting creates an atmosphere of chaos congenial to the theme of breakdown which runs through the play.

The disordered setting is surely an appropriate backdrop for projecting a sense of cosmic chaos. O'Casey implies that the universe of *Shadow* is at best godless; at worst, it is presided over by malevolent forces. When Minnie is taken, Seumas invokes higher and higher deities to protect himself even if it means sacrificing her. His appeal to Saint Anthony, "Holy Saint Anthony grant that she'll keep her mouth shut," . . . is followed by further appeals to stronger powers: "God grant she won't say anything," and "God grant she'll keep her mouth shut.". . . The cowardly and self-serving quality of these prayers is emphasized by the Biblical form of the subject and verb and the colloquialism of the object. Ironically, however, the prayers are granted. Minnie is permanently silenced, shot accidentally in cross-fire between Irish patriots and Black and Tans. If God has indeed answered Seumas, He is petty and irrational and His presence in the universe is far from consoling. Of course it is more probable that Seumas's prayer bears no relation to Minnie's accidental death. Seumas himself explains that event in terms of "the tappin' on the wall.". . . There does not appear to be much difference between imaginary noises and God's intervention in either Seumas's or O'Casey's minds. The effect of equating the two, however, is to deny the presence of God in the universe of *Shadow*. (pp. 54-5)

Granted that God has been banished from *Shadow*, it follows that sincere religious belief is irrelevant because it does not correspond to the play's metaphysical reality. O'Casey's Christians, however, are rarely sincere. Often, as in *Shadow*, the self-consciously Christian characters are hypocrites. Religion offers people like Seumas and Grigson a convenient way of sugar-coating their hostility and aggression.... The religion of Ireland as revealed in *The Shadow of a Gunman* is violence decked out in Christian trimmings.

This coupling of Christianity and violence has a political side. Seumas's oft-quoted speech on the state of Ireland convincingly suggests that the religion of violence is more than a private aberration, it is a political disease afflicting the whole society. (p. 55)

Shadow of a Gunman is about living under conditions of social instability and collapse.... The fact that Minnie is shot accidentally in cross-fire between the Irregulars and the Black and Tans illustrates the murderous quality of both sides....

One of the meanings of the title which the play dramatizes so well is the long shadow cast over all the action, however innocuous, trivial, or apolitical, by the "troubles."...

By superimposing the slum poverty on the "troubles" and the religious chaos, O'Casey provides *The Shadow of a Gunman* with a very credible external reality in which to locate the domestic and personal symptoms of breakdown. It is certainly true that the predatory qualities of the characters abet the religious, political and economic disintegration which *Shadow* dramatizes. The play thus suggests the interrelationship between religious collapse, political upheaval, economic oppression and individual manifestations of brutality. Undeclared war describes the social and the political situation; it is also a good metaphor for the exploitative personal relationships between the characters. (p. 56)

The life of the tenement is contagiously and effortlessly destructive. Through some fatal mixture of personality and environment, decent characters like Mrs. Henderson and egotists like Tommy Owens turn into unpleasant bullies.

Mr. Gallogher and Mrs. Grigson are interesting but minor examples of O'Casey's theme of exploitation. Its fullest treatment is reserved for the sacrifice of Minnie Powell. In one sense, Minnie offers herself. She takes the bombs of her own free will to save Donal and, at the same time, she also manages to save Seumas. In another, profounder sense, Minnie is set up as sacrificial victim.

Minnie's action in this light is not so much a matter of rational decision as of impulsive gesture based on several seemingly trivial and harmless, yet mistaken, beliefs.... Minnie's beliefs are ... a complicated and dangerous amalgam of passion, patriotism, propaganda and romantic fantasy. Minnie is too unreflective a character to sort out her beliefs and discard the illusions. Although Donal appreciates the falseness of some of Minnie's beliefs, particularly the ones that involve him, he does not attempt to separate fact from fancy. In effect, Donal encourages Minnie's fantasies. At first, they make him feel important; during the raid, they protect him.... She is the victim of a chance bullet, her own romantic illusions, the patriotic madness of her society and the cowardice and selfishness of Donal and Seumas. (p. 58)

[Donal's] complicity and Minnie's memory both fade as Donal takes stage centre for a final Shelleyian thrust of words.

Ah me, alas! Pain, pain, pain, ever, for ever! It's terrible to think that little Minnie is

dead, but it's still more terrible to think that Davoren and Shields are alive! Oh, Donal Davoren, shame is your portion now till the silver cord is loosened and the golden bowl be broken. Oh, Davoren, Donal Davoren, poet and poltroon, poltroon and poet....

Not only have the phrases become more measured and poetic, but the pronouns of his previous speech have been translated into nouns. Rather than Donal expressing himself, Donal the poet is watching Donal the man expressing himself. And it is Donal, not Minnie, who is chief in his mind. As his immediate response yields to aesthetic distancing, Donal refashions Minnie's death into a lament for himself. Thus Minnie's death, like her life, is exploited.

From all that has been said, it seems fair to conclude that in *The Shadow of a Gunman,* O'Casey goes to considerable pains to present a thoroughgoing picture of breakdown. The sacrifice of Minnie Powell, the exploitative domestic relationships in the tenements, the economic deprivations, the murderous political strife, the religious hypocrisy and the vacuum in the sky unmistakably convey a sense of chaotic conditions and man's inadequate responses.

Belying these manifestations of breakdown, however, is the unquenchable talk of the play's tenement dwellers. By its very exuberance, it seems to express affirmation. But the talk, in spite of its exuberance, is the best illustration of how the characters are locked into the prevailing breakdown. Although everyone in the play talks, no one seems to care consistently whether or not his words have precise and literal meaning. For Maguire, language is a diversionary tactic. For Gallogher, Owens, Grigson, Shields and Davoren himself, talk is a form of escape from the slums, from the "troubles" and from a nagging sense of their own impotence. The flow of words induces a drugged stage of well-being in them where all sense of the necessary relationship between words and action is lost.

When action does occur, it tends to explode unexpectedly somewhere off stage. Maguire's fate and Minnie's sacrifice are violent examples of the failure of language to connect to action in this play. Maguire waltzes on and off stage talking about butterflies; he leaves a bag without telling anyone that it contains bombs. Later, he is reported killed in an I.R.A. action. In retrospect, his talk seems intentionally misdirected, while his true purpose is unaccompanied by any explanations. Meanwhile, Minnie goes off to die for the gunman on the run, her fantasy Donal who has nothing in common with the real Donal that O'Casey sets before the audience. Her final words, coming from offstage, ought to illuminate her action. But they are discredited slogans that bear no relation to reality. Maguire's and Minnie's words are, in different ways, strangers to their actions. (pp. 58-9)

Donal and Seumas finish as they began, talking irrelevantly. Donal's poetry floods the play with words as he attempts to bridge art and life like his model Shelley. But Donal's poetry proves hopelessly escapist. He is unable to come to terms with Minnie's death, hiding instead behind the soothing alliteration of "poet and poltroon." Seumas's religious commentary, like Donal's poetry, is spread over the whole play. From the beginning, Seumas uses it as a vehicle for expressing his anger and his jealousy rather than his holiness. When, at the end, he explains the traumatic events by "the tappin' on the wall," he shows his religious vocabulary to be nothing more than a noisy gloss for superstition. The implications of Maguire's and Minnie's actions are dissipated in this unceasing yet empty talk. Donal and Seumas, like Maguire and Minnie, are unwilling or unable to connect language and action. In this way, the misuse of language contributes a major share to the play's expression of chaos.

O'Casey has thus locked his characters into negative patterns of behaviour and thrown away the key. The most vital characters like Minnie are destroyed and weaker characters like Donal understand yet cannot alter the fact that their energies are being dissipated and perverted. No character escapes the general demoralization because the world O'Casey creates in *Shadow* is in all its aspects hostile to life. (pp. 59-60)

> Bernice Schrank, "Poets, Poltroons and Platitudes: A Study of Sean O'Casey's 'The Shadow of a Gunman'," in MOSAIC: A Journal for the Study of Literature and Ideas *(copyright © 1977 by the University of Manitoba Press; acknowledgment of previous publication is herewith made), Vol. XI, No. 1 (Fall, 1977), pp. 53-60.*

*   *   *

O'HARA, John   1905-1970

O'Hara was an American novelist, short story writer, essayist, and critic. His chosen milieu is often small town America, which he has recreated in the fictional Gibbsville. The protagonists of O'Hara's novels are depicted in their struggle for financial and social dominance in prose noted for its objective and understated style. His short story collection *Pal Joey* was made into a successful Broadway musical. (See also *CLC*, Vols. 1, 2, 3, 6, and *Contemporary Authors*, Vols. 5-8, rev. ed.; obituary, Vols. 25-28, rev. ed.)

ARTHUR VOSS

[John O'Hara] was concerned mainly with depicting manners and customs in the tradition of Sinclair Lewis, Lardner, and Fitzgerald. (p. 279)

[The stories of *Pal Joey*, with] their malapropisms, bad grammar and spelling, and slang, ... would seem to derive most immediately from Ring Lardner's *You Know Me Al*. Joey, although perhaps somewhat more sophisticated, possesses much the same quality of egotism, vulgarity, brashness, and naïveté, despite a certain shrewdness in small things, as Lardner's baseball protagonist. If he is not an altogether admirable character, Joey is not contemptible either. (p. 280)

[The stories he wrote in the 1960's, late in his life, are] better, on the whole, than [his] earlier ones. By and large they have more substance, more story quality, more interesting characters, more penetrating social observation, and more significant implications. Like O'Hara himself, many of his characters have grown older, and there is more concern than in the earlier short fiction with rendering thoughts and feelings, particularly those having to do with how a character has lived his life and what he has or has not made of it. These characters, especially when they suffer disappointment, deterioration, or defeat, are often presented so as to evoke our sympathy, but it should also be noted that the number of unsympathetic characters in the later stories is not inconsiderable—vulgarians, scoundrels, degenerates, unfaithful wives, philanderers, and worse are held up to

view, though usually with more subtlety and restraint than in the often heavily ironic and sardonic exposés of such persons in the earlier stories. (pp. 281-82)

But O'Hara is probably consistently at his best in the many stories which are primarily character studies. ... He made them seem very real, not so much through penetrating deeply into them psychologically as by showing in detail what they say and do in relation to their environments and to the other characters in the story. Often he restricted himself to a minimum of auctorial exposition and description, relying heavily on dialogue instead to tell his story, and he had a very fine ear for the speech of his characters, no matter what their occupation or social station. (p. 282)

The general [critical] indictment against O'Hara contains a number of specific charges: He was a limited writer who was too flatly and literally realistic, too preoccupied with social distinctions and trivial details, and unable to transcend his realism as Hemingway did. He wrote too rapidly and discursively; he ought to have revised and polished more. His stories need more of such elements as humor, emotion, symbolism, imagery, mystery, and often they need more point. They may be vivid and plausible, but they do not have enough truth. There is undoubtedly some basis for these criticisms, but taken altogether they perhaps asked O'Hara to be something he was not. ... [O'Hara is praised] more for short stories than for his novels, in recognition that he possessed not inconsiderable talents ... as a literary craftsman and social historian. (p. 283)

> Arthur Voss, in his The American Short Story: A Critical Survey *(copyright 1973 by the University of Oklahoma Press), University of Oklahoma Press, 1973.*

MALCOLM BRADBURY

[O'Hara's work is] a fiction of social absurdity.

For O'Hara's fiction was deeply consistent with the man, as it must be: it is a materialistic fiction, built on the patent solidity of society, the weight of things, the detailed appurtenances of possession, the measure and symbolic value of goods. O'Hara, in correspondence with Fitzgerald, once noted that they were both parvenu authors, and it is of course to the parvenu that social substance is most substantial, class and rank most real. ...

O'Hara's novels and stories, found excessively frank in their time, postulate a coordinated, respectable and essentially monogamous society, held by code and habit and desire, and struggling within it an essentially adulterous humanity. His first novel starts in an unsatisfactory marital bed, and so, in a sense, does all life in the O'Hara universe. Caught between the two—substantial, virtuous society and practical sexuality and angst—is that recurrent O'Hara type, the respectable reprobate. ...

His work shares the dominant literary attitudes of his time; it is touched with that mixture of radicalism and nostalgia central to the mood of the early to mid-century American novel, and something of the self-made intellectuality also characteristic of the period. His temper was shorter than that of many of his peers, and his anti-intellectuality ... more assertive, leading to stronger declarations that what he possessed was, well, ultimate craft: the gift of getting dialogue right, observation precise, structure under control. Even his sense of grievance was reasonably typical; there was arrogance and defiance as well as social aspiration that passed, as with Fitzgerald, deep into the tenor of his writing. Perhaps the most striking difference from the rest of his rather incestuous generation is in the rhythm of the career. O'Hara was the writer as worker, and the work intensified as time went on. . . .

O'Hara's is not an unexamined realism. . . . [He] became increasingly concerned with speculation about technique, and particularly about his modes of outward presentation of inward states; the result is a careful realism, in special and singular economy, one that O'Hara perfected long before he commented on it. . . .

O'Hara at his best depended on tight lines of control. He never possessed technique in any Jamesian or experimental sense; his claim was to "craft" in a journalistically professional form.

But he could write with an extraordinary, clear purity, which is most articulate as a tone. It comes out as a mode of apparent indifference, a hard surface given to the text through a predominance of dialogue or a continuous functionality of scene, through the abstraction of psychological inwardness from the characters, through a particular way of spatializing the public and the private, the narrative overview and the inward moves of being. This offended critics who made humanism a requisite of a fictional text . . . , but of course compassion or involvement is not necessarily absent from the mode. We feel that O'Hara's characters are both given substance and drained of it by living in a world that is solid and harsh; we feel him creating to suppress, to limit what might be said in order to reveal this. The famous oblique endings of the stories work in this way. . . .

O'Hara worked best with a very special marriage of accumulated, dense social detail, a given wealth of society, and a sparse and limited mode of writing; this is why he so frequently succeeds most in the short stories. . . . O'Hara's refusal to overdress, to go for metaphor in style, or for a total logic in narrative, and his insistence on distilling a precision from a story, are the essential notes [in his best stories]. The social surface is solid; the narrative presses continuously with a deducible logic; the anxieties underlying the experience are elicited; the text stays cool. Reality is both there and not there, as in all good realism; and if we want to judge that realism still has a stylistic currency, that there is an appropriate balance still to be won from this form of anxious social reconciliation, then we do well to look hard at O'Hara.

Malcolm Bradbury, "A Respectable Reprobate," in The Times Literary Supplement (© *Times Newspapers Ltd. (London) 1976; reproduced from* The Times Literary Supplement *by permission), May 28, 1976, p. 633.*

JOHN UPDIKE

"Selected Letters of John O'Hara" . . . cannot but sweeten the reputation of a notoriously irascible and hypersensitive author. (p. 200)

These letters, even when they scold and complain, turn outward, toward the social envelope. Though he strikes an egotistical pose, it is hard to think of another significant twentieth-century fiction writer who was less of an egoist, less of an autobiographical self-celebrator. His interest in

other people and their lives is so unfeignedly keen that anything about them, any window-glimpse into their psychologies and social predicaments, will serve him for a story. The action in his stories is often surprisingly slight; he considerately refuses to manipulate characters beyond what their systems will naturally stand. (p. 204)

O'Hara's ability and willingness to portray women has not been often enough complimented. Compared to the women of his fiction, Hemingway's are mere dolls. Indeed, if there is an American male author who has set a greater variety of believable women on the page, or as effortlessly projected himself into a female point of view, I haven't read him. Their disadvantaged position and the strength of the strategies with which they seek advantages are comprehended without doctrine, and without a loss of heterosexual warmth. (p. 213)

Humanity in all its divisions was present to him; his gifts of curiosity and empathy were so strong that one must ask what, if anything, his art lacked. Love of language might be an answer—language as a semi-opaque medium whose colors and connotations can be worked into a supernatural, supermimetic bliss. . . . Tuned to less than highest pitch, his prose and dialogue just run on. . . . But the interest of the human life in his mind's eye was so self-evident to him he saw no need to *make* it interesting. A thing was itself, and rarely reminded him of another. He is resolutely unmetaphorical, and language seldom led him with its own music deeper into the matter at hand. Hemingway's flatness had about it a willed point, a philosophical denial of depth; O'Hara's was serenely post-philosophical. His best short stories have a terrific delicacy, and the calm compositional weirdness of a Degas or an Oriental print. . . . O'Hara was crazy about writing, and his writing has the innocence of enthusiasm. . . . What innovations his art contains—including his once scandalous sexual frankness— were forced upon him, one feels, by his reverence before the facts of life. (pp. 213-14)

John Updike, "The Doctor's Son," in The New Yorker (© *1978 by The New Yorker Magazine, Inc.), November 6, 1978, pp. 200-14.*

*   *   *

OLSON, Charles   1910-1970

Olson was an American poet, essayist, and critic. He is the mentor of the Black Mountain poets and with his 1950 essay "Projective Verse" established the principles for the Projectivist school of poetry. Although his poetry bears the influence of both Pound and Williams, Olson was a unique and powerful creative force in contemporary poetry. (See also *CLC,* **Vols. 1, 2, 5, 6, 9, and** *Contemporary Authors,* **Vols. 15-16; obituary, Vols. 25-28, rev. ed.;** *Contemporary Authors Permanent Series,* **Vol. 1.)**

THOM GUNN

Charles Olson . . . exists in the world of factions—of manifestoes and extravagant gestures. He appears to be influenced by such rebels against orthodoxy as Pound and the Rimbaud of *Les Illuminations.* So far so good, I suppose: Pound and Rimbaud were geniuses who succeeded, against all probability, in expanding the boundaries of poetry. In Olson, however, the habit of scholarly detail inherited from Pound clutters the imagination, and the habit of recklessness in imagination (inherited maybe from Rimbaud) cancels out any possible consistency or relevance in the scholarly details. These twin disasters come about, I suspect, because he has little interest in the sensible world except as a handle on which to hang bits of poetry. . . . If we want the explanation of his technique, we may find it in his essay on "Projective Verse," printed in *The New American Poetry 1945-1960* . . . , which though it has been very influential, it would not be unfair to describe as the worst prose published since *Democratic Vistas.* This passage opens with the statement of a rule:

> ONE PERCEPTION MUST IMMEDIATELY AND DIRECTLY LEAD TO A FURTHER PERCEPTION. It means exactly what it says, is a matter of, at *all* points (even, I should say, of our management of daily reality as of the daily work) get on with it, keep moving, keep in, speed, the nerves, their speed, the perceptions, theirs, the acts, the split second acts, the whole business, keep it moving as fast as you can, citizen. And if you also set up as a poet, USE USE USE the process at all points, in any given poem always, always one perception must must must MOVE, INSTANTER, ON ANOTHER.

The description of this psychological process was first made several hundreds of years ago, and the recommendation of it as a specifically poetic process was made at least as early as the start of the nineteenth century, but it is the complete lack of qualification, the absolutism of his demand, that distinguishes Olson's enunciation of it as a rule for writing poetry. . . . "Put down anything so long as you keep writing" would be a fair enough paraphrase. The result is *The Distances,* which consists of performances as flat and inept as the feeble rhymes that are printed daily in [newspapers]. (pp. 595-96)

> *Thom Gunn, in* The Yale Review *(© 1961 by Yale University; reprinted by permission of the editors), June, 1961.*

MARJORIE G. PERLOFF

Olson's essay ["Projective Verse"] begins with this diagram:

> (projectile   (percussive   (prospective
> vs.
> The NON-Projective

To Creeley, this terminology and mode of presentation was enormously exciting, a way of breaking out of the "closed system," of "poems patterned upon exterior and traditionally accepted models." . . . [This vocabulary] occurs in Pound's *Antheil and the Treatise on Harmony.* In this essay, Pound praises the composer-theorist Antheil for his understanding that "music exists in time-space; and is therefore very different from any kind of plastic art which exists all at once." . . . The "monolinear," "lateral," and "horizontal" action of . . . "musical mechanisms" is, in Pound's words, "like a projectile carrying a wire and cutting, defining the three dimensions of space." . . . The *projective element* in music—its locomotive quality—is defined as the fourth dimension.

The notion of the poem as projectile, a mechanism or force projected through time-space, is thus not as revolutionary

as Olson's admirers have professed it to be. The synonymic use of "projectile" and "percussive," for that matter, makes little sense until one has read Pound's *Antheil,* in which he devotes a whole section to the role of percussion in the "time-spacing" created by "musical mechanisms." . . . (pp. 287-88)

In the first two pages of his essay, Olson defines "OPEN verse" and discusses "COMPOSITION BY FIELD" under three headings: its "*kinetics,*" its "*principle,*" and its "*process.*" . . . Note that although . . . Olson singles out Robert Creeley and Edward Dahlberg as the fellow writers who most influenced his theory, the text of "Projective Verse" itself suggests that their concepts as well as Olson's were in turn derived from the critical writings of Pound and Williams. (p. 288)

Such indebtedness is not, in itself, a fault; Williams himself, after all, derived many of his critical concepts from Pound and then adapted them to his own purposes. The difference is that Olson consistently insinuates . . . that his theory of poetry is revolutionary. Yet his main deviation from the Pound-Williams aesthetic is that he muddles their concepts.

Take, for example, the tripartite division into the *kinetics,* the *principle,* and the *process* of projective verse. The division sounds impressive but what is its real point? If poetry is a "high energy-construct" (Rule 1), clearly its form will be determined by the content or energy to be conveyed from poet to reader (Rule 2). Why the first is *kinetics* and the second *principle* is never made clear. The third division —the "process of the thing"—seems to be no more than a corollary of (1), for if the poem is an "energy-discharge," it follows that one perception must immediately and directly lead to a further one (Rule 3). This is *kinetics* all over again. Or *process* if you want to call it that. Olson's three-step definition is, in short, merely pretentious, a device used to convince the reader that the argument in question is proceeding logically or that, at the very least, it is highly complex. (pp. 290-91)

Olson is again following Pound and Williams in his insistence that the basic unit of prosody can no longer be considered the foot, that, as Pound said in Canto LXXXI, "To break the pentameter, that was the first heave." In the "new poetry," the basic unit becomes the *line* or breath group of artfully arranged syllables. Olson's emphasis on the centrality of syllable and line thus has ample precedent. But his conclusion is his own:

> Let me put it baldly. The two halves are:
>   the HEAD, by way of the EAR, to the SYLLABLE
>   the HEART, by way of the BREATH, to the
>   LINE. . . .

This formulation, like the distinction between *kinetics, principle,* and *process* discussed above, has more manner than matter. . . . [The formula could] be reversed, and in any case it hardly seems to matter which of the two—syllable or line—is HEAD or HEART. (pp. 292-93)

The necessity of "getting rid of the lyrical interference of the individual as ego" and of avoiding the traditional mimetic role of poetry is one of Olson's obsessive themes. In "On Poets and Poetry" (1953), for example, he defines the image "as a 'thing,' never so far as we know, such a non-animal as symbol," and in the "Letter to Elaine Feinstein" (1959), which serves as a postscript to "Projective Verse," he declares that in the past few centuries, "representation was never off the dead-spot of description. Nothing was happening as of the poem itself—ding and zing or something. It was referential to reality."

If this allegedly *new* concept of the image as thing, as object relating not to any external reality but only to other objects within the field of the poem, has a familiar ring, it is because Olson's "objectism" is merely Pound's "objectivism" in not very new dress. (p. 294)

[Although] Olson uses the analogy of "clean wood" rather than of granite or marble—Pound's favorite building materials—to define poetry, the doctrine is really the same. Williams summed it up in his famous phrase, "No ideas but in things". . . . (p. 295)

"Projective Verse," one concludes, is hardly the breakthrough in literary theory it is reputed to be. It is essentially a scissors-and-paste job, a clever but confused collage made up of bits and pieces of Pound, Fenollosa, Gaudier-Brzeska, Williams, and Creeley. One could argue, of course, that Olson repeatedly acknowledges his debt to "the work of Pound & Williams," and that he admittedly uses their poetics as a springboard from which to chart the directions the "new poetry" should take. But this is not quite what happens. We have already seen that Olson claims his "objectism" to be a "more valid formulation for present use" than the "objectivism" of his Masters. In the years following the publication of "Projective Verse"—years in which Olson began to publish his own poetry—he became increasingly testy about his relationship to Pound and Williams. (pp. 295-96)

Evidently, Olson's aim [in "I, Mencius, Pupil of the Master . . ."] is to use the typographical spacing and verse technique of the *Cantos* to criticize Pound's unfortunate return to the "closed verse" of traditional poets. But despite its parody rhymes . . . , its recurrent metal images, or its witty allusions . . . , "I, Mencius" is no more than a superficially clever poem. For one thing, Olson's own Rule #3—"ONE PERCEPTION MUST IMMEDIATELY AND DIRECTLY LEAD TO A FURTHER PERCEPTION"—is not observed in this poem, which basically restates the same theme over and over again. (p. 299)

[Despite] Olson's repeated insistence that "contemporary workers go lazy RIGHT HERE WHERE THE LINE IS BORN," his own prosody is not in any way remarkable. In ["I, Mencius,"] for example, it is not clear that the line always ends "where its breathing, shall come to, termination." . . . Olson insists that "only he, the man who writes, can declare, at every moment, the line its metric and its ending," but in that case, "only he, the man who writes" can know *why* the line ends when it does. . . . One finds . . . no sense of inevitability in Olson's verse line, no principle which may be said to govern the way syllables must be combined to constitute lines. The poet simply breaks off where he happens to break off. . . .

[During] the sixties, Olson became such an oracle, even if to a relatively small coterie, that he could and did say almost anything—banal, confusing, contradictory, meaningless—and get away with it. (p. 300)

[We] might conclude by looking at a late Olson poem so as to see to what extent Olson has managed to MAKE IT NEW.

My text is, appropriately I think, a late Olson poem entitled "from The Song of Ullikummi," which bears the subtitle: "(translated from Hurrian and Hittite and read at Spoleto 1965 to honor the presence of Mr. Ezra Pound)." At this festive occasion, one gathers, Olson finally wanted to make peace with his "inferior predecessor." Like his first Master, he would base his poem on an ancient myth, only he would go one step further than Pound by choosing an obscure Hurrian myth, wholly beyond Pound's own scholarly range.

"From The Song of Ullikummi" is based on Hans Güterbock's 1951 translation of the incomplete epic, which is in turn based on the following myth. The god Kumarbis has dethroned his father Anus but is in turn threatened by Anus's second son, the storm god. Kumarbis sends his messenger, Imbaluris, to the Sea to seek her advice. She summons Kumarbis to her house and feasts him. As a result of her advice, Kumarbis leaves his native Urkis and goes to a place where he meets a huge rock. He has intercourse with this rock and bears a son called Ullikummis, who grows into a gigantic pillar of diorite. He rises from the sea like a tower until his height is 9,000 leagues and his girth the same. To the consternation of the gods, he reaches up to heaven. A conflict between Ullikummis and the storm-god now ensues.

Olson's poem is based on the first twenty-two lines of the first tablet. The Güterbock text prints the Hittite transcription of the Hurrian myth on the left side of the page and the English translation on the right. . . . (pp. 301-02)

In his version, Olson omits the statement of epic theme, the reference to the conflict between Kumarbis and the storm god, and the description of the journey. His subject, rather, is the act of intercourse itself, yet, although his poem deals only with this one event, it is more than twice as long as the relevant portion of the original narrative. (p. 303)

[The] lines are somewhat reminiscent of Pound: the retelling of ancient myth in contemporary idiom, the casual free verse, the juxtaposition of foreign text with its English equivalent. Yet the differences outweigh these superficial similarities. Whereas Pound usually juxtaposes different myths, playing off one against another to create a new image, Olson harps with tiresome monotony on the same theme:

> the fucking
> of the Mountain
>   fucked the mountain went right through it and
> came out the other side. . . .

And, although he often copies the Güterbock translation verbatim, . . . in the few cases where he does make changes in the parent text, it is in order to turn a neutral narrative statement into a cute sexual reference. . . . [Note] that the wit, which does not rise above the most banal locker-room joke, is fraudulent in that Olson depends upon our not being able to read the Hittite. . . . (pp. 303-04)

The novelty of [the] linguistic juxtapositions rapidly wears off once we know what the Hittite means. If a poem is meant to be, in Olson's words, "a high energy-construct" or "energy-discharge," it is difficult to justify the essential repetitiveness of "from The Song of Ullikummi." Nor does the "FORM" of this particular poem seem to be "AN

EXTENSION OF CONTENT," for as we can see by looking at the parent text, the same content can be and is presented in very different form. One would be grateful if, in keeping with the doctrine of "Projective Verse," the "PERCEPTION" of the opening line—"fucked the Mountain"—ever led to a "FURTHER PERCEPTION," but Olson seems to find the notion of a god fucking a rock so titillating, so enchanting, that he can think of nothing else, and the poem ends as it began. . . .

One can object at this point that it is unfair to judge Olson by this relatively unimportant poem, that the *Maximus Poems,* say, or "The Kingfishers" would give us a different image of the poet. No doubt there is some truth in such an objection—Olson did write better poems than "Ullikummi" —but we must take the poem seriously because Olson himself took it very seriously indeed. (p. 305)

"Ullikummi" . . . simply manifests in particularly blatant form Olson's central imaginative failure. Pound and Williams, one should recall, talked of prosody only after long and ardous experiments with different verse forms, line units, and syllable combinations; theirs was what Eliot liked to call "workshop criticism." Olson, on the other hand, began by announcing that the syllable and the line were the "HEAD" and the "HEART" of the new prosody and hoped that no one would notice that, in his own poetry, he let the lines fall where they may. Again, whereas Pound's and Williams' objectivist theories were the natural outgrowth of their experiments with imagery, Olson simply announced that the "objects in field" that compose a poem must refer to nothing outside themselves, only to discover that in his own poetry, references to external reality became increasingly obtrusive. (pp. 305-06)

> *Marjorie G. Perloff, "Charles Olson and the 'Inferior Predecessors': 'Projective Verse' Revisited," in ELH (© copyright 1973 by The Johns Hopkins University Press), Summer, 1973, pp. 285-306.*

THOMAS F. MERRILL

Charles Olson wrote "The Kingfishers" in 1949 when his "stance toward reality" was quickening. Soon he would codify that stance and the principles of its expression in two position papers, "The Human Universe" and "Projective Verse," but in "The Kingfishers" we have perhaps the most dense rendering of the Olson posture. Later, in *The Maximus Poems,* the density will attenuate and the method will lose some of its aggressive presence, but in this earlier, briefer effort we have the advantage of a concentrate. The poem is Olson distilled, form obediently extending from content, a reliable index to the dogmatic complexity of its author. As Olson himself once put it [in *Letters for Origin*], "If you don't know Kingfishers you don't have a starter." . . . (pp. 506-07)

"The Kingfishers" is, to use a term Olson borrowed from Franz Kline, a "marvelous maneuver," the result of ". . . that wonderful sense that one does what one knows before one knows what one does." In "The Kingfishers" Olson did what he only later fully knew [as he indicated in marginalia], and the poem's consistency with intellectual positions he was to codify in the future is testimony to the trustworthiness of what Olson has called "blind obedience" to "personage," that is, the belief that "each of us is more than a physiology or a will . . . [that] we are also an obedi-

ence. And what we obey—have to obey—is something we are in the hands of, not in our own hands alone. I refer to the life in us." (p. 507)

[M. L. Rosenthal's] reading shows a considerably greater acquaintance [than many other critics] with Olson's concerns and his methodology. Isolating the three major motifs that run through "The Kingfishers" (the ancient symbol 'E''; the quotation from Mao; and the overall symbol of the kingfisher), he acknowledges [in *The New Poets: American and British Poetry Since World War II*] the "crucial issue" of the poem as the "betrayal of humanly meaningful modes of life that were discovered before the emergence of the modern state." Aside from the word "betrayal," which perhaps intrudes an overly moral ingredient into Olson's organic view of cultural history, Rosenthal's précis is not inconsistent with the cultural position which Olson's works and marginalia yield. (p. 509)

In Jung, as in [Brook Adams, whose *The Law of Civilization and Decay* was important to Olson], Olson finds a principle of energy, racial or psychic, which is both within and beyond man—an energy precisely equivalent to what he labels the "life in us"—available for obedience. . . .

Adams' "racial energy," Jung's "archetypal anima," and Melville's creative "recovery" of primordial energy through image and feeling supply an outline of the cultural point of view animating "The Kingfishers." It is a view which recommends the repossession of a lost, pre-Socratic "stance toward reality" (elsewhere called by Olson the "will to cohere") which unburdens man of the abstractions of Greek rationalism by placing him in a posture obedient to the rhythms of the "life in us." The particular intensity of "The Kingfishers" generates from Olson's conviction that the "recovery" is now at hand as a real cultural possibility for America. . . . (p. 510)

Like his literary guru, Melville, Olson feels himself in a revolution of "recovery rather than advance" and senses the inadequacy of the term *writer* to comprehend his quest. "I find it awkward to call myself a poet or a writer," he confesses. "If there are no walls there are no names. . . . I am an archeologist of morning. And the writing and acts which I find bear on the present job are . . . from Homer back, not forward." "The Kingfishers" is a product of that anthropological commitment to the recovery of a pre-Greek orientation, and it is no dishonor to consider the poem less an utterance of Olson the poet than the potent statement of Olson the archeologist.

Not only does the poem open with the ruins of ancient Angkor Vat, take us through a series of quick cuts of Mayan ritual, and investigate relics and burial vaults, but it closes with a paraphrase of Rimbaud's "Fêtes de la Faim" which turns out ultimately to be a prophetic declaration of Olson's intention to launch an archeological expedition of his own. . . . [The] residue of the ancient Mayan Empire, particularly . . . the stone hieroglyphs, . . . originally caught his interest as the expression of a civilization "anterior" to the Greek in which Western civilization is rooted. . . . Olson is convinced that the energy which nourished their great civilization can be repossessed through the latent power of the glyphs and also through the love, sensed in the very flesh, of the present-day Maya. (pp. 511-12)

Almost within the year, Olson would be off to Mexico where in Campeche and Yucatan he would find confirmation of the assumptions worked out in advance in "The Kingfishers." . . .

"The Human Universe" explicitly relates Olson's taste for Mayan civilization to his position:

> I have found that the hieroglyphs of the Maya disclose a placement of themselves towards nature of enormous contradiction to ourselves. . . . Man has made himself an ugliness and a bore. It was better to be a bird, as these Maya seem to have been, they kept moving their heads so nervously to stay alive, to keep alerted to what they were surrounded by. . . . O, they were hot for the world they lived in, these Maya, hot to get it down the way it was—the way it is, my fellow citizens. . . .

The way it "was" and "is" (could be) is the orientation from which Western man has been alienated since the advent of Greek humanism (logic, classification, and idealism), a humanism (dubbed "discourse" by Olson) which has estranged man "from that which was most familiar." (p. 512)

The poem opens with an ontological dogma: "What does not change / is the will to change." The line finds a specific context later . . . in material Olson quotes from Plutarch; its appearance here is as a controlling text. While assuming the Heraclitean axiom exploited by Plutarch that all is flux, its emphasis rhythmically and conceptually falls on the word "will," the "*will* to change" (italics mine). Olson's explicit definition of will, "the innate voluntarism to live. . . . the infinitive of being," proposed in *The Special View of History* . . . would rule out any notion that human existence is helplessly at the mercy of change. To the contrary, Olson insists that "man does influence external reality," . . . but he consistently points out that there are at least "two sorts of will" which he identifies at the cultural level as the "will to cohere" and the will to "disperse," and at the individual level as the "will of power" and the "will of achievement." . . .

"Power" and "achievement" are terms borrowed from Keats, and the will of power, as Olson explains it, "tries to make it by asserting the self as character. The second makes it by non-asserting the self as self. In other words the riddle is that the true self is not the asserting function but an obeying one, that the actionable is *larger* than the individual and so can be obeyed to." . . . Olson thus assimilates Keats's terms into his principle of "blind obedience" to "personage" and, although the "life in us" is now called the "actionable," the principle that one ought to assume an obedient rather than an assertive role toward natural process remains the same. Olson links his position even closer to Keats's by incorporating into it the principle of negative capability. . . . (p. 513)

The changeless "will to change," then, might be seen as a recommended position in the face of universal flux, a position that is comfortable with mystery, content in process, and devoid of "irritable reaching after fact and reason." It is a position in which the will is obedient to the larger force of process, neither assertive nor egocentric, and yet one which "achieves" because it taps the energy of the "actionable." It is the kind of flexible position that Brooks Adams sees in successful civilizations. . . . (pp. 513-14)

The announcement that opens "The Kingfishers" is thus both an explanation and a challenge. It accounts for the rise and fall of civilizations, but it also advises that the cultural consequences are in man's control: he can choose to assert or obey, disperse or cohere, impose or achieve. The energy of the poem generates from the conflict between these options. (p. 514)

Fernand, the enigmatic center of interest, is presumably an archeologist of sorts himself. Although he is profoundly disturbed by the eroded value of kingfisher feathers, it is not clear whether his concern is aesthetic, economic, or even pedantic. . . . The central enigma of Fernand, however, originates from the undercutting of his apparent aesthetic concern by an oddly materialistic diction.

If the conceptual impact of Fernand is diffuse, his kinetic presence is nevertheless potent. We sense the genuineness of his concern, we feel the depth of his disillusionment with the present, and we grasp the urgency of his appeal. We could explain away the conceptual untidiness of the aesthetic-economic tension as a concession to realism— that's the way people talk at parties—but a more plausible reconciliation of these aesthetic and economic concerns is available in the Brooks Adams excerpt [cited] earlier: "When a highly centralized society disintegrates, under the pressure of economic competition, it is because the energy of the race has been exhausted." Within the context of Adams' cultural theory the cessation of the export of feathers is not merely an economic phenomenon but announces the exhaustion of racial energy. "Why did the export stop?" thus becomes a cultural puzzle of considerable metaphysical weight and suggests that archeology holds promise of a solution. (pp. 514-15)

[However,] the moral seems to be that such mysteries as feathers and E's are impervious to a discursive, analytical stance because their real significance is rooted in a primordial matrix. . . . The epistemological assumptions of one culture may be useless in sounding the assumptions of another. . . . (p. 516)

The concluding section of Part I is appropriately philosophic—even didactic. Principles which up to this point have been presented for intuitive and visceral absorption are now more conceptually defined through the borrowings from Plutarch. In addition to the Plutarch material, however, Olson adds some significant embellishments from Norbert Wiener's *Cybernetics; or, Control and Communication in the Animal and the Machine,* the subtitle of which is directly quoted in the poem. From Wiener's book Olson takes the term "feedback" and declares it a law. In *Cybernetics and Society* Wiener defined feedback as "a method of controlling a system by reinserting into it the results of its past performance," but Olson's interest in the term is in its application to epistemology: as the technique man employs for obedience to "nature's force." In a universe of process, of incessant change, man must assume a posture which will tap rather than obstruct the inherent energy of that change. (pp. 520-21)

The law of feedback is most demonstrable in man's creative acts. There his obligation is to create or "feed back" objects that are "equal to the real itself," and that is why Olson insists that "art is the only twin life has—its only valid metaphysic." . . . (p. 521)

In a universe of ever-shifting relationships, where one

moment's description of a thing is nullified by the new constellation of the next moment, reality is indeed a hopelessly elusive thing; "the too strong grasping of it" obviously "loses it," and the only conceivable way of dealing with it is through corresponding motion. For this reason Olson's work may to some seem circular and repetitive, a charge Olson readily admits. His art, as it "twins" reality, must keep moving abreast with what is going on, forging ahead in a circular envelopment of the subject, never emending, never changing, but, true to the process of his activity, keeping up with the moment and "feeding back" what comes at him fresh at the threshold of the skin. This is the law of feedback, the law of Olson's art. (p. 522)

The narrator's plea [in Part II] . . . is that we forbearingly look into the whiteness of the face of the Mayan ruins with candor, and that in our examination we allow tolerance for "the dryness of the place" (no Eliotic desiccation here, but literally the well-documented dryness of Campeche and Yucatan which made the cultural success of the Maya so spectacular, particularly their achievement in domesticating maize).... In "The Human Universe" Olson concedes that the descendants of the Maya "have gone down before the poundings of our way" and are "poor failures of the modern world, incompetent to arrange that, in the month of June, when the rains have not yet come far enough forward to fill the wells, they have water to wash in or to drink." ... (p. 523)

We should not excuse the conquistadors' destruction of Mayan idols on grounds that the idols were "black" from sacrificial "human gore." To the contrary, we are requested to "hear, where the dry blood talks / where the old appetite walks." Rather than blinding our understanding with moral judgments, we should "look" with candor beneath the dark violence of Mayan ritual and "hear" the primordial reality of "the old appetite." The appetite can still be found; it "hides" in the "eye" of the present-day Maya and "runs in [their] flesh / chalk [the chalk of the glyphs]."

The curious line "whence it arose" seems bafflingly to suggest that the "old appetite" hidden in ancient Mayan culture somehow "arose," presumably to some otherworldly reality. "The Kingfishers" itself provides little assistance toward clarifying this enigmatic phrase, but in "The Praises," which Olson considered a companion piece to "The Kingfishers," the phrase appears again in conjunction with the myth of how the Sun, originally mortal, is enticed into the heavens by the Moon. Olson's admitted euhemerism causes him to conjecture in "The Gate and the Center," "How many generations does it take to turn a hero into a God?" and it would appear as though he tentatively intended to connect anthropological history and religious mythology. (pp. 523-24)

Olson's apparent admiration for the "old appetite" and his disdain for those who would excuse the conquistadors' destruction of the Mayan culture on the grounds that it was violent, bloody, and harsh reinforces the fact that what he culturally values is not ethically but aesthetically admired. "Art is the only morality," . . . he once wrote to Cid Corman, and this conviction helps us to appreciate the kinetic tension with which aesthetic and moral virtues are counterpoised in the final two stanzas of Part II. . . . Primordial power is measured against social "enlightenment" in a kind of Heraclitean acknowledgment that "it is by disease that health is pleasant; by evil that good is pleasant; by hunger, satiety; by weariness, rest." The oppositions imply an inevitable trade-off: beauty at the expense of justice and vice versa. "Dirtiness" becomes law, presumably, when the oppositions are not seen as natural conditions of the flux but as pressing either/or options. The law, as Olson instructs us, is "feed-back"—"staying in process," remaining "obedient" to the "actionable," and avoiding all "irritable grasping after fact and reason." "If man is active," Olson says, "it is exactly here where experience comes in that it is delivered back, and if he stays fresh at the coming in he will be fresh at the going out." The failure of the attention to safeguard that freshness results in "slime," the "fetid nest," "maggots," and all the other ready images of pejorocracy.

It is no wonder, then, that the final part of "The Kingfishers" sarcastically disavows its culture's classical roots, both temperamentally and syntactically, on the basis that it "can take no risk that matters, / the risk of beauty least of all." For Olson, at least, the ending is a forcefully personal one. Whatever others choose to do, he has found his "kin," the Maya, to whom he freely commits himself. With Rimbaud, he fixes his taste to phenomena, "la terre et les pierres," and dedicates himself to the search for honey among the stones. (pp. 524-26)

As if cleaving to its own injunction, "not accumulation but change," "The Kingfishers" does say the same things over and over in its sections, but each time from a different vantage point of space, time, and perception. We have seen recurring figures metamorphize in response to the changed conditions in which they are reconceived: a "pool" changes to a "nest"; from "nest" it changes to a vessel for time; finally it reappears as a burial vault. Similarly, "slime" transposes into "rejectamenta," then to "mongolian louse," then to "maggots," and finally to a generalized "what crawls below." No matter what the figure, the poet's obedience to the energies flowing through him in the feedback process assures its coherence—even its reality. Restricting his responsibility to the act of "attention," to "staying fresh at the coming in and the going out," he remains confident all the while that if he does only this the poem will take care of itself. This is the logic, of course, of "composition by field" and the rationale behind Olson's admission that when he writes a poem, "I don't know what I am up to! And must stay in that state in order to accomplish what I have to do."

"The Kingfishers" was written before "The Gate and the Center," "The Human Universe," *The Special View of History,* and Olson's other statements of cultural position. It preceded Olson's knowledge of the metaphysics of Whitehead which so significantly structures his later work and thought. Nevertheless, the poem's intuitive obedience to the stance toward reality codified for Olson six years later by Whitehead is such that it is a passage from *Process and Reality* (unknown to Olson at the time "The Kingfishers" was written) that best summarizes its theme:

> The social history of mankind exhibits great organizations in their alternating functions of conditions for progress, and of contrivances for stunting humanity.... The art of progress is to preserve order amid change, and to preserve change amid order. Life refuses to be embalmed alive. The more prolonged the

halt in some unrelieved system of order, the greater the crash of the dead society.

Marginalia in Olson's copy of "The E at Delphi," scribbled in ten years after he wrote "The Kingfishers," reveals the confirming impact of his subsequent knowledge of Whitehead. Ammonius' allusion to the famous Heraclitean remark, "It is not possible to step into the same river twice," receives Olson's arrowed note, "Add Whitehead." (pp. 526-28)

The point is that Olson's natural progress seems to be from felt intuition to codified exposition without appreciable loss of the content's integrity: from "The Kingfishers," say, to *The Special View of History*. All this is by way of reaffirming that Olson, as poet-archeologist-teacher-metaphysician, was the master of the "marvelous maneuver"; he did what he knew before he knew what he did. (p. 528)

> Thomas F. Merrill, "'The Kingfishers': Charles Olson's 'Marvelous Maneuver'," in Contemporary Literature (© 1976 by the Board of Regents of the University of Wisconsin System), Vol. 17, No. 4, Autumn, 1976, pp. 506-28.

PHILLIP E. SMITH II

One of the important topics in Olson's work is the relationship of the idea of culture to the idea of community. As he worked on *The Maximus Poems* in the early 1950's, Olson came to believe that modern poets should follow the advice of William Carlos Williams in his essay, "Descent," and resist the inherited culture, history, and mythology of Western Europe in favor of the local immediacy of one's own person and place. Olson interpreted the dominant ideas of Western culture as leading to egoism and the will to power. Against them he insisted modern man should employ a communitarian "alternative humanism" which would result in the "will to cohere." (pp. 13-14)

[In "To Gerhardt,"] Olson draws upon the myth of the death of the European corn-god in order to insist on the necessity of sacrificing the cultural tradition ranging from Homer to Pound.

Olson writes as a man who has already found his poetic stance by rejecting the limitations of previous poetry and culture. . . . (p. 16)

The unity of humanism in place as well as person is the great accomplishment of *The Maximus Poems*. . . . [Olson brings] together the ideas of culture and community. Olson's descent into the poetic and real "ground" of Gloucester brings him not only the sense of locality, or polis, but also a sense of coherence based on local identity. . . . Olson's alternative humanism opposes such simplistic and reductive inherited categories as hierarchies, gods, and mass man. They distort the thoughts and lives of people who would undertake a cultural revolution. (pp. 20-1)

Olson hoped that he might educate his readers to become involved and aware working people who, knowing their European heritage of corporate capitalism, slavery, and slaughter of native Americans, could, with "the polis in their eye," create a new and more perfect community. (p. 21)

> Phillip E. Smith II, "Descent into Polis: Charles Olson's Search for Community," in Modern Poetry Studies (copyright 1977, by Jerome Mazzaro), Spring, 1977, pp. 13-22.

SHERMAN PAUL

[There] is evidence in the eleven plays collected [in *The Fiery Hunt and Other Plays*]—play, dance, dance-and-verse, opera—that Olson knew the various theaters of the classic Greeks, of Noh, of the masque, and of such exemplary contemporary companies as the Yiddish Art Theatre. . . .

Olson was impatient with "straight theatre," which he felt was too much concerned with "contemporary realism." he wanted "enlargements and poets' treatment," a drama, [George Butterick explains in his Introduction], antedating Greek comedy and tragedy, emphatically given over to language and movement and to the single actor. . . . From the start his predilection was for a minimal company: for the single actor who exemplified heroism, danced the Man . . . and for the very few who were necessary to dance out his moral equations. . . .

I call [*The Fiery Hunt and Other Plays*] primary because what . . . makes them notable is their singular emphasis on dancing the Man and, in doing so, dancing out Olson's own developing fable. Anyone familiar with "Apollonius of Tyana" will have remarked Olson's didacticism and the extent to which the dance patently fables him. Now, reading these plays, he will find that this is not unusual but characteristic. Olson defined man, in Vedic fashion, as a "dancing thinker," but in respect to him we might modify this to "dancing pedagogue," bringing over the insistence on single intelligence and adding the insistence on the *work* to be done. (p. 624)

All of these plays are occasional . . . in being clearly the result of Olson's occasions. For example, "The Fiery Hunt," a remarkable finished work, enacts the problem of father(s) and son which was such a critical matter in Olson's career. (p. 625)

Of the plays written at Black Mountain College, two, companion pieces, . . . are especially fine: "Apollonius of Tyana" and "The Born Dancer." The first, "A Dance, with Some [Many] Words," dramatizes Olson's second-birth and self-shaping, the vocational choice that he had made in undertaking *The Maximus Poems*, that great poem of place. Thematically it is the richest of Olson's dance-dramas, the only one hitherto published and well-known. The second, treating Nijinsky, is appropriately pure dance, and dance here, with a brilliance not to be found in any of the others, itself becomes Olson's projective speech. It tells of Olson's respect for the human body, of his awareness of sexuality in the growth of consciousness, and of his hatred of all that impedes its proper (*tropic*) development. (pp. 625-26)

None of Olson's later work is moved by the intensity that informs the early work. In these plays of the 1960's, Olson is a parodist-social critic, somewhat removed from the art-work, often moved by disgust. In "Telepinus" ("a Christmas Entertainment for Manhattanville"!) Telepinus, the Hittite god of fertility whose name heavily puns, still seems to be angry and withdrawn, reluctant to do the work of the solstice. In his speeches he refers to the "futile masses". . . . In "Fluff" ("a 'Temperament' of Four Natures"), a characteristic speech is the following of Lady 1: "I am / wiggle / ass / Doris / Day / I am pastry / in your stomach / I am / bullshit / all over." Hyacinthus says, "I use / democracy // . . . I don't believe / in anything. . . ."

This brief play collapses into "rottenness"; the grossness of the characters overwhelms the author who ends it all in a brawl, "literally, a vulgar dirty mess." Olson, the black humorist, writer of satyr plays?

Even the "Wild Man Fragment," resuming Olson's most serious theme, breaks off in hopeless hopefulness. The wild man, who is "nature" and has "native (neolithic) powers," lives in fear of "much today which / is [hostile]." His antagonist is "Pointed Beard" ["scientist modernism commercial-success present intellectual best (exponential IBM computer future), the full miserable self-autonomy of the intellectual as it now is"]. These stock characters . . . define for us, as our critical situation, the endless opposition of Nature and Culture. They identify Olson's allegiance and the large theme—the great theme of myth—his work addresses. Curiously, they provoke little action; the enterprise is almost static. (pp. 626-27)

> Sherman Paul, "Dancing the Man," in boundary 2 (copyright © boundary 2, 1978), Winter, 1978, pp. 623-27.

*   *   *

OSBORNE, John   1929-

Osborne is an English playwright and screenwriter. His first play, *Look Back in Anger*, established him as an "angry young man" of British drama. In this and in subsequent work Osborne views contemporary social problems with an uncompromising eye, exposing hypocrisy and exploring subjects, such as homosexuality, considered taboo in traditional theater. Critics have complained that his verbal brilliance and thematic daring are not matched by technical control. Osborne collaborated with Anthony Creighton on the play *George Dillon*. (See also *CLC*, Vols. 1, 2, 5, and *Contemporary Authors*, Vols. 13-16, rev. ed.)

JOHN SIMON

What Osborne has tried to do [in *Luther*] is to write a genuine English Brechtian play, modeling himself largely on *Galileo* (which possibly is not one of Brecht's best works and certainly not one of the best models), but he has produced only a brazen simulacrum. It is hollow in the sense that Osborne's Martin Luther is not a complex, rousing, captivating, charismatic leader. . . . (p. 21)

Two factors contribute largely to the hollowness of the protagonist. One is that Osborne tried very carefully to stick to historical data and put together the preponderant part of Luther's speeches out of the reformer's actual preserved utterances. But here several difficulties arise: not enough intimate material by and about Luther is recorded, what there is does not necessarily provide suitable speeches and incidents for a play, and Osborne's selections from the available sources are not always the most judicious. . . . Above all, dramatic and verbal invention is mandatory even in a historical play; Brecht, for that matter, had no compunction about making up all but a few basic facts of the Galileo story.

The other reason for this hollowness is Osborne's insistence on making something negative, doubting, unsure under the arrogance, the key to Luther's revolt. Even if that were all there was to it—and I cannot help feeling that this rebellion without cause, or nearly, is more characteristic of Osborne than of Luther—it does not make for strong drama or a convex, alive hero. The very father-son conflict in

Luther is not commandingly developed, yet that is the farthest Osborne sticks his nose into Lutherian nosography.

As for the shallowness, it stems from Osborne's inability to make the people, places, and issues come to life. Since Brecht is the model, where is the portrait of an age (real or imaginary, it matters not) that we get in *Mother Courage;* where is the dramatic pot running over with hot, bubbling incidents, minor characters, curious inventions? What could be more schematic and stolidly conceived than Osborne's Knight who is supposed to convey Luther's betrayal of the peasants; what could be more perfunctory and unintegrated than the sudden emergence and disappearance of a Mrs. Luther?

But, of course, this is Osborne's weakness: he writes dazzlingly about single characters who fulminate in deprecation and imprecation, who can scorch and blast a whole human landscape with their tirades; but when it comes to interrelating characters, presenting complementary or conflicting views with equal vivacity and conviction, Osborne's powers flag. (pp. 21-2)

> John Simon, "'Luther'" (1963-64), in his Uneasy Stages: A Chronicle of the New York Theater, 1963-1973 (copyright © 1975 by John Simon; reprinted by permission of Random House, Inc.), Random House, 1976, pp. 21-2.

JOHN SIMON

John Osborne's *A Patriot for Me* is about as unnecessary a play as I have ever seen. (p. 218)

Altogether, Osborne is a perfect example of a playwright who voices the mood of a particular moment in history: *Look Back in Anger* was, to a degree, the expression of English working-class anger against the upper classes, which at last could be reviled with impunity. But it was even more the venting of a self-destructive rage such as overtakes a country that sees itself fallen from political eminence to feeding on memories. And to men too young to have lived them, such memories become a source of especial irritation. Osborne had not so much written a play as tapped a vein.

But there was something that he genuinely possessed: a gift for raillery, invective, lacerating tirades whose victims could be anyone or anything, and whose power, though rhetorical rather than dramatic, could nevertheless buffet the stage. When the time of heroes and statesmen is passed comes the time of the jeerer; Osborne became the beloved Thersites of the British theater. As the climate changed, he did his best to change with the times, and became more and more successful, wealthy, upper class and conservative. But his one true note—his fulminations—no longer fitted the new perspective. England, its upper crust somewhat reshuffled, was becoming a homogeneous place again, and with Osborne safely ensconced in his room at the top, nothing remained for him to do except inveigh against the middle class (*Inadmissible Evidence*) or the lower class (*The Hotel in Amsterdam*).

In the latter play and in *Time Present*, Osborne goes to absurd lengths to find something to assail, even as his development into a reactionary proceeds apace: in *A Bond Honoured* even God comes off scot-free. In *A Patriot for Me*, the only thing Redl, on the verge of suicide, can harangue against is—the Spaniards! His psychologically and dramatically unwarranted attack on them is surely the most gratuitous farewell speech ever written. In future Osborne plays the characters may be reduced to denouncing cigarettes or the London telephone directory; the objects of invective have become so remote or stale that a late Osborne play is just a bunch of sour gripes.

A Patriot for Me seems to deal with ambition and self-indulgence fighting it out against the background of a similarly schizoid but also narrow-minded and corrupt society. It is some kind of dance on top of the volcano, some sort of *Walpurgisnacht* hurtling into *Götterdämmerung,* in which social orders, races, sexes, even fellow homosexuals oppose, torment and persecute one another—but of all these things Osborne tells you no more than a high-school sex orientation lecture tells about human relations. (pp. 218-19)

What Osborne cannot do is write about tenderness and love, hetero- or homosexual. (p. 219)

Feeble vignettes succeed one another: *A Patriot for Me* is as superficial a passing parade as *Luther.* . . . The wit is pathetic ("You were born with a silver saber up your whatnot") and only the pathos is good for a laugh ("It's the time of night when people die. People give up"). Loosely and flaccidly, the play follows a fascinating career, and ends with a bang from a Browning and a whimper from Osborne. (pp. 219-20)

You might expect a play whose high point is a drag ball to be a bore; what you would not expect is that even the drag ball is a drag. (p. 220)

> John Simon, "'A Patriot for Me'" (1969), in his Uneasy Stages: A Chronicle of the New York Theater, 1963-1973 (copyright © 1975 by John Simon; reprinted by permission of Random House, Inc.), Random House, 1976, pp. 218-20.

JOHN LAHR

Osborne's craft has always been overrated. His ability to manage plot and invent startling stage images is marginal; his language, that brute verbal overkill which sizzled the '50's and early '60's has turned from taut, sometimes beautiful explosions of rancorous poetry to more theatrical badinage in the last decade. All his texts suffer from a literary sloppiness which mirrors his own intellectual disarray. His adaptation [of *The Picture of Dorian Gray*] isn't so much 'executed' as excreted. Osborne had an opportunity to bring new theatrical life to a tale whose longeurs and elusiveness put the vehicle into disrepair even as a novel. But just to red-pencil the novel as he does and then mount it on stage is to turn the theatre into a library instead of a playing area. Epigrams are dramatic events on the page; but on stage, they pall without the counterpoint of action. Reading Wilde's novel requires at least one's eyes are open. The stage adaptation can be completely comprehended with one's eyes shut—the true test of dismal theatre. (p. 24)

> John Lahr, in Plays and Players (© copyright John Lahr 1975; reprinted with permission), April, 1975.

ANDREW K. KENNEDY

There appears to be something improvised, even haphazard, in the way Osborne moves from one play-style to another. There are no long-deliberated changes from one mode of language to another (as in Eliot), nor does there seem to be a compelling inner movement (as in the gradual

compression of language in Beckett and Pinter). Yet one can see in Osborne's zig-zagging line of development two main play-forms—the room-based and the open-stage play —and two distinct stage languages—histrionic self-expression and the dialogue of characters intended to be socially, or historically, representative. The tension between these two modes of language keeps recurring in both types of play. Sometimes Osborne attempts to create an interplay between the two modes of language within a double or shifting structure: in *The Entertainer* through connecting Archie Rice's domestic talk with his music hall 'turns', in *Luther* through the shift from the private interior of Act I to the 'epic' propensities of the other two acts. The histrionic monologuist keeps re-entering the large-scale 'open' plays; and the dialogue of more or less monologue-centred plays keeps expanding (or thinning out) to catch, in almost gratuitous sketch-like scenes, the *language,* the up-to-date idiom, of this or that *contemporary* cartoon type. . . . In all this we find versatile inventiveness at the cost of imperfect artistic control. And we recognise Osborne's at once generous and anxious urge to embody *both* the inner and the outer world; to express troubled psychic states and to represent all kinds of 'interest'—voices, social movements, scenes. In brief, the urge towards wholeness.

Yet it is precisely in his language that Osborne has been least able to develop, to match his ideal conception of a drama that is at once personal and social or communal. There is a recurrent loss of 'felt life' in his dialogue of relationship, group, and large-scale public events, both in the contemporary and the historical or quasi-historical plays. (In the latter Osborne has found it particularly difficult to give life to 'the potentially fascinating dialectic' between an ideology or an institution and the principal character—the potential Brechtian direction.) By contrast, he has given a new voice to the isolated or wounded character, the play seen through a temperament, the line from Strindberg. (pp. 194-95)

In a witty simplification, Mary McCarthy wrote that Osborne 'like a coloratura or countertenor, finds that he is limited to parts of experience, as it were, already written for his voice's strange timbre'. In other words, Osborne cannot extend the range of his dramatic language—though he keeps straining to do so—through a personal creative limitation. Yet, is it not possible that such a limitation is intensified by the difficulty, in our time, of creating a language that has dramatic life *both* on the personal and on the communal plane? (p. 196)

Osborne's drama, which keeps striving towards some balance of the personal and social in the dialogue itself, repeatedly makes one conscious of an acute imbalance. Frequently, the imbalance is exactly what is being dramatised. In the early and contemporary plays the hyperarticulate character (George Dillon, Jimmy Porter) defines himself by rejecting, with ribald contempt, the language as much as the values of a group (the clichés of the Elliot family, the genteelisms of Alison and her sort). In a later play like *Inadmissible Evidence* Osborne goes much further—towards a curiously externalised form of solipsism: the self-alienated monologue of Bill Maitland absorbs solid clusters of vocabulary from the social world—technology, legal jargon and so on—only to spit them out again as alien stuff. (p. 198)

There is much in Osborne's dramatic language that seems to connect with the desire to 'hear the words out loud', in order to reach some certainty (if only the reassurance of 'I talk, therefore I am'—as Mary McCarthy suggests). Histrionic rhetoric in particular is inseparable from the *feeling* that words are self-authenticating. Further, Osborne is essentially a verbal dramatist.... Perhaps it is no accident that the term 'old-fashioned'—also used by Osborne about the form of his first play—is now applied to his 'allegiance to words', in a context that makes it clear that Osborne is aware of the shrinking area of meaning through words. The power of language is asserted against its felt decline. The texture of Osborne's rhetoric itself embodies this tension— the attempt to gain new theatrical vitality for what is, after all, an 'old-fashioned' language. (p. 204)

[There] is considerable stylistic variation in feeling in Osborne's rhetoric of self-dramatisation, both in particular speeches and from one play to another. It may not be what Eliot called 'an improvement in language', but it does amount to a revitalisation of rhetoric.

The limitations of Osborne's rhetoric seem to be these: it is an over-externalised rhetoric, which cannot accommodate 'thinking aloud' or genuine inwardness: it has 'no time for' pauses and silences, reflection and implicit self-seeing.... It is a rhetoric which amplifies a mediocre speaker, or intensifies a naturalistically based idiom; it does not create a new dramatic language capable of expressing unexpected states of mind and experience—though that might be too much to expect. At the same time the energies of this rhetoric seem to be too much at the mercy of moments of empathy releasing the right kind of verbal paroxysm—with the risk of sheer exhaustion. By now Osborne himself seems to have got tired of rhetoric. *Inadmissible Evidence* was the last play where rhetoric was consistently expressive; the later plays either avoid, or (as in *Time Present*) look back on that style fitfully.

It is probable that Osborne would be more at home in a theatre which still had a central rhetorical convention— somewhere between Elizabethan drama and Victorian melodrama. As it is, his persistent naturalism has tended to inhibit; and his 'restless search for a style' has only rarely— in *The Entertainer* and in *Inadmissible Evidence*—led to a roughly satisfying fusion between the structure of the play and texture of the dialogue—releasing and controlling a 'full-blooded' theatrical language. (pp. 211-12)

> *Andrew K. Kennedy, in his* Six Dramatists in Search of a Language: Studies in Dramatic Language *(© Cambridge University Press 1975), Cambridge University Press, 1975.*

E. G. BIERHAUS, JR.

Why [*Look Back in Anger*] no longer generates [its early] enthusiasm is the purpose of this essay, for if we respond to *Look Back in Anger* at all today we do so because it is an event . . . , not because it is a play that sucks us into its world and compels us to accept that world on its own terms. (p. 47)

Look Back in Anger deals with a social theme; it is clearly dependent upon its dramatic antecedents (most notably a conventional plot packaged in a well-made play); and its characters are conscious of class, that is to say they are traditional rather than innovative. Yet . . . it introduces a new element into drama, an element of such proportions that it has been changing the form of drama (though not its substance) ever since.

I want to discuss this new element (actually, it is an old element that Osborne rediscovered), but before doing so I want to explain why the modern response to *Look Back in Anger* is more respectful than enthusiastic. We must first see how predictably the play rolls along without extending itself beyond the perimeters of a thousand prior well-made plays before we can truly appreciate the new element it introduces.

For our response to a play to be enthusiastic, our minds and our emotions must be engaged by what we are seeing or reading. . . . Although *Look Back in Anger* continues to engage our emotions, it fails to engage our minds. After watching or reading it, we feel dissatisfied and disappointed. There are, I think, three reasons for this intellectual failure: the play's transparent structure, its arbitrary motivations, and its bogus characterizations. (pp. 47-8)

In *Look Back in Anger* the transparency of its disguises is so obtrusive that we become intellectually isolated from it before it is half over. For example, a telephone call from Helena prepares us for the Act I curtain, and a telephone call from the hospital where Hugh's mother is dying prepares us for the Act II, scene 1, curtain. Moreover, Cliff's exit in Act I to buy cigarettes is unconvincing: its dramatic convenience undercuts any believability it might possess. And Cliff's exit before Jimmy's return in Act II, scene 2, is such a reversal that even Osborne feels compelled to rationalize it in a stage direction. . . . These disguises are so blatant that we aren't even permitted the mental satisfaction of penetrating them. (p. 48)

Seeing through a play to its structure as we do in *Look Back in Anger* is as disturbing as seeing a stage hand pass by an open window during performance. When the magic tricks are obvious, one feels embarrassed for and contemptuous of and bored by the magician.

Equally as unreliable in this play are the motivations of its characters. They are often as arbitrary as the French scenes are capricious. At some point, a motivation of every character is suspect. Characters have a habit of adopting one stance then another without a convincing reason, sometimes without any reason at all. (p. 49)

[Predictability] is ubiquitous in this play. Its characters don't grow: they regress, although I suppose it can be argued that regression is at least a *change*. (p. 51)

The major problem with *Look Back in Anger* is that it wants stature. Its present and passing worlds are the same, with one exception: Jimmy, Alison, Cliff, and Helena have all the Edwardian aspirations, but none of the graces. The world of this play is not so much angry as barren. . . . In lamenting the passage of the Edwardian world, Jimmy laments indeed the passing of his own. The Edwardian world, however, was real; even as a referent in dramatic dialogue it stands for something. But the world of *Look Back in Anger* stands for nothing. It is sterile. Its characters talk a lot, but they don't *say* anything. What this play needs is silence.

We can, I think, attribute these arbitrary motivations and opposing stances (and quite possibly the transparent structure) to the play's faulty characters. *Look Back in Anger* is a love story that is untrue to itself. The actual lovers in this play are Jimmy and Cliff. Alison and Helen—and Madeline —are included to make its world more universal and respectable (plays in 1956 were still censored by the Lord Chamberlain), and to give Jimmy an opportunity to show off his masculine superiority. Despite these subterfuges, however, the real love affair in this play is homosexual. When Jimmy and Cliff interact, the stage lights up with "revolutionary fire." . . .

This, of course, throws the play completely out of focus because the action that isn't there is really the action that's taking place, while the action that's taking place is really only a substitute for the action that isn't there. (p. 52)

Jimmy wants to create his own world, to re-order relationships: he wants Alison to be his mother and he wants Cliff to have his babies. Since this is impossible, he makes everyone suffer. The character of Jimmy Porter is so unremittingly selfish, savage, and, at last, destructive that not a shred of humanity adheres to it. Goethe remarks somewhere that "One cannot always be a hero, but one can always be a man." Poor Jimmy can't even be a man. For dramatic characters in realistic drama, this is fatal.

Because a genre throws its own details into relief, any failure of these details is inevitably amplified. If Jimmy Porter is to be successful, one has to care about him. And we don't. We don't care about him because his constant solipsistic rhetoric cuts off our response. When you get as much affection as Jimmy gets from his world, you have to give something in return. But he never does. He shows us no contrasts and no costs, concomitant components in a changing character. But Jimmy doesn't change. Ultimately, therefore, we don't care about him because he can't risk himself: he has no self to risk.

Why then is *Look Back in Anger* an important play? What makes it a landmark? The answer is paradoxical: anger. That which prevents our intellectual response to Jimmy is also the very characteristic which engages our emotions. If *Look Back in Anger*'s link with the past is the well-made play, its link with the future is anger: vituperative, vicious, and direct. There are no contrasts within Jimmy Porter because his whole character is a contrast with the surface courtesies of his Edwardian predecessors. In that world where animosity was always dignified, "a vulgar wrangle was unknown."

Jimmy may be indirect about love, but he's eloquently explicit when angry. That much of his anger is misplaced does not diminish the impact of its being *expressed*. When cornered—as he is throughout the play because his sexual preference is denied expression—Jimmy sucks in his breath, relaxes that stiff upper lip that hasn't spoken a coarse word on stage since the Elizabethans, and lashes out. He takes on everyone and exhausts them all. Indeed, it is precisely because Jimmy's anger is so open that audiences and readers respond to him in spite of themselves. (pp. 53-4)

Look Back in Anger is already an anachronism. But it is also a landmark. And what it marks, namely that anger is a viable dramatic alternative to repression, is worth celebrating. *Look Back in Anger*'s greatest achievement is its emancipation of drama from the restrictions of past generations. Just when we expected emotional outbursts in the theatre to be forever off stage or in impeccably good taste, this play crept upon us, leaving us stunned, drained, almost disbelieving. Jimmy Porter is not an "Eminent Victorian," nor was he "born out of his time". One honors him more, and

the play he dominates, by calling him an angry young man. (p. 55)

E. G. Bierhaus, Jr., "No World of Its Own: 'Look Back in Anger' Twenty Years Later," in Modern Drama *(copyright © 1976, University of Toronto, Graduate Centre for Study of Drama; with the permission of* Modern Drama*), March, 1976, pp. 47-55.*

LAWRENCE R. RIES

Osborne's plays present characters who flail about somewhat violently but always futilely in a hopeless world. His heroes have moved beyond hope and have accepted the despair that has infected much of modern society. Archie Rice, in *The Entertainer,* is a characteristic Osborne hero driven towards despair by the modern spirit. He tries to keep alive an art of the past, vaudeville, but the sense of identity that was formerly necessary has been destroyed. Archie says, "We all had our own style, our own songs." But his father answers him, "They don't want real people any more." When the individual's identity and sense of purpose is gone, he is left with the incapacity to act. For this reason, Archie's spirit is essentially nihilistic. . . . Archie has given in to the malaise of the age, and is beyond the point of reasserting himself. . . . Archie's daughter Jean is the voice of the present who offers hope through social and moral commitment. She has taken part in a demonstration against the prime minister in Trafalgar Square, and thinks the answers to the world's problems lie in the personal sense of commitment. Osborne presents a sympathetic picture of Jean at the beginning of the play, but the strength of the "social salvage unit" comes to appear quite shoddy in contrast to Archie's open pessimism as the drama develops. (p. 27)

Lawrence R. Ries, in his Wolf Masks: Violence in Contemporary Poetry *(copyright © 1977 by Kennikat Press Corp.; reprinted by permission of Kennikat Press Corp.), Kennikat, 1977.*

*   *   *

OTERO, Blas de   1916-

Otero is a Spanish poet. His early poetry is marked by its anguished and isolated tone, reflecting the young poet's struggle with the question of God and of faith. Later in his life, however, Otero overcame his sense of alienation and expanded his poetic concerns to include the social and political problems of contemporary Spain. He is generally considered one of the finest and most influential poets of the postwar generation in Spain.

HARDIE ST. MARTIN

Blas de Otero reaches back to the roots of Spain for his poems. In his earlier work words exploded with savage passion in love poems to a withdrawn God and in poems about death—poems became tender and more lyrical when a woman or sad little girls came into them—, but the poetry he was now doing was loaded with quiet indignation and anguish. . . . The poet is possessed by an Unamunesque preoccupation with himself, with God—if such a being exists—and eternal peace. . . . Peace, in this world, must replace hunger, suffering, injustice.

Common oppression joins men. Now that the smoke has lifted from the ruin laid round by the Spanish Civil War the poet has to examine reality like other men. . . .

Otero's approach sometimes takes the form of popular or traditional song—sometimes he imitates its rhythms and sometimes he inserts bits or even just echoes of an actual song in his poems—and sometimes he draws the reader with a conversational tone. The violence that follows out of wasted love for God in his earlier poetry gives way to a more mature calmness in his later work. Driven out of himself to a more human kind of poetry by a hard historical circumstance, from the sadness and desperation of private concern to a deep interest in his fellowman, the poet's wild anger becomes less concentrated and more compassion comes into his words. There is also hope. (pp. 7-8)

Many things happen to words in Otero's poetry. One senses a strange transformation in language. The poet has control in an opposition between him and his material. Dislocations, enjambments and sudden breaks at the end of a line are used to make images and feelings work on more than one level at the same time, as in "Letters and Poems to Nazim Hikmet" where he speaks

> . . . about things that don't exist: God
> is eavesdropping behind the door . . .

What an amazing God is this that does not exist yet eavesdrops behind prison-cell doors! The irony grows by suspending the word "God" at the end of one line and dropping it suddenly on the next line. It also drops like a mask behind which the enemy is hiding.

He can surprise with a sudden twist of phrase. For instance, the expected "cogidos de la mano" (holding hands, hand in hand) is made over into the pathetic "cogidos de la muerte" (holding deaths, death in death). . . . The poet sees something with the sharp insight of a child and the thing is familiar and brand new at once. Otero also makes us look in a fresh way at phrases or lines he borrows from other poets (Quevedo, Machado, Vallejo). In his work each sound looks for the companion that will follow it and once found they cannot exist without each other. (pp. 9-10)

Otero listens to the unusual logic of his imagination and there is a thread of irrationality in many of his poems that attract us like the dark fierce moments in Blake or Rimbaud. The inexplicable and the clear are inseparable in some of his poems. His poetry has a sort of baroque interior (not cluttered up in his better poems) in contrast to the baroque exterior of Lorca and some of his generation. Immediate impact on the reader seems to have been the poet's early aim but the later poems are stronger in a subtle way, more disciplined, working on the reader through a simplicity comparable, at its best, to Antonio Machado's. (pp. 10-11)

Hardie St. Martin, "A Poet in Time," in Twenty Poems by Blas de Otero, translated by Hardie St. Martin (copyright © 1964 by the Sixties Press), Sixties Press, 1964, pp. 7-12.

GEOFFREY R. BARROW

In Historias fingidas y verdaderas Blas de Otero renounces the lyric in favour of prose, avoids crisp denunciation and protest and rejects a clear and distinct syntax. In place of the assertive confidence that has dominated his writing during the last decade, he raises doubts as to his poetic identity; instead of faith in a revolutionary immensa mayoría, he engages in intensive self-scrutiny. The tension of the work lies in the depiction of conflicts within the personality of the poet. A psychological reality is expressed in prose pieces that are a projection of states of mind, of fears, memories and dreams, as well as a personal record of daily life. The prose is now contorted and compressed, now casual and rambling. The lack of serenity is mirrored in this prose style and in an often private symbolism that point to a fragmented and purposeless everyday life and project a disintegrated world picture.

The section on Cuba and the autobiographical pieces in the work suggest that the immediate catalysts for this prise de conscience are Otero's visit to an Hispanic revolutionary socialist state and the approach of middle age. At the same time, the roots of this intimate journal lie in contradictions already latent in the poet's work. The discrepancies between revolutionary idealism and a tedious, futile, wandering existence; between nostalgia for the tranquility of Vizcaya, his patria chica, and the actual problems of Spain; between idealistic, moral criticism and the course of historical events emerge as sources of tension. The poet's social marginality, his practical inability to effect any social change, is implicit. The total effect is that of paradox, specifically, the paradox of exile, of indefinite suspension. . . . (pp. 39-40)

Historias fingidas y verdaderas is Otero's first venture into prose apart from a handful of prose fragments in Ancia and En castellano and was written concurrently with the last poems to be included in Que trate de España. It represents an important stage in the disintegration of traditional poetic forms begun in Pido la paz y la palabra. The brevity of the prose pieces and their recourse to the sound effects, imagery and density of expression usually associated with verse preclude them from being considered as a legitimate effort to develop an authentic prose style. True, there is a tendency toward the anecdotal, descriptive, and expository, but the work is essentially experimental. It marks a transformation of the lyric, a further slackening of poetic convention, not a premature termination of Otero's development as a lyric poet.

The movement toward a greater formal freedom already demonstrated in Otero's poetry by the gradual introduction of free verse, the occasional suppression of punctuation and the use of collage technique is now taken a step further. The prose pieces vary in length from less than a dozen lines to almost three pages and the flexible arrangement of paragraphs permits a variety of formal structures. . . . There is no single dominant principle of organisation. . . . Discursive autobiographical accounts appear beside impressionistic sequences, cinematographic montages and newspaper-like press releases, not to mention arguments and commentaries. Otero is rethinking his notions of literary form and genre in order to render the whole of his many-sided personality. Diversity of form is one way of coping literarily with inner tensions and contradictions.

On another level, the uncertainties of Otero's syntax and diction represent an uncannily accurate reproduction of the inflections and rambling irrelevancies of everyday speech, with the stress upon speech rhythms as the basis for prose. . . . [Free] associations, ellipses and paratactical constructions help to free the sentence from the restrictions of logic and convention. This is more than just the integration of a number of already existing techniques derived from surrealism. It is an act of resistance, an assertion of the value of freedom and spontaneity over formal, technical craftsmanship. (pp. 40-1)

Otero constantly questions his function, allegiances, and antecedents, either directly or by allusion and pastiche. He is intricate to the point of self-contradiction, but this lack of a consistent mask, the obsessive doubts and negations of his poetic identity, gives his writing a peculiar range and depth. His theory of poetry swings between the ethical and the aesthetic although he comes close to losing faith in literature itself. Such uncertainties reflect the troubled relationship of authorship to authority, the isolation of the poet and the collapse of a shared community to which both writer and reader belong.

Linking the cause of poetry with that of politics, Otero asserts the ethical or utilitarian function of literature. He is trying to re-establish a lost unity between poet and audience in which the personal and the collective become one. (p. 41)

No consistent political theory of art emerges from [his] scattered and piecemeal statements. The dream of revolution serves as an ideal upon which values can be based but there is no understanding of the dialectical evolution of the new world from the old and the precise role of the poet in this transformation. Moreover, there is in *Historias fingidas y verdaderas* a vacillation between the figure of the poet as revolutionary, however visionary and utopian, and that of the poet as aesthete, a curious coexistence of extreme political and poetic tendencies.

Several accounts of the nature and function of poetry convey a belief in the autonomy of the poem which suggests Otero has turned aesthete, specialist, and refuses to see further than his specialisation. He claims that the poetic image preserves what is lasting and essential in everyday experience, capturing an immanent or transcendent reality that it alone can convey.... The process of naming is a consuming interest of the poet and is evidence of an attempt to create a poetic world abstracted from the phenomenal world. What 'is' is differentiated from what 'exists.' ... This is an assertion of the poet's power to create a world that captures the essence of phenomenal reality yet exists independently, not a playful tautology uttered by the poet posing as confidence man.

The belief in poetry as an instrument of knowledge and truth becomes a kind of religion which allows Otero to reject his empirical self and maintain that his true self is only to be found in the poem.... [The] work of art is granted some form of ultimate reality or divinity and the creative process becomes a means to salvation.... There is the utmost concentration on the poem's peculiar demands but the process is ultimately magical and intuitive. In an almost mystical manner, the poet gives himself up to the absolute reality that transcends him, although elsewhere the process is considered to be more conscious and painful.

Ironically, the figure of the poet as anti-poet, fatigued and disgusted with literature, is a measure of his dedication to his art. Even though he admits to a fanatical compulsion to write, he often aspires to reject the rigour and sacrifice required.... [He projects] the figure of the poet as sufferer, his suffering being a token of effort and seriousness. Nevertheless, Otero's ambivalent attitude toward written literature hides a real criticism of writing as a formalised technique. (pp. 42-3)

The continuing need for poetry is unquestioned. What is criticised is the social marginality of the poet, his poor reception, which is seen as a consequence of written culture. Otero recognises the potential of the electronic media and song to propagate speech rather than writing, to make the poet speak again. He also recognises the distance between what is possible and what actually exists.

The common denominator of Otero's diffidence and uncertainty about the poet's relationship to his public, of his doubts about written culture, and of his shifting between extreme political and poetic tendencies is the condition of interior exile. The poet's rootlessness is revealed as much by the frequency with which his prose turns upon itself to explore the nature and function of poetry as by his extraordinary number of references to other writers and artists.... Like Ezra Pound, Otero strives to create his own system of values, his own canon of what should be known, admired and imitated. Lacking the assurance of a common tradition, the displaced poet gathers sustenance from a desperate and eclectic search for technical forerunners and spiritual companions. (pp. 44-5)

There is also a political dilemma in which the poet on the one hand seeks escape and support in a quest for absolute values that would shore up his doubts and uncertainties, while on the other he engages in a desperate attempt to protest against the world, register its omnipresent evil and gather strength from a willed optimism. The aesthetic dilemma resulted in an effort to renovate a poetic tradition and a plea for cultural pluralism. The political dilemma is symbolised by the figure of the *vagamundo,* the displaced and disoriented figure of the poet lacking any clear and consistent political philosophy.

The attention given to memories and dreams, childhood, places visited and distant loves marks an attempt to recover a lost innocence, an attempt frequently frustrated by the intrusion of hostile elements. (p. 45)

A quest for absolute values lies behind Otero's concern with childhood memories, recollections of amorous moments, townscapes drawn from his travels, surrealistic explorations of irrational dreams and stylised pictorial visions. The continuing influence of Machado is suggested by the balconies, mirrors, parks and water images that provide a means of access to a timeless world perceived by the intuition. This lonely withdrawal into contemplation is epitomised in "Vivir para ver" ... where, recalling Salinas, Otero erects the bastion of the poetic imagination against a corrosive reality. Only by closing his eyes to insulate himself from the outside world is the poet able to see. Yet Otero rarely manages to completely disassociate himself from historical reality.... Hostile elements continually prevent the poet from resurrecting lost paradises of youth and innocence.

In contrast with this private search for absolute values, Otero succumbs to absolute political creeds and, influenced especially by his contact with Cuba, supports the cause of a world-wide socialist revolution. He affirms his solidarity with the broad masses of the Spanish people, with North Vietnam, and with the young.... More important, he espouses collectivism because it offers escape from his own solitude.... The idealistic tendency, moral outlook, piecemeal facts, and secular millennialism of Otero's politics, however, mark a primitive level of political awareness and bear the stamp of revolutionary romanticism.

Apart from an oblique attack on censorship, the object of

Otero's protest is the condition of the Spanish working class, the *inmensa mayoria* with which he has allied himself for over two decades.... Reference points are dissolved and the poet's subjects are considered in a largely indeterminate social situation. The miners are monumentalised figures, the migrant labourers are characterised impressionistically by their suitcases and regional accents, and the rural workers are only identified symbolically as "la boca desdentada." The cornerstone of Otero's critique is that in Spain, nothing changes.... There is no understanding of the concrete social and economic structures of wealth and power except in "De playa a playa" ... where the poet mounts a brief attack against American monopoly capitalism.

The political impotence Otero experiences, his practical inability to effect any social change whatsoever, explains his attraction to secular millennialism and Christian ethics. The broad moral stance adopted in the third-person self-portrait, "Manifiesto" ..., exemplifies his leaning toward ethical referents such as *desidia, falsedad, envidia sin causa,* and *odio sin pretexto.* Yet such a moral outlook is naive since it points to certain idealistic expectations of the poet as if his class enemy had always stuck to promises of fair play. Otero's idealism also appears in his image of the approaching millennium, already foreshadowed by the Cuban Revolution and soon to be achieved in Spain.... Such a belief in imminent redemption alongside the portrayal of present realities is revolutionary utopianism, an attempt to arrive at once at the new world without understanding the dialectical evolution of the new from the old. The existing order will be inverted and the broad masses of the Spanish people will be the dominant figures of a new order. This is the politics of the optative. Otero adds to his idealisation of the *inmensa mayoria* and his blunting of the antagonistic contradictions operating in society an image of history made by the masses and impelled by some unknown force.... But the masses are never seen as explicitly conscious of their role in history and the implication that they will one day achieve the millennium suggests that, in present terms, the only class in which Otero can place his hope is written off as hopeless. (pp. 46-8)

The anguish of Otero's political dilemma, prevented by circumstance from achieving escapist absolutes and by utopian ideology from addressing himself to the concrete problems of popular life, is personified in the figure of *el vagamundo.* This is the familiar modern exile, wanderer, uprooted man with his immediate Spanish antecedent in Alberti's *hombre deshabitado.* Otero's creation of the personae of *el vagamundo* and the autobiographical third-person, *el hombre,* exemplifies the ontological problems of a poet suspended between a world he rejects and one that does not yet exist. Waiting, tedium and purposelessness are recurrent themes, as is the dogged will of the poet to survive.

Otero's aimless wandering is recorded in prose pieces with such characteristic titles as "Los días y los temas," "Ciudades," "Seguir siguiendo," "Al azar," "Diario," "Pasar," "Andar," and, of course, "El vagamundo." He casts himself as an impotent spectator, detached from mankind, sunk in solitude and introspection, penning irrepressibly his random impressions. The minutiae of observed reality are transcribed along with memories, reflections and asides to evoke the final emptiness and tedium of his travels, his fragmented daily existence. The erratic and unexpected development of the prose conveys bewilderment and indecision. The physical picture of the poet ... and his repeated awareness of his own death suggest the weariness of self-imposed exile. True, there is much wit and humour in the work.... But solitude and lack of direction as frequently bring forth desperate self-justifications, pleas for peace, and a willed and fragile optimism.

It is premature to decide whether *Historias fingidas y verdaderas* marks a temporary setback in Otero's development as a political poet. The tortuous contradictions, vacillations between progressive and reactionary political tendencies, hermeticism, and introspection point to disenchantment as well as signalling the paradox of a civilised and sensitive poet who strives after revolutionary solidarity with the people. The primitive level of political awareness is an historically necessary weakness in a Spain beset with the traditional failure of liberalism, controlled by censorship, and where the only dissent permitted is that couched in ethical language. Out of his desire to be faithful to several gods Otero has produced a literary work that is, notwithstanding its documentary importance as a poet's journal, fundamentally inauthentic, shattered rather than made taut by its unresolved contradictions. Yet the profusion of reflections upon writing, literary tradition, poetry, the poet and his audience signify an effort to struggle with and overcome an ideological and aesthetic crisis. (pp. 48-9)

> *Geoffrey R. Barrow, "A Hidden Paradox: Blas de Otero's 'Historias Fingidas y Verdaderas'," in* Hispanofila, *May, 1975, pp. 39-49.*

*   *   *

OZ, Amos   1939-

Oz is an Israeli novelist, short story writer, editor, and essayist. His work is rich in symbolic and allegorical overtones: the geographic characteristics of modern-day Jerusalem become in his fiction a symbol of human isolation; the persecution of the Jews at the hands of the Christians during the Crusades alludes to the current crisis in the Middle East. Both the depth of his thematic concerns and the consistent high quality of his prose mark him as one of the finest writers in Israel. (See also *CLC*, Vols. 5, 8, and *Contemporary Authors*, Vols. 53-56.)

HANA WIRTH-NESHER

The development of the novel and the rise of modern cities have taken place concurrently. As society has tended more and more to become concentrated in what we call cities, the novel has been a major literary response, concerning itself with the complex interaction among individuals in groups and between individuals and society. (p. 91)

Because the city as a dense heterogeneous society tends to instill in its inhabitants the sense of a threatening "other," the modern Jewish novel becomes a classic example of how the city functions symbolically in modern literature. Like Leopold Bloom in Joyce's *Ulysses,* who roams the streets of Dublin as an outsider because he is a Jew, the characters ... [in] Amos Oz's *My Michael,* ... never lose their sense of strangeness in the urban environment. (p. 93)

[In] Jerusalem, despite its centuries of civilizations, it is the hills that always dominate, that appear ready to envelop and crush the city at will, and that outlast each layer of shards and stone. The winds of the Judean hills, sweeping over the city like God's whirlwind in the book of Job, overawe man's pretensions and dwarf even the most bold and brilliant of his structures.

In this setting of gold and silver domes and stone bulwarks and in this meeting place of the Levant and the West, . . . Oz has situated the events of his novel, *My Michael.* . . . [The] novel is the first person narrative of Hannah Gonen, an Israeli born young woman who leaves her studies in literature to marry an aspiring geologist, Michael. The rest is a tale of frustration. Michael, Hannah soon discovers, is a sterile, excessively earnest academic whose obsession with identifying rocks she finds incomprehensible and his goals for scholarly publication and university advancement petty. Hannah can find no outlet for her sensual longings—her husband seems distant and dull, and the city treats her with stony indifference. The novel is a record of her disappointments, neuroses, and fantasies. (p. 100)

The city of Jerusalem is not merely background in this novel; it plays a dominant role in that its characteristics are intertwined with the psychology of the central consciousness. It is important to note here the geography and terrain that Hannah Gonen inhabits in the Jerusalem of the 1950's. First, it is a divided city. . . . Surrounding the city topographically are the Judean hills, vast stretches of bare, dramatic hills that bring cool winds to the city and are covered, for the most part, with shadows and rock, not forest. . . . The city itself in its totality is heterogeneous, a mixture of Jew, Moslem, and Christian. (pp. 100-01)

What all of this means is that Hannah Gonen lives in a city that may be fairly homogeneous as a section but is heterogeneous organically. Unlike the "other" of ethnic neighborhoods accessible to all in a city like New York, Jerusalem has an invisible hostile area hidden behind hills and walls. But it clearly remains a threatening "other" whose presence is felt even in the parts it does not inhabit, by the force of memory, guilt, and fear. And even in the modern Jewish city of Jerusalem, a variety of cultures dwell side by side. (pp. 101-02)

In Jerusalem, social and spatial features will overlap even more dramatically than in other cities, chiefly because the layout of the city is a constant reminder that its inhabitants are at war and that one group is physically almost completely surrounded by the other. . . . The hills themselves are indeed dominant in all of Hannah's meditations about her life. . . . For Hannah, "In the after glow of sunset the Jerusalem hills seemed to be plotting some mischief." . . . At nightfall in Jerusalem, "at the ends of the streets you can glimpse the brooding hills waiting for darkness to fall on the shuttered city." . . . In her fantasies, these hills are brooding not only as natural phenomena but as enemy territory: "Worn commando uniforms with creases. A blue vein stands out on Halil's forehead. . . . Aziz uncurls and throws. The dry shimmer of the explosion. The hills echo and re-echo . . ." . . . .

But there are other meaningful spatial dimensions of the city. Hannah Gonen lives in an urban area where dwellings are visible miles away, because they cling to bare hills, but at close range they are mysterious, because Middle Eastern architecture frequently means inner courtyards and outer walls. . . . She also lives in a city that, because of its ancient roots, has a visible modern outer layer and centuries of hidden layers beneath the surface. That her husband

Michael is a geologist adds a note of irony to Hannah's predicament: he too is seeking mysteries beneath the earth's surface, but they are the secrets of natural materials, not of the needs and forces of man. Furthermore, Michael is incapable of translating his work metaphorically to search for the inner needs of humans, in this case of his wife's mind. (pp. 102-03)

But the outstanding emotion that Jerusalem elicits from Hannah is that of being lost. . . . (p. 103)

Nor is she able to see her small region, modern Jerusalem in the State of Israel, as part of a visible whole. Spread over a number of hills, some of which reach into Arab territory, Jerusalem seems infinite, a borderless city. . . . The paradox about the city for Hannah is that on the one hand the section of it that she inhabits is too familiar—"Maybe it's a pity that Jerusalem is such a small city that you can't get lost in it," she says to Michael as they immediately identify their location after a taxi ride in the rain—while on the other hand, as a total city in her mind, it contains so much that is unknown that she feels immeasurably lost. (pp. 103-04)

It is clear that Oz is using Hannah to depict the isolation and fear that many Israelis feel partially as a country in a state of siege and partially as a small enclave of Western culture in a vast area of cultures and landscapes unlike what they have known. . . .

Both the social and spatial aspects of Jerusalem in this novel express symbolically the awe and insecurity of its inhabitants, particularly during the period during which the novel takes place. Hannah Gonen continually asks existential questions that finally lead her to imagine self-annihilation. Jerusalem, as a Biblical visionary city and as a modern metropolis with borders and neighborhoods, serves as a perfect image for that frame of mind. (p. 104)

Hana Wirth-Nesher, in Modern Fiction Studies *(© copyright 1978, by Purdue Research Foundation, West Lafayette, Indiana), Spring, 1978.*

JOHN BAYLEY

Amos Oz has no alternative in his novels but to tell us what it means to be an Israeli. *The Hill of Evil Counsel* is a trio of interlinked narratives set in Jerusalem at the time just before the founding of the Israeli state. The third story—"Longing"—is told in the form of letters from a bacteriologist to a woman doctor in New York. . . .

Oz is a writer of great humanity and sensitivity. He conveys with a kind of light exactitude the atmosphere of the time; the physical feel of the town, and above all the consciousness of his narrator correspondent, and his reluctance to lose the Europeanness which is all he has, and the modes of understanding that go with it. . . . So effectively skillful and tactful is the composition that its symbolic overtones are only present in a complex mixture of excitement and disquiet, just as the title itself—"Longing"—suggests an ironic query the more potent for being uninsistent. . . .

In each of the three narratives a boy is present who is loosely identified with the author himself at that age, and his vision of things—solipsistic, romantic, historically innocent—exercises an effect of liberation, in itself slightly ironic, on the claustrophobic dedication of the scene; even though the child himself is of course dedicated, he hardly knows to what. One of the admirable things about Oz's novels is the humor in them, a humor which formulates itself in having taken, and accepted, the narrow measure of the Israeli scene. Unlike much ethnic writing his does not seek to masquerade as *Weltliteratur*. It is Jewish literature acquiescing amusedly in its new militantly provincial status. The symbolic needs humor to keep it sweet, and Oz is a master of the kind of ludicrousness deployed so effectively in [Bellow's] *Mr. Sammler's Planet*. . . . (p. 35)

> *John Bayley, in* The New York Review of Books *(reprinted with permission from* The New York Review of Books; *copyright © 1978 Nyrev, Inc.), July 20, 1978.*

LIS HARRIS

[Oz's novels and novellas] are studded with interesting details about Jewish life in general and Israeli immigrant life in particular, but they share a peculiar emotional flatness and shed a curiously dim light on lives that on the surface are all excitement. . . . "The Hill of Evil Counsel," . . . a collection of three long stories with interwoven themes and characters, is of a piece with the rest of his work, though the last story, "Longing," gets a bit deeper below the skin of the main character than the others do.

All three stories take place during the last days of the British Mandate, in a ragged, sun-bleached, lower-middle-class neighborhood on the outskirts of Jerusalem. In the first (and title) story, it is May, 1946. The full-scale war that will erupt two years later is a shadowy threat that the neighborhood's mostly Polish and Russian immigrants (who want at all costs to avoid more disruption in their lives) prefer not to contemplate. . . . [The family Oz writes about consists of] Dr. Kipnis, a diffident, middle-aged veterinarian; his bitter, bleakly hysterical wife, Ruth, who constantly taunts her husband with idealized memories of her haute-bourgeoise Warsaw childhood; and their sensitive, dreamy son, Hillel (who turns up under another name in the other stories). . . . Typically, Oz drops the wife just when she starts to get interesting. [He has her run off with an admiral, a well-known roué]. Plot development seems to bore him, and it is not unusual for him simply to abandon his characters when their lives threaten to become too complicated.

In the second story, "Mr. Levi," which appears to take place some months after the first, the tension of a prewar national state of mind is palpable. . . . Mr. Levi is an unpleasant but believably authoritative middle-aged resistance fighter (about whom we learn almost nothing), who is smuggled into the house of what seems to be the family that we have just read about in the previous story, now miraculously reunited. No mention whatever is made of the mother's nocturnal escapade. . . . It is a bit disconcerting . . . to see the mother calmly setting the family tea cart and passing bowls of oranges when just a few pages earlier we have witnessed her doppelgänger "racing deep into the desert, across mountains and valleys, and onward, to Baghdad, Bombay, Calcutta" with the belching admiral in his silver Rolls-Royce. (pp. 79-80)

"Longing" is about a middle-aged Viennese-born doctor named Emanuel Nussbaum, who is dying of cancer. Nussbaum lives next door to the (or a) veterinarian. The story is written as a series of confessional letters that Nussbaum sends to his former mistress, a doggedly unsentimental, blunt psychologist (from Nussbaum's descriptions of her, she seems rather heartless, but I'm not sure Oz intends

that) who has emigrated recently to New York. In the first two stories, Oz captures a strong sense of place and mood but conveys little of what anyone is feeling, except for the not particularly riveting yearnings of the young boy. In this one, the main character is at least given the chance to recall the strong currents of his life, although in a kind of epistolatory-résumé style. (p. 80)

[Oz] seems unwilling or unable to come to grips with his characters' feelings about the fragility of either their past lives or their present ones. It is as if he were writing a war play in which no one exhibited fear or terror or ever mentioned guns, blood, or death. Perhaps, being a Sabra, he simply takes those things for granted. But when the closest he can come to describing fear is to anthropomorphize nature, as he does in "Mr. Levi" . . . it trivializes both the depth and the magnitude of the collective national recovery that all his work strains to convey. (p. 81)

> *Lis Harris, "O Pioneers!" in* The New Yorker *(© 1978 by The New Yorker Magazine, Inc.), August 7, 1978, pp. 79-81.*

A. S. BYATT

[Amos Oz] can write with delicate realism about small lives, or tell fables about large issues, but his writing, even in translation, gains vitality simply from his subject matter.

The Hill of Evil Counsel contains three long tales about the last two years of the British Mandate in Palestine, the uncertain, shifting, hopeful, terror-ridden years before the war, and the declaration of the independent Jewish State. . . . If Israel is to become both rubble and flowering desert, the fate of Jerusalem is even more problematic: Amos Oz shows us this only obliquely through the histories, hopes, extravagant dreams and anxieties of his families. . . .

Amos Oz's translator, Nicholas de Lange, works closely with him, and it is possible, even in translation to gauge how the shifting style betrays the shifting composition of the thoughts, fears, weak and powerful hopes of the isolated people in Jerusalem. The language shifts from Old Testament grandeur to Old Testament diatribe; from composed Yiddish humour to that peculiar claustrophobic chatter that one gets in Jewish novels which come from Europe and America as well. . . . It is a book about contradictions and an unkind climate and it is, like the society it prefigures, ferociously alive.

> *A. S. Byatt, "Yearning for Jerusalem," in* The Times Literary Supplement *(© Times Newspapers Ltd. (London) 1978; reproduced from* The Times Literary Supplement *by permission), October 6, 1978, p. 1110.*

J. JUSTIN GUSTAINIS

As a seamstress who takes different pieces of cloth and sews them into a quilt, Amos Oz writes short pieces of fiction which together form a quilt in the reader's consciousness. Just as the quilt may be of many colors but still one garment, Oz's stories speak of many things but still pay homage to one central idea: universal redemption through suffering. Although the concept is hardly unique to either Judaism or Zionism (two perspectives influencing Oz's writing), the point may be made that the Jews have the longest history of suffering as a people and therefore have one of the stronger claims to the redemption which suffering is alleged to bring. (p. 224)

Without belaboring the point, it seems to me that Oz shows in all his work that the people who endure the suffering imposed by others and by themselves will triumph, will be redeemed. The damned are those who forsake their burden. Oz's work would be valuable for this alone, but it contains much more. He writes in a spare, simple style which masks the great complexity of thought. He writes from both the head and the heart. (p. 225)

J. Justin Gustainis, in Best Sellers *(copyright © 1978 Helen Dwight Reid Educational Foundation), October, 1978.*

P

PALAZZESCHI, Aldo 1885-1974

Palazzeschi was an Italian poet and novelist. Originally allied with the futurist school, Palazzeschi broke with this group early in his career and established himself as a unique and strongly individual artist. He is best known for his novel *The Sisters Materassi*, which reveals Palazzeschi's fine sense of humor and traditional prose style. He received the Feltrinelli dei Lincei Accademi, Italy's highest literary award, in 1957. (See also *Contemporary Authors*, obituary, Vols. 53-56.)

DORIS GRUMBACH

It takes Palazzeschi a long time to tell this simple story [*The Sisters Materassi*], for his subsidiary interests are varied, and he is often sidetracked by complex metaphor and simile. These stylistic tangents are worth his time and reader's, and they enrich a novel already full of interest. But his primary concern is with character, both dominant and recessive. Like Proust he submits good to evil and microscopically examines the results. And like Proust again, the struggle between the two is unevenly weighted because eccentricities of character and personality outbalance the strength of moral decision. . . .

One is rather impressed by [Palazzeschi's] entire objectivity. The Materassis and their beautiful, evil nephew are, like the Guermantes, specimens worthy of exact and loving investigation and display, and, in their way, they are as fascinating and worthwhile to the reader.

> *Doris Grumbach, "The Squander of Innocence,"* in Commonweal *(copyright © 1953 Commonweal Publishing Co., Inc.; reprinted by permission of Commonweal Publishing Co., Inc.), July 31, 1953, p. 425.*

PAUL PICKREL

After a long descriptive introduction that even Sir Walter Scott might have found a bit leisurely, *The Sisters Materassi* is a brillant examination of . . . the symbiosis of emotional relationships. . . .

The moral insight in Mr. Palazzeschi's book does not result from the fact that he writes of a society rich in moral insight. His stodgy, unintrospective, provincial characters are moral enough. . . ; but they would never understand the compassionate, sophisticated, humorous breadth of view he brings to bear upon their situation. *The Sisters Materassi*

derives its stature from its author, as, in the end, all novels must. (p. xvi)

> *Paul Pickrel, in* The Yale Review *(© 1953 by Yale University; reprinted by permission of the editors), Autumn, 1953.*

ERNEST JONES

[*The Sisters Materassi*] is leisurely in a pleasantly old-fashioned way. . . . It lingers throughout on the details of the dailiest kind of life and out of them creates an entire little world, all wonderfully alive, for Signor Palazzeschi knows exactly what he is about and is sure of his power. This long-drawn out and unclimactic account of the fatuities of the Materassis, lingerie makers to wealthy Florentines, and of their selfish and selfless devotion to a worthless object, their beautiful, captivating, and amoral nephew, is reminiscent of the novels of Italo Svevo. But with a difference. The buffoonery of a Zeno, the folly of an Emilio Brentani destroy them spiritually. Signor Palazzeschi, though he never loses sight of the spiritual and moral idiocy which animates the self-sacrifice of his victims, sees their folly as conferring on them a perverse minor triumph. Their entirely material and curiously sexual passion for Remo reaps for them the spiritual benefit of being able to continue life on some level meaningful to them when money and the object of passion are gone. In this sense, and as a study of the material destruction of those ripe for destruction the novel is first-rate.

Technically it is remarkable for the way in which, on occasion, the careful realism is deliberately violated by the introduction of passages of grotesquerie which point up in comic horror the monstrousness of the victor and his victims. (pp. 712, 714)

The portrait of Remo, the temperate and calculating prodigal, is superb. . . . It is possible to construe him, given the date of *The Sisters Materassi*, as a sly parable on Fascist youth, though on its surface the novel is set in a political vacuum into which nothing penetrates but the immediate material concerns of the characters. His existence is all *Kraft durch Freude,* and although his important affiliations are with motorcars, in his radiant and meaningless beauty he reminds one of a figure on a party poster. (p. 714)

> *Ernest Jones, in* Partisan Review *(copyright © 1953 by Partisan Review, Inc.), November-December, 1953.*

THOMAS G. BERGIN

[*Il codice di Perelà* (1911) is one of Palazzeschi's] earliest books and his first great success. Perhaps there are technically "better" novels in the canon—there are certainly some of more robust fiber (how could it be otherwise when the protagonist of this ambiguous allegory is made of smoke?)—but it seems to me that this quasi-Pirandellian exercise in wistful mischief can tell us as much as any other about the author's talents, attitudes, and direction. Perelà, it will be remembered, born of a fireplace with three attendant mothers, enjoys—if that is the word—a brief and educational sojourn in our world of flesh and blood. At first all goes well: ladies court him and politicians exalt him, deeming his silence oracular. But then comes the reversal of fortune and Perelà, still all but wordless and of course blameless, is vilified, condemned, and eventually compelled to vanish into insubstantial ether. Had the book appeared thirty years later all critics worth their salt would have recognized in Perelà an authentic Christ figure. And so we might still consider him were it not for the author's manner, as airy as the substance of the vaporous transient who, for all the smoky light he may shed on human mores, keeps reminding us that he is "molto leggero." It is all very "buffo" and if there are dark shadows in the corners, well, we don't have to look. (pp. 56, 58)

If *Perelà* is, at least in appearance, as light and feathery as the smoke-man himself, the same cannot be said of *Sorelle Materassi*, a robust structure of good nineteenth century dimensions and an all but Manzonian style to adorn it. It remains, after forty years, the author's best known book and most critics would agree that this is as it should be. The novel may be seen as a story of involuntary involvement and its price, or as a triumph, however sad, of wayward heart over calculating head, or even, as has been suggested, as an allegory of the conflict between nineteenth century order and twentieth century emancipation. Seeing the smug and severe sisters betrayed by instincts they do not know they possess and exploited by selfish yet somehow irresistible youth, one can only say that the novel is as searching a study of the perverse pathos of life as any Italian novelist has given us....

[*Stampe dell' ottocento* recalls] the sights and characters of the author's childhood [and] is the kind of book that Italian men of letters like to write and write very well. It might be compared to Cicognani's *L'età favolosa* or some of the early chapters of Parini's *L'uomo finito* or, leaving Tuscany, Zuccoli's *L'occhio del fanciullo*. But if the genre is traditional, *Stampe* has its own distinctive flavor; it is not as aggressively intellectual as Papini's recollections nor as programmatically nostalgic as Cicognani's. Nostalgia there is, but it is underplayed, all but patronized. Nor is it the work of a "solipsist"; little Aldo is inevitably at the center but the focus is rather on the "cose viste." ... (p. 58)

Within this triangle of fantasy, realism, and reminiscence the remaining works find their place.... *Roma* (1953) is, ostensibly at least, a novel of the old-fashioned sort, presenting sympathetically a noble old Roman family at grips with today's world. There is a whiff of D'Annunzio in this somewhat baroque saga and, coming out as it did in the full tide—or rather against it— of Resistance literature, *Roma* found some detractors. I suspect an obliquely polemical intent here; as Palazzeschi had not been deceived by the pretensions of bourgeois society in his youth, nor seduced by the allure of Fascism in later years, so now he is not to

be carried away by the new freedom but rather, with consistent low key perversity, elects to champion the old values. ... The short stories (the best known collection is *Il palio dei buffi*, 1937) are of the same mixture; many are stories of "buffi" ("odd fellows"), some realistic to the point of pathos, others portraying Pirandellian obsessions, yet others essentially comic. Fantasy goes as far as it can in *Bestie del '900* (1951), in which all the protagonists are animals (Trilussa had prepared the public for this kind of Aesopian commentary), but Palazzeschi's anthropomorphism is distinctively subtle. (p. 59)

Palazzeschi's success as a prose writer has tended to obscure his really considerable achievement in the field of poetry. As all critics have noted, he began as a *crepuscolare* but somehow not quite like the others of that school; he later embraced *futurismo*—but somehow with a difference, finally emerging to make a *parte per se stesso*. And if, in critical telegraphese, we may define the *crepuscolari* as sentimental and the *futuristi* as strident, we can see how, in the case of Palazzeschi, the sentimentalism is regularly seasoned by an ironic self-awareness and even a sense of fun, while on the futuristic side the pyrotechnics are moderated by a certain *sens de mesure* and a good ear.... The ability to suggest mysteries of haunting resonance in simple everyday things is a truly poetic secret and Palazzeschi has mastered it.... The language in which these tenuous images are set forth is simple, the rhythm frequently suggests a nursery rhyme, but in the manipulation of assonance, rhyme, alliteration, and repetition one sees the hand of a master. (pp. 59-60)

Palazzeschi is a writer who, even with the evidence of sixty-odd years of literary activity open for our inspection, remains difficult to pigeon-hole. As a novelist he seems to have no particular motivation—social, political or philosophical. He is no reformer, no doctrinaire moralist—and no hedonist either. He does not attempt to excite us with the spectacular nor titillate us with the scabrous; even his *personaggi* are of no great stature. His prose has, normally, a Manzonian stateliness—sentences may easily run to a dozen lines—which he can vary, when it suits him, with a laconic, elliptical dialogue not unlike that of Hemingway, but he clearly writes as it comes to him, without any dedication to the *bello stile* as such. One can only describe him as a faithful and interested observer of life, thoroughly aware of its absurdities, gifted in recording them—and always compassionately. Pancrazi noted, speaking of the odd folk that make up *Il palio dei buffi*, that Palazzeschi could thoroughly enjoy the eccentricities of his gallery but never permitted amusement to slip into mockery. More than most novelists, I think, he writes to please himself, and this gives his work a special quality of purity. In an insensitive man such an attitude might have led to the arid cultivation of art for art's sake.... [In Palazzeschi] a cool detachment does not stop sympathy; he scrutinizes, questions, even challenges convention without ever rejecting it. (p. 60)

Thomas G. Bergin, "The Enjoyable Horrendous World of Aldo Palazzeschi," in Books Abroad *(copyright 1972 by the University of Oklahoma Press), Vol. 46, No. 1, Winter, 1972, pp. 55-60.*

*   *   *

PERSE, St.-John (pseudonym of Alexis Saint-Léger Léger) 1887-1975

A French poet, Perse first published his verse under a pseu-

donym to conceal his identity as a diplomat. He was a political exile during the Second World War, and during this period his work is imbued with a sense of solitude and loss. His poetry reflects his love of nature and explores the sensual exchange between man and his surroundings, presented in a highly wrought, almost classical verse style. Perse collaborated with the artist Georges Braque on a volume entitled *Birds*. (See also *CLC*, Vol. 4, and *Contemporary Authors*, Vols. 13-16, rev. ed.; obituary, Vols. 61-64.)

CONRAD AIKEN

[In *Pluies,* a] magnificent poem, which is at once a kind of litany, or litany of litanies, and an allegorical history of mankind, a history in terms of metaphor, the poet drives his tandem of methods with complete mastery. The *whole meaning,* the history of man in terms of rain, or the interpretation of him in terms of rain—rain as the fertilizer, rain as the purifier, even as the principle itself of life and change—gives a majestic centripetal design to the poem, and a tremendous sense of controlled richness, but it is also of such a nature, even more so than in the case of *Anabase,* as to make the utmost possible use of incidental, but directed, improvisation. With the beginning of each of his nine canticles the poet can return, as it were, to his base, his central theme, only then to allow himself, in the long, rich, flexible triads, the dispersed exfoliation of imaginative reference, the sheaves of image and metaphor, which so wonderfully evoke a sense of the many-corridored, many-layered, many-echoed and many-faceted past of man. Here too the use of highly affective language, and what at moments seems an almost "blind" symbolism, is precisely what contributes most to the poem's remarkable projection of the racial unconscious: it isn't *about,* it becomes and is, our sad rich dreadful glorious disastrous foul and beautiful history. We emerge with it, shedding and altering; and at the end, after a prayer to rain, it is as if by a ritualistic achieving of self-knowledge we had released ourselves from what is binding or shameful and were now free to go forward again. Surely this is one of the finest poems of the century. (pp. 321-22)

> *Conrad Aiken, "Perse, St. John" (originally published in a different version under a different title in* The New Republic, *April 16, 1945), in his Collected Criticism (reprinted by permission of Brandt & Brandt), Oxford University Press, New York, 1968, pp. 320-23.*

ROGER LITTLE

However much one may see seeds of Perse's style and imagery in the earliest published work, and see the same forceful guiding hand behind all the poems, a development is [clear].... [It] is a gradual move away from a specific preoccupation with the physical, through broader connotations of the material image, towards a gesture of speculation on the metaphysical. It is a shift in emphasis rather than of subject, which remains essentially grounded in this world.

Early suggestions of an interest in the in-between states on which Perse is to build so much offer only in retrospect a basis for wider application. Reading *Eloges,* for example, the immediate reaction is to the physical and sensual qualities of the poems. The plenitude of the land and solitude of the sea are posited explicitly, without the poet delving into the nature and implications of their point of meeting. Hal-

cyon expanses of purity stand in opposition to the 'végétales ferveurs' of the poet's tropical island home. Distinctions were sharp, brilliant colours reflecting the child's clear-cut ideas, brought up as he was with a sure sense of hierarchy and propriety in all things.... (p. 785)

If the child has an instinctive liking for the doorstep (and how often children seem to concentrate their games at this point midway between safety and adventure) ... it is *Exil* that brings us face to face with its full poetic significance. It is *Exil,* too, ... that specifies and elaborates upon the conjunction of threshold and beach.... [It] is on the shore—the threshold—of the New World, though essentially on any shore in the world, that Perse can construct his poem out of the very quicksand ambivalence of the site. (p. 786)

Both *Exil* and *Amers* are played out at the edge of the sea, and both derive much of their central imagery from the fact. But in most of the other poems too the critical shore is mentioned or its equivalent proposed. If it starts essentially as an expression of *la poésie des départs* with which Perse was to sympathize so much ... it did not remain at that stage.... Ideas and epithets of distance recur more and more often in Perse's output, and that of departure and travel becomes the very framework for the majestic epic of oriental spaces, *Anabase.* As an expression of the nomadic nature of man's spirit, it epitomizes the very notion of *la poésie des départs* while avoiding any of the superficiality or Romantic exoticism into which the genre has all too often slipped. Reinforced by all the overtones of poetic creation and profound spirituality, the poem concludes triumphantly.... The precarious restlessness is something accepted as a force for good. To stand still is to atrophy, to die. Consequently it is seen as an integral part of the human condition that however splendid and satisfying the immediate environment may appear, we are always aware of an urge to 'fare forward'. We are always in a state of exile, and none more so than the man who uses his faculties to the full, since he is more fully receptive to the present, but also more acutely aware of his unfulfilled potential.

Although *Anabase* shows an important manifestation of the same idea, the terms are necessarily different since the poem is set inland, although starting beside the sea. The series of American poems includes, apart from *Exil* and *Amers* which take place on the sea-shore itself, a number of references to its importance.... The poet's own position is clearly allied to that of the special intercourse of land and sea, or of any equivalent image evoking ambiguity, insecurity, and at the same time creativity, poetry being born of the conjunction of such forces, in themselves nothing, but being sublimated through the art of words. (pp. 787-89)

The extension of [the] newly found positive aspect of the sea shore as the threshold to new vistas of plenitude can well be seen by reference to *Amers.* The multiplicity of connotation in the title itself suggests that of the poem: apart from the 'Seamarks' of the translated title, there are echoes of bitter gall, of 'amour' (sometimes spelt 'am*er*' in medieval French) and of 'mer' itself. From the poem, with its central imagery revolving around the sea and love, the title could be a crossing of *mer* with *amour.* It is truly Persean that an actual word with even wider associations, and just as appropriate, should have been used. But lurking also is what Miłosz called 'l'amer amour de l'autre monde'. (pp. 789-90)

[The] constantly repeated notion of being on the verge of some marvellous discovery, whether of a rare plant or bird or of some mystical insight, provides intense excitement, and captivates by its immense enthusiasm for life in all its forms. . . . [There] is a double view of the relationship between things and the sea: if things pay homage or lemming-like disappear into the primeval element, it is the sea, 'elle-même voyageuse', which allows things to be appreciated for what they are. . . . The sea is in its turn the threshold, as we have seen, to that sort of 'super-reality' in which things play their part, both as themselves and as images of metaphysical counterparts. . . . Both spatial and temporal concepts are included in a sort of 'pan-time', partaking of both immensity and eternity. . . . The maieutics of threshold and beach sharpen sensitivity so as to allow an over-all appreciation of its significance. Only an attachment to concrete phenomena can permit any exploration of mystery and abstraction.

Not only in space, but also in time Perse shows a predilection for the threshold of day and night, and again these are gradually assembled into a broader conception of man standing on the verge of eternity. Any mystical tendency which this might suggest is, as in other fields, subordinate to the physical bases of the idea. The mention of dawn or dusk comes so frequently to Perse's pen that elaboration seems scarcely necessary. What is true of the spatial images of the threshold is also true of the temporal. . . . But dawn and dusk are not the only fulcrum-points of the fourth dimension. Noon and midnight are also springboards to something greater, and are frequently evoked in Perse's work. . . . Corresponding to the four main points of the day —dawn, noon, dusk and midnight—which are all temporal 'thresholds' in Perse's world, are their equivalent seasons in the course of the year: the solstices and equinoxes. Again links are forged with broader connotations, with the doorstep itself, with love, and with the intoxication of creation. . . . (pp. 790-92)

[Perse] is far more attracted to spatial than to temporal extension. . . .

The virtue, then, of threshold, beach, dawn, and noon is a precariousness which heightens awareness. In itself, each 'threshold' remains unchanged, stated unequivocally as valid for its own sake. But like a catalyst in a chemical reaction, it must be present for the reaction to take place. The sublimation occurs without denying or denaturing the area of space or time which lies on either side of the threshold, yet with a very complete exploration of both the contents and limits of either direction. The dialectic is a form of dualism in which both elements are *positive*. . . . [Perse's] quest for order leads him from the precarious here and now into universal history and geography, but also into that spiritual infinity which alone can suggest a sense and pattern in existence. (p. 792)

> Roger Little, *"The Image of the Threshold in the Poetry of Saint-John Perse,"* in The Modern Language Review (© *Modern Humanities Research Association 1969), October, 1969, pp. 777-92.*

JOHN D. PRICE

[For Perse] symbolic and individual man, that is Man the species and man the solitary male human being, share many of the same qualities, and . . . these vary little throughout the poetry. Furthermore, it is in the light of his own conception of himself as a man that Perse perceives the outside world, the 'other' that, whether woman, earth, sea or muse, takes on a feminine aspect. (p. 555)

[By] placing between himself and the world a screen of praise, Perse maintains both his solitude and his liberty, preserving himself from involvement with a kind of diplomatic immunity. This situation is that of man throughout Perse's work; 'gardé par le sourire et par la courtoisie' . . . , he can tour the world at his leisure; his relationship with it is held at one remove, and he cannot be imprisoned in the immobility that he holds to be so dangerous to the human species. . . . All senses at the ready, he proceeds in search of the new and the unknown.

Man's role in relation to his fellow-men is seen in [*Anabase*] as one of creating order, either physical in the building of towns, or legal in the formulation of laws. This order can be inhabited by those for whom it is created, but not by its creator himself, who moves on to repeat the exercise elsewhere.

In *Amitié du Prince* the preoccupations of the major character are more spiritual and artistic. His public daytime role is sparsely described, simply as being 'd'être là' . . . , and to keep watch. . . . A more detailed account is given of his night-time activities; then he satisfies his sexual appetite, sings 'ses plus beaux chants de Prince' and pursues a spiritual debate with himself. . . .

The association, by virtue of their non-public character, of sexual, artistic, and spiritual activities is again strongly made in *Anabase,* and here once more man asserts his domination over them, returning at dawn to his daytime role. . . . (p. 556)

[The] night-time pursuits are kept totally separate from man's public and daytime occupation, and man exercises his mastery over the temptations and delights they offer in order to pursue his nomadic path and his public function as builder and establisher of order.

In the *Exil* tetralogy, however, it is clear that this public function has ceased, and this fact allows the spiritual preoccupations evident especially in *Amitié du Prince* to play a wider and fuller role. The 'Étranger' becomes the 'Poète'; instead of building towns and founding laws, the latter, while still fundamentally concerned with the creation of order and the discovery and acceptance of the new, is engaged on a spiritual quest, saluting a new age and relaying his message of hope to the rest of humanity. . . .

It can now be seen in what ways Perse's conceptions of the individual man and of humanity are the same: both go forth to conquer . . . , refusing either to submit or to involve themselves with the things and forces they observe around them: distance, freedom and praise are maintained to the end. Secondly, both individual man and Man are distinguished from the static society of men who inhabit the towns created for them, trapped in the routine of their habits and their customs. Perse's heroic conception is of a nomad rather than of a settler, of a hunter rather than a farmer, and remains constant throughout his work. (p. 557)

In direct contrast with individual man, the individual woman is associated primarily with staticity, with the pauses in man's nomadic life. From the first it is she who stays at home while the man pursues his wanderings. . . . In that pre-war poetry that describes not a childhood but the life of an adult, the woman's role is purely sexual; as we have seen, she had no part to play in man's public or day-time life.... [However], she has an association with man's other nocturnal pursuits. This parallel is used once more in *Exil* to introduce the first of the symbolic women to appear in the poetry, the Muse figure of the 'Mendiante'.... Unlike the physical women who appear in this tetralogy—the poet's mother and his mistress, 'sur l'autre rive' . . . , and the 'Étrangère'—who remain locked within their houses, in the latter case even refusing to contemplate the New World, the 'Mendiante', like man, is a wanderer, 'partout-errante'.... She is, also like him, a threshold creature, and at this site of ambiguity opening on to the outside and the unknown she brings to the nomad the spiritual and poetic newness that he now seeks.

There is another equally important difference in the characteristics accorded to femininity once this is seen as symbolic rather than physical: whereas the women of *Anabase* were sterile in the sense that man never contemplated the thought of childbirth, the symbolic forces are prolific with freshness and the unknown. The characteristics of the 'Pluies' illustrate this aspect of symbolic femininity very well.

Two very different sorts of force are brought to the town that the rains invade: there is on the one hand the violent and renewing, freshening strength of nature, symbolized by the vegetal complexity and disorder of the banyan tree, and on the other a possible form to contain this force, a form associated with gardens, the order man gives to or imposes on nature. Since it is not merely the city that is refreshed by the rains, but also the institution of language, the form is also seen as the metre, the rhythm to be imposed.... (pp. 557-58)

The domination of the female by the male, whatever the characteristics of the former, is the one constant element of the relationship between the two principles. (p. 558)

[The] 'Amante' and the 'Amant' are ambivalent figures, at once individuals meeting in a particular spatio-temporal situation, and representatives of Perse's view of humanity....

The poet's physical enjoyment of the woman's body [in *Amers*] is akin to the sensual delight he takes in living things in general, and implies no lasting involvement with the woman as a person. Later the physical sense of 'Amant' modulates rather abruptly into a more spiritual one, as the canto ends with a paean to the 'amants', 'seuls et libres, sans caution ni gage', who, whether male or female, are attributed the male—or more correctly, human—qualities of detachment and wandering. Thus the question of the personal fate of the 'Amante' is eluded, forgotten or, to take a more sympathetic view, transcended in this shift to an avowedly symbolic plane of thought. (p. 559)

In spite of the femininity of its force and fecundity, the sea symbolizes the spiritual reservoir within man, and it is therefore only to be expected that at the very centre of this most feminine of symbols we should find the ultimate personification of the male principle of order: 'Dieu l'Indivis gouverne ses provinces'.... It is precisely this principle that we have seen to animate man on his twin journeys through the material and spiritual domains of his existence, and the symbolic placing of it at the centre of 'la Mer iden-

tifiée à l'Être universel, s'y intégrant infiniment et y intégrant l'homme lui-même' is Perse's ultimate affirmation of his optimism about man's destiny.

Throughout the poetry then, and in spite of the varying qualities that are classified or personified under the sign of woman, the relationship between male and female remains constant, a reflection of Perse's view of man as triumphant nomad....

At the centre of the metaphysical picture that is presented in *Amers* is this conception of man as a nomad going from victory to greater victory, yet remaining emotionally detached from the fate of his enterprises. It is an attitude of the greatest optimism, and that it is consciously taken and asserted is evident from a number of prose texts.... Perse has written that *Amers* was intended specifically as an expression of this optimism.... It is therefore, on the poet's own admission, a one-sided view of man's destiny—just as one-sided, though obviously in the opposite direction, as the one he attacks. As such, it is difficult to reconcile with the avowed ambition of *Amers,* which in the same 'Note' is described in the following words: 'Reprise de la grande phrase humaine, à son plus haut mouvement de mer, pour une réintégration totale de l'homme sur ses deux plans complémentaires'—these being of course the material and spiritual domains into which Perse's world is characteristically divided. For how can we have a 'réintégration totale de l'homme' if a whole part of human experience and human possibility is systematically excluded and ignored?

The excluded part is that which, taken by itself, can lead to the nihilism that Perse rejects, and of which it is convenient to call one aspect, that of human experience, suffering.... Perse identifies his thesis and his synthesis, and does not bother to present an antithesis. (pp. 560-61)

[By] refusing, in this particular poem that is supposed to be an exaltation of the human condition, to depict or to refer to at any length, that part of human experience that might oppose such a view, Perse *undervalues* and renders suspect the very grandeur he is trying to celebrate. There is, one strongly suspects, in all human enterprises worthy of the name, a time for the gritting of the teeth, for wishing one had never started out; man's greatness can only be truly meaningful if he overcomes suffering and the difficulties that beset his path, and to exclude these from consideration both demeans the ultimate victory that Perse wishes to evoke, and renders it less credible....

[Perse] fails totally, in *Amers,* to depict the only background against which his heroic conception of man can have meaning, which is the essential ambiguity of the human condition—essential if only because there is so much of it, and so much variety through the dimensions of time and space, that almost any attitude of life, optimistic or pessimistic, can find evidence in its support. (p. 562)

One of the reasons for this imbalance, for this non-depiction of the totality of human experience and possibility lies in the separation of the symbolic and the individual levels of existence in *Amers,* and the fact that most of its action takes place on the former level. (p. 563)

[Almost] all the characters of *Amers,* with the possible exception of the 'Amants' at certain points of their dialogue, contemplate the drama of human destiny from some distance, separated even from each other. As we have seen, the dissatisfaction with man's progress felt by the various feminine figures in *Amers* does not in any way cast doubt upon his future triumphs. The symbolic view of 'Man' is completely separate from the men who live in the town that seeks renewal, and by divorcing the two notions of symbolic and temporal realities, as he does characteristically throughout his work, Perse is able to prevent any dissatisfaction with the latter from clouding his belief in the former, and thus avoids the real drama of human destiny. There is no direct confrontation between the two levels, no attempt to integrate the realities of human suffering and evil into the symbolic view of man, no dramatic development in any dialectical sense, and no conflict: *Amers,* describing a religious ritual rather than the human condition, is a work that can satisfy only the converted.

Coming to these rather negative conclusions about the most ambitious poem written by one of the world's most gifted poets is all the more painful when one contrasts *Amers* with some of his earlier work, and more especially with the *Exil* tetralogy. In these four poems an individual man is stripped to the bone of his detachment and the action is explicitly rooted in subjective experience, using this as a starting point for more symbolic and metaphysical speculation, rather than presenting these on their own as objective truth. Such symbolic figures as appear are related to an individual human being, to a particular spatio-temporal situation, rather than floating in an unrelated and ill-defined eternity. And in these poems, written at a time of enforced staticity in exile, Perse is confronted by precisely those problems and that part of human experience from which his carefully adopted diplomatic immunity normally shields him. In particular he is led to consider the fate of individual human beings, his mother, the 'Étrangère' and of course himself. . . . (pp. 563-64)

It is of course the case that he overcomes these difficulties, and the possible temptation of pessimism, by redonning his habitual mask of praise. . . . However, because the difficulties have been admitted and presented, because the world described is identifiably that of a human individual related to other members of the species, we feel that this triumph has substance. . . .

[It] is at least partly this systematic exclusion of the depiction of human suffering and evil, and this divorce between symbolic and temporal reality that are responsible for the feeling that is commonly experienced by the reader of *Amers* once he has ceased to be impressed and even overwhelmed by the formidable prosodic mastery of the poem; the feeling that the work is, in its essence, hollow. . . . (p. 564)

> *John D. Price, "Man, Women, and the Problem of Suffering in Saint-John Perse," in* The Modern Language Review *(© Modern Humanities Research Association 1977), July, 1977, pp. 556-64.*

ROGER LITTLE

[There is] an affinity between Perse's poetry and the great sacred texts. This involves not only a wealth of legitimate interpretations and a sense of revealed truth, firmly rooted in Perse's case in physical realities, but also a carefully woven and infinitely pleasurable pattern of sound and inflexion. The establishment of this highly wrought texture and Perse's refusal of any preordained orthodoxy are what most clearly distinguished his work from Claudel's, and

these two factors are crucial in recognizing Perse's very individual voice. The other aspect that singles him out is the one most often noted: his celebration of the world and its ways, and his ennoblement of even the humblest tasks and objects which fulfil their potential.

The quest for self-fulfilment indeed guides Perse's mind through its own labyrinth, with the outside world as a constant foil and fund of imagery, to an ecumenical vision of physical and spiritual totality, the peaceable eye at the centre of violent natural forces. He is an accomplisher rather than an innovator, blending many traditions and seeming to be a pioneer more because some of those traditions had long been out of fashion than because of any intractable extremism or hollow belief in originality for its own sake.

> *Roger Little, "The Eye at the Centre of Things," in* The Times Literary Supplement *(© Times Newspaper Ltd. (London), 1977; reproduced from* The Times Literary Supplement *by permission), October 7, 1977, p. 1155.*

[The brief texts in *Song for an Equinox*] can be taken doubly: as a nostalgic recapitulation of the themes and forms that Perse explored and perfected during more than half a century of labor, or as a relatively easy and altogether pleasing initiation into the mysteries of the *oeuvre*. (p. 10)

> Virginia Quarterly Review *(copyright, 1978, by the* Virginia Quarterly Review, The University of Virginia), *Vol. 65, No. 1, (Winter, 1978).*

*   *   *

PINCHERLE, Alberto
See MORAVIA, Alberto

*   *   *

PINTER, Harold   1930-

A major British playwright, Pinter has also produced poems, short stories, screenplays, dramatic sketches, and criticism. His work is noted for its brilliant handling of dramatic mood and tension. The superficial, banal dialogue characteristic of his plays reveals the dramatist's fascination with the way people communicate, which for Pinter transcends the limits of language. Pinter's plays have at their core a fabric of irrationality and absurdity; this serves to highlight his persistent theme of the ambiguity of truth and ways of knowing. (See also *CLC*, Vols. 1, 3, 6, 9, and *Contemporary Authors*, Vols. 5-8, rev. ed.)

JOHN RUSSELL TAYLOR

The technique of casting doubt upon everything by matching each apparently clear and unequivocal statement with an equally clear and unequivocal statement of its contrary —used rather crudely in some parts of [his first play, *The Room*]— . . . is one which we shall find used constantly in Pinter's plays to create an air of mystery and uncertainty. The situations involved are always very simple and basic, the language which the characters use is an almost uncannily accurate reproduction of everyday speech (indeed, in this respect Pinter, far from being the least realistic dramatist of his generation, is arguably the most realistic), and yet in these ordinary surroundings lurk mysterious terrors and uncertainties—and by extension, the whole external world of everyday realities is thrown into question. Can we ever know the truth about anybody or anything? Is there any absolute truth to be known?

However, this is to anticipate. In *The Room* the hand is not yet entirely sure and the mystifications are often too calculated, too heavily underlined. The suppression of motives, for example, which in later plays comes to seem inevitable, because no one, not even the man who acts, can know precisely what impels him to act, here often looks merely an arbitrary device: it is not that the motives are unknowable, but simply that the author will not permit *us* to know them. So, too, the melodramatic finale.... [Rose, in this play], belongs to that group of characteristic Pinter figures from his first phase (that in which he wrote 'comedies of menace'), those who simply fear the world outside. The plays of this group—*The Room, The Dumb Waiter, The Birthday Party,* and *A Slight Ache*—all take place in confined surroundings, in one room in fact, which represents for their protagonists at least a temporary refuge from the others (it is tempting, but not really necessary, to see it in terms of Freudian symbolism as a womb-substitute), something they have shored up against their ruins. The menace comes from outside, from the intruder whose arrival unsettles the warm, comfortable world bounded by four walls, and any intrusion can be menacing, because the element of uncertainty and unpredictability the intruder brings with him is in itself menacing. And the menace is effective almost in inverse proportion to its degree of particularization, the extent to which it involves overt physical violence or direct threats. We can all fear an unexpected knock at the door, a summons away from our safe, known world of normal domesticities on unspecified business (it is surely not entirely without significance that Pinter, himself a Jew, grew up during the war, precisely the time when the menace inherent in such a situation would have been, through the medium of the cinema or of radio, most imaginatively present to any child, and particularly perhaps a Jewish child). But the more particularized the threat is, the less it is likely to apply to our own case and the less we are able to read our own semiconscious fears into it. (pp. 235-36)

[In *The Birthday Party*], the element of external violence has not altogether disappeared, but the heavy (if cloudy) symbolism of *The Room* has vanished, and instead we get a real comedy of menace which is funny and menacing primarily in relation to the unrelieved ordinariness of its background. The very fact that Stanley, Meg, and her husband Peter are believable figures living in a believable real world intensifies the horror of Stanley's situation when the intruders come to break into his comfortable humdrum life and take him away. But, it might be said, the arrival of McCann and Goldberg takes it out of the real everyday reality: whatever we may have done in our lives, it is unlikely to be anything so terrible and extraordinary that two professional killers would be hired to deal with us. The answer to that is that this might well be so if Stanley's offence were ever named, or the source of his punishment explained. But this is not the case: the menace of McCann and Goldberg is exactly the nameless menace with which Stanley cruelly teases Meg before they arrive.... Just as she can be terrified by this nameless threat of retribution for unknown crimes, so we can be terrified when the same fate actually overtakes Stanley. With his habitual dexterity in such matters Pinter manages to rig the scene of Stanley's breakdown in such a way that we never know what the guilt to which he finally succumbs may be: every conceivable accusation is thrown at him, one way and another.... Something for everyone, in fact: somewhere, the author seems to be telling his audience, you have done something—think hard and you may remember what it is—which will one day catch you out. (pp. 237-38)

The ambiguity, then, not only creates an unnerving atmosphere of doubt and uncertainty, but also helps to generalize and universalize the fears and tensions to which Pinter's characters are subject. The more doubt there is about the exact nature of the menace, the exact provocation which has brought it into being, the less chance there is of anyone in the audience feeling that anyway it could not happen to him. The kinship with Kafka, particularly *The Trial*, is obvious.... Pinter has not omitted to provide a footnote to *The Birthday Party* in a one-act play he wrote immediately afterwards, *The Dumb Waiter*. In *The Birthday Party* the hired killers (if they are hired killers) appear as all-powerful and inscrutable: where Stanley is the menaced, they are menace personified, invulnerable beings, one might suppose, from another world, emissaries of death. But no, *The Dumb Waiter* assures us, hired killers are just men like anyone else; they only obey orders, and while menacing others they themselves can also be menaced. (pp. 238-39)

The fact that the people being menaced [in *The Dumb Waiter*] are precisely those whose business it is usually to menace others, hired killers, offers an extra twist of irony, but does not make any essential difference to their situation. It does, however ... [cast] doubts on the safety and integrity of the room itself. Without any physical intrusion whatever, the menace may be lurking already inside the room ... ; it is no good simply keeping our minds closed to outside influence, for even inside there the seeds of destruction may already be planted. (pp. 239-40)

[*A Slight Ache*] marks the end of the 'comedy of menace' phase in Pinter's work, though ironically just when he was moving out of it the phrase was coined and has become almost unavoidable in discussion of Pinter, though generally applied to work which does nothing to merit the title. For these early plays, however, the description is admirably exact. Menace is unmistakenly present: the central characters ... are all prey to unknown dangers, unspoken threats, and finally an unpleasant fate (all the more sinister for remaining undefined) overtakes them all. But comedy is present, too, usually in the earlier scenes, but nearly all through in *The Dumb Waiter*. Evidently, on one level at least, Pinter has learnt a lot from the master of controlled horror, Hitchcock, many of whose bravura effects are achieved in precisely this way, from making some horrible reality emerge out of a piece of light and apparently irrelevant comedy. But Pinter's comedy rarely even seems irrelevant: it is 'about' the same things as his scenes of terror, the inability, or he has implied, the unwillingness of human beings to communicate, to make contact with each other. If it is terrifying to open the door to a strange knock, it is equally terrifying to open your mind to someone else, for once he is in you never know what he may do.... Consequently, in ordinary conversation Pinter's characters twist and turn, profoundly distrustful of any direct communication, and even when they attempt it are generally constitutionally incapable of achieving it: hardly ever in his work does one encounter two people of the same level of intelligence in conversation—there is nearly always one leaping ahead in the exchange while another stumbles confusedly along behind—except at the lowest end of the scale, where both are so stupid that communication is virtually impossible anyway. And out of these confusions and conversational impasses Pinter creates his characteristic forms of comedy.... (pp. 241-42)

[If his revue sketches] are plays in miniature, they are plays with many differences from what has gone before. There is no menace, no battle between the light and warmth of the room and the invading forces of darkness and disruption from outside.... They are just tiny cameos in which two or more characters are put into relation with each other and allowed simply to interact; they are all, in a sense, about failures of communication, or more properly perhaps the unwillingness to communicate.... (p. 243)

[Later,] the emphasis in his work comes to be placed much more squarely on the relationships between characters, their attempts to live together without giving up too much of themselves. (It might be remarked, parenthetically, that if no character really wants to communicate with the others in Pinter's plays he nearly always wants the other to communicate with him, and much of the tension in the dialogue comes from the constant evasions, the slight revelations and drawings back involved in this endless skirmishing on the threshold of communication, with each character determined to find out more than he tells.) ... [Though] the earlier plays are certainly not tied to a moral of any sort, they are slightly impeded in the presentation of people just being, existing, by the exigencies of plot, which require them to be menaced and to succumb.... [But in *A Night Out* and *The Caretaker*], the characters, the one mysterious external menace removed, can get on with precisely the job this statement envisages for them: just existing.

It is, in fact, tempting to see Pinter's progression from the earlier plays to the later in terms of a closer and closer approach to realism. In the early plays the quiet, often wryly comic tone of the opening scenes is gradually replaced by something much more intense and horrific, and something considerably farther away from mundane considerations of likelihood. The probability of what happens, indeed, is never at issue: it is clear from the outset that this is a private world we have been permitted to enter, and as such, whatever relations with any outside world of objective reality we may imagine we perceive, it has its own consistency and carries its own conviction.... Menace, [in *The Birthday Party*], is a matter of situation: it does not come from extraordinary, sinister people, but from ordinary people like you and me; it is all a matter of circumstances whether at some point I suddenly become the menace in your life or you the menace in mine, and not anything inherent in either of us.... [In] *The Dumb Waiter* he comes closer still [to reality] by elaborating the point about the normality of those who menace when they are outside the context in which their menace is exerted, and by leaving the violence implied in the final tableau instead of having it directly enacted on the stage. From here it is a short step to *A Slight Ache,* in which the nominal menace is completely passive and the real disruptive force exists in the mind of the menaced. There is no violence here at all, because no violence is needed.

The point at which this gradual change seems to crystallize in a single decision is in *The Caretaker,* where again we have the room, but no outside menace, simply a clash of personalities on the inside, and again we have to have one of the inhabitants displaced by another. (pp. 244-46)

[In *The Caretaker*] for the first time psychological realism overtly won out; these ... are people existing, making their own decisions, creating the circumstances of their own lives, and not in any sense the puppets of fate, as were in many respects the characters of *The Room, The Birthday Party*, and *The Dumb Waiter*. *The Caretaker* still works completely in terms of a private myth, as they did, but it gains in richness and complexity by also working completely, as they did not, on the quite different level at which comprehensible motivation comes into play: for the first time we can sensibly consider (if we want to) why the characters do what they do as well as, more obscurely, why what happens has the effect it does on us. (p. 246)

[The] style of *The Caretaker* is much more direct than that of Pinter's earlier plays. Everything that Aston says—suitably enough, considering his mental condition—is perfectly clear and unequivocal. And though Mick's mental processes are devious the intention behind everything he says is clear, even when he is talking apparently at random just to unsettle the old man.... Only Davies is subject in his conversation to the characteristic Pinter ambiguity, and this is here symptomatic not of the general unknowability of things, but of a specific intention on the character's part to cover his tracks and keep people guessing about himself.... (pp. 247-48)

In fact, [*The Caretaker*] seems to be built upon a proposition new in Pinter's work, one which he has expressed as 'simple truth can often be something much more terrifying than ambiguity and doubt'. (p. 249)

Little by little the desire for verification has shifted from the audience into the play they are watching; instead of watching with a degree of mystification the manoeuvres of a group of characters who seem perfectly to understand what they are doing but simply offer us no means of sharing that understanding, we are now required to watch understandingly the manoeuvres of people who do not understand their situation but are trying laboriously to establish the truth about it. And this truth goes beyond the mere verification of single facts (except, perhaps, in the comedies) to a quest for the how and the why, the who and the what, at a deeper level than demonstrable fact. This involves a new preoccupation with the means of communication, since the question comes back, will people tell the truth about themselves, and if they will, can they? (pp. 257-58)

Significantly, the only people in Pinter's plays who appear to tell the whole truth, into whose minds indeed we are permitted to look, are madmen.... Between *The Room* and *The Dwarfs* we have in effect run the complete dramatic gamut from total objectivity to total subjectivity, and discovered in the process that there are no clear-cut explanations of anything. At one end of the scale no motives are explained and everything remains mysterious; at the other as many motives as possible are expounded for us, and if anything the result is more mystifying than before. It is only from a middle distance, as in *The Caretaker* and *A Night Out,* that we can see a picture simple enough to hold out the possibility that we may understand it, that we are given enough in the way of motive to reach some provisional conclusions on the characters and their actions. It is a perfect demonstration of the conspiracy on which normal human intercourse relies, and incidentally of the knife-edge on which dramatic 'realism' rests: if we were told a little less about what is going on it would be incomprehensible, but if we were told a little more the difficulty of establishing any single coherent truth would be just as great.

In fact, the great paradox of Pinter's career, by the normal standards of the theatre, is that the more 'realistic' he is, the less real. With most dramatists the sort of compromise by selection which permits us to feel we have a sufficient understanding of the characters and motives in *The Caretaker* and *A Night Out* is the nearest they get to reality; it seems like reality because in life we often assume much the same (generally on quite insufficient evidence) and anyway the idea that we can safely make such assumptions is reassuring. But in his other works Pinter has, to our great discomfort, stripped these illusions from us: we cannot understand other people; we cannot even understand ourselves; and the truth of any situation is almost always beyond our grasp. If this is true in life, why should it not be true in the theatre? (pp. 258-59)

[Instead] of regarding Pinter as the purveyor of dramatic fantasy he is usually taken for, we might equally regard him as the stage's most ruthless and uncompromising naturalist. The structure of his characters' conversations, and even the very forms of expression they use, are meticulously exact in their notation of the way people really speak (and this is as true of his best-educated characters as of his least ...), while in his minutely detailed study there is seldom room for the easy generalization, even in his most explicit plays, *The Caretaker* and *A Night Out*. But to label him simply as a naturalist so truthful that his audiences have refused to recognize themselves in the mirror leaves several important elements in his drama out of account.

First, there is his mastery of construction, which is anything but naturalistic—life never shapes itself so neatly. Not only can he handle to perfection the one-act form, working up little by little to one decisive climax, but he can also sustain a three-act drama with complete mastery. . . . [This] is not to say that he writes what we usually mean by the 'well-made play', with its formal expositions, confrontations, and last-act revelations; for him much of the point of life is that we usually do come in half-way through a story and never quite catch up, that the two vitally concerned parties never do meet, that letter which will explain all and round things off neatly is probably never opened. And so instead his plays are usually built on lines easier to explain in musical terms. They are, one might say, rhapsodic rather than symphonic, being held together by a series of internal tensions, one of the most frequent being the tension between two opposing tonalities (notably the comic versus the horrific, the light or known versus the dark or unknown) or two contrasted tempi (in duologue there is usually one character considerably quicker than the other in understanding, so that he is several steps ahead while the other lags painfully behind). The resolution of these tensions used to be in a bout of violence, when one key would at last establish an unmistakable ascendancy (usually the horrific would vanquish the comic, the forces of disruption establish a new order in place of the old), but in the later works Pinter has shown new skill and resourcefulness in reconciling the warring elements or ending more subtly and equally convincingly on a teasingly unresolved discord.

This musical analogy points also to the other element in his drama which effectively removes it from the naturalistic norm; what, for want of a better word, we might call his orchestration. Studying the unsupported line of the dialogue

bit by bit we might well conclude that it is an exact reproduction of everyday speech, and so, bit by bit, it is. But it is 'orchestrated' with overtones and reminiscences, with unexpected resonances from what has gone before, so that the result is a tightly knit and intricate texture of which the 'naturalistic' words being spoken at any given moment are only the top line, supported by elusive and intricate harmonies, or appearing sometimes in counterpoint with another theme from earlier in the play. It is this which gives Pinter's work its unusual and at first glance inexplicable weight and density; until we understand the process we are unable to account reasonably for the obsessive fascination the most apparently banal exchanges exert in his plays.

If Pinter's plays are the most 'musical' of the New British drama, however, it follows that they are the most poetic, because what else is music in words but poetry? . . . [His] works are the true poetic drama of our time, for he alone has fully understood that poetry in the theatre is not achieved merely by couching ordinary sentiments in an elaborately artificial poetic diction, . . . or writing what is formally verse but not appreciable to the unwarned ear as anything but prose. . . . Instead he has looked at life so closely that, seeing it through his eyes, we discover the strange sublunary poetry which lies in the most ordinary objects at the other end of a microscope. At this stage all question of realism or fantasy, naturalism or artifice becomes irrelevant, and indeed completely meaningless: whatever we think of his plays, whether we accept or reject them, they are monumentally and inescapably there, the artifact triumphantly separated from the artist, self-contained and self-supporting. Because he has achieved this, and he alone among British dramatists of our day, the conclusion seems inescapable that even if others may be more likeable, more approachable, more sympathetic to one's own personal tastes and convictions, in the long run he is likely to turn out the greatest of them all. (pp. 259-61)

> *John Russell Taylor, "A Room and Some Views," in his* Anger and After: A Guide to the New British Drama *(© 1962 by John Russell Taylor; reprinted by permission of A. D. Peters & Co. Ltd.), Methuen and Co. Ltd., 1962, pp. 233-61.*

JAMES R. HOLLIS

Harold Pinter has listened to the labored pulse of his century, limned its temper, and perhaps more importantly, recreated its frightening silences. In a time which Tiutchev adumbrated as the "hour of wordless longing," Pinter serves us well by reminding us that we live in the space between words. (p. 1)

Dramatic irony emerges from the disparity between expectation and result. . . . But Pinter's irony goes beyond "dramatic" or "Sophoclean" irony; it is existential irony. Pinter's plays may be ironic at many levels but their most pervasive irony arises from our confrontation with the world we actually live in but do not recognize. We ascribe anonymity to the characters and situations of Pinter's drama precisely because they are too familiar, too disconcertingly close to where we live. . . . [The] audience is implicated in the irony of Pinter's work in a fashion which is not superficially apparent but which accounts for the discomfort heroes and heroines always feel at the moment of *anagnorisis*. Thus the deepest ironic intent of Pinter's work is to make strange that which is familiar and to make familiar that which is strange. (pp. 7-8)

But even though Pinter's plays often seem bizarre and rather mysterious, they are nevertheless overtly realistic in their mood and movements. His characters, for example, are clearly upper, middle, or working-class types although that is not to say that they are typological or allegorical. Even though the problems of any single character may be paradigmatic, they are also distinctly individual. Pinter's characters are not pasteboard figures demanding a one-to-one identification with some allegorical backdrop; rather, they are open and incomplete as all men are open and incomplete. The abyss over which they seem to teeter is surely the same abyss which Heidegger describes as "the openness of Being." Pinter does not dehumanize his characters as Beckett and Ionesco sometimes do; they remain "human, all-too-human." (pp. 8-9)

Pinter seems to be the only playwright to fuse the absurdist consciousness with overtly conventional realism to achieve a dramatically viable amalgam. In *A Slight Ache,* for example, the audience readily enters into the world of the play because it seems comfortably familiar. Soon they realize themselves caught as the wasp is caught in the marmalade and, having committed themselves, must wait upon the conclusion. Then the playwright has his audience from the outset and they must see the matter through. Thus the afternoon tea becomes a horrifying ritual of divestiture without ceasing to be an afternoon tea as well. (p. 9)

Pinter is an original and creative talent. It is true that he has imbibed the vapors of the "masters" [such as Beckett, Ionesco, and Genet], and it is true that they have informed his vision, but the vision was there in the beginning. . . . Pinter is not then an absurdist in the strictest sense although he seems to be doing many things that the absurdists are doing. There are points of influence perhaps, but Pinter's voice is distinct and individual. (pp. 9-10)

Pinter perceives similar problems of communication as Beckett but employs a different strategy of dramatization.

Pinter employs language to describe the failure of language; he details in forms abundant the poverty of man's communication; he assembles words to remind us that we live in the space between words. . . . The effect of Pinter's language, then, is to note that the most important things are not being said, that the dove that would descend to speak the procreative word still hovers amid the precincts of silence. (p. 13)

Language is obviously important in Pinter's effort to get himself across to us, but we must also recognize the many occasions when it is through silence that he communicates. There are many ways in which Pinter uses silence to articulate, but the first, and perhaps most common, is simply *the pause.* The pause occurs when the character has said what he has to say and is waiting for a response from the other side, or it occurs when he cannot find the words to say what he wants to say. In either case he has attempted to span the chasm that exists between him and those around him. He is caught up short; he has reached the limits of language and now waits in silence for something to happen.

There are other occasions in the plays of Pinter when the silence is hard to hear because there are so many sounds being made at the same time. (pp. 14-15)

This is *the silence which emerges when the most important things are left unsaid.* (p. 15)

Pinter's characters typically manifest the exhaustion of their capacities and of the forms by which they live. Although they may fill the air with words, *the silence of these characters is the result of their having nothing to say.* Ionesco has effectively parodied this cultural phenomenon by eliciting nonsense syllables from his characters. Pinter has tried to do the same thing the hard way, that is by using the normal speech of the characters to reveal the poverty, the emptiness of their lives. These are characters who finally exercise their power of speech but find themselves, like the orator in Ionesco's *The Chairs,* filling the air with gibberish to camouflage the fact that they have nothing important to say. (p. 16)

Pinter's gift has been to create dramatic representations of silence as a presence. . . . While there is much in Pinter which is of significance to the discerning observer of contemporary artistic expression, perhaps nothing is more important than Pinter's endeavor to forge a poetic out of the silence which surrounds us. (p. 17)

One of the central metaphors in Pinter is "the room." The room is suggestive of the encapsulated environment of modern man, but may also suggest something of his regressive aversion to the hostile world outside. (p. 19)

The Room conveys a drab lower-class environment without the implicit sentimentalism of social reformers. This is not to say that Pinter is insensitive to the condition of his characters but that their psychological peril is his focus rather than their social deprivation. Thus the social environment is supplanted by the psychological environment and the psychological environment is the product of the needs and weaknesses of those characters. (pp. 29-30)

As much as the barrenness of the room, the entry of Riley, the violence of Bert may contribute to the metaphoric atmosphere of the play, it is clear that language is the means through which Pinter articulates the nameless and says what one finds hard to say. Through his uncanny ear for the syntax and rhythms of common English speech, Pinter is able to reproduce the sundry kinds of silence which we often do not consciously hear. (p. 30)

The language of *The Room* and [of] other plays . . . is the standard speech of the working classes, a patois informed by the daily fare of sex and violence in *News of the World* and the "telly." Why then does Pinter's conventional transference of this speech to dirty little people in grubby little rooms seem so unconventional? What strikes us as strange in Pinter is often due to the failure of our memory. If, for example, we find ourselves overhearing a conversation on a subway, we expect that there will be numerous gaps or pauses, many sentences left hanging. . . . If one were to transfer such conversations to the stage that which we take for granted would suddenly seem strange. Such a playwright would hardly seem a realist until we chanced to recall that our everyday existence is charged with just such mystery. (pp. 30-1)

One of the ways in which Pinter permits silence to work upon our consciousness is to have the characters engage in seemingly insignificant but compulsively repetitive activities. At first these acts may seem slightly strange or slightly humorous; but as they continue, they become forms of expression for emotions too profound to utter. Stanley's beating of the drum ends the first act [of *The Birthday Party*] and the second act begins with McCann slowly and mechanically tearing a newspaper into equal strips. Both characters are channeling and expressing their fears and aggressions. (p. 35)

The systematic undercutting of . . . fact is characteristic not only of *The Birthday Party* but of the other works in the Pinter corpus. It is not that the characters are lying (though we do not know that they are not lying); it is simply that we can only see the truth over their shoulders. . . . As the separate testimonies to the "truth" accumulate in Pinter's plays, the "truth" becomes even more uncertain and the "facts" of the matter begin to call each other into question. (p. 36)

[For example, in *The Birthday Party*, we] never know for certain that Goldberg and McCann are killers; perhaps they are from an asylum and are trying to return a patient. We never know who Stanley is; it is likely that he is using an alias and perhaps even his musical career is part of his cover identity. *The Birthday Party* resists all allegory. Pinter has left too many loopholes for the one-to-one identification which allegory demands. To allegorize Pinter one must also assume the author to have a preconceived plan for the play. In the [Kenneth] Tynan interview on BBC, Pinter expressly declared that he did not. Rather he explained, the idea grew out of the concrete situation. The characters, in effect, make the idea of the play and not the reverse. . . . *The Birthday Party*, then, is not a tissue of systematic signification, the requirement of allegory, but an elaboration, an exfoliation of existential givens. (pp. 41-2)

Pinter possesses a heightened sense for the dramatic which one sometimes also finds in the Hitchcock film. Our attention is focused on the most mundane details even while we know that something more important is afoot. (p. 44)

The Dumb Waiter has a number of motifs in common with *The Room* and *The Birthday Party*. But most importantly, in all three someone sits anxiously within a room and regards each intrusion into that room as the externalization of a threat long felt but unsusceptible to complete articulation. For this reason the sundry silences of the three plays are perhaps more important to our understanding of those characters than whatever they may say overtly. (p. 49)

[Although it is as tempting in this play as in the others,] it is not necessary to allegorize *The Dumb Waiter* to feel the compelling power of Pinter's dramatization of men ignorant of their assignment. It is not necessary to identify the mysterious voice with the Deity to understand man's suspicion that there is a power that is not so much malevolent as detached and unconcerned about those dancing on the killing ground beneath. There seem finally two ways of responding to the absence of answers to a man's questions. He may continue his frustration by asking himself additional questions until he has pushed himself to the abyss. Or he can simply continue to play the game and hope he does not stumble along the way. Gus and Ben personify this central dilemma. (p. 50)

The limitation of set in *The Dumb Waiter* and the other plays of "the room" metaphor obviously goes beyond the need to pare costs, beyond any desire to heed the so-called classical unities. It is rather a strategy to compress a situation, to focus on its central tension as a means of making manifest the Angst-ridden isolation of the characters in those rooms. What one may wish to make of those characters in those situations becomes the problem. Those who avoid allegory have Pinter's blessing. (pp. 50-1)

Pinter's theatre is consequently given to psychological realism rather than to social realism. His preoccupation is with the isolated individual and not the machinations of mace or mitre or suffering masses. But he is, paradoxically, more the realist than the realists. He cuts his "slice of life" thinner and thereby makes it more nearly translucent. Though he may portray a mad society, the basic commitment of the realist is to reason—the reasoned analysis, the reasoned solution. Pinter has no necessary obligation to reason, for his province is the psyche where there are things unaccountable to ratiocinative man. (p. 52)

Previously in Pinter one never discovered what any character's personality really was. The characters were all too frightened to undertake any probing self-analysis. In *A Slight Ache* (1959) we see at last characters who discover the truth of their identities. (p. 53)

The process by which Pinter takes Edward from a cocky, self-assured author to a snivelling dog that cowers before a man who does not speak is as subtle as it is terrifying. Edward's monologues are in fact dialogues, not between himself and the visitor but between himself and himself. He is engaged in questioning himself, and he finds that the answers are destructive. In the dialectic of examination, he discovers the synthesis, the final term, is emptiness. (p. 58)

Other themes which Pinter dramatized in *A Slight Ache* [in addition to this central theme of vacancy] include the psychological stratagems of projection and reaction formation, and the theme of blindness. (p. 59)

All of these themes have exercised Pinter's imagination [in other plays,] but they converge most successfully in *A Slight Ache*. (p. 60)

Pinter returns repeatedly to several themes which, expressed in problematic terms, seem central to the articulation of his vision. The problem of verification, for example, remains crucial to all of his plays. . . . The problem of identity recurs as well. . . . These themes are merged in some of Pinter's later plays as *a struggle for possession*. The struggle is to find and possess the truth, or as Kierkegaard might say, to stand in absolute relationship to it. But the struggle is also to find and possess the real person, the embodiment of the truth. *The Caretaker* merges these themes and is perhaps Pinter's masterpiece thus far. (p. 70)

[The] themes which preoccupy Pinter—the room as a haven from the threatening world outside, the search for the truth, the quest for identity, and the struggle for possession—attain their most engaging synthesis in *The Caretaker*. *Night School* and *The Collection* [which explore similar themes] thus serve as five-finger exercises for what most observers agree to be Pinter's greatest achievement. . . .

The three careworn characters of *The Caretaker* are at various junctures along the circuitous path of this quest for identity. (p. 77)

Davies seems rootless, without a history or stable identity. His isolation is conveyed by his evasive answers to the questions. All identifying details seem lost and one wonders if Davies has ever known where he came from. The halting phrases, the confused pauses betray his fragmented consciousness. Davies has lost his way. He cannot retrace his steps or begin anew. (pp. 81-2)

Even the most banal aspects of existence seem fraught with

serious implications for Davies because he is trying desperately to learn the game so that he can play it too. At every turn, however, he is defeated by language. Language is either too much for him or not enough for him; it either bewilders him or tells him the obvious. Either way he does not communicate to others nor understand fully what they are saying to him.

Because of the confusion about his own identity, about his "standing" in the world, Davies does not trust language at all. He cannot bring himself to say what he wants to say and so stammers around the subject. (p. 84)

Act two represents the fulcrum of the play. It is the occasion in which the triangular relationship begins to take shape and in which Davies begins to try to play the game. (pp. 86-7)

Each of the characters of *The Caretaker* nurses a private illusion.... Each wants to make his way in the world. While Aston and Mick are important to the story, it is clear that Davies is the central character. (pp. 89-90)

Davies is more buffoon than tragic hero, yet there are aspects of his character that approximate the classical *hamartia*. His "flaw" is to miscalculate, to misread the silent communion between brother and brother. (p. 90)

The apartment of *The Caretaker* may be seen as an expanded version of "the room." This time, however, the intruder is not the threat but the one threatened. (p. 91)

Again the vehicle through which the values of the play are made manifest is language. (p. 92)

Pinter has tried to do the most difficult of things, to talk about whatever it is we cannot talk about and for his effort, he is told that he lacks thematic content. Pinter gives voice to the silences, somethings poets have tried to do since Orpheus, and he is told that there is no lyricism in the proletarian paeans of Davies, Mick, and Aston.

The difficult trick which Pinter tries to turn in *The Caretaker* is to show the way in which the language succeeds in revealing most profoundly by seeming to fail.... It is in the "edging around" that the real conflicts of the play emerge. (p. 93)

There are other ways in which Pinter communicates by seeming not to communicate. The recurrent references to the Buddha statuette provide one example. The real symbols of the play, the shoes, the shed, et. al. are so mundane that one naturally expects the Buddha to function symbolically as well; but it does not. One could see it as the ordered center of a disordered universe but that takes us nowhere.... The point behind all of these non-symbols is that the symbols, the referents, the guidelines are not functioning. Davies wants to make his way in the world, to make the "right connections"; and he seeks the deeper explanation behind the phenomenal appearances, but there is none. (pp. 93-4)

It is in the sundry recitals of silence, then, that Pinter's recurrent themes are integrated and articulated. (p. 94)

It is easy to feel out of one's depth with the plays of Pinter. One always faces the question "what is this about?" or "what is he doing?" ... When Pinter's drama is at its best, it is true that the audience may wish to evaluate what is going on; but their involvement is not so much rational as

non-rational. Insofar as the nameless anxieties that haunt the characters are validly, that is to say dramatically, rendered, the observer is drawn into the same circle of anxiety. We are not all itinerant caretakers, of course; but we are all, in our own way, care-taken wanderers. If we rationalize while watching Pinter's plays, it is more likely that we are trying to hypostatize into categories the encircling metaphors of the play, to beat off their seductive gestures with our reasoned principles. (pp. 94-5)

Pinter's two act play *The Homecoming* (1965), reveals an assured craftsman who knows what he wants to do and is doing it. For many *The Homecoming* is not as satisfying a play as *The Caretaker*, but there is little doubt that *The Homecoming* is a rich fusion of the previous themes of the search for a secure home, the poverty of the self, and the struggle for possession. (p. 96)

Critic John Warner has argued that *The Homecoming* is a dramatization of the plight of contemporary man in the time of the eclipsed gods and their sorry substitutes, Science and Rationalism. Consciously or unconsciously, then, the characters of the play represent their fellows in a search for psychic wholeness. (p. 108)

The issue of morality has often been raised in connection with *The Homecoming*. At the superficial level, *The Homecoming* is a shocking play, an affront even to the morality of those who live in a morally fluid age. But the characters of *The Homecoming* are no more concerned with moral issues than a dog is self-conscious about his relationship to a fire hydrant. That is not to dismiss the characters as being merely animals. Rather they are dramatizations of a region of the human consciousness which lies below volition and is amoral in character.... They, like those who went before and like those who shall follow, are about the business of coming home, the return to the proximity of the source. (p. 110)

The Homecoming suggests the possibility that [Pinter's] silences are widening and are extending themselves toward the expression of compelling human archetypes. For all their refusal to leave "this world," Pinter's characters nevertheless strain for something beyond. The transcendental motive need not take its grounding in a specifically theological, philosophical, or cultural pattern to be authentic. Lenny tells us in *The Homecoming* that neither the known nor the unknown merits our reverence. But the silence which ensues from such a confession need not necessarily be arid. Neither is it necessary to conclude that to arrive home is to have completed one's venture. If the Pinter corpus can develop beyond *The Homecoming*, if the ensuing forms continue to be "original," if the silences continue to be procreative, then he will have demonstrated that "the way home is the way forward." (p. 111)

The silences of the last plays [*Silence* and *Landscape*] differ only in degree, not in kind from the silence which surrounded Rose, the Birthday Boy, and Davies. Throughout the corpus, characters try and ostensibly fail in their efforts to fling linguistic bridges across the abyss. But the abyss widens or deepens and the ballistic potential of their language is again outdistanced. Thus, the silence deepens.... While the early characters moved in a generally realistic environment, however strange and unreal that environment often seemed, the last characters do not move about very much at all. Their isolation is intensified, literalized; their movements and gestures toward each other are mechanical and rigid. Their discourse is more fragmentary than before. They begin somewhere near where Davies ended. Their conversation proceeds at different levels and rarely is there a point of intersection. Each seems caught in the prison of himself, in the strictures of an unrelieved past, and blessed (or cursed) with only a partial insight into the nature of his condition. (pp. 112-13)

As Pinter follows the direction of his vision, as he moves ever toward the OM, he runs the risk of replacing drama with apotheosis, of trading the stage for the temple. (p. 113)

For all the static qualities of *Landscape* and *Silence,* however, there is movement still. Bodies are turgid and comparatively immobile, but spirits yet move through deepening shades of silence. For all their truncation, for all their visions and memories *manqué,* these characters ... are embarked. They cannot go home again; they cannot see what they are heading toward; they are, however, irretrievably embarked. If they may not then go with the protective word, they must journey with broken words through regions of silence. For all the chaos and discordancy of their silences and ours, a poetic of the highest order emerges, a dramaturgy become thaumaturgy. (p. 121)

Pinter's concern is not with the "struggling proletariate" of the social realists or even with an abstract notion of "man," but rather with the concrete experience of being human. His characters are found neither at the barricades nor behind the threatened panoplies of power. They are lonely, frightened individuals who have returned to the privacy of their rooms to have a think. They are kings and counselors without their regalia. They are all, under the skin, shivering creatures who fear the silences around them. ... There is, finally, no hortative moral to draw from Pinter's plays, no deontological road map to guide us though his work does remind us that the dream we dream is communal. (pp. 122-23)

Perhaps Pinter's greatest contribution is to rediscover the wordless quality of our language, to recover what Rilke called the "language where languages end."

Pinter's particular achievement has been to sustain linguistically the sort of tensions which seem to drive his characters from within. The fragmentary sentence, the phrase left hanging, the awkward pause, become outer manifestations of the inner anxiety, the deeper uncertainty. The discordant clash of language in, say, *The Caretaker,* is indicative of the discord that arises not only between character and character but within each of the characters. The fumbling efforts at conversation which ensue indicate the desperate need the characters have to make themselves known. (p. 123)

Many of Pinter's characters, on the contrary, go to some length to evade being known by others. ... [This] evasion arises out of the character's fear that if he reveals himself, if he comes clean, he will be at the mercy of those who know him. (pp. 123-24)

The subtle beauty of Pinter's quotidian language arises from its capacity to tell us more about the characters who use that language than they are capable of telling us themselves. Like all lyric poets, Pinter's first obligation is to the *how* of communication and not to the *what.* If such mundane language seems mysterious and terror-ridden, it is only because the lives of men who use a worn-out language are mysterious and terror-ridden. The realist usually sets out to employ the language of common men and succeeds in reproducing only what he thinks is the language of common men. Paradoxically, Pinter's success in attuning our ear to the everyday modes of discourse makes it possible for us to recover the strangeness, the mystery inherent in common human experience. (pp. 124-25)

The kind of hearing necessary to experience Pinter's drama fully is not a simple matter, for Pinter's language is not the rhetoric of direction but the rhetoric of association. One word can, like a pebble in a pond, send out an infinite number of circles. One word may not only lead to another but will more often stir some forgotten experience of pain or pleasure; however, that which ensues is not more language but more silence. (p. 127)

> *James R. Hollis, in his* Harold Pinter: The Poetics of Silence *(copyright © 1970 by Southern Illinois University Press; reprinted by permission of Southern Illinois University Press), Southern Illinois University Press, 1970.*

JOHN SIMON

The least of *The Homecoming*'s troubles is that it does not make sense. This only stirs the interpreters, professional and amateur, to greater heights of interpretative madness. Ambiguity and implication are, of course, valid and potent artistic devices, but if the whole scenario, on almost all levels, has to be supplied by the critic or spectator, who then is the playwright? Pinter's play, like all his others, depends on tricks of diametrical reversal, going from one extreme to the other and saying vague, hostile nothings that can be made menacing, portentous or deep.

The basic flaw of *The Homecoming* is that it is totally formulaic and predictable: every character, sooner or later, becomes the opposite of himself. (p. 345)

These instant contradictions extend to the whole play. ... Now, people are often inconsistent, but they are not schematically self-contradictory. Nor are they, and this is the second big flaw here, all profoundly repulsive or utter nullities. But those are the only kinds of characters you tend to find peopling (or, rather, insecting) a Pinter play. Pitiful worms or poisonous adders: nobody you can care about in the least; not even when, as invariably happens, the worms lengthen into adders, and the adders shrivel into worms.

This leaves the language. But there hardly is any in Pinter: only commonplaces, repetitions, insults, non sequiturs and pauses. This too is a language, I grant you, but is it a language for human beings? ... [But] the pauses, ah, those famous Pinter pauses! How minimal can minimal art get? That is where you, dear spectator, fill in the play. And if others can have *their* interpretations, you won't be caught with your mystagogic pants down either, by gum. ... As for all those gratuitous pauses, if they serve any purpose, it is to stretch Pinter's meager, stunted inventions into full-length plays. (pp. 346-47)

Most noteworthy is the play's intense though latent homosexuality. Once again the motif of the same woman (and what a beastly woman!) shared by two or more men somehow involved with one another—in rivalry, kinship or lovehate—appears; just as it did in *The Servant, Accident,* and *The Basement,* among others. And as so often is the case with homosexual sensibility, the action oscillates between affectlessness and sadomasochism. Instead of a casebook on *The Homecoming,* I'd like a case history on its author. (p. 347)

John Simon, "'The Homecoming'" (1971), in his Uneasy Stages: A Chronicle of the New York Theater, 1963-1973 (copyright © 1975 by John Simon; reprinted by permission of Random House, Inc.), Random House, 1976, pp. 345-47.

GARETH LLOYD EVANS

If we seek, in twentieth-century criticism, for anything approaching the extent of the detailed verbal analysis of Pinter's plays, we find it only in commentaries on Yeats, Eliot and Christopher Fry. In short, we find it in poetic dramatists in whose language the technical and aesthetic resources of poetry and verse are used to a very high degree. (p. 166)

Pinter's language is generally regarded by the intelligent theatregoer and by some perceptive critics as a remarkable evocation of 'real speech'. It is often declared to be the embodiment of the way *we* speak—half-inarticulate, stumbling, leaving questions completely or half-unanswered, lacking clarity—generally of meaning, often of articulation. Both 'real' language and Pinter's version of it, are a long way from that of the 'well-made' play and even from the studiously-constructed naturalistic drama of, say, Galsworthy and Shaw. Indeed it is easy to conclude that Pinter's language is a particular antithesis of Shaw's, having nothing of its sinewy articulateness, its directness, its wit, its socratic poising of question and answer, statement and counter-statement, its almost embarrassing lucidity. (p. 167)

At face value, certainly, Pinter 'sounds' like people speak. . . . [When] Pinter (as in *No Man's Land*) writes 'educated', balanced, apparently intellectually superior characters, they still manage to sound inconsequential. (pp. 167-68)

Compare the language of a well-made play with a Pinter play, and a contrast is apparent—verbal purpose, direction as opposed to apparent ad hoc verbal activity. We may, indeed, push the matter a little further and declare that his plays do not, in the conventional sense, 'end' at all. They stop.

But although we seem to recognize, in . . . real speech, the Pinter timbre, we should, if we listen carefully, also realize that it lacks, unquestionably, a kind of tension which Pinter habitually possesses. This, in itself, should warn us against a too close association between the real and the written. Pinter's language is as taut as a bow-string—it contains a potential that the real neither has nor intends. (pp. 168-69)

One very important facet of [Pinter's uniqueness] is that the language is eminently written for the actor—he is a player's playwright—as a kind of code. This is not to say that other dramatists, using very different modes, are not aware of the requirements of the actor. However, Pinter is unique in expressing his awareness in this extraordinarily precise way.

Yet, however much a close examination of Pinter's language reveals a sophistication of concept and technique, it is difficult still not to feel the tang of 'real' speech in it. . . .

Pinter is no more and no less successful in depicting the speech patterns we recognize in the disaffected, the under-privileged, as in Davies, than he is with the sophisticates in *Old Times,* or the pompous (with a trace of Jewish incantation) in Goldberg. We recognize them all. We swear we have heard people who sound like this. (p. 170)

[However, it] is extraordinarily difficult to visualize Pinter's characters; they are, until an actor becomes them, particularly disembodied. No one on this earth looks like a Pinter character.

The difficulty of visualizing them or assessing what they are like or what motivates them is due to the fact that a Pinter person is not complete—it is a piece of ore that we experience, and a small piece at that. . . . In fact the range of emotions covered is very small and though he uses the speech-characteristics of different social and professional classes, the characters who speak this speech are too partially-formed to represent their class—they sound as if they come from this or that class, but they do not in any other way relate to it. What Pinter has done has been to endow very fragmentary dramatis personae with the apparent characteristics of totally-rounded characters, and he has done it by creating a language which to a degree 'impersonates' the real, but which very often has its own ritual and rules, its own life. . . .

And, indeed, even when we are, in the hands of this supreme verbal magician, lulled into believing that what we hear is 'real', inside the speech a certain stylization is at work. (p. 171)

The effect, in reading the text, is as if you were coming across or, more accurately, being led into, a short or extended poetic image. It is poetic because of the technical resources of rhyme, repetition, rhythm and out-of-the-ordinary verbal resonance; it is an image because although the impersonation of real speech is always, to a degree, present, what is being said is a key which unlocks a door to what is unsaid. (pp. 172-73)

The development of Pinter's expertise and sensitivity with language has not meant a departure from this basic 'metaphorical' writing but a subtilizing and complicating of it in structure, tone and implication. In *The Homecoming* there occurs not the first but, up to that point, the best manifestation of that development, for in it there is a complete and superb integration of dramatic language with the language of theatre. Throughout his career Pinter has been acutely aware of, and has utilized, inanimate objects, stage-furniture, and made them into extra dramatis personae. The newspaper, the spectacles and the electric light in *The Birthday Party* [are examples]. . . . Even when there is no one dominating object, the reader and the theatregoer are made to feel, every time an object is handled or even mentioned, that it means significantly more than mere touch or mention. Nothing, so to speak, is wasted—the realistic bric-à-brac of the well-made play seems, by comparison, museum'd and inert: in Pinter inanimate objects seem always on the point of coming to life. . . . Each time, in *The Room,* a stage-direction occurs, an extra dimension is added not just to the action of the play, but to the elusive meaning that lies behind the words. (p. 173)

The customary notion of a Pinter play is that it sidles inconsequentially from an unimportant point A to an indeterminate point X, Y or Z—it does not matter which. In fact the verbal image-building which has been noted produces an episodic structure. . . . The movement of a Pinter play on stage is very much one of ebb and flow. The extended images represent points of crisis, but between their appearances there lie areas of relaxation. (pp. 173-74)

Pinter's plays are 'about' certain states of feeling (rather more, indeed, about feeling than thinking) which are presented to us in human embodiment—it is a kind of allegorical writing. The feeling *is* the character just as surely as, in a mediaeval play, the vice or the virtue *is* the character—the message *is* the medium. . . .

Many of Pinter's plays are, to a degree, concerned with one or other of the seven deadly sins and these are embodied in characters, though he does not, like the earlier playwrights, often depict or assume or imply the existence of virtue. Good Deeds, we may say, has little to do with Pinter's Everyman, but Lust, Pride, Avarice have.

It is, therefore, as wrong to assess a Pinter 'character' and the language it uses in customary psychologically realistic terms as it is to conceive of a dramatized mediaeval Vice or Virtue in those terms. (p. 174)

Older critics would claim that his work is poetic because it uses, though in ways that are often covert or disguised, many of the conventional resources of poetic communication—rhythm, associative value of words, image-making, tonal effect. He is poetic in the deeper sense that no specific and clear literal meaning can be abstracted from the majority of his plays. In a very obvious sense you not only change a Pinter play if you try to translate it into different terms, you destroy it in the way you would destroy any work of art and, moreover, you find you are no nearer the heart of a mystery. (p. 175)

The allusive and the elusive predominate in Pinter—unlike naturalistic prose-drama where it is either non-existent or of marginal effect. Unlike so many of his contemporary prose-naturalistic colleagues Pinter neither seems in any sense to want to lead men to action nor to relate his events and characters to explicit contemporary actualities; he exhibits no anger, looking either backward or forward, about the establishment, and he seems not to have considered the social causes of underprivilege and tried to root them out.

Pinter incites the imagination, troubles the spirit, and excites the emotions. None of his plays, while we are actually watching them, engage us in any 'issue', moral or otherwise —the 'experience' given us with dramatic subtlety, verbal sophistication and a complete awareness of theatrical possibilities is too strong to allow us to engage ourselves with anything else. It is only afterwards when, in any case, we are often trying to pin down meaning, that the question of 'issues' may arise—as, for example, the 'morality' of *The Homecoming*.

Pinter is not concerned with the actualities of man in society but, taking on the traditional function of the poet, with some of the realities of what man is. He uses, as many poets have done, the sense-data of the contemporary world as a sharp salt, but it is no more.

When we enter into a Pinter room we have to accept a format which embraces states of feeling rather than impersonates the real world, which is self-sufficient and has very much more the status of an image rather than of an actuality. (pp. 175-76)

> *Gareth Lloyd Evans, "Harold Pinter—The De-*

ceptive Poet," in his The Language of Modern Drama *(© Gareth Lloyd Evans, 1977), J. M. Dent & Sons, Ltd, 1977, pp. 166-76.*

* * *

PLATH, Sylvia   1932-1963

Plath was an American poet, novelist, and short story writer. A leading member of the confessional school of poetry, Plath explores in her verse the horror and chaos that lurk beneath the appearance of sanity. Her violent, despairing poetic vision is presented in verse distinguished by technical control and brilliant imagery. Plath also published under the pseudonym Victoria Lucas. (See also *CLC*, Vols. 1, 2, 3, 5, 9, and *Contemporary Authors*, Vols. 19-20; *Contemporary Authors Permanent Series*, Vol. 2.)

GEORGE STEINER

It is fair to say that no group of poems since Dylan Thomas's *Deaths and Entrances* has had as vivid and disturbing an impact on English critics and readers as has *Ariel*. Sylvia Plath's last poems have already passed into legend as both representative of our present tone of emotional life and unique in their implacable, harsh brilliance. Those among the young who read new poetry will know 'Daddy', 'Lady Lazarus', and 'Death & Co.' almost by heart, and reference to Sylvia Plath is constant where poetry and the conditions of its present existence are discussed. (p. 211)

To those who knew her and to the greatly enlarged circle who were electrified by her last poems and sudden death, she had come to signify the specific honesties and risks of the poet's condition. Her personal style, and the price in private harrowing she so obviously paid to achieve the intensity and candour of her principal poems, have taken on their own dramatic authority.

All this makes it difficult to judge the poems. I mean that the vehemence and intimacy of the verse is such as to constitute a very powerful rhetoric of sincerity. The poems play on our nerves with their own proud nakedness, making claims so immediate and sharply urged that the reader flinches, embarrassed by the routine discretions and evasions of his own sensibility. Yet if these poems are to take life among us, if they are to be more than exhibits in the history of modern psychological stress, they must be read with all the intelligence and scruple we can muster. They are too honest, they have cost too much, to be yielded to myth.

One of the most striking poems in *The Colossus*, 'All the Dead Dears', tells of a skeleton in the Cambridge museum of classical antiquities. . . . The motifs touched on are those which organize much of Sylvia Plath's poetry: the generation of women knit by blood and death, the dead reaching out to haul the living into their shadowy vortex, the personage of the father somehow sinister and ineffectual, the poet literally bled and whistled clean by the cruel, intricate quality of felt life. (pp. 211-12)

[A] penchant for the Gothic effect seems to me to weaken much of Sylvia Plath's earlier verse, and it extends into her mature work. She used Gothicism in a particular way, making the formal terrors an equivalent to genuine and complex shocks of feeling, but the modish element is undeniable. Her resources were, however, more diverse. Possessed of a rare intensity and particularity of nervous response—the 'disquieting muses' had stood at the left side of her crib 'with heads like darning-eggs'—Sylvia Plath tested different symbolic means, different modes of concretion, with which to articulate what rang so queer and clear inside her. It is almost silly to argue 'influences' when dealing with a young poet of this honesty and originality. But one can locate the impulses that helped her find her own voice. Wallace Stevens for one.... Or Emily Dickinson, whose authority gives a poem like 'Spinster' its spiky charm.... The tactile, neutral precision of D. H. Lawrence's observations of animal and vegetable is recognizable in 'Medallion' and 'Blue Moles'. These poets, together with Andrew Marvell and the Jacobean dramatists, seem to have meant a lot. But the final poem in *The Colossus,* a seven-part garland 'For a Birthday', is unmistakable. In at least three sections, 'Dark House', 'Maenad', and 'The Stones', Sylvia Plath writes in a way that is entirely hers. Had one been shown only the last six lines, one would have known—or should have—that a formidable compulsion was implicit and that a new, mature style had been achieved:

> Love is the bone and sinew of my curse.
> The vase, reconstructed, houses
> The elusive rose.
>
> Ten fingers shape a bowl for shadows.
> My mendings itch. There is nothing to do.
> I shall be good as new.

Undoubtedly, the success of this poem arises from the fact that Sylvia Plath had mastered her essential theme, the situation and emotive counters around which she was henceforth to build much of her verse: the infirm or rent body, and the imperfect, painful resurrection of the psyche, pulled back, unwilling, to the hypocrisies of health. It is a theme already present in *The Colossus* ('Two Views of a Cadaver Room'). It dominates, to an obsessive degree, much of *Ariel.* ... It requires no biographical impertinence to realize that Sylvia Plath's life was harried by bouts of physical pain, that she sometimes looked on the accumulated exactions of her own nerve and body as 'a trash / To annihilate each decade'. She was haunted by the piecemeal, strung-together mechanics of the flesh, by what could be so easily broken and then mended with such searing ingenuity. (pp. 213-15)

This brokenness, so sharply feminine and contemporary, is, I think, her principal realization. It is by the graphic expression she gave to it that she will be judged and remembered. (p. 215)

The progress registered between the early and the mature poems is one of concretion. The general Gothic means with which Sylvia Plath was so fluently equipped become singular to herself and therefore fiercely honest. What had been style passes into need. It is the need of a superbly intelligent, highly literate young woman to cry out about her especial being, about the tyrannies of blood and gland, of nervous spasm and sweating skin, the rankness of sex and childbirth in which a woman is still compelled to be wholly of her organic condition. Where Emily Dickinson could—indeed was obliged to—shut the door on the riot and humiliations of the flesh, thus achieving her particular dry lightness, Sylvia Plath 'fully assumed her own condition'. This alone would assure her of a place in modern literature. But she took one step further, assuming a burden that was not naturally or necessarily hers....

[So] far as I know there was nothing Jewish in her back-

ground. But her last, greatest poems culminate in an act of identification, of total communion with those tortured and massacred. (p. 216)

Sylvia Plath is only one of a number of young contemporary poets, novelists, and playwrights, themselves in no way implicated in the actual holocaust, who have done most to counter the general inclination to forget the death camps. Perhaps it is only those who had no part in the events who *can* focus on them rationally and imaginatively; to those who experienced the thing, it has lost the hard edges of possibility, it has stepped outside the real.

Committing the whole of her poetic and formal authority to the metaphor, to the mask of language, Sylvia Plath *became* a woman being transported to Auschwitz on the death trains.... In 'Daddy' she wrote one of the very few poems I know of in any language to come near the last horror. It achieves the classic act of generalization, translating a private, obviously intolerable hurt into a code of plain statement, of instantaneously public images which concern us all. It is the 'Guernica' of modern poetry. And it is both histrionic and, in some ways, 'arty', as is Picasso's outcry.

Are these final poems entirely legitimate? In what sense does anyone, himself uninvolved and long after the event, commit a subtle larceny when he invokes the echoes and trappings of Auschwitz and appropriates an enormity of ready emotion to his own private design? Was there latent in Sylvia Plath's sensibility, as in that of many of us who remember only by fiat of imagination, a fearful envy, a dim resentment at not having been there, of having missed the rendezvous with hell? In 'Lady Lazarus' and 'Daddy' the realization seems to me so complete, the sheer rawness and control so great, that only irresistible need could have brought it off. These poems take tremendous risks, extending Sylvia Plath's essentially austere manner to the very limit. They are a bitter triumph, proof of the capacity of poetry to give to reality the greater permanence of the imagined. She could not return from them. (pp. 217-18)

George Steiner, "Dying Is an Art," in his Language and Silence *(abridged by permission of Atheneum Publishers; copyright © 1967 by George Steiner), Atheneum, 1967 (and reprinted in* The Art of Sylvia Plath: A Symposium, *edited by Charles Newman, Indiana University Press, 1970, pp. 211-18).*

A. E. DYSON

One immediately felt [reading *The Colossus*] a highly distinctive new voice, and sensibility—something cool, refreshing, healing, like the personality of the poet herself; but something darker, too, at the heart. The title poem is significantly named; a sense of the huge and continuing dominated her sensibility. But the grandeur of nature oppressed, as well as fascinated her: apprehensions of lurking menace, more likely to test endurance than joy, are seldom absent. In 'Hardcastle Crags', the young woman who walks at night through a bleak landscape is offered nothing, unless it be the satisfaction of pitting flesh and blood against the iron of the universe itself.... (p. 204)

In battling with the encroachments of rock, wind, the sea which is 'brutal endlessly', a temporary, almost humdrum heroism may be earned, as poems like 'Point Shirley' and 'The Hermit at Outermost House' suggest; but nature outlasts man, and wins again in the end....

When Sylvia Plath encountered a landscape that had been tamed and reduced by man, she responded as to a type of trifling. Walking in Grantchester Meadows, since Rupert Brooke the very Touchstone of English nostalgia, she notes that 'Nothing is big or far'. The birds are 'thumb-size', the cygnets 'tame', the Granta 'bland', the water rats 'droll'. Even the students, lost in a 'moony indolence of love', are unmenaced, and therefore somewhat unreal. 'It is a country on a nursery plate', a pretty place, but Sylvia Plath was more at home when she sensed behind nature its naked inhospitality to man.

Wind and sea were only the more natural of the forces she detected waiting to batter or supplant the human race, or patiently take over when it was gone. In 'Ouija', there is an eerie evocation of 'those unborn, those undone' as they crowd into the seance room, drawn to the living by envy. . . . (p. 205)

In 'Mushrooms', the quality of menace is even more chillingly detected, in the sinister, almost cancerous proliferation of fungus. This macabrely ironic vision of a form of life infinitely lower than man, simply waiting in endless patience to 'Inherit the earth', has the vividness of science fiction at its best, without being in the least sensational. (The associations which the word 'mushroom' have for us since Hiroshima may enhance the effectiveness, which is not, however, dependent upon them.) In 'Sculptor', by a further surprising stroke, the forms the sculptor is about to create are felt as bodiless realities waiting to use him for incarnation, after which they will both dwarf and outlast him. . . . (p. 206)

The affinity which Sylvia Plath felt with the dead and the alien was not unlike a form of pity; a conviction of kinship with everything that lives or has lived, however inaccessible or sinister. Her feeling for animals is similar in kind, not only in 'Frog Autumn' and 'Mussel Hunter at Rock Harbour', but in one of the most moving of her earlier poems, 'Blue Moles'.

One further theme running through *The Colossus* was her occasional sense of being teased by glimpses of better worlds, also lurking just beyond the surface of things, but now in the realm of acknowledged fantasy. (p. 207)

[It was] in the last two years of her life that [a] kind of miracle occurred; the dark undercurrent of her experience became a new and fierce possession, and a terrible beauty was born. Between *The Colossus* and the very late poems, there was a period when her earlier mode took on a new, almost ethereal quality in poems such as 'I am Vertical', where a longing for death more explicit than anything expressed earlier is transmuted, however, by an altogether refreshing and spring-like quality of style. And then, something further happened; it seems as though having mastered form, she transcended it, and the central drama of her troubled consciousness was wholly released. In 'Daddy', violence erupts through the poem's powerful rhythm, which seems generated, however, by the actual experience of the poem, and imbued with organic life. The rhythm is hinted at in the first stanza, temporarily lost in the second, recovered powerfully but still fitfully in the next six; and then from stanza nine onwards it takes over completely, as though generated by the creative ferment itself. And in two of the other unforgettable poems of this period—'Lady Lazarus' and 'A Birthday Present'—something altogether

exalted and ecstatic controls the verse. In literary terms, one is aware of the influence of Robert Lowell, and of Sylvia Plath's close friend of genius, Anne Sexton; but the label 'confessional' poetry, which has already been used to link them, seems more inadequate, even, than labels usually do. Certainly much of the greatest poetry since the Romantics (since Shakespeare, indeed) has dealt with the deranged mind; with the paradox of wisdom and folly, of true vision wholly alienated from the rational mind. In Sylvia Plath, it is as though the poet finds in personal experience a depth of derangement, but then, in the magnificent sanity of creation, transmutes this into a myth for her age. (pp. 208-09)

In Sylvia Plath's last poems, as in the work of Robert Lowell and Anne Sexton, we are reminded that the Modern Movement, as Kafka himself exemplified it, is not dead, but still with us; that its mutations are if anything more terrifying than those we have learned to accept in Yeats, Eliot and Joyce; that an art which *does* confront our present nuclear world fully and totally must be an art on the brink of the abyss; that perhaps the creative mind exploring its innermost anguish is the only mirror art can hold up to us today.

The paradoxes of Sylvia Plath's last poems are inexhaustible. In 'Lady Lazarus' she faces with bitter irony our modern response to the miraculous, but in a poem where the miracle of dignity, at least, is achieved. At moments, it seems almost as if the writer's unhealed suffering is required for the poem's aesthetic success. (p. 210)

> *A. E. Dyson, "On Sylvia Plath," in* The Art of Sylvia Plath: A Symposium, *edited by Charles Newman (copyright © 1970 Charles Newman and the estate of Sylvia Plath), Indiana University Press, 1970, pp. 204-10.*

ROBERT BOYERS

Crossing The Water is an extraordinary book, not promising merely nor dazzling as one might have expected of a poet who was later to write the poems in *Ariel*, but perfectly satisfying in the way that only major poetry can be. That her achievement here may be spoken of in terms more orthodox than one could legitimately apply to *Ariel* is but one of the facts the promoters of the legend will have to deal with—how distressing it must be, for some of them at least, to confront a Plath largely in control even of her most terrible associations, and deliberately fashioning a voice by working through the poetry of Stevens, Frost, Lowell, Roethke, and others. The figure of the demon-lady with red hair eating men, and everything else, "like air," is considerably attenuated in the perspective of this new volume. Though one was always grateful for the dozen or so magnificent poems in *Ariel*, one may now be grateful that they can be read in a broader perspective wherein we shall more resolutely attend to the poems themselves rather than to the figure of the poet haunting the margins.

The items included in *Crossing The Water* were written, or so at least the dust-jacket of the volume informs us, "in the period between the publication of *The Colossus* (1960) and the posthumous book *Ariel* (published in England in 1965)." A number had appeared in periodicals before the poet took her life in 1963, but very few writers and critics had taken notice of them in discussing her career. It was as if, with *Ariel*, one had all one needed to reach some proper estimation of the poet. . . . We see clearly now that *Ariel* was by no means enough, that we wanted some assurance of substantiality and permanence in our impression of such poems as "Tulips," "Lady Lazarus," and "Daddy." Already too many of us had come to think of these poems we have so often read aloud and heard recited to us as instances in some peculiar event we had lived through and wondered over, but which seemed more and more remote from conventional poetic experience. In part, of course, it is the propensity of our youth and literary cultures to convert disturbed people into heroes that was responsible, but the *Ariel* poems themselves had no small hand in encouraging us to think of them as extraordinary primal events without antecedent or analogue. *Crossing The Water* may be discussed less feverishly, and one does not hesitate to describe it as a book with a number of great poems, a number of less ambitious but beautifully realized poems, and several immature pieces each of which calls to mind a particular poetic voice imperfectly assimilated.

One need only be familiar with the work of a few poets to speak of Plath's failures in *Crossing The Water*. In poems like "Who," "Dark House," "Maenad," and "The Beast," the hand of Roethke is unmistakably heavy on the page. To read [such] lines in a Plath poem is to have our attention forcibly turned *from* the intrinsic relations among the poem's constituent elements *to* a mode of comparison that has little to do with Plath, but a great deal to do with Roethke's compelling ingenuity and uniqueness. . . . (pp. 96-7)

The presence of Stevens is ordinarily less obvious in Plath, whether one examines *The Colossus* or the present volume, but how startling it is to come upon . . . a poem called "Black Rook In Rainy Weather." . . .

It is as though Plath had sat down to write the poem fresh from an intensely involving session with "Thirteen Ways Of Looking At A Blackbird" and a few shorter lyrics in the *Opus Posthumous,* such as "The Course Of A Particular." Again, one draws attention to these things not to score points on Sylvia Plath but to suggest emphatically how thorough was her absorption in the poetry of her time and how difficultly she forged what is by all accounts an original voice. In her memorable work one hears that voice practically alone—nothing alien clings to it, nothing interferes with its inwardness and that special resonance which is the imprint of a driven and strangely passionate sensibility. (p. 98)

So fine are the best poems [in *Crossing The Water*] that they cannot fail to impress a trained reader with their distinctive authority and linguistic abundance. . . . In these poems the Sylvia Plath whom we have learned to speak of as a case, a clinical item in a running catalogue of the century's abuses, has transformed her character into a fate, an emblem of the singular personality gorgeously projecting itself into a universe of alien things allowed their otherness. Though the project of *Ariel* involved an insistent appropriation and evisceration of this otherness, this peculiar thinginess in the object and human universe through which the poet moved like a devouring angel, the project of the major poems in *Crossing The Water* falls short of so encompassing an enterprise. What we so admire in the present volume is the formal verbal apparatus which makes possible the evocation of a conflict without altogether dissolving the initiating elements in that conflict. The ardor of immediate

perception co-exists here with the hunger to use that perception and transform its objects into something that they are not, but the tension is manageable, and the objects retain their identities. In *Ariel,* a poppy observed had inevitably to be changed into something it could call to the mind only of a furious and distracted sensibility, into a bloody mouth, in fact, or "little bloody skirts." A warmly upturned smile in the concerned face of a loved one would turn to a fish hook, ominous and seductively sinister. There are conversions of this sort in a number of poems in the new book, but they are relatively few, and they seem almost out of place here. Frequently the poet will play with the far-flung association or the grotesque extension of an already unpleasant image, but it is the original image itself she cares for here, its special character and irreducible resonance. (pp. 98-9)

[In the opening stanza of "Widow"] we suspect the poet of contriving an occasion for a display of hysteria such as we have known in *Ariel,* a display in which a series of wondrous metamorphoses will tell us a great deal about the processes of an intelligence conceived almost abstractly, as if it were nothing but process devoid of determinant content. We see though, in succeeding stanzas, that this is not to be the case in "Widow," for it is carefully directed towards the establishment of a vital tension between the reality of the widow, the essence of the condition the word itself traditionally invokes, and the poet's emotional relationship to that condition as dictated by her own needs. What she does here is to imagine what the condition must really be like, to insist upon a mode of imaginative relation, in fact, in which the needs of the self will be deliberately restrained. To speak in such a context of responsible imagination is not at all misguided, nor ought it to invite critical reprisal, as if the merest mention of responsibility were to introduce into a specifically aesthetic domain a moral dimension not at all warranted or conceivably welcome. One may speak of responsible imagination, after all, without any reference to realities external to the poem. The question of propriety here refers exclusively to elements set in motion within the poem itself, and the loyalty to experience one feels moved to comment upon in reading *Crossing The Water* is a loyalty to a particular experience whose dimensions the poem initially describes or suggests. . . . How unafraid the poet is to inhabit this almost otherworldly dimension of the widow's loss, to give expression to a grief anachronistic in its single-mindedness. (pp. 99-101)

Often in going through *Ariel* one thought of the late R. P. Blackmur's reflection on Robert Lowell's earliest work, to the effect that in it there is nothing loved unless it be its repellence. Blackmur never really understood what Lowell's first volumes were about, and just so does his observation miss the mark if too rigidly applied to Plath. Still there is some truth in the observation taken in relation to *Ariel* where one necessarily thinks of *Crossing The Water* in other terms. If Sylvia Plath does not love the widow she describes, her compassion for and insight into her condition are at least considerable. Always, of course, the impulse to cry me me me is present, but the determination not to clearly masters any such impulse, and one must be moved by the drama the poet enacts among her warring desires. . . . [One] trained in the excesses and hungers of *Ariel* would not expect . . . lines like these [in "Two Campers in Cloud Country"]:

It is comfortable, for a change, to mean so little.
These rocks offer no purchase to herbage or people:

How restrained the sentiments in such assertions and yet how tense the voice that utters them, how unlike comfort are the attendant emotions. If from nothing else in the poem, a reader would know for sure of the tension that rings just in the background of every utterance by listening to the final words:

> Around our tent the old simplicities sough
> Sleepily as Lethe, trying to get in.
> We'll wake blank-brained as water in the dawn.

For Sylvia Plath it was no easy matter to love what did not openly include her or that did not yield to her will, and she did no doubt court repellence precisely so that she might justify her poetic and personal excesses. The image of her acquiescently pondering a blank-brained awakening is then no emblem of an easy regression, but the expression of a determined wish to be, occasionally, nothing at all, and thereby to inhabit a various universe according to the principle of a negative capability. "The horizons are too far off to be chummy as uncles," the poet observes, and the line may stand in a sense for the impression one takes of the entire volume. It measures the poet's capacity to endure limited distance and otherness, to resist the temptation to suffocate everything in her fervent embrace. (pp. 101-02)

As one reads through the *Ariel* poems one is taken not by any sense of mystery but by a sense of inevitability that grips one by the throat, occasionally perhaps by the fingers of the hand, and drags him along to an ending that was never really in question, no matter how dazzlingly circuitous the route. There is an element of mystery in *Crossing The Water* that is very different indeed, and one may locate its source at just that point where the object refuses to yield in its intransigeant otherness and insists upon a range of potential meanings or associations that lead not in a straight line but in several directions at once. And this mystery is no mere rhetorical affair, but at least equally an affair of a spirit which can still afford a limited generosity. Suffused as so many poems in this volume are by this genuine current of mystery playing over the surfaces of objects and persons, it is no wonder that even ritualistic enactments incorporated by the poet are touched with a gentleness, a tentativeness one will hardly identify with *Ariel*. One need look no further than the poem "Candles," in fact, to see a perfectly glorious manifestation of this gentleness, this tentativeness, an alternation of sombre sentiment and delicate perception that constitutes a fabric as fine as anything Sylvia Plath has given us. . . . (pp. 102-03)

How pleasant to be able to say of such a poem that the Lowellian echoes are unmistakable, and that they do not matter a bit, that so totally has the poet taken possession of her materials and transformed them that the life and breadth of all she has touched are enlarged and enhanced. And as to the craft that makes such a poem what it is, how just it is to observe that mere quotation is nearly sufficient —analysis of dynamics may well take a back seat to a mode of pleasure we may not have thought possible where Sylvia Plath was concerned. (p. 104)

> Robert Boyers, "On Sylvia Plath," in Salmagundi (copyright © 1973 by Skidmore College), Winter, 1973, pp. 96-104.

GENE BALLIF

[I think] that the so called "religious" motifs of [Plath's] "Mystic" have nothing to do with religion or religious spirituality or the supernatural as commonly conceived, but rather with the only variety of religious experience she knew and perhaps believed she ever would know: the "mystical union" of her "great love" and the creative mania that seized her up in the wake of its rupture and left her with a sense of something worse than "total neutrality," a sense of utter annihilation.

> This is a case without a body.
> The body does not come into it at all.
>
> It is a case of vaporization.

—as "The Detective" wittily puts it. Clearly, the only gods Plath worshipped were poetry and her husband, and from the moment she fell in love we see that husband and poetry were one. (pp. 239-40)

A word about the "religious" motif in "Medusa" as compared with that in "Mystic." The two are quite different poems, of course, but it seems to me that the "remedies" interrogated in the later poem suggest a connection. The "Communion wafer" of "Medusa" had also appeared as "Communion tablet" in "Tulips," where it was associated with a kind of death that was not unwelcome. The religious allusions in both "Medusa" and "Mystic," however, evoke something repellent, something dreaded, scorned, and refused; and though in the later poem the refusal seems muted by an Eliotic presence (echoes of "Ash Wednesday" and "Marina" haunt the first eight lines, for example, and the first "remedy," patently suggestive of Eliot's conversion, is followed by "Memory?"—a key word in *Four Quartets*); the voice that "would like to believe in tenderness" cannot. What the ecclesiastical language in both poems connotes is a crippled, imprisoned, parasitic existence that inevitably implicates the mother and, just as inevitably, the daughter's fear of that "total negation of self" she thought she'd faced the worst of. (pp. 245-46)

"Mystic" is Plath's to-be-or-not-to-be poem, whose final lines suggest that, like Hamlet, she defers felicity a while in favor of a readiness for the hope of day-to-day living. . . . (pp. 246-47)

To call ["Mystic"] "confessional" would be misleading, so ingeniously does it evade confession, and if the letters help reveal what its pressure of disguise comes out of, they don't elucidate the process of its art. Paradoxically, its obscurities are vivid and sharp, obliterating distinctions with an acid edge; the images its images beget seem to move live a multiple-exposure film sequence, fluent, surreal, sea-shifting, like a liquid translucent palimpsest. "Medusa," one could say to suggest what troubled her bond with her mother, is a palimpsestuous poem. . . . Composed under duress of contending emotions, it suffers from the conditions of its own brilliance. Plath's strenuous hand here renders the aegis of Athena a trophy too cloudy to ensure steady and lucid reflections, as if to fix the features of the Gorgon too closely were to run the risk of fixing one's own. How is a reader to apprehend what so clearly doesn't want to be apprehended clearly? It is hard to approach such heavily guarded self-exposure. (p. 248)

A poem like "Daddy" has to be read for what it is on its surface before it can take root in imaginations that sense in it something else. What it is on that level has proved to be so much for so many of its readers, however, that one begins to look for cultural explanations of the sort George Steiner gave when over a decade ago he remarked that the late poems are "representative of our present tone of emotional life" [see excerpt above]. By the time she wrote "Daddy" and "Lady Lazarus," Plath's personal situation had pushed her to psychic extremes one can readily associate with the last half of the Sixties; but the continued popularity of those poems among the young suggests something more, and other, than a tribute to her achievement. One assumes that the twin themes of parricide and suicide have connections and significances as profound and enduring for our culture as ever they did for the Greeks and Romans, and as they've no doubt always had in some form or other for every culture. Yes, but *what* form, one wants to ask, and why? Our forms in particular seem formless—anesthetic and hysterical in emotional tone, cerebral and mindless, dehumanized by their own vitality. Even some of Plath's best poems seem to me tainted with a dram of these evils, notwithstanding their intensities of feeling, style, and apprehension. Their obscurities, moreover, vivid and suggestive as they are, tend to turn them into *jeux de qui* and *jeux de quoi*. Her themes may be timeless and her methods uniquely personal, but there is something in what she does and does not convey that continues to make her the most misunderstood and controversial of American poets. Cultists, New Feminists, necrophiliac reviewers, and in some ways even the "dissenters" among her audience might be the mere fringe of the cultural anarchy her poetry flourishes in. I suppose even some of her most intelligent and appreciative readers would admit, as I do, to split feelings about her that tend to interfere with efforts to understand what she means. Perhaps that has something to do with why Hardwick said of her poems that "there is no question of coming to terms with them"—and one reason why some of us keep having to try. (pp. 258-59)

> *Gene Ballif, "Facing the Worst: A View from Minerva's Buckler," in* Parnassus: Poetry in Review *(copyright © by* Parnassus: Poetry in Review*), Fall-Winter, 1976, pp. 231-59.*

LORNA SAGE

This selection [*Johnny Panic and the Bible of Dreams*], made by Ted Hughes, of Sylvia Plath's miscellaneous prose—published stories, articles, a few passages from the notebook-journals—is probably the best that can at present be done to pad out the record. . . .

[The] notes from Cambridge (1956) are the most remote, not just in time. They reek of closet-theatre, and are full of self-disliking yet somehow cosy parentheses—"as I have so often boasted cleverly", "see, how dangerous", "always patching masks". She sounds bored with the gothic contents of her consciousness; the motifs are all there (Lazarus, the cold moon, father/lovers, birth-damaged babies, stillborn poems) but devoid of passion or even interest, as though she had grown weary of rehearsing them. It was perhaps a defensive pose; however, it seems to have stuck, and obviously had to be unstuck—"My God, I would love to cook and make a house, and surge force into a man's dreams, and write"—before these gruesome relics could work their miracles in the later poems. . . .

More interesting, if less paraphrasable, are the pieces from 1961-62 which record some of the events that went into "The Bee Meeting" and "Berck Plage". The tone is very

different, though how far it's representative is impossible to tell. It would be cheering to think that it was since these were professional notes, ready-tailored to be used for poetry, shorn of self-analysis. She hardly needed to make notes about herself—what she did need was visual recall, the "soap-coloured oak" and "raw date" on Percy B.'s coffin; the different veils, the cow parsley and angry bees zinging "as at the end of long elastics". There are some interesting contrasts between her private tone and her bardic finalities: "The end, even of so marginal a man, a horror", says the journal of her dead neighbour. "This is what it is to complete. It is horrible", says the poem, placing him centre stage, but at the same time merging him with all the dead, especially Daddy. Or again, there is the prosaic grave as a "narrow red earth opening", compared with the "naked mouth, red and awkward" that gapes in the verse. The poetry and the prose seem at last to have sorted themselves out—as though now that she was writing poems that pleased her, she no longer needed to compose sub-lyrics in her journals. The closer she got to simply gathering material, the better her prose. . . .

She is surprisingly inept at inventing structures, even ordinary plots, taking refuge instead in archaic, would-be wry, O. Henry "twists" to rescue directionless narratives. Only four or five of the stories take on a full fictional identity, and then it's done through large-scale mythic patterns rather than the discreet adjustments that usually belong to the form. For example, the only endings she can make work seem to be death or waking out of a hallucination, or both at once, as in the title story, "Johnny Panic". There, and in a companion piece, "The Daughters of Blossom Street", she manages something like the metamorphosed autobiography of *The Bell Jar*, turning a brief job she had in 1958 as secretary to a psychiatrist at Massachusetts General Hospital into a cold, gleeful vision of the sharable nightmare. . . . Even here, though, there are signs of self-consciousness and the worry about pastiche, since the heroine arrives at her "bible", her collection of dreams, by stealing them out of people's files.

Indeed, in so far as the stories have—or suggest—a theme, this is it. Perhaps because they are so often hesitant, dependent, ill at ease, they reveal even more clearly than her poems her fear that for all her isolation, she was a psychic parasite. "Day of Success", which tries to dislaim any such parasitism, must be one of the creepiest instances: an attempt at a woman's magazine story (unpublished until last year) about a young wife and mother coping with her writer-husband's sudden breakthrough into realms of money and fame. It is saccharine-sweet, and entirely (deliberately?) fails to hide its bitterness. . . . It's terrible stuff, with the feeblest of happy endings, a parody of the zest with which she threw herself into the role of housewife and insisted on an exaggerated separation of roles in the earlier part of her marriage. . . .

This collection of prose belongs to the semi-created level of [Plath's] work, but even here she has the power to set off like firecrackers problems that go way beyond the often dull or scrappy style.

> *Lorna Sage, "Death and Marriage," in* The Times Literary Supplement *(© Times Newspapers Ltd. (London) 1977; reproduced from* The Times Literary Supplement *by permission), October 21, 1977, p. 1235.*

SIMON BLOW

[*Johnny Panic and the Bible of Dreams*] is only of interest if discussing why Sylvia Plath should ever have wanted to write prose—so inferior (*The Bell Jar* included) is it to her verse—thus this publication must have a purely technical fascination, for even Plath addicts cannot have grown so indiscriminate as to swallow these writings whole. . . .

She thought that fiction, by obliging a writer to create outside himself, would train her to objectivity, and yet in all but a very few of these stories does she not write of death, the dying or the dead. In prose her death obsession never shakes off an adolescent curiosity and yearning, and in one story, 'The Daughters of Blossom Street', she hints at a suspiciously unattractive asset to an early death. Young Billy takes a fatal header while running up and down unlit stone stairs, and Plath puts into a character's mouth, 'I think that boy's a lucky boy. For once in his life he's got sense. For once in his life, I think that boy's going to be a hero'. Later she reflects that Dotty was quite right to think that, as posthumous fame is heaped on the boy through dying young. This is unattractive in the light of Sylvia Plath's own death by suicide at thirty, and the fame that has grown from it and surrounded her since.

But, in fairness, she did do her best to exorcise her demons by writing stories and a part of her was quite serious when she said that her aim was to be a top-paid storyteller of *The New Yorker* or *The Ladies' Home Journal*, only it wasn't for her. Plath's suicide put her private neuroses into the public domain and in the majority of these stories they are all too visible and prevent the fiction from taking on any life of its own. (p. 42)

From two articles published in this collection she seems to have been on the defensive over her poetry, as if she thought that the success she craved could never come from what would be judged a minor form when set against the vast territory of fiction. 'For me, poetry is an evasion of the real job of writing prose', she wrote and she tortured herself for ideas and an original style. Very occasionally she got there, as in a story like 'The Fifteen-Dollar Eagle' where for once she is able to stand aside and observe, but she couldn't keep it up, and soon enough she is back to death and more death. Perhaps were Sylvia Plath alive it would be possible to see these stories differently, but in that event it is doubtful that such a book would ever have come about. (pp. 42-3)

[However] the book ends with two prose pieces that served as notes for three of her poems. These are of interest since it is Sylvia Plath's poetry that ultimately must hold us, not her suicide and the inflated legend that has sprung from it. To compare the prose with the verse is to see how a formless, unshaped talent was transformed by its rightful medium into something positive and durable. (p. 43)

Simon Blow, "Sylvia Plath's Prose," in Books and Bookmen *(© copyright Simon Blow 1978; reprinted with permission), June, 1978, pp. 42-3.*

MARGARET ATWOOD

"Johnny Panic and the Bible of Dreams" is a minor work by a major writer. . . . [It will interest] any reader sympathetic enough to Plath's work to have read most of it already and to be interested in foreshadowings, cross-references, influences and insights. . . . [It's a prose catch-all]

and as such it ought to round out one's knowledge of the writer and, perhaps, offer some surprises. Luckily it does both. . . .

It was a shock akin to seeing the Queen in a bikini to learn that Sylvia Plath, an incandescent poet of drastic seriousness, had two burning ambitions: to be a highly paid travel journalist and to be a widely published writer of magazine fiction. . . . To this end she slogged away in the utmost self-doubt and agony, composing more than 70 stories, most of which were never published, and filling notebooks with the details of what she thought of as real life: styles of clothing and interior decoration, mannerisms of acquaintances, sketches of the physical world that she believed she had no talent for observing. (Poetry she considered a mere escape, a self-indulgence, an indulgence in self, and as such unreal, because she was not totally convinced of her own worth or even of her own existence.)

It's easy to sneer at such ambitions, and the editor [Ted Hughes] does not altogether resist the temptation, though his disapproval is gentle and underlined by a statement of crushing validity: Sylvia Plath's genuine medium was poetry. Of course this is true; but her desire for journalistic success, which seems so incongruous in view of the final excellence of her achievement, must be placed in context. Sylvia Plath became famous only after she was dead. . . .

On one level "Johnny Panic" is the record of an apprenticeship. It should bury forever the romantic notion of genius blossoming forth like flowers. Few writers of major stature can have worked so hard, for so long, with so little visible result. The breakthrough, when it came, had been laboriously earned many times over. But there's more to "Johnny Panic" than juvenilia. The writing varies widely in quality and interest, or rather in the quality of the interest; for although the young Sylvia Plath squeezed out some fairly dismal stories, as most young writers do, all the pieces presented here are revealing.

Some things stand brilliantly on their own: two short later essays, "America! America!" and "A Comparison"; several of the notebook entries; the title story, which foreshadows "The Bell Jar"; and "Tongues of Stone." Two pairs—notebook entry, short story—demonstrate the transformation from observed real life to fiction; in both cases the notebook entries have a spontaneity that the stories, in their desire to be literary, almost lose. There are some straight formula pieces, most notably "Day of Success," which is about a young wife and mother who keeps her dashing playwright husband by being domestic. At first sight these stories are merely no more deplorable than other such 1950's set pieces, but on second reading they cause pricking of the thumbs.

Even when she was trying to be trite, Sylvia Plath could not conceal the disconcerting insights into her own emotional mainsprings that characterize her poetry. The unevenness of the stories is often the result of a clash between the chosen formula and the hidden message that forces its way through, seemingly despite the writer. (p. 10)

The stories are arranged chronologically but in reverse order. This creates an archeological effect: the reader is made to dig backward in time, downward into a remarkable mind, so that the last, earliest story, "Among the Bumblebees" (a wistful story about a little girl's worship of her father who dies mysteriously), emerges like the final gold-crowned skeleton at the bottom of the tomb—the king all those others were killed to protect. Which it is. (p. 31)

Margaret Atwood, "Poet's Prose," in The New York Times Book Review (© 1979 by The New York Times Company; reprinted by permission), January 28, 1979, pp. 10, 31.

* * *

POIRIER, Louis
See GRACQ, Julien

* * *

PYNCHON, Thomas 1937-

Pynchon is an American experimental novelist and short story writer often associated with the black humorists. His labyrinthine, encyclopedic novels reflect the formlessness of contemporary history and depict the powerlessness of the individual before contemporary technology and a seemingly imminent apocalypse. In his novels all events seem to be linked to vague conspiracies, his protagonists becoming involved in vain quests to seek the root of these mysteries. Considered by many critics to be the most important American novelist to emerge in the past twenty years, each of his three novels has garnered a major literary prize, most notably a National Book Award for *Gravity's Rainbow*. (See also *CLC*, Vols. 2, 3, 6, 9, and *Contemporary Authors*, Vols. 17-20, rev. ed.)

JOHN VERNON

Chance meetings in Pynchon's novels are exploited as parodies of realism by being accepted as part of the normal, necessary order of events. A line of action that is entirely arbitrary, that is taken by chance, links perfectly with others that are stumbled upon, and all of them lead somehow to the right place. Yet this right place, whether it be V. or a full disclosure of the Tristero system, is never finally reached. The clues that Oedipa Maas assembles about the Tristero in *Lot 49* are all happened upon accidentally, through a Jacobean play, a lavatory wall, a chance meeting with another character in a labyrinthine munitions plant, and so on. The atmosphere of a multitude of possibilities is created, an infinite proliferation of plot lines; yet the one that is followed is the only one, the right one, the way out; and yet again, it brings us no closer to an answer, an identity, a V., a meaningful pattern, than we were to begin with. (p. 65)

John Vernon, in his The Garden and the Map: Schizophrenia in Twentieth-Century Literature and Culture (© 1973 by The Board of Trustees of the University of Illinois; reprinted by permission of the author and the University of Illinois Press), University of Illinois Press, 1973.

GORE VIDAL

I find it admirable that of the nonacademics Pynchon did not follow the usual lazy course of going for tenure as did so many writers—no, "writers"—of his generation.... The fact that he has got out into the world (somewhere) is to his credit. Certainly he has not, it would seem, missed a trick; and he never whines.

Pynchon's first novel, *V.*, was published in 1963.... Cute names abound. Benny Profane, Dewey Gland, Rachel Owlglass. Booze flows through scene after scene involving members of a gang known as The Whole Sick Crew. The writing is standard American. (p. 119)

From various references to Henry Adams and to physics in Pynchon's work, I take it that he has been influenced by Henry Adams's theory of history as set forth in *The Education of Henry Adams* and in the posthumously published "The Rule of Phase Applied to History." For Adams, a given human society in time was an organism like any other in the universe and he favored Clausius's speculation that "the entropy of the universe tends to a maximum" (an early Pynchon short story is called "Entropy"). (p. 120)

Pynchon's use of physics is exhilarating and as an artist he appears to be gaining more energy than he is losing. Unlike the zero writers, he is usually at the boil. From Adams he has not only appropriated the image of history as Dynamo but the attractive image of the Virgin. Now armed with these concepts he embarks in *V.* on a quest, a classic form of narrative, and the result is mixed, to say the least.

To my ear, the prose is pretty bad, full of all the rattle and buzz that were in the air when the author was growing up, an era in which only the television commercial was demonically acquiring energy, leaked to it by a declining Western civilization. (pp. 120-21)

With *The Crying of Lot 49* (1966) Pynchon returns to the quest, to conspiracy. Cute names like Genghis Cohen, an ancient Hollywood joke. Bad grammar: "San Narcisco lay further south," "some whirlwind rotating too slow for her heated skin." A lot of booze. Homophobia. Mysteries. It would appear that most of the courses Pynchon took at Cornell are being used: first-year physics, psychology, Jacobean tragedy—but then his art is no doubt derived "from experience and not much of that." (p. 121)

The first section of *Gravity's Rainbow* is called "Beyond the Zero." Plainly a challenge not only to *l'écriture blanche* but to proud entropy itself. Pynchon has now aimed himself at anti-matter, at what takes place beyond, beneath the zero of freezing, and death. This is superbly ambitious and throughout the text energy hums like a . . . well, dynamo.

The narrative begins during the Second War, in London. Although Pynchon works hard for verisimilitude and fills his pages with period jabber, anachronisms occasionally jar (there were no "Skinnerites" in that happy time of mass death). The controlling image is that of the V-2, a guided missile developed by the Germans and used toward the end of the war (has Pynchon finally found V.? and is she a bomb?). (p. 122)

England. Germany. Past. Present. War. Science. Telltale images of approaching . . . deity? Two characters with hangovers "are wasted gods urging on a tardy glacier." Of sandbags at a door, "provisional pyramids erected to gratify curious gods' offspring." And "slicks of nighttime vomit, pale yellow, clear as the fluids of gods." Under deity, sex is central to this work of transformation. (p. 123)

Eventually, the text exhausts patience and energy. In fact, I suspect that the energy expended in reading *Gravity's Rainbow* is, for anyone, rather greater than that expended by Pynchon in the actual writing. This is entropy with a vengeance. The writer's text is ablaze with the heat/energy that his readers have lost to him. Yet the result of this exchange is neither a readerly nor a writerly text but an uneasy combination of both. Energy and intelligence are not in balance, and the writer fails in his ambition to be a god of creation. Yet his ambition and his failure are very much in the cranky, solipsistic American vein. . . . (pp. 123-24)

Gore Vidal, in The New York Review of Books *(reprinted with permission from* The New York Review of Books; *copyright © 1974 Nyrev, Inc.), July 15, 1974 (and reprinted in his* Matters of Fact and of Fiction: Essays 1973-1976, *Random House, 1977).*

JAMES ROTHER

[Let] us postulate one overriding function of this contraption called *V.*, namely to call attention to history not as a nightmare from which we're trying to awake, but as a fantasy into which we've been mythically herded. It should be pointed out that *V.* proposes no history at all, not even a fake one, since to be historical is to be fictional in the least rewarding sense.... Such history-oriented fictions—and it makes no difference whether the history is personal or public, social or psychological—all accept the whims of chronology, the arbitrary daydream of events poised in sequence. Yet we have every reason to believe that this long-accredited view of the universe is as false as the Ptolemaic Disneyland it managed to replace, that it is only in our contrived histories of what never was that events could not stall into psychic tableaux, pockets of occurrence. Far from being the metaphorical vehicle of experience, time is simply its tenor; and far from being endlessly fluid, it stalls constantly, folding itself neatly into synchronisms whose *raison d'être* lies hidden in the accidents of consciousness that give rise to their perception. Thus *V.* is everyone and no one, eternal and non-existent; she is *Cherchez la femme* and Sweet Cheat Gone, maximum Vicissitude and maximum Velocity. Indeed, she must be considered what one of Pynchon's anti-figures, Dnubietna, engineer-poet of the Anglo-Maltese school ..., observes history to be: a "step-function." For where all characters are one character and all history reincarnates the fraud that each of us has been here before regressing to lives we've never lived, what we experience as fiction becomes inseparable from those patterns of recurrence which to us are everyday "reality." (pp. 29-30)

What has disappeared from the scene is the writer whose imagination of reality dominates our fictional rehearsals of that reality. In the golden age of omniscient narration, the authorial stance always resembled Hamlet on the battlements soliloquizing with a ghost. Writers postured, they gesticulated, they sent their egos into whatever combat nature or society saw fit to engage them with.... But Dickens and Thackeray created their heroes without novels and novels without heroes without realizing that they themselves were postmodern; writers like Pynchon and Barthelme—the first to employ cybernation in the service of literature—not only know they are postmodern but have manufactured a universe which knows it is too. It is as though a complex mechanism had been designed specifically to build another mechanism whose only purpose was to observe itself in the act of being a machine. (pp. 30-1)

James Rother, in boundary 2 *(copyright © boundary 2, 1976), Fall, 1976.*

ROBERT MARTIN ADAMS

On its surface, *V* is an incredibly active novel, with an immense cast of characters as vigorously in motion as a swarm of paramecia in a drop of swamp-water. They penetrate the sewer systems of Manhattan, yo-yo up and down the East Coast, rattle around Egypt, Florence, Malta, and South Africa; they change appearances, change identities, couple like rabbits, group and regroup, diffuse and drop out of sight as fast as motes in a beam of sunlight. The activity isn't completely pointless, since plots and semi-connected actions form and reform, sometimes unbeknownst to the participants, sometimes accidentally; but often all pretense of sequential behavior disintegrates in a whirl of miscellaneous partying, a picturesque but gratuitous act. In the end, the various plots don't cohere, the individual actions are spaced out. Why does Paola Maijstral feel she has to enter a black whorehouse in order to become, or in spite of the fact that she is, the preferred girl of McClintic Sphere? Why after a spell there does she feel inclined to go back to Pappy Hod, with whom life seems distinctly less preferable? These things, and many others, happen, but without apparent motivation, or at least only with such motivation as the reader wants to impute to the character after the event. Uncertainty and actual provocation are built into the structure of the fiction.... [The] plot (in the sense of "what happens to the characters," and even in the sense of "how the characters' inner life develops") is not the vehicle of the book's main interest. Its function, and the function of all that frantic, superficial activity, is to distract and impede, not to express. One can't say that it does or doesn't function in other ways as well; there's an uncertainty principle at work as we read, in that no action is so far-fetched or remote that it can't, perhaps later, tie up on some level with another; and the construction isn't so tight that what looks important can't be simply forgotten or erased by a coincidence.

In any event, all the hurry and scurry in the novel—drunken brawls, promiscuous beddings-down, aimless wanderings, mistaken identities, weird acts of violence, and arbitrary linkages—lead nowhere. For one tale that is tied up in pink ribbon—probably sardonic—like that of Paola and Pappy, there are dozens that the author leaves hanging in mid-air, without bothering to conclude them.... And apart from all the characters who simply split off the action and disappear, the action plot itself is meaningless. Profane, the schlemiel-Redeemer, makes the point about all his "experience" at the end of the book, when he says "offhand" (but he means "in deepest seriousness"), "I'd say I haven't learned a goddamn thing."

What is important to the book takes place outside the realm of the characters' actions, and to a large extent outside their comprehension; and it's only indirectly, semi-allegorically connected with Stencil's search for V. That is more in the nature of a private anxiety, since the woman in whom the principle of V was momentarily embodied, insofar as she was an individual at all, was dead well before the action of the novel starts.... The search for V is therefore pointless and obsessive as it's carried on after the war; it goes beyond the person, beyond even the several perhaps-conspiracies of which she may have been an intermittent agent, into her existence as a malignant or at best indifferent principle of nature.... The fact that a number of other people can get caught up in a search-program as flimsy as Stencil's shows by strong implication how loosely they're attached to the texture of everyday life. Yet the fact is that everyday life itself includes alien and even hostile elements, as is shown most gruesomely in the discovery after her death and dismemberment that the lady largely consisted of inanimate prosthetic materials—a wig, a glass eye, false teeth, a wooden foot, a star sapphire imbedded in her navel. Thus, though the search for V as protracted by Stencil is insane, her reported nature ties her closely to a theme running through the entire book, the encroachment and usurpation of the inanimate world on the animate. V as a physical principle needn't be sought anywhere because she (it) is present everywhere; V as a person can't be sought, because she is dead. There's a potent unspoken connection here. (pp. 170-72)

As a sensitive schlemiel, Benny Profane is at hopeless odds with all natural things, a Redeemer limp and helpless against encroaching evil; he sees it but is helpless to do anything about it. This is why—against superficial probability—he is such a magnet for women who want to protect, mother, and be personally intimate with him. Yet hardly any of this vision of a world gradually depersonalizing relates more than hazily to the narrative. Reified people are simply a condition of the world within which the novel takes place, and Stencil's preference for connecting it with lady V (or Vernichtung or Valletta, or Victoria, or vortex, or all of them) is hardly shielded at all from the suspicion that it's a private obsession. Stencil's search and the structure of the world are like two giant vortexes the tips of which meet in the paper-thin plane of the narrative action.

Stencil, junior, has the interesting mannerism of referring to himself only in the third person, as if he were an outline to be filled in; it's a revealing individual mannerism, but the condition it bespeaks is general, striking in him mainly because he has such a phantom-image of what his life must contain. Nobody remarks his transparency because nobody is more opaque than he is; on the contrary, his insane energy contrasts with their random jittering, catches them up and organizes them for a moment, before moving on and out. (p. 173)

The V of V's that Pynchon uses as an epigraph to his novel intimates the narrowing of the ordering mind to a point of monomania, the simultaneous reduction of life to a single point of vitality, and so the limiting of kindly intent among or between human beings to an automatic gesture of self-defeat—like a secular saint walking through life under the name "Profane." . . . Pynchon's characters are [thin and flat]; the arabesques of their activity are strictly limited, and behind them—bad if it's only an obsession, worse if it's something more—is the encroachment of an inanimate, impersonal, inhuman power. It speaks in Pynchon's prose, which is frequently colored gray by scientific and technical terminology; it speaks even more coldly in a constant fascination with abstract and impersonal process. Pynchon's outline-characters caper across an ice-cold universe. Their relation to Joyce's outline-figures (who yet never fail to be full of other outlines) is neither intimate nor immediate. But in the sense of a fragile and fearful existence maintained against the grain of an ostentatiously pointless plot, they are a true Joycean development. Like Joyce's personae, they swim the waters of a sea thick with the plankton of learning both vulgar and encyclopedic; and the fable they unfold has no more to do with morality than with politics or religion. Heroes and villains of the book are its underlying patterns, the real plot is our ability to see them; and in that respect, rather than in other, more immediate characteristics, the book declares its parentage.

"Oneiric chill," a phrase used somewhere in *V* for a specific purpose, characterizes the book as a whole, and carries over with special relevance to *Gravity's Rainbow*—an extraordinary tour de force of paranoid fantasy, cloak-and-dagger romance, and technological poetry. . . . As in *V*, there's no following the chain of events; it isn't a chain but a Jackson Pollock of wiggling lines, blobs, blurs, and smears. Many words are spoken, but only rarely by individuals; thoughts and impressions occur, but are rarely localized behind any specific pair of eyeballs. What the novel represents is not what happened over a period of time to a few chosen individuals, but the nightmare of the disintegrating European mind in the final stages of a war that was as much enacted as fought. There's no order or economy or coherence to this story. . . . In its erratic and tangled course, the novel blossoms into extravagantly decadent orgies, narrows down to Keystone-Cop chases, turns to brutally sadistic animal episodes, and always, always weaves developing technologies and corporate mergers, chains of command and task-force terminology into the weft of human intentions. (pp. 174-75)

The deciphering of novel by reader parallels the persistent, paranoid effort of the "characters" (but they are transparent cutouts, not true characters) to decipher the twisted and tormented face of Europe; a collective message works its painful way toward consciousness. The world is a palimpsest, but the topmost message is not letters at all, it is a tangle of squirming, semi-animate shapes. (p. 176)

Pynchon has written, in *Gravity's Rainbow,* an appallingly intelligent, deeply disbelieving, almost unreadable parable of the modern world; it has the frigidity of a nightmare, along with a nightmare's lurking suspicion that there's another and worse nightmare lurking behind this one. You can't even trust your sense of horror. The book perhaps suffers, like those of Joyce, from too slavish a devotion to the principle of imitation—chaos is altogether chaotic and void is bleakly vacant; like Joyce's novels, too, it defies all principles of economy, and sometimes its black humor is a little jejune. But in the large it's a deeply moving and very serious book. (p. 178)

Though it's deeply rooted in specific locales and a limited period of time, *Gravity's Rainbow* again reminds us of Joyce in suggesting behind the immediate scenario a timeless and universal process. People intrude on objects only peripherally and blunderingly, objects advance on people inexorably, and people cooperate with this process by calmly converting others or themselves into objects. In a book that's saturated with sex, mostly the kinky varieties to be sure, some of the most passionate and sensitive writing is devoted to a celebration of the special molecular affinities of different families of plastics. The book's perspectives are inhumanly long. Pynchon appears to have less than no interest in morals, in politics, in religion, in what used to be called "human nature." He doesn't write an "art novel" properly so called, a realistic novel, a novel of ideas, a horror story, a psychological study, or a science-fiction fable—though traces of all these ingredients are perceptible. Though the phrase doesn't characterize it very closely, *Gravity's Rainbow* could be called a visionary apocalyptic novel, Joycean less in specific techniques than in its scope, penetration, and cold perspective. (pp. 178-79)

Robert Martin Adams, in his AfterJoyce: Studies in Fiction After "Ulysses" *(copyright © 1977 by Robert Martin Adams; reprinted by permission of Oxford University Press, Inc.), Oxford University Press, New York, 1977.*

ALFRED Mac ADAM

When we read a Pynchon text we may be disconcerted by it, but we usually find ourselves comfortable with at least one of its elements: setting. In fact, Pynchon's *mise en scène* may be the only reason for calling his books novels. He is as archeologically precise about places and things as Flaubert, although he should probably be compared to the Flaubert of *Salammbô*. In that text, Flaubert transports Emma Bovary's problems back to Carthage, rendering both Emma and the setting abstract. Pynchon, on the other hand, creates a false familiarity in the mind of the reader which makes him forget that what he is reading is not a study of people in a historical setting but the clash of personified ideas surrounded by the things of the twentieth century. Flaubert and Pynchon are opposites that converge: Flaubert makes the alien familiar by recreating the problems of the nineteenth-century bourgeoisie in Carthage and Pynchon makes the familiar strange by having his personifications collide in a setting we know only too well.

This disjunction between character and setting is the first indication that Pynchon is a satirist, that he is reworking satire as a modern-day disciple of Petronius, Apuleius, or Voltaire might. In addition to this use of a pasteboard, *trompe-l'oeil* setting, there are three other aspects of his work that support a reading of them as satires: his characters are associated with ideas or *idées fixes*, his scenes take precedence over his plots, and his characters' psychological development is reduced to a minimum. The difference between satire and, for example, novel may be seen in two areas: character and plot. Novelistic plots, as Fielding suggests in *Tom Jones*, both echoing and modifying Cervantes, tend toward history writing, and it would not be unreasonable to suggest that the particular form of history used as the model for novelistic plots is the developmental sort we associate with Hegel. (pp. 555-56)

We cannot become "intimate" with characters in either satire or romance because they never acquire psychological depth. In both genres, character is subordinated to some greater concept, either ideas, in the case of satire, or archetypes, especially those associated with fertility, death, regeneration, or sterility in the case of romance. In both genres, characters are impenetrable, not human, and this alien quality is only mitigated by occasional outpourings of sentiment or flashes of wit. The relationship between satire and romance, with regard to character, is interesting because of the antithetical nature of the two genres: romance tends toward the noble, the heroic, and the superhuman, while satire tends toward the roguish or ordinary. (pp. 556-57)

The juxtaposition of romance and satire is also important for understanding Pynchon's esthetic enterprise because he appropriates one of romance's principal plots, the quest, and uses it for satiric purposes. . . .

All three of Pynchon's texts are ironic quests, but *V*, his first, is the most mysterious. It is a search for something or someone, V, but what V is is never made clear. The search ends in mystery and death, and all the reader knows at the end is that the enigma concerns the existence or nonexistence of something "out there," something that either possesses meaning or not. But whatever it is must be at all costs ascertained, and this idea of a mystery-to-be-resolved is what defines the reader's situation in all three of Pynchon's satires. *V* is arranged in such a way that, as a totality, it seems to be defying the reader to find a system of meaning. This dare, this either/or crux, is in fact the result

of yet another juxtaposition, that of faith and paranoia, and it is through this juxtaposition that Pynchon makes his readers participate in his texts as though they were characters. (p. 557)

The reader of *V*, or so it would seem, cannot help but create meaning as he reads. Despite what may be warnings to the contrary, the reader will inevitably forge both meaning and unity, a plot that signifies, out of a series of chapters from disparate but related stories. The fact that the text is bound as a volume virtually guarantees this creation of meaning, although this very act is one of the pitfalls the author is preparing for his meaning-bound readers. The book begins in 1955 and ends in 1919, a reversal which suggests that time in the text does not have the same relationship to space and meaning it has in romance, where plots are often, as in *Parzifal*, linked to the changes of the seasons. . . .

There are, naturally, other texts that resemble *V*, other texts in which episodes are heaped together in such a way that it is the decision of the reader to determine the presence or absence of meaning. Huxley's *Eyeless in Gaza*, Marc Saporta's *Composition Number 1*, Julio Cortázar's *Hopscotch*, or Guillermo Cabrera Infante's *Three Trapped Tigers* might be examples. In all of these books, as in *V*, the reader is the most important character, whose principal problem is the invention or discovery of meaning in the text. Whether he will exist in doubt and disregard the problem of meaning completely, or whether he will postulate a meaning for the text, is his dilemma. (p. 558)

The clash of faith and paranoia, grace and fulmination is the subject of *The Crying of Lot 49*. *Gravity's Rainbow* takes an element present in both *V* and *The Crying of Lot 49*, the international corporation, and identifies it as the occult, meaningful system "out there," although while the system is supposed to possess meaning, it is never made clear just what its meaning is, as if meaning could be divorced from intentionality. All we learn in the three books is that the corporation, the Yoyodyne corporation which appears first in *V* and reappears in the other two texts, stands on both sides of all political, social, and ethical fences. In *Gravity's Rainbow*, the protagonist discovers he is actually the "product" of the company, and in *The Crying of Lot 49* we learn that Pierce Inverarity, the dead man who may be the invisible force behind Oedipa Maas's quest, is an owner of Yoyodyne Inc. . . .

The Crying of Lot 49 reveals both Pynchon's sense of literary genres and his attitude toward meaning in literature. This slim volume mediates between two very large-scale enterprises, *V* and *Gravity's Rainbow*, and may be taken as the ironic rewriting of the romance plot of enlightenment (a parody of either *The Golden Ass* or perhaps *La Nausée*) or as a detective fiction in which the detective, like Oedipus, is both the investigator and the object of investigation. Whether by chance or by design, *The Crying of Lot 49* stands as a pivotal text in Pynchon's oeuvre: it restates the central issue of *V*, to make order of confusion or remain in doubt, in the shape of a classical satire, a narrative interspersed with verse interludes, here in the form of songs. This model provides the structure for *Gravity's Rainbow*, the spectacular difference being that of scale. (p. 559)

The most typical of all the devices in Pynchon's repertoire is his use of trick names: how are readers supposed to react to a woman named Oedipa? The Sophoclean or Freudian association is inevitable, and baffling, but an understanding of the device as a device and not as the knot which, once unraveled, opens the way to some deeper meaning, may make Pynchon's esthetics more comprehensible. Our task is to understand the device, not to decipher it. Pynchon's onomastic punning produces a kind of Brechtian "alienation effect," reminding the reader that what he is reading is a fiction, that the words here are only words. (pp. 559-60)

Pynchon seems to have modeled his text on a short story by Jorge Luis Borges, "The Approach to Al-Mu'tasim" (1935) from the *Ficciones* (1944) collection.... Borges's story is a bogus book review in which Borges, or his narrator, pretends to be writing about *The Approach to Al-Mu'tasim,* by one Mir Bahadur Alí, "the first detective novel written by a native of Bombay City," a text damned (apocryphally) by the English essayist Philip Guedalla as "a rather uncomfortable combination of those allegorical poems of Islam which rarely fail to interest their translators and those crime fictions which inevitably baffle John H. Watson and refine the horror of human life in the most irreproachable hotels of Brighton" (translations mine). The copy Borges reviews also bears a spurious prologue by yet another English literary figure, Dorothy Sayers, just to make its credentials all the more "irreproachable."

The plot is simple: an Islamic Indian kills a Hindu in a riot. He flees and while hiding finds a horrible man who mentions in passing a few mysterious names. The next day the unnamed protagonist sets out to investigate those names. The search, the quest for whatever lies behind those names, which would seem to be the "good," leads the protagonist, like Kim, over all of India, to all levels of life. In the last scene he approaches the final name, Al-Mu'tasim, an encounter Borges does not describe. He does note that in the second, revised edition, the one he reviews, the text is rendered allegorical: Al-Mu'tasim becomes a symbol of God, the search a search for Him. Pynchon appropriates this story or plot summary and fleshes it out, although it seems he prefers the earlier, less obviously allegorical version, where Al-Mu'tasim's identity is still ambiguous. (pp. 560-61)

Unless we revise *The Crying of Lot 49* and make it too into an allegorical quest for God, we must be content with uncertainty. We can never, if we eschew allegorization, know if Tristero and the W.A.S.T.E. system are good or evil, and we accept the fact that we will never know who is bidding for lot 49 at the end of the narrative. We agree that there is nothing more to the story than unresolved mystery.

Borges resolves the "lady or the tiger" crux Pynchon leaves undecided because he wants to maintain the pose of the book reviewer and because he wants to show the *disponibilité* of any literary plot, its susceptibility to interpretation. Both Pynchon and Borges deploy their material in their own way, but both are rewriting the same plot, the quest. (p. 561)

One way, then, of approaching *The Crying of Lot 49* is to dismiss the reader's quest for meaning from the inquiry. Instead of dispelling ambiguity for the sake of coherence or intellectual security, the reader would focus his attention on how the text deploys its devices and how it translates the satiric tradition. We might begin with character: Mucho Maas, Metzger, Hilarius, and the others stand as foils for

Oedipa Maas; she is chosen to be Pierce Inverarity's executrix, they are not. None of them is meant to be the *pharmakos.* . . . These characters are only updated types. For the Panglossian pedant of traditional satire, Pynchon substitutes the mad psychoanalyst. The rest of Oedipa's male companions embody one or another profession, from lawyer to disc jockey, each in his way caricaturing all members of his profession. The rock groups and the Yoyodyne chorus stand as ironic commentators on the action, their traditional role in satire.

Another fixture of satire reworked here is the relentless outpouring of information. Pynchon includes an inordinate amount of scientific knowledge about such matters as entropy and the calculus theorem abbreviated as "dt" or "delta-t." Entropy, divorced both from physics and communication theory and translated into literary speculation, defines the relationship between a text and a tradition. A text may simply reiterate the given patterns of a literature as long as there is enough energy in the system, the complex relationship between readers and writers, to sustain it. But somewhere in the business of literary production the system begins to lose energy—epics, for example, are today only sporadically written and even more rarely read. In order to revitalize the process, some agency recombines elements present in the tradition so that work may go on. This would seem to be the role of the individual author: he cannot contribute new elements to the process, but he certainly can recombine them in a new way, or, more importantly, infuse new power into the system by means of irony. (pp. 562-63)

The importance of irony in this revitalization cannot be overemphasized. And Pynchon's irony is derived primarily from juxtaposition: he wants romance and satire to clash and to create a situation in which the reader will realize that both genres are nothing more than fictions, not mirrors of the age or imitations of life. . . .

In this sense, Oedipa Maas is a metaphor for the reader, just as Pierce Inverarity may be understood to represent the artist. His name, as suggestive as hers, renders both roles sexual, the artist being the masculine, the reader feminine. His given name, Pierce, complements this sexual division of labor by evoking the phallic stylus violating the white purity of the page, while his last name, Inverarity, hints at such concepts as inveracity and inversion, the illusory or lying aspect of writing. The text constitutes the communion of these two archetypes, the writer who leaves of himself only the misleading traces of his will . . . , and the reader who executes it, seeing it in an extraordinarily dark glass. Oedipa follows Pierce's map, and it is through this act that the calculus concept becomes a literary metaphor: she charts his course as if it were the trajectory of a projectile instead of a literary plot. . . . She sacrifices her life in order to carry out his ambiguous will, but without her sacrifice, entropy would once again threaten the system. Without the participation of the reader, the text would cease to exist. (p. 563)

Oedipa's role as reader and interpreter is alluded to throughout *The Crying of Lot 49,* but perhaps the most significant instance occurs at the beginning of chapter 2, when she first comes to San Narciso, Pierce Inverarity's city in southern California. She associates Pierce's realm, as she observes it from above, with a printed circuit: "there were to both [San Narciso and the printed circuit] outward patterns a hieroglyphic sense of concealed meaning, of an intent to communicate." ... What the actual message is, what the meaning is of the circuit or city, which both stand as signs in an unknown script, is the plot she sees spread out before her. Just as in one version of Borges's story the search is its own justification and not the outcome of the search, the searcher, in this case, the reader, would seem to be the real object of the quest. Oedipa, in the same passage, senses the adumbration, the shadow of Pierce . . . , and the narrator calls it "an odd, religious instant," vaguely horrifying yet wonderful. Suddenly the geometry of the scene changes: instead of looking down on San Narciso, Oedipa is in the middle of things, the eye of a hurricane. . . . Oedipa is variously looking down at a man-made landscape, an artifact as artificial as a literary plot, or standing at the center of a silent whirl, excluded from communication, divorced from the Word, yet tantalized by the possibility both may exist. Fixtures taken from a literary tradition concerned with producing awe through language are here made grotesque: if there is a divinity in this text, it is Pierce Inverarity, Proteus, wearing one more disguise.

Another romance device revitalized through irony here is the interpolated tale. Here it is Richard Wharfinger's Jacobean drama *The Courier's Tragedy*, a bogus text worthy of comparison with Mir Bahadur Alí's *The Approach to Al-mu'tasim*. We notice that the play constitutes a gathering point for two of *The Crying of Lot 49*'s principal themes, the Echo and Narcissus relationship between Oedipa and Pierce (which is a motif: San Narciso, the Saint Narcissus of Wharfinger's play, and Echo Courts, the motel in San Narciso where Oedipa stays), and the concept of language as a failed system of communication, one which has only a shadow existence, an "intent to communicate" (just as road systems, printed circuits, urban design all seem to be attempts to say something, although what that may be is

unknown), while true communication can only take place between those linked by bonds other than language, those who have been initiated into secret societies. Of course, what is communicated among the initiates is not a message but the fact of communality, which would make them like circuits through which an electric current would flow. Wharfinger, much sicker than his namesake "Sick Dick," member of yet another rock group, wrote, according to Driblette, his twentieth-century director, another "reworker" analogous to Borges and Pynchon, only to entertain. . . . The interpolated play, like its traditional counterparts, reflects and comments on the major action: *The Crying of Lot 49* is entertainment and it entertains, like Gothic romance, by posing mysteries, enigmas not to be resolved but to be enjoyed for their own sake.

It is perhaps as entertainment that all satires should be read instead of being defined, as they have been, as literature's commentary on society's foibles. Satire may use its didacticism as an *apologia pro vita sua,* but to reduce Swift, Pope, and Peacock to the level of censor is to trivialize their texts as esthetic enterprises. What Pynchon attempts to do in his writings is to create a literature that destroys the concept that art must mirror life. His texts constantly point out their own artificiality, their identity as literature, and consistent with this mockery of the dictates of literary realism is a turn toward intellect, to the mind as creator of unreal systems, especially philosophy and theology. (pp. 564-66)

The ideology of satire, as Pynchon writes it, is not to reform the reader, who would then, presumably, reform the world, but to reclaim for literature one of the purposes essential to all rhetorical exercises: to delight. (p. 566)

Alfred Mac Adam, "Pynchon as Satirist: To Write, to Mean," in The Yale Review (© *1978 by Yale University; reprinted by permission of the editors), Summer, 1978, pp. 555-66.*

Q

QUEEN, Ellery [joint pseudonym of Frederic Dannay (1905-) and Manfred B(ennington) Lee (1905-1971)]

Americans Dannay and Lee created both novels and stories around their character Ellery Queen and contributed some of the finest mystery and detective fiction to the genre. They are five-time recipients of the Edgar Award and have compiled several anthologies of memorable pieces from *Ellery Queen's Mystery Magazine.* **(See also** *CLC,* **Vol. 3, and** *Contemporary Authors,* **Vols. 1-4, rev. ed.; obituary for Manfred B. Lee, Vols. 29-32, rev. ed.)**

NEWGATE CALLENDAR

["A Fine and Private Place"] exhibits all of the virtues and defects of the Queen books. It is full of stale literary devices, such as a simply preposterous diary. The writing is arch and labored. ("I'd better totter off and tuck my lil ole self into beddy-snooky-bye.") Any character capable of delivering this sentiment deserves all that is coming to her . . . But if Ellery Queen doesn't write too well, he can plot. In this story—about the murder of a jinx-haunted supertycoon and a wife who inherits under curious circumstances —there is the usual rash of well-planted clues, real or fake; and the *outré* paraphernalia of the murderer; and a couple of familiar characters, now growing older. There always will be a market for this kind of old-fashioned puzzle. (p. 38)

Newgate Callendar, in The New York Times Book Review (© 1971 by The New York Times Company; reprinted by permission), June 20, 1971.

Only recently did I begin to like the Queen detective novels. I always admitted, of course, the extraordinary plotting ability of the authors, and the amazing capacity to plant a million clues while being perfectly fair with the reader. But, I confess it, Ellery himself put me off: there was always something of the Philo Vance about him which I didn't like. . . .

[Both *Calamity Town* and *The Dragon's Teeth*] are excellent. . . . I found in them virtues I did not expect. The detection in both cases is not too difficult, and when you have solved the crime you can sit back and enjoy what is a delectable brace of psychological dramas. The personality of the hero is less intrusive than before or since, and the ma-

noeuvring among the characters excellently done and highly contributive to tension. It is not often that a writer (or writers in this case . . .) whose forte is pure detection can contrive an atmosphere so well. (p. 187)

The Spectator (© 1973 by The Spectator; reprinted by permission of The Spectator), August 11, 1973.

FRANCIS M. NEVINS, JR.

[Dannay's and Lee's early books], from *Roman Hat* through *The Spanish Cape Mystery* (1935), are generally bracketed together as Queen's First Period. The obvious hallmark of this period is the recurrence of adjectives of nationality in the titles. Another, more significant but less obvious, is the overpowering influence of [S. S. Van Dine], which began to melt away around 1932 and had almost totally vanished . . . by 1935. The Ellery of these first "Problems in Deduction" is a polysyllabic literatus wreathed in classical allusions and pince-nez—in short, a close imitation of Philo Vance or, as Manfred Lee in recent years called him, the biggest prig that ever came down the pike. For those who don't like First Period Queen—a group that apparently includes the authors themselves, to judge from interviews near the end of Lee's life—these novels are sterile, lifeless, relentlessly intellectual exercises, technically excellent but unwarmed by any trace of human character nor by any emotion other than the "passions of the mind." For those who love Period One, including myself and most Queenians, these books are splendid *tours de force* of the artificer's art and are nowhere near totally devoid of interest in human character or concern with fundamental issues. (pp. 6-7)

It's convenient to date the beginning of Queen's second period from *Halfway House* (1936) since this is the first of Ellery's cases not to contain an adjective of nationality in the title. But the new title format is merely symptomatic of changes in substance. The main influences on Dannay and Lee in this period were the women's slick magazines, to which they began to sell around the middle of the decade, and Hollywood, where they worked as script writers for Columbia, Paramount and M-G-M in the late Thirties. Compared with the early masterworks, the novels of Period Two suffer from intellectual thinness, an overabundance of feminine emotion, and characters cut out of cardboard with the hope that they would be brought to life by movie performers. On the other hand, with the broader perspective that accompanies the passage of time we can see the entire second period as a series of steps in the progressive humanization of Ellery and the Queenian universe and as the necessary preparation for the great synthesis of Period Three. (p. 7)

Queen's third period, which many would judge the crown of his career, opens with *Calamity Town* (1942) and embraces twelve novels, two books of short stories and sixteen years. In this period there was nothing Queen would not dare. We find complex deductive puzzles; achingly full-drawn characterizations; the detailed evocation of a small town and of a great city, each of which comes to life on the page; the creation of a private, topsy-turvy, Alice-in-Wonderland otherworld; explorations into the historical, psychiatric and religious dimensions; hymns of hate directed at McCarthyism and other brands of political filth; a gently sketched middle-age love story; a nostalgic re-creation of Ellery's young manhood. We find all this and so much more within a sequence of strict detective stories. . . . (pp. 8-9)

The hallmarks of Period Four are, on the one hand, an undiminished zest for radical experiment within the strict deductive tradition, and on the other hand, a retreat from attempts at naturalistic plausibility coupled with a reliance on stylization of plot and character and the repetition of dozens of motifs from the earlier periods. (p. 12)

[No] major mystery writer anywhere was more influenced by S. S. Van Dine than was Queen. But in several significant respects Queen altered the Van Dine structure for the better. First of all, even in his earliest novels Queen proved himself far more skillful at drawing character, writing vividly, and plotting with finesse. Second, Queen dropped the first-person narrative employed by Van Dine and thereby gained the flexibility of being able to write scenes at which no official is present. But most important of all was Queen's innovation of fair play, of providing the reader with all the information needed to solve the case along with or ahead of the detective. Fair play was not a ground rule of the game as Van Dine played it, and in fact most of Vance's solutions depend on intricate, and often debatable, psychological analyses of the suspects. Ellery's solutions on the other hand are based on rigorous logical deductions from empirical evidence, which, unlike the mental data from which Vance proceeded, was as accessible to the reader as to the detective, a point emphasized by Queen's famous "Challenge to the Reader" device. (pp. 18-19)

The Tragedy of X must be ranked among the supreme masterpieces of the Golden Age of detective fiction, a book of staggering complexity, stunning ingenuity and dazzling fairness to the reader. Queen used this novel to introduce two motifs that were to become hallmarks. First is a distinctive murderer-victim relationship whose exact nature I can't specify lest I spoil several early Queen novels for those who haven't yet read them; the *locus classicus* of this motif being Conan Doyle's *The Valley of Fear,* I will refer to it as the Birlstone Gambit. . . . Queen employed the motif over and over during the early Thirties, then dropped it at the end of Period One. The second motif introduced in *X* was left virtually untouched for almost two decades but became literally synonymous with the Queen canon during the Fifties and Sixties: I mean, of course, the classic Queenian device of the Dying Message. . . . Drury Lane and several others, one of whom will be dead within min-

utes, discuss the last moments of life in a conversation which is [central to Queen's work]. . . . The discussion culminates in Lane's words: "There are no limits to which the human mind cannot soar in that unique, godlike instant before the end of life." That statement suggests that beneath the criminous surface of *X* Queen is seriously concerned with power and the love of power, and indeed these themes recur in the book in several forms, such as the murderer's silent intimate relationships with his victims over the years in which he is shaping their destruction, Longstreet's sadistic lust for power over the men and women in his milieu, the motives behind Lane's own investigations, and the god-like power of the dying. And if we prescind from serious literary intent and simply look at the large number of sharply etched characterizations, and the vivid evocations of time and place (and especially of the transportation network made up of the streetcar, the ferry and the shortline passenger train, all three near extinction today), and the integration of the milieu into the plot and of each of the plot's myriad details into a rationally harmonious mosaic, we will find so many more reasons why *The Tragedy of X* must appear in any listing, however short, of the supreme achievements of crime fiction, and why it will be read with awe long after our grandchildren are dust.

The Tragedy of Y (1932) is no less dazzling than *X* in perfection of structure and technique and in its blending of serious intent with the deductive puzzle. In it Queen created a milieu fully worthy of the doom-haunted Eugene O'Neill. . . . (pp. 27-9)

[The Hatters, the doomed family in *The Tragedy of Y,* are] not merely a group of figures in a detective novel but a paradigm of American society, its members rotting with greed and sadism and inertia, consenting for the sake of expected legacies to be dehumanized in love-hate relationships with each other and with the bitch goddess of wealth and property who rules the roost. But the sickness in the Hatters is not curable by surgery or social revolution; it is not some naturalistic venereal disease but a disease of human nature and the human condition, the gift of a dark god. (p. 30)

The Tragedy of Y is, like its predecessor, one of the most stunning detective novels ever written, and also like *X* it introduces two motifs that have come to be distinctively identified with Queen. One is distrust and despair of human nature, which will reappear throughout the Canon but with especial force during the McCarthy-haunted Fifties in such books as *The Origin of Evil* and *The Glass Village.* The other is the motif of manipulation. . . . And over and above the brilliance of *Y* as a detective novel stands the power of its black vision. . . . Although rooted in a genre that has traditionally been oriented to reason, order and optimism, *Y* evokes depths of tragic despair that are virtually without parallel in the history of crime fiction. (pp. 30-1)

[*The Tragedy of Z*] is by no means one of Queen's greatest achievements, being far less dazzling and full-bodied than the masterworks. Except for one brief scene, Lane is kept offstage until almost halfway through the book, and the presence and first-person narration of Patience Thumm are woefully inadequate substitutes. Compared with the great novels of 1932, *Z*'s plot is both simplistic and flawed. . . . But the faults are more than compensated for by the bone-chilling bizarrerie of the two sequences in the death house (which are both suspenseful and effective as outcries against capital punishment), and by the unobtrusively brilliant planting throughout the book of clues to be collated by Lane at the denouement. Though not one of Queen's most distinguished novels, *Z* is a highly intriguing work that repays more than one reading.

Which is more than can be said for the last of the Barnaby Ross tetralogy. *Drury Lane's Last Case* (1933) has some excellent ideas but is marred by haste, disorganization, coincidence, artificiality, incredible motivation, and a staggering number of holes in the plot.... Although murder doesn't rear its head until the final quarter of the book, there is so much intellectual puzzlement throughout that no one cares. (pp. 32-3)

[*The Greek Coffin Mystery*] may blow your mind, especially if you're unfamiliar with the complexities of the formal deductive puzzle. Although it's not perfectly flawless in all its thousands of details, the flaws are virtually imperceptible without several careful readings. In short, *The Greek Coffin Mystery* is probably the most involuted, brain-crushing, miraculously well constructed detective novel published in the United States during the Golden Age. (p. 36)

There is more abundant carnage in [*The Egyptian Cross Mystery*] than in any other deductive novel by Queen or anyone else, but the bloodbath, far from being gratuitous, serves two purposes. Within the deductive framework, the profusion of headless and crucified bodies is a precondition to the ingenious variations of the Birlstone Gambit on which the solution rests. Looking outward to the experiment with larger meanings, the physical horror of the murders is necessary to Queen's analogies between the Tvar-Krosac vendetta and its equivalent in macrocosm, war. If we look at the parallels Queen draws between the fugitive Tvars and nation-states (each brother's alias, for example, is the name of a city in a distant country), and at the fratricidal elements of the plot, and at the staggeringly vague and inadequate motives for the carnage, we will appreciate that buried within *Egyptian Cross* are the aborted remains of what might have become a powerful anti-war novel.

Technically the book is less than perfect, with much of the counterplotting in the middle chapters only distantly related to the story as a whole—a defect I call the Hollow Center. There are also a few unplugged holes at the end.... But with an exceptionally large and well-handled cast and a richly involuted plot and the vivid evocation of several socially, economically and geographically disparate milieus, *Egyptian Cross* must be ranked one of the better Queen novels of Period One. (pp. 37-8)

The solution of [*The American Gun Mystery*] is eminently fair to the reader, but once again depends on the Birlstone Gambit. Furthermore the killer's motive is a woefully weak one, and Ellery never explains how he managed to get his first victim into the position required for his plan. The novel also suffers from a Hollow Center, with the boxing counterplot that fills out the middle chapters unrelated to the basic storyline. And last but not least, Queen's unfamiliarity with film history and technique leads to the incorporation of several sizable cinematic gaffes into the plot structure. But despite its flaws *American Gun* is still a richly rewarding detective novel; if it does not strike one as an untouchable masterpiece, this is largely because Queen's own best work has helped raise the standards so high.

In *The Siamese Twin Mystery* ... Queen again attempted to infuse a philosophic dimension into the formal deductive puzzle, with notable success on both levels. (pp. 39-40)

The Siamese Twin Mystery is not as richly plotted as the earlier Queen novels; were it not for the fire sequences the book would be no more than a novelet. But Queen does not pad. The detection and the fiery background are necessary to each other and to Queen's theme of the power and emptiness of reason in the face of death. Purely on the puzzle level, Queen supplies some truly dazzling variants on the false confession gambit, and sets out (for the first time in a novel about Ellery and his father) a series of magnificently involuted Dying Message devices. *Siamese Twin* is by far Queen's best book of 1933 and one of the best of all his Period One works. (pp. 41-2)

Ellery's solution [in *The Spanish Cape Mystery*] is relentlessly logical and scrupulously fair, but one can sense Queen's realization that he is fast exhausting the possibilities of the formal deductive puzzle. For this is the fourth of his novels since 1932 that rests on another version of the Birlstone Gambit, and the wary reader of earlier Period One work should be able to spot the gambit, and the murderer it entails, before he has finished fifty pages. A more significant pointer to Queen's dissatisfaction is the beginning of a change in Ellery's world-view that parallels a shift in Queen's view of his craft. In Chapter 15 Ellery expresses his credo up to this point: "My work is done with symbols ... not with human beings.... I choose to close my mind to the human elements and treat it as a problem in mathematics. The fate of the murderer I leave to those who decide such things." This of course is the classic stance of the scientist who develops Cyclon B or napalm and leaves the practical consequences of his brainwork to the practical men. But at the end of the book Ellery realizes that he has exposed a murderer whose act was justified if any crime ever was. "I've often boasted that the human equation means nothing to me. But it does, damn it all, it does!".... [With] *The Spanish Cape Mystery* Queen closes out Period One—one of the greatest sustained endeavors in the history of crime fiction—and begins the movement away from the pure problem of deduction and in the direction of the novel that incorporates such a problem. (pp. 49-50)

[We] can see the whole of Period Two [late 1935 to 1939] as a transitional stage, as a series of steps in the progressive humanization of Queen's universe. Under the guidance of his two new markets he learned to infuse greater life and warmth into his characters, including Ellery himself; to master the presentation of a woman's viewpoint ... ; and to develop a skill with character and relationship approximating his finesse with clue and counterplot. In short, Queen in Period Two worked at "opening up" the formal deductive puzzle, making room within its intellectual rigor for more of the virtues of mainstream storytelling. His experiments of the late 1930's were to come to full fruition, integrated into the most devious of puzzle plots, with the great novels of Period Three.

It's convenient, and conventional, to regard *Halfway House* (1936), the first Queen novel to break the chain of nationality-titles, as the beginning of the second period. However, this novel preserves both the subtitle "A Problem in Deduction," which had appeared in all of Ellery's book-length adventures of Period One, and the Challenge to the Reader, which had appeared in most of them.... But as long as the movement away from the work of 1929-

1935 is recognized as a gradual evolution and not a sudden change of course, there's no harm in considering *Halfway House* the first novel of Period Two. (pp. 51-2)

If *Halfway House* was not vastly different from the works of 1929-1935, Queen's next novel is so unlike its predecessors as hardly to seem the product of the same author. In *The Door Between* (1937) deduction takes a back seat to intuition, the stress is on characterization and relationships, and for the first time in the Queen canon one finds "love interest" on every page. . . . [It's] probably the best Queen novel of Period Two. (pp. 54-5)

At the denouement [of *The Door Between*] Ellery explains the crime to the satisfaction of everyone but himself, then later reveals, to the murderer alone, a second and even more stunning solution. This two-solutions device is employed here for the first time in a Queen novel, evoking intellectual, moral, and sheerly human ambiguities with an intensity worthy of Simenon.

As a formal puzzle *The Door Between* can't stand up against the best novels of Period One. . . . But as a simultaneous imitation and parody of the Rinehart/Eberhart "women's mystery novel" it's an excellent job, full of strokes of satiric genius like putting a hard-boiled private eye in the traditional role of idiot hero. As a study of character and atmosphere the book breaks little new ground . . . , but it's more vivid and convincing in these respects than many of Queen's earlier efforts. *The Door Between* is not in itself major Queen but it is a major stride forward on the road to Period Three. (pp. 56-7)

The plot [of *The Devil to Pay*] is nowhere near Queen's best and nowhere near complex enough for a Queen novel, although it's competent and adequate in most respects. The characterization and dialogue, however, are somewhat less than adequate. Even Ellery becomes no more than a mold for a B-picture leading man; change his name to Charlie Brown and, except for the denouement scene, you'd never know he was supposed to be the detective of Queen's earlier novels. (p. 58)

The Four of Hearts boasts a number of skillfully planted clues, an exceptionally well-concealed murderer, and a gorgeous plot bristling with legal points that are best discussed in the learned obscurity of a footnote. On the negative side, a great deal of the material in the book is not strictly relevant to the grand design. Here more than in any other single novel, Queen threw every conceivable ingredient into the mixture: a wacky-humor opening, three separate and distinct love stories, a barrage of movieland patter, and a quite serious multiple murder scheme. Queen's attitude toward the Hollywood milieu varies from chapter to chapter, and he makes us see the movie capital as in turn absurd (the initial chapter), sick (the funeral sequence), and warmly wonderful (the Paula Paris aspects). The abrupt changes of tone from farce to grief to light romance to rigorous rationality are grating at times, and there's a certain meant-to-be-made-into-a-movie aura about the book that prevents one from taking it with full seriousness. But the disunity of tone is functional at least to the extent that it enables Queen to plant clues unobtrusively in the chapters one is most tempted to read with a relaxed mind; re-reading those chapters, we can learn a great deal about the murderer's reactions to unforeseen developments by taking a close look at dialogue which, the first time around, we passed off as Hollywood banter. *The Four of Hearts* is by no means the apex of the Queen canon, but it provides us with a divertingly cockeyed view of the big movie studios of the Thirties and with a wild roller-coaster ride through the celluloid Wonderland.

The main setting of Queen's next novel is New York rather than Hollywood, but the tone of *The Dragon's Teeth* (1939) still comes straight out of movieland, specifically from the screwball comedy films of the late Thirties, the kind that Carole Lombard used to star in. The book is something of a quickie, the chapter titles are atrocious puns as they were in *The Devil to Pay,* and Ellery is still little more than a receptacle for the personality of a movie actor; but there are plenty of fascinations herein for the Queen addict, and if you don't expect a *Greek Coffin* or a *Cat of Many Tails* you can have a lot of fun with it. (pp. 61-2)

Queen's second collection of short fiction, *The New Adventures of Ellery Queen* (1940), recapitulates his development from the end of Period One to the end of 1939. The book as a whole lacks the unity of style and content of the first volume of *Adventures* or the later *Calendar of Crime,* and the individual stories range from the magnificent to the indifferent, but the best tales in *New Adventures* rank with Queen's greatest work at less than novel length, and more than that no one can ask from a book of short fiction.

Crown of the collection is that peerless classic "The Lamp of God" [also published as "House of Haunts"]. . . . Having never written a detective novelet before in his life, Queen calmly turned out here one of the half dozen greatest works of all time in that form, then dropped the form for almost a quarter of a century. (p. 64)

"The Lamp of God" is the second stunning example of a Queen specialty we have seen before at short-story length in "The Adventure of the Glass-Domed Clock" and shall see again at book length in *The King Is Dead*: titanic misdirection concealing a blindingly simple solution. It is also one of the finest pieces of atmospheric writing in the mystery genre, evoking a physical and a metaphysical chill that rise off the page into the reader's bones. Queen here proved himself a genius at summoning up the howling fear that the world has been abandoned to the demonic, and then at exorcising the panic of chaos through the rigorous exercise of reason—which is, I submit, the fundamental ritual underlying detective fiction.

The religious dimension of the story deserves some comment. Queen significantly describes Ellery as "that lean and indefatigable agnostic," and Ellery says of himself: "If I were religiously inclined . . . if I, poor sinner that I am, possessed religious susceptibilities, I should have become permanently devout in the past three days." And elsewhere in the tale he comments: "No riddle is esoteric . . . unless it's the riddle of God; and that's no riddle—it's a vast blackness." Finally, Ellery speaks of "chance, cosmos, God, whatever you may choose to call it," giving him the instrument for understanding the truth: on one level, human reason, on the other, its analogue the sun, the light, the lamp of God. This novelet, then, is Queen's explicit treatment of a theme that is central to several of his later masterpieces, including *Ten Days' Wonder, The Player on the Other Side* and *And On the Eighth Day*: theomachy, the battle of (in a non-literal sense) gods, of light against darkness as in Zoroastrianism, of sun against cold, of reason against the absurd. (pp. 65-6)

Several commentators on mystery fiction have written of *Calamity Town* as if it were a simple-minded tribute to the goodness of an unspoiled American community. Actually, however, Queen's Wrightsville is a fairly realistic microcosm of the United States, with plenty of rot and inhumanity and strife alongside all the grace and bucolic peace.... No one in this novel is overwhelmingly good, and almost no one is overwhelmingly bad, but some are clearly better than others.... (pp. 112-13)

Calamity Town is not only a novel of society but also and perhaps even primarily a novel of nature, and the rhythms of nature are at the heart of the book. The central imaginative pattern of the novel is a dialectic. *One: In the midst of life, death....* *Two: In the midst of death, life....* Out of the horror of the full truth, revealed by Ellery on Mother's Day, comes the possibility of happiness for two young people and a baby. Ellery's explanation is itself counterpointed by quotations from Walt Whitman, the poet of nature's rhythms. The action of the novel covers nine months, the cycle of gestation. (p. 113)

[Even] though the book ends on notes of hope, Queen gives us no cause to believe that this is anything more than another moment in the eternal alternation of nature's rhythms....

The superb evocation of Wrightsville marks a tremendous advance over the picture of Hollywood in *The Four of Hearts,* which didn't work because its different facets canceled each other out. In *Calamity Town* Queen employs even more divergent facets than in the *Four* but remains in full control, playing them creatively upon each other so that they mutually reflect and illuminate. (p. 114)

There Was an Old Woman (1943) is clearly unlike almost everything Queen had done in the Thirties, and in some ways is even more radical than *Calamity Town.* Previous Queen novels had integrated the formal deductive problem into the woman's mystery (*The Door Between*), the Hollywood novel (*The Four of Hearts*), and regional Americana (*Calamity Town*). This time Queen decided to merge the complex puzzle with a relatively new development in crime fiction, the way-out wacky mystery, which had been practiced by ... others in the late Thirties and early Forties. Queen took this approach, molded it into highly personal form, and wound up with the first sustained specimen of his private brand of black humor. (p. 117)

Frederic Dannay described this aspect of the Queen canon as "Ellery in Wonderland." The technique rests on plunging the quintessential man of reason into a milieu as mad as the underside of Carroll's rabbit-hole and requiring him to forge some sort of order out of the chaos. The Wonderland theme first appeared in Queen's 1934 short story "The Mad Tea-Party," which is still Dannay's favorite among Ellery's short adventures, probably because of this very Wonderland aspect. The theme recurs every so often in Queen's two Hollywood novels of the Thirties and in the drinking-bout sequence of *The Dragon's Teeth.* But *There Was an Old Woman* is the first Queen novel to which the theme is central. (pp. 117-18)

Unhappily Queen's vision of the Absurd occupies only part of the book. The balance consists of a convoluted formal deductive problem, for purposes of which the absurd gargoyles of the Wonderland scenes simply shed their grotesque qualities and take their places as figures in a typi-

cally solid Queen plot.... As a result, *There Was an Old Woman* must ultimately be judged a fascinating two-books-in-one, at odds with itself at every step, with some fine individual sequences in both the novel-of-the-Absurd and the detective-story sections, but never adding up to an integrated whole. (pp. 120-21)

[In *The Murderer Is a Fox*] Ellery's loving and meticulous reconstruction of the exact events of June 14, 1932 in the house of Bayard and Jessica Fox is carried out with the historian's intellectual tools and generates the same sense of excitement that spurs the conscientious historian in his search for truth. To merge the detective story and historical reconstruction is a diabolically difficult feat.... But Queen skirts all the pitfalls.... The book culminates, as do a large number of Queen novels since, in a false or partial solution which is followed by the true, final and stunning solution, although here as in *The Door Between* Ellery's ultimate solution rests not on reasoning but on intuition in the Maigret manner.

The Murderer Is a Fox does not have the thematic unity or imaginative design of a *Calamity Town,* but in no other novel does Queen communicate so well the excitement of the quest for truth. I suspect this is why Ellery's ultimate solution is left completely unverifiable, for the truth historians seek is also unverifiable and in the search for historical truth is no analogue to the device of the murderer's confession in detective fiction.... *The Murderer Is a Fox* [is] noteworthy for its depiction of historical thinking in action.... (pp. 122-23)

Throughout [*Ten Days' Wonder*] Diedrich Van Horn is clothed in the attributes of deity: tremendous power, apparently limitless goodness, awesome knowledge. However, the solution reveals him as a being of monstrously evil nature and with an unerring ability to manipulate weak mortals to his own designs. At the end of the final, thunderous interview, Ellery forces Diedrich to kill himself. The god has been found out to be not the good and loving being he seemed but a moral monster, manipulating the trapped creatures under his sway, coldly determined to degrade and destroy the puny human beings who have usurped his divine prerogative. Therefore the forces of reason and humaneness demand the death of God. (p. 136)

Very few mystery writers have ever dared to mingle crime fiction with cosmic drama. *Ten Days' Wonder* is Queen's most sustained and successful attempt up to that time to do so, a dazzlingly rich work embracing dimensions that seemed utterly incompatible with the genre until Queen showed that it could be done. It is a nearly inexhaustible book, and certainly ranks among his half-dozen finest novels. (pp. 137-38)

At the beginning of *Cat of Many Tails* ... Ellery has renounced his habit of intervening in the lives of others, and has returned to the ivory tower of the novelist.... [He] dreads being again responsible for others' lives. Deeper down seems to be a residue of sullen resentment at being bested (except for a purely intellectual victory that came too late) by his adversary in *Ten Days' Wonder.* And at the deepest level of Ellery's mind we may sense something of the guilt and despair at the death of God of which Nietzsche spoke so eloquently.

So Ellery has dropped out, detached himself from the mess and horror of the real world, performed an "inner emigration.'' The theme of detachment has recurred time and time again in the Queen canon. In *Calamity Town* it was exemplified in Aunt Tabitha, who ran out on the Wright family in its crisis, and in *There Was an Old Woman* it was embodied in the escapist Horatio Potts. But in *Cat of Many Tails* the theme is directly connected with Ellery himself. (p. 138)

The atmosphere is full of impending holocaust, with references to Hiroshima, the Nazi death camps, the Cold War, the quadripartite division of Vienna, the first Arab-Israeli conflict, the anti-Communist witch hunts, and the threat of nuclear destruction. . . . But the international headlines that daily remind each man of his own mortality have been dwarfed by local headlines conveying the same message. A mass murderer is at large in the city. He has strangled six victims in less than three months. . . . As usual in third-period Queen, the full explanation is finally topped by an even fuller and more stunning solution. And, as in *Ten Days' Wonder,* Ellery is shattered by that solution.

There are other similarities between the two contiguous novels. The murder method in both is strangulation, the ''player on the other side'' in both is several times compared to a god, and in both Ellery's failure to comprehend has cost others their lives. The difference, however, is that in *Cat of Many Tails* Ellery learns wisdom. In key scenes at the beginning and middle and end of the book he receives instruction from a father-figure: first from his physical father, who is instrumental in making Ellery involve himself again; then from the titan Prometheus, founder of civilization according to Greek mythology, who appears to Ellery in a dream after the carnage of the Cat riots; finally from Dr. Bela Seligmann, the great Viennese psychiatrist, the ''grandfather of the tribe,'' who has seen all the terrors in the world and in the heart of man. (pp. 138-40)

But although Queen in *Cat of Many Tails* shows a fastidious contempt for humanity, the abstract mass, the mob, he also shows how much he loves the individuals he has created by the fullness of life which he has infused into almost all of them (the single exception being Jimmy McKell, the millionaire reporter, who is so glaringly artificial it hurts). Even the Cat's victims, none of them ever seen alive but only talked about by others, become as real as the living people, each one carefully delineated and distinguished, a person rather than a statistic. And from the interweaving of the lives of the victims and their survivors and the scores of officials and the thousands of bystanders . . . emerges the portrait of the city as a fully rounded character in its own right. Queen evokes countless aspects of life in the city from the racial turmoil (a short but prophetic encounter with an outraged black father in a Harlem stationhouse) to the struggle against the stifling heat, from the chaos of a full-scale riot to the delights of popular radio programs like *The Shadow* and *Stella Dallas.* And besides portraying the city in vivid detail and penetrating deeply into the hearts of his major characters, Queen also integrates thousands of tiny fictional elements into a unified mosaic embodying a very personal vision of existence. *Cat of Many Tails* is the most abundant novel Queen ever wrote, stands with *Calamity Town* at the pinnacle of his work, can be read and re-read with unceasing satisfaction, and offers permanent testimony to what can be accomplished within the framework of the mystery story. (pp. 141-42)

Not only is *The Origin of Evil* by far the best of Queen's Hollywood novels, it's one of his best books of the Fifties also. The plot is full of distinctively Queenian elements— murder by psychological shock as in *The Door Between,* a killer who uses another person as his living weapon as in *Ten Days' Wonder,* the solution within a solution, the ''negative clue'' device, and the series of seemingly absurd events connected by a hidden logic as in *Ten Days' Wonder, Cat of Many Tails* and *Double, Double.* The religious motifs of *Ten Days' Wonder* return in low-key with the appearance of not one but two Diedrich-like manipulators, each playing upon the other, one referred to as ''the invisible god'' and the other as ''the god of events.'' As in *Ten Days' Wonder* the truth turns out to be devilishly complex; in fact my only serious objection to the story is that the murderer's plot *requires* the presence of a master detective to unravel certain complexities the killer wants to be discovered, although Ellery's entrance into the case is totally unexpected and accidental.

But, as usual since *Calamity Town,* Queen is up to more than just a good detective novel. The subject of *The Origin of Evil* is clearly stated in the title, and the answer to the title's implicit question is, quite simply, human nature. (pp. 147-48)

[Every] major character in the novel except Ellery and his nemesis is compared over and over again to various animals, [and] the imagery of the jungle recurs every few pages. Both the killer's adopted name and his plot are grounded in Darwinian biology with its themes of the endless struggle for survival and of ''nature red in tooth and claw.'' The player on the other side turns out to be quite literally ''the old Adam,'' and at the end of the novel the old Adam is not only unbeaten but has become the intimate and familiar of Ellery himself. This union of apparent opposites seems especially apt when we recall Ellery's all-too-human reaction of moralistic outrage and contempt when he learned of Delia's sexual habits, despite his very clear desire to have her himself. No man can call another animal, for the same nature stains us all. (pp. 148-49)

[The] major trouble with this book is that Queen's treatment of the Korean war and of impending nuclear holocaust is completely at odds with his grim view of man. The conflict in Korea is portrayed not as one more monument to man's power-hunger and blood-lust but in the standard propaganda terms of the filthy Commies from the North attacking their peaceful democratic neighbors in the South. And the threat of World War III is presented literally as a hoax, a publicity gimmick dreamed up by a young would-be actor to get himself into the movies (the actor quite fittingly winds up volunteering for the crusade against evil in Korea). We must remember, of course, that in those days when Joe McCarthy ruled the land, thousands of Americans had their careers ruined for raising doubts about matters such as these; and it seems clear that in 1951 Queen was not yet ready to put his body on the line. So if *The Origin of Evil* fails to cohere thematically, the reign of terror in which it was written is more to blame than Queen. (pp. 149-50)

Unfortunately the same structural defect that plagued *There Was an Old Woman* also pops up in *The King Is Dead.* In the earlier novel Queen couldn't integrate a serious deductive plot into the topsy-turvy milieu, and in the later he can't make an organic whole out of a locked-room puzzle, a serious psychological study, and a fable about fascism and revolution. Nevertheless the suspense and the misdirection and the central clue and many other aspects of the book are all of the highest order. Even when a Queen novel fails as a whole, it never lacks wondrous parts.

The following year Queen again tried something completely different and again ran into technical snags he couldn't lick. The challenge he set himself in *The Scarlet Letters* . . . was to create a complex milieu and breathe life into a very small cast of characters and generate an atmosphere of intense urgency, but without employing any strictly criminous elements until the last two chapters of the book. However, he fell into the trap of letting the book's novelistic and deductive aspects collide and smash each other up, and the net result is another fascinating failure. (pp. 158-59)

[With its] excellences of story and character and setting, the first three-quarters of *The Scarlet Letters* is superb reading. But once we come to the murder and the traditional apparatus of mystery fiction, the novel suddenly becomes incredibly weak (though the weaknesses are apparent only in retrospect). Ellery's solution is based on reasoning so gossamer and speculative as to suggest Maigret or a character in Woolrich rather than the logical successor to Sherlock Holmes. That Queen has subtly evaded almost all the legal problems raised by the solution should be obvious even to nonlawyers. . . . But worst of all is that once we learn the answers, we see that Queen has misled us monstrously in the body of the book. Although we have seen and been told, over and over, how much like clandestine lovers Martha and Van Harrison were acting, the revelation of their true relationship makes utter nonsense of all her observed and reported behavior. Equally infelicitous is Queen's treatment of the satanic manipulator theme, which simply can't work where the villain is a fully fleshed naturalistic figure with no intimations of the more-than-human such as Queen properly added to the corresponding figures in *Ten Days' Wonder* and *The Origin of Evil*. Finally, even though the murderer's entire plan depends on Ellery and Nikki learning certain facts prior to the murder, he does absolutely nothing to point them towards those facts, which Ellery uncovers by sheer good luck. (pp. 160-61)

But for all its flaws, there are enough good things in *The Scarlet Letters*—prose, social observation, depiction of character and time and place—to require a reading and repay a re-reading. Nowhere near the best of Queen, it's still distinctly and unmistakably Queenian. (p. 161)

Vicious and absurd categories like "guilt by association" and "Fifth Amendment Communist" became common currency [during the McCarthy Era], and trials or hearings to determine whether one was "subversive" were held on a grand scale, without even the semblance of Due Process safeguards. The theatre, film and literature were extremely hard hit, and even mystery fiction which is generally considered an apolitical genre was hurt when Dannay's friend Dashiell Hammett was jailed for 6 months. It was in this atmosphere of terror that Queen wrote . . . *The Glass Village* (1954), which two decades later still stands out as a breathtakingly readable book and which has "dated" not one iota. (p. 162)

Or, to relate *The Glass Village* to a central Queen motif, we might call it a study in due process on the other side of the rabbit hole. Queen had dealt with legal themes many times before but had seldom gotten his law straight; this time, by creating a context in which the legal procedure *has*

to be ridiculously wrong, he turned out the finest law novel of his whole career.

It's also one of his best detective stories of the Fifties, complete with bizarre clues, the functional equivalent of a dying message, and a full measure of inspired misdirection. (p. 165)

[In] *The Fourth Side of the Triangle* (1965), Queen attempted the offtrail experiment of a novel set in the present but filled with characters and attitudes more appropriate to the crime fiction of the early 1920's, with Ellery the nominal detective but incapacitated and offstage for most of the book and unsuccessful when he finally does some detecting. The experiment was not a howling triumph but the fact that Queen was still experimenting, still not content with a formula after more than 35 years of mystery writing, is more significant than the specific weaknesses of this book. (p. 187)

With *Face to Face* (1967) Queen not only returned to the simon-pure detective novel but put Ellery squarely at center stage—a combination he had not employed since *The Player on the Other Side*. The result was a novel that in a curious way is *Player's* mirror image. For in *Player* the physical murderer was known from the outset and the problem was to locate the manipulator who was using him as a weapon, while in *Face* the manipulator's identity is clear at once and the task is to deduce whom *he* used as his living weapon. (p. 192)

What is most memorable about *Face to Face* . . . is not the identity of the woman who pulled the trigger for Armando but Queen's treatment of her in human terms. . . . [The] mingled compassion and revulsion for her which Queen evokes at the climax, [a] sense of moral ambiguity . . . , seems to me the most fully human aspect of Queen's work in the Sixties; and the fusion of this ambiguity with splendid technical expertise raises *Face to Face* to high rank within the Canon. (p. 194)

Readers who find the adventures of Ellery Queen too artificial and intellectualized and remote from the real world should be overjoyed by *Cop Out,* which in essence is an average-grade swiftpaced hardnosed paperback original that just happens to be in hard covers. . . . What is Queen's name doing on a novel containing naturalistic, credibly evil gangsters, knowledgeable details of police routine and suburban bourgeois living, voyeurism, fellatio, excremental allusions in abundance, and a finger-search up a suspect's vagina? Although none of these elements is objectionable in itself, their combined appearance in a Queen novel seems [out of place]. . . . The book does contain a few distinctly Queenian elements, such as the allegorical character-names, the theme of manipulation (in a minor key), and the county-name Taugus which harks back to *Inspector Queen's Own Case*. Everything else in it could have been done by almost any competent journeyman mystery writer. Dannay told me several times that the objective in *Cop Out* was to do something utterly and completely different from anything Queen had ever done before. In this the authors succeeded. (pp. 203-04)

[Among other technical flaws in *The Last Woman in His Life*] is Ellery's ludicrous lecture to his father on the elementary facts of homosexuality, a subject with which I should think a thirty-year police veteran would be sufficiently conversant. The reason for all this over-obviousness is that Queen is deliberately aiming the book at the great ignorant majority to whom homosexuals are simply fags, fairies or fruits. Technically faulty as his approach is in whodunit terms, Queen deserves a great deal of credit not only for making the "pervert" in *The Last Woman* a person we can empathize with but for making his "perversion" one of the book's few decent acts. (p. 206)

Queen returned to near the top of his form in *A Fine and Private Place* (1971), which is the supreme manifestation of his tendency to build his recent novels around a leitmotif. In *The Player on the Other Side* it was a chess game, in *The House of Brass* it was greed for worthless things, in *The Last Woman in His Life* it was sex confusion. This time the leitmotif is the figure 9. (p. 207)

A Fine and Private Place is brim-full of the ingredients we have come to know as Queen hallmarks—the self-enclosed chessboard milieu, the satanic manipulator, the adversary's mocking notes to the investigators, the false solution followed by the truth. But most Queenian of all is the fantastic dozens upon dozens of variations on the concept of nineness that Queen lovingly plants in his pages. Most obvious of these are the many allusions to pregnancy, the growth of a fetus, and childbirth—the entire crime, the murderer's brainchild, is conceived and developed like a human baby. Perhaps the least obvious 9-motif is that by beginning and ending the novel with the same three words (words, as it happens, connoting fatherhood), Queen shapes the entire book into a figure that curls back on itself: a 9 of sorts, a fetus of sorts. I will not further spoil the pleasures of nine-hunting in store for readers but will assure them that the mind-blowing dazzlement of the most lavishly involuted Queen novels blazes in full glory in *A Fine and Private Place*.

As always in late Queen, the echo phenomenon is distinctly noticeable. . . . Once again Queen has taken full advantage of the right to borrow from himself without self-plagiarism.

If only the book's last twenty pages were as satisfying as what came before them! Unfortunately the solution is weakened by certain flaws built into the structure. For example, Queen here demonstrated a brilliant way of breaking the old rule that the murderer must be a major character, not a walk-on part; but the result is that there are literally no suspects on whom the wary reader can fasten and only one person who could possibly be the murderer. An even more damaging flaw is that the murderer's master plan requires of Ellery and his father at certain key points a whopping amount respectively of stupidity and failure to communicate—qualities with which each obligingly comes through at all the proper moments. (pp. 208-09)

But this is only to say that once again Queen's reach has exceeded his grasp. All carping aside, *A Fine and Private Place* must be ranked with *The Player on the Other Side* and *Face to Face* as one of Queen's three finest detective novels of the past fifteen years. And no one but Queen could have conceived it. (p. 209)

Francis M. Nevins, Jr., in his Royal Bloodline: Ellery Queen, Author and Detective *(copyright © 1974 by The Popular Press), Bowling Green University Popular Press, 1974.*

R

RANSOM, John Crowe   1888-1974

Ransom, an American poet, critic, and man of letters, was a major proponent of New Criticism. Like most southern writers of his period, his principle theme was the decay of southern lifestyles, beliefs, and integrity. The most significant body of his poetry was written between 1915 and 1928 when he was associated with the Fugitive Group. Most of the work in his *Selected Poems*, for which he won the National Book Award, is from this period. He is also remembered as a member of the agrarian movement, which sought to defend traditional southern values from encroaching northern industrialism. (See also *CLC*, Vols. 2, 4, 5, and *Contemporary Authors*, Vols. 5-8, rev. ed.; obituary, Vols. 49-52.)

MURIEL RUCKEYSER

John Crowe Ransom has done a strange thing [in rewriting "Conrad in Twilight,"]: he has made an extension and a transformation. Even while the method is maintained. So that time and choice, which can bear the rhyme away, have with this poem borne it back again in a different life. . . .

Years after "Conrad in Twilight," its first life, the poem has taken on a second life whose meaning is based on—and contradicts—the first. "Master's in the Garden Again" speaks for a further stage of life. It is a declaration, and a celebration; it is offered to the reader as a transparency with a key. (p. 187)

The strength of the new poem is very close to the qualities of Hardy, Hardy old and seen by Ransom in "Old Age of an Eagle," an essay which first appeared in the *New Republic* in 1952. These qualities, established by admiration and a kind of identity declared and built, will be in the poem as it climbs and rouses past its dripping scene. (pp. 187-88)

The poem sets the scene at once; although "Conrad in Twilight" jumped straight into dialogue, now we are given autumn ("Evening comes early"), the exchange (that is, true dialogue), and the man and woman, the lovers in bonds, conjugate. In the old days, the woman leapt right in, nagging:

> Conrad, Conrad, aren't you old
> To sit so late in your mouldy garden?

This time, Conrad is called both "dear man" and "surprise" (well, perhaps *he* is not called surprise, perhaps it is

the warning voice of nagging practicality that is surprised by her own thoughts, but I think Conrad is dear man, and surprised, as he is later thinker and master and champion). He is mood; she is "intrusion." (p. 188)

It is possible to be put off early in this poem by what seems like bumpiness, coyness, dated diction. Ransom himself has warned us of this in other poems by other poets. The music he claims is one he has described in the Hardy essay: he uses the folk line, or dipodic line, with its symmetry and a syncopation in a line whose musical expectation is so strong that the pause which can be produced is in itself strong, too. This is a clear and country music on which Ransom counts, and he has provided it with two chief sounds to carry the range of this wide-ranging poem: the long ā established in *exchange* and *late* and carried through to the last sound of the last line, and the long ō that begins with *bold* and *cold* and takes us to *blow* and all the variant o's and ow's sounding out toward the end. (pp. 188-89)

In the first "Conrad" it was a matter of tea and slipper and a blazing log at home. In the old poem, autumn was "teasing" and the poem ended with a described autumn.

Here, in part ii of the new poem, we have another couplet setting the scene, which is the action of the man, a still, negative persevering in the face of what seemed to be only a warning of lateness, cold, damp, his own creakiness. But it darkens—

> Nor the autumn's blow for an instant swerved

and then the described autumn, as it was the earlier poem,

> Autumn days in our section
> Are the most used-up thing on earth

and then the Biblical "or in the waters under the Earth." Used-up is what the persevering is about, *that* is what she has been calling him under the names of solicitude, *that* is what he has been refusing to be, even when it looked as though he could only be by sitting there. The black wet tatters of the year are here. Beyond them

> The show is of death. There is no defection.

Now a curious thing happens. We are beyond the old poem, and beyond the old life. There is something that is used-up, and the poet knows what it is. It is the old life itself. And there is something more. What comes next, in the

466

bringing-together of gardens? What have these all turned into? What comes once the show of death has been produced before us? It is produced, in full strength "no defection" and in full music, *show* being recognizable as a key sound in this poem. (p. 190)

The dialogue is between man and the Power. The Hardy Power, the cruel weather, It with a capital I, and I with a capital all there is to deal with It. The children are gone, fallen, dead by suicide because they are too "menny," anyway lost. And no more the querulous

> "O did It lay them low,
> But we're a poor sinner just going to dinner."

The heart itself is transformed, no longer tell-tale heart but

> See the tell-tale art of the champion heart.

Now the incantation takes up speed and action, the sound begins to swing. . . . Feeling has now been dealt with by assertion. . . . Ransom has spoken of "the metaphysical Powers arrayed against him"; here they are as one Power. The development of parallel feelings in this poem—no, conjugate feelings—lets me suspect that the wife has her chance for some parallel in the house, although it must come out of her "pity's sake" that works for his health as he sits out his mood for the health of his garden. There is her condemnation to the house, but he has come through; the garden's condemnation in the metaphor, although we know what winter is.

Ransom is not going to allow the metaphor to take over. His "that time of year thou may'st in me behold" is around him, being dealt with. But what happens? what is happening?

> A pantomime blow, if it damns him to do,
> A yell mumming too.

It has already "happened," though, in decision and in sound. And with the choice of the man, the garden has chosen. . . .

> But it's gay garden now,

and the acting-out, the singing, the making, which has done it to this garden, grants us a last invocation

> Play sweeter than pray, that the darkened be gay.

Here are the bravery, the irony, the honesty, the surprisingly banal moments, the music—and the maudlin, daily, saving life in Ransom's quickened poetry. . . . And the first poem of this garden, after all this lifetime with its poems, is transformed to the early and late of this second poem, with its darkness and play, its ease of irony as the poet moves along, full (as he said of Hardy) of "fierce folkish humor." (pp. 191-92)

Afterthought: I am still haunted by what happens to the woman in the poem and to the vowels that deepen and deepen into the undersounds of the climax. (p. 192)

> *Muriel Rukeyser, in* New World Writing, *edited by Steward Richardson (copyright © 1964 by J. B. Lippincott Company), Lippincott, 1964.*

JASCHA KESSLER

[Here] is a poet of middling ambition and gifts, with a stubborn individuality, a poet who has been a most learned and lifelong critic and theoretician of the art, who knows how to think deeper into poetry than anyone you may name, but also how to write simply, more clearly, dispassionately and genially, with ease and wit, than anyone in the business has managed to do in our critic-besotted "academic" time.

Endurance has been the central problem of the arts in the 20th century, and we all know how it obsessed Hemingway and has come to haunt the aged Pound. Ransom, instead of going on and on like Pound in the face of his own doubts of five decades, has chosen to refine his work, selecting and rewriting and rethinking his poems one by one.

This third selection [in the third revised edition of "Selected Poems"] seems to have brought the process down to the point where he has defined his own essence: what he has finally left in glows like a great cabochon: it is the purest of his poetry. And it is very likely to shine long in the dark confusions of our changing fashions (and readers) in the contemporary world.

This is an extraordinary book, and will be a useful key to many, not only for Ransom's treasury, but into the always-hidden secrets of poetry.

> *Jascha Kessler, "A Master Poet Analyzes His Work," in* The Los Angeles Times *(copyright, 1969, Los Angeles Times; reprinted by permission), September 28, 1969, p. 49.*

STANLEY KUNITZ

[John Crowe Ransom never deviated] from his love for the graces of a civilization and from his faith in the rituals and sanctions of a tradition. This is not to say that he was a conventional writer or thinker—his sensibility was much too keen, his mind much too fine, for sterile conformism.

His spare output of poems, exquisitely tuned, oblique, ardent but understated, leavened by irony, is the gift of his that we treasure most, because it delights us and because it encourages us to believe in the possibility of perfection. (pp. 251-52)

> *Stanley Kunitz, in his* A Kind of Order, A Kind of Folly *(© 1935, 1937, 1938, 1941, 1942, 1947, 1949, 1957, 1963, 1964, 1965, 1966, 1967, 1970, 1971, 1972, 1973, 1974, 1975 by Stanley Kunitz; reprinted by permission of Little, Brown and Co. in association with the Atlantic Monthly Press), Atlantic-Little, Brown, 1975.*

W. POTTER WOODBERY

The greatest stumbling-block to understanding ["The Equilibrists"] is the moral contradiction that holds Ransom's lovers in their state of equilibrium, the curious duality of their allegiance to both chastity and passion. . . . The lovers are not caught in a struggle to resist a lesser for a higher good, whether that higher good be the things of the spirit or the pleasures of the flesh. Instead, they perform a delicate balancing act, maintaining a fine equipoise between two equally desirable but mutually exclusive values. What set of ethical attitudes would allow for the serving of such contrary masters?

Most attempts to explain the poem founder on this problem. [Robert] Buffington supposes that the lovers are husband and wife but that one of them has a former mate who is now dead. (pp. 51-2)

Bernard Bergonzi, in another important reading of the poem, acknowledges that both passion and abstinence are affirmed, but he divides the allegiances to each between the lovers and the poet. . . . In his attempt to explain the poem, Mr. Bergonzi invokes the medieval tradition of *amor courtois,* that secular rival to orthodox Christian morality which celebrated erotic love at the expense of the conventional ideal of chastity. The "sin" of Ransom's lovers, rather than being fornication or adultery, is a sin against this secular ideal of erotic love: "By not consummating their love, or at least by allowing themselves to become separated, the two lovers had sinned *against* the religion of love itself, a concept familiar in medieval literature." . . . Not only does this interpretation destroy the equipoise that is part and parcel of the lovers' moral attitude, passion here taking precedence over chastity, but it also misreads the poet's response to the lovers, which develops . . . from anger at their strictness to an appreciation of their tortuous but beautiful equilibrium.

I should like to venture an additional explanation of the poem, drawing somewhat differently than Mr. Bergonzi does upon the courtly love tradition. It is true that for Andreas Capellanus the goal of loving was, in C. S. Lewis's phrase, "actual fruition." Elsewhere in the literature of *amor courtois,* however, we find a deliberate encouragement of sexual restraint even to the point of rejecting consummation as the ultimate goal of courtship altogether because of the effect that such restraint has in sustaining and increasing passion. . . . It is a short step from the desire to strengthen and prolong passion as a preliminary to actual coition to the pursuit of an intense, unconsummated passion that has become the sole reason for loving.

Denis de Rougemont, who has called this phenomenon "The Love of Love" (to distinguish it from the love of one person for another), traces it through the love lyrics of the Troubadours writing in southern France during the twelfth century. (pp. 52-4)

It is to the Troubadours that we largely owe our view of love in western culture, he maintains, and the tremendous impact of these poets upon our erotic sensibilities can be explained by the fact that they speak to a frightening but inescapable impulse in western man: the secret longing for death. The Love of Love, as de Rougemont sees it, is in fact not a love of Love at all but reveals an unspoken infatuation with death. Provençal love poetry arose simultaneously with the flourishing of a neo-Manichaean heresy known as Catharism and, M. de Rougemont believes, is a symbolic expression of the heresy's basic doctrines. Essentially a Gnostic heresy, Catharism espoused a dualistic philosophy. The soul at birth falls from a transcendent realm of perfection and Light into the dark, woeful existence of life in the body. Physical creation is thoroughly evil, and the hope of escaping its fetters is man's only hope of knowing the good. The Cathars owed the polarized metaphors of darkness and light as well as the preference for death over life to their Manichaean antecedents. As M. de Rougemont puts it, "Every dualistic—let us say, every Manichaean—interpretation of the universe holds the fact of being alive in the body to be the absolute woe, the woe embracing all other woes; and death it holds to be the *ultimate* good, whereby the sin of birth is redeemed and human souls return into the One of luminous indistinction." . . . (pp. 54-5)

Provençal love poetry, if M. de Rougemont's thesis is correct, is an occult liturgy for the worship of death. The pains and sorrows of unsatisfied love are welcomed as a kind of mortification of the flesh which serves to purge the lover of earthly attachments. . . . The idealized lady of the lyrics is a poetic symbol of the Absolute, and the perpetual yearning for her represents the longing of a soul for union with that Absolute that is possible only in death. The exclusive command that she holds over the affections serves to protect the soul from unworthy attachments. And finally, the stasis of the lover in his state of perpetual desire, forever frozen as he is on the near side of active consummation, anticipates the final stillness of death. (p. 55)

The poem promises at its start a love story. . . . We enter the scene of an action already in progress. The medieval couple (the imagery conclusively establishes the specific setting of their tale) are presently separated by the wanderings of the knight, if he may be called that. But things had not always been as they are now: the man and woman had once been lovers or, to be more precise, near lovers. . . . But their amorousness had stopped just short of consummation. Whereas her body was ready for love, her mouth, that had before so warmly kissed but then so coldly forbade, had uttered the cold, gray words of denial: "Arise [from the bed of love], / Leave me now, and never let us meet, // Eternal distance now command thy feet." . . . Hence the present wanderings of the lover-knight.

No sooner has this exposition been unveiled, however, than the direction of the poem takes a sharp turn. Because of the impasse of the lovers, frozen as they are between passion and its denial, the plot comes to a sudden halt. Conflict is the lifeblood of any narrative, but conflict that is in motion, that builds to a climax and issues ultimately in resolution. The equilibrium of Ransom's lovers precludes any progress in the action. We shall never know the victor in this duel of spirit and flesh because the antagonists are too equally matched. The plot germ perishes in this ethical stalemate. What had promised to be a simple love story begins to take on the shape of something entirely different. The focus of the poem now shifts to the attitude of the poet towards the lovers in their plight, and he struggles to comprehend their curious predicament. At this point, it begins to be clear that the principal business of the poem is not to spin a tale at all but rather to let us share with the poet his education in the nature of erotic love. The illumination finally granted him, he puts in lines made "to memorize" their doom. . . . The lovers offer, as it were, an exercise to be learned, and the epitaph of the final stanza is as much a memory lesson as it is a memorial. Putting aside our narrative expectations is essential if we are not to be sidetracked by questions regarding the actual fate of the lovers. The grave to which the poet relegates them . . . is not a literal grave. This death to which they come in the poem exists only in the probing fancy of the poet and is not a real event in their personal history. As we shall soon discover, it is the metaphorical death to which the relentless logic of their idea of love impels them.

The attitude of the poet toward the plight of the lovers passes through two phases. His initial attitude, which will ultimately be abandoned, is the attitude of common sense. What business have lovers to speak of honor? No more, to be sure, than the proverbially dishonest thieves! . . . Chastity may very well be meritorious in a cloister, but on the couch of love it is at best a dubious virtue. The turning point comes in stanza 9. Before this point, he can find nothing good to say about their equilibrium. . . . But then, his view of the lovers undergoes a sudden reevaluation. His reassessment of their predicament requires a harder, more tough-minded attitude—one only "for those gibbeted and brave": "Man, what should you have?/ . . . Would you ascend to Heaven and bodiless dwell?/ Or take your bodies honorless to Hell?" . . . Both questions are rhetorical, and in each case the unstated answer is "No." The function of the next two stanzas on Heaven and Hell is not to provide speculation about the actual destiny of the lovers, but instead to demonstrate that upsetting the balance between chastity and passion, in whatever direction the equilibrium might be resolved, would be ruinous. The tone of each stanza is heavily ironic. The thin, bodiless existence of the celestial lovers ("Sublimed away") . . . reveals the moral consequence of choosing chastity over passion and calls to mind the icy spinsters and effete young men who populate Ransom's poems and who, through their flight from eros, deceive themselves into thinking that they have found perfection on earth and have successfully escaped the iniquity of flesh. The agonizing carnality of the damned . . . discloses the consequence of choosing passion over chastity and the futility of a rapacious carnal appetite that, once satisfied, must repeatedly feed all over again. The final attitude of the poet toward the lovers is embodied in the epitaph he composes for their symbolic tomb, the location of which, significantly, is neither in Heaven nor in Hell. This reassessment by the poet keeps the balance between restraint and desire intact and celebrates the beauty of their fine equilibrium:

> Equilibrists lie here; stranger, tread light;
> Close, but untouching in each other's sight;
> Mouldered the lips and ashy the tall skull.
> Let them lie perilous and beautiful. . . .

The insistence that chastity be given its due is clearly faithful to the Manichaean premise of the Provençal love lyrics: life in the flesh is a life of woe. (pp. 56-9)

That the Manichaean love philosophy of Provence does not embrace the alternative of abnegating eros altogether, however, requires some explanation. How can we account for the Troubadours' insistence that at least passion (if not coitus) have its due as well? . . . The strategy of asceticism is ineffectual because the temptations of the flesh are not alone in binding the soul to its earthly existence. The mastery of the world through knowledge, which Schopenhauer recommends, is a deceptive victory. Knowledge deceives with the illusive hope that man's short spell on earth can be made reasonably noble and good and that eros can be conquered. The false promise of asceticism ignores the truth that earth is a place so thoroughly tainted that the blight reaches even into the courts of reason. The soul in Gnostic thought is not pure Light but Light that has been befouled by its contact with matter. As Ransom puts it in "The Swimmer" (perhaps his most explicitly Manichaean poem), not only "eggs and meat," but even Christians spoil. The perpetually unconsummated passion for the lady of the Provençal lyrics keeps alive that nostalgia for the Transcendent which guarantees our disenchantment with all earthly fulfillments, whether fleshly or spiritual. . . . For this reason, the "flames" of Ransom's equilibrists are equal in radiance to their "ice," and their dual allegiance to passion and chastity elevates them above the sub-lunar world of the here and now to an experience of transport that can ultimately be consummated only in death. (pp. 60-1)

The equilibrists will have no consolation, whether conjugal or illicit; they prefer instead the perpetual hunger of a perilous longing which is the condition of their joy and which they know (indeed, actually desire) will never be relieved by consummation.

Passion also means passivity. To suffer is to surrender action for inertia, to substitute (in the arena of love) dalliance for the sexual climax. . . . The Troubadours, it was found, often encouraged the indefinite postponement of the act of love itself. Stopping love in a moment of penultimate blissfulness, their lovers remain, like Keats's forever unravished Grecian bride, in a sublime stillness. Likewise, Ransom's equilibrists twirl in a spinning motion . . . , whose center contains no motion at all. (pp. 62-3)

Ransom's metaphor for their equilibrium—two polarized stars—recalls the Manichaean doctrine that the least spoiled particles of Light had been transformed into stars. If life in the flesh is a life of woe, we may take comfort in the promise that "A kinder saeculum begins with Death." . . . Ransom's equilibrists reach their apotheosis only in a vision of their doom. (p. 63)

The statement of Ransom's poetry on the man-woman relationship resurrects the love myth of Provence. We find in "The Equilibrists" the strongest evidence of that resurrection, though auxiliary themes appear, as has been shown, in other of Ransom's poems. The criticism of Ransom's poetry has largely concerned itself with the poet's techniques, especially with his use of irony and tone. There are certain psycho-philosophical attitudes implicit in his verse, however, which the mask of irony is not always successful in concealing and for which we must hold the poet accountable. . . . [The] Manichaean presuppositions of the verse are unmistakable, and the systematic exposition of them brings into focus a dimension of Ransom's poetry that heretofore has gone unexplored. (pp. 64-5)

> *W. Potter Woodbery, "The Sword Between Them: Love and Death in Ransom's 'The Equilibrists'," in* The Southern Literary Journal *(copyright 1977 by The Department of English, University of North Carolina at Chapel Hill), Spring, 1977, pp. 51-65.*

RICHARD GRAY

[Ransom's] appreciation of Allen Tate, written in honor of Tate's sixtieth birthday, . . . leads us into the heart of his own attitude toward experience. For in this essay Ransom offers the reader a detailed examination of the *character* of his subject, as much as of his literary achievement. He makes us see what he thinks of Tate not only as a poet and novelist but also as a man, and what he thinks of him is defined in principle in the opening sentence: "The poet, the thinker, the whole man—Allen Tate's personality is greatly distinguished in our time." "The whole man": that is essentially how Ransom presents Tate, and all whom he admires. No praise could be warmer from a person for whom the ideal of human completeness remained a source of continual inspiration—such inspiration, in fact, that it would not be too much to say Ransom's entire work depends on a comparison between this ideal and the sense of fragmentation he associated with more recent events.

Ransom's conception of the whole man does not involve any simplification of experience. On the contrary, its complex and specific nature is constantly emphasized. This is the result, largely, of his belief in the dual nature of the human personality, its indebtedness to both the reason and the sensibility. The reason, as Ransom sees it, man employs in his attempts to understand experience, to discover and use the universal patterns latent in the "world's body." The sensibility on the other hand simply enables him to enjoy experience, the fine qualities of particulars, including all those that cannot be absorbed into any pattern formulated by the rational element. So far what Ransom has to say may sound thoroughly commonplace, a hardly individualized version of a generally held idea. What distinguishes his argument, though, is that he manages to relate this conventional distinction to his comparative analysis of agrarian and industrial societies, and to do so in detail. The thesis that nearly all of his writing sets out to prove, in one way or another, is that only in a traditional and rural society—the kind of society that is epitomized for Ransom by the antebellum South—can the human being achieve the completeness that comes from exercising the sensibility and the reason with equal ease. With the rise of science and industrialism, the thesis continues, these two elements have become dissociated. Science and industry demand control of nature, and in pursuance of this man has had to exploit his reason and deny his sensibility. The image of the whole man, consequently, has been replaced by a concept of personality that emphasises its "appetitive and economic" functions at the expense of everything else.

In the course of his career Ransom has managed to apply the implications of this change to his analysis of several kinds of human activity, including the broad activities of work and leisure. Labor in a traditional society, for example, is described in essay after essay as performing "one of the happy functions of human life." This, so the argument goes, is because agriculture is the major form of employment in that society; and agriculture satisfies not just the reason of man, by supplying him with the requisite "material product," but his sensibility as well. . . . For like most of the Agrarians, Ransom insists that the cultural forms characteristic of any particular system are integrally related to the forms of its economic life, and so the "right attitude to nature" that rural labor is said to promote is extended into a definition of its artwork as well. The arts in a traditional community satisfy the two sides of human nature just as its agrarian experience does, in the sense that they demonstrate "the power of the material world to receive a rational structure and still maintain its particularity." Belonging essentially to what is called a "classical" mode of imitation, they manage to reflect both the constant and the contingent elements in life; whereas the artistic forms generated by an urban society cannot help but betray a bias in favor of one element or the other.

An inevitable consequence of Ransom's commitment to the idea of a unity of personality is that his discussion of one function of the consciousness tends to fade imperceptibly into a discussion of its other functions, so his essays on aesthetics are often transformed into essays on ethics about halfway through. And this particular tendency is reinforced by Ransom's own insistence that the only satisfactory system of morality—the kind of system, essentially, that is characteristic of a rural environment—is one that appeals to the aesthetic sense as much as the conscience. The beautiful and the good then become inseparable. . . . [For example, he maintains that] the traditional man commits himself to the principle of courtship so as to train the instincts *and*

so as to enjoy the subtler forms of pleasure it makes available to him—the detached contemplation of the object of desire, for instance, and the carefully discriminated and graded series of excitements that precede the final union. It is an enormously sophisticated interpretation of the scope of emotional experience. . . . (pp. 56-8)

Ransom is ingenious enough to extend the imputation of crudity to his analysis of the spiritual differences obtaining between agrarian and urban communities, this despite the fact that it was the charge of religious backwardness and crudity, leveled at the time of the Scopes trial, that initially stimulated his interest in his region. Indeed, there is a touch of characteristic bravado in the way Ransom insists that the very fundamentalism for which the South was mocked is a mark of its achievement. His argument is not a difficult one to grasp, although it is possibly more difficult to swallow. It depends on a rather pragmatic approach to religion, which insists that those varieties of belief are good which promote a "working definition of the relation of man to nature." The more thorough the definition is, apparently, the better the religion until one arrives at that variety which manages to hold in equilibrium two diverse interpretations of the human role—one of which depicts nature as "usable and intelligible," the other of which insists that it is "mysterious and contingent." God, according to this form of belief, can be understood, but only partly. He can be obeyed, and yet still remain mysterious and unpredictable. The ideas are, of course, contradictory. Ransom insists, though, that they can be reconciled in experience because they both grow naturally out of the practice of agriculture. . . . (p. 58)

[The majority of Ransom's poems] describe the dissociations for which a society expressing itself in "a series of isolated perfections" is responsible. There are, for example, the lovers in "Eclogue," the failure of whose relationship is directly ascribed to the fact that they are "one part love / And nine parts bitter thought." Their lack of inner integrity, the suggestion is, has prevented them from enjoying a complete relationship. And there are the lonely protagonists of so many of the poems, like "Miriam Tazewell," whose alienation stems from an inability to relate the complexities of their interior being to the abbreviated definitions of identity available in the world around them. In these and similar cases an alternative system of value—in which wholeness and consequently an integration of the inner and outer worlds does seem possible—is not made explicit, as it is in the essays. But it is nevertheless there, in the idioms of the verse. This is because poetry at its best, according to Ransom, should devote equal stylistic attention to what he calls "structure" and "texture." By "structure," Ransom explains, he means the totality of the poem, the "logical object or universal" that appeals to the reason; and by "texture" is meant "the tissue of irrelevance" and particularity that caters more to the demands of the sensibility. "A beautiful poem," according to these criteria, "is one that proceeds to the completion of a logical structure, but not without attention to the local particularity of its components." Obviously, Ransom would consider it arrogant to claim that he achieves this beauty in his verse, but it is clear enough that he aims for it. Almost from the beginning of his poetic career, he has tried to articulate a form which involves the simultaneous evocation of contradictory responses, catching the complex and yet unified reaction of the complete man to experience. And where the attempt has been successful, as it has been in many of his poems, the result has been a type of discourse that demonstrates its positives in its methods of expression. (pp. 58-9)

["Antique Harvesters"] is perhaps Ransom's most famous piece, and the fame is, I believe, quite justified. For in it he locates the meaning of his regional experience. He indicates, that is to say, the context of inherited belief on which his own work depends, and establishes the imaginative significance of his region for him—as a place where unity of consciousness is still possible and even likely. The South, in the poem, represents both a resource and a myth; and the poem itself consequently belongs at the center of his life's work. The fact that this is so—that "Antique Harvesters" has a centrality that none of Ransom's other poems possesses—is more or less suggested in the opening lines, which have the density and gravity of ideas brooded over for a very long time. . . . The poem is set on the banks of the Mississippi during the autumn, a season that as in the Keats ode reminds man of his mortality but also allows him to see that mortality as part of a general cycle of growth and decay. It is too a time of pause, offering him an opportunity to consider his harvest, material and spiritual. One thing gained from the land is suggested by the opening description of the old men, and that is endurance, the mildness of those who are as "dry" and "spare" as the earth they love. Another is suggested by the reference to the raven with its "sable" wings—an intimation of death and human limits, the humility acquired in any engagement with the soil. And, as if this were not enough, the third stanza of the poem introduces something else yielded by the land. For, as the old men talk and the descendants of long generations labor in the field, the sense of a usable past and a traditional life style becomes unavoidable. (pp. 60-1)

With the appearance of the hunters, a new feeling of ritual begins to enrich Ransom's portrait. Certainly, the more romantic associations this feeling dictates are tempered by the mundane detail, but the feeling is still present, and powerful enough to be carried over into the subsequent description of the harvesters. For when the poet returns after a while to these laborers in the field, they are addressed as if they were participants in a rite as well. Their activities, as described in the concluding stanza of the poem, seem to be as decorous and significant as the ceremonial of the chase that interrupted them—the only difference being that in this case the activities are directed toward the honoring of "our lady" the earth rather than a simple fox. . . . The ending is a thoroughly appropriate one, a convincing demonstration of the scope of Ransom's dualism. It affirms the dignity of the antique harvesters, the sense of decorum and heroism with which their commitment to the land is accepted; and yet it does so without rejecting the original recognition of the facts in the case of the farm laborer, or in the case of any man destined to work and then die. Nothing of that firm grasp on the actual demonstrated by the opening of the poem has been lost, but a great deal has been added to it and gained.

This gain is registered among other things in the staple idiom of the verse, which offers a characteristic reflection in word and manner of the contraries of thought on which the argument depends. The very title, "Antique Harvesters," gives a clue to this, referring as it does both to the concepts of tradition and ritual and to a particular event in the farming year. And throughout the following discourse equal weight is given to these two terms of reference: elevated and romantic metaphors, such as the description of the fox as a "lovely ritualist," are drastically qualified by the "dry, grey, spare" setting in which they appear, and the occasional use of an elegant or archaic word is braced by a sustained commitment to the colloquial. The result, as in a couplet like

> The horse, the hounds, the lank mares coursing by
> Straddled with archetypes of chivalry,

is an interplay of contradictory terms so complex that it almost defies analysis. And of course, that it should defy *immediate* analysis at least is part of Ransom's intention, since what he wishes to do essentially is to express the possible coexistence of these terms rather than their separateness. Agriculture, the premise is, brings the ceremonious and the mundane levels of experience together by transforming ordinary life into significant ritual. Its activities, and the moral and religious practices it encourages, supply the basis for that sense of tradition and even chivalry that surrounds all those who participate in them. This is the *donnée* of "Antique Harvesters," making it—to the extent that Ransom succeeds—not so much a portrait from life as a minor historical myth, in which the notion of unity of consciousness is proposed and then firmly attached to the Southern and agrarian idea.

This reading of the rural life, which identifies it at once with the decorous stance and the commonplace gesture, helps to resolve what would otherwise be a puzzling ambivalence in Ransom's agrarian argument—the argument we find developed in his essays. When he is arguing along strictly economic lines, he seems to offer an idea of agrarianism which approximates to the one suggested by the mundane or "low" set of terms in "Antique Harvesters." He insists on the importance of subsistence farming, and even proposes government aid in the form of bounties and free land for those willing to be their own producers and consumers, carpenters and builders. But, when other considerations to do with the quality of life are introduced, he tends to present a more aristocratic image, related to the "high" set of terms used in the poem. Emphasis is then placed on the belief that an agricultural society is a traditional one, promoting quite sophisticated codes of expression and behavior. . . . [The] self-contradiction is more apparent than real. "Antique Harvesters" demonstrates this more decisively than anything else, because it brings together qualities that Ransom discovered in the agrarian experience and elsewhere tended to deal with separately; its basis in hard work, that is, and the ritualized forms of conduct to which it leads, the onerous details of agricultural labor and the sense of ceremony that this labor fosters. As usual with a writer who delighted in turning his opponents' accusations back upon themselves, the argument is a sophisticated and very deliberate one, but no amount of sophistication can disguise one thing—the fact that its roots are in the Southern inheritance. For what Ransom does essentially in his work is to draw on the idea of the good farmer *and* that of the fine planter and then devise an imaginative alternative composed of elements from both. His version of the complete man represents a resolution of traditional conflicts— an idea of the good life which depends on his region for much of its content, but on him for its coherence. (pp. 61-3)

Richard Gray, in his The Literature of Memory: Modern Writers of the American South *(copyright © 1977 by Richard Gray), Johns Hopkins University Press, 1978.*

RENAULT, Mary   1905-

Renault is a British novelist. Her work often deals with the historical and political events of ancient Greece. Critics note her ability to render a historical epoch with clarity and credibility. (See also *CLC*, Vol. 3, and *Contemporary Authors*, Vols. 81-84.)

W. C. McWILLIAMS

[*The Charioteer*] is the most sensitive and accurate treatment of homosexuality I know of; modern in setting, it has all the sense for a real issue that one looks for in Renault's historical fiction. (It is also a useful antidote to her *The Persian Boy*, which is far below her usual standard; admirers should stick to . . . her earlier books.) (pp. 271-72)

> W. C. McWilliams, in Commonweal *(copyright ©*
> *1973 Commonweal Publishing Co., Inc.; reprinted*
> *by permission of Commonweal Publishing Co.,*
> *Inc.), December 7, 1973.*

HUGH KENNER

Despite her bibliographies and factual afterwords, Miss Renault setting out to re-create a Greek reality isn't your ordinary taxidermist, intent on matching the colors of the glass eyes. No, she's a male impersonator. . . .

Classical Greece, where homoerotic relations were unencumbered by moral disesteem, has set her imagination free repeatedly. . . .

Part of [the] secret [of "The King Must Die"] is that Miss Renault varied the formula. Dispensing with [her main persona], she made her Ralph-figure, Theseus, the protagonist and first-person reminiscer. . . . Part of it is the fructive ambiguity of legend. Theseus . . . doesn't hamper with historicity the way Plato or Alcibiades do, and it's possible for the novelist to enchant with guesses at the kind of real events that might have turned into the legends we have.

But the book's chief secret is the way the author's feelings have responded to the opportunities of a world so strange she feels free in it . . . .

She has written no other such book. . . . To be firm about that is not to reproach her with failure, but to insist on the credit she deserves for her transcendent book. The god, she tells us in it many times, spoke repeatedly to Theseus. Not only to Theseus.

> Hugh Kenner, "Mary Renault and Her Various
> Personas," in The New York Times Book Re-
> view (© 1974 by The New York Times Company;
> reprinted by permission), February 10, 1974,
> p. 15.

With sympathetic imagination and masterful scholarly poise, the author sifts fact and legend [in *The Nature of Alexander*] to give this forthright account of the enigmatic genius of the 4th century B.C., Alexander the Great. Drawing on sources as primary as one can find, and combining both admirable historical perspective and disarming common sense, this biography is also an engrossing narrative. . . . Not only is this first-rate scholarship, it is also a brilliant, handsome, and moving work. (p. 75)

> Virginia Quarterly Review *(copyright, 1976, by*
> *the* Virginia Quarterly Review, The University of
> Virginia), *Vol. 52, No. 3 (Summer, 1976).*

Our tour-guide for Renault's seventh foray into Ancient

Greece [*The Praise Singer*] is reminiscing Simonides of Keos, master poet of that era. . . . Renault makes [the time period] familiar with her usual, effective you-are-there approach—a great deal of casual shoptalk and reference to odd customs. Simonides goes everywhere, meets everyone, and is always at the scene of major events. . . . Though afflicted with the regulation nasty daddy, he is an unusual narrator for Renault, being both ugly and heterosexual, but his narrative tone of voice is just like that of her other heroes—a bit fey, a bit coy, but as strangely readable as ever. Another for Renault's host of fans, and if not her best, far from her worst. (p. 1089)

> Kirkus Reviews *(copyright © 1978 The Kirkus*
> *Service, Inc.), October 1, 1978.*

*   *   *

REXROTH, Kenneth   1905-

Rexroth, generally acknowledged to be one of the major living American poets, is also a critic, essayist, translator, and playwright. Although associated with the San Francisco Renaissance and the Beat poets, he is a craftsman who defies rigid categorization. An intimate voice is characteristic of his poetry, and it is a credit to his craftsmanship that this intimacy seems natural, not merely poetic artifice or sentimentality. Rexroth is also a skilled translator of non-Western verse into English. (See also *CLC*, Vols. 1, 2, 6, and *Contemporary Authors*, Vols. 5-8, rev. ed.)

RUBY COHN

[The four verse plays in *Beyond the Mountains*] are based on extant Greek tragedies, but in form they are modeled on Japanese Noh plays. Like Noh plays, they contain few characters in rich costumes, as well as Chorus and Musicians, and each drama is climaxed by a dance. As in Noh plays, too, Rexroth's stage is almost bare, but his language is more profuse in imagery. Rather than the duologues of Noh, Rexroth uses the three speaking parts of Classical drama.

The first of Rexroth's plays is called *Phaedra,* and it presents the basic story of Euripides' *Hippolytus.* (p. 263)

In an Author's Note, Rexroth explains that "Phaedra and Hippolytus achieve transcendence but are destroyed by impurity of intention." Rexroth is probably drawing on the Zen teachings behind Noh, in which the dance leads to *yugen,* a kind of transcendence. In the American play, however, the deaths of the lovers seem dictated by Greek myth rather than a search for transcendence; Phaedra impales herself upon a sword, and Hippolytus is trampled to death by a bull. The final words of the Chorus are full of gnomic morality that the drama has not theatricalized: "Impure intention is damned / By the act it embodies. / Each sinned with the other's virtue. / They go out of the darkness, / Onto a road of darkness. / The wind turns to the north, and / The leaves rattle. An unknown / Bird cries out. And the insects / Of a day die in the starlight." The wisdom is sententious and the images facile; they have not been earned in action.

Iphigenia at Aulis again follows the story of Euripidean tragedy, with different nuances. Rexroth's Iphigenia, who has been her father's mistress, and who kindles the desire of an innocent Achilles, has a vocation for transcendence. Therefore it is she who sends her lover off to Troy, and she who forces her father to sacrifice her. Though we scarcely need Rexroth's note that "Iphigenia marches straight to transcendence," the note implies that this is a noble fate, whereas the play gives us a distastefully manipulative woman.... The closing words of the Chorus contrast the fate of Iphigenia with that of Helen: "Aeneas and Odysseus / Wander, lost in a new world. / Helen dies in a brothel." But the contrast is more vivid than the play, in which events are stated without dramatic development.

The titular *Beyond the Mountains* is composed of two plays, *Hermaios* and *Berenike*. Despite the exotic Hellenism of the names, however, the plot is that of the *Oresteia*. (pp. 264-65)

[Rexroth's character] types are reminiscent of Yeats.... And even though Greek myth is more familiar than Celtic myth, Rexroth lacks the atmospheric tension evoked by Yeats' dialogue. It would be otiose to compare Rexroth with the greatest English-language lyric poet of the twentieth century, but the American's determination to load his lines with passionate images undercuts the static intensity of the Noh-form he has chosen. The short lines carry too heavy a load of images to drive the drama. As dialogue poems, however, they present piquant variations on Greek tragedy. (p. 265)

> Ruby Cohn, "Kenneth Rexroth," in her Dialogue in American Drama (copyright © by Indiana University Press), Indiana University Press, 1971, pp. 263-65.

BRYAN WILSON

[Kenneth Rexroth in his *Communalism: From Its Origins to the 20th Century*] takes the Judeo-Christian tradition rather than the Marxist as his starting point [and] is under no illusions about these modern communes, which he sees as often little more than crash pads for an uncommitted, floating, and perhaps work-shy population, who are merely opting out of the everyday world....

Mr Rexroth writes fluently, but behind his easy style there is more scholarship than he chooses to reveal (there are no footnotes, and no bibliography). One may not concur with every judgment, and one may doubt the occasional statement of fact, but a wide knowledge of the sources is always apparent. He has not chosen to offer any analysis of the structural similarities between movements, nor does he draw at all on the now well developed sociology of communitarian movements, but the reader looking for a general account of communes will find this an extremely readable book. Communal groups are often alike in the nature of their organisation, in the problems of social control, relationships, and authority, and description without an analytical framework could be tediously repetitive; it is much to Mr Rexroth's credit that, in spite of this, he sustains our interest in a narrative that never flags.

> Bryan Wilson, "The Communer Belt," in New Statesman (© 1976 The Statesman & Nation Publishing Co. Ltd.), January 2, 1976, p. 18.

JULIAN SYMONS

[An Autobiographical Novel by Kenneth Rexroth is a] detailed account of his first twenty-one years by a man who appears to have total recall of almost everything that has happened to him. It is easy to see why Kenneth Rexroth was regarded almost with reverence by a whole generation of West Coast poets, for he had exemplified in his youth their idea that all life is movement and that all movement should be free....

An Autobiographical Novel is a wonderfully entertaining book. It is also a specifically American odyssey, which has no counterpart in any English life of the period.

The figure who emerged from [a] stewpot of emotional and cultural self-education ... [was] very American: a tough-minded man strongly sceptical about accepted ideas and attitudes, an idealistic anarchist prepared to place personal freedom far above the idea of order, a believer in art as the noblest form in which such freedom could be expressed....

Some words of reservation are in order. The book has not been written but dictated, and it is not free of deplorable words like "totalized" and "situational", nor of clichés about "gracious and mellow people" or "one of the finest human beings I've met in my life". There is a maddening absence of dates, particularly irritating in passages which begin "that spring" or "that winter" without identifying the year.

There are occasions when one feels that a later Rexroth is speaking for the youthful one.... The title also is a little puzzling. Does it mean that passages in the book are deliberately invented? One would prefer not to think so.

When the words of reservation have been said, however, this remains a fine book, illuminating both about the author and the period in which he grew up. Kenneth Rexroth is a genial polymath (he has translated poetry in six languages) who is also a bohemian and a mystic, a scholar and at times a bit of a bum. It is not likely that he will ever be widely regarded in England as an important poet, but nobody could read this autobiography without feeling that he is an admirable man.

> Julian Symons, "The Education of an American," in The Times Literary Supplement (© Times Newspapers Ltd. (London) 1977; reproduced from The Times Literary Supplement by permission), March 25, 1977, p. 332.

DOUGLAS DUNN

British readers may have heard of Kenneth Rexroth as a father-figure of the Beats. That role has been exaggerated, even by grateful Beats themselves. Insufficient credit has been granted to Rexroth's identity as an old-fashioned, honest-to-God man of letters of downright independence of mind....

Rexroth and his books are American in a way few people know enough about. He is of the America that can be caricatured or dismissed only through prejudice....

What Rexroth evokes in his rambling, lucid, magnanimous book [*An Autobiographical Novel*] is his own growing up through precocious perception and experience of American radicalism, middle-class life, American literature, and the excitements of European modernism. It is a story of American promise and its decline. His childhood was remarkable by any standards; the book, I suspect, is called 'a novel' for the reason that he rubbed against the well-known or the great so consistently for it to look, in retrospect, like a succession of embarrassing fictional coincidences. It could not have been better if he had invented it. (p. 789)

Of the entire radical or politically agitated view of literature, and the fates of their exponents, Rexroth has much wisdom to offer, worth attending to as the wisdom of a poet who has more first-hand experience than most who pronounce on the subject. His temper is too independent, too scholarly, for cut-and-dried allegiances. He turns his back on Eliot and Pound. He has the irritating habit—for the mediocre, that is, the literary side-takers—of liking some but not all of certain poets or movements. Like all good examples in modern poetry, he has been seen as a figure instead of as a creator; as a representative rather than a participant. That he is all four of these persons at once comes as a sweet discovery from a reading of his work instead of from side-glances at other people's estimates of his reputation. (p. 790)

> *Douglas Dunn, "A Forgotten America," in* The Listener *(© British Broadcasting Corp. 1977; reprinted by permission of Douglas Dunn), June 16, 1977, pp. 789-90.*

EMIKO SAKURAI

Kenneth Rexroth has been trying for decades to accomplish what has been regarded as an impossible task—rendering Japanese and Chinese poems into acceptable English verse without losing the effects of the original. And he comes nearer to achieving the impossible with each new volume. [*One Hundred More Poems from the Japanese*] is a sequel to *One Hundred Poems from the Japanese*. . . . The new volume differs from the old in several aspects. With the exception of the haiku and some classic nature poems, the theme is always love—earthy, frankly sensual love. A girl in contemporary poems sings with astonishing candor the joy of lovemaking. The sorrow of parting at dawn and yearning for the lover are conveyed with subtlety and delicate beauty in the ancient tanka and with directness and sensuality in the folk songs and the modern tanka of poetess Yosano.

Stylistically, the translations are generally less concentrated than previously, when Rexroth was striving for maximum compression. The retranslations of poems from the [earlier] collection show some dilution of the original intensity because of the addition of extra lines. . . . With the revised renderings, however, Rexroth achieves his other goal of creating poems that can stand as poetry in English. Utmost compression can lead to incomprehension in translations, since the original overtones cannot be adequately conveyed. In the accuracy of rendering and overall artistry, the present volume far surpasses the previous one. (pp. 180-81)

One Hundred More Poems from the Japanese contains some of the best renderings of Japanese poetry to date. . . . [Rexroth's] success with the present book enforces many critics' view that only poets can produce acceptable translations in verse. (p. 181)

> *Emiko Sakurai, in* World Literature Today *(copyright 1978 by the University of Oklahoma Press), Vol. 52, No. 1, Winter, 1978.*

*   *   *

RICH, Adrienne   1929-

An American poet, critic, essayist, and translator, Rich was a National Book Award winner with *Diving into the Wreck*. Her development of a relaxed form of free verse combined with formal diction has been seen by many critics as revolutionary and distinctive in American poetry. Her later work is inti-mately connected with her interest in the feminist movement. (See also *CLC*, Vols. 3, 6, 7, and *Contemporary Authors*, Vols. 9-12, rev. ed.)

ANNE BERNAYS

[*Of Woman Born*] is a disturbing book. In a footnote on page 76 the author, a poet and critic, writes: "I never read a child-rearing manual . . . that raised the question of infanticide."

This strikes me as an observation so inappropriate to the subject at hand—motherhood—that it raises doubts as to whether reality and wish have not been hopelessly lost in one another, and throws a good many of Rich's insights into serious question.

All mothers have, at one time or another, experienced a murderous kind of rage toward their children. While it is the proper business of child-rearing books to deal with *feelings* of rage (along with other disagreeable and guilt-producing emotions like melancholia, frustration, boredom, lethargy, despair, and the desire to flee), it seems to me that a discussion of the *act* of murdering your own baby doesn't belong in Doctor Spock any more than husband-or wife-killing belongs in a marriage manual.

Ms. Rich, when asked why her poems never speak of her children, replies: "For me, poetry was where I lived as no one's mother, where I existed as myself." Is Rich asking us to believe that when she is a writer she is not a mother, and vice versa? It seems as if Ms. Rich is either unable or unwilling to incorporate the experience of motherhood into the part of her that creates not bodies but poems. The one turns off, the other turns on, and never the twain shall overlap. (p. 89)

The pervasive tone of this book suggests that the author has been grievously used, as if, like Rosemary in Ira Levin's novel, she had been drugged and then raped by the devil.

Ultimately, the poignancy of Rich's message reaches us. We want desperately to console her for having suffered her "primal agony"—which we are nevertheless unable to share.

Subtitled *Motherhood as Experience and Institution, Of Woman Born* is convincing only when it catalogues and analyzes the outrages society commits on the mother, from the brutal mechanics of obstetrical care to the politics of patriarchy, whose strategy it is to keep Mother down. . . . Rich has done a scholarly job of reading and absorbing, and of documenting her various accusations. There is no question about it: mothers don't have it as good as fathers. Fathers have money, freedom to move around, power, daily diversion, professional and political clout, general esteem. But society has reserved the second-class section for *all* women, not just mothers—for old women and little girls, the nonmarried and the lesbians. Why single out mothers? Mothers, after all, have something no one else has: their children. Rich's book is about motherhood—curious there is so little in it about children. The experience was traumatic for her; the institution reminds her of a prison. . . .

It is hard to finish reading Ms. Rich's book without feeling she has been unfair to her own extraordinary gifts as a writer. In many ways it is a barren book—the very opposite of Mother. (p. 90)

Anne Bernays, "Motherhood: A 'Primal Agony'?" in Harvard Magazine *(copyright ©, 1977 Harvard Magazine, Inc.; reprinted by permission), January-February, 1977, pp. 89-90.*

DAVID KALSTONE

[Rich] has for a long time been interested in American life as registered and suffered by those not in power, those not directly responsible for it, and especially women.... Rich has also written about isolated pioneer figures, whose "unarticulate" lives preserved qualities gone underground—qualities which she, in her poetry, would like to make available to the present. Increasingly in the 1970s that interest has taken on a political cast in connection with the women's movement and feminism. Her prose study, *Of Woman Born: Motherhood as Experience and Institution* (1976)—parts autobiography, history, anthropology—is the most ambitious sign of her commitment to expressing and investigating the unexpressed feelings of women. But it is important to remember that this has been a long-standing concern of Rich's poetry. People who frame questions about the effect of her ideological commitment upon her poetry are, I think, looking in the wrong direction. Part of the ideological commitment is *to* poetry and the special powers of its language to probe and reveal. (pp. 137-38)

The final line of ["From an Old House in America"]—"Any woman's death diminishes me"—alludes to Donne's famous line. Its shock value drains away fairly quickly on second reading. Rich knows, of course, that Donne's meditation doesn't refer to the death of men alone, and her own version seems less "true" than simply being a signal, a semaphore, saying that certain kinds of language from the past just won't do. The line is a deliberate narrowing of focus, an unsubtle way of talking about a subject Rich treats with as much point and with more complexity in images which in this same poem precede the "put-down" of Donne. The subject of this poem is women's dream of isolation. The loaded gun [which was a sexual image in "Face to Face"] is that of the watchful frontier woman at her stockade, and Rich imagines, with a great deal of psychological penetration, that this dream also "snares" a woman's pride. It may be like a "suicidal leaf" (the half-rhyme "life" close to the surface) ready for combustion under the burning-glass.

I have used this example for two reasons. First, to cite one instance of the way Rich's feminism has come forward in her recent writing. Second, and more important, to suggest that the shock value of a line like "Any woman's death diminishes me"—and our agreement or disagreement with its place as *poetry*—should not blind us to the fact that elsewhere in the same work Rich is continuing a task more effective as poetry and more profoundly political. Rich's images—like the "loaded gun" of "Face to Face" and "From an Old House . . ."—often attach themselves in the mind to feelings of ardor and tension. Sometimes, as in "Face to Face," the poem is pitched toward a meeting or a reconciliation. The main action takes place in stillness, an isolated concentration to find the "old plain words," the "God-given secret," which will, in the meetings dreaded and desired, both explode and reach out for understanding. In the later assertiveness of "From an Old House . . ." the "loaded gun" defines boundaries of self, a stockade within which exploration and attention to the self are taking place. No immediate release is promised. But in both these exam-

ples, Rich is straining toward a charged language which will make the self, at last, palpable. (pp. 140-41)

Composing in charged phrases shifts attention to her images, draws the pulse of the poem to them and away from verbs. In many of Rich's poems the images—close to the truth of dreams—rest close to one another in a complexly realized present.... Rich appropriates the manner to the coil and recoil of emotions. Her ardor transmutes traditional modernist materials. Above all, she puts them at the service of dialogue. What marks her ... is the explicit demand her speakers make not only to understand but *to be understood*. They fight off the notion that insights remain solitary, unshared, dribble off into the past. What's more, her poems, however public in reference, proceed in a tone of intimate argument, as if understanding—political as well as private—is only manifest in the tones with which we explain ourselves to lovers, friends, our closest selves. Whether this radical intensity can be attained and sustained is the question George Eliot asked in *Middlemarch,* and the one Rich asks again and again as her poems make the attempt. (p. 142)

[In her] period of apprenticeship Rich was guided by instinct to the literary modes and postures through which she could express a smouldering and independent nature—one which impressed itself more directly in later work. It is interesting how, in the mannerly tones of her Frostian narratives, she goes intuitively to the core frustration of women dwindling into marriage. She is also not blinded by the glittering surround of heroic figures to whom she is in other ways drawn. In "Euryclea's Tale" (1958), impersonating Ulysses's old nurse, or in "The Knight," playing the critic of heroes herself, she is marvelously penetrating about the burdens and derelictions of traditional warriors. "Who will unhorse this rider / and free him from between / the walls of iron" ("The Knight"). "I have to weep when I see it, the grown boy fretting / for a father dawdling among the isles" ("Euryclea's Tale").

Yet still we see the knight "under his crackling banner / he rides like a ship in sail." And Euryclea, baffled and resentful on the part of the boy Telemachus, still can think of Ulysses's vagrancy in more romantic terms.... (p. 144)

The ambush here is the storyteller's own susceptibility to all facets of the story, to the all-encompassing light in which Ulysses's travels may be viewed.... (p. 145)

In taking on earlier literary modes and historical figures, Rich very often found an angle of the subject which allowed her to enter the scene guardedly. But the time she wrote "Antinoüs: the Diaries" it was with a measure of self-disgust. Only later, when they were no longer part of the inherited "poetry of furs and manners"—and through the strange economy of a poet's memory—was she to welcome back those glints of richness as signs, not of a transmitted love of surfaces, but as answering to the hidden resources of the spirit. Modulated, in a different key, a chastened opulence was to be one way of talking about the sunken treasure of personality—the lost, the suppressed, the unspoken—in Rich's more disciplined, radical poems. For example, in "Diving into the Wreck" (1972), one way of talking about confusions of history and sexuality, the damages, the riches rotting and waiting to be unlocked, was to imagine them among shifting underwater forms, "the silver, copper, vermeil cargo," the sea-creatures "swaying their crenellated fans," "the ribs of the disaster / curving their assertion / among the tentative haunters."

But when she published *Snapshots of a Daughter-in-Law* (1963), Rich was using her "literary" skills ("The Knight," "Euryclea's Tale" and "Antinoüs: the Diaries" were all collected in this volume) in an irritated way. She had found her subject: fighting free of what sheltered her, others' homes, others' books and language; but she had not found her own way of speaking. In the forthright title poem, the "snapshots of a daughter-in-law" are part of a highly literary strategy, ironically like "The Waste Land," testing traditional poetic representations of women against deflating modern instances of women's daily experiences, inner strengths and resentments. . . . (pp. 145-46)

The literary irritation is twinned with a mounting bitterness far more central, the discovery of "the silent isolation of minds in marriage," as Helen Vendler puts it. (pp. 146-47)

Distinctions fall away—Yeats's dictum that the poet must choose between perfection of the life and perfection of the work, for example. The pain and conflict which Rich records in her account would energize her work for years to come. . . . With *Snapshots*, Rich began dating each of her poems by year, a way of limiting their claims, of signalling that they spoke only for their moment. The poems were seen as instruments of passage, of self-scrutiny and resolve in the present. (pp. 147-48)

Necessities of Life is a remarkable collection. In its mainly pastoral setting, the New England woods, Rich plays out, with freedom and feeling, a number of contradictory roles, which in the urban domesticity of *Snapshots* and in her later books had and would conflict with one another. In *Necessities of Life* she seems to enjoy a precarious immunity, the chance to experience a various self. . . . The title poem acts out, metaphorically, with wry satisfaction, the rebirth of a tough little self. . . . (p. 151)

It is strange then that the assertive self of some of these poems [in *Necessities of Life*] does not penetrate the poems of love and marriage; that those poems are lyrics of disintegration and the fine winnowing of self. *Necessities of Life* is in a delicate equilibrium, fully open to those rich and contradictory feelings. What is more astonishing is that it closes with a poem which breaks that pattern. The poem . . . is "Face to Face" and in it, almost for the first time, Rich anticipates bringing together both the energies of the solitary ego and the energies of dialogue, of a lovers' relationship. The poem hopes for the nourishment of a marriage through the charged revelation of the inner life. . . . What language [the lovers] were to speak was yet to be discovered.

The books which follow *Necessities of Life* seem driven by the craving for new ways of talking, so that the asserted, palpable self might be accepted as the basis of relation between lovers, husband and wife, friends. . . . Gone the old instinct that the ego must dwindle in relationships. Her poems lie like wishes on the pages. They make the further implicit claim . . . that the recharged and regenerated selves are the only true basis of political change. Both her radicalism of the late 1960s and her feminism in the 1970s, at their most convincing, rest on self-scrutiny and individual growth. *Leaflets*, *The Will to Change* and *Diving into the Wreck* ask to be read less like books of detachable polished poems and more like journals—patient, laconic, eloquent

but dating themselves, provisional instruments of passage in the present. One doesn't turn back. (They are, for example, not the kind of journals into which one hundred new poems could be dropped retrospectively, as was the case in the second edition of Robert Lowell's *Notebook*.)

It is striking how many of these poems are about fresh starts, as if that position had to be re-imagined constantly to keep up the intensity of the verse, bypass disappointments, overcome the pain of broken connections. (pp. 154-55)

Rich had, in *Leaflets*, begun to write *ghazals*, a form borrowed from the Urdu poet Ghalib, and anticipating the fluid play of images she described in "Images for Godard." The *ghazal* had a minimum of five couplets, each free-standing and independent of the others. "The continuity and unity flow from the associations and images playing back and forth among the couplets in any single *ghazal*." Each of her *ghazals* was dated, as were the letters, "pieces" and finally "films" and "photographs" which make up *The Will to Change*. To cut images as free as possible from ordinary temporal sequence became Rich's aim, convinced as she was that "In America we have only the present tense." Syntactical irregularities became a means of self-interrogation, as in this scene in an old house [in "The Blue Ghazals"]:

> To float like a dead man in a sea of dreams
> and half those dreams being dreamed by someone else.
>
> Fifteen years of sleepwalking with you,
> wading against the tide, and with the tide. . . .

These sentence fragments raise ghosts of questions and conclusions. Being incomplete, they expose fears and loyalties at the same moment, and their grammar suggests how such emotions float entwined and unresolved in the mind. (p. 159)

"Diving into the Wreck" [presents] adventures behind the common definitions of sexuality and beyond the damages done by acculturation and conditioning. It is here also that Rich makes her strongest political identification with feminism, in her attempts to define experiences unique to women or to define the damages done by false definitions of sexual identity. Into her images she has been able to concentrate much of what has always been in her poetry: what it is like to feel oppressed, betrayed and unfulfilled. The explicit identification with feminism sometimes sets poems off balance. But this is a matter of presentation and not—as some critics have suggested—because Rich has radically changed the direction or interests of her writing. (p. 162)

Rich's poems are bound to be restless, bound to be looking constantly for new beginnings, because they will never resign themselves to solitude.

The pressure under which she writes has led her in new directions. Her prose study *Of Woman Born* represents several years of study and finally brings together materials from anthropology, history and from her own life as both child and mother. . . . [It grows] out of the tensions between the sexes which her poems have always explored, asking this time—and appropriately in prose—whether they are ingrained in the biological differences between men and women or historically conditioned. The central effort of feminism, but here explored through the special experience of motherhood, the way she has felt it and the way it has been defined in Western societies. (pp. 163-64)

[It] is clear that Rich's sustained prose effort and large historical framework will take some of the pressure off what she expects of individual poems. Especially in the early 1970s, one could hear in Rich's poems the growing frustrations and anger accumulated by re-imagining again and again the fresh starts, the efforts at reconciliation. Titles like "Burning Oneself In" and "Burning Oneself Out" speak for themselves. "The Phenomenology of Anger" (1972) acts out some of women's deepest nightmares and cravings for violence, but it also speaks Rich's special frustration as an image-maker, all those years hoping for dialogue.... Even redirecting her violence, there is . . . at the back of Rich's mind a suppressed dream of dialogue and regenerated selves.

And twinned with the anger in these recent poems, there is also an enlarged awareness—a new voice, I think, in Rich's work—of the tragedy wrought into human relationships and into the attempts at dialogue and exchange. There are two particularly important examples: on the level of social injustice, her "Meditations for a Savage Child" and, less general, a poem of blunted love, "Cartographies of Silence." "Meditations for a Savage Child" is a remarkable poem based on the documents Truffaut also used so movingly in his film *L'Enfant Sauvage,* the records of the French doctor, J. M. Itard (now published as *The Wild Boy of Aveyron*). Itard had observed and partly "civilized" a savage child in the late eighteenth century. Rich, perhaps following Truffaut, introduces excerpts from the doctor's accounts as points of departure for each of the five sections of her poem. Unlike Truffaut, who chose to play the part of Itard in his film, Rich often takes on the role of the child, or ponders what he has to teach her, as she engages in a series of meditative exchanges with the voice of Itard. The poem is partly a long historical register of Rich's own divided spirit. Itard is an adversary but not an enemy , as they gaze across the ambitious ruins of Enlightenment philosophy. In the solicitous elegance of his prose, she finds words which have been emptied of their meaning: humanity, administrators, protection of the government—the roots of much which would have once engaged her own ardor. But in the mysteries of childrearing, of miseducation, she locates everything which defeats that ardor. (pp. 164-66)

In its very title "Cartographies of Silence" sends us back to the ardor for a knowledge of human relationships which has animated much of Rich's work. But the poem itself turns an appraising, sad eye on the large energies involved in a career so fervently directed outward. It is hard to know, now that some of Rich's force and passionate intelligence has been directed into prose, just what role poetry will come to play in her life and in her writing. Critics have in the past pointed out how much, in her commitment to the notation of present feelings, the pain of the moment, Rich has given up the traditional retrospective and shaping functions of verse. Poems like "Meditations for a Savage Child" and "Cartographies of Silence" show that whatever she has relinquished she has given up purposefully, that she understands the price of her ardor without giving up her rights to it. (p. 169)

> *David Kalstone, "Adrienne Rich: 'Face to Face',"* in his **Five Temperaments: Elizabeth Bishop, Robert Lowell, James Merrill, Adrienne Rich, John Ashbery** *(copyright © 1977 by David Kalstone; reprinted by permission of Oxford University Press, Inc.), Oxford University Press, New York, 1977, pp. 129-69.*

MYRA STARK

A woman in a patriarchal society such as ours, Rich has said, "in which males hold dominant power and determine what part females shall or shall not play," is defined by powerlessness. In her poetry Rich probes the effects of such a society on women and moves toward personal and political ways of breaking out of it. An early poem, "Aunt Jennifer's Tigers," examines the life of a woman dominated, indeed "terrified by men." Creating in her needlepoint tigers a vision of masterful and assured life, Aunt Jennifer cannot escape the powers that confine her: her hands even after death are "still ringed with ordeals she was mastered by." "Snapshots of a Daughter-in-Law" explores the lives of women whom men "dominate, tyrannize, choose, or reject," women who gain identity only through their relationships to men. The poem presents the consequences of such powerlessness: minds "moldering like wedding-cake" . . . ; energies turned inward or erupting angrily at other women; women who either die as complete adults at fifteen or are labelled and dismissed as "harpy, shrew and whore." "Time," Rich reminds us, "is male" and selects for praise women who are beautiful and nurturing, who shave their legs and iron their clothing—and that of others. . . . (p. 34)

But Adrienne Rich does more in her poetry than merely examine the consequences of powerlessness. "What it means to be a man, what it means to be a woman . . . is perhaps the major subject of poetry from here on," she has said. A number of Rich's major poems deal with this process of discovery—with woman's search for an authentic self and a freely chosen life. Both the themes and the imagery of these poems reflect the author's concern with the subject of power.

"The Roofwalker," from *Snapshots of a Daughter-in-Law,* focuses on these birth pangs. It contrasts the life the poet has rejected with the life she is struggling to bring into being. The old life is represented by a traditional image; a woman reading in the lamplight seen against cream wallpaper. The metaphor, recalling Erickson's belief that women are defined by their inner space, suggests an existence secure, protected, if essentially vicarious. But such a life is one which the poet" "didn't choose"; the space is "a roof I can't live under." . . . To present her search for the new life, Rich chooses an untraditional metaphor—the construction worker. Engaged in a dangerous and difficult occupation, the roofwalkers are builders and doers, powerful "Giants," men who master their environment with strength and tools. The poet, too, is a construction worker. In "When We Dead Awaken: Writing as Re-Vision," Rich speaks of women becoming their own midwives, "creating themselves anew." But the endeavor to build a new life leaves her feeling naked and exposed, just as the roofwalkers are depicted as silhouetted against the sky, alone and vulnerable. Even her tools "are the wrong ones." The choice of imagery reveals the nature of the life she is seeking. It is to be an existence created consciously by choice, constructed, not like the old life, unthinkingly accepted. If the creation is perilous, it is also heroic.

"Diving Into the Wreck" is a more recent poem which also explores the birth of the transformed self. The underwater ruin, a metaphor for the dead self and the dead civilization which created it, is the scene for the primal search. The archetypal descent into the underworld takes place, however, complete with the apparatus of modern technology. The diver is equipped with body armor, knife, mask, camera, and a book of myths. Like "The Roofwalker," the poem stresses the powerful nature of the diver's mission, her courageous exposure to the unknown element. Learning to surrender to the sea, the poet discovers the ability in her body to survive in the new element. (pp. 34-5)

Rich's metaphors for the birth of the transformed self—the construction worker raising a new roof, the diver descending into blackness—are characteristic of her poetry in that they are drawn from the tools and technology of our time. In "Trying To Talk To a Man," the explosive and difficult relationship between the man and the woman is developed through the image of bomb testing. Just as the emergencies —"laceration, thirst"—are transferred from the public and technological world to the personal one, so is the power of the process. Addressing the man, Rich says, "Your dry heat feels like power" . . . ; the ultimate testing is internal, the danger is in "ourselves." (p. 35)

A number of poems use an untraditional metaphor for the soul's journey, drawn also from the world of modern technology—the helicopter. Lying on a blanket in the forest during a moment of happiness and peace, the poet in "In the Woods" views "My soul, my helicopter" leaving her body in a Whitman-like flight. . . . In "Snapshots of a Daughter-in-Law" the poet hails the new woman who plunges "breasted and glancing through the currents, / at least as beautiful as any boy / or helicopter, / poised still coming, / her fine blades making the air wince." . . . The image is of flight and freedom, and discovery, but the stress is on the poets and energies released in the process.

What emerges from a reading of such poems, poems which must be viewed as attempts "to create something / That can't be used to keep us passive," is a redefinition of the nature of power. Traditionally women's fragmented lives have dissipated their energies; their position has denied them power. . . . Rich spoke of the times "When I'm in a group of women where I have a sense of real energy flowing and of power in the best sense—not power of domination but just access to sources . . ." This definition of power "in the best sense" as energies released, not as domination achieved, provides the impetus behind a number of Rich's poems which focus on the lives of strong and competent women.

In "Planetarium," Rich celebrates Caroline Herschel, the astronomer, "levitating into the night sky / riding the polished lenses," discovering in her ninety-eight years, eight comets. The absorbed and intent woman, "in the snow / among the Clocks and instruments / or measuring the ground with poles" . . . becomes a model and a hope for the poet who is herself searching to "translate pulsations / into images for the relief of the body / and the reconstruction of the mind." . . . Just as Caroline Herschel worked with electrical energies and impulses, the poet sees herself "bombarded," standing in the "direct / path of a battery of signals." . . . The powerful woman holds out a hope for the poet of the possibility of success. (p. 36)

"I Dream I'm the Death of Orpheus" presents the poet as "a woman in the prime of life, with certain powers," having developed, for example, "the nerves of a panther." . . . But these powers are "severely limited" by the unseen authorities. The poet is condemned to feel "the fullness of her powers / at the precise moment when she must not use

them." Her "mission" is clear: "if obeyed to the letter" it will "leave her intact." Yet the confusions and ambivalences inherent in her situation bewilder and frustrate her.

One aspect of the powerful women in [these] poems is their penetrating clarity of vision. . . . But the poet in these . . . poems, is not only a seer, she is also a woman on a quest. . . . The poet is strengthened in this quest for the new self and the new life by the women who are centers of power and energy in the poems. That they exist and can be invoked is perhaps the reason the "mission" can be undertaken at all.

The poetry of Adrienne Rich, then, concerned with discovering what woman has been and can be, is necessarily involved with the subject of power: with the examination of the results of women's powerlessness; with a redefinition of the nature of power; with the search for new sources of power for women; and with a celebration of the passing of power from men alone to both men and women. (pp. 36-7)

> *Myra Stark, "The Poetry is the Power," in* Poet and Critic *(© Department of English, Iowa State University), Vol. 10, No. 2, 1978, pp. 34-7.*

MARGARET ATWOOD

"Diving Into the Wreck" . . . was fueled by an immense pounding energy, a raw power, "raw" in the sense of "wound." It was played on a kettle drum with an ax, to a warehouse filled with riot casualties. By contrast, "The Dream of a Common Language" is played on the piano, at evening, beside a half-open window. There are one or two other people in the room, friends of the player, and perhaps some strangers listening outside. The music is subdued but intense, and it is only after you have been hearing it for some time that you realize the player is half-blind and is missing several fingers. These are poems written *despite,* poems of willed recuperation. Pain is no longer their theme but a given condition they are trying to transcend; the best word for what they have is perhaps not "power" but "authority."

This book will probably be labeled "feminist" and even "lesbian." Both labels apply, though like all labels they are too often used merely for slotting items into pigeonholes so they can be safely dismissed. Adrienne Rich, however, is not easy to dismiss, and her poems, even when they insist on such labels, escape from them. "Twenty-one Love Poems," for instance, seems at first to be a cycle of poems tracing an affair between two women, yet it eludes such simple definition. For although the sequence is insistently rooted in the mundane details of such an affair, conducted amidst the specifics of a city—"the Discount Wares, the shoe-store," "the rainsoaked garbage, the tabloid cruelties / of our own neighbourhoods"—it begins to open both outward and inward, until by its end the dialogue with the lover has become a frightening monologue, the speaker's conversation with her "own soul." The figure in the final poem is not a "lesbian" or a "feminist" or anything with such familiar features. It's pure Rich, a portentous presence, half dark, half light, moving imponderably in moonlight across a space formed by a great circle of stones. (p. 7)

These poems are by an older poet, and possibilities, especially possibilities for heroism, have contracted in the face of the actual. Miss Rich is now asking: How, given the world and its history—which in her eyes must be seen as a history of oppression for all women and many men—how, given violent and shoddy America, can anyone live and affirm? (pp. 7, 42)

The real interest is in women and their histories, both personal and mythical. In this universe, helicopters have no place; instead there are images of caves, moonlight, subversive witchcrafts practiced in "the kingdom of the sons," curing, growing. The voice of these poems no longer says, "I could be as good as a man," but "Men are not good enough"; or, more clearly, "I want to be a woman, as fully as possible." History has not feared women becoming men, but women becoming women; thus all women are still "unfinished," "halfborn," their lives throughout history stunted and denied. Again and again, the figure of the scavenger recurs, as a "slippered crone" going through trashbaskets, as the poet leafing through her own past, searching letters and memorabilia for clues, or, finally, as a woman retreating from "argument and jargon" to the kitchen, where she arranges treasured scraps on the table, forming them into a design.

To save, to salvage from the past what can be salvaged—this, not the incandescent demolition of such earlier poems as "Autumn," is the task Miss Rich now sets herself. (pp. 42-3)

> *Margaret Atwood, "Unfinished Women," in* The New York Times Book Review *(© 1978 by The New York Times Company; reprinted by permission), June 11, 1978, pp. 7, 42-3.*

LAURA E. CASARI

Poet Adrienne Rich, in *Of Woman Born*, chose the topic of motherhood "because it was a crucial, still relatively unexplored, area for feminist theory." . . . She thoroughly documents the powerlessness of women in a patriarchal culture and vividly depicts its results. Aware that literature on prepatriarchal cultures is scarce, Rich offers her analysis of its importance along with her vividly depicted experience of motherhood, an experience potentially desirable, but destroyed by the institutions in patriarchal culture. This combination of historical material and personal experience makes starkly clear that we have lost, in taking women's freedom from them, much that our culture sorely needs. (p. 206)

Rich has written with precision of the plight of women in a patriarchy; with the assurance and power of the freed woman, she offers women the strategy and vision necessary to collectively build a world "truly ours." (p. 207)

> *Laura E. Casari, "Woman Freed," in* Prairie Schooner *(© 1978 by University of Nebraska Press; reprinted by permission from* Prairie Schooner*), Summer, 1978, pp. 206-07.*

STEPHEN YENSER

Adrienne Rich's [*The Dream of a Common Language: Poems 1974-1977*] frustrates oblique approaches and defies moderate responses. Breathtakingly beautiful and moving for the most part, it is sometimes depressingly narrow and mean. Nor is there enough between to allow one to relax into qualified judgments without misrepresenting the book. Even when the good and the bad float in the same medium, they rarely dissolve into the merely interesting or the mediocre. Still, *The Dream of a Common Language: Poems 1974-1977* is a unified project, not just a collection of poems, and it is sobering to contemplate the possibility that

Rich could not have accomplished the best without doing her worst.

The unity of the volume springs from what we might think of as a pair of interrelated myths that it articulates bit by bit. One of them . . . concerns female identity. (p. 83)

[If] being a whole woman means being able to apprehend the self as a whole, Rich has made herself into one. Her thoughts and feelings are sensations. (p. 84)

When Rich turns from women's struggles with themselves to the oppressive society her eloquence turns to rant. . . . Men, "all of them," according to Rich's Paula Becker, feed on women, who seem sometimes to love men but must actually be dissembling. In short, the male is a "predator," a "parasite."

Some of these judgments are offered in contexts that might permit qualification, but Rich is not interested in hedging. . . . Rich has begun to solve the problem of the imperfect world by dividing human nature into two parts and identifying the worthwhile part with her group. The knot that we might have thought human nature was, is actually a fiction, the result of tying together in our minds the female virtues and the male vices. . . . (pp. 85-6)

It would seem that you could cross horses with griffons before you could combine Rich's intelligent sensitivity with her flagrant simplisms. Yet here they are together. Either the latter must be calculated gestures that warp and provoke in order that they might be attended to at all, in which case they are on a par with television commercials and political harangues and fail her own test for preservation . . . , or they are cries of excruciating occasions, reckless expressions of terror, hatred, and longing that have a certain dramatic truth, in which case they deserve preservation but can hardly be thought steps on the way to any truly common language. This is an important book grievously flawed. (p. 86)

> *Stephen Yenser, in* The Yale Review *(© 1978 by Yale University; reprinted by permission of the editors), Autumn, 1978.*

*   *   *

ROETHKE, Theodore   1908-1963

Roethke was a major twentieth-century American poet. His work strongly conveys the physical presence of nature and the human body in dynamic descriptive imagery. *The Far Field* is generally considered his best and most representative work. He was awarded the Pulitzer Prize in Poetry in 1954 for *The Waking*. (See also *CLC*, Vols. 1, 3, 8, and *Contemporary Authors*, Vols. 81-84.)

KENNETH BURKE

Roethke can endow his brief lyrics with intensity of *action*. Nor is the effect got, as so often in short forms, merely by a new spurt in the last line. No matter how brief the poems are, they progress from stage to stage. Reading them, you have strongly the sense of entering at one place, winding through a series of internal developments, and coming out somewhere else. (pp. 69-70)

Thus, though you'd never look to Roethke for the rationalistic, the expository steps are . . . ticked off as strictly as in the successive steps of a well-formed argument. And thanks to the developmental structure of such poems, one never thinks of them sheerly as descriptive: they have the vigor, and the poetic morality, of action, of form unfolding. (pp. 70-1)

[You] will rarely find in his verse a noun ending in "-ness" or "-ity." He goes as far as is humanly possible in quest of a speech wholly devoid of abstractions. (p. 73)

If Roethke adheres to his present aesthetic, there are more [abstract] . . . expressions in ["Burnt Norton,"] one Quartet of Eliot's, than Roethke's Vegetal Radicalism would require for a whole lifetime of poetizing. (p. 74)

[We can use] Kantian distinctions to specify a possible criterion for a purified poetic idiom. The ideal formula might be stated thus: *A minimum of "ideas," a maximum of "intuitions."* In this form, it can sum up the Roethkean aesthetic. (pp. 75-6)

[We] can see in Roethke's cult of "intuitive" language: a more strictly "infantile" variant of the Dantesque search for a "noble" vernacular; a somewhat suburban, horticulturist variant of Wordsworth's stress upon the universal nature of rusticity; and a close replica of Lawrence's distinction between the "physical" and the "abstract."

With "prowess in arms" (*Virtus*) he is not concerned. The long poems, still to be considered, are engrossed with problems of welfare (*Salus*), though of a kind attainable rather by persistent dreamlike yielding than by moralistic "guidance of the will." As for *Venus,* in Roethke's verse it would seem addressed most directly to a phase of adolescence. The infantile motif serves here, perhaps, like the persuasive gestures of sorrow or helplessness, as appeal to childless girls vaguely disposed toward nursing. The lost son's bid for a return to the womb may thus become transformed into a doting on the erotic imagery of the "sheath-wet" and its "slip-ooze." And in keeping, there is the vocabulary of flowers and fishes (used with connotations of love), and of primeval slime. (pp. 81-2)

Now let us ask what kind of selectivity is implicit in Roethke's flower images (with their variants of the infantile, rustic, and physical).

In particular, what is a greenhouse? What might we expect it to stand for? It is not sheer nature, like a jungle; nor even regulated nature, like a formal garden. . . . But there is a peculiar balance of the natural and the artificial in a greenhouse. All about one, the lovely, straining beings, visibly drawing sustenance from ultimate, invisible powers—in a silent blare of vitality—yet as morbid as the caged animals of a zoo.

Even so, with Roethke the experience is not like going from exhibit to exhibit among botanic oddities and rarities. It is like merging there into the life-laden but sickly soil.

To get the quality of Roethke's affections, we should try thinking of "lubricity" as a "good" word, connoting the curative element in the primeval slime. Thus, with him, the image of the mire is usually felicitous, associated with protection and welcome, as in warm sheath-like forms. Only in moments of extremity does he swing to the opposite order of meanings, and think rather of the mire that can hold one a prisoner, sucking toward stagnation and death. Then, for a period of wretchedness, the poet is surprised into finding in this otherwise Edenic image, his own equivalent for Bunyan's slough of despond.

Flowers suggest analogous human motives quite as the figures of animals do in Aesop's fables (except that here they stand for relationships rather than for typical characters). The poet need but be as accurate as he can, in describing the flowers objectively; and while aiming at this, he comes upon corresponding human situations, as it were by redundancy. Here was a good vein of imagery to exploit, even as a conceit: that is, any poet shrewdly choosing a theme might hit upon hothouse imagery as generating principle for a group of poems. Yet in this poet's case there was a further incentive. His father had actually been a florist, in charge of a greenhouse. Hence, when utilizing the resources of this key image for new developments, Roethke could at the same time be drawing upon the most occult of early experiences. Deviously, elusively, under such conditions the amplifying of the theme could also be "regressive," and in-turning.

The duality, in the apparent simplicity, of his method probably leads back, as with the somewhat mystic *ars poetica* of so many contemporary poets, to the kind of order statuesquely expressed in Baudelaire's sonnet, "*Correspondances,*" on mankind's passage through nature as through "forests of symbols," while scents, sounds, and colors "make mutual rejoinder" like distant echoes that fuse "in deep and dusky unity." (pp. 82-3)

What, roughly, then, is the range of meaning in Roethke's flowers? In part, they are a kind of psychology, an empathic vocabulary for expressing rudimentary motives felt, rightly or wrongly, to transcend particular periods of time. Often, in their characters as "the lovely diminutives," they are children in general, or girls specifically. . . . The preconscious, the infantile, the regressive, the sexual—but is there not in them a further mystery, do they not also appeal as a pageantry, as "positions of pantomime," their natural beauty deriving added secular "sanctification" from the principle of hierarchy? For the thought of flowers, in their various conditions, with their many ways of root, sprout, and blossom, is like the contemplation of nobles, churchmen, commoners, peasants (a world of masks). In hothouse flowers, you confront, enigmatically, the representation of status. By their nature flowers contribute grace to social magic—hence, they are insignia, infused with a spirit of social ordination. In this respect they could be like Aesop's animals, though only incipiently so. For if their relation to the social mysteries were schematically recognized, we should emerge from the realm of intuitions (with their appropriate "aesthetic ideas") into such "ideas of reason" as a Pope might cultivate ("whatever is, is right" . . . "self-love, to urge, and reason, to restrain" . . . "force first made conquest, and that conquest, law" . . . "order is heaven's first law" . . . "that true self-love and social are the same"). A Roethke might well subscribe to some such doctrine, notably Pope's tribute's to "honest Instinct"—but in terms whereby the assumptions would, within these rules of utterance, be themselves unutterable. (pp. 85-6)

Some of the short pieces come close to standard magazine verse. . . . But mostly, here, we want to consider the four longer pieces: "The Lost Son," "The Long Alley," "A Field of Light," and "The Shape of the Fire."

Roethke himself has described them as "four experiences, each in a sense stages in a kind of struggle out of the slime; part of a slow spiritual progress, if you will; part of an effort to be born." At the risk of brashness, we would want to modify this description somewhat. The transformations seem like a struggle less to be born than to avoid being undone. Or put it thus: The dangers inherent in the regressive imagery seem to have received an impetus from without, that drove the poet still more forcefully in the same direction. . . . His own lore thus threatened to turn against him. The enduring of such discomforts is a "birth" in the sense that, if the poet survives the ordeal, he is essentially stronger, and has to this extent *forged himself* an identity.

The four poems are, in general, an alternating of two motives: regression, and a nearly lost, but never quite relinquished, expectancy that leads to varying degrees of fulfillment. In "Flight," the first section of "The Lost Son," the problem is stated impressionistically, beginning with the mention of death ("concretized," of course, not in the name of "death," which would be at the farthest an abstraction, at the nearest an abstraction personified, but circumstantially: "At Woodlawn I heard the dead cry"). When considering the possible thesaurus of flowers, we were struck by the fact that, in the greenhouse poems, there was no overt reference to the use of flowers for the sick-room and as funeral wreaths. Deathy connotations are implicitly there, at the very start, in the account of the Cuttings, which are dying even as they strain heroically to live. And there is the refuse of "Flower Dump." But of flowers as standing for the final term of human life, we recall no mention. Roethke has said that he conceives of the greenhouse as symbol for "a womb, a heaven-on-earth." And the thought of its vital internality, in this sense, seems to have obliterated any conscious concern with the uses to which the products of the florist's trade are put. In any case his present poem, dealing with a lyric "I" in serious danger, fittingly begins in the sign of death.

The opening stanza, however, contains not merely the theme of deathlike stagnation. There is also, vaguely, talk of moving on. . . . And throughout the opening section, with its images of rot and stoppage, there is likewise a watching and waiting. Even a rhetorical *question* is, after all, subtly, in form a *quest*. Hence the call for a sign ("Out of what door do I go, / Where and to whom?"), though it leads but to veiled oracular answers ("Dark hollows said, lee to the wind, / The moon said, back of an eel," etc.), transforms this opening section ("The Flight") into a hunt, however perplexed. (pp. 86-7)

[Though the second section] is but a series of restatements, it has considerable variety despite the brevity of the lines and despite the fact that each sentence ends exactly at the end of a line. And the Grammatical shifts, by dramatizing the sequence of topics, keep one from noting that the stanza is in essence but a series of similarly disposed images (symbolizing what Roethke, in a critical reference, has called "obsessions"). (p. 89)

The third section, "The Gibber," might (within the conditions of a lyric) be said to culminate in the *act* that corresponds to the attitude implicit in the opening scene. It is sexual, but reflexively so: the poet is disastrously alone. . . . Against a freezing fear, there is a desperate cry for infantile warmth: "I'm cold. I'm cold all over. Rub me in father and mother." The reflexive motif is most direct, perhaps, in the lines: "As my own tongue kissed / My lips awake." The next lines (Roethke has called them a kind of Elizabethan "rant") culminate in a shrilly plaintive inventory of the hero's plight:

All the windows are burning! What's left of my life?
I want the old rage, the lash of primordial milk!
Goodbye, goodbye, old stones, the time-order is
　going,
I have married my hands to perpetual agitation,
I run, I run to the whistle of money,

the lamentation being summed up, by a break into a different rhythm:

Money　money　money
Water　water　water

Roethke's Vegetal Radicalism is not the place one would ordinarily look for comments on the economic motive. Yet you can take it as a law that, in our culture, at a moment of extreme mental anguish, if the sufferer is accurate there will be an accounting of money, too. It will be at least implicit, in the offing—hence with professional utterers it should be explicit. So, the agitation comes to a head in the juxtaposing of two liquidities, two potencies, one out of society, the other universal, out of nature. (And in the typical dichotomy of aestheticism, where the aesthetic and the practical are treated as in diametrical opposition to each other, does not this alignment encourage us to treat art and the rational as antitheses? For if money is equated with the practical and the rational, then by the dialectics of the case art is on the side of an "irrational," nonmonetary Nature.) (pp. 90-1)

Though the second section was *entitled* "The Pit," here actually is the poem's abysmal moment, after which there must be a turning.

Hence, section four, "The Return." Recovery in terms of the "father principle." Memory of a greenhouse experience: out of night, the coming of dawn, and the father. After the description of the dark, with the roses likened to bloody clinkers in a furnace (an excellently right transition from the ashes theme at the close of the previous section to the topic of steam knocking in the steam pipes as a heralding of the advent), the movement proceeds. . . . (p. 91)

And after talk of light (and reflexively, "light within light") the poem ends on his variant of religious patience and vigil, as applied to the problem of super-egoistic rationality:

A lively understandable spirit
Once entertained you.
It will come again.
Be still.
Wait.

There has been a coming of light after darkness, a coming of warmth after cold, a coming of steam after powerlessness, a coming of the father and of his super-egoistic knock —and now at the last a more fulsome coming is promised. And within the rules of this idiom, "understandable" is a perfect discovery. It is perhaps the only "intellectualistic" word (the only word for "rational") that would not have jarred in this context.

All four of the long poems follow this same general pattern. (p. 93)

All told, to analyze the longer poems one should get the general "idea" (or better, mood or *attitude*) of each stanza, then note the succession of images that actualize and amplify it. Insofar as these images are of visible, tangible things, each will be given its verb, so that it [will] have sufficient incidental vividness. But though, in a general way, these verbs will be, either directly or remotely, of the sort that usually goes with the thing (as were dogs to bark, or pigs to grunt), often there may be no verb that, within the conditions of the poem, the noun objectively requires.

For instance, at the beginning of "The Shape of the Fire," there is a line "A cracked pod calls." As an image, the cracked pod belongs here. It is dead, yet there is possibility of a new life in it. Hence, topically, the line might have read simply "A cracked pod." Similarly, there is the line, "Water recedes to the crying of spiders." If spiders stand in general for the loathsome, the line might be translated formalistically: "The principle of fertility is overcome by the principle of fear." However, though pods may rattle, and spiders may weave or bite or trap flies, pods don't call and spiders don't cry.

In considering this problem most pedestrianly, we believe we discovered another Rhetorical device which Roethke has used quite effectively. That is, whenever there is no specific verb required, Roethke resorts to some word in the general category of *communication*. Thus, though "shale loosens" and "a low mouth laps water," a cracked pod calls, spiders and snakes cry, weeds whine, dark hollows, the moon and salt say, inanimate things answer and question and listen or are listened to. To suggest that one thing is of the same essence as another, the poet can speak of their kissing, that is, being in intimate communion (a device that has unintended lewd overtones at one point where the poet, to suggest that he is of the essence of refuse, says, "Kiss me, ashes," a hard line to read aloud without disaster, unless one pauses long on the comma). The topic is clouds? Not clouds that billow or blow, but that would just *be*? The line becomes: "What do the clouds *say*?"

There are possible objections to be raised against this sort of standard poetic personifying, which amounts to putting a communicative verb where the copula is normally required, or perhaps one could have no verb at all. But it does help to suggest a world of natural objects in vigorous communication with one another. The very least these poetic entities do is resort to "mystic participation." The poet's scene constitutes a society of animals and things. To walk through his idealized Nature is to be surrounded by figures variously greeting, beckoning, calling, answering one another, or with little groups here and there in confidential huddles, or strangers by the wayside waiting to pose Sphinxlike questions or to propound obscure but truth-laden riddles. One thus lives as though ever on the edge of an Ultimate Revelation. (pp. 96-8)

[Similes] are very rare in Roethke. The word "like" appears, unless we counted wrong, but three times in the four long poems; "as," used as a synonym for "like," occurs not much oftener. Indeed, one way to glimpse the basic method used here is to think, first, of simile, next of metaphor, and then (extrapolating) imagine advancing to a further step. Thus, one might say, in simile, "The toothache is like a raging storm," or metaphorically, "The raging tooth." Or "beyond" that, one might go elliptically, without logical connectives, from talk of toothache to talk of ships storm-tossed at sea. And there one would confront the kind of *ars poetica* in which Roethke is working.

The method may be further extended by the use of a word in accordance with pure pun-logic. Thus, if in "reach" you

hear "rich," you may say either "reach me" or "rich me" for the reach that enriches. ("Rich me cherries a fondling's kiss.")

Much of this verse is highly auditory, leaving implicit the kind of tonal transformations that Hopkins makes explicit. And often the ellipses, by weakening strictly logical attention, induce the hearer to flutter on the edge of associations not surely present, but evanescently there, and acutely evocative (to those who receive poetry through ear rather than eye). (pp. 98-9)

Though Roethke's lines often suggest spontaneous simplicity, and though the author has doubtless so cultivated this effect that many lines do originally present themselves in such a form, on occasion the simplicity may be got only after considerable revision. (p. 100)

[By] eschewing the "rationality" of doctrine (a "parental principle" which one may situate in identification with father governments or mother churches, or with lesser brotherhoods themselves authoritatively endowed), the poet is forced into a "regressive" search for the "superego," as with talk of being "rubbed" . . . "in father and mother." Eliot could thus "rub" himself in dogma, borrowed from the intellectual matrix of the church. But Roethke, while avidly in search of an essential parenthood, would glumly reject incorporation in any cause or movement or institution as the new parent (at least so far as his poetic idiom is concerned). Hence his search for essential motives has driven him back into the quandaries of adolescence, childhood, even infancy. Also, . . . the search for essence being a search for "first principles," there is a purely technical inducement to look for definition in terms of one's absolute past; for a *narrative* vocabulary, such as is natural to poetry, invites one to state essence (priority) in *temporal* terms, as with Platonist "reminiscence"—an enterprise that leads readily to "mystic" intuitions of womb heaven and primeval slime.

The battle is a fundamental one. Hence the poems give the feeling of being "eschatological," concerned with first and last things. Where their positivism dissolves into mysticism, they suggest a kind of phallic pantheism. And the constant reverberations about the edges of the images give the excitement of being on the edge of Revelation (or suggest a state of vigil, the hope of getting the girl, of getting a medal, of seeing God). There is the pious awaiting of the good message—and there is response to "the spoor that spurs."

Later poems repeat the regressive imagery without the abysmal anguish. Thus, in "Praise to the End!" our hero, expanding in a mood of self-play . . . follows with snatches of wonder-struck childhood reminiscence mixed with amative promise:

> Mips and ma the mooly moo,
> The like of him is biting who,
> A cow's a care and who's a coo?—
> What footie does is final.

(pp. 104-05)

[In] the theme of childhood reverie, as ideally reconstructed, the poet can contemplate an Edenic realm of pure impulsiveness.

Yet perhaps it is not wholly without *arrière-pensée*. For is the motivation here as sheerly "regressive" as it may at first seem? Is not this recondite "baby-talk" also, considered as rhetoric, one mode of lover-appeal? And considering mention of the wink and the bite in connection with talk of the fall, might we not also discern an outcropping of double meanings, whether intended or not, in reference to a "mooly man" who "had a rubber hat" and "kept it in a can"? The cloaking of the utterance in such apparent simplicity may not prevent conception of an adult sort here, particularly as the lines are followed immediately by talk of "papa-seed." (pp. 106-07)

Though Roethke has dealt always with very concrete things, there is a sense in which these very concretions are abstractions. Notably, the theme of sex in his poems has been highly generalized, however intensely felt. His outcries concern erotic and auto-erotic motives generically, the Feminine as attribute of a class. Or, though he may have had an individual in mind at the moment, there is no personal particularization in his epithets, so far as the reader is concerned. He courts Woman, as a Commoner might court The Nobility (though of course he has his own "pastoral" variants of the courtly, or coy, relation).

But because his imagism merges into symbolism, his flowers and fishes become Woman in the Absolute. That is what we would mean by "personification."

By "personalization," on the other hand, we would mean the greater *individualizing* of human relations. (Not total individualizing, however, for Aristotle reminds us that poetry is closer than history to philosophy, and philosophy seeks high generalization, whereas historical eras, in their exact combination of events, are unique.) In any case, we have seen one recent poem in which Roethke has attempted "personalization" as we have here defined it: "Elegy for Jane (My student, thrown by a horse)." Though not so finished a poem as "The Visitant," it conveys a tribute of heart-felt poignancy, in a pious gallantry of the quick confronting the dead, and ending:

> If only I could nudge you from this sleep,
> My maimed darling, my skittery pigeon.
> Over this damp grave I speak the words of my love:
> I, with no rights in this matter,
> Neither father nor lover.

Perhaps more such portraits, on less solemn occasions, will be the Next Phase? Meanwhile, our salute to the very relevant work that Roethke has already accomplished, both for what it is in itself, and for its typicality, its interest as representative of one poetic way which many others are also taking, with varying thoroughness. (pp. 107-08)

> *Kenneth Burke, "The Vegetal Radicalism of Theodore Roethke," in* Sewanee Review *(reprinted by permission of the editor, © 1950 by The University of the South), Winter, 1950, pp. 68-108.*

JOHN D. BOYD

There is a widespread emerging consensus that Roethke must be judged, along with Robert Lowell, as one of the two American poets of his generation most likely to achieve a durable, major reputation. (p. 409)

For most readers the verse which best represents this poet, and which compels one to return to him again and again, is that body of poems in which a thriving microcosm is set in motion: the poems about orchids and geraniums, about bats, night crows, field mice and summer storms, about a girl thrown by her horse, a small boy waltzed to giddy joy (or is it terror?) by his tipsy father. Above all, it is the so-called "greenhouse poems," in which one finds the special Roethkean voice. These are the poems that prompted John Berryman, in a moving elegy on the death of Roethke, to lament, "The Garden Master's gone," and led Kenneth Burke, in one of the earliest and best essays we have, to celebrate Roethke's "vegetal radicalism" [see excerpt above]. Roethke himself spoke of "the greenhouse, my symbol for the whole of life, a womb, a heaven-on-earth" confirming what would be evident enough without such corroboratory evidence: that from Roethke's childhood experiences around a greenhouse in Michigan, run by his father, he evolved a set of poetic images and symbols, a vocabulary, a tone, a way of apprehending the natural world, which were to serve him steadily (some would say obsessively) through the rest of his career. (pp. 409-10)

[It] is largely through the formal or structural properties of these poems that Roethke has worked magic upon his somewhat unpromising materials. . . .

[Many] elements, some of them nonstructural, helped Roethke forge a uniquely energized descriptive poetry. Berryman felt that "all previous poets' attention to plants has been casual. Flowers and weeds alike writhed and lived on the page [in Roethke] as they never had before." Some of the means by which Roethke created this writhing life are fairly obvious even on casual reading, and some have been noted by critics: the symbolic suggestiveness of Roethke's plants, by which parallels between the plant and human worlds are so often implied; the proliferation of strong action verbs, by the use of which a world we ordinarily perceive as quiescent and static becomes dynamic; the resolutely concrete and sensory vocabulary . . . ; the heavy charge of rich sense impressions, so reminiscent of Keats; and, finally, the unmistakable Roethkean tone, an apparently detached, almost clinical preciseness, which yet manages to convey a hushed, breathless mystery and excitement. . . .

Roethke's vegetative world partakes of a life force partly its own, partly its fictively defined observer's; as in so much romantic and post-romantic literature, the sense of aliveness that critics have savored here is the product of an interpenetration or coalescence of subject and object. (p. 411)

[We] say something substantial about the greenhouse poems when we note that they owe much of their "writhing life" to this crackling atmosphere of contending opposites. One manifestation of this is the somewhat covert presence of a living authorial voice, uniting the clinical and the compassionate, the enthralled. Another . . . is the omnipresent tension between the forces of life and death. . . . (p. 412)

Roethke unites in an especially dramatic way "the general, with the concrete; the idea, with the image; the individual, with the representative." . . . The emotive atmosphere of these poems is deeply ambivalent; the empathy by which we share the joy of invincible growth is blended with the pain of struggle, the revulsion of decay and death. . . . Even humor is sometimes oddly mixed with horror and disgust, creating a kind of whimsical macabre. . . . Other contraries abound: the static and the dynamic, the active and the passive, stillness and movement, struggle and surrender, motion in contrary directional patterns. The greenhouse itself, locale and symbolic microcosm for the whole sequence, "blends and harmonizes the natural and the artificial," while it "still subordinates art to nature." (pp. 412-13)

Roethke has shown infinite care and inventiveness in shaping his materials. The poems have an air of felicitous improvisation, a function, no doubt, of several factors: brevity, the flexible free verse, the offhand, colloquial idiom, and the primitivism implicit in the subject matter. Nevertheless, each poem has a remarkable inner logic, which an appreciative reader intuits rather than observes. Each poem has been allowed to define and shape its own uniquely appropriate formal coherence from within, in accordance with its own subject and theme. Because of the peculiarity of these themes, one hesitates to pun by using the term "organic unity," but the brief description I have just given of the formal dimension of the greenhouse poems might almost serve (indeed, *has* served) as a good Coleridgean definition of that term. And it does serve to define their formal qualities, as well as their themes. (pp. 413-14)

[The dynamism of the greenhouse world] is sufficient to define something of the distinctiveness (perhaps uniqueness) of Roethke's efforts, in relation to other literary treatments of plants. The further point needs to be urged that in these poems the *organization* generates its own dynamism, which (1) contributes significantly to our impression of relentless energy, already salient in the poems' content alone, and (2) enriches our understanding of the manifold possibilities for expressing in poetry the artist's delight in form, our awareness of the variety of formal resources available to him.

The only critic who seems to have understood this quality in Roethke's greenhouse poems was Burke. . . . (p. 414)

Always we can locate more than one, sometimes a great many [formal patterns in these poems], and always they illustrate precisely what Coleridge meant by "organic form": each pattern seems to have "grown" from the particular materials at hand, never imposed arbitrarily from without. This organic unity, while it occurs in some other Roethke poems, is by no means his invariable strength. Its absence has been deplored in many of the later, Yeatsian poems; critics have sought doggedly to find it in the controversial sequences in and following the *Lost Son* volume, but there is no consensus yet as to their success. (p. 418)

[Sound patterns] are conspicuously active in every one of the greenhouse poems. Roethke was always an alliterative poet, and the density of phonetic devices is especially heavy in this sequence, so that we are sometimes reminded of Hopkins, or of Anglo-Saxon verse, both of which apparently were important stylistic influences on Roethke. Besides alliteration (and internal consonance), we find a conscious, controlled use of assonance and internal rhyme. Both patterns (consonant and vowel repetitions) are rife in "Orchids," as in all the others. Roethke will sometimes play with an assonance or consonance pattern (or both at once) involving a series of sounds. . . . (p. 420)

Often the sound patterns are used to reinforce other patterns of progressive development within the poems. . . . [However, even] when this shaping of sound sequences to accommodate other patterns is absent, the sequences are one more means of fusing the lines of the poem into a whole which has continuity and momentum.

Even the meter is occasionally if not consistently func-

tional. The poems are all in free verse, and the general shape is varied from one poem to the next: sometimes the lines are uniformly short, sometimes uniformly long, sometimes freely fluctuating in length. Often a pattern of line expansion or contraction is correlated with meaning: in "Root Cellar" the lines fluctuate with unusual regularity, evoking the breathing vegetation so eerily described. In "Weed Puller," the longest line is "Those lewd monkey-tails hanging from drainholes,—"; in "Orchids" the longest line, "The faint moon falling through whitewashed glass," is soon followed by a series of lines in which there is a definite ritardando, in keeping with the intensifying hush and spookiness:

> Lips neither dead nor alive,
> Loose ghostly mouths
> Breathing.

> (pp. 421-22)

[There is considerable sophistication of form] in these remarkable little poems. . . . Roethke was as careful about the arrangement of his poems in the sequence as he was about the shape of each individual poem. . . . (p. 424)

> *John D. Boyd, "Texture and Form in Theodore Roethke's Greenhouse Poems," in* Modern Language Quarterly (© 1971 University of Washington), *December, 1971, pp. 409-24.*

ANTHONY LIBBY

Roethke remains, despite shadows of doubt about his ultimate value, a seminal voice in contemporary poetry. He must be one of the most uneven poets ever called "great" in serious critical writing. He consistently explored new territory only to retreat into the security of old and often secondhand styles. He could be as false to his deepest visions as he was to his unique voice. But if his poetry sounds with echoes from the past it also reverberates into the future. For all his occasional clumsiness Roethke is a poet's poet. . . . [He was] a dominant influence on most of our recent mystical or oracular poets, poets of transcendent landscapes and magical transformations. (p. 267)

The rivers of [Roethke's] "North American Sequence" appear in such physical detail that we wonder at first whether physical description is the whole aim of the poetry. In a way it is; Roethke wants us to feel the objects in his poetry as he leads us to the revelations he will not always articulate, or cannot articulate, lacking . . . precision with abstract language.

If some critics have understood "North American Sequence" too much in terms of a traditional mystical opposition between spirit and matter, Roethke's imprecision is at least partly to blame. . . . Actually Roethke seeks an interpenetration of sense and spirit. "A body with the motion of a soul" . . . , the body fully itself with its own spiritual grace, immersed in the flow of being where "All finite things reveal infinitude." . . . Like Bly and Dickey, Roethke is an earthbound mystical poet, a champion of the senses. . . . Final knowledge is to be sensed, not spiritually intuited. In describing the end of the mystical progression in "The Far Field," Roethke suggests something like Eliot's "still point of the turning world"; but he does it with a realistic physical image: "I have come to a still, but not a deep center, / A point outside the glittering current." . . . (p. 273)

Roethke is not, however, always so firm in his resistance to that transcendence which implies separation from the physical. . . . Eliot may have intruded more upon his consciousness than he liked. Often, especially in his last poems, he seems to accept the tenets of Eliot's other-worldly mysticism, and the concomitant tendency toward abstraction, the use of purely symbolic terms to define a non-sensual state. But his abstractions lack the subtle force of Eliot's. In *Four Quartets* the image of the rose, though it lacks any real sensual referent, concentrates the force of the entire poem. When Roethke, in "The Rose," writes of "the rose in the sea-wind," the image not only derives too obviously from Eliot's symbol, it seems contrived and flat, an oddly dead flower in the otherwise beautifully vital sequence.

Roethke's problems with abstract language and symbolism cannot, of course, all be blamed on Eliot, who is too often held personally responsible for the academic excesses of modern American poetry. Roethke's tendency toward abstraction and symbolic overload appears even in the Williams-influenced flower poems of *The Lost Son*—for instance, "Cuttings (later)," which unlike the first "Cuttings" loses a rich suggestiveness when Roethke plugs it into theological concepts both trite and vague. Even without Eliot's influence, the temptation toward vitiating symbolism would probably have increased as Roethke's theological imagination became more complex, more pedantic. But he remained, partly because of Williams's influence, at least theoretically aware of the dangers of abstraction. (pp. 273-74)

Some of Roethke's finest lines can be as abstract as anything in Eliot. But in general he is less comfortable with logical argument than Eliot, a weakness especially evident in his final poetry, in the highly "lit'ry" and artificial language of the "Sequence, Sometimes Metaphysical" in *The Far Field*. Since his abstractions tend to accompany an uncharacteristic yearning for transcendence from the world of sense, it is hardly surprising to find Eliot's ultimate abstraction, "God," in much of this poetry. (pp. 274-75)

Despite his history of mental illness Roethke was not usually so much a manic depressive as such an orthodox mystic as St. John of the Cross, who experiences first the absolute despair of the dark night, then the sudden, absolute ecstasy of union. For Roethke, such a dichotomy, like the opposition between "God" and the world, could not convincingly be sustained. The imagery of his most effectively mystical poetry, poetry not of transcendence but of physical immersion, combined darkness and light in a union ambiguously beautiful; and it was that dark revelation which Roethke's poetic descendants had begun to explore even as he himself fell away from its difficult truths. (pp. 275-76)

When Roethke's final poems fail it is often because they seek—through abstract statement and the clichés of orthodoxy—too easy a resolution of his ambivalence toward the mystical experience. But the final abstractions of "In a Dark Time" are partly redeemed by its deeply resonant closing phrase, "free in the tearing wind.". . . Roethke explains this passage by saying that the mystical experience is "no moment in the rose garden," that "God himself, in his most supreme manifestation, risks being maimed, if not destroyed." The mystic who participates in the divine consciousness must suffer the same danger. This [is an] unusually contemporary version of mysticism, in

which dark night and ecstatic vision have become simultaneous, inextricable from each other. . . . Unlike the traditional transcendent mystic, the contemporary visionary often locates himself not in an imagined area of cosmic peace but at the center of a storm. This is Roethke's "steady storm of correspondences" but also the storm of irreducible particulars. The locus of vision is the point of maximum tension among all the world's dualities, the breaking point of a pattern constantly threatening to fly apart. The turmoil that characterizes Roethke's vision here anticipates Bly's plunge "Into the wilds of the universe" . . . or Plath's electroshock revelation in "Mystic": she is "Used, utterly, in the sun's conflagrations."

The imagery that attends such mystical experience is properly ambiguous, more dark than light. . . . Phrases like "dark water" occur throughout [poets such as Roethke, Bly, and Plath], and the idea of immersion in that water informs their mystic imaginations. . . . [Often], as in Roethke's "A Field of Light," it must be read as literal. In "dead water," under "a fine rain," the speaker falls into "a watery drowse.". . . Roethke characteristically uses such terms to describe his gentler visionary states. Though the end of "Field" announces a vision not of unity but of "the separateness of all things," the description carries an overriding sense of union: "I moved with the morning." Variants of this line (like "I rock with the motion of morning" . . .) occur frequently in Roethke. . . . (pp. 276-77)

Often the solid world is imagined wholly as water. . . . But the sense of earth in watery flux is not always soothing, especially when the poet confronts the final implications of unifying immersion. (p. 277)

Throughout "North American Sequence" water that does not already surround the poet threatens and promises to submerge him, as he correspondingly internalizes it; in "The Far Field," as the water approaches the poet feels within himself "a weightless change, a moving forward / As of water quickening before a narrowing channel," and there follows the meditation on the "thought of my death."

This immersion, the flow into water or into earth, "flying like a bat deep into a narrowing tunnel" . . . implies a new mysticism, one opposed to the mysticism of transcendence not only because it is described in immediately physical terms and because it suggests a deep ambivalence in its imagery of darkness and its more literal suggestions of death. Because the water which receives the poet has usually become internalized, the image of movement into watery darkness also suggests, unlike images of transcendence, a movement into the depths of the self, and "down into the consciousness of the race.". . . (pp. 278-79)

Jung's influence on Roethke has been misunderstood, or understood too much in terms of logical dualities by critics who emphasize the orthodox aspects of Roethke's mysticism. . . . Except in his last and most theologically conventional poems Roethke seldom falls into . . . simple progressions. Because he tends to discover a paradoxical light within the darkness, not beyond it, his poetry, like Bly's and Dickey's, constantly involves images of dark light, "bright shade," "shimmering" illuminations in shadow. Like Plath and Bly, Roethke's favorite light seems to be the shimmering moon, as coldly dark as it is light. (pp. 279-80)

Sometimes stones are made animate, like the laughing stones in "A Field of Light," but more often stones remain stones, dead but paradoxically heavy with spiritual resonance. Confronting this lithic preoccupation, critics tend to discover death wishes in Roethke as well as Plath. But to identify with stones is not necessarily escapist or self-destructive; it can be the logical end of a particularly visceral sort of mysticism, mysticism which depends on physically experiencing spiritual abstractions. Though the lithic experience seems as close to the experience of unchanging timelessness as the resolutely earthbound poet can come, at the same time stones, especially Roethke's and Plath's stream-washed stones, are physically part of the constant flow of matter, dissolving and dissolving in accord with the earth's deepest reverberations. . . .

[Stones] form part of a constellation of images (often surrealist) of darkness, dim moons, water, death, and transformation. (p. 280)

Roethke's women often play a mythic and implicitly mystical role. . . . [But they] often seem ill-suited to the task of guarding dark secrets. Rather than being powerful they appear childishly vulnerable, soft and furry like the baby animals and plump birds which quiver about them. Though some of Roethke's love poems are evident triumphs, many, especially toward the end, degenerate into pop love-song cliché, frequently involving the wind. As his words go limp, heavily precious sentimentalism takes over. Like the "essayistic" language of much of the philosophical poetry, here sentimental language creates the effect of excessive abstraction; the vitality of individual experience becomes lost in generalizing triteness. It remains fairly clear . . . [that] Roethke uses women—as he uses animals in his meditations—as "mediators" in his journey to the spiritual heart of nature. But to succeed in this aim—even disregarding the idea that women may be less appropriate for such an instrumental role than animals—requires more control of tone, and more psychological self-assurance, than Roethke usually possesses.

The second stanza of "The Pure Fury," which could be offered in evidence of the awkwardness of Roethke's philosophical abstractions, also exemplifies the inadequacy of his abstract women, though here the problem is not exactly sentimentality. . . . [The] woman described in this poem [has been called] an anima figure, but she seems too foolish and insignificant for that rather heavy role, more stereotype than archetype. . . . (pp. 281-82)

Perhaps inevitably, Roethke's most forceful and enlightened woman is not the figure of a lover but an intelligent mother-figure. "Meditations of an Old Woman" not only contains an attack (in "Fourth Meditation") on spiritually pretentious clichés about women but it creates a clearly female being who is fully individuated and as human as Roethke. . . . She is a convincing representation, partly because not simply archetypal, of a basic female force that Roethke successfully evokes in few of his poems. . . . Reduced to archetype, this woman is related to the fulfilling natural force Roethke will later seek in "North American Sequence" where, as W. D. Snodgrass has written, the final aim is entry "into water as woman, into earth as goddess-mother." The actual means of that entry remain ambiguous; as "Enshroud" and "Terrible" suggest, Roethke's female is as potentially ominous as she is enlightening, when he confronts her fully. In this respect she resembles Bly's women who guard the secrets of dark waters under the earth, the Great Mothers whose current violent

reappearance in our racial psyche he describes at length in his essay "I Came Out of the Mother Naked." (pp. 282-83)

Roethke could not, of course, be expected to travel so far into [the] surrealist vision [as Bly and Plath]. . . . His unique value lies partly in his ability to develop much of the poetic and spiritual vocabulary they have carried further and to articulate the vision at a time when it seemed far more eccentric than it seems now. That vision—the animism, the "body consciousness," the particularly corporeal approach to mystical contact, with the evolutionary and apocalyptic imagery that logically follows—has become almost commonplace in poetry now. This happens not entirely because of Roethke's influence; the vision is at least in its large outlines collective; fragments of it keep turning up. . . . In the darkness beneath the waters Roethke saw something extensive enough to touch us all, something ancient that calls forth terror and ecstasy, but something at the same time new, and newly come to the deep dreams of our deepest poets. (pp. 287-88)

> *Anthony Libby, "Roethke, Water Father," in* American Literature *(reprinted by permission of the Publisher; copyright 1974 by Duke University Press, Durham, North Carolina), November, 1974, pp. 267-88.*

C. E. NICHOLSON and W. H. WASILEWSKI

A pervasive interest in the poetry of Theodore Roethke is that man creates the world he perceives, hence Roethke accepts as axiomatic the reciprocity between the external, perceptible, world and the faculties of the human mind. "Interlude" develops this theme while offering a comment on the creative process itself.

In the opening three lines of the poem, Roethke presents a vitalistic conception of nature, alluding unobtrusively to the physical properties of man by introducing the term "hand" in a colloquial phrase. A familiar referent describing the uncontrollability of "air," "hand" is among the indices of meaning providing an interpretation for "the rush of wind." . . . Since the verbs imply violence, injury and disarrangement ("tender leaves" are despoiled, "confusion" exists), what emerges is an anthropomorphic image of the wind, the wind according to the demands of his individual perception, encourages the reader to understand an external force within the context of human nature. His reason for doing so becomes clear in the remainder of the poem.

Foreground established, Roethke introduces the poem's *characters*. "He waited for the first rain in the eaves." Central to an understanding of the piece, the "we" eludes explicit identification and might be approached more profitably as a strategy; for it is an attempt to depict man (generically, the poet specifically) confronting the energizing forces of nature, perceiving the disparate elements of reality and finally seeking to harmonize his view by forming a Gestalt. Thus, at the end of the first stanza, the reader sees man posed in expectation "for the first rain"—man, who has been both observer and participant in the diaphanous interval between order and "confusion" awaits the ensuing storm so that he may continue translating nature's performance into poetic form.

The tempest increases in intensity. . . . Despite the dangers inherent in the upheaval, the poet-*seer* desires it to continue, for this is both dynamizing agent and raw material for his poem. Expectation becomes muted however, as the poem observes that the moment is passing. . . .

The wind lay motionless in the long grass.
The veins within our hands betrayed our fear.

(pp. 26-7)

Invested with human qualities, functioning as a violent instrument transforming the world from order with "confusion," [the wind] now lies still, corpselike. . . .

There is [a] significant reason for the expression of "fear." Namely, it is the poet's cry for the loss of the wind as a source of poetic inspiration. Expectation defeated, the *interlude* of revelation passed, Roethke ends his poem—the closure itself serving as a final tribute to the creative function of the wind. (p. 27)

C. E. Nicholson and W. H. Wasilewski, in The Explicator *(copyright © 1978 by Helen Dwight Reid Educational Foundation), Spring, 1978.*

*   *   *

ROTH, Henry   1906-

Roth, an American novelist and short story writer, is known primarily for his only novel, *Call It Sleep*. The book is generally considered a modern American classic, though it was widely ignored when it first appeared in 1934. A naturalistic novel about the early life of a young immigrant Jew, it is one of the most intensely realized visions of a child's view of a fearsome world ever written. Roth has virtually abandoned writing since *Call It Sleep*, producing only a handful of stories for magazines. (See also *CLC*, Vols. 2, 6, and *Contemporary Authors*, Vols. 11-12; *Contemporary Authors Permanent Series*, Vol. 1.)

WALTER ALLEN

The 'thirties, in America even more than in England, was the period of socially conscious fiction and of much theorizing about what was called the proletarian novel. Inevitably, *Call It Sleep* was seen as an attempt at a proletarian novel; or it was judged that it would have been a better book if it had been a proletarian novel. . . . (p. 443)

Call It Sleep must be the most powerful evocation of the terrors of childhood ever written. Lost, bewildered, friendless, the small boy David scuttles through the streets of the Lower East Side like a frightened little animal lost in a jungle inhabited by the larger carnivores. We are spared nothing of the crudeness of cosmopolitan slum life and living. . . . And all the terrors the boy experiences in the streets of New York are brought together, symbolized, in his fear of the tenement houses in which he lives, the dark, rat-infested cellars with their overwhelming suggestion of mindless and brutal animality, the sweating stairways to be tremblingly climbed to the topmost apartment, which means warmth and security because his mother is there, and, finally, the roof above, the escape to which is freedom.

Yet though the squalor and filth, the hopelessness and helplessness of slum-life are remorselessly presented and the cacophony never ceases—this must be the *noisiest* novel ever written—*Call It Sleep* does not strike one as primarily a novel of social protest, an exposure novel, like Farrell's *Studs Lonigan*, to which many reviewers of the first edition compared it. . . . Indeed, there is a sense in which the Schearls are in the slums but not of them. Roth shows this beautifully in his dialogue. He renders with what seems quite horrible fidelity the mutilations of English as spoken by the immigrant slum-dwellers, Jewish, Hungarian, Italian, Irish alike. . . . David, too, speaks like this when he is speaking English—but not when he is at home with his parents, talking in Yiddish. Then he, and they, speak a remarkably pure English, the English of people of cultivation; and we see them in a wholly new light. In this way, Roth makes us sharply aware, as no other novelist except Willa Cather has done, in a book like *My Antonia*, of the degradation, the diminution in human dignity, that was one aspect of the immigrant's lot as he moved from a society with a traditional culture to another with no culture at all. (pp. 444-45)

There is another obvious difference between this novel and the American novels of social protest of the 'thirties, of which *Studs Lonigan* may be taken as representative. In those novels, the characters strike one as being wholly conditioned by their economic and cultural circumstances; they are almost excretions of their environment. This is anything but true of Roth's characters. Despite the conditions in which they live, they are dominating figures. . . .

But the real center of the novel is the boy David, and Roth seems to me to plunge us into a child's mind more directly and more intransigently than any other novelist has done. We experience the child's instantaneous apprehension of his world. Roth captures, too, better, I think, than it has ever been done in English before, what might be called a child's magical thinking, which is closely allied to the thinking of the poet. With David, we are a long way from either Tom Sawyer or the boy Studs Lonigan; his world is not that of simple fantasy or make-believe but one he creates with the desperate, compulsive imagination of the poet. (p. 446)

[To] have written *Call It Sleep* is itself enough to make any man's reputation. In it, Roth shows himself a master of the novelist's art, a master of sympathy, humor, detachment and deep poetic insight into the immigrant's lot and into the mind of childhood. Place, time and people are alike uniquely and unforgettably evoked, so that to read *Call It Sleep* is to live it. (p. 447)

Walter Allen, in his afterword to Call It Sleep *by Henry Roth (reprinted by permission of Michael Joseph Ltd.), Avon Books, 1964, pp. 442-47.*

WILLIAM FREEDMAN

Call It Sleep is the kind of book one feels a bit reluctant to write about, at least to "criticize," in the icy sense of that term. To criticize, to analyze, is in a sense to freeze, and Henry Roth's great and only novel becomes too much a part of one's immediate and intimate experience for that. It is, of course, the very personal quality of the book that assured its consignment to obscurity during the golden age of the proletarian novel. Though *Call It Sleep* may be such a work in the sense that it deals with a working-class Jewish immigrant family in Brownsville (and the Lower East Side of New York) shortly after the turn of the century, it is a book about very particular and very painfully real people with very particular and real problems, fears and guilts. (p. 107)

This may mean that the novel offers us no patentable answer to the sufferings of David and his parents, but it does bring us into contact with them as identifiable human beings and establishes an intimacy that I, for one, have too rarely enjoyed in the reading of fiction. (pp. 107-08)

Autobiographical though the book may be, it is first of all the product of a highly gifted, creative, literary imagination, and the fact that it was the only sustained achievement of what surely must have seemed an inexhaustible literary mind is every reader's loss. . . . Perhaps one of the reasons for its premature exhaustion was its overexertion in this one great work, for in *Call It Sleep* Roth has produced a literary *tour de force*. He has framed with rare success a story of profound social and psychological realism in a mythopoeic outline of symbolic death, redemption and rebirth and rendered both through a subtly complex and symbolic system of light and dark imagery. (pp. 109-10)

Roth's novel takes us through an agonizing two-year period in the life of young David Schearl—from his sixth to his eighth years—and relives for us the world of his daily experience, a world beset by unsubsiding fears and recurrent attacks of guilt. David has a compelling need to belong, yet he is withdrawn into the frightened confines of his own painfully vivid imagination. He is alienated from his peers; rejected by his father; and petrified by the normal sexual experiences of childhood, his father's seething violence, the prospect of retribution for his guilt (both real and imagined), the largeness and chaos of his physical world, and above all the dark. It is the dark that comes to symbolize all that is ugly and intolerable in David's experience, all that threatens him and from which he seeks to escape. It first and most saliently looms before him in the specter of the cellar. . . . (p. 110)

The cellar not only crystallizes all his childhood fears in one horrifying symbol: it, or rather a different cellar, is also the scene of his last and greatest guilt. It is the place to which he leads his revered friend and stands sentry while Leo "plays bad" with his cousin.

But darkness is characteristic of more than merely cellars. It is also what David most acutely senses and best remembers about the closet in which he is invited to indulge in lewd sex play by the crippled girl upstairs. And it is also the identifying feature of his despised father, his "dark face," his "black hair," "ink-black hand," "dull black shoe," black milk-wagon horse, and his black whip. Gradually the quality of darkness spreads like an inky stain over David's imagination and comes to stand for everything that threatens him—not only the cellar, the closet, and his father, but Luter, the man who attempts to seduce his mother, sex, sin, guilt, death, and even the devil himself. (pp. 110-11)

Naturally enough, light is David's salvation, and like its antithesis it is an expanding symbol which characterizes and eventually comes to stand—in the boy's mind and in the reader's—for everything that is redemptive, everything that offers reprieve, however brief, from the torments of darkness. . . . [Most] significantly it is the light of God in a variety of transforming manifestations, the source of purification, redemption, and salvation. (p. 111)

The book to which *Call It Sleep* is perhaps most frequently compared is Joyce's *Portrait of the Artist,* but the comparison is more apt than is realized by those who make it. For in a very real sense these moments of mystical transformation, of blinding radiance, are moments of imaginative transcendence, experiences through which David momentarily transcends the chaos of his physical universe. Only after such experiences as these is he able to order and deal with his world and accept it for what it otherwise too painfully is. (p. 112)

Light must be found in the midst of darkness. The imagination does not literally create, it transforms, and what it transforms are the very materials which Roth has transfigured in *Call It Sleep*—the fears, the anguish, the pain, and the ugliness of life—here a young boy's life on the Lower East Side. The important point, though, is that Roth has transfigured his raw materials without distorting them out of recognizable shape. For the myths of redemption and rebirth are implicit in the story of David Schearl, and both are rendered largely by means of a symbolic image pattern that is part of David's own conscious awareness and that is viewed symbolically by his own fertile imagination as well as by the reader. Such a fusion of myth, symbol, and profound realism does more than raise *Call It Sleep* far beyond the level of most of the proletarian fiction that once obscured it. It makes Roth's novel one of those too rare works of fiction that we can both live and admire, simultaneously. (p. 114)

> William Freedman, "Henry Roth and the Redemptive Imagination," in The Thirties: Fiction, Poetry, Drama, *edited by Warren French (copyright © 1967 by Warren French), Everett Edwards, Inc., 1967, pp. 107-14.*

TOM SAMET

[There has] been nearly unanimous agreement among critics that the . . . closing episodes [of *Call It Sleep*] witness a radical transfiguration of David Schearl. Whether the terms of the [protagonist's] conflict are defined as political, psychological, or religious, all of Roth's interpreters argue that *Call It Sleep* traces a movement from terror and alienation to tranquility and reconciliation. (p. 569)

The terms recur again and again [in the interpretations]: redemption, reconciliation, salvation, vision, transcendence. . . . [I would like to suggest that] David's moments of illumination are essentially bogus—images of betrayal rather than of salvation. And the tranquility which he wins from terror is something far more marginal, tentative, and equivocal than has generally been recognized. Dazzled by Roth's verbal fireworks, much as David is dazed by the light from the car tracks, most critics have failed to understand David's actual domestic predicament and the defined dramatic action of the novel's ending. It is, after all, "only toward sleep" that David can extract coherence from the chaotic nightmare of his waking world; it is only in the numbed withdrawal, the fuzzy half-consciousness of sleep that terror is held at bay. The question nags; if the critics call it redemption, why does Roth call it sleep?

The world of Roth's novel is curiously insular. The Schearls are immigrant Jews and the people among whom they live are immigrant Jews. Their alienation is so extreme that they have no clear conception of the forbidden and forbidding world from which they are alienated. The society that surrounds them is hostile—that much they understand—and David's few thrusts into alien territory result in experiences of confusion and pain. Inhabitants of a kind of cultural island, Roth's Jews have their own religion, their own teachers, their own tenements, their own language—all of which isolate them from the world which encircles but rarely touches them. They are walled-in and American life is walled-out. (p. 570)

This quality of cultural introversion is one of the remarkable aspects of *Call It Sleep*. From an urban Jew writing in the thirties one might reasonably expect a bitter examination of the failures of American life, a harsh judgment upon the seductive land which had promised so much and delivered so little. Some such judgment is surely implicit in the bleak ghetto landscape against which the action is set. . . . But the indictment of American life is never *more* than implicit. Roth's social judgments are hidden because, in a very real sense, the society that he is judging is hidden—concealed largely beyond the view of David Schearl, through whose consciousness the world of the novel is created. The central focus of *Call It Sleep* is not upon the "Golden Land"; nor is it upon that social frontier where the alien and impotent encounter the entrenched and powerful, where the drama of failure is acted out. The novel is concerned instead with the radically estranged, and with the permanently separate world in which they live. (p. 571)

[The] domestic world to which David flees is as terrible and menacing as the world outside, and a novel that begins with a child's persistent need to find in his home a refuge from the streets, ends with his desperate flight to the streets from the terrors of home. (pp. 571-72)

Threatened by the world outside and the world within, David is paralyzed. Fear and guilt are the major components of his experience. . . . David is terrorized by his father, who seems to him an omnipotent and inexplicably malign God: "Who could answer his father? In that dread summons the judgement was already sealed." . . . Albert Schearl (unlike Kafka's confident and successful father) is a man profoundly alienated from family and society, driven by guilt and suspicion, who projects his own sin onto his son. Posed against the menacing father, and completing the Oedipal triangle, is the soft, yeilding, protective Genya: "The comfort of being against her breast outstripped the farthest-flung pain." . . . (p. 572)

To some extent the relationship between Albert and David is corollary to the father's social predicament. What I have said concerning the cultural isolation of the Schearls applies more fully to David and Genya than to Albert, whose position as head of the family forces him to function—and malfunction—in the larger world outside. In this world he is an eternal alien, and his life is an endless series of abrasions. He has no friends and cannot hold a job. . . . Contrasting with the perpetual friction of his experience in urban America is the idealized memory of life on the Austrian farm. . . . For Albert Schearl the price of existence in industrial America is nothing less than a total loss of personal identity. He is tormented by the imagined coherence of the life which he has abandoned and by the radical discontinuity between domestic and commercial life in the New World. (pp. 572-73)

Schearl's private sense of persecution mirrors a larger historical situation. The humiliations which he suffers in his journey from an Austrian farm to an American printing-shop correspond to the humiliations of modern man in his migration from farm to factory. Ultimately, of course, it is David who is the victim of his father's bitterness and alienation. What the father suffers in real and imagined indignity, the child suffers in physical and emotional cruelty. Impotent in society, the father becomes an omnipotent tyrant in the home; society's abused child turns that abuse against his own son. (p. 573)

Knowing of [his] parricide, we are compelled to view Al-

bert less as a victim of social alienation than as the unconscious creator of his own defeats, a man whose sense of persecution . . . betrays a terrible need to be punished. More importantly, the story of the parricide helps to illuminate the complex relationship between Albert and David, to explain not only the tyranny and terror which David must confront, but also the terms of his struggle for salvation. (p. 576)

In persecuting his son, Albert inflicts upon David the punishment for his own crime of parricide.

The belief that David is not his son releases Albert from the fear of retribution by removing the imagined instrument of that retribution. . . . It is one of the moving ironies of *Call It Sleep* that only in their complementary fantasies—of childlessness and of fatherlessness—can Albert and David Schearl approach one another. David's imagined escape from the anguish of identity prefigures the retreat into sleep which alone can appease the cruel contradictions of his world.

The trouble with David's fantasy is that it offers no permanent refuge from terror. He cannot be "somebody else" forever. Those critics, therefore, who find in the novel an achieved serenity, a completed pattern of reconciliation, have invariably emphasized David's visionary imagination, his essentially religious nature, and a series of "mystical experiences" which he undergoes. . . . And according to most critics it is in the blurred half-consciousness which follows David's second experience of the streetcar's subterranean light that he achieves the vision which unifies, reconciles, redeems. (pp. 577-78)

Certainly it is true that David is granted a vision—a vision which brings into kaleidoscopic conjunction his fears, his sense of God, and the cacophony of the streets. But that David is reconciled or redeemed by the experience seems to me doubtful. David confuses the current of the car tracks with the purging coal of Isaiah, but there is no reason to conclude that Roth is guilty of the same confusion. At the end of the novel the electric rail remains what it has always been—not a source of divine or visionary power, but an electric rail. And David, first duped into shoving metal between the tracks by the threats of a gang of gentile thugs, by the mocking promise that he will see "all de angels" . . . , is once more betrayed by an alien and hostile world.

Each of David's earlier ventures into that world had ended in disaster. . . . In this world of decayed houses and supple confusions, unnatural vices and impudent crimes, this world where beauty is lost in terror, it is hardly surprising that signs are taken for wonders.

According to one critic, *Call It Sleep* "belongs in the company of the great *Bildungsroman*," and perhaps in some narrow sense this is true. Certainly David's consciousness responds to his world and grows through his experience. . . . At the end of *Call It Sleep*, however, David is carried by a policeman up the dark stairs to his home. The presence of the policeman—authority symbol of an alien society—underlines the fraudulence of David's experience at the streetcar tracks. . . . David is not, after all, a young man entering adulthood, but a child of eight. . . . (pp. 578-80)

David does indeed move chaotically *toward* maturity, but

that maturity lies far beyond the time of the novel. And although it is true, as [has been pointed] out, that the milk ladle thrust between the lips of the streetcar tracks is a sexually charged image, that image does not represent David's experience or acceptance of adult sexuality. What kind of maturity—what kind of manhood—one must finally ask, is possible for an eight-year-old boy? Whatever tranquility David has achieved, whatever truce he has made with terror, he must still resolve the complicated anxieties of adolescence. We are told that David seeks "some sign, some seal that would forever relieve him of watchfulness and forever insure his well-being." . . . Far from affirming the validity of David's mystical moment, this merely reminds us that he is still a child. Such wishes are infantile fantasy; there are no magical signs or seals; the painful struggle against "the dark and his father" cannot be won with such tokens.

By the end of *Call It Sleep* a good many changes have taken place. Albert is subdued and ashamed in the novel's final scene, and he can now accept as his own the son whom he had earlier rejected. . . . David is at last able to feel "a vague, remote pity" . . . for his father. These are significant achievements, genuine victories won through

suffering. But no shame can purge Albert of his guilt, and no pity can release David from the long struggle for selfhood which still confronts him. Indeed, there is something mildly disturbing about David's "strangest triumph, strangest acquiescence" . . . as if acquiescence were the condition of his curious and compromised triumph. *Call It Sleep* witnesses neither transfiguration nor redemption, but strategic retreat. The electric current, the bogus vision, cannot alter the permanent facts of David's intractable world. In the end he is carried home . . . to the parents with whom he must continue to struggle for survival and salvation. David remains trapped between the dark outside and his father within. For the moment there is only sleep to knit up the ravelled sleeve of care, to offer refuge from cruelty and confusion. (pp. 580-81)

Tom Samet, "Henry Roth's Bull Story: Guilt and Betrayal in 'Call It Sleep'," in Studies in the Novel, *Winter, 1975, pp. 569-83.*

*   *   *

RUIZ, José Martínez
See AZORÍN

S

SCHAEFFER, Susan Fromberg   1941-

Schaeffer is an American novelist, poet, and critic. (See also CLC, Vol. 6, and Contemporary Authors, Vols. 49-52.)

JOSEPH PARISI

Susan Fromberg Schaeffer is that rarity: a fine novelist *and* poet. Where others pad slim and fragile volumes with material better kept from a candid world, this prolific author fills a 144-page book in which each poem exemplifies intelligence heightened and transmitted through vivid imagination, brilliant imagery, and remarkable formal integrity. How she can sustain such power, poem after poem, makes one marvel at her craft. *Granite Lady* comprises an immense range of subjects in an exceptional variety of treatments. She dramatizes growing up with fear, from the child's point-of-view; growing old and the state of senility; the quiet horrors of death, before and after the grave; the terrors of loss, impermanence, dislocation; natural disasters and psychic convulsions; and the miscellaneous griefs that callousness and neglect provoke. Her recurring theme is survival in the face of seemingly insurmountable odds. Her method: the odd perspective, the unexpected angle of vision, the hallucinatory fantasy, the fairy tale bent to sinister degrees. These poems force us to live the traumata of her characters' lives and often to relive our own.

Under the heading of "Glimmerings", a series of poems presents vignettes of childhood. Worlds but vaguely remembered by the adult spring instantly back from memory into life. In this uncharming nursery-tale atmosphere, the inanimate is always alive. . . . (pp. 239-40)

Other poems are deliberately confusing at first to convey the frightening aspects of the Brobdingnagian universe confronting the most sensitive young. In *The Mother's Curses,* the fears and insecurities are handed down through the generations, despite attempts to break the crippling pattern. . . . Another section, "Lightning Storm", turns to the marriage hearse. The highly original *Spat* describes blow by blow a quarrel using a fantastic jewelry-box metaphor. The *Housewife* finds herself in a frustrating replay of youth. Father is replaced by husband, and through an inversion and "shrinkage" her home has become like her girlhood dollhouse, only now the children "play with us / Like dolls." She asks: "Do others feel like this? Where do they go?" *The First Madam,* the enigmatic treatment of a

Freudian case history in *The Picture: Wolves in the Tree,* and several of the other poems are beyond paraphrase, and probably outside mere rational consideration. But the words, even when meaning is ambiguous and obscure, still have an unsettling, evocative force. . . . [These] poems do so much at once, they won't be pinned down. Their complexity of motion, wild inversions, shifts in tone and emotional configuration, subtlety of nuance, and rich associative progressions must be experienced. They continue to give up new meanings, provoke different feelings with each re-reading.

In short, what I'm trying to say is: Susan Fromberg Schaeffer is a *poet.* And *Granite Lady* is an extraordinary achievement. (p. 241)

> *Joseph Parisi, in* Poetry (© *by The Modern Poetry Association; reprinted by permission of the Editor of* Poetry), *July, 1975.*

CAROL J. ALLEN

[*Alphabet for the Lost Years*] has two distinct parts although formally there are three sections in the volume. The first and more successful contains meditations on objects and emotions from the Arch to the Zzz of bees and sleepers. The focus on abstractions gives this alphabet an intellectual detachment that mutes the "cry of the human" heard in much contemporary poetry. No first-person pronouns here, and yet there is a mind at work and anguish, however disguised, in poems on Dementia, Hate, Jealousy. . . . The language is spare, the short lines grouped in couplets or triplets. But their control is balanced and occasionally upset by dependence on sound effects. . . . The second half of the book collects more personal poems. Perhaps the most successful is "Tulips, Again." Here Schaeffer plays with various metaphors of shape . . . much as she does in the alphabet poems, but with less detachment. Her last lines skillfully bring together the variations with a typical use of repetition. . . . Though in general the second half of the volume is less provocative than the first, "Tulips, Again" combines the playful and the serious in a manner characteristic of Schaeffer's best poems. (p. 319)

> *Carol J. Allen, in* Prairie Schooner (© *1977 by University of Nebraska Press; reprinted by permission from* Prairie Schooner), *Fall, 1977.*

LYNNE SHARON SCHWARTZ

Time in Its Flight is built around the marriage of Edna, a spirited Boston teen-ager of quite original attitudes, and the morose but passionate John Steele, a dedicated Vermont country doctor.

Set in the latter half of the past century, the book is a chronicle of the burgeoning Steele family in its passages through joy and adversity, births, illnesses, and death, with accompanying probes into the meaning of time, change, mortality, and other imponderables. When these large themes are embodied in action or event, the results are admirable, but they are too often pursued in an expository, didactic manner.

Schaeffer has a teeming imagination, and scatters ideas, anecdotes, and descriptions with a prodigal hand (the portrayal of nineteenth-century New England rural life is in fact educational, offering meticulous details about domestic customs, farm lore, fads, superstitions, tidbits from magazines and newspapers); unfortunately, only a portion of these contribute to any formal design or movement. Similarly, Schaeffer's attempt to render a photographic reality of affectionate family life (children underfoot, pancakes sizzling) yields tedium. When Schaeffer is not patronizing her characters or reminding the reader how lovable they are in all their quirkiness, her writing can be taut and vigorous. . . . (p. 35)

> *Lynne Sharon Schwartz, in* Saturday Review *(© 1978 by Saturday Review Magazine Corp.; reprinted with permission), June 24, 1978.*

WEBSTER SCHOTT

"Time in Its Flight" illustrates Tolstoy's idea about happy families. They are boring.

Not that Susan Fromberg Schaeffer intends it. She livens things up with epidemics, marriages, a suicide by hanging, insanity, a murder trial, philosophy via daguerreotypes, reports of the American Civil War and 20 or 30 deaths. None of this helps much. Mrs. Schaeffer, who did better with "Anya" and "Falling," is a prisoner of her romantic fatalism. . . .

"Time in Its Flight" will satisfy if you need to kill time or want to know how the rural rich once lived in America. But it's a poor intellectual companion. It's capriciously organized and confusing without purpose. Susan Schaeffer's heroes speculate sophomorically about time and opposites, and the author worries as much about costumes as she does about the people inside them. Her characters are incidental to their environment. Her most vivid scene has John and Edna contemplating their losses after their children have departed. "Time in Its Flight" cries for such moments of insight. It's usually panorama and chatter.

> *Webster Schott, "Happy Family," in* The New York Times Book Review *(© 1978 by The New York Times Company; reprinted by permission), August 13, 1978, p. 34.*

*   *   *

SEFERIADES, Giorgos Stylianou
  See SEFERIS, George
*   *   *

SEFERIS, George (pseudonym of Giorgos Stylianou Seferiades; also transliterated as Georgios Stylianou Seferiadis)   1900-1971

Seferis, a Nobel Prize-winning Greek poet, was also a distin-

guished translator and critic. Seferis combined Greek mythology with modern poetic techniques and is generally credited with the renovation of twentieth-century Greek poetry. His work has been likened to the Symbolists, who were early influences. Odysseus is a recurring image in his work, that eternal wanderer being Seferis's symbol of spiritually dispossessed modern man. (See also *CLC*, Vol. 5, and *Contemporary Authors*, Vols. 5-8, rev. ed.; obituary, Vols. 33-36, rev. ed.)

EDMUND KEELEY

[The funeral of George Seferis] proved to be a more or less spontaneous public event, not to say political demonstration, of a kind normally reserved in Greece for the passing of popular prime ministers illegally out of office. The drama and symbolism of it—thousands of young people raising the victory sign at the poet's grave, shouting "immortal", "freedom", "elections", and singing an early Seferis lyric . . . would surely have surprised the poet himself even more than it may have surprised his readers in England and America. Less than three years before his death . . . , Seferis declared, in one of the few interviews he allowed to appear in print:

> I am sorry to say that I never felt I was the spokesman for anything or anybody. . . . I've never felt the obligation. . . . Others think they are the voices of the country. All right. God bless them. . . .

When Seferis published a volume of poems dedicated to the people of Cyprus in 1955—his first volume since the death of Sikelianos—critics in Greece, quick to dress him in the mantle of national poet, either celebrated the publication as an eloquent defence of Greek interests in the Cyprus dispute or criticised the poet for beginning to write what was understood to be propaganda in verse form. The new volume was, in fact, typical of the kind of poetry that Seferis had been writing since the middle 1930s and especially during World War II, "political" poetry only in the broadest sense of the term: a persona brooding over the *"new idiocies of men/or of the gods"* that had brought on renewed suffering, fearful always that he is *"fated to hear newsbearers coming to tell him"* that the latest war is *"all for an empty tunic, all for a Helen"* (as he puts it in his 1955 poem alluding to Euripides' heroine). The persona of the Cyprus volume is much the same as that of "The Last Stop", written ten years earlier, at the end of World War II, just as the poet was returning to Greece from Italy after his long service with the Greek Government-in-exile. . . . (p. 37)

What the critics of the Cyprus volume failed to recognise was that the poet had succeeded in transcending propaganda—and anything approaching it—by taking the same large view, by giving expression to the same mythologising sensibility that had characterised his vision of the contemporary predicament (including that of his own nation) since *Mythistorima*, the 1935 volume of mythologised history that had established his as the most important new voice in Greek letters. It was understandable that the narrow response to the Cyprus volume might irritate the poet enough to make him dismiss any sort of public role for the kind of poet he chose to be. At the same time Seferis remained Greek through to his bones. [He] continued to be a "national" poet in his capacity for dramatising personal preoccupations in those terms that help to define the enduring qualities of his nation, for example, its landscape, its legends, its demotic traditions in literature. (pp. 37-8)

Seferis's irritation regarding the public role he was supposed to play became acute after the Nobel Prize award of 1963 moved him on to an international stage. He was now not only poet laureate, but the first Greek Nobel laureate of any kind, with a fame that quickly spread far beyond national boundaries. And if those of his countrymen who never read poetry sometimes confused him with a Greek soccer star of similar name and renown, many of those who knew better began to look to him for the sort of prophetic leadership that nobody else was providing. . . . But whatever Seferis's private sentiments, he remained adamant at first about avoiding public pronouncements. (p. 38)

If the official attitude towards Seferis in the months following his statement [against the régime, March, 1969,] was essentially one of pretending that he was too senile to be taken seriously, the attitude of intellectual circles in Athens, from students to fellow writers, was one of homage that soon approached adoration. "The Poet" became "Our Poet." It was not merely that Seferis had finally acceded with full heart to his expected role of laureate-spokesman, but as the first independent man of mind with the courage to speak out on an international stage against the régime and the drift of its ambitions, he served to free others with less opportunity for courage and a smaller platform. The immediate result of his influence was the coming together of a group of writers, with disparate political affiliations but a common distaste for the Junta, a rather motley but nevertheless committed intellectual underground that produced a strong anti-régime statement supporting Seferis's position, and, eventually, a volume of anti-régime stories, poems, and essays entitled *Eighteen Texts,* with the lead contribution Seferis's latest poem, "The Cats of St. Nicholas." . . .

[An effect of the volume was] to put Seferis at the centre of opposition to the régime's control over the intellectual life of the country, to make him gradually the unacknowledged leader of dispossessed students and the silent voice of those with no public outlet for their own brooding sense of injustice—until the feeling he had engendered found an ultimate release in the surprises of his funeral. (p. 40)

> *Edmund Keeley, in* Encounter *(© 1972 by Encounter Ltd.), March, 1972.*

A writer like Seferis may suffer in a minority language many disadvantages in his lifetime, but, if he is a great writer, as Seferis was, surely he puts the rest of the world at a disadvantage until it learns that language. Meanwhile, we must do what we can with the devices of translation and literary gossip. It is worth noticing that the harmonious rumble of his prose is almost as difficult to reproduce in English as his poetry.

> *"Poet on a Pony," in* The Times Literary Supplement *(© Times Newspapers, Ltd. (London) 1974; reproduced from* The Times Literary Supplement *by permission), January 4, 1974, p. 4.*

WALTER KAISER

[The publication of this translation of *A Poet's Journal: Days of 1945-1951*] represents an act of personal homage on the part of each of us to one of this century's greatest poets and most civilized men. (pp. vii-viii)

[No] one, under whatever circumstances, can fail to be moved by the intimacy and intensity of these journal entries, which take us so completely into the heart and mind of the poet and his creative act, in a way that few other such documents do. There are other great literary journals in this century—Gide's, Woolf's, Camus's, Pavese's—and there are also collections of letters which help us better to understand an author. But I cannot think of many which expose quite so clearly the naked thought and sensibility out of which poems have grown. Generally, the closest we seem to get to the genesis of literary works is in documents such as the canceled version of *The Waste Land.* This journal, however, reveals to us the deep inner sources of Seferis's poetic achievement. It possesses that candor of revelation and that rare numinous quality which we associate with James's notebooks and the letters of Keats and Rilke. (p. viii)

With [his title], Seferis joins hands with, and pays tribute to, the greatest of his predecessors in modern Greek literature, Constantine Cavafy, a number of whose most personal and powerful poems begin with the same title, though of course with different dates. And indeed, if any spirit haunts these pages, it is that of Cavafy—Cavafy the European, Cavafy the Greek, the lonely exile, the skeptical political observer, the chronicler of history, the forger of language, the celebrant of love, the man of memories, the witness and martyr (in his tongue the same word signifies both) of the decline of Greek civilization.

Seferis's journal, or more precisely that portion of it printed here, begins shortly after the liberation of Greece by the Allies at the end of World War II. (p. ix)

[Following the war, Seferis] and his wife Maró went off for two months to a house appropriately named Galini—the Greek word for calm, peacefulness, serenity—on the island of Poros near the coast of Argolis.

It is here on Poros that the first of the three central preoccupations of this journal begins. Seferis seems to have had some intimation of what was about to happen to him. "I am starting," he writes, "on a long, very dark voyage, and I'm deeply wounded by my land." Nursing that wound, thinking to escape everything, he comes to the Galini only to discover that his voyage has brought him to the great poem his whole life had been preparing him for. To the reader who knows that poem, "Thrush," these are pages of endless fascination through which one can chart the gradual emergence of this work which, as Seferis says, sums up all the past years and brings to fulfillment ideas for verses he had for some time been jotting down at random in his journal. One finds those "ideas"—phrases, rhythms, images, thoughts—hidden away in this diary from its earliest pages; many of them eventually take their final form in the "Thrush," others are employed even later in *Three Secret Poems.* His experience of the Galini, "the house by the sea," which gave him as he later said "for the first time in many years the feeling of a solid building rather than a temporary tent," leads him down Proustian paths to speculate on the houses he has known and lost during his lifetime, and these memories become the genesis of the plangent threnody on houses that forms the opening section of the "Thrush." So too, we see him go off one day for a swim and come upon the sunken wreck which provides his poem with its title and one of its basic images. In the same way, we follow his increasing preoccupation with the light—"the most important thing I've 'discovered' since the time the ship that brought me home entered Greek waters." The presence of the sea and the insistence of the "angelic and black light'' become more and more overwhelming for him, until in the end he has to close the shutters of his room to block them out in order to finish his poem. As one follows the daily life and thought this journal records, one watches the elements of Seferis' poem take root and flower; one feels the febrile tension of the poetic process, the moments of illumination, the heavy fatigue of creation, inspiration's ''sudden flaring up and dying down like green wood burning''; until finally one experiences the drained sense of relief as the poem is completed on the last day of October. If the name of the house on Poros seems strangely to echo the culminating word of Seferis' first great poem, so too the last experience he records on the island echoes an image and a hope expressed in that same poem, ''Mythistorema,'' over a decade earlier. For as he leaves Poros at the beginning of December, the sight of the first almond tree in flower performs a kind of benediction on these weeks of introspection and creativity.

The second great preoccupation or theme of this journal is Cavafy, to whom Seferis' thoughts return again and again. This should not of course be surprising, since Cavafy's achievement can never be far distant from the thoughts of any modern Greek poet; it is something that everyone who would fashion poems in that language must somehow come to terms with. . . . Yet the subject was only to prove increasingly refractory for him. In some very basic way, his experience of life obliged him ultimately to reject the great art of Cavafy in favor of the humbler, earthy, analphabetic, vital prose of Makriyannis. But one s ould recognize that such a rejection, if that is even the proper word for it, comes paradoxically only at the ultimate stage of admiration. . . . Nonetheless, in April 1950 he copies into this journal some of the extensive notes he had assembled. . . . Fragmentary and undeveloped though they are, they remain extraordinarily suggestive and provocative, with the insights that only one great poet can have about another. At times they come close to expressing Seferis' own *ars poetica*. Throughout these critical observations, one is conscious that their special luminosity derives from a lifetime of reading and experience, of asking what it means to be a Greek, of steadfast fidelity to the Muse of poetry. (pp. x-xii)

It is hardly an exaggeration to claim that [the] destruction of Smyrna [his birthplace] was the determining historical event in Seferis' life: it is this that made him feel permanently and profoundly *heimatlos*, this that gives all his poetry its sense of irredeemable alienation, this that demanded his lifelong search for his identity as a Greek. (p. xiii)

The burden of emotion in [the] final pages is almost intolerable. Returning to the place of his beginnings, Seferis feels that his life has come full circle and that all his past is both summed and summoned up. ''At every step, memories stir within me overwhelmingly; a constant, almost nightmarish piling up of images; incessant invitations from the dead.'' . . . ''Memory,'' he wrote in one of the two beautiful poems he composed during his visit to Skala, ''wherever you touch it, hurts.''

But Memory, as Greeks have always known, is also the Mother of the Muses. Out of the experiences so vividly recorded in this journal, the repository of memory, some of Seferis' finest poetry was created. The chronology of events and experiences . . . is, in the last analysis, unimpor-

tant. ''I didn't have in mind,'' Seferis explains,'' 'to write the story of my life, day by day.' Day by day we live our life; we don't write it.'' What matters is rather the unique sensibility which shines out of every page. Often Seferis' perceptions have the painful sensitivity of an open wound, ''pulsing in the midst of life,'' and there are entries here written in blood. Often his perceptions are given instantaneous form and shape by his intense mythopoeic awareness, and there are moments when we behold the raw stuff of life miraculously transmuted in the alembic of this poetic imagination. Often his perceptions are endowed with lengthening shadows in the receding perspective of memory. But always, his mind and heart are open to receive whatever life proffers, however rewarding, however painful. And courage is not the least of the qualities that make these pages so memorable. (pp. xiii-xv)

Like all the most significant journals, it tells us not so much what its author did day by day as who he was and who he became as those days went by. It bestows on us, ultimately, the gift of himself, preserving for all time the lineaments of the living, experiencing man and his singular honesty in facing the light of day. As such, these daily jottings are precisely what he so touchingly called them: ''the footprints one leaves behind as he passes.'' (p. xv)

> *Walter Kaiser, in his introduction to* A Poet's Journal, *by George Seferis, translated by Athan Anagnostopoulous (copyright © 1974 by the President and Fellows of Harvard College; excerpted by permission of the author and publishers), Cambridge, Mass.: The Belknap Press of Harvard University Press, 1974, pp. vii-xv.*

EUGENE CURRENT-GARCIA

Originally entitled *Days of 1945-51,* [the] portion of Seferis's voluminous diary [published as *George Seferis: A Poet's Journal*] was first made ready for publication in Greece in 1967 because, he said, its pages stood out ''almost by themselves, among the many that we use to help our memory in various ways.'' Memory, which Seferis himself found inescapably painful, thus becomes the keynote of the book, woven like a dark thread binding together each of its dominant themes, yet paradoxically evoking and shaping his most moving poetic utterances. (p. 311)

[At] the end the great poet sums up, in a dramatic crescendo of feeling, what he meant by saying that these pages stood out by themselves among many such which the artist uses to help the memory ''in various ways.'' One of those ways may be seen in the poetry itself, which for many years Seferis had fashioned out of the raw stuff of life recorded in his diary. As a native Greek poet he could hear echoes of Homer and see evidences of ancient as well as modern Greece all around him. Thus . . . he enjoyed a certain advantage over foreign contemporary poets like Pound and Eliot, who also draw on Classical mythology for their substance. . . . [He made the fullest use of that advantage] by making his mythic gods and heroes come alive in a vividly realistic setting; so that in his poems the ancient and modern worlds, and the roles of past and present become intermingled and identified as Seferis draws ''a continuous parallel between contemporaneity and antiquity'' to give shape and significance to present day futility and anarchy. (p. 314)

[Just] as Stratis-Odysseus serves as the poet's voice, so Elpenor in *Mythistorema* and later poems stands for his weaker companions—typically, a ''figure who reveals the weakness of a spirit that so frustrates his captain and . . . makes the voyage agonizing and endless." Elpenor is a Homeric "sub-hero," a minor character and a man of little substance; but Seferis develops the brief mention of him in Books XI and XII of the *Odyssey* into a full-fledged "portrait of pervasive mediocrity," most fully presented in the "Argonaut" section of *Mythistorema* (No. 4) and in the middle section of "Thrush," his most ambitious poem. Elpenor, therefore, is also a central figure in Seferis's poetry, one who, the poet himself explained, "symbolizes those to whom we refer in daily conversation with the expression: 'the poor devil.' However, let us not forget that these guileless men, exactly because they are 'easy,' are often the best carriers of an evil which has its source elsewhere." . . . [These] modern Elpenors are even more sharply dramatized in the poem "Thrush," where Elpenor takes center stage as a hot, sensual would-be seducer of Circe ("whom not even Odysseus could master without a god's help") and is put down and humiliated by Circe's hard, realistic dismissal of his sentimentalized recollection of lost, bygone beauties and fragmented memories of lovely moments. (p. 315)

> *Eugene Current-Garcia, "Days with George Seferis: A Review Essay," in* The Southern Humanities Review *(copyright 1975 by Auburn University), Summer, 1975, pp. 311-17.*

*   *   *

SIMON, (Marvin) Neil   1927-

Simon is an American playwright and screenwriter who has enjoyed tremendous popular success. He is a master of the one-liner; however, many critics feel that this style reduces his characters to mere vehicles for the delivery of his jokes. His plays are excellent entertainments, but many critics contend he could do more serious work with his verbal talents and gift for dialogue. (See also *CLC*, Vol. 6, and *Contemporary Authors*, Vols. 21-24, rev. ed.)

BRENDAN GILL

I begin to perceive that I may have been unfair to Neil Simon in pursuing over the years a theory about him which has been, after all, entirely inside my head and not his, and which I have therefore had no reason to grow impatient with him for failing to live up to. The awkward fact of the matter is that I have thought I could detect a certain figure in the brightly colored wall-to-wall carpet of his work, but Mr. Simon has now made it plain that the figure isn't there and never *was* there; moreover, he has proceeded to pull the carpet itself right out from under me. . . . After Mr. Simon's dazzling "Barefoot in the Park," which, though but an airy, negligible anecdote, filled a whole evening with delight, I wondered whether he wasn't going to lead comedy in a new direction—one in which a continuous free association of homely, amusing small talk would take the place of the usual carefully carpentered box of self-triggering gags and predictable sudden reversals of fortune. It was evident that Mr. Simon had what amounted to a genius for badinage, and it occurred to me that he could elevate this into an art form of his own, blessedly free of the Victorian clutter that has hobbled the comedies of most of his Broadway contemporaries. To my dismay, Mr. Simon has shown no interest in becoming a sort of Beckett of banter. His plays have grown ever more cautious and better made, which is to say more old-fashioned, and his latest hit, "Last

of the Red Hot Lovers," . . . is by far the most old-fashioned play in the Simon canon. With this one, he strikes me as marching straight back into the nineteenth century; it is a curious development, but I have learned my lesson, and wild horses could not drag from me a portentous generalization about it. . . .

[Simon] holds "Last of the Red Hot Lovers" to be something new for him; he calls it a serious comedy, and I fear that he intends to display a still greater degree of seriousness in the future. It is a grave misreading of his gifts, for Mr. Simon's so-called seriousness has a banality of insight not easily to be distinguished from that of soap opera. When he tries to dramatize his no doubt deeply felt emotions in respect to old age and death, to say nothing of such abstractions as goodness and decency, he rises with difficulty to the level of a high-school essay. . . . Mr. Simon's clumsy grapplings with Real Life are being saluted as signs of a newfound compassion and a new breadth of vision on the part of the mature playwright. They are nothing of the sort. . . . "Last of the Red Hot Lovers" is a very funny play . . . but it is also synthetic, and compassion and breadth of vision would have been thoroughly out of place in it. (p. 64)

> *Brendan Gill, in* The New Yorker *(© 1970 by The New Yorker Magazine, Inc.), January 10, 1970.*

JOHN SIMON

When will playwrights learn that it takes more than a string of funny lines to make a comedy? Actually, Neil Simon's *The Gingerbread Lady* purports to be more than a comedy, and the lines, for the most part, are less than funny. Less than funny for several reasons. 1) They traipse over the same old terrain, from sex-starvation to unquenched-thirst jokes, from kinky-sex to show-biz in-jokes, from Mafia to Polish jokes. (There are no elephant jokes.) You may not have heard precisely these jokes before, but your surprise is no greater than at hearing the triumphal march from *Aida* played on water glasses. 2) There are too many of them. Hardly ever is anyone, regardless of age, background, or calling, allowed to speak in anything but funny lines. Whether he is touched, anguished, or crushed, it is all converted into jokes. They end by tripping one another up, and a joke slipping painfully on the peel of the previous joke is no laughing matter. 3) The jokes do not, except superficially, rise out of character or an individual way of looking at the world. (p. 301)

Jokes are not really funny in a vacuum; or at most are funny only one at a time. . . . Jokes must grow out of some meaningful human soil, must tell us something also about the teller, about a society, about life itself. They need the resistance of a hard surface off which to bounce: bits of dialogue, realities, that are not funny. And if the play is to have any value, they must aim at something more ambitious than a mere detonation in the auditorium—something, perhaps, resembling the truth. (pp. 301-02)

[Simon in *The Gingerbread Lady* has failed to provide his] character with dimensions, let alone stature. Whether this particular person is saved or goes under interests us only insofar as she is sufficiently particularized and developed for us . . . ; or conversely to the extent that her predicament is seen in the context of show business, society, or some other larger force that brings the individual to her knees. (p. 302)

John Simon, "'The Gingerbread Lady'" (1970-71), in his Uneasy Stages: A Chronicle of The New York Theater, 1963-1973 (copyright © 1975 by John Simon; reprinted by permission of Random House, Inc.), Random House, 1976, pp. 301-03.

JOHN SIMON

[*The Sunshine Boys* is a play] where gagwriting is ostensibly subordinated to pathos, and underlying the comedy is a supposedly serious theme.... The significant plot concerns a once famous vaudeville team, Lewis and Clark.... (p. 444)

The story is exiguous but presumably will serve as scaffolding for the exploration of such great topics as What Was the Glory of Burlesque?, Where Has That Old-time Humor Gone?, What Is to Become of Beloved Entertainers Grown Aged?, Is Greasepaint Thicker Than Friendship in the Theater? and Can Man Laugh Away His Mortality? There may be one or several worthy plays in this, but none can survive burial alive under 10-Gags-10 per minute—some new, more old, a few funny, many dreadful, but all of them marching, skipping, somersaulting at you without respite. The humor itself is sternly limited in scope: insult jokes, speaker's-stupidity jokes, geriatric sex jokes, and show-biz in-jokes. Although [Clive Barnes] has compared this alleged comic masterpiece favorably to Molière and Shaw, one glance at *Don Juan* and the difference slaps you in the eye.

To Simon, the basic unit of playmaking is the joke. Not the word, the idea, the character, or even the situation, but the gag. It kills him if here and there a monosyllable resists funnying up, if now and then someone has to make a move that won't fracture the audience. Note how many lines in *Don Juan* don't try in the least to be funny—which is why those that really are hit us, and why life and thought are allowed elbow room in the play. (p. 445)

John Simon, "'The Sunshine Boys'" (1972-73), in his Uneasy Stages: A Chronicle of The New York Theater, 1963-1973 (copyright © 1975 by John Simon; reprinted by permission of Random House, Inc.), Random House, 1976, pp. 444-45.

CATHARINE HUGHES

God's Favourite ... is another of Simon's attempts to be taken seriously on the way to the bank....

[Simon's problem is that he is clever] but here as elsewhere, very little of the humour flows from the characters; the efforts at profundity are shallow and unrewarding. Jokes all too often fall back on quick references to brand names (Lemon Pledge furniture polish, Perdue chicken, Bic Banana pens), TV shows ('Hollywood Squares') and the like. It is a cheap, easy and regrettably, all too frequently accepted, substitute for genuine humour. (p. 35)

Catharine Hughes, in Plays and Players (© copyright Catharine Hughes 1975; reprinted with permission), February, 1975.

HAROLD CLURMAN

"Constant pleasure," said Voltaire, "is no pleasure." The geyser of gag lines in Neil Simon's latest spurt, *California Suite*, is virtually incessant.... Occasionally I heard a spot of dialogue which struck me as particularly bright but, when I left the theatre, I could not remember the stuff....

There is hardly any character or psychology ... not immediately recognizable, and [virtually] no complexity of situation.... The scenes are sustained by jocular repartee rather than living speech. If we were to take this show seriously—if anyone can—I would be obliged to say that the attitude toward the personages involved is not only shallow and vulgar but basically callous. There is moreover an element of smug hypocrisy in the compost, for in each instance we are assured that everybody really loves everybody and there are no hard feelings. Fun is fun, so everyone, including the author, is forgiven.

If there are those who would maintain that I am being priggish about all this because I fail to acknowledge the grain of "truth to life" in these sketches, I can only reply that if such is the fact, my most bilious suspicions about the state of our civilization would have been confirmed. And they are not comic! (p. 30)

Harold Clurman, in The Nation (copyright 1976 by the Nation Associates, Inc.), July 3, 1976.

JULIUS NOVICK

[Simon delightedly immerses] himself in the minutiae of modern American upper-middle-class existence, which no one conveys with more authority—or, anyhow, more assiduity—than he.... Simon can see the eternal, if at all, only as an aspect of the temporal; for him, "the troubles of our proud and angry dust" means that the cleaning lady didn't come in this morning.

The problem with Simon for serious critics is that he is good enough to make them angry that he isn't better. There is something very real and recognizable in his work—something that leads them to demand from him more perspective on the world he writes about than he has. Along with the something real in his work is something very glib; and, paradoxically, it is the reality that makes the glibness so frustrating to contemplate....

Neil Simon's work is a true expression of his constituency—that is why it is so successful. How you feel about him is inseparable from how you feel about the people he depicts. (p. 53)

Julius Novick, in The Humanist (copyright 1976 by the American Humanist Association; reprinted by permission), September/October, 1976.

JOHN SIMON

Chapter Two is being heralded as a deepening of Neil Simon's art. It is certainly every bit as much deepening as it is art. The play is admittedly based on Neil Simon's and Marsha Mason's courtship and marriage. George Schneider, a novelist, has lost his beloved wife from cancer; Jennie Malone is an actress who has lost a rather less beloved husband by divorce. Pimping for George is his younger brother, Leo, a theatrical agent; pimping for Jennie is her chum Faye, a queen of the soaps. Against all sorts of likelihood, George and Jennie meet, love, and marry, and start having difficulties, because George is afraid that happiness with the absolutely perfect Jennie means unfaithfulness to the memory of the absolutely perfect Barbara. Finally, though, things settle down blissfully, while Leo and Faye, both unhappily married, try their hand at some unsuccessful and ludicrous adultery. They, clearly, are intended as some sort of comic relief from the supposedly serious drama of George and Jennie, but they end up as standard

Neil Simon characters making sure that the play does not get too "high" for the audience.

There's no danger of that, however. As one of the characters observes, "I have already tried transcendental meditation, health foods, and jogging, and I am now serenely, tranquilly, and more robustly as unhappy as I have ever been." I quote this for two reasons. First, because it is merely an updated version of the Horatian *naturam expelles furca, tamen usque recurret:* try to drive Neil Simon out of Neil Simon with a pitchfork, and he comes rushing right back in. But also, there is the fact that, a few days later, I can no longer remember whether it is the hero or heroine who speaks that line. The characters in Simon are interchangeable because, with minor differences, they are all Neil Simon: accumulations of wisecracks, machines that chop life down to one-liners, and humanoid contraptions, miserable for the sake of being comically miserable. This might even be all right if you did not have the feeling that the author so unabashedly adores them for being that and no more than that. (pp. 155-56)

Simon's characters have no ideas, and do not exist in any sort of existential or social context. . . . It may be that farce writers have usually dealt with obsessive characters in a rather sealed-off space; in that case, I can only say that Simon's obsessions strike me as less compelling, less real even, than most good farceurs'. (p. 156)

> *John Simon, in* The Hudson Review *(copyright ©*
> *1978 by The Hudson Review, Inc.; reprinted by*
> *permission), Vol. XXXI, No. 1, Spring, 1978.*

*   *   *

SINCLAIR, Upton   1878-1968

Sinclair was an American novelist, journalist, essayist, and playwright known for his radical criticism of social injustices. His work exposes many forms of human exploitation, but focuses often on the wrongs inflicted by industry. Though prolific in his literary output, Sinclair remains best known as the author of *The Jungle*. He won a Pulitzer Prize in 1942 for *Dragon's Teeth*, and has written under the pseudonyms of Clarke Fitch, Frederick Garrison, and Arthur Stirling. (See also *CLC*, Vol. 1, and *Contemporary Authors*, Vols. 5-8, rev. ed; obituary, Vols. 25-28, rev. ed.)

WALTER B. RIDEOUT

Both in life and in writings Sinclair has attempted, as did Dickens, to be the persuading intermediary between the contending classes. With admirable sweetness of temper, considering his lack of success, he has continued to argue that the owning class should perform a revolution by consent, that the capitalist should give up his profits and power in exchange for citizenship in an industrial democracy. But in the novels that he has so prodigally brought forth year after year since the publication of *The Jungle*, the lamb of his Christian spirit has rarely been able peacefully to lie down with the lion of his Marxian vocabulary. As a result, although Sinclair is the only one of the Socialist novelists who continued . . . to write Socialist novels, his is the classic case among them for unresolved discrepancies between his fictional structure and the "message" that he is trying to convey. . . . (pp. 36-7)

Despite his artistic limitations . . . Upton Sinclair has built up over half a century a body of work which is a whole tradition in itself. The outstanding Socialist novelist of the first

two decades, in the lonely twenties he almost *was* radical American literature. In the thirties the young Leftists, when they were not damning him as a "social fascist" in accordance with some current "Party line," admitted that his novels and tracts had been and still were instrumental in teaching them the facts of capitalist life. But Sinclair's work, from *The Jungle* onward, had always pushed out from radical circles into the wide ranges of the whole reading public to inform them of the social and personal irresponsibility of capitalists, the disruption of the middle class, the struggle of labor to organize, and the martyrdom of radicals. In the forties his moderately Socialist tales of Lanny Budd and a stricken century sold to hundreds of thousands of American citizens, who found them the easiest way to learn what historical events had prepared the Second World War and were preparing the "Peace." If Sinclair has never been a great creative novelist (what is Lanny Budd beyond a mirror of history?), he has been something else of value— one of the great information centers in American literature. Few American novelists have done more to make their fellow citizens conscious of the society, all of it, in which they live. (p. 38)

> *Walter B. Rideout, in his* The Radical Novel in
> the United States 1900-1954: Some Interrelations
> of Literature and Society *(copyright © 1956 by*
> *the President and Fellows of Harvard College;*
> *excerpted by permission of the publishers), Cam-*
> *bridge, Mass.: Harvard University Press, 1956.*

PETER A. SODERBERGH

[Obituaries asked us] to remember "Uppie" for three achievements: (1) the Federal interest in food inspection stimulated by his 1906 work *The Jungle;* (2) his EPIC (End Poverty in California) program of the early Depression years; and (3) the anti-Nazi novel, *Dragon's Teeth* (1942), for which he won the Pulitzer Prize. It was recalled also that for a generation Sinclair was one of the most feared and vilified homegrown Victorian Socialists in modern history. (p. 173)

Generally overlooked has been Sinclair's running battle with Hollywood, which reached its peak in the 1930's. No other private citizen outside movie circles has provoked the film colony into such a frenzy. . . . All his adult life Sinclair was trying to tell America something: That social injustice could be redressed only by public faith in, and a total realization of, the concept of economic equality. Such a message is more palatable today. Between the two World Wars it reeked of that virulent strain of Anarchism which many Americans felt would demolish cherished institutions. For the better part of a decade Sinclair, the middle-aged word-merchant from Pasadena, was the personification of that destructive force in the minds of his wealthy neighbors in nearby Hollywood. (pp. 173-74)

Had movie-makers seen Sinclair as something more than another eccentric busybody with radical daydreams they might have felt less ambushed in 1934. Evidence that he was dead serious was there for all to see well beforehand. (p. 175)

When Sinclair scored the "ignorance and prejudice, deliberately created and maintained by prostitute journalism," in *The Brass Check* (1919), it should have been fair warning that Hollywood could not be far behind. It was only a matter of time until the man who called Los Angeles the "City of Black Angels'' focused on the city's best-known commodity: The movies.

Sinclair chose books as his weapons: *Money Writes!* and *Oil!*, both published in 1927. In the former, a scathing survey of the state of American literature, he was unsparing. He deplored the ''cinema excrement'' that oozed forth in the name of art. (pp. 175-76)

Sinclair saw his novel *Oil!* as a portrait of the ''moral and political breakdown of our ruling classes.'' Into it he poured every ounce of talent and conviction at his command. The result was a brilliant example of Sinclair at his best, if one cared for Sinclair. In terms of what was ''acceptable'' thinking in America in the 1920's his hero, J. Arnold ''Bunny'' Ross, did everything wrong. Ross rejected the idealism of World War One, operated in the darkness between Socialism and Radical Bolshevism, financed a ''Red'' newspaper, betrayed his own middle class affiliations by slashing out at Big Businessmen, was unashamed of his religious cynicism and sexual experiments, sought to establish a labor college to give meaning to education, castigated super-patriots for burning ''radical'' literature, and married an unpolished Jewess with Bolshevik inclinations. Clearly, this was autobiographic projection of the most obvious, and compelling, sort. ''Bunny'' Ross caused reactions which showed America for what it really was.

Reserved for Hollywood were short sections of merciless prose. That they were peripheral to the main thrust of *Oil!* made them no less devastating. (pp. 176-77)

Among other things, Sinclair's two books seemed to be saying something to the motion picture industry. Hollywood producers and stars were making too much money. Sinclair equated them to ''steel kings,'' suggesting thereby that movie people, too, would have to surrender their holdings and powers to the common good. (p. 178)

There was a brief accommodation between the two adversaries in 1932 when M-G-M adapted Sinclair's pro-temperance novel *The Wet Parade* (1931) to the movies. Sinclair thought it was ''a very good motion picture.'' The key year for both Sinclair and Hollywood, in terms of their inevitable duel, was 1933. (pp. 178-79)

By and large, despite minor reverses between 1931 and 1933, the film industry fared better than most segments of our stricken society. Sinclair, empathetic with the plight of the average citizen, believed that the extravagant conduct and gaudy affluence of Hollywood's elite were a ''mocking affront to the common man.'' The common man was not sufficiently offended to boycott his favorite brand of amusement, but that did not deter Sinclair from seeking ways to reform his exploiters. (p. 180)

[The monograph] *I, Governor of California and How I Ended Poverty* had been printed 200,000 times by July 1934. In it Sinclair the Altrurian proposed his simplistic and appealing ''End Poverty in California'' platform, which became known as the EPIC plan. It was difficult to ignore EPIC, even if one wished to. Sinclair, better organized [in his campaign for governor] than people suspected, had twenty-one campaign offices in Los Angeles proper [and several elsewhere].

[It was Sinclair's] tax plan that concerned the studios. He obviously had labeled them as fugitives from adequate taxa-

tion and was planning his pursuit. ''The world in which we live is going to be remade,'' Sinclair promised, ''and never again will those who seek private advantage be masters either in politics or industry.'' While in New York in September 1934—a trip which included a friendly chat with Franklin Roosevelt—Sinclair was quoted as saying that California ought to ''rent one of the idle studios and let the unemployed actors make a few pictures of their own.'' Evidently that was the remark which galvanized Hollywood attitudes. The producers could take no more lying down. Sinclair had to be stopped, whatever the cost. In the words of the man who was their nemesis: ''the war was on.'' (p. 185)

Led by M-G-M, the ''Stop Sinclair'' campaign may have been a classic example of media misuse, but it was effective. ''The full force of motion picture industry . . . has been thrown into the crusade to keep Upton Sinclair out of the Governor's chair in Sacramento,'' reported the New York *Times* Hollywood correspondent. (p. 186)

It became apparent by mid-October 1934 that Sinclair was losing the early lead he held over seventy-three-year-old Frank Merriam. Gradually the ''power of graphic persuasion'' so rigorously applied by Hollywood and their journalistic allies swung large blocs of popular opinion against EPIC. (pp. 188-89)

Ten days after Merriam's election Sinclair, the inveterate pamphleteer, was hard at work on his interpretation of the rise and fall of EPIC. It was published in 1935 as *I, Candidate for Governor and How I Got Licked.* (p. 189)

Sinclair bore Hollywood no lasting grudge and was dealt no permanent psychological wounds by his experience. He was delighted when Walt Disney purchased the rights to a fantasy he wrote in 1936, *The Gnomobile,* and he lived to see it play in theaters everywhere in 1967. When he spoke of his ''great adventure'' he spoke not of Hollywood but of the manner in which the EPIC movement had redirected ''the whole reactionary tone'' of California toward a more progressive political spirit. By 1936 he was back in harness, somewhat relieved that he had ''coughed up that EPIC alligator'' and regained his privacy. Before his death he would write forty-two major works and earn his place in our tiny band of Dissenters. (pp. 190-91)

Peter A. Soderbergh, ''Upton Sinclair and Hollywood,'' in The Midwest Quarterly *(copyright, 1970, by* The Midwest Quarterly, *Kansas State College of Pittsburg), Winter, 1970, pp. 173-91.*

JOHN DEEDY

Sinclair's [*Boston*] is a fascinating, if flawed work—baldly partisan pieces frequently are—a cut below *The Jungle* and others of his books. (p. 475)

For those reading [*Boston*] for the first time, the story moves on two levels—that of the Sacco-Vanzetti case itself, and that of a wealthy Boston family that is touched by events. . . .

[You'll] enjoy renewing contact with Upton Sinclair, that intense, junior Bernard Shaw with the American-Socialist vision. Sinclair writes with insight and passion—style and wit, as well. I challenge anyone not to chuckle at his portrayal of the Boston of the Brahmins and the old *Transcript,* the newspaper that served the city's most proper. (p. 476)

John Deedy, in Commonweal (copyright © 1978 Commonweal Publishing Co., Inc.; reprinted by permission of Commonweal Publishing Co., Inc.), July 21, 1978.

* * *

SINGER, Isaac Bashevis 1904-

Singer is a Polish-born novelist, short story writer, translator, and journalist who writes primarily in Yiddish. Much of his fiction deals with his East European Jewish heritage, and magic, mysticism, and peasant folk traditions are frequent motifs in his work. A master storyteller, Singer does his best work in his novellas and short stories. Winner of the 1978 Nobel Prize for Literature, Singer is generally conceded to be the greatest living Yiddish writer. (See also CLC, Vols. 1, 3, 6, 9, and Contemporary Authors, Vols. 1-4, rev. ed.)

TIMOTHY EVANS

[Singer's] stories have taken him out of category altogether since the time . . . when he could still be considered a Yiddish modern primarily concerned with the life of the *shtetl*. In *Passions,* as in *A Crown of Feathers,* postwar and contemporary settings predominate. In these collections, and in *Enemies,* [a] novel, Singer has marked a period in his work. And though he is careful to maintain, as always, an appeal from his art to the life and experiences of medieval Polish Jewry, Singer's obsession with the memory "of a world that is no more" has shifted into a new key.

Passions seems to deepen the new tendencies he has discovered in his work. He notes the expansion of his subject, which now includes all the Jews of Eastern Europe, "specifically the Yiddish-speaking Jews who perished in Poland and those who emigrated to the U.S.A." But we get no further than his lead story before we discover that the quick don't mingle any the less with the dead here than in his earlier work. . . . [In] a *shtetl* story, "Two Corpses Go Dancing," in which the Evil One warned that "the world is full of dead ones in sable capes and fur coats who carouse among the living." Singer vindicates him right away in *Passions,* leading off his collection, and sounding its common chord, with "Hanka," which records his discovery of a dancing corpse in contemporary Argentina. But the terms of the discovery have been adjusted. Hanka traces her death-in-life to the physical confinement she endured as a girl in hiding from the Nazis—"if you lie in a grave long enough, you get accustomed to it and you don't want to part from it." And so, to anyone at all familiar with the pressures and stresses of the "survivor pathology," Singer's tale will seem as plausible as a case study. Where once he used his narrative wit to question the old world picture, he tends increasingly to transvalue the *shtetl* world, translating its materials into modern imaginative usage.

"Hanka" proves the possibility of such an undertaking; its necessity can be inferred from the story's subtheme. It plays through all these stories. "There are circumstances when you are torn away like a leaf from a tree and no power can attach you again. The wind carries you from your roots," and you become, like Singer's characters, like Singer himself, "*Na-v'nad*—a fugitive and a wanderer." A condition of displacement so radical as to blur the distinctions between life and death can form a ground for the idea that "the past is not dead—it's not even past," and this is part of the displacement theme's function in Singer's recent work. Having always relied on an extraordinary skill of reference, he now applies his customary materials—sacred stories, Hasidic lore, cabalistic motifs, folk tales—to the description of a world in which they would seem to have no force at all. And yet, in dreams, in memories, in moments of transcendence that cannot be explained, the past returns, the dead reveal themselves as never having died at all. "If I hadn't known I was in Brownsville," says Sam Palka, "I would have thought I was in Konskowola." (pp. 527-28)

But epiphanies are in their nature fugitive experiences, and *Passions* unsentimentally puts them in their place as stations along the way of an imaginative pilgrim who has known since his boyhood that he could expect to "find no place for myself in the world." Although he touches down, in the collection, at Argentina, Portugal, Israel and Miami, Singer's wanderings here follow, in the main, the path that took him from the *shtetl* to Warsaw and from Warsaw to New York with so many of his people. He has followed them where they have gone, always listening to them, and he shares their testimony with us. But they are still "a riddle to the world and often to themselves," and Singer remains a man for whom "there's no explanation for anything." And if, in *Passions,* he finds his end in his beginning, hasn't nostalgia sustained the Jews throughout the term of their continuing exile? Most of his Polish settings turn up in the final third of the book, and he brings his collection to rest in a very familiar study house in the *shtetl,* where Zalman the glazier and Levi Yitzchok come to exchange stories with Meyer the Eunuch, who always has the final word. "Everything can become a passion," he concludes here, "even serving God."

Or, even, telling stories: here is passion in the art, an imaginative providence as prodigal as ever, a talent in its prime, a writer to be rejoiced in. (pp. 528-29)

Timothy Evans, in Studies in Short Fiction (copyright 1976 by Newberry College), Fall, 1976.

ANDREW BERGMAN

Isaac Bashevis Singer picks up [in "A Young Man in Search of Love"] where his previous memoir, "A Little Boy in Search of God," left off: with the young author in the tenacious arms of his much older lover (and landlady), Gina, and with him trying, through a bit of starvation, to duck the draft. Here again, we are in the world of prewar Yiddish Warsaw, which, we know, is about to be obliterated by history. And we are also, of course, in the exhilarating good company of Mr. Singer, churning with restless skepticism, moral passion and erotic preoccupation. . . .

Mr. Singer's companions and loves, responding to a master's slightest nudge, bound out of his memory and onto the page. He fills his account with gentle humor, capturing quite wonderfully a young man's extravagant self-absorption and urgent need for answers. (p. 59)

Andrew Bergman, in The New York Times Book Review (© 1978 by The New York Times Company; reprinted by permission), April 30, 1978.

EDWARD HIRSCH

Isaac Bashevis Singer's new books, a memoir [*A Young Man in Search of Love*] and a novel [*Shosha*], are two more rescue operations in his ongoing literary raid on the vanished world of prewar Poland. Although *A Young Man in Search of Love* follows the conventions of autobiography, and *Shosha,* those of fiction, the impulse behind both narratives is to recapture a lost world, to render the rich interior and exterior lives of people responding to unique circumstances. In the foreground of each book, an ambitious young author . . . encounters a heterogeneous blend of worldly and unworldly Jews. In the background, a heavy German blade hovers overhead. Singer writes from the other side of that fallen Nazi knife; it has been his remarkable achievement to penetrate its steel surface, to capture the uncapturable. (p. 34)

In both life and art, Singer is seeking "tangled situations and genuine dilemmas." His search for love has also become a quest for God: "For me, religion and love, even sex, are attributes of the same substance."

This central spiritual quest, revealed in a wealth of tangled plots and moral dilemmas, has infused Singer's most important work. . . .

Shosha is filled with the usual Singer questions about demonic possession, free-floating souls, an archive of spirits, a world rife with secret powers and occult mysteries. But mostly it is a testament to the haunting power of the past. (p. 35)

Edward Hirsch, in Saturday Review (© 1978 by Saturday Review Magazine Corp.; reprinted with permission), July 8, 1978.

ALAN LELCHUK

[In "Shosha"] many Singers appear in one way or another —the journalist, the rabbi's son, the children's writer, the European refugee. (p. 1)

There is a nice variety of characters in "Shosha." Singer's method of narration, moving from one small dramatic scene to another, encourages such variety. This method . . . demands fast-paced plot, simple story line with ingenious reverses and character sketched in broadly. Reading Singer is an easy experience, something like reading the bare outline of a Bellow novel, without the latter's intense fleshing out. . . .

Besides amusing character, there is convincing setting, Warsaw, 1930's. The Warsaw scenes are drawn with a knowledge of place and atmosphere lacking in Singer's recent ventures into the American scene, and they hark back to his finer work, as in the memoir "In My Father's Court." Here the hectic street life of the Polish ghetto, with neighborhood interplay of Jewish gangsters and prostitutes mingling with Hasidic families and workers, is effectively done. . . . There is much dialogue here. When the talk involves the adventures of everyday life it is alive with humor and irony; when it travels to the upper airs of metaphysics and occultism—the existence of God, good and evil, the transmigration of souls—it is solemnly uneventful. Singer's Warsaw scenes are resonant with a felt reality and capture poignantly a real, if provincial, culture. When it comes to transforming *shtetl* life into serious art, however, Singer does not have the wit of Sholem Aleichem or the force of Babel. . . .

Happily, [the protagonist's] Aaron Greidinger's swarm of women, his benevolent harem, takes up a good part of the book and is part of an erotic theme—or dream—obviously dear to the old patriarch's heart (Singer's). With a father who stands at the lectern all day saying, "It is forbidden," it is not surprising that Greidinger seeks transgression, wherever possible. This particular erotic pattern, with its

convenient precedent in the Bible, is a favorite of Singer's, dramatized best, to my mind, in the energetic novel "The Magician of Lublin." . . . [There] is more passion in descriptions of food and eating in "Shosha" than there is in the descriptions of sex. One gets the sense that the play of the erotic—so well *felt* in "The Magician"—is here a remembrance of past powers, a passion paid lip service to. Perhaps something else, too. At one point counselor Feitelzohn advises the young writer, "The main thing is, don't spare the schmaltz. Today's Jews like three things—sex, Torah, and revolution, all mixed together. Give them those and they'll raise you to the skies." In "Shosha," there is that mix.

A crucial theme in this novel, one that was dramatized superbly in Singer's wonderful short story "Gimpel the Fool," concerns innocence that borders on saintliness, which, in its childlike acceptance of all things in this world, will defeat evil and achieve redemption. It is embodied here in the figure of Shosha herself, a girl of 9 who speaks like a child of 6 when we first meet her, who is left back in school two years and is considered "a little fool" and who never does grow up as she gets older. The early scenes, in which the immature Shosha puts all her innocent faith in the precocious rabbi's boy, are filled with a fine evocation of childhood, where the world is a big uncharted territory and intimacy the only guide. As a caterpillar crawling about there, protected by Aaron, Shosha is alive with the questions and delights of a child. But as the butterfly who is Aaron's betrothed and wife, Shosha is overly predictable, uninspiring. And Aaron Greidinger fails to probe into his complicated motives for returning to Shosha, stopping at surface explanations to himself and others. (p. 22)

[Singer] is basically a simple writer—not deceptively simple, like Agnon. His most appealing scenes and characters seduce the reader, rather than provoke, stimulate, educate. This is no small power in a writer. For it means the ability to take a conventional situation, hold it up for his audience to see, then twist it about to show them a new and unexpected view. (pp. 22-3)

A problem in "Shosha," as elsewhere in Singer, is his failure to confront fully a difficult dilemma. Late in the novel, Betty Slonim admonishes the hero, "You're both a godless lecher and a fanatical Jew—as bigoted as my great-grandfather! How is it possible?" And Aaron Greidinger replies, "We are running away and Mount Sinai runs after us. This chase has made us sick and mad." But the hero here does not become sick and mad—though he has bouts with sickness and madness—as perhaps his temperament and circumstance dictate. Instead, the author permits him to exit quietly from Poland and eventually take up life anew in America, while an *external* madness (Nazism) has obliterated the other characters. The way out for Singer is the dream, the fantasy, the mythic, not the real. The predicament is not examined with the seriousness he proposes. Singer is best when he offers us childlike dreams of innocence and salvation ("Gimpel"), parables of erotic//religious torment ("The Magician of Lublin") or historical recreations of false wonder and miracle ("Satan in Goray"). "What are writers?" Aaron Greidinger wonders aloud. "The same kind of entertainers as magicians." And while Feitelzohn immediately disputes that, saying Aaron is a serious young man, there is much truth in the hero's assessment, so far as his creator is concerned. Singer's aim is to entertain, and by this standard, he fully succeeds in "Shosha." (p. 23)

Alan Lelchuk, "Sex, Torah, and Revolution," in The New York Times Book Review (© 1978 by The New York Times Company; reprinted by permission), July 23, 1978, pp. 1, 22-3.

ALEX SZOGYI

[In *Enemies: A Love Story* Singer created a masterpiece of Jewish amatory surrealism that] painted the madness of the flesh against a backdrop of imminent world destruction. . . . [*Shosha* is] a quintessential tale of the Jewish soul in perpetual exile. [Like *Enemies,* it] portrays lust roaming through a decaying world, specifically, prewar Warsaw—only this time with such intense attention to realistic detail that we are transported into the realm of caricature.

The characters here—as in the author's previous works, are haunted by dybbuks of their own choosing, avatars of their own worst selves. And their tragedy is that their fate never seems grand or heroic enough for their passions. The result is Chekhovian irony: Everything is seen through the prism of absurdist opera glasses. . . .

[Aaron's] strength and his weakness is his deep and abiding love for one person—the half-mad, haunted Shosha. In trying to give her the support she needs to live, he senses that by sacrificing himself and marrying her he may save her from herself. (This harks back to those 18th-century picaresques, like *Tom Jones,* where the hero never forgets his love for a poor girl as he hacks through the jungle of ambition.) (p. 21)

[Betty Slonim and Sam Dreiman,] wild cartoons of types we all recognize, are the finest characters in the novel, and the tale of Betty's intrusion into Tsutsik's life provides the best and funniest moments in the complicated narrative.

In fact, their long flirtation often reads like a Woody Allen parody. It has that same abrupt, painfully truthful quality that zigzags back and forth between comic and tragic perception—an effect attributable to Singer's positive genius for describing the wildness of women caught in the throes of ambition and sexual dilemma. . . .

Throughout the book, Singer plays with two notions of love. One is the life-giving and preserving deep love of someone for his chosen bride, and he includes every obligato for this ancient emotion; the other is total promiscuity. No matter which option they choose, though, the characters all end up unhappy. . . .

Yet despite this unhappiness, Singer seems to be saying, the world can be explored today only by sensually tasting the variety of life's spices. Before Hitler, before still another dispersal into the diaspora, the old values could be maintained. But now modern man must search in a different way. To be sure, he must continue to hope for a meaning, but meaning will be given in terms of sexual revelation rather than through any form of Divine message. (p. 22)

Alex Szogyi, "Eros and Exile," in The New Leader (© 1978 by the American Labor Conference on International Affairs, Inc.), August 14, 1978, pp. 21-2.

PAUL BERMAN

"What can one do? How is one to live?" the narrator of *Shosha* asks, and though the setting of this novel is Warsaw

of the Twenties and Thirties, before the war had given shape to the modern world, the existential dilemmas of philosophy and love behind these questions seem entirely modern. Love is so confusing that Tsutsik, the narrator, conducts affairs with five different women at once, and when he does settle down, it is with Shosha, the moronic and physically stunted sweetheart of his childhood, as if in demonstration of love's inner illogic. Matters of philosophy, which are closer to Tsutsik's heart, prove even more troublesome. He wishes he could find some universe of value and meaning in religion, wishes he could dig up out of the past some useful concept from Jewish mysticism, wishes he could salvage some significance from the old stetl. The only alternatives his friends can offer from the present are Stalin, or Trotsky, or the ideas of a cafe philosopher whose masterwork is a book called, marvelously, *Spiritual Hormones.* But none of this will do. Not unlike Isaac Bashevis Singer himself, one supposes, Tsutsik seems doomed to be a man at a spiritual loss.

All this makes for an entertaining novel, for though Singer is an earnest writer, his earnestness steps lightly, and in any case he provides plenty of amorous women and unexpected turns in Tsutsik's writing career to move things along. But entertaining or not, the novel labors under the growing shadow of Hitler, which ultimately overtakes the story and brings it to a grimly abrupt ending. There are no spiritual hormones, Singer seems to be saying. There are no solutions to existential dilemmas. There is not even a stetl to yearn for anymore, only the rootlessness of the modern world. (p. 94)

Paul Berman, in Harper's (copyright © 1978 by Harper's Magazine; all rights reserved; reprinted from the September, 1978 issue by special permission), September, 1978.

ROBERT ALTER

Shosha is Isaac Bashevis Singer's most personal novel. . . .

A blurb-writer might say that *Shosha* "recaptures" the Warsaw of Singer's youth, but the book has no nostalgic softness because it is so consciously a novel about the process of remembering—remembering as the source and perhaps the justification of all literary activity, remembering as the mind's intimation of time stopped or time reversed and thus a token of performance in a violent chaotic universe. The cast of significant characters is limited, but in many scenes . . . Singer conveys a sense of the teeming particularities of Polish-Jewish life reminiscent of the best things in his two compendious family chronicles, *The Manor* and *The Family Moskat.*

The pursuit of the past is translated into a central principle of plot in Greidinger's relationship with Shosha. She was his intimate childhood friend in the poor and pious Jewish neighborhood of Krochmalna Street, and when he rediscovers her as an adult, still a slip of a girl, scarcely full-grown, retarded in mind as well as in body, she seems to him the embodiment of arrested, or perhaps perpetuated, childhood. . . .

Now, all of this verges on allegory, and that is a basic problem of the novel. Shosha's very name fits into the design: it suggests the Hebrew word for rose, . . . the rose that does not wither, that is beyond the ravages of time. To possess this fragile flower, Greidinger is prepared to sever his social connections with the world of Yiddish writers, to neglect his material well-being, even to sacrifice his life. . . . To be sure, the eternally innocent Shosha has her poignant moments in the novel, but she strikes this reader at any rate as too vague, too much a mere idea, and the overwhelming attraction she holds for the intellectual Greidinger is no more than intermittently credible. In order to create a plausible relationship between two such disparate figures, a novelist would have to have the psychological genius of a Dostoevski or the insight into the metamorphic power of imagination of a Nabokov. Singer's own gifts lie elsewhere —in the evocation of cultural character-types and settings, in the embodiment of metaphysical speculation in the destinies of fictional personages.

And yet, Singer, here as elsewhere, is so *beguiling* a writer that one readily forgives the flaws of his work. The sketchiness in the psychological definition of character is abundantly compensated for by the writer's ability repeatedly to dramatize, in the full concreteness of the fictional moment, the movements of the contemplative mind as it ponders man's imponderable place in the infinite scheme of things. In this regard, *Shosha* at its best recalls one of Singer's finest stories, "The Spinoza of Market Street." (p. 20)

Metaphysical speculation, anchored in . . . individual character and situation, retains something of its intrinsic intellectual breadth but is both enlivened and ironically qualified by a wry sense of the discrepancies between systems, concepts, logical reasoning, on the one hand, and the stubborn particularities of existence, on the other. As a writer of metaphysical fiction, Singer is thus the exact obverse of J. L. Borges. Borges creates *ficciones* that are ingenious parables devised to unsettle conventional notions of time, space, extension, causation, identity. Singer, faithful to the Yiddish literary tradition from which he derives, adheres mimetically to the gritty surfaces of a closely observed world but surrounds that world with vertiginous mental prospects against which human lives and their impedimenta waver, wobble, vanish, only to reappear with an assertive irreducibility. (p. 21)

Singer may have made a tactical error in introducing Shosha as one symbolic "answer" to the quandary of human transience, but in other ways the novel succeeds in plangently rendering the process of questioning the place of man in the frightful flux of being, and that is what gives conviction to this literary pursuit of a vanished past. (p. 22)

> *Robert Alter, in* The New Republic *(reprinted by permission of* The New Republic; © *1978 by The New Republic, Inc.), September 16, 1978.*

MAUREEN HOWARD

[Singer's] fables and stories, the inspired characters, rabbis, charlatans, whores, so good, so evil, are out of a world that can never be parochial, a world out of our childhood legends, out of medieval romance, out of episodic sagas. They are the stories that were once told to sustain life and community of an evening in any house, any town.

But being at least partially literary in origin, Singer's tales are also more sophisticated than we first imagine. It's astonishing how difficult it is to construe his work. As we read, we may conjure up Freud, the archetypal meanings of sudden death and transfiguration. But we are left, more than with any contemporary writer except perhaps Borges, with the story, the pure story. In Singer's balance of innocence and sophistication is really where his magic lies.

In a well known interview, Singer once said that he wrote "as if," meaning that he wrote about a lost world of Jewish culture as if the second world war had not held overwhelming tragedy for the Jewish people. And that was further extended to his feeling that it is quite natural and healthy in the face of such knowledge to go on living and writing. As we look at Singer's work now, in the continuing stories we can see that there is never a touch of self-pity or pomposity. There's not one nostalgic note for the days of piety and poverty, because the problems of our secularism and our human frailty, our loss of faith, our loss of faith in both God and a shaky rational world, remain [immediate and passionate]. . . .

[Singer] writes as if words themselves were not questioned in high literary circles, as if we had been lectured and analyzed in our modern fiction quite enough, as if, given the possibility of thorough destruction, stories still matter.

> *Maureen Howard, "Isaac the Fool," in* The New Republic *(reprinted by permission of* The New Republic; © *1978 by The New Republic, Inc.) October 21, 1978, p. 16.*

LEON WIESELTIER

Singer the novelist has always seemed much less accomplished than Singer the writer of short stories. The novels have been shapeless, even slovenly, and *Shosha* is no exception. Not the stories, however. These are uncommonly vigorous and carefully fashioned. . . . [The collection entitled *Gimpel the Fool*] contains Singer's best work, his boldest and liveliest inventions. And it belies at once his familiar disclaimer that he is only a storyteller. He is not. His tales are thick with speculation and prejudice, and both are damaging.

Singer's fiction sets out always from the experience of suffering. Theodicy is its plot. His people seek reasons for their pain, and—save for the somewhat inscrutable Rabbi Bainish of Komarov in "Joy"—they usually do not find them. What they find instead are ideas, a vast profusion of dangerous doctrines to do the work of the faith that has gone unrewarded. Singer's people are what they believe, or do not believe. They do not all, of course, possess the amazing resilience of Gimpel, who is so credulous he is sublime. Many turn dramatically to heresy, which they do not always quite understand.

There is, indeed, a great measure of human truth in the ordinariness of these adopted heterodoxies. . . . There is, unfortunately, also a certain philosophical insouciance about them. Singer plays too fast and too carelessly with his warring world views. There are too many imponderables, too much sheer, lingering mystery. All this obsessive heaven-storming comes to seem mannered, and even mischievous. . . . What delights Singer most is the very spectacle of the struggle; he is sardonically amused by the inadequacy of his addled Jews' resources. He hobbles the devout and then laughs.

He discredits even their defections. For Singer's wronged believers demand not illumination so much as license. They yearn to sin. And it is in his rapt fascination with sin that Singer's sly modernism is disclosed. The sacrilegious practices of the Sabbatians and the abominations of the eighteenth-century false messiah Jacob Frank join here with the Satanism of Baudelaire and the criminality of Dostoevsky to produce a central vision of numinous vice; it is as if inspired depravity is the only religious expression that remains. And the most numinous vice, the outrage that will best engage the angry, hidden God, is fornication. . . . Singer's eroticism is a matter of principle and it is vivid and inexhaustible. He revels in his voluptuaries in their caftans, taunting the Lord of the Universe in the fleshpots of Galicia. (pp. 6, 8)

Singer seems to detest women. . . . [The] women in his narratives are always less than characters; they are only mere sites of iniquity—no more than creation's most savory forms of pork. It is not a mysticism of love that Singer expounds, but rather a kind of vulgar theological prurience. He has mistaken manhood for grace.

Misogyny is not all that confounds Singer's grand vision of salvation by sin. In *A Young Man in Search of Love*, a rather casual chronicle of the obstreperous desires of his youth, Singer alludes to "the great adventures inherent in Jewish history—the false Messiahs, the expulsions, the forcible conversions, the Emancipation, and the assimilations. . . ." Illusion, disorder, transgression, apostasy: in these are to be found the florid romances of Jewish experience. Not a word, however, of what was surely the most unlikely and daring Jewish adventure of all—the adventure of a life in *halakha*, of allegiance to the law in even the direst adversity, of individuals and communities fired by tradition's discipline and willing to remain steadfast unto death. Of those Jews who would seek release from the rabbinical way Singer writes with asperity, even scorn. He is not alive to their special strength. They appear in his works caricatured, as blind, bumbling, craven votaries of a bizarre and frozen culture. And it is this proud and bilious indifference to the character of piety that further vitiates Singer's thirst for its collapse. . . .

[He] has taken an extraordinary vengeance in literature: a joyless, acid portrait of Jewish life surrendered to demons and doubt, a grotesque congeries of the uncanny and the perverse. Singer moves straight from the disappointments of reason to the raising of tables. His comedy is often brilliant, and just as often cruel. And it agrees nicely with that facile infatuation with the demonic that currently prevails in American culture, not least among American Jews. (p. 8)

> *Leon Wieseltier, "The Revenge of I. B. Singer," in* The New York Review of Books (*reprinted with permission from* The New York Review of Books; *copyright © 1978 Nyrev, Inc.*), *December 7, 1978, pp. 6, 8.*

EDWARD ALEXANDER

[The] wide appeal of Singer's stories among readers ignorant of, and indifferent to, Jewish religion, Jewish history, Jewish peoplehood, is a literary fact of the first importance because it disproves the fashionable literary prejudice which holds that writing about Jews is an insuperable obstacle to universal appeal. Critics who have blithely assumed that it is the natural destiny of the human race, or of that part of it which reads books, to puzzle over Blake's Zoas and Yeats' gyres and Pound's socio-economic ravings, are invariably brought up short at the prospect of reading books about Jews because, they maintain, the concerns of Jews are not those of universal humanity. (p. 8)

Singer's tremendous success among critics as well as among ordinary readers seems to illustrate the truth of Cynthia Ozick's contention that, contrary to the apostles (to the

Jews, anyway) of universalism, great literature never consciously seeks to be "universal." . . . (p. 9)

Hopeless and helpless before [the inevitability of the Holocaust], nearly all of the Jews in [*Shosha*] live only for the present, pursuing pleasure without regard for truth or value. (pp. 9-10)

The self-destructive futility of hedonism is hardly a new theme in Singer's novels. But, whereas in the earlier novels the distance established by moral judgment between the novelist and his hedonists was clear and distinct, here it is blurred by what we may suppose to be a kind of nostalgia for his own youthful experiences and aspirations. . . .

[Whereas] in *The Magician of Lublin* and *Enemies* each of the hero's women represented some distinct portion of his fragmented life, in *Shosha* the multiplication of lovers seems more a virtuoso performance than a structural and thematic device. (p. 10)

Ultimately, despite the unseemly relish with which [Aaron] dwells on what must finally be repudiated, this is also the view of the narrator and his creator as well. It is clear not only that sexuality stands in diametrical opposition to Judaism, but that it derives much of its demonic force from the power of what might be called anti-Judaism. . . .

In *Shosha*, it is primarily (not exclusively) religion which resists hedonism. Religion reacts to the imminence of the Holocaust not by living in and for the present, but by dwelling on the past. "In Germany, Hitler had solidified his power, but the Warsaw Jews had celebrated the festival of the exodus out of Egypt four thousand years ago." The very fact that they live thus in the past implies their belief in a future. (p. 11)

Both the memoir [*A Young Man in Search of Love*] and the novel serve to remind us that Singer is that rarity among modern Jews, an intellectual who seems never to have been tempted by leftist sloganeering and utopianism. *A Young Man in Search of Love* gives us an unsavory picture of a cadre of leftist bullies. . . .

Singer acknowledges that he, too, worshiped idols, the idol of love (as we have already noted) and the idol of literature. Both books dwell on the special difficulties of the Yiddish writer, who felt isolated and frustrated not only because his choice of such a vocation made him a *meshumad* (apostate) in the eyes of the religious, but, also, because he was "stuck with a language and culture no one recognized outside of a small circle of Yiddishists and radicals." Here was a sort of double exile. (p. 12)

Even when Aaron finds his proper subject—the false messianism that Singer's own first novel dealt with—he senses that the literary vocation cannot provide a substitute for the life-giving bread of the Jewish religion from which he has separated himself. . . .

In its defiance of time and change, Aaron's attachment to Shosha symbolizes his idea of the aim of literature: "to prevent time from vanishing." Ultimately, however, it was not time and change which destroyed Shosha and so many of Aaron's friends and their world but the external violence of the Holocaust. For the writer who tells the story of the novel, literature has become the instrument for preserving the memory, and even resurrecting the souls, of the dead.

This elegiac sense is largely absent from *A Young Man in*

Search of Love. The book is more a series of anecdotes—some of them brilliantly rendered—than the autobiography of a mind. It is also lacking in contour, sense of proportion, and narrative development. The book simply stops rather than concluding, and the complete absence of dates from what purports to be a factual account is frustrating. (p. 13)

> Edward Alexander, "The Nobel Prize for I. B. Singer," in Judaism (copyright © 1979 by the American Jewish Congress), Winter, 1979, pp. 8-13.

*   *   *

SINGH, Khushwant   1915-

Singh is an Indian novelist, historian, short story writer, essayist, journalist, and editor. His major themes are the religious traditions, moral problems, and sociopolitical tensions of Indian life. Familiar with Western culture as well as Punjabi, Singh wrote almost exclusively in English. *Train to Pakistan* **is generally considered his major fictional work. (See also** *Contemporary Authors***, Vols. 9-12, rev. ed.)**

SANTHA RAMA RAU

[In "I Shall Not Hear the Nightingale," Khushwant Singh has again] chosen a period of recent Indian history in which hatred, bloodshed and terrorism were close to the surface of Indian life, and handles them with the same authority that he displayed in his first novel.

Khushwant Singh is direct to the point of brutality, unsentimentally observant, and in his bold characterizations he is ready to explore the least appealing aspects of human nature and relationships. His humor—expertly integrated with an essentially sad and cynical story—is wild, broad, unsparing. Unlike most Indian novelists who exhibit either prudishness or a respectable reticence about sex, his love scenes—or rather, sex-scenes—are startlingly explicit. All these signs of a bounding literary vitality surround a story of two Indian families, one Sikh, one Hindu, and the disruptive events, personal and national, that engulf them. (p. 26)

Once again Khushwant Singh has proved himself an accomplished and commanding novelist. (p. 27)

> Santha Rama Rau, "Two Families at the Crossroads," in The New York Times Book Review (© 1959 by The New York Times Company; reprinted by permission), December 13, 1959, pp. 26-7.

PHOEBE LOU ADAMS

Khushwant Singh is unusual among the Indian novelists published in this country in that his novels deal directly with violence. . . . [*I Shall Not Hear the Nightingale*] is set in 1942 and is the story of a Sikh family divided over loyalty to the British raj. (p. 98)

The novel takes no sides politically. The English deputy commissioner is represented as a decent man trying to enforce reasonable laws, while Sher Singh's trigger-happy idiocy is all his own invention and no fault of the Indian party officially seeking independence. What the author sets out to portray is the confusion of mind among people who have given up, or are about to give up, their loyalty to one regime but have not yet found a substitute for it. . . . The author himself offers no solution.

Mr. Singh is a businesslike writer, not given to frills or subtlety. Even so, the novel is not entirely sober. There are mischievous caricatures of minor officials and fawning tradesmen and a scandalously funny episode in which the family's mistreated boy-of-all-work takes a Rabelaisian revenge. Mr. Singh gives the impression of being an artless and sometimes clumsy writer, but his major characters come to life, and their mistakes have the power to make the reader's conscience itch. (pp. 98-9)

> Phoebe Lou Adams, "Men Without a Country," in The Atlantic Monthly (copyright © 1960 by The Atlantic Monthly Company, Boston, Mass.; reprinted with permission), January, 1960, pp. 98-9.

VASANT ANANT SHAHANE

Khushwant Singh, as a short-story writer, pursues and practices the art of the short story in its early twentieth-century mold and narrative form. His stories reveal a distinct narrative structure and an almost traditional development of the plot which recalls, and approximates, the early phase of the Italian *novella* or German *novellum*. Although his stories are not tales in the traditional sense, they exemplify many narrative elements of the tale. Although his stories tend to be episodic in structure and intent, the unfolding of the dominant theme characterizes all of his stories. Episodes seem to be dexterously strung together to make the essential point or to delineate character or bring out the significance of action. Action and episode dominate the stories. This dominant characteristic accounts for their being within the traditional mold and conventional pattern.

Singh's stories derive their structure from the plot which is based on conflict or crisis in character and situation. The development of action in his stories is sequential and is marked by progression in time rather than in space. The stories are episodic in some measure since episodes, or units of action, often seem to dominate other elements in the story such as character, theme, symbol. The action is unfolded in a series of complications which evoke curiosity and create suspense. A conflict in situation and character is created, developed, and resolved through a succession of scenes. The resolution of the conflict brings out the point of the story which is sometimes a surprise, sometimes an unexpected tragicomic outcome or revelation; but it is always a fitting finale to the interesting sequence of events. Khushwant Singh's stories display a linear development in sequence, a geometrical design, the lines advancing in straight, though different, directions only to find the ultimate point of resolution.

His stories and techniques cannot be described as modern because they do not transcend the traditional narrative and episodic structure and enter the arena of modernity either of the "luminous halo" indicated by Virginia Woolf or of segments of space-time polarity. (pp. 32-3)

The definitions or descriptions of the novel as a "dramatic poem" or the short story as a "poetic playlet" are inapplicable to Khushwant Singh's novels and to his short stories primarily because the basic quality of his creative mind is not that of a poet but that of a satirically and comically inclined writer of fiction. . . .

The compression of a maximum of life within a minimum of space, which is an essential element of the modern short story, characterizes Khushwant Singh's stories of social import. He is a humorist and realist in one, and his stories reveal this dual artistic power. (p. 33)

Irony is one of the main characteristics of Singh, and his stories illustrate this quality. (p. 34)

"The Mark of Vishnu" is a strikingly original and significant story, and it has found a place in many anthologies of Indo-Anglian and English stories. Though many anthologists seem to admire "The Mark of Vishnu," I believe it suffers from inherent weaknesses of structure, theme, and symbol. First, the title "The Mark of Vishnu" is overweighted with religious and moral significance for the thin body and narrative content of the story to bear as its symbolic heading; second, the irony arising out of the symbolic significance is partly misconceived. (p. 37)

"The Mark of Vishnu" has a powerful theme and an extraordinarily gripping narrative content; yet the irony, which is the keynote of the story, is not quite brought out.... The ironic meaning emerging from the two levels of meaning of the title is the principal motif of the story. The mark of Vishnu is a symbol of divine preservation, whereas the actual "V" mark, dug by the *Kala Nag's* fangs, since it is fatally destructive, is the very reversal of the original Hindu symbol. The issue is presented between superstition and reason, popular belief and corporal reality, pagan faith in animal deity, and the sheer aggressive beastliness of the animal world; yet the question remains whether the problem is appropriately presented.... The sheer scientific, biological, bodily reality, of the natural poisonousness of the fangs of the cobra is pitted against the superstitious-cum-religious belief of the Hindus that the cobra is divine.... Ganga Ram's blind devotion to the *Kala Nag,* as presented by Khushwant Singh, seems a little unconvincing inasmuch as it is an exaggerated portrayal of a perhaps vanishing Hindu tradition and belief. (pp. 38-9)

Khushwant Singh's art of the short story is marked by a preponderant comic spirit which assumes various shapes and forms.... Singh is a skilled craftsman in unmasking the central character in a story; in the process, he is mildly satirical, or farcical or lively and light-hearted. This process operates extensively in Singh's stories, and man's absurdities are constantly exposed and held up to ridicule. (p. 39)

The quality of experience and its presentation in stories such as "My Own My Native Land" are journalistic and reportorial in nature, which develops into a pattern in Singh's fiction. The experience seems to merely touch the surface of life and does not form part either of sensibility or sensation, the two principal strands in modern English and American fiction.... Singh's stories, though masculine in spirit, do not belong to the world of sensation. They contain qualities which are associated with the essays of Addison and Steele, the perceptive comments on social and individual mores, a fine sense of humor, and a not-too-obtrusive moral intention. Though they lack the urbanity and surface graces of Addison's essays, they embody and encompass his delectable satirical art, his liveliness and humor. (pp. 50-1)

In analyzing some of the sociologically and psychologically motivated short stories of Singh, the critic should recognize and interpret the interplay of means and ends.... Sometimes the characteristics of the central figure undergo a change, but this is only a means of creating the total effect, which is the author's ultimate objective. Thus, the interplay between means and ends constitutes a growth which is almost parallel to the development of the story's structure. (p. 53)

Although Khushwant Singh is a pronounced realist, he quite often confronts the supernatural. His treatment of the intangible, inexplicable, and supernatural elements of human experience and its differentiation from the actualities of existence brings out his view of the complexity of life and the danger of oversimplifying it. He portrays characters and situations that are outside the boundaries of the rational and yet seem truer than real-life characters and commonly prevailing situations. (p. 59)

[Singh] does not quite create what may be termed as "formula" stories, though the elements of ideological and structural manipulation in them are unmistakable. Stories such as "The Great Difference" are essentially sociological and, therefore, approximate to the pattern of the formula story. The accepted pattern of the "well-made tale," too, is relevant to stories such as "Rats and Cats in the House of Culture" and "The Constipated Frenchman." The predominant quality of Khushwant Singh as a short-story writer is his comic spirit, informed by the sense of incongruity and by the bewildering phenomena of contradictions in life. Modern man is up against the absurdities that life presents and though the sense of the absurd has in part led to the formulation of the philosophy of existentialism, which has given birth to writers such as Kafka, Singh is not attracted to this philosophical approach. He is primarily preoccupied with the incongruities of life in a lighter vein and with the comic spirit that is generated from the schism between what men are and what they seem—by the gulf that divides appearance from reality. His short stories communicate elements of experience in which darkness is distilled into light and in which the comic is creatively transmuted into essence. (p. 67)

Train to Pakistan (1956) is one of the finest realistic novels of post World War II Indo-Anglian fiction. It is Khushwant Singh's supreme achievement, which he is unlikely to excel. This realistic masterpiece contains, among other things, a well-thought-out structure, an artistically conceived plot, an absorbing narrative, and imaginatively realized characters. It has many notable features such as an unobtrusively symbolic framework, meaningful atmosphere and a powerful, unvarnished naturalistic mode of expression or style.

The predominant quality of *Train to Pakistan* is its stark realism, its absolute fidelity to the truth of life, its trenchant exposition of one of the most moving, even tragic, events of contemporary Indian history, the partition. It is also marked by its special naturalistic *mores.* The individual in Khushwant Singh's fictional world is silhouetted against this vast, panoramic background, the great human catastrophe of the partition of India and the ghastly and inhuman events which followed it. Khushwant Singh's art is revealed in not merely probing deep into the real but in transposing the actual into symbol and image. His art of realistic portrayal cannot be described merely as an exercise in the bookkeeping of existence; in effect, it is a creative endeavor of transcending the actual, asserting the value and dignity of the individual, and finally, of expressing the tragic splendor of a man's sacrifice for a woman. (p. 68)

[The train] indicates the harrowing processes of this change, the awful and ghastly experience of human beings involved in a historical, impersonal, and dehumanized process. The train suggests the fate of individuals, the destinies of the two newly formed nations, consequent upon a political decision and the miseries, sufferings and privations which issue from it. Second, the train is also a symbol of the machine age, an era dominated by science and technology. (p. 69)

[The] train is a dual symbol: it symbolizes life and action but it also stands for death and disaster. (p. 70)

Singh's art of portraying and transmitting atmospheric effects is amply shown in scenes of the trains from Pakistan.... The use of the words "ghost" and "ghostly" forms part of the accentuation of experience and expression. Adjectives in Khushwant Singh are filled with subtle meaning, and single nouns, like little "drops," contain oceans of meaning. Thus, the significance of the title, *Train to Pakistan,* is woven into the narrative substance of the novel. It also indicates the process of the connection between meaning and symbol. (p. 72)

Train to Pakistan has an almost conventional structure since it grows out of a chronological sequence of time. Yet the structure is not purely traditional because it is superseded by an intangible current of values and also an evolving form. It is not circumscribed by the areas of action and character, but transcends them and enters the area of value judgment.... Thus the synthesis of reality and value is one of the remarkable qualities of *Train to Pakistan.* ...

Train to Pakistan alternates between the dramatic novel and the novel of character, between growth in space and movement in time and, therefore, simultaneously develops both of these dimensions. (p. 73)

Train to Pakistan is surely part of the march of the novel toward realism, but it also goes beyond it in the area of values, the field so subtly and superbly explored by great novelists such as Tolstoy and Dostoevsky. It embodies the exploration of new concepts of reality. *Train to Pakistan,* in spite of its predominantly realistic mores, tends toward prophetic fiction. Paradoxically, it is prophetic because it is so innately realistic. The exploration of the human world and its related values in *Train to Pakistan* is more profound and more moving than perhaps the most erudite and expert commentary on aspects of twentieth-century civilization. (p. 74)

It is Khushwant Singh's deep and ethical humanism that governs his portrayal of the real and the actual. *Train to Pakistan,* therefore, is no mere realistic tract, nor is it a bare record of actual events. On the contrary, it is a creative rendering of the real, and it reaffirms the novelist's faith in man and renews artistically his avowed allegiance to the humanistic ideal. (pp. 103-04)

The symbolistic pattern in the novel, though prominent in places, is overshadowed by the realistic strain. Religious festivals—Baisakhi and Christmas—symbolize the regeneration of man, but the effect is hardly sustained by the sequence of events. Birds too are symbols of the renewal and joy of life, and it is surely ironic that Sabhrai would not, after all this ado, hear the nightingale. The monsoon, which is an atmospheric rhythm, also symbolizes renewal of life in a cyclical pattern, but even its effect in short-lived.

The basic theme, interlinked with symbol, is that of love as a solver of the problems of life—human, social, cultural, and political....

A dichotomy between the inference of the title and the im-

plications of the content is created in *I Shall Not Hear the Nightingale.* The title signifies the poetic intention of the novelist, whereas the substance of the novel is dominated by dialogue and descriptions of individual, social, and political situations, and by the complications that arise from them. The tension arises out of the difference between the novelist's desire to make a poetic communication about life and his actual performance in capturing merely the physical reality of India in ferment. The schism between symbol and theme, poetical ideal and realistic treatment, is a significant feature of the novel's form.

However, the schism is not deep, and the dichotomy between Khushwant Singh's intention to make a poetic communication about life and his realistic portrayal is resolved by his mode of presentation of lifelike characters. Fictional characters look in two directions, out toward life and in toward art. The characters in *I Shall Not Hear the Nightingale* look toward life and become lifelike, not artlike. In this process, the dichotomy between the poetic intention and the realistic achievement is resolved since the realm of life is all-inclusive and covers the area of the passion of life and prose of everyday existence. (p. 124)

[The motif of love is] the basic principle, the sine qua non of *I Shall Not Hear the Nightingale* and, by implication, of Khushwant Singh's attitude toward, and evaluation of life. (p. 125)

Khushwant Singh's nonfiction is pervaded by his view of life, which reveals his "acceptance" of the world with all its bizarre associations. His view of the world shows his positive acceptance of things as they are and thus becomes the kernel of his realistic creed.... Singh's literary talent is versatile, and his comic pose makes him appear sometimes a hedonist and at other times a supercilious social historian. But the fact remains that Khushwant Singh is deeply religious in his basic approach to life, and his inner craving for moral elevation is an act of the will. (p. 141)

Singh's essays are in part personal and in part objectively expository and are marked by liveliness, gentle irony, and an irrepressible comic spirit. His historical sense is often combined with his perception of contemporary relevance, and this movement, backward and forward in time, gives his essays their essential vitality. (p. 142)

[In some of his essays, the] description is almost idyllic, and the poet in Singh bursts out in lyrical expansiveness. But the question arises whether it is genuine and whether this lyrical strain is in accord with the dominant realistic trend in his writing. It seems to me that there is no inevitable conflict or contradiction between the poetical and the realistic elements in fiction and that these apparently contradictory tendencies can coexist and even contribute to the totality of effect in art. (p. 144)

[The] satirical mode is only one aspect of Singh's creative art; certainly, it is not the most important one. He, of course, holds the mirror to India's, and the world's, "Monsters and Monstrosities"; but he also knows that the world is not monopolized by monsters only. There are also angels. As a realist, he faces the monsters, exposes them, ridicules them, and makes them the target of his rapier thrusts and biting irony. As a humanist, he realizes and acknowledges the principle that man will supersede all the monsters and establish the supremacy of the moral law. Man is the crowning glory of creation, and, though he is partly beast, he is also partly angel. In moments of crisis, the angelic in man will triumph over the beastly element in him. This is indeed the moral triumph of man so forcefully demonstrated in *Train to Pakistan.*

Singh's criticisms and comments on life and personalities aim at reaching the humanistic ideal. The novelist is harmoniously combined with the social critic in his creative self. I think he occupies a special position in his adherence to, and interpretation of, Realism. His creative faculty is preoccupied, not so much with the individual as an isolated entity or with society in the mass, as with the main issue of maintaining the balance between them. The far sighted realist must try to keep the balance between the claims of sociological presentation and the virtues of psychological analysis. Singh's realism thus becomes part of his moral universe. It is tinged with and mellowed by his deep humanistic faith; therefore, it is free from the disastrous effect of Mrs. Grundy, who equates "realistic" with "pornographic." Khushwant Singh's realism is singularly free from this blemish because it is profoundly permeated with moral values. As a creative writer, Singh is an embodiment of the synthesis of the realist and the humanist—which is indeed the essence of his achievement. (pp. 150-51)

An extremely interesting aspect of Khushwant Singh's achievement as an author, of fictional and nonfictional prose, is his use of the English language.... This particular variety of English, sometimes called "Indian English," has been admired by certain linguists, and quite paradoxically denounced as "Babu English" by certain others, particularly by purists. (p. 152)

Another significant aspect of Khushwant Singh's use of language and style is his realistic, down-to-earth idiom, transposed from Punjabi to English, which is a pronounced expression of the quality of his mind and his view of life. He unconsciously, almost inevitably, revolts against the deceptively soft and sweet style of the Romantics and what he believes to be its fake exterior.... Singh's style also seems to be part of the general trend in style that has been influenced by the belief that there is a close connection between serious intention and "unvarnished" realism. The identification of realism or naturalism with the exploration of the more dreary and darker side of life rules out the use of figurative language. (pp. 153-54)

Singh specializes in the use of Indianisms which faithfully depict the gestures, attitudes, and the vernacular of Punjabi villagers. The Punjabi rustic dialect abounds in the use of four-letter words. (pp. 156-57)

These deviations from the norms of native speakers of English or, alternatively, the literal English translations of typical Indian modes of expression or usage, characterize not merely Khushwant Singh's special modes but also his attitudes and value patterns. I admire the delicate and rare combination in Singh of the faithful translator of Punjabi expressions into English and the suave, urbane, cultured, Westernized writer who frequently quotes French and Italian.... Khushwant Singh the typical Punjabi rustic has come to terms admirably with Khushwant Singh the highly educated, Westernized, cosmopolitan, cultured person. In this peculiar synthesis lies the extraordinary vigor and urbanity of his style, the down-to-earth worldliness, and the visionary gleam of his art as a creative writer of great passion and power. (p. 158)

Vasant Anant Shahane, in his Khushwant Singh *(copyright 1972 by Twayne Publishers, Inc.; reprinted with the permission of Twayne Publishers, A Division of G. K. Hall & Co., Boston), Twayne, 1972.*

K. R. SRINIVASA IYENGAR

Khushwant Singh's most enduring work has been done in the field of Sikh history and biography, and his full-length portrait of Ranjit Singh vividly brings out the leader, the ruler and the man.... [His first novel] *Train to Pakistan* projects with pitiless precision a picture of bestial horrors enacted on the Indo-Pakistan border region during the terror-haunted days of August 1947. (p. 498)

As a piece of fiction, *Train to Pakistan* is cleverly contrived, and the interior stitching and general colouring is beyond cavil.... It could not have been an easy novel to write. The events, so recent, so terrible in their utter savagery and meaninglessness, must have defied assimilation in terms of art. Khushwant Singh, however, has succeeded through resolved limitation and rigorous selection in communicating to his readers a hint of the grossness, ghastliness and total insanity of the two-nation theory and the Partition tragedy.... [The] novel adequately conveys them both. (pp. 501-02)

[In *I Shall Not Hear the Nightingale*] Khushwant Singh observes as with a microscope, and records his findings without any squeamishness; and his analysis of the complex of relationships within the family and in the wider world, and his unravelling of the tangle of conflicting loyalties, show both understanding and skill. Humour is blended with brutality, mere sentiment is eschewed, and the picture that emerges is arresting as well as amusing.... Although not as tightly constructed as *Train to Pakistan* and although lacking its consistency of tone and power of articulation, *I Shall Not Hear the Nightingale* has a vivid sense of time, place and the social milieu; and the figure of Sabhrai wholly redeems the dimness and murkiness of the general atmosphere. The fever of sensuality is easier to describe than the radiance of Faith, and this is the reason why Sabhrai almost 'steals' the novel. (pp. 502, 504)

K. R. Srinivasa Iyengar, in his Indian Writing in English *(© 1962, 1973, K. R. Srinivasa Iyengar), Asia Publishing House, 1973.*

* * *

SLADE, Bernard 1930-

Slade, an American playwright and screenwriter, is best known for his comedy *Same Time, Next Year*. (See also *Contemporary Authors*, Vols. 81-84.)

JOHN SIMON

To all but the most fastidious, I can warmly recommend Bernard Slade's *Same Time, Next Year*. A two-character play similar in theme to *Avanti*, and in quality to *The Voice of the Turtle*, it is genuinely funny, often moving, and slyly perspicacious throughout. If it does not rise into the domain of art, it at least never stoops to facile salaciousness, obvious vulgarity, or straining for laughs, like the current Schisgal, McNally, and Simon plays....

This is what the commercial theater ought to be based on: plays that are entertaining, undemanding, adroit, but also respectful of human truths.... (p. 65)

John Simon, in New York *Magazine (copyright © 1975 by NYM Corporation; reprinted with the permission of* New York *Magazine), March 31, 1975.*

HAROLD CLURMAN

[What sustains *Same Time, Next Year*] is not its sentimental base—though that is what makes it "cozy"—but its steady stream of funny lines. For example, the woman explains that her husband was in the service during the war for four years—three of them as a POW. A yak! Funnier still, the man mentions that his wife never travels by plane. "Is she afraid of flying?" the woman asks. "No, of crashing," he answers.

Since the action stretches from 1951 to 1975, we observe the alteration of manners and customs through the period. For instance: the man, still troubled by his conscience, has consulted a "shrink"; his talk is now peppered with Freudian jargon. More strikingly, when the woman arrives in 1961 she no longer wears the usual housewife's outfit but appears in blue jeans and an American Indian headband; she has also become a student at Berkeley. The first words out of her mouth on this occasion are "Shall we fuck?" Then again, and this is surely funny, in one of the intervals designating the passage of time, we hear—besides songs, news items, etc.—a Nixon radio broadcast in which he speaks of those loyal and upright public servants, Haldeman and Ehrlichman.

There is in that aspect of the play a further touch of political history. The woman has not only become four-letter-word forthright in speech but "radicalized." She is shocked to learn that her lover voted for Goldwater and scandalized when she hears him wish for Vietnam to be wiped off the earth. "Why?" she exclaims. Because, he tells her, his son was killed in the war there. She falls on his neck in tears. So there is more to the show than just gags: every possible string of popular appeal is plucked.

Does it make sense to take this comedy "seriously"? Perhaps it should simply be set down as sub-Simon frivolity. But at the end of the first act I could not forbear thinking: this is all false, foolish, foul—and undoubtedly a tremendous hit. (pp. 413-14)

Harold Clurman, in The Nation *(copyright 1975 by the Nation Associates, Inc.), April 5, 1975.*

J. W. LAMBERT

A contemporary American comedy of manners, *Same Time, Next Year* . . . [is] concerned with that most difficult of dramatic values, affection. . . . [It] uses an improbable plot device on which to hang reflections of the world and of jumbled private emotions: in this case the illicit meeting, for one night in every year, of a married man and a married woman briefly escaping from their own spouses and daily trials. We look in on them in a motel cabin once every five years from 1951 to 1976, catching up with changing fashions in American society, sharing their unabated family frets. It is all very lightly done by Bernard Slade. . . . [The] point of it all—a point more easily appreciated and more highly valued by 'ordinary' theatregoers than by metropolitan sophisticates—is the way in which, through the exchange of news and family photographs, the momentary sharing of apprehensions—far more than through sex, fun though that remains—these two build a lasting bond. (pp. 43-4)

J. W. Lambert, in Drama, *Winter, 1976.*

LUCY HUGHES-HALLETT

Same Time Next Year is set in an hotel room in California at five-yearly intervals between 1951 and 1976. An adulterous couple meet there for an annual clandestine weekend while the audience eavesdrops and watches them work through the social history of America's last quarter century. Between them they toy with all the major fads and philosophies to have swept the western world in the period. (p. 37)

With such a format, characterisation is bound to give way to caricature and the plot becomes little more than a linking device for a series of sketches, but against all odds the play holds together. Bernard Slade manages to make his characters likeable. They may not be anything special, indeed a more colourless couple could scarcely be imagined. They're naïve, conventional and not very bright, but their helpless normality makes them touching. They love their children and show each other photographs, neither of them really wants a divorce, they fumble nervously, dressing under the bedclothes at their first encounter, and each year they feel a bit shy at first. They tell each other stories about their respective spouses which reveal comfortable family lives in the background beside which their annual transgressions are of no real significance. Here are no Anna and Vronsky, just two decent people having a bit of a break from the kids. (p. 38)

Lucy Hughes-Hallett, in Plays and Players *(© copyright Lucy Hughes-Hallett 1976; reprinted with permission), December, 1976.*

* * *

STUART, (Hilton) Jesse 1907-

Stuart, an American novelist, short story writer, and poet, writes primarily about the poor people of Appalachia. Much of his fiction has a distinct oral character, replete with the mountain dialect and mannerisms of his narrator. A short story master with a strong sense of narrative and well drawn characters, he is sometimes accused of being unselectively prolific. Many critics, however, believe that his work is underrated by the critical community as a whole. (See also *CLC*, Vols. 1, 8, and *Contemporary Authors*, Vols. 5-8, rev. ed.)

LEE PENNINGTON

[Stuart has a distinct vision of life which permeates all of his novels.] There is the dark world. . . . It is the world which Stuart sees around him—Kentucky or Appalachia—but is representative of the universal and the characters who live in the dark world are universal men. The dark world is dead or is dying. And at this point the Stuart cycle begins.

From the dark world, or the dying world, comes a world of light and all the symbolic overtones contained therein. But the world does not, cannot, act alone. There must be a force, the life force, which generates from the death a substantial rebirth. That force is youth and in a symbolic sense is the savior of the culture and of mankind.

Time in the cycle becomes involved in what we have spoken about before—the oneness, the single entity, the past, present and future, just as the symbolic force is a part of all existence, a part of all mankind. There is most often a symbolic woman, one who is the essence of freedom and of youth, and that woman becomes the natural mother of the new youth, the new world of light.... She produces the oneness in the child who is of culture and of time, all culture and all time.

Within the vision we face death but always with the hope of a rebirth and we are left with a conscious understanding of the nature of the hope. We realize that the dark world was a result of our own doing and that the light world is the result of our being.

There is the fight and the importance of the struggle, perhaps similar to the one experienced in the works of Ernest Hemingway, except that with Hemingway the end result of the fight is not important and with Stuart the end result is. The end is important with Stuart because it also indicates a beginning, a new beginning through rebirth, and if not a rebirth of the individual character, at least a rebirth of his being, his soul, his memories, through the symbolic youth. With Stuart, however, it is only those who perform the battle well who are granted the rebirth. The living dead never realize their destinies.

Further, there is Stuart's use of parallel structure, a structure [finely developed and keenly executed].... (pp. 151-52)

Stuart selected the dark hills and the people of the dark hills because the hills are the home of the people of the darkness, and these sons and daughters of darkness are symbols for a far greater concept concerning the nature of man. The people, like the concept of man in the Twentieth Century, are lost, lonely and forgotten. Yet, from the dark hills and the people of darkness can come a world of light. (p. 152)

> *Lee Pennington, in his* The Hills of Jesse Stuart *(copyright © 1967 by Lee Pennington), Harvest Press, 1967.*

J. R. LeMASTER

Although the Agrarian Movement was in its heyday while Stuart was a student at Vanderbilt, he had mixed emotions about the actual achievements of the group. As he says, he liked very much what the Agrarians were advocating, but not what they were doing: "Their farming was on paper. I went to one professor's home and he had a few tomatoes in a little garden and these plants were poorly cultivated. At my home, we farmed: we knew how to do it. We made a living and some to spare farming our Kentucky hills and valleys, We were not 'gentleman farmers'." ... The Fugitives were bound together by virtue of their being southerners. They were literary intellectuals who were intensely aware of cultural decadence in the South, a view they shared with William Faulkner, and much of the decadence they blamed on the old antebellum ideal of a Jeffersonian society. On the other hand, the Agrarian Movement actually cultivated Jeffersonian idealism, even though it counted Ransom, Tate, Warren, and Davidson among its members. Stuart is right about what the Agrarians stood for. They fostered an overwhelming sense of place and believed that human success and happiness depend upon establishing and maintaining a right relation with nature, with the land. They opposed industrialization as dehumanizing and in general favored an imaginatively reconstructed pre-Civil War South. The Agrarian Movement arose and flourished during the Great Depression and probably must be viewed in that context. Nonetheless, the Fugitive sense of the decadence of the times and the Agrarian sense of the importance of place have been central to almost everything Jesse Stuart has written in the last forty years. (pp. 20-1)

He is a rhapsodic or bardic poet [in *Man with a Bull-Tongue Plow*], and he is still feeling his boyhood love for Robert Burns.... [One] finds that he knows he is out of the mainstream of poetry, even in the thirties: "I do not sing the songs you love to hear." Also in the same poem one suspects that he knows his form to be out of vogue: "And these crude strains no critic can call art." ... For the most part, *Man with A Bull-Tongue Plow* is a celebration of agricultural or agrarian existence, although it becomes increasingly philosophical near the end.... Significantly, in the first half of the collection one hears much about Robert Burns, but in the latter half Burns is dropped and in his place one hears much about Donald Davidson. (p. 21)

Stuart finds dozens of ways to symbolize the life process, including the sprouting of seed into plants and the floating of a leaf on a stream of water. Whatever the way, the life of the individual is always absorbed into the life of the whole, and the life of the whole is always is turn observed in the individual.

The poet's concern is the greater American culture, along with the kind of sensibility shaped by that culture, and that such is the case does not depend entirely for its support upon what he says about the symbols in *Album of Destiny*. He has his characters speak about the things that most interest him as a poet. (pp. 22-3)

In a long celebration of pioneer ancestors, Stuart draws numerous contrasts between life in a golden past and life in twentieth-century America. In some instances he does this as a direct attack on the values of the present. [He addresses] lines, for example, ... to stalwart pioneer mothers who bred a race of hearty and courageous Americans, as opposed to twentieth-century women who have turned whorish.... He pits the old against the new, and in his creating of a golden past one always suspects that he has in the back of his mind more than a prewar South, or even a pioneer America. Somewhere much farther back in time he imagines a unified existence similar to the one Eliot pictures before "dissociation" set in, an existence symbolized in Judeo-Christian tradition by the Garden of Eden before the Fall.

Disapproving of the direction he saw American culture taking in the thirties, Stuart admonishes youth to do something about it.... He also admonishes the poet to enlist his services in a battle against growing decadence.... The greatest fault in "Songs of a Mountain Plowman" is that the poet feels so strongly about his subject matter that he cannot sustain the slightest pretense of objectivity. In far too many instances, he clearly breaks down and records his own deep-seated sense of desperation over America.... However poor the poetry in it, "Songs of a Mountain Plowman" stands as the strongest evidence we have of the poet's beliefs about the state of American culture in the thirties. (pp. 25-7)

[One] is forced to conclude that Stuart has not changed his beliefs, The Fugitive-Agrarian synthesis or fusion which characterizes the poems has in fact not changed, and that in spite of the poet's acute awareness that American culture has changed drastically. *Album of Destiny* was followed by *Kentucky Is My Land* ..., a collection which at first glance appears to be without a conscious plan. But when one looks a second time he finds that *Kentucky Is My Land*

is made up of poems about the poet's bronze-skinned figures of the earth, and that these are placed between two
long prose poems, both unquestionably about America and
American culture. The poems in this collection are characteristic of most, if not all, of Stuart's writing in that they are
highly autobiographical. In this case, there are poems about
the poet, about his wife, and about his daughter.

The first of the long prose poems, and the one from which
the collection gets its title, is structured on a metaphor in
which Kentucky is the heart of America, which in turn is
the body. In terms of the metaphor, the health of the heart
determines the health of the body, and the circulatory system stands as a symbol of the poet's attempt to change the
direction of cultural development in America. Once he has
established the Kentucky-America relationship, Stuart
writes of the birth of a child in a pastoral world, in the
poet's world of W-Hollow on the literal level. However, as
he creates this world the reader is impressed that it is an
unreal one, another Eden, or the world of a golden age long
gone by. In the pages that follow, one watches the child
grow into the world about him, absorbing the smells, tastes,
sights, sounds, and touch of it until he is at one with it. . . .
When the child has grown to manhood, he travels in all
directions from the heart of America and rejects what he
finds in favor of Kentucky. . . . Toward the end of the
poem one discovers that what the poet's child of nature is
rejecting is, in the aggregate, all of modern America. Disillusioned by industrial city streets, he returns to his pastoral
world and there becomes the poet's archetypal man for a
new America.

In the metaphor of the heart and body lie two other important considerations. In the first place, the man of nature,
like the blood in the circulatory system, comes and goes.
Again like the blood, when he leaves the heart of America
he carries the life of the body with him. . . . He is further
like the blood in that he returns to the heart for cleansing
and renewal; thus Stuart's poem symbolically becomes an
agrarian effort as well as an agrarian statememt. In the second place, in the circulatory system one finds an appropriate symbol for all of Stuart's poetic efforts. His intentions
have always been that he would evoke symbols from his
natural world of Eastern Kentucky, and that they in turn
would travel outward in much the same way that the blood
travels from the heart.

"The Builder and the Dream," coming at the end of *Kentucky Is My Land*, is a symbolist poem, and in writing it the
poet is everywhere cognizant of *The Waste Land*. Following the example of Eliot, he invokes the Fisher King from
ancient Grail legend in the form of one Ben Tuttle—who
symbolically succeeds in abolishing the wasteland and
thereby fulfills his dreams of a post-wastland existence. At
the same time, he symbolically fulfills the poet's dream of a
post-wasteland America. In various versions of the Grail
legend, productivity of the land depends upon the condition
of the Fisher King. In existing *Perceval* versions of Grail
texts, the land is laid waste when the Fisher King is disabled, and it is made fertile and productive again when the
health of the Fisher King is restored. Logically, the Fisher
King is the most appropriate symbol Stuart could find to
represent what he considers to be the problem of man's
essential oneness with earth. (pp. 27-9)

A symbolist poem can never be a closed world—by mere
virtue of its being symbolist. Because it is a symbolist

poem, that Jesse Stuart may or may not be Ben Tuttle
makes no difference. It does make a difference that Ben
Tuttle, as one of those Americans gone soft . . . , has a
dream about restoring denuded forest lands. And of even
greater significance is that when he does something about
the dream he is also doing something about himself—the
fact is that he is changing the conditions of his existence.
(pp. 29-30)

Although the language is not always convincing, "The
Builder and the Dream" is a very important poem. In Ben
Tuttle the poet succeeds symbolically in destroying the
modern American sensibility, and in Ben Tuttle's deed, the
wasteland culture of modern America. Beyond these
things, and even more important, is that he succeeds symbolically in supplanting the fractured sensibility with a unified one and the fractured culture with one in which man
feels at home.

[*Hold April*] is largely a celebration of the rites of
spring. . . . The basic themes of the collection are man's
oneness with the earth, the old and the new, and mutability.
On the other hand, in *Hold April* Stuart is more willing than
he is in any other collection to accept life as it is. (pp. 30-1)

In *Hold April* there is a new sense of humility. . . . [But]
nowhere is there, as in Whitman, a celebration of America's teeming cities. His vision has not changed, although he
has momentarily become less vocal about his concerns over
modern American culture. (pp. 31-2)

The most recent evidence of where Stuart stands as a poet
is to be found in a typescript of satirical poems entitled
"Birdland's Golden Age." . . . The satirical poems began
in 1965 because of the way President Johnson was handling
the war in Viet Nam, and although Stuart continues to add
poems to the group he has been reluctant to submit it for
publication as a collection. As far as the poet of "Birdland's Golden Age" is concerned, however, modern American culture has nearly run its course, and we presently
stand on the verge of anarchy. . . . The destiny of America
is very much the poet's concern, as it was in the thirties.
Only his method of treating his subject has changed. After
being a lyric poet on the one hand, and occasionally a symbolist on the other, he adopts the extremes of satire in order
to handle what he views as critical conditions. . . . According to the poet, our present madness has gone too far, and
we are consequently in need of being purged or purified. . . . (pp. 35-6)

Not only has America gone mad, but Appalachia, in the
midst of the madness, has become a doomed tree. Even
there the poet sees little hope. . . . He sees Appalachian
highways cluttered with discarded beer cans as one of many
symbols of a growing decadence. . . . Whether Stuart has
given up on his beloved Appalachia remains to be seen. His
recent fiction would generally indicate that he has not, although one might interpret his 1973 novel *The Land beyond
the River* as the strongest possible evidence that he has.
One thing is certain: during an unusually long career as a
writer he has cherished the region. But beyond that, having
arrested the American frontier there in his consciousness,
he has long held Appalachia before the remainder of America as a model for national existence.

Accompanying the poet's shift of attitude and method in
"Birdland's Golden Age," there is also a dramatic shift in
form. The sonnet, which for years has stood for the ulti-

mate in orderliness in his work, has diminished in importance. In place of the sonnet one finds poems with shorter lines, and poems in which there is obviously less effort on the poet's part to use measure or meter. But in spite of the radical changes in technique and form, there is still plenty of evidence that Stuart cannot give up on Appalachia. Although he includes Appalachia in his satire on America, recognizing that it too needs to be purged, he does so with love, viewing his method as corrective. He attacks strip-mining, corrupt politics, and the welfare program, but in "Birdland's Golden Age" (in contract to what one reads in the essay "My Land Has a Voice," for example) Appalachia will remain Appalachia only if the wounds are healed.... (pp. 36-7)

Stuart's satire, directed at the ills of modern America, is not limited to general issues. Prominent people are satirized as examples of what is wrong with America. The list includes such names as Presidents Truman, Eisenhower and Johnson, Lady Bird Johnson, Billie Sol Estes, Billy Graham, John L. Lewis, and many more. The incidents recounted by the poet concerning these people comprise present American decadence. (p. 38)

In "Birdland's Golden Age," in spite of the change in method, Jesse Stuart is saying essentially what he has always been saying—that man has lost his once-harmonious existence in nature, that he has lost his love for the land, and that ultimately man must survive in nature's balances or not at all. In short, Stuart is an oddity in American poetry. Over a long career he has consistently employed his art in the service of the state, and for that reason he is one of a few modern poets fit for Plato's republic. As a moralist, he has conducted a love affair with his country, and his poetry is chiefly a record of that. At any rate, since the Great American Depression, and since the Fugitive-Agrarian synthesis took place in his thinking, he has constantly sung one song. (p. 39)

> *J. R. LeMaster, "Jesse Stuart's Poetry as Fugitive-Agrarian Synthesis," in* Jesse Stuart: Essays on His Work, *edited by J. R. LeMaster and Mary Washington Clarke (copyright © 1977 by The University Press of Kentucky), University Press of Kentucky, 1977, pp. 19-39.*

WADE HALL

[When] a man writes honestly, without pretension or distortion, about the way people look, act, and think, he produces fiction that is believable and humor that is natural and organic. This is the essence of Jesse Stuart's humor: it is an element as basic to his works as the winds that blow through the beech trees of W-Hollow.... Stuart's humor emerges from his subject matter and is sustained by it. There are few quick laughs in his works. Rather, his humor evokes the constant amusement of man observing man in the natural act of being himself. From regional raw materials Stuart has, therefore, shaped fiction and nonfiction that transcend locale and speak to man's comic (and tragic) condition everywhere. (p. 90)

To an outlander the people of Eastern Kentucky must have appeared culturally retarded, primitive, and definitely odd. However, Stuart has never written with the intention of ridiculing them because of their way of life. When he sketches a man drunk in a cow stall, he is holding up a mirror in which his readers may see their own absurd excesses. It is the way of serious humor that first one laughs at someone else, then gradually realizes that he is laughing at an aspect of himself. The accidents of language, looks, and dress—as all humorists know—derive from a common human nature.

But it is the apparently unique way of life in Appalachia that has made it an appealing literary subject to outsiders. The folk life with its superstitions and old-fashioned customs has been a Stuart hallmark. From beginning to end, it has informed his prose with color and vitality and a tone of comic realism. (p. 91)

Although the locale of Stuart's works may be outside the chief currents of American life, his humor is related directly to two main movements, local color and the humor of the Old Southwest. Hamlin Garland once defined local color literature as having "such quality of texture and background that it could not have been written in any other place or by anyone else than a native"—a quality unmistakable in Stuart's work. Like the local colorists of the late nineteenth century, Stuart delineates vividly the people and the customs of a particular region. Like them, he often blends humor and pathos in a single story or character. Grandpa Tussie in *Taps for Private Tussie,* for example, is a mixture of comic and pathetic elements. But Stuart seldom allows his stories to sink to the pathetic level of Bret Harte's sketches of life in the mining camps of the far West, which typically end in a fountain of tears. The Kentucky humorist's sure control of his materials (and his emotions) commands the reader's respect for his characters—even when they go down to defeat. (pp. 91-2)

Dialect was an important flavoring device of the local colorists, but it was frequently used as an end in itself or to cover up basic structural and stylistic weaknesses and a superficial knowledge of subject matter. The humor of Stuart's writings is enhanced by his judicious use of a dialect that suggests the sound and tone of hill country speech while staying clear of the pitfalls of exaggeration and affectation in phonetics and syntax. Stuart characters speak a simple but expressive language filled with natural metaphors and similes. (p. 92)

[His] books often contain a roughness (sometimes bordering on crudeness) demanded by his coarse materials.... A Southwestern humorist would have been hard pressed to compile a bloodier catalog of physical abuses [than occur in Stuart's accounts of fights].

Another feature of Old Southwestern humor found in Stuart is the tall tale. A man for whom reality is meager and sordid can relish at least momentary glory in a dream world of exaggeration.... [And Stuart's rip-roaring braggarts] are transformed by imagination into mythic heroes whose exploits are as fantastic as Mike Fink's.

Stuart also employs the frontier humorist's technique of using a participant in a story as the narrator. The recurring boy narrator, Shan Powderday, often sounds like a Kentucky Huck Finn. And like Mark Twain's yarnspinners, Stuart's Old Op (in *The Good Spirit of Laurel Ridge*) will launch into a lengthy digression whenever a random remark triggers his memory. Another form of frontier humor is the hoax, a favorite sport of backwoods pranksters, which provides the plot for "Powderday's Red Hen," a story of two boys who fabricate an elaborate lie about a hen that crows and curses.

Another point of similarity between the Kentucky writer's

characters and those of the earlier frontier is that both enjoy the same kinds of entertainments. In addition to hunting, their most popular sport, his characters engage in such activities as frog-trouncing, described vividly in "Frog-Trouncin' Contest." Hangings were also popular entertainments. In "Another Hanging" Stuart has a storyteller recall "one of the best hangin's this country has ever seen." Surrounding the grim center of attention there is a carnival atmosphere, with young people courting, children cavorting, and families enjoying picnic lunches.

A humor based on discomfort, like that of George Washington Harris's Sut Lovingood, is present in much of Stuart's works. (pp. 93-5)

Jesse Stuart's participation in the main currents of American humor has been largely accidental and uncontrived. Similarities between his work and the earlier humor exist because, like the local colorists, he has focused on particular people and the ways that set them apart from ordinary Americans. And, like the Old Southwestern humorists, he has tried to write about them honestly and simply. He has tried to tell the truth about people who have been caricatured and misunderstood.

Although Stuart's works feature strong narrative lines, it is perhaps in characterization that his strength as a humorist lies. [He] has created a memorable gallery of comic characters—people who are usually the more amusing because they are not self-consciously humorous. Suspicious of the law and outsiders but also generous and duty-bound, patriotic in time of war but prone to chafe under military discipline, these are independent people who make a separate peace and return home AWOL. They are hardworking —perhaps pipe-smoking—women, indulgent of their men's occasional indiscretions and excesses and hardy enough to keep house and stand by their men, if need be, in the woods and fields. They are men who love a good drink of moonshine liquor and welcome a contest of wits with the revenue agents. They are essentially a proud people who may seem backward and unprogressive. (p. 95)

In addition to his grotesques, Stuart has filled a hall with Gothic portraits. . . . For strangers to Stuart's world, his fiction rooted in fact (as much of it is) seems like comic invention or exaggeration.

The humor in Stuart's books has come from many directions. Political and religious elements of the hillman's life, for example, have provided him with an extensive reservoir of material. Politics has always been a deadly serious business in Kentucky, sometimes leading to bloody, even fatal, encounters at the polling places. (p. 96)

Hill people, even when they don't belong to a church, are apt to be as partisan in their religion as in their politics; and Stuart derives much humor from such denominational allegiances. Rivalry is keen, especially between the Baptists and the Methodists, and sometimes exists within the splinter sects of a single denomination.

Stuart's religious people sometimes speak in unknown tongues and handle snakes, and they eagerly anticipate revival meetings. They are usually opposed to movies (perhaps even television), dancing, drinking, and card playing. They frequently practice baptism by total immersion (in a nearby creek) and perform the scriptural ceremony of foot washing. According to the author's count, there are at least

eight "Baptist heavens"—presumably each splinter group has its own.

Stuart's human comedy of man's mortality is enacted against the backdrop of the ever-greening, ever-fresh, enduring earth, and the irony of man's proud attempts to reshape and possess it is a constant theme in the Appalachian writer's work. Stuart delights in poking fun at feuding, land-grabbing, deed-coveting people who do not know how to live in right relationship to the land. (p. 97)

An important aspect of man's relationship to the earth is his affinity for animals. The Kentucky writer's sympathetic characters are fond of a menagerie of animals. . . . (p. 98)

The natural background in his works—the woods, fields, sky, pasturelands, rivers, and the creatures that inhabit them—is not, of course, "humorous," not even the minnow battling the Goliath snake. Only man can be humorous, for only he can exercise a will to become something other than he is, could, or should be—and then be aware of the discrepancy. And only man can fail to live in a right relationship to nature. Animals have no choice. But man, the crowning achievement of creation, is reminded of his fragile transience every time the world is recreated by a new sunrise. (p. 99)

In no single book is Jesse Stuart's classic sense of the comic so much in evidence as in *Foretaste of Glory,* one of his most successful works but often ignored or underrated by critics. In this novel he bares the frailties of man that make him generally a choice butt of humor and specifically an appropriate object of satire. Here is displayed dramatically the disparity between what man pretends to be and what he actually is—the gap that is the fertile field of humor.

On September 18, 1941, in the river town of Blakesburg, the trumpet of the Lord apparently sounds—and catches just about everyone unready for glory. Although the heavenly display that causes the panic is actually the aurora borealis or nothern lights, the people fear that Christ has returned to judge them; and despite whatever respectable fronts they may possess, they know that He will find out their secret sins. Consequently, they scurry about frantically trying to put their lives and houses in order before they are called to account. . . . But the world does not end. And when the sun comes up on September 19, the people resume their old ways and familiar coverups. They sink into the hypocritical grooves from which they were insanely jarred into a short-lived morality. They go back to being as human—and as laughable—as ever. In the end, a false foretaste of glory has done nothing to change their natures. (pp. 99-100)

[In "The Reaper and the Flowers"] Stuart takes the foibles and shortcomings and vices that all flesh is heir to, exaggerates them in the person of Uglybird, and invites his readers to join the citizens of Blakesburg in laughter—so that they may acknowledge their problems and failings and remedy them or at least momentarily forget them. And he has made available the catharsis afforded by humor as well as by tragedy. Jesse Stuart, like all good men of humor, is essentially a moralist, who, in Mary Washington Clarke's words, is in the business of "driving out evil with laughter." (pp. 101-02)

Wade Hall, "Humor in Jesse Stuart's Fiction,"
in Jesse Stuart: Essays on His Work, *edited by*

*J. R. LeMaster and Mary Washington Clark
(copyright © 1977 by The University Press of
Kentucky), University Press of Kentucky, 1977,
pp. 89-102.*

JIM WAYNE MILLER

In Jesse Stuart's short story "This Farm for Sale" Dick Stone decides to sell out and move into town. He authorizes his old friend Melvin Spencer, a well-known local real estate agent, to sell his hill farm. Spencer is really a poet. . . . [In his advertisements he] describes the nuts and berries and other wild fruits growing on the Stone farm— the hazelnuts, elderberries, pawpaws, and persimmons— and the jellies and preserves Mrs. Stone makes from them. He describes the tall cane and corn growing in rich bottomland beside the Tiber River, which is full of fish; the broad-leafed burley tobacco; the wild game in the woods; the house constructed of native timber. Spencer's advertisement causes Dick Stone to see his farm with new eyes. He says to his family: "I didn't know I had so much. I'm a rich man and didn't know it. I'm not selling this farm!"

A vivid illustration of the poet's function, Stuart's story suggests the complex relationship between word and thing, the magical power of language, artistically used, to transform and clarify our perceptions and to heighten our experience. "This Farm for Sale" may be taken as a key to the proper understanding of all Stuart's work—the poetry, the fiction, the autobiographical and biographical accounts. In this celebration of a farm and the life a family lives on it we have on a small scale what Stuart has written large in all his works. For as creator of W-Hollow, the fictional place, Stuart is celebrator of a land, a people, their way of life, and their values. Stuart is to W-Hollow and to us what Melvin Spencer is to the Stone farm and family.

As a poet, Stuart differs from most of his neighbors in the Cumberland foothills in his ability not only to see but to say what he sees, not only to feel but to express his feelings. But it is not just his personal feelings that the poet expresses. The poet, according to Emerson (in "The Poet"), tells us "not of his wealth, but of the commonwealth." This is precisely what Melvin Spencer does in Stuart's "This Farm for Sale." Dick Stone owns the farm but he is not yet in possession of the best part of it, which cannot be had except through a certain vision of it. Melvin Spencer gives Stone—and all others who read his advertisement—this vision. And through his rendered vision of a land, a people, and their way of life, Stuart apprises readers not of his wealth but of the commonwealth. (pp. 103-04)

Spencer's language not only presents an integrity of impression, organizing the Stones' perceptions as they have not been organized previously, but his language has the effect of legitimizing or certifying the life of the family on the farm. His language assists them in establishing a relationship to the farm they have not had. As a result of their altered perceptions, the Stones now possess their farm more surely than ever.

Stuart's "This Farm for Sale" suggests the relationship between naming and possessing. The poet is a namer, and naming, even in its simplest form, is a profound act. Naming objects, framing them in words, unleashes the transfiguring effect of word on thing. The act of naming may be relatively simple, no more than an enumeration. . . . But naming may be a more elaborate act, involving an array of the capabilities of language in the process of catching human experience in a web of words. Naming is one way of taking ultimate possession of objects or experience. In writing the stories, novels, and poems that create the world of W-Hollow, Jesse Stuart has been involved in an elaborate act of naming and thus of taking possession.

It is the act of naming which accounts for the tendency to repeat, catalog, and elaborate detail in Stuart's work. (p. 105)

The physical terrain about which Stuart writes is not all there is to W-Hollow, for mere physical locality is not *place,* a word implying human involvement and participation in a locality. It has been suggested that "the catalyst that converts a physical locality into a 'place' is the process of experiencing it deeply, and of engaging with it in a symbolic relationship." In a process aided by language Dick Stone experiences the conversion of a locality—his farm— into a place. Stone's place—and any place—is locality humanized, nature and human nature merged or linked. . . .

In Stuart's descriptions and characterizations of people he typically merges nature and human nature. Quite often his people are rendered by metaphors and similes that image their physical features in terms of details from their surroundings. (p. 107)

The success of Stuart's merging of nature and human nature varies from poem to poem, from story to story. Sometimes the technique of deriving physical descriptions and personal qualities of individuals from their immediate natural surroundings seems mannered and predictable. One simile or metaphor may strike the reader as more apt than another. But the cumulative effect, nevertheless, is the creation of a living world in which the connection between people and the land is close and organic; in which people are aware of their dependence on the land. (pp. 108-09)

While the examination of philosophical and intellectual problems is foreign to Stuart's concrete and spontaneous approach, a philosophy is implicit in his work. And Stuart suggests, in his depictions of people and their relationship to the land, that human beings derive more than just their livelihood from the land. The values they hold and live by are also rooted in the soil and in the way it is worked. Not surprisingly, Stuart is disturbed by the interruption of this connection brought on by the decline of the subsistence farm and by the institution of the Soil Bank. (p. 109)

Stuart is clearly critical of what he considers an unnatural relationship to the land, a relationship that lacks the proper give-and-take of the traditional farmer, for whom farming is not just a way of making a living but also a way of life. Stuart has understood, in his life and in his work, that place can be possessed spiritually only by giving oneself to it. The spiritual possession of America, accomplished, paradoxically, by the giving of self, is the theme of Frost's "The Gift Outright," whose familiar, aphoristic first line is: "The land was ours before we were the land's." (p. 110)

Land, physical terrain, is so fundamental to Stuart's experience that he visualizes the structure of a novel as a range of mountains. His central character is the highest ridge, while the minor characters are mere foothills. This way of conceiving of his characters suggests the degree to which he identifies people with place. In this connection it is instructive to consider that in what is taken to be his least successful novel, *Daughter of the Legend*, Stuart writes about a place and a people other than those he knows best.

But where he has worked with his own materials, his people in their place, Stuart has created a world whole and complete. W-Hollow is there, a world alive, existing not as a dead transcript of reality but as a vision, possessing a dimension lacking in a transcript. W-Hollow is itself a reality created through language. "Words," Emerson says, "are signs of natural facts." The natural facts of W-Hollow are present in Stuart's work in abundance. But just as "particular natural facts are symbols of particular spiritual facts" (Emerson's "Nature"), Stuart's created world is a symbol, the embodiment of a tradition, a set of values, the spirit of a place. (p. 112)

The W-Hollow world does not deny age and death. But even the very old remain children of the earth. Like the earth itself, Stuart's people can be very old and yet seem young. (pp. 113-14)

Stuart turns the slightest incidents into symbols. It is this sort of symbol making that causes the world of W-Hollow to be a multileveled, resonant reality. Stuart's people shape the land and are, in turn, shaped by it. His people derive their strength from the very land that demands of them strength of character and spirit. They are so subtly attuned to the land that they seem at times to be an embodiment of the land's qualities, its moods and spirit—just as the grandfather in "Another April," very old and yet youthful in spirit, resembles the earth—old and yet young and fresh on the first of April. The land bears everywhere the mark of the people who live on it, while the people seem to be an outgrowth of the land, as natural there as an outcropping of rock, weathered and shaped by the seasons. It is this symbiosis of land and people, nature and human nature, which makes W-Hollow, Stuart's fictional place, not so much a locality in northeastern Kentucky as it is a symbol of human spirit. W-Hollow is a part of the American experience, and an important part, revealed and rendered through the transforming power of language, just as Dick Stone's farm is revealed to him by Melvin Spencer's words. (p. 114)

The world of W-Hollow is a community conceived on a human scale, not so large that people have lost their sense of relationship to one another or to the land itself. Drawn into this world we undergo the experience of Dick Stone who, hearing his farm described by a poet, realizes for the first time how much he has, how rich he is. Just as Melvin Spencer gives Dick Stone the most precious part of his farm through the transfiguring power of language, Stuart gives us through his work a vision of the earth and our relationship to it. This is Jesse Stuart's gift outright, and it is priceless. (p. 115)

> *Jim Wayne Miller, "The Gift Outright: W-Hollow," in* Jesse Stuart: Essays on His Work, *edited by J. R. LeMaster and Mary Washington Clarke (copyright © 1977 by The University Press of Kentucky), University Press of Kentucky, 1977, pp. 103-16.*

*   *   *

STYRON, William   1925-

Styron is a Pulitzer Prize-winning American novelist, short story writer, and playwright. The public controversy surrounding *The Confessions of Nat Turner* has somewhat ob-
scured the critical acclaim received by his previous work. *The Long March*, for example, is often described as a small masterpiece. A southern writer, Styron has often been compared to Faulkner because of his dense imagery and rhetorical style. (See also *CLC*, Vols. 1, 3, 5, and *Contemporary Authors*, Vols. 5-8, rev. ed.)

IHAB HASSAN

[*Set This House on Fire* is] an ambiguous novel of outrage, one that also happens to be artistically flawed.... [It] treats, in distraught and melodramatic fashion, the regeneration of Cass Kinsolving. The regeneration of Cass, bumbling, guilt-ridden drunkard that he is, dates from his murder of a degenerate rapist, Mason Flagg. We move in a foggy world which the narrator describes as "a grotesque fantasy of events lacking sequence and order . . .". We are witness to the degradation of Cass at the hands of Flagg who forces him to paint pornographic pictures, to perform before an audience as a seal, and to sing bawdy songs on all fours. Flagg violates Cass's dignity, and to make doubly sure he rapes Cass's beloved Francesca. Violence, however, begets violence; Cass breaks open Flagg's skull with a stone. But the murder, although it may be of questionable justice, proves to be a redemptive act; victim and assailant do not become one. By concealing the murder, Luigi, the police corporal, forces Cass on his own resources; he robs him of the luxury of self-recrimination, the ease of guilt. In his darkest hour, Cass mutters: "And as I sat there . . . I knew that I had come to the end of the road and had found nothing at all. There was nothing. . . . I thought of being. I thought of nothingness. I put my head into my hands, and for a moment the sharp horror of *being* seemed so enormous as to make the horror of nothingness less than nothing by its side . . ." This is the brief moment of outrage for Cass, brief because he ends by accepting the burdens of freedom. But *Set This House on Fire* remains a flawed book by a very gifted writer, and one of its moral flaws is that while it brings us artificially close to the facts of violence, it ends by evading them. (pp. 243-44)

> *Ihab Hassan, in* The American Scholar *(copyright © 1965 by the United Chapters of Phi Beta Kappa; reprinted by permission of the publishers), Vol. 34, No. 2, Spring, 1965.*

WELLES T. BRANDRIFF

[During *The Long March*] Mannix has been physically disabled and is about to be socially ostracized (at least by a part of society). But there has been no comparable emotional crisis. That inner compartment of the mind where a man reacts emotionally to the external world has not undergone any great change. Mannix is still the tortured man that he was before the march began, and, more significantly, he is still the deluded man.

The same thing cannot be said about Culver, however. His illusions have disappeared by the end of the march. He is no longer deluded by the thin veneer of order called civilization, for he has seen the chaos and disorder which seethe just beneath its surface. And as the forces of disorder prepare once again to crack open this veneer (this time in the form of the Korean War), his inner world of emotional order and serenity crumbles before their onslaught.

The most significant theme in this novel, then, deals with the thin, fabricated veneer called civilization, and one man's growing awareness of the essential disorder which lies just beneath the surface of this veneer. It also concerns the state of psychological disorder into which Culver slides, as he gradually becomes aware of the presence of this disorder.

The development of this awareness, and its by-product of psychological disorder, is paralleled by the development of a foundation of symbolism, the specific function of which is to underscore the contrast between surface order and subsurface disorder. This groundwork of symbolism, though constructed of varying individual symbols, is cemented together by an adhesive of sound. And it is this recurring motif of sounds which provides the narrative with such strong symbolic support. (pp. 54-5)

Although the inverted time order is certainly important, the most significant symbolic event in the first chapter is undoubtedly the introduction of the sound motif. A phonograph that plays only "Haydn, Mozart, and Bach" sounds somewhat unusual, but in this particular case it goes far towards pointing out the need for order in Culver's life. For although music itself is the imposition of order on sound, these three men have, in turn, imposed an ultimate order on music. (p. 55)

The character of the sound motif changes sharply after Culver's recall into the Marine Corps, signaling the transition from the old world of order to this new world of forced marches and endless tactical problems, "of frigid nights and blazing noons, of disorder and movement. . . ." Moments after having heard about the mortar accident, while the shock of revelation grips the characters in a tableau of suspended action and "awesome silence . . . back off in the bushes a mockingbird commenced a shrill rippling chant and far away, amidst the depth of the silence, there [seemed] to be a single faint and terrible scream." Those sounds that fit in the order of things are still there for all to hear, but for one who will listen carefully, there is also the sound of death and disorder. It is only a faint thread of sound far off in the background, but it is there nonetheless.

Later on, Culver hears—or imagines he hears—an "echo, from afar, of that faint anguished shriek he . . . heard before. . . ." (p. 56)

[At another time, on radio watch], his imagination begins to play tricks with the sounds of the radio signals. "Cracklings, whines, barks and shrieks—a whole jungle full of noise"—echoes through his mind "like the cries of souls in the anguish of hell. . . ." The "faint fluting of a dance-band clarinet" is strung briefly across his earphones and it seems very much out of place. . . . It is important to note that Culver thinks of the fluting of the clarinet—and not the other sounds—as the "thread of insanity. . . ." It is the jungle sounds which are most appropriate for the type of world he is coming gradually to know.

Styron has begun to define mid-century civilization in far more specific terms by this point in the novel. The world he describes is characterized by disorder and violence. There is always war, although it does not often appear in the form of a hot war. It is the time of not-peace called the cold war. There is an enemy who is "labeled Aggressor" although there is "no sign of his aggression. . . ." He is an invisible, "spectral foe" who poses a threat to peace yet rarely ever commits himself. In a faint echo of the sound motif, Styron compares the state of the nation (and world) to a "distant bleating saxophone" which seems "indecisive and sad . . . neither at peace nor at war." (p. 57)

Culver has become the disillusioned man by the end of the march, for the veneer of civilization has cracked open, laying bare the chaos underneath. For the first time in the narrative, he has a clear understanding of the nature of the modern war-world in which he is forced to exist. . . . (p. 58)

In the past, Culver has always felt that peace and order are the reality and war merely a temporary interruption to this state. Appropriately, the Haydn passage has been used symbolically to underscore this belief. As his concept of reality changes, however, so too does the nature of the sound motif. By the end of the story, the sounds have changed in form and intensity from the soothing ordered notes of a Haydn passage to the chaotic shriek of the wounded and the roar of not-so-distant thunder.

The shattering of his illusion plunges Culver deeper than ever into a psychological morass of despair and disillusionment. . . . He has come to realize that he has never known "serenity, a quality of repose . . . but . . . that, somehow, it had always escaped him." He has come to the point, finally, where he can admit to himself that he has "hardly ever known a time in his life when he was not marching or sick with loneliness or afraid." (p. 59)

> *Welles T. Brandriff, "The Role of Order and Disorder in 'The Long March',"* in English Journal *(copyright © 1967 by The National Council of Teachers of English), January, 1967, pp. 54-9.*

RICHARD PEARCE

[The] feeling of war as the condition of life pervades all of Styron's works: in *Lie Down in Darkness*, Peyton Loftis commits suicide on the day the bomb is dropped on Nagasaki; in *Set This House on Fire* Cass Kinsolving traces the beginning of his self-destructive striving to his experiences in World War II, which drove him to the psychiatric ward. And even *The Confessions of Nat Turner*, although set a full century earlier, is informed by the spirit of the battlefield.

Besides being inescapable, war is outrageously unreasonable. The enemy is undefined; heroic action becomes clownish and self-destructive. . . . What Styron shows in his most convincing fiction is, first, that beneath the calm and affluent exterior of modern life lies a violent potential, and, second, that this violence has a capricious life of its own and erupts as a senseless surprise, often in the form of an accident. He was feeling his way toward this vision in *Lie Down in Darkness* where, despite the influence of Faulkner, his characters are moved not by the logic of history but by ahistorical, irrational, and undefinable energies which burst through the mannered and manicured surface of their lives to drive them apart, frustrate connection, and deny psychological and aesthetic resolution. (pp. 6-7)

Styron, in dramatizing war as the condition of life, developed a postwar perspective close to that of Heller and the next generation. Or perhaps it would be more accurate to turn his own phrase and see him as a "bridge" between two generations. With most writers of his generation [such as James Jones and Norman Mailer,] he shares a faith in literature as a way to knowledge and order, and a faith in Christian humanism as a way to salvation. With Heller, Vonnegut and the next generation he shares an apocalyptic, or neo-apocalyptic, view which denies the possibility of knowledge, order, or salvation. (p. 8)

The modern experience of apocalypse lacks a temporal or linear dimension. It is ahistorical and nonrational. It does not follow from anything, cannot be explained causally, cannot be justified morally, and does not look forward to a golden age of peace. It is an experience of violent and perpetual ending. Such an experience pervades the worlds of Peyton Loftis and Cass Kinsolving; both of these novels are charged with violent and irrational energies. [*The Long March*] reveals a world dominated by indefinable capricious forces; but, more importantly, it dramatizes the impotence of reason in explanation and moral guidance. The universe of the novel is dualistic, but there is no way of telling the forces of good from the forces of evil; and this is epitomized in the confrontation between Colonel Templeton, whose orders are both capriciously destructive and morally necessary, and Captain Mannix, whose rebellion is at once profoundly humanitarian and necessarily dehumanizing. The weaknesses in Styron's writing, especially in parts of his otherwise powerful *Set This House on Fire* and in the primary conception of *The Confessions of Nat Turner,* seem to arise when Styron substitutes a traditional, rational, and, in context, simplified apocalypse for the terrifying one he imaginatively discovered.

Styron also shares with the earlier generation a desire to see the world in heroic proportions; hence his use of myth in evoking the downfall of the Loftis family in *Lie Down in Darkness,* the crucifixion of Mannix in *The Long March,* the hubris of Cass in *Set This House on Fire,* the martyrdom of Nat Turner in *The Confessions.* But in each case the subject of his fiction is denied its heroic potential. *Lie Down in Darkness* remains a domestic tragedy, Mannix is turned into a clownish perpetrator of the very violence he rebels against, Cass is humiliated and must finally renounce his strivings. Except for *The Confessions of Nat Turner,* where I think Styron was working counter to his best imaginative instincts, the forces against which his characters contend cannot be confronted heroically. This is just their malicious quality. They end by reducing the protagonist, comically, by humiliating him. They are just like the forces that "shanghaied" young Styron into the "clap shack." (pp. 8-9)

The senseless surprise, the absurd humiliation, and the final realization that it was all a mistake effect the ultimate violation in Styron's world. We should remember that violation is the end result of violence; it is an unjustified infringement . . . , primarily physical but finally psychological. (p. 9)

Styron's heroes [according to Ihab Hassan] follow in the tradition of Ivan Karamazov and Ahab, as "metaphysical rebels," struggling against a world which God created as "perpetually unjust," and perpetuating the unjust violence in the dialectic of their rebellions. Metaphysical rebels, yes, but not quite in the mold of Ivan or Ahab, for there is an unreasonable and indefinable force in the modern world which undermines their kind of heroic rebellion. (p. 10)

Lie Down in Darkness [is] a remarkable achievement of imagination, observation, and control. A large cast of characters are, for the most part, fully imagined. The locale and manners of Tidewater society are sensitively observed and recorded. The novel, a collage of flashbacks from the day of Peyton Loftis' burial, is skillfully put together. And there is a rich range of style and pace in the narrative, the descriptions, and the dialogue, which includes a final tour de force in Peyton's interior monologue on the day of her suicide.

Lie Down in Darkness bears Faulkner's imprint, despite Styron's deliberate efforts to eliminate it. The structure, the key symbols, and many of the characters recall *The Sound and the Fury,* and the funeral procession seems to derive from *As I Lay Dying.* . . . In *Lie Down in Darkness,* despite the literary allusions, there is almost no sense of passing time, no real connection between the present and a past that contained its communal and sustaining values. And despite the preponderance of flashbacks the novel is all present. Unlike Faulkner, who shows us a present rising out of an ambiguous past, Styron shows us a past that is part of the ambiguous present. (p. 11)

[The] hearse carrying Peyton's body to the cemetery will remain central: it will serve, in its realistic detail and comic irrelevancy, to ground remembrance and rhetoric in the chaotic and sweltering reality of the present moment. (p. 12)

If the hearse continually brings us back to the present moment in time, it also brings us back to the present position in space. . . . The hearse serves to stall us, to fix us, in the mundane present. And if, with its implacable reminder of Peyton's death, it begins to suggest a meaningful connection between past events and the present moment, the connections are never made for us in the fabric of the novel and are in fact undermined by the continual insistence of physical irrelevancy. There is no connection between the places where the hearse—accidentally—stops and any places in the lives of the main characters. Nor is there any connection between the physical details so sharply reported in these scenes and any details in the main story line—and the contrast is enforced by the contrast in tone, pace, and diction. The continual insistence of irrelevancy in the present makes flight into the past—for either escape or meaning —futile. While Faulkner fractured his narrative and the objective continuum of time in *The Sound and the Fury* to discover meanings in the subjective time patterns of his characters, Styron fractures his narrative to destroy whatever connections of causality and meaning might be gained by his flights into the past. (pp. 12-13)

Lie Down in Darkness is structured to undermine causal connections between past, present, and future. . . . With no causal connections, no organic nexus, there are no physical, emotional, psychological, or ethical directions. . . . [The] modern experience of apocalypse goes beyond this and expresses a total nihilism and chaos; there is neither a sense of ending nor a sense of beginning, nor can the warring powers be ethically designated. (p. 15)

Peyton's story is not one of the loss of innocence, as so many critics conclude. There is nothing for her to lose. She is desperately striving for an emotional, psychological, and ethical center. . . . [In] her world, torn by the forces driving her mother and father, there is no center that Peyton can reach toward or run away from. New York is not a rejection of her home; the novel opens and closes with the train which joins New York and Port Warwick, making them part of the same fabric. (p. 16)

The powerful interior monologue which concludes the story of Peyton Loftis works in a way that is diametrically opposed to its prototype in *Ulysses,* and serves to distinguish Styron's and Joyce's worlds. It does not give us a sense of formal or psychological unity, but is fully expressive of Peyton's apocalyptic experience. While Molly Bloom is almost continuously inert, Peyton is continually in motion. The frantic emotional and physical pace of this section contrasts dramatically with that of all the other narrative lines in the novel, especially the one carrying the hearse to the cemetery. Peyton is driven from Tony's to the bar to Lennie's to Berger's to Harry's, and finally to Harlem, where she jumps out of a bathroom window; the violence of her energy is reinforced by the repeated references to the atomic bombs which have just been dropped on Hiroshima and Nagasaki. And her irrational physical movement is complicated by her stream of consciousness, which is not really a stream, for the recollections do not seem to flow from one association to the next; they seem to explode out of her wild unconscious—disconnected moments of the past driven irrationally into the present. The violent energy is also expressed in the images that surface, especially the flying birds and the sense of drowning. The birds symbolize innocence, purity, freedom, and also the avenging furies of her conscious and unconscious guilt. Drowning is a symbol of orgiastic forgetfulness and of renewal. But, more important, together the images of flying and drowning evoke the contradictory and centrifugal movement that dominates the novel, the force that drives Milton and Helen apart and denies Peyton a stable center of emotional and moral reference.

Peyton's suicide ends with a note of resurrection: "Myself all shattered, this lovely shell? Perhaps I shall rise at another time, though I lie down in darkness and have my light in ashes." This is not in character for Peyton, despite the religious influence of her mother. And Styron must have sensed this, for he ends the novel with an entirely different kind of religious experience [a Negro Baptism]. . . . The experience of the baptism recalls the Book of Revelation, and the militant Gabriel connects it with the experience of irrational warfare that boils just beneath the surface of the novel. . . . The realistic detail and the comic irrelevancy of this scene make it a parody of the religious resolution of *The Sound and the Fury.* The baptism does not wash away the sins of the world, as Ella Swan believes, nor does the religious experience offer any hope of resurrection or even of endurance. Instead it exposes the reality existing beneath the polished suburban surfaces and southern manners, and gives ultimate expression to the forces tearing apart the world of Peyton Loftis.

[In *The Long March,* Styron found] a form which expressed the human situation with conciseness and clarity, and in which he could affirm the values of Christian humanism in a way that was consistent with his vision. (p. 19)

[In the image of the soldier precariously suspended by his heels ten stories above the street by two drunken pranksters, Styron found a metaphor for the human situation.] In an environment that is urban, military, and dark, man is surprised, ambushed, senselessly assaulted—not to the end of defeat or destruction, not to any end at all. He is suddenly and capriciously turned upside down, turned from a man with potentials of dignity and heroism into a helpless clown acutely aware of life's terror. This terror is caused not by a hostile power or even by an indifferent universe, but by a wanton sporting with individual life—"Imagine being that high upside-down in space with two drunks holding onto your heels."

The Long March is similar in many ways to Melville's *Billy Budd.* In both works the thematic conflict is between the innocent individual and the representative of social necessity. In both works social law is made manifest in a military order. In both works the hero's instinctive reaction to human injustice has immediate destructive consequences for his associates and for himself. Both works end in a martyrdom that is in fact socially just. But the difference between *The Long March* and *Billy Budd* is signal; the view of life after World War II is sharply differentiated from that of earlier periods. Melville dramatizes the tragic price of human preservation and social harmony; Captain Vere, as he condemns Billy, is deeply aware of this price. Colonel Templeton knows that military order and soldierly discipline are necessary on the battlefield, but despite his sensitivity, integrity, and realistic logic, the end he serves is not a human harmony, as it was with Vere. (pp. 20-1)

[*Set This House on Fire* (1960)] continuously penetrates the meretricious physical, social, and psychological façade of American life. Moreover, it dramatically contrasts the façade with the senselessly violent irrationality it covers. (p. 25)

A weakness of *Set This House on Fire* may derive from Styron's faith in the traditional forms of novel writing and in the redemptive possibilities of Christianity. Both the narrative dialogue and the plot are strongly linear, and in both there is a promise of fulfillment. But the powerful experience Styron evokes is not linear; it denies the possibility of epistemological, theological, and psychological progress. The total effect of the novel, however, accommodates its weakness, and reinforces its main theme, which is the contrast between meretricious and worn-out forms and the irrational and destructive energies which will not be contained by them. (p. 26)

It is absolutely consistent with the nature of the novel for Cass's undirected striving to culminate in a sequence of actions out of a grade B movie—the rape, the murder, the chase to the cliff top—in a meretricious form that gives a false sense of excitement, resolution, and meaning. But the real culmination is the recognition that the murder of Francesca was an accident . . . and that Cass's revenge was a mistake. The real culmination, then, is an experience of accident, mistake, or random violence, which is totally incongruent with the logic of the melodramatic scene enacted by Mason, Francesca, and Cass. And the recognition should remind us of the incongruity between the disconnected violations in Cass's dreams, recollections, and his life as an expatriate, on the one hand, and on the other, his pattern of quest and redemption.

Opposed to and lying beneath the forms which offer a false sense of meaning and hope lies a violence that has a capricious life of its own, and which is expressed in violations that are absolutely unreasonable. . . . In *Set This House on Fire* it is manifested by allusions to totalitarianism in the references to World War II. . . . That totalitarianism is only alluded to, that it escapes clear articulation, makes it all the more frightening. For the most terrifying form of total violation is when the power is unseen, unseeable, unknown, and unknowable. (pp. 34-5)

What makes the assailant or the power unseeable and unknowable is that it is literally formless and totally contradictory. Cass strives for the pure form of artistic harmony and of the God of love and salvation, but the power that energizes his world is an anti-form, like the Beast of Revelation.

Most critics see Cass as having found salvation—love and harmony—in the reconciliation with his family, in the pastoral retreat, in the acceptance of his own limitations as an artist. But it seems to me that Styron was working intellectually at odds with his imaginative discoveries. He shows Cass's house set on fire. And what he exposes in the images, energies, and conflicting patterns of the novel is the perpetual conflagration, the eternal apocalypse suppressed beneath the meretricious surface of American life and the false hopefulness of Christianity. (pp. 35-6)

Nat Turner [in *The Confessions of Nat Turner*] is inspired by two Gods. A Negro slave educated by a benevolent white master and enjoying the relative ease of a house servant, he is turned into a fanatic by the God of Ezekiel, who comes to him in a vision, and inspires him to lead a vengeful and slaughterous revolt against the slavemasters of Southampton County, Virginia. And he is redeemed by the voice of the murdered Margaret Whitehead, coming to him in his prison cell and speaking to him in words of love from the New Testament. Both the Old Testament God of vengeance and the New Testament God of love turn Nat Turner away from the social reality of slavery in the American South. As in *Set This House on Fire,* the *deus ex machina* serves as an ethical, psychological, and artistic evasion. (pp. 36-7)

The challenge which Styron set for himself in this novel was one that no white southern writer had ever accepted, to "enter into the consciousness of a Negro in the early decades of the 19th century," in fact to become the unique individual of Nat Turner by narrating the story of his rebellion from his point of view. (p. 37)

In Styron's first two works there is no *deus ex machina* and no redemption. In *Set This House on Fire* there is enough in the novel to counteract the pattern of redemption.... But in *The Confessions of Nat Turner,* while the rebellion is social, the redemptive pattern is dominant. And the movement toward redemption undermines the basis for rebellion. The outspoken criticism in *Ten Black Writers Respond* may be misguided in taking Styron to task for distorting history; a writer is under no obligation to be true to the facts, especially when the facts are so few and uncertain. But they are right in seeing Styron's Nat Turner as being oblivious to the social reality which he claims to respond to. And they are also right in seeing that Styron shows the flaw to be not within the system of slavery but within the mind of the rebel. (p. 39)

What I am pointing to here is a weakness in the novel that derives from Styron's ambivalence, which kept him from fully realizing either the social or the psychological possibilities.... One of Styron's outstanding strengths as a novelist is in his descriptions, his evocations of place, which worked so well either to reinforce or to counterpoint the dramatic scenes in his earlier works, but in this novel they betray his uncertainty. Another of his strengths is in his handling of action, but here it leads to a simplification of his psychological insights. (p. 40)

Styron shows Nat Turner to be motivated by the sublimation of his desire for the white woman of his dreams, who finally takes the form of Margaret Whitehead.... Louis Rubin makes an even better case for Styron when he interprets Nat Turner's real rebellion to derive not so much from his bondage or his exploitation but from society's depriving him of his right to love and be loved. (p. 41)

Both Styron's observation and Rubin's interpretation tell us much about the potential of Nat's characterization, but unfortunately the novel is not developed to realize these complex insights or to make us feel their emotional impact. Margaret Whitehead is a paper character, cut from the pattern of southern romance. And her relation with Nat is too transparent a device, designed to reveal impulses which Styron ... defines as, "historically speaking, those of the traditional revolutionary—that is to say puritanical, repressive and sublimated." Nat Turner is a weak character not because of Styron's "racism," nor because it is impossible for a white man to create a successful black revolutionary. It is because Turner, billed as a unique and complex character, is diminished or explained away by such simplified psychology. This is not to say that Styron was wrong in seeing the traditional revolutionary as puritanical, repressive, and sublimated, just that he did not go far enough in developing this potential. (pp. 41-2)

The challenge that exercised Styron's imagination was to enter the consciousness of Nat Turner, to tell the story from his point of view. We are led to wonder whether Styron might have developed Nat Turner more convincingly and more interestingly [by choosing a different vantage].... A secondary character—black or white, historical or contemporary ... might develop the ironies and the clashes of perspective, might deepen and expand the scope of the novel, might leave Nat Turner an engaging enigma. (pp. 42-3)

Richard Pearce, in his William Styron *(American Writers Pamphlet No. 98; © 1971, University of Minnesota), University of Minnesota Press, Minneapolis, 1971 (revised by the author for this publication).*

ARDNER R. CHESHIRE, JR.

A man on his judgment day, reflecting on his moral responsibility for past actions and the possibility of redemption—this is an important motif not only in *The Confessions of Nat Turner* but in Styron's two other novels as well. (p. 110)

[Particularly] in *The Confessions of Nat Turner,* the recollective character of the hero's meditation on past experience provides the structural key to the novel. When *The Confessions of Nat Turner* is viewed from this perspective, the existential questions that Styron poses are placed in sharp focus, and the novel transcends the many heated arguments concerning the relationship between black characters and a white author and the institution of slavery in the Old South.

Nat's confession is much more than a series of flashbacks; it is a recollection of past experience. (p. 111)

Nat's confession has all the distinguishing characteristics of a recollection as defined by [Gabriel Marcel]. Faced with a spiritual discontinuity (his inability to pray or to feel the presence of God), and an existential discontinuity (his imminent death), Nat attempts, through recollection, to understand the fundamental orientation of his being and to establish a new relationship with God. He comes to see through his meditation that his redemption depends, and always has depended, not only on rebelling against and being free of the system of chattel slavery, but on participating in the fellowship of Being, on moving away from isolation and estrangement toward a loving relationship with another human being. The story of Nat Turner is one of a man in quest of himself and communion with others and with God, a quest that almost fails initially because of his misplaced fidelity to his white masters, and later, because of his inability to see the world in nonabstract, human terms. (p. 112)

Nat remembers that [after he was sold to Reverend Eppes] he "began to sense the world, the *true* world, in which a Negro moves and breathes. It was like being plunged into freezing water." He continues to stay with this crazed preacher only because of "the gloomy comfort of Ecclesiastes"—the book of the Bible which Camus used as a starting point for *The Myth of Sisyphus,* and which Nat undoubtedly uses as the starting point for his later belief in absolute, existential freedom.

Though Eppes is supposed to carry out Sam Turner's promise to make Nat a free man at age twenty-five, the preacher sells him instead to an illiterate small farmer named Tom Moore. The promise of freedom, which had so helped to sustain Nat, is taken away. He suddenly realizes that he exists, and always has existed, in a closed system which denies him the right to be an individual. . . . From the moment he is sold by Eppes, Nat banishes his first master from his mind "as one banishes the memory of any disgraced and downfallen prince." Nat's childlike faith in white authority is destroyed, but at this point he is unable to reflect on past experience in any philosophical way. He is too filled with hate. Not until he is in jail does he come to understand that his misplaced fidelity to white authority made it impossible for him to achieve an authentic identity or to enter into a loving relationship with another human being.

In Part III of *The Confessions of Nat Turner,* "Study War," Nat swings from submission to violence and attempts to transcend the chaos of his existence through a quest for complete existential freedom. Having read and talked only about the Bible all his life, Nat understandably expresses his intense desire for freedom through Old Testament rhetoric, and he plans the details of his rebellion using the prophetic books of the Old Testament. The Old Testament God of retribution replaces Sam Turner in Nat's reordered world. . . . (p. 114)

Underlying Nat's biblical rhetoric, however, is a philosophy of personal commitment, action, and choice rather than any reliance on authority. The decision to rebel against his white masters is his and his alone. Throughout "Study War," Styron undercuts the idea of Nat's being controlled by God. He clearly indicates that Nat's visions always occur when he is in a weakened condition from fasting or when he has been driven almost to a frenzy by punishment or sexual desire. . . . It seems quite clear that Nat himself freely chooses to rebel against the condition of slavery; God does not command or guide him. . . .

Having chosen to fight for his freedom, Nat is now faced with a moral dilemma which becomes the central issue in the section "Study War": what to do about the few white people for whom he has sympathy. The success of his insurrection demands that they be killed, but something inside Nat recoils at the idea of such a completely heartless slaughter. . . . Despite Nat's hatred of the white man, his obsession with freedom, and the precedents for slaughter he finds in the Old Testament, he has misgivings about taking human life so indiscriminately. (p. 115)

Though Nat convinced his followers that murder was essential to their freedom, he cannot kill the very man who holds him as chattel. This is the case because in the seconds before he first raises his axe, Nat actually *sees* Travis for the first time. (pp. 115-16)

[As Nat kills Margaret,] he is thinking of [her] not as a person but as an abstraction, as a most treasured and holy part of the white man's imagination, which he, a slave all his life to the white man, defiles.

After killing Margaret, Nat is suddenly aware that his intense hatred for the white man and his burning desire for freedom have caused him to lose his humanity. Before the murder he saw the world only in terms of his quest for freedom, as an object that was real only insofar as he conceived of it as such. Now he sees for the first time that he is not morally autonomous. (pp. 116-17)

Styron said in an interview . . . that after the murder Nat "was suddenly overtaken by his own humanity. It is partially why the revolt fails." (p. 117)

With the exception of his murder of Margaret, Nat believes that what he did was not wrong. Given a choice between slavery and freedom again, he would choose freedom, even if that choice meant others would die. . . . Despite his lack of remorse, he does feel a sense of loss and incompleteness. Through recollection, however, Nat comes to understand why he feels such emptiness: he realizes that he has never entered into the redemptive fellowship of Being. From his early adolescence at Turner's Mill until his capture by the whites after his insurrection, Nat remains a being apart. (p. 118)

[The] idea of a true dialogue with Margaret does not even push its way into Nat's conscious thought until he is about to die. Only then can Nat break the taboos of his slave society and express love and passion for a white woman.

Nat's redemption as a man results from his awareness, through recollection, that he must enter into a loving relationship with another human being. . . . Through recollection, he has broken down the barriers between himself and another person and moved to a higher level of participation where unity of being is recaptured. This loving experience with Margaret leads to a feeling of reconciliation with God. It is, paradoxically, a transcendence through immanence. Nat thinks that he reaches God (a Christian God of love and mercy) through his communion with another human being.

There are two main problems with this redemptive ending. First, it is autistic. Though Nat believes that he briefly fuses his spirit with Margaret's, she is, of course, quite dead. Though dramatically powerful, this redemptive moment is at first intellectually troubling. Second, as Alan Holder has pointed out, "Having built such a case against her (Margaret), the book is asking too much of us to accept Margaret as an incarnation of Christly love and the agent of Nat's redemption. We are given a spiritual happy ending that is decidedly forced." Nevertheless, despite these objections, there is perhaps another, more satisfying way of viewing the end of the novel. (p. 120)

From Nat's point of view, Margaret does appear worthy of being his Thou in an I-Thou relationship. Through such an interpretation it becomes possible to accept the redemptive ending of the novel. It makes it possible for us to see Nat as Styron surely does—as an authentic human being who through recollection has transcended the voids of submission to authority and solipsism and achieved redemptive communion. (p. 121)

Ardner R. Cheshire, Jr., "The Recollective Structure of 'The Confessions of Nat Turner'," in The Southern Review *(copyright, 1976, by Ardner R. Cheshire, Jr.), Vol. XII, No. 1, January, 1976, pp. 110-21.*

RICHARD GRAY

Since the time he started writing, it seems to have been [Styron's] conscious aim to perpetuate the great tradition in Southern literature, and to assume the throne left vacant by William Faulkner by producing something that, in terms of both its themes and its historical scope, could merit comparison with *The Sound and the Fury, Look Homeward, Angel,* and *All the King's Men.* . . . Styron's first published book, *Lie Down in Darkness,* [was] treated with almost universal respect and had epithets like "brilliant," "major," and "tragic" showered upon it. *Lie Down in Darkness,* as befitted its author, had ambition written over its every page—it represented a deliberate stab at greatness—and the fact that Styron could back his ambitions up with an extraordinarily seductive style (by turns descriptive, lyrical, and elegiac) more or less guaranteed its initial success. It was almost too easy, thanks to the prodigious brilliance of its language and the intricacy of its narrative structure, to read more into the book than was actually there.

Not that *Lie Down in Darkness* is a poor or uninteresting novel—far from it. It is, I believe, a fascinating and to some extent a perceptive one because—whether Styron intended it or not—it presents us with such an honest account of the author's own predicament. It is, in a way, profoundly autobiographical; . . . the area of autobiography it deals with bears upon Styron's problems as a *Southern* writer. . . . *Lie Down in Darkness* concerns itself with one family, the Loftis family, living in Port Warwick, Virginia. In actual clock time it covers the events of one day, during which the body of the older daughter, Peyton Loftis, is brought back from New York for burial. But, in describing this particular day, the author reaches back continually into the past to investigate the circumstances leading to Peyton's death, which came at her own hands; and in the process the book becomes an intensive exploration of the family's almost effortless self-destruction. . . . [The] various members of the Loftis family constitute one another's Hell; their home life is a kind of prison house from which they are unable and, because of their mutual dependence, unwilling, even, to escape. (pp. 285-86)

Styron's manner of telling the tale affects our reception of it. The overall framework of return he uses for the narrative, the complex layers of memory through which the characters speak to us, above all the powerful sense of reenactment attaching itself to almost every thought and gesture—all this makes us feel that the dark backward and abysm of the old world lies just below the surface of landscape and consciousness, waiting for an appropriate moment to reappear. Further, it makes the Loftis family seem just as much imprisoned in *time* as they are by each other—or, to be more accurate, imprisoned in times passed. Theirs is "a land of the dying," Styron explains to us at one point in the novel, a Hades inhabited by half-remembered ghosts; and it requires no great stretch of the imagination, really, to see

the Loftises themselves as ghost-haunted people, driven in some cases beyond endurance by voices from out of their past. (p. 286)

[The] question Styron seems to be asking in *Lie Down in Darkness* is briefly this: When the old institutions become irrelevant and the old myths obsolete, *and when our habits of thought and feeling continue nevertheless to be shaped by them*—how then do we change the situation? How can we create new institutions and new myths when our usual means of altering things—our minds and hearts, dictating the scope of our actions—are among the things to be altered? How do we will an act of defiance if our wills have been conditioned by the very forces we would defy? I have stated the problem oversimply, of course, in order to make it clear. (p. 288)

Styron never answers this question during the course of the book, nor is any satisfactory solution ever implied; and the reason for this, I think, is very simple. For all his perceptiveness in locating the problem, he, William Styron, the creator of the Loftis family, is as caught up in that problem as any of his creations are. He depends, to the point of parody, on the earlier *literary* tradition of the South just as Milton, Helen, and Peyton Loftis all depend on its broader cultural tradition. The most immediate and important debt Styron owes is (predictably enough, perhaps) to William Faulkner [as he readily admitted]. . . . [The] book amounts almost to an elegy, or imitative tribute, to the father figure of modern Southern literature. There, in the portrait of the Loftises, is the dissolving family familiar to us from *The Sound and the Fury:* the alcoholic father, the neurotic, selfish mother, the idiot child, and the older child who wanders around a strange Northern town for much of one day, clutching a timepiece, and then shortly afterward commits suicide. There, also, are the Negro characters performing the function of chorus, commenting on the Loftises just as they do on the Compson family, and coming together in a revival scene at the end of the action to round it off on an unexpectedly hopeful note. The narrative framework of Styron's book, involving a family's journey to inter a coffin, is modeled on *As I Lay Dying;* Peyton Loftis is modeled on Temple Drake in *Sanctuary,* another Southern belle turned nymphomaniac (she even crosses and uncrosses her legs nervously, just as Temple does!); Milton Loftis's father is modeled on the platitudinous Mr. Compson. And so on. . . . The result is a story that has an almost overpowering feeling of *déjà vu* about it, that is full of echoes and vague remembrances—the shadowy presence of all the characters and situations it imitates and, in a sense, memorializes. Is Styron himself aware of this dimension of the novel? It is difficult to say, although my guess, based on the available evidence, is that he probably is. Does he know what he could do to change it? That is an easier question to answer, because it is clear from the world he imagines that he does not. *Lie Down in Darkness* never escapes, for more than a moment, out from under the shade of William Faulkner and the magnolia blossom. . . . It represents a cul-de-sac—a beautiful, spell-binding cul-de-sac admittedly, but a cul-de-sac nonetheless; and the gravity of its language, the brilliance of its structure—the impeccable nature, even, of its own self-reflexiveness—should never blind us to the fact that nearly everything in it is borrowed.

The two books that Styron wrote during the next nine years register no significant advance on *Lie Down in Darkness,* at least as far as this problem of liberation from the past is concerned. (pp. 288-89)

The Confessions of Nat Turner [is the book], I think, in which he has begun to find the answers he needs—both to his own problems as a Southern writer of the second, post-"renaissance" generation, and to the larger questions facing anyone who inherits, however unconsciously, a particular way of organizing and figuring experience. Its subject is that ultimate victim of the past, and the roles and mythologies the past bequeaths, the American Negro slave. Its method, as Styron puts it, is that of "a meditation on history"; since the story is based on an actual slave revolt that occurred in Virginia in 1831 and the supposed "confessions" made by its leader, Nat Turner, after his defeat and eventual capture. In this way, Styron places himself squarely at the center of the Southern tradition—and not, as in *Lie Down in Darkness,* merely to commemorate that tradition but so as to develop it, carry it a stage further. History—the relationship of past to present in the writer's own experience and in the lives of his characters—is as much the motivating force in this book as it is in Faulkner's work, say, in Ransom's or in Warren's. The only difference is that it is now what James Baldwin has called the "common history" of white and black that comes under scrutiny; and this change, far from being a superficial one, signals other changes of approach and interpretation that enable Styron to achieve a radically fresh understanding of familiar material. In a sense the *Confessions* represents the most significant attempt made over the last twenty years to fashion something new out of the creative inheritance of the region. . . . (pp. 290-91)

In practical terms, the process of self-emancipation described in the *Confessions* . . . is left unfinished, equivocal; and the real, which is to say the only completed, liberation occurs not in the life of the protagonist but *in the consciousness, the mind and spirit, of the writer*. The freedom won in the book, and by the book in a sense, is an imaginative rather than an active, political one—a matter of private and, in fact, literary experience to which the writer's craft, his own act of writing bears witness. Perhaps it will be obvious enough already just how, in the *Confessions,* Styron achieves this freedom—by developing for the first time *beyond* his tradition, adding to the existing monuments, rearranging them and so endowing them with an original value. For the familiar ghosts of Southern literature—the great plantation, the gentleman farmer, the plantation lady, and the Southern belle—they are all there as usual. But they have all been made unfamiliar now, severed from their old connections. This time it is the underdog who presents them to us, the victim whose suffering has made their elegant games and playacting possible. We see them with altered vision, as if the past were being redeemed and revalued for us as we read. . . . Many other novels and poems may have described the exotic setting of the *Confessions* for us, but Styron's novel places it in a new, and profoundly disturbing, light.

Of course, a simple change in narrative point of view, however significant it may be historically, does not go all the way to account for this metamorphosis. Even more important, in a sense, is the use Styron makes of the accepted structures of Southern writing. His general attempt to re-write history—by engaging event with myth, yesterday with today, and by establishing what is essentially a symbiotic relationship between his characters and their environment—is familiar. . . . [Many writers] have seen it as their main purpose to reconcile their ideas or beliefs with the received facts and legends of history. The difference in Styron's case, however, and it is a crucial one, is that these strategies are now being used not for nostalgia's sake nor even to demonstrate the virtues of precedent, ceremony, and ritual but so as to further the cause of a carefully formulated, highly sophisticated form of radicalism. Traditionalism in Styron's hands becomes, effectively, an agent of revolution, the kind of plea for immediate, drastic, and even violent change that one is more inclined to associate with political writers such as Cleaver, or visionaries such as Emerson and Thoreau, than with the likes of Robert Penn Warren, Thomas Wolfe, and William Faulkner. One way of charting the course Styron has taken, in fact, is to say that Faulkner and his generation could never have written something like the *Confessions,* if only because it is the sort of book that measures itself in terms of its distance from them and their work. It predicates a certain tradition, in other words, a particular orthodoxy from which it has developed and with which it can establish a definite, objective relationship; and that tradition is made up as much from the novels, plays, and poems of the "renaissance" as from the broader, social and cultural, patterns of the South. Without necessarily endorsing the aims of the *Confessions,* though, or sharing in the impulses that led Styron to write it, Faulkner and his contemporaries would, I believe, have understood the novel; they would have seen how it has grown out of their own work and, in growing, taken on a separate, distinct life of its own. The *Confessions* uses its given inheritance and then transcends it so as to present us with a broadly inclusive, yet cross-grained and self-evidently personal portrait of *all* our lives in history; and that, as Styron's predecessors would probably have recognized, is really the best that can be said about any Southern book. (pp. 304-05)

Richard Gray, in his The Literature of Memory: Modern Writers of the American South (*copyright © 1977 by Richard Gray*), *Johns Hopkins University Press, 1978.*

T

TATE, (John Orley) Allen   1899-1979

Tate was an American poet, critic, novelist, and man of letters. A member of the "Fugitive Group" of artists, Tate created a poetry that reflected the concerns of his fellow Fugitives: the life and landscape of the agrarian South inform all of his work. Tate's best poetry presents a world where the mythical and historical past serve allegorically to illuminate simple, personal experience. (See also *CLC*, Vols, 2, 4, 6, 9, and *Contemporary Authors*, Vols. 5-8, rev. ed.)

CLEANTH BROOKS

[Tate grounds] his quite various speculations on art, letters, society, manners, morals, and human behavior . . . on a total view of man; that is to say, on religion, and specifically the view of man given in the classical-Christian tradition. Thus, Tate can set forth an ethics, an aesthetics, a concept of proper social order, and an idea of history that are thoroughly consonant with one another. Tate's writings do not, to be sure, give off the reek of the conscious system builder. But from any thoughtful reading of his works in verse and prose, of his fiction and his nonfiction, there arises the sense of a remarkable coherence. (pp. 686-87)

[Tate] located and articulated his essential ideas while he was still a very young man. Think of that remarkable essay "Religion and the Old South." The ideas contained in this seminal essay state, in what anthropologists and other scholars of symbolism would call "compact" form, much of what the later poetry and prose would extend, articulate, and develop. In compact form, the essay contains the essence of "The Ode to the Confederate Dead," "The Mediterranean," and even "The Seasons of the Soul." It also contains "Literature as Knowledge," "Three Types of Poetry," and those magnificent late essays "Poetry Modern and Unmodern" and "A Southern Mode of the Imagination." It prefigures quite clearly the theme of Tate's novel, *The Fathers*. But I am being too general, and I am also getting ahead of the game.

To be more specific: By 1930 Tate had already discovered what is reductive and destructive in Hegel and Hegelianism. Hegel destroys human history by turning it into a paradigm: in his system, rationalism devours sensibility and the universal devours the particular. As Tate puts the matter more generally: "Abstraction is the death of religion no less than the death of everything else."

For Tate, that "everything else" includes man himself, whose unity as a whole being is lost when human history becomes transformed into an abstract series of events. . . . [In] "Religion and the Old South" his analogy has to do with the distinction between an actual horse and mere horsepower. He points out that the religious view will never be satisfied with anything less than the whole horse, whereas modern civilization tends to discard everything but the horsepower.

The young essayist, however, never takes a holier-than-thou nor a sanctimonious more-religious-than-thou attitude. He views the split in the horse as the consequence of a split in the human mind which now views the horse with modern, post-Cartesian eyes. Like the man at the cemetery gate in the "Ode to the Confederate Dead," he is well aware that the catastrophic split has already occurred and may well be irremediable. The essay is here primarily concerned with reviewing the consequences. Thus, the tone is predominantly descriptive rather than hortatory. (pp. 687-88)

[What] emerges early in Tate's work [is] his basic belief in man as a total being whose view of reality, if it is to be true to the reality of which he himself is a part, must take account of spirit and flesh, sensibility and reason, and not settle for some abstract account devised to satisfy the mind about the nature of material objects and their relation to each other. (p. 688)

The language in Tate's poetry and his fiction . . . [judges] the situations described—by its accuracy, by its discriminations, by its ability to bring to focus and unity the disparate and even warring elements. This is precisely what we expect of a poet, for in poetry, proper focus is indispensable. It is typically in poetry that reason and sensibility—head and heart—speak, and in doing so, become one unified voice. That unified voice is not simply rational man, or practical man, sentimental man, or animal man. (p. 690)

Tate tells us in the concluding paragraph of the essay "Poetry Modern and Unmodern" that he himself first experienced "the shock to the twentieth-century sensibility out of which modernism developed," not through reading Yeats, Eliot, and Pound, but through reading James Thomson, the author of *The City of Dreadful Night*. Tate points out that the issues were not really defined for him in Thomson's book. Thomson's "inflated rhetoric and echolalia merely adumbrated the center of psychic and moral interest" that was to be later articulated by poets such as Yeats and Eliot. As regards his own poetry, Tate goes on to say: "It remained [for me] to find the right language and to establish a center from which it could be spoken; for the poet is never wholly aware of his subject until his language is able to speak it, and to render it to the entire human being, to both the sensibility and the intellect, at that focus of awareness at which he does not know whether he is thinking or feeling." This is spoken specifically about the poet, but it applies to us all. No human being is truly aware of a situation until he can render it in a language that is at once intellectual and emotional.

So, at the end of this magnificent, late essay, we come back again to the division in modern man—to the rift between reason and emotion, the gap that is peculiarly the task of the poet to bridge. It is the same chasm that the great Romantic poets such as Wordsworth and Coleridge strove to bridge, with, I believe, only partial success. This has also been the special task of the great twentieth-century poets such as Yeats, Eliot, and Tate—though their analysis of the problem has differed rather sharply from that of, say, a Wordsworth, and accordingly they have had to employ very different strategies.

I have just invoked the names of Yeats and Eliot. Let me take this occasion to declare that no modern poet has been concerned more intensely with the unity of being than has Allen Tate—not even Yeats, for whom it was the true center of concern. Let me say further that no poet has been more concerned with the importance of recovering a living tradition—not even the author of "Tradition and the Individual Talent."

I have stressed Tate's attempt to find a language that could bring reason and emotion together in one unified experience. "Retroduction to American History" and "Causerie" are sardonic comments on a culture that has failed to bring them together. But a related task for this poet was to bring present and past into experiential relationship; that is, to bring the traditional to bear upon the contemporary. . . . Tate was not retreating from an unpleasant and unpoetic present day into a delightful and, therefore, "poetic" past. (pp. 691-92)

[In the essays cited above, Tate explained that] modernity involves a profound sense of the past, but with a final commitment to the present. Unless there is a sense of tradition, there can be no real modernism. . . . History, for Tate, is important, and because he is a southerner, the history of southern culture has a special significance.

As I have already remarked, for Tate history is a matter of concrete particulars, an account of real men and women, of actual circumstances and events. When history is run through a Hegelian meatgrinder, say, or maybe a Marxist grinder, Tate has not been willing to accept what has come out as history. For he would deny that anyone possesses a privileged view of history—would deny that any political party or group of intellectuals really knows how history will finally come out. (*Faith* that certain things lie beyond the grave, or a belief that the New Jerusalem does exist in eternity—beyond the realm of time—are very different matters.) But for most modern intellectuals, the New Jerusalem lies not in eternity but in the realm of time; that is to say, it is a secular city with flesh-and-blood citizens, a place to which a correct understanding of history can deliver us,

more or less on schedule. Tate clearly distrusts all guide books and roadmaps for getting to the secular New Jerusalem, presumably because he regards the secular New Jerusalem to be a mirage. As early as 1930, when he published "Religion and the Old South," the essay in which he indicated that Hegel actually destroyed history when he reduced it to an intellectual process, he observed that "sad, more concrete minds may be said to look at their history in a definite and now quite unfashionable way." Clearly, he numbered among these "sad, more concrete minds," his own. (p. 692)

[Tate] very early found an essential difference between the Old South and the rest of the country in their quite different orientations toward the future and the past. The Old South was semifeudal, agricultural, and backwardlooking; indeed, as he once actually calls it, a "traditional European community." The first settlers of Virginia and the Carolinas were no Pilgrim Fathers; they were not possessed by a messianic mission; nor were they bent upon building the perfect society in the American wilderness. If those indifferences render the Virginians and Carolinians a less noble band, nevertheless, the absence of messianic purposes is precisely Tate's point—a point that I would like to bring to a special focus of my own. Millennialism [the belief that we can produce the perfect society, here and now] never got the grip on the Old South that it fastened, for better or worse—perhaps one should say, for better *and* worse—on the rest of the country.

This is not to say that Tate regards the society of the Old South as perfect. In fact, he has some sharp criticisms to make of its quality and character. To name just a few; it had the curse of slavery; it was insufficiently intellectual; it failed to produce a genuine literature. Tate would add that it was not fully capable of understanding its own true virtues: that is to say, the eighteenth-century rationalistic political ideas it brought over from Europe, and its religion—whether the deism of the Virginia planters or the dissenting evangelical protestantism of the back country—were not appropriate to the semifeudal, patriarchial, society that rapidly developed in the South between 1607 and 1860.

Was the Old South in fact the kind of society that Tate describes? Or is his concept built up out of the speculations and fantasies of a young man of the 1920s? The historians who have come into prominence in the 1960s and 1970s thoroughly vindicate Tate's basic conception. (p. 693)

The classical-Christian tradition—where I locate Allen Tate's work—sees millennialism and utopianism as heresies —falsifications of history and oversimplifications of human nature. They have developed out of ancient gnosticism. But we delude ourselves if we think of them as harmless aberrations of the mind. Not so: they have power to warp and destory. Unless we understand why Tate sees in such forces of modernity an implicit threat to civilization and to man himself, we shall miss the passion and the sense of tragedy in Tate's poetry, and in his great novel, *The Fathers*.

The world revealed in Tate's poetry is in danger of destruction—perhaps as never before. But the prime threat is not the hell bomb. It lies within man himself, that now divided creature whose heart and head are hardly on speaking terms anymore. It is man who poses the serious threat not only to himself but to everything else. What is the testimony of Tate's poetry? What does it say? (pp. 694-95)

If space permitted, one might present the whole of the magnificent "Ode to the Confederate Dead." The world in which the dead men lived was completely human. They felt that they belonged to causes and purposes larger than themselves, causes to which they could wholly submit themselves. They believed that they had a meaningful place in history, whereas the man at the cemetery gate, though he envies the dead men the faith in which they lived and died, cannot attain it any more than could J. Alfred Prufrock or Stephen Dedalus. (pp. 695-96)

Read in its entirety, *The Seasons of the Soul* develops almost every element of Tate's vision of modern life. It says in finely developed and articulated poetry all that he had adumbrated in his earliest essays on the state of the culture of the West.

In what is perhaps the finest first novel (and in this case, also, the finest last novel) ever written, Tate sums up his philosophical and historical judgment as it is specifically focused upon the South. The Buchan family is destroyed in the Civil War, but not merely by fire and sword. It is destroyed from within. The Buchan family had lived by custom, taste, and family tradition. Each member knew without going through any painful reference to rule or principle what conduct was expected of him or her. But this reliance on unthinking taste has left it thoroughly vulnerable to change—particularly when that change comes to the person of a charming, unprincipled, completely rootless young man, George Posey, who seeks the hand of the daughter of the house.

Major Buchan, the kindly, guileless patriarch, is especially vulnerable. He cannot understand George Posey anymore than he can understand the forces of modernity that are at work on the national scene. He still thinks that statesmen are gentlemen of principle and honor, and that wars are fought by soldiers who respect the rights of the civilian population.

Tate has been scrupulously fair to Posey. He is not made an obvious villain: no more is Major Buchan made a saint—though in his innocence, he approaches moral blindness. In short, Tate has been too fine an artist to turn the story into a neat moral fable. Yet the novel does dramatize the weakness as well as the virtues of the civilization of the Old South when confronting a great industrial-commercial power. (pp. 696-97)

[Faulkner's] Sutpen is far closer in spirit to George Posey than he is to Major Buchan. Sutpen and Posey are antitraditional. They are both ambitious, "new" men. Both consider themselves hard-boiled realists, though actually they are at the mercy of their own undisciplined emotions. . . . If the victorious North represented in general this new ethic and this new dynamic, it should be noted that Posey and Sutpen possess them too.

Yet even in *The Fathers* Tate does not preach or argue. He presents. He witnesses to the truth as only a great artist can witness—through imaginative forms. . . . [He is] an acute, if impassioned, critic of our culture. I admire his sense of history and his insight into what is true and abiding in mankind. (p. 697)

> *Cleanth Brooks, "Allen Tate and the Nature of Modernism," in* The Southern Review *(copyright, 1976 by Cleanth Brooks), Vol. 12, No. 4, Autumn, 1976, pp. 685-97.*

RADCLIFFE SQUIRES

Any consideration of the pastoral mode today involves us in questions of very awkward accommodation. As a matter of fact, there are two traditions not susceptible of extension into modern literature, at least not in any pure manner. These are the epic and the pastoral. . . . Both epic and pastoral conceive of human character as being perfectly revealed in action. Homer and Theocritus clearly believed that was so; we do not. It is questionable whether even Virgil could quite believe Homer's credo, and we are very likely to approve of the *Aeneid* at those moments when a psychological strangeness subsumes the heroic movement. We do not believe in action as the great revealer, largely because we cannot feel sure that meaningful action is possible. Hence, adaptations of epic in modern literature convert action to symbol, and the symbol itself is subjugated to quarrelsome oppositions, is diluted by irony, and, finally, is no revealer at all, but is in fact itself revealed by such devices as stream of consciousness. We believe in the major tragedy and major triumph of the epic pole of man's being, but we do not credit an analogue of action.

If it was accurate to mention the major tragedy and triumph of the epical pole of man's being, it is accurate to speak of the minor bliss and fulfillment of the pastoral pole of man's being. Yet we are speaking of essence, not reality.

One can hardly disagree with the usual definition of pastoral verse: rustic in setting and simple in thought and action. But while one does not disagree with the definition, neither is he noticeably informed by it. Let me suggest that the difficulty of definition is that we have no poetry that is not in some way pastoral, or, to put it another way, we have no examples at all of pastoral poetry. What I mean by that outrageous remark is this: Pastoral poetry aims at yielding an impression of innocuous happiness, which we desire; it aims at paraphrasing an animal energy, which we admire; it aims at creating a freedom of being, which we yearn for, would escape to if we could, but in which we cannot believe, and, seeking, cannot find. We cannot believe or find because we cannot remove time from action and cannot remove mind from existence. Neither can we achieve complete freedom without inclining toward a licentiousness which, like pornography, is not at all free or adventurous but stylized, heartless, and dead. At best, then, pastoral poetry gives intimations of a state we apprehend in imagination but cannot accept in reality. It gives what form can be given to our sophistries of Edens, our superstitions of blessed isles, our love of dolphins moving, our sentiments about past cultures, especially those that, like Theocritus' dear, nonsensical meadows, never existed. In short, we can have, to borrow Empson's title, *some versions of* pastoral. Pure pastoral we cannot have. Indeed, one may wonder to what extent a pure pastoral poetry was possible for Theocritus or any of the other ancients. The main drift of the classical lyric was not pastoral. (pp. 733-34)

[Any] important poetic consciousness yearns toward a pastoral vision at the same time that it yearns toward its polar opposite, an epical vision, neither of them quite possible. Allen Tate is no exception, for we can observe how in his early and middle work his aspirations divide between a desire for a perfect world, which poets always seem to think they deserve, and a wish to assert through action and will a change upon the world as it actually is. I suggest this division (rather than fashionable aesthetics) led him to embrace in his early career a belief in "dissociation of sensibility." That was a worry he later abandoned, but not for a long time. In the meantime, this division tended to direct the course of his poetry. It lies behind his "Ode to the Confederate Dead," a poem in which the natural world moves on about the narrator, beyond him, offering inklings, but no sure prophecy, no heroic home, while he himself is powerless to implement his will to act. He can only react, and, even so, the manner of reaction finally reduces will to veleity, while the minor fret of aggravated sensibility remains. Therefore one way to see the "Ode" is as a poem about the blunting of the epic will. There are many poems in which the pastoral will or desire is equally blunted. (pp. 734-35)

I believe for Tate the separation from the timeless world of the pastoral aspect of life and poetry meant loss of humanity. Surely, it is at least partly for that reason that he could, in the 1930's, throw himself passionately into a movement for which he had few practical hopes. I refer to the Agrarian Movement. The whole picture of the movement is, of course, complicated by the historical milieu of the Great Depression, by wounded southern pride, and, perhaps, by a certain amount of desperate impudence on the parts of the advocates. But I have uncovered little to suggest that Tate thought Agrarianism would really prevail. Nor did he or any of the Agrarians except Andrew Lytle think of being a farmer—dirt or gentleman. Why then all the energy, the public debates, the quarrels, the cruel and hasty words? I submit that their passion was at base an artist's passion and one which rehearsed Blake's indignation at the abstractions of an industrialism that called human innocence into doubt.

The same abstract malignity that questions innocence also questions experience. Or, to put it another way, to doubt the spirit is to doubt the flesh, and to doubt the pastoral is to doubt the epical. This attendant doubt surfaces in such poems as "Aeneas at Washington" and "The Mediterranean." For these are both poems wherein the burden of history ultimately divorces man from history, giving him as a consolation prize a "sense of history." They are poems that wrench their triumph from a recognition that there is no triumph. In the magnificence of his despair Tate could go even further, creating marvelous poems about the enemy of poetry, that narcissistic abstractionism in which he perceives Alice submerged in the looking-glass. . . . She possesses "eyesight," rather than vision. The horridness of the picture derives from the separation of consciousness from a natural world. Such poems come from deciding to look the devil in the eye, something no one has to do, but if he does it and is not destroyed, he may be strengthened.

When World War II came, Tate saw it as the inevitable extension of industrialism with totalitarianism as its inevitable expression. To defeat Germany, he felt, America would have to become even more fascistic than Germany. He envisioned our young pro-consuls of the air destroying the lama, which is to say, he envisioned the death of innocence, freedom, and possibly of poetry. The poems of this time . . . were either strident in their denunciation or woebegone in their defeat. Yet a remarkable alteration occurred in his outlook. In "Seasons of the Soul" he confronted, almost for the first time, his own past, both at the level of fearful nightmare, which he had done before, and at a level of relative innocence, which he had not done before. . . . The cave imagery for Tate, who was once fond of spelunking around Sewanee, incorporates the submerged

self, its memory, atrament, cryptic omens, the self's whole past experience to be comprehended at last in ways it could not have been comprehended in that past when past was present. That which happened in the serial drift of accident cannot be recaptured in memory, but it can be truly known in the imagination. That which existed in space rather than time, he tells us of his youth, can be transfigured first into time and then further transfigured into timelessness. Though "Seasons of the Soul" suggested changes in Tate's viewpoint, it nevertheless continued his old theme of an inability to convert feeling into action in the world, that theme which pervades "Ode to the Confederate Dead." "In bloody time of war / Who will know the time?" he asks. Only an ungenerous critic would want to judge "Seasons of the Soul" as anything short of being a very nearly perfect poem. Still, it is a penultimate poem in the sense that the changes in Tate's conceptions, which it adumbrates, were only fully realized a decade later in the terza rima poems of an unfinished sequence, "The Maimed Man," "The Swimmers," and "The Buried Lake." These are intricate poems; the symbolism is of a tremulous echoing, rather than of a fixative order. Yet it is fair to say that the poems are as easy to understand as they are difficult to explicate. They are, all three of them, poems of confrontation with the self, a lost or almost lost self. This self must be shaken free of an ancestral past which the poet had labored under, as one remarks in such earlier poems as "Records" and "Sonnets of the Blood." In "The Maimed Man," Tate adduces an early self, an incomplete self whom he must know better before he can move through him with the help of poetry into a poet's freedom. He must "rehearse / Pastoral terrors of youth still in the man." . . . ["The Swimmers"] is Tate's version of pastoral, an American pastoral with terror inseparable from the beauty. He had never before quite been able or willing to admit the propriety of that fusion. (pp. 737-41)

Cleanth Brooks has spoken of ["The Buried Lake"] as a great religious poem and a great love poem. That is altogether true of its public face. I would add that for Tate, and, surely, we are always at least dimly aware of what a poem is doing for its creator, it is a poem that creates a home for the poet. That is to say, it is, in an essential way, a pastoral poem. And I note with awe that this pastoral home is created within the self before it is created and envisioned without. That act of creation, no matter how much it depends upon a buried lake of good and evil, corruption and purity, or on the ministrations of St. Lucy, is one that ultimately is created by the poetic will. And so the poem combines the element of will and the element of desire. The epic element creates the pastoral.

My envoi to the subject takes the following turn. Tate had, from his early maturity, known that such a confluence or relationship was possible and desirable in art. He had seen, in his essay "Tension in Poetry," that any extreme, classical or romantic, was not so beautiful or true as finding a position between the extremes and drawing power from both. In that knowledge he joins Blake and his reverence for pastoral and epic, though he called them innocence and experience, contraries necessary to progression. He joins Yeats and his obsession with the interacting subjective and objective facets of the self, and T. S. Eliot whose poetry bisects the line of self and non-self, of time and eternity. (pp. 742-43)

Radcliffe Squires, "Allen Tate and the Pastoral

Vision,'' in The Southern Review *(copyright, 1976, by Radcliffe Squires), Vol. 12, No. 4, Autumn, 1976, pp. 733-43.*

THOMAS R. WEST

Allen Tate published in 1938 a splendid novel that places the social and aesthetic vision in a living circumstance. The setting of *The Fathers* is Virginia and Georgetown at the breaking up of the Union. The story is told through the elderly Lacy Buchan's recollections of his boyhood. His father, Major Lewis Buchan, sums up the antebellum Southern social order. George Posey, who marries Lacy's sister Susan, reflects the modern temperament; as a destructive presence in the Buchan family, he is an instance of the forces that were beating in upon the Old South. In Major Buchan, substantial feeling and moral will are one. He is a whole man and a gentleman; he gets his gentlemanly completeness from his perfect relationship to a full and sustaining environment, though it is on the verge of crumbling. He exemplifies the Southerner whose character, Tate had said in *Stonewall Jackson*, is in his property—and that can mean also in the kin and community within which his property locates itself. The Buchans, remembers the narrator, seemed to suffer their domestic troubles and the political crisis as a single event, for "as in all highly developed societies the line marking off the domestic from the public life was indistinct.'' The community contains manners and ceremonies for the expression of the important feelings, and the "personal'' sphere as we know it hardly exists, or hardly articulates itself. The moral and emotional lives of the antebellum Virginians, acted out through precise community rituals and customs, become in effect impersonal and have dignity.... [The major] joins the private to the public order and lives ceremoniously within the dense and mannerly composite, ceremoniously restrained even in his revelation of his own distress. (pp. 58-60)

George Posey, although of an established family, has been raised outside the system of understandings that have perfectly tempered the major. George must be personal, and shape himself through his own will and passions. Tate might have said of him that he lives by the angelic imagination, trying to grasp the essences by an autonomous thrust of the will, as the major lives by the symbolic imagination and contents himself with the truths his surroundings provide him.... George's [feelings], while forceful, have little power of direction and growth. His will is energetic, but it is the energy of spasm rather than of consistent purpose. His feelings have violence without depth or perception.... George represents ... the alliance between the apparent opposites of science and primitive lust, for in his eagerness to seize upon existence George reduces it by cold rationality to its usable terms. (pp. 60-1)

The Fathers is a stunning novel, and a remarkable testing out of social philosophy in an imagined living situation. It is in one way a curious accomplishment. Its author has been a spokesman for a literary school that has sounded, perhaps not quite by its own intention, almost as though it would deny to ideas the right to have an explicit independent place within an artistic work. The most admirable figure, Major Buchan, is a gentleman in whom thought is totally contained within tradition, manners, and experience. Yet ideas command *The Fathers*: careful speculative observations made by the narrator on the events he recalls give the themes, and the characters are representations of them.

While Tate has a pleasing skill at bringing back the texture of life in an era that is past and peopling it with real human beings, it is the ideas that give the novel its greatest strength.

The sensibility possessed by Major Buchan is indivisible. His exquisitely polished manners, his spareness of open gesture, his impersonality—the traits that in another person would be the results of reason and a strenuous moral will—derive in Buchan's case from that brand of feeling we call taste and from the massive feeling that constitutes his sense of his social heritage. (pp. 62-3)

Thomas R. West, in his Nature, Community, & Will: A Study in Literary and Social Thought *(reprinted by permission of the University of Missouri Press; copyright 1976 by the Curators of the University of Missouri), University of Missouri Press, 1976.*

DENIS DONOGHUE

Allen Tate's work in poetry, fiction, and criticism touches American life at nearly every point of consequence and continues to exert moral pressure even when the causes it serves are already mostly lost. Many of his poems take up arms against his fated enemies: the North; the forces in the Old South that made the New South inevitable; the ideologies of positivism and naturalism, which Tate regards as vandalism. The "Collected Poems'' is the definitive manual of these wars....

I find it significant that the new "Collected Poems'' contains about 30 early poems more than the corresponding section of Tate's standard selection, "The Swimmers and Other Selected Poems'' (1971). In a note to "The Swimmers'' Tate said that by an "early'' poem he meant a poem he had written before 1922, when he first read Eliot.... In his novel "The Fathers'' (1938) the narrator reports that, "in my feelings of that time there is a new element—my feelings now about that time.... There is not an old man living who can recover the emotions of the past; he can only bring back the objects around which, secretly, the emotions have ordered themselves in memory.'' Tate's earliest poems are such objects, and they are recovered in the "Collected Poems'' for that reason, like the memories recited in his "Memoirs and Opinions'' (1976).

After 1922, Tate's work took on a lot of freight—preoccupations in history, politics, religion and literature. Some of these were a consequence of his birth in Kentucky: he would have found it impossible to ignore the South, the nature of tradition, the family, the "antique courtesy'' of myth. Other themes were congenial to a poet of Tate's temper: time, death, belief, errancy of feeling, will and intellect. In essays and, by implication, in poems, Tate has been speaking of a possible harmony of feelings, will and intellect, but he knows that in practice they exhibit mostly chaos. He has described various forms of excess, beginning with the refusal or the failure "to represent the human condition in the central tradition of natural feeling.'' Another exorbitance is "the thrust of the will beyond the human scale of action.'' And a third excess is "the intellect moving in isolation from both love and the moral will, whereby it declares itself independent of the human situation in the quest of essential knowledge.'' That last adjective, "essential,'' explains why Tate calls such an exorbitant imagination "angelic''; it represents a claim upon essence without the mediation of existence, and it is a form of spiritual pride. Against these forms of vanity, Tate sets the symbolic imagination, and his text for its working is Dante.... (p. 13)

I name these few themes in default of a complete list: such a list would constitute not only Tate's history but much of the moral history of the modern world. But I name them also to account for the difficulty of Tate's poetry, where it is difficult.... I do not know whether or not Tate's poems have been conceived in joy, but most of them come with an air of tension, if not desperation. Like many other American poems, they assume that they have to do all the work by themselves.

Given Tate's sense of modern life, his preoccupations and his feeling for grand causes mainly lost, his poems cry out for structures and forms commensurate with the chaos of their substance; or, the same thing in other terms, cry out for a masterful rhythm equal and opposite to the chaos it encounters. Some of his poems fail to reach their rhythm, and in these what we feel at every point is turbulence and frustration.... Such poems bring to bear upon their provocations an order, or a set of orders, chiefly theoretic, hypothetical, archaic or chivalric; good in general and worthy in any case but not good enough in the particular case. So the poetry senses its doom in advance, takes up burdens it has no hope of sustaining. I am thinking of "Sonnets of the Blood" (1931) and other poems as late as "The Maimed Man" (1952), poems which are moving and desperate because, achieving so much, they cannot achieve themselves.

It is well known that Tate resorted to other poets in the hope of finding himself and his own voice. Before 1922, his masters were mainly those he named in the note to "The Swimmers"; after 1922, they were chiefly Eliot, Yeats, Hardy and in certain moments Hart Crane. (pp. 13, 45)

Tate's poetry has resorted to many kinds of music. The first risk is ventriloquism, when one of Tate's poems sounds like Tate reading one of, say, Eliot's poems. A more desperate risk is inarticulateness, when the music sinks. The great occasions are those when a poem achieves its rhythm, and Tate's voice comes powerfully through its commotion. I am thinking of "The Mediterranean" (1933) for a relatively early instance, and of "The Swimmers" and "The Buried Lake" (1953) for the grand achievements. In the first, Virgil helps Tate to assume every burden in the case, and the achieved rhythm takes in its surge the sense of human action in which Europe and America are about equally implicated. Twenty years later, Tate's guide was Dante. The *terza rima* of "The Swimmers" and "The Buried Lake" is a remarkable achievement, commensurate with the grandeur of their themes....

[The example of Dante in "The Buried Lake"], as of Virgil in earlier poems, has given Tate the conviction that he is not compelled to do all the work by himself. Whatever the mood of the poet, his poem is at peace with its mixture of knowledge and ignorance, reason in madness....

One of the gratifications of the "Collected Poems" is to find an exasperated spirit, in the later poems, taking things a little easy. As Wallace Stevens wrote of another occasion, the mind lays by its trouble and relents. (p. 45)

> Denis Donoghue, "Moving and Desperate," in The New York Times Book Review, (© 1977 by the New York Times Company; reprinted by permission), December 11, 1977, pp. 13, 45.

HILTON KRAMER

For readers of a certain age—I have in mind those who, like myself, first came to modern poetry (and to the criticism written to defend and elucidate it) in the years just after the Second World War—the publication of Allen Tate's "Collected Poems 1919-1976" ... is an event that stirs a good many memories and associations. Scarcely 20 years had passed since the appearance of his first books in 1928—the year of both "Mr. Pope and Other Poems" and "Stonewall Jackson: The Good Soldier"—yet in those first years after the war Mr. Tate already seemed a venerable survivor of several lost worlds. The Nashville of the Fugitives, the New York of the young Malcolm Cowley and Kenneth Burke and E. E. Cummings, like the Paris of Gertrude Stein and Ford Madox Ford; had receded into the mists of literary legend....

It seemed slightly incredible ... that this embattled exponent of the New Criticism—for so was Mr. Tate generally regarded in the academic controversies of the time—could the same writer who had once belonged to the worlds that had produced Hemingway and Hart Crane and "I'll Take My Stand."...

[Throughout the complex history of New Criticism], Mr. Tate was never a writer easy to take hold of. For the New Criticism enjoined us to concentrate our attention on the poem itself—when it ventured into discussions of fiction or drama, it seemed to treat them too as poetic structures—and not to be bemused by the distractions of literary history, or indeed history of any sort. (p. 3)

The odd thing about all this, so far as Mr. Tate's own writings were concerned, was that he had been all along a writer—as poet, critic, novelist and biographer—deeply immersed in the materials of history, and there could never be any question of separating *his* literary achievements from their attachment to the historical imagination. Only by means of a certain pedagogical magic and a classroom atmosphere of extreme casuistry could the author of "Ode to the Confederate Dead," of that fine novel "The Fathers" (which Arthur Mizener once described as "the novel 'Gone With the Wind' ought to have been") and "Reactionary Essays on Poetry and Ideas" be separated from the iron grip of history. It was done, of course, but the result, I think, was to blur his distinction, especially his distinction as a poet. The New Criticism may have enhanced our appreciation of his powers of literary artifice, but it diminished our understanding of the vision that such artifice was designed to serve. In this respect, the most blatant of Mr. Tate's political and historical essays often prove a better guide to the poetry than the most accomplished explications of his language and structure. (pp. 3, 36)

Returning to the poetry again on the occasion of this new "Collected Poems," one is indeed keenly aware that "time and history" is its central concern and "man's attachment to the past" its major theme, but it is a particular history that so impresses itself on our imagination—the history of a lost world carried in the mind of a Southerner, a classicist and an artist exiled to a Northern culture in which the imperatives of industrialism, philistinism and bourgeois capitalism reinforce a sense of irretrievable defeat.

The tragic dimension of Mr. Tate's poetry, which we feel most profoundly in the poems written in memory of friends —especially in "Seasons of the Soul," written in memory of John Peale Bishop, and "The Eye," written for E. E. Cummings—as well as in the better-known "Ode to the Confederate Dead," the irony of which is in its not being an ode at all, is to be found precisely in this consciousness of exile from a history that holds the poet in its power. All that can be retrieved from this history, and from the sense of defeat that is inseparable from it and which in the end is indistinguishable from the scenario of existence itself, is what the artist makes of it. Is this, perhaps, why the poems written in memory of friends who were also poets seem to carry a special power?

It is, in any case, in this sense of history—the most encompassing of Mr. Tate's lost worlds—that we find the source of both the politics that may appall us and the poetry that moves and instructs us. . . . This is a poetry that is formal, elegant, "metaphysical"; and coming to it today from an immersion in the newer, looser, more solipsistic modes of contemporary verse, it too conjures up a lost world—a world of flawless, well-made structures and meters that flatter and educate the ear. But it is also a poetry of knowledge, a poetry confident in its assumption that poetry has something to tell us about our experience, about history, that only poetry can tell us. Mr. Tate's very long and distinguished career is, in its way, a kind of parable on the poet's vocation, for his poetry is often wise as well as beautiful in ways that his prose is not. It is the poetry that will live. (pp. 36-7)

Hilton Kramer, "Allen Tate: Lost Worlds," in The New York Times Book Review (© 1978 by The New York Times Company; reprinted by permission), January 8, 1978, pp. 3, 36-7.

*   *   *

THEROUX, Paul   1941-

Theroux is an American novelist, short story writer, travel writer, poet, and critic. His work often deals with the conflict between romantic idealism and reality, frequently in exotic settings such as Africa, Malaysia, and the Near East. Critics have generally praised the craftsmanship of his construction and his rich style while lamenting his occasionally unresolved themes and insubstantial characterizations. (See also CLC, Vols. 5, 8, and Contemporary Authors, Vols. 33-36, rev. ed.)

MICHAEL IRWIN

The first thing to say about [*The Consul's File*] is that it makes excellent reading. The stories span a wide range of mood and theme. At one extreme there is comedy—a forty-five-year-old Englishwoman blandly commandeering the title role in the local drama society's production of *Suzie Wong*; at the other there are revenge, rape, murder and a ghost or two. Paul Theroux appears to be equally at ease with any of these subjects. He is a natural short-story writer. Repeatedly he contrives a plot that is compact, interesting and unpredictable. His surprise endings have an organic quality: they do not trimly dispose of what has gone before, but ask the reader to reinterpret it. The narration is quick, clear and restrained; the stories are left to speak for themselves. The general standard is high but I particularly enjoyed "Pretend I'm Not Here", "Diplomatic Relations" and the deftly structured "The Autumn Dog".

The Consul's File was surely intended to add up to something a good deal more than the sum total of its parts. Names, places and institutions recur; a major character in one episode will take a minor role in another. Presumably the stories were designed to be mutually reinforcing, and to convey, cumulatively, a sense of the day-to-day life of the town. But this secondary objective is not fully achieved. Most of the tales have been previously published in magazines, and Paul Theroux does not seem to have sufficiently modified and cross-related them for their new context. There are awkward discontinuities. . . . While *The Consul's File* does generate a sense of community atmosphere it could and should have generated more. The recurring characters tend to remain shadowy: they have too little to say and do. There is no feeling for the *work* of the place. We hear of rubber trees giving place to oil palms, but never see either. The ghost-stories are jolly enough in their own right, but aren't easily reconciled with the rest of the collection. The gin-drinkers at the Club never talk about ghosts.

Paul Theroux avoids gratuitous local colour and keeps exposition to a minimum usually getting a story started with a few short assertions. In general this is a virtue: his book has none of the officious cosmopolitanism that disfigures so many novels set Abroad. But it can also be said that he leaves some stories underexplained. The reader who has visited Malaysia, who knows something about the relationships between Indians, Chinese, Malays, Americans and Englishmen, will perhaps not only understand the stories better, but be able to fill in some of the gaps that make the collection rather less than an imaginative whole.

Michael Irwin, "The Maugham the Merrier," in The Times Literary Supplement (© Times Newspapers Ltd. (London) 1977; reproduced from The Times Literary Supplement by permission), June 3, 1977, p. 669.

ANTHONY BURGESS

To Somerset Maugham it was the F.M.S., to Henri Fauconnier *Malaisie*, to myself Malaya; to the American writer Paul Theroux . . . it is Malaysia. It is recognizably the same place in all its nominations, and there is nowhere in the world quite like it. I wrote about it from the viewpoint of a Colonial Education Officer, Fauconnier from that of a French rubber-planter who loved the Malays and was learned in their language. Willie Maugham, who knew the country least, has unfairly effected a literary near-monopoly of it. In Theroux's new volume of stories ["The Consul's File"], narrated by a young American consul who appears in each of them, the Ayer Hitam Dramatic Society puts on an adaptation of "The Letter," and old British expatriates try to behave like Maugham eccentrics. Maugham is always around somewhere, even in the post-Vietnam age, sardonically sipping gin *pahits* on the club veranda, observing exilic adulteries, defiled by mold on the termite-eaten shelves of the Carnegie Library. (p. 1)

But there is also the more terrible Malaya that Maugham heard of but never saw. He merely picked up the story about a Malay woman who imparts lethal hiccups to the man who deserts her (somebody in Theroux's book picks up that story from Maugham and retails it as local folklore). . . .

Such tales must, to readers who don't know Malaya, sound like fanciful shockers. After my six years out there, I can only nod sagely and shiveringly at Theroux's terse narrations. But I must not give the impression that Theroux is merely trying to titillate with choice exotica. His book is a rounded and many-sided (there's a fine Asiatic contradiction for you) portrait of a typical Malayan town. . . .

"The Consul's File" has, to this British reader, a great deal of exotic charm, but the exotic resides in that new breed—the American in Southeast Asia. . . . This American has written as good a Malaysian book as that masterpiece by Henri Fauconnier, "La Malaisie." We always had odd Frenchmen lurking about, taking notes. I remember meeting Jean Cocteau, who called Kuala Lumpur *Kouala l'impure.* He was right. The whole damned country is glamorous with impurity, and Paul Theroux has caught a great deal of it. (p. 18)

> *Anthony Burgess, in* The New York Times Book Review (© *1977 by the New York Times Company; reprinted by permission), August 21, 1977.*

DONALD DAVIE

"The war did not destroy the English—it fixed them in fatal attitudes. The Japanese were destroyed and out of that destruction came different men; only the loyalties were old—the rest was new." Thus the thirty-six-year-old New Englander Paul Theroux, pursuing his studies of the post-Imperial British, this time in Malaysia, Somerset Maugham country. The short stories in *The Consul's File* should be popular. How to cope, or more precisely how *not* to cope, with losing an empire—for an updated Somerset Maugham the subject has everything: nostalgia, pathos, irony, and (not too frequently of course, but the more tellingly) gusts of delicious guilt and right-thinking anticolonialism. Even the appropriate tone, scenario, and idiom are common stock—credits to Graham Greene. Given these advantages, an adroit practitioner like Paul Theroux could hardly go wrong. Nor does he; *The Consul's File* can be recommended as a thoroughly good read. And yet it is, or it ought to be, intolerably depressing. . . .

[None] of the lives that the stories introduce us to—of Anglicized Malays and Indians, Americanized Chinese, Americans passing through, British (and the odd American) planters, doctors, and government surveyors and so on—ever escapes [a] dispiriting diagnosis of their situation as futile, insignificant, and undignified. Even the human and marital relations among them, not just the inter-racial ones either, are blighted and doomed. . . .

To make no . . . bones about it, I think Paul Theroux is bad medicine for any Englishman who even half attends to what he is reading, and only a little less bad for any American who cares about what England has become and what may be expected of her. He nourishes some of our worst weaknesses and saps what remains of our strength. But in saying so I rely on my own conviction that what has been weakest about us for a long time is the rationalistic lie, not the romantic one. In any case, however, are these the demands that can be made of "art"? And isn't Paul Theroux the storyteller an artist? That's as may be; I speak of the effect he will have. (p. 28)

> *Donald Davie, in* The New York Review of Books *(reprinted with permission from* The New York Review of Books; *copyright © 1977 Nyrev, Inc.), November 10, 1977.*

ANNE TYLER

From the start, Paul Theroux's ["Picture Palace"] takes us by surprise. In the first place, it's less exotic than most of his books, which tend to be set in far-off countries and to be peopled by characters who are foreign at least in outlook, if not in fact. It lacks the snap and crackle of, say, "The Family Arsenal," his best-known novel, and draws its energy instead from internal events: the unfolding and shaking out of old memories, the slow evolution of character over years and years.

There's also the surprise of finding that "Picture Palace" is not what the first few pages lead us to expect. That is, it's not, thank heaven, one of those books about famous but bored, crotchety, eccentric old artists gracelessly enduring the young biographer/sycophants who are nibbling around the edges of their lives. It's true that Maude Coffin Pratt is a well-known photographer, and that young Frank Fusco is busy ferreting out all her old pictures for a grand retrospective; and it's true that she refers to Fusco as a "barnacle" and to the retrospective as "taxidermy." But what makes the difference is that the art, here—Maude's photography—is more than just a convenient peg to hang a plot on. In fact, "Picture Palace" is, among other things, a serious reflection on the relationship between art and the artist: what art adds to the artist's life and what it subtracts.

For Maude, photography is first a means to an end. She sees her camera as license to stare, unobserved, in a family where staring is impolite. Then she sees it as a way to capture the attention of her brother Orlando. Orlando is the center of Maude's world, her only love, and she unashamedly dedicates a large portion of her life to trying to seduce him.

This incestuous fixation is the book's one flaw. It seems contrived, magnified; it's a clearer "why" for Maude's photographic career than we need to have. And although Mr. Theroux succeeds wonderfully in adopting the voice of a first-person woman narrator—apparently working on the assumption that women aren't all that different from men, which seems reasonable enough to me—he fails to make us visualize what Orlando's attraction is. . . .

At any rate, given this obsession, we're shown how it leads Maude to take spectacular leaps as a photographer, chasing fame so that Orlando will notice her. She photographs E. E. Cummings, D. H. Lawrence and Paul Robeson; she also photographs black servants, blind people and a pathetic "Pig Dinner" at which circus acrobats perform in the nude. . . .

There is something convincing and satisfying about the way this life work of Maude's creeps up on her. And she has some marvelously peevish remarks to make about her art, which she appears to view as some sort of shaggy, burdensome beast determined to shamble after her. For Maude, it's an either/or proposition: either she sees or the camera sees, but never both. "None of my pictures came out," she says on one occasion, "which was why I remembered it so clearly." Photography diminishes her experience, or supplants it, or steals it away from her, or conceals the fact that she *has* no experience. She is like those tourists who miss Europe because they've been too busy taking pictures of it. Yet the pictures are experiences in themselves; we're the ones who gain. (p. 10)

Essentially, Maude is the only character in "Picture Palace." You can hardly count her family members, who seem pale beside her; or the obtuse Frank Fusco; or the bewildering number of real personages (Graham Greene, Hemingway, Eliot, and on and on) who make cameo appearances. But Maude is strong enough to sustain the whole book—slangy, tough, blunt, single-minded. Her tactics in pursuing Orlando are so unprincipled that you first gasp and then laugh. She has something snide to say about everyone from Truman Capote to "Jack Guggenheim." And not a one of her colleagues escapes her sharp tongue. . . . We may shake our heads over Maude, but we can never doubt her reality. She is always, without a missed beat, a believable woman; she makes "Picture Palace" a vibrant and compelling book. (p. 25)

> *Anne Tyler, "The Artist as an Old Photographer," in* The New York Times Book Review (© *1978 by The New York Times Company; reprinted by permission), June 18, 1978, pp. 10, 25.*

NICHOLAS GUILD

It is refreshing to find a story that touches on the relationship between art and life and still manages to avoid the narcissism which so often drenches such productions, giving you the uneasy feeling that the writer is hiding behind some half-open door, peering in as you read to see if your face is registering the proper degree of respectful sympathy. *Picture Palace* succeeds partly because Maude's discussions of her craft seem convincingly to be about photography—there is no sense that picture snapping is some heavy-handed metaphor for fiction writing—and partly because Maude really believes in the impersonality of art—the camera is, after all, a device for recording the external world—but principally because Theroux for the most part has a very firm grasp of what he is about. What he has given us is a superbly crafted, elegantly controlled novel in which most of the booby traps this sort of story sets for a writer are evaded with an easy finesse that almost makes one forget that they were ever there.

I should hate to suggest, however, that *Picture Palace* is nothing more than a fictionalized discussion of what the jargon calls the "creative process"; it is also, even primarily, about a wounded life. (p. G1)

The book is not, however, without flaws. The long sequence at the beginning, in which Maude has dinner with Graham Greene, strikes one as rather pallid, and here and there in the opening pages the comedy is a little overplayed—rather surprising in a novel in which elsewhere the tone of the protagonist's narration, a certain flinty puckishness that signals Maude's refusal to become the captive of circumstance, is one of its chief strengths. . . .

But what is vastly more important is the novel's overall success. Theroux has a wonderful sense of style and pace, and his story builds in complexity without ever becoming cumbersome. The achievement is very real. (p. G4)

> *Nicholas Guild, "Portraits of a Lady," in* Book World—The Washington Post (© *The Washington Post), June 25, 1978, pp. G1, G4.*

VICKI GOLDBERG

It was bold of Theroux to make Maude a photographer [in *Picture Palace*], and that she is believable as one is a remarkable feat, since artists are notoriously hard to draw. In a story of self-deception, photography is a near perfect metaphor for imperfect perception. . . .

The plot's quite a creaky business in *Picture Palace*, but it hangs on a marvelously constructed and nicely realized

metaphor of vision and blindness. At age eleven, snapping her first photograph, Maude suddenly cries, "I can't see!"—because her thumb is on the viewfinder. This is a tidy way of remarking that the self constantly gets in the way of vision, and throughout the book Maude's desires blind her for a time to important facts that the reader has already guessed.

Maude herself is a vigorous, rackety, memorable creation, though badly flawed. Her tenacity, cunning, and self-doubt would be quite sufficient to fuel an artist's career. Unhappily, Maude is less convincing as woman than as photographer. Even an elderly and famous woman hell-bent on eccentricity would scarcely think that critics who praised her as a credit to her sex were "calling attention to my tits, which they promptly put in the wringer of art criticism." Or berate a young man for keeping pornographic pictures of "Kenny's great hairy ass or his dripping tool." This is impossibly graphic and a bad mistake. . . .

Still, Theroux's knowledge of photography gives Maude space and focus. Her attitudes are sharp and contemporary: Snapshots are the true American folk art; good photographs are found rather than created; photographers can be "meticulous assassins." . . .

What keeps the reader reading is Theroux's dexterous, energetic style. He can overwrite or misjudge—the incest angle is the weakest aspect of *Picture Palace*—but he seems almost incapable of writing a dull sentence. He can conjure up the British in wartime, "obsessed with their own fortitude, making a virtue of the national vice—their love of a plucky defeat." . . .

Picture Palace itself is rather like one of Maude's photographs—inventive on the surface, deftly composed, full of minor revelations. But Maude, a serendipitous subject, is unevenly lit, and whole areas of figures in the background are poorly resolved. Only technique and pizzazz pull off the picture; both Maude Pratt and her creator have a fine command of the one and a generous supply of the other.

> *Vicki Goldberg, "Images of a Lifetime," in* Saturday Review (© *1978 by Vicki Goldberg; reprinted with permission), July 8, 1978, p. 32.*

KARL MILLER

Mr. Theroux's *Picture Palace* examines the relationship between the personal life of an artist and the art it produces (or, as we shall see, doesn't produce). The story is told by a celebrated photographer, Maude Coffin Pratt . . . , who is engaged, as the sole surviving tenant of the family house on Cape Cod, in looking through her old pictures, piled in the adjacent windmill. With her is trendy Frank Fusco, who is mounting a Maude Pratt retrospective, bedizened with stereophonic sound effects. This work causes charming, ill-natured Maude to resuffer her past life. . . .

Orlando is her brother, and her designs on him are thwarted when she finds that, having been prepared by her for incest, he chooses to commit it with her sister Phoebe instead, in the windmill. Maude witnesses and records their embrace, and then, for a term, goes blind, staying on, Agonistes, at or around the mill with these slaves of passion, her screwing siblings. For all its fast moving, this is a densely literary book.

It is also a romantic book, evoking as it does a commitment

which takes two people out of the world, a commitment which Maude aims at and misses. . . .

Orlando to the windmill—the book may be alluding to Virginia Woolf, and to the well-known seaside house and lighthouse in her fiction, so that it is surprising that she should be among the few celebrities of the period who do not put in an appearance in the book as Maude's subjects. . . .

Early in the book discomfort ensues with the feeling (mine anyway) that Maude is a man. She is aggressive, assassin-like, is rarely civil, wants to punch Frank in the mouth, and belches her disapproval of his retrospective in his face. She is meant to be hermaphroditic, longing to turn male and mustached with age. But it occurred to me that some of her pugnacities were less like those of any conceivable Yankee virago than like those of her compatriot Robert Frost, as they have been recalled by the disenchanted. Then Frost himself turned up in person on the page: an "utter egomaniac," "the biggest son-of-a-bitch I was ever to photograph," "monologuing to a group of admirers, a whopping earache of complaints against his family." But Maude is not very different, more son-of-a-bitch than bitch. *Picture Palace* explores the wilder shores of American androgyny, and a conception which transcends both sex and shore—that of the famous and cantankerous old artist who gets to punch the world in the mouth.

The writer's habit of allusion and his recruitment of real people demonstrate that Maude inhabits an Anglo-American literary culture. . . .

Where the novel does well is in its sketching of the art, cult, and history of photography. Fox Talbot is remembered, Julia Cameron is revered, the American virtuosi of the twentieth century are paraded and disparaged: I was sorry there was no homage to the best of all photographers, Lartigue. You feel that the pictures credited to Maude would have been worth taking. Though the novelist overdoes the shame of a Florida banquet where businessmen are diverted by Arbus freaks and bareback riders from a local circus, the *Pig Dinner* shots come to life in the mind, as do her *South Yarmouth Madonna*, her Cuba pictures, her rogues' gallery of eminent writers. Meanwhile the clichés of the Camera Club—"Honest Face," "Drunken Bum," "Prostitute in Slit Skirt Standing near *Rooms* Sign"—provide a very funny page.

The novel presents an egomaniac in a darkroom meditating on the impersonality of art and holding that "subject is everything." It tries to show that Maude's exhibited, retrospective pictures fail to express that other subject which calls the shots, and that the secrets locked in the shots no one knows affirm her true self, and the failure of its loving endeavors. The book's account of the proximity between these two failures, however, is unable to convey that the art for which she is known does not display her, and that the undisplayed incest picture does. The importance assigned to this emblem of Maude Pratt's romantic agony is the most conventional, the least idiosyncratic, element in the book. Perhaps there is another thing that could be said about its sources, about the matter of convention. *Picture Palace* is a romantic fable which has history in it, and living people, and it may be that it also has in it a reading of Doctorow's *Ragtime*. (p. 25)

> *Karl Miller, in* The New York Review of Books
> *(reprinted with permission from* The New York

Review of Books; *copyright © 1978 Nyrev, Inc.),*
August 17, 1978.

PAUL BAILEY

Paul Theroux's brilliant new novel ends with a startling scene. Maude Coffin Pratt, a famous American photographer, is attending the private view of a retrospective exhibition of her life's work. . . . With the arrival of the young man who has organised the the the show, it becomes deafening. Maude realises that it is he, Frank Fusco—the toadying recipient of a Guggenheim fellowship—who is the hero of the hour. The artist herself is a mere onlooker. She remains where she always was—on the periphery.

Picture Palace is a very funny book about a very sad human being. Maude is a perpetual spectator, fated to record what she cannot experience. (pp. 275-76)

Her lens at the ready, she mingles with the mighty. . . . Hers is a vicarious existence, like a certain kind of novelist's—almost, one might say, like Paul Theroux's. He's a bit of an onlooker, too.

Picture Palace works splendidly on the surface, like Maude's talent. What it lacks as a work of art is what she lacks as an artist: an essential empathy. She tells us she cares, but not convincingly: she's only *there* when things happen. The people—the *real* people of fiction, as distinct from Theroux's Manns and Eliots—are shadowy, insubstantial. The novel would be better if they weren't. One wants this solitary figure to function among recognisably complex individuals, seen with something other than a camera. One would like her to be *there* when things *aren't* happening. One would like her to be *there* with truly imagined characters. . . . It's a difficult place to get to, that there. I'd feel happier with this clever book if I could say, in all honesty, that Paul Theroux knew something of its whereabouts. (p. 276)

> *Paul Bailey, "That There," in* New Statesman
> *(© 1978 The Statesman & Nation Publishing Co.
> Ltd.), September 1, 1978, pp. 275-76.*

WILLIAM H. PRITCHARD

Paul Theroux is simply a wonder, and [*Picture Palace* is] a remarkable piece of work. In reviewing . . . *The Family Arsenal* . . . I spoke of how it (and its very fine predecessor, *The Black House*) each featured a desperate man endowed with great sensitivity, irony, and visionary or novelistic powers of forecast and apprehension. I also noted that both novels were consistently entertaining. . . . *Picture Palace* is even bolder and more daring than the last two, partly because its narrator . . . is a tough seventy-year-old photographer named Maude Coffin Pratt who is both desperately wrong about things . . . and righter about them than anybody else can be, the way artists are "right" about things. . . . The book undertakes a very complicated and satisfyingly dialectical exploration of blindness, sight, insight, vision and revision—which exploration is the equivalent to the moral and political argument of *The Family Arsenal,* or the anthropological and mystical one of *The Black House.*

An exploration, but not an argument, for one never feels after reading Theroux that one has learned something about the Nature of . . . of whatever. An even better word for it is "entertainment," and some of the most entertaining things about *Picture Palace* are the set-pieces in which Maude encounters famous modern artists—like D. H. Lawrence or T. S. Eliot or Frost or Raymond Chandler—and "does them" (play is made with sexual force of this expression) into art, storing them in an old windmill on Cape Code, but more truly in the picture palace of her mind put on display by this novel. . . . With prose like [Maude's description of Graham Greene,] Theroux convinces us that words are worth a thousand pictures.

The Family Arsenal was chock-full of London cockney tough-talk; *Picture Palace* is equally idiomatically alive, page by page, as Maude satirizes the new photographers with their highest priced equipment. . . . *Picture Palace* shares with Susan Sontag's recent *On Photography* many moral and cultural reservations (to put it mildly) about taking pictures, but Theroux feels rather more inwards with the activity than does Sontag, and he is a lot more fun, as when Maude makes a scornful list of photographic clichés. . . . (pp. 527-28)

It's true that incest is the most heavily-used of literary themes, but it seems to me no more damaging here, with its theatrical heightening of experience, than in Faulkner or Ivy Compton-Burnett. It's all just a story, dazzlingly and intensely told, with the great modern fictional classics—James and Conrad and Ford and Faulkner, and Graham Greene too—giving Theroux ballast for the idea that the telling is enough. I think it is, because he never lets up, never writes a paragraph of filler or "transition" which has less than his full presence as a writer behind it. *Picture Palace* is another impressive testimony that as a steadily producing writer of long and short fiction, travel books, essays and reviews—of "letters" generally—no American writer matters more than this gifted and possessed word-man. (p. 529)

> *William H. Pritchard, in* The Hudson Review *(copyright © 1978 by The Hudson Review, Inc.; reprinted by permission), Vol. XXXI, No. 3, Autumn, 1978.*

*　　*　　*

THURBER, James　　1894-1961

Thurber, a short story writer, cartoonist, essayist, and dramatist, is generally considered the outstanding American humorist of this century. A distinctive stylist both in his prose and his cartoons, Thurber satirized the events of middle-class life and the relations between the sexes. His portrait of the bewildered modern man beset by the world's mundane woes appeared so consistently in his work as to become the stereotypical Thurber man. (See also *CLC*, Vol. 5, and *Contemporary Authors*, Vols. 73-76.)

JULIAN MOYNIHAN

In a tribute to Mary Thurber written after her death in 1955 and reprinted in *Alarms and Diversions* Thurber testified to the life-long occupation of his mind by a sense of confusion apparently brought on by his formidable mother's addiction to practical jokes involving elaborate disguises and sudden shifts of identity. Images of this confusion—Mitty's autism, the 'chronic word garblings' of lady conversationalists in the party pieces, the famous drawings of the seal in the bedroom, the House-Woman and the enormous inscrutable rabbit blocking life's path to the Goal—proliferate in his work, suggesting that he wrote and drew with a firm professional hand to exorcize a deep uncertainty which was often

dangerously close to sheer panic. And yet, because he was an authentic artist, Thurber's invention has given a shape and face to the unconfessed dreams and *angst* of all but the most robust men. . . .

Thurber's attitude toward his favourite subjects was always complicated and sometimes ambiguous. In celebrating the modern sex war he regularly portrayed Woman as just a little bit taller, tougher, surer and faster on the draw than her opponent, and he agreed with 'those wiser men who spoke of the female with proper respect, and even fear.' At the same time he called himself a feminist and backed the feminine conspiracy on the cogent grounds that women sought to seize power in order to prevent the world from being blown to fragments. Another of his obsessions was language. An inveterate wordgamesman and dictionary reader he brooded and wrote a good deal about the 'disfigurations of sense and meaning' which accompany Cold War propaganda tactics and about the 'carcinomenclature of our time' fostered by the adulteration of common speech by professional and technological jargons. . . . Thurber's whimsy is often more relevant to issues in the great world than first appears. . . .

As Yeats once remarked, the peculiar heroism of modern artists is chiefly manifested in their unflinching attentiveness to the world's and the self's chaos as revealed to them by the contents of their own minds. Thurber had a good measure of this heroism. . . .

> *Julian Moynihan, "No Nonsense," in* New Statesman *(© 1962 The Statesman & Nation Publishing Co. Ltd.), December 14, 1962, p. 872.*

LOUIS HASLEY

Beyond question the foremost humorist of the twentieth century, James Thurber was a divided man. With minor exceptions he did not explore the century's large social and political problems. War, religion, crime, poverty, civil rights—these were not his subjects. Instead he struck at the immemorial stupidities, cruelties, and perversities of men that lie at the root of our ills. A disillusioned idealist, he satirized mean behavior to sound the clearest note of his discontent. Yet he considered himself an optimist or near kin to one. He insisted that the perceptive reader would detect in his work "a basic and indestructible thread of hope." (p. 504)

Aside from relatives and family servants, he gives us artists and intellectuals like himself, isolates in our time, self-exiled by a temperament alien to the world and at the same time treated contemptuously by that world. Validity might then be dismissed as an irrelevance because we are faced with two conflicting sets of ideas. It was the study of man, however, that absorbed Thurber, and the proof of his right to the title of artist lies in his ability to universalize his subjects.

The world of James Thurber is conjugal, social, artistic, and psychological, as it is in his favorite author, Henry James. It is, of course, less genteel, less sinister, less subtle, less refined, less elaborate than in James, but it fits the pace of life in today's journalistic offices and studios, as well as its upper-middle-class social gatherings that are viable only with plentiful alcoholic stimulation. Here the artist-intellectuals and their long-suffering spouses communicate among themselves, having only tangential contact with this or that "outsider" from the practical world of affairs.

James Thurber found man a frightening subject, although a large part of his best work was in perceptive, affectionate, admiring tribute to [relatives,] friends and *New Yorker* associates. . . . (pp. 504-05)

In a civilization in which women were winning the battle of the sexes, Mitty the non-hero [in "The Secret Life of Walter Mitty"] is among the defaulters by virtue of allowing his wife to dominate him. He achieves secretly a kind of compensatory victory by indulging in interludes of stream-of-consciousness fantasy, triggered whenever the immediate outside event threatens to run him down—fantasy in which he vividly and heroically figures as a man among men. The story is a masterpiece of associational psychology in its shuttling between the petty, humiliating details of his outer life and the flaming heroism of his self-glorifying reveries. He becomes the prime exemplification of the Thurber man, as critics have called him, a figure of the little man such as appears prominently in other Thurber stories to the end of World War II. This man is likewise brilliantly celebrated in many of Thurber's sophisticatedly primitive cartoons, which are necessary adjuncts to the full appreciation of the people whom Thurber envisioned. Similarly, Mrs. Mitty is the practical, no-nonsense, hard-headed wife ("the Thurber woman") who bosses her husband about as she might an irresponsible child. (p. 506)

If Mitty has only an escapist's psychological victory, Martin's triumph [in "The Catbird Seat"] is complete and unalloyed; but both are widely considered exceptions in the female-dominated world of James Thurber. Still a third "exception" occurs in the fable, "The Unicorn in the Garden," wherein the man, whom the wife tries to have put in the booby-hatch, manages to have her put away instead. In the series of drawings called "The War Between Men and Women," it is the women who surrender to the men. Perhaps the number of such "exceptions" is sufficient to puncture the legend of the monolithic triumph of women over men in Thurber's world. (pp. 506-07)

In its contempt and grotesquerie, ["The Greatest Man in the World"] is equaled only by Ring Lardner's story "Champion" . . . in depicting a blind and indiscriminate hero worship by the American public, with a secondary indictment of the press in pandering to the debased tastes of its masses of readers. The nation's political leaders likewise share guilt with the press. . . .

In the realm of slangy satire, "The White Rabbit Caper" is a hilarious take-off on radio mystery stories as written for children. An animal story with clever dialogue that teems with puns and is touched with rare fantasy, it is one of the funniest pieces Thurber ever wrote. At another extreme is "A Call on Mrs. Forrester," a beautifully imagined and sensitive account of a visit by the narrator to the charming Marian Forrester, the central character in the novelette, *A Lost Lady,* done in the manner of its author, Willa Cather. (p. 507)

Given Thurber's passion for brevity, clarity, and conciseness, and his satirist's desire to teach, it was reasonable that the fable as a form should exert a magnetic attraction upon him. That his didacticism was intentional many of the morals readily show. . . . Though most of the fables are universal in their cast, several are geared to political relevance in our day. . . . The most fully worked out and best realized symbolically is "The Rabbits Who Caused All the Trouble," an allegory of the operation of the Big Lie among nations and a satire of imperialistic, protective invasion. Ultimately the most charming and probably the most enduring of the fables is "The Unicorn in the Garden," a parable justifying the imagination and its sense for beauty, telling us that only those who can see a unicorn can truly see reality.

Dogs, mechanisms, language, women, marriage, and sex are the subjects about which Thurber wrote most of his delightful personal essays. (pp. 508-09)

One of the passions of James Thurber was his devotion to language. He battled often and zealously against obfuscation, against "the carcinomenclature" of "an agglomerative phenomenon of accumulated concretations." What he insisted on was clarity, accuracy, and sense. He blamed the merchandisers and the "political terminologists of all parties" for the continuing debasement of our language, asking instead that it be used with dignity and grace. Some of this advocacy is straight, but much of it is woven lightly and wittily into a great variety of situations and contexts, including word games. . . . (pp. 509-10)

Thurber was continuously preoccupied with relations between the sexes, bringing to the subject an extensive knowledge of modern psychology supported by a keen observation of what went on in the society around him. . . . The most characteristic of his women are business-like, matter-of-fact, dominating if not domineering, unintellectual, somewhat parasitical, and given to exasperating oversimplifications. Their husbands, feeling vaguely injured and resentful for having allowed the women to take command, must assume some small share of the responsibility with the wives for the quarrels—quarrels which are usually encouraged alcoholically during or after parties. . . . As to sexuality itself, Thurber temperamentally maintains (like Ade, Marquis, Lardner, and most literary humorists) a diffident distance and a decorously dressed posture. (p. 510)

A "sure grasp of confusion" is one of Thurber's hallmarks. . . . The various "confusion pieces," demonstrating the often perverse irrationality in human endeavor, must be rated among the most humorous of all of Thurber's blends of the absurd and the commonplace.

During the last ten years of his life, Thurber turned more and more to serious treatments of literary subjects and people. His spirit followed a less creative, more critical turn, and while he never yielded wholly to despair, the note of gloom is unmistakable. Art, he declared, was "the one achievement of Man which has made the long trip up from all fours seem well advised." But the present time, he said, meaning around 1960, "is one of formlessness in literature, in drama, and in comedy as well as in speech." Comedy, he asserted in a piece called "Magical Lady," "has ceased to be a challenge to the mental processes. It has become a therapy of relaxation, a kind of tranquillizing durg." . . . In pointing up the decline of comedy, he calls attention to the prevalence of horror jokes and comics, sick comedians, and a *Zeitgeist* that is manic. (pp. 511-12)

Turning to a final category, we cannot fail to recognize Thurber's eminence in the portrayal of actual people. There is, first of all, the volume that has the rightful claim to be considered his best, the somewhat burlesque autobiography, *My Life and Hard Times.* Despite its autobiographical basis, it is the most consistently creative and humorous of all his books. (p. 512)

Thurber's style is an enviable model of twentieth-century American—supple, witty, unmannered, sensitive to words, marked by humor that ranges from the quiet to the explosive, and by inspired metaphor. . . . About the only device of humor that crops up with regularity is some form of paronomasia—elaborate punning or word play, often done with song lyrics, as in "I want a ghoul just like the ghoul that buried dear dead Dad." Confusion is sometimes served by a snowballing technique or by exaggeration, as in "The Night the Ghost Got In." That night the police answered a burglar alarm from the Thurber residence by "a Ford sedan full of them, two on motorcycles, and a patrol wagon with about eight in it and a few reporters."

Thurber once declared in a letter to this writer, "I almost never plan the use of a literary device, but just take it when it comes along." Of course a number of them occasionally came along, several of which are the incongruous catalogue, the *reductio ad absurdum,* the comic neologism, understatement, altered clichés, nonsense, alliteration, slang, parody, literary allusion, and invective.

Thurber was, it must be conceded, a fastidious stylist with psychological depth, subtlety and complexity; with a keen sense of pace, tone, ease, and climax; and with imagination that often wandered into surrealism. He handled minor tragedy with unparalleled expertness. Revisions were frequent and painstaking, a given piece often being revised ten or (as with "Mitty") fifteen times. (pp. 512-13)

The areas of contemporary life which he left unexplored are extensive, as indicated at the outset of this essay. There are no lengthy sustained, creatively structured works. He was a critic of manners only (as were James and Jane Austen!). Aside from the fantasy pieces, his writing in one way or another confined to his experiences, which show an almost provincial concern with a narrow band of society. . . . And except for certain engaging eccentricities in his subjects, his nostalgia provides a *nil nisi bonum* principle of selection. (p. 513)

On the score of attitudes to women he was ambivalent. Half-satirically he admitted that men had made a mess of things and that women would have to take over. In *Lanterns and Lances,* published the year of his death, he drops the satire and says flatly, "If I have sometimes seemed to make fun of Woman, I assure you it has only been for the purpose of egging her on." Throughout his work there is a distrust of science and reason, for which men are principally responsible; it would seem, therefore, that Thurber subscribes, though in no unmasculine way, to the more intuitive and human approaches to reality which characterize the feminine makeup.

He was chary of ultimates. His writings set this life in no perspective of religious or anti-religious conviction. Escapist that he admitted to being, one feels that he kept religious questionings and promptings closely in check. (p. 514)

Thurber's widow, Helen Thurber, in the . . . Foreword to the posthumous *Lanterns and Lances,* is intent also on refuting any attribution of final hopelessness to her late husband. "It was not too long before his death that he wrote the lines: 'Let us not look back in anger, nor forward in fear, but around in awareness.' He showed all three at times—anger certainly, fear perhaps—but he always put awareness above the others. That, I think, is the real key to James Thurber as a person and as a writer."

And with that expert testimony, why not let the record stand until better comes along? (p. 515)

Louis Hasley, "James Thurber: Artist in Humor," in South Atlantic Quarterly *(reprinted by permission of the Publisher; copyright 1974 by Duke University Press, Durham, North Carolina), Autumn, 1974, pp. 504-15.*

KENNETH HURREN

The temptation to tangle with an analysis of the late James Thurber's gay and anguished humour is generally irresistible to reviewers confronted with such excerpts from the work of this inconsistently gifted man as may, from time to time, be offered upon a stage. It probably will, however, be resisted by me. This is partly because analysis entails rationality, and I doubt whether that is quite the thing to bring to any question involving humorous taste; partly because I can see the folly of attempting a task in which so many devoted students have failed; partly, too, because I have no really confident view of Thurber, whose fancies sometimes entertained me immoderately, but whose reputation had, I think, to survive some of the most unfunny and aimless pieces of writing and drawing ever put between covers; but mostly, perhaps, because Thurber *intended* the stuff to be between covers (either in magazines or in books) and however it goes in the theatre has little relevance to its real quality.

This is not to say that some of it doesn't take pretty vivaciously to the boards: a show some years ago called *A Thurber Carnival* managed to turn a lot of the stories and observations of the minutiae of American living into engaging sketches and I remember it with affection. (p. 22)

Thurber [was] a sporadic comic genuis and . . . a warm and compassionate observer of human frailty, echoing the bewilderment, the perplexity and the unquiet desperation that occasionally besiege us all. (p. 23)

Kenneth Hurren, "One Man's Thurber," in The Spectator *(© 1975 by The Spectator; reprinted by permission of* The Spectator*), July 5, 1975, pp. 22-3.*

*   *   *

TRAVEN, B.   1890-1969

Traven was an American-born short story writer, novelist, and screenwriter. He wrote in German and translated his own work into English, a method which accounts for the sometimes fragmentary and incorrect use of English in his fiction. Traven was deliberately vague about his background; however, since his death some facts have emerged. He lived in Mexico for most of his life and that country serves as the setting for most of his fiction. Because his recurring theme is the exploitation and degradation of the working classes, Traven has been linked with Marxist, socialist, and anarchist doctrines. He avoids dogmatism, however, espousing a form of humanism in the tradition of Thoreau. (See also *CLC,* Vol. 8, and *Contemporary Authors,* Vols. 19-20; obituary, Vols. 25-28, rev. ed.; *Contemporary Authors Permanent Series,* Vol. 2.)

ALAN CHEUSE

Traven's spare but resonant narration, which harks back to the old wisdom tales of Indian-American mythology, has much in common as well with that alienated (Brecht called it "distanced") mode of presentation which we have come to associate with technologically produced works of cinematic art.

"The Kidnapped Saint" will give readers new to the Traven canon ample opportunity to discover this distinctive style at its best. The eight stories in the collection will in fact be new to all but the most intrepid Traven followers (and some will be new even to them). (p. 34)

In addition to these tales, with their remarkable fusion of deep empathy and the self-conscious distance that always prevents us from turning Indian passion to gringo pastoral, the collection contains the first seven (and most successful) chapters of a novel previously unpublished in the United States, "The White Rose," Traven's uneven satire on the American entrepreneurs who ravaged Mexico's petroleum reserves before President Cardenas nationalized them at the outbreak of World War II. . . . [In a previously unpublished political essay, "In the Freest State in the World,"] the young Traven, apparently writing as "Ret Marut," fiery anarchist editor of the revolutionary Munich journal "Der Ziegelbrenner," gives a stirring account of what seems to be his own capture and near-execution by right-wing police. . . .

Traven's penchant for such disguises has made great headaches for scholars. . . . But, as any reader trained to keep his gaze from wandering from the screen should know quite well by now, it is the stories themselves, whether fables of the downfall of avaricious gringos or tributes to the native wisdom of peasants bereft of modern technology that remain the sites where the true Traven treasure abides. (p. 36)

> *Alan Cheuse, in* The New York Times Book Review (© *1975 by The New York Times Company; reprinted by permission), October 19, 1975.*

MICHAEL L. BAUMANN

[Most] Traven scholars now agree: that Traven had been an itinerant actor and anarchist writer by the name of Ret Marut in pre-World War I Germany. . . .

[Both] circumstantial and internal, or textual, evidence seems to confirm the identity of the two men: Ret Marut disappeared from Germany in the early 1920s (he probably left Europe in 1922 and landed in Mexico toward the end of that year); B. Traven's stories began to appear in German magazines early in 1925, their manuscripts having been sent to Germany from Mexico; Traven's novels, the manuscripts of which were likewise sent to Traven's German publishers from Mexico, started coming out in April 1926; Traven clearly expresses ideas in his novels found also in the writings of Ret Marut, and he often does so in Ret Marut's own words and style. It is difficult, in other words, to doubt that the two authors *were* one and the same man. (pp. 404-05)

[However] we do not know who that man was before he became Ret Marut, since we do not know where Marut-Traven was born or where he spent his childhood and early manhood. (p. 405)

But if we leave aside the question of Traven's origin—that is, of who Ret Marut was—for the moment because we cannot answer it, and turn to Traven's literary output, we make a curious discovery. We find that nearly half of that output deals with Americans in Mexico. Of the early

Traven novels, only *The Death Ship* takes place in Europe —and at sea near Europe—and *its* protagonist is an American sailor. (All of the later novels—and all of the stories— take place on the North American continent.) Certain Germanic traits are found throughout Traven's writings, yet the peculiarly American character of the first half of Traven's literary output cannot be denied either: the laconic American humor, the pride in and love of America that underlie all of the bitter criticism of this country, the hatred of servitude, the fierce, Puritanical indignation at injustice, the many thematic and tonal resemblances to mainstream American authors. . . . [Where] did Red Marut, who had been deeply involved, emotionally and intellectually, in the social and political problems of Germany from 1917 to 1921 . . . , suddenly find his so strangely authentic American voice? For in these early novels and stories he describes the lives of American *lumpenproletarians* in Mexico with an intimacy that can only have been acquired over a period of years spent in Mexico, just as the knowledge of Mexico—and of the United States—that went into Traven's only nonfiction work, *Land des Frühlings*, must have taken a good many years to come by.

Yet three of Traven's early novels were ready for publication by 1925, two and a half years, at best, after Ret Marut had set foot on Mexican soil—according to one source, Traven's novels were ready for publication as early as 1923 —and the others followed in rapid succession, so that by 1929 Traven had published five novels, a collection of short stories, and the above-mentioned nonfiction work. . . . Three of the early novels, as well as the more important of his short stories, are narrated by an American called Gales (or Gale), and Traven later either hinted or said outright that these novels and stories are autobiographical. Traven thus implied that he himself had been Gales. Yet it seems highly improbable that one man could have had all of the adventures described in Traven's early fiction in a matter of two and a half years *and* that he could have turned them into novels and stories at almost the same time. Besides, Ret Marut was living in Germany when some of those adventures were taking place in Mexico. (pp. 405-06)

Since readers generally agree that the events described in the early Traven novels are not invented but based on real experiences, the question becomes: whose experiences are they? A Swiss reader, Max Schmid, has suggested that they are those of an "*Erlebnisträger*," or a "carrier of the experience." . . . In the stories and novels narrated by Gerard Gales, Gales is evidently the *Erlebnisträger*, not Marut-Traven. The real Gales, then, must have been one of the many transient Americans drifting about Mexico during the 1910s and 1920s. He may well have been a Wobbly (which would explain why the original title of *Die Baumwollpflücker* was *Der Wobbly*). Marut-Traven must have met him soon after arriving in Mexico. . . . According to this theory, Marut-Traven recognized the literary value of the *Erlebnisträger*'s diaries, or of that man's attempts to turn his adventures into fiction. Somehow Marut-Traven obtained those manuscripts and translated them into German. He also rewrote, as he translated, and he worked his own ideas into the texts. Then he marketed those manuscripts in Germany and became, upon the publication of *Das Totenschiff*, a famous author. Such is the theory; needless to say, it has not yet been proven.

That Traven wrote in German, whatever the source of his

material may have been, we know today. We know that he wrote all of his works in German, even if he rewrote *some* of his novels and stories in English for American publishers. But both Traven's German and his English have puzzled some of his readers, and a look at how Traven uses these two languages would appear to be in order.

If we start with Traven's German prose, we find that, in some of the novels and stories told by an American and in certain other novels and stories told by an omniscient author, there seem to be an unconscionable number of Anglicisms: unaltered English or American words, American expressions or idioms worked into the German sentence, and bilingual coinages. Otherwise, Traven's German prose is clean, simple, direct, forceful, and, by and large, correct. (pp. 407-08)

Traven's Anglicisms do not necessarily violate the German language, not even when he introduces American idioms or uses words that do not exist in German. . . . Still, we may ask how and why these incongruities wandered into Traven's German prose. Three possible explanations have occurred to me: (1) that—on the assumption that Marut-Traven was born and raised in North America—American expressions flooded back into his consciousness as he wrote about Americans in Mexico; (2) that Marut-Traven deliberately used American expressions, either because he wanted to give his German prose an exotic flavor, or because he wanted to throw future literary bloodhounds off his track; (3) that the material which Marut-Traven used in his novels and stories was not his own but borrowed from an American, namely, from the *Erlebnisträger,* and that, rewriting this material in German somewhere in the Mexican bush, Marut-Traven did not have access to an English-German dictionary.

It is, of course, the third explanation that makes most sense. (It does not exclude the other two.) An American adventurer who had already been in Mexico during the 1910s and had recorded his experiences there in his own idiom would have used such expressions as I have mentioned. If that American happened, furthermore, to be a German-American, he might have recorded his experiences in a mixture of German and American English. Ret Marut would then either have translated the American *Erlebnisträger*'s manuscripts or turned them into adequate German, leaving those American or English words for which he found no German equivalents. Or, again, if that American happened to be a German-American, he might even have recorded his experiences in German and inadvertently sprinkled American expressions into his prose. Ret Marut would then merely have corrected the style, worked his own philosophic reflections into the novels and longer short stories, and perhaps made no changes at all in the less significant anecdotes.

Such a hypothesis would explain why so many manuscripts were ready for publication in 1925: the American had written their first drafts after years spent in Mexico before 1922. Marut-Traven revised the manuscripts and, either accidentally or on purpose, let the Americanisms discussed above slip into the German prose. If he let them slip in on purpose, i.e., if Marut-Traven knew what he was doing and why he was doing it, then he certainly succeeded in giving his German prose an exotic flavor. Needless to say, Traven was no James Joyce in the matter of mixing languages, but he appears to have been able charmingly to handle a good many colloquial American expressions. (pp. 410-12)

[*The Death Ship*] has enough Germanic oddities in it to make us goggle-eyed.

Traven's malapropisms in English are of three kinds: (1) those that miss being full-fledged idioms, (2) those that miss being genuine colloquialisms, slang expressions, or curses, and (3) metaphrases. The third kind predominates. (p. 412)

Traven, finally, is guilty of a fourth kind of malapropism in English: he structures whole sentences according to German syntax. One such Germanic monster should be enough to show what I mean: "What you were doing, where you were sailing, and on what ships you were at that time, I have not asked you" (pp. 413-14)

[The] American version of *The Death Ship* suffers a sea change in transit from Germany to North America, and the problems posed by American idiomatic usage are not solved.

One explanation for the Germanic quality of Traven's English—on the assumption that Ret Marut himself actually wrote the English versions of those texts of Traven's novels and stories that were published in America as "original" English texts, such as *The Death Ship*—may be that Marut-Traven, after having written in German for many years, found it difficult to switch back to English. (p. 414)

Yet for all of Traven's incorrect use of American English, it seems fair to say that this linguistic weakness does not detract from the vitality, narrative drive, and emotional impact of a novel like *The Death Ship.* What it does lead us to suspect, however, is that the author of the novel, Marut-Traven, was not Gerard Gales, the "American sailor" whose story is told in *The Death Ship,* since the "Gales" of the novel is demonstrably not at home in the idioms of English. Nor can we believe that Marut-Traven can ever have been the Gerard Gales of *The Cotton Pickers, The Bridge in the Jungle,* "The Night Visitor," and the other stories of which Gales is the narrator or protagonist. If the adventures related in these realistic novels and stories happened in the early 1920s—in the American version of *The Death Ship* . . . we are made to believe that the year Gales misses his ship in Antwerp is 1922—and if the narrator was in truth an American sailor (and, according to other novels and stories, an American cotton picker, oil rigger, bum, etc.), he would surely have known his own language, or at least his own slang, in 1934, the year *The Death Ship* was published in the United States, or, more properly speaking, in 1925, the year Traven offered to rewrite, in German, his own original English-language version of that novel. . . . But either "Gales" was not *telling* his own stories because a gentleman with a heavy German accent who had recently arrived in Mexico from Germany was telling them *for* him, or the real Gales had never written those manuscripts in English because, as a German-American, he had written them in German. Whatever the final explanation may be, the *Erlebnisträger* hypothesis would appear to force itself upon us as soon as we reflect on Traven's peculiar use of the English language.

If we did not already know that Traven had been an intellectual, not an uneducated worker, when he was Ret Marut, then what we have seen of his language habits would throw the proletarian past Traven gave himself into further doubt. For a real American sailor would at least curse more pungently than Traven's sailor does. However, what we have seen of Traven's language habits may, at the same time that it recommends the *Erlebnisträger* interpretation, also strengthen our belief in Traven's claim that *he* was an American. The English or American expressions in Traven's German prose point to an American background—although not to precisely the background Traven so frequently sketched for himself. That there are many American expressions in the prose of those of Traven's novels and stories *not* narrated by Gales, that these American expressions, in other words, are found also in the *second* half of Traven's literary output, suggests that the American background is not the exclusive property of the *Erlebnisträger*. This is important for the evaluation of any other evidence we may have of Traven's alleged or real identity as an American, such as his interest in American drifters abroad, his fairly intimate knowledge of America itself, and his relation to earlier American writers. His use of language suggests that two Americans (perhaps both of them German-Americans) had something to do with the creation of at least the early part of B. Traven's literary output: one, an anarchist intellectual who had spent many years in Germany before arriving in Mexico, the other, an adventurer and, probably, an Industrial Worker of the World. Alone, this conclusion may not be much, but added to our other findings, it brings us significantly closer to the unriddling of the B. Traven mystery. Our object, as literary critics, is not, after all, to discover the true identity of Ret Marut (or of the *Erlebnisträger*), but to provide a basis for our work. If we know why Traven is more at home in German than in American English, we can stop giving the American editions of his novels and stories the kind of critical attention we ought to be giving only to the German editions, except where we have what seem to be two separate versions of one novel, as in the case of *Das Totenschiff* and *The Death Ship*. And if we know that Traven's knowledgeability about the United States in his early work is due to the experiences of a second person, namely, an American Wobbly (and perhaps also to *some* personal acquaintance with "den States," on the part of Ret Marut himself), then we shall be most willing, as critics, to find a place for Traven in the literature of this country, and, as fellow Americans, to acknowledge happily that he *was* an American, to recognize a claim he made so often and so tenaciously. That Traven was also a European, with linguistic and cultural roots in pre-World War I Germany, has already explained, and will continue to explain, those aspects of his work that his North American heritage cannot explain. . . . (pp. 415-17)

Michael L. Baumann, "Reflections on B. Traven's Language," in Modern Language Quarterly *(© 1975 University of Washington), December, 1975, pp. 403-17.*

MICHAEL L. BAUMANN

[*Land des Frühlings (Land of Spring)*] is a Traven source book: here we find, in the form of theory, argument, and statements of fact, Traven's principal ideas, as well as material similar to that which went into his novels and stories. Here we find Traven's fierce indignation, his anger at the inequities of a world he did not make, and his intense involvement in the fate of the underdog. Here we meet Traven the idealist and impatient philosophical anarchist, the observer of nature, the humorist, the lyrical and sentimental 19th-century Romantic, and the 20th-century ironist. And we get to know a side of the man that Traven deliberately distorts in his novels and denied vis-à-vis the

biography hounds who came to Mexico to ferret out the secret of his identity: the educated, voracious, and critical reader, the intellectual whose roots go down deep into the soil of both European and American history and culture. (p. 75)

The book is specifically addressed to the German working-class reader, who cannot be expected to know much about Chiapas, or even about Mexico. Traven, a very methodical teacher, instructs this reader not only in the lore of Chiapas, but also in that of Mexico, the United States, Europe, and the world. And in so doing, he discusses literally hundreds of separate topics and ideas. . . . He weaves a number of arguments into his text and concludes them with prophecies and visions. In this way *Land des Frühlings* becomes a book about the fate of man. If Chiapas, as Traven tells us at the beginning of the book, has a climate "similar to the late spring of Central Europe," we understand, towards the end, that all of Mexico is, in Traven's eyes, the land of a new beginning for man—Traven calls it "Newland"—and that, for him, the entire North American continent is the real land of spring.

Traven gives the title of his book another dimension when he suggests that the ruins of man's first civilization may be found . . . underneath the jungles of Chiapas and under the rubble caused by earthquakes and volcanic eruptions. He proposes, furthermore, that Chiapas may, indeed, be the cradle of mankind, that man may have originated in Chiapas and spread to the other continents from that South-Mexican state. This would make Chiapas the "land of spring" for us all. It would also make the Indian race the *Urrasse*, the primordial race of mankind. Traven says that the Indian race "carries in its individuals the traits of all of the other human races on earth," and he attempts to document his case with archaeological evidence. (pp. 75-6)

[Traven] prizes the Indians' communal sense above all other virtues. In his eyes, the Indians are the only genuine Christians on earth, though he does not call them that. (p. 77)

The difference between the two types of ethos, the white man's and the Mexican Indian's, is dramatically illustrated in Traven's fiction. . . . And in all of these works Traven makes every effort to have his white readers understand the Mexican Indians' simple demands, their human dignity—and their communal sense.

Although Traven finds it difficult to describe that communal sense, he returns to the notion of the communal sense again and again and sets it off against European and American individualism. The phrase "communal sense" becomes an almost chiliastic invocation in *Land*. Communal life, life organized in communes and made possible by people who are rational and generous enough not to be constantly in each other's hair, or, worse, at each other's throats, has been the dream of most philosophical anarchists, including Traven. (p. 80)

In *Land*, Traven violates one of the principles of anarchist thinking by breaking the sometimes spoken but more often unspoken commandment not to formulate blueprints for a better society. (In his fiction, Traven keeps this commandment almost from first to last; he breaks it only in his very last novel in 1960, in the visionary *Aslan Norval*, which formulates an economic project—the building of a canal across the United States—designed to save America and the American way of life.) In *Land*, Traven suggests countless measures for Mexico to cure its ills, and some of his suggestions come close to being blueprints for a better society. (p. 81)

At the end of the book, the reader may have a hard time deciding which Traven, the idealist or the realist, is more persuasive, but whatever his decision, he will admire, and perhaps even love, the idealist.

There are other Travens in *Land des Frühlings* that should be mentioned, and among them is the observer of nature, continually awed by what he sees. (He appears in the novels, too, most prominently, perhaps, in *The Cotton Pickers*.) This Traven is a true follower of Thoreau. (p. 82)

Land des Frühlings is obviously basic Traven. Whatever we may be looking for, intimate contact with the author, adventures in Chiapas, the history of Mexico and of its people, an outline of hope, not only for Mexico, but for the United States and mankind, the vision of a poetic sensibility, at once European and American, or the themes of the novels and stories, we will find it in this classic Traven work. Fascinating in its own right, but useful also as a key to his fiction and personality, *Land des Frühlings* is, surely, the most important book Traven wrote. (p. 85)

> *Michael L. Baumann, "B. Traven: Realist and Prophet," in* Virginia Quarterly Review *(copyright, 1977, by the* Virginia Quarterly Review, The University of Virginia*), Vol. 53, No. 1 (Winter, 1977), pp. 73-85.*

JOHN M. REILLY

The narrator's repudiation of the popular formula for success, which he repeats at length throughout [*The Death Ship*], links his tale with the specific demystification of many novels that are anti-bourgeois and symptomatic of the authors' estrangement from prevailing cultural ideals. On the other hand the efforts to set us straight about the real work of sailors leads to the radical core of this story of the proletarian at sea.

Presenting himself as homeless and stateless the narrator, thus, represents the common man contending with the bureaucracy of the modern nation, but cast back upon his own individual resources he, more importantly, epitomizes the proletarian in a modern, industrial society.... In telling us of the operations of the death ship, the narrator again demystifies. This time in such a way as to show that market relations dominate political relations, though it is necessary for the fact to be concealed. Here, then, is the setting in which the free proletarians labor. They are particularized by detail of life aboard the death ship, but at the same time they are representative of the more completely mystified participants in production relations ashore.

The absence of a certain name for the narrator marks him as a man without roots in any other way of life, while his attitude shows him to be without nostalgia. (pp. 112-13)

This clear-sighted narrator's repudiation of the illusions of romance not so incidentally makes reference to the literature as well as the life it represents. Working in the stokehold he observes that "there were no hairy apes around with lurking strains of philosophy for stage purposes." Similarly the chartless voyage of the death ship to nowhere in particular constitutes a rejection of the traditionally inherent symbolism of a sea voyage.... In place of [the] conventions of sea romance *The Death Ship* provides devices appropriate to the narrator. The Yorikke, the death ship itself, has life.... In industrial life nature seems to have been subdued and is ordinarily not perceived at all, but the machine is the focus of the work which gives rise to social life. So, too, it is the appropriate object for the imagination of the anti-romantic proletarian seaman.

One echo of prior sea literature rings positively in *The Death Ship*. That one is from Melville. As Ishmael called the whaler his Harvard, so the narrator of Traven's tale says no man could have a better college than the Yorikke. Beyond that there is also in Traven's novel, as in Melville's, the significance of a crew taken from all the world's continents and the sense of solidarity with them in work. And like Ishmael, Traven's narrator has a close companion lost in shipwreck. Alongside these parallels the difference between Melville's and Traven's novels stands out clearly. In *The Death Ship* there is no Ahab, a human embodiment of the overreaching force of American expansion. The only nexus is the production/work process. What was Ahab has become technology.

But finally the most important departure from the Melvillean pattern, as well as from other sea literature, is in Traven's narrator himself. As the Yorikke's voyage goes nowhere, so, too, the narrator goes nowhere with his thoughts and speech, because there is nothing for him to learn about life at sea. He knows it all when his tale begins. The familiar first-person narration implies development as the speaker learns from experiences and the auditor/reader interprets significance. Traven's narrator discovers no meanings in his experience. (pp. 113-14)

There are no quiet sections in *The Death Ship*, no passages given over to pondering. The narrator is always talking at the audience, always asserting views long held about his reality, and always inserting his humanizing presence into descriptions of events so that there is scarcely room for the audience to think independently. The narrator seizes the center of the novel and it is his hard-boiled and comic attitude that produces the book's world-view. One hardly feels the presence of an author, so completely has the voice of the narrator taken over.

This is, of course, a positive achievement. For what it means is that Traven has extended the process of demystification to literature itself. Not only has he repudiated the illusions of sea literature, the romantic content and devices, but he is also working to dispense with the illusions that are at the heart of realistic literary technique. The tendency of literary realism is toward the production of autonomous narratives on the analogy with plays performed within the proscenium arch. Events are understood to be apart from author and audience both, following a logic inherent in a world we cannot enter but only observe. The characters do not speak to us directly, and we are discouraged from possible doubts that characters or events are wrong by the supposition that the story is the author's world, private property. *The Death Ship* narrator works against this tendency by his strong presence and continuous awareness that he is telling a tale, making a book instead of an independent world. For all his certitude the narrator invites readers into his story or to at least engage with him in appraising events. Much of this is achieved by comic tone, a hand on the shoulder to encourage us in dropping the conventional pitying response to stores of working-class life, and much is the result of our recognition that the narrator's views grow out of practical life. (pp. 114-15)

In departing from the illusions of literary realism [Traven] created a vehicle that effectively carries the class outlook of the proletariat. *The Death Ship* is without the aura that envelopes "art" in our society and weakens its effect on readers' consciousness, because the narrator speaks a popular language in a popular style. Perhaps he is the child of Melville's Ishmael, but he is also the brother of Sam Spade, and like Sam he speaks as people really do when they are free of illusion. (p. 115)

> *John M. Reilly, "The Voice of 'The Death Ship'," in* The Minnesota Review *(© 1977 by The Minnesota Review), Fall, 1977, pp. 112-15.*

*   *   *

TRILLING, Lionel   1905-1975

Trilling was an American critic, novelist and essayist. The philosophy of Matthew Arnold he explored in his first book, *Matthew Arnold*, led to his adoption of that writer's concept of maintaining a "disinterested" mind. Trilling logically approached and dissected popular theories, ideals, and culture in his writings. His novel, *The Middle of the Journey*, manifests his belief that faults are inherent in the artistic liberal imagination. As a result, Trilling tries to reveal the author's responsibility to portray the complex nature of life. (See also *CLC*, Vol. 9, and *Contemporary Authors*, Vols. 9-12, rev. ed.; obituary, Vols. 61-64.)

JACQUES BARZUN

[A distinct view of life is discernable in Trilling's works, revealed in the proposition that he] developed and illustrated throughout that galaxy of essays he published during the last 35 years. It is this. Intuition and perception alike show not merely that life overflows ideologies and coercive systems—so much is obvious: there would be no systems and ideologies if life were not impossibly hard to regiment. The contention is rather that the only things worth cherishing in life are necessarily destroyed by ideology and coercion from their first onset. In other words, variety and complexity are but different names for possibility; and without possibility—freedom for the unplanned and indefinite—life becomes a savourless round of predictable acts. There is then no point to literature or thought; there is in fact no literature and no thought, but a mere ideological echo of a diminished life.

For a critic, the best way to sustain the possibilist mind was clearly through the examples of literature, the lessons conveyed not by or out of an abstract of meanings, but out of the love and pleasure of literature itself; out of the fears and passions literature holds and radiates, out of the illusion of timelessness it inspires—feelings and illusions which can only be felt spontaneously; awakened, perhaps, but unlearned, and which constitute the chief freedom of the mind.

This is the "word" that Trilling felt he must utter and illumine, as indeed he did with ever-widening powers of reference and interconnection. To the very last, as in his Harvard Lectures entitled *Sincerity and Authenticity* (1972) and his Jefferson Essay *Mind in the Modern World* (1974), his affirmations were opposed not solely to overt schemes of social and political repression charged with philanthropic intent, they opposed equally all other fixities professing to

be sufficient or complete, whether derived from natural science, depth psychology, or peremptory moralising.

That this outlook is not a disguised anarchism, a longing for an unconditioned life, is shown in its first full exposition in the volume of essays that has given a new phrase to the language, *The Liberal Imagination* of 1950. That imagination was once expansive and generous, but time and circumstance had reduced it to a mere animus propelling certain judgments triggered by certain words and images. (p. 84)

To these reflex acts and ready-made ideas, Trilling gave in effect the rejoinder that so often marked his teaching and his conversation: "It's complicated. . . . It's much more complicated. . . . It's very complicated." The positive counterpart was, also in effect: "Continue to think and feel, and to will only what you have first fully imagined. . . ." To that imagining, literature, especially the novel, is the great inciter. The great novels are also the books that in his time Trilling could count on his readers knowing or being willing to take up. . . .

Yet there can be no doubt that Trilling's teaching of the great books that are not novels played an important part in the formation of his thought. He differed from his peers (as we flatteringly call them) in two important respects: first, he had to reread at least once a year the works that most intellectuals sooner or later reduce to handy clichés, their own or the conventional ones. (p. 85)

[He] was virtually alone among critics in not having been reared on the French critical tradition. He read the language with difficulty and escaped the force of those writers that gave Irving Babbitt, T. S. Eliot and their followers formulas from the 1890s to adapt to the 1920s: the great troop of analysts from Rémy de Gourmont and Léon Hennique to André Gide and Ernest Seillière. Of course, Trilling read Eliot and Babbitt, but they did not "take" in the proper way, the ground not being prepared by a first-hand knowledge of the French poets and men of letters.

A different tradition more than filled this gap—the English liberal tradition that includes Mill and Arnold but is not restricted to them, whatever modern opinion may say. There is Burke and Hazlitt, Bagehot and James Fitzjames Stephen, Ruskin and Morris, Yeats and even Walter Pater in his radical early days. Since the turning of liberalism on its head that I have referred to, it is increasingly difficult to make oneself clear by referring to thinkers as "liberal" or "conservative", especially when the new criteria of social democracy, which are irrelevant historically, are added to the diagnostic list. What is clear is that the men I have just cited exhibited in their time a self-critical liberalism of the kind that Trilling thought indispensable. When he deplored the lack of an intelligent conservative tradition in American literature, he meant the absence of discussion about premises and consequences such as is found in England in the liberals themselves—Mill as well as Bagehot, Stephen, and the rest. In the United States, even before the contentious 1930s, the party lines were so drawn that only headlong advocacy or a bland assumption of moral unanimity was to be found. The truth was that, as always in the nature of important ideas, "it's much more complicated, it's very complicated."

So imaginative a vision of our 20-century predicaments and automatisms deserved to be shown in a piece of imaginative literature, and Trilling seized the earliest chance to make the attempt. The result was his novel *The Middle of the Journey*.... Some months after its first appearance, it attracted attention because its central figure drew upon the life and character of Whittaker Chambers, who in our day used to haunt the College campus. After the trial of Alger Hiss, inferences were made about other persons in the story; but as their creator said in the Introduction to the reissue, the attributions are groundless.

Nor is it because of the link with a nameable hero (or villain) that the work marks a moment in our century's intellectual history, like *Fathers and Sons* or *L'Education Sentimentale;* it is because it depicts the aberration of reason and deadening of sensibility that I have been trying to suggest in discursive terms. It would take more than an essay of quasi-personal reminiscence to suggest further how *The Middle of the Journey,* whose title from Dante's opening line reminds us of the descent into Hell, was related in the author's mind to the vast subject of art in its modern role of angry prophet and exclusive saviour. Liberal unimaginativeness about society and eager advanced views in art go hand in hand, and the principle of perpetual displacement by a new avant-garde encourages the taste for restless change. A corrective judgment can only resist fashion by being comparative, that is to say, historical, but this is incompatible with taking pleasure in obsolescence. The product of all these sentimentalities is the culture-philistine, whom Nietzsche pinned on a labelled card a century ago. Multiplied since by access to (a half-) education and by the mass diffusion of art and thought, this new type of culture consumer finds a literature written for him, serving his predilections by contrived shock, routine political dissent, and sadistic assaults on the Old Philistine, long since dead, but theatrically still necessary.

It is at this point that, in Trilling's work ... the maxim that literature is a criticism of life is given its continuation and counterpart: life is and ought to be a criticism of literature. (pp. 85-6)

One wishes in vain that he had embodied his perception of types and attitudes in other novels and that he had lived to finish the Memoir he had just begun about the middle of *his* journey—the 1930s and '40s. The absence of other novels is not to be explained by native bent or turn of mind. Trilling's desire to write fiction was strong. He wrote some short stories, including the superb and much anthologised "Of This Time, Of That Place", where the reader will find in the depiction of two diversely blinkered minds, who meet tangentially in the clear consciousness of a third, a prophetic refutation of the recent theories about the superiority of madness.... The main reason why Trilling did not write more novels is that teaching leaves too little energy and unbroken time for self-absorption, let alone for writing on the large scale. (p. 86)

[There] must have been in Lionel Trilling's work an opposition of some kind between the desire to show the complexity that thought must attain in order to do reality justice and the need for lucid simplifying which teaching undergraduates or reviewing books for general readers entails. The tension was there, and it was at times painful. It was the price paid for living in our odd demotic culture and working in an institution dedicated to art and intellect yet bound by the written or spoken word. (p. 87)

The outcome of this struggle was Lionel's characteristic style. It is not to everyone's taste, especially if one approaches prose with pre-established patterns of how it should sound and break up its cargo of thought. But whoever is willing to let the long roll and retreat and fresh surge of Trilling's thought carry him from outset to destination will find that it is clear, firm, undeviating despite its wave-like movements, and unambiguous in its delivery of the particular complication it proposes to establish....

Lionel Trilling was bent on developing the large consequences of the often hidden relations and implications for life that he found in literature. (p. 88)

> Jacques Barzun, "Remembering Lionel Trilling," in Encounter (© 1976 by Encounter Ltd.), September, 1976, pp. 82-8.

MARK SHECHNER

[Much] of what was fresh in American writing after the war came down in the fertile precipitate of ideas and attitudes released into [writers' and intellectuals'] thought by the chemistry of socialism on the wane. (p. 4)

It was in the post-war climate of stalemate and reassessment that Lionel Trilling came to prominence as a spokesman for ambivalence, moral realism (that is, the acceptance of "good-and-evil"), ideas in modulation, and the tragic view of life. He emerged in the forties as a pivotal figure among the New York intellectuals. (p. 8)

The Middle of the Journey, in its muted way, is ... an account of spiritual death and rebirth, and the cycle of depression and revival in general is etched deeply into the larger movement of Trilling's work.... [The] entire emotional vista opened up by both psychoanalysis and modern literature was [extremely important] to Trilling. Trilling was aware of the precedents; psychoanalysis, as he understood it, was a codification of the great surge of self-discovery and self-healing that marked the literature of the nineteenth-century. Mill in particular served him as a model of interior regeneration, and not only his *Autobiography* but the essays on Bentham and Coleridge stood behind the lessons on politics and the emotional life that Trilling himself delivered to his own generation in *The Liberal Imagination.* (p. 9)

Trilling's case against the liberal imagination as he found it in the 1930s ... [and] his estimate of its intellectual shallowness is well known and generally accepted by now, even if the general recoil from ideology that liberalism's shortcomings appeared to justify is no longer celebrated as quite the wisdom it once seemed to be.... The dominant themes of Trilling's political and cultural thought in the forties grew in tandem with his interest in psychoanalysis; it is clear that his adoption of Freud was a special feature of those attitudes toward the progressive culture that were the polemical heart of *The Liberal Imagination....* (pp. 9-10)

Freudian man was a step upwards from liberal man in complication and mysteriousness, and was, in effect, his contradiction: he had an unconscious mind whose purposes were not always in accord with either his conscious will or his class interest; he was given to entertaining contrary ideas and emotions at the same time and to tormenting himself with his own ambiguities; he was prone to irrational fits of melancholy or guilt and to performing unexplained rites of apology and expiation for crimes he had not committed, and he had a fondness for self-defeat that made his failures seem more genuine expressions of will than his successes. How unlike the utilitarian man of liberalism, who maximizes pleasure at every meager opportunity, and how much closer to the neurotic hero of contemporary fiction, who confirms the modern character that Hegel called the "disintegrated consciousness!". . . One thing psychoanalysis and contemporary fiction agree on is the alienation of modern consciousness from the wellsprings of will and desire, and for Trilling, the sufficient measure of liberalism's imaginative bankruptcy was its refusal to countenance the irrational component in human nature. (p. 10)

But that did not amount to a charge of political bankruptcy, for though Trilling despaired of liberalism's capacity to ameliorate the material conditions of life, nowhere did he venture an estimate of its political ideas or programs comparable in scope or trenchancy to his assessment of its imagination. Coming from a writer whose reputation owed so much to the climate of contemporary politics and who was so widely accepted as a political intellectual, Trilling's books yield surprisingly little concrete political thought. (pp. 10-11)

[This] deflection of attention from the world to the intellectuals and their perception of it was Trilling's way of detaching himself from the liberal mainstream to become its critic. . . . Trilling's finest essays were snapshots of the contemporary intellectuals in the act of observing and defining reality. His essays in *The Liberal Imagination* on Dreiser ("Reality in America") and the Kinsey Report are superb definitions of American and liberal styles of social knowledge, and if one learns little from them about the actualities of reality in America, one learns a great deal about the ideology of social perception in a society founded upon rationalized optimism. One also learns from Trilling something about the emotional impact of ideas and programs, what they feel like and what qualities of life they purvey. What we would recall most vividly of the thirties were its ideological failures and their devastating consequences for those who had committed their lives to its prevailing myths. (pp. 11-12)

Both the strengths and limitations of Trilling's approach to the politics of culture are evident in *The Middle of the Journey*, his sole effort at yoking political thought to literary views in order to illuminate politics, rather than to venerate literature. That book was an attempt to bring to the politics of contemporary culture a sort of synthetic Victorian sensibility, an impasto of attitudes that Trilling had concocted for himself out of Mill, Arnold, Forster, Freud, and Keats, and to disclose the deadness at the core of liberalism by demonstrating how paradoxically stultifying was the embrace of its unremitting optimism upon the human heart. (p. 12)

In later years Trilling himself observed that his intention had been to write a book about death, and about the refusal of intellectuals schooled in the liberal tradition to countenance it, because it lay outside the domain of their progressive fantasies. Or, as he would ask rhetorically in pointing up the way all things are politicized when dogma commands the imagination, "Was there not a sense in which death might be called reactionary?" John Laskell, Trilling's somewhat retiring spokesman in *The Middle of the Journey*, has recently lost the woman he loved to a sudden illness and has himself just recovered from a dangerous attack of scarlet fever. In his convalescence he visits the rustic Connecticut home of Arthur and Nancy Croom, vigorous, cheerful, and enlightened progressives who can scarcely pronounce the word death let alone draw tragic lessons from the presence of this walking *memento mori* in their midst. Arthur Croom is protected from depression by what Laskell calls "the armor of idealism." Laskell, however, needing to talk about his brush with death and to explore the meaning of that experience, finds that he is isolated from his friends and their sprightly intelligence, for he has looked into the abyss and seen there the end of ideology. He is joined at the Crooms' by another apostate from the Left, Gifford Maxim, a repentant Communist, indeed, secret agent turned staunch necessitarian or law-and-order man, whose political views have shifted radically to the right without surrendering an ounce of their millenarian zeal. Laskell thinks of him as "the man of the far future, the bloody moral apocalyptic future that was sure to come." As we now know, Maxim is modelled upon Whittaker Chambers, whose transformation from espionage agent to prosecution witness won him a starring role in the soap opera of America's post-War revulsion against Communism. Though the plot of *The Middle of the Journey* is full of turns, including another sudden death, which supposedly puts to the test everyone's ideas about class, character, and "reality," the book is essentially a conversation piece; the moral element that Trilling was so intent upon pushing is contained in the by-play among these four, the Socratic dialectics of competing ideas whose overall purpose is to cast all ideas into doubt.

The Middle of the Journey just coruscates with intelligence and dialectical sparkle, and it remains the most illuminating document we have of the recoil of the political imagination from dogma under the pressure of the chastened realism of the late thirties and early forties—that fall into the quotidian that was the new era's particular form of disillusionment. Maxim, Laskell, and the Crooms are sharply drawn representative figures who stand for political positions and processes that engaged, and ruined, so many intellectuals in the thirties. But the book is first of all about *the imagination* under the sway of social ideas, or, as Trilling would entitle a monograph later in his career, about "mind in the modern world." It is a book about the mind and about those parts of it that take their cue from and find expression in political ideas. It is especially about that region of mind that is given neither to pure will nor pure idea, where the historical sense intersects the return of the repressed, and richly "overdetermined" motives take shape as political views. The politics of *The Middle of the Journey* is largely a politics of the mind and of character; the book's historical dimension is drastically foreshortened, and the context of actual events and circumstances so generalized as to be unimportant. (pp. 12-13)

I don't want to oversell the book or claim for it more literary merit or thematic depth than I think it really has. To my mind it is more a document than a realized piece of fiction; its value lies in its grasp of an historical moment and of a generation's disillusionment and conversion, out of which came not only a revised and subdued politics but a reconstituted aesthetics as well. The crisis of the late thirties meant as much to art as it did to a politics, and *The Middle of the Journey* reflects not only the triumph of the will in repose over the will in action, of ideas in modulation over the logic of the next step, but of sensibility over agit-prop and modernism over realism. . . .

Laskell has *no* character to speak of, only ideas, and it is true that he lacks either depth or definition, but there is a minimal character here, and certainly a strange one. The "disintegrated consciousness" that Trilling would later attribute to the modern character is apparent in Laskell, though in relatively benign form. Consider Laskell's situation: he is a dangling man. . . . His chief possessions are ideas, though he holds them with no great passion or conviction. . . . It is very much to the point that Laskell has been ill and is presently recuperating, for though we are told that he has been grappling with scarlet fever, *we know* that he has really been stricken with history and is recovering from the past. (p. 14)

For all its apparent interiority and concern with the self, *The Middle of the Journey* can't be taken for a psychological novel. . . . *The Middle of the Journey* is very much about the dilemmas of consciousness; the forces in contest are ideas, not instincts, and the inner dynamics of character are simple and shallow. . . .

The Middle of the Journey's link to psychoanalysis, then, lies neither in its ideas nor in its aesthetic strategies but in the deeper rhythm of experience that plots its moral curve; the rhythm of illness and recovery, or crisis and conversion that sets us to talking about ideological movements and revolutions in the language of disease and health. Laskell, Maxim, and the Crooms all suffer from ideas—they are literally sick with modern thought. (p. 15)

[The] novel was, for Trilling, the definitive cultural document, the very measure of the *Zeitgeist,* and he was open to the thought that the contemporary decline of novelistic passion and the breakup of the synthesis of philosophy and precise social observation in modern fiction might well betoken nothing less than the much-advertised decline of the West. (pp. 15-16)

Where Trilling stood apart from the general mood was not in his bleak diagnosis—even announcing *the* death of *the* sexual will was not so unique—but in the prescription for relief. He distinguished himself from both the Reichians (for whom *the* sexual will was also distressed) and the liberals and unreconstructed Marxists in his vote for psychoanalysis and the novel as correctives to the general malaise. . . . He was out to form, as he would put it, a "modern self," a resilient ego that would be equal to the demands of the age, and he attempted the transformation by immersing himself in literature and assimilating the exemplary monuments of unaging intellect. Though the formation of a reinvigorated but durable self was a personal quest, Trilling always treated it as the project of his generation through the neat rhetorical gambit of turning the experiencing "I" into a "we," thus both disguising the personal stakes involved and playing up the shared aspects of the crisis. The essays in *The Liberal Imagination* can be read both as chapters in a moral autobiography and showcases for the acculturated ego in the process of its self-reconstruction.

It seems an odd choice to seek emotional renewal for oneself, let alone for one's culture, through the agency of, of all things, *the* novel. . . . [For Trilling], the modern crisis was not primarily a crisis of conditions, however awful they might be, but of emotions and imagination; it was to the impoverished inner life that the lessons in *The Liberal Imagination* were addressed. And it was in the novel, especially the great nineteenth century novels that are the richest examples of that genre, that Trilling saw the modern social imagination working at its highest pitch. (pp. 16-17)

But we should keep in mind that Trilling was almost always talking about himself, and that the essay in which his most exalted claims for the novel are made, "Art and Fortune," is also a spiritual autobiography in miniature, done according to the Romantic paradigm. Ostensibly a meditation on the death of the novel, it is really about the death and rebirth of "the will," and there can hardly be any doubt about whose will is at issue. Moreover, in claiming for the novel the power to renovate the will, Trilling seems to have had in mind not only his own intimate relation to books but the example of Mill, whose youthful bout with depression was cured by the reading of Marmontel's *Mémoires* and whose convalescence and emotional re-education were abetted by therapeutic doses of Wordsworth. To reflect back upon *The Middle of the Journey* after reading *The Liberal Imagination* is to perceive the central weakness of Trilling's novel, which is his allowing John Laskell to speak for his convictions without giving Laskell the benefit of his vital experiences, that is to say, his reading. Laskell's recovery from liberal ideas, unmediated by anything but his post-operative meditation upon a bedside rose, rather than something more substantial . . . is never credible. (p. 17)

Indeed, the problem of abstraction is general throughout the book, and is not just a flaw in the characterization of Laskell. By removing the action from some natural arena of conflict to a house in rural Connecticut—that is, to a world apart—Trilling was able to write a sort of moral pastoral whose characters are largely representative abstractions. (pp. 17-18)

Connecticut is not a metaphor for the world but for the seminar room, and the odd collection of friends and haphazard acquaintances who gather at the Crooms' has nothing to work out but ideas, for nothing dramatic is at stake. To throw the emphasis of dramatic action upon the collision of ideas in isolation, as Trilling does, is both to play up their historical importance *and* to exaggerate their political value. (p. 18)

[Trilling's] most influential books, like *The Liberal Imagination* and *The Opposing Self,* are books of exemplary lives, exemplary minds, really, intellectual and therefore moral models whose ways of balancing pressures and reconciling tensions shine forth as salutary cases. James, Keats, Austen, Forster, Arnold, Mill, Orwell, and, especially, Freud, to rename the central figures in the pantheon, are heroes of thought, whose heroism consists of a judicious balancing of claims, a skeptical adherence to the cultural donnée, and a qualified acceptance of the conditioned nature of social existence. They are, in a phrase, mature adversaries of culture. (p. 19)

[In] view of Trilling's ardent declarations of admiration and intellectual indebtedness, perhaps nothing is so remarkable about him as the discrepancy between his zeal for Freud and his use of him. While many of Trilling's essays on literature and culture over the years may be read as applied Freud, they are largely applications of his character and his outlook rather than his ideas about the constitution of the mind. Indeed, the reader who has been struck by the discrepancy might feel justified in wondering whether such lionizing of Freud was not done at the expense of psychoanalysis as such, for it is plain that the figure of the man in Trilling's thought greatly overshadowed the method. (p. 20)

[*Civilization and its Discontents*] was the indispensable book for Trilling, who considered it a milepost in the cultural history of the West for its conclusion that discontent was built into the condition of man in culture and therefore inevitable, and much of what passes for Freudian thought in Trilling's writing is really applied *Civilization and its Discontents*. (p. 21)

[Psychoanalysis itself] was not uniformly compelling for Trilling, and if he neglected to apply it with all the rigor and zeal that has been demonstrated by more recent practitioners, it is not because he misunderstood its interpretive strategies but because he lacked enthusiasm for the diagnostic reduction of complex feelings and perceptions. As a partisan of literature he was distressed by the psychoanalytic practice of analyzing downward in pursuit of reality among the infantile, the somatic, the irrational, and the unconscious levels of being. (pp. 23-4)

[What] passes in Trilling for balance or negative capability or a full and judicious view of situations is sometimes just a pulling of punches. Even a passing familiarity with psychoanalysis and its explanatory capabilities makes it relatively plain that Trilling was often guilty of turning away from his insights and finessing conclusions about the inner dimensions of fiction that the logic of inquiry entitled him to draw.

Only once did Trilling take the wraps off his psychoanalytic curiosity and allow himself the freedom of his insights. That was in the essay, "The Poet as Hero: Keats in his Letters" (in *The Opposing Self*), in which he brought to bear the authority of Freudian ideas to argue for Keats's geniality, his passion, and his courage. Not incidentally, the Keats essay is, in my judgment, Trilling's most splendid essay on a single author and his work. (p. 25)

Lionel Trilling may have been a friend of literature but he was no fan of poetry, and his writing demonstrates amply that the novel, with its vistas and textures and examinations of character in society, suited his aesthetic and moral intuitions far better than did poetry, with its preference for the self in isolation and its traffic in those portions of the emotional life that lie below "character," that is, below scruples, judgment, values, reason, and the social instincts.

After the Keats essay, not only were there no more ventures into applied psychoanalysis—save, of course, the meditations on *Civilization and its Discontents*—but no more encounters with poetry. That side of the self that poetry and psychoanalysis hold in common was not the side that Trilling cared to pursue, at least not in public, and as James and Austen bulked larger in his thoughts, poetry diminished to the vanishing point. . . . The century shapes up in Trilling's portrait as the exclusive domain of its great novelists. . . .

Trilling was captivated by the *idea* of the inner life, much as he was by the idea of politics or the idea of death; he Hegelianized psychoanalysis for the same reasons he Platonized politics: to refine out the cruder elements and isolate the essential ideas. (p. 28)

In reading Trilling, one often feels that he is holding too much at bay, as though his first consideration were to deny extremes. Certainly the habits of balance, skepticism, and

irony that stood him in good stead during a decade of dogma and intellectual vulgarity also served to cut short lines of inquiry to which he was committed in principle but unwilling to put into practice. His first priority was to defend "mind" against whatever forces threatened to overwhelm it, even when those forces were not ideological or moral orthodoxy or unreason, but the mind's own natural propensity to explore. . . . To see one pressure behind Trilling's criticism as the attempt to fashion a moral self out of parts collected from books should not necessarily undercut his judgments but rather bring them into sharper relief. Once we grasp the idea, for example, that such self-construction was a work of deliberate and skillful artifice and that the adopted literary elements could become the very scaffolding of the ego, we can more plainly recognize the basic emotional premise of a book like *Sincerity and Authenticity*: that the culture of authenticity that took hold in the sixties posed a vital threat to those, like Trilling, who had assembled their social egos at other times according to different rules. . . . (p. 29)

Trilling *is* elusive, especially in the face of efforts to pin down his ambiguities and link up his positions to his historical situation and to what he would call his "will." What is not ambiguous is his role in the post-War redefinition of liberalism, for he must be included among the intellectuals who transformed the prevailing rhetoric of liberalism from one of social progress and justice to one of sensibility and depth, all the while tidying up the depths by purging them of whatever was embarrassing, childish, or undignified. For the intellectuals, Trilling pointed the way from Henry Wallace to Adlai Stevenson, and from a politics of quantities that spoke of masses and dreamed of the greatest good for the greatest number, to one of qualities, that counselled personal self-development and individual self-restraint.

Trilling's brands of modulation and synthesis were a boon to his criticism; the range of voices and the purchase on ideas they brought him gave him a grasp and flexibility matched by few of his contemporaries. But such intellectual syntheses as he could effect, including the blending of psychoanalysis and liberalism, were often made at considerable cost, usually to the radical features of the original ideas. Thus psychoanalysis was asked to surrender its critical edge, while liberalism was called upon to forego its progressive fantasies. (p. 32)

Mark Shechner, "Lionel Trilling: Psychoanalysis and Liberalism," in Salmagundi: Special Issue on Lionel Trilling *(copyright © 1978 by Skidmore College), Spring, 1978, pp. 3-32.*

DENIS DONOGHUE

It was common for critics to maintain, during the years in which Trilling wrote his major books, that the relation between the individual artist and society was a relation between virtue and vice, or at least a relation between the highest aesthetic purity and the worst conditions which an indifferent society would impose upon a pure intention. Society was deemed to be a bourgeois conspiracy of the worst to thwart the best: the artist was regarded as a holy man in the degree of his victimage. Artist and critic were supposed to huddle together for comfort in the storm, since their motives were equally noble. The storm was a monster compounded of money and aggression.

Trilling was never persuaded by these common assumptions, and he turned their rhetoric upside down. I do not imply that he put his talent at the disposal of a mass society or that he tried to take the harm out of the standard social purposes; but he did not encourage the artist to take spiritual comfort from the grossness of material conditions or to regard himself as a victim of social alienation. Trilling did not interpret the relation between artist and society in terms so favorable to the artist that society could only be construed as barbarism and the artist as a tragic hero. He continued to urge upon the artist a concern for social consequence even when the particular society in question merited every rebuke it received. He did not turn away from society or from the values of responsibility, companionship, and mutuality which the concept of society almost desperately entailed. He never encouraged the artist to think that he might dispense with society, despise its purposes, and find within himself a sufficient moral authority. . . . Trilling set out to attach to the sentiment of society an aura of conscientiousness and value. He described the idea of society as if it had, by comparison with the individual people who compose it at any moment, not of course historical priority but logical priority; not priority of time but privilege of idea and feeling. He persuaded his readers to find even in the imperfections of society a perfection lost, abused, but not destroyed. The mind engaged in the understanding of society is encouraged to see, even in the monstrous lineaments offered to its attention, a sequence of human possibilities. At a time when other critics were repudiating the idea of society as a source of value because particular societies were demonstrably corrupt, Trilling kept the lines of communication open. (pp. 161-63)

Trilling used not the general mind of society but a particular mind compounded of his own major purposes and the purposes he ascribed to the best intentions of a possible society rather than of the particular society in question and in force. Such a mind could not be entirely American, since it would not release itself from the hope of living in an answerable society and making a home for itself in forms domestic, moral, and historical. A hundred reasons prevented the mind from being entirely European, reasons of responsibility and temper, despite the attributes which enabled Trilling to keep the peace somehow between Arnold and Freud. (pp. 163-64)

It is my impression that Trilling insisted upon the validity of mind as an integral force and held himself aloof from the necessitarian argument. The idea of society, like the idea of mind, was a matter of conviction; if you released yourself from responsibility, you insisted upon providing the force of conscience from your own moral resources, perhaps enriched by your aesthetic sense. If you acted upon the assumption that mind is merely a function of the governing codes, you chose slavery in preference to freedom. Trilling was severe upon these motives: they were either abject or arrogant; they pretended that mind could float free from society or that the least evidence of a movement of mind was a delusion. . . . Trilling [speaks of] the mind's dependence upon society and [says] that "only the greatest minds can even seem to be free of this dependence—and they but seem to be." But while it is probably true that "all human values, all human emotions, are of social growth if not of social origin," there are certain intellectual processes which arise from a refusal to obey this truth. I have in view the act which Arnold feared and distrusted, "the dialogue of the mind with itself," a dialogue which began when "the

individual, absorbed in separate interests, withdrew from the service of the commonwealth.". . . The modern version of that dialogue often issues as the mind's attendance upon the heuristic possibilities of language, since these arise from the grammatical and phonetic character of the language rather than from circumstances directly social or political. The names of Beckett, Borges, and the Joyce of *Finnegans Wake* stand for such possibilities. Trilling's sympathy did not embrace those activities, presumably because he distrusted their claim upon the ostensibly unconditioned character of language. A self-engendered style is always willful. Trilling disapproved of self-sufficiency, which he considered "the classic advice of philosophy in a disorganized society." It meant, in another formulation, "self-cultivation in loneliness, in the face of the degeneracy of the world, with reference to some eternal but ill-defined idea." Trilling also distrusted that action without end or purpose which is sometimes promoted as role-playing: he thought it a bogus abundance, a willful setting out to look for life, as though there were not enough life already to hand. Skeptical of anything we do or any experience we seek merely for the sake of knowledge, Trilling valued consciousness as a human power, but only as a means to another end. He was not one of those critics who represent consciousness as the supreme act, the sublime form of intelligence, an act more opulent than any end it might propose. In Trilling's work consciousness is respected as a means, an instrument, but the end is given as social consequence. (pp. 164-66)

Perhaps this explains why Trilling's mind was especially sensitive to the moment in which a person's feeling moves from one level of awareness to another, registering new and heavier burdens: acknowledgment of different levels, as of different burdens, entailed assent to temporal conditions and mediations. In his fictions Trilling was particularly inclined to represent moral decisions as movements from one level of awareness to another. In "The Other Margaret" there is a moment in which the young girl recognizes for the first time the fact of responsibility; it marks her entry upon the moral life. I read the recognition as a private intimation corresponding to the public act by which one participates in politics and society, the burden of *The Middle of the Journey*. Indeed there is a paradigm in Trilling's novel which points to the crucial moment in which one phase of feeling turns into another. (p. 166)

I have remarked that Trilling is a critic not of consciousness but of power, and for the same reason he insists upon referring to consciousness as mind. He does not take pleasure in the latitude, the mobility, the imperative nature of consciousness: he is not a critic of, say, the persuasion of Georges Poulet, who regards the act of consciousness as the ultimate human sign. Poulet's account of consciousness is always expansive: he does not care what consciousness does so long as it does not die. Trilling's understanding of consciousness is more pragmatic, more administrative, turned toward the near future in which urgent work must be done. He is interested not in the possibilities of mind but only in its consequences. . . . Trilling thought of mind as concerned with the imposition of order upon general experience, the reduction of multiplicity to unity, and the determination of choices. He judged mind upon its results. (pp. 167-68)

Trilling maintained that our contemporary ideology reveals a disaffection from history, as if amnesia were a virtue. The mind, he said, is increasingly discredited on the grounds that its activity is necessarily indirect: "It cannot be in an immediate relation to experience, but must always stand merely proximate to it." Thus far the theme is fairly common. The philosopher Merleau-Ponty, for instance, has spoken of certain great works in this century which express "the revolt of life's immediacy against reason." Trilling spoke . . . of the "contemporary ideology of irrationalism" which celebrates "the attainment of an immediacy of experience and perception which is beyond the power of rational mind." "In our day," he argued, "it has become just possible to claim just such credence for the idea that madness is a beneficent condition, to be understood as the paradigm of authentic existence and cognition." I share Trilling's sense of a crisis in modern society as a perturbation in the relation between mind and experience, but I wonder to what extent Trilling's argument was forced upon him by his settling upon a certain terminology. . . . It is well established that Trilling associated mind with the idea of order and even with the idea of hierarchy, "the subordination of some elements of thought to others." He put the force of his authority in favor of objectivity, meaning "the respect we give to the object as object, as it exists apart from us," the fullest recognition of "the integral and entire existence of the object."

It is not surprising, then, that he was deeply suspicious of those forms of consciousness for which the word *mind* seems blunt, and for which we find ourselves resorting to the more daring concepts *imagination* and *genius*. We want an understanding of consciousness which takes risk in its stride. Trilling was suspicious of those powers not chiefly in themselves but in their consequences at large: he did not think they would provide the authority of a valid culture. He would admit them, I feel, only as a critical force bearing upon the administrative function of mind, keeping its orders and hierarchies lively by keeping them under scrutiny. He spoke of genius as "a unique originating power of mind," and showed himself responsive to its manifestations when they appeared in literature as action and power, but he did not include its qualities in the ideal form of a true society. I assume that he wanted to think of a society's intellectual resources as held to some extent in common rather than in a few exceptional people. He wanted the artist to embody the highest form of the common mind, including a degree of critical force and scruple found in the common mind only on its strenuous occasions. He did not want the artist's mind to differ in kind from the common forms of intelligence: he thought it an advantage, for example, that an artist's mind could maintain a consecutive argument just as scrupulously as the mind of a scientist, a philosopher, or a schoolmaster. . . . The idiom of mind was more congenial to Trilling than the idiom of genius and imagination because mind could be translated into practical terms and put to work in society; imagination and genius could not be put to work, or could be only indirectly and in forms too wayward to be trusted. (pp. 169-70)

To Trilling the hardest question turned upon the presence of will in society: he did not favor an ethic of inertia, but he could find a justification for will only when its defeat, in the long or the short run, was inevitable; then it might be entertained as critique, lest the official purposes of society weary of themselves. (p. 172)

I have been maintaining that Trilling's theme is the mutual

bearing of mind and society. Society is never represented as a mere aggregate of philistines; mind is never represented as if its freedom were absolute and its activity unconditioned. The happiest situation is one in which spirit and matter, self and circumstance, make a harmony together and mind acknowledges its responsibility to society. This situation rarely obtains, as Trilling knew when he referred in *The Liberal Imagination* to "the chronic American belief that there exists an opposition between reality and mind and that one must enlist oneself in the party of reality." He resented the common assumption that reality is merely "external and hard, gross, unpleasant," and that mind is respectable only when it resembles that reality and reproduces the sensation it affords. Trilling refused to make the mind a sacred object or to think it omnipotent. (pp. 172-73)

In his early essays he invoked mind with some confidence: he could not believe that a society would deprive itself of the power embodied in consecutive thought, the relation between one image and another, the response of a practical intelligence to the facts of a case. But in later essays he felt that society was indeed depriving itself of this power and of the security of purpose it certified. . . . Trilling's understanding of mind presents it . . . as the distinctively human attribute, the disinterested act of intelligence propelled by a sense of experience held in common, the speech of people who share the common experience. It is not the dialogue of the mind with itself, since that dialogue has lost or set aside its sense of general human nature and the universal conditions in which life is lived. Mind is the power used by "a man speaking to men" about the continuities of shared experience in the hope of understanding it. Trilling was aware of the exorbitance of mind, "the desiccation of spirit which results from an allegiance to mind that excludes impulse and will, and desire and preference." But he refused to disown mind for that or any other reason. In fact his later essays are designed to circumvent the low repute in which mind is held and to ensure that the work of mind is carried out by resorting, if necessary, to a more congenial terminology. The new word is *culture*.

But the word we need at once is *society*. In *Sincerity and Authenticity* Trilling refers to society as "an entity whose nature is not to be exactly defined by the nature of the individuals who constitute it." Society is "a concept that is readily hypostatized—the things that are said about it suggest that it has a life of its own and its own laws. An aggregate of individual human beings, society is yet something other than this, something other than human, and its being conceived in this way, as having indeed a life of its own but not a human life, gives rise to the human desire to bring it into accord with humanity." The repetition of *human* and *humanity* reflects the desperation in Trilling's rhetoric, the need to recite these syllables as if to recite them were to make them tell upon our consciences. Trilling is referring to the modern meaning of *society,* for the moment, and taking for granted the low repute in which it is held. In that sense the laws which originally reflected the fellowship and mutuality of people living together are now deemed to have forgotten their origin and become forces in themselves, independent and therefore monstrous. Conventions which were once amenities have lost their responsiveness: they are now chains. . . . Trilling assumes that mind has always known its human bearing and that the temptation to release itself from the claims of feeling, impulse, and will is merely occasional: generally this knowledge makes mind what it is and keeps it true to its vocation. Culture is the process by which a forgetful Society is reminded of its human responsibility and recalled from the monstrous forms it has taken. (pp. 173-76)

It seems to me that when Trilling speaks of society's being brought into accord with humanity, the evidence he produces is invariably an image or an idea or a set of ideas. Ideas are certainly the chief instruments of the cultural process in Trilling's version: "By culture we must mean," he writes in *The Liberal Imagination,* "not merely the general social condition to which the novel responds but also a particular congeries of formulated ideas." If the work of Culture were to be successful, it would establish the presence of ideas in society as having about the same authority as that of beliefs and doctrines in religion. Society would authenticate its conscience by virtue of its ideas: it would be a secular version of the City of God. In *Beyond Culture* Trilling describes the work of Culture as the attempt to "make a coherent life, to confront the terrors of the outer and the inner world, to establish the ritual and art, the pieties and duties which make possible the life of the group and the individual." The energy of Society must be transformed into human images: events must become experiences. (p. 176)

It is clear that by Culture Trilling meant High Culture, an action with ideas as its content and an urbane style as its form and bearing. The actions of Popular Culture are not observed, presumably because Trilling thinks them of little interest or imperfect and fitful in their bearing upon society, effecting only a simpleminded and perhaps corrupt transformation of society. I assume that there is a direct relation between his insistence upon High Culture and his equal insistence upon the unbroken circumference of the self: in both cases Trilling's tone is severe because he is maintaining a position under continuous attack. In the past few years it has become unfashionable to speak of the self as a circle defined by an irrefutable center. Trilling's insistence was widely taken as proof that he was dismally out of touch with contemporary ways of feeling. (p. 177)

[It may be useful] to represent Trilling's major books in a narrative sequence, because they reveal a certain development, not a change of attitude on his part but a more explicit set of strategies to cope with a changing situation. It has been alleged that he merely turned Tory and adopted the morality of inertia rather than participate in the spirit of the age. The truth is more complex. In his early essays Trilling maintained the hope of a mutual relation between society and the individual mind. He took for granted the integral self, and he considered its highest form disclosed in mind: the most serious acts of the mind were directed upon the public objective world and took their morality from the universally respected good of society. Mind acted upon reality: reality was not merely given—it was received by mind and modified by the spirit of that reception. The pure of heart were those who maintained a social conscience and did not merely cultivate their sensibilities. The grand themes were social, personal, historical, political; the most pressing arguments were ideological. Ideally there would be a fine adjustment of pressure between mind and society. But in frequent practice the adjustment was disturbed, mind was intimidated by society, browbeaten by institutions, conventions, impersonations, monsters of the marketplace.

But there remained another possibility: mind could define itself and establish its character by opposition to the imperatives of society. This is the official theme of *The Opposing Self,* in which Trilling reflected upon the self which emerged at the end of the eighteenth century, exhibiting an "intense and adverse imagination of the culture in which it has its being.". . . Keats is the hero of *The Opposing Self* because he is the purest example of that conflict, holding in balance "the reality of self and the reality of circumstance." Mutual support is the best condition, but mutual tension even to the degree of opposition and conflict will answer nearly as well, because it keeps both terms alive. In *The Opposing Self* Trilling praises the adversary mind in Keats, Tolstoy, Dickens, Jane Austen, James, and Orwell. He is not distressed to find the self quarreling with society, because the quarrel is good for each participant.

In his later books, especially in *Beyond Culture,* Trilling was dispirited to see that the hard-earned achievements of an opposing self were now mass-produced and sold in cheap plastic imitations, the rhetoric of a counterculture which he could not help despising. The rhetorical flourishes of the counterculture seemed cheap, glib in their easily acquired alienation, their borrowed sentiments. I think that Trilling was outraged by the vulgarization of a motive which he sometimes felt in himself, the dream of freedom representing itself as a rage for unconditioned spirit. He protested against unconditioned spirit, and perhaps protested so vehemently because he had to resist its temptation in himself: in any case he rebuked those who went the low road by simply disengaging themselves from the daily concerns of society. (pp. 178-80)

Disengagement from society was to Trilling a grave scandal even though it was a natural temptation, offering a holiday in reality. There is a passage in "On the Teaching of Modern Literature" in which he expounds the implications of modern literature in these terms and represents it in ways which are, I think, misleading. Trilling quotes Thomas Mann as saying that his fiction could be understood as an effort to free himself from the middle class. He then goes further: the aim of modern literature as a whole is "not merely freedom from the middle class but freedom from society itself." "I venture to say," he continues, "that the idea of losing oneself up to the point of self-destruction, of surrendering oneself to experience without regard to self-interest or conventional morality, of escaping wholly from the societal bonds, is an 'element' somewhere in the mind of every modern person who dares to think of what Arnold in his unaffected Victorian way called 'the fulness of spiritual perfection.'" Up to this point the argument seems to me sound, but Trilling goes on to warn the teacher that "if he is committed to an admiration of modern literature, he must also be committed to this chief idea of modern literature." "I press the logic of the situation," he goes on, "not in order to question the legitimacy of the commitment, or even the propriety of expressing the commitment in the college classroom (although it does seem odd!), but to confront those of us who do teach modern literature with the striking actuality of our enterprise." I think he presses the logic exorbitantly. Even if we grant that the end of modern literature is to achieve freedom from society, the end is never reached. . . . In any case the chief idea to which Trilling refers is merely an idea, and it must make its way in the world against the force of other ideas and interests and against the more sullen dogged force of those states of being which do not entertain ideas at all. Besides, the idea abstracted from a novel or poem is not the same as the idea when it is involved in the texture, density, and organization of the work: an idea is nothing more or less than a motif when it is implicated in the structure of the work. And since Trilling was anxious about the consequences of his idea in the world at large, it is necessary to remark that a reader of a novel or poem does not go out into the world and act upon an idea, even a chief idea, he has encountered in his reading. He is much more likely to act upon his prejudice, habit, routine, all those persuasive imperatives which he has received without the labor of taking thought. . . . Literature is not important for what it can do: it cannot cure a toothache. In the idiom of action literature never goes beyond gesture: it is always a play, or a play within a play; its intensities are always virtual, a mime of passion. But literature is not reduced or humiliated by this consideration: the fact that it keeps itself within parentheses and refuses to compete in any direct sense with the forces engaged in society means that it stays true to its nature as a vision of life —not life as lived but life as seen, known, felt, suffered, understood. It is my impression that Trilling pressed his logic too far on this occasion not because he misunderstood the action of ideas in literature but because the idea in question was this particular one. (pp. 180-82)

The occasion on which Trilling expounded these matters most directly was the essay "Hawthorne in Our Time," in which he distinguished not so much between Hawthorne, James, and Kafka as between our diverse understanding of their tempers and achievements. He maintained—not very convincingly—that we have lost interest in James because we have turned against his conviction "that the world is *there*: the unquestionable, inescapable world; the world so beautifully and so disastrously solid, physical, material, 'natural.'" We have decided that James is not one of us, after all, because he does not share our intransigence; he takes undue pleasure in the world, and yields to it for that reason. I find this argument unpersuasive not because I do not recognize a feeling at large in the world which is indeed what Trilling describes it as being but because I cannot see any evidence that James has fallen in our esteem for any such reason. (p. 182)

In Trilling's argument Kafka is the modern hero because he refuses to yield his imagination to the apparent intractability of the world. Kafka gives very little recognition to the ordinary world "as we know it socially, politically, erotically, domestically": he does not concern himself with the relations between one person and another, or with cases of conscience, or with morality. The modern consciousness requires, according to Trilling, "that an artist have an imagination which is more intransigent than James could allow, more spontaneous, peremptory, and obligatory, which shall impose itself upon us with such unquestionable authority that 'the actual' can have no power over us but shall seem the creation of some inferior imagination, that of mere convention and habit." We are preoccupied by "the ideal of the autonomous self." Trilling is outraged by modern willfulness, our alleged contempt for conditions and circumstances, the "angelism" with which we insist upon direct access to spirit and essence. Essence means, in that insistence, the immediacy of our experience, and spirit is the attribute that makes the insistence what it is, our autonomous identity. Trilling is pointing to a force that is undoubtedly active in contemporary feeling. But I wonder why he finds

it necessary to represent Kafka in such terms. Kafka is not interested in miming our daily activities, but he does not ignore "the actual" or encourage us to ignore society. It is an essential principle of his art to conceive social institutions at such an advanced stage of reification that they are already congealed in their monstrous forms: they are systems rather than *societas*. Trilling admires Kafka's art but with reluctance, I think. I suggest that the reason is not that Kafka scorns the actual detail of our lives but that he does not hold out the possibility of redeeming the monstrous forms of society. (pp. 183-84)

Kafka is crucial in Trilling's criticism because he represents an outer limit of his sympathies. Consider these sentences in which Trilling reflects upon "the extraordinary aesthetic success which Kafka consistently achieves": "Aesthetically, it seems, it is impossible for him to fail. There is never a fault of conception or execution, never an error of taste, or logic, or emphasis. As why should there be? An imagination so boldly autonomous, once it has brought itself into being, conceives of nothing that can throw it off its stride. Like the dream, it confronts subjective fact only, and there are no aesthetically unsuccessful dreams, no failed nightmares." It is a revealing passage, starting with that "aesthetically" in which the adverb imposes a limiting judgment while its official assertion is appreciative. Trilling drives a wedge between aesthetics and morality by associating the first with dream and nightmare, irrefutable but narrow activities, and by implication associating those values to which Kafka is indifferent with nearly everything of density and substance in a serious life. (p. 184)

I have been maintaining that Trilling was unwilling, even in a grim time, to find the poetic experience in dissociation from the texture of society and that he insisted upon attaching even to an imperfect society an aura of inherited value. But if nearly every social institution harbors corruption, where is a scrupulous image of society to be found? He can hardly say, with Plato's disputant in *The Republic,* "Not here, O Ademantus, but in another world." And yet there is a sense in which, given such desperate conditions in practice, Trilling points beyond them not to any particular society but to the idea of a society, an idea sustained only by his need of such a thing. He can also point in another direction, toward Language: or, rather, toward a certain kind of language, a certain style, *eloquentia*. This is "the mind of the old European society" to which [R. P. Blackmur] referred, "taken as corrective and as prophecy." It is a corrective by virtue of the tradition it embodies, at once a rhetoric, a poetic, and a politics: it is a prophecy by virtue of its persistence as a working possibility. But of course it is beautiful only in its potentiality.

Normally we do not think of Lionel Trilling as a critic of language in the sense in which we apply that description to R. P. Blackmur, Leo Spitzer, or Erich Auerbach. Close intensive reading of a text is never the substance of Trilling's work, though it may have occupied his preparatory hours: he disposes of a poem's language before he deals with it in any explicit way. The poetic experience reaches him of course in language, but he does not settle upon it professionally until the language has ventured into the public world in the form of ideas. Indeed it may be one of the limitations of his criticism that its author is content with a strictly instrumental theory of language and that he has circumvented the questions raised by modern linguistics and hermeneutics. But the explanation is probably simple enough. Trilling values in language chiefly its self-forgetful character, the nonchalance with which it sometimes takes its nature for granted and turns toward something more interesting, the ideas and attitudes which make for life and death. He suspects any manifestations of language which call attention to themselves as constituents rather than as instruments, or which appeal to a particular class of reader rather than to readers in general. What Trilling values in language corresponds to what he values in society: reasonable energies at work, fair purposes and consequences, more nonchalance than self-consciousness, and just enough tension to foster and maintain vitality. For the same reason Trilling distrusted every version of formalism: the forms he valued were transparent rather than opaque, functional rather than problematical. A form offers itself as a problem when its motives are not sustained by forces in the world at large and the available analogies are deemed useless. In both language and form Trilling values those procedures which can be construed as corresponding to a certain way of life, reasonable, cultivated, urbane. The rhetorical function of criticism is to maintain the correspondence. (pp. 185-86)

> *Denis Donoghue, "Trilling, Mind, and Society," in* Sewanee Review *(reprinted by permission of the editor; © 1978 by The University of the South), Spring, 1978, pp. 161-86.*

*   *   *

TRYON, Thomas   1926-

Tryon, an actor turned novelist, has written several best-selling novels. (See also *CLC*, Vol. 3, and *Contemporary Authors*, Vols. 29-32, rev. ed.)

PETER ACKROYD

There is a line which has resounded through B-films, soap-operas and pulp fiction and it goes something like this: "Ned, wait! . . . Are you familiar with what are commonly referred to as the Greek mysteries?" There is a pregnant pause, and Ned whispers, in a tone somewhere between shock, anguish and determination, "No! And that won't stop me!" My first quote is taken verbatim from Mr Tryon's new novel (he is already famous for *The Other,* the other one), but I must admit to writing the second quote myself. The Ned is Theodore Constantine and indeed he doesn't let it stop him; his abysmal ignorance of classical ritual accounts for most of the plot of *Harvest Home,* and he wouldn't know a vegetation symbol if one got up and tickled him. . . . Who is Widow Fortune, and why does she keep crying "Drat!" and "Where in the nation!"? Is there something which the villagers will not or cannot reveal? And why is everything so damned rural? Read on, Mr Tryon keeps hinting, and you may see something nasty.

And indeed, eventually, we do. At first there is only the occasional glimpse of darkness visible; the villagers mutter about something called the "Waste" and at one of their simple country fairs there are enough phallic symbols to make an academic blush. But Tryon writes very discreetly, and the first climax comes almost without warning. . . .

The story in question has something to do with the Earth-Mother and the Eternal Return; English schoolboys of the more respectable kind have been studying this sort of thing for years, and it may be that familiarity breeds *noblesse*

oblige. But, whatever his education, Mr Tryon is a shade portentous about these perfectly harmless pagan rites; he reacts to them as an American dame would react to Stonehenge, and his final Dionysian touches are too bloodstained to be interesting. I know that America is a matriarchal society but this, Mr Tryon, is ridiculous.

> *Peter Ackroyd, "Read Without Rest," in* The Spectator *(© 1974 by The Spectator; reprinted by permission of* The Spectator*), February 9, 1974, p. 171.*

Harvest Home is a marketable concoction of sex, witchcraft and literary pretension, enormously long and unbelievably silly. It is the second, more ambitious and rather more distasteful novel of a Hollywood actor turned writer; its atmosphere resembles those inept horror films especially made for television and shown at furtive hours. . . .

The Cold Comfort Farm names . . . are misleading: that isn't at all the flavour of the book. The lumbering efforts at thoughtful observation are a diversion, too. . . . Its real concern is with hysteria, cruelty, and adolescent fantasies of perverse sex. (p. 219)

> *The Times Literary Supplement (© Times Newspapers Ltd. (London) 1974; reproduced from* The Times Literary Supplement *by permission), March 1, 1974.*

WEBSTER SCHOTT

Thomas Tryon seems to have been born with a silver story in his mouth. He spins best-selling novels: "The Other," "Harvest Home," "Lady." He probably has written another best seller in "Crowned Heads"—a tale with the impact of "The National Enquirer" crossed with "The Day of the Locust."

The places are right: Los Angeles, New York City, the undiscovered paradises of Mexico and Crete. And Tryon's characters, four of Hollywood's ex-crowned heads bear so much resemblance to real people in remembered situations that his fiction seems to merge with fact. I assume that "Crowned Heads" draws from dozens of actual lives—Greta Garbo, Mickey Rooney, Freddie Bartholomew, Stan Laurel, Gloria Swanson, Marilyn Monroe—in order to create its splendid illusions. But in the manner of his fellow semi-nonfiction novelists, Tryon dodges identification. (p. 6)

There's something for everyone in "Crowned Heads." Tryon plays to the senses. He presses sex, but it always leads to something deeper. He watches manners, introduces details, covers settings with a Peeping Tom passion. His stories ripple with plots and subplots. (pp. 6-7)

> *Webster Schott, in* The New York Times Book Review *(© 1976 by The New York Times Company; reprinted by permission), July 11, 1976.*

WILLIAM WALSH

In spite of what we must technically call Thomas Tryon's prose, his study of a Garbo character, a child prodigy, a failed actress and a decrepit Ronald Colman type, from Hollywood figures who are loosely associated in a particular film, has a curious, even an unaccountable readability. It appeals to that part of one's nature, at least if you were brought up on the films rather than the television, which rejoiced as the organ disappeared and the credits flicked up at the prospect of well-organised, nicely balanced dreams, of appalling acting, primitive morality, and the kind of suspense which could be relied on not to shock your susceptibilities but only to caress your expectations. The plots of the four *contes* of which *Crowned Heads* is composed certainly conform to this last point. Fedora-Garbo arranges her own immortality with the aid of an unknown daughter. Bobbit the child prodigy has an even more fantasy-saturated life after his childhood career is over than he ever did during it. Willie, the old charmer, comes to a grisly end, crucified in his own private chapel by a trio of teen-aged monsters. Lorna, the second-rank star, comes to her drink and drug-sodden conclusion in a sexually charged bout with a rattlesnake. This Lorna part of the novel seems to me much the most effective, bringing out in an intimate and painful way the corrupting effect of having to purvey the fantasies that simply titillate others. (p. 61)

> *William Walsh, in* Books and Bookmen *(© copyright William Walsh 1976; reprinted with permission), December, 1976.*

[*Crowned Heads* features] four tangentially related Hollywood stars [and] may be the best "Hollywood novel" you will find. Mr. Tryon convincingly depicts what becoming a film star can do to a person, and his characters are beautifully drawn. He does a masterful job of introducing cliché elements while avoiding the clichés themselves. The final section, "Willie," is an exceptionally powerful example of foreshadowing and growing suspense. (p. 17)

> Virginia Quarterly Review *(copyright, 1977, by the* Virginia Quarterly Review, The University of Virginia*), Vol. 53, No. 1 (Winter, 1977).*

*   *   *

TURCO, Lewis   1934-

Turco is an American poet, playwright, essayist, and editor. He is noted for his skillful use of traditional poetic constructions, particularly in *Awaken, Bells Falling: Poems 1959-1967*, and *The Inhabitant*, which are generally considered his best works. (See also *Contemporary Authors*, Vols. 13-16, rev. ed.)

[*Awaken, Bells Falling*] is a full and varied book, showing off the range of Turco's talent and the variety of his mind. His view of things is quiet and dark; he accepts rather than affirms, acknowledges rather than celebrates. But the poems have a solidity beyond acceptance, for he knows the music of the day's events and remembers the way the ordinary can often glow and blaze. Whether he writes of a pumpkin, a Christmas tree, the death of a president or an ordinary evening in Cleveland, he writes with compassion and precision. If death too often overshadows life, and pain, life's joys, nevertheless Lewis Turco finds his singing voice in suffering, finds reason to live and love in despair. These are good poems by a poet of a real ability. (p. cxlix)

> Virginia Quarterly Review *(copyright, 1968, by the* Virginia Quarterly Review, The University of Virginia*), Vol. 44, No. 4 (Autumn, 1968).*

HYATT H. WAGGONER

Turco as poet has tended to preserve and rework Modernist attitudes in our post-Modernist period, and Turco as critic has—how consciously I don't know—taken on the role of valiant defender of the timeless verities of the poet's art against all those who promote confusion by putting first what is properly secondary, for instance by writing "confessional" poetry or striking a "prophetic" stance. (p. 50)

[In] Turco's latest poems, the effects of a warming trend in the poet's mental weather is evident, so that his next volume may be expected to surprise those who have not followed the newest poems as they have appeared in the magazines. The "new" Turco may well appear to be attired and equipped not with greatcoat and club but more in the fashion of Whitman. . . . (p. 51)

Images of winter, of silence, and of either a cold darkness or a cold whiteness suggest, and sometimes establish, the prevailing mood of *Awaken, Bells Falling*. Quite often they seem to echo early Stevens or early Frost, or both at once. In the title poem the climactic passage in "The Whiteness of the Whale" in *Moby-Dick* is, consciously or unconsciously, drawn upon to enrich the suggestions of the images. Reading "Winter; / allcolor; whiteness. . . ." we can't help remembering how Melville put it: the whiteness of the perpetual arctic snow was "the colorless all-color of atheism." When we read the final lines of the poem—". . . Bells fail in the streets; / the hall empties us into ice, / / sheeted, sheer as mirrors, unreflecting."—we find ourselves in the not too different world of Stevens, who thought one must have a mind of winter to survive. (pp. 51-2)

In so cold and threatening a world as Turco inhabits in this book, artifice can be both shield and weapon, or greatcoat and club. For me, though, the finest poem in the volume shows much less of that "easy virtuosity" that August Derleth called attention to in a review of Turco's earlier volume. It is not primarily such verbal play as we have in the lines just quoted that gives "Burning the News" its power. There is nothing euphuistic about lines like "The smoke of Asia / drifts among the neighbors like mist. . . ."

Where *does* its power come from? From the vision behind and in the words, perhaps? . . .

The title he gives his non-review [of my book, *American Poets from the Puritans to the Present*], "The Ghost of Emerson," refers both to a claim made by and the organizing idea in my book—roughly, Emerson's centrality in the development of American poetry—and to Turco's own personal "response." Like Eliot meeting the ghost of Dante during the London blitz, Turco encountered the ghost of Emerson and came to think of the encounter as a revelation, or series of revelations. (p. 53)

An example of [a poem influenced by these Emersonian revelations] is "Mary Moody Emerson, R.I.P.," which strikes me as a finer poem than anything in *Awaken* with the possible exception of "Burning the News." (p. 55)

"I Am Peter" is a very personal, very autobiographical, poem . . . while still avoiding the "confessional" qualities Turco has so often said he despised. It is also, it seems to me, a very fine and moving poem, some miles along the road beyond most if not all of the earlier work.

Both the poem on Emerson's Aunt Mary and "The Pilot" seem to me to exemplify Emerson's idea of the poetic imagination, which suggests, among other modern variants, Buber's notion of "dialogue"—an "I-Thou" relation, made possible only by imagination and will, to use the old terms, rather than an "I-It" form of *scrutinizing*. In "The Pilot," especially, the poet's "angle of vision" has changed and he is really, it seems to me, doing what Emerson meant by "sharing the circuit of things through forms," making the "forms . . . translucid," so the light can shine through. (p. 56)

Hyatt H. Waggoner, "The 'Formalism' of Lewis Turco: Fluting and Fifing with Frosted Fingers," in Concerning Poetry (copyright © 1969, Western Washington State College), Fall, 1969, pp. 50-8.

WILLIAM HEYEN

The Inhabitant (1970) is the collection of poems that Lewis Turco has been heading toward for a long time. As his books have appeared his work has not only gotten better, but has changed. (p. 115)

Most of the work in Turco's First Poems (1960) is too stiff metrically, or too pretty, or too ingenious, or too heavily moral and wise. Depending on your tolerance for "promising" first volumes, you're likely to consider Turco's apprentice work "very pleasant to hear," as did Donald Justice when he wrote a Foreword for First Poems, or as merely a sort of unpromising game "exhibiting the most ordinary of all kinds of skill," as did James Dickey when he reviewed it. . . . What most concerns me here is the strenuous and irritating morality of the book, something the poet *had* to grow out of. Nothing is more aggravating in poetry than the presentation of conventional wisdom unless it is the presentation of conventional wisdom conventionally. It is not just that some of Turco's early poems are didactic, poems of statement, poems with some of the excesses of newspaper obituary verse, but that behind them is a sort of puritanical fury that demands that every action, everything that happens to anyone at any time anywhere should and must yield its drop of meaning. Meaning everywhere, but not a drop to think. Turco wasn't willing to allow a poem to well up from its own subtle sense of itself, wasn't willing to allow it to do what it wanted to do.

In any case, apprentice work, it seems to me, does become interesting as its potential is or is not fulfilled with more mature poems, and this is reason enough for its publication. (pp. 115-16)

Awaken, Bells Falling: Poems 1959-1967 (1968) represents a great step forward. This third collection—an impossible-to-get-hold-of chapbook, The Sketches, was published in 1962—has already arrived. Most of the poems are finished and satisfying. Occasionally the sermonic tone of First Poems still breaks through and is offensive, but for the most part skill, awareness, and curiosity brought these poems into being rather than the constant puritanical rage for a sign. Turco's voice is less insistent. Authorial intrusion is at a minimum. The sensibility behind these poems has made an intelligent decision, a decision of the intelligence, and is willing to allow its subjects to Be rather than constantly Become. An example of the book's method and belief is its shortest poem, "School Drawing":

> There is a road: no
> one is walking there. Brown
> paper, black paper triangles
> wrangle with the air
> to make a windmill

striping a crayon
sun. A black arrow points
away from the blades that turn in
fire. It is burning,
and there is no wind.

This means what it says, no more and no less. Turco has gone back to the innocence of words here. The fire of illumination in this book, as in "School Drawing" and "Burning the News," burns up the old ways we've had of bringing a scaffolding of meaning to a poem. The crutches are in flames, says Turco. Poems dwell on the edge of mystery. . . . The subject of this poem is the Being of the drawing, not what Turco thinks it means or what I think it means. Turco is now willing to allow his subject to surface when and how it pleases. He is willing to suggest rather than state. He has gotten past trying to prove anything. And this kind of poem, I must insist, is neither flippant nor shallow. It is motivated, in Turco at least, by a complex of emotional needs. . . . (pp. 116-17)

His poems in this third book, then, are aware of themselves as bearers of consciousness, awareness, intelligence, but are not as strident or methodical or militant as First Poems. The poems now, in fact, are metaphors for what seems to be a developing vision. Poetry now . . . "explains why/ . . . even as it explains nothing." I don't think Turco realized the complexity of this truth during the time First Poems was being forced into shape. (pp. 117-18)

[What] I feel reading The Inhabitant is a deep and strong sense of my own existence, my own loneliness in time. The twenty-eight poems . . . dramatize the Inhabitant's developing consciousness of his domestic world in terms that are near and clear. Images of emptiness, absence, loss, boredom, fatigue, monotony, darkness, stagnation, and corrosion dominate. But Turco turns so much domestic dross into poetry, and the effect of this book is strangely uplifting. The poems are a record of a nameless man's willingness to allow his world to be.

In The Inhabitant Turco moves to a concept of the "still-point" not as the fruition of a life of mystical straining or as one of the strange momentary joys of our lives, but as a necessity, a defensive gesture, our minds defending us, against ourselves, as Stevens says in one of his "Adagia." (pp. 118-19)

"The Playroom" is a deep and rewarding poem. It takes the Inhabitant's awareness into the moving realm of his relationship with his daughter. "The Portrait of a Clown," which follows "The Playroom"—both poems are spatially, technically, and thematically at the dead center of the book—is a companionpiece, a sequel. It again poses the questions unresolved by "The Playroom": how can the Inhabitant be his child's world? how can he save her from pain? how can he make his own world suffice? The answer is not programmatic or definite, but the Inhabitant is on the verge of knowing. . . . [From] here on The Inhabitant is intent on capturing the stillness that is real, now, the moment you are reading this. If objects are symbolically extended forward and backward in time, if the Inhabitant's mind is still at play, he senses that he is indulging himself. If the universe is evolving, changing, there is a sense in which it is, at any moment, during any day of total consciousness, deathless, as still in time as Zeno's paradoxical arrow.

The Inhabitant's struggle (and, since we seem to enter

"The Door" in the first poem, ours) is to accept his world and to become his own "true flesh," as Turco puts it. . . . ["The Dwelling House"] is a summary of where he has come from. As it ends it recalls Stevens in "Final Soliloquy of the Interior Paramour." . . . [Here] Turco takes us to an eye-to-eye contact with one another, naked together, *naked,* unsponsored and free. (pp. 120-21)

The Inhabitant walks from attic to cellar of his home listening to his furniture declare its own plain songs. As was [Poe's] Roderick Usher, the Inhabitant is hypersensitive and feels the sentience of all things. But the House of Usher, of course, disappears under the tarn of time; Turco's house seems, finally, to flourish in the here and now. . . . He wants to fix his time, order it. His effort is . . . to love, to love the dark and beautiful contingency of his experience. (p. 122)

[Turco moves] toward that world, beyond the explanations of old gods, where the Inhabitant comes to stillness and joy. This spiritual progress, I take it, is part of what Conrad Aiken means when he calls *The Inhabitant* a poetry of "whole meaning." This book is a whole world, not a slice of life, and one of the fascinating things about where Turco's break with his past has taken him is that the world he has opened for himself is dynamic, self-propagating, endless. There are numberless things that Turco can now allow to be themselves. . . . It seems to me that this is a good test of any aesthetic, any world view: can it take everything into account? . . .

Many of the poems here are wonderfully realized, satisfied with themselves, not straining to be more, finished. The perceptions of many are deeply intelligent and moving. (p. 123)

> *William Heyen, "The Progress of Lewis Turco,"*
> *in* Modern Poetry Studies *(copyright 1971, by Jerome Mazzaro), Vol. 2, No. 3, 1971, pp. 115-24.*

DAVID G. McLEAN

Those who frequent the small world of the little poetry magazines know Lewis Turco as a champion of the classical virtues of form and craftsmanship. In a 1968 essay entitled "Defining the Poet," Turco wrote, ". . . a poet is an artificer of language, and . . . a poem is an artifice of language." For Turco, the poet is always primarily the artificer, the maker, *not the seer.*

This is an unpopular position to defend in light of today's strong neo-romanticism and also in light of America's [Emersonian] poetic tradition. . . . For Emerson, the poet is the visionary who mystically intuits truth and who then unself-consciously expresses this truth in the form which its inner nature dictates. But Turco, always suspicious of visionaries, attributes much of the inferior poetry of the present popular American poets to an easy and undisciplined adherence to that philosophy.

In *The Inhabitant,* Turco's latest collection of poems, the inhabitant, in a sense, represents the American poet caught in the classical vs. romantic crossfire. In "The Living-room," he encounters what may be the visionary muse as it mystically appears as a singing skull. The inhabitant yearns to hear the singing of the skull; but he hears nothing, even though "he is a lover of song." He is tempted "to pretend that he has heard," but he rejects the subterfuge. It is only then that he hears the music. Thus his "inspiration" comes

not from the vision but, as is later suggested in "The Kitchen," originates in the factual world about him. . . . (pp. 65-6)

The message is clear, although we do a disservice to *The Inhabitant* if we imply that the book is excessively didactic. It is not.

The poems of *The Inhabitant* lead the reader, along with a visitor who may be the inhabitant's other self, into the inhabitant's home—or symbolically his unconsciousness. Beginning with "The Door," the visitor moves through the rooms and furniture of the house until he is totally absorbed in the inhabitant's world. It is a world of half-light and shadow, heavy with the anticipation of death, revealing in the concluding poem, "The Dwelling-House," not death but a re-birth that allows him to see the world free and naked. . . .

[These poems] collectively comprise a single experience, as the unity of the prosody stresses. The poems dealing with the furniture and other appendages of the inhabitant's home are divided into stanzas based upon word-count. These furniture poems are arranged alternately with poems about the house itself, which are written as "prose-poems." A mechanical repetition of two such prosodies might ordinarily lead to a monotonous and heavy-handed formalism, but the variety possible in these two particular forms serves to avoid that pitfall while still maintaining a desirable cohesiveness.

However, successful as is the collection as a whole, few, if any, of the individual poems rival the best of Turco's earlier works such as "The Pilot" or "The Forest Beyond the Glass." Perhaps nearest to them is "The Cat," one of *The Inhabitant's* most striking poems. (p. 66)

Tightly structured and rich in an unlabored symbolism, "The Cat" illustrates the craftsmanship to which Lewis Turco is so dedicated. (p. 67)

> *David G. McLean, in* Agora, *Spring, 1972.*

R. DICKINSON-BROWN

Lewis Turco's poems get better, book after book. *The Weed Garden . . .* is Turco's best. The finest of the twenty-one syllabic poems here are almost as good as anything new I have read in years. But these poems have an elusive and cryptic profundity; to understand them it is first necessary, unfortunately, to understand some of the weaknesses in Turco's work. A good deal of the best poetry of our century is syllabic. . . . The success of these poems depends in part, I believe, upon the fusion of innovations of rhythmic perception with the almost inherent characteristics of English iambic tendency, stopped lines, rime and off-rime. Turco's practice is looser. It resembles the work of Marianne Moore, and it verges easily into slackness and dullness. As with Moore, Turco's virtues are often not in rhythm. . . . (pp. 286-87)

In addition, Turco is something of an ornamentalist. He plays with obsolete and invented words: "A twilleter fuzzes / against a burning lamp." And he is given to silly and exasperating puns. In "Mary Moody Emerson R.I.P.," "Ralph Waldo / shrugged and put down to whim this / relative moodiness." This is, doubtless, a love and delight of language, but I confess I find it a waste of time and talent. . . . [These qualities of Turco's poems] are the junk of experience, done when there is nothing else to do.

Turco's characteristic procedure is built in part, but finally improves, upon these habits. His poems are laid out in a series of deft and sometimes slick, slightly surrealistic settings. . . . [Many of his] details are empty, pretty swirls of ornament and setting, not the real thing; they are perception at a superficial, routine, and graceful level.

But Turco is an intelligent and alert poet. . . . [At its best, this] is hard, complete poetry, in which the details have become the meaning, and none functions ornamentally or superfluously; they are scarcely even illustration, so fully do they signify. Such a pattern of progression exists in most of these and the rest of Turco's poems. The real writing comes at last.

There are two common themes in Turco's poems. . . . [The first, a distinction between human and wild,] has been a commonplace for more than two centuries, and the particular quality of feeling here is also in Wallace Stevens, Yvor Winters and others; there is little originality in Turco's marking of it, but it is very well executed. The other "theme" in *The Weed Garden* gathers more slowly and imperfectly, because it is original, and imperfectly understood by the poet himself. The theme is presented in the conclusion to "Home Thoughts." . . . (pp. 287-88)

Turco is writing about an evolution toward fusion with the universe. It may be natural to see a kind of neo-Emersonianism here, but there is none. There is a concept of people evolving themselves into their own god, and so becoming the universe—and destroying the distinction [between human and wild] marked in "The Orchestra." Turco needs to articulate his idea better and to implement it more, if we are to make much of it, and then it may prove only an eccentricity. But at the moment we have before us an interesting, developing idea in the work of a talented and neglected poet. (pp. 288-89)

> *R. Dickinson-Brown, "Lewis Turco's Best Book of Poems," in* Modern Poetry Studies *(copyright 1974, by Jerome Mazzaro), Winter, 1974, pp. 286-89.*

FELIX STEFANILE

Turco seems to have the whole of the English lyric tradition at his fingertips, and though this is not entirely a good thing —too much tinkle here and there, here a bit of Keats, there a bit of Mother Goose—I belong to the old school, and see in this bravura the commitment of a poet to craft. I trust poets who show clear influences, and I don't trust the groggy, toneless, "spontaneous" mutter of much that goes by the name of verse today among the younger, studiously untutored poets of the confessional school. (p. 297)

I would like to see Turco . . . return to the inspiration of "The Sketches," the sequence that forms the middle third of [*Pocoangelini: A Fantography*]. There, in a handful of character vignettes—A. R. Ammons called them "an autobiography of biographies"—we have a poet who is direct, clear-seeing, musical, and quite real. Poems like "Guido the Ice House Man," "Ercole the Butcher," and "Mrs. Martino the Candy Store Lady" speak to the human condition with grace, always a strong point with Turco, and warmth. Just as importantly, I think the resistance of the subject matter—real people, often simple, not particularly highly endowed—works well with this poet's tendency to treat his material with too much "fanciness." A tension is set up between the nubbiness of the material and the neatness of Turco's technique:

> When you come to the best of quiet doors,
> there Guido sits with his hat pulled down
> and his lids pulled down,
> and the shadows down, down to his knees
> like an awning's ghost—

Precision of language, and to be envied. (pp. 297-98)

> *Felix Stefanile, in* Italian Americana *(copyright © 1975 by Ruth Falbo and Richard Gambino), Vol. I, No. 2, Spring, 1975.*

* * *

TYLER, Anne   1941-

Tyler is an American novelist and short story writer. Her fiction is generally concerned with familial relations and focuses on the themes of isolation, thwarted ideals, and the problem of communication between individuals. (See also *CLC*, Vol. 7, and *Contemporary Authors*, Vols. 9-12, rev. ed.)

JIM HUNTER

[At the end of] *The Clock-Winder*, the domestic settlement and content which have been achieved are seen slightly distanced, through the subdued distress of Peter, hitherto offstage. 'He's just back from Vietnam,' they say of him. 'Everyone murmured, as if that explained things.'

Miss Tyler's book is quite apolitical. . . . [It] is warmly and shrewdly written, the characters are persuasive, and there is a salutary sense that bourgeois life is not necessarily rotten to the core. The novel will give pleasure and perhaps restoration to its readers, who will be mostly middle-aged and middle-class: and it has every right to do so. Nevertheless, for a writer as alert as Miss Tyler evidently is to produce a book as graceful and cheering as this does involve some sort of withdrawal from horrors of which non-fictional Americans today are not allowed to be unaware, and the inspiration which shows us the happy ending through the cool eyes of the war veteran was perhaps a twinge of conscience. (p. 157)

> *Jim Hunter, in* The Listener *(© British Broadcasting Corp. 1973; reprinted by permission of Jim Hunter), February 1, 1973.*

LYNN SHARON SCHWARTZ

The family as a sealed unit, with an imperious grip on its members through the twin traps of heredity and environment, is the subject of [*Searching for Caleb*]. . . . The Pecks, a well-to-do Baltimore clan, are skillfully traced from the founding father down four generations to the single young descendant. The shape of the family tree, as one character notes, is a diamond. Outsiders brought in by marriage do not thrive: the insular Peck personality, a mélange of mediocrity, loyalty, emotional evasion, and impeccable respectability, smothers them or drives them away. In a wry reversal of the thesis that "you can't go home again," *Searching for Caleb* asks instead whether you can ever really get away. The Peck renegades, after the trauma of breaking family ties, are left passive, dry, and remote—still dominated, it would seem, by the tyranny of chromosomes.

Anne Tyler's tone is understated, ironic, and elliptical, which suits her characters well. *Searching for Caleb* rarely gives us heights and depths of emotion or the excitement of discovery, but it does offer the very welcome old-fashioned virtues of a patient, thoughtful chronicle. (p. 28)

Lynn Sharon Schwartz, in Saturday Review (© *1976 by Saturday Review/World, Inc.; reprinted with permission), March 6, 1976.*

WALTER SULLIVAN

Anne Tyler goes at her work with as much gusto as Margaret Drabble, but on a smaller scale and in a style that is more tightly controlled. Miss Tyler has learned a great deal about her craft . . . since her first novel was published, but she has retained a kind of innocence in her view of life, a sense of wonder at all the crazy things in the world and an abiding affection for her own flaky characters. (p. 120)

Miss Tyler is concerned with the quality of human existence. She turns her characters loose to live as they will, and the choice that each makes is a testimony to life's infinite variety. . . . [In addition to profundities,] there is joy in the surface, the remarkable accuracy with which Miss Tyler depicts the world, the unobtrusiveness of her technical skill, and the wit and perception with which she creates her people and establishes her conflicts. Within the boundaries she has set for herself she is almost totally successful. (pp. 121-22)

Walter Sullivan, in Sewanee Review (*reprinted by permission of the editor;* © *1977 by The University of the South), Winter, 1977.*

ANATOLE BROYARD

"Earthly Possessions" . . . is just another one of those slightly stale, wry books that so many women writers seem to be turning out: A heroine who is a rueful optimist or cheerful pessimist, takes us on a long walk through the world in order to point out its incongruities. A Michelin guide to desolate panoramas, dismal accommodations, poor fare. A woman laughing out of the other side of her mouth. . . .

Charlotte is the nearest thing to a character in "Earthly Possessions," yet she is only a hope chest of negatives, a woman on the run from boredom toward an empty ambiguity. Her mother and father are the caricatures we have come to expect from contemporary fiction, what E. M. Forster called "flat characters." Her father silently takes old-fashioned formal pictures of the people in his small town and her mother is merely fat, as if she could make up in quantity what she lacks in quality. There is nobody in the book for Charlotte to bounce off and so she merely rolls around until she stops. (p. 12)

Anatole Broyard, in The New York Times Book Review (© *1977 by The New York Times Company; reprinted by permission), May 8, 1977.*

ROGER SALE

> I was born right here in Clarion; I grew up in that big brown turreted house next to Percy's Texaco. My mother was a fat lady who used to teach first grade. Her maiden name was Lacey Dabney.

This paragraph opens the second chapter of Anne Tyler's *Earthly Possessions*, and it is very arch. What do I know about "that" house, or Clarion, or Percy, that I should be thus invited in; if I accept the invitation, what can I make of someone who calls her mother "a fat lady," or who imagines, without seeming herself to care, that I need to know the fat lady's maiden name? Nor do matters improve when she starts speaking of herself:

> These were my two main worries when I was a child: one was that I was not their true daughter, and would be sent away. The other was that I *was* their true daughter and would never, ever manage to escape to the outside world.

Thus twelve years, or, as it turns out, thirty-five, of Charlotte Emory's life are reduced to a cartoon, and by her own hand, the possible anguish is then lost.

If what Anne Tyler had intended were a cartoon, then all might be well. . . . [But] *Earthly Possessions*, at least in its best moments, is a straightforward realistic novel about Charlotte Emory's abduction by Jake Simms, a pathetic young man who is trying to rob a bank just as Charlotte is standing in line to draw out her savings so she can at last leave home. The robbery fizzles, Simms takes Charlotte as hostage by bus to Baltimore and then by car to the South. All the coy parts of the novel, the writing that is at once glib and strained, come not in the story of the getaway but in alternating chapters which describe Charlotte's past as one of the depressed and zany inmates of "that big brown turreted house." To add to the awkwardness, Tyler won't let Charlotte allude in the present to anything in her past until the retrospective chapters can explain the references.

We have had enough, perhaps, of titles . . . themselves arch, novels that even at their best deprive the private lives they describe of dignity with a nervous or cute prose. Tyler's novel could have been called *Charlotte and Jake*, and, had it been, she might better have seen how much her patient and unhurried dialogue can reveal all we need to know about Charlotte's past just by showing us the person she is. [The] best effects of the writing are cumulative. . . .

Jake comes increasingly to rely on Charlotte's blankness, which he gradually understands as her trust of him. Tyler is excellent at making this blankness expressive; at the beginning, for instance, it is unnerving that neither of them mentions sex, but slowly Tyler shows that this is the result of Charlotte's being so absorbed in the trip that she seems in a cocoon, while Jake is too involved in his own determination to fail. . . .

[In] the alternating chapters, even near the end of the novel, the characters are still habitually given to false summarizing. . . . Knowledge comes slower and harder in the best of the novel, and there is no way to summarize it; I only wish Anne Tyler had retrieved *Charlotte and Jake*, the fine short novel that got lost in *Earthly Possessions*. (p. 39)

Roger Sale, in The New York Review of Books (*reprinted with permission from* The New York Review of Books; *copyright* © *1977 Nyrev, Inc.), May 26, 1977.*

GILBERTO PEREZ

Anne Tyler's *Earthly Possessions* is written in the first person, the narrator a housewife of thirty-five who, having lived all her life in the same house in Clarion, Maryland, informs us in the first sentence of the book that she has decided to leave her husband. Just as she is about to get cash for the trip, she is kidnapped by a bank robber. . . . [The] character's own assessment of her situation [is that of an] outrageous joke. Miss Tyler does well a peculiarly feminine mode of self-belittling, sardonic humor, something like Carol Burnett's. (p. 611)

I'm not sure Miss Tyler is aware that the alternating chapters of [*Earthly Possessions*], though all in the first person, are really in two different voices: the retrospective and the eyewitness first person, one may call them. We accept the convention, in an eyewitness account of ongoing events, that the narrator will come to find out things unexpected at the beginning, as indeed Charlotte does in her experience with the bank robber. But in a retrospective account, a summing up of past events from the perspective of the present, we feel cheated unless we get some sense all along that the narrator knows how things will turn out. (p. 612)

Gilberto Perez, in The Hudson Review *(copyright © 1977 by The Hudson Review, Inc.; reprinted by permission), Vol. XXX, No. 4, Winter, 1977-78.*

U

UNGARETTI, Giuseppe   1888-1970

An Italian poet, translator, and critic, Ungaretti is one of the major poets of the twentieth century. Considered by many to be the father of modern Italian poetry, he adapted the conventions of French blank verse to the Italian lyric, thus revitalizing that form. A concise craftsman, he concentrated on the power of the individual word, freeing his poetry of florid rhetoric. His work is often concerned with the spiritual quest of modern man, conveyed in a dreamlike, impressionistic manner with very personal imagery. (See also *CLC*, Vol. 7, and *Contemporary Authors*, Vols. 19-20; obituary, Vols. 25-28, rev. ed.; *Contemporary Authors Permanent Series*, Vol. 2.)

GLAUCO CAMBON

[The "I" of "I fiumi" (The Rivers)] defines itself more strongly and completely than anywhere else in *L'allegria*. (p. 584)

Bits of personal history rise to the surface, whether the persona evokes his lost Africa or his more recently abandoned Paris. Mostly, though, in the other poems it is a nonhistorical self that emerges (or seeks resubmersion in the All), with fragments of memory floating around. But in "I fiumi" the "I" takes stock of its whole history; it repossesses its vital ambience; it momentarily finds the "innocent country" elsewhere so poignantly missed, and strikes roots in its native soil without having to surrender its mobility. It is a historical self. Accordingly, the poem takes shape as a total epiphany rather than as a fragmentary illumination. It does not merely pierce and subvert, it orders and recapitulates— a rare operation for any modern poet whose beginnings must be subversive. Not just the moment out of time, the timeless instant; but the duration, the river of time, which one can also ply backwards, toward the source. . . . [The] action of *recognizing* himself has sprung in the persona from [the] reviewing-reliving of his own past. Memory, the Bergsonian *mémoire* as opposed to the inertial opacity of *matière*, equals consciousness and is conceived as the liberating force, in sharp contrast to later phases of Ungaretti's work where memory will be equated with guilt and phobia, "Caino" in *Sentimento del tempo* providing the clearest example. . . . There (as in "Alla noia," where memory is apostrophized as "sad mockery" and "darkness of blood") memory is the negative existential principle, the doom from which deliverance is sought, and the poet opposes it to innocence (as in his essays).

Here instead, in "I fiumi," memory is the cleansing of consciousness, and it appears as individual as well as historical, ethnic memory which extends backward into prenatal memory—a kind of *historical anamnesis* (notice the pointed reference to Plato's concept in Ungaretti's *Ragioni d'una poesia* . . .). . . . [In] "Risvegli" anamnesis deranges the persona who . . . risks losing himself utterly, and has to come back to himself in an "awakening" that is the opposite of the existential recognition attained in "I fiumi". . . . And in "Girovago," anamnesis takes the form of déjà vu, leading to disenchantment and estrangement, for every new place the persona visits turns out to have been only too well known from earlier, indefinable phases. Not so in "I fiumi," where anamnesis is the natural projection of individual consciousness and thus helps the self to find, to recognize himself, by constituting his history as an offshoot of his prehistory. In "Risvegli" the persona has placed himself this side of the dark beyond which is his prehistory; he is "lost with his memory" in pursuit of "those lost lives" (*quelle vite perse*), all right, but the prenatal reaches are glimpsed and exorcised; the demonstrative word applied to them is a distancing one, *quelle* (those), while the qualifying adjective, *perse* (lost), implies an irrecoverable loss, a kind of existential waste from which the reconnoitering self recoils in fear, to fall back upon the reassurance of familiar things. Anamnesis can be a disquieting, even a shattering revelation.

In "I fiumi," on the contrary, the hammering iteration of the demonstrative adjective *questo* (this) and its cognate adverb *qui* (here) conveys firm proximity, showing that the persona has placed himself right in the middle of everything that could have otherwise remained disturbingly beyond his reach. . . . Things are within the persona's grasp, indeed he feels that here he has really recognized himself as an intimate part of the universe. The heightening repetition of *questo*, always at the beginning of a line . . . structures the poem hieratically; anaphora results in litany. . . . Thus a form of stability counterpoints the flowing of fluvial imagery and the protean changes of the persona in the first part. The cue comes from the first two lines of the poem:

> Mi *tengo* a *quest* 'albero mutilato
> abbandonato in *questa* dolina

> I *hold* on to *this* mutilated tree
> forlorn in *this* glen

Here the cardinal word *questa*, though already emphasized by close repetition, is still embedded in mid-line; it will emerge to dominant initial position later on, at the crucial moment of recognition ("Questo è l'Isonzo," This is the Isonzo). So much for the supposed lack of structure in Ungaretti's poetry—if anybody were still willing to credit that hoary imputation. (pp. 584-86)

Ungaretti's choice of current speech to the exclusion (in the *Allegria* phase) of courtly diction, his rejection of traditional prosody in favor of a free rhythm, his concentration on what is elemental in word and structure, make of *L'allegria* not so much an avant-garde experiment in free verse as a return to the literary source of Italian poetry. Paratactic, idiomatic, imbued with a religious solemnity (as witness the ceremony of symbolic death and baptismal rebirth which is enacted in stanzas 2, 3 and 4 to culminate in the vaguely Christlike figure of the acrobat walking on water), verbally pared down to austere simplicity, attuned to harmony with creation: "I fiumi" rejuvenates Italian poetry.... Ungaretti's career will complete the cycle by going on from the Gothic to baroque, from Saint Francis and Jacopone to Petrarch, the Petrarchists of Europe, and Leopardi, in a personal rehearsal of the whole literary history of Italy and Europe that is marked ... by the transition from ... assertive to hypothetical modes, from austerity to tense luxuriance.

Thus the whole style of *L'allegria* ... amounts to a feat of cultural anamnesis. (pp. 586-87)

Never again, in the course of his long creative career, would Ungaretti find such an ecstatic, calm voice, such a vision of oneness with the elements. Compare the steadiness of "I fiumi" with the demonic restlessness of the persona's rhetorical stance in *Sentimento del tempo* pieces like "La pietà" or "Caino." Or again, compare the effortless quality of diction in "I fiumi" (whose scarcity of acknowledged variants seems to indicate a massive accession of grace) with the rather labored, if poignant, style of "Canzone" in *La terra promessa*.... In "I fiumi" verbal and existential innocence is a gift; in "Canzone," instead, it appears as a glimpsed idea of distant perfection, strenuously pursued. (pp. 587-88)

Ungaretti's development as a poet after *L'allegria* could be seen as the loss of innocence and the constant endeavor to regain it; which helps us to understand why his valuation of the fundamental word *memory* and semantic equivalents changed so drastically from "plus" to "minus" in the course of his career. When we realize how peculiar Ungaretti's personal destiny was, and how cogently his imagination used it to make it exemplary, so that the four rivers of his individual history could become, rather than four accidental countries, the four rivers of a unique Eden, we shall see why his achievement grows with the passing of time. (p. 588)

> *Glauco Cambon, "'The Rivers': Ungaretti's Anamnesis," in* Books Abroad *(copyright 1970 by the University of Oklahoma Press), Vol. 44, No. 4, Autumn, 1970, pp. 584-91.*

ANDREW WYLIE

Ungaretti's poems are of their time to such an extent that within the volume that collects *Vita d'un uomo*, four divisions are easily seen. These divisions are: *L'allegria*, in which a spare and hard language describes the trenches of World War I; *Sentimento del tempo*, in which a more peaceful time generally gives rise to a quieter language: *Il dolore* and *Un grido e paesaggi*, in which the sheer size of World War II was enough to shatter any semblance of fragility; *La terra promessa*, *Il taccuino del vecchio*, and the latest poems, which join the previous languages of war and peace for our time.

Of all Ungaretti's works, the most peaceful are furthest from us now. But how much peace is there in these poems? Very little; even in *Sentimento del tempo* and the poems since *Taccuino*, there is often an extremely violent language.

What Ungaretti has done in his poetry is similar to what the Viennese school did to the musical tradition. Like magnets brought close at the same poles, words stand next to their surrounding words in tension.... [This] is a matter of experimental time [alteration in tempi, of varying degree, intensity, and interval]. (p. 611)

Within each line, we experience a certain logic of the flow, only to have that logic "surprised" at the beginning of the next line.

Now [this] process can occasionally be seen in Ungaretti's early work, for instance in the beginning of "Veglia" (Watch): "Un'intera nottata / buttato vicino / a un compagno / massacrato". This is a common method in the later *Sentimento del tempo*, and is one reason why the poems in that volume are, as a whole, the least violent in Ungaretti's work.

But already, as in "Agonia" (Agony), there is something different: "Morire come le allodole assetate / sul miraggio" ("To die like larks parched / on the mirage"). Here the lines are no longer divided at the point of greatest degree of alteration, which instead occurs between "larks" and "parched."

Now take the beginning of a still later poem, "Tu ti spezzasti" (You Shattered): "I molti, immani, sparsi, grigi sassi / Frementi ancora alle segrete fionde / di originarie fiamme soffocate" ("The many, monstrous, scattered, grey rocks / Still shuddering in secret slings / Of choked natal flames"). Here there's a great density of alteration *within* the lines, with less time to grasp alteration than there was in the Pound, or in "Veglia." When we hear "The many," we think: "The many—*what*?" But instead of "The many rocks," which is what we might expect, we have "The many, monstrous." So we hear that and think: "The many, monstrous—*what*?" But again, instead of the noun for which we're waiting, there's another adjective.

If dislocation of syntax accounts for the density of alteration in the first line, in the second and third lines alteration is dependent rather on the unexpected coupling of words— "secret" with "slings," "choked" with "natal" and "flames." Unless we've read the poem before, we don't remember words joined like this, so we can't expect them. They are all the more surprising because they are joined within the same line.

Words stand next to their surrounding words in tension: between each adjective and its noun, between each noun and its verb, is a high degree of alteration, with the logic of the flow repeatedly broken. This density of alteration gives violence even in a slow tempo.

So if these poems are of their time, and if there are distinctly separate voices between one division and another—between the poems of one war and another, between the poems of one "peaceful" interval and the next—there's still unity. We do not live under the old order; poetry that reflects our time must break that order. So now that "only the improbable and violent are important," this is a new unity. Ungaretti's poetry is true to his time; we are living his violence now. (pp. 612-13)

> Andrew Wylie, "*Ungaretti's Poetry and Experimental Time,*" in Books Abroad (*copyright 1970 by the University of Oklahoma Press*), *Vol. 44, No. 4, Autumn, 1970, pp. 611-13.*

TAKIS PAPATZONIS

[On first reading Ungaretti's poetry,] I was greatly moved by his delicate poetic sensibility, by the aesthetic beauty of his immaterial forms which seemed to belong austerely to "pure poetry," by the masterly technical elaboration with which he combined deeply moving emotions and situations. Parallel to this was the absence of every device of rhetoric of inflation. Instead, I found a classical brevity, a condensation achieved by masterful dexterity, which gave to his poems the impression of musical epigrams. . . .

In the genius of Ungaretti, and in the new form which he was giving to the Italian lyric, I met something unprecedented, a renovation syncronized with new directions. (p. 616)

[I have read] Ungaretti, though a victim of his age, nevertheless represented the transition from a rhetorical and lyrical babbling to an austere and laconic style. Even so, this theory goes, Ungaretti had achieved nothing more than an "infertile formalism," in contrast to the perfections achieved by the newer Montale and Quasimodo.

Permit me to disagree with these arbitrary divisions, this false dividng line of the thirties. The flow of aesthetic evolution has been uninterrupted; no period has been isolated from another; and the age . . . has produced poets and writers who are among the glories of any literature—Rilke, Mallarmé, Appollinaire, Valéry, Claudel, Eluard, Yeats, Joyce, Eliot, Pound, Lorca, Caváfis, Sikelianós, and the Kazantzákis of the *Odyssey*—to mention many, but not all. Equal to these, in worth and importance, is Giuseppe Ungaretti. He is anything but a victim of his age, and his work demonstrates that poetry has flowed unimpeded in the seven decades of our century in a uniform pursuit of whatever is beautiful in its myriad forms. His entire work is proof against the falsity of this imaginary barrier of the thirties. Further still: if the work written after the thirties is to survive, it will be because it has been nurtured on the masterpieces of the immediate past. Great periods of literature are not barriers or dividing lines; rather they are floodlights that illuminate vast regions of both past and future.

Ungaretti refined the innate musicality of Italian poetry, made it more immaterial, transmuted vulgarity and rhetoric into a sober and disciplined formal harmony of almost mathematical proportions. He must be placed, in value and importance, by the side of Apollinaire and Mallarmé and Valéry, among the great renovators of modern times to whom future generations will owe a great debt. (p. 617)

> Takis Papatzonis, "*Ungaretti: The Great Renovator of Modern Italian Poetry,*" in Books Abroad (*copyright 1970 by the University of Okla-*

homa Press), *Vol. 44, No. 4, Autumn, 1970, pp. 616-17.*

TOM O'NEILL

[Ungaretti's] sense of guilt, of corruption in the nature of man— . . . man who, without the help of God's grace, cannot hope to redeem himself, which is at the centre of Jansenist doctrine [—is] to be found explicitly stated on more than one occasion in the critical writings of the poet. . . .

This sense of guilt is to be seen in the consciousness of the fleetingness of time, in the transiency of human existence. (p. 61)

[Jansenist doctrine] is a point of departure from which [Ungaretti] will move out in search of an order and permanence on a spiritual level which will find correspondence in a search for order and permanence on an artistic level in the poetic form. The aim of the poet will be to achieve in his poetry that state of grace which, when achieved, will remove the sense of guilt in him and restore him to his original state of innocence before the Fall and give him once more a sense of *measure* which, given the link between life and poetry in Ungaretti, is never merely equated with a simple aesthetic metrical game. (pp. 62-3)

[Ungaretti's] destruction of the traditional metres of Italian poetry is not so much a destruction as a *purification* of that tradition in order to build it afresh. This reconstruction is seen . . . in the reintroduction of punctuation and traditional versification in *Sentimento del tempo* but . . . it is a reconstruction which is already present *consciously* in the poems of *L'Allegria* in the return to the individual word, the *parola* . . . according to the poet, the basic rhythmic unit of the Italian language. (p. 63)

[Right] from the outset of his poetic career there is in Ungaretti a concern for form and tradition and it is his concern for these, through a purification of them, that constitutes to a great extent his originality in these early years. . . .

[The] consciousness of the fleeting nature of time and, along with this, the sense of guilt, of Jansenist mark, which has been individuated right from the outset in Ungaretti's poetry . . . is constituted by a search for stability and permanence. . . . If immortality of the body is not possible, immortality of the spirit is through form. (p. 64)

[The crisis expressed in the poetry of *Sentimento del tempo*] was much more than just a personal one but in the years of Fascism in Italy and of general spiritual upheaval in Europe as a whole, was the crisis of an age, the crisis of a society. (p. 65)

[Valery's perception that even the most ancient and best ordered civilization is mortal and fragile enough to perish by accident is] alien to Ungaretti, not only by nature but also by the faith he has in the power of poetry which, in its essence, is essentially faith in the single word. . . . (p. 66)

Evidently the concern for form and and tradition that has characterized the poetry of Ungaretti from the outset has . . . moved beyond the personal sphere in which the poet, platonically, was merely concerned with the perpetuation of the man, through his works, to a much more embracing sphere, namely that of saving the works themselves, now threatened. The aim of the poet is now, through his poetry, to rebuild and recreate civilisation. Poetry now takes on more than ever a moral content and the concern for form, if it becomes predominant, does so because it is now clear to the poet that it is precisely form that is the highest expression of civilisation. (pp. 66-7)

Nor . . . is this merely an empty, rhetorical concern for form . . . but it is a concern through form, for the very existence of civilisation itself. . . .

Clearly there has been a distinct evolution in the poetry of Ungaretti over the years and if it still takes its roots very much in the personal events of the poet's life, it is clearly no longer meant to be merely an expression of a personal situation, if indeed it ever had been, but one of more universal significance: more, it is meant to be one of civic significance—not in the narrowly nationalistic sense as in the poetry of the late Nineteenth century—but civic in the sense that it celebrates and perpetuates the highest ideals and aspirations of man—civic in the sense indicated by Eliot in *Tradition and the individual talent*. . . . (p. 68)

[The poems of *La terra promessa* can be seen] as a perpetuation and a renewal—in a personal key—of all that is of value in civilisation by drawing inspiration from that same civilisation's literary heritage. It is this concern that dictates Ungaretti's choice of the traditional and most beautiful poetic vehicles in Italian, the *canzone* and the *sestina*, and it is this same concern that sends him for his subject-matter back to the Classical inheritance of Italy in Aeneas and Dido. (p. 70)

> Tom O'Neill, "The Problem of Formalism in Ungaretti's Poetry," in Italian Quarterly (copyright © 1970 by Italian Quarterly), Fall, 1970, pp. 59-73.

MARGARET BROSE

Ungaretti endows his verbal structures with thematic force [in *L'Allegria*]; the syntactic and semantic encodations converge in such a way that the former becomes a transcription of the latter. Encoded within the poems' structural patterns lies *L'Allegria*'s central myth of Edenic harmony and cosmic immersion: the "paese innocente". The convergence is in fact threefold: syntax and semantics both parallel Ungaretti's psychological experience of Edenic unification in the trench. The most striking characteristics of that experience are the poet's sense of identification with his fellow soldiers and all natural phenomena, on the one hand, and the sense of spatial and temporal immobility, on the other hand. These two conditions are transcribed thematically into a static Edenic vision of universal harmony. Their structural counterparts are, respectively, metaphor and parataxis.

By metaphor I refer to the immediate and synthetic verbal representation of relations of identity; by parataxis, the syntactical representation of a world without spatial or temporal periodicity. Metaphor is in *L'Allegria* the dominant paratactical stylistic device.

Classical rhetoricians such as Aristotle and Quintillian regarded metaphor as a poetic trope. In recent years metaphor has been viewed as one of the fundamental principles of language formation and phenomenological apperception. *L'Allegria* is "metaphorical" in both respects (as are mystical and primitive perceptions of reality). There is little consensus, however, as to the exact form and function of metaphor as trope; or for example, as to whether such rhetorical figures as metonymy and synecdoche are distinct tropes or

are simply forms of metaphor. There is a similar lack of consensus with regard to the nomenclature applied to *L'Allegria*: its basic syntactical construction has been described as *analogia, metafora, comparazione, similitudine,* and *apposizione*. Yet all of these terms designate a relationship of similarity between two things: a relationship of metaphor. (pp. 45-6)

Metaphor in *L'Allegria* . . . encompasses all the rhetorical devices used to describe one thing in terms of something else. The basic perspective employed is that of analogy. One might even say that the perspective is two-dimensional, and that in *L'Allegria* the metaphors operate on two levels: generality (essence) and specificity (attribute). All phenomena are perceived in terms of a general similarity: participation within a universal harmony; analogy in terms of consubstantiality. This is, so to speak, a "deep-structure" metaphorical relation. There are, moreover, those phenomena which are perceived also in terms of a particular analogous aspect: a specific similarity between two specific dissimilars. This would be a "surface-structure" metaphorical relation. All phenomena are analogous in essence; some phenomena have analogous attributes.

One might also describe these two dimensions in terms of "explicit" and "implicit" metaphorical constructions. Those figures in *L'Allegria* which refer to a specific similarity between two things are stated explicitly. They are, properly speaking, similes, the two terms being joined by the connective *come*. However, many of the figures in *L'Allegria* express a general relationship—a similarity not of any one attribute, but ascription of a general essence. Here the relationship is given implicitly: the two terms are not described as "like" each other in any particular aspect but are presented in a mutually interdependent relationship; their interaction depends upon a "deep-structure" metaphorical identification. This implicit metaphor usually takes the form of two substantives joined by the preposition *di*. These categories do not constitute a binary opposition ("specific-explicit" figures versus "general-implicit" figures, for example), since any two things which share a specific similarity also share a general similarity of essence. The designations of "specific" and "general" are not, therefore, mutually exclusive: they are intended only to suggest that all those phenomena not participating in an overt simile, participate nevertheless in a universal harmony. The distinction between explicit and implicit metaphors, however, is both syntactically and semantically manifest.

L'Allegria's explicit metaphors are "similes", which are descriptive forms of metaphor. (pp. 47-8)

A simile . . . is not only discursive and logical, it is semantically unilateral: both its terms are restricted to their literal senses. My designation of *L'Allegria*'s similes as "surface-structure" metaphors implies, therefore, both overt syntactical connectives and restricted, unilateral semantics. This explains in part why the "essential" (or "radical") metaphor is a richer rhetorical figure: syntactically it is compressed while semantically it is extended onto both literal and figurative levels. The implicit or essential metaphors of *L'Allegria*'s ("substantive-*di*-substantive") all exhibit this syntactic compression and semantic extension. To achieve a similar density, *L'Allegria*'s similes must rely upon a startling juxtaposition of the two terms' literal senses only. Essential metaphors are naturally catachrestic, similes only so by design. The fact that many of *L'Allegria*'s similes approach catachresis reveals the depth of Ungaretti's metaphoric perception of reality at that period. (p. 48)

In *L'Allegria* there are well over fifty similes (explicit metaphors). The majority appear in the chapters "Il Porto Sepolto" and "Naufragi", those poems written between December, 1915 and August, 1917 while Ungaretti fought in the trenches of Carso.... The chronology is not unimportant: it suggests that a heightened metaphoric perception occurred within the trench. All five of *L'Allegria*'s chapters contain similes, as indeed do Ungaretti's other collections. In "Il Porto Sepolto" and "Naufragi", however, the similes occur with greater frequency (twenty-seven and nineteen times respectively) and greater force. Their strength as imagery derives from the catachrestic union of the two terms: from the novelty or unexpectedness of their juxtaposition. Since the two terms of a simile have only literal signification, their confrontation is one-dimensional or "horizontal"; a metaphor, on the other hand, contains bilevel signification (literal *and* figurative) and its terms interact "vertically" as well as horizontally. The similes in "Il Porto Sepolto" and "Naufragi" explore the limits of their one dimension, and the two terms are usually startlingly dissimilar.... To this end, Ungaretti often compares something animate to something inanimate, or an abstract to a concrete entity....

Only two of the twelve poems in "Ultime", Ungaretti's pre-war poems, contain similes, and these are discursive and heavily modified. (p. 49)

The only two similes in "Prime", Ungaretti's post-war poems, are even less striking. This chapter marks the transition between *L'Allegria* and *Sentimento del Tempo*, but lacks the strength of both. Only three of "Prime"'s seven poems retain the laconic style of *L'Allegria;* the remaining four are especially discursive prose poems. The two similes of the chapter appear in prose poems; or, rather, they disappear within the diffusive prosaic matrix. (pp. 50-1)

The chapter "Girovago" contains war poems written after Ungaretti's trench experience. The poems exhibit some of the same weaknesses as those in "Ultime" and "Prime", but with this important difference: "Girovago" retains that aura of cosmic *communitas* experienced within the trench. Although neither of the two similes in "Girovago" presents a particularly unusual comparison, they both effectively evoke that mood of innocence and awe which accompanied Ungaretti's revelation of universal harmony. (p. 51)

Ungaretti's similes are most impressive in the chapters "Il Porto Sepolto" and "Naufragi", those poems actually written in the trench. Here they most approximate the "essential" metaphor syntactically and semantically. A simile normally tends toward the discursive mode. In "Il Porto Sepolto" and "Naufragi", however, it assumes a more compressed form, without extensive modification, while still obeying laws of logic and grammar: here its syntax is most integrative. In these two chapters the simile is also at its most catachrestic semantically, its two terms being drawn for the most part from different classifications and realms of experience: their comparison provokes, therefore, a revelation of what Shelley called a "before unapprehended" and often fantastic relation of similarity.

The simile in "Il Porto Sepolto" and "Naufragi" mirrors Ungaretti's experience in the trench: in that spiritual and physical wasteland he perceived a bond of similarity and fraternity between all things no matter how ostensibly dissimilar. In that world of spatial and temporal immobility a revelation of *communitas* was achieved, instantaneous and intense. Ungaretti's sense of identity with other phenomena is not restricted to objects or animals which, like birds, bear some conventional metaphorical relation to men. This is not to imply, however, that "Il Porto Sepolto" and "Naufragi" are devoid of such similes. Many of the figures used by Ungaretti to suggest the identification of men with natural phenomena are posited upon rather manifest aspects of similarity, especially those drawn from the animal and vegetable kingdoms. (p. 52)

The most effective similes in "Il Porto Sepolto" and "Naufragi" function much this way. A "vertical" (or paradigmatic) movement of meaning between two parallel situations, one literal and one figurative, is denied; to compensate, Ungaretti exploits the "horizontal" (or syntagmatic) distance between the terms' literal or contiguous meanings. The semantic distance that the two terms must traverse in order to meet on grounds of similarity evokes unexpected vistas of dissimilarity. The power of the simile resides in what is left unsaid: in this way it best approximates a metaphor's parallel levels of signification. When the comparison is too accessible, we question neither the manifest similarity nor the latent dissimilarities. When, on the other hand, the stated similarity is incongruous and uncommon, we are forced to inquire how the two terms are similar and, thus, how they are not: a Pandora's box is opened.

Many similes in "Il Porto Sepolto" and "Naufragi" compare a tangible and intangible term, thus assuring an *a priori* element of incongruity. (p. 53)

The verb in *L'Allegria*'s similes is of great importance. The verb is generally an active transitive verb, and usually in the first person singular, present tense. The verb defines the specific similarity between the two terms, and evokes by contrast their dissimilarities. When the verb is in the first person singular, it also defines the poet's interaction with those phenomena. In the war-poem chapters "Il Porto Sepolto" and "Naufragi", the verb is always metaphorical and often metamorphic: either emblematic of a particular metaphorical identification between two phenomena other than the poet himself, or the vehicle for Ungaretti's own metamorphosis into some non-human phenomenon.

Metaphorical relations between two phenomena are established by means of Ungaretti's interaction with them. Because of this, the similes in these two chapters are never abstractions; they are immediate and concrete.... [The] two terms of the simile are instantaneously telescoped into the *present* and *presence* of the poet. The similes become "concretized" because even if one of the terms is intangible or abstract, the ground of their analogy depends upon a verb of concrete action. The tangibility of the one term is transferred to the second by means of the verb. In these similes the verb not only describes a metaphorical relation, it is actually a "metaphor" by itself: it functions semantically on two levels, referring to two parallel objects or situations. In reference to one, the verb's meaning is literal, in reference to the other, figurative.

It is this bilevel signification which ... differentiates a metaphor from a simile. (pp. 55-6)

Ungaretti's practice of using verbs metaphorically approaches what Aristotle calls making a metaphor "graphic". For Aristotle, the liveliness of a metaphor is greatly increased when the "hearers *see* things", by which he means "using expressions that represent things as in a state of activity". Most of the Homeric examples of "graphic" metaphors cited by Aristotle show inanimate objects endowed with life by means of the actions they perform. Many inanimate phenomena in *L'Allegria* are, by means of an active verb, endowed with similar metaphorical life. (p. 56)

In the construction "noun-of-noun", an attribute or impression becomes a substantive rather than an adjective: it is, therefore, as a grammatical *entity,* separate from and equal to the object once incorporating it. (p. 62)

[In] Ungaretti's "animistic" vision in *L'Allegria,* all phenomena and their attributes are perceived as autonomous and participating equally in a cosmic harmony. The "noun-of-noun" construction abounds in *L'Allegria,* where it substantivizes attributes and succinctly fuses abstract and concrete entities. Just as the metaphorical verbs in *L'Allegria* permit Ungaretti to interact with abstract and inanimate phenomena, the metaphorical "noun-of-noun" construction permits interaction between the phenomena themselves. (p. 63)

Giuseppe Ungaretti's *L'Allegria* is "paratactical" in its syntax, metrics, and semantics. But it is especially the "noun-of-noun" construction which permits interaction among entities, concrete and abstract, and substantivizes attributes. Metaphorical relationships are instantaneously and graphically represented—mirroring *L'Allegria*'s atemporal, immobile vision which precludes predication and periodicity.... [This is] a stylistic device inherited from the Symbolist poets and adopted by Ungaretti to express his vision of universal harmony....

In *Sentimento del Tempo* the underlying vision is of hierarchical separateness and the rhetoric is hypotactical. (p. 65)

[What] is parataxis in *L'Allegria* becomes hypotaxis in *Sentimento*.... Hypotaxis is based on periodicity, the product of time, and thus perfectly mirrors Ungaretti's growing obsession with time after 1919. *L'Allegria*'s vision of ecstatic cosmic immersion gives way to *Sentimento*'s experience of disunion and death, and to Ungaretti as witness to his own isolation and transience. (p. 66)

The majority of *L'Allegria*'s some sixty implicit metaphors ("noun-of-noun") are found in the second chapter, "Il Porto Sepolto", written in the trench.... [Most] "noun-of-noun" metaphors in "Il Porto Sepolto" join two independent entities. Their union is all the more effective therefore: there are no immediate syntactical or semantic indications as to which noun is subordinate to the other.

This type of metaphor is initially experienced as neither "horizontal" (as in a syntactical progression) nor "vertical" (as in metaphorical bisignification): it is an immobile, immediate fusion of two entities into a new whole. It is, therefore, paradigmatic of the cosmic fusion felt by Ungaretti throughout his trench experience.... Metaphorical language is both epiphanic and epistemological: it reveals relationships and provides knowledge of the world. (pp. 67-8)

"Prime", *L'Allegria*'s last chapter, marks the "first" poems of Ungaretti's second period and a decisive falling-away from the Edenic vision of cosmic harmony expressed by the metaphors and parataxis of *L'Allegria.*

The parataxis of *L'Allegria* is not arbitrary. It is, perhaps, the syntactical mode best suited to express an epiphanic experience of harmony. It is the mode of prayer. (p. 71)

L'Allegria's metaphors and parataxis create illuminations: they "figure" forth the ultimate harmony of the world. This interpretation seems consonant with Ungaretti's own perceptions. (p. 72)

[He has said] that modern poetry seeks to transcend time.... Poetry seeks, by means of the word, to recreate eternal Edenic harmony, now lost to mankind since the Fall. The poetic word seeks to recapture its "originaria purezza". Poetry's mission is religious, according to Ungaretti, and "la poesia è testimonianza d'Iddio". In the beginning the word was the world. Since the Fall, word and world are severed. The poet seeks to rejoin them, to *know* the world through the word, to transcend the Copernican crisis of the unknowability of the universe and the non-referentiality of language. By means of the word ... word becomes world. The poetic act creates a promised land. Poetry is, simultaneously, epiphany and epistemology. (pp. 72-3)

Margaret Brose, "Metaphor and Simile in Giuseppe Ungaretti's 'L'Allegria'," in Lingua E Stile *(reprinted by permission of Società editrice il Mulino, Bologna), March, 1976, pp. 43-73.*

WAIN, John 1925-

Wain is a British novelist, poet, short story writer, essayist, and editor. His fiction and much of his early poetry humorously attack the British class system, though he is more concerned with human dignity than with broad social injustice. Wain's poetry has recently come under attack for its lack of forcefulness. (See also *CLC*, Vol. 2, and *Contemporary Authors*, Vols. 5-8, rev. ed.)

JASCHA KESSLER

[Wain's] verse way [in "Letters to Five Artists"] is to combine the sonorously slack and portentous tones of late Eliot with the informal chat of Auden and the broken eye-rhythms of W. C. Williams. All on the surface, you see, for easy scanning. Not exactly a pastiche though; a synthesis, rather, of what these poets have left for the serious poet writing in England today: a means of talking intelligently about what matters—the fate of the single spirit in this world. . . .

[Exile among Barbarians] is the general theme of the book; the great poet whose works were all youth and love, the flesh, and was forced to live out his days in a bitter, rude place by imperial edict, and who came to see our lives' essence in the flow of water, water which changes like our lives. By singling out five artist friends and thinking of them Wain puts together a world for himself, enough of a world at any rate to live by, invisible and evanescent as it may be. . . .

It is a unified vision, if a sad one. The only trouble is that the book as a whole lacks force and attractive energy. I fail to find much trace of the unseen field of force that a thinking mind leaves in its wake: poetry, in short. Instead, there is a general feeling that, yes, the poet knows what he wants to say, and can't say it in prose because prose would sound pretentious (like so many of our "philosophers" and pundits and gurus from sociology and "psychology").

And I suspect that what he has to say to his friends (and to us) is simple: that there is not much to go on with, but that you must be praised because you do after all go on, even making something from it . . . because you are creators, loving and suffering and joying in work. But Wain's speech in poetry is ponderous, too, laudatory, elegiac, philosophical and so on. But not, unfortunately, anywhere very interesting.

Jascha Kessler, "Eavesdropping on Letters to Friends," in The Los Angeles Times *(copyright, 1970, Los Angeles Times; reprinted by permission), May 17, 1970, p. 42.*

TERRY EAGLETON

Feng, it seems, was the original of Shakespeare's Claudius, and [John Wain's *Feng*] takes him as the protagonist of the Hamlet drama. . . . Feng's inner life, such as it is, remains strikingly tedious; he comes through in his prose-monologues as a garrulous bore. Nothing in the poem really comes alive: it's a savage, violent society and a harrowing plot, but all this is curiously tamed and toned down, filtered through a sensibility too equable, domesticated and undramatic to be adequate to the turbulent demands of the subject-matter. When Wain writes 'I felt their needs drawn through my flesh like wires', it's difficult to believe that he really feels it, anywhere below the cranium. The theme of the poem is POWER (its capitals)—power in that abstract sense characteristic of bourgeois liberalism. Wain seems to dislike POWER, although it's not clear what he feels about the power propping up the society which permits liberals like himself to protest against POWER. (pp. 78-9)

Terry Eagleton, in Stand *(copyright © by Stand), Vol. 17, No. 1 (1975-76).*

LAWRENCE R. RIES

The proper place to begin a study of Wain's poetry is with the examination of his basic premise: human goodness and love shall outlast violence and brutality. He is willing to admit to man's instinctive selfishness . . . , but human interaction ultimately transcends and overcomes petty individual inadequacies. Wain traces the source of the violence in the world to mechanization, industrialization, and the consequent dehumanization of modern society. Western civilization, he says, no longer breeds loving, feeling individuals but automatons who, having lost their identity, are ready to pass on to others the psychological violence of which they themselves are victims. Violence breeds greater violence, and the destructive forces that are loose in the world must be brought under control. Finally, he examines the artist's role in a world of violence. In a predictably evasive manner, he insists that the artist must not escape from his responsibilities by submission to the forces of destruction, but must rise above the violence and in this way withstand the onslaught of the darkness.

Again and again it is evident that poems written from the neohumanistic conviction are means of escape rather than of confrontation. As if in answer to those poets who have committed themselves with more abandon, these poets see small hope for those who struggle against violence. . . . With the poetry presently under discussion, I feel there is no real desire for new insights, or new understanding of violence, but only an intellectual evasion of its implications.

John Wain assumes the role of spokesman for the neohumanistic position with some vigor both in his poetry and in his critical remarks. He has made it quite clear that he considers those poets who are searching into the secret recesses of the psyche in an attempt to come to terms with the modern consciousness inferior to those whose assumptions about human nature are more stable and who are thus able to suggest cures for the illness. . . . [The fault] lies not with Wain's humanism but with the narrow and crippling limitations he imposes upon it. He carries this to such a point that he accuses those who hold skeptical or cynical attitudes towards the modern world of inventing their pessimism. . . . (pp. 131-32)

Wain does not exhibit a continuing evolution of theme from his early poetry to his later. His style, on the other hand, developed markedly in *Wildtrack* (1965) and *Letters to Five Artists* (1970). . . . [He] seems to use an expanding style to compensate for a static, overburdened theme. (p. 132)

The victory of humanity over violence becomes a major theme in Wain's poetry, and he sees the vocal assertion of the human element over everything else as a primary function of the artist: "The artist's function is always to *humanize* the society he is living in, to assert the importance of humanity in the teeth of whatever is currently trying to annihilate that importance." The early poems of *A Word Carved on a Sill* show the poet striving to write according to this prescription. . . .

["When It Comes" illustrates] a major failing in Wain's humanistic stance, for while expressing sentiments of private compassion, [it fails] to come to terms with the situation at hand. The poet's emotions are not directed towards the violence and savagery that is visited upon the hundreds of thousands of suffering human beings, but he thinks of those who are not yet born, those who will never have to suffer. Although our first response might well be, "What a compassionate man this poet is!" the tone of the poem suggests that its object is not the suffering of others, but the ennobling of the self through high-minded thoughts in the face of death. (p. 133)

The forces of violence are seen [in "Patriotic Poem"] as ineffective against the ennobled human spirit reinforced by patriotic concerns. But Wain again reneges somewhat on his commitment, for in this triumph of humanity over the base powers of war, the people surrender an element of their individuality to their country:

> Rises the living breath of all her children;
> And her deep heart and theirs, who can distinguish?

The repetition of such sentiments as this soon degenerates into humanistic doggerel, and the humanism runs very thin. He attempts to elevate humanity in both these poems, but the price ultimately is too high. It is usually at the cost of some greater virtue that he is able to extol the lesser.

This compromise is unfortunate, for at times Wain achieves

a remarkable poetic insight into the psychic violence of the modern condition. "To a Friend in Trouble" brings together elements found in Gunn and Plath in an effective fusion. The loss of love in this poem is traced to the loss of other values, and this relation is expressed in a series of violent images. . . . [The] loss of love is not a personal event but one in which all who live in the modern world share. . . . Wain rises to greater compassion in this poem than in "When It Comes" because he admits his own helplessness and participation in the selfishness of the world without becoming self-indulgent. (pp. 133-34)

This poem is held together by a fine tension exemplified by the ambiguous role of the speaker as both observer and participant. But Wain does not often lower himself to the role of participant; he is more frequently seen as the detached observer making moral judgments upon the world. It is in this position that he undoes the fine touches of a poem like "To A Friend in Trouble." (p. 135)

Two of Wain's most impressive poems explore violence as a destructive force from which the world must turn away. "A Song about Major Eatherly" and "On the Death of a Murderer" trace the disintegrating effects that violence has, not upon its victims, but upon those who initiate such action and also upon those who observe it. Violence is seen as a chain of reaction whose destructive effects cannot be stopped once set in motion.

"A Song about Major Eatherly" examines the gradual metamorphosis into a madman of the man who supposedly piloted the plane that dropped the bomb on Hiroshima. "Good news," says the poet, "It seems he loved them after all." . . . The "good news" is that Major Eatherly took upon himself the moral burden of his actions and rescued himself from the greater spiritual destruction. In piloting the plane that carried such devastation to its goal, he had resigned his humanity, for he had allowed himself to be used as an instrument rather than as a man. . . . There is, however, danger in this acknowledgment, for those who had earlier seen this action as a great patriotic act now must respond out of guilt, for in accepting himself as guilty, Eatherly is also pointing a finger at that society that produced and suppported his actions. He the destroyer then becomes a victim in his own society. . . . Eatherly's atonement is not a symbolic act. He is no scapegoat, for his repentance does not take away the common guilt; it rather increases it and calls forth greater violence in his hostile imprisonment. . . . (pp. 137-38)

The emotions that Wain expresses in this poem are easy to participate in, almost too inviting. And such emotions are exceedingly difficult to attack from a humanistic standpoint. However, it is precisely at this point that we can show why and how the neohumanistic response to violence is evasive. William Bradford Huie's book *The Hiroshima Pilot* exploded the myth that Eatherly piloted the plane that dropped the bomb and later was driven to self-destructive criminal acts through guilt for his part in the bombing. In reality, Eatherly commanded the advance weather plane (he was far away from Hiroshima when the bomb was dropped), and his conversion to pacifism grew more out of his earlier psychological problems that were intensified by his deep resentment that he was not given any publicity or fanfare for his role in the Hiroshima bombing than from a sense of profound moral guilt. . . . Wain is not guilty of purposefully distorting the truth, but I believe it exposes a humanistic laziness in his overall mentality, that in finding a mythologized story that fits his moral outlook, he adopts that as fact and uses it as a moral sledgehammer.

Again and again the poem is marred by the poet's compulsion to philosophize and moralize, as though he were unable to make his point through mere presentation. . . . And at the very end the poet shows that his sympathies are neither with Major Eatherly nor with the society that he represents; the humanizing impact, which he imposes upon the reader too energetically, is that the bomber pilot has taught us to reject violence. . . . (p. 138)

[In] a poem like "On the Death of a Murderer," in which Wain himself is the horrified analyst of modern violence, he feels compelled not to let his observation stand on its own merits and he intervenes with offensive nonpoetic explanations and recommendations. Rather than integrate his message into the expressive part of his art, he frequently sets off sections of didactic verse within a poem in order to emphasize his theme. His moral concerns appear to be so great that he fears they may be lost in the artistic process. Certainly we can expect Wain, who has shown himself to be an astute critic in his own right, to be more aware of the relation between propaganda and art, and the necessity for integrating the two; and he should be conscious of how his refusal to subordinate the former to the latter affects his poetry.

It is perhaps this tension in his artistic credo that induces him to write poems about his own art and the art of others. One third of *Weep before God* is a long poem called "A Boisterous Poem about Poetry." A more recent book of poetry, *Letters to Five Artists,* discusses the lives and art of five friends. . . . In both of these works Wain philosophizes about his own theory of art and poetry, and his recommendations are an obvious defense of his own poetical position. They are more philosophical reflection than poetry, and he continuously praises those who share his own particular view of the creative artist. (p. 141)

"A Boisterous Poem about Poetry" is a response to the malaise of the late 1950s in which many were asserting that British poetry had exhausted itself. . . . Wain suggests that the gloom-mongers were too willing to entomb the spirit of modern poetry. . . . There are serious poets and fickle poets, the accomplished and the uninitiated. His distinctions rest upon strange grounds, for it is the amateur poet, according to Wain, who concerns himself with the dark side of life: violence, cruelty, sorrow, despair. . . . The serious poet, on the other hand, is an ameliorator, who observes an unbalanced situation and sets out to rectify it. In his role as healer and savior, the serious poet is somehow able to call on the hidden resources of language to effect his ends, while the poet with his "bag of despair" can only "rattle on tin cans / And claim that [he is] singing." . . . (pp. 141-42)

In "Introductory Poem" to *Letters to Five Artists,* he suggests that the artist must not be preoccupied with understanding the violence in which his world is drowning. The poet . . . is a lyrical recorder who must make others lament and weep over, not understand, such violence. . . . (p. 143)

The deficiency in Wain's philosophy is that the major problems of mankind are not confronted, or, if they are, only obliquely. Poetry becomes, from his point of view, an assertion of optimism, a refusal to open one's eyes in the dark. . . . Wain's uncompromising humanism demands the affirmative voice even when events might lead elsewhere. By rejecting analysis and inquiry for indiscriminate assertion, his humanism must be seen as less than adequate for our moment. (p. 144)

> *Lawrence R. Ries, "John Wain: The Evasive Answer," in his* Wolf Masks: Violence in Contemporary Poetry *(copyright © 1977 by Kennikat Press Corp.; reprinted by permission of Kennikat Press Corp.), Kennikat, 1977, pp. 130-50.*

PHOEBE PETTINGELL

Wain can be as quixotic as our own Southern "Fugitive" poets (whose work he intensely admires). Like Allen Tate's Aneas, he has "an infallible instinct for the right battle on the passionate side." Unfortunately, he sometimes lacks the irony that would save him from the excess of insisting, "only in the sphere of art is humanity able to rise totally above its failures and inadequacies." One is also embarrassed to be told that in reading poetry, "we see our imperfections mirrored in our splendors, and we accept ourselves, at last, in peace and thankfulness." (p. 19)

When he concentrates on the work of individual poets, he is superb. He displays empathy and insight in discussing the influence the family history of Milton's patrons had on *Comus,* or the effect of *Eddas* on the subjects and style of the early Auden. His magnificent tributes to Philip Larkin and William Empson's poetry are alone worth the price of [*Professing Poetry*]. Most of all, Wain is attracted to those poets who recognize the need for "roots going down into the instinctual and primitive" to temper our sterile reasoning—for the sense of lifegiving ritual in our lives that art conveys through form. (pp. 19-20)

> *Phoebe Pettingell, in* The New Leader *(© 1978 by the American Labor Conference on International Affairs, Inc.), July 3, 1978.*

JASCHA KESSLER

John Wain, elected [to the Oxford Chair of Poetry] in 1973, offers nine lectures in "Professing Poetry," a charming introduction about his relation to Oxford, and an appendix of his recent poems that gives us examples to judge him by. . . . His style is straightforward: You know what he thinks all the time, and, like Johnson, he offers firm arguments, stating his positions on art, poetry and politics unequivocally. Of very few commentators may that be said; he belongs, in short, in Edmund Wilson's company. (p. 1)

In "On the Breaking of Forms," and "Poetry and Social Criticism," Wain shows us his own position: individualist, anti-state, common sense, the middle ground today where privacy survives, if precariously. These lectures are powerful attacks against propaganda, social utilitarianism and/or esoteric freedoms and dogmas. Wain is a sort of old-fashioned liberal, which is reactionary indeed today, here as in the English welfare state. He argues for our inherited language, which is what we all speak, unless we are speaking the masses Newspeak.

"Professing Poetry" is everywhere interesting and accessible; nowhere difficult or academic: It wears its learning lightly. Its forceful opinions have been earned by hard labor and show us a man worth hearing. Wain has something important to teach about poetry. Wide though the gulf between England and America be today, we should listen to him and learn. (p. 8)

Jascha Kessler, "Wain on Poetry without Pontification," in The Los Angeles Times Book Review *(copyright, 1978, Los Angeles Times; reprinted by permission), August 6, 1978, pp. 1, 8.*

SUSAN WOOD

[John Wain] typifies the very best of what one might call "Englishness"—good sense, moderation, a feeling for language, erudition without pretension, and wit.

The essays [in *Professing Poetry*] cover a wide variety of topics related to poetry and poets, and what comes through in all of them is Wain's deep love for poetry, his delight in sharing with us what he finds valuable. This is true particularly in the essays that deal with the work of individual poets—Auden, Emily Dickinson, Philip Larkin, William Empson and Edward Thomas. He has a knack for going right to the heart of a poet's work, placing it in the context of intellectual and social history without being stuffy about it, without taking anything away from the poem as poem. His insights, if not radical, are fresh and lively. . . .

Wain's is a basically conservative spirit, as indicated by his championship of form and his feeling that poetry should not become a means of social criticism. It is difficult to fault his stance against art as propaganda. . . .

Scattered throughout the essays are also passing remarks that make one smile with delight at their wit or gracefulness. . . . [For example:] "a poem conveys a great deal just by how it walks on to the stage, and it is possible to fall in love with a poem, as with an actress, just by seeing it move."

The volume closes with a selection of Wain's own poems written during the same period—poems of feeling, grace and humor that confirm one's faith in his criticism. (p. E3)

Susan Wood, in Book World—The Washington Post *(© 1978 The Washington Post), October 8, 1978.*

D. A. N. JONES

The Pardoner's Tale tells the stories of two men, both "forty-ish", who cannot help falling madly in love, sometimes despairingly, sometimes with great success. The lineaments of gratified desire are persuasively drawn. Precise details of plot and character dissolve into an amorous haze, spreading delight. . . .

The two stories are ingeniously linked. . . . [The] linking method has been deliberately designed to make it difficult for John Wain's narrative to carry conviction, to suspend the reader's disbelief: he has met this self-imposed challenge and succeeded triumphantly. . . .

We remember [Chaucer's] pardoner, the "full vicious man" who could tell "a moral tale", and priggishly accused others of riggishness so that they would guiltily buy his pardons. The ambiguities of the title offer a field for enjoyable speculation. Perhaps Giles, the novelist, is a sort of pardoner: certainly, he brings about the resolution of Gus's story in a spirit of forgiveness. Perhaps, the dying old lady is as vicious as Chaucer's pardoner, when she tells the story of her life: certainly, she has no concept of forgiveness. At any rate, John Wain's novel is written in a warmly forgiving spirit; and this, together with its engaging riggishness, contributes to the reader's delight.

D.A.N. Jones, "Forty-ish and Riggish," in The

Times Literary Supplement (© *Times Newspapers Ltd. (London) 1978; reproduced from* The Times Literary Supplement *by permission), October 13, 1978, p. 1140.*

*   *   *

WAKOSKI, Diane   1937-

Wakoski is an American poet often linked with the confessional school. In her work she explores highly personal experiences, predominant themes being pain, loneliness, and lost love. Her alternating tones of humor and anger, however, save her work from maudlin sentimentality. (See also *CLC*, Vols. 2, 4, 7, 9, and *Contemporary Authors*, Vols. 13-16, rev. ed.)

GERALD BURNS

The byplay in Wakoski's [*The Man Who Shook Hands*], getting around to the story of the man who shook hands, is bad Ponge. But the story is wonderfully moving, not from the digressions ("motion which suspends motion") but from the *good* Wakoski knack of taking the time to get it right. In writing time usually means space; while she mentions the "bourgeois" fear that one will be misprised or laughed at, she doesn't mention the equally bourgeois fear that one taxes a reader with too many words. She takes the time, and that is a fraction how she can write good long-line poems. (p. 303)

Her trouble in art used to be the brutality or too merely literary embarrassment (not to mention a kind of betrayal) of conducting her life in public. . . . Reading her is a mixture of the pity she really seems to want and the admiration she extorts. . . .

Lovely poems follow, a few of the line-ends more interesting for her interest in Olson . . . yet Olson comes upon a good thing, tricks himself into an insight, while dancing it (maybe in a digression), and Wakoski is like a novelist, talking until enough is said. . . .

[She] practices spontaneous and get-yourself-out-of-this-mess poems and is busily self-renewing, that Sexton domesticity turned healthy. So the danger for her as a writer is that one feels *warmly* toward her for being such an entertainer, and how is she to take that? (p. 304)

Gerald Burns, in Southwest Review *(© 1978 by Southern Methodist University Press), Summer, 1978.*

PETER SCHJELDAHL

[Miss Wakoski's] poems are professionally supple and clear and often feature a kind of sardonic humor, but their pervasive unpleasantness makes her popularity rather surprising. One can only conclude that a number of people are angry enough at life to enjoy the sentimental and desolating resentment with which she writes about it. Notable among her themes is an anti-male rage that seems the opposite of liberating: Miss Wakoski isn't mad at men who oppress her, she's mad at men who fail to fulfil her exacting romantic fantasies. "I could no more give up my idea of finding the perfect man than I could give up poetry," she writes in an oddly defiant introductory essay. "Are they not the same concept, the same spirit, the same holy quest, for beauty. . . .?"

The eponymous subject of ["The Man Who Shook Hands"] is a fellow who took leave of the poet after a night together by shaking hands, a lapse in erotic etiquette brooded on so obsessively that one keeps expecting it to hatch something, but it never does. . . .

Nor does Miss Wakoski show the least inclination to sisterly feeling. All her many heroes are male. Her hatred of her mother is expressed with hair-raising harshness. Her repeated railings against fate for making her (in her own eyes) physically plain suggest a crude sexual competitiveness assumed to be in the nature of things. The last line in the book is "How I hate my destiny," and ultimately irritating is the level of consciousness Miss Wakoski brings to her troubles, a level high enough, one would think, to trigger some growth or extension, or at least some rueful laughter. But perhaps she would regard any such transcendence as a betrayal of her "holy quest," which, as a result, goes nowhere. (p. 15)

> *Peter Schjeldahl, in* The New York Times Book Review (© *1978 by The New York Times Company; reprinted by permission), August 13, 1978.*

*   *   *

WELDON, Fay   1933-

Weldon is a British novelist, playwright, and scriptwriter who writes about the problems of contemporary women. Her humanist approach transcends radical feminism, exploring the frailties and insecurities which plague both sexes. (See also *CLC,* **Vols. 6, 9, and** *Contemporary Authors,* **Vols. 21-24, rev. ed.)**

D. A. N. JONES

Fay Weldon has a dashing, unconventional way of writing a novel; but there is something familiar about *Female Friends.* "Female friends" is a favourite locution of Thackeray's. I took down *Philip,* to check, and found much else in common. . . . Both authors are fond of the present tense, of chatting to the reader, of offering little homilies. Thackeray also sometimes puts his dialogue in the form of a dramatic script, just as Fay Weldon does. Their subject-matter is similar, too: the sufferings of women, particularly at the hands of other women, their mothers and their female friends. This has been an enjoyable theme for certain male writers since Thomas Middleton's *Women Beware Women.*

In *Female Friends,* the women who need to beware of each other are called Grace, Marjorie and Chloe (the narrator). Girls of very different backgrounds with very different— and most interesting—mothers, they come together in a country village during the 1940 evacuation. The narrative hops back and forth in time, as the three girls, grow up, meet disagreeable men, and become mothers in unusual ways. . . .

Chloe's vision of the males in this book is somewhat blurred. Although she sharply observes the bad things they say or do to women, she becomes implausible when she tries to guess about their motives, to report their political conversation, to describe their activities in their pubs and businesses. Males are frequently seen as a breed of large, hard-to-handle but covetable pets. . . .

[It is said that] "female friends are not to be trusted". Chloe is inclined to agree:

> Fine citizens, we make, fine sisters! Our loyalties are to men, not to each other. We are divided amongst ourselves. We have to be, for survival's sake.

The main idea—an exhortation to women to pull together— is put over very well, even if one feels that there is more female unity around than Chloe supposes.

> *D.A.N. Jones, "Warnings for Women," in* The Times Literary Supplement (© *Times Newspapers Ltd. (London) 1975; reproduced from* The Times Literary Supplement *by permission), February 28, 1975, p. 213.*

VICTORIA GLENDINNING

The majority of novel-readers, one is told, are women; it would be interesting to know what proportion, and what kind of women, prefer fantasy—daydreams of an impossibly different life—to stories which reflect everywoman's lot. Fay Weldon's *Remember Me* is in the second category. Not only does the reader learn what style and colour are the clothes worn by the [characters], . . . but where they bought them. . . . Food, furniture and household linens are given the same attention. Fay Weldon is a successful television playwright, which may account for her eye for settings and for setpieces: breakfast, a dinner party, moments in the day crosscut between three households. . . .

Role-playing is emphasized by a persistent Happy Families technique: "Up gets Margot, the doctor's wife. . . ." Proper names are reiterated as in a game. . . .

Reading *Remember Me* is rather like gossiping about friends of friends. The characters are real, in that one knows the most intimate things about them; and yet they are schematic, reduced, as are people known only through an informant—or through the television screen. Only Madeleine's teenage daughter—fat, graceless, addicted to Sugar Puffs—seems properly solid; but in the end she too bursts into a cacophony of self-definitions: "I am Hilary, daughter of a dead mother, child of a lost father. . . ."

Those who are not alienated by these inner incantations may be so by the banality of some of the authorial comments. . . . Some insights, less global, are on that account more interesting: many married men, for example, must secretly feel like the doctor, about money, that his wife "did not quite realize the difficulty with which it was earned, nor her good fortune in being allowed to spend what was by rights his and his alone".

"Oh I am the doctor's wife, mother of the doctor's children, feeder of the doctor's cat." Oh I am the reviewer, and I can see that this is an intelligent but not a first-class novel; and oh I am a woman novel-reader, and for all my critical remarks I read about these people and their stereotyped conflicts and their sex-lives and their lifestyles with an avidity way beyond the call of duty.

> *Victoria Glendinning, "The Muswell Hill Mob," in* The Times Literary Supplement (© *Times Newspapers Ltd. (London) 1976; reproduced from* The Times Literary Supplement *by permission), September 24, 1976, p. 1199.*

MARTIN AMIS

Fay Weldon's novels have so far moved pretty confidently up the social scale. From the girls-together scruffiness of "The Fat Woman's Joke" and "Down Among the Women," she has progressed via the TV-executive and careerperson stratum of "Female Friends" to the stockbrokers suburbia of "Remember Me." In ["Words of Advice"] Miss Weldon finally strikes it rich, and is ushered into the presence of her first millionaire.

Her first millionairess, too, naturally. Miss Weldon's world has always been assertively, almost parodistically, matriarchal; she writes as if *men* had the hormones; when things happen, you may be sure that women make them do so. (p. 13)

Gemma is the chief puppeteer. She is also the chief monologist in this generally rather garrulous novel, punctuating the maneuvers with a detailed account of her formative years. (You feel, during these speeches, that Weldon is writing flat out for Gemma: they certainly share a taste for didacticism and the epic simile.) Gemma's history is directed at the long-suffering ear of Elsa, whose socio-sexual prospects it is clearly meant to allegorize and, ultimately, to define. Yes, the Weldon woman still carries the same albatross: the Weldon man. He will either be a pitiful lapdog—who will at least look after you, and defray your infidelities —or an arty maverick—who will awaken you, then break your heart and very possibly your back too. "Sex," says Weldon, who has plainly mused thoroughly on this topic, "is not for procreation; it is for the sharing out of privilege."

What, then, has privilege done to Miss Weldon's world? Most obviously, it has stylized it. Miss Weldon has never been much of a socially "concerned" writer (for which many thanks) and although her eye for the hardware of status remains unblinking, she is not particularly interested in the moral significance of wealth. Rather, she sees the moneyed life as being *suspended*, freed from the banal contingencies of our own daily huff-and-puff. It is, as they say, no accident that the most naturalistic scene in the book is a glimpse of Victor's abandoned wife, chugging enjoyably along in middle-class obliviousness—a milieu much closer, one suspects, to Miss Weldon's natural habitat. As a result of this spry distancing, anyway, "Words of Advice" is a raffish, open-ended novel, in which all kinds of cockeyed notions, crooked parallels and unassimilated themes can be harmlessly let out to play. (pp. 13, 52)

Stylization, however, inevitably puts style under the limelight, and Weldon's prose—normally a crisp and functional performer—makes a somewhat bashful leading lady. As she aspires more and more identifiably to the wise, otherworldly manner of Muriel Spark, it becomes clear that Miss Weldon's intention is to flirt quite candidly with cliché, to let language reflect the dutifully trite ponderings of her characters. But whose clichés are they? . . . Naïve people often have naïve thoughts—but aren't they often vividly naïve? I suppose Miss Weldon should know, since she is ever-ready to dispense timely adages whenever the action pauses to catch its breath: "The good we do lives after us . . . what are good times without the bad? . . ." . . . These strides toward the lectern are curiously out of place among Miss Weldon's devil-may-care ironies, and point to larger flaws.

Cliché spreads inward from the language of the book to its heart. Cliché always does. Miss Weldon may have climbed the social scale, but she now seems absurdly remote from its lowlier representatives. Even when it is your intention to show people pathetically conditioned by their experience, you can't have dumb secretaries saying things like "I'll look it up under 'superstitions' in Occult Weekly" and "Everything can be filed. It said so in Lesson Six, Office Routine." Unsurprisingly, when Miss Weldon chooses to gouge some "real" emotion out of these mock-ups, she

starkly announces that this is what she is doing—we get "real sorrow" and "real affection" within a few lines. Similarly, in a novel where the heroine is a psychosomatic cripple (all she has to do is "want" to walk, etc.) the last thing you expect, outside pulp fiction, is that she will actually get up and *walk*. But that's what Gemma actually does—in an attempt to join Elsa in the customary dash from the menfolk which supplies Miss Weldon with her codes. "'Run!' cries Gemma . . . 'You must. You must run for me and all of us.'" Social mobility should of course, be available to all but, as we've seen, it remains a risky business. (p. 52)

Martin Amis, "Prose is the Leading Lady," in The New York Times Book Review (© *1977 by The New York Times Company; reprinted by permission), October 2, 1977, pp. 13, 52.*

ERIC KORN

As Fay Weldon debatably remarks (to extract [a phrase from *Little Sisters*] from the hail of marmoreal aphorisms that rattle across each page): "Sexual passion, requited, invigorates the parties concerned and enhances rather than diminishes the response to the outside world . . . romantic love, on the other hand, seems to work as a slow poison". Eventually all this knowingness dulls the edge of intelligence. There are entertaining cameos [in her novel] . . . but they are only bubbles on the glassy surface. Though Fay Weldon's tool is the engraver's, after a while it cuts no ice.

Eric Korn, "Blowing Bubbles," in The Times Literary Supplement (© *Times Newspapers Ltd. (London) 1978; reproduced from* The Times Literary Supplement *by permission), February 24, 1978, p. 227.*

MARY HOPE

Fay Weldon's myth-making and mannerisms are curiously unsatisfactory, like walking on to a step which is not there. She juggles many a spinning word around a slight tale of trendy beautiful people and swinging 'sixties beautiful objects. . . .

Somewhere [in *Little Sisters*] there is a moral or two about the inevitable interchangeability of People and Things when Sex is around, but the convolutions of style get in the way, or anyway my way, of any desire to work it all out. There is a crudity of tone underlying the archness and Mrs Weldon fails to distance herself from the dross she derides. (p. 24)

Mary Hope, in The Spectator (© *1978 by* The Spectator; *reprinted by permission of* The Spectator), *March 4, 1978.*

AMANDA HELLER

"Praxis," we are informed, means turning point, culmination, action, even orgasm. It is also the given name of Praxis Duveen, a blowsy Everywoman. . . .

[She is] an extravagant failure as a wife and mother [who] eventually commits a celebrated murder from which she emerges both an apostle and a victim of the women's movement.

The story of her various rises and falls makes a witty commentary on fifty years' worth of changing notions about women's place. *Praxis* is not merely a feminist fable, however. This tough and enjoyable novel is, at bottom, a celebration of the modern art of survival. (p. 94)

Amanda Heller, in The Atlantic Monthly (copyright © 1978 by The Atlantic Monthly Company, Boston, Mass.; reprinted with permission), December, 1978.

*   *   *

WIEBE, Rudy   1934-

Wiebe is a Canadian novelist, short story writer, and critic whose didactic works probe the spiritual issues of Christian faith. (See also CLC, Vol. 6, and Contemporary Authors, Vols. 37-40, rev. ed.)

INA FERRIS

Rudy Wiebe's *The Blue Mountains of China* centres upon the problem of belief—the sustaining relationship of the self to something beyond itself. As a Christian, Wiebe perceives this problem primarily in terms of the relationship to the divine, and his task is to convince the contemporary, secular reader that this relationship must be taken seriously. (p. 79)

Questions about plot, structure and point of view embodied in Wiebe's narrative strategy serve as mediations for the spiritual themes probed by the fiction. Wiebe's characters, exiled in the wilderness, search for the Promised Land that will transform existential chaos into meaningful form. The novel itself, multiple and fragmented, highlights the absence of such integrative vision and engages the reader in his own struggle in a narrative wilderness. Working through dissonance and disjunction, Wiebe subjects the reader to a process of relentless disorientation. The senses are assaulted by disconnected images—a cow's bulging eye, a coruscating chandelier, a leg oozing black pus—and the mind struggles to assimilate the sharply differing settings—a sand-assaulted well in the desert of Paraguay, a silent snow-covered street in Moscow, a crowded lice-infested basement in China. As the novel's disparate voices succeed one another, point of view switches abruptly. Dramatic shifts in narrative distance and mode typically accompany these alterations of perspective, so reinforcing the general sense of unpredictable and unstable narrative process.

Blue Mountains opens, for example, with the calm reminiscence of the aged Frieda Friesen narrating events from her childhood and adolescence on the prairie. Her secure faith, her sense of a self sustained by the divine, emerges immediately: "What I tell I remember only through God's grace." Frieda sees and accepts her life as a whole, convinced that "it all comes from God, strength and sickness, want and plenty." . . . This belief determines her narrative stance, accounting for the detached perspective, the even tone and the curiously impersonal language that modulates only rarely into the language of specific personal response. (pp. 79-80)

The next chapter plunges us into a radically different narrative mode: "The cell had one opening: the door. Three half steps long, nearly two wide, thirteen rows of sweating stone floor to ceiling." . . . As setting switches from the expanse of prairie to the confinement of a dark cell, narrative focus narrows suddenly and moves to a concentrated, internal perspective. The reader is now in Russia, in 1929, in prison, in the mind of young Jakob Friesen. Where Frieda's mode of narration allowed the reader to remain outside the experiences being recorded, the narrative now pulls the reader into the fiction. Calm recollection of the past gives way to a tormented experience that is present tense in impact; the language of minimal response is exchanged for a language soaked through with the perception of a particular psyche. Psychological realism, probing deeply into a consciousness, supplants the autobiographical method of the relation of events. Vertical movement displaces horizontal, and the narrative slows down. Frieda's chapter covered twenty years; Jakob's chapter—five times longer—covers only a few weeks. As the prose becomes denser, Wiebe stretches language in an attempt to express the simultaneity of experience, to capture the diverse pressures converging on the vulnerable Jakob whose once "solid sure" world has collapsed, leaving him to confront dark, fearful forces deep within.

Such jolting shifts are typical of narrative process in *Blue Mountains*. Frieda's story is the only recurrent strain and constitutes the only approach to conventional continuity and form. But Wiebe undercuts the reassurance this engenders by breaking up her story, introducing it not only in portions but at irregular intervals. Moreover, he avoids providing it with a firm sense of closure—a further installment is always possible. Frieda's narration ends well before Wiebe's narrative, and her story—the only one rendered in direct first person—takes its place among the other personal and partial perspectives that make up the bulk of the novel. This polyvocal technique, while reflecting the multiplicity and subjectivity of modern reality, functions primarily to focus the problem of point of view itself, to raise questions about the possibility of an authentic, integrative vision.

Like point of view, structure also becomes reflexive. The basic narrative unit is the test of self, a unit complicated and extended with each experiential formulation as Wiebe experiments with a range of possible self-definitions, from young Jakob Friesen's self-destructive self-assertion to David Epp's futile yet constitutive self-sacrifice. Built out of these units, the novel resembles a kaleidoscope in which the same central elements recombine continually into new configurations. These individual configurations compose a discontinuous sequence that counteracts the sense of significant linear progression inherent in the narrative act. In effect, Wiebe generates a structure that is a question about structure. Temporal sequence can neither reveal the significant relationship between episodes nor body forth the form capable of containing them. By deliberately disrupting conventional teleological expectations, Wiebe questions traditional linear structures that not only render the temporal intrinsically significant but make it the bearer of atemporal values. Consequently, his antilinearity places in doubt the time structures the human mind erects, particularly that of history, and works to undercut the sense of time as history—the traditional time of the novel as a genre. (pp. 80-1)

As the novel's central image of journeying stresses process not completion, activity not action, so the cumulation of the basic narrative units in *Blue Mountains* signifies the novel's search for form, translating into narrative terms the existential problems explored in the fiction. The narrative questions in effect constitute a metatheme—a secular version of the novel's main theme that engages the reader directly and turns his experience into a confrontation of the central concerns of the fiction. Faced with the rapidly shifting perspectives, the reader experiences—as a result of technique itself—a secular analogue to the spiritual search for a centre dramatized in the novel's action. Such technique is not a simple mimesis of the uncertain modern world, nor is Wiebe writing a self-conscious novel. Rather, he engenders a genuine displacement, a translation, that creates a secondary level of the narrative at once thematically resonant and rhetorically functional. This level turns the reader's consciousness into the ultimate concern of the fiction by involving it in the process of sense-making. And Wiebe ensures that the reader will experience its full complexity by creating a dense and compelling fictional world that pulls in the reader, forcing participation even as it obstructs the formation of ready interpretation and decertainizes response.

The novel is a powerful imagination of different minds. Wiebe's concrete method establishes the existential focus and combines with his antilinearity to generate the maximum impact of each experience as experience. Released from significant sequence, each episode is cut off from past and future and becomes an intense present intensely rendered. With no central plot to place the episode in an overall scheme, each assumes equal weight and comes uniquely and fully into focus. Wiebe probes in depth, thoroughly imagining the specific human medium of each experience. His vivid, flexible prose economically creates the interior world of the characters, and the detailed evocation of conflicting internal forces jostling with the pressures of external event, of the formative past fusing with the problematic present, brings the mind under exploration to a full, concrete realization. (p. 82)

The density and interiority of these experiences inhibit generalization, make judgment difficult. Yet even as Wiebe keeps generalization and judgment off-balance, he insists on their necessity. The dominant concrete focus of the novel exists in tension with a pull toward abstraction; through the latter Wiebe generalizes his narrative exploration and brings to bear upon the existential moment his moral themes and transcendent realm of meaning. The same antilinearity, for example, that isolates the episodes and encourages the emergence of the moment in all its concreteness works also to generate a level of abstraction that implies the insufficiency of the purely existential approach. Antilinearity, as noted earlier, implicitly denies the significance of temporal sequence and so of history. But when combined with the pervasive Biblical typology of the novel, it does more than this: it redefines history as figural—a reenactment of Scripture. Through Biblical allusion Wiebe weaves in a possible perspective, reminds the reader that an interpretive act is required. But the emphasis here, as in all of Wiebe's narrative strategies, is on exploration, and he persists in unsettling and complicating response. In drawing on Biblical typology, he does not merely translate ancient structures and images into contemporary idiom but rather transforms the inherited paradigm so that the relationship of the fictional version to the model becomes a question not a statement. (pp. 82-3)

The complex effect of *Blue Mountains* depends on its sustaining this tension between the concrete and abstract levels of the fiction. Here two narrative impulses—authenticity and perspective—confront one another, reflecting in secular terms the conflicts between mundane experience and religious idealism experienced by characters within the fiction. In David Epp's chapter, for instance, circumstantial realism plays off against the possibility of a deductive

structure informed by an ideal: the louse and the Last Supper exist on different levels of perception. Wiebe's doubleness of vision does not preclude choice but reveals its full difficulty, as in his comic presentation of Sam Reimer, the failed visionary. Although Wiebe's comedy here shades into satire exposing the hollowness of contemporary society, he mitigates against this clear and simplifying direction of decision through the central Quixotic concept that allows a more complex confrontation of real and ideal.... Through such interplay Wiebe offers possibilities for interpretation, suggests levels of significance without defining a particular significance. This exploratory, open technique signals the deep awareness of the difficult conditions of belief for the modern mind that makes *Blue Mountains* so impressive an imagination of this problem.

But Wiebe cannot, finally, affirm his existential mode with its potentially subversive, experimental technique. The final chapter, "On the Way," presents a striking reversal of method and perception as Wiebe brings his novel to a resolution, pointing explicitly to *the* way. Despite the suggestions of process and journeying in its title, "On the Way" is dominated by a technique that stabilizes and encloses the fiction: the kaleidoscope is not only stilled but fixed into an exemplary pattern. Exploration gives way to assertion; Wiebe pulls structure toward closure and moves point of view toward definition. Insistently constructed as a conclusion absorbing the entire novel, the final chapter summons characters from earlier chapters (or recalling earlier chapters) and moves them at one time toward one place. The reader is similarly drawn in and directed, for the setting and historical moment (Canada, 1967) allow no retreat from the fictional experience. The whole narrative converges on a single point—John Reimer, carrying his cross across Canada, enveloped in Christ images and granted an authority and integrative power withheld from the rest of the narrative. The ambiguities of structural relationships in earlier portions are now replaced by the clarity of a centripetal structure defining Reimer as the locus of significance. Point of view, withdrawing from its characteristic subjectivity, adopts an external perspective and reinforces the implications of structure by making Reimer the focus and authenticating his testimony. Wiebe's individuating, internal method of characterization is replaced by a generalizing, external approach that turns character into type. Reimer himself is a symbol functioning on the abstract level of idea and ideal that now takes over as narrative dominant.

Through this decisive shift in method Wiebe signifies the inability of his existential mode to resolve the questions he raises. Itself incoherent, it cannot grant coherence; based on a commitment to the individual and the concrete, it cannot penetrate experience to reveal its essence. Undercutting his own earlier narrative strategies, Wiebe now redefines reality as essence, not experience, and deliberately thins existential context to concentrate on its underlying forms. (pp. 83-4)

Rather than generating a perception of essence, the final chapter conveys a sense of attenuation, verges on cliché and common place that obscure the significance of Wiebe's effort. The crux of the problem is John Reimer who bears the burden of the synthesis Wiebe attempts. To support this weight Reimer must be a compelling presence. But he remains an unrealized intention, a willed figure who is unable to animate the imagination. Reimer functions as theoretical conception rather than symbolic force integrating the experience of the narrative. He emerges as a rational, imposed and self-conscious symbol, relying heavily—and inappropriately—on statement. This reliance on discursive forms dissipates the emotional power essential to support his role and points to the basic weakness underlying his creation. (p. 84)

His thinness becomes especially clear when he comes in contact with old Jakob Friesen, betrayer of his son, survivor of prison camps and a man who believes he believes nothing. Old Jakob brings with him the most powerful episodes of the novel and his words, evoking experiences that the reader has shared, resonate as John Reimer's fail to do. When Friesen counters Reimer's statement of faith with his own doubt ("It helped her exactly nothing,") his assertion is charged with the memory of the dramatic episodes it conjures up; it brings vividly to mind their anguish, bewilderment, courage and despair. John Reimer, cut off from the fictional power upon which Jakob Friesen draws, speaks a pale language by comparison. His statement remains statement. And his purely symbolic action appears, in the context of the difficulties of experience and action we have previously encountered, as facile and inadequate. Reimer himself must give this action force, but he cannot do so. Undercut by an inappropriate rationalism, set off from the experiential context that must support his structural role, Reimer lacks the concentrated suggestiveness necessary to turn him into a compelling symbol capable of absorbing and illuminating the problems raised by the exploration of the preceding chapters.

The failure of this final chapter is as significant as the effort it represents. Wiebe's attempt to expand the possibilities of the novel by pushing it beyond its traditional roots reveals how deeply his own artistic gifts draw upon those roots. Religious idealism may support the conscious aesthetic structuring the final chapter, but the authentic voice of the chapter belongs to a fugitive from another mode—to old Jakob Friesen. Despite the depth of his own religious convictions, Wiebe's imagination is essentially secular and novelistic, animated less by the transcendent Christian vision than by the powerful pull of, in his own words, "the world that is now . . . where everybody else it's hurting is living." (p. 85)

> *Ina Ferris, "Religious Vision and Fictional Form: Rudy Wiebe's 'The Blue Mountains of China'," in* MOSAIC: A Journal for the Study of Literature and Ideas *(copyright © 1978 by The University of Manitoba Press; acknowledgement of previous publication is herewith made) Vol. XI, No. 3 (Spring, 1978), pp. 79-85.*

GEORGE WOODCOCK

I thought of *War and Peace* when I read . . . Rudy Wiebe's *The Scorched-Wood People*, which too, on a very different scale, is about war and defeat in a vast country. Rudy Wiebe, whose ancestors lived many generations in Russia, has always struck me as being similar in many ways to Tolstoy, not in any way the equivalent in stature or in sheer artistry, but on his own smaller scale irradiated with the same kind of rather primitive religious concerns, and just as prone as the great Leo Nicholaevich to subordinate his innate sense of form to a compelling didactic motive. (p. 98)

The scorched-wood people are, of course, the *bois brulés*, as the Métis were originally called. In his novel Wiebe is not concerned, except for a few reminiscent references to the pre-1869 past that are necessary for background, with the entire span of Métis history. He has written a tale about the two rebellions, of 1869-70 and 1885, in which the Métis unsuccessfully defied the centralizing power that entered Canada with Confederation and is the enemy of all Canadians who believe in personal freedom. (pp. 98-9)

Unfortunately Rudy Wiebe has been unable in *The Scorched-Wood People* to separate the purpose of historical fiction, which is to give us a plausible image and feeling of the past, from that of the historical moralist, which is to apportion blame, signal merit and formulate lessons. He feels too deeply about his subject to detach himself in the Flaubertian manner, yet at the same time he seeks to give some plausible fictional rendering of his feelings. He tries to do so through the device of a committed narrator who comments on the events as they occur, in fairly regular chronological sequence. But this very device, used to achieve a degree of verisimilitude, turns out to be the least convincing feature of *The Scorched-Wood People*. The narrator is a Métis oral poet, and we are led to identify him with Pierre Falcon, the most famous of the Métis bards, who was present at the skirmish of Seven Oaks in 1816, when he composed his famous song which became something of an anthem of the Métis "nation." (p. 99)

But it very soon becomes evident that Wiebe is little concerned with the history of the Métis, which he deals with very cavalierly, and much more with the iniquity of their fate. However, the real heart of the book, which creates its curiously frenetic atmosphere and provides an unstructured continuity far more compelling than the narration line, is the personality of Louis Riel, whose role as a religious visionary clearly fascinates Wiebe.

The publicity relating to *The Scorched-Wood People* presents it as an epic of Louis Riel and Gabriel Dumont, but little justice is really done to Dumont, either in terms of historical accuracy or in terms of a sympathetic portrayal of the man. . . . Only [Dumont's] courage emerges in *The Scorched-Wood People;* the intelligence and the grandeur are somehow lost. (pp. 99-100)

Yet at the same time Rudy Wiebe, the chronicler of Mennonite religious agonies, has convincingly projected the spiritually tortured and divided Riel, and as a study of Riel as visionary hovering on the edge of insanity *The Scorched-Wood People* is often profound and always understanding. But the failure to portray convincingly a whole man like Dumont mars the book from beginning to end, and *The Scorched-Wood People* is a disappointing book for those whose expectations are at the level of *The Blue Mountains of China*. (p. 100)

> *George Woodcock, "Riel & Dumont," in* Canadian Literature, *Summer, 1978, pp. 98-100.*

*   *   *

WIESEL, Elie(zer)   1928-

Wiesel is a Hungarian-born American novelist, journalist, short story writer, and essayist who writes chiefly in French. A survivor of Auschwitz and Buchenwald, he draws his themes from many areas of Judaic concern. He writes of the Holocaust, of the Soviet Jewry, and of the Six Day War, often incorporating elements of history and of Hasidic legend into his fiction. (See also *CLC*, Vols. 3, 5, and *Contemporary Authors*, Vols. 5-8, rev. ed.)

KENNETH TURAN

To a great many of his readers, Elie Wiesel is much more than just a writer. He is a symbol, a banner, and a beacon, perhaps *the* survivor of the Holocaust. More than outliving Auschwitz and Buchenwald, Wiesel, starting with a slim, terrifying volume called *Night* in 1958, has written about that experience and its aftershock with an anguished power that no living writer has matched. Reading his books—there have been more than a dozen—one feels the inexpressible nausea and revulsion that a simple recitation of statistics never manages to arouse. He seems to own the horror of the death camps, or rather, the horror owns him.

Yet even a writer as single-minded as Wiesel must eventually branch out, and this he has done. In 1972, he published *Souls on Fire*, a masterful, joyous retelling of the legends surrounding the Hasidic masters of Eastern Europe, and now comes *Messengers of God*, described as the successor to *Souls* and the result of ten years work, in which Wiesel recreates the stories of some of the Bible heroes, from Adam through Job.

As a reteller of tales, Wiesel has few flaws. His is a deliberate, elegant style, consciously elevated and poetic, and if he occasionally tries to pack too much into a sentence, to jam it too full of significance and meaning, it is an error easy to forgive.

Wiesel's primary purpose in writing *Messengers*, he tells us, is to at once humanize and contemporize the heroes of the Old Testament, to remind us that "they are human beings: people not gods."...

There is much intriguing, perceptive reasoning here, many captivating reinterpretations of legends, as when Wiesel concludes of Cain and Abel that the former killed the latter "to push immanent injustice to its ultimate absurd conclusion, as if to shout to God: Is that what You wanted?" Yet the impression remains that Wiesel tends to push the contemporaneity too hard.

One of the most striking things about *Messengers of God* is the way Wiesel takes the stories and legends and the very existence of Biblical figures like Abraham, Isaac and Jacob to be the literal truth. Wiesel is the direct descendent of the pious sages he wrote of in *Souls on Fire*—he believes....

Having done extensive research in . . . Midrashic literature, Wiesel deftly guides us among the boggling tidbits that the rabbis in their zeal extracted from the Holy Word. No point, it seemed, was too minor to elaborate on endlessly....

Fascinating, simply fascinating, and it is no wonder that Wiesel could not resist adding his own modern words to this great tapestry. Even if he has not completely succeeded, the attempt has a special grace of its own.

> Kenneth Turan, "An Elegant Teller of Tales," in Book World—The Washington Post (© The Washington Post), August 8, 1976, p. F7.

BERNARD MANDELBAUM

[The seven short stories in *Messengers of God: Biblical Portraits and Legends*] are gems of mystery and suspense that draw upon material from the Bible and the vast ocean of rabbinic legend and commentary. God plays a central role in each episode, yet the characters Wiesel vividly portrays are the biblical Adam, Jacob, Moses, Job, who pul-

sate with complexities and paradoxes, strengths and weaknesses known to everyman. The author is not one to idealize biblical heroes. Jacob's deceptiveness and fear of real challenge are shown to be the consequence of experiences that are so poignantly rendered they throw light on the reader's own struggle for self-discovery. At the same time, Wiesel relates these characters' own experiences to his traditional concerns: the nature and destiny of the Jewish people, the holocaust, the mystery of God's way with man. In so doing, he has been at pains not to minimize the darkness in life and the enigma of man's behavior, and he also offers guidance. (p. 35)

> Bernard Mandelbaum, in Saturday Review (© 1976 by Saturday Review/World, Inc.; reprinted with permission), October 2, 1976.

MICHAEL J. BANDLER

Elie Wiesel is inexorably linked with the Holocaust, a storyteller determined to keep the world from forgetting the lessons of the immediate past. But there is another side to him—that of Biblical and Talmudic scholar—known largely to his students and lecture attendees. It is this facet which is limned in [*Messengers of God: Biblical Portraits and Legends*, a] series of capsule reflections on Biblical household names. . . . By blending ancient texts with commentaries and legends, Wiesel removes the patriarchs and prophets from the pantheon—as it were—and enables us to see them as ordinary men, with all their shortcomings and strengths—a contemporary view of what they were in their time, as well as what they would become in ours. (p. 153)

> Michael J. Bandler, in Commonweal (copyright © 1977 Commonweal Publishing Co., Inc.; reprinted by permission of Commonweal Publishing Co., Inc.), March 4, 1977.

JACK RIEMER

[*Messengers of God: Biblical Portraits and Legends*] is a strange creative achievement. At one level all he has done is collect and retell old legends. He has simply transmitted some of the many tales that the Jewish tradition has woven around the biblical figures. His book looks like an anthology of previously published material.

But at another level the words "all he has done is retell" and "simply transmitted" in the preceding paragraph are colossal understatements. For what he has really done is take the midrashim, the thousands of disparate, disorganized, disjointed commentaries on the biblical stories that are scattered all through rabbinic literature and weave them into hauntingly beautiful and coherent psycho-biographies and into models and mirrors of ourselves. Somewhere in this book Wiesel has a metaphor about what midrash does to Bible that also expresses what Wiesel has done to midrash. He says: "Midrash is to Bible as imagination is to knowledge." He means by that that the biblical stories are the base, the bare bones, around which midrash creates new realities. (p. 220)

And now see how gradually, imperceptibly, but surely the whole focus of our reading has changed. Suddenly we realize that we are not just playing detective games with a cryptic tale or doing intellectual exercises with a resilient text—we are confronting ourselves in the biblical-midrashic mirror. (pp. 220-21)

[To] make us see ourselves as we really are by means of the

ancient words, is no "simply," no "merely" as we thought at first reading. It is art, and creative achievement of the highest order. It is the kind of art that draws us, pains us, and makes us grateful. To read this book is an esthetic and an intellectual experience, but much more than that, it is a voyage of self-discovery and self-recognition. Its pages can be read at two levels, as commentary on the ancient words and as commentary on our own situation, and perhaps they are the same. (p. 221)

Jack Riemer, in Commonweal *(copyright © 1977 Commonweal Publishing Co., Inc.; reprinted by permission of Commonweal Publishing Co., Inc.), April 1, 1977.*

* * *

WILLIAMS, Tennessee   1914-

Twice a winner of the Pulitzer Prize in Drama, Williams is one of the most important American playwrights of the twentieth century. His work is characteristically concerned with the conflict between the illusions of an individual and the reality of his situation, most notably in *Cat on a Hot Tin Roof* and *A Streetcar Named Desire*. Because loneliness and disappointment are so typical in his work, he has often been criticized for having a limited perception of the human condition. His later work is generally considered to be of uneven quality, none of it meeting the standards of his prize-winning plays. In addition to drama, Williams also writes novels, short stories, and screenplays. His fiction is criticized for being sketchy and undeveloped. (See also *CLC*, Vols. 1, 2, 5, 7, 8, and *Contemporary Authors*, Vols. 5-8, rev. ed.)

JOHN SIMON

For some time now, any number of epigones have been turning out better imitation Tennessee Williams plays than Williams himself has written lately. As a result, Williams was forced to abandon self-imitation for self-parody and produce several rather unsuccessful Williams pastiches. But *In the Bar of a Tokyo Hotel* does not even qualify as poor parody: it makes *The Seven Descents of Myrtle* look, by comparison, like a triumphal ascent of Parnassus. It is a play by a man at the end of, not his talent (that was long ago), but his tether—a man around whom the last props of the dramatic edifice have crumbled and who, in an impotent frenzy, stamps his feet on the few remaining bricks. That someone who was a major American and world dramatist should come to this is a tragedy almost unparalleled in the annals of literature, never mind drama; it would have been a fit subject for a play by the former Tennessee Williams.

In a sense, to be sure, Williams has always been a confessional playwright—and even a confessional being, going from psychoanalysis to Catholicism. But the trouble with his quasi-confessional plays is that they are not honest confessions. In them, Williams appears either as a middle-aged hysterical woman (archetype: Blanche DuBois), or as a sensitive, oversensitive young man, a little too good (*Orpheus Descending*) or too wicked (Sebastian in *Suddenly Last Summer*) for his milieu. These are the two sides of the same trick coin (it always comes up tails): on the one hand, the fear of aging and death and the insatiable hunger for sex as both specific and panacea; on the other, the artist's victimization by society or his own overexacting vision. While Williams was in command of his art, these disguises and fragmentation hardly mattered. Now, in this play, he comes closer to fusing the two falsely complete personas into his

one genuinely incomplete one; but, alas, he still lacks the guts to do it, and besides it is too late. (p. 197)

John Simon, "'In the Bar of a Tokyo Hotel'" (1969), in his Uneasy Stages: A Chronicle of the New York Theater, 1963-1973 *(copyright © 1975 by John Simon; reprinted by permission of Random House, Inc.), Random House, 1976, pp. 197-99.*

M. A. CORRIGAN

Tennessee Williams' writing reveals a striking preoccupation with the problem of time. Like other modern dramatists, he has juxtaposed past and present, created worlds of fantasy, and employed mythical substructures in order to suspend the irrevocable forward direction of time in his plays. Williams frequently expresses the conflict between real and ideal in temporal terms; time, often as arch-enemy, is ranged with fact, necessity, body, mortality, and locked in combat with eternity, truth, freedom, soul, immortality. Williams' dramas are marked by a thematic obsession with time and its effect on human life to such a degree that his whole career can be viewed from the perspective of his changing attitude toward time. (p. 155)

Three major periods, coinciding approximately with the last three decades, emerge in a consideration of Williams' plays from the standpoint of the time theme. *The Glass Menagerie, Camino Real,* and *Night of the Iguana* exemplify the characteristic stance toward time that Williams adopts in each period; each of these plays, moreover, employs a different technique to achieve an arrest of time.

The events of *The Glass Menagerie* are enactments of Tom Wingfield's memories; his monologues, addressed directly to the audience, frame the play's seven animated "tableaux" and mediate between past and present. In reliving the events surrounding the visit of his sister's "gentleman caller," Tom conveys to the audience the effect of the past on the present and endows the past with timeless significance. . . .

Williams asks for non-realistic lighting in the play, in order to set off the events occurring in memory. A general dimness gives the effect of ethereality. Williams also specifies that "the light upon Laura should be distinct from the others" and resemble the light upon a madonna in a religious painting. At one point, he calls for special light upon Amanda: "the light upon her face with its aged but childish features is cruelly sharp, satirical as a Daumier print." Such lighting reflects Tom's emotional response to the other characters: his memory canonizes Laura and criticizes Amanda. (p. 156)

What is unique about the Wingfields is their retreat from the world of daily existence. Each of them has a fantasy world which is infinitely more real than the world of the St. Louis tenement. . . . (p. 157)

The play also makes extensive use of music, which, in framing each scene, serves as a mediator between the present situation of the narrator and his memories of the past. There are, in addition, three distinct musical themes played at intervals during the drama: Laura's theme, "The Glass Menagerie," which is light, delicate, and poignant; the nostalgic fiddling associated with Amanda's reveries; and the "theme three" adventure music which calls Tom to his wandering future. The music in all three cases is symbolic of the illusions which dominate the three main characters.

The techniques which emphasize memory and illusion in the drama reinforce the theme of the escape from time which controls the action. The survival tactic practiced by the Wingfields is to retreat from reality into a timeless world of their own making. . . . Laura's retreat can not be dismissed as lightly as Amanda's nostalgia and Tom's puerile dreams. Withdrawal from the world is a matter of necessity, not choice, for her. (pp. 157-58)

The picture of life presented in *The Glass Menagerie* is a disturbing one: the only defense against the relentlessness and cruelty of life in time is the ultimately unsatisfactory retreat into a world of illusion. None of the Wingfields has the capacity to "fight back." Amanda in her reveries is an incurable romantic whose practical schemes are doomed to failure. Laura is an object of pity; she backs away from life, not because she wants to, but because nature has ill-equipped her to fight for survival. Tom literally runs away, only to learn that his dreams were illusions and that reality mocks him wherever he goes. Williams, however, celebrates the attempt to flee the present as a noble failure. (p. 158)

Mind or spirit, in the form of Amanda's recollections, Tom's dreams, or Laura's fantasy, imposes itself on the recalcitrant material of experience and achieves, if only for a moment, a purity and beauty normally denied to those who are earthbound and timebound.

Most of the plays which Williams wrote during the 1940s depict the defeat of the light of spirit by the darkness of matter. His first play, *Battle of Angels,* is explicitly built on a set of dichotomies: light vs. darkness, imagination vs. practicality, life vs. death—or, in terms of the plot, the young free-spirited wanderer and the woman he impregnates vs. the woman's moribund husband and the hostile townspeople. If the hero, Val Xavier, has a "fault," it is pausing to fall in love; his lovers, past and present, prevent his escape from responsibility. When Williams rewrote the play, under the title *Orpheus Descending*, he retained the Manichean structure and added a set of classical analogies. Williams' mythological allusions suggest the utter incapacity for change or progress in the human situation. Like Orpheus, Val is an innocent alien, a visitor from a better world, who is destroyed by the evil forces which pervade this world. The only way to preserve one's purity, implies Williams, is to stay free of human ties.

Williams sets up similar struggles between matter and spirit in *Summer and Smoke* and *A Streetcar Named Desire*. . . . Body and soul are irreconcilable opposites; in any direct clash, body or matter necessarily wins. In these early plays Williams presents the plight of human beings struggling with their dual natures and hemmed in by their mortality. Those who submit to the conditions of mortal existence are viewed as corrupt; those who defy them in pursuit of a timeless ideal are eventually destroyed by the corrupt anyway. No compromise between pure spirit and base matter is possible in a world in which the realities of timebound existence place limitations on the spirit's capacity to be free.

Most of the plays which Williams wrote during the 1950's assert the spirit's capacity to be free in the face of heavy odds. Time is still the enemy, but those who strive to overcome it are victors, not necessarily on a literal level, but very clearly on a spiritual plane. In changing from a Mani-

chean to a modified Pelagian stance, Williams enlarges the possibilities for heroism. At least, in the middle plays, one's choices are related, not irrelevant, to the outcome of one's life. Although Williams, unlike the Pelagians, does not deny the existence of original sin, he does extol the ability of man to rise by sheer force of will power above the limitations his mortality imposes upon him. *Camino Real* reveals how Williams' attitude toward the plight of humanity in time alters to offer the possibility for greatness to man.

Williams suspends the rules of strict chronology and causality by adopting in *Camino Real* a structure based on association. He writes in the play's foreword that his aim is to give the audience a sense of "the continually dissolving and transforming images of a dream." (pp. 158-59)

[Like so many of Williams' characters], the characters in *Camino Real* are wanderers, rootless, displaced persons. . . . Camino Real is a way station, albeit a most depressing one, on the journey from birth to death. Williams uses the opening lines from Dante's *Inferno* as the play's epigraph. The inferno experienced by the characters on the Camino Real is caused by the inevitable change and dissolution which accompany time's forward motion. . . .

As demanded by the stage directions, the legendary characters wear modern clothes with only vestigial touches of the period costume. The combination of contemporary and historical costuming suggests that each character represents a legend or myth that is still operative in the present. The drama indicates which is the saving myth. *Camino Real* is a paean to dreamers and idealists of all ages. The only way out of the plaza is through the Terra Incognita, and the only characters to take that route are Byron, Don Quixote, and Kilroy—romantics all. (p. 160)

Camino Real in offering the Terra Incognita as a remedy for the pain of being human, denies the possibility of a resolution in time of the problems posed by mortality. By including the Casanova-Marguerite subplot, Williams avoids complete escapism. Even as Don Quixote and Kilroy leave to follow their dreams, Casanova and Marguerite remain on the Camino Real to find "salvation" in their mutual love. Williams' point is obvious: idealism can conquer the limitations of mortality, love can make them bearable.

Pelagianism provides the philosophic framework of Camino Real. . . . [The] Pelagian stance in the modern drama is the exaltation in the last act of the energy and competence of man, alone and without aid. . . . Whether or not the gesture of defiance in *Camino Real* really succeeds in overcoming the limitations of the world, time, and necessity is irrelevant. The act of defiance itself is courageous, heroic, and therefore worthwhile.

A tinge of Pelagianism is also evident in *Cat on a Hot Tin Roof* and *Suddenly Last Summer,* in which Williams commends characters who rebel against their present situation, whether with good or bad results. One play of Williams' middle period is noteworthy, both for its emphatic treatment of time as the source of man's problems and for its obvious Pelagianism. Unlike Williams' memory play and dream play, *Sweet Bird of Youth* uses a conventional technique and structure. (pp. 161-62)

In Williams' Pelagian world man exercises free will, but only within the narrow sphere of deciding whether to face reality and the burden of time. . . . Williams does not suggest that human beings can alter their destinies in time.

Williams' dramas of the sixties and seventies, however, reveal a different approach to the human predicament. His later characters discover the significance of their existence and the possibility of control by immersing themselves in time, rather than by escaping or defying it. In *Night of the Iguana, The Milk Train Doesn't Stop Here Anymore, Kingdom of Earth,* and *Small Craft Warnings,* it is not the "loners," but those who need each other, not the defiers, but the accommodators, who are set up as ideals. And in the later plays there is no doubt that the archetypal sin-suffering-atonement-redemption pattern is *fully* realized. (pp. 162-63)

The attempt to break down the barriers of time does not so obviously affect Williams' techniques in *Night of the Iguana* as it does in *The Glass Menagerie* and *Camino Real.* Nevertheless, *Night of the Iguana* resembles *Camino Real* in that the Costa Verde functions as a kind of Never-Neverland, placed on a hill overlooking, but somehow apart from the time-drenched world below. On this hill each character strives to come to terms with time and the duality of human nature, though earthbound, strives for the infinite. The play is like *The Glass Menagerie* in that memory is an important part of each character's conception of himself. . . . More than the iguana is freed before the night is over, for all the characters learn to abjure the past to which they are tied. (pp. 163-64)

Although the classical myth of Orestes defines the basic dramatic situation of *Night of the Iguana,* the Christian myth provides the key to the resolution of the drama. More is involved in the play's Christian perspective than the simple equation of Shannon tied in his hammock and Christ nailed to the cross, both "atoning" for the transgressions of mankind, although this relationship is clearly implied by Williams. The religious ritual structure of sin-suffering-atonement-redemption works itself out, not in Shannon's assumption of the role of Christ-figure, but in his progress toward a truly Christian outlook on the world. Shannon has always been willing to "suffer" and "atone"; he does it every eighteen months with a vengeance. What makes this encounter different from all others is the new knowledge of what must come after atonement, of what constitutes a redeemed life. Shannon comes to this realization largely through his contact with Hannah.

While Shannon conscientiously sets himself apart from the mass of men in his search for God, Hannah offers him a different approach to this search, based upon her own experience: find God in ministering to the needs of others. (p. 165)

An author who updates myths can break down the barriers between past and present. If he stresses "the eternal return of the same," the effect of the myth may be to undermine the importance of timely existence. But myths may also be used to define basic human situations or problems confronted differently by each age and existentially by each individual. It is this latter function which the myth serves in *Night of the Iguana,* the message of which is the necessity of finding one's place in the present. The characters of the play, as Williams says . . . , "reach the point of utter despair and still go past it with courage." Their despair results from the burdens placed on them by their mortality

and by the changes which accompany the passage of time. The drama consists in their coming together, enlightening, and helping each other through this "dark night of the soul."

The characters of Williams' later plays resolve their problems, not by taking refuge in an idealized past or in imaginative leaps, but by courageously accepting present reality and assuming responsibility for the future. . . .

In the first stages of his career, whether he is depicting the defeat of the forces of light by the forces of darkness or exalting the energy of self-sufficient man. Williams adopts an essentially negative attitude toward time. He views the inexorable march of time as destructive of man's work and dreams. The quest in *The Glass Menagerie* and *Camino Real* is for what is untouched by time. By contrast, in Williams' later plays the forward march of time—in extending to human beings the opportunity to create anew, to change and progress—is a source of meaning. The courage to become is what the characters of Williams' later plays seek and find. . . .

That the later plays of Williams embody a more satisfying philosophy of living is no guarantee of their dramatic worth. Indeed, Williams' earlier plays are generally considered his best. Yet there is a paradox involved in Williams' attempt in his early plays to fashion for the stage actions which are supposedly devoid of human meaning in order to prove the significance of what cannot be humanly enacted. For it is the *plaza* which comes to life on stage, and the Terra Incognita which is doomed to remain without artistic form. (p. 166)

Just as the lack of a philosophy that comes to terms with man's temporality and mortality does not necessarily make a bad play, so the embodiment of a philosophy that provides a viable rationale for living does not of itself insure success. All that can be said is that given two plays of similar dramatic merit, the one in which mortality is seen as a source of insight rather than a hindrance to vision is the one that will be more humanly satisfying. . . . [It] is only from *Night of the Iguana* on, that Williams' characters have confronted time to find its human significance. (p. 167)

> *M. A. Corrigan, "Memory, Dream, and Myth in the Plays of Tennessee Williams," in* Renascence *(© copyright, 1976, Marquette University Press), Spring, 1976, pp. 155-67.*

MICHAEL LASSELL

Memoirs, which Williams consistently refers to as a "thing," moves back and forth between the near and distant past, between the struggle for success and the struggle to retrieve it. Quite legitimately, Williams may be capsulizing, rarefying facts to manageable size and form, presenting the essence rather than the graph of actuality. The author's life, as he sees it, is made accessible through the medium of written expression; we do not come to see what it is like to be Tennessee Williams, but what it is like to see Tennessee Williams more or less as he is willing to be seen. But no matter how faithful to events a writer may wish to be, memoirs are a compromise; they exist as aesthetic works apart from fact as surely as they may represent an attempt to unite objective and subjective impulses in literary form, and *Memoirs* exists, unassailable, immune to charges of faulty, truncated, or manufactured memory. . . .

What is most remarkable about *Memoirs* is its frankness, especially related to sexuality, and, paradoxically, its guarded tone.

Williams' highly touted openness about his homosexuality is both commendable and dangerous: commendable because he has chosen to make this important part of his life known (which precluded his residence at a major American university theatre) and dangerous because his attitude toward homosexuality is likely to confirm any number of armored stereotypes. Williams attributes the genesis of his homosexuality to childhood illness and to a classic Freudian family situation: overbearing mother and distant father, a model long suspect within the psychiatric profession itself. He experienced a not uncommon guilt that made early expression of his homosexuality impossible, a guilt, however, that persists in maturity. . . . (p. 79)

Memoirs fails on at least one level, an aesthetic level primarily, but in such a way as to affect our reception of the life and its work. The failure is in the tone of the book and is related to Williams' perception of the role of writing and of language. Perhaps this is not a failure in the usual sense, but an evident resistance to or disregard of recent speculation about language. Williams has made an attempt to incorporate formal "advances" in his plays, juxtaposing new presentational theatrical techniques against an essentially representational vision and illustrative purpose. The relationship to writing has not changed.

Williams writes, he says, to come out of himself: writing as therapy, confession, purgation. He believes that every writer must draw from the material of his own life to create art in which the personal experience is treated in such a way as to be of greater significance than the author alone. All of Williams' work is autobiographical in some measure; *Memoirs* reveals how much it is. All artists, of course, draw from their own experience, whether it be physical or imaginative, but the impulse to universalize (central to Williams' process), to submit experience to metaphor in an attempt to expand significance, is becoming increasingly archaic. Certainly, Williams has created vivid aesthetic masks for his life in his best plays, *Streetcar* and *Cat* for example, but he sacrificed the poignant reality of *The Glass Menagerie* in order to do so. . . . [Williams] invests his masks with too much power, divesting himself of a certain responsibility for the very animation that gives the masks meaning.

Williams seems to have a complete, almost naïve faith in the power of language to communicate, to express, to represent his intention. . . . This belief in the efficacy of words to effect an identity of intention and expression places a burden on the book, the play, the story, the poem that may be too heavy for the aesthetic "artifact" to bear. Williams seems to write from the assumption that the audience will find in the work itself all it needs to understand or feel what is going on, what is meant to be going on. For Williams, the fragile balance among artist, object, and observer tilts toward that of the artist and his work of art. In a sense, Williams closes his writing before it becomes public; he does, perhaps, too much. The audience may therefore experience a Williams' piece as effect rather than cause, as response rather than stimulus. It is as if he does not trust his audience, is unwilling to authenticate any response except the one he wishes us to have. Thus, Williams' metaphoric constructs are sometimes justifiably open to the charge of ob-

vious, heavy-handed symbolism; the symbols reverberate only within limits set by the author. The irony of his situations falls leaden as often as it startles because, perhaps, it is underscored by an intruding author and not by the created events. Williams' language, too, is closed; he does not leave enough unsaid.

This same vision creates a disarming detachment in *Memoirs,* where Williams attempts to speak directly to his audience, ostensibly without the intermediary of an aesthetic mask. Characteristically, however, he erects a screen between himself and the reader that serves the function of the aesthetic artifact. The result produces an extraordinary effect; Williams goes into great, untidy detail about his illnesses, his shock therapy, his sexual relationships, yet these details fail to resonate. *Memoirs,* for all its candor and humor, lacks the passion of the best plays. It is as though Williams does not trust us to pull the details together into the portrait he wishes us to have. (p. 80)

Increasingly, one suspects that Williams has quite clear-headed objectives in *Memoirs*—that he wishes to present a being represented by experience and by predilection. He wishes to counter his image as a Romantic sot, so he presents a Williams immune to the sentiments that surround being in love and trying to write about it. Williams seems to have a penchant for such fictive biography; Tennessee, after all, is not his home state but that of his paternal ancestors. (p. 81)

In *Memoirs,* Williams has written not so much an autobiography, but a novel about a writer named Tennessee Williams. Williams emerges as a *character* in his own life rather than an autonomous being, a character who expresses himself in memoirs just as his characters express themselves in his plays as masks and mask-wearers. . . . The aesthetic nature of the *Memoirs* and its narrator suggests that if this character were not in fact sickly, he would have to be invented as a hypochondriac.

If *Memoirs* is by nature almost useless as factual history and somewhat confused in purpose (confessional or creative?), what is its value or use? . . . Williams' image of himself is both useful and valuable in its relation and applicability to his less obviously autobiographical work; the book increases our understanding of both the work and the process. By itself, it is generally well-written. It raises a number of social issues related to sexuality, fame, and the role of the artist. It provides new perspectives on other luminaries. It provides a great deal of detail that fills in the cartoon of Williams' reputation, and it is in large measure through the detail that we come to understand the relationship between Williams' life and art: what details are chosen? how are they used in *Memoirs* and then in the plays or fiction? how is Williams' life different from art, his art different from his life? *Memoirs* is a kind of map with which we can further explore the territory of Williams' mind, work, and method. (pp. 81-2)

[*Moise and the World of Reason*] is a perfect "companion piece" to the *Memoirs* and cannot be understood on perhaps its most significant level without it. This level is the relationship of *Moise* to the totality of Williams' work and its centrality to his vision. It may be possible to assume without biographical information that the old playwright in *Moise* is meant to represent Williams himself. With *Memoirs,* however, that old "derelict" emerges without further embellishment as the same character who narrates the auto-biography.

But Williams has rationed his own biography and distributed some of its excess to other characters in *Moise*. . . . [The incidents in *Moise*] are Williams' experiences as revealed in *Memoirs,* and *Moise* begins to come across as a subtle self-portrait, as unromanticized as *Memoirs* is indulgent. It is as if Williams came to present himself by assigning three sets of his own psychic patterns to three distinct characters, the sum of which is Tennessee Williams. . . .

Small Craft Warnings is the play that figures prominently in the "present" of *Memoirs,* the play, it turns out, that the old playwright in *Moise* was using as a vehicle for an off-Broadway come-back. After reading *Memoirs,* it is almost gratuitous to see Williams at the center of all the characters in *Small Craft Warnings.* . . .

In *Memoirs,* in *Moise,* in *Small Craft Warnings* we find direction by finding indirection out. If Williams realizes the extent of his revelation in *Memoirs* and the nature of its real success, he may come upon the breakthrough in his writing that critics, public, and playwright are demanding. By being more specifically personal, less ostensibly "creative," Williams has produced in *Memoirs* a work that comes closer to subtlety and to art than a good many of his more self-consciously "aesthetic" enterprises; we see the mask and the face behind the mask and realize it may have been the face that interested us all along. The myth is in the man; the works are allusions to himself. (p. 82)

> *Michael Lassell, "Williams on Williams," in* yale/theatre *(copyright © by* Theater, *formerly* yale/theatre *1976), Fall, 1976, pp. 78-82.*

JOHN WHITTY

Williams has written some of the most moving dramas of the modern theatre. He is such a grand old man that I suppose no one will tell him when a play simply stinks. And that is what *This Is (An Entertainment)* does—rankly and raucously.

If this *were* merely an entertainment, we might try to respond in kind, but . . . [this is] an empty pretentious script. . . .

It is of course possible to satirize politics and even revolution, as Dürrenmatt has done in grotesque tragicomedies, but Williams's revolution is simply irrelevant to his single character in a densely populated play. It is of course possible to laugh at a munitions maker as a crawling, sex-starved cuckold, but such figures would look better in *Daily Worker* cartoons than on [a] set. It is even possible to share the zest of a Countess for several lovers, but not when she mislays her children as easily as her cigarette lighter; and not when she buys that amatory zest with the profits of her husband's munitions. Are these objections too realistic for a play insistently called an entertainment? To avoid them, Williams should not violate the boundaries of fantasy. . . . (p. 406)

> *John Whitty, in* Educational Theatre Journal *(© 1976 University College Theatre Association of the American Theatre Association), October, 1976.*

MARY ANN CORRIGAN

In *A Streetcar Named Desire* Williams synthesizes depth characterization, typical of drama that strives to be an illusion of reality, with symbolic theatrics, which imply an acceptance of the stage as artifice. In short, realism and theatricalism, often viewed as stage rivals, complement each other in this play. Throughout the 1940s Williams attempted to combine elements of theatricalist staging with verisimilitudinous plots and characters. His experiments either failed utterly, as in *Battle of Angels* in which neither literal nor symbolic action is convincing, or succeeded with modifications, for instance . . . in *The Glass Menagerie.* In *A Streetcar Named Desire* Williams is in control of his symbolic devices. They enable the audience not only to understand the emotional penumbra surrounding the events and characters, but also to view the world from the limited and distorted perspective of Blanche. (p. 385)

The conflict between Blanche and Stanley is an externalization of the conflict that goes on within Blanche between illusion and reality. The illusion sustaining her is her image of herself as a Southern belle, a fine, cultured, young lady. The reality is a lonely woman, desperately seeking human contact, indulging "brutal desire" as an affirmation of life. Blanche's "schizoid personality is a drama of man's irreconcilable split between animal reality and moral appearance." This drama is played out not only in Blanche's mind, but between Stanley and Blanche as well. Stanley strips away Blanche's illusions and forces her to face animal reality. In doing so, he demonstrates that reality is as brutal as she feared. She has no choice but to retreat totally into illusion. Thus, the external events of the play, while actually occurring, serve as a metaphor for Blanche's internal conflict.

In pitting Blanche and Stanley against one another, Williams returns to his oft-told tale of the defeat of the weak by the strong. But, for a change, both figures represent complex and morally ambiguous positions. Blanche is far from perfect. She is a liar, an alcoholic, and she would break up the Kowalski marriage if she could. Despite his rough exterior, Stanley genuinely loves and needs his wife, and he cannot be blamed for protecting his marriage against the force that would destroy it. The ambiguity of Blanche and Stanley makes them more realistic than many of Williams' characters, who are often either demons (philistines with power, wealth and influence) or angels (helpless, sensitive, downtrodden artists or women). Although Williams depicts both positive and negative personality traits in Blanche and Stanley, his attitude toward the two characters changes in the course of the play. In the beginning Williams clearly favors Stanley by emphasizing his wholesome natural traits, while dwelling on Blanche's artificiality. But such, we learn, are the deceptive appearances. The more Williams delves into Blanche's inner life and presents it on stage, the more sympathetic she becomes. Stanley's true nature also becomes apparent, in its negative effect upon her psyche, and, in the end, she is the undisputed moral victor. (pp. 392-93)

Williams remains as much as possible within the conventions of verisimilitude in using theatrical devices to reveal Blanche's distorted vision of reality. The audience is, however, aware that baths and light bulbs have a meaning for Blanche apart from their functional existence. The further Blanche retreats from reality, the more Williams distorts the surface realism of the play. (pp. 393-94)

The characters of his early one-act plays, of *The Glass*

Menagerie and of *A Streetcar Named Desire* who doggedly cling to an imaginative vision of what life ought to be, while resolutely ignoring what life is, are invested with a dignity denied those who accommodate themselves to imperfect existence. The theme of the necessity of illusions lends itself to theatricalist treatment, since the non-objective world, which is far more important to Williams' characters than the objective one, must somehow be made tangible on stage. Williams' use of theatrical devices to objectify thoughts and feelings is much more sophisticated in *A Streetcar Named Desire* than in his hitherto most successful play, *The Glass Menagerie*. In the earlier play Williams thought he needed a screen to depict exact and obvious equivalents for his characters' thoughts. In *A Streetcar Named Desire* he relies more upon the suggestive qualities of costuming and staging to communicate psychological tendencies more subliminal than thought. *The Glass Menagerie*'s musical themes, particularly the sentimental fiddling and the jolly roger tune, reflect not so much the characters' inner lives, as the author's ironic perspective on them. On the other hand, in *A Streetcar Named Desire,* the nightclub music and the Varsouviana convey the emotional states of the characters at each stage of the action.

The realism of *A Streetcar Named Desire* distinguishes it from *Summer and Smoke* . . . , with which it is superficially related. In *Summer and Smoke* the conflict is between two abstractions; in *A Streetcar Named Desire,* it is between two people. . . . [In *Summer and Smoke*] John, who represents first Body and later Soul, lacks the ambiguity that makes Stanley a good dramatic character and a worthy opponent for Blanche. Stanley is as much a bundle of contradictions as his antagonist. His strength, brutality, and virility are balanced by his vulnerability to Blanche's attacks, his awkward attempts at tenderness, and his need for his wife's approval. The unexpected character changes of *Summer and Smoke,* the "turnabouts" necessary to demonstrate the proposition that Body and Soul are irreconcilable, have no parallel in *A Streetcar Named Desire.* The only event of any significance in *Summer and Smoke,* Alma's transformation, is not depicted on stage; it occurs between the acts. By contrast, Blanche's gradual emotional collapse is presented stage by stage. When Williams can no longer convey the disintegration of her mind by depicting only objective reality, he resorts to distortion of verisimilitude in order to present subjective reality. Blanche does not mechanically move from one extreme to the other; she suffers and undergoes—on stage. The difference between *A Streetcar Named Desire* and *Summer and Smoke* is not, as an occasional critic has suggested, between a melodramatic and a "subtle" presentation of the same action, but between a play that finds adequate expression for the conflicts between and within individuals and one that sidesteps such conflicts completely.

Williams achieves his most successful revelation of human nature in its totality in this play in which he distorts the realistic surface as little as possible and only when necessary. The audience accepts as believable the direct depiction of Blanche's fantasies because the necessary touchstone in recognizable reality is consistently maintained. . . . *A Streetcar Named Desire* reveals an unerring sense of when and how to combine realism and theatricalism. (pp. 394-95)

> Mary Ann Corrigan, "*Realism and Theatricalism in 'A Streetcar Named Desire*,'" in Modern Drama (copyright © 1976, University of Toronto,

Graduate Centre for Study of Drama; with the permission of Modern Drama*), December, 1976, pp. 385-96.*

CHARLES MAROWITZ

What has always fascinated me about Tennessee Williams, particularly in his early work, is the sense that the plays are never about what they appear to be about. They contain an opposing duality. In *Glass Menagerie,* Amanda Wingfield's mannered gregariousness is constantly at odds with Laura's fragile introversion; just as Tom's poetic yearnings tug against the Gentleman Caller's traditional American drive for 'getting on'. In *Streetcar Named Desire,* Blanche du Bois' gentility is virtually at war with Stanley Kowalski's primitive aggression—just as it ultimately clashes with *her* Gentleman Caller Mick, in a last act dénouement reminiscent of that in *Menagerie.* In *Cat On A Hot Tin Roof,* Maggie's materialist thrust is pitted against Brick's passivity. It is as if the secret centre of every Williams play is a dramatisation, by proxy, of the interplay that characterises certain kinds of homosexual relationships; active partners and passive partners; doers and done-to. What gives the early plays a curious kind of force is that heterosexual relationships are being dramatised from the standpoint of homosexual experience. In a way I cannot adequately explain, Williams captures (I believe by accident), the character of two opposing life-forces; one, thrusting and materialistic; the other, submissive and spiritual.

Because art works best when it wears masks, the disguises that Williams' characters wear give them an extra dimension: a sense of operating above and beyond their particular concerns. (p. 26)

When Williams began writing for the stage, in the mid-'forties, the American theatre would not permit the degree of explicitness which is, at present, the rage of almost every western theatre capital. He was obliged to use artistic subterfuge in order to transmit his experience and this gave his work greater depth. In his later work, when permissiveness was the by-word, and Williams could deal with all his obsessions without inner censorship, the plays became squat and murky—curiously lacking the deeper texture of the earlier work. In that early work, the plots were part of Williams' disguise. The need to disguise put a greater pressure on him to invent and, in relationships like Stanley's and Blanche's, Amanda's and Laura's, in the narrative structure of a play like *Suddenly Last Summer* and even a short work like *Something Unspoken,* the events themselves have a resonance which does not rely upon the language employed by the characters who inhabit them.

In the later period, Williams begins to depend more and more on direct statement or dialogue whose inference is abundantly clear which, in theatrical terms, is the equivalent of direct statement. For this reason, *The Red Devil Battery Sign* strikes me as forced and self-conscious. It's not that the political equation drawn by the play (which concerns an affair between an omnipotent senator's daughter and a mariachi) is not convincing (which it isn't) but that the frame-of-reference of Williams' characters does not legitimise his political commentary. Sexual politics and power politics do interconnect, but in order to accept the equation, one needs a more persuasive political framework for the dramatic characters. Without it, one feels that Williams is telling one story (the one he's really concerned about, impetuous promiscuity in an exotic Texan Setting) and only making reference to the political parallel in order to give that tale a greater significance. (pp. 26-7)

No one quite forgives [Williams] for not producing another *Streetcar Named Desire*—which is gruesomely unfair. *Orpheus Descending* was a fine play and even so small-scale a work as *Period of Adjustment* had virtues which only Tennessee Williams could have produced. Williams writes too much, which is another way of dealing with writer's block—the conventional one being not to write at all. My admiration for the man (and the talent) is so great I am quite prepared to sweat out all his five-finger exercises in the hope that the next full-fledged concerto will eventually arrive. . . . It is not more plays that we need from Tennessee Williams, but a new insight into the experience the writer is attempting to deal with in those plays, and that is achieved (sometimes) by reflection rather than proliferation. (p. 27)

> Charles Marowitz, "Tennessee Revisited," in Plays and Players (© copyright Charles Marowitz 1977; reprinted with permission), September, 1977, pp. 26-7.

MICHAEL ANDERSON

The storm-waters are rising around the farmstead somewhere in rural Mississippi when Lot, coughing ominously, comes back to the family home with his new bride; everyone has fled except his half-brother Chicken, who sits morosely in the kitchen downing liquor from an earthenware jug when he is not carving indecent figures on the wooden table or entertaining his new sister-in-law by hurling a startled cat into the flooded cellar. . . .

[*Kingdom of Earth*] reminds one occasionally of Pinter, but more frequently of Victorian melodrama, hinging as it does upon that old standby, a disputed inheritance. . . .

[The] Southern air is heavy with symbolism, too: the farmstead . . . stands for the corrosive influence of long-dead parents. . . . Chicken, loutish and sensual, relishes only the physical pleasures of life and never penetrates far beyond the culinary regions of the house. . . . Lot, pouring sherry wine from a cut-glass decanter in the tarnished opulence of his mother's parlour, embodies a feminine search for some kind of other-worldly refinement: in Tennessee Williams's over-heated world even his sickness is a gesture of defiance in the face of Chicken's rude health.

Kingdom of Earth is sub-titled 'The Seven Descents of Myrtle', but it might well have been called 'Southern Comfort Farm'. Williams himself, apparently, has called it 'my comic melodrama', and indeed it is difficult to know how seriously the author wants us to take this play. The brooding atmosphere, the sudden eruptions of violence, the hostility to brute masculinity, are familiar from his other plays, but here they tip over into the sort of luxuriant excess that makes one suspect the author has his tongue in his cheek: as an exercise in Mississippi Gothic there can't be much to beat Lot's macabre end: having plundered his mother's wardrobe, preserved in the marital bedroom, he struggles into the whitest of her gowns and, pale and gasping, expires before his incredulous wife. (p. 39)

> Michael Anderson, in Plays and Players (© copyright Michael Anderson 1978; reprinted with permission), April, 1978.

RICHARD GRAY

[Tennessee Williams takes] familiar characters, situations, and themes and then weaves them into a baroque conceit possessing neither original substance nor extrinsic value. The world so imagined hardly exists—or, at least, hardly deserves consideration—on any other level than the decorative: it offers us a group of charming grotesques, preserved in amber. What is Southern about it, really, is not a certain quality of perception, a sense of engagement between past and present, the public and the private, myth and history: but a turn of phrase or personality, a use of the bizarre and sensational for their own sake, which has the net effect of creating distance. For regionalism is substituted a form of local color, and a very precious and slightly decadent form at that, in which the gap between drama and audience seems deliberately widened so that the latter can revel without compunction in a contemporary "Gothick" fantasy. (p. 258)

[Williams] himself, I think, remains less than fully aware of [this reductive process]. Of course, Williams does have some suspicion of what he is doing, as his references to his own literary exhibitionism indicate. But these references are scattered and nearly always discreetly qualified. More to the point, they have never prevented him from reaching for some larger theme in his plays—and reaching in such a way, unfortunately, as to emphasize his limitations rather than go beyond them. Far from helping to charge his rich style with a vision equal to it, all his occasional ventures into moral statement tend to do is to remind us how very much he depends on the romantic commonplace; our attention is directed above all to the passing of time, the fragility of innocence, the loneliness of the sensitive person in a brutal world. This can hardly provide the sort of framework he requires, within which each play's images could be satisfactorily accommodated; and without it the audience is left to experience those images at random, to enjoy, in a fairly casual way, a series of Gothic—. . . largely *Southern* Gothic—effects. Often, if we look closely at the different elements in the series, we can even see from exactly where they came. Many of the characters, for example, seem when examined to trail the shadow of Yoknapatawpha behind them. . . .[There] is nothing intrinsically strange or suspect about this kind of borrowing: Faulkner is so much a part of the South by now that it would have been stranger, in a sense, if Williams had tried to ignore him. But there is, surely, something suspect and even wrong about the *manner* of this borrowing. For all Williams has been able to do with his adopted characters, really, by way of making them new is to vulgarize and dilute. His people (like his tropes, his settings) have been deprived of the functions and meanings assigned to them in their original context, and they have assumed no satisfactory fresh ones to replace them. They are there in the plays for the interest they inspire as exhibits, curios of human nature, and that is just about all they are there for. Thus, Williams's predatory women are not dangerous and frightening as Faulkner's are, a subversive commentary on sexual and family relationships; they are just neurotics, and rather silly neurotics at that. His girl-children are not mythic, Southern avatars of the Earth Goddess, merely Gothic pinups. And, as for his aristocratic young men, they are treated with the kind of approval, and taste for the pathetic or bizarre detail, that recalls the literature of the *fin de siècle* more than anything else. The funereal mansion, the intimations of incest, violence, and miscegenation, the brooding over the past and the desperate attempt to recover some of its memories: many, if not all, of the familiar elements of Southern writing reappear, but only, we must suspect, for the local excitement they can produce—to punctuate the narrative and, possibly, to intrigue. Yoked together as they are here, the most that Williams is able to create out of them is an exotic, broken world—a place that may provoke our lively curiosity at first but which, precisely because it is so very much less than the sum of its constitutent parts, is likely to leave us feeling a little cheated. (pp. 259-60)

> *Richard Gray, in his* The Literature of Memory: Modern Writers of the American South (*copyright © 1977 by Richard Gray*), *Johns Hopkins University Press, 1978.*

* * *

WRIGHT, Judith 1915-

An Australian poet of international stature, Wright is also a biographer, critic, and short story writer. Her traditional lyric poetry reflects her Australian heritage and is most noted for its excellent descriptive imagery. (See also *Contemporary Authors*, Vols. 13-16, rev. ed.)

VAL VALLIS

Judith Wright's collection of talks given "because she was invited" has as its first concern poetry in general. [*Because I Was Invited*] also presents a further group of poets treated in the manner of her previous book *Preoccupations in Australian Poetry*. The great merit of that book lay in her rejection of the usual critical approach, with its emphasis on style and technique at the expense of theme and philosophy. . . .

In the broadest sense the issue of conservation underlies the entire work. Blake's strictures on the evils of "single vision" are central to her argument. . . .

For all the seriousness and the prophetic content of her message these talks are never sermons. She is too good a poet to generalize. Her detail is always concrete, sharp, significant, whether in quotations selected from the poets she discusses, incidents that have occurred in the melancholy grind of teaching her poetry in schools, or facts painstakingly amassed. . . .

[Her first book, *The Moving Image*,] with its formidable introductory title poem is the work of a practised poet. . . .

[The title poem] was composed after the other poems in the book. It is richer in universal statement than in particulars, many of its key themes and images having been presented in sharper focus in such poems as "Northern River", "Dust", "Country Town", and "The Company of Lovers" (itself a poem veering to the universal rather than, as so often, sending "a shaft trembling in the central gold"— Judith Wright's own image . . .). . . . Indeed, the most commonly heard objection to her poetry as it progressed was that its author "had gone too philosophical". . . .

[I would rate *Alive, Poems 1971-72* highly], if only for its return to those flashing images drawn from ordinary domesticity that reverberate in the reader's mind. . . . And who in English since Hardy or Mew (except Judith Wright herself elsewhere) has written a love elegy as inevitable as "Lake in Spring" in that volume? The slimness of this book belies its value: the work is a careful distillation of years of criticism and love.

> *Val Vallis, "Doing Philosophy's Job," in* The Times Literary Supplement (© *Times Newspapers Ltd. (London) 1976; reproduced from* The Times Literary Supplement *by permission), April 9, 1976, p. 432.*

PETER PORTER

Judith Wright is a poet of resonant plainness. Much too plain in the past, for my taste—but her two recent books [*Alive* and *Fourth Quarter*] suggest that she is verging on new shores of amazement. This is partly horror at the efficiency with which her fellow-countrymen are raping their country and partly the intensity of growing old. Hymning a good wooden house and its familiar and loved objects, she asks, 'Who'd live in steel and plastic / corseting their lives / with things not decently mortal?' The decency of mortality is a theme she exploits with great richness. . . .

English readers could gain insight into the ambiguous nature of Australia by reading Miss Wright's poems. All Australian poetry tends towards the condition of nature poetry, and her unemphatic accounts of the innocent terrain and its contending overlords are excellent guides to the continent. From insects, creatures and simple rituals, she builds up a case for an Arcadian future. Alas, she knows there is scant hope of its coming to pass. But she also knows that the struggle is older than White Australia. (p. 33)

> *Peter Porter, in* The London Observer (*reprinted by permission of The Observer Limited), May 7, 1978.*

MARGARET GIBSON

Selected from work over a span of 30 years, Wright's poems [in *The Double Tree: Selected Poems, 1942-1976*] bear witness to her commitment to "poetry's ancient vow to celebrate lovelong / life's wholeness." She is Australian, and her bond to her native land and its once pastoral wildness is evident, expressed in lyric poems of skilled prosody. In her later work, the vow to celebrate radiance is harder to keep. As she sees the destruction to wildlife, water, and land, she is more convinced of human destructiveness, aware of the murderous heart as well as the passionate heart. She looks at opposites, seeking unity and form as "the compass heart swings seeking home / between the lands of life and death." Throughout we follow this poet's pilgrimage, respectful of her loving bonds to family, duty, passion, growth, and art. (pp. 1273-74)

> *Margaret Gibson, in* Library Journal (*reprinted from* Library Journal, *published by R. R. Bowker Company, a Xerox company; copyright © 1978 by Xerox Corporation), June 15, 1978.*

Z

ZATURENSKA, Marya 1902-

Zaturenska is a Russian-born American lyric poet. She won the 1938 Pulitzer Prize in Poetry for *Cold Morning Sky*. (See also *CLC*, Vol. 6, and *Contemporary Authors*, Vols. 13-16, rev. ed.)

BABETTE DEUTSCH

An almost palpable darkness hovers over many of the lyrics of Marya Zaturenska, which move from the innocent fairyland of a romanticized child's world toward a place peopled by haunted men and women, and their fearful, august companions, demons, angels, sibyls, gods. Her lyricism lacks the austere quality of Louise Bogan's. That she has read the metaphysicals with a fond attentiveness, the epigraphs and the names of her poems bear witness, as does the tone of those religious lyrics which have the quality of pastels. But her dream-charged imagery, twined with roses and with serpents, belongs to another country of the mind. She may briefly recall to us the forgotten beauties in the old book of nature, bid us "Remember Paradise and its perfect climate," more often she will suggest "the Gothic terror". Her poetry has an old-fangled quality, even as she acknowledges the risk we run when we listen to the voice of the past, or glances at the fact that "disaster lies in wait / For the heart and for the state." (p. 267)

> *Babette Deutsch, in her* Poetry in Our Time *(copyright © 1963 by Babette Deutsch; 1963 by Doubleday; reprinted by permission of Babette Deutsch), revised edition, Doubleday, 1963.*

ROBERT PHILLIPS

It was T. S. Eliot who asserted, "The most individual parts of the poet's work may be those in which the dead poets, his ancestors, assert their immortality most vigorously." In other words, a healthy tradition is capable of modifying itself continuously in the guts of the living, giving rise to fresh statements and new implications.

This surely is true of the work of Marya Zaturenska, whose new book [*The Hidden Waterfall*] is firmly rooted in the many conventions of lyric poetry, but which startles with its freshness. In her choice of matter as well as of mode, Miss Zaturenska is a true lyric poet—that is, pertaining to the lyre and relating to madrigals, airs, and sonnets (i.e., "little songs"). It is appropriate that one poem in this, her eighth collection, concludes with the lines, "Renewed are the sea's advances. / Resume, resume, the old dances, / And the song with the old refrain, / Renew our life again!" It is a book in which the poet literally sets some of the most serious "old refrains" of traditional poetry dancing new jigs. As such, it is pure Zaturenska. The imagination of Miss Zaturenska has never been lured by the fashionable or the trivial. Instead of the topical, she attempts to write of the timeless. Even her earlier poems involving the Second World War (from *The Listening Landscape*) were banished when she assembled her *Collected Poems* eight years ago, as if even that event were but a footnote in the true history of mankind.

Marya Zaturenska has long been one of America's natural sources of power and light; her second collection, *Cold Morning Sky*, full of magic and mystery, shadow and epiphany, won the Pulitzer Prize when she was a young woman. Even then her work was fully mature. It always gave, for instance, the impression of being directly spoken by the individual poet herself. Her work has never imitated others; her influences are thoroughly assimilated. . . . Subjective, highly emotional, in even her new adaptations from the Italian, the voice is always that of Marya Zaturenska, not that of some assumed persona.

Because Miss Zaturenska's work is so emotional, and because emotions are rarely sustainable, her poems are relatively brief. The ambitious, extended poem like *The Waste Land* or *Paterson* is not for her. The longest in the present collection is just over fifty lines. But when her poems do approach greater length, there is about them the same trance-like quality of the brief lyric, as if the whole were one spontaneous flash of inspiration, springing full-panoplied from the poet's head and armed with its own internal music and inevitable form.

Moreover, since she writes within the tradition of deeply-felt, deep-imagined poetry, it is natural that most of her poems deal with the universal concerns—love, sorrow, religion, death. But if her subject matter seems restricted, her responses to it are not. *The Hidden Waterfall* displays an impressively broad play of the imagination as well as a highly individual, but controlled, use of rhythm and sound. It is in these matters, her personal idiom, that she is distinguished (in both senses) from the handful of other known American lyricists of the century—Teasdale and Millay, Leònie Adams and Bogan, as well as Roethke.

Another trait of her idiom is an ability to surprise in the region of rhyme. She pairs and slant-rhymes sky/endlessly, unspeakable/impossible, it/forget, age/heritage. The result is music of a subtle sort. Like Robert Frost's, her verses rhyme but do not jangle.

Miss Zaturenska rarely takes traditional material without hammering it into a shape all her own. In one of the finest of these new poems, "Cordelia's Song," the familiar figure of Lear on the heath becomes, in her version, "the lost man in the rain"—a more diminished vision, but a very human one.... Miss Zaturenska's is nearly a post-mythic world—informed by legend, but imagined beyond it. Hers is a universe in which the golden apples already have fallen, the azure-breasted birds already have flown.

Lastly, *The Hidden Waterfall* is so original because of the poet's personal passions which supply subjects and allusions exclusively hers. (pp. 98-9)

The collection divides into four sections, but it is in the first, "A Shakespearian Cycle," that Miss Zaturenska has written her finest and most original work since her *Collected Poems*. With a song each for Prospero, Perdita, Cordelia, Marina, Ophelia, and Miranda, she recreates six individual and difficult *psychescapes*. (p. 99)

Depending upon such intensity, and writing within such restrictions, the poet of course runs risks. In a small number of these new poems, Miss Zaturenska cannot sustain the pitch. Sentiment shifts into sentimentality, as in "Another Snowstorm," a poem about old age and the approach of death. Other faults of the volume might be her persistence in archaic inversions and a tendency to overuse certain images. There are, for instance, a few too many islands in the book's mainstream (perhaps these are personal symbols of isolation and of solitude, or—in Jungian terms—symbols of the refuge from the menacing assault of the "sea" of the unconscious).

But these are small faults in a generous gathering. Confronted by the book's music and truth, one is tempted to say of Marya Zaturenska what she herself has said of Christina Rossetti: "Your quiet gifts rang purest gold, / Rang finest silver, and were loved, were heard." In an age of cacophony, it is rare pleasure to encounter a poet so dedicated to song. (p. 100)

> *Robert Phillips, "A True Lyric Poet," in* The Ontario Review *(copyright © 1975 by* The Ontario Review*), Spring-Summer, 1975, pp. 98-100.*

*   *   *

ZUKOFSKY, Louis   1904-1978

Zukofsky was an American poet, critic, translator, and novelist who, with William Carlos Williams and others, helped establish the Objectivist movement. His major work is the multivolumed poem sequence *A*, which utilizes a wide range of forms and themes in an attempt at an exhaustive examination of American culture and poetic thought. An uncompromising practitioner of his theories of poetry, Zukofsky was relatively unnoticed by the general public until late in life, though throughout his career he was praised by fellow poets. (See also *CLC*, Vols. 1, 2, 4, 7, and *Contemporary Authors*, Vols. 9-12, rev. ed.; obituary, Vols. 77-80.)

BURTON RAFFEL

As Zukofsky notes in his preface [to *Catullus*], it is the

sound of the Latin which has come to interest him—not however as Latin sound, but as a challenge, a kind of dare. He has done what he said he would do, namely construct Latin sounds in English. It works, in Catullus 8; though the effect is somehow strange, it is more than acceptable. (p. 439)

> Who we favor—whom—put to us? Caeli, *tibby:* now to your
>
>   (know bees?)
> perspective egregious "best" unique ah me kitty ah,
> come wasting on my eyes t'her reared at flame my medulla's
> Seize fay licks, Caeli, see as *in* and more potence.

This is Catullus 100—but is it English? (I do not mean: is it poetry? If it is not English, then it is not a translation into English. Period.) ... I'm told, reliably, that English schoolboys do this sort of thing all the time. Zukofsky does it, here, almost all the time: Catullus keeps sounding like this, for page after page:

> Furius, "Little Villa" has no nod for Auster,
> flaw to oppose a taste naked to Favonius,
> nor sighs with Boreas, out Apheliotes,
> worms eat and mill it fifteen thousand two hundred.
> O vent them horrible, I'm out quite, pestilent mm.

To whom is this translation of Catullus 26 of any use? The Latinist can read Catullus in Latin; he does not need, nor presumably is he interested to read, that "o ventum horribilem atque pestilentem" can be aped (but not translated, no) as "o vent them horrible, I'm out quite, pestilent mm." The non-Latinist wants to know, as well as he can, what Catullus said and how he said it. Can he get anything—*anything*?—from this? (p. 440)

Page after page of [*Catullus*] runs on in this never-never world of phonetic aping. In the middle of some of the gibberish one sometimes comes across a line, or several lines, of brilliant *translation*: Catullus 101, after beginning "Mulled hosts their countries yet mulled there by a core of wake tossed ...," for "Multas per gentes et multa per aequora vectus ...," and after continuing for most of the poem in this same sterile vein, suddenly coalesces in two oddly beautiful lines: "Now do mind inter here our how precious gift more our parent home / traditional trysts tears, my renewed death offerings ..." I don't care that this too apes the Latin sound ("nunc tamen interea haec"); it is English, and it is poetry, and I like it. Sometimes, but not often, a whole poem coalesces in this way, and the page sings:

> Diana, sum us in faith a-
> like pure girls and boys we greet you,
> Diana, pure boys and girls, as we
>   sing to you as you count us.
> O Latonia, most to my
> great lord Jove his own child, o his,
> for whom your proper mother lay
>   beside Delian olive ...

These are the first lines of a beautiful Catullus 34, a poet's translation. (pp. 441-42)

Several facts must be faced. Catullus ... is terribly difficult to translate. No one has done the whole job terribly well; in the nature of things, no one is likely to.... The best that one can do is to translate beautifully what one can, and leave the rest. Certainly, to try to translate Catullus, of all poets, into some rigid framework like heroic couplets, or the sonnet form, is madness, procrustean, doomed. To abandon English for pages at a time, in an even madder attempt to turn English into Latin, is still worse, and this, alas, is what Zukofsky has mostly done. Most of his book is unreadable; most of this book was not meant to be *read,* in any realistic sense of the word. It is much more the kind of musical game being played by John Cage, in music, and by many many practitioners of concrete poetry. As musical game, it has a kind of organized charm—but Zukofsky does not offer it as a musical game, he claims much more for it. Nor is he entirely sure, all the time, whether he wants to translate or play sound-games. (p. 444)

No one could, I think, have done this book better than Zukofsky has done it, but no one should have done this book: it does not perform, and it is neither translation nor Catullus. (p. 445)

> Burton Raffel, *"No Tidbit Love You Outdoors: Far as a Bier: Zukofsky's 'Catullus',"* in *Arion (copyright © 1969 by the Trustees of Boston University), Autumn, 1969, pp. 435-45.*

THOMAS A. DUDDY

[The beginning of Zukofsky's *A* is] richly assertive of the poem's "subject": aurality and its relation to measure. Aurality, where words seen literally as the *dynamics* of the poem are in kinetic relation between their occasions as sounded "meanings" (speech) and as configured sounds (music); measure, the abstract law from which aurality is suspended (mathematics). And so *A* begins in motion, with words "playing" the finite fugal structures of Bach, with words "played" against the measure (the isolated "A" subtly dislocating the iambic tetrameter line with an unfamiliar downbeat).... What is unique about the work is not that is is *about* music or that it is "musical" or that it was intended for musical setting (though it is often all these), but that it is a poetry *reaching out* toward a system of measure which, in this sublunary world, is best exemplified by music, and best of all by Bach. Zukofsky's "music" is a music in respectful proof of the "caged/'silence'" from which it issued, the *mathémata,* the science or knowledge, which both propels the poem into being and receives it at its close. Music here is epistemology.

It is the implementation of this concern with aurality and measure which most distinguishes the poet from those other moderns to whom he is, in many ways, a blood relative. Like Ezra Pound, Williams, and Charles Olson, Zukofsky is given to the use of so-called "anti-poetic" materials, to the epic-long, continuing poem, and like them, too, he is "difficult," which is to say that he is difficult to "explain." But the principle of organic form we find more or less operative in the Pound/Williams line is significantly modified by a classical disposition toward a strictly articulated measure. Both the *Cantos* and *Paterson* were allowed to spill over beyond their original intentions.... I doubt very much, however, that Zukofsky will exceed his plan of twenty-four movements to *A*, not only because twenty-four is generically right (the number which organizes Homeric epic), but also because the poem thus far demonstrates too respectful a working-out of numerical method.... [The reader feels] that within the density of "information" which the poet submits, there is yet a means to keep, literally, time with the poem. Quantity is thus a useful descriptive grammar:

"A"-18 is executed almost entirely in eight-word lines; eight quatrains made up of two-word lines open *"A"-19* and are followed by twenty-five pages of skinny Spenserian stanzas (twelve two-word lines and then one three-word line), the last two lines of which (*"raz'd* nine/so soon twenty") modulate the poem into *"A"-20,* where "nine" and "twenty" act as private structural keys; and *"A"-21,* a translation of Plautus' *Rudens,* is conceived, except for the speeches of the chorus, in five-word lines. No matter what the count is *of*—whether of words, syllables, or accents, it must, of course, be *heard* (though "measure, tacit is," "aurality is meaning.") and heard not mechanically, but as a felt recognition of design. The effect of a poetry so thoroughly encased in sound (Zukofsky's technique includes a command of all the conventional sound effects of poetry) and sound so precisely suspended from measure is that it helps to secure each part of the poem to its own discrete occasion and gives to the work, as it were, knowledge of its own finitude. So that while *A* is a reminder that poetry is, like life, a process (both volumes of the poem end with "continues"), its devotion to measured forms suggests that it has a morality of intention more "objective," more an assertion of authorial choice, than that which organic life could give it. (pp. 251-53)

A proposes as "content" an intricate configuration of facts or particulars (the acquired pictorialness of "images" precludes its use here) in support of its formal dynamic. In this sense, *A* is "about" Bach, the violin, poetry, Celia (the poet's wife and a composer), Paul (his son and a violinist), and other particulars, both private and public, of the poet's world. It is typically, moreover, the musical fact which serves to *define* that world. (p. 253)

[It] is important not to confuse the particular "stereoscopic" view of experience as music with the Romantic's translation of experience into moral law. Zukofsky is not suggesting that we will see harmony everywhere, even among our garbage cans, if only we see things his way; he is ornamenting the formal concern of his poem—the primacy of sound in epic poetry and the laws (aesthetic, not moral) to which sound refers. The music, then, is autonomous, not transcendental, and its "meaning" is locked into discourse. Music—literally, "the art of the Muse." The relevant Muse in *A* is Calliope, not Orpheus. (p. 254)

Less an elaborate pun than an extended display of half-rhyme, the *Catullus* may ... be seen as an English imitation of the phonetic shape of Catullus' Latin. "Meaning," and the general disposition of thought is, of course, present, but it is obviously of secondary importance; it is not always "clear," and it enters through re-located points in the sound.... Given the poet's regard for the auditory sense of language and his wish, as he has said in a recent interview, to "keep the noises as close to the body as possible," his *Catullus* seems a remarkably fresh re-breathing of Catullus. It makes those conventional attempts to "capture" "spirit," "tone," "meaning" seem like so many supplantations of the original.

Just as the *Catullus* is, in large part, a denial of the referential value of language and an assertion, instead, that "aurality is meaning," the *Autobiography* belies conventional expectation by being not a reference book about the poet's life (Zukofsky is, in a sense, our only anti-confessional poet), but by being a blue print for the musical production of some of his poems (what a poet's life is, after all, *about*). . . . The work must be performed, heard, to be understood. Beyond the pleasure of its *meaning,* beyond, too, the pure charm of the work's conception, the *Autobiography* is instance of that stage in the writer's formal dynamic in which words, no longer reaching toward music's measure, have, through projection of their own implications, been assimilated into it. The measure of Zukofsky's life is in that union. (pp. 255-56)

[His is] a suggestion that American poetry may be seeking what it never really has had—a workable classicism of its own. What *A* offers to that possibility is a circumstance in which technique mediates between the large American voice, on the one hand, with its "statements," its social concern, and the intimate lyric voice, on the other, with its privacy, its feelings. Zukofsky's classicism is not aestheticism, not art compromising reality, but art dealing from "the structure of its own house." It is all very much like music. (p. 256)

> *Thomas A. Duddy, "The Measure of Louis Zukofsky," in* Modern Poetry Studies *(copyright 1973, by Jerome Mazzaro), Vol. 3, No. 6, 1973, pp. 250-56.*

KENNETH COX

A bare and unpretentious way of speaking, brevity of phrase and concentration on the matter nearest to hand: such features of a language of survival are those [Louis Zukofsky's] work has chiefly tended to establish. Its intrinsic qualities are richer and deeper. . . .

At the age of 22 he conceived the idea of a poem that should run concurrent with his life, predetermined by number of sections or movements but undetermined as to form or content, the determined but unforeseeable course of history. He called it "A" and finished it after he had turned 70. (p. 11)

He shared Pound's conception of poetry as something semi-musical but in some respects his native gifts were more like Joyce's. He had a deep sense of dedication, great technical skill and little imagination. He combined an extremely keen literary sense with a grasp of large intellectual structure. He too had the strength to be sentimental as well as comic. His sense of rhythm was however delicate and restricted rather than powerful. In compensation he had a swiftness and subtlety of thought and feeling which earned him in his youth Pound's superlative: *the most intelligent man in America* and later Guy Davenport's: *the poet wisest in his time about love.*

It is not possible to give a simple description of Zukofsky's writing because he wrote differently as different parts of his work required. The diversity of his pace and tone has perhaps been masked by the general austerity of his style. Microscopic in his attention to detail, he saunters, ambles, dances, turns, leaps. His phrasing tends to be conceptual and abbreviated, connexions are often tenuous or undetectable, and some of his meaning bears the relation to experience algebra bears to arithmetic. Delighting in quirks and quibbles he had an extraordinary capacity for seeing different aspects of a whole as one. He would for example, modelling a movement of his poem on Bach's chaconne and englishing a verse of Mallarmé's, change one letter to bring a word into line not only with subatomic physics but with a concept of medieval Jewish philosophy. It is no use arguing about it: some minds work like that.

Zukofsky's poetry has been called 'experimental' and certainly he exploited to their limits devices he invented himself or found suggested in the work of others, but nothing he did was accidental. He must have learned much from trying to teach English to engineers. Cutting the inessential, rejecting the plausible, accepting the indefinable and subordinating detail to totality, Zukofsky makes most other writing look windy or overcharged. (p. 12)

> *Kenneth Cox, "Louis Zukofsky," in* Agenda, *Summer, 1978, pp. 11-12.*

Appendix

THE EXCERPTS IN CLC-11 WERE REPRINTED FROM THE FOLLOWING PERIODICALS:

Agenda
Agora
American Literature
The American Poetry Review
American Prefaces
American Quarterly
The American Scholar
Américas
Arion
Arizona Quarterly
The Atlantic Monthly
Best Sellers
Book World—The Washington Post
The Bookman
Books Abroad
Books and Bookmen
boundary 2
Bulletin of Hispanic Studies
Busara
Canadian Forum
Canadian Literature
Canadian Review of American Studies
The CEA Critic
The Centennial Review
Chicago Review
The Christian Science Monitor
College English
Commentary
Commonweal
Concerning Poetry
Contemporary Literature
The Critic
Critical Quarterly
Critique: Studies in Modern Fiction
Cross Currents
The Dalhousie Review
Diacritics
Drama
The Drama Review
Educational Theatre Journal
ELH
Encounter
English Journal
L'Esprit Créateur
Essays in Criticism
Essays in Literature
The Explicator
Forum for Modern Language Studies
The French Review
French Studies
Genre
The German Quarterly
Harper's
Harvard Magazine

Hispania
Hispanofila
The Hollins Critic
The Hudson Review
The Humanist
The International Fiction Review
The Iowa Review
Italian Americana
Italian Quarterly
Journal of Commonwealth Literature
Journal of European Studies
Journal of Modern Literature
Journal of Popular Culture
Journal of Spanish Studies: Twentieth
  Century
Judaism
Kentucky Foreign Language Quarterly
Kentucky Romance Quarterly
Kirkus Reviews
Library Journal
Lingua e Stile
The Listener
London Magazine
The London Observer
The Los Angeles Times
The Los Angeles Times Book Review
Midstream
The Midwest Quarterly
The Minnesota Review
Modern Drama
Modern Fiction Studies
Modern Language Notes
Modern Language Quarterly
The Modern Language Review
Modern Poetry Studies
Monatshefte
Moons and Lion Tailes
MOSAIC: A Journal for the Study of
  Literature and Ideas
The Nation
National Review
Die Neuren Sprachen
The New International
The New Leader
New Mexico Quarterly
The New Republic
New Statesman
Newsweek
New York Herald Tribune Book World
New York Magazine
The New York Review of Books
The New York Times
The New York Times Book Review
The New Yorker

Nouvelle Revue Française
The Ontario Review
Open Letter
Papers on Language and Literature
Parnassus: Poetry in Review
Partisan Review
Phylon
Plays and Players
PMLA
Poet and Critic
Poetry
Prairie Schooner
Publishers Weekly
Renascence
Review
Revista de Estudias Hispanicos
Revue des Langues Vivantes
Rivista di Letterature Moderne e
  Comparate
Romance Notes
Romanic Review
Salmagundi
Saturday Night
Saturday Review
Scandinavian Studies
Science Fiction Studies
Sewanee Review
Shenandoah
South Atlantic Quarterly
The Southern Humanities Review
The Southern Literary Journal
The Southern Review
Southwest Review
The Spectator
Stand
Studies in Short Fiction
Studies in the Novel
Symposium
Texas Studies in Literature and Language
Thoth
THOUGHT
The Times Literary Supplement
The Tulane Drama Review
Twentieth Century Literature
University of Toronto Quarterly
The Village Voice
Virginia Quarterly Review
West Coast Review
Western American Literature
Western Humanities Review
World Literature Today
Yale French Studies
The Yale Review
yale/theatre

THE EXCERPTS IN CLC-11 WERE REPRINTED FROM THE FOLLOWING BOOKS:

Adams, Laura, ed., Will the Real Norman Mailer Please Stand Up? *Kennikat, 1974.*

Adams, Robert Martin, AfterJoyce: Studies in Fiction After "Ulysses," *Oxford University Press, 1977.*

Aiken, Conrad, Collected Criticism, *Oxford University Press, 1968.*

Balakian, Nona, and Simmons, Charles, eds., The Creative Present: Notes on Contemporary American Fiction, *Doubleday, 1963.*

Biasin, Gian-Paolo, Literary Diseases: Theme and Metaphor in the Italian Novel, *University of Texas Press, 1975.*

Bigsby, C.W.E., ed., Edward Albee: A Collection of Critical Essays, *Prentice-Hall, 1975.*

Bracher, Frederick, The Novels of James Gould Cozzens, *Harcourt, 1959.*

Braudy, Leo, ed., Norman Mailer: A Collection of Critical Essays, *Prentice-Hall, 1972.*

Brée, Germaine, ed., Camus: A Collection of Critical Essays, *Prentice-Hall, 1962.*

Brée, Germaine, and Guiton, Margaret, An Age of Fiction: The French Novel from Gide to Camus, *Rutgers, 1957.*

Brodin, Dorothy, Marcel Aymé, *Columbia University Press, 1968.*

Brophy, James, D., W. H. Auden, *Columbia University Press, 1970.*

Bruccoli, Matthew J., ed., Just Representations: A James Gould Cozzens Reader, *Harcourt, 1978.*

Bufithis, Philip H., Norman Mailer, *Frederick Ungar, 1978.*

Cohn, Ruby, Dialogue in American Drama, *Indiana University Press, 1971.*

Deutsch, Babette, Poetry in Our Time, *Doubleday, 1963.*

Donoghue, Denis, The Third Voice: Modern British and American Verse Drama, *Princeton University Press, 1959.*

Doyle, Paul A., Pearl S. Buck, *Twayne, 1965.*

Drew, Fraser, John Masefield's England: A Study of the National Themes in His Work, *Fairleigh Dickinson University Press, 1973.*

Driver, Sam N., Anna Akhmatova, *Twayne, 1972.*

Enright, D. J., Conspirators and Poets, *Chatto & Windus, 1966.*

Esslin, Martin, ed., Samuel Beckett: A Collection of Critical Essays, *Prentice-Hall, 1965.*

Evans, Gareth Lloyd, The Language of Modern Drama, *J. M. Dent & Sons, Ltd., 1977.*

Farrell, James T., Literature and Morality, *Vanguard, 1947.*

Field, Leslie, and Field, Joyce, eds., Bernard Malamud: A Collection of Critical Essays, *Prentice-Hall, 1975.*

Finholt, Richard, American Visionary Fiction, *Kennikat, 1978.*

Fisher, Joan, and Gaeng, Paul A., eds., Studies in Honor of Mario A. Pei, *University of North Carolina Press, 1972.*

Fowlie, Wallace, Dionysus in Paris: A Guide to Contemporary French Theater, *Meridian Books, 1960.*

French, Warren, ed., The Thirties: Fiction, Poetry, Drama, *Everett Edwards, 1967.*

Friedman, Melvin J., Samuel Beckett Now, *University of Chicago Press, 1970.*

Frohock, W. M., The Novel of Violence in America: 1920-1950, *Southern Methodist University Press, 1950.*

Gardiner, Harold C., ed., Fifty Years of the American Novel, *Scribner's, 1951.*

Gide, André, Autumn Leaves, *trans. by Elsie Pell, Philosophical Library, 1950.*

Gilman, Richard, Common and Uncommon Masks: Writings on Theatre 1961-1970, *Random House, 1971.*

Glen, Duncan, ed., Hugh MacDiarmid: A Critical Survey, *Scottish Academic Press Ltd., 1972.*

Glicksberg, Charles I., The Literature of Nihilism, *Bucknell University Press, 1975.*

Gray, Richard, The Literature of Memory: Modern Writers of the American South, *Johns Hopkins University Press, 1978.*

Guicharnaud, Jacques, with Guicharnaud, June, Modern French Theatre, *Yale University Press, 1967.*

Harrison, Gilbert A., ed., The Critic as Artist: Essays on Books 1920-1970, *Liveright, 1972.*

Hollis, James R., Harold Pinter: The Poetics of Silence, *Southern Illinois University Press, 1970.*

Hook, Andrew, ed., John Dos Passos: A Collection of Critical Essays, *Prentice-Hall, 1974.*

Iyengar, K. R., Indian Writing in English, *Asia Publishing House, 1973.*

Kalstone, David, Five Temperaments: Elizabeth Bishop, Robert Lowell, James Merrill, Adrienne Rich, John Ashbery, *Oxford University Press, 1977.*

Kazin, Alfred, Bright Book of Life: American Novelists and Storytellers from Hemingway to Mailer, *Atlantic-Little, Brown, 1973.*

Kennedy, Andrew K., Six Dramatists in Search of a Language: Studies in Dramatic Language, *Cambridge University Press, 1975.*

Kenney, Edwin J., Jr., Elizabeth Bowen, *Bucknell University Press, 1975.*

Kermode, Frank, Puzzles and Epiphanies: Essays and Reviews 1958-1961, *Routledge & Kegan Paul, 1962.*

Kilroy, Thomas, ed., Sean O'Casey: A Collection of Critical Essays, *Prentice-Hall, 1975.*

Knight, G. Wilson, The Christian Renaissance, *Methuen and Co. Ltd., 1962.*

Kostis, Nicholas, The Exorcism of Sex and Death in Julien Green's Novels, *Mouton, 1973.*

Kuehn, Robert E., ed., Aldous Huxley: A Collection of Critical Essays, *Prentice-Hall, 1974.*

Kunitz, Stanley, A Kind of Order, A Kind of Folly, *Atlantic-Little, Brown, 1975.*

Leavis, F. R., For Continuity, *The Minority Press, 1933.*

LeMaster, J. R., and Clark, Mary Washington, eds., Jesse Stuart: Essays on His Work, *University of Kentucky Press, 1977.*

Littlejohn, David, Black on White: A Critical Survey of Writing by American Negroes, *Viking Penguin, 1966.*

Magny, Claude-Edmonde, The Age of the American Novel: The Film Aesthetic of Fiction between the Two Wars, *trans. by Eleanor Hochman, Ungar, 1972.*

Malin, Irving, ed., Contemporary American-Jewish Literature, *Indiana University Press, 1973.*

Mann, Thomas, Nachträge, Dem sechzigjährigen Hermann Hesse, *S. Fischer Verlag, 1974.*

Mann, Thomas, Reden und Aufsätze II, Hermann Hesse zum siebzigsten Geburstag, *S. Fischer Verlag, 1960, 1974.*

Mercier, Vivian, The New Novel: From Queneau to Pinget, *Farrar, Straus, 1971.*

Moore, Gerald, Seven African Writers, *Oxford University Press, 1970.*

Morgan, Edwin, Hugh MacDiarmid, *British Council, 1976.*

Nevins, Francis M., Jr., Royal Bloodline: Ellery Queen, Author and Detective, *Bowling Green University Popular Press, 1974.*

Newman, Charles, ed., The Art of Sylvia Plath: A Symposium, *Indiana University Press, 1970.*

O'Connor, William Van, ed., Forms of Modern Fiction, *Indiana University Press, 1948.*

Pearce, Richard, William Styron, *University of Minnesota Press, 1971.*

Pennington, Lee, The Hills of Jesse Stuart, *Harvest Press, 1967.*

Ravenscroft, Arthur, Chinua Achebe, *British Council, 1969.*

Richardson, Stewart, ed., New World Writing, *Lippincott, 1964.*

Rideout, Walter B., The Radical Novel in the United States 1900-1954: Some Interrelations of Literature and Society, *Harvard University Press, 1956.*

Ries, Lawrence R., Wolf Masks: Violence in Contemporary Poetry, *Kennikat, 1977.*

Sartre, Jean-Paul, Literary and Philosophical Essays, *trans. by Annette Michelson, Rider, 1955.*

Schwartz, Ronald, José Maria Gironella, *Twayne, 1972.*

Shabane, Vasant Anant, Khushwant Singh, *Twayne, 1972.*

Simon, John, Singularities: Essays on the Theater 1964-1973, *Random House, 1976.*

Simon, John, Uneasy Stages: A Chronicle of the New York Theater, 1963-1973, *Random House, 1976.*

Smith, Brian-Keith, ed., Essays on Contemporary German Literature: German Men of Letters, Vol. IV, *Oswald Wolff, 1966.*

Squires, Radcliffe, The Loyalties of Robinson Jeffers, *University of Michigan Press, 1956.*

Steiner, George, Language and Silence, *Atheneum, 1967.*

Strong, L.A.G., John Masefield, *British Council, 1964.*

Symons, Julian, Mortal Consequences: A History—From the Detective Story to the Crime Novel, *Harper, 1972.*

Taylor, John Russell, Anger and After: A Guide to the New British Drama, *Methuen and Co. Ltd., 1962.*

Updike, John, Picked-Up Pieces, *Knopf, 1977.*

Vernon, John, The Garden and the Map: Schizophrenia in Twentieth-Century Literature and Culture, *University of Illinois Press, 1973.*

Vidal, Gore, Matters of Fact and Fiction: Essays 1973-1976, *Random House, 1977.*

Voss, Arthur, The American Short Story: A Critical Survey, *University of Oklahoma Press, 1973.*

Warren, Robert Penn, ed., Faulkner: A Collection of Critical Essays, *Prentice-Hall, 1966.*

Weinberg, Helen, The New Novel in America: The Kafkan Mode in Contemporary Fiction, *Cornell University Press, 1970.*

West, Thomas R., Nature, Community, & Will: A Study in Literary and Social Thought, *University of Missouri Press, 1976.*

Woodcock, George, Poets and Critics: Essays from "Canadian Literature" 1966-1974, *Oxford University Press, 1974.*

Zioltowski, Theodore, ed., Hermann Hesse: A Collection of Critical Essays, *Prentice-Hall, 1973.*

Cumulative Index to Critics

CRITIC INDEX

CRITIC INDEX

CRITIC INDEX

CRITIC INDEX

CRITIC INDEX

CRITIC INDEX

CRITIC INDEX

CRITIC INDEX

CRITIC INDEX

CRITIC INDEX

CRITIC INDEX

CRITIC INDEX

CRITIC INDEX

CRITIC INDEX

CRITIC INDEX

CRITIC INDEX

CRITIC INDEX

CRITIC INDEX

CRITIC INDEX

CRITIC INDEX

CRITIC INDEX

CRITIC INDEX

Cumulative Index to Authors

AUTHOR INDEX

AUTHOR INDEX